THE POWER OF MUSIC

The Power of Music

An Exploration of the Evidence

Susan Hallam and Evangelos Himonides

https://www.openbookpublishers.com

© 2022 Susan Hallam and Evangelos Himonides

This work is licensed under an Attribution-NonCommercial-NoDerivs 4.0 International license (CC BY NC ND 4.0). This license allows reusers to copy and distribute the material in any medium or format in unadapted form only, for noncommercial purposes only, and only so long as attribution is given to the creator. Attribution should include the following information:

Susan Hallam and Evangelos Himonides, *The Power of Music: An Exploration of the Evidence*. Cambridge, UK: Open Book Publishers, 2022, https://doi.org/10.11647/OBP.0292

In order to access detailed and updated information on the license, please visit https://doi.org/10.11647/OBP.0292#copyright

Further details about CC BY-NC-ND licenses are available at http://creativecommons.org/licenses/by-nc-nd/4.0/

All external links were active at the time of publication unless otherwise stated and have been archived via the Internet Archive Wayback Machine at https://archive.org/web

Digital material and resources associated with this volume are available at https://doi.org/10.11647/OBP.0292#resources

Every effort has been made to identify and contact copyright holders and any omission or error will be corrected if notification is made to the publisher.

ISBN Paperback: 9781800644168
ISBN Hardback: 9781800644175
ISBN Digital (PDF): 9781800644182
ISBN Digital ebook (EPUB): 9781800644199
ISBN Digital ebook (azw3): 9781800644205
ISBN Digital ebook (XML): 9781800644212
ISBN Digital (HTML): 9781800646766
DOI: 10.11647/OBP.0292

Cover image by Tabitha Lincoln, all rights reserved. Cover design by Anna Gatti.

Contents

Author Biographies	xiii
Susan Hallam	xiii
Evangelos Himonides	xiv
Preface	xvii
1. Introduction	1
Music, Its Functions and Origins	2
Transfer of Learning	7
Methodological Issues	9
Ways of Engaging with Music and Varying Levels of Commitment	11
Music Therapy	13
Interpreting the Research Findings	13
2. Music and Neuroscience	15
Neuroscientific Methods	17
Changes in the Brain following Musical Activity	18
Comparisons between Musicians' and Non-Musicians' Expertise	19
The Automation of Skills as Expertise Increases	25
Bimanual Motor Coordination	26
Multisensory Learning	29
Neurological Differences Relating to Genre and the Instrument Played	30
Studies with Child Musicians and Non-Musicians	33
Genetic and Maturational Effects versus Training Effects	37
Intervention Studies	38
Overview	42

3. Aural Perception and Language Skills	43
Explanations of the Relationships between Music and Language	46
Comparisons between Musicians and Non-Musicians	55
Research with Children	62
Research with those with Auditory or Language Impairments	72
Overview	77
4. Literacy and Related Language Skills	79
Correlation Studies and Comparisons between Musicians and Non-Musicians	80
Intervention Studies	83
Children Facing Challenges with Literacy Skills	90
Are Pitch or Rhythm Programmes More Effective in Enhancing Literacy?	96
Reviews, Meta-Analyses and Conclusions	101
Spelling	102
Writing	103
Overview	105
5. Music, Spatial Reasoning and Mathematical Performance	107
Comparisons between Musicians and Non-Musicians, and Correlation Studies	110
Musical Interventions and Spatial-Temporal Reasoning	114
The Relationships between Spatial Skills and Mathematics	119
The Relationships between Music, Spatial Skills and Mathematics	122
Musical Engagement and Mathematical Performance	123
Overview	130
6. The Impact of Musical Engagement on Memory	133
Visual Memory	134
Research with Children	140
Verbal Memory	141
Research with Children	145
Working Memory	148
Research with Adults	149

Research with Children and Young People	154
Older Adults	159
Reviews and Meta-Analyses	167
Overview	169
7. Executive Functioning and Self-Regulation	**171**
Research with Adults	175
Research with Children	181
Research with Older People	190
Reviews of the Literature	194
Overview	197
8. Intellectual Development	**199**
Nature or Nurture	201
Correlational and Comparative Research with Adults	202
Correlation and Comparative Research with Children	206
Intervention Studies	210
Music and Emotional Intelligence	215
Studies with Older Adults	217
Reviews and Meta-Analyses	219
Overview	221
9. Musicians and Creativity	**223**
Neurological Studies of Creativity	225
Correlational and Comparative Research on Musicians	227
The Personality of Musicians and Creativity	230
Intervention Studies	232
Creativity in Later Life	234
Reviews and Meta-Analyses	235
Overview	235
10. General Attainment	**237**
Correlation and Comparative Studies	237
Large-Scale Research	241
Research with Disadvantaged Populations	247
Intervention Research	248
Reviews and Meta-Analyses	251

Explanations for the Research Findings	253
Neurological Studies	254
Length of Engagement with Music	255
Type, Nature and Quality of Musical Training	256
The Role of Executive Functions in Attainment	257
Personality Factors	257
Motivation	258
Overview	259
11. Music and Studying	261
Listening to Music prior to Completing a Task	261
Background Music	269
The Nature of the Music	270
Preferred Music, Familiarity and Liking	276
Preference for Music of One's Own Culture	279
The Nature of the Task To Be Completed	279
Background Music and Memory	279
Background Music and Attention	284
Reading Comprehension	286
Second-Language Learning	288
Background Music and English as a Second Language	289
Individual Differences	290
Musical Expertise	290
Gender	292
Personality	292
Background Music and Metacognition	294
The Impact of Background Music on Children's Behaviour and Task Performance	296
Background Music and Primary-School Children	297
Background Music and Older Students	300
Research with Children with Emotional and Behavioural Difficulties, ADHD and Developmental Difficulties	301
Children with Attention Deficit Hyperactivity Disorder and Attention Deficit Disorder	301
Emotional and Behavioural Difficulties	303

Older Adults and those with Cognitive Impairment	304
Reviews and Meta-Analyses	307
Explaining the Impact of Background Music on Cognitive Performance	309
An Explanatory Framework	316
Overview	317
12. Re-Engagement and Motivation	**319**
Motivation	319
Motivation Developed through Engagement with Music	322
Children and Young People Facing Challenging Life Circumstances	325
El Sistema and *Sistema*-inspired Programmes	326
Raised Aspirations and Motivation for Learning	326
Self-Beliefs	331
School Attendance and Positive Attitudes towards School	332
Emotional and Behavioural Difficulties	333
Transferable Skills	334
Music Interventions Unrelated to *El Sistema*	334
School Attendance and Attitudes towards School	339
The Integration of Young People with Special Educational Needs into Mainstream Education	340
School-Based Music Therapy Interventions for Children with Emotional and Behavioural Difficulties	342
The Role of Rap and Hip Hop in Therapy in School Contexts	347
Music Programmes for Young Offenders	353
Music Programmes for Adult Offenders	361
Choirs	362
Projects Using Gamelan	363
Assorted Music Therapies	365
Overview	372
13. Personal, Social and Physical Development	**375**
Personal Development	375
Music and Identity	375
Music and Personality	377

Self-Beliefs	384
Self-Beliefs, Deprivation and Disaffection	387
Children with Special Educational Needs and Disabilities	389
Ensemble Participation	390
Musical Preferences and Self-Esteem	391
Social Development	392
Musical Ensembles and Teamwork	397
School Climate	400
Sistema Programmes	401
Prosocial Skills and Empathy	403
Interventions for Children with Special Educational Needs and Disabilities	405
Physical Development	406
Music, Locomotor Performance and Coordinated Motor Skills	408
Overview	410
14. Psychological Wellbeing	413
The Use of Music to Support Emotional Stability and Manage Moods	418
Singing	425
Wellbeing in Young Children	430
Music and Wellbeing in School-Aged Participants	432
Music and Wellbeing in Adolescents and Young People	437
Actively Making Music	444
Music and Wellbeing in Adults	447
Participation in Musical Activities	449
Attendance at Music Festivals	451
Music and Wellbeing in the Older Generation	453
Music, Wellbeing and the COVID-19 Pandemic	465
The Impact of the Pandemic on Music Professionals	475
Overview	477
15. Music and Physical and Mental Health	479
The Role of Music in Psychological and Physical Health	480
Music, Stress and the Immune System	484

Active Music-Making and the Promotion of General Good Health	486
Music, Health and the Older Generation	488
Music, Dementia and Care in the Home	497
Reviews of the Relationship between Music Therapy and Dementia	499
Music, Public Health and Music on Prescription	501
The Role of Community Music and Creative Workshops	503
Music, Brain Plasticity and Movement	505
Breathing	509
Speech Impairment	510
Music in Hospital Settings	511
Music and Mental Health: Stress, Anxiety and Depression	519
Mental Health Care in Children, Adolescents and Young People	523
Insomnia	525
Music, Trauma and Abuse	527
Severe Mental Ill-Health	538
Overview	549
16. Music, Inclusion and Social Cohesion	551
Music and Conflict	555
Music and Refugees	560
Social Inclusion	566
Overview	571
17. Music in Everyday Life	573
Music and Leisure	574
Listening to Music	576
Attending Live Musical Events	577
Actively Making Music	578
Socioeconomic Status	579
Music in the Arts	581
Listening to Support Everyday Activities	581
Music and Driving	582
Music at Work and to Accompany Mental Activity	583

Music and Exercise	584
Music, Commerce and Consumption	585
The Economics of Music	588
Music and Non-Human Species	589
Overview	591
Reflections on an Exploration of the Evidence for the Power of Music	593
Bibliography	597
Index	805

Author Biographies

Susan Hallam

Professor Susan Hallam (MBE) studied the violin at the Royal Academy of Music prior to becoming Principal 2nd violin in the BBC Midland Light Orchestra and Deputy Leader of Orchestra da Camera. She studied for her BA in psychology externally with London University and for her MSc in the Psychology of Education and her PhD at the Institute of Education, University of London. She is currently Emerita Professor of Education and Music Psychology at University College London, Institute of Education. She is a past editor of the Psychology of Music and Music Performance Research. She has been Chair of the Education Section of the British Psychological three times and is an Academician of the Learned Societies for the Social Sciences. She has been awarded lifelong honorary membership of the British Psychological Society and the International Society for Music Education. In 2020 she was awarded a Music & Drama Education Lifetime Achievement Award.

Her research interests in music include practising, performing, musical ability, musical understanding and the wider impact of engagement with music. She is the author of numerous books related to music including: *Instrumental Teaching: A Practical Guide to Better Teaching and Learning* (1998); *The Power of Music* (2001); *Music Psychology in Education* (2005); *Preparing for Success: A Practical Guide for Young Musicians* (2012) (with Helena Gaunt); *Active Ageing with Music* (2014) (with Andrea Creech, Maria Varvarigou and Hilary McQueen); *The Impact of Actively Making Music on the Intellectual, Social and Personal Development of Children and Young People: A Research Synthesis* (2015); *The Psychology of Music* (2018); and *Contexts for Music Learning and Participation: Developing and Sustaining Musical Possible Selves* (with Andrea Creech and Maria

Varvarigou). She is editor of *The Oxford Handbook of Psychology of Music* (*2009, 2016*) (with Ian Cross and Michael Thaut); *Music Education in the 21st Century in the United Kingdom: Achievements, Analysis and Aspirations* (*2010*) (with Andrea Creech); and *The Routledge International Handbook of Music Psychology in Education and the Community* (*2021*) (with Andrea Creech and Donald Hodges).

Evangelos Himonides

Dr Evangelos Himonides held the University of London's first ever lectureship in music technology education and now holds the country's first ever Chair in Technology, Education, and Music. Evangelos works at University College London, where he leads a number of courses and supervises doctoral and post-doctoral research. At postgraduate level, he has led and now serves the MA in Music Education programme at UCL, with courses in 'Music Technology in Education' and 'Choral Conducting, Leadership and Communication'. At undergraduate level, Evangelos developed UCL's first ever music-related course in the Institution's near two-century history, which is called 'Interactions of Music & Science' and offered under the innovative Bachelors of Arts and Sciences (BASc) programme. He is fellow of the RSA and Chartered Fellow (FBCS CITP) of the British Computer Society. As a musician, technologist and educator, Evangelos has had an ongoing career in experimental research in the fields of Psychoacoustics, Music Perception, Music Cognition, IT, Human-Computer Interaction, Special Needs, the Singing Voice & Singing Development. Publications currently number over two hundred in high-profile international journals, such as Frontiers of Psychology and Cognitive Science, Psychology of Music, IJME, RSME, Journal of Voice, Logopedics Phoniatrics Vocology. Evangelos has been working on numerous funded research projects for leading UK Research Councils such as the AHRC, ESRC, EPSRC, grant-making foundations/charities such as The Paul Hamlyn Foundation, RNIB, the AmberTrust and the Esmée Fairbairn Foundation, government agencies/departments (such as DfES, QCA) and also the European Union.

Evangelos is associate editor for the Journal of Music, Technology and Education (Intellect), associate editor of Frontiers in Psychology, past associate editor for the Journal Logopedics Phoniatrics Vocology

(Informa Healthcare), reviews editor for Psychology of Music (SAGE), editor of the Society for Education and Music Psychology Research (SEMPRE) Conference Series, and section editor for 'technology' for the Oxford Handbook of Music Education. Evangelos has co-edited, with Andrew King, two key volumes in Technology, Music and Education, published by Routledge.

As a sound engineer and researcher, Evangelos has recorded in numerous venues (including York Minster, St.Paul's, RCM), with various artists such as Derek Lee Ragin (Farinelli), Vanessa Mae (SONY BMG) and Jarvis Cocker (Pulp) and for numerous media productions (for the BBC, Ch5, Discovery Channel, RTL, CBS, PBS, History Channel).

Evangelos has developed the free online technologies for Sounds of Intent, Inspire-Music and the Online Afghan Rubab Tutor. In his spare time, Evangelos likes to record music, play guitar, and handcraft musical instruments in order to raise funds for his charitable work.

Preface

This book was written to provide an update to *The Power of Music: A Research Synthesis of the Impact of Actively Making Music on the Intellectual, Social and Personal Development of Children and Young People* (2015). As the evidence was collated, it became clear that much more research had been undertaken since the original book was produced and that that research was focused on a much wider age range with particular expansion in work with older age groups. It was therefore decided to expand the book to include research across the lifespan covering a wider range of issues, particularly those relating to health and wellbeing as these have become more important in the research agenda in recent years. The title referring to an exploration of the research was selected to make it possible to take account of all kinds of research, from large-scale population studies to single case studies, correlation studies, experiments and evaluations of interventions with a focus on both listening to and actively making or creating music. Some interventions that have several different outcomes are mentioned in more than one chapter. As there has been much controversy recently as to whether music can have any impact, particularly on cognition, it was felt to be important to include examples of individual research projects for the reader to be able to draw their own conclusions about the impact of music rather than relying on a summary, although an overview is provided at the end of each chapter. This means that the book is not always an easy read. Some of the research is extremely complex and takes time to understand. It is hoped that, despite this, the reader will be enabled to make an informed decision about the power of music in a range of areas across the lifespan.

1. Introduction

The speed of change in electronic media in the latter part of the 20th century revolutionised access to and the use of music in people's lives. Music can be accessed in many ways, through radio, CDs, DVDs, TV, tablets, SMART technologies, computers and phones, and can be downloaded to enable the creation of personal playlists. This can be achieved with very little effort, but this was not always the case. Historically, people could only access music through participating in religious or other social events. These changes have made it possible for individuals to use music to manipulate their moods, arousal levels and feelings, and create environments which may change the way that other people feel and behave. Music can be used to aid relaxation, overcome powerful emotions, generate moods appropriate for carrying out routine activities, prepare for social activities or stimulate concentration. In short, music can be used to promote wellbeing. In young people, it supports the development of identity and self-presentation. Alongside this, technological advances in research techniques have increased our understanding of the way that music can benefit the intellectual, social and personal development of children and young people.

The chapters in this book explore the ways that music can benefit children and young people, as well as the wellbeing and health of the general population. This introductory section sets out what we know about the functions and origins of music; the transfer of learning; methodological issues; ways of engaging with music with varying levels of commitment; music therapy; and issues related to the interpretation of research findings.

© 2022 S. Hallam & E. Himonides, CC BY-NC-ND 4.0   https://doi.org/10.11647/OBP.0292.01

Music, Its Functions and Origins

There is evidence for engagement with music pre-homo-sapiens (Turk, 1997). A bone flute estimated to be about 50,000 years old has been found in a Neanderthal burial site and this may have been predated by singing. In China, bone flutes have been found dating back to 6000 BCE, stone flutes from 1200 BCE, and a system of classification of instruments according to the materials that they were made of from 500 BCE (Zhenxiong et al., 1995). Such evidence of the early use of instruments has been found in several cultures (Carterette and Kendall, 1999).

Despite the evidence of musical activity in early humans, there is no consensus as to whether music has evolutionary significance, although the arguments for its evolutionary role are strong. For instance, Miller (2000) has argued that music exemplifies many of the classic criteria for a complex human evolutionary adaptation, pointing out that no culture has ever been without music (universality); musical development in children is orderly; musicality is widespread, all adults can appreciate music and remember tunes; we have a specialist memory for music; specialised cortical mechanisms are involved; there are parallels in the signals of other species—for example, birds, gibbons and whales—so evolution may be convergent; and music can evoke strong emotions which implies receptive as well as productive adaptations.

Considering the possible functions of music, Huron (2003) set out the following theoretical positions:

- mate selection—music performance may have arisen as a courtship behaviour;
- social cohesion—music may create or maintain social cohesion through the promotion of group solidarity and altruism;
- group effort—music may contribute to the coordination of group work;
- perceptual development—music may contribute towards the more general development of sound perception;
- motor skill development—singing with movement and other music-making provides opportunities to refine motor skills;

- conflict reduction—music may reduce interpersonal conflict within groups through shared activities unlikely to provoke argument or dispute;
- safe time passing—music may provide a way of passing time which avoids engagement with possible dangerous situations;
- transgenerational communication—music may have originated as a useful mnemonic device for passing on information from generation to generation.

Those supporting a sexual selection theory—for example, Miller (2000)—argue that male musical performance influences female choice of mate. This might also apply to males' choice of mate and could explain why music becomes so important in adolescence. Other theories propose that music has evolved from emotional or impassioned speech, or indeed was an imitation of bird song (Cross, 2003, 2009, 2016; Huron, 2003). Some have suggested that music evolved through the mother-child relationship—in particular, soothing and comforting behaviour, which developed into lullabies. This is supported by evidence that systems for processing sound develop while the foetus is still in the womb and are fully operational for processing music at birth (Gaston, 1968; Parncutt, 2009). Dissanayake (1988) further suggests that the musicality of mother-infant interaction might lay the foundations for a grammar of the emotions.

There is considerable support for the role of music in promoting social cohesion. For instance, Sloboda (1985) speculates that music-making is rewarding because participating in it generates social bonding and cultural coherence. This is supported by the role of music in a wide range of ceremonies (Roederer, 1984). It has survival value in that synchronising the moods of many individuals can support them in collectively taking action to strengthen their means of defending themselves from attack (Dowling and Harwood, 1986). Moving together rhythmically may reinforce this process (Kogan, 1997). This approach suggests that music reinforces groupishness—the formation and maintenance of group identity—as well as collective thinking, synchronisation and catharsis (the collective expression and experience of emotion; Brown, 1991). This is supported by Weinstein and colleagues (2016), who demonstrated that small- and large-scale bonding could occur in choirs of 20 to 80 people and larger groups of over 200. These findings corroborate evolutionary accounts which emphasise the role of music in the social bonding of large groups which other primates are not able to manage.

Cross (2003), drawing on the work of Smith and Szathmary (1995) and Mithen (1996), suggests that the appearance of homo sapiens is marked by the emergence of a flexible cross-domain cognitive capacity which:

> 'is uniquely fitted to have played a significant role in facilitating the acquisition and maintenance of the skill of being a member of a culture—of interacting socially with others—as well as providing a vehicle for integrating our domain-specific competences so as to endow us with the multi-purpose and adaptive cognitive capacities which make us human' (2003: 52).

This intrinsically transposable aboutness of music (2003: 51) allows its many meanings to change from situation to situation. This may be exploited in infancy and childhood as a means of forming connections and interrelations between different domains—social, biological and mechanical. Musical activity may simultaneously be about movement, mood, emotion and mastery embodied in sound, affording the opportunity to explore cross–domain mappings.

Not all authors agree that music has evolutionary purpose. Some suggest that music, along with the other arts, has no evolutionary significance and no practical function (Barrow, 1995; Pinker, 1997; Sperber, 1996). Music is condemned as an evolutionary parasite. Pinker (1997) argues that music is bound to the domain of language, auditory scene analysis, habitat selection, emotion and motor control, and merely exploits the capacities that have evolved to subserve these areas. Music is an evolutionary by-product of the emergence of other capacities that have direct adaptive value. It exists simply because of the pleasure that it affords; its basis is purely hedonic.

In the 21st century, music has a multiplicity of functions which operate at several levels: that of the individual, the social group and society in general (Radocy and Boyle, 1988; Gregory, 1997). Merriam (1964) recognises ten major musical functions: emotional expression, aesthetic enjoyment, entertainment, communication, symbolic representation, physical response, enforcing conformity to social norms, validation of social institutions and religious rituals, contributions to the continuity and stability of culture, and contributions to the integration of society.

There is extensive evidence of the key role that music plays in the lives of individuals (Sloboda et al., 2009). Music can generate feelings of wellbeing, can facilitate working through difficult emotions, and is frequently linked to spirituality (Juslin and Sloboda, 2001). It is widely used for exploring and regulating emotions and moods (Juslin and Laukka, 2004; North et al., 2004; Saarikallio, 2011; Shifriss & Bodner, 2014) and can be effective in inducing positive affective states (North et al., 2004), achieving desirable moods (Vastfjall, 2002) and also for coping with negative moods and emotions (Miranda and Claes, 2009; Shifriss & Bodner, 2014). The most common activity for mood regulation is listening to music (Saarikallio and Erkkilä, 2007). Even adolescents who play an instrument report that the best activity for mood regulation is listening to music alone (Saarikallio, 2006). In adolescence, music makes a major contribution to the development of self-identity. It plays an important role in teenagers' lives and they spend many hours listening to it (Bonneville-Roussy et al., 2013; Bosacki and O'Neill, 2013; Greasley and Lamont, 2011). Teenagers listen to music to pass time, alleviate boredom, relieve tension and distract themselves from worries (North et al., 2000; Tarrant et al., 2000; Zillman and Gan, 1997). Music is seen as a source of support when they are feeling troubled or lonely, acting as a mood regulator and helping to maintain a sense of belonging and community (Schwartz and Fouts, 2003; Zillman and Gan, 1997). It is also used in relation to impression management needs. By engaging in social comparisons, adolescents are able to portray their own peer groups more positively than other groups in their network and are thus able to sustain positive self-evaluations. Music facilitates this process (Tarrant et al., 2000).

At the individual level, music has also been seen as a vehicle for emotional expression, conveying ideas and emotions which might be difficult to communicate in ordinary verbal interchanges. Music elicits physical responses, can aid relaxation or stimulate activity, and is particularly effective in changing moods (Thayer, 1996). Listening to music provides opportunities to experience aesthetic enjoyment and be entertained, while making music can be seen as a source of reward and intellectual stimulation, providing interesting and challenging activities at the rehearsal stage, and opportunities to demonstrate expertise and musicianship in performance which, if successful, can lead to enhanced self-esteem.

In small groups, music is a means of communication. Making music is a social activity in that creating, interpreting, performing and hearing music all depend on shared social meanings. Music can serve to provide shared experiences and understandings which assist in binding together social groups, supporting their identities. This is apparent in its use in children's games and also in adolescence, where music becomes one of the central aspects of young people's chosen youth culture. Music is also used in work contexts. It can facilitate the appropriate level of stimulation for mental or physical activity and may also serve to ensure that individuals literally work in time together. Emotional expression can also be important at the group level, for instance, in protest songs. It provides a means of expressing feelings towards subjects which are taboo or where there are inhibitions regarding the expression of emotions—for example, love, and not only romantic love but the love of God or a country, school or institution. Music fosters prosocial behaviour, a shared sense of success, physical coordination, shared attention, shared motivation and group identity (Weinstein et al., 2016). It creates and strengthens social bonds amongst interacting group members through endorphins, which are released during synchronised exertive movements in singing or playing together and are involved in social bonding across primate species (Tarr, Launay and Dunbar, 2014).

In society as a whole, music provides a means of symbolic representation for ideas and behaviours. It can represent the state, patriotism, religion, bravery, heroism or rebellion. It can encourage conformity to social norms through songs or alternatively may incite challenges to those social norms. It provides validation of social institutions and religious rituals and plays a major part in ceremonial occasions including weddings, military functions, funerals and sporting events. Music also contributes towards the continuity and stability of culture, as individuals respond in similar ways to the music of their own culture, while the social nature of musical activity invites and encourages individuals to participate in group activities, reducing social isolation.

The power of music is reflected in the way that there have been—and continue to be—attempts to exert control over it. In Nazi Germany, music was carefully selected for use at mass rallies to generate appropriate patriotic emotions. In the USSR, the music of Shostakovich was censored by the Soviet government. During the Cultural Revolution in China, Western music was denounced as decadent and forbidden. In Iran, when Ayatollah Khomeini was in power, tight restrictions were placed on particular types of music. In white-dominated South Africa, centres of African music were demolished, while musicians living in exile continued to influence the attitudes of the world against the prevailing political system through their music. In the Western world, criticism of hard rock music by the establishment and its purported effects have been well documented (Martin and Segrave, 1988). Music also reflects the values, attitudes and characteristics of a society. For instance, Weber (1958) suggests that the Western classical tradition reflects a drive to rationalise and understand the environment. Technological advances impact on the way that music-making develops, as does the extent of contact with—and influence of—other musical cultures (Nettl, 1975), and the development of musical literacy. The latter extends what can be passed onto future generations, while oral cultures restrict what can be remembered (Sloboda, 1985).

Transfer of Learning

The transfer of learning from one domain to another depends on similarities between the processes involved. Transfer between tasks is a function of the degree to which the tasks share cognitive processes. Transfer can be near or far, and is stronger and more likely to occur if it is near. Salomon and Perkins (1989) refer to low and high road transfer. Low road transfer depends on automated skills and is relatively spontaneous and automatic—for instance, in processing music and language, or using the same skills to read different pieces of music or text. High road transfer requires reflection and conscious processing—for instance, adopting similar skills in solving different kinds of problems.

Some musical skills, near and low road, are more likely to transfer than others—for instance, those relating to the perceptual processing of sound, timing, pitch, timbre and rule-governed grouping information, fine motor skills, emotional sensitivity, conceptions of relationships between written materials and sound, reading music and text, and memorisation of extended information, music and text (Norton et al., 2005; Schellenberg, 2003). Far transfer may occur in relation to the impact of making music on intelligence and attainment. High road transfer may also occur in relation to the skills acquired through learning to play a musical instrument—for instance, being able to recognise personal strengths and weaknesses, being aware of a range of possible strategies (task-related and personal) relating to motivation, concentration, monitoring progress and evaluating outcomes.

Throughout this book, the ways that transfer can occur in relation to skills developed through active engagement with music—and the ways these skills may impact on intellectual, social and personal skills—will be explored. The impact of music on wellbeing and health will also be considered, with particular reference to the impact of music on emotions. Consideration will be given to the extent to which learning to control emotions through music can support the development of more general change in behaviour.

Research exploring the impact of music on cognitive skills has a long history, going back to the 1970s. However, there was a surge of interest following the discovery of the so-called Mozart effect, where 20 minutes of listening to Mozart was claimed to enhance intelligence (Rauscher et al. 1993; 1995). This was later discredited by a range of studies (Cabanac et al., 2013; Hallam, 2001; Schellenberg and Hallam, 2005), which suggested that music could change arousal levels which, in turn, affected performance on cognitive tests. Since then, much research has been undertaken to explore whether active engagement with music can enhance cognitive ability. For reviews, see (for example) Benz et al. (2016); Bugos (2019); Hallam (2015); Holmes (in press); Jaschke et al. (2013); Miendlarzewska and Trost (2014); Moreno (2009); Rauscher (2009); and Schellenberg (2016). This research will be explored in detail later in this book.

Methodological Issues

Research exploring the ways in which active engagement with music has an impact beyond the development of musical skills has been undertaken within a number of disciplines adopting different research paradigms. The designs and methods adopted vary widely, as do the sample sizes.

Much early research considering the impact of engaging with music on other skills was based on correlation studies undertaken with professional or young musicians with varying levels of expertise. This has been criticised on the basis that showing a relationship between musical skills and other skills does not demonstrate causality. This is particularly the case with neuroscientific studies (Schellenberg, 2019). Some research has compared the performance of groups identified as musicians or non-musicians. This research has been—and continues to be—useful in highlighting possible areas of transfer. What it is unable to do is identify the direction of causality, although studies using multiple regression analyses are able to take into account possible confounding factors.

Experimental studies, where the outcomes of musical interventions are compared with those where there is no musical intervention or an alternative intervention, offer the possibility of establishing causality. Such studies vary in the length of the intervention, the range of measures adopted to measure outcomes, the age of the participants, and the nature of the activity of the control or alternative intervention group. In an ideal scientific study, participants are randomly assigned to intervention and control groups. In longitudinal research, where follow-up may be weeks or months later, it can be difficult to sustain participation and there is a high likelihood of dropout. This is reduced if participants self-select the activity that they wish to undertake, but this then constitutes a confounding factor, as those selecting a musical activity may share particular characteristics—for instance, high levels of intelligence or particular personality characteristics. The context of musical interventions and their natures are also critical in determining impact. Different outcomes might be expected in relation to whole-class general music lessons or individual instrumental lessons. The quality of the teaching and the relationships between learners and teachers are also likely to be important. The extent of variability in research design and implementation tends to produce conflicting evidence. Qualitative research, including interviews, focus groups, and ethnographic/case studies, is able to provide insights into the perceptions of participants and the contexts within which music may have a wider impact. However, it has been criticised as being too subjective. All of these methods of undertaking research have the potential to enhance our understanding of the nature of transfer of musical expertise to other domains and skills—albeit in different ways.

Systematic reviews are typically used to appraise, summarise, and communicate the results and implications of large bodies of research, such as that relating to the transfer of musical skills to other domains. They can help in overcoming bias, which may be associated with single research projects and the lack of generalisability in studies conducted with one type of population. Systematic reviews aim to rigorously identify and evaluate research, and provide objective interpretation and replicable conclusions. Systematic reviews may include a meta-analysis—a specific statistical strategy for assembling the results of several studies to provide a single estimate of the size of impact. Meta-analyses draw on existing experimental research, using complex statistical analysis to reanalyse data to assess the impact of interventions across many studies. They adopt different criteria for the studies selected for inclusion. Greater numbers of criteria which studies need to meet in order to be included lead to the exclusion of more research. Perhaps because of this, meta-analyses frequently produce conflicting outcomes. Those adopting meta-analytic approaches are very critical of research which does not adopt the strict methodological requirements of randomised controlled trials, where individuals are randomly allocated to groups. They also argue that control groups should participate in alternative interventions rather than no intervention. Meta-analyses have been severely criticised. For instance, Ansdell and DeNora (2014) argue that too much important information is lost when music is forced into before–after, yes–no grids of variables and outcome assessments.

An inclusive research strategy was adopted in accessing the literature to be included in this book. Academic databases relevant to neuroscience, psychology, education and music were searched, in addition to web-based searches to locate relevant grey literature. Analysis of located documents frequently led to further relevant material. The following chapters will synthesise the findings from a wide range of studies, to further develop our understanding of whether the skills gained through actively participating in making music can transfer to other skills and, if so, what circumstances might support this. The book also examines the evidence relating to listening and making music, and its impact on wellbeing and health. Each chapter synthesises the research findings from all of the studies, focusing on one aspect of transfer or impact, and drawing conclusions as appropriate.

Ways of Engaging with Music and Varying Levels of Commitment

People can actively make music or listen to it, although both means of engagement require listening. Listening to music or speech requires the processing of an enormous amount of information rapidly without conscious awareness (Blakemore and Frith, 2000). An idealised view of musical listening is that it is a focused activity undertaken solely for the purpose of deepening understanding and appreciation of the music. In practice, most listening takes place alongside other activities, including those relating to travel, studying and physical activity, including relaxation and taking exercise (Sloboda et al., 2009). Like these activities, listening does not necessarily preclude listening with full attention (Herbert, 2012). Listening can have benefits in terms of its impact on mood, emotions and arousal levels.

Actively making music can take many forms, from informal interactions in the home between children and parents to formal instrumental lessons. Recently, there has been greater recognition of the importance of informal learning, both for the acquisition of musical skills and creativity and for the personal and social benefits which may emerge (Hallam et al., 2016; 2017). Formal music tuition in schools may include whole-class teaching of instruments, ensemble work, or focus on singing, the theory of music, listening or the history of music. Those singing or learning to play an instrument through individual tuition may also join ensembles out of school, which increases their time commitment to music alongside any individual practice that they may undertake. Any intellectual, personal or social benefits emerging from active engagement with music will depend on the type of activity, the level of commitment of the learner and the quality of the teaching, both musically and in terms of the rapport between teachers and learners. The role of individual preferences, context and the diversity in how different people interact with music need to be taken into account when carrying out research and interpreting findings. This is frequently not the case. Many studies do not assess whether the participants have actually learned any musical skills. It is frequently assumed that participation alone will ensure that musical skills have been acquired. If they have not, then there is no reasonable prospect of transfer to other skill areas.

The level of commitment to music is another important factor in the possible impact of music in people's lives. Music constitutes a leisure activity for many people, either through listening to or making music. For some, singing or playing is a serious leisure activity, while for others it is merely recreational. Similarly, listening is (for some) a hobby to which they devote considerable time and energy, while for others it constitutes casual engagement. Those who attend live music performances tend to have a higher level of musical experience and rate music as more important in their lives than non-attenders. Attending a live music event suggests a greater level of commitment than listening to recorded music. The main reasons for attending live events include hearing a particular artist or style, learning about new music, affirming or challenging existing musical tastes, and personal and social reasons, such as engaging in social interaction and being part of a community (Pitts and Burland, 2013; Pitts and Spencer, 2008).

For some amateur musicians, music shares many characteristics with the work of professional musicians—it can be seen as an extremely serious leisure activity, while others see it merely as a hobby they engage with for personal amusement (Gates, 1991). Reported reasons for participation in active music-making include a love of music, the desire to develop skills and respond to challenges, and opportunities to meet with like-minded others. Musical activities also provide pleasure, relaxation and an opportunity for self-expression (Cooper, 2001; Taylor and Hallam, 2008). Taylor (2010) argues that amateur musicians seek affirmation, validation and verification of their musical selves as part of a community of practice in a similar manner to their professional counterparts. However, for amateurs this is less well defined and they strive to attain a group affiliation based on a cultural ideal of musical competence (Taylor, 2010). Rewarding membership of a community of practice can develop through group lessons (Wristen, 2006), where mastering new repertoire in the company of others can facilitate the enhancement of self-confidence (Coffman and Adamek, 1999; 2001).

Despite the many differences in forms and levels of engagement, music can have a considerable impact on subjective wellbeing. Wellbeing can be enhanced through listening while undertaking other tasks, or through using music to change moods and emotions. However, music does not always have positive effects. It can cause distress when it is not to the liking of a listener and is out of their control.

Music Therapy

In addition to the listening to and making of music undertaken by the population as a whole, music has been used therapeutically. The role of music in health and healing has been recognised for more than 30,000 years. It is referred to in the Bible and the historical writings of ancient civilisations in Egypt, China, India, Greece and Rome. Music therapy can provide positive psychological, physiological, cognitive and emotional benefits to patients, and has done since its development as a profession in the United States following the two world wars. Music was used to relieve the perception of pain of those with severe injuries, and medical staff noted the benefits to health and wellbeing. Since then, it has developed considerably to encompass music-making with individuals and groups, work in hospitals and planned listening to support those with mental health issues. Since the increased availability of music, individuals have been able to use music therapeutically to manage their own moods and emotions (DeNora, 2000; 2007).

Interpreting the Research Findings

There is now an extensive body of research exploring the wider benefits of music. In interpreting these findings, it is important to be judicious in suggesting what they may mean for policy and practice (Linnavalli et al., 2018). Currently it is not possible to say with any great confidence that any particular musical intervention will lead to any specific outcome—be it intellectual, personal or social—although it is clear that making music can support the development of a wide range of skills and have an impact on creativity. Making music is generally pleasurable, providing a rewarding experience and a sense of achievement for participants, although there are exceptions to this. Its frequent social context also leads to a sense of belonging and it can be engaged with throughout the lifespan. It is clearly worth continuing to try to understand the circumstances under which music is beneficial, and for whom.

2. Music and Neuroscience

Music has played an important role in neuroscience, enhancing our understanding of the brain and how it functions. The human brain contains approximately 100 billion neurons, many of which are active simultaneously as we process information. Neurons communicate with each other through nerve impulses, which allow information to be processed and analysed. Each neuron has axons and dendrites, both of which transmit nerve impulses. Axons pass nerve impulses away from the cell body, dendrites towards the cell body. Each neuron has approximately a thousand connections with other neurons. When we learn, there are changes in the growth of axons, dendrites and the number of synapses connecting neurons—a process known as 'synaptogenesis'. When an event is important enough or is repeated sufficiently often, synapses and neurons fire repeatedly, indicating that this event is worth remembering (Fields, 2005). In this way, changes in the efficacy of existing connections are made. As learning continues and particular activities are engaged with over time, myelination takes place. This involves an increase in the coating of the axon of each neuron, which improves insulation and makes the established connections more efficient. Effectively, the neurons become wired together. This enables better connections within specific brain regions, and also improves the functioning of broader neuronal pathways connecting separate brain regions, which are needed for many human activities (sensory, cognitive and motor). Pruning also occurs, a process which reduces the number of synaptic connections, enabling fine-tuning of functioning. Through combinations of these processes, which occur over different timescales, the cerebral cortex self-organises in response to external stimuli and the individual's learning activities (Pantev et al., 2003). Overall, the evidence from neuroscience suggests that each individual has a specific learning biography, which is reflected in the way the brain processes information (Altenmuller, 2003: 349).

The brain has three main parts: the cerebrum, cerebellum and brainstem. The cerebrum is the largest part of the brain; the cerebellum is located under the cerebrum, while the brain stem acts as a relay centre, connecting the cerebrum and cerebellum to the spinal cord. The cerebrum is divided into two halves: the right and left hemispheres. They are connected by the corpus callosum, which transmits messages from one side of the brain to the other. Each hemisphere controls the opposite side of the body, but not all functions of the hemispheres are shared. Generally, the left hemisphere controls speech, comprehension, and mathematical and literacy functions, while the right hemisphere controls creativity, spatial ability, artistic and musical skills. For most people, the left hemisphere is dominant for hand use and language. The brain is also separated into the frontal, temporal, occipital and parietal lobes. The frontal lobe is associated with executive functions and motor performance, while the temporal lobe is associated with the retention of short- and long-term memories and processing sensory input, including auditory information and language comprehension. The visual processing centre is the occipital lobe, while the parietal lobe is associated with sensory skills.

Music has played an important role in neuroscience, facilitating the study of neural plasticity, as training in music is complex and multimodal, and musicians and those aspiring to become musicians spend many hours practising and are committed to engagement with music over long periods of time (Pantev and Herholz, 2011). Making music draws on many brain functions, including those related to perception, action, cognition, emotion, learning and memory. It has therefore been an ideal tool to show how the human brain works and how different brain functions interact. The findings from the neuroscientific study of musicians have led to greater understanding of cortical plasticity (Barrett et al., 2013; Dalla Bella, 2016; Habib and Besson, 2009; Herholz and Zatorre, 2012; Jäncke, 2009; Merrett et al., 2013; Münte et al., 2002; Rauschecker, 2001; Strait and Kraus, 2014; Wan and Schlaug, 2010; Zatorre and McGill, 2005).

Neuroscientific Methods

Recently, technology has changed the way that neuroscience has been able to study the brain. Previously it largely relied on studying individuals suffering from damage to the brain, exploring how the damage affected particular behaviours. Common assessment techniques which are adopted now include:

Electroencephalography (EEG), which measures electrical activity generated by the synchronised activity of thousands of neurons, allowing the detection of activity within particular cortical areas, even at subsecond timescales. EEG measures event-related potential (ERP). An event-related potential (ERP) is the measured brain response that is the direct result of a specific sensory, cognitive or motor event. It is any stereotyped electrophysiological response to a stimulus. Evoked potentials and induced potentials are subtypes of ERPs. Other types of ERP include:

- Frequency-following response (FFR) is an evoked potential generated by periodic or nearly periodic auditory stimuli. As part of the auditory brainstem response, the FFR reflects sustained neural activity integrated over a population of neural elements.

- Gamma-band activity (GBA) comprises an EEG frequency range, from 30 to 200 Hz, and is distributed widely throughout cerebral structures. GBA participates in various cerebral functions, such as perception, attention, memory, consciousness, synaptic plasticity and motor control.

- Early left anterior negativity (ELAN) is an event-related potential in electroencephalography (EEG), or a component of brain activity that occurs in response to certain kinds of stimuli. It is characterised by a negative wave that peaks at around 200 milliseconds or less after the onset of a stimulus, and most often occurs in response to linguistic stimuli that violate word category or phrase structure rules.

- Early right anterior negativity (ERAN) is a potential in electroencephalography, or a component of brain activity that occurs in response to a certain kind of stimulus.

- Mismatch negativity (MMN) is an element of an event-related potential to an odd stimulus in a sequence of stimuli. It is most frequently studied in relation to auditory or visual stimuli. In the case of auditory stimuli, the MMN occurs after an infrequent change in a repetitive sequence of sounds. It is usually evoked by either a change in frequency, intensity, duration, or real or apparent spatial locus of origin.
- Magnetic resonance imaging (MRI) is a type of scan that uses strong magnetic fields and radio waves to produce detailed images of the inside of the brain.
- Voxel based morphometry (VBM) is a technique using MRI that allows investigation of focal differences in brain anatomy, using parametric mapping. The brain images are smoothed so that each voxel represents the average of itself and its surrounding areas.
- Functional magnetic resonance imaging (fMRI) is a brain-scanning technique that measures blood flow in the brain when a person performs a task. fMRI works on the premise that neurons in the brain which are the most active during a task use the most energy. A haemodynamic response allows the rapid delivery of blood to active neuronal tissues.
- Magnetoencephalography (MEG) is a functional neuroimaging technique for mapping brain activity by recording magnetic fields produced by electrical currents occurring naturally in the brain, using very sensitive magnetometers.
- Transcranial magnetic stimulation is a non-invasive procedure that uses magnetic fields to stimulate nerve cells in the brain.

Changes in the Brain following Musical Activity

As individuals engage with different musical activities over long periods of time, permanent changes occur in the brain. These changes reflect what has been learned and how it has been learned. They also influence the extent to which developed skills transfer elsewhere. Extensive active engagement with music induces cortical reorganisation, producing functional changes in how the brain processes information. If this occurs early in development, the alterations may become hardwired and produce permanent changes in the way information is processed (Schlaug et al., 1995a; 1995b). Indeed, there is evidence that Western classical musicians have increased neuronal representation specific for the processing of the tones of the musical scale (Pantev et al., 2003). The largest cortical representations are in musicians who have been playing their instruments for the longest period of time. Overall, the evidence suggests that active engagement with music has a significant impact on brain structure and function (Merrett et al., 2013; Norton et al., 2005). Playing a musical instrument also seems to speed up brain maturation. For instance, Hudziak and colleagues (2014) found more rapid cortical thickness maturation in areas implicated in motor planning and coordination, visuospatial ability, and emotion and impulse regulation following musical training.

Comparisons between Musicians' and Non-Musicians' Expertise

A long-standing strand of research has explored the differences between the brains of musicians and non-musicians and those with different levels of musical expertise. The first (now seminal) studies provided evidence of larger auditory and somatosensory cortical areas in adult musicians compared with non-musicians (Pantev et al., 1998; Elbert et al., 1995). Recent criticism of this approach has drawn attention to the lack of clarity in classifying musicians and non-musicians. Musicians vary widely in their areas of expertise and the levels that they achieve, while so-called non-musicians may be very experienced listeners. Despite these issues, this strand of research has enhanced our understanding of the differences which emerge in the brain related to musical training, starting in childhood or adulthood through to professional levels of expertise (Herholz and Zatorre, 2012; Huotilainen and Tervaniemi, 2018; Munte et al., 2002; Tervaniemi, 2009).

Certain pieces of research exploring the differences between musicians and non-musicians, or the functional changes due to musical training, have highlighted the differences in very basic cortical and subcortical processing—for instance, the response latencies and amplitudes of responses to random, musical or language sounds. Musicians demonstrate higher fidelity of brain stem responses in conveying temporal and frequency information present in the sounds that they are exposed to (Wong et al., 2007). This fidelity increases quickly over a period of a year when children are actively engaged in making music (Skoe and Kraus, 2013).

The differences between musicians and non-musicians are in evidence at different levels of the auditory pathway, from the brainstem (Kraus and Chandrasekaran, 2010; Strait and Kraus, 2014) through to the primary auditory regions (Bermudez et al., 2009; Gaser and Schlaug, 2003) and subsequently to higher levels of auditory processing. Low-level neural enhancements are likely to have a considerable impact on higher-level processing because the ability of the cochlea and the brain stem to replicate the content of a sound, and to deliver it accurately to higher-level cortical processes, forms the basis of all sound processing. This, in turn, leads to better performance in listening to speech embedded in noise or hearing masked sounds (Strait et al., 2010; Strait and Kraus, 2011a; 2011b; Slater et al., 2015). Overall, trained musicians have greater volume and cortical thickness in the auditory cortex regions, which are most likely to be responsible for fine pitch categorisation, discrimination and temporal processing. There are structural differences at the level of the primary auditory cortex and auditory association areas (Schlaug, 2009). For example, Gaab and Schlaug (2003) compared brain activation patterns between musicians and non-musicians while they performed a pitch memory task. Both groups showed bilateral activation of the superior temporal, supramarginal, posterior middle and inferior frontal gyrus, and superior parietal lobe. However, the musicians showed more right temporal and supramarginal gyrus activation, while the non-musicians had more right primary and left secondary auditory cortex activation. Since the performance of both groups was matched, these results suggest that the processing differences are related to musical training. Non-musicians may rely more on brain regions important for pitch discrimination, while musicians may prefer to use brain regions specialising in short-term memory and recall to approach pitch memory tasks.

Schneider and colleagues (2002) used magnetoencephalography to compare the processing of pure tones in the auditory cortex of 12 non-musicians, 12 professional musicians and 13 amateur musicians. They found neurophysiological and anatomical differences between the groups. The activity evoked in the primary auditory cortex after stimulus onset in the professional musicians was 102% larger than in the non-musicians, and the grey-matter volume of the anteromedial portion of Heschl's gyrus was 130% larger.

Koelsch and colleagues (2002) compared event-related brain potentials in response to harmonically inappropriate chords in musical experts and novices. Such chords elicited an early right anterior negativity (ERAN), which was larger for musical experts than for novices, probably because the experts had more specific musical expectancies than the novices. When chords were presented with a deviant timbre, they elicited a mismatch negativity. This did not differ across the groups, indicating that the larger ERAN in the expert musicians was not due to a general enhanced auditory sensitivity, but to specific changes in the brain related to the processing of harmony, learned through experience with music.

Also focusing on aural processing, Shahin and colleagues (2003) investigated whether the neuroplastic components of auditory evoked potentials were enhanced in musicians in relation to their musical training histories. Highly skilled violinists and pianists and non-musicians listened to violin tones, piano tones and pure tones, the latter of which was matched in fundamental frequency to the musical tones. Compared with non-musicians, both musician groups evidenced larger responses to the three types of tonal stimuli. These results suggest that the tuning properties of neurons are modified in the auditory cortex in relation to the extent of acoustic musical training.

Similarly, Tervaniemi and colleagues (2006) compared the neural and behavioural sound encoding of non-musicians and amateur band musicians. They explored auditory event-related potentials to changes in basic acoustic features, frequency, duration, location, intensity, gap and abstract features, melodic contour and interval size. There were statistically significant differences in response to location changes but not to other feature changes. This suggests that, when compared with non-musicians, even amateur musicians have neural sound processing advantages if the acoustic information is relevant to their musical genre.

Non-musicians seem to need more neuronal resources for processing auditory information, relative to musicians. This is evidenced by stronger activation of primary auditory regions. For instance, Besson, Faïta and Requin (1994) presented musicians and non-musicians with short musical phrases that were either selected from the classical musical repertoire or composed for the experiment. The phrases terminated either in a congruous or harmonically, melodically or rhythmically incongruous note. The brain waves produced by these endnotes differed greatly between musicians and non-musicians, and also as a function of the participant's familiarity with the melodies and the type of incongruity. The findings additionally showed that the musicians were faster than the non-musicians in detecting the incongruities.

Functional magnetic resonance imaging scans (fMRI scans) have been used to study grey and white matter in the brain. Grey matter contains most of the brain's neuronal cell bodies and includes regions of the brain involving muscle control and sensory perception—for instance, sight, hearing, memory, emotions, speech, decision-making and self-control. Structural differences in the grey matter of several cortical areas, including the motor, somatosensory and auditory areas, have been observed between musicians and non-musicians. Luders, Gaser, Jancke and Schlaug (2004), using a voxel-by-voxel morphometric technique, found grey-matter volume differences in motor, auditory and visual-spatial brain regions when comparing professional keyboard players with a matched group of amateur musicians and non-musicians. These differences are related to cortical folding, indicating a greater cortical surface or longer distances between the cortical areas of, for example, fingers. This suggests that a larger patch of cortical surface is reserved for finger control in musicians than in non-musicians.

Similarly, Groussard and colleagues (2014) compared the brains of non-musicians and amateur musicians, the latter playing an instrument for up to 26 years. Musical training led to greater grey-matter volume in different brain areas in the musicians. The changes appeared gradually in the left hippocampus and right middle and superior frontal regions, but later included the right insula, supplementary motor area, left superior temporal and posterior cingulate area. Together, these regions are implicated in many functions including verbal memories, bodily awareness, emotional experiences, control of movement, language, memory and impulse control. To ensure that the findings were linked with musical training and not normal brain maturation, the researchers controlled for age and educational level.

There are indications that musicians exhibit increased grey-matter volume in the inferior frontal gyrus when compared to non-musicians (Sluming et al., 2002). Voxel-based morphometry and stereological analyses were applied to high-resolution three-dimensional magnetic resonance images in 26 male orchestral musicians and 26 non-musicians who were matched for sex, handedness and intelligence. The wide age range of the participants, from 26 to 66, enabled the researchers to undertake a secondary analysis of age-related effects. The findings revealed increased grey matter in Broca's area in the left inferior frontal gyrus in the musicians. Overall, there was a significant age-related volume reduction for only the non-musicians in the cerebral hemispheres and dorsolateral prefrontal cortex subfields bilaterally, as well as in the grey-matter density in the left inferior frontal gyrus. There was a positive relationship between years of playing and the volume of grey matter in musicians who were under 50 years old. The authors suggested that orchestral musical performance promoted user-dependent retention, and possibly the expansion of grey matter involving Broca's area.

Similarly, James and colleagues (2014) used optimised voxel-based morphometry to perform grey-matter density analyses on 59 age-, sex- and intelligence-matched young adults with three distinct, progressive levels of musical training intensity or expertise. The findings showed a functional difference between areas exhibiting increase versus decrease of grey matter as a function of musical expertise. Grey-matter density increased with expertise in areas known for their involvement in higher order cognitive processing, such as those concerned with executive function, working memory and auditory processing. In contrast, grey-matter density decreased with expertise in areas related to sensorimotor function. This decrease may have reflected high levels of automatisation of motor skills in those with greater expertise. A multiple regression analysis showed that grey-matter density predicted accuracy in detecting fine-grained incongruities in tonal music.

Changes in white matter have also been observed in the brains of musicians. White matter is composed of the nerve fibres, axons, which connect nerve cells and which are covered by myelin, an insulating layer that forms around nerves, consisting of protein and fatty substances. It is this which gives the white matter its colour. Myelin speeds up the communication between cells. Musicians have greater anisotropy, a phenomenon varying in magnitude according to the direction of measurement, which suggests that they either have a larger number of fibres or greater myelination or both. Such findings have been observed in corticocortical connections, where neurons in one cortical area communicate with neurons in other cortical areas, but also in corticomuscular connections, where neurons communicate with muscles (Bengtsson, Nagy and Skare et al., 2005). Some research has shown that musicians have greater amounts of substances in their brains related to neuronal metabolism. The brain relies almost entirely on circulating glucose rather than storing energy as glycogen. The majority of this glucose is used to maintain synaptic function and the resting potential of neurons. When there is an increase in these substances, it suggests more active use of, for example, auditory cortical areas (Aydin et al., 2005).

Musicians have a larger corpus callosum than non-musicians (Schlaug et al., 1995a). This phenomenon is particularly evident in male musicians (Lee et al., 2003). Greater midsagittal size of the corpus callosum has also been found (Lee et al., 2003; Oztürk et al., 2002; Schlaug et al., 1995). Musicians have more and/or thicker neuronal tracts between the left and right motor and somatosensory areas. These structural differences may relate to a range of functional differences between musicians and non-musicians (Fauvel et al., 2014). The amount of musical practice is also associated with greater integrity of the corticospinal pathway (Bengtsson et al., 2005).

Individuals with absolute pitch—the ability to categorise tones into pitch classes without reference to other sounds—have been the focus of some pieces of research. For instance, Loui and colleagues (2012) showed that those possessing absolute pitch had increased functional activation during music listening, as well as increased degrees, clustering and local efficiency of functional correlations, with the difference being highest around the left superior temporal gyrus. Similarly, Loui and colleagues (2011) observed hyperconnectivity in bilateral superior temporal lobe structures linked to having absolute pitch. Furthermore, the volume of tracts connecting the left superior temporal gyrus to the left middle temporal gyrus predicted absolute pitch performance. Using *in vivo* magnetic resonance morphometry, Schlaug and colleagues (1995a) measured the anatomical asymmetry of the planum temporale. Musicians with absolute pitch revealed stronger leftward planum temporale asymmetry than non-musicians or musicians without absolute pitch. These results indicate that having absolute pitch is associated with increased leftward asymmetry of the cortex subserving music-related functions. Similarly, Bermudez and colleagues (2009) used multiple methods to compare 71 musicians, 27 with absolute pitch, with 64 non-musicians. They found functional evidence which indicated the importance of a frontotemporal network of areas, which were heavily relied upon in the performance of musical tasks. There was a difference between the musicians and those with absolute pitch in that there was a significantly thinner cortex in a number of areas—including the posterior dorsal frontal cortices—that have been previously implicated in the performance of tasks involving absolute pitch.

The Automation of Skills as Expertise Increases

As musicians' expertise develops, many of their skills become automated. This means that neurological differences between musicians and non-musicians become harder to interpret, since some tasks reveal less neural activity in musicians because of their automatisation (Jancke et al., 2000), while others show more brain activity (Kleber et al., 2010; Nikjeh et al., 2008; 2009). Simple motor tasks tend to become automated while complex tasks, even those related to auditory processing, may require more neurological resources (Gaab and Schlaug, 2003).

In a review, Zatorre and colleagues (2012) pointed out that, while brain imaging had identified structural changes in grey and white matter that occurred with learning, ascribing imaging measures to underlying cellular and molecular events was challenging. Perceptual or motor systems with extended representation in the brain as a result of musical training may process information more efficiently, using fewer neuronal resources, than less specialised systems. Enhanced efficiency might be manifest in lower blood flow demands in skilled musicians as compared to non-musicians when performing complex motor sequences. Functional neuroimaging studies do not always present findings consistent with observed anatomical differences. Musicians can exhibit either lower or more localised activation in the primary motor cortex than non-musicians, and more variable levels of activation in motor association regions (such as the premotor and supplementary motor areas). Such inconsistencies may reflect higher order cognitive processes—for example, tonal processing, working memory and syntax—that are required for performance. This may lead to increased density in associated brain regions. Other processes (for instance, sensorimotor functions and basic motor control) are likely to be automated, requiring fewer resources and less brain volume (James et al., 2014). This may also explain inconsistencies between visible structural changes and increased or decreased activation in musicians in primary auditory and motor regions. Using event-related potentials, Trainor and colleagues (1999) compared the responses of adult musicians and non-musicians to infrequent changes to the last note of a five-note melody, which either altered the contour or the interval. The findings suggested that contour processing was more basic, while interval processing was more affected by experience. This, again, indicates that it is not always obvious whether training is associated with increased or decreased activation in underlying brain regions.

Bimanual Motor Coordination

Pianists have provided a particular focus for research exploring bimanual motor coordination. Automatisation of these processes means that training is not systematically associated with increased brain volume. For example, a decrease in striatal volume is observed in skilled pianists as a function of greater efficiency in motor performance (Granert et al., 2011). Haslinger and colleagues (2004) compared professional pianists with musically naïve participants as they carried out in-phase, *mirror* and anti-phase, *parallel* bimanual sequential finger movements during functional magnetic resonance imaging. The tasks included the performance of two different kinds of externally paced bimanual finger tapping, involving the index to little finger of both hands. In one condition, participants had to carry out parallel finger movements starting either with the index finger of the right and the little finger of the left hand, or vice versa. The task then consisted of continuous, bidirectional finger movements sequentially involving the index, middle, ring and little finger of one hand versus little, ring, middle and index finger of the other hand. The second task demanded the performance of mirror-like finger tapping. The corresponding fingers of both hands, index–index, middle–middle, ring–ring, little–little always had to be moved simultaneously in bidirectional, sequential order. A resting condition without finger movements served as a control. These tasks correspond to bimanually playing scales, which constitutes part of pianists' regular practice routines. Musicians and non-musicians showed significantly different functional activation patterns, suggesting increased efficiency of cortical and subcortical systems for bimanual movement control. This may be fundamental to achieving high-level motor skills, allowing the musician to focus on the artistic aspects of musical performance.

Similarly, Krings and colleagues (2000) performed functional magnetic resonance imaging with professional piano players and non-musicians during an overtrained complex finger movement task, using a blood oxygenation level dependent echo-planar gradient echo sequence. Participants performed a complex finger opposition paradigm using the right hand, with self-paced light touches of a thumb pad to a finger pad without looking at the hand. The order of tapping was 5-4-3-5-4-2-5-3-2-4-3-2, omitting one subsequent finger in each run. The pattern was repeated. During rest periods, participants were asked to relax. The task was practised before the scanning session to avoid learning effects during the scan. Activation clusters were seen in the primary motor cortex, supplementary motor area, premotor cortex and superior parietal lobule. There were significant differences in the extent of cerebral activation between the groups, with pianists having a smaller number of activated voxels. This suggested that long-term motor practice led to a different cortical activation pattern in pianists. They needed to recruit fewer neurons to complete the same movements.

Using self-paced bimanual and unimanual tapping tasks which reflect typical movements made in playing the piano, Jäncke and colleagues (2000) measured haemodynamic responses, applying functional magnetic resonance imaging in two professional piano players and two carefully matched non-musician participants. The primary and secondary motor areas were activated to a much lesser degree in professional pianists than in non-musicians, suggesting that the long-lasting extensive hand-skill training of the pianists led to greater efficiency. This was reflected in the smaller number of active neurons needed to perform given finger movements. Similarly, Meister and colleagues (2005) compared pianists and non-musicians as they performed simple and complex movement sequences on a keyboard with the right hand. In non-musicians, complex motor sequences showed higher fMRI activations of the presupplementary motor area and the rostral part of the dorsal premotor cortex compared to simple motor sequences, whereas the musicians showed no differential activations. This suggested that a higher level of visuomotor integration was required in a complex task in non-musicians, whereas the musicians employed the rostral premotor network during both tasks. Neural plasticity, as a result of long-term practice, mainly occurs in caudal motor areas, but the slowly evolving changes during motor-skill learning may extend to adjacent areas, leading to more effective motor representations in pianists.

Also focusing on a complex right-handed finger tapping task, Hund-Georgiadis and von Cramon (1999) investigated blood-flow-related magnetic resonance signal changes and the time course underlying short-term motor learning in ten piano players and 23 non-musicians. A functional learning profile, based on regional blood oxygenation level, was assessed. All participants achieved significant increases in tapping frequency during the 35-minute training session while in the scanner, but the pianists performed significantly better than the non-musicians and showed increasing activation in the contralateral primary motor cortex throughout motor learning. Concurrently, involvement of secondary motor areas—such as the bilateral supplementary motor, premotor and cerebellar areas—diminished relative to the non-musicians throughout the training session. Extended activation of primary and secondary motor areas in the initial training stage during the first seven to 14 minutes, as well as rapid attenuation, were the main functional patterns underlying short-term learning in the non-musician group. Attenuation was particularly marked in the primary motor cortices as compared with the pianists. When the tapping sequence was performed with the left hand, transfer effects of motor learning were evident in both groups.

Involvement of all relevant motor components was smaller than after initial training with the right hand. This suggests that the involvement of primary and secondary motor cortices in motor learning is dependent on experience.

Using similarly complex unimanual and bimanual finger tasks, Koeneke and colleagues (2004) studied cerebellar hemodynamic responses in highly skilled keyboard players and non-musician participants. Both groups showed strong haemodynamic responses in the cerebellum during task conditions. However, non-musicians showed generally stronger haemodynamic responses in the cerebellum than the keyboard players, suggesting that long-term motor practice leads to different cortical activation patterns. The same movements required less neuronal activity. Palomar-García and colleagues (2017) found reduced connectivity between the motor areas that control both hands in musicians compared with non-musicians. This was particularly evident in those whose instruments required bimanual coordination. The effects were mediated by the number of hours of practice.

Multisensory Learning

Structural differences in the brains of musicians and non-musicians extend beyond the auditory pathway and motor circuitries to the parietal regions. These regions seem to be involved in multisensory encoding and integration. Music performance is one of the most complex and demanding cognitive challenges that human beings undertake. It requires precise timing of a number of hierarchically organised actions, as well as precise control over pitch interval production, implemented variably depending on the instrument involved (Zatorre et al., 2007). Structural differences due to musical training extend to motor and sensorimotor cortices, to premotor and supplementary motor regions, and involve subcortical structures such as the basal ganglia and the cerebellum. This neuronal circuitry is engaged in motor control and fine motor planning—for example, finger movement—during musical engagement, as well as in motor learning (Schmidt and Lee, 2011). Musicians have stronger connectivity between the right auditory cortex and the right ventral premotor cortex than non-musicians. The longer the period of time playing an instrument, the stronger the connection

(Palomar-Garcia et al., 2017). Lahav and colleagues (2007) used functional magnetic resonance imaging to explore whether the human action-recognition system responded to sounds found in a complex sequence of newly acquired actions. They chose a piece of music as a model set of acoustically presentable actions and trained non-musicians to play it by ear. They then monitored brain activity in participants while they listened to the newly learned piece. Although they listened to the music without making any movements, activation was found bilaterally in the frontoparietal motor-related network, consistent with neural circuits which have been associated with action observations and may constitute a human mirror neuron system. Presentation of the practised notes in a different order activated the network to a much lesser degree, whereas listening to equally familiar but motorically unknown music did not activate this network. These findings suggest that there is a hearing–doing system that is highly dependent on the individual's motor repertoire and that this network is established rapidly, with Broca's area as its hub.

Neurological Differences Relating to Genre and the Instrument Played

Neural changes are specific to the particular musical activities undertaken (Munte et al., 2003). Functional auditory responses are strongest in the areas reflecting each musician's instrument, demonstrating timbral specificity related to their training (Pantev et al., 2001). The processing of pitch in classical string players, who have to create different pitches with no guidance from frets, is characterised by longer surveillance and more frontally distributed event-related brain potentials attention. Drummers whose focus is rhythm generate more complex memory traces of the temporal organisation of musical sequences, while conductors demonstrate greater surveillance of auditory space as they listen to and balance the sounds of the various instruments in the ensemble that they are conducting (Munte et al., 2003).

Compared with non-musicians, string players have greater somatosensory representations of finger activity, the amount of increase depending on the age of starting to play (Pantev et al., 2003). Pianists, violinists and non-musicians are differentiated by the particular form and shape of the motor cortex, violinists and pianists both needing to be able to move their fingers quickly (Bangert and Schlaug, 2006), while trumpet players have greater functional activation in the cerebellum (which coordinates voluntary movements), the dominant sensorimotor cortex and the left auditory cortex (Gebel et al., 2013). This may be because trumpet players need to be sensitive to the relationship between their embouchure and minute sequential differences in sound. In relation to players of wind instruments, Choi and colleagues (2015) found significant changes in cortical thickness in lip-tongue related areas and resting-state neuronal networks, and differential activation in the precentral gyrus and supplementary motor areas in comparison with non-musicians.

The functional reorganisation of the motor cortex reflects differential usage between instrumentalists. When comparing the regions containing the hand representations of pianists and violinists, large anatomical differences in the precentral gyrus have been revealed (Bangert and Schlaug, 2006). String players require highly developed fine motor skills, particularly in the left hand, while keyboard players require highly trained fine motor skills in both hands, but particularly the right hand, which frequently supports melody and has more challenging technical passages than the left-hand accompaniment. Most keyboard performers exhibit a configuration known as the 'Omega sign' in the left more than the right hemisphere, whilst most string players show this only on the right. The prominence of this sign is related to the age at which musicians began to play an instrument and the cumulative amount of time they spent practising. Greater cortical representations of fingers in violinists' left hands, as compared with right hands, have been found using magnetoencephalography (Elbert et al., 1995).

Instrument-specific neuroplasticity extends to perception. Timbre-specific neuronal responses are observable in different groups of instrumentalists. For example, string and trumpet players reveal stronger evoked cortical responses when presented with the sound of their respective instrument (Pantev et al., 2001). This is particularly evident in the right auditory cortex (Shahin et al., 2003). Musicians also display increased gamma-band activity induced by the sound of their own instrument as compared to other instruments (Shahin et al., 2008). These findings are supported by functional imaging evidence from violinists and flautists (Margulis et al., 2009), which suggests that instrument-specific plasticity is not restricted to the primary auditory cortex but forms a network including association and auditory-motor integration areas. Such experience-specific plasticity has been shown at the level of the brainstem (Strait et al., 2012).

Some research has explored whether the style or genre of music might shape auditory processing. Tervaniemi and colleagues (2016) studied the auditory profiles of classical, jazz and rock musicians, with particular reference to genre-specific sensitivity to musical sound features. The participants watched a silent video and were instructed to ignore the sounds. The researchers recorded the accuracy of neural encoding of the melody. All groups showed a cortical index of deviance discrimination, but the strength of the responses varied. Automatic brain responses were selectively enhanced to deviance in tuning in classical musicians, timing in classical and jazz musicians, transposition in jazz musicians, and melody contour in jazz and rock musicians. The jazz players had larger mismatch negativity (MMN) amplitude than all other experimental groups across the six different sound examples, indicating a greater overall sensitivity to auditory outliers. Enhanced processing of pitch and the sliding up to pitches were only found in jazz musicians. A more frontal MMN to pitch and location (compared to the other deviations) was observed in jazz musicians, and left lateralization of the MMN to timbre in classical musicians. Overall, the characteristics of the particular styles or genres of music learned influence a musician's perceptual skills and the brain's processing of them.

Training, listening experiences, musical styles and genre all shape musicians' brains (Vuust et al., 2012). Folk musicians exhibit early right anterior negativity in inferofrontal brain regions in response to chords which deviate from the conventions of Western music, indicating differences in their expertise compared with non-musicians (Brattico et al., 2013). Musical expertise in more than one music culture can modify chord processing by enhancing responses to ambivalent or incongruous chords.

Focusing on communication between musicians, Vuust and colleagues (2005) explored how jazz musicians exchanged non-verbal cues when they played together. The musicians received and interpreted cues when performance departed from a regular pattern of rhythm, suggesting that they enjoyed a highly developed sensitivity to subtle rhythmic deviations. Pre-attentive brain responses—recorded with magnetoencephalography to rhythmic incongruence—were left-lateralized in expert jazz musicians and right-lateralized in non-musicians, suggesting functional adaptation of the brain to a task of communication, similar to that required for learning language.

Studies with Child Musicians and Non-Musicians

There has been considerable research focusing on the structural and functional changes which occur in children's brains as a result of engagement with music. Enhancement of brain responses to musical sounds can occur early in development. Four-month-old infants exposed to melodies played on either guitar or marimba for just over two hours over the course of a week exhibited MMN selectively to the sound to which they had been exposed (Trainor et al., 2011). The effects of musical training during development extended to brainstem responses when processing speech in noise (Strait et al., 2013). Trainor and colleagues (2012) studied six-month-old Western infants, who were randomly assigned to six months of either an active participatory music class or a class in which they experienced music passively while playing. Active music participation resulted in earlier enculturation to Western tonal pitch structure, larger and/or earlier brain responses to musical tones, and a more positive social trajectory. Neural-level changes also occur in children participating in musical playschool activities designed to develop a love for music through active engagement with making music, singing and musical instruments. Putkinen and colleagues (2013) explored the relationship between informal musical activities at home and electrophysiological indices of neural auditory change detection in two- to three-year-old children. Auditory event-related potentials were recorded in a multi-feature paradigm that included frequency, duration, intensity, direction, gap deviants and attention-catching novel sounds. Correlations were calculated between these responses and the amount of musical activity at home reported by the parents. The neurological findings implied that there was heightened sensitivity to temporal acoustic changes, more mature auditory change detection and less distractibility in children when there were more informal musical activities in their home environment.

One strand of research has focused on the effects of training with the Suzuki method, where children learn to play by ear and through imitation. The method is implemented rigorously wherever it is adopted, which makes it easier to make comparisons between studies. One study with four- to six-year-old children revealed changes in auditory evoked responses to a violin and a noise stimulus. The musically trained group showed faster responses to violin sounds than the non-musician group (Fujioka et al., 2006). These changes were accompanied by enhanced performance on a musical task and improved working memory in a non-musical task. Another study adopting the Suzuki method tracked and recorded brainwave patterns. The research included adult professional violinists, amateur pianists and four- and five-year-old children studying the piano. Measures were taken before the children commenced music lessons and one year later. The adult musicians showed robust enhancement of induced gamma-band activity specific to their musical instrument, with the strongest effects in the professional violinists. Induced gamma-band responses are associated with attention, expectation, memory retrieval and the integration of top-down, bottom-up and multisensory processes. The children receiving piano lessons exhibited increased power of induced gamma-band activity for piano tones with one year of training, while children not taking lessons showed no effect (Shahin et al., 2004; 2008).

In a similar study, Trainor and colleagues (2009) found larger induced gamma-band responses in five-year-old children learning to play instruments. Responses to musical sounds were larger in adult musicians than in non-musicians, and developed in children after one year of musical training (but not in children of the same age who were not engaged in music lessons). Trainor and colleagues concluded that musical training affected oscillatory networks in the brain which are associated with executive functions, which in turn can enhance learning and performance in several cognitive domains.

Standard musical training has been linked to greater mismatch negativity responses to melodic and rhythmic modulations in children between 11 and 13 years of age who have received musical training (Putkinen et al., 2014), while structural changes in the brain have been found in relation to reading musical notation. Bergman and colleagues (2014) undertook a longitudinal study with 352 children and young people between the ages of six and 25, carrying out neuroimaging investigations with 64 participants on two or three occasions, two years apart. Those playing an instrument had larger grey-matter volume in the temporo-occipital and insular cortex areas, previously reported to be related to reading musical notation.

Structural differences in grey and white matter have also been found in children who engage in music, particularly during early childhood, compared with those who do not (Groussard et al., 2014; Habibi et al., 2018; Huotilainen and Tervaniemi, 2018; Pantev and Herholz, 2011). Schlaug and colleagues (2009) found that after just over two years of musical training, five- to seven-year-old children who were committed to music practice showed increased size of the anterior part of the corpus callosum. Similarly, Hudziak and colleagues (2014) assessed the extent to which playing a musical instrument was associated with cortical thickness development among healthy children and young people. Over a two-year period, 232 young people aged six to 18 underwent MRI scanning and behavioural testing. While there was no association between cortical thickness and years playing a musical instrument, a later follow-up showed that music training was associated with an increased rate of cortical thickness maturation in areas implicated in motor planning and coordination. Similarly, Habibi and colleagues (2018) investigated the effects of music training on children's brains, comparing children engaged with musical training and others involved in either sport or no regular after-school activity. Two years after training, the children in the music group showed brain changes related to enhanced auditory processing skills.

A different approach was adopted by Hyde and colleagues (2009). They tested two groups of children who had no prior formal musical training. The instrumental group consisted of 15 children aged six years old who had weekly half-hour private keyboard lessons and who continued lessons for 15 months. The comparison group consisted of 16 children who were almost six years old, who did not receive any instrumental music training but participated in a weekly 40-minute group music class in school consisting of singing and playing with drums and bells. The children underwent a magnetic resonance imaging (MRI) scan twice, at the beginning of the research and again 15 months later. The second scan showed that the children learning to play instruments had areas of greater relative voxel size, within the motor areas, the corpus callosum and the right primary auditory region (in contrast to the comparison group). Overall, the study demonstrated regional structural brain plasticity in the developing brain that occurred with only 15 months of instrumental musical training in early childhood. The study demonstrated that the type of musical training is important in the transfer of musical skills (Hyde et al., 2009).

In a cross-sectional study, Ellis and colleagues (2012) explored the impact of age-related maturation and training using functional magnetic resonance imaging (fMRI) and linear regression techniques. The participants, aged five to 33, had a range of hours of musical practice from none to 21,000. Age-related effects common to melodic and rhythmic discrimination were present in three left hemisphere regions: the temporofrontal junction, the ventral premotor cortex, and the inferior part of the intraparietal sulcus—regions involved in actively attending to auditory rhythms, sensorimotor integration, and working memory transformations of pitch and rhythmic patterns. In contrast, training-related effects were localised to the posterior portion of the left superior temporal gyrus/planum temporale, an area implicated in spectrotemporal pattern-matching and auditory–motor coordinating transformations. A single cluster in the right superior temporal gyrus showed significantly greater activation during melodic as opposed to rhythmic discrimination. In a second study (Ellis et al., 2013) using the same sample, an fMRI study explored how relative hemispheric asymmetries in music processing, making *same or different* discriminations, were shaped by musical training as assessed by cumulative hours of instrumental practice. A peak in the supramarginal gyrus was characterised by a leftward asymmetry in partial correlation with participants' cumulative hours of practice, controlling for age and task performance. The findings suggested a direct link between the amount of time spent practising an instrument and the importance of this region in auditory working memory.

Starting musical training before seven years of age seems to have a particularly strong effect in stimulating brain changes (Barrett et al., 2013; Penhune, 2011; Zatorre, 2013). Structural differences in the corpus callosum between musicians and non-musicians—and the extent of hand representations in the motor cortex—are greater for musicians who begin training before seven years of age (Amunts et al., 1997; Elbert et al., 1995; Schlaug et al., 1995a; 1995b). Early training is also associated with greater auditory cortex and brain-stem responses to tones (Pantev et al., 1998; Wong et al., 2007). This is confirmed even when the amount of training is controlled for (Bailey and Penhune, 2010; Watanabe et al., 2007). Musicians who begin their training when they are very young display better sensorimotor synchronisation skills when compared with those starting at ages older than seven. This difference is underpinned by brain connectivity in terms of white matter and structural differences in terms of grey matter (Bailey and Penhune, 2012; Bailey et al., 2014; Steele et al., 2013).

Genetic and Maturational Effects versus Training Effects

Overall, cross-sectional studies suggest that there are structural and functional differences in the brains of musicians and non-musicians, and that engagement with music leads to behavioural changes which are underpinned by changes in the primary and secondary auditory and motor cortices, as well as in sensorimotor and multimodal integration areas. The age of starting engagement with music and the intensity or duration of that engagement may account for the extent of brain differences, suggesting that there may be a causal link between musical training and changes in the brain. However, the observed differences could be caused by existing predispositions or genetic factors. At the extreme end, these include those with difficulties in processing sound (for instance, those who are tone deaf or suffer from congenital amusia);Dalla Bella et al., 2011; Kirnarskaya, 2009; Peretz and Hyde, 2003; Williamson and Stewart, 2013) and at the other extreme those who exhibit exceptional skills—for instance, prodigies or musical savants (McPherson and Lehmann, 2018; Simonton, 2017). Individual anatomical and functional properties of the brain, or genetic predispositions for learning, might impact on the learning of musical skills (Zatorre, 2013). These might explain discrepant findings in neuroplasticity and have implications for research, which needs to take account of individual differences (Foster and Zatorre, 2010; Golestani et al., 2011; Merrett et al., 2013). There are also issues relating to maturational effects which are not always addressed, although there are exceptions to this (Ellis et al., 2012; 2013).

To summarise, studies which compare the brains of musicians and non-musicians can show neurological differences structurally and functionally between the two groups. The age at which musical engagement begins and its intensity or duration can account for some differences, but cannot demonstrate a causal link. Differences might be accounted for by genetic factors or predispositions. Longitudinal or short-term intervention studies can address these issues.

Intervention Studies

Short-term intervention studies can demonstrate causality. For instance, Chen and colleagues (2012) used fMRI to investigate the formation of auditory-motor associations while participants with no previous musical training learned to play a melody. Listening to melodies before and after training activated the superior temporal gyrus bilaterally, but neural activity in this region was significantly reduced on the right when participants listened to the trained melody. Learning to play a melody involves acquiring conditional associations between key presses and their corresponding musical pitches, and is related to activity in the dorsal premotor area of the superior frontal gyrus. When playing melodies and random sequences, activity in the left dorsal premotor cortex was reduced in the latter compared to the early phase of training. Learning to play the melody was also associated with reduced neural activity in the left ventral premotor cortex. Participants with the highest performance scores for learning the melody showed more reduced neural activity in the left dorsal premotor area and the ventral premotor cortex. Overall, these findings demonstrated that auditory-motor learning is related to a reduction in neural activity in the brain regions of the dorsal auditory action stream, which suggests increased efficiency in the neural processing of a learned stimulus.

There is evidence that the brain responds relatively quickly to new activities. Measuring event-related potentials (ERPs), Bangert and colleagues (2001) found that audio-motor coupling occurred following a 20-minute piano lesson. In another study, eight-year-old children with just eight weeks of musical training differed from controls in cortical ERPs (Moreno and Besson, 2006), while music training for 25 minutes over a seven-week period led to changes in electroencephalogram (EEG) frequencies associated with enhanced cognitive processing (Flohr et al., 2000).

Transcranial magnetic stimulation (TMS) has also revealed changes in hand cortical representation resulting from short-term training of novel fine motor skills (Pascual-Leone et al., 1995). Cortical motor areas were tracked targeting the contralateral long finger flexor and extensor muscles in participants learning a one-handed, five-finger exercise on the piano. In a second experiment, the researchers studied the different effects of mental and physical practice of the same five-finger exercise on the modulation of the cortical motor areas, targeting the muscles involved in the task. Over the course of five days, as participants learned the one-handed exercise in two-hour daily practice sessions, the cortical motor areas targeting the long finger flexor and extensor muscles enlarged, and their activation threshold decreased. Such changes were limited to the cortical representation of the hand used in the exercise. The research also studied the effect of increased hand use, without the requirement to learn the five-finger exercise, in participants who played the piano for two hours each day using only the right hand. In these participants, the changes in cortical motor outputs were similar but significantly less prominent than for those who learned the new skill.

Similarly, Lappe and colleagues (2008) reported ERP changes in young adults after two weeks of music training. Later, Lappe and colleagues (2011) divided non-musicians into two groups and provided them with two weeks of musical training. In the sensorimotor group, training consisted of learning to play a musical sequence on the piano. In the other group, the non-musicians detected errors in performances after listening to the stimuli played by other participants. Following the sensorimotor training, participants showed enhanced detection of incorrect pitch or timing, as compared to listening. This difference was accompanied by a larger brain response to pitch and duration deviations, indicating greater enhancement of musical representation in the auditory cortex fostered by sensorimotor training. Similar results showing greater benefits of auditory-visual multimodal training (as compared to unimodal training) have also been reported (Paraskevopoulos et al., 2012).

To summarise, short-term changes in behaviour and brain activity can be observed as a result of a brief period of musically related training. Sensorimotor and multimodal training, typical of learning to play a musical instrument, are more efficient in engendering neuroplastic changes than unimodal training. This effect is likely to be underpinned by brain changes occurring between auditory, motor and sensorimotor integration regions involving both feed-forward mechanisms capable of predicting the outcome of motor activity and feedback mechanisms for monitoring performance (Herholz and Zatorre, 2012).

Practice can lead to dramatic improvements in the discrimination of auditory stimuli. Carcagno and Plack (2011) investigated changes in the frequency following response (FFR) after a period of pitch discrimination training. Twenty-seven adult listeners were trained for ten hours on a pitch discrimination task using one of three complex tone stimuli: a static pitch contour, a rising pitch contour or a falling pitch contour. Behavioural measures of pitch discrimination and FFRs for all the stimuli were taken before and after the training phase for participants, as well as for an untrained comparison group. Those receiving training showed significant improvements in pitch discrimination as compared to the comparison group for all trained stimuli. These findings indicate that even relatively low-level processes in the mature auditory system are subject to experience-related change. Similarly, Bosnyak and colleagues (2004) found change in the functional brain attributes used for discriminating small changes in pure tones, measured by EEG in non-musicians after training over 15 sessions. Menning and colleagues (2000) used sequences of pure and deviant tones to train participants' discrimination skills over a three-week period. Participants had to detect deviant tones, differing by progressively smaller frequency shifts from the standard stimulus. Frequency discrimination improved rapidly in the first week and was followed by small but constant improvements thereafter. The results suggested a reorganisation of the cortical representation for the trained frequencies.

Schulte and colleagues (2002) designed a melody perception experiment—involving eight harmonic complex tones of missing fundamental frequencies—to study short-term neuronal plasticity of the auditory cortex. The fundamental frequencies of the complex tones followed the beginning of the virtual melody of the tune Frère Jacques. The harmonics of the complex tones were chosen so that the spectral melody had an inverse contour when compared with the virtual one. After a baseline measurement, participants were exposed repeatedly to the experimental stimuli for one hour a day. All reported a sudden change in the perceived melody, indicating possible reorganisation of the cortical processes involved in the virtual pitch formation. After this switch in perception, a second measurement was taken. Cortical sources of the evoked gamma-band activity were significantly stronger and located more medially after the switch in perception. The results revealed that the primary auditory cortices were involved in the process of virtual pitch perception, and that their function was modifiable by laboratory manipulation.

Adopting a different approach, Loui and colleagues (2009) explored brain activity occurring when participants learned a new musical system. Participants listened to different combinations of tones from a previously unheard system of pitches based on the Bohlen-Pierce scale, with chord progressions that form 3:1 ratios in frequency, which is different from the 2:1 frequency ratios found in existing musical systems. Event-related brain potentials elicited by improbable sounds in the new music system emerged over a one-hour period. The findings demonstrated that humans use a generalised probability-based perceptual learning mechanism to process novel sound patterns in music.

Functional neuroimaging yields results which are less consistent and more difficult to interpret. Pitch-related learning tasks are associated with either decreased (Jäncke et al., 2001; Zatorre et al., 2012) or increased activation (Gaab et al., 2006) of the auditory regions. Similar discrepancies are observed following short-term sensorimotor training: for instance, piano-like instrumental learning. Here, listening to melodies before and after training was associated with either increased activation of action observation regions (for instance, the premotor region, Broca's area and the inferior parietal region; Lahav et al., 2007), or decreased activation of the dorsal auditory action pathway (Chen et al., 2012). These findings reflect those encountered in cross-sectional studies, where musical training manifests itself in increased or decreased activation. In certain circumstances, learning seems to improve efficiency in encoding or processing information, thus requiring less neuronal resources.

The ways that we learn are reflected in specific brain activity. In an intervention study, students aged 13 to 15 were taught to judge symmetrically structured musical phrases as balanced or unbalanced using traditional instructions about the differences, including verbal explanations, visual aids, notation, verbal rules and playing of musical examples, or participating in musical experiences including singing, playing, improvising or performing examples from the musical literature. Comparisons between the two groups revealed activity in different brain areas (Altenmuller et al., 1997). Similarly, Tervaniemi and colleagues (2001) have shown that musicians who play by ear and improvise may learn to process complex musical information differently to and more accurately than classically trained musicians, leading to corresponding differences in auditory neural responses. It seems that the way musical skills are acquired has a direct influence on brain development.

Overview

The evidence from neurological studies relating to engagement with music suggests that the human brain has remarkable plasticity and changes in response to training or the demands of the environment. Active engagement with making music provides a rich aural and sensorimotor experience which can shape the structure and functions of the human brain. As the skills needed to become an expert musician are acquired, an association between fine motor movements and specific sound patterns is developed, which is based on real-time multisensory feedback. This creates changes in the brain which are in evidence when comparisons are made between non-musicians and musicians involved in different musical activities. These changes are found in children and adults after a few months of musical training. As musicians become more expert, interpreting the findings from neurological studies becomes more complex, because of the way that many aural and motor skills become automated, thus requiring less neural activity. Despite these challenges, it is clear that music has made a major contribution to our understanding of plasticity in the brain, as well as demonstrating the role of learning in developing expertise (albeit in interaction with existing genetic predispositions).

3. Aural Perception and Language Skills

Language and music are unique human forms of communication. In everyday life, we utilise complex linguistic systems to process sound in the environment (Kraus and Slater, 2016). The environment is full of events where it is necessary to segregate sounds into streams where several sound sources are present at the same time (Bregman, 1994) and it is necessary to differentiate between those which are relevant and those which are irrelevant.

Being able to process sound has high survival value, and hearing is the first sense to develop. The foetus in the womb can respond to sound as early as 19 weeks into pregnancy (Moon and Fifer, 2000; Graven and Browne, 2016). Learning the melodies, timbres and rhythms of the music and language of an individual's culture begins in the mother's womb during the third trimester of development. At this point, the foetus can discriminate the speech of their mother from that of a stranger, and the speech of their native language from a non-native language (Kisilevsky et al., 2003; Kisilevsky and Hains, 2009). Foetuses also respond differently to music and speech (Kisilevsky et al., 2004; Granier-Deferre et al., 2011).

The impact of prenatal auditory experience can be observed among newborns when infants show a strong preference for their mother's voice over the voice of another female (DeCasper and Fifer, 1980; Cooper and Aslin, 1989), their mother's language over a foreign language (Moon et al., 1993; 2012), and specific passages of speech (DeCasper and Spence, 1986) or music (Hepper, 1991) which were presented to them during the final weeks of pregnancy. Some have proposed that this early recognition of music and speech has evolved as a cross-cultural adaptation to support mother-infant interactions (Huron, 2001; Tarr et al., 2014; Freeman, 2000; Fritz et al., 2009; Gregory and Varney, 1996).

Advances in technology—for instance, magnetoencephalography—have been used to record foetal and neonatal cognitive functions by non-invasively recording the magnetic fields produced by active neurons in the brain. During the later weeks of pregnancy and the first months of life, the cognitive capabilities related to the recognition of emotion and language acquisition develop rapidly. The newborn can process emotional information and speech sounds which form the basis of the child's development in relation to social tasks and native language (Huotilainen, 2010).

Early interactions between adults and infants include the use of infant-directed forms of language and music which are preferred by infants; Trainor (1996; 1989) refers to this infant-directed speech as a type of musical speech, while Koelsc and Masataka (1999) and Fernand and Siebel (2005) suggest that the early developing brain processes language as a type of music. It has been proposed that singing develops directly out of motherese (infant-directed speech consisting of exaggerations, elevated pitch, slow repetitions and melodic elaborations of ordinary vocal communication; Dissanayake, 2004; Falk, 2004; Mahdhaoui et al., 2009; Saint-Georges et al., 2013). Motherese and singing have simple melodic arches which are cognitively easier to process than words. Both are therefore able to support mother-infant communication and language development while newborns are at a relatively early stage of neurological development (Bouissac, 2004).

Infants prefer singing to speech. For instance, Nakata and Trehub (2004) studied six-month-old infants who were presented with extended audio-visual recordings of their mother's infant-directed speech or singing. Cumulative visual fixation and initial fixation on the mother's image lasted longer for maternal singing than for maternal speech. Furthermore, movement reduction, which tends to indicate intense engagement, accompanied visual fixation more frequently for maternal singing than for maternal speech. The repetitiveness of maternal singing may promote moderate arousal levels which sustain infant attention, in contrast to the greater variability of speech, which may result in cycles of heightened arousal, gaze aversion and re-engagement. The regular pulse of music may also enhance emotional coordination between mother and infant. Bosseler and colleagues (2016) found that the exaggerated pitch contours of infant-directed speech resulted in differences in brain activity linked to online statistical learning in sleeping newborns. Karzon (1985) found that young infants could discriminate three-syllable sequences when the suprasegmental characteristics typical of infant-directed speech emphasised the middle syllable. This pattern of results suggests that the exaggerated suprasegmentals of infant-directed speech may function as a perceptual catalyst, facilitating discrimination by focusing the infant's attention on a distinctive syllable within a series of polysyllabic sequences.

Learning to comprehend and communicate through language places heavy demands on the auditory system. Understanding the stress patterns of a child's native language helps him or her to segregate continuous streams of syllables into words. This ability is present from birth (Mampe et al., 2009). The neonatal brain stores auditory experiences of speech and music as memory traces (Partanen et al., 2013a; 2013b). Exposure to music before birth has an impact on the brain, which helps the newborn to make sense of a range of sounds and auditory scenes immediately after birth. The newborn needs to learn the phonemes of his or her native language quickly and effectively so that he or she can construct a map of them in the first year of life (Kuhl, 2004). This is crucial for the development of language skills.

To function effectively, the auditory system requires high- and low-level cognitive skills. In humans, the process begins in the cochlea, where information about the acoustic characteristics of particular sounds is presented. This information is then subject to time and frequency processes, subsequently progressing to higher levels in the auditory system. High-level cognitive skills are required to make sense of auditory information. These skills include memory, attention and predictive processes. Such processes are vital in speech perception; for instance, being able to segregate sounds into streams when listening to speech within noise, the perception of music, and learning native and other languages. As we saw in Chapter 2, there is a large body of evidence that active engagement with music in childhood produces structural changes in the brain and its functioning—changes which are related to the processing of sound (Elbert et al., 1995; Huotilainen and Tervaniemi, 2018; Hutchinson et al., 2003; Pantev et al., 2001; 2003; Pascual-Leone, 2001; Schlaug et al., 1995a; 1995b). How easily individuals are able to process sound depends on their prior experiences with it (Krishnan et al., 2005; Krizman et al., 2012; White-Schwoch et al., 2013). Knowledge related to auditory processing is acquired through exposure to particular environments and is applied automatically whenever an individual listens to music or speech (Bigand and Poulin-Carronnat, 2006). This process begins in the womb and continues throughout infancy.

Research on aural processing and its relationship with language has taken several forms beyond that undertaken in neuroscience. Some has considered the relationships between language and music in terms of processing but also skill levels. Another strand of research has focused on aural perception—including comparisons of musicians with non-musicians, adults and children—while some research has considered how music might help those with difficulties in processing sound. The following sections will consider these issues.

Explanations of the Relationships between Music and Language

Language and music share many characteristics, including the use of the auditory domain as the input path and the organisation of perceptual elements into structured sequences (Patel, 2003). Understanding the relationship between musical training and speech perception has proved challenging. Early work focused on hemispheric specialisation. For example, Bever and Chiarello (1974) suggested that language was based in the left hemisphere and music in the right. In the 1990s, technological developments in neuroimaging revealed partial neural overlap between the two domains (Patel, 2008), although clinical studies of those with brain damage revealed separate deficits in music and language (Peretz and Coltheart, 2003). Despite this, there is evidence of common brain regions for processing music and language (Herdener et al., 2014; Koelsch et al., 2002) but this does not necessarily imply that there is shared processing circuitry, as the findings of such research are open to different interpretations (Kunert and Slevc, 2015). However, research focusing specifically on shared neural circuitry has indicated neural overlap for the processing of speech and music (Besson et al., 2011; Bidelman et al., 2013; Bugaj and Brenner, 2011; Chandrasekaran et al., 2009; Degé and Schwarzer, 2011; Gordon et al., 2014; Kraus and Chandrasekaran, 2010; Kraus and White-Schwoch, 2016; Overy, 2003; Patel and Iversen,

2007; Rogalsky et al., 2011; Sammler et al., 2007; Schulze et al., 2011; Tallal and Gaab, 2006; Wong et al., 2007). Despite this, the extent and nature of the overlap continues to be hotly debated (Norman-Haignere et al., 2015; Patel, 2016; Peretz et al., 2015). One area of controversy is whether the brain networks involved are separate or whether the neural resources are shared (Kunert and Slevc, 2015; Norman-Haignere et al., 2015; Peretz et al., 2015). A further issue is that the ease with which shared processes operate depends on the individual's prior experiences with sound, including music (Bigand and Poulin-Carronnat, 2006; Elmer et al., 2014; Krishnan et al., 2005; Krizman et al., 2012; Patel, 2016; White-Schwoch et al., 2013). The strongest evidence for neural overlap and cross-domain experience-dependent plasticity is in the brainstem, followed by the auditory cortex. The evidence and the potential for overlap becomes less apparent as the mechanisms involved in music and speech perception become more specialised and distinct at higher levels of processing (Ogg and Slevc, 2019).

The relationship between language and musical abilities might be explained in terms of signal processing in the dorsal auditory stream, which is domain-general. This suggests that there is overlap between the perceptual processing of linguistic (Kotz and Schmidt-Kassow, 2015; Kotz and Schwartze, 2010), musical, affective and prosodic sensory information (Fruhholz, Trost and Kotz, 2016). The dorsal circuit integrates auditory and motor processes, providing a neural mechanism for speech development, articulation, articulatory sequences and the encoding of new vocabulary, phonological short-term memory and the feed-forward function (Buchsbaum et al., 2005; Hickok and Poeppel, 2007). The putamen also plays a pivotal role in human motor cortico-basal ganglia thalamo-cortical circuitry, but is also involved in the perception of beats involving local gamma-band oscillations (Merchant et al., 2015). This circuit is involved not only in sequential and temporal processing, but also in rhythmic behaviours such as music and dance, where audition plays a crucial role. The circuit is usually involved in the control of voluntary skeletomotor movements, and includes the supplementary motor cortex and the putamen as the fundamental cortical and neostriatal nodes, respectively.

Two theoretical positions—Hickok and Poeppel's (2000; 2007) neuroanatomical model and Patel's OPERA hypothesis—have underpinned much research. Hickok and Poeppel (2000; 2007) argue that progress in understanding the nature and extent of overlap has been limited because of the failure to consider the effects of different tasks when mapping speech-related processing systems. They outline a dual-stream model of speech processing in which a ventral stream processes speech signals for comprehension, and a dorsal stream maps acoustic speech signals to frontal-lobe articulatory networks. The model assumes that the ventral stream is largely bilaterally organised, while the dorsal stream is strongly left-hemisphere dominant. The OPERA model proposed by Patel (2011) includes overlap in subcortical and cortical networks but adds precision (the music must place higher demands on the networks than language); emotions (the music must elicit strong positive emotions); repetition (the musical activity must be repeated frequently); and must be associated with attention. The model suggests that there is anatomical overlap of the neural areas that process acoustic features in both speech and music, but that music requires greater precision than speech and places higher demands on overlapping neural areas. It also suggests that musical training requires repetition so that the neural areas are continually activated which, in turn, leads to enhanced attention.

In early life, speech and music processing have been shown to rely on overlapping neural substrates (Kotilahti et al., 2010; McMullen and Saffran, 2004; Perani et al., 2011). Brandt and colleagues (2012) have argued that, without the ability to hear musically, it would not be possible to acquire language. They suggest that music serves as a scaffold to learn speech, supported by the mother's use of motherese as she interacts with her child (Fernald, 1989).

Musical and language processes might have similar developmental underpinnings in infants and children but be modularised in adults. As newborns do not understand syntax and the meaning of words, they focus on the acoustic features of voices and the prosodic features of language (rhythm, speed, pitch and relative emphasis). The processing systems may become differentiated as they become more familiar with speech and cognitive maturation occurs (Koelsch and Siebel, 2005). Koelsch (2011) suggests that there is an emergent modularity. Speech and music processing both depend on perceptual categorisation. In speech, the focus is primarily on timbral contrasts, while in music the focus is on distinguishing differences in pitch. The sounds of vowels and sound frequencies are spread along continua. Acquiring musical and language skills requires individuals to learn to separate the sounds in each continuum into separate vowels or pitches. In addition, it must also be possible to separate variation within a category—for instance, sound variation produced by different speakers from variation that constitutes a change of category. Patel (2008) suggests that these challenges are likely solved by a shared system. If there is a shared sound-category learning mechanism, it would suggest comparable individual differences in language and musical abilities. Some support for this comes from research with individuals classed as 'tune deaf' which has shown that poor musical performance tends to be associated with deficits in processing speech sounds' (Jones et al., 2009).

There may be a sensitive period for musical training. Support for this comes from findings that musicians who begin training early show better task performance and greater changes in auditory and motor regions of the brain than those who start later in childhood (Bengtsson et al., 2005; Elbert et al., 1995; Gaser and Schlaug, 2003a; Koeneke et al., 2004; Penhune, 2011; Schneider et al., 2002). Those who have absolute pitch—the ability to identify or produce musical pitch without recourse to any reference tones—offer further support as, typically, those with absolute pitch begin training before the age of six, with almost no examples of absolute pitch in those commencing musical activity after nine years of age (Baharloo et al., 1998). However, auditory learning and plasticity remain possible after sensitive periods (Strait et al., 2010). During a sensitive period, learning is largely a bottom-up process that is triggered by exposure to auditory input, and is optimised because underlying neural circuits are still developing and are extremely sensitive to input received. Following a sensitive period, learning is largely a top-down process that depends on attention to enhance the salience of features in order to encode them. The process involves changing the structure and efficiency of pre-existing circuits to optimise processing. Music training may support the developmental trajectory of top-down control over speech processing (Strait et al., 2014; White et al., 2013).

The most recent research approaches draw on the clinical evidence of music-related deficits in neurologically impaired individuals, while also exploring the processing of music in healthy people, using neurocomparative music and language research (Sammell and Elmer, 2020). Particular areas of interest have been the role of general attention (Perruchet and Poulin-Charronnat, 2013), rhythm, neuronal entrainment, predictive coding and cognitive control (Slevc and Okada, 2015). For instance, Sammell and Elmer (2020) suggest that temporal attention can be influenced by external rhythmic auditory stimulation and that this benefits language processing, including the processing of syntax and speech production. Such research starts from the proposition that speech and music have similar acoustic (Reybrouck and Podlipniak, 2019; Tsai and Li, 2019) structural features (Boll-Avetisyan et al., 2020; Daikoku, 2018; Fotidzis et al., 2018; Lagrois et al., 2019; Lee et al, 2019; Myers et al., 2019; Silva et al., 2019; Snijders et al, 2020).

Processing systems for language and music share the challenge of extracting a small number of categories that are meaningful from a flow of acoustically variable signals. The analysis skills used in language processing, phonological distinctions, blending and segmentation of sounds are similar to the skills necessary for the perception of rhythmic (Lamb and Gregory 1993; Lipscomb et al., 2008), harmonic and melodic discrimination (Anvari et al., 2002; Barwick et al., 1989; Lamb and Gregory, 1993). The processing of timing cues is emerging as particularly important in leading to better segmenting of the sounds of speech and quicker recognition of distinctive units of spoken language (Kraus and Chandrasekaran, 2010; Overy, 2003; Tallal and Gaab, 2006). Reybrouck and Podlipniak (2019) argue that some sound features and their common preconceptual affective meanings may reflect joint evolutionary roots of music and language that continue to the present day—for instance, musical expressivity and speech prosody. Recent neurophysiological models assume that speech and music processing, as well as the role of rhythm in language development, are based on the synchronisation of internal neuronal oscillations with temporally regular stimuli (Goswami, 2019; Lakatos, et al., 2019; Large et al., 2015; Poeppel and Assaneo, 2020). For instance, Lakatos and colleagues (2019) argue that rhythms are a fundamental and defining feature of neuronal activity in humans. Rhythmic brain activity interacts in complex ways with rhythms in the internal and external environment, through the phenomenon of neuronal entrainment. This has been proposed as having a role in many sensory and cognitive processes. Auditory senses are faced with many rhythmic inputs. Entrainment couples rhythmic brain activity to external and internal rhythmic events, serving fine-grained routing and modulation of external and internal signals across multiple spatial and temporal hierarchies. Lakatos and colleagues (2019) propose a theoretical framework, explaining how neuronal entrainment dynamically structures information from incoming neuronal, bodily and environmental sources. For instance, Doelling and Poeppel, (2015) suggest that the brain exploits the temporal regularities in music to accurately parse individual notes from the sound stream using lower frequencies or entrainment, and in higher frequencies to generate temporal and content-based predictions of subsequent musical events associated with predictive models.

One strand of research has focused on the patterning of strong and weak syllables or beats that make up rhythm, pulse and prosodic stress (Breen et al., 2019; Frey et al., 2019; Myers et al., 2019; Richards and Goswami, 2019; Snijders et al., 2020). The rhythmic patterning of both speech and music has been proposed to draw on domain-general abilities which are required to perceive and process the temporal features of sound (Jones, 2019; Kotz et al., 2018). Richards and Goswami (2019) explain that prosody, particularly the hierarchical structuring of stressed and unstressed syllables, provides reliable cues to the syntactic structure of speech (Selkirk, 1984) and may therefore facilitate the acquisition of syntactic language organisation (Cumming et al., 2015). Early disturbances of this rhythm-syntax interface may hinder normal language acquisition, leading to developmental language disorders. Richards and Goswami suggest that basic processing of rhythmic prosodic cues may provide a key foundation for the scaffolding of higher aspects of language during development.

A further strand of research has focused on the common auditory processing of temporal regularities (Boll-Avetisyan et al., 2020; Fotidzia et al., 2018; Lagrois et al, 2019; Reybrouck and Podlipniak, 2019). These are thought to promote higher-level linguistic functions (Breen et al., 2019; Frey et al., 2019; Fotidzis et al., 2018: Richards and Goswami, 2019; Rossi et al., 2020; Snijders et al., 2020), possibly through neuronal entrainment (Myers et al., 2019). For instance, Lagrois and colleagues (2019) found that so-called 'beat deaf individuals', those who have beat-finding deficits in music, showed deficits in synchronising tapping with speech rhythm, and more generally, in regular tapping without external rhythms. This pattern of deficits may arise from a basic deficiency in timekeeping mechanisms that affects rhythm perception across domains. Similarly, Boll-Avetisyan and colleagues (2020) used multiple regression analyses and found that musical rhythm perception abilities predicted rhythmic grouping preferences in speech in adults with and without dyslexia, while Fotidzis and colleagues (2018) found that musical rhythmic skills predicted children's neural sensitivity to mismatches between the speech rhythm of a written word and an auditory rhythm. A further strand of research has explored top-down modulations of common auditory processes by domain-general cognitive and motor functions in both perception and production (Christiner and Reiterer, 2018; Daikoku, 2018; Lee et al., 2019). For instance, Jung and colleagues (2015) demonstrated that rhythmic expectancy is crucial to the interaction of processing musical and linguistic syntax, while Silva and colleagues (2019) demonstrated top-down adjustment of music and language perception through behavioural modelling. They found that listeners placed break patterns in ambiguous speech-song stimuli differently, depending on whether they believed that they were listening to speech prosody or contemporary music. Similarly, Tsai and Li (2019) found that the strength with which an ambiguous stimulus was perceived as song rather than speech depended not only on the acoustics of the stimulus itself, but also on the sound category of the preceding stimulus, while Mathias and colleagues (2019) showed that pianists gradually anticipated the sounds of their actions during music production, similar to the mechanisms of auditory feedback control during speech production (Hickok, 2012; Palmer and Pfordresher, 2003). Overall, this research suggests that the listening context, the listener's own motor plans and statistical and domain-specific expectations may influence the top-down anticipation and perception of acoustic features in speech and music.

Myers and colleagues (2019) summarise the current state of knowledge about neuronal entrainment in speech envelope tracking, reflecting quasi-regular amplitude fluctuations over time. Speech envelope tracking is neural and occurs simultaneously at multiple time scales corresponding to the rates of phonemes, syllables and phrases (Giraud and Poeppel, 2012; Gross et al., 2013). They argue that the slowest rate, corresponding to prosodic stress and rhythmic pacing in the delta range, constitutes a particularly strong source of neuronal entrainment which is crucial for normal language development.

Jung and colleagues (2015) demonstrated that rhythmic expectancy is crucial to the interaction of processing musical and linguistic syntax, supporting the incorporation of dynamic models of attentional entrainment into existing theories, which have proposed a sharing of neural resources between syntax processing in music and language (Patel, 2003), and a dynamic attention network that governs general temporal processing (Large and Jones, 1999). Their findings suggest that the interaction of music and language syntax processing depends on rhythmic expectancy, supporting emerging theories of music and language syntax processing with dynamic models of attentional entrainment.

Some research has examined domain-general top-down modulations of music and language from the perspective of perception and production, focusing on the continuous interaction between bottom-up and top-down processes in line with significant trends in predictive coding (Erickson and Thiessen, 2015). For instance, Koelsch and colleagues (2019) suggest that music perception is an active act of listening. When listening to music, we constantly generate plausible hypotheses about what could happen next. Actively attending to music resolves uncertainty. Within the predictive coding framework, Koelsch and colleagues (2019) present a formulation of precision filtering and attentional selection, which explains why some lower-level auditory—and even higher-level syntactic—music processes elicited by irregular events are relatively exempt from top-down predictive processes. They provide evidence for the attentional selection of salient auditory features, which suggests that listening is a more active process than traditionally conceived in models of perception. To examine predictive mechanisms in music, Fogel and colleagues (2015) presented listeners with the beginning of a novel tonal melody of five to nine notes and asked them to sing the note they expected to come next. Half of the melodies had an underlying harmonic structure designed to constrain expectations for the next note, based on an implied authentic cadence within the melody. Each authentic cadence melody was matched to a non-cadential melody in terms of length, rhythm and melodic contour, but differing in implied harmonic structure. On average, participants showed much greater consistency in the notes sung following authentic versus non-cadential melodies, although there was significant variation in consistency for both melodies, suggesting that individual differences were important.

Examining perceived relationships between perceptions of speech and song through the speech-to-song illusion, Margulis and colleagues (2015) presented native-English-speaking participants with brief spoken utterances that were repeated ten times. The speech-to-song illusion occurs when a brief phrase is repeated several times and then begins to be perceived as song. The illusion exposes a border between the perception of language and the perception of music. The phrases used were either drawn from languages that were relatively difficult for a native English speaker to pronounce, or languages that were relatively easy for a native English speaker to pronounce. Participants rated the utterances before and after the repetitions on a five-point Likert-like scale as ranging from sounds exactly like speech to sounds exactly like singing. The speech-to-song illusion occurred more readily if the utterance was spoken in a language difficult for a native English speaker to pronounce. This suggests that speech circuitry was more likely to capture native and easy-to-pronounce languages, and more reluctant to relinquish them to perceived songs across repetitions.

Some research has explored the processing benefits of rhythmically highly regular stimuli such as songs. For instance, Rossi and colleagues (2020) investigated whether meaning was extracted from spoken and sung sentences in a similar way. Participants listened to semantically correct and incorrect sentences while performing a correctness judgement task. Neural mechanisms were assessed with several methods. The combined results indicated similar semantic processing in speech and song.

The findings of the effects of general rhythmic processing skills on higher-order linguistic abilities are currently being investigated in the context of first language acquisition (Ladányi et al., 2020). Christiner and Reiterer (2018) found that links between musical aptitude, phonetic language abilities, and imitation of foreign speech in pre-school children were mediated by domain-general working memory resources. While this does not preclude auditory perceptual connections between music and language, the findings suggest that there may be more complex interactions which have not yet been identified.

Miles and colleagues (2016) suggest that two different aspects of music and language depend on the same two memory systems. One brain system, based in the temporal lobes, helps humans memorise information in both language and music—for example, words and meanings in language, and familiar melodies in music. The other system, based in the frontal lobes, helps humans unconsciously learn and use the rules that underlie both language and music, such as the rules of syntax in sentences, and the rules of harmony in music. The findings suggest that one set of brain structures underlies rules in both language and music, but also that a different brain system underlies memorised information in both domains.

Over time, the research exploring the relationship between music and language has progressed from exploring the mapping of music and language functions in the brain to trying to understand the mechanisms involved. Much further investigation is required before there is a clear understanding of this. Future research needs to take account of individual differences and the nature of the tasks studied, as neural overlap might be task-dependent. Differences in listening tasks may limit the extent to which any clear conclusions can be drawn about the underlying neurobiology of music and speech.

Comparisons between Musicians and Non-Musicians

Altenmüller (2003) proposed that cortical activation during music processing reflects the individual's auditory learning biography (their personal musical experiences accumulated over time). He suggests that the complexity of neural networks is enhanced depending on the complexity of auditory information experienced. Musical training leads to the development of mental representations of music, which may involve different cerebral substrates to those required for other types of aural processing. These representations can take several forms, including auditory, sensory motor, symbolic or visual. This means that, to process the same level of auditory information, professional musicians use larger and more complex neural networks when compared with non-musicians.

A considerable body of research has developed which has focused on making comparisons between sound processing in musicians and non-musicians. In such research, musicians tend to be identified in terms of playing an instrument or being involved in formal singing activities. Non-musicians are defined as not engaging in music-making in these ways, although they may engage with music in other ways. Despite the crudity of this distinction, much research has been undertaken on this basis, with participants of all ages, from children to seniors. This research has demonstrated that musicians have enhanced abilities to process pitch and temporal sound information (Chobert et al., 2011; 2014; Kishon-Rabin et al., 2001; Kraus and Chandrasekaran, 2010; Magne et al., 2006; Marques et al, 2007; Micheyl et al., 2006; Moreno et al., 2009; Schon et al., 2004; Strait et al., 2010; Tervaniemi et al, 1997; van Zuijen et al., 2005; Zendel and Alain, 2009). They have improved performance on a range of listening skills (Hyde et al., 2009; Pantev et al., 2001; Patel and Iverson, 2007; Tallal and Gaab, 2006). They have enhanced auditory attention (Strait and Kraus, 2011; Strait et al., 2014), better processing of the metric structure of words when they are presented in sentences (Marie et al., 2011b) and better discrimination and identification of moraic units of timing and other language features (Sadakata and Sekiayama, 2011). Musicians can classify voiced sounds, vowels, more easily and quickly than non-musicians (Bidelman et al., 2014), and have advantages in relation to the processing of linguistic syntax (Fiveash and Pammer, 2014) and in making judgements about grammar (Patston and Tippett, 2011). They are better able to distinguish rapidly changing sounds (Gaab et al., 2005), harmonic differences (Corrigall and Trainor, 2009; Musacchia et al., 2008; Zendel and Alain, 2009), temporal novelty (Herdener et al., 2014) and tonal variations in non-native speech sounds (Chandrasekaran et al., 2009; Cooper and Wang, 2010; Kühnis et al., 2013; Marques et al, 2007; Martinez-Montes et al., 2013; Perfors and Ong, 2012; Wong et al., 2007; Wong and Perrachione, 2007; Yang et al., 2014). They can perceive speech better than those without training when it is accompanied by noise (Parbery-Clark et al., 2009a; 2009b; 2011), and can identify syllables presented when spectral information is degraded (Elmer et al., 2012), identify whether sentences in a foreign language which is tone based are the same or different (Marie et al., 2011a; 2011b) and predict the ability to perceive and produce subtle phonetic contrasts in a second language (Slevc & Miyake, 2006). They are also better than non-musicians at the perception and processing of vocally expressed emotion (Bhatara et al., 2011; Lima & Castro, 2011; Strait et al., 2009; Thompson et al., 2004).

At the subcortical level musicians demonstrate more robust and quicker auditory brainstem responses to music (Lee et al., 2009) and speech (Bidelman et al., 2009; Bidelman & Krishnan 2010). For instance, Musacchia and colleagues (2007) demonstrated that musicians, compared to non-musicians, had earlier and larger auditory and audiovisual brainstem responses to speech and music stimuli. The strength of the brainstem response was related to the number of years of musical practice. Similarly, Wong and colleagues (2007) examined brainstem encoding of linguistic pitch and found that musicians show more robust and faithful encoding compared with non-musicians. The extent of subcortical consonant discrimination in noise perception is also enhanced in musicians (Parbery-Clark et al., 2012). Finally, musicians have an increased neural capacity for the perception and processing of vocally expressed emotion (Strait et al., 2009a; 2009b) and have high-functioning peripheral auditory systems. The quality of aural encoding is related to the amount of musical training (Wong et al., 2007) and also the nature of instrumental requirements.

As was demonstrated in Chapter 2, there are subtle differences between musicians in their aural processing, depending on the instrument that they play. For instance, Rauscher and Hinton (2011) used four discrimination tasks with adults aged 16–63—musicians and non-musicians—and found that auditory discrimination was better in the musicians. This was particularly true of the string players as compared with percussionists, probably as a consequence of the many years of subtle tonal discrimination required to play a stringed instrument. The findings demonstrated that expertise in playing a musical instrument selectively improved discrimination thresholds corresponding to the skills emphasised by training on that instrument. Similarly, Brattico and colleagues (2013) established that responses to sound are modulated by expertise in more than one music culture, as is typical of Finnish folk musicians, while Tervaniemi and colleagues (2006) found that amateur musicians still had advantages over non-musicians in their neural and behavioural sound encoding accuracy. In a later study, Tervaniemi and colleagues (2016) found that classical, jazz, and rock musicians exhibited automatic brain responses which were selectively enhanced to deviants in tuning, classical musicians, timing, classical and jazz musicians, transposition, jazz musicians, and melody contour, jazz and rock musicians. Another study found different brain responses to six types of music featured by classical, jazz, rock and pop musicians and non-musicians. Jazz and classical musicians scored higher in a musical aptitude test than band musicians and non-musicians, especially with regards to tonal abilities. Jazz musicians had a greater overall sensitivity to auditory outliers, processing of pitch and sliding up to pitches (Vuust et al., 2012).

Greater left-hemisphere lateralisation has been shown in musicians in comparison with non-musicians when they are presented with musical stimuli (Bever and Chiarello, 1974; Hirshkowitz et al., 1978; Besson et al., 1994; Schlaug et al., 1995a). This is consistent with more efficient verbal processes. This asymmetry has been proposed to potentially be related to language and pitch processing skills. Ohnishi and colleagues (2001) assessed cortical activation during a passive listening task and also found greater activation of the planum temporale and the left dorso-lateral prefrontal cortex in musicians than in non-musicians. The authors also found a negative correlation between the degree of activation in the left planum temporale and the age of commencement of musical training. Non-musicians demonstrated right dominant secondary auditory areas during the same task. Further, the degree of activation in the left posterior dorsolateral prefrontal cortex and the left planum temporale correlated significantly with absolute pitch ability. Fujioka and colleagues (2006) also observed a greater left-hemisphere lateralisation in four- to six-year-old children who received music lessons over the period of a year when listening to violin tones, as compared with children receiving no music lessons.

The auditory expertise gained over years of music training finetunes the auditory system (Strait and Kraus, 2011a; 2011b) strengthening the neurobiological and cognitive underpinnings of speech and music processing including enhancing neural responses to changes in pitch, duration, intensity and voice onset time. Musicians' enhanced perceptual skills play a role in enhancing language skills (Bever and Chiarello, 2009; Gaab et al., 2005; Hutka et al., 2015; Jakobsob et al., 2003;

Strait et al., 2014; Tallal and Gaab, 2006; Zatorre and Belin, 2001; Zattore et al., 2002). This increased sensitivity and attention to speech seems to be supported, in part, by right-hemisphere processing (Jantzen et al., 2014). Musicians' pitch expertise appears to extend from music to the language context with no significant differences between domains (Alexander et al., 2005; Bidelman et al., 2011; Delogu et al., 2010; Lee and Hung, 2008; Marie et al., 2011; Mom and Zuo, 2012; Weidema et al., 2016). Musicians are also better at recognising vocally expressed emotion. For instance, Pinheiro and colleagues (2015) investigated the effects of musical training on event-related potential correlates of emotional prosody processing. Fourteen musicians and fourteen non-musicians listened to 228 sentences with neutral semantic content, differing in prosody: one third with neutral, one third with happy and one third with angry intonation, with intelligible semantic content and unintelligible semantic content. The findings suggested that auditory expertise can have an impact on different stages of vocal emotional processing.

Fujioka and colleagues (2004) found that people with no formal music education processed both contour and interval information in the auditory cortex automatically. They designed stimuli to examine contour and interval information separately. In the contour condition, there were eight different standard melodies, each consisting of five notes, all ascending in pitch. The corresponding deviant melodies were altered to descend on their final note. The interval condition used one five-note standard melody transposed to eight keys from trial to trial, and on deviant trials the last note was raised by one whole tone without changing the pitch contour. There was also a control condition, in which a standard tone and a deviant tone were presented. The results suggested that musical training enhanced the ability to automatically register abstract changes in the relative pitch structure of melodies.

Language and music depend on rules and memorised representations. Miranda and Ullman (2007) examined the neural bases of these aspects of music with an event-related potential study of note violations in melodies. Rule-only violations consisted of out-of-key deviant notes that violated tonal harmony rules in unfamiliar melodies. Memory-only violations consisted of in-key deviant notes in familiar well-known melodies. These notes followed musical rules but deviated from the actual melodies. Finally, out-of-key notes in familiar well-known melodies constituted violations of both rules and memory. All three conditions were presented to healthy young adults: half were musicians and half non-musicians. The results revealed a double dissociation, independent of musical training, between rules and memory. Both rule violation conditions, but not the memory-only violations, elicited an early, somewhat right-lateralised anterior central negativity consistent with previous studies of rule violations in music, and analogous to the early left-lateralised anterior negativities elicited by rule violations in language. In contrast, both memory violation conditions, but not the rule-only violation, elicited a posterior negativity, a component that depends, at least in part, on the processing of representations stored in long-term memory, both in language and in other domains. The results suggest that the neurocognitive rule memory dissociation extends from language to music, further strengthening the similarities between the two domains.

Harding and colleagues (2019) recorded the EEG of 28 participants with a range of musical training, who listened to melodies and sentences with identical rhythmic structure. The results showed that participants with only a few years of musical training had a comparable cortical response to music and speech rhythm. However, the cortical response to music rhythm increased with years of musical training, while the response to speech rhythm did not, leading to an overall greater cortical response to music rhythm across all participants. It seems as if task demands shape asymmetric cortical tracking across domains.

Focusing on sound discrimination, Parbery-Clark and colleagues (2012) established that musicians have an increased ability to detect small differences between sounds. They showed that this conferred advantages in the subcortical differentiation of closely related speech sounds (for example, /ba/ and /ga/), distinguishable only by their harmonic spectra. By measuring the degree to which subcortical response timing differed for the speech syllables /ba/, /da/ and /ga/ in adult musicians and non-musicians, they showed that musicians demonstrated enhanced subcortical discrimination of closely related speech sounds. Further, the extent of subcortical consonant discrimination correlated with speech in noise perception. Similarly, Ott and colleagues (2011) determined whether musical expertise led to an altered neurophysiological processing of subsegmental information available in speech signals. They analysed neurophysiological responses to voiced and unvoiced consonant-vowel syllables and noise-analogues in 26 German-speaking adult musicians and non-musicians. The findings showed that musicians processed unvoiced stimuli, irrespective of whether these were speech or non-speech stimuli, differently to non-musicians. Zuk and colleagues (2013) examined the perceptual acuity of musicians to the acoustic components of speech necessary for intra-phonemic discrimination of synthetic syllables. Musicians and non-musicians were compared on discrimination thresholds of three synthetic speech syllable continua that varied in their spectral and temporal discrimination demands. Musicians demonstrated superior discrimination only for syllables that required resolution of temporal cues. In addition, performance on the temporal syllable continua positively correlated with the length and intensity of musical training.

Musicians are also better at processing intervals than non-musicians. Comparisons between eleven musicians aged 21-33 and ten non-musicians aged 19-29 years who were required to detect infrequent changes to the last note of a five-note melody—which either altered the contour or the interval up or down—showed that contour processing was more basic and less affected by musical experience (Trainor et al., 1999).

The benefits of musical training have been shown to continue throughout the lifespan. Bidelman and Alain (2015) showed that musical training can offset the decline in auditory brain processing that frequently accompanies normal ageing. They recorded brainstem and cortical neuroelectric responses in older adults as they classified speech sound along an acoustic phonetic continuum. Those who had only had modest musical training had higher temporal precision in speech-evoked responses and were better at differentiating phonetic categories. Even limited musical training can preserve robust speech recognition late in life.

As considered in Chapter 2, comparisons between musicians and non-musicians cannot demonstrate causality. Differences in aural processing could be present at birth or appear at any stage of development due to genetic programming, while differences in language skills could have developed through diversity in educational opportunities or home circumstances.

However, the fact that most enhancements are greater the longer the period of training suggests that musical experience is the cause (Ho et al., 2003; Lee and Noppeney, 2015; Musacchia et al., 2008; Norton et al., 2005; Pantev et al., 1998; Seither-Preisler et al., 2014; Strait and Kraus, 2014; Wong et al., 2007), although the nature of the particular musical activities may be important, as may the intensity and commitment to engagement with music. The issue of causality can best be resolved by intervention studies. These usually take place in research with children.

Research with Children

There have been reports of the benefits of music for language development, extending from early years through childhood (Tierney and Kraus, 2013; White et al., 2013) in addition to benefits for auditory skill development, including auditory discrimination and attention (Putkinen et al., 2013) and language skills including pitch perception (Linnavalli et al., 2018; Nan et al., 2018; Yang et al., 2014).

One strand of research has focused on infants and preschool children. For instance, Zhao and colleagues (2016) examined the effects of a laboratory-based intervention on music and speech processing in nine-month-old infants who were exposed to music in triple time (a waltz) in a social context. Infants, with the aid of caregivers, tapped out the musical beats with maracas, or their feet, and were bounced in synchronisation to the musical beats. The intervention incorporated key characteristics of typical infant music classes to maximise learning. It was multimodal, social, and offered repetitive experiences. A control group experienced similar multimodal, social, repetitive play, but without music. Following the intervention, the infants' neural processing of temporal structure was tested using tones in triple time and speech with foreign syllable structures. After 12 sessions, the infants' neural responses to temporal structure violations in music and speech were assessed. Compared with infants in the control group, the infants exposed to the music intervention improved their detection and prediction of auditory patterns, demonstrating enhanced temporal structure processing in music and speech, musical pitch and the processing of timing. The intervention enhanced the infants' ability to extract temporal structure information and to predict future events in time, a skill affecting both music and speech processing.

Similarly, Trainor and colleagues (2012) reported neural-level changes in six-month-old infants randomised to engage in active participatory music classes for six months or a class in which they experienced music passively while playing. Active music participation resulted in earlier enculturation to Western tonal pitch structure, larger and/or earlier brain responses to musical tones, and a more positive social trajectory. Also working with six-month-old infants, Gerry and colleagues (2012) found that random assignment to six months of active participatory musical experience accelerated the acquisition of culture-specific knowledge of Western tonality, in comparison to a similar level of passive exposure to music. The infants assigned to the active musical experience showed superior development of prelinguistic communicative gestures and social behaviour compared to infants assigned to the passive musical experience. The findings showed that infants can engage in meaningful musical training when appropriate pedagogical approaches are used, and that active musical participation in infancy both enhances culture-specific musical acquisition and impacts the development of social and communication skills.

Another comparable study is that of Snijders and colleagues (2020), who investigated whether infants could learn words from ecologically valid children's songs. Forty Dutch-learning ten-month-olds participated in the research to explore whether infants could segment repeated target words embedded in songs during familiarisation, and subsequently recognise those words in continuous speech in a test phase. The infants participated in both song and speech sessions. The findings showed that 10-month-old infants could indeed segment words embedded in songs. Working with children participating in Head Start provision, Yazejian and colleagues (2009) evaluated the effects of a supplementary preschool classroom music and movement curriculum on language skills. The participating children made greater gains in communication skills than children in a comparison group, although there were no differences in receptive language or phonological awareness.

A study with children aged two to three by Putkinen and colleagues (2013) found a relationship between informal musical activities with parents at home and auditory event-related potentials linked to sound discrimination and attention. They showed that children with higher levels of musical activity had heightened sensitivity to temporal acoustic changes, more mature auditory change detection, and less distractibility. The children in the research who also attended a music-focused playschool until the age of four or six displayed more rapid development of neural responses than those who gave up the activity. A related cross-sectional study showed enhanced control over auditory novelty processing in musically trained school-aged children and adolescents (Putkinen et al., 2015).

Similarly, the Soundplay project in the UK worked with children aged two to four years old, using a combination of methods including observation, music, language tracker tools, interviews and written reports compiled by early years practitioners, parents and workshop leaders. They found that, after participating in the project, children who had been identified as being at risk of developmental delay achieved higher than average development in language skills (Pitts, 2016). In Australia, Williams and colleagues (2015) investigated parent-child home music activities in a sample of 3031 Australian children participating in a national longitudinal study. The frequency of shared home music activities was reported by parents when children were two to three years old and a range of social, emotional and cognitive outcomes were measured by parent and teacher report and direct testing two years later (when the children were four to five years old). A series of regression analyses found that the frequency of shared home music activities had a small significant association with children's vocabulary, numeracy, attentional and emotional regulation, and prosocial skills. Taken together, these studies provide causal evidence of the role of music training and less formal musical activities in shaping the development of important neural auditory skills in young children.

We can also consider studies looking at older children: Trainor and colleagues (2003) found that four-year-olds who had received Suzuki training had a better developed auditory cortex and were better able to discriminate between sounds. Fujioka and colleagues (2006) recorded auditory evoked responses to a violin tone and a noise-burst stimulus in four- to six-year-old children in four repeated measurements over a one-year period using magnetoencephalography, and found that the children who had participated in music lessons throughout the year showed a clear musical training effect in response to the violin stimuli, when compared with the untrained children. Similarly, Shahin and colleagues (2004) measured auditory evoked potentials in response to piano, violin and pure tones twice in a group of four- to five-year-old children enrolled in either Suzuki music lessons or non-music controls. Where children were learning to play an instrument—piano or violin— auditory evoked potentials observed for the instrument played were comparable to those of children who were not musically trained and approximately three years older in chronological age, suggesting that the neocortical synaptic matrix is shaped by an accumulation of specific auditory experiences, and that this process is accelerated in those who have musical training. The children playing the piano also exhibited increased power of induced timbre-specific gamma-band activity for piano tones with one year of training in comparison with non-musicians (Shahin et al., 2008).

Using event-related potential and behavioural measures in a longitudinal design, Nan and colleagues (2018) showed that musical training conferred advantages in speech-sound processing in 74 Mandarin-speaking children aged four to five years old, who were pseudo-randomly assigned to piano training, reading training or a no-contact control group. Six months of piano training improved general auditory word discrimination, as well as word discrimination based on vowels, compared with a control group. Although the reading group yielded similar trends, the piano group demonstrated unique advantages in comparison with the reading and control groups in consonant-based word discrimination and in enhanced positive mismatch responses to lexical tone and musical pitch changes. The improved word discrimination based on consonants correlated with enhancements in musical pitch among the children in the piano group. The results suggested strengthened common sound processing across domains as an important mechanism underlying the beneficial impact of musical training on language processing.

Some research has focused on the development of musical skills and auditory discrimination in school-aged children (Elbert et al., 1995; Hutchinson et al., 2003; Pantev et al., 2001; 2003; Pascual-Leone, 2001; Schlaug et al., 1995a; 1995b). This has provided evidence that musical training enhances auditory processing in children who, prior to training, exhibited no pre-existing differences (Chobert et al., 2014; François et al., 2013; Kraus et al., 2014b; Moreno et al., 2009; 2011; Norton et al., 2005; Tierney et al., 2013). Making music has been shown to strengthen children's auditory encoding of speech (Chobert et al., 2014; Magne et al., 2006; Strait et al., 2011a; 2011b; 2013; Tierney et al., 2013) and auditory discrimination and attention (Chobert et al., 2011; Koelsch et al., 2003; Moreno et al., 2009; Putkinen et al., 2013), as well as leading to structural changes in auditory cortical areas in the brain (Hyde et al., 2009; Seither-Preisler et al., 2014).

For instance, Hyde and colleagues (2009) tested two groups of children who had no prior formal musical training. The instrumental group consisted of 15 children aged six years old who had weekly half-hour private keyboard lessons over a period of 15 months. The control group of 16 children, who were almost six years old, did not receive any instrumental music training, but participated in a weekly 40-minute group music class in school, consisting of singing and playing with drums and bells. Structural brain changes in motor and auditory areas, of critical importance for instrumental music training, were correlated with behavioural improvements on motor and auditory musical tests. Children who played and practised a musical instrument showed greater improvements in motor ability and in auditory melodic and rhythmic discrimination skills. Changes in the right auditory area underlay improved melodic and rhythmic discrimination. Similarly, Putkinen and colleagues (2014) conducted a longitudinal study of more than 120 school-aged children and showed that children who received formal musical training displayed enhanced development in neural responses related to pre-attentive neural sound discrimination and auditory attention. The musically trained children also showed superior performance in tests of executive functions.

Huotilainen and Tervaniemi (2018) investigated longitudinal brain development in children starting a musical hobby. At age seven, when most of the children in the music group had just started their training or were about to start, there were no group differences in the brain responses compared with children of the same age starting other hobbies. Two years later and beyond, enhanced auditory brain responses had developed in the music group, while no such development was observed in the brain responses of the control group. In a later study, Putkinen and colleagues (2020) studied nine- to fifteen-year-old children who had or had not participated in musical training. Using auditory event-related potentials, they showed that the musically trained children demonstrated enhanced sound encoding.

Not all of the intervention studies with music have shown positive outcomes. For instance, working with seven- and eight-year-old Spanish children who were learning to speak English as a second language, Fonseca-Mora and colleagues (2015) showed that all of those participating in a phonological training program benefited from that training, but additional musical support had no clear benefits.

Strait and colleagues (2012) explored the encoding of speech in quiet and noisy backgrounds in musically trained and non-trained children. Thirty-one children with normal hearing between the ages of seven and thirteen participated. Those classified as musicians had received private instrumental training from at least the age of five, and had practised consistently for at least four years. The musically trained children outperformed the non-musicians on speech-in-noise perception overall and demonstrated less auditory brainstem response degradation with the addition of background noise than non-musicians. Perceptual, speech-in-noise, cognitive, auditory working memory and attention performance correlated with the extent of the musicians' musical training. Similarly, Slater and colleagues (2015) followed a cohort of eight- to nine-year-old school children for two years, assessing their ability to perceive speech in noise before and after musical training. After an initial assessment, participants were randomly assigned to one of two groups. One group began music training immediately and completed two years of training, while the second group waited a year and then received one year of music training. The research showed that speech-in-noise perception improved after two years of group music training.

Several studies have compared the impact of music versus painting or equivalent visual stimulation. In an early study, Moreno and Besson (2006) tested whether eight weeks of musical training affected the ability of eight-year-old children to detect pitch changes in language. Twenty non-musician children listened to linguistic phrases that ended with prosodically congruous words, or with weak or strong pitch incongruities. Reaction times, error rates and event-related brain potentials were recorded for the final words. For both groups, the weak incongruity was the most difficult to detect, but performance was not significantly different between groups. However, the amplitude of a late positive component was largest in response to strong incongruities, and was reduced after training only in the music group. These results suggest that a relatively short exposure to pitch processing in music exerted some influence on pitch processing in language.

In a later longitudinal study, Moreno and colleagues (2008; 2009) studied event-related potentials in 32 eight-year-old non-musician children over nine months, while they performed tasks designed to test the hypothesis that musical training improves pitch processing in music and speech. Following initial testing, the children were pseudo-randomly assigned to music or to painting training for six months, and were tested again after training using the same tests. After musical—but not painting—training, children showed enhanced reading and pitch discrimination abilities in speech. The results revealed positive transfer from music to speech, showing that short periods of training can have strong consequences on the functional organisation of children's brains.

A further study (Moreno et al., 2011a) researched 64 children, half of whom received visual art training and the other half music training. To undertake the training, two computerised training programmes were developed and administered. The training programmes had the same learning goals, graphics and design, duration, number of breaks and number of teaching staff. The only difference was the content of the training. The music curriculum was based on a combination of motor, perceptual and cognitive tasks, and included training in rhythm, pitch, melody, voice and basic musical concepts. The training relied primarily on listening activities. The curriculum in visual art emphasised the development of visuospatial skills relating to concepts such as shape, colour, line, dimension and perspective. The children engaged in the training programmes in two daily sessions of one hour each, five days a week, for four weeks. The programmes were projected onto a classroom wall and conducted in groups, led by a teacher. The findings showed that training in music listening skills transferred to verbal ability. After the music training, the children exhibited enhanced performance on vocabulary knowledge. There was no significant increase in verbal or spatial skills following visual art training, although there was a trend towards improvement in spatial skills.

Similarly, Chobert and colleagues (2014) randomly assigned non-musician children to music or painting training and recorded neural responses to syllables that differed in vowel frequency, vowel duration and voice onset time. This was done three times: before training, after six months and after twelve months. While no cross-group differences were found before training, enhanced pre-attentive processing of syllabic duration and voice onset time was found after twelve months of training in the music group only. These results suggest that active musical training can lead to improvements in aural processing. Similarly, over a period of two years, François and colleagues (2013) assigned eight-year-old children, matched for cognitive abilities, sex, age, grade at school and socioeconomic status, to music or painting lessons. Prior to the study, the two groups of children performed similarly on a test where they had to identify whether three syllable nonsense words were present within a five-minute-long string of syllables. After one year of training, the music group performed better than the painting group in speech segmentation skills, with the difference increasing over the two-year period.

Another strand of research has considered the impact of second language training versus music training in enhancing aural processing. For instance, in a comparative study of the impact of second language learning (French) and musical training, Moreno and colleagues (2015) recorded event-related potentials for French vowels and musical notes in 36 four- to six-year-old children. The children demonstrated improved processing of relevant trained sounds, and an increased capacity to suppress irrelevant, untrained sounds. After one year, training-induced brain changes persisted, hemispheric changes appeared and there was increased EEG complexity at coarse temporal scales during music and French vowel tasks in widely distributed cortical regions. These findings showed that musical training increased diversity of brain network states, which supported domain-specific music skill acquisition and music-to-language transfer effects. Similarly, Carpentier and colleagues (2016) conducted a 28-day longitudinal study of monolingual English speaking four- to six-year-old children randomly selected to receive daily music or French language training. Children completed passive

EEG music-note and French-vowel auditory detection tasks before and after training. Comparison of pre-training with post-training showed that musical training was associated with increased EEG complexity at coarse temporal scales during music and French vowel tasks in widely distributed cortical regions. The findings demonstrated that musical training increased the diversity of brain network states to support domain-specific music skill acquisition and music-to-language transfer effects.

Further evidence for the benefits of musical training on language comes from Yang and colleagues (2014), who examined whether children's experience of music training related to language skills in Chinese (their first language), English (their second language) and their performance on a musical achievement test. Seventy-seven children who had received formal musical training out of school, beginning in semester three, were categorised as musicians, and the remaining 173 children were classed as non-musicians. The children's musical skills over the 11 semesters of the study improved when they received training, and their performance in their second language (English) was also enhanced, although performance in their first language was not.

In a correlational study, Milovanov and colleagues (2008) explored the relationship between musical aptitude and second-language pronunciation skills in school-aged children. Children with good linguistic skills had better musical skills than children with less accurate linguistic skills. ERP data showed that children with good linguistic skills showed more pronounced sound-change evoked activation with music stimuli than children with less accurate linguistic skills. These findings implied that musical and linguistic skills could partly be based on shared neural mechanisms. In a regression study, Swaminathan and Schellenberg (2020) used a sample of six- to nine-year-old children to test the links between musical expertise and language ability, speech perception and grammar. The analyses revealed that language abilities had significant partial associations with musical ability but not with music training. Further, rhythm discrimination was a better predictor of language skills than melody discrimination. The authors concluded that links between music and language arise primarily from pre-existing factors and not from formal training in music.

Music training can alter the course of auditory development as late as adolescence. Tierney and colleagues (2015) investigated the effects of in-school music training versus another in-school training programme not focusing on the development of auditory skills. They tested adolescents on neural responses to sound and language skills before they entered high school, pre-training, and again three years later. They showed that in-school music training begun in high school prolonged the stability of subcortical sound processing and accelerated the maturation of cortical auditory responses. Phonological processing improved in both the music training and active control groups, but the enhancement was greater in adolescents who underwent music training.

Not all of the research supports the proposition that singing supports speech development. For example, Snijders and colleagues (2020) found that ten-month-old infants were able to segment words in children's songs—but they performed equally well at segmenting infant-directed speech. Similarly, Rossi and colleagues (2020) found no differences between speech and songs in a study on semantic processing in healthy adults.

Taken together, these data suggest that the presentation of verbal material as song may not be sufficient to enhance vocabulary learning or language comprehension in healthy individuals.

Children from Deprived Backgrounds

Some research has focused on children who have been perceived as 'at risk' because of their deprived backgrounds. For instance, Kraus and colleagues (2014) used a randomised controlled trial to investigate whether community music participation could induce a change in auditory processing in children from deprived backgrounds. The programme provided free music instruction to children who were considered to be at risk. The participants were 44 children with a mean age of eight years, living in gang reduction zones in Los Angeles. The children were randomly assigned to participate in or defer musical participation for one year. Participants attended music classes twice weekly for three to ten months. Students began in music appreciation classes, where they learned pitch-matching and rhythm skills, musical styles and notation, and basic vocal performance and recorder playing.

Students then progressed to instrumental instruction. Students were given their own instruments and participated in group-based instrumental classes for four hours per week. The children who were more committed to the music intervention, who attended more and participated to a greater extent in the classroom activities, developed stronger brain encoding of speech than those who were less engaged. The children who completed two years of music training had a stronger neurophysiological distinction of stop consonants and neural mechanisms linked to reading and language skills. One year of training was sufficient to elicit changes in nervous system functions. Greater amounts of instrumental music training were associated with larger gains in neural processing. The research showed that participation reinforced literacy skills and enhanced the neural encoding of speech cues—important for reading—and the perception of speech in noisy backgrounds (Kraus et al., 2014a; 2014b; Kraus and Strait, 2015; Slater et al., 2014).

Similarly, in an *El-Sistema*-inspired project, Habibi and colleagues (2016), as part of an ongoing five-year longitudinal study, investigated the effects of a music training programme on the auditory development of children, over the course of two years, beginning at age six to seven. The children in the music group were compared with two groups of children from the same socioeconomic background, one involved in sports training and the other not involved in any systematic training. Prior to participating, children who began training in music did not differ from those in the comparison groups in any of the assessed measures. After two years, the children in the music group, but not in the comparison groups, showed an enhanced ability to detect changes in tonal environment, and an accelerated maturity of auditory processing as measured by cortical auditory evoked potentials to musical notes.

Research with those with Auditory or Language Impairments

When the auditory system does not have full acoustic input, as in the case of hearing deficits or congenital deafness, the development of skills related to audition is damaged. Working with deaf children, Rochette and colleagues (2014) compared the auditory perception, auditory cognition and phonetic discrimination of 14 profoundly deaf children who completed weekly music lessons between the ages of eighteen months and four years, and 14 deaf children who did not receive musical instruction. The trained children showed better performance in auditory scene analysis, auditory working memory and phonetic discrimination tasks. Multiple regression analysis showed that success on these tasks was at least partly driven by music lessons.

While cochlear implants can support hearing, they cannot deliver complete auditory information to the cochlea. The input is small and distorted, and has an impact on communication skills. However, children who receive a cochlear implant by 12 months of age demonstrate normal language growth rates and achieve age-appropriate receptive language scores three years after the implant. Later implants lead to significant language delay, evident three years after the implant. The development of speech follows a similar pattern to that of normal hearing children, but is delayed (Leigh et al., 2013). Some research has explored whether musical interventions can help these children. For instance, Torppa and colleagues (2014a) assessed word and sentence stress perception, discrimination of fundamental frequency, intensity and duration, and forward digit-span twice over a period of 16 months. Twenty-one early-implanted children and age-matched normal-hearing children aged four to 13 years participated. Children with cochlear implants who had been exposed to music improved with age in word stress perception, intensity discrimination and digit-span. Their performance was equivalent to the natural-hearing children, while later-implanted children performed less well. Overall, the findings suggested that music was a valuable tool for the rehabilitation of implanted children.

A further study (Torppa et al., 2014b) researched the interplay between singing and cortical processing of music in children with cochlear implants. The findings showed an augmented development of neural networks for attention, and more accurate neural discrimination associated with singing. In addition, Torppa and colleagues concluded that musical playschool also supported learning with other children, as it offered more efficient use of mirror neurons, especially as the children with cochlear implants participated alongside their normal-hearing peers. The emotional and social aspects of the group in musical playschool may also impact on learning outcomes, through the provision of a positive and inspiring environment.

Similarly, Good and colleagues (2017) studied 18 children with cochlear implants aged six to 15, who received either six months of individualised piano lessons or six months of individualised painting lessons. Measures of music perception and emotional speech prosody perception were obtained pre-, mid- and post-training. Music training led to improved performance on tasks requiring the discrimination of melodic contour and rhythm, incidental memory for melodies and emotional speech prosody perception. Art training did not lead to the same improvements. Good and colleagues concluded that music training may be an effective supplementary technique for supporting auditory rehabilitation following cochlear implantation.

Children born very premature have an increased likelihood of sensory, cognitive and motor deficits. Mikkola and colleagues (2007) used neurocognitive tests with very pre-term children at one and five years old and suggested that they may have altered primary auditory processing. They suggested that the early auditory environment within the intensive care unit and during later hospitalisation might play a role in the decreased auditory, attention and learning skills of prematurely born infants. To ameliorate such deficits, Virtala and Partanen (2018) developed interventions focusing on music. They found that music-making and parental singing promoted infants' early language development and auditory neural processing.

There is some evidence that aphasia can be rehabilitated through music. Sparks and colleagues (1974) used melodic intonation therapy, which involves sung intonation of propositional sentences in such a way that the intoned pattern is similar to the natural prosodic pattern of the sentence when it is spoken. Eight severely, but not globally, impaired right-handed aphasic subjects with left hemisphere damage (resulting from cerebrovascular accidents) participated. Each patient acted as their own control. The participants had shown no improvement in verbal expression for at least six months, during which time they had received other language therapy. Recovery of some appropriate propositional language occurred for six of the eight patients as a result of melodic intonation therapy.

It has also been argued that music may aid the development of listening skills and support children with learning difficulties (Hirt-Mannheimer, 1995; Humpal and Wolf, 2007; Wolf, 1992). Music has helped children with developmental disabilities (Mendelson et al., 2016) and those with particularly low reading levels (Cogo-Moreira et al, 2013).

Infants of dyslexic parents show some minor differences in auditory processing compared with infants of parents without dyslexia. These can be observed in infancy using neurological measures. In a review of research on auditory processing deficits in individuals with dyslexia, Hämäläinen and colleagues (2013) showed that measures of frequency, rise time and duration discrimination, as well as amplitude modulation and frequency modulation detection, are most often impaired. It may be that infants with dyslexic parents and children with symptoms of dyslexia might benefit from training of their auditory systems to overcome the possible differences in auditory processing early in life. Indeed, musical interventions have been found to be successful in helping children with dyslexia overcome some of these difficulties (Flaugnacco et al., 2015). Children who show delayed language development at three and four years of age are at risk of dyslexia, although many children who eventually are diagnosed as dyslexic have perfectly normal language development. However, early language difficulties and a diagnosis of language impairment in childhood is predictive of reading disabilities in the later school years, and during adolescence and adulthood.

Atypical entrainment to rhythmic prosodic cues due to deficits in fine-grained auditory perception may constitute a risk for the development of speech and language disorders (Goswami, 2011; Ladányi, et al., 2020). If this is the case, then increasing the regularity of stimuli, or strengthening individual rhythmic abilities with the aim of improving neuronal entrainment, may enhance development. Some research has suggested that song could be used for improving speech processing in individuals with language processing deficits, including dyslexia (Vanden Bosch et al., 2020) as music-based training effects in dyslexia have already been demonstrated. Enhancing the auditory skills of children with dyslexia can be achieved by attendance at musical play school (Overy, 2000; Overy, 2003).

Children with developmental language disorders have been shown to be impaired not only in language processing (including syntax), but also in rhythm and metre perception. Sammler and Elmer (2020) suggest that there may be a role for rhythm-based processing in language processing and acquisition. Frey and colleagues, in a longitudinal study using EEG, demonstrated that six months of music training positively influenced the pre-attentive processing of voice onset time in speech in children with developmental difficulties, while Przybylski and colleagues (2013) tested the influence of external rhythmic auditory stimulation on syntax processing in children with specific language impairment and dyslexia. Children listened to either regular or irregular musical prime sequences, followed by blocks of grammatically correct and incorrect sentences. They were required to perform grammar judgements for each auditorily presented sentence. Performance of all children, including controls, was better after regular prime sequences than after irregular prime sequences. The benefit of the regular prime was stronger for children with specific language impairment than for dyslexic children. The results suggest that rhythmic structures, even in non-verbal materials, may boost linguistic structure processing. Regular music therapy can also help children with Rett syndrome, a genetic brain disorder associated with problems with language and coordination. It can improve receptive language, and verbal and nonverbal communication (Chou et al., 2019).

Music-making—whether playing an instrument or singing—is a multimodal activity that involves the integration of auditory and sensorimotor processes. The ability to sing in humans is evident from infancy and does not depend on formal vocal training, although it can be enhanced by training. Wan and colleagues (2010) reviewed the evidence on the therapeutic effects of singing, and how it might potentially ameliorate some of the speech deficits associated with conditions such as stuttering, Parkinson's disease, acquired brain lesions and autism. Singing may help children who stutter by reducing stress and using melodic architecture to help in the formation of longer verbal phrases (Clements-Cortès, 2012; Wan et al., 2010).

Overview

The previous sections and recent reviews (Benz et al., 2016; Engel et al., 2019; Hallam, 2015; 2017; Hämäläinen et al., 2013; Jäncke, 2012; Patel, 2008; Sammler and Elmer, 2020; Wan et al., 2010; White et al., 2013) provide considerable and compelling evidence that musical training sharpens the brain's early encoding of sound, leading to enhanced performance on a range of listening and aural processing skills. Active engagement with music in childhood produces structural changes in the brain related to the processing of sound, which can develop over quite short periods of time. Making music supports the development of aural processing systems, which facilitate the encoding and identification of speech sounds and patterns which, in turn, enhance language skills. The earlier that active participation takes place, the greater the length of participation, the level of commitment and its intensity, and the greater the impact. Musical experience and training also enhance emotional perception and a range of cognitive skills. The benefits of musical engagement occur without the conscious awareness of the participants and have been demonstrated with a range of different groups across the lifespan. Despite this, it is not possible to say with any certainty which musical activities are the most beneficial. For young children, informal music-making in the home and more formal activities in playschools have both been found to be effective. Later, school music education can have an impact, as can instrumental tuition. The particular instrument played and the genre engaged with lead to very specific neural and behavioural changes.

Overall, enhancing auditory cognition requires sufficient training, high levels of personal motivation, rewarding musical experiences, supportive learning environments and a range of high-quality formal and informal learning experiences. The most effective learning approaches will depend on the age and individual characteristics of the learner. The identification of optimal musical interventions is important to enable the further development of conceptual understanding and the enhancement of aural processing, as well as the amelioration of problems with aural processing and language.

4. Literacy and Related Language Skills

Literacy is generally defined as the ability to read and write, but more broadly has been considered as the ability to identify, understand, interpret, create, communicate and compute, using printed and written materials in a variety of contexts. This chapter will focus on how active engagement with music may support literacy, with a particular emphasis on reading and the skills required to become a competent reader. It will also consider research on writing and spelling.

The evidence for an association between music training, musical skills and reading skills is typically explained by near-transfer theories. Reading requires the development of decoding and comprehension skills. Comprehension requires basic word-decoding skills, as well as higher-level cognitive processes such as memory and attention (Sesma et al., 2009). Active engagement with making music may have a differential impact on decoding and comprehension. Decoding is the ability to apply knowledge of letter-sound relationships, including knowledge of letter patterns, to enable the correct pronunciation of unfamiliar words. It is strongly associated with auditory skills (Ahissar et al., 2000). In order to be able to decode written material, readers have to be aware of the sounds related to the written word, i.e. phonics. Phonological awareness is an important precursor to early reading (Bradley and Bryant, 1983). Children need to develop phonological awareness to begin to be able to translate written text into sound. Phonological awareness is the ability to analyse and manipulate language on two levels. At the word level, phonological awareness refers to the ability to manipulate and analyse larger phonological units (for instance, rhyming and blending words). At the phoneme level, phonological ability refers to the ability to analyse and manipulate individual sound units (phonemes) within a word. It has repeatedly been shown that phonological awareness is an important predictor of later reading ability (Pratt and Brady, 1988; Bruck, 1992). Successful decoding occurs when a learner uses knowledge of letter-sound relationships to accurately read a word.

Correlation Studies and Comparisons between Musicians and Non-Musicians

One strand of research on the role of music in the development of literacy skills has focused on comparing musicians with non-musicians. A second strand has examined the relationship between musical skills and literacy.

Comparisons between musicians and non-musicians have revealed that musicians exhibit advantages in making judgements about grammar (Patston and Tippett, 2011), are better at correctly pronouncing irregularly spelled words (Jakobson et al., 2008; Stoesz et al., 2007), and remembering lyrics (Kilgour et al., 2000), novel words (Dittinger et al., 2016) and short excerpts of speech (Cohen et al., 2011). They have a larger vocabulary (Forgeard et al., 2008a) and in one study showed enhanced comprehension of complicated passages of text (Thompson et al., 2012). Those who have had musical training demonstrate enhanced speech perception on a wide range of different tasks. For instance, they can perceive speech better than those without training when it is accompanied by noise (Parbery-Clark et al., 2009a; 2009b; 2011), can identify syllables presented when spectral information is degraded (Elmer et al., 2012), identify whether sentences in a foreign tone-based language are the same or different (Marie et al., 2011a; 2011b), and predict the ability to perceive and produce subtle phonetic contrasts in a second language (Slevc and Miyake, 2006). They are also better at phoneme perception (Kuhnis et al., 2013). Children with four years of music lessons, aged nine, have been found to be more accurate and fast in accurately discriminating syllables that varied in duration and frequency than those not having lessons (Chobert et al., 2011). Cross-sectional studies have shown that preschool and school-aged children and adults with musical experience are able to make stronger distinctions between speech syllables than non-music students (Kraus and Nicol, 2014; Parberry-Clark et al., 2012;

Strait and Kraus, 2014; Zuk et al., 2013). Having musical skills also enhances the ability to interpret affective speech rhythms (Thompson et al., 2004); eight-year-olds with musical training outperform those with no training on music and language tasks (Magne et al., 2006). In research with 250 Chinese elementary-school children, Yang and colleagues (2014) examined the relationship between long-term music training and students' development of first language, second language and mathematics. The musician children outperformed non-musicians on musical achievement and second language development. Although music training appeared to be correlated with the children's final academic development of first and second languages and mathematics, it did not independently contribute to the development of first language or mathematical skills.

Correlation studies are able to identify if there are relationships between musical skills and various skills related to literacy, including verbal and auditory working memory. Studies with preschool children, aged four to five years, have found relationships between musical skills, phonological awareness and reading development (Anvari et al., 2002). There is a positive relationship between phonological awareness and musical ability in preschoolers, children aged five to six, and older children (Lamb & Gregory, 1993; Milovanov et al., 2008; Milovanov and Tervaniemi, 2011; Peynircioğlu et al., 2002), while Loui and colleagues (2011) worked with children aged seven to nine years old and showed a significant positive correlation between pitch perception and production, and phonemic awareness. There are also relationships between the development of auditory skills in early childhood and informal musical activities (Putkinen et al., 2013a).

Moderate relationships have also been found between tonal memory and reading age (Barwick et al., 1989), while the magnitude of neural responses to speech harmonics is correlated with reading ability (Banai et al., 2009). Schellenberg (2006) found that length of music training predicted measures of reading even after controlling for intelligence, while Chandrasekaran and Kraus (2010) linked poor reading ability with deficiencies in processing essential sound elements. Corrigall and Trainor (2011), examining the association between length of music training and reading ability in 46 six to nine-year-old children enrolled in music lessons, found that length of training correlated significantly with reading comprehension but was not associated with word decoding scores. The length of music training was robustly associated with reading comprehension, even after age, socioeconomic status, auditory perception, word decoding, general intelligence and the number of hours spent reading each week were taken into account. There is a relationship between individuals who are tone deaf and phonological processing, word discrimination and syllable segmentation (Jones et al., 2009).

Swaminathan and colleagues in a series of studies (2017; 2018; 2019) explored a range of relationships between music and other skills. In 2017, they reported that the relationship between music training and reading in adults was facilitated by general cognitive—rather than auditory—skills. In 2018, also working with adults, they assessed reading ability, comprehension and speed, music-perception skills, melody and rhythm, general cognitive ability, non-verbal intelligence, short-term memory, working memory, family income and parents' education, and found that reading ability was associated positively with music training, English as a native language and general cognitive ability. The association between reading and music training was significant after socioeconomic status, native language and music perception skills were controlled for, but when general cognitive abilities were held constant, there was no longer an association between reading and music training. These findings suggest that the association between reading ability and music training is a consequence of general cognitive abilities. In 2019, an association between rhythm aptitude and speech perception was found in a sample of six- to nine-year-old children. Musical training was associated positively with performance on a grammar test, musical ability, IQ, openness and age. Regression analyses revealed that language abilities had significant partial associations with musical ability and IQ but not with music training. Rhythm discrimination was a better predictor of language skills than melody discrimination. Musical ability predicted language ability independently of IQ.

Not all correlational studies have shown a positive relationship between music and literacy skills. Establishing the main and subsidiary beats in a musical selection has not been found to be a significant predictor of reading in third- and fourth-grade students (Chamberlain, 2003), while Hartas (2011) found no relationship between parent-reported frequency of singing songs and rhymes or playing music at three years and teacher-rated performance on literacy. The strongest relationships with children's learning outcomes were between family income and mother's educational level.

Intervention Studies

Learning to read requires word decoding skills These skills are strongly associated with auditory skills. The auditory analysis skills used in language processing, phonological distinctions, blending and segmentation of sounds are similar to the skills necessary for the perception of rhythmic (Lamb and Gregory, 1993; Lipscomb et al., 2008), harmonic and melodic discrimination (Anvari et al., 2002; Barwick et al., 1989; Lamb and Gregory, 1993). Learning to become an expert reader involves dynamic cross-modal processes, beginning with the mapping of letters and sounds, culminating in skilled reading, which involves the simultaneous processing of phrases, sentences and larger multiple sources of information from the text and their integration with contextually relevant background information from the reader's own experiences (Gellert and Elbro, 2017; Perfetti and Stafura, 2014). The dynamic and multiplex process of reading has been argued to be similar to the entrainment seen in musical ensembles, where individuals segregate and integrate concurrent streams of information (Ragert et al., 2014). Reading requires integrative attending and activates an amodal interface, where internal and external goals and experiences intersect.

A range of intervention studies have explored the impact of active engagement with music on phonological awareness and reading skills. Research findings, which attempts to demonstrate causality between musical engagement, phonological awareness and reading, have been mixed. Arts-enriched programmes that include music have led to improvements in school readiness in relation to receptive vocabulary (Brown et al., 2010) and literacy (Phillips et al., 2010) when compared to non-arts programmes. In a school-based arts programme which included music, Gardiner and colleagues (1996) showed that children with a lower score on literacy at baseline achieved similar scores on reading tests after one year of visual arts and music training, as compared to controls.

Some research has focused on the impact of music on sound processing, as it relates to phonemic awareness. In a study of preschool children's informal musical activities at home, Politimou and colleagues (2020) found systematic associations between rhythm perception/ production and phonological awareness, while melody perception was related to the acquisition of grammar. Similarly, Eccles and colleagues (2020) evaluated the effect of varying durations of music instruction over a single academic year on the phonological awareness and early literacy of young children aged five to seven, compared with children who only received class music. The children with greater exposure to music showed greater improvement in phonological awareness. Douglas and Willats (1994) found that group training involving singing and the use of percussive instruments improved decoding.

Good and colleagues (2002) worked with kindergarten children who participated in a weekly music intervention lasting 30 minutes which consisted of singing, body percussion activity, movement, instrument playing, singing and the use of graphic notation. On completion of the programme, the music group exhibited significantly higher phoneme segmentation fluency as compared with controls. Similarly, Degé and Schwarzer (2011) showed that preschool children who were randomly assigned to intensive training in music (ten minutes each day for five days each week, for twenty weeks) showed improvements in phonological awareness that were identical to changes in other children who received lessons in perceiving and segmenting speech sounds. A control group who received sports training showed no improvement.

Also working with kindergarten children, Moritz and colleagues (2013) explored whether musical activity could support the acquisition of reading skills before formal reading instruction began. They found that rhythm skill was related to phonological segmentation skills at the beginning of kindergarten, and that children who received more music training during kindergarten showed a wider range of phonological awareness skills at the end of kindergarten than children with less training. Furthermore, kindergartners' rhythmic ability was strongly related to their phonological awareness and basic word identification skills in second grade. Schon (2014) has also shown that phonological awareness can be influenced by several months of rhythmic training which, in turn, improves reading skills. In a preschool setting, Elliot and Mikulas (2014) investigated the effectiveness of an integrated music curriculum on language and literacy skills in a year-long study, which employed a pre- and post-treatment design with a control group. Students in the treatment group received instruction using an integrated music curriculum as part of their preschool instruction. The findings showed that the students in the treatment group had significantly greater gains in language and literacy, with an effect size of 0.24. In a similar study, Vidal and colleagues (2020) tested 44 children aged three to four years old with a phonological awareness test, prior to and after an intervention period lasting a full school year with weekly music or visual arts classes. Following the interventions, both groups improved, but the music class students outperformed those in the visual art classes, showing larger differences before and after the intervention.

Working in a community setting, Linnavalli and colleagues (2018) studied whether a low-cost, weekly music playschool provided for five- to six-year-old children would have an impact on linguistic abilities. Sixty-six children were tested four times over two school years on phonemic processing, vocabulary, perceptual reasoning and inhibitory control. The children attending music playschool were compared to their peers who were attending dance lessons or not attending either activity. Attendance at music playschool significantly improved the development of children's phoneme processing and vocabulary skills.

In a series of studies, Rauscher and colleagues (Rauscher, 2009; Rauscher & Hinton, 2011) explored whether children receiving Suzuki violin instruction performed better on phonemic awareness tasks than control groups. Seventy-five musically naive five-year-olds participated. Lessons were provided for 45 minutes per week for 16 weeks. Prior to instruction, there were no differences in the children's performance on a reading test, but following the intervention the children receiving music lessons scored significantly higher on letter-word calling and phonemic awareness than the other groups.

Adopting a training programme which included a range of activities, Gromko (2005) studied five- to seven-year-old children who received four months of music instruction for 30 minutes once a week. The instruction included active music-making with movement emphasising a steady beat, rhythm and pitch, as well as the association of sounds with symbols. The children who received the music instruction showed significantly greater gains in phonemic awareness when compared to a control group. Learning to discriminate differences between tonal and rhythmic patterns and to associate their perceptions with visual symbols seemed to transfer to improved phonemic awareness. Similarly, Welch and colleagues (2012) evaluated the impact of a music programme which linked literacy activities with a range of musical activities including chanting, clapping, copying and composing rhythms, and improvising using rhymes and alliterative or unusual vocabulary. Children participating in the musical activities showed on average 8.4 months of reading improvement compared with 1.8 months for those in the control group. In a later study, Welch and colleagues (2020) evaluated a six-month specialist singing project undertaken with young disadvantaged children in London, where professional singers provided focused mentoring—relating to a specialised programme of singing and vocal activities—to generalist primary-school teachers. The mentored classroom-based singing activities resulted in significant improvements in children's singing, changes in reading and aspects of executive function related to inhibition and phonological working memory.

Using painting as a comparison activity, Moreno and colleagues (2009) conducted a longitudinal study with 32 non-musician children over nine months. Following the first testing sessions, non-musician children were pseudo-randomly assigned to music or to painting training for six months and were tested again after training using the same tests. After musical—but not painting—training, children showed enhanced performance in reading. In a further study of eight-year-old-who were assigned pseudo randomly to six months of music or painting tuition, the children in the music group showed larger pre- to post-test improvement in reading irregularly spelled words (Moreno et al., 2009). A further study with pseudo-random assignment of four- to six-year-olds to four weeks of daily, computer-controlled lessons in listening to music or visual arts, children in the music group had larger pre- to post-test increases in vocabulary (Moreno et al., 2011a; 2011b). The music group also showed greater improvement on a task that required them to match arbitrary symbols with words, a skill that is a prerequisite for learning to read (Moreno et al., 2011b). Similarly, Chobert and colleagues (2011; 2014) conducted a longitudinal study over two school years with non-musician children randomly assigned to music or painting training. Neurological responses to syllables that differed in vowel frequency, vowel duration and voice onset time were recorded three times over the course of the study. The results highlighted the influence of musical training on the development of phonological representations in normally developing children. Also using painting as a comparison activity, François and colleagues (2013) assigned children, matched in terms of cognitive abilities, sex, age, grade at school and socioeconomic status, to music or painting lessons for a two-year period. Before the start of the study, the two groups of children performed similarly on a test where they had to identify whether three-syllable nonsense words were present in a five-minute string of syllables. After one year of training, the music group performed better than the painting group, with the difference increasing over the two-year period.

Nan and colleagues (2018) studied 74 Mandarin-speaking children aged four to five years old who were pseudo-randomly assigned to piano training, reading training or a no-contact control group. Six months of piano training improved behavioural auditory word discrimination in general, as well as word discrimination based on vowels, when compared with controls. The group receiving reading training yielded similar trends; however, the piano group demonstrated unique advantages over the reading and control groups in consonant-based word discrimination. All three groups improved on general cognitive measures, including tests of IQ, working memory and attention. Focusing on adolescents, Tierney and colleagues (2015) investigated the effects of in-school music training, versus a school training programme that did not focus on the development of auditory skills. Participants were tested on neural responses to sound and language skills before they entered high school, before the training and again three years later. In-school music training begun at secondary school prolonged the stability of subcortical sound processing and accelerated maturation of cortical auditory responses. Phonological processing improved in the music training and control groups, but the impact was greater in the adolescents who underwent music training.

In an interesting study which directly related rhythm to reading, Lipscomb and colleagues (2008) provided a form of reading rhythm training to children in third grade who participated in four sessions each week for 12 weeks, where they read lists of words at varying *tempi*. This led to a dramatic improvement in reading fluency.

Children from low socioeconomic backgrounds tend to fall progressively further behind their higher income peers over the course of their academic careers. Music interventions have been proposed as a way to help low-income children to improve their academic attainment. Some research has pursued this line of enquiry. For instance, Register and colleagues (2004) examined the effects of a music therapy programme designed to teach reading skills versus a television programme designed to support literacy skills on the early literacy of kindergarten children aged five to seven years from low socioeconomic backgrounds. Each class was assigned to one of four treatment conditions: music only, video only, music and video or a control group with no activity. Children's literacy was assessed using standardised tests and teacher assessment. The 'music and video' and 'music only' groups achieved the highest increase in the mean scores of four out of seven literacy subtests. The 'video' group scored significantly better on phonemic segmentation than the other groups. Strong correlations were found between letter-naming and initial sound-fluency tests. However, children were more off-task in the video condition than the music condition. Children in the 'music' and 'video' enrichment groups showed gains in four out of the eight tests used to measure progress. Slater and colleagues (2014) used a controlled, longitudinal design to assess the impact of group music instruction on English reading ability in 42 low-income Spanish-English bilingual children aged six to nine in Los Angeles. After one year, children who received music training retained their age-normal level of reading performance, while a matched control group's performance deteriorated, consistent with expected declines in this population. While the extent of change was modest, the outcomes nonetheless showed that music can help to counteract the negative effects of low socioeconomic status on children's literacy development. In a similar study, Barbaroux and colleagues (2019) studied the impact of a classical music training programme, Démos, on the cognitive development of children from low socioeconomic backgrounds. The children were presented with standardised tests before the start of the programme, and again after 18 months of music training. The findings showed that the Démos music training improved reading precision.

Not all of the research has found a positive impact of musical training on literacy (Bowles, 2003; Kemmerer, 2003; Lu, 1986; Montgomery, 1997). Some findings have been difficult to interpret. For instance, Rauscher (2014) provided at-risk preschool children with weekly piano instruction, computer instruction or no instruction for two years. No effects were found in relation to verbal, memory or reading tests. Similarly, Piro and Ortiz (2009) focused on the way that learning the piano might impact on the development of vocabulary and verbal sequencing in second-grade children. Forty-six children who had studied the piano for three consecutive years participated, with 57 children acting as controls. At the end of the study, the music learning group had significantly better vocabulary and verbal sequencing scores. However, they had already been playing the piano for two years with no initial differences in reading between their skills and those of the control group. These findings are difficult to interpret. The authors suggested that no enhancement had occurred because effects may take a long time to appear, because the age of tuition was important, or because the summer holidays immediately prior to testing may have lowered initial scores. The tuition itself may also have changed over time.

Lukács and Honbolygó (2019) evaluated the transfer effect of general elementary-school music education on the development of linguistic abilities. The relationship between specific musical auditory skills, phonological awareness and reading was investigated in 30 second-grade children who either attended a class with an intensive music curriculum or a class with a regular curriculum. The findings indicated no significant differences between the children experiencing intensive music education or the normal curriculum. Overall, one year of Kodály-based classroom music education was not sufficient to yield improvement in musical and linguistic abilities, although phoneme deletion accuracy was associated with tonal memory, suggested by a similar quasi-experimental pre- and post-test design with measurements taken across a period of two years. Kempert and colleagues (2016) tested the effects of two interventions: a consecutive combination of musical and phonological training, and phonological training alone. The participants were 424 German-speaking children aged four to five years old. The findings demonstrated a positive relationship between musical abilities and phonological awareness. While the phonological training produced positive effects, adding musical training did not contribute significantly to the development of phonological awareness. This may have been because of differences in the initial level of phonological awareness of the participants.

Overall, there may be a range of reasons for the differences in the research findings. The types of training adopted differ and there may be differences in the quality of their delivery. There is a large age range in the participating children's ages and they are likely to be at different stages in their developing literacy, although experimental designs are able to take account of this to some extent. The development of phonological skills may be important early on in the process of developing literacy skills and these may be enhanced with shorter periods of musical engagement, whereas longer training may be needed to influence decoding and ultimately understanding.

Children Facing Challenges with Literacy Skills

One strand of research has focused on children with difficulties in reading. The evidence for the importance of rhythmic training is especially strong for poor or dyslexic readers (Overy, 2000; 2003; Tallal et al., 1993; Thomson, 1993). Huss and colleagues (2011) have shown that dyslexics have lower performance than normal-achieving readers on tasks involving musical metrical structure. This is supported by a range of studies showing that children with dyslexia have difficulties with keeping a beat (Corriveau et al., 2007; Corriveau and Goswami, 2009; Goswami et al., 2002; Tierney & Kraus, 2013b; Wolff et al., 1990). While children with dyslexia have impaired rhythmic processing skills, especially for rhythm production, they have normal pitch-processing skills (Overy, 2000; 2003; Overy et al., 2003).

Musical interventions emphasising the development of rhythmic skills seem to have the greatest impact for children facing challenges with literacy. For instance, working with children in kindergarten, Bolduc (2009) compared the effects of two music programmes. One programme employed musical activities to increase interest in reading and writing in those with special educational needs, while the other was primarily designed to enhance musical abilities. The programme that focused on enhancing reading and writing was more effective in enhancing phonological awareness than the one designed to enhance musical abilities. Similarly, Standley and Hughes (1997) evaluated the effects of music sessions designed to enhance the pre-reading and writing skills of 24 children, aged four to five, who were enrolled in early intervention programmes or programmes for children with particular needs.

The intervention lasted for just over seven weeks and included two 30-minute music lessons per week for a total of fifteen lessons. In the autumn, musical activities were designed to teach writing skills and, in the spring, reading skills. Children receiving the normal kindergarten curriculum without music involvement acted as controls. All participants were tested before and after the intervention. The findings demonstrated that music significantly enhanced print concepts and the pre-writing skills of the children. Replicating this work, Register and colleagues (2001) studied 50 children aged four to five years old enrolled in early intervention programmes or programmes for children with particular needs. The intervention and control group both received two 30-minute music sessions each week for an entire school year. The differentiating factors were the structure and components of the musical activities. The autumn sessions for the experimental group were focused on writing skills while the sessions in the spring taught reading and literacy concepts. Music sessions for the control group were based purely on thematic material, which was determined by the classroom teacher with the purposeful exclusion of all pre-literacy concepts. All participants were tested at the beginning and end of the programme. The findings demonstrated that the music sessions significantly enhanced both groups' abilities to learn pre-writing and print concepts, but the experimental group showed significantly higher results on logo identification and a word recognition test after the intervention. Working with older children, aged six to eight, Nicholson (1972) studied the impact of a music intervention on children categorised as slow learners. After music training, the experimental group exhibited significantly higher reading performance, scoring in the 88th percentile versus the 72nd percentile. After an additional year of musical training, the reading scores of the experimental group were still superior to those of the control group.

Drawing on a theoretical framework which emphasised pulse as the underlying organisational feature common to music and language, Long and Hallam (2012) investigated the impact of an intervention on children aged eight to ten years old. The rhythm-based music intervention involved an entrainment strategy in which groups of children rapidly developed music-notation reading skills while synchronising stamping, clapping and chanting actions in time with a musical accompaniment for ten minutes each week. The intervention groups received the rhythm-based music intervention for ten minutes each week for six weeks. The effects of the rhythmic training were assessed before and after the intervention, and measured reading behaviour and rhythmic performance. A control group was matched on reading comprehension and rhythmic performance. There were statistically significant effects on reading comprehension scores for those children with lower attainment in reading, but not for normal-attaining children. This research demonstrated that children with reading difficulties can benefit from specific rhythmic musical training which was carried out alongside their normal-attaining classmates. In a similar study, Long (2014) recruited 15 children aged nine to ten who had been identified as weak readers by their school. The intervention consisted of ten minutes of rhythm-based exercises and was administered at the start of the children's usual weekly curriculum music lessons. The children's school music teacher was trained to deliver the intervention in two sessions, with a gap of one week between them. Following participation in the intervention, statistically significant gains occurred in the children's reading comprehension, reading accuracy and reading rate. An analysis of reading fluency revealed significant gains in the prosodic features of reading behaviour, including syllable division, grammatical structure and phrase contours. The rhythmic training emphasised group interaction, which also led to the children reporting positive changes in their sense of wellbeing. This research showed that interventions can be effective when delivered to a whole class by a class teacher. The intervention required mental anticipation and inhibitory control by participants, in order to lift one foot while striking the other against the floor in synchrony with the strong beat of the musical accompaniment and the actions of the other children. The entrainment activity applied the theoretical modelling of normal anti-synchrony—as one foot comes up, the other goes down (Clayton et al., 2005)—and a stable hierarchical distribution of cognitive attention (Clayton et al., 2005; Jones, 1976; Jones and Boltz, 1989; Jones and Yee, 1997). Overall, the children were required to plan ahead, synchronise, monitor and integrate multi-level physical coordination, which in turn required anticipatory and inhibitory control, while keeping time with the musical accompaniment and the other children. The teacher also modelled reading simple staff notation and chanting the alphabet letter names of music notation in a monotone, which was synchronised in time with stamping and clapping actions. During the training, in addition to reading pitch, the note durations were varied and rests were added. Following the intervention, the children demonstrated statistically significant gains in reading comprehension, accuracy and rate of reading. Comprehension and rate of reading had large effect sizes, with a moderate effect size for accuracy. The mean change in reading accuracy for the intervention group was 1.83 in standardised scores and, for the control group, 0.45 in standardised scores. The mean change in reading comprehension for the intervention group was 5.82 in standardised scores and, for the control group, 3.49 in standardised scores. There was no statistically significant difference in rate of reading. Using the same music programme for ten minutes each week over a ten-week period with groups of ten children, 354 in total, who had lower-than-average reading scores in the first year of secondary school (eleven- to twelve-years-old), Hallam (2018) found that those randomly allocated to intervention groups showed statistically greater improvement in reading accuracy and comprehension than controls, but not in reading rate. The differences in reading accuracy were equivalent to 1.38 in standardised scores and, for reading comprehension, 2.33 in standardised scores. Similarly, Bonacina and colleagues (2015) developed computer-assisted training, called rhythmic reading training, where reading exercises were combined with a rhythmic background. Participants took part in nine bi-weekly individual sessions of 30 minutes. The intervention had a positive effect on reading speed and accuracy, and significant effects were also found for the reading speed of short and long pseudo-words, high-frequency long words, and text reading accuracy.

Not all of the research has demonstrated overwhelmingly positive effects of music interventions for those who find literacy challenging.

For instance, Bhide and colleagues (2013) compared the effects of a musical intervention for poor readers with a software intervention based on rhyme training and phoneme-grapheme learning, and found that both interventions had similar benefits for literacy, with large effect sizes. Some music interventions have had very small effects. For instance, working in Brazilian schools in an attempt to improve reading skills, Cogo-Moreira and colleagues (2013) studied children aged eight to ten with reading difficulties. Two hundred and thirty-five children with reading difficulties in ten schools participated in a five-month, randomised controlled trial in an impoverished zone within the city of São Paulo, to test the effects of a music education intervention while assessing reading skills and academic achievement during the school year. Five schools were chosen randomly to incorporate music classes, while five served as controls. Two different methods of analysis revealed mixed results. Positive results were found for the rate of correct real words read per minute and phonological awareness. There were also improvements in Portuguese and mathematics throughout the school year but, overall, the effects were relatively small.

Children with dyslexia have been studied over a number of years. The core deficit underlying developmental dyslexia has been identified as difficulties in dynamic and rapidly changing auditory information processing, which contributes to the development of impaired phonological representations for words. Overy (2003) argued that the underlying causes of the language and literacy difficulties experienced by dyslexic children are linked to deficits in timing, as they exhibit timing difficulties in language, music, perception and cognition, as well as motor control. Based on these ideas, Overy and colleagues (2003) designed a programme which was administered to 15 dyslexic children aged seven to eleven, and 11 control children, aged seven to ten. The children were tested on musical aptitude and their scores were compared. The results showed that the dyslexic group scored higher than the control group on three tests of pitch skills, but lower than the control group on seven out of nine tests of timing skills. Particular difficulties were noted on one of the tests involving rapid temporal processing, in which a subgroup of five of the dyslexic children was found to account for all of the significant errors. There was also a correlation between spelling ability and the skill of tapping out the rhythm of a song, both of which involve the skill of syllable segmentation. These results suggest that timing presents a particular difficulty for dyslexic children and that they may be helped using targeted interventions.

Since this early research, a range of studies have considered issues relating to dyslexia. Even short-term rhythm instruction has brought about positive effects (Habibi et al, 2014). Seven—month-long training has been shown to lead to an increase in phonological awareness and reading skills (Flaugnacco et al., 2015). Habibi and colleagues (2016) tested the efficacy of a specially designed cognitive music training method which included a series of musical exercises involving (jointly and simultaneously) the sensory, visual, auditory, somatosensory and motor systems, with special emphasis on rhythmic perception and production, in addition to intensive training on various features of musical audition. Two separate studies were carried out—one in which children with dyslexia received intensive musical exercises concentrated over 18 hours during three consecutive days, and the other in which the 18 hours of musical training were spread over six weeks. Both studies showed significant improvements in several untrained, linguistic and non-linguistic variables. The first study yielded significant improvement in categorical perception and the auditory perception of the temporal components of speech. The second study revealed improvements in auditory attention, phonological awareness, reading abilities and repetition of pseudo-words. These benefits persisted for six weeks after training. Flaugnacco and colleagues (2015) carried out a prospective, multi-centre, open randomised controlled trial with children with dyslexia aged eight to eleven, consisting of test, intervention and re-test. After the intervention, the music group performed better than the control group in tasks assessing rhythmic abilities, phonological awareness and reading skills. The findings showed that music training can modify reading and phonological abilities even when they are severely impaired.

Thomson (2014) explored the perception of amplitude envelopes in speech and non-speech, and the necessity of this skill for parsing the sounds represented as letters in literacy in a group of school children with dyslexia. A six-week rhythm-based intervention had positive effects on phonological awareness and literacy equal to those of a control intervention on phonemic awareness, while Frey and colleagues (2019) investigated whether six months of active music training was more efficient than painting training in improving the pre-attentive processing of phonological parameters based on durations that are often impaired in children with developmental dyslexia. Comparisons were made with a typically developing group of children matched on reading age. The results showed a normalisation of the pre-attentive processing of voice onset time in children with developmental dyslexia after music training, but not after painting training. Working with adults, Boll-Avetisyan and colleagues (2020) assessed the reading and musical abilities of dyslexics and age-matched controls, and presented them with a rhythmic grouping task. They listened to speech streams with syllables alternating in intensity, duration or neither, and indicated whether they perceived a strong-weak or weak-strong rhythm pattern. The findings showed that the adults with dyslexia had lower musical rhythm abilities than those without dyslexia. Lower musical rhythm ability was associated with lower reading ability. However, speech grouping by adults with dyslexia was not impaired when musical rhythm perception ability was controlled for. Rhythmic grouping was predicted by musical rhythm perception ability, irrespective of dyslexia. Overall, the results suggested associations among musical rhythm perception ability, speech rhythm perception and reading ability in adults with dyslexia. Cogo-Moreira and colleagues (2012), in a review of research on dyslexia and music, found no randomised controlled studies and argued that it was therefore impossible to draw any conclusions.

Are Pitch or Rhythm Programmes More Effective in Enhancing Literacy?

As researchers have explored the extent to which active engagement with music may support the development of literacy skills, there has been ongoing debate about the kind of interventions which may be the most successful. Most musical programmes include pitch and rhythm activities, but some research has focused on trying to assess whether rhythm or melody is more important in supporting literacy skills. One approach to considering this has been to examine the relative skills of those with poor musical or literacy skills. For instance, Sun and colleagues (2017) examined whether phonological impairments were evident in individuals with poor music abilities. Twenty individuals with congenital amusia and 20 matched controls were assessed on a pure tone-pitch discrimination task, a rhythm discrimination task, and four phonological tests. The amusic participants showed deficits in discriminating pitch and rhythmic patterns that involved a regular beat. As a group, these individuals performed similarly to controls on all of the phonological tests but eight. Amusics with severe pitch impairment, as identified by the pitch discrimination task, exhibited significantly worse performance than other participants in phonological awareness. A regression analysis indicated that pitch discrimination thresholds predicted phonological awareness beyond that predicted by phonological short-term memory and rhythm discrimination. In contrast, the rhythm discrimination task did not predict phonological awareness beyond that predicted by pitch discrimination thresholds, suggesting that accurate pitch discrimination is critical for phonological processing. Patscheke and colleagues (2019) also investigated the separate effects of training in rhythm and pitch on phonological awareness in preschool children aged between four and six years old. Participants were randomly assigned to either a non-music training condition, a sports programme or a music training condition which was either based on rhythm or pitch. All groups were trained three times a week for twenty minutes per session over a period of 16 weeks. Phonological awareness was tested before and after the training phase. Following training, only the pitch programme showed a positive effect on phonological awareness concerning rhyming, blending and segmenting. Lamb and Gregory (1993) also found that pitch perception was associated with reading ability in five-year-olds after controlling for non-verbal ability, while Barwick and colleagues found that pitch perception was associated with reading ability in seven- to ten-year-old reading-disabled children after controlling for general intelligence. Similarly, Besson and colleagues (2007) examined pitch processing in dyslexic children and found that they had difficulties discriminating strong pitch changes that were easily discriminated by non-dyslexic readers. Rautenberg (2013) studied the effects of musical training on decoding skills in German-speaking primary school children and found that rhythmical abilities were significantly correlated with decoding skills, reading accuracy and reading prosody, while tonal skills were not related to reading skills.

As the research with children experiencing difficulties with literacy has shown, programmes with a focus on rhythm have been particularly effective in enhancing reading skills (Boll-Avetisyan et al., 2020; Fotidzis et al., 2018; Hallam 2018; Long, 2014; Long and Hallam, 2012; Overy, 2003; Overy et al., 2003). There is a relationship between tests of auditory-visual rhythmic pattern-matching and reading ability in eight- and nine-year-olds (Rudnick et al., 1967; Sterrit and Rudnick, 1967), while rhythmic skills may be a better predictor of reading ability than pitch-based skills (Douglas and Willatts, 1994; Huss et al., 2011; Strait, et al., 2011a; 2011b; Swaminathan and Schellenberg, 2020), although not all of the research supports this.

Cultural factors play a role in how individuals perceive metrical structure, including beat perception (Tierney and Kraus, 2013b) and the perception of complex rhythms (Hannon and Trehub, 2005). The human ability to perceive and entrain to a beat flexibly and accurately is spontaneous and universal across cultures (Savage et al., 2015; Bégel et al., 2017), although there is individual variability in sensorimotor synchronisation, including the phenomenon known as beat deafness (Nozaradan et al., 2016)—an individual's inability to distinguish musical rhythm or move in time to it. By nine months of age, the coordination of rhythm and syllable structure is usually sufficiently supportive for the infant to segment speech streams into syllables (Morgan and Saffran, 1995). Rhythmic movement may play a role in this process. While many children naturally move in time to a beat, enculturation plays a major role in this process (Repp and Su, 2013; Manning and Schutz, 2013). Jones and colleagues (2006) propose the pitch-time entrainment theory, which argues that timing in the brain can be understood as a response to regular or irregular rhythmical events. Children display entertainment—the patterning of body processes and movements to the rhythm of music—typically by four years of age (Trainor and Cirelli, 2015) but it takes longer to adjust to tempo. This does not usually occur until seven to eight years of age (Kurgansky and Shupikova, 2011).

Reading ability and phonological awareness are related to a variety of rhythmic abilities, including reproduction of rhythmic patterns (Rautenberg, 2015), tempo reproduction (Moritz et al., 2013), tapping to the beat of music (David et al., 2007), discrimination of stimuli based on amplitude rise times (Goswami et al., 2011; Leong et al., 2011) and temporal patterns (Overy, 2003; Strait et al., 2011). Furthermore, children who have language-learning impairment tap more variably to a beat (Corriveau and Goswami, 2009). Musical training improves verbal ability (Moreno et al., 2011), speech segmentation (François et al., 2013), sentence processing (Moreno et al., 2009) and syllable processing (Chobert et al., 2014), while training in beat synchronisation has been shown to improve reading fluency (Taub and Lazarus, 2012). Overall, it seems that rhythmic training may enhance learning to read. Neurological evidence revealing a direct link between cortical and behavioural measures of rhythmic entrainment supports this (Nozaradan et al., 2016).

Tracking rhythm patterns seems to play a vital role in both music and speech perception, both of which are important for acquiring reading skills. Beat induction, where humans can derive a pulse from most music even when it is not explicit, has been suggested to serve the development of auditory scene analysis and language (Patel, 2008). In particular, the supplementary motor area known to be involved in the articulation of speech and the preparation of movement, is engaged when performing music, imagining listening to music or imagining performing to music (Herholz and Zatorre, 2012; Brown et al., 2015). It also plays an important role in planning music during performance, in terms of rhythm and melody sequencing (de Manzanö and Ullén, 2012). The link between the basal ganglia and the supplementary motor area along the dorsal route supports the finding that the ability to synchronise with a beat is positively correlated with better pre-reading skills, such as the segmenting of speech streams and better neural encoding of speech and language (Carr et al., 2014; Tierney and Kraus, 2014; Kraus and Slater, 2016), better subcortical neural timing in adolescents (Tierney and Kraus, 2013a) as well as better cognitive and linguistic skills (Tierney and Kraus, 2013b). The integration of sensory and motor information may provide a mechanism for predicting sequence timing (Large et al., 2015), such as the processes that ensure smooth flow in a conversation.

Tierney and Kraus (2013c) propose that two theories—the temporal sampling hypothesis and dynamic attending theory—suggest that rhythm in music and the envelope of speech may be tracked biologically through the same mechanism. The temporal sampling hypothesis proposes a neural mechanism for the tracking of speech amplitude over time (Goswami, 2011) suggesting phase-locking of slow neural oscillations in the delta and theta range. The mechanism selectively samples low-frequency information in the amplitude envelope which is crucial for the segmentation of speech sounds. Dynamic attending theory proposes a similar set of neural oscillators that phase-lock and resonate to the temporal structure of music, leading to an attentional focus that changes in relation to the rhythmic structure of a piece of music (Velasco and Large, 2011). Speech is inherently temporal, with boundary lengthening and pauses enhancing the experience of language as a temporal phenomenon (Moberget and Ivry, 2016). The metrical, intonational and pitch components of grammar are experienced as prosody (Ferreira and Karimi, 2015).

Some studies have reported the importance of both rhythmic and pitch perception in the development of reading skills (Atterbury, 1985; Forgeard et al., 2008). Atterbury (1985) found that reading-disabled children aged seven to nine could discriminate rhythm patterns as well as controls, but were poorer in rhythm performance and tonal memory than normal-achieving readers. Anvari and colleagues (2002) studied 50 four- and 50 five-year-olds and found that both rhythm- and pitch-perception skills predicted early reading performance in four-year-olds, even after taking account of variance due to phonological awareness. In five-year-olds, only pitch perception predicted early reading performance, after accounting for phonological awareness. Tsang and Conrad (2011) studied 69 children with and without formal music training. The trained children out-performed the untrained children on pitch discrimination, rhythm discrimination and phonological skills, although the two groups performed the same on tests of word identification, timbre discrimination and receptive vocabulary. Jones and colleagues (2006) have shown that pattern structure, particularly initial patterns of pitch and time, involving small pitch intervals is important and that listeners rely heavily on global pitch structure and rhythm for language processing.

There are a range of possible reasons for the differing outcomes of the research, including the different methods used to assess reading, the nature of the musical interventions, whether they support the development of pitch, melodic or rhythmic skills, and the prior musical and literacy experiences of the participants. Where musical activities involve learning to read notation, there may be direct transfer to reading text. Singing has also been proposed as one possible way in which musical activity improves literacy, as it involves reading predictable text, segmenting words into syllables so that lyrics can be matched to music, or recognising patterns (Butzlaff, 2000; Forgeard et al., 2008). Other possible explanations for the impact of musical training on reading performance relate to changes in concentration and motivation that aid children in focusing for long periods of time, helping them to persevere (Butzlaff, 2000).

Reviews, Meta-Analyses and Conclusions

There have been a number of reviews of the research considering the relationship between musical engagement and literacy. Taken together, they indicate that there are a number of similarities between learning to read text and music. The auditory analysis skills used in language processing, phonological distinctions, and the blending and segmentation of sounds are similar to the skills necessary for music perception of rhythmic and melodic discrimination. The five sub-skills underlying reading acquisition—phonological awareness, speech in noise perception, rhythm perception, auditory working memory and the ability to learn sound patterns—are linked to music experience. Temporal attention can be influenced by rhythm, which benefits syntax processing and speech production. Music and written text both require the reading of notation from left to right, and the conversion of notation into specific sounds. The reviews agree that music education can contribute to literacy development in all children, including those who find the development of literacy skills challenging (Bolduc, 2008; Bugaj and Brenner, 2011; Sammler and Elmer, 2020; Schön and Tillman, 2015; Tierney and Kraus, 2013a).

Rolka and Silverman (2015) carried out a systematic review analysing research on music and dyslexia. Twenty-three studies were included. Some focused on the challenges of studying music—in particular, problems with reading notation—although most explored how music could be used to improve literacy skills, or to test for neural processing of auditory information, offering the potential to inform early diagnosis. The findings from the review revealed that music training was seen as a remediation tool to improve literacy skills for children with dyslexia, although the specific type of music support to achieve predictable outcomes require further investigation.

Meta-analyses have had mixed results. Butzlaff (2000) carried out two meta-analyses; the first included 29 studies examining the correlation between music instruction and reading performance, and the second six intervention studies. The first demonstrated a significant, positive relationship between music instruction and performance on reading tests; the second yielded no reliable effects. In contrast, Standley (2008) in an analysis of 30 experimental studies found a strong overall effect, while the meta-analysis of Gordon and colleagues (2015), based on 13 studies, found that music training led to gains in phonological awareness skills, while transfer effects for rhyming skills became stronger with increased hours of training. No significant transfer effect emerged for reading fluency measures.

To conclude, taken together, the evidence set out in this chapter, along with research reviews and meta-analyses, suggests that active engagement with music can have a positive effect on children's literacy. A variety of musical activities appears to contribute to these benefits, although the exact nature of those which are most effective remains to be established. Differences in the outcomes of the research may depend on its rigour, the age and general life experiences of the participants, the assessment measures used and their reliability and validity, and the nature and quality of the musical instruction.

Spelling

There has been much less focus on the impact of active engagement with music on spelling compared with reading. In an early study, Douglas and Willatts (1994), working with seven- and eight-year-olds, found positive correlations among tests of pitch and rhythmic aptitude, and vocabulary, reading and spelling. When vocabulary scores were taken into account, the association between rhythm and spelling abilities remained, but those between pitch aptitude and spelling disappeared, suggesting the importance of rhythm in relation to spelling. Overy (2003) found a positive effect of music lessons on spelling performance, with children with poor spelling skills benefiting the most, while Hille and colleagues (2011) tested 194 boys who were in Grade 3 (aged eight to nine) in Germany, just over half of whom had learned to play a musical instrument. The boys who played an instrument showed better performance in spelling, an effect which occurred independently of intelligence test scores (there being only a weak correlation between spelling mistakes and non-verbal measures of intelligence). Examination of data from those who performed poorly on spelling showed that those who played an instrument were under-represented. Only 27 percent of boys in the lowest quartile played an instrument, whereas 61 percent of boys in the highest quartiles were active musicians. Singing in a choir or taking part in a course entitled First Experiences With Music was not associated with spelling performance, suggesting that it was the skills developed through playing an instrument which had the potential for transfer. Currently, there is insufficient research on the relationship between actively engaging in musical activities and spelling skills for us to draw any firm conclusions.

Writing

As with spelling, little attention has been paid to the influence of active engagement with music on writing. An exception was a study where children from economically disadvantaged homes participated in instruction which focused on the concepts of print, singing activities and writing. The children in the experimental group showed enhanced print concepts and pre-writing skills (Standley and Hughes, 1997). Register and colleagues (2001) replicated the study of Standley and Hughes (1997), evaluating the effects of a music intervention using a curriculum designed to enhance the pre-reading and writing skills of 25 children aged four to five who were enrolled in early intervention programmes and a programme for children with exceptional needs. Intervention and control groups received two 30-minute music sessions each week for an entire school year. The autumn sessions for the experimental group were focused on writing skills, while the spring sessions taught reading and book concepts. Music sessions for the control group were based on thematic material, as determined by the classroom teacher, with purposeful exclusion of all pre-literacy concepts. All participants were pre-tested at the beginning of the school year and post-tested before the school year ended. The findings showed that music sessions significantly enhanced both groups' abilities to learn pre-writing and print concepts, although the experimental group showed statistically significantly higher results on logo identification and word recognition following the intervention.

Some research has focused on whether learning to play a musical instrument can enhance the development of fine motor skills, which may contribute towards the development of handwriting. Neuroscientific studies have shown changes in the cortical representation of fingers during intensive keyboard practice sessions over periods as short as five days and as long as two weeks (Pascual-Leone, 2001).

Orsmond and Miller (1999) compared the fine motor abilities of children who participated in two years of piano instruction and those who had never received formal music training. A significant improvement in fine motor skills was found only for the children who received the piano lessons, and a significant difference in the speed of response was found between the two groups at the end of the two years of instruction. The innumerable opportunities to assess, refine and time their motor responses to specific stimuli during musical practice, and the availability of constant evaluative feedback (sound) may allow musicians to improve the accuracy and speed of perceiving and responding to relevant stimuli. Similarly, Costa-Giomi (2005a) compared the fine motor abilities of children from low-income families who participated in two years of piano instruction and those who had not received formal music training. A significant improvement in fine motor skills was found for the children receiving the lessons. The children in the experimental group were supplied with acoustic pianos and practised, on average, for up to three-and-a-half hours weekly (Costa-Giomi, 2005b). The motor proficiency of the two groups was comparable at the start of the project (Costa-Giomi, 1999). The findings suggested that the improvement in motor proficiency was mainly caused by differences in a speed subtest which required children to react quickly to catch a rod that was sliding down against a wall. Scores in tasks that measured hand-eye coordination and dexterity were not affected by the lessons. Costa-Giomi concluded that music performance requires accurate and quick motor reaction to visual, aural and kinesthetic stimuli, which improves accuracy and speed in perceiving and responding to stimuli.

To conclude, while there is relatively little evidence, it appears that learning to play a musical instrument contributes to the development of fine motor skills, which may support the development of handwriting.

Overview

Taken together, the evidence suggests that active engagement with music can have a positive effect on children's literacy. The enhancement of aural skills improves phonological awareness, which supports the decoding of written material into sound, while rhythmic activities, in particular, seem to support reading skills—particularly for those who are experiencing difficulties with literacy. There is too little evidence to draw any conclusions relating to the role of learning to play a musical instrument on spelling or handwriting.

5. Music, Spatial Reasoning and Mathematical Performance

Historically, there has long been interest in the relationship between acquired musical skills and performance in mathematics. It has been assumed that there is a strong connection between music and mathematics, as many musicians play from notation and are constantly required to adopt quasi-mathematical processes to subdivide beats and turn rhythmic notation into sound. More recently, there has been interest in the relationship between music and spatial-temporal reasoning, which contributes to some areas of mathematical understanding. Spatial-temporal reasoning is the ability to transform mental images in the absence of a physical model (Rauscher et al., 1997; Shaw, 2000). It involves the ability to manipulate and understand complex shapes through mental imagery, as the individual develops and evaluates patterns which change in space and time. Cooper (2000) viewed spatial-temporal reasoning as an abstract model of cognition consisting of several elements, including pattern-seeking, recognition, retention and recall; visualising imagery; perceiving figures as wholes; generating a whole image from a fragment; grasping the whole of a problem; understanding spatial relationships from multi-perspectives and among internal movement of parts; maintaining orientation within space; and mentally manipulating shapes within two- or three-dimensional space. The key features used in spatial-temporal reasoning include the transforming and relating of mental images in space and time, the use of symmetries to compare physical and mental images, and temporal sequencing (Grandin et al., 1998). These skills are high-level mathematical abilities which are useful in learning proportional reasoning (Grandin et al., 1998; Shaw, 2000) and induce advanced understanding of mathematical concepts such as fractions, proportions, symmetry and other arithmetic operations (Tran et al., 2012). Developing spatial-temporal thinking may also be related to geometrical skills.

Early mathematical skills tend to be one of two types: number knowledge or number operation (Griffin, 2004). The latter is linked with the formulation of mental number lines, which enable children to understand magnitudes, relations between them and arithmetic operations (Jordan et al., 2008; Gunderson, 2012). Mental number lines are linked with spatial-temporal reasoning. The development of a mental number line is fundamental for mathematical understanding and facilitates performance, especially in arithmetic (Ramani and Siegler, 2008; Booth and Siegler, 2008; Van Nes and Doorman, 2011; Gunderson et al., 2012). Spatial skills have also been linked with spatial structuring, which is important in determining quantities, as well as comparing and calculating them (Butterworth, 1999; Mulligan and Mitchelmore, 2009). Undertaking such tasks early in development occurs unitarily. This takes time and can also lead to errors. Most children gradually learn to organise objects in ways that enable them to count more accurately and efficiently. This helps them to understand the decimal system. Spatial awareness contributes to the development of patterning, while the temporal element might be used in structuring and strategy choice.

Explanations for the relationship between music and spatial-temporal reasoning have been sought in neuroscience. Two main approaches have developed. The first concerns connectivity, and proposes that the processing of music and spatial tasks is underpinned by overlap in brain functions (Fiske, 1996). In contrast, near-transfer theory suggests that music and spatial-temporal reasoning share some processes, and the development of one leads to the development of the other (Rauscher, 2009; Schellenberg, 2004). Explanations for the links between music and spatial-temporal reasoning relate to connectionism—the development of neural connections (Sporns, 2011)—and modular theory, which is related to near-transfer (Jordan-DeCarbo and Nelson, 2002). The connectivity proposal has been supported by Shaw (2000), who suggested that musical and spatial processing overlap in the brain and, as a result of these cortical connections, the development of certain kinds of musical and spatial abilities (especially spatial-temporal abilities) is intertwined. Near-transfer suggests that several kinds of thinking are required in order to learn and make music. Both are multi-dimensional processes. A range of spatial skills might be improved because of the practice required in making music (Jordan-DeCarbo and Nelson, 2002).

Particular interest in the relationship between music and spatial reasoning skills developed following a study by Rauscher and colleagues (1993), who claimed that after listening to Mozart's 'Sonata for Two Pianos (K448)' for ten minutes, adult participants showed significantly better spatial reasoning skills than after periods of listening to relaxation instructions designed to lower blood pressure, or listening to silence. The mean spatial reasoning scores were eight and nine points higher after listening to the music than in the other two conditions. However, the effect only lasted for ten to fifteen minutes. Early attempts to replicate the phenomenon were unsuccessful (Chabris, 1999; Steele et al., 1999). Using a logical rather than spatial reasoning task, Newman and colleagues (1995) tested 114 students before and after listening to either eight minutes of Mozart's music, relaxation instructions or silence, and found that all participants showed a practice effect with no particular enhancement in the music group. Similarly, Rideout and Laubach (1996) tested four female and four male undergraduates on two equivalent spatial tests, following either the presentation of Mozart's 'Sonata for Two Pianos in D Major' or a non-musical activity. EEG was recorded during, at baseline and at two task performance periods. Correlations were generated between task performance and EEG variables. Performance improved significantly following the presentation of the music. In a later study, Rideout and colleagues (1998) studied 16 participants who showed reliable improvement on a paper-folding and cutting task after listening to Mozart's 'Sonata for Two Pianos in D Major'. The enhanced performance was also noted for 16 other participants after listening to a contemporary musical selection with similar musical characteristics. In both cases, the control procedure included ten minutes of listening to a relaxation tape. Similarly, Wilson and Brown (1997) examined the effect of Mozart's music on 22 college undergraduates who had listened to a selection of Mozart's music. Each participant performed a pencil and paper maze task after a ten-minute presentation of each of three listening conditions: a piano concerto by Mozart, repetitive relaxation music and silence. Limited support for the previously obtained enhancing effect of listening to Mozart's music was revealed in measures of performance accuracy on this spatial task, whereas no effect was found for either the number of maze recursions or the overall quality of maze solutions. Hetland (2000b) carried out two meta-analyses and found that music significantly enhanced performance on a variety of spatial tasks, but that music other than Mozart also enhanced spatial-temporal performance over a short period of time.

Some research has explored the so-called Mozart effect on children. For instance, as part of the BBC programme *Tomorrow's World*, a replication of Rauscher's study was undertaken with over 6,000 ten- and eleven-year-old children (Hallam, 2001). They were tested after they listened simultaneously to either contemporary pop music by Blur or Oasis, the same piece of music by Mozart that was used in Raucher's study, or a talk given about experiments. After being assigned at random to one of the three listening experiences, each child completed two tests of spatial abilities. No statistically significant differences were found between the performance of the three groups on the two tests of spatial reasoning. A reanalysis of the data using a different statistical approach by Schellenberg and Hallam (2006) showed that performance on one of the tests—square completion—did not differ as a function of the listening experience, but performance on the paper-folding test was superior for children who listened to the popular music compared to the other two groups. This was interpreted in terms of the arousing effects of the popular music, which the children also enjoyed, leading to an increase in their motivation.

This mixed, although mainly negative, evidence relating to the Mozart effect led to research focusing on the role of music when it was played alongside the completion of a range of different intellectual tasks. The impact of background music is considered in more depth in Chapter 11.

Comparisons between Musicians and Non-Musicians, and Correlation Studies

One strand of research has compared the performance of musicians with non-musicians on spatial-temporal reasoning tasks, while a further strand has compared performance on mathematical tasks. Neuroscientific research into brain structures has confirmed that the areas of the brain where spatial reasoning occurs are more pronounced in adult musicians, and that the processing of music and spatial-temporal tasks activates similar neural structures. Sluming and colleagues (2002) found that musicians achieved better results than controls on a line orientation test and were better in finding the middle of a line (Patston et al., 2006). Skills used in these two tasks may be related to the ability to manipulate the mental number line. Taking account of the importance of the concept of mental number line for the development of mathematical thinking, it is possible that active engagement with music enhances this process (Siegler and Booth, 2005; Ramani and Siegler, 2008).

There is considerable evidence from research with professional musicians or those training to become professional musicians that they have better spatial-temporal reasoning abilities than non-musicians, including mental rotation. Pietsch and Jansen (2012) compared students of music, sports and education, and demonstrated better performance on mental rotation tasks among the first two groups, while Sluming and colleagues (2007) found that members of orchestras outperformed controls in mental rotation tasks. They suggested that this was linked with more pronounced development of Broca's area in the brains of the musicians, while Mark (2002) showed that the areas of the brain which are activated whilst performing music and spatial-temporal tasks are proximate.

Musicians are better at a range of visuospatial search tasks. Patston and Tippett (2011) administered a language comprehension task and a visuospatial search task to 36 expert musicians and 36 matched non-musicians in conditions of silence and correct or incorrect piano music playing in the background. Musicians performed more poorly on the language comprehension task in the presence of the background music compared to silence, but there was no effect of background music on the musicians' performance on the visuospatial task. In contrast, the performance of non-musicians was not affected by the music on either task. This suggests that, when musicians process music, they recruit a network that overlaps with the network used in language processing. Musicians have better reaction times to selective and divided visual attention tasks (Rodrigues et al., 2013). They are better at matching a set of coloured blocks to a visual image (Stoesz et al., 2007), have better memory for line drawings (Jakobson et al., 2008), and are more accurate when asked to mark the centre of a horizontal line (Patston et al., 2006) and when asked to judge the orientation of a line (Patston et al., 2007). These findings might be particularly important in linking music with mathematics, as the ability to visualise a horizontal line and localise a middle and proportional distance on it is closely related to the notion of the mental line used for a variety of mathematical operations (Gunderson et al., 2012). However, Helmbold and colleagues (2005) compared 70 adult musicians and 70 non-musicians matched for age, sex and level of education on their performance on different aspects of primary mental abilities including verbal comprehension, word fluency, space, flexibility of closure, perceptual speed, reasoning, number and memory—they found no significant differences except for flexibility of closure and perceptual speed, where the musicians performed reliably better than non-musicians.

Pannenborg and Pannenborg (1915) compared individuals with varying degrees of musical talent and found only a slightly higher level of mathematical ability in those with high levels of musical ability. In contrast, Haecker and Ziehen (1922) administered a self-report questionnaire via the internet to 227 musical and 72 unmusical male participants, who were doctoral-level members of the American Mathematical Association or the Modern Language Association. The questionnaire assessed musicality, music perception, music memory and musicianship, music performance and music creation. The mathematics group did not exhibit higher levels of either musicality or musicianship. The mathematicians reporting high-level music performance ability did not report significantly greater musicality than did the literature or language scholars. Similarly, Haimson and colleagues (2011a; 2011b) recruited participants from the online membership of the American Mathematical Society and the Modern Language Association and presented them with a questionnaire assessing skills in musicality and musicianship. Members of both groups reported relatively low levels of musicality with no statistically significant differences between them. Revesz (1954) also found that reported levels of interest or aptitude for mathematics in musicians were low.

Vaughn (2000) meta-analysed studies comparing mathematics achievement in students with and without self-selected music study, and only reported a very small positive association between mathematics and musical engagement. Working with fourth-grade children, Haley

(2001) investigated the effects of participating in an instrumental music programme, band or orchestra on their academic achievement. The children were placed into three groups. The first consisted of children who had studied an instrument prior to the introduction of band and orchestra in fourth grade, the second consisted of children just beginning to study an instrument and the third consisted of children with no experience of instrumental instruction. The findings showed that students who had studied an instrument prior to fourth grade had higher scores in mathematics achievement than did students in the other groups.

Comparing performance in reading and mathematics in two schools with different levels of music education, one with an outstanding music programme and the other with no music programme, Deere (2010) carried out a survey. Students experiencing high-quality music education had higher Tennessee Comprehensive Assessment Program (TCAP) reading and mathematics scores in the fourth grade. There was also a high correlation between music education and TCAP scores in reading and mathematics. In the eighth grade, where musical education was of high quality, students also reported higher TCAP reading and mathematics scores.

In a study with young children, Williams and colleagues (2015) investigated parent-child home music activities in a sample of 3031 Australian children participating in *Growing Up in Australia: The Longitudinal Study of Australian Children*. Frequency of shared home music activities was reported by parents when children were two to three years old. A range of social, emotional and cognitive outcomes were assessed by parent and teacher report and direct testing two years later, when the children were four to five years old. A series of regression analyses found that frequency of shared home music activities had a small significant partial association with measures of children's numeracy. The findings suggested that there may be a role for parent-child home music activities in supporting children's mathematical development.

Catterall and colleagues (2000), using the NELS:88 data, studied low socioeconomic status students who exhibited high mathematics proficiency in twelfth grade and found that 33 percent were involved in instrumental music compared with 15 percent who were not involved. Miksza (2010) extended this research, examining the potential relationship between participation in high-school music ensembles and extra musical educational outcomes, including achievement in mathematics, using data from the Education Longitudinal Study of 2002. The sample of 12,160 students was representative of white and minority high-school students from 603 rural, suburban and urban schools across the United States. The students who belonged to school music ensembles had higher scores in standardised mathematics tests. The study controlled for socioeconomic status but not mathematical performance prior to any music training. Similarly, Bergee and Weingarten (2020) used multi-level mixed modelling to test the extent to which students' music achievement scores were related to their reading and mathematics achievement scores. Of the four levels examined—individual students, classrooms, schools and districts—only individuals and districts accounted for a significant portion of the total variance in achievement scores. There was a strong relationship between music scores and reading/mathematics achievement. In higher education, Barroso and colleagues (2019) aimed to identify the cognitive and affective factors related to mathematics and music theory that best explained undergraduate music theory achievement. The findings suggested that mathematic scores and music theory confidence were important predictors of grades in undergraduate music theory examinations.

Musical Interventions and Spatial-Temporal Reasoning

While the research comparing musicians and non-musicians, and that showing relationships between music, spatial-temporal reasoning and mathematics is important, it is not able to demonstrate causality. To demonstrate causality, it is necessary to carry out experimental intervention studies where the impact of musical engagement is compared with the impact of other activities or no activity. Rhythm may be particularly important, as infants engage in significantly more rhythmic movement to music and other rhythmically regular sounds than to speech, and also to some extent exhibit tempo flexibility (Zentner and Eerola, 2010).

General music instruction—including singing, movement and playing percussion instruments—has been shown to assist four- to six-year-old children in the development of spatial ability (Bilhartz et al., 1999). Zafranas (2004) studied 61 kindergarten children who received two piano or keyboard lessons weekly during one school year. Following piano or keyboard instruction, participants improved significantly in hand movement, gestalt closure, triangles, spatial memory and arithmetic, but not in matrix analogies. Similarly, Gromko and Poorman (1998) investigated the effect of music training on 15 preschoolers' performance on subtests of the Wechsler Preschool and Primary Intelligence Scale. For the three-year-olds in the study, this musically intellectually stimulating environment resulted in an increase in the ability to perform spatial-temporal tasks.

Rauscher and colleagues (1997) assigned 78 students from three preschools to music, computer or no instruction groups. The instruction groups received training in one of the following: piano or keyboard (either individually or coupled with group singing lessons), group singing lessons only or computer instruction. The children were pre- and post-tested using one spatial-temporal reasoning task, object assembly, and three spatial recognition tasks (geometric design, block design and animal pegs). There were no differences between groups in pre-test scores, but after instruction the children in the piano group scored significantly higher on the spatial reasoning task compared to children in the other conditions. There were no differences amongst the groups on the spatial recognition tasks. The computer group, singing and no-instruction groups did not improve significantly over time on any of the tests. Later studies (Rauscher, 2002; Rauscher and Zupan, 2000)—which were undertaken over three years with upper-middle-income children who were provided with eight months of weekly 40-minute keyboard instruction in groups of eight to ten beginning in either kindergarten, aged five, or first grade, aged six—scored higher on two spatial-temporal tasks, puzzle-solving and block-building compared to children who did not receive music instruction. No enhancement was found for a pictorial memory task. However, these effects were not maintained when music instruction was terminated, although when lessons resumed in second grade the same children's scores increased again, surpassing the levels that they had reached before the lessons were terminated. The children who received instruction over a period of three years scored higher on the spatial-temporal tasks compared to children who had not received instruction. While the scores of the keyboard group improved every year, although not significantly, after kindergarten the scores of children who began instruction in the second grade did not improve, suggesting that it was important that the training began early. Rauscher and La Mieux (2003) also reported that children who received keyboard lessons, singing training or rhythmic instruction scored higher than controls on spatial reasoning tasks. Further studies examined the effects of musical instruction on spatial-temporal reasoning in middle-income elementary-school children (Rauscher and Hinton, 2011). Two groups—a music group and an animated reading group—received 40 minutes of lessons in groups of eight to ten for nine months. At the end of the study, the children who received the keyboard lessons scored significantly higher on spatial-temporal reasoning tasks than those who received the animated reading lessons, although the improvement for the keyboard group was only for the girls.

Working with elementary-school students, Johnson and Davis (2016) investigated the effects of a programme combining musical ensembles in residence with regular classroom music instruction on students' auditory discrimination and spatial intelligence. In combination with regular, sequential general music classes, participants in the programme received two half-hour lessons each week from musical ensembles in residence, lasting for four consecutive years. The chamber ensembles provided aural models for reinforcing fundamental concepts. Data were collected from a stratified, random sample of students in grades two and four to five receiving the experimental programme, and from demographically similar comparison schools which did not receive any regular music instruction. A total of 684 elementary students participated in the study. Children participating in the programme with the chamber music ensembles showed consistent and statistically significantly greater scores in both auditory discrimination and spatial intelligence measures.

Holmes and Hallam (2017) examined the potential of active music-making to improve mathematics achievement in primary-school pupils. In a quasi-experimental design, 60 children aged five or six participated in the music programme, while the same number of pupils from parallel classes made up two control groups. Lessons contained a variety of musical, predominantly rhythmical activities, based on popular nursery rhymes. Spatial-temporal skills were tested at the beginning and the end of the study. Throughout the intervention, pupils were assessed on musical skills, as well as general and specific mathematical skills. A strong relationship between musical and spatial-temporal skills was found in both age groups. The younger group scored higher than their peers on a picture test and a puzzle test. The results for the older children were also higher for the music group in both spatial-temporal tests. Some enhancement in mathematics in the intervention group was found, although there was no significant contribution of spatial-temporal abilities to general mathematics achievement.

One strand of research has focused on preschool children from deprived backgrounds participating in Head Start programmes (Rauscher, 2003, Rauscher et al., 2005). In the first study, 87 Head Start children were randomly assigned to one of three groups—piano, computer or no instruction—for 48 weeks over two years. At the end of the intervention, the children who received music instruction scored significantly higher than control groups on visual and auditory tasks that required spatial and temporal skills. Performance on an arithmetic task also improved following music instruction. A second study focused on whether different types of music instruction had different effects. Over 100 Head Start children of mixed ethnicity were assigned randomly to one of four conditions: piano, singing, rhythm or no instruction. All of the children in the music groups received weekly individual instruction for a period of 48 weeks over two years. The data from the three music groups replicated the data from the first study. The children in the music groups scored significantly higher at post-test on tasks requiring spatial and temporal skills. The rhythm group scored significantly higher than the piano and singing groups on temporal and arithmetic tasks. A third study was conducted to determine whether the effects endured after instruction stopped. The scores of the Head Start children who received lessons in the first and second studies were compared with three groups of grade-matched children participating in Head Start who did not receive music instruction, at-risk children not involved in Head Start, and middle-income children who did not receive music instruction. The children who had received music instruction in the first study continued to score higher than all of the other groups of children, with the exception of the age-matched middle-income children, on three of the four tests two years after instruction had ended. The data from the children who participated in the second study when they progressed to kindergarten showed that the singing, piano and rhythm groups scored higher than the Head Start and at-risk children on five of the tests. In addition, the rhythm group scored higher than the singing and piano groups on an arithmetic subtest, and scored significantly higher than the middle-income children on the temporal, arithmetic, mathematical reasoning and numeracy tasks. These findings suggest that rhythm instruction has the strongest impact on a range of mathematically related tasks. Rauscher and Hinton (2011) summarised the results from several of these studies and showed that music groups had higher scores on arithmetic and spatial abilities following musical interventions, although they were equivalent initially (Rauscher, 2014).

Several research projects have been undertaken within the context of the *El Sistema* approach to musical engagement, a structured extracurricular orchestral programme. For instance, Osborne and colleagues (2015) studied pupils from a low-income neighbourhood participating in *El Sistema* and showed that they had greater improvement in spatial reasoning, verbal and mathematical skills than comparison groups. Further evidence for music being responsible for enhanced spatial reasoning in at-risk children comes from an Israeli study, in which a two-year music training intervention of two to three hours per week was introduced in some after-school centres for at-risk children, but not in other centres (Portowitz et al., 2007). Children participating in the intervention showed larger improvements in remembering and reproducing a complex line drawing.

The most effective music interventions for enhancing spatial temporal reasoning in all children seem to be based on rhythm (Hetland, 2000a; Holmes, 2017; Holmes and Hallam, 2017; Rauscher and Le Mieux, 2003). Children in the early years of primary school seem to benefit the most from such interventions (Costa-Giomi, 2004; 2013; Graziano et al., 1999; Holmes, 2017; Holmes and Hallam, 2017; Rauscher, 2002, Rauscher and La Mieux, 2003; Rauscher and Zupan, 2000; Schellenberg, 2004). The optimal length of interventions that is required for there to be a sustainable impact has not been conclusively established. Rauscher and Zupan (2002) showed improvement in spatial-temporal skills which continued throughout a four-year programme, whilst Rauscher (2000) suggested that there was a need for programmes to last for at least two years to achieve lasting change. The underpinnings of such accelerated progression in disadvantaged and other pupils are not yet clear, and these enhancements might be mediated by the development of general cognitive abilities. It is also possible that these programmes raise participants' motivation, self-efficacy, and perseverance. Overall, the majority of studies have shown that spatial-temporal skills can be improved by musical training. Interestingly, when other related cognitive abilities have been assessed—for instance, pictorial memory (Rauscher and Zupan, 2000), spatial recognition (Rauscher 1994; 1997), and number recall (Rauscher and La Mieux, 2003)—there has been no significant improvement related to musical engagement.

Not all of the research has shown an impact of music on spatial reasoning. For instance, Hanson (2003) investigated the effects of a sequenced Kodály literacy-based music programme on the spatial reasoning skills of kindergarten students. Fifty-four kindergarten children participated. One group of children received Kodály music instruction, a second group computer instruction and a third group no intervention. The programme lasted for seven months. Spatial-temporal reasoning, spatial reasoning and a nonspatial measure were assessed. The analysis revealed no statistically significant differences in pre-, post- or gain scores for any of the measures.

The Relationships between Spatial Skills and Mathematics

Children engage with arithmetic long before they experience formal mathematics education. Some number processing is present prior to the development of language. Preschool children understand estimation and comparison of quantities often before they can count or use number terminology. They have a sense of ordinality (Kaufmann, 2008) and use and develop strategies and procedures in solving problems (Bisanz et al., 2005). Very young children can discriminate between small groups of items containing different numbers of objects. Understanding increasing quantity by adding objects and decreasing quantity by removing them depends on observing ordinal relations among numbers (Bisanz et al., 2005). This skill is related to addition and develops earlier than subtraction. Children gradually develop greater accuracy until they can provide exact solutions to arithmetic problems. This is usually achieved by four to five years old. They also begin to develop rules and concepts that inform and constrain their growing ability to manipulate numbers (Bisanz et al., 2005). Krajewski and Schneider (2009) developed a three-phase model of this process: basic numeric skills, quantity number concepts and number relationships. At the third level, visual-spatial skills play a vital role, while non-verbal representations of magnitudes are essential for problem-solving (Rasmussen and Bisanz, 2005). This model supports a strong relationship between spatial skills (Cheng and Mix, 2014), the visual–spatial components of working memory and the development of mathematical abilities.

Alternatively, Spelke (2008) proposes a broader model which outlines three main systems which support young children's mathematical learning: a system for representing small exact numbers of objects, up to three; a system for representing large approximate numerical magnitudes—for example, about 20—and a system for representing geometric properties and relationships. Each system is malleable and relatively independent in young children, but as basic concepts and mathematical operations develop, children learn to connect the three systems. Linking representations of numbers with representations of space helps in creating mental number lines, which are central to understanding relationships between numbers and calculations.

Spatial structuring is essential for many mathematical activities of a numerical or geometrical nature. Van Nes and de Lange (2007) propose that the ability to imagine a spatial structure relates to a specific magnitude, and to mentally manipulate it helps in understanding quantities and the process of counting and also speeds up that process. Van Nes and Dorman (2011) describe the mathematical skills which rely on spatial structures as composing and decomposing of quantities; counting and grouping; part-whole knowledge in addition, multiplication and division; comparing a number of objects; patterning; building a construction of blocks; ordering, generalising and classifying;

and more sophisticated mathematical operations; for instance, algebra, proving, predicting, and mental rotation of structures.

Booth and Siegler (2008) examined whether the quality of numerical magnitude representations of first-grade children with a mean age of 7.2 years was correlated with, predictive of and causally related to their learning of arithmetic. The children's pre-test numerical magnitude representations were correlated with their pre-test arithmetic knowledge, and were predictive of their learning of answers to unfamiliar arithmetic problems. The relation to learning to solve unfamiliar problems remained after controlling for prior arithmetic knowledge, short-term memory for numbers and mathematics achievement test scores. In addition, presenting randomly chosen children with accurate visual representations of the magnitudes of addends and sums improved their learning of the answers to problems. Representations of numerical magnitude are both correlationally and causally related to arithmetic learning. These abilities are engaged not only in geometry, but also in number sense, comparing and calculating quantities, and effectively using strategies to solve problems.

Similarly, Gunderson and colleagues (2012), using two longitudinal data sets, found that children's spatial skills and mental transformation ability, at the beginning of first and second grades, were a predictor of improvement in linear number-line knowledge over the course of the school year. Spatial skill at age five predicted performance on an approximate symbolic calculation task at age eight. This relationship was mediated by children's linear number-line knowledge at age six. Similarly, working with 760 preadolescent college students and high- and low-ability college bound youths, Casey and colleagues (1995) found that spatial skill (as measured by the Vandenberg Mental Rotation Test) was highly related to success in mathematics. For all of the female samples, mental rotation predicted mathematics aptitude even when verbal aptitude scores were entered into the regression first. For the male samples, the relationship varied as a function of the ability of the sample. Overall, spatial skills are widely used in many levels of mathematical thinking and their development is considered a strong predictor of achievement in mathematics at primary school and other stages of education.

The Relationships between Music, Spatial Skills and Mathematics

Another strand of research has studied the relationships between music, spatial skills and mathematics. Understanding ratio enables children to calculate fractions, divisions and proportions, while pattern recognition is used in spatial-temporal tasks and in a broad variety of mathematical tasks. Schlaug and colleagues (2005) suggested a link between these skills and using rhythmic notation, while Gordon (1993) saw the link as being through the processing of structures of sound. Geist and colleagues (2012) argue that music is children's first patterning experience and helps engage them in mathematics even though they do not recognise this.

Research has provided evidence for the relationships between music, spatial-temporal reasoning and mathematics. For instance, McDonel (2015) found strong correlations between musical aptitude, rhythm achievement and scores in numeracy tests. However, the sample size was very small, so the findings have to be interpreted cautiously. Spelke (2008) compared performance in tasks measuring performance on the three main systems supporting young children's mathematical learning: representing small exact numbers of objects, large approximate numerical magnitudes, and representing geometric properties and relationships in students aged five to seventeen with no music training, with sports training, with training in other art forms and with music training which was considered on three levels of intensity: moderate, intense and highly intense. The first experiment, with children who had low levels of music training, did not show that such instruction enhanced any core mathematical skills. The second experiment included students with mixed levels of music training. Here, the children with intense music instruction outperformed the others in all tests related to spatial awareness. In the third experiment, students with extensive music training achieved higher scores in tests of sensitivity to geometry, including a task which assessed children's ability to relate numerical and spatial magnitudes, and involved operations on a mental number line. Researching these relationships is complex, because musical training may be associated with some aspects of mathematics but not others. For instance, Bahna-James (1991) found that high-school students' music theory grades correlated with their grades in algebra, geometry and precalculus, but not with grades on an advanced mathematics course on logic. Similarly, Bahr and Christensen (2000) reported that performance on a mathematics test and a musicianship rating scale correlated in areas where music and mathematics shared structural overlap in pattern recognition and symbol usage, but not for other areas of mathematics, where there was no overlap. However, not all of the research supports this. For instance, Helmbold and colleagues (2005) failed to demonstrate any advantage for musicians in pattern recognition.

Holmes and Hallam (2017), working with primary-school children showed correlations between music and only some, rather than all, mathematical skills related to spatial reasoning, while changes in mathematical skills reliant on memory were much smaller. This finding suggests that the development of spatial skills may act as a moderator between rhythmic instruction and attainment in mathematics. There were correlations between spatial reasoning scores and music performance. These were high for a picture test and a puzzle test score. Correlations between music score, the two puzzle tests and various mathematical performances showed strong correlations with some but not all mathematical tests. The strongest correlations were with two- and three-dimensional shapes. There were lower or no correlations with addition, subtraction, counting and number recognition.

Cranmore and Tunks (2015) adopted a qualitative approach asking 24 high school students to share their direct experiences with music and mathematics, as well as their perceptions of how the two fields were related. Participants were divided into four groups based on school music participation and level of achievement in mathematics. Most of the students saw mathematics as a foundation for musical ability, suggesting a different direction to most previous studies. Rhythm was perceived to have the most connections with mathematics.

Musical Engagement and Mathematical Performance

Some studies have concentrated on the impact that learning music might have on the development of specific cognitive skills which are considered useful in acquiring mathematical understanding; for instance, notions of proportions, fractions and patterns. Gardiner and colleagues (1996) showed that children participating in an arts programme—which included seven months of supplementary music lessons with a lower score on mathematics at baseline—outperformed controls in terms of mathematics achievement. Those participating for the longest period of time had the highest scores overall. As all of the groups participated in music and other arts, it was not possible to conclude that it was the music element that produced the effect.

Whitehead (2001) examined the effect of Orff Schulwerk music instruction on the mathematical scores of middle- and high-school students. Subjects were randomly placed into three groups: a full treatment group which received music instruction for 50 minutes five times each week, a limited treatment group which received 50 minutes of instruction once a week and a no treatment group which received no music instruction. After 20 weeks, the full treatment group showed higher significant gains in mathematics than the other two groups. The limited treatment group showed limited mathematics improvement and the no treatment group showed the lowest gain.

Ribeiro and Santos (2017) aimed to verify the efficacy of non-instrumental musical training on numerical cognition in children with low achievement in mathematics. Using cluster analysis, they examined whether children with low scores on numerical cognition would be grouped in the same cluster pre- and post-musical training. Primary-school children were divided into two groups according to their scores on an arithmetic test. Testing with a battery of numerical cognition tests revealed improvements for the children with low achievement in mathematics, especially for number production capacity, compared to normative data. The number of children with low scores in numerical cognition decreased after the intervention.

Neville and colleagues (2008) examined the differences in results between four groups of preschoolers who received music training; attention training; no training and general teaching delivered in a small group; and no training and general teaching in a large class. Music instruction was delivered daily and included listening to music, making music, moving to music and singing. The intervention lasted for eight weeks. A statistically significant change was recorded in numeracy and visual cognition for the music group and the attention group. Children from the music group performed especially well in verbal counting and estimating magnitudes. Similarly, Geoghegan and Mitchelmore (1996) investigated the impact of a weekly early-childhood music programme on the mathematics achievement of preschool children aged four to five. The group of children involved in musical activities scored higher on a mathematics achievement test than the control group, although home musical background may have been a confounding factor. The children who listened more frequently to adults singing and to their own music collection at home performed better than other children.

Cheek and Smith (1999) examined whether the type of music training was related to the mathematics achievement levels of eighth-grade students. Data were collected from the Iowa Academic Achievement Tests of Basic Skills and through a survey on participants' music background, including type of musical instrument, number of years of school music lessons, number of years of private lessons and demographics. No significant difference was found between the mathematics scores of students who did and did not receive private music lessons. However, students with two or more years of private lessons had a significantly higher mean mathematics score than students with no private lessons. Furthermore, students who had keyboard lessons had significantly higher mathematics scores than students who had music lessons on other instruments.

In an innovative study, Kvet (1985) investigated whether significant differences existed in sixth-grade reading, language and mathematics achievement between students who were excused from regular classroom activities for the study of instrumental music and students not studying instrumental music. Over 2000 sixth-grade students participated. The analyses showed that there was no significant difference in sixth-grade reading, language and mathematics achievement between those who were excused from regular classroom activities for the study of instrumental music and those not studying instrumental music.

Focusing on emotions related to mathematics as well as achievement, An and colleagues (2014) studied 56 third-grade elementary students in a pre-post-test control group design, which was utilised to examine changes between two groups of participating students in mathematics achievement and dispositions, including beliefs about success, attitude, confidence, motivation and usefulness. The students in the music group received music-mathematics integrated lessons, while the students in the control group received traditional lecture- and textbook-based mathematics instruction. Analysis of the results demonstrated that, despite statistically equivalent pre-test scores prior to the intervention, after the intervention the music group students had statistically significantly higher positive mathematics disposition scores than their non-music-group peers. This suggests that there are advantages for teachers in utilising music-themed activities as a context for offering students the opportunity to learn mathematics in a challenging yet enjoyable learning environment.

While the evidence for the impact of musical activity on mathematics performance is mixed, some authors have proposed that there may be a link between the use of fractions and proportions in rhythm, and point out that the processing of these requires mathematic specific skills (Shaw, 2000; Schlaug et al., 2005; Jones, 2011). For instance, Courey and colleagues (2012) examined the effects of an academic music intervention on conceptual understanding of music notation, fraction symbols, fraction size and equivalency in third-graders from a multicultural, mixed socioeconomic public-school setting. Sixty-seven students were assigned in their class to their general education mathematics programme or to academic music instruction for 45 minutes, twice a week for six weeks. The academic music students used their conceptual understanding of music and fraction concepts to inform their solutions to fraction computation problems. Statistical analysis revealed significant differences between experimental and comparison students' music and fraction concepts, and fraction computation following the intervention, with large effect sizes. Students who began instruction with less fraction knowledge responded well to the intervention and produced post-test scores similar to their higher achieving peers. Similarly, Azaryahu and colleagues (2019) examined the effect of two integrated intervention programs representing holistic versus acoustic approaches to teaching fraction knowledge. Three classes of fourth-grade children attended 12 lessons on fractions. One class attended the *MusiMath* holistic programme focusing on rhythm within the melody, while the second class attended the academic music acoustic programme (Courey et al., 2012) which used rhythm only. The third class of children received regular mathematical lessons on fractions. Students in both music programmes learned to write musical notation and perform rhythmic patterns through clapping and drumming as part of their fraction lessons. They worked toward adding musical notes to produce a number fraction, and created addition–subtraction problems with musical notes. The music programme used a 4/4 time signature with crotchets, quavers and semiquavers. In the mathematics lessons, the students learned the analogy between musical durations and half, quarter and eighth fractions, but also practised other fractions. Music and mathematics skills were assessed before, immediately following, and three and six months after the intervention. The analysis indicated that only the *MusiMath* group showed greater transfer to intervention trained and untrained fractions than the comparison group. The academic music group showed a positive trend on trained fractions. Despite this, both music groups outperformed the comparison group three and six months after the intervention on the trained fractions. Only the *MusiMath* group demonstrated greater gains in untrained fractions. Similarly, Hamilton and colleagues (2018) describe a pilot study which aimed to determine whether understanding in mathematics, and specifically, fractions, equivalence, ordinance and division improved when music and musical rhythm were used in lessons. The preliminary data suggested that students responded positively to this novel method of teaching in terms of engagement but also test performance.

Focusing on piano keyboard skills, Johnson and Edelson (2003) developed an activity for teaching children aspects of mathematics through musical concepts, including the use of musical instruments and musical symbols, to expand the concepts of serial order, fractions, sorting, classification and ratios. They concluded that music had the potential to assist in developing mathematical skills. Also using piano keyboard lessons but combined with a video game, Graziano and colleagues (1999) demonstrated that preschool children given six months of piano keyboard lessons improved dramatically on spatial-temporal reasoning, while children in appropriate control groups did not improve. The researchers also developed a *Spatial* maths video game which was designed to teach fractions and proportional mathematics. It was extremely successful in a study involving 237 second-grade children, aged six to eight years old. The children participating in the piano keyboard training as well as the maths video game scored significantly higher on proportional mathematics and fractions than children who experienced non-musical training along with the maths video game. Lim and colleagues (2018) investigated future teachers' experiences and perceptions of using a virtual reality game for elementary maths education. The virtual reality game was designed and developed to integrate a musical activity, beat-making, into the learning of fractions. The mathematics education students who participated perceived that the concept of fractions was effectively represented via beat-making in the virtual reality game.

Wentworth (2019) explored the effectiveness of an integrated approach to music and mathematics in high school. Four lessons were taught to an intervention and control class to determine how mathematically motivated music instruction affected students' understanding of operations of functions, composition of functions, inverse functions, domain and range. A pre-post-test design was used to determine the effect on achievement of the integrated lessons; a questionnaire was also given out, to identify differences in students' mathematical perceptions, self-efficacy and determination. The intervention group demonstrated significantly greater gains overall. Three major differences were identified between the groups—the intervention group used function notation more frequently than the control group; the control group demonstrated confusion between composition of functions and inverse functions, while the intervention group did not; and the intervention group showed more mathematical work for the applications portion of the test than the control group. The integrated instruction led to comparable and, in some cases, significantly better mathematics outcomes than the control group, giving students an increased willingness to work with mathematical applications both on the post-test and moving forward.

Not all of the research has shown that music has a positive effect on learning mathematics. For instance, Costa-Giomi (2004) worked with nine- to ten-year-old children from low-income families, who were involved over three years with weekly individual piano lessons. All of the children who participated in the study were given an instrument so that they could practise at home. Self-esteem and musical understanding were enhanced for the music group, but their academic achievement in mathematics and English was no different from a control group.

The quality of the musical input is crucial in any transfer of skills. This was illustrated in a three-year study to explore whether group music instruction could improve the test scores of economically disadvantaged elementary-school children (including almost 600 kindergarten to fifth-grade students from four elementary schools). One school provided 30 minutes of keyboard lessons per week, another a 40-minute lesson every six days, while the remaining two schools acted as controls. All lessons were in groups of 20 to 25 pupils. Participants were pre-tested with two subtests measuring verbal abilities, two measuring quantitative abilities and one measuring spatial-temporal abilities. Tests were then repeated at 9, 18 and 27 months. During the first two years of the study, there were difficulties in the implementation of the music programme, and it was only at the end of the study when the children had received one year of high-quality tuition that there were any gains (Rauscher, 2005).

Similarly, Yang and colleagues (2014) examined the relationship between long-term music training and child development based on 250 Chinese elementary-school students' academic development of first language, second language and mathematics. They found that the musician children outperformed the non-musician children only on musical achievement and second language development. Although music training appeared to be correlated with children's final academic development of first- and second-language learning and mathematics, it did not independently contribute to the development of the first language, nor all mathematical skills. The authors argued that other variables might be important; for example parents' level of education.

Two experiments by Rickard and colleagues (2012) also revealed inconclusive results. The first was based on an already existing music programme for ten- to thirteen-year-olds. Comparing participation in drama, art or music groups, there was some improvement in the music group on a non-verbal IQ test but not in academic achievement. A second musical intervention, provided externally over six months, included playing music with percussion instruments, composing, improvising, playing in a group, singing, active listening and analysis of a wide range of styles. As the programme was introduced in a private school, all of the students were of middle or high economic status. Three groups participated in music, drama or an additional activity. Students from the music group achieved better results in mathematics but this result was also in evidence in the drama group. The authors argued that the age of the children may have been a factor in the outcomes of the research.

Cox and Stephens (2006) compared high-school students with different numbers of music credits in relation to their mean mathematics grade point averages, or their mean cumulative grade point averages. Students were then separated into two groups based on the number of music credits. Those who had earned at least two music credits per grade level were placed into Group A. This included ninth-graders with two or more music credits, tenth graders with four or more music credits, eleventh graders with six or more music credits, and twelfth graders with eight or more music credits. The remaining students were placed into Group B. The group A students performed better than the group B students but the differences were not statistically significant, although there was a slight upward trend in grade point average as the number of music credits increased. Lower grade point averages were non-existent as music credits increased.

Overview

There have been a number of reviews of the impact of music on cognitive skills, including spatial reasoning and mathematics. In relation to spatial reasoning, Hetland (2000a) reviewed 15 studies and found a strong and reliable relationship and concluded that music instruction led to dramatic improvement in performance on spatial temporal measures. She commented on the consistency of the effects and likened them to differences of one inch in height or about 84 points on the SAT (p. 221). She showed that the effects were likely to be stronger among younger children, three to five years than those aged six to twelve years. Similarly, Črnčec and colleagues (2006) reviewed the evidence on the impact of music teaching on spatio-temporal reasoning skills and found that there was a consistent effect, although improvements in associated academic domains, such as arithmetic, had not been reliably shown. More recent research(as reviewed above) generally supports a positive role for music in developing spatial temporal reasoning skills, the consistency of the findings suggesting a near transfer, automated effect. Where spatial temporal skills are well developed the wider and more appropriate the choice of strategies and the more efficient and less erroneous mathematical operations. Rhythm-based instruction seems to be the most conducive for the improvement of spatial temporal reasoning skills, followed by learning to play the piano. Singing leads to smaller changes.

Focusing on the impact of engaging with music on a broader range of academic skills and educational attainment, including mathematics, Hodges and O'Connell (2007) suggest that a moderate position needs to be taken. At one extreme, the data support the contention that music improves academic performance, but at the other extreme there is no basis for saying that music instruction has no effect on academic achievement. Hodges and O'Connell argue that human learning is so complex that any simplistic explanations must be rejected. They suggest that some music experiences have a positive impact on academic performance under certain circumstances. What is neglected is the impact that an individual teacher can have. Excellent teachers who are enthusiastic and who relate well to students may make a greater difference to educational outcomes than particular methods used, although if the overall quality of tuition is poor it can have a negative impact. A more recent systematic review also suggests that the findings are inconclusive and contradictory (Jaschke et al., 2013). Jaschke and colleagues attribute this to differences in research design, the analytical methods used, the nature of the musical interventions and differences in neural activation during the processing of these tasks. Recent meta-analyses have come to similar conclusions about the challenges faced by research and some have concluded that overall, music does not have an impact on children's cognitive skills including mathematics (Sala and Gobet, 2020).

To conclude, the evidence suggests that active engagement in musical activities enhances a range of spatial processing skills, particularly in young children. These skills may support the development of some simple mathematical skills, mediated by line number knowledge, but do not transfer to all mathematical skills. There remain many questions about the type of training that may be effective, that involving rhythm seems a likely candidate; how long training needs to be sustained, the type of mathematical activities which may be most influenced by musical activity, and the overall quality of the training on offer.

6. The Impact of Musical Engagement on Memory

Memory is the faculty of the brain by which data or information is encoded, stored and retrieved when needed. There are several different types of memory, which broadly fall into three groups: sensory memory, short-term memory and long-term memory. Sensory memory is very short, typically acting for less than half a second, and accurately retains material for that time, acting as a buffer for stimuli received through the five senses. Iconic memory refers to immediate visual memories, echoic memory to auditory memories and haptic memory to the sense of touch, while olfactory memories relate to smell and gustatory memories to taste. Short-term memories are slightly longer than sensory memories but still disappear after a few minutes. Short-term memory holds information briefly until it is needed. The term 'short-term memory' is often used interchangeably with the term 'working memory'. Short-term memory is temporary and has limited capacity, as the information being processed is either lost or entered into long-term memory.

Long-term memory is the brain's system for storing, managing and recalling information. It is complex and serves different functions. Long-term memories include anything from an event that occurred five minutes ago to something from 50 years ago. There are many different forms of long-term memories. Sometimes they are conscious, requiring us to actively think in order to recall them. Other memories are unconscious and appear without an active attempt at recollection. The most common forms of long-term memory are explicit memory (the intentional recall of information), declarative memory (the retention and recall of important facts, dates and information), episodic memory (enabling memory of first-hand experiences in one's life), semantic memory (the storage of vocabulary, names and general knowledge), implicit memory (sometimes referred to as unconscious memory where information from a moment in time cannot be specifically recalled), procedural memory (memory for how to do things), auditory memory (which helps to retain information based on the sounds an individual has heard), visual spatial memory (which enables memory for spatial objects and their manipulation), and working memory. The latter has been more controversial than other forms of memory. Cowan (2014), after reviewing the evidence, suggests that it is the retention of a small amount of information in a readily accessible form which facilitates planning, comprehension, reasoning and problem-solving. In the research on the impact of making music on working memory, mention is often made of executive control skills that are used to manage information in working memory, and the cognitive processing of that information. Overall, there continues to be debate about the actual nature of working memory, although there is agreement that similar research findings are obtained when specific test methods are adopted. This chapter reports the findings from research on the impact of music on visual memory, verbal memory and working memory, although, as will be seen, much of the research explores several different aspects of memory simultaneously.

Visual Memory

One strand of research has explored the impact of musical training on visual cognition. Early work focused on memory for musical notation. For instance, Sloboda (1976) demonstrated that musically trained adults showed significantly greater capacity to maintain musical notation in short-term memory than non-musicians. George and Coch (2011) investigated the neural and behavioural aspects of visual memory in college-aged, non-professional musicians and non-musicians. Behaviourally, the musicians outperformed the non-musicians on standardised subtests of visual memory. Event-related potentials were recorded in standard visual paradigms, where participants responded to infrequent deviant stimuli embedded in lists of standard stimuli. Electrophysiologically, the musicians demonstrated faster updating of working memory in the visual domain. These findings demonstrated that long-term music training was related to improvements in visual working memory. Similarly, Brochard and colleagues (2004) used a neuropsychological task in which participants had to detect the position of a target dot relative to vertical or horizontal reference lines which flashed onto a screen. In the perception condition, the reference line remained on the screen until the dot was displayed, while in the imagery condition, the line disappeared before the target dot was presented, requiring participants to keep a mental image of the reference line. In both conditions, musicians had shorter reaction times compared to non-musicians, suggesting that the musicians had enhanced visuospatial abilities. The authors concluded that the enhanced performance of the musicians resulted from their long-term reading of musical notation, which requires fine-grained recognition of the positions of notes on the stave and also efficient attentional processes. This explanation is supported by Kopiez and Galley (2002), who suggested that patterns of saccadic eye movements can be used as an indicator of mental processing speed. The specific demands of reading musical notation, particularly if it is begun at an early age, may modify the way visual information is processed by the nervous system. Kopiez and Galley (2002) and Gruhn and colleagues (2006) compared saccadic eye movements during oculomotor tasks in adult musicians and non-musicians, and reported more efficient oculomotor strategies in the musicians, which they argued may be associated with complex visual processes involved in the long-term practice of reading musical notation, alongside more efficient attentional processes. Gruhn and colleagues (2006) point out that there is some evidence (Biscaldi et al., 2000; Currie et al., 1991; Kinsler and Carpenter, 1995; Sereno et al., 1995) that there is a strong association between attention and saccadic eye movements. The control of eye movements requires highly complex mental processes, involving many cerebral areas (Tatler and Wade, 2003). All modalities of attention have an impact on the oculomotor system (Kimmig, 1986).

Rodrigues and colleagues (2007) compared the performance of musicians who were members of a symphony orchestra or symphonic band with non-musicians, in tasks involving visual attention. They used a multiple-choice reaction-time test which consisted of specific motor responses to various luminous stimuli. The test was applied twice in order to assess divided visual attention ability. The second time, it was used alongside other continuously and randomly changing visual stimuli presented in video form. The participants were asked to respond verbally to each change. The musicians showed a higher percentage of correct responses when the test was applied alone, but not when the test was applied together with other changing visual stimuli, although the musicians showed shorter reaction times for verbal responses to stimuli changes. The authors suggested that musicians may have augmented divided visual attention ability compared to non-musicians, which they ascribed to ensemble rehearsal. They argued that the professional activities of musicians are characterised by constant demands of divided visual attention, including dealing with several kinds of visual stimuli simultaneously—for instance, the musical score, the conductor's gestural instructions and the body movements of other musicians—while also playing their own instrument.

Patston and colleagues (2006) compared right-handed musicians and non-musicians in a line bisection task, which entailed marking the centre of 17 horizontal lines, varying in length from 10 to 26 cm, displayed randomly on a page. Neurologically intact right-handers showed a slight but reliable tendency to bisect about two percent to the left of the centre on this task (Hausmann et al., 2002) a phenomenon attributed to dominance of the right hemisphere for visuospatial attention (Oliveri et al., 2004). In contrast, Patston and colleagues (2006) demonstrated that musicians showed a slight rightward bias, while non-musicians showed greater deviation to the left. The musicians also bisected the lines more accurately and with fewer intermanual differences than the non-musicians. The researchers suggested that musicians may develop an increased ability for the left hemisphere to perform cognitive functions that are typically right-hemisphere dominant, resulting in more balanced spatial attention. In a later study, Patston and colleagues (2007a) compared reaction times and accuracy between musicians and non-musicians in response to stimuli presented to the left and right of a vertical line. Both groups performed more accurately with the left-sided stimuli, but the musicians were significantly more accurate than non-musicians for the right-sided stimuli, and overall had faster reaction times. This suggested a more balanced attentional capacity in musicians, as well as enhanced visuomotor ability. They may also have an advantage on line and dot tasks of the type used in this study and that of Brochard and colleagues (2004), because they are familiar with these components—they are similar to those required for reading musical notation, although the placement of the lines vertically rather than horizontally means that the tasks are not truly equivalent. Patston and colleagues (2007b) also studied the lateralisation of visuospatial attention using interhemispheric transfer time. Musicians and non-musicians responded to stimuli presented to the left and right visual fields while being submitted to electroencephalography. Non-musicians showed significantly faster responses in the right to left direction than in the opposite direction and a shorter latency in the left than in the right hemisphere. In contrast, musicians exhibited no directional difference between hemispheres and no hemispheric difference in latency, indicating more bilateral neural connectivity. Patston and colleagues concluded that the bimanual training of musicians facilitates additional myelination that results in more balanced connections between the hemispheres than normally found in those without musical training.

Stoesz and colleagues (2007) investigated visual processing of local details in musicians and non-musicians, utilising disembedding and constructional tasks. They used the group embedded figures test, where a series of 25 complex figures is presented, each containing one of nine targets hidden in the design. The task is to examine each test figure and outline the hidden target as soon as it is identified. In a second study, two tests were used: a block design subtest, which requires the participant to replicate a geometric pattern presented on a card using the top surfaces of several coloured blocks, and secondly a task involving copying possible and impossible drawings of objects. The musicians outperformed the non-musicians on the embedded figures test, the block design subtest and the task of copying drawings of physically impossible objects. These findings suggest enhanced visual processing of local details. There was a correlation between the block design scores and the accuracy scores for the impossible figures, but not for the possible figures. Local processing ability did not correlate with drawing ability per se. Stoesz and colleagues concluded that a relative strength in local processing contributed to the superior performance of the musicians on the drawing task. They suggested that the enhanced visual processing of local details may reflect training-induced changes in the frontoparietal system involved in controlling exploratory eye movements and shifts in visual attention—skills that are important for reading musical notation (which requires the detailed analysis of visual details).

Suárez and colleagues (2016) carried out a cross-sectional study exploring the relationship between music training and visual working memory in adult musicians and non-musicians. Twenty-four musicians and 30 non-musicians matched for age, gender, years of formal education and verbal intelligence performed several working memory tasks. The musicians outperformed the non-musicians in tasks related to visual motor coordination, visual scanning ability, visual processing speed and spatial memory. Similarly, Jakobson and colleagues (2008) studied visual memory in pianists and non-musicians using a visual design learning test, which required participants to try to learn and remember a sequentially presented set of 15-line drawings of simple geometric figures, each containing two elements (for example, a circle and a line). Participants were asked to draw all the figures that they could remember, after each of the five learning trials and after a delay. A test of delayed recognition was also administered. The results suggested superior visual memory in musicians, since they outperformed non-musicians on the fourth and fifth learning trials and on the delayed recall and delayed recognition tasks. After controlling for general intelligence, the group difference on the delayed recall tasks persisted. The researchers suggested that the observed relationship between visual memory and musical training may be related to improvement in processes supporting attention to visual details, to the increased skill of musicians at holding and manipulating visual images in working memory—which confers an advantage during the encoding process—or to superior use of high-level, strategic memory processes.

Some research has focused on processing speed—for instance, Bugos and Mostafa (2011) examined the effects of music instruction on information processing speed. Using neuropsychological tests, the paced auditory serial addition task and the trail-making test, they examined the role of music on information processing speed in 14 musicians and 16 non-musicians. The musicians performed better on both tests, suggesting that musical training has the capacity to enhance the processing speed of auditory and visual content. Brain-imaging studies have also suggested more efficient visual processes in musicians. For instance, Platel and colleagues (1997) showed activation of an associative visual area in musicians during a pitch-discrimination task, while Schmithorst and Holland (2003) investigated the relationship between musical practice and cerebral processing relating to melody and harmony. The findings showed that musicians and non-musicians used different neural networks to process these elements. In the musicians, the inferior parietal areas were activated only during melody and harmony perception. These have been identified as involved in general visuospatial processing. In a study comparing male symphony orchestra musicians with non-musicians, there was increased density of grey matter in Broca's area in the musicians—an area important for spoken language and visuospatial localisation (Sluming et al., 2002). More recently, Sluming and colleagues (2007) showed enhanced performance on a visuospatial task by orchestral musicians, compared to non-musicians. This was also associated with increased activation in Broca's area.

Not all of the research with adults has shown enhanced visual memory in musicians. For instance, Cohen and colleagues (2011) showed that, while musicians had superior auditory recognition memory for musical and non-musical stimuli compared to non-musicians, this was not the case for the visual domain. For both groups, memory for auditory stimuli was inferior to memory for visual objects. Although considerable musical training is associated with better musical and non-musical auditory memory, this does not increase the ability to remember sounds to the levels found with visual stimuli. This suggests a fundamental capacity difference between auditory and visual recognition memory, with a persistent advantage for the visual domain. Using a very different task, Brandler and Rammsayer (2003) asked 35 adult musicians and non-musicians to indicate, from memory, the location of buildings on a city map that they had previously studied. There were no statistically significant differences between the performance of the musicians and non-musicians on this task. Chan and colleagues (1998) also found no benefit of musical training in relation to a visual task where the participants—60 female college students from the Chinese University of Hong Kong—had to draw from memory ten simple figures that they had been asked to memorise. Thirty of the participants had had at least six years of training with a Western musical instrument before the age of 12, while 30 had received no musical training. The participants were matched in terms of age, grade point average and years of education. There were no statistically significant differences between the musicians and non-musicians in the proportion of drawings that they were able to create.

Research with Children

Another strand of research has focused on visual memory in children. For instance, Degé and colleagues (2011b) tested the effect of a two-year extended music curriculum on secondary school children's visual and auditory memory. The curriculum consisted of learning to play a musical instrument, participating in an orchestra, auditory perception and music theory training. Ten-year-old children who had just started the programme and children without training were tested on visual and aural memory at the start of the programme and two years later. Prior to the training, there were no differences between the groups, but the children participating in the musical training improved significantly from time one to time two in visual and auditory memory, while the children not receiving training did not. These effects were apparent even when a range of confounding variables was taken into account, including intelligence, socioeconomic status, extra-curricular schooling, motivation to avoid work and musical aptitude.

It seems that musical training generally has a positive impact on aural memory in children but this is not necessarily the case for visual memory. Ho and colleagues (2003), working with a group of Chinese children, showed that those with music training did not demonstrate better visual memory than their non-musician counterparts. When the performance of these children was followed up after a year, changes in visual memory were not significantly different between the groups. Similarly, Roden and colleagues (2012; 2014a) examined the effects of a school-based instrumental training programme on the development of visual memory skills in primary-school children. Participants either took part in a music programme with weekly 45-minutef instrumental lessons in small groups at school, or received extended natural science training. A third group of children did not receive any additional training. Each child completed visual memory tests three times over a period of 18 months. No differences between groups were found in the visual memory tests. Similarly, Rickard and colleagues (2010) explored the effect of increasing the frequency and intensity of a classroom-based instrumental training programme on visual memory across a two-year period. Data from 142 participants aged eight to nine were analysed. Eighty-two children were allocated to the intensive string-music training programme; 68 acted as a control group and participated in their usual music classes. The intensive music training had no effect on visual memory, although an improvement in visual perceptual ability was observed in the first year.

To conclude, there are a number of reasons why the evidence relating to visual memory is inconsistent. First, there is no reason why music, which essentially requires enhanced aural skills, should have any impact on visual skills. Only if musicians are required to read musical notation is it likely that there would be any impact on visual skills. As some musicians play by ear, this is not always the case. Second, in the research, visual memory has been assessed using different methods, including reaction times and recall accuracy. Third, participants in some studies (Chan et al., 1998; Ho et al., 2003) were Chinese. The Chinese language is written in symbols rather than letters, which may have led to experimental and control groups already being skilled in processing complex visual signs. Fourth, the participants in the research were of very different ages. Fifth, the levels of musical experience in those classified as musicians varied, and sixth, the nature of the musical training itself was different, particularly the extent to which it involved learning to read musical notation.

Verbal Memory

Research has compared the performance of musicians with non-musicians on a variety of verbal tasks. For instance, Parbery-Clark and colleagues (2009a) investigated the effect of musical training on identifying speech in noise, which is a complex task requiring the integration of working memory and stream segregation, as well as the detection of time-varying perceptual cues. Sixteen musicians and 15 non-musicians aged 19 to 31, all with normal hearing, participated. The musicians outperformed the non-musicians on hearing speech in challenging listening environments. In a second study, Parbery-Clark and colleagues (2009b) compared subcortical neurophysiological responses to speech in quiet conditions and in noisy conditions, for a group of highly trained musicians and non-musician controls. Musicians were found to have a more robust subcortical representation of the acoustic stimulus in the presence of noise. They demonstrated faster neural timing, enhanced representation of speech harmonics and less degraded response morphology in noise. Neural measures were associated with better behavioural performance on a hearing-in-noise test, in which musicians outperformed the non-musician controls. These findings suggest that musical experience limits the negative effects of competing background noise, thereby providing biological evidence for musicians' perceptual advantage for speech in noise.

Other studies have found similar results. For instance, Strait and Kraus (2011b) assessed the impact of selective auditory attention on cortical auditory evoked response variability in musicians and non-musicians. The outcomes indicated strengthened brain networks for selective auditory attention in musicians. Strait and colleagues (2010) administered a standardised battery of perceptual and cognitive tests to adult musicians and non-musicians. Tasks included those which were either more or less susceptible to cognitive control—for instance, backward versus simultaneous masking—and more or less dependent on auditory or visual processing: for instance, auditory versus visual attention. The findings indicated lower perceptual thresholds in musicians specifically for auditory tasks that related to cognitive abilities, such as backward masking and auditory attention. The results suggested that long-term musical practice strengthens cognitive functions and that these functions benefit auditory skills. Further, the intensity of the enhancement of verbal memory and auditory attention was related to the start of musical training and how long it lasted (Kraus and Chandrasekaran, 2010).

Cohen and colleagues (2011) compared professional musicians and music students with non-musicians on their verbal and visual memory. The musicians were significantly better than non-musicians at remembering familiar music, unfamiliar music, speech and environmental sound clips, but there was no difference between the two groups on their performance on tests of visual memory. Also working with music students, Kilgour and colleagues (2000) studied whether music training acted as a mediator for the recall of spoken and sung lyrics, and whether the presentation rate of materials was important rather than the inclusion of melody. In the first experiment, 78 undergraduates, half with music training and half without, heard spoken or sung lyrics. Recall for sung lyrics was superior to that for spoken lyrics for both groups. In the second and third experiments, presentation rate was manipulated so that the durations of the spoken and the sung materials were equal. With presentation rate equated, there was no advantage for sung over spoken lyrics. In all of the experiments, those participants with music training outperformed those without training. Overall, the results suggested that music training leads to enhanced memory for verbal material. Similarly, working with 15 highly trained pianists and 21 non musicians, Jakobson and colleagues (2008) studied non-musical perceptual and cognitive abilities. The musicians showed superior immediate and delayed recall of word lists and greater use of a semantic clustering strategy during initial list-learning than non-musicians. The group differences in delayed free recall of words persisted even when IQ was controlled for.

Brandler and Rammsayer (2003) tested the psychometric performance of 35 adult musicians and non-musicians on different aspects of primary mental abilities, verbal comprehension, word fluency, space, closure, perceptual speed, reasoning, number and memory. The only statistically significant differences were found in relation to verbal memory and reasoning. Performance on verbal memory was reliably higher for the musicians than for the non-musicians, but the non-musicians performed significantly better on subscales of a culture-free intelligence test. This supports the notion that long-term musical training exerts beneficial effects on verbal memory. This is probably because it leads to changes in cortical organisation.

In research exploring attention, Puschmann and colleagues (2019) required participants with varying amounts of musical training to attend to one of two speech streams while detecting rare target words. The findings showed that the duration of musical training was associated with a reduced distracting effect of competing speech on target detection accuracy. More musical training was related to robust neural tracking of both the speech stream to be attended to and the speech stream to be ignored, up until the late cortical processing stages. The findings suggested that musically trained persons were able to use additional information about a distracting verbal stream to limit interference by competing speech.

One strand of research has compared musicians' performance as opposed to non-musicians' performance in detecting pitch change in spoken sentences in both native, French (Schön et al., 2004) and unfamiliar (Portuguese—Marques et al., 2007) languages. Similarly, Deguchi and colleagues (2012) studied the effects of familiarity of intonational contour and the presence of meaningful context, using behavioural and electrophysiological data from Italian musicians and non-musicians. Performance was compared in a pitch incongruity detection task using sentences in native, Italian and foreign (French) languages and in jabberwocky, meaningless sentences formed by pseudo-words. To examine whether these differences depended on enhanced auditory sensitivity to pitch, the frequency discrimination threshold for tones was obtained using a psychophysical procedure. Musicians were more accurate than non-musicians at detecting small pitch changes in all languages, showing a smaller response bias. Overall, the findings confirmed musicians' advantage in the detection of subtle pitch changes, not only with tones but also with speech sentences, in both native and unfamiliar languages. Such effects seemed to emerge from more efficient pitch analysis acquired through musical training.

Enhancements of short-term memory related to music may also support linguistic functions. Ludke and colleagues (2014) randomly assigned 60 adult participants to one of three listen-and-repeat learning conditions: speaking, rhythmic speaking or singing. Participants in the singing condition showed superior overall performance on a collection of Hungarian language tests after a 15-minute learning period, as compared with participants in the speaking and rhythmic-speaking conditions. These differences were not explained by age, gender, mood, phonological working memory ability, or musical ability and training. The researchers suggested that a 'listen and sing' learning method could facilitate verbatim memory for phrases spoken in a foreign language.

The relationship between musical expertise and language processing is well documented, but there is less evidence of language-to-music effects. Bidelman and colleagues (2013) used a cross-sectional design to compare the performance of musicians to that of tonal language

(Cantonese) speakers on tasks of auditory pitch acuity, music perception and general cognitive ability, including fluid intelligence and working memory. While musicians demonstrated superior performance on all auditory measures, comparable perceptual enhancements were observed for Cantonese participants, relative to English-speaking non-musicians. These results suggest that tone language background is associated with higher auditory perceptual performance for listening to music. Musicians and Cantonese speakers also showed superior working memory capacity relative to non-musician controls, suggesting that in addition to basic perceptual enhancements, a background of tonal languages and music training might also be associated with enhanced general cognitive abilities. The findings support the notion that tonal language speakers and musically trained individuals have higher performance than English-speaking listeners in the perceptual cognitive processing necessary for basic auditory—as well as complex music—perception. These results illustrate bidirectional influences between the domains of music and language.

Research with Children

Early work exploring the relationship between musical training and verbal memory was carried out with Asian participants. For instance, Chan and colleagues (1998) showed that learning to play a musical instrument before the age of 12 enhanced the ability to remember words. Participants with musical training could remember 17 percent more verbal information than those without musical training. Music training in childhood may therefore have long-term positive effects on verbal memory. Ho and colleagues (2003) supported these findings in a later study of 90 boys aged six to fifteen. Those with musical training had significantly better verbal learning and retention abilities. Duration of music training, learning to play an instrument and verbal learning performance correlated positively, even after controlling for age and education level. Those with musical training learned approximately 20 percent more words from a 16-word list. Their retention was also better after 10- and 30-minute delays. A follow-up study compared children from the same cohort who had just begun or continued their music training for one year, and those who had given up playing. Children in the beginner and advanced training groups significantly increased verbal learning and retention performance. This was not the case for those who had discontinued training, although their verbal memory performance remained stable at least nine months after ceasing to play an instrument. Ho and colleagues concluded that music training seemed to have long-term enhancing effects on verbal memory.

While these studies demonstrate a relationship between musical training and verbal memory, they do not demonstrate causality. For this, intervention studies are required. In further work with Chinese participants, which focused on children aged four to five years old, Nan and colleagues (2018) studied 74 Mandarin-speaking children who were pseudo-randomly assigned to piano training, reading training or a no-contact control group. Six months of piano training improved behavioural auditory-word discrimination in general, as well as word discrimination based on vowels, compared with controls. The reading group yielded similar trends. However, the piano group demonstrated unique advantages over the reading and control groups in consonant-based word discrimination. All three groups improved on general cognitive measures, including tests of IQ, working memory and attention.

In a typical intervention study, working with kindergarten children, Hallberg and colleagues (2017) investigated the effects of instrumental music instruction as opposed to no tuition. The children received five hours of instrumental instruction for five weeks using the Suzuki method and were tested on working memory efficiency, visuospatial processing and controlled attention. The only statistically significant difference between the two groups related to attentional control, which was enhanced in those having instrumental music instruction. Rickard and colleagues (2010) researched 142 children from nine primary schools, 82 of whom (aged eight to nine) participated in an enhanced school-based music programme. The remainder of the children acted as controls and received standard class music lessons. The children were tested three times within the first two years of the study, and in the third year a subset of the control sample was tested again. Verbal learning and immediate recall scores significantly increased after one year of enhanced school-based music training. No such increase was found in the control group. However, these advantages disappeared in the second year, although in the second year of the study there was significantly enhanced visual perception for the music training group. Similarly, Roden and colleagues (2012) examined the effects of a school-based instrumental training programme on the development of verbal memory skills in primary-school children aged seven to eight years old. Participants either took part in a music programme with weekly 45-minute sessions of instrumental lessons in small groups at school, or received extended natural science training. A third group of children did not receive any additional training. Each child completed verbal memory tests three times over a period of 18 months. Children in the music group showed greater improvements than children in the control groups after controlling for their socioeconomic background, age and IQ. Overall, the evidence suggested that children who have musical training develop efficient memory strategies for verbal materials. This is likely to be because playing music requires continued monitoring of meaningful chunks of information. Individual notes are combined into meaningful melodic phrases which have a quasi-syllabic structure, and are based on temporal frameworks that have metric structures which are parallel to stresses on syllables in language (Patel and Daniele, 2003). This is supported by evidence that the auditory cortex is structurally and functionally shaped through the individual's experiences with sound (Fritz et al., 2007). Fujioka and colleagues (2006) recorded auditory evoked responses to a violin tone and a noise-burst stimulus from four- to six-year-old children on four occasions over a one-year period, using magnetoencephalography. Half of the children participated in music lessons throughout the year, while the other half had no music lessons. A clear musical training effect was expressed in a larger and earlier peak in the left hemisphere in response to the violin sound in musically trained children compared with untrained children. This transition could be related to establishing a neural network associated with sound categorisation and/or involuntary attention, which can be altered by musical learning experiences.

 Also working with primary-aged children, Piro and Ortiz (2009) adopted a quasi-experimental approach to examining the effects of a scaffolded music instruction programme on the vocabulary and verbal sequencing skills of two cohorts of second-grade students. One group of 46 children studied piano formally for a period of three consecutive years as part of a comprehensive instructional intervention programme.

The second group of 57 children had no exposure to music lessons, either at school or through private study. The findings showed that the experimental group had significantly better vocabulary and verbal sequencing scores following the intervention than the control group. In an interesting study, Brodsky and Sulkin (2011) focused on children's hand clapping and reported positive effects of a classroom hand-clapping intervention on verbal memory. They examined whether children who spontaneously engaged in hand-clapping song activity demonstrated improved motor or cognitive abilities. The study also investigated the outcome of a two-group, eight-week classroom intervention. The study found that children who were more skilful at performing hand-clapping songs were more efficient in first grade, while those in second grade who spontaneously engaged in hand-clapping songs were advantaged in bimanual coupling patterns, verbal memory and handwriting. Classroom hand-clapping song training was more efficient than music appreciation classes in developing non-musical skills among participating children. Adopting an experimental design, Martens and colleagues (2011) focused on the effect of musical experience on verbal memory in 38 individuals with Williams syndrome, aged 6 to 59. Participants who had engaged in formal music lessons scored significantly better on a verbal long-term memory task when the stimuli were sung than when they were spoken in comparison to those who did not have formal lessons, who showed no benefit for either the sung or spoken conditions.

Working Memory

Working memory is the time- and capacity-limited storage of task-relevant information, which generally requires mental manipulation, flexible use or inhibition of distractors, or all of these. It is different to short-term memory, as it requires mental manipulation of encoded information or the inhibition of goal-irrelevant stimuli. From a neuroscientific perspective, working memory also requires the integrity of the medial-temporal lobe regions, whereas short-term memory does not. In addition, there is strong evidence linking behavioural measures of working memory to both localised and distributed patterns of neural oscillations (Yurgil et al., 2020). Working memory is typically studied using behavioural tasks that require the implementation of a combination of stored information, manipulation of that information and interference including the N-back (Ding et al., 2018), backward digit-span (Clayton et al., 2016; George and Coch, 2011; Zuk et al., 2014), reading span (D'Souza et al., 2018; Franklin et al., 2008) and operation span tasks (D'Souza et al., 2018; Franklin et al., 2008). The N-back task presents participants with a sequence of visual or auditory stimuli. The participant then maintains the information while deciding whether each subsequent stimulus item matches the stimulus that came a specific number of letters previously (Owen et al., 2005). In the backward digit span task, participants are presented with a series of digits, then asked to report the sequence of digits in reverse order (Hester et al., 2004). The central executive component of working memory has been argued to play an important role in the performance of span tasks, particularly backward span. Both forward and backward span tasks recruit the central executive resources necessary for successful task performance (Hester et al., 2004). For the reading span task, a number of sentences are presented one sentence at a time. As the number of sentences increases, so does the memory load required to perform the task. Where two sentences are presented sequentially, after each sentence, the participant writes the sentence verbatim and the last word of each sentence in order (Daneman and Carpenter, 1980). Finally, the operation span task requires participants to memorise a sequence of unrelated words while simultaneously performing a series of mathematical operations. After all of the operation word strings are presented, the participant writes all of the words that were displayed in the order of presentation (Turner and Engle, 1989). The reading span and the operation span require participants to hold information while working on a secondary task, which can cause interference. Each of these tasks fulfils the criteria of maintenance and manipulation of information, which may occur with differing levels of interference (Aben et al., 2012).

Research with Adults

Oechslin and colleagues (2013) used functional magnetic resonance imaging with non-musicians and amateur and expert musicians, who listened to a comprehensive set of specifically composed string quartets with hierarchically manipulated endings. Two irregularities at musical closure were implemented, differing in salience but within the tonality of the piece. Behavioural sensitivity scores of both transgressions perfectly separated participants according to their level of musical expertise. The functional brain imaging data showed compelling evidence for stepwise modulation of brain responses by expertise level in a fronto-temporal network hosting universal functions of working memory and attention. Additional independent testing evidenced an advantage in visual working memory for the professionals, which was predicted by musical training intensity. Similarly, George and Coch (2011), using event-related potentials and a standardised test of working memory, investigated neural and behavioural aspects of working memory in college-aged, non-professional musicians and non-musicians. Behaviourally, the musicians outperformed the non-musicians on standardised subtests of phonological and executive memory. Event-related potentials were recorded in standard auditory oddball paradigms, where participants responded to infrequent deviant stimuli embedded in lists of standard stimuli. Electrophysiologically, the musicians demonstrated faster updating of working memory in the auditory domain and allocated more neural resources to auditory stimuli, showing increased sensitivity to the auditory standard deviant difference and less effortful updating of auditory working memory.

Halpern and Bower (1982), in a pilot study with 12 musicians and 12 non-musicians, briefly presented visually similar melodies that had been rated as good or bad, followed by a 15-second retention interval and then recall. The musicians remembered good melodies better than bad ones while the non-musicians did not distinguish between them. In one study, six musicians and six non-musicians were briefly presented with good, bad and random melodies, followed by immediate recall. The advantage of the musicians over the non-musicians decreased as the melody type progressed from good to bad to random. In a second study, seven students and professional musicians divided the stimulus melodies into groups. For each melody, the consistency of grouping was correlated with the memory performance found in the first two experiments. The findings showed that the musicians used musical groupings, while a simple visual strategy was used by the non-musicians.

Talamini and colleagues (2016) requested musicians and non-musicians to perform a digit-span task that was presented aurally, visually or audiovisually. The task was performed with or without a concurrent task in order to explore the role of rehearsal strategies, but also to manipulate task complexity. The musical abilities of all participants were also assessed. The musicians had larger digit-spans than non-musicians, regardless of the sensory modality and the concurrent task. In addition, the auditory and audiovisual spans, but not the visual alone, were correlated with one subscale of the music test. The findings suggested a general advantage of musicians over non-musicians in verbal working memory tasks, with a possible role of sensory modality and task complexity. Similarly, Hansen and colleagues (2013) administered a digit-span test, a spatial span test and a musical ear test to non-musicians, amateur musicians and expert musicians. The expert musicians significantly outperformed the non-musicians on the digit-span test. These scores were also correlated with musical scores and those on a rhythm subtest. No cross-group differences were found on the spatial span test. Fennell and colleagues (2020), in a complex experimental study with 22 non-musicians and 30 musicians, presented participants with a memory element, three nouns, a melody or a dot matrix, followed by a sentence and then a comprehension question on each trial. After participants answered the comprehension question, they had to judge whether a second memory element was the same as the first one. The musicians performed more accurately on working memory tasks, particularly those related to verbal and musical working memory.

D'Souza and colleagues (2018) compared musicians, bilinguals and individuals who had expertise in both skills, or neither. One hundred and fifty-three young adults were categorised into one of four groups: monolingual musician, bilingual musician, bilingual non-musician and monolingual non-musician. Multiple tasks relating to cognitive ability were used to examine the coherence of any training effects. The findings revealed that musically trained individuals, but not bilinguals, had enhanced working memory. Neither musical or language skill led to enhanced inhibitory control.

Okhrei and colleagues (2016) explored the performance of the working memory of musicians and non-musicians in tests with letters, digits and geometrical shapes. The participants were students who, for ten to fifteen years, had been engaged in regular musical practice (classed as musicians), and their peers, who had no previous musical experience (classed as non-musicians). A computerised working memory test for letters, digits and shapes, with successive presentation of stimuli, was applied. The musicians and non-musicians did not differ in the overall number of mistakes and latency of responses in all subtests for letters, digits and shapes. The left hand made significantly more mistakes than the right in both groups, but this regularity was more typical in non-musicians. The righthand responded faster than the left while carrying out all subtests in both groups, but such a motor asymmetry was more evident for non-musicians. In the main, musicians did not demonstrate an increase in latency of responses with task complexity, while non-musicians did. Overall, the efficiency of working memory test performance did not differ among musicians and non-musicians, but the musicians had tighter interhemispheric cooperation during the memory test, indicated by less motor asymmetry. Musicians had almost equal latency of responses regardless of task complexity, while non-musicians required more time for responding to stimuli during growing task complexity.

Investigating specific aspects of working memory that differed between adult musicians and non-musicians, Suárez and colleagues (2015) compared the performance of 24 musicians and 30 non-musicians matched for age, gender, years of formal education and verbal intelligence on several working memory tasks. The musicians outperformed non-musicians in tasks related to visual motor coordination, visual scanning ability, visual processing speed and spatial memory, although no significant differences were found in phonological and visual memory capacity. The findings support the view that musical training is associated with specific and not general working memory skills.

Ding and colleagues (2018) investigated to what degree the number and duration of notes in a sequence influenced the tonal working memory of participants with or without professional musical training. A forward tonal discrimination task tested the maintenance of tonal information, while a backward N-back tonal task probed the running memory span of tonal information. The findings showed that the number of notes, but not the duration of notes, in a tone sequence significantly affected tonal working memory performance for musicians and non-musicians. In addition, within a minimum musical context, musicians outperformed non-musicians on a N-back tonal task but not a forward-tone sequence-discrimination task. These findings indicate that the capacity of tonal working memory is determined by the number of notes, but not the duration of notes, in a sequence to be memorised, suggesting a different mechanism underlying tonal working memory from verbal working memory. Musicians held more items in memory for both tonal and atonal auditory stimuli, but retained items longer than non-musicians only for tonal stimuli.

Focusing on the role of attention, Pallesen and colleagues (2010) measured activation responses dependent on blood oxygenation level in musicians and non-musicians during working memory performance relating to musical sounds, to determine the relationship between performance, musical competence and generally enhanced cognition. All participants easily distinguished the stimuli. The musicians performed better, as reflected in reaction times and error rates. They also had larger activation responses dependent on blood oxygenation level than non-musicians in the neuronal networks that sustain attention and cognitive control, including regions of the lateral prefrontal cortex, lateral parietal cortex, insula and putamen in the right hemisphere, and bilaterally in the posterior dorsal prefrontal cortex and anterior cingulate gyrus. The relationship between task performance and the magnitude of the response was more positive in the musicians than in the non-musicians, particularly during the most difficult working memory task. The results confirm previous findings that neural activity increases during enhanced working memory performance. The results also suggest that superior working memory task performance in musicians relies on an enhanced ability to exert sustained cognitive control. This cognitive benefit in musicians may be a consequence of focused musical training. Similarly, Strait and colleagues (2011b) assessed the impact of selective auditory attention on cortical auditory evoked response variability in musicians and non-musicians. The outcomes indicated strengthened brain networks for selective auditory attention in musicians in that they, but not non-musicians, demonstrated decreased pre-frontal response variability with auditory attention. Musicians' neural proficiency for selectively engaging and sustaining auditory attention to language indicates a potential benefit of music for auditory training.

Research with Children and Young People

Not all of the research has been with professional or expert musicians. One strand of research has focused on children. Behavioural investigations of children have shown that music training and musical aptitude are associated with enhanced auditory working memory. For example, in a longitudinal study of six- to eight-year-old children, half of the sample was randomly assigned to biweekly keyboard training for six weeks, while the other half received no training. Following the intervention, only the training group demonstrated a significant improvement in working memory capacity, measured with the backward digit-span task (Guo et al., 2018).

Christner and Reiterer (2018) tested preschool children's abilities to imitate unknown languages, to remember strings of digits, to sing and to discriminate musical statements. Their intrinsic, spontaneous singing behaviour was also assessed. The findings showed that working memory capacity and phonetic aptitude were linked to high musical perception and production ability as early as age five, suggesting that music and foreign language learning capacity may be linked from childhood. Early developed abilities may be responsible for individual differences in both linguistic and musical performances. Working with kindergarten children, Hallberg and colleagues (2017) studied the impact of instrumental music instruction on cognitive processes in children who were taught the violin using the Suzuki method for five weeks, with a total of 15 hours of instruction. This group was compared with a control group. Assessments were made using the Stanford-Binet five working memory and visuospatial subscales and the Kiddie Connor's Continuous Performance Test attention subscales. There were no statistically significant differences in the means of pre- and post-change scores between the groups on the Stanford-Binet five subscales, but there was an effect for the combined Kiddie Connor's Continuous Performance Test measures and one effect for a specific subtest, hit response time. These findings demonstrate that attentional control, a psychological process necessary in academic learning, may be enhanced with instrumental music instruction when engaged within early childhood.

In a longitudinal study, Bergman and colleagues (2014) analysed the association between musical practice and performance on reasoning, processing speed and working memory. Three hundred and fifty-two children and young people between the ages of six and twenty-five years old participated in neuropsychological assessments and neuroimaging investigations on two or three occasions, two years apart. Multiple regression analysis revealed that playing an instrument had an overall positive association with working memory capacity, visuospatial working memory, verbal working memory, processing speed and logical reasoning across all three time points, after correcting for the effect of parental education and other after-school activities. Those playing an instrument also had larger grey-matter volume in the temporo-occipital and insular cortex areas previously reported to be related to musical notation reading. The change in working memory between the time points was proportional to the weekly hours spent on music practice for both of the working memory tests but not for reasoning ability. These effects remained when controlling for parental education and other after-school activities. Similarly, Lee and colleagues (2007) examined the effects of music training in children aged 12 and young adults on a forward digit-span, a backward digit-span, a simple spatial span and complex spatial span tasks. The young adults performed better than the control group with respect to the digit-span and non-word span tests, while the children performed better than the control group in all of the span tests. In a similar study, Roden and colleagues (2014a) investigated the influence of group instrumental training on the working memory of children learning instruments through a German *Sistema*-inspired programme. A quasi-experimental design was used with children receiving musical training, compared with those receiving natural science training or no training. The music group received weekly lessons for 45 minutes on musical instruments of their choice. The maximum group size was five and the children could undertake practice at home. The children were tested at three points over the course of 18 months with a battery of tests, including seven subtests which addressed the central executive, the phonological loop and the visuospatial sketchpad components of Baddeley's working memory model. The music group showed a greater increase on every measure of verbal memory, verbal learning, delayed recall and recognition than the science and control groups. There were large effect sizes. These differences remained when the statistical modelling took into account age and measured intelligence.

Working with 42 school-aged children, Strait and colleagues (2011) assessed auditory working memory and attention, musical aptitude, reading ability and neural sensitivity to acoustic regularities. Neural sensitivity to acoustic regularities was assessed by recording brainstem responses to the same speech sound presented in predictable and variable speech streams. The research revealed that musical aptitude and literacy both related to the extent of subcortical adaptation to regularities in ongoing speech, as well as to auditory working memory and attention. Relationships between music and speech processing were specifically driven by performance on a musical rhythm task, highlighting the importance of rhythmic regularity for both language and music. These data suggest common brain mechanisms underlying reading and music abilities, which relate to how the nervous system responds to regularities in auditory input.

In a longitudinal study, Saarikivi and colleagues (2019) investigated the development of working memory in musically trained and untrained children and adolescents, aged nine to twenty. Working memory was assessed in 106 participants using digit-span forwards and backwards tests and two trail-making tests. The tests were administered three times—in 2011, 2013 and 2016. The findings showed that the younger musically trained participants, in particular, outperformed their untrained peers in the trail-making tests and the digit-span forwards tests. These all require active maintenance of a rule in memory or immediate recall. In contrast, there were no group differences in the backwards test (which requires manipulation and the updating of information in working memory). These results suggest that musical training is more strongly associated with heightened working memory capacity and maintenance than enhanced working memory updating, especially in late childhood and early adolescence.

Ireland and colleagues (2018) developed age-equivalent scores for two measures of musical ability, a rhythm synchronisation task and a melody discrimination task, that could be reliably used with schoolchildren aged seven to thirteen, with and without musical training. These tasks were administered to children attending music or science camps. Children's paced tapping, non-paced tapping and phonemic discrimination were measured as baseline motor and auditory abilities. The musically trained children outperformed those without music lessons, although the scores decreased as difficulty increased. Older children performed the best. Years of lessons significantly predicted performance on both music tasks, over and above the effect of age.

Degé and Schwarzer (2017) aimed to investigate whether an enhanced articulatory rehearsal mechanism might explain higher verbal memory scores in musically trained children compared with untrained children. They tested 39 ten- to twelve-year-old children, 19 of whom were musically trained and 20 untrained. Verbal memory was assessed with two-word lists. Children memorised one word list under normal conditions and the other word list when they had to repeat an irrelevant word over and over again (articulatory suppression). Gender, socioeconomic status, intelligence, motivation, musical aptitude and personality were controlled for. There was a significant difference between musically trained and untrained children in favour of the musically trained children in verbal memory in the normal condition. However, in the articulatory suppression condition, the advantage of musically trained children disappeared. The authors concluded that an enhanced verbal rehearsal mechanism might be responsible for the better verbal memory in musically trained children.

James and colleagues (2019) undertook a cluster randomised controlled trial focused on musical instrumental practice, in comparison to traditional sensitisation to music. Over the last two years of primary school, 69 children aged 10 to 12 received group music instruction by professional musicians twice a week as part of the regular school curriculum. The intervention group learned to play stringed instruments, whereas the control group was sensitised to music via listening, theory and some practice. Broad benefits manifested in the intervention group as compared to the control group for working memory, attention, processing speed, cognitive flexibility, matrix reasoning, sensorimotor hand function and bimanual coordination. Learning to play a complex instrument in a dynamic group setting impacted development more strongly than classical sensitisation to music. The results highlighted the added value of intensive musical instrumental training in a group setting within the school curriculum.

Escobar and colleagues (2020) investigated the perception of speech in noise in 49 young musicians and non-musicians, who were assigned to subgroups with high or low assessed working memory based on performance on the backward digit-span task. The effects of music training and working memory on speech-in-noise performance were assessed on clinical tests of speech perception in background noise. Listening effort was assessed in a dual task paradigm and through self-report. There was no statistically significant difference between musicians and non-musicians, and no significant interaction between music training and working memory on any of the outcome measures. However, a significant effect of working memory on speech-in-noise ability was found. This suggests that music training does not provide an advantage in adverse listening situations, either in terms of improved speech understanding or reduced listening effort. While musicians have been shown to have heightened basic auditory abilities, the effect of this on speech in noise and listening effort may be more subtle. Regardless of prior music training, listeners with high working memory capacity were able to perform significantly better on speech-in-noise tasks.

Some research has shown no effect of music training on working memory. For instance, Banai and Ahissar (2013) researched whether the pattern of correlations between auditory- and reading-related skills differed between children with different amounts of musical experience. Children in the third grade with various degrees of musical experience were tested on a battery of auditory- and reading-related tasks. Very poor auditory thresholds and poor memory skills were abundant among children with no musical education. For these children, indices of auditory processing were significantly correlated with and accounted for up to 13 percent of the variance in reading-related skills. Among children with more than one year of musical training, auditory processing indices were better, but reading-related skills were not correlated with them. Very poor auditory and memory skills are rare among children with even a short period of musical training, suggesting that musical training could have an impact on both. The lack of correlation in the musically trained population suggests that a short period of musical training does not enhance reading-related skills of individuals with normal auditory processing skills.

Overall, as outlined in the previous section, cross-sectional studies have shown that higher working memory capacity is associated with better scores on rhythmic subtests of musical aptitude in children as young as five. Where children were randomly assigned to music training or control conditions, there was a causal effect of training on working memory capacity. The evidence for a close relationship between musical practice and working memory suggests that training, rather than any predisposition, produces changes in working memory capacity, although associations between working memory capacity and measures of musical aptitude suggest that training-related advantages are not independent of existing abilities. Musical training and musical aptitude may both affect memory performance among children.

Older Adults

The experiences that individuals have throughout their lifetime influence the quality of their cognitive ageing. In older individuals, former and current musical practices are associated with enhanced verbal skills, visual memory, processing speed and planning functions. Participating in making music does not have an age limit (Thaut and Hodges, 2019). Adults can take up musical activities, or resume or continue activities pursued earlier in life in their older years. This can have several benefits: supporting further learning, assisting in slowing cognitive decline and supporting rehabilitation. For instance, taking piano lessons for six months has been shown to enhance levels of concentration, attention and planning in 60- to 85-year-old adults, compared to a control group. The piano lessons were individualised, and consisted of motor dexterity exercises and learning music theory. Participants were tested on cognitive and working memory measures at three points in time: pre-training, post-training and following a delay of three months. The experimental group obtained significantly higher scores post-training on a trail-making test and digit symbols than the untrained controls, indicating an improvement in visual scanning, perceptual speed, and working memory (Bugos et al., 2007). Similarly, Bugos (2010) examined the effects of active piano-playing instruction compared with music-listening instruction on executive function in healthy older adults, aged 60 to 85. Seventy adults were matched by age, education and estimated intelligence in two 16-week training groups (group piano instruction or music-listening instruction). Participants completed a battery of cognitive assessment tests pre- and post-instruction to assess processing speed, verbal fluency, planning and cognitive control.

Forty-six participants completed the study. There were no statistically significant differences between the groups on measures of executive function. Both groups demonstrated an increase in scores, although those learning to play the piano had significantly enhanced processing speed, verbal fluency and cognitive control. In a later study, Bugos (2019) focused on motor skills. Participants were randomly allocated to piano, percussion or music-listening groups, and undertook 16 weeks of training with three hours of practice per week. The groups were matched for age, education, intelligence and musical aptitude. In the piano and percussion groups, improvements in processing speed, visual scanning and working memory were recorded. All three music conditions led to improved rhythmic accuracy and hand synchronisation. Similar results have been reported after older adults have sung in a choir, engaged in group music-making or played percussion instruments (Hallam et al., 2014; Hallam and Creech, 2016).

Fauvel (2014) compared the performance of musicians and non-musicians in middle and late adulthood on long-term memory, auditory verbal short-term memory, processing speed, non-verbal reasoning and verbal fluency. The musicians performed significantly better than non-musicians on measures of processing speed and verbal short-term memory. Both groups displayed the same age-related differences. In relation to verbal fluency, musicians scored higher than controls and displayed different age effects. A second study showed that when musical training started in childhood or adulthood, it was associated with phonemic, but not semantic, fluency performance. Musicians who had started to play in adulthood did not perform better on phonemic fluency than non-musicians. The current frequency of training did not account for musicians' scores on either of these measures. Overall, the findings yielded little evidence of reduced age-related changes owing to musical training. Phonemic fluency was the only variable that exemplified a positive effect in ageing.

The influence of music on memory applies to listening to music as well as participating in musical activities (Varvarigou et al., 2012; Hallam and Creech, 2016). For instance, Degé and Kerkovius (2018) investigated the effect of a music training programme on working memory, verbal and visual, and as part of central executive processing in older adults. The experimental group was trained in drumming and singing, while one control group participated in a literature training programme and a second group was untrained. Twenty-four female participants, aged 70 years old on average, were randomly assigned to either a music, literature or untrained group. The training lasted for 15 weeks. At the start of the programme, the three groups did not differ significantly in age, socioeconomic status, music education, musical aptitude, cognitive abilities or depressive symptoms. Following the programme, there were no differences between the groups on central executive function but there was a potential effect of music training on verbal memory and an impact of music training on visual memory. Musically trained participants remembered more words from a word list and more symbol sequences correctly than both control groups.

Musical improvisation was used by Diaz Abraham and colleagues (2020) to study its impact on verbal memory in older adults. Two types of verbal memory were evaluated prior to the intervention: one neutral, the other emotional. The participants were exposed to musical improvisation in the experimental condition, while two control groups carried out rhythmic reproduction or experienced a rest condition. Memory performance was evaluated through immediate and deferred free recall and recognition tests. The memory performance of those with five or more years of training (defined as musicians) and non-musicians was compared. There was a significant improvement in neutral verbal memory among participants involved in musical improvisation. They remembered more words than those in the control conditions. Differences were also found according to the musical experience of the sample, with musicians outperforming non-musicians.

Parbery-Clark and colleagues (2011) compared older musicians and non-musicians on auditory and visual working memory, and the ability to perceive speech in noise. They found that the musicians were significantly better at perceiving speech in noise and performed better in auditory, but not visuospatial, working memory capacity tasks. The research also revealed a linear relationship between auditory working memory and speech-in-noise performance, suggesting that these two functions were related. Similarly, Grassi and colleagues (2018) reported that older adult musicians outperformed older adult non-musicians on auditory and visuospatial working memory tasks, as well as auditory discrimination, although the groups did not differ on tests of short-term memory. Amer and colleagues (2013) also reported that older adult musicians outperformed older adult non-musicians on several tests of executive function, including visuospatial working memory.

One strand of research has explored the impact of different levels of long-term engagement with music on cognition. For instance, Hanna-Pladdy and MacKay (2011) evaluated the association between musical instrumental participation and cognitive ageing. Seventy older healthy adults, aged 60 to 83, participated in varied musical activities and completed a comprehensive neuropsychological battery. Three groups — non-musicians, those with low musical activity(one to nine years through the lifespan) and those with high musical activity over ten years — were compared. Participants were matched on age, education and history of physical exercise. Those with at least ten years of musical experience had better performance on non-verbal memory, naming and executive processes in advanced age relative to non-musicians. Years of musical activity, the age of commencement of that activity and type of musical training predicted cognitive performance. In a later study Hanna-Pladdy and Gajewski (2012) researched 70 older adults aged 59 to 80, musicians and non-musicians, who were assessed on neuropsychological tests and general lifestyle activities. The musicians scored higher on tests of visuospatial judgment.

Another strand of research has tested the potential of music intervention programmes to reduce the deleterious effects of ageing on cognition. For instance, Hars and colleagues (2013) investigated whether six months of music-based multi-task training had beneficial effects on cognitive functioning and mood in 134 older adults aged over 65 who were at increased risk of falling. The intervention group consisted of 66 older people who attended once-weekly hourly supervised group classes of multi-task exercises, executed to the rhythm of piano music, or a control group of 68 individuals with delayed intervention who maintained usual lifestyle habits for six months. A short neuropsychological test battery was administered at the start of the intervention and after six months. It included the mini mental state examination, a clock-drawing test, a frontal assessment battery, and anxiety and depression scales. For those participating in the musical activities, there was an improvement in sensitivity to the interference subtest of the frontal assessment battery, a reduction in anxiety level, an increase in the mini mental state assessment score and a reduction in the number of participants with impaired global cognitive performance. Overall, six months of once-weekly music-based multi-task training was associated with improved cognitive function and decreased anxiety in community-dwelling older adults.

Engagement with music has also been found to reduce the risk of dementia. For instance, Verghese and colleagues (2003) examined the relationship between leisure activities and the risk of dementia in a cohort of 469 participants aged 75 years of age and over, who resided in the community and did not have dementia at the beginning of the research. They examined the frequency of participation in leisure activities at enrolment, and measured cognitive activity and physical activity in terms of the number of days of the week when activity took place. A range of possible confounding factors were controlled for including age, sex, educational level, presence or absence of chronic medical illnesses, and baseline cognitive status. Over a follow-up period of five years, dementia developed in 124 participants, Alzheimer's disease in 61, vascular dementia in 30, mixed dementia in 25 and other types of dementia in 8. Among leisure activities, reading, playing board games, playing musical instruments and dancing were associated with a reduced risk of dementia. A one-point increment in the cognitive activity score was significantly associated with a reduced risk of dementia but a one-point increment on the physical activity score was not. The association with the cognitive activity score persisted after the exclusion of participants with possible pre-clinical dementia at the start of the research. The findings were similar for Alzheimer's disease and vascular dementia. Increased participation in cognitive activities at the start of the research was associated with reduced rates of decline in memory. Overall, participation in leisure activities was associated with a reduced risk of dementia. In a co-twin study, Balbag and colleagues (2014) showed that twins who played an instrument were 64 percent less likely to develop dementia than their co-twins. The research examined the association between self-reported playing of a musical instrument and whether or not both twins developed dementia or cognitive impairment. Controlling for sex, education and physical activity, playing a musical instrument was significantly associated with less likelihood of dementia and cognitive impairment. In a review, Schneider and colleagues (2018) concluded that playing a musical instrument was a potential protective mechanism against cognitive decline among older adults.

Some studies have shown improvements in cognition and working memory in patients with dementia after active singing interventions (Maguire et al., 2015). Singing groups engaged in three vocal music sessions each week including familiar, nostalgic and nonfamiliar, novel, vocal music selections in four 50-minute singing sessions. The programme progressively exercised individual vocal ranges, vowel placements respiratory patterns and recruited cognitive engagement through melodic structures, musical architecture and story development. Participants were predominantly Caucasian, aged 70 to 99 years old, and from two groups: one living in assisted accommodation, the other in secure-ward dementia accommodation. Each group was divided into singers and listeners. Participation in the singing groups was voluntary. Levels of participation were assessed throughout the programme from no attention to dozing off, through to brief periods of attention but not singing. The category participation included singing for most of the time, singing all of the time and singing with enthusiasm. The music was varied each month and focused on four separate musical genres: Valentine's day, patriotic, musical theatre and folk patriotic. The music was selected and arranged to incorporate relaxing, rhythmical elements, rich harmonies, increased vocal range and exercise along vocal lines and word articulation. Deep breaths, appropriate posture and vocal resonance were consistently coached and promoted throughout all sessions. Two of the weekly vocal music sessions were live music sessions with a vocal music leader who sang and played piano accompaniment. The other session consisted of a 50-minute taped DVD recordings. A norovirus outbreak in the assisted living group led to a quarantine period of one month in the middle of the study, resulting in no access to any participants during this time.

Analysis of the data showed that the independent residents had significantly higher scores than those with dementia. Singers with dementia had significantly higher scores than listeners by the end of the study. There was no significant difference between the clock-drawing ability of singers and listeners with dementia initially, but singers scored significantly higher after engaging with the singing. Overall, the findings for those living independently and the dementia groups showed that singers had significantly higher satisfaction with life scores than those listening to music. The norovirus outbreak may have affected the scores of the independent-living participants, as they had lower scores on the mental state examination and the clock design test score. The findings showed that an active singing programme, using an innovative approach, led to significant improvement in cognitive ability in individuals with dementia. Similarly, Pongan and colleagues (2017) aimed to determine the efficacy of choral singing versus painting sessions on chronic pain, mood, quality of life and cognition in patients with Alzheimer's disease. Fifty-nine patients with mild Alzheimer's disease were randomised to a 12-week singing or painting group. Chronic pain, anxiety, depression and quality of life were assessed before, immediately after and one month after the sessions. Both singing and painting interventions led to significant pain reduction, reduced anxiety, improved quality of life, improved digit-span and inhibitory processes. However, depression was reduced only in the painting group, while verbal memory performance remained stable over time in the singing group but decreased in the painting group. Overall, the findings suggest that singing and painting interventions may reduce pain and improve mood, quality of life, and cognition in patients with mild Alzheimer's disease, with differential effects of painting for depression and singing for memory performance. Also focusing on singing, Camic and colleagues (2013) worked with ten people with dementia and their family carers in a singing-together group for ten weeks. Measures of mood, quality of life, dementia, behavioural and psychological problems, activities of daily living and cognitive status were measured at pre-, post- and ten-week follow-up. Engagement levels were monitored during the sessions and care partners were asked to rate each session. Additional qualitative information was obtained through interviews pre- and post-intervention and at follow-up. The results showed that the dementia sufferers were deteriorating slowly over the course of the study on all measures, but that they and their carers' quality of life remained relatively stable. Engagement levels during the programme were very high, and attendance excellent. The interviews provided strong support for the intervention, having promoted the wellbeing of all participants.

In a randomised controlled study, Särkämö and colleagues (2014) compared the effects of three different interventions on working memory on a group of patients with dementia. Each participant was assigned to one of three 10-week group-based interventions: singing, listening to music or usual care. The findings showed that participants in the singing group showed a temporary improvement in working memory, as measured by backward digit-span. Also using a randomised controlled study, Narme and colleagues (2014) studied 48 patients with Alzheimer's disease or mixed dementia, and compared the effects of music versus cooking interventions on their emotions, cognition and behaviour, as well as on their professional caregivers. Each intervention lasted for one hour, twice a week for four weeks. The findings showed that music and cooking interventions led to positive changes in emotional state and decreased the severity of behavioural disorders, as well as reducing the stress levels of the caregivers, but there was no benefit to the participants' cognitive status.

Mansky and colleagues (2020) carried out a post-hoc observational analysis of the Zurich disability prevention trial. Past and present musical-instrument playing was correlated with mini mental state assessment and a visual analogue scale using linear regression at baseline and mixed model linear regression over one year. Two hundred community-dwelling adults were included. Just over 48 percent of participants had played a musical instrument, 35 percent had played in the past and 13.5 percent continued to play. At the start of the programme, those currently playing an instrument had a higher adjusted mini mental state assessment score than those who had never played. Over a 12-month period, those who had continued to play showed significantly more improvement from baseline in the mini mental state assessment than those who had never played. This association remained significant even after restricting the analysis to those participants who had not undertaken higher education. Over time, no differences were observed for the visual analogue scale, although past players had the largest decline in health-related quality of life at 12 months. Overall, present and past musical-instrument playing was able to assist in preserving cognitive function in community-dwelling older adults. An ongoing study is being undertaken by James and colleagues (2020) in Hannover and Geneva over a 12-month period with elderly people receiving either piano instruction or musical listening awareness. Testing is being carried out at four time points: prior to the research, and after 6, 12 and 18 months, following training on cognitive and perceptual motor aptitudes, as well as wide-ranging functional and structural neuroimaging and blood sampling. The researchers hope to show that musical activities can diminish cognitive and perceptual motor decline.

Overall, the research to date suggests that music training may protect against age-related decline in working memory and can improve performance among older adults who show decline in working memory. Importantly, music training may be useful in the prevention and treatment of dementia, although the benefits may be more related to general wellbeing rather than cognitive enhancement. Not all the research shows that engaging with music can help to stave off dementia. Kuusi and colleagues (2019) examined the causes of death of Finnish professional classical musicians, performing artists and church musicians between 1981 and 2016 and showed that overall, there appeared to be a protective effect of music for health, although there was increased mortality in alcohol-related disease among female performing artists and in neurodegenerative diseases among male performing artists.

Reviews and Meta-Analyses

Reviews of the role of active music-making on visual, verbal and working memory have had mixed findings. On the basis of their review, Franklin and colleagues (2008) concluded that the benefits of music training on working memory were not limited to the auditory domain but could lead to enhanced verbal working memory. Strait and Kraus (2011a) suggested that the auditory expertise gained over years of consistent music practice fine-tuned the human auditory system, strengthening the neurobiological and cognitive underpinnings of both music and speech processing, subsequently bolstering the neural mechanisms that underpin language related skills, such as reading and hearing speech in background noise. In a later review, Kraus and colleagues (2012) examined the biological underpinnings of musicians' auditory advantages and the mediating role of auditory working memory. They reported associations between working memory performance, music training or aptitude, and neural encoding of speech. Moreno and Bidelman (2014) argued that some programmes that aimed to impact on the non-auditory functions necessary for higher order aspects of cognition, including working memory (for instance, visual arts), may not yield widespread enhancement. They suggested that musical expertise uniquely taps and refines a hierarchy of brain networks, which subserve a variety of auditory, as well as domain-general, cognitive mechanisms. From this, they inferred that transfer from specific music experience to broad cognitive benefit might be mediated by the degree to which a listener's musical training fine-tuned lower and higher order executive functions, and the coordination between these processes. Dumont and colleagues (2017), in a review of five studies, reported mixed results. One experimental study showed improved performance in those who had participated in formal music lessons, but the remaining four studies, although reporting positive or partially positive results, were limited in the rigour of their methodology. Overall, there did seem to be potential benefits of active engagement with music, but methodological limitations did not allow clear conclusions to be drawn. On the basis of their review, Benz and colleagues (2016) argued that music training could have positive effects, but that these were frequently restricted to the auditory domain.

In a meta-analysis examining the effects of music training on a range of cognitive skills, Sala and Gobet (2017b), using random effects models, showed a small overall effect size but slightly greater effect sizes with regard to memory-related outcomes, although overall there was an inverse relationship between the size of the effects and the methodological quality of the design of the studies. In a later meta-analysis, Sala and Gobet (2020) reanalysed data from 54 previous studies including a total of 6,984 children. They found that music training appeared to be ineffective at enhancing cognitive or academic skills, regardless of the type of skill—verbal, non-verbal, speed-related, participants' age or duration of music training. Studies with high-quality designs showed no effect of music education on cognitive performance.

Three meta-analyses were carried out by Talamini and colleagues (2017), who focused on short-, long-term and working memory. The studies involved young adult musicians and non-musicians using tonal, verbal or visuospatial stimuli. The 29 studies in the analyses included 53 memory tasks. The results showed that musicians performed better than non-musicians on tasks involving long-term memory, short-term memory and working memory. A further analysis included a moderator: the type of stimulus presented (tonal, verbal or visuospatial). This was found to influence the effect size for short-term and working memory, but not for long-term memory. The musicians' advantage in terms of short-term and working memory was large with tonal stimuli, moderate with verbal stimuli, and small or null with visuospatial stimuli. The three meta-analyses revealed a small effect size for long-term memory, and a medium effect size for short-term and working memory, suggesting that musicians perform better than non-musicians in memory tasks—although this advantage was moderated by the type of stimuli.

Baird and Samson (2015) reviewed the literature on music cognition in dementia, pointing out that different types of memory are not impaired in the same ways in dementia. They argued that little rigorous scientific investigation had been undertaken, and that large-scale randomised control studies had questioned the specificity of the effect of music and found that it was no more beneficial than other pleasant activities. However, they acknowledged that music was unique in its power to elicit memories and emotions, which could provide an important link to an individual's past and a means of non-verbal communication with carers. Walsh and colleagues (2019)—in a meta-analyse which focused on cognitive impairment or dementia as the outcome, and included studies with learning to play a musical instrument as the main intervention—found a 59 percent reduction in the risk of developing dementia for those playing a musical instrument. However, they advised caution in interpreting the findings, as the evidence base was limited by its size and methodological issues.

Overview

The evidence presented in this chapter suggests that active engagement with making music can have positive effects on some aspects of memory. The effects are strongest when they relate to the aural skills which active engagement with music is acknowledged to enhance: memory for music and stimuli presented verbally. The evidence for the impact on visual skills is less strong and is likely to depend on the extent to which musicians' skills include reading musical notation. Musicians tend to have greater working memory capacity than non-musicians, but measures of musical expertise suggest that training-related advantages are not independent of existing abilities. Musical training and musical aptitude may both affect memory performance among children.

7. Executive Functioning and Self-Regulation

Executive functions enable individuals to optimise performance on a range of tasks. They improve concentration, facilitate planning, help with the prioritisation of information, and promote flexibility in changing strategies, switching between tasks, and adapting to change (Diamond, 2013). Most models of executive functions postulate three related but separable components: inhibition or inhibitory control; shifting, cognitive flexibility or switching; and updating or working memory updating (Diamond, 2013; Gould, 2014; Lehto et al., 2003; Logue et al., 2012; Miyake et al., 2000). Inhibition or inhibitory control requires the control of thoughts or behaviour to override a response which has priority over other possible responses. Cognitive flexibility requires an individual to change perspective or switch between task demands, while updating requires individuals to maintain, add, delete and manipulate items within memory. These executive functions develop through childhood and adolescence and can be improved with practice (Diamond, 2013; Diamond et al., 2007; Miyake et al., 2000). Overall, executive functions include the activities of working memory and involve the control of actions, thoughts, emotions and general abilities including planning, solving problems, and being able to adjust to novel or changing task demands (Diamond, 1990; 2002; Lezak, 2004; Zelazo, 2004). Because of the plasticity of the brain, they continue to develop over the lifespan, although Friedman and colleagues (2008) argue that they are influenced by a highly heritable (99%) common factor and that there are additional genetic influences unique to particular executive functions. Supporting this, they presented data from a multivariate twin study examining why participants varied in each of the three elements of executive functioning and why these abilities were correlated but separable. Other research has shown that the development of executive function is complex, as neural changes are affected by synaptic proliferation, pruning, myelination, neurofilament and neurotransmitter levels. Each of these has its own developmental trajectory until, over time, the neural networks settle into more stable states. Performance on three complex executive functioning tasks has been shown to improve until at least age 15, although the pace of improvement slowed with increasing age and varied across tasks (Best et al., 2011). Understanding executive functions is important, as they impact on the quality of life and performance in school and in the workplace, and have been shown to improve with practice (Diamond, 2013; Diamond et al., 2007). This means that there is the possibility that they can be trained.

Executive functions can be measured in several different ways. Inhibition control can be assessed by a range of tests, including the Stroop test and the stop-signal task. The Stroop test requires participants to read colour words—for example, red, blue or green—presented on a screen, and then to say the colour of the font aloud. In congruent trials, the colour of the font is the same as the word, while in incongruent trials, the colour of the font does not match the word. In neutral trials, a string of asterisks appears. The Stroop effect is the difference in the average of correct responses between incongruent and neutral trials. In the stop-signal task, participants are required to fixate on a cross in the centre of a screen, which is replaced by either a square or a circle. They are instructed to push left as quickly as possible if they see a square, and to push right as quickly as possible if they see a circle. On a quarter of the trials, participants are presented with the shape, then hear a stop signal (a beep from the computer), and are instructed to withhold any response when they hear that signal. On each trial where there is a stop signal, the onset of the stop signal is adjusted until participants can correctly inhibit it for half of the responses. Performance is measured as the stop-signal reaction time—an estimate of how long it takes to inhibit an already initiated response.

Cognitive flexibility, or set-shifting, assesses the ability to shift from one task to another. Participants are shown a set of five cards each with a different figure on it. The figures switch around with each element. For example, in one problem the figures on the cards might be three green stars, one red circle, two yellow blocks, four yellow crosses and two red crosses. The participant sees four of the cards lined up in a row, and one by itself below. He or she is told to match that card to one of the four above, but not told the rule for matching. The participant does not know whether to match by shape, colour or number. Feedback is only given on whether the participant is right or wrong in the match made. Through trial and error, the participant needs to work out the rule. The score is how many correct sorts are made.

The updating or working memory element of executive function tends to be assessed using various digit-span tests. For instance, in the forward test the participant repeats a series of numbers in the order that they are given. In the reverse digit-span, the numbers have to be repeated backwards. In spatial spans, the assessor touches a series of blocks in a particular order. The participants have to copy that order or reverse it. The Tower of Hanoi test can also be used to assess working memory. It requires the participant to rearrange disks to match a model while following specific rules; for instance, not putting a large disk on top of a smaller one. The goal is to complete the task in as few moves as possible. These various tests have been used in research with adults and children—both young and older people.

There has been great interest in whether making music might enhance executive functions. When musicians engage in making music, they read and decipher musical notation, recall music from memory and may improvise new material. They produce musical sounds while also planning ahead, keeping notation and rhythms in mind until they are performed. They must monitor their performance but also attend to the auditory streams produced by other performers so that they can flexibly coordinate and adjust the sounds that they are producing to match those of the group (Okada and Slevel, 2018). Managing this complexity may enable individuals to become more effective in managing equally complex tasks in other situations (Cabanac et al., 2013). Musical activities, formal and informal, promote analytical thinking, planning and prioritising, attention, problem-solving and other executive functions (Serpell and Esposito, 2016). Each of the three components of executive functioning has been linked to musical activity. For instance, overriding expectations and unexpected resolutions of musical ambiguity may draw on general inhibitory control mechanisms (Slevc and Okada, 2015). Shifting is implicated in ensemble-playing, where musicians must coordinate their own playing with others in the group (Jentzsch et al., 2014; Palmer, 2013). Playing with others requires being able to flexibly shift between auditory streams (Loehr et al., 2013) and also adjust dynamically to the other members of the ensemble (Loehr and Palmer, 2011; Moore and Chen, 2010). Updating is crucial in reading musical notation, particularly in sight-reading, as musicians need to look ahead in the score to prepare for what to play next. Expert sight-readers typically look at least four notes ahead of where they are playing (Drake and Palmer, 2000; Furneaux and Land, 1999; Goolsby, 1994). This requires constant updating of the contents of working memory, holding in memory what is being played and what is still to be played. Indeed, there is evidence that being able to sight-read well is related to non-musical measures of working memory capacity (Meinz and Hambrick, 2010).

Music has been used to enhance executive functions, as it is a multifaceted activity. Learning to play an instrument usually, although not always, requires the learner to read music, translate printed notation into planned motor sequences, develop fine motor coordination and hold a great deal of information in memory (Peretz and Zatorre, 2005). Formal music practice involves controlled attention for long periods of time, keeping musical passages in working memory, encoding them into long-term memory, decoding musical scores and translating them into motor programmes. These activities draw on complex cognitive functions which have been illustrated in brain-imaging research (Stewart et al., 2003). Schon and colleagues (2002) investigated the brain areas involved in reading musical notation using functional magnetic resonance imaging. They compared reading musical notation to reading verbal and numerical notation. Professional musicians were required to play musical notation, read verbal information and read the numbers displayed on a five-key keyboard. The three tasks revealed a similar pattern of activated brain areas. Playing an instrument is also related to an increased rate of cortical thickness maturation in the dorsolateral prefrontal cortex and orbitofrontal cortex, areas often involved in executive functions (Hudziak et al., 2014). Musically trained children also show greater blood-oxygenation-level-dependent responses in a task-switching paradigm in the bilateral ventrolateral prefrontal cortex and supplementary motor area (Zuk et al., 2014)—regions linked to executive functioning (Nachev et al., 2008; Nee et al., 2013).

Listening to or tapping complex polyrhythms—for instance, tapping four against three—requires inhibitory control and is associated with activation in Broadmann Area 47, an area of the brain which is implicated in the processing of syntax in oral and sign languages, musical syntax, and the semantic aspects of language. It is also associated with activity in the anterior cingulate cortex, which is implicated in empathy, impulse control, emotion and decision-making (Vuust et al., 2006; 2011). Stewart and colleagues (2003) scanned musically naïve subjects using functional magnetic resonance imaging before and after they had been taught to read music and play a keyboard. When participants played melodies from musical notation after training, activation was seen in a cluster of voxels within the right superior parietal cortex, consistent with the view that music-reading involves spatial sensorimotor mapping.

Research with Adults

Much of the research with adults has been based on correlations examining the relationship between levels of musical expertise and performance on various tests of executive function. Some of this research has used continuous measures of musical expertise, while other research has compared the performance of musicians with that of non-musicians. As seen in Chapter 6, a range of studies have demonstrated that musicians may have advantages in performance in working memory compared with non-musicians. This has been demonstrated on measures of auditory and visual working memory (Franklin et al., 2008; Fujioka et al., 2006; George and Coch, 2011; Lee et al., 2007; Pallensen et al., 2010; Parbery-Clark et al., 2011). Other research has explored other elements of executive functioning. For instance, Hansen and colleagues (2012) administered digit- and spatial-span tests and a musical ear test to non-musicians and amateur and expert musicians. The expert musicians significantly outperformed the non-musicians on the digit-span test. Digit-span forward scores were also found to be correlated with musical ear test scores and scores on a rhythm subtest. However, there were no differences between the groups on the spatial-span task. Similarly, Strait and colleagues (2010) administered a standardised battery of perceptual and cognitive tests to adult musicians and non-musicians, including tasks which were more or less susceptible to cognitive control and more or less dependent on auditory or visual processing. The outcomes indicated lower perceptual thresholds in musicians, specifically for auditory tasks, including auditory attention. There were no group differences for simultaneous masking and visual attention tasks. Overall, long-term musical practice strengthened those cognitive functions which benefited auditory skills. Also focusing on auditory skills, Clayton and colleagues (2016) investigated whether musicians would outperform non-musicians in recognising a speech target in a multi-talker, cocktail-party-like environment. Executive function assessment included measures of cognitive flexibility, inhibition control and auditory working memory. The musicians performed significantly better than the non-musicians in spatial hearing and measures of auditory working memory. A multiple regression analysis revealed that musicianship and performance on a multiple-object tracking task significantly predicted performance on the spatial hearing task, confirming the relationship between musicianship, domain-general selective attention and working memory in solving the cocktail party problem.

Some research has focused on the role that music might play in enhancing attention. For instance, Medina and Barraza (2019) explored the relationship between long-term musical training and the efficiency of the attentional system. They compared performance on the alerting, orienting and executive attentional networks of professional pianists compared with a matched group of non-musician adults. The executive attentional network was more efficient in musicians than non-musicians, although there were no differences in the efficiency of alerting and orienting networks between the groups. The findings showed that the efficiency of the executive system improved with years of musical training, even when controlling for age. The three attentional networks of the non-musicians were functionally independent, while for the musicians the efficiency of the alerting and orienting systems were associated. Similarly, Pallensen and colleagues (2010) examined working memory for musical sounds and found that, in comparisons between musicians and non-musicians, the musicians had heightened activity in neuronal networks that sustained attention and cognitive control, including the prefrontal regions and the supplementary motor area. The relationship between task performance and activation patterns was strongest in the musicians during the periods when the load on working memory was the heaviest. Also focusing on attention, Román-Caballero and colleagues (2020) investigated attentional and vigilance abilities in expert musicians with a measure which allowed the assessment of the functioning of the three networks that are concerned with alerting, orienting, and executive control—along with two different components of vigilance (executive and arousal vigilance). Forty-nine adult musicians, from 18 to 35 years old, were matched on an extensive set of confounding variables with a control group of 49 non-musicians. The musicians showed advantages in processing speed and the two components of vigilance, with some specific aspects of musicianship (such as years of practice or years of lessons) correlating with these measures.

Another strand of research has considered the relationship between executive functions, music training and bilingualism. For instance, Moradzadeh and colleagues (2015) investigated whether musical training and bilingualism were associated with enhancements in specific components of executive function: namely task-switching and dual task performance. One hundred and fifty-three participants belonged to one of four groups: monolingual musician, bilingual musician, bilingual non-musician or monolingual non-musician. The findings demonstrated reduced global and local switch costs in musicians compared with non-musicians, suggesting that musical training can contribute to increased efficiency in the ability to shift flexibly between mental sets. The musicians also outperformed the non-musicians on dual task performance, but there was no cognitive advantage for bilinguals relative to monolinguals, nor an interaction between music and language. The findings demonstrated that long-term musical training, but not language training, was associated with improvements in task-switching and dual task performance. Similarly, Moreno and colleagues (2014) explored executive functions in musicians, bilinguals and controls. Participants completed a visual go/no go task that involved the withholding of key presses to rare targets. Participants in each group achieved similar accuracy rates and response times, but the analysis of cortical responses revealed significant differences. Success in withholding a prepotent response was associated with enhanced stimulus-locked neural activity. This was particularly the case for the musicians when compared with the bilinguals. The findings showed that bilingualism and music training have different effects on the brain networks supporting executive control over behaviour. A small amount of research has examined the differences in executive functioning between different types of musicians. For instance, percussionists have been found to outperform vocalists and non-musician controls on an integrated visual and auditory—plus continuous performance—test of inhibition (Slater et al., 2017).

Much of the research has revealed inconsistency in terms of the impact of musical activity on the different elements of executive functioning. For instance, Zuk and colleagues (2014) carried out an experiment with 30 adults with and without musical training using a standardised battery of executive function tests. Compared to the non-musicians, the musicians showed enhanced performance on some measures of executive function, cognitive flexibility, working memory and verbal fluency, but not on inhibition or shifting. Similarly, Helmbold and colleagues (2005) studied the psychometric performance of 70 musicians and 70 non-musicians on different aspects of primary mental abilities: verbal comprehension, word fluency, space, flexibility of closure, perceptual speed, reasoning, number and memory. No significant differences were found between the musicians and non-musicians except for flexibility of closure and perceptual speed, where the musicians performed reliably better than non-musicians. In research with older adults, Amer and colleagues (2013) also found inconsistency. They investigated whether long-term music training and practice were associated with enhancement of general cognitive abilities in late-middle-aged to older adults. Professional musicians and non-musicians matched on age, education, vocabulary and general health were compared on a near-transfer task involving auditory processing, and on far-transfer tasks that measured spatial span and aspects of cognitive control. The musicians outperformed the non-musicians on the near-transfer task, on most but not all of the far-transfer tasks, and on a composite measure of cognitive control. The results suggested that sustained music training or involvement was associated with improved aspects of some elements of cognitive functioning in middle-aged to older adults, but not all.

Using a continuous assessment of musical expertise, Slevc and colleagues (2016) investigated the relationship between musical ability and executive functions by evaluating the musical experience and ability of a large group of participants, and exploring whether this predicted individual differences on inhibition, updating and switching in both auditory and visual modalities. Musical ability predicted better performance on both auditory and visual updating tasks, even when controlling for a variety of potential confounds, but musical ability was not clearly related to inhibitory control and was unrelated to switching performance. Similarly, Okada and Slevc (2018a) used a large test battery of tasks related to working memory, inhibitory control, and cognitive flexibility, as well as an assessment of musical training. One hundred and fifty participants completed the tests. Overall, the data showed a positive relationship between individual differences in musical training and working memory updating ability, but no relationship with inhibition or shifting. The authors suggested that the inclusion of intelligence as a covariate may have eliminated any positive association between musical training and tasks assessing inhibition. Similarly, Brooke and colleagues (2018) administered an executive function battery of tests containing multiple tasks assessing inhibition, shifting and working memory updating, as well as a comprehensive, continuous measure of musical training and sophistication to 150 undergraduates. Overall, these data showed a positive relationship between individual differences in musical training and working memory updating ability, but no relationship with inhibition or shifting. The differences in the tasks used to assess shifting—or the use of comparisons between musicians with non-musicians rather than the use of continuous musical measures—may account for some of the inconsistencies in findings. In relation to inhibition, measures of intelligence may have acted as mediators.

Working with Chinese participants, Chen and colleagues (2020) examined the relationship between musical training and inhibitory control through the go/no go response inhibition and Stroop tasks by using event-related potentials. In the go/no go task, participants had to press a keyboard button in response to white shapes, while they had to inhibit responding to purple shapes. In the Stroop task, participants were presented with Chinese colour words, printed in different colours. The behavioural results showed that the music group had enhanced performance compared with the control group in the Stroop task, while the groups performed similarly in the go/no go task. The results showed that individuals that received music training had stronger conflict-monitoring and motor-inhibition abilities when completing the interference control task. As musical training appeared to enhance inhibitory control, it was suggested that it might support those with psychiatric disorders such as addictions, attention deficit hyperactivity disorder and obsessive-compulsive disorder, all of which have been shown to involve deficits in inhibitory control.

Some research has highlighted differences in performance depending on the nature of the tasks. For instance, Fischer and colleagues (2013) tested 16 healthy adults on performed magnitude and pitch comparisons on numbers sung at variable pitch. The stimuli and response alternatives were identical, but the relevant stimulus attribute, pitch or number differed between tasks. Concomitant tasks required retention of either colour or location. The findings showed that the spatial association for pitch was more powerful than that for magnitude. There appeared to be no automaticity of spatial mappings in either stimulus dimension.

Travis and colleagues (2011) expanded the area of investigation beyond executive functioning to develop a unified theory of performance. They compared professional and amateur classical musicians matched for age, gender and education on reaction times during the Stroop colour-word test, brain waves during an auditory event-related potential task, paired reaction-time tasks, responses on a sociomoral reflection questionnaire, and self-reported frequencies of peak experiences. Professional musicians were characterised by lower colour-word interference effects, faster categorisation of rare expected stimuli, a trend for faster processing of rare unexpected stimuli, higher scores on the sociomoral reflection questionnaire, and more frequent peak experiences during rest, tasks and sleep. The authors suggested that the findings could be interpreted as effectiveness being influenced by the level of mind-brain development and emotional, cognitive, moral, ego and cortical development, with higher mind-brain development supporting greater effectiveness in any domain.

Working in a health context, Siponkoskhifors and colleagues (2020) explored the use of musical activity for those with traumatic brain injuries, particularly where there were impairments of executive functioning. Forty patients with moderate or severe traumatic brain injuries were randomly allocated to receive a three-month neurological music therapy intervention, either during the first or second half of a six-month follow-up period. Neuropsychological testing, motor testing and magnetic resonance imaging were performed at baseline, and at three and six months. The findings showed that general executive functioning and set-shifting improved more in the first group than the second over the first three-month period, and the effect on general executive functioning was maintained in the six-month follow-up. Voxel-based morphometry analysis of the structural magnetic resonance imaging data indicated that grey-matter volume in the right inferior frontal gyrus increased significantly in both groups during the intervention versus control periods, which also correlated with cognitive improvement in set-shifting. These findings suggest that neurological music therapy can enhance executive functioning and induce fine-grained neuroanatomical changes in prefrontal areas in those with traumatic brain injuries. Furthermore, Kuriansky and Nemeth (2020) have developed a musical intervention for work with children who have experienced environmental trauma, which can lead to deficits in executive functioning.

Research with Children

Some research has indicated that participation in formal early music education classes is linked with better self-regulation skills. Winsler and colleagues (2011) compared a group of three- to four-year-old children receiving weekly music and movement classes (Kindermusik) with a group who had not experienced any structured early childhood music classes. Those enrolled in the music classes showed better self-regulation than those not enrolled, as measured by a battery of tests that required children to wait, slow down and initiate or suppress a response. The Kindermusik children were also more likely to use a range of positive self-regulatory strategies, including private speech, during an attention task, and singing or humming during a waiting task. Parent-child music therapy efficacy studies have also indicated that joint active music participation supports improved child-parent interactions, and enhances impulse control and self-regulation skills (Malloch et al., 2012; Pasiali, 2012). Galarce and colleagues (2012) reported enhanced self-regulation in terms of speaking inappropriately to others, while Brown and Sax (2013) found that an arts-enriched programme, including music, helped emotional regulation skills in low-income children when compared to non-arts programmes.

Several studies have explored the relationships between active engagement with music and executive functions in preschool children. For instance, Bugos and DeMarie (2017) studied the effects of a short-term music programme including creative activities, bimanual gross motor training and vocal development on preschool children's inhibition. Thirty-six preschool children were randomly assigned to musical activities or Lego training. Results pre- and post-programme on a matching familiar-figures test—requiring inhibition and visual discrimination—indicated fewer errors post-training by the music group compared to controls. Overall, the findings showed that music interventions involving vocal activity and improvisation on pitched and non-pitched instruments enhanced inhibition on a matching familiar-figures test, but not on the day-night Stroop test, after a six-week-long intervention with 90 minutes of weekly musical training, compared to children who undertook Lego training.

Similarly, the development of inhibition was observed in a study of Finnish children who, after undertaking musical activities at home, showed greater attention to other tasks, while their brains responded less strongly to auditory distractors compared to their peers (Putkinen et al., 2013). Working with 120 school-aged children, Putkinen and colleagues (2014) conducted a longitudinal study and showed that children who received formal musical training showed superior performance in tests of executive functions, while Putkinen and colleagues (2015) found that musically trained preschool and school-aged children attending a musical playschool showed more rapid maturation of neural sound discrimination than a comparison group. In China, Shen and colleagues (2019) examined whether musical training enhanced executive function in preschool children who had not undergone previous systematic music learning. Participants were 61 preschool children from a university-affiliated kindergarten in North China. The experimental group underwent 12 weeks of integrated musical training including music theory, singing, dancing and roleplay, while the control group performed typical daily classroom activities. The three components of executive function—inhibitory control, working memory and cognitive flexibility—were assessed. Executive functions were tested before and after musical training. The results showed that the children's executive functions could be promoted by music training. In further tests undertaken 12 weeks later, the effects were sustained.

In a highly controlled study, Moreno and colleagues (2011a) assigned 71 four- to six-year-old children to either a computerised music training programme or a computerised visual arts training programme. The two programmes had the same learning goals, graphics, design, duration, number of breaks and number of teaching staff. The music curriculum was based on a combination of motor, perceptual and cognitive tasks, relying primarily on listening tasks, and included training in rhythm, pitch, melody, voice and basic musical concepts. The visual art curriculum focused on the development of visuospatial skills. The children engaged in the training programme in two daily sessions of one hour each for five days per week. After four weeks of daily training, the children who received the music training showed greater gains in inhibitory control than the children who received visual arts training, as well as a greater index of brain plasticity on no go trials in a go/no go task. The children in the music group also showed greater improvements in the ability to identify geometric figures on the basis of colour while ignoring irrelevant variation in shape. These changes were positively correlated with changes in functional brain plasticity during an executive function task. However, there was no difference in reaction times between the music and visual arts groups.

In a similar, longitudinal study in the Netherlands, Jaschke and colleagues (2018) examined cognitive skills in 147 primary-school children aged six to seven, randomly allocated to music, visual art or passive control groups. The music group significantly outperformed the other groups in planning, inhibition and verbal intelligence. Neuropsychological tests assessed verbal intelligence and executive functions. The findings showed that the children in the visual arts group performed better on visuospatial memory tasks as compared to the three other conditions. However, the test scores on inhibition, planning and verbal intelligence increased significantly in the two music groups over time as compared to the other groups.

In a quasi-experimental study where children were able to self-select to take music lessons, Roden and colleagues (2014a) worked with children aged seven to eight years old over an 18-month period. Those who self-selected to take music lessons on an instrument of their own choosing outperformed children who received science lessons on two tasks assessing updating ability: a counting-span test and a complex-span test. Working with older children aged nine to twelve, with different lengths of time spent having music lessons, Degé and colleagues (2011) assessed five different executive functions: set-shifting, selective attention, planning, inhibition and fluency. Significant associations emerged between the months of having music lessons and all the measures of executive function.

Adopting an approach where no musical notation was used, Guo and colleagues (2018) investigated the effect of a six-week instrumental practice programme playing the keyboard harmonica. Forty children aged six to eight years old were randomly assigned to either the experimental group or an untrained control group. Cognitive measurements included verbal ability, processing speed, working memory and inhibitory control. After the six-week training, only the experimental group showed a significant improvement in the digit-span test, especially the digit-span backward test that measures working memory. No significant influences were found on the other cognitive tests.

Saarikivi and colleagues (2016) investigated whether individual differences in executive functions predicted training-related changes in neural sound discrimination. They measured event-related potentials induced by sound changes, coupled with tests for executive functions in musically trained and non-trained children in two age groups (9 to 11 and 13 to 15). High performance in a set-shifting task, indicating cognitive flexibility, was linked to enhanced maturation of neural sound discrimination in both musically trained and non-trained children. Musically trained children with good performance showed large neural responses to sound in both age ranges, indicating accurate sound discrimination. In contrast, musically trained low-performing children showed an increase in sound responses with age, suggesting that they were behind their high-performing peers in the development of sound discrimination. In the non-trained group, only the high-performing children showed evidence of an age-related increase in neural responses, while the low-performing children showed a small increase with no age-related change. These findings suggest an advantage in neural development for high-performing non-trained individuals. There was an age-related increase in response only in the children who performed well in the set-shifting task, irrespective of music training, indicating enhanced attention-related processes in these children. This research provided evidence that, in children, cognitive flexibility may influence age-related and training-related plasticity of neural sound discrimination.

Also studying primary-aged children, James and colleagues (2019) performed research on 69 children aged ten to twelve. The children received group music instruction by professional musicians twice a week as part of the regular school curriculum. They learned to play stringed instruments. In contrast, a control group was sensitised to music through listening, theory and some practice. There were benefits for the intervention group as compared to the control group for working memory, attention, processing speed, cognitive flexibility, matrix reasoning, sensorimotor hand function and bimanual coordination. The findings highlighted the added value of intensive musical instrument training in a group setting within the school curriculum. Working with 27 musically trained and untrained children aged nine to twelve, Zuk and colleagues (2014) found that the musically trained children were better at shifting but not at inhibition or updating. They showed enhanced performance on measures of verbal fluency and processing speed, and significantly greater neural activation during rule representation and task-switching in regions of the brain known to be involved in executive functions (compared to musically untrained children).

Focusing on older children aged 10 to 13, with or without musical training, Kausal and colleagues (2020) assessed attention and working memory, while brain activity was measured with functional magnetic resonance imaging. Participants were presented with a pair of bimodal stimuli, auditory and visual, and were asked to pay attention only to the auditory, only to the visual, or to both at the same time. Both groups had higher accuracy on items that they were instructed to attend to, but the musicians had overall better performance on both memory tasks across attention conditions. The musicians showed higher activation than controls in cognitive control regions, such as the frontoparietal control network, during all encoding phases. In addition, facilitated encoding of auditory stimuli in musicians was positively correlated with years of training and higher activity in the left inferior frontal gyrus and the left supramarginal gyrus, structures that support the phonological loop.

Working with adolescents, Gonzalez and colleagues (2020) examined whether there was a relationship between time spent in musical training and executive function. Adolescents between the ages of 14 and 18 completed three tests of executive function: the Tower of Hanoi test to assess working memory, the Wisconsin Card Sort test to assess cognitive flexibility, and the Stroop task to assess inhibition. They also completed a musical experience questionnaire, which included their lifetime musical practice hours. The adolescent musicians were found to have improved inhibitory control relative to non-musicians, while inhibition scores correlated with music practice time. No other elements of executive function were found to be associated with musical training. These findings suggest that the impact of musical training may not be the same for all executive functions and that there may be unique associations between certain types of training and inhibitory control.

A few studies have worked with mixed age groups. For instance, Holochwost and colleagues (2017) examined whether music education was associated with improved performance on measures of executive functions. Participants were 265 school-aged children from first to eighth grade. They were selected by lottery to participate in an out-of-school programme offering individual and large ensemble training on orchestral instruments. Executive functions were assessed through students' performance on a computerised battery of common executive function tasks. The findings showed that, relative to controls, students in the music education programme exhibited superior performance on multiple tasks of inhibitory control and short-term performance. The largest differences in performance were observed between students in the control group and those who had participated in the music programme for two to three years, although conditional effects were also observed on three of the executive function tasks for students who had been in the programme for one year. Similarly, Hudziak and colleagues (2014) assessed the extent to which playing a musical instrument was associated with cortical thickness development among 232 healthy youths aged six to eighteen over a two-year period. While there was no association between cortical thickness and years playing a musical instrument, follow-up analysis revealed that music training was associated with an increased rate of cortical thickness maturation within areas implicated in motor planning and coordination, emotion and impulse regulation.

In another mixed-age study, Nutley and colleagues (2013) focused on children and young people aged between 6 and 25. In a longitudinal study with testing two years apart, they demonstrated that musical practice had a positive association with working memory capacity, and visuospatial and verbal processing speed and reasoning skills at all time points, after taking into account parental education and participation in other school activities. Those participating in musical activities had larger grey-matter volume in the temporo-occipital and insular cortex—areas which are known to be associated with the reading of musical notation. Changes in working memory were proportional to the number of hours spent in weekly practice, but this did not apply to measures of verbal reasoning. It may be that reading notation is important in the development of at least some executive functions as it requires visuospatial working memory, rapid information processing, visuospatial decoding and a constant updating of musical notation.

In some research where comparisons have been made between music training and other interventions, similar effects have been found. For instance, using second-language learning as a control, Janus and colleagues (2016) compared the effects of short-term music training and tuition in French on executive control. They pseudo-randomly assigned 57 four- to six-year-old children matched on age, maternal education and cognitive scores to a 20-day training programme offering instruction in either music or conversational French. The children were tested on verbal and non-verbal tasks requiring executive control. All of the children improved on these tasks following training. Children in both groups had better scores on the most challenging condition of a judgement task about the correct grammar of a sentence, where it was necessary to ignore conflict introduced through misleading semantic content. Children in both training groups also showed better accuracy on an easier condition of a non-verbal visual search task at post-test, but the children in the French training group showed significant improvement on the more challenging condition of this task. This research showed that, while music may be able to enhance executive functioning, it is not alone in being able to do so. Similarly, Habibi and colleagues (2018) compared children receiving music training with those receiving sports training or those not enrolled in any systematic after-school training. The children with music training showed stronger neural activation in regions involved in response inhibition during a cognitive inhibition task, compared with those in the no-activity control group, despite no differences in performance on behavioural measures of executive function. However, no such differences were found between music and sports groups. Also using sport as a comparison group, Sachs and colleagues (2017) investigated the effects of music training on executive function with functional magnetic resonance imaging and several behavioural tasks, including the colour-word Stroop task. The 14 children involved in the ongoing music training, aged eight to nine years old, were compared with two groups of children with comparable general cognitive abilities and socioeconomic status: one involved in sporting activities, the other not involved in music or sports. During the Stroop task, the children with music training showed significantly greater bilateral activation in trials that required cognitive control compared to the control group, despite no differences in performance on behavioural measures of executive function. No significant differences in brain activation or in task performance were found between the music and sports groups. The results suggest that systematic extracurricular training is associated with changes in the cognitive control network in the brain, even in the absence of changes in behavioural performance, whether the intervention is music- or sports-based. Taken together, these studies indicate that, while music may be able to support the development of executive functions in children, it is not alone in being able to do so.

Not all of the research has found positive relationships between musical training, executive functions and self-regulation. For instance, Schellenberg (2011) found no link between music lessons and most of the measures of executive function, which were assessed in trained and untrained musicians aged nine to twelve years old. The musically trained children had higher digit-span scores, which remained when a range of socioeconomic factors were taken into account, but there were no differences on any other measures. Overall, the association between musical training and executive function was negligible. Similarly,

Mehr and colleagues (2013) conducted two randomly controlled trials with preschool children investigating the cognitive effects of a brief series of music classes, as compared to a similar visual arts class or to a no-treatment control. Parents attended classes with their children, participating in a variety of developmentally appropriate arts activities. After six weeks, the children's skills were assessed on four cognitive areas: spatial navigational reasoning, visual form analysis, numerical discrimination and receptive vocabulary. Initially, the children from the music class showed greater spatial navigational ability than children from the visual arts class, while children from the visual arts class showed greater visual form analysis ability than children from the music class. However, a partial replication attempt comparing music training to a no-treatment control failed to confirm these findings, and the combined results of the two studies were negative. Overall, children provided with music classes performed no better than those with visual arts or no classes on any assessment. Similarly, Grinspun and colleagues (2020) conducted an empirical study, in which a sample of 61 second-grade school students from two elementary schools— one from Ghent, Belgium and the other from Santiago, Chile—were administered a musical aptitude test and an attention and inhibitory control test. There was no statistically significant effect of musical experience on sustained attention, cognitive flexibility or audiation. In a study which explored the impact of different musical activities, Norgaard and colleagues (2019) studied 155 seventh- and eighth-grade middle-school band students, who were divided into groups based on the type of musical training that they received. The key area of interest for the researchers was whether the students learned to improvise. Both groups received two months of instruction in jazz phrasing, scales and vocabulary, but only the experimental group was taught to improvise. All instruction was part of the warm-up routine in regular band classes. All students were tested before and after instruction on cognitive flexibility and inhibitory control. The findings showed that improvisation training had different effects on executive function depending on the students' grade levels. In seventh grade, the results showed that improvisation training enhanced the students' abilities to inhibit irrelevant information, although this change was only marginally significant. There was no effect of inhibition with eighth-grade students but there was a significant change in cognitive flexibility. It may have been that their advanced technique allowed them to be more engaged directly with tonal jazz improvisation compared to the seventh-graders. The real-time evaluation of their musical output according to tonal convention may have resulted in them making quick adjustments to their performance. This may have contributed to enhanced cognitive flexibility. In a study of similar complexity, Bowmer and colleagues (2018) investigated the effect of weekly musicianship training on the executive function abilities of three- to four-year-old children in a London preschool, using a two-phase experimental design. In Phase One, 14 children took part in eight-weekly musicianship classes, provided by a specialist music teacher, while 25 children engaged in nursery free-play. The children receiving the musicianship training improved on measures relating to planning and inhibition skills. In Phase Two, the musicianship group continued with music classes, while a second group began music classes for the first time and a third group took part in an art intervention. There were no significant differences in performance improvement between the three groups during Phase Two, although performance differences between groups were nearing statistical significance for a peg-tapping task.

Research with Older People

Some research has supported the beneficial effects of music training on executive functions in older musicians. For instance, Hanna-Pladdy and MacKay (2011) studied 70 older healthy adults—aged 60 to 83—varying in musical ability who completed a comprehensive neuropsychological battery. The groups (non-musicians and low- and high-activity musicians) were matched on age, education and history of physical exercise, while the musicians were matched on their age of starting to play an instrument and formal years of musical training. The musicians were classified in a low-level musical group with one to nine years of experience, or a high-level musical group with more than ten years of musical activity, based on their years of musical experience throughout their lifespan. The findings showed that participants with at least ten years of musical experience performed better on non-verbal memory, naming and executive processes in advanced age relative to non-musicians. Several regression analyses evaluated how years of musical activity, age of commencing musical training, type of training and other variables predicted cognitive performance. Similarly, Hanna-Pladdy and Gajewski (2012) researched 70 age- and education-matched older musicians and non-musicians, aged 59 to 80. They were assessed on neuropsychological tests and general lifestyle activities. The musicians scored higher on tests of phonemic fluency, verbal working memory, verbal immediate recall, visuospatial judgement and motor dexterity, although they did not differ in the level of other general leisure activities from the non-musicians. Level of education best predicted visuospatial functions in the musicians, followed by recent musical engagement which offset low levels of education. Early age of engaging with musical activity, less than nine years old, predicted enhanced verbal working memory in musicians, while the analyses for other measures were not predictive. Recent and past musical activity predicted variability across both verbal and visuospatial domains in ageing, implying that early age of musical engagement, sustained and maintained during advanced age, may enhance cognitive functions and act as a buffer to age and education influences. Similarly, Strong and Mast (2019) examined similarities and differences in the cognitive profiles of older-adult instrumental musicians and non-musicians. They compared neuropsychological test scores among older adult non-musicians, low-activity musicians (those with less than ten years of lessons), and high-activity musicians (over ten years of lessons), controlling for self-reported physical and social activity, years of education and overall health. Significant differences among groups were found on tasks of visuospatial ability, naming and executive functioning. No significant differences were found on tests of attention, processing speed or episodic memory. The findings support the late-life cognitive benefits of early musical training, but only in some cognitive domains, including language, executive functioning and visuospatial ability.

Some research has adopted self-report methods to study the impact of making music in older age. For instance, Gembris (2008) carried out a questionnaire study with members of senior amateur orchestras with an average age of 71 years old, and found music was seen as helping them to cope and deal with difficult situations. Participants in singing activities (Clift et al., 2008) and a wide range of other musical activities (Creech et al., 2014) have reported that making music stimulates cognitive capacity, including improving their attention, concentration, memory and learning. Executive functions, such as attention, inhibition, planning, monitoring and meeting new challenges have also been self-reported as improved in relation to musical activity (Hallam and Creech, 2016; Varvarigou et al., 2012).

An intervention study with older adults aged 60 to 85 (Bugos et al., 2007) who were randomly assigned to six months of individual piano lessons or a non-lesson control group found that the music group outperformed the control group on a test that assessed processing speed in matching symbols with digits. There were significant improvements in attention, concentration, planning, cognitive flexibility and working memory. For these benefits to be maintained, regular practice and tuition were needed, as decline followed when the activities ceased. Another study further supported the benefit of group piano lessons on executive functions such as verbal flexibility and inhibition control in 24 older adults (Bugos, 2010). The improvement in executive function was significantly greater in those receiving music tuition compared to a music appreciation group consisting of 22 older adults who learned about musical elements while listening to music. However, both groups demonstrated significantly improved executive performance. In a similar study, Bugos and Kochar (2017) found that older adults who had short-term piano lessons improved on category-switching in a verbal fluency task. The research aimed to evaluate the efficacy of a short-term music programme on executive functions in healthy older adults. Thirty-four adult participants with little to no formal music training were recruited, and completed a battery of standardised cognitive measures at three time points: before training, after completion of a control time period and after training. The piano training programme included 30 hours of focused music theory, finger dexterity exercises, bimanual coordination exercises, technical exercises, performance duets and standard piano repertoire. The findings showed significantly enhanced verbal fluency and processing speed following training, although no difference was found in verbal memory performance. In a further study, Bugos (2019) examined the effects of bimanual coordination in music interventions on cognitive performance in healthy older adults aged 60 to 80. One hundred and thirty-five participants completed motor measures and a battery of standardised cognitive measures, before and after a 16-week music training programme with a three-hour practice requirement. All participants were matched by age, education and estimate of intelligence, and allocated to one of three training programmes: piano training, fine motor, percussion instruction, gross motor and music-listening instruction. The findings revealed significant enhancements in bimanual synchronisation and visual scanning and working memory abilities for fine and gross motor training groups as compared to the listening group. Pairwise comparisons revealed that piano training significantly improved motor synchronisation skills as compared to percussion instruction or music listening. These findings suggest that active music performance may benefit working memory and that the extent of the benefits may depend upon coordination demands. In another study using piano lessons, a four-month weekly group piano lesson designed and implemented by a professional music teacher and pianist resulted in improved performance on a Stroop test in 13 older adults. This cognitive improvement was not observed in 16 older adults in the control group (Seinfeld, 2013).

Also focusing on the type of activity, Biasutti and Mangiacotti (2017) investigated whether cognitive training based on rhythmic musical activities and music improvisation exercises could have positive effects on executive functions in older participants. Thirty-five residents in a residential home with mild to moderate cognitive impairment and healthy ageing were randomly assigned to an experimental group which participated in cognitive music training composed of 12 biweekly 70-minute sessions, and a control group which attended 12 biweekly 45-minute sessions of gymnastic activities. A neuropsychological test battery was administered at baseline and at the end of the programme. There was significant improvement for the experimental group on a mental state examination, a verbal fluency test and a clock-drawing test, while the control group did not show any significant improvements. No improvement was found in performance on an attentional matrices test for the music group, although those participating in the gymnastics activities showed a significant reduction in performance.

Evidence from neuroscience has shown that there are differences in the frontal cortex of musicians and non-musicians (the area of the brain which is implicated in the regulation of attention; Gaser and Schlaug, 2003; Sluming et al., 2002). Musical engagement increases grey-matter density in the frontal brain areas which are involved in controlling musical tasks (Hyde et al., 2009), while musicians who continue to engage in music-making beyond 60 years old show less or no degeneration of grey-matter density in the frontal cortex. Practising a musical instrument seems to help to prevent deterioration of executive functions involving monitoring and planning (Sluming et al., 2002). Alain and colleagues (2019), using an electroencephalogram, investigated the effects of music-making on inhibition control and interference in 60 healthy older non-musicians, who received three months of musical, visual art, or no training. The music-based intervention included the use of body percussion, voice and non-pitched musical instruments, as well as learning basic music theory and melody and harmony concepts by singing simple songs. The training was provided by a professional music teacher. Transient differential neural activities were observed in frontocentral sites in both intervention groups, but there was no improvement on task performance. Using electroencephalography, Moussard and colleagues (2016) used a visual go/no go task and demonstrated that a group of 17 older musicians exhibited a neural response, indicating a conflict-detect signal or inhibition of a prepotent response in the central midline sites between go and no go conditions, compared to a group of 17 older non-musicians.

Reviews of the Literature

Reviews of the literature have drawn different conclusions relating to the role of music in enhancing executive functions. Moreno and Bidelman (2014) concluded that research has demonstrated the robust, long-lasting biological benefits of music training to auditory function—the behavioural advantages conferred by musical experience extend beyond enhancements to perceptual abilities and impact non-auditory functions necessary for higher-order aspects of cognition (for instance, working memory). They suggest that findings indicate that alternative forms of arts engagement—for instance, visual arts training may not yield such enhancements, suggesting that musical expertise uniquely refines a hierarchy of brain networks, subserving auditory as well as domain-general cognitive mechanisms. They argue that transfer from specific music experience to broad cognitive benefit might be mediated by the degree to which a listener's musical training enhances lower- and higher-order executive functions, and the coordination between them. They argued that understanding the impact of music on the brain will provide a more holistic picture of auditory processing and plasticity, and may also help inform and tailor remediation and training programmes designed to improve perceptual and cognitive benefits. Whether these structural changes lead to higher intelligence, better memory or stronger cognitive processing in childhood continues to be debated. In a later review, Moreno and Farzan (2015) concluded that music training leads to robust and long-lasting benefits to behaviour which extend to inhibitory control and its neural correlates. Other forms of art engagement or brain training do not appear to yield such enhancements. They suggest that music uniquely taps into brain networks which are concerned with inhibitory control. Miendlarewska and Trost (2014) go further and suggest that rhythmic entrainment is the essential mechanism supporting the learning and development of executive functions which, in turn, may underlie enhancements in reading and verbal memory.

In their review, Loui and Guetta (2019) point out that music, as an intrinsically creative art form, requires bottom-up and top-down perceptual processing, attention and integration of executive functions. Attention is a subset of executive functioning and underpins goal-directed processes including conflict-monitoring, task-switching, and working memory. Considerable research has addressed the effects of musical training on these executive functions, but Loui and Guetta argue that the findings from this research have been mixed and inconclusive. Similarly, Okada and Slevc (2018b) argue that, as the relationships between musical ability and executive functions have mostly been demonstrated by correlational studies, the relationships could have a range of different explanations. Musical experience could draw on some or all aspects of existing executive functions, while musical training could improve executive functions more broadly, or the observed relationships could merely reflect selection bias, where individuals with pre-existing skills that are useful for music-learning are more likely to pursue and persist in continued music lessons. Alternatively, both explanations might be relevant, as music lessons may exaggerate pre-existing differences. While these issues continue to be debated, there is agreement that musical experience draws on particular cognitive abilities, so that the relationships between musical experience and cognitive abilities should reflect the specific abilities that are critical to musical experience. However, it is difficult to know exactly which, if any, executive functions are reliably related to musical experience.

Focusing on issues relating to ageing, Sutcliffe and colleagues (2020) note a lack of intervention studies with random assignment of participants to conditions and a lack of well-matched control conditions. These factors make it difficult to draw firm conclusions. They argue that, while music training might be a valuable tool for supporting healthy neuropsychological ageing and mental wellbeing, well-controlled intervention studies are necessary to provide clear evidence. Similarly, in their review focusing on older adults, Koshimori and Thaut (2019) suggest that the cross-sectional and correlational studies undertaken with musicians have shed light on the potential benefit of formal musical training on executive functioning and brain changes in the prefrontal area. Task-based studies have consistently demonstrated that individuals with formal musical training have differential brain activity during executive function tasks relative to those without musical training. However, these studies do not allow any direct and causal effects of music training on executive functioning or brain changes to be demonstrated. Furthermore, the specific effects of different types of musical training on executive function, brain structure and function in the prefrontal area are still unclear. Examining the evidence related to playing the piano, they concluded that this activity may have beneficial effects on executive functions in healthy older non-musicians because it is a complex process, requiring the coordination of multiple sensory modalities, motor control, monitoring, working memory, inhibition and attentional shifting. However, the sample sizes of some of the studies were frequently small and there were often additional methodological limitations. This meant that the findings had to be interpreted with caution.

Overview

Drawing firm conclusions about the impact of musical activity on executive functioning is challenging for a range of reasons. Some studies only investigate one cognitive process. Different assessment tasks are used to measure the same executive function, which makes comparisons difficult. While correlation studies are useful in identifying areas for further research, they tend to use different ways of categorising individuals into groups of musicians and non-musicians, or assessing different levels of musical expertise. Research has been undertaken with infants through to the elderly, sometimes with mixed-age groups, leading to the possibility of a wide range of confounding factors. The evidence also shows that musical interventions can have different effects on the three elements of executive functioning. Different research projects have shown benefits for working memory, inhibition or cognitive flexibility, although it is clear that some elements of executive functioning can be enhanced by musical training. It might be that the beneficial effects of musical experience would be more pronounced in populations with relatively lower executive functions, such as young children, elderly adults or patients with neuropsychological issues.

Overall, the evidence from studies of children, adults and older adults relating to the impact of actively making music on executive functions is inconclusive. For more definite conclusions to be drawn, more attention needs to be given to the type of programme adopted, the nature of its musical content and the quality of its delivery to the participants. Ideally music lessons should incorporate skills that build on one another with gradual increases in complexity. To enhance executive functions, activities might usefully include reading musical notation, sight-reading, playing in an ensemble and practice with complex polyrhythms. They should also start when children are young and continue over many years, ideally throughout the lifespan.

Generally, the jury is still out on the possible impact of music training on executive functions. Future research needs to attempt to establish more clearly which executive functions may be implicated in transfer and whether these relate to skills which have become automated or are related to those requiring conscious cognitive processing or a combination of these. Chapter 9 will consider the relationship between executive functions and measured intelligence. Music has an advantage over many other possible interventions for enhancing executive functioning, as it is generally an intrinsically motivating activity, frequently offering opportunities for enjoyable social interactions. Many aspects of music training—reading music, practising and playing in ensembles—are likely to engage executive functions and because many people enjoy music lessons for their intrinsic value, music training may provide a relatively easy to implement naturalistic executive training programme.

8. Intellectual Development

The term intelligence is used in everyday life to identify differences between individuals in the way that they are able to learn and carry out particular tasks. Beyond this general everyday usage, there is no clear agreement amongst the scientific community regarding the nature of intelligence. The first test of intelligence was developed in France by Binet and Simon (1916), to differentiate children's ability to learn in order to subsequently help teachers tailor instruction to meet children's needs. This test included the ability to name objects, define words, draw pictures, complete sentences, compare items and construct sentences. Statistical analysis of data from use of the test revealed that responses were highly correlated, leading Spearman (1938) to suggest that there was a single underlying general intelligence factor which became known as 'g'. This factor is generally accepted to relate to abstract thinking, including the ability to acquire knowledge, adapt to novel situations, and to benefit from instruction and experience. Terman (1916) developed an American version of Binet's test, the Stanford-Binet Intelligence Test, which is similarly made up of tests of vocabulary, memory of pictures, naming of familiar objects, repeating sentences and following commands. There is also evidence for specific intelligences. One such distinction is between fluid intelligence—which refers to the capacity to learn new ways of solving problems and learning— and crystallised intelligence, which refers to accumulated knowledge. Crystallised intelligence increases with age, while fluid intelligence tends to decrease with age. Since these initial conceptualisations, many types of intelligence have been proposed. For instance, Thurstone (1938) proposed seven clusters of primary mental abilities, word fluency, verbal comprehension, spatial ability, perceptual speed, numerical ability, inductive reasoning and memory. More recently, Sternberg (1985) proposed a triarchic theory of intelligence which includes analytical, creative and practical intelligence. In contrast, Gardner (1983) proposed eight intelligences: linguistic, logico-mathematical, spatial, musical, kinaesthetic (related to movement), intrapersonal (personal insights), interpersonal (interacting with others), and naturalistic (relating to plants and nature).

Research exploring the impact of musical activities on intelligence has tended to focus on general intelligence, although there are exceptions to this. One of the most commonly used tests in this research is the Wechsler Adult Intelligence Scale (WAIS). This consists of 15 different tasks, including working memory, arithmetic ability, spatial ability and general knowledge about the world. The WAIS-IV yields scores in four domains: verbal, perceptual, working memory and processing speed. Tests of non-verbal reasoning, which do not rely on literacy skills, have also been developed. Raven's Progressive Matrices (1981) is one of the most commonly used. Each element requires the testee to identify a missing element that will complete a pattern.

More recently, the concept of emotional intelligence has emerged. This can be traced back to the work of Thorndike (1920), who referred to the concept of social intelligence, which was described as the ability to understand and manage people. Gardner (1983), within the framework of multiple intelligences, elaborated the concept to include intrapersonal and interpersonal intelligence, the former relating to the capacity to understand oneself and to use such information to regulate one's own life, and the latter to the capacity to understand the intentions, motivation and desires of others. Currently there are two constructs of emotional intelligence. Ability emotional intelligence focuses on the ability to process emotional information and use it to navigate the social environment (Mayer et al., 2001), although it has further evolved to include the abilities to accurately perceive emotions, to access and generate emotions so as to assist thought and understand emotions and emotional knowledge, and to reflectively regulate emotions so as to promote emotional and intellectual growth (Mayer et al., 2004). In contrast, trait emotional intelligence, or trait emotional self-efficacy, concerns emotion-related self-perceptions. Trait emotional intelligence was proposed by Petrides and Furnham in 2001 and is conceptualised as an aspect of personality measured through self-report. Daniel Goleman's book (1996) popularised the concept of emotional intelligence, with the model he proposed being seen as combining ability and trait emotional intelligence. Empathy is typically associated with emotional intelligence, because it relates to an individual being able to connect their personal experiences with those of others. The role of music in the development of empathy is discussed in Chapter 12.

Nature or Nurture

An ongoing and contentious debate about intelligence is whether it is determined by genetic or environmental factors. Clearly, if intelligence is determined by genetic factors alone then musical interventions will have no impact. Nowadays, it is increasingly recognised that measured intelligence (IQ) is determined by both genetic predisposition and environmental factors, although whether these operate additively or interact with each other continues to be fiercely debated. Considerable research has been undertaken to attempt to identify a gene or genes responsible for intelligence. This research has shown that intelligence within the normal range is a polygenic trait—in other words, influenced by more than one gene, and in the case of intelligence, at least 500 genes.

Traditional additive genetic models have shown intelligence to have extremely high heritability levels, while other research has shown that it is extremely malleable. Sauce and Matzel (2018) suggest that intelligence has unusual properties that create a large number of hidden gene environment networks which allow for the contribution of high genetic and environmental influences on individual differences in IQ. They argue that current research methods underestimate gene environment interplay and inflate estimates of genetic effects, which in turn deflate estimates of the impact of the environment. They provide evidence which shows cognitive gains in children through adoption and immigration, and changes in heritability across the life span. They also present evidence for gains in population IQ over time relating to societal development, for a slowdown in age-related cognitive decline and for gains in intelligence from early education. They acknowledge that the high heritability of intelligence could have emerged from independent genetic effects, while high malleability could have arisen from independent environmental effects, but suggest that these cannot account for individual differences and conclude that gene environment interplay is key to understanding intelligence given the present state of evidence.

Brain imaging has provided the basis for research on the neurobiology of intelligence by highlighting the important functional and structural anatomical regions implicated, grey-matter volume and thickness, and white-matter integrity and function in the temporal, frontal and parietal cortices (Goriounova and Mansvelder, 2019). Genome-wide association studies have made it possible to show that 98 percent of associated genetic variants are not coded into functional protein and are likely to have a regulatory function at different stages of neural development. Those genes that do produce functional proteins are implicated in a range of neuronal functions, including synaptic function and plasticity, cell interactions and the metabolism of energy. Recent research in cellular neuroscience has shown positive correlations between dendritic size, action potential speed and IQ, but there is much that is still not understood about what underpins individual differences in intelligence.

Considering the relationship between music, language and intelligence, Jung and Haier (2007) developed a model parietofrontal integration theory, which highlights the structural links common to these areas specifically in shared neural structures, such as the prefrontal cortex, the anterior cingandulate and a region within the temporal lobes. This research, along with that indicating the malleability of intelligence, suggests that music interventions may be able to enhance intelligence. Also exploring genetic and environmental influences between music and IQ, Mosing and colleagues (2016) undertook a co-twin study based on more than 10,500 twins. Phenotypic associations were moderate, although the relationship disappeared when controlling for genetic and shared environmental influence. A twin highly trained in music did not have a higher IQ than an untrained twin. The findings strongly suggested that the associations between musical training and IQ were not causal.

Correlational and Comparative Research with Adults

Correlational studies have shown that engagement with music can enhance some skills which contribute to scores on intelligence tests. The evidence suggests that the longer the training, the greater the impact (Corrigall et al., 2013; Degé et al., 2011a; Schellenberg, 2006), and that the relationships between musical training and intelligence remain when a range of confounding variables related to family background are taken into account (Corrigall et al., 2013; Degé et al., 2011a; Schellenberg, 2006; 2011a; 2011b; Schellenberg and Mankarious, 2012). For example, Schellenberg (2011b) studied 196 undergraduates ranging in age from 17-26 years old, either with at least eight years of extracurricular private music lessons or with no lessons. The musically trained participants had higher scores than their untrained counterparts on the IQ composite score, and on its verbal and non-verbal subtests. These advantages were evident even when gender, parents' education, family income and first language were held constant. Similarly, Corrigal and Schellenberg (2013) studied the relationships between cognition, personality, participation in music lessons and length of participation. One hundred and eighteen adults and 167 children aged ten to twelve completed personality and cognitive ability tests. Cognitive ability was associated with duration of musical involvement, even when demographic variables were controlled for.

Swaminathan and colleagues (2017) examined whether the link between intelligence and musical expertise was better explained by formal music lessons or musical aptitude. Musically trained and untrained adults completed tests of non-verbal intelligence, Raven's Advanced Progressive Matrices and musical aptitude. They also provided information about their music lessons and socioeconomic status. Duration of music training was associated positively with socioeconomic status, non-verbal intelligence, and melodic and rhythmic aptitude. Intelligence and music aptitude were also positively associated. The association between musical training and intelligence remained after controlling for socioeconomic status but disappeared after controlling for musical aptitude, although musical aptitude had a strong correlation with intelligence, even after accounting for music training and socioeconomic status. The association between music training and intelligence may arise because high-functioning individuals are more likely than other individuals to have a strong aptitude for music, and therefore to take music lessons.

Some research has focused on particular aspects of intelligence. For instance, Anaya and colleagues (2017) assessed the visuospatial sequence learning and memory abilities of long-term musicians. They recruited 24 highly trained musicians and 24 non-musicians, who completed a visuospatial sequence learning task and receptive vocabulary, non-verbal reasoning, and short-term memory tasks. The findings showed that the musicians had enhanced visuospatial sequence learning abilities relative to non-musicians. They also performed better on the vocabulary and non-verbal reasoning measures. The large difference observed on the visuospatial sequencing task remained even after controlling for vocabulary, non-verbal reasoning, and short-term memory abilities. Criscuolo and colleagues (2019) explored the relationships between general intelligence, executive functions and musical expertise. One hundred and one Finnish healthy adults grouped as musicians, amateur musicians and non-musicians were administered the Wechsler Adult Intelligence Scale III, the Weschler Memory Scale III and the Stroop test. After being matched on a range of variables, the musicians exhibited higher cognitive performance than non-musicians on all of the tests. Linear regression showed significant positive relationships between executive functions, working memory and attention, and the duration of musical engagement, after controlling for possible confounding variables.

Focusing on fluid intelligence, Meyer and colleagues (2018) administered a test battery including measures of episodic memory, working memory, attention, executive function and processing speed to 72 undergraduate students with a range of musical expertise. Three groups of students were identified:

- an expert group who had begun musical training at age ten or younger and had engaged with music for ten years or longer. They self-rated between three to five on two Likert scales relating to sight-reading skills and improvisation skill;
- musical amateurs, who included those with more than one year of musical training;
- non-musicians, who had less than one year of musical training and typically no training at all.

The findings showed that the musicians with extensive experience scored significantly higher in fluid cognition, attention and working memory tests of executive functions and processing speed than did the non-musicians and the less well-trained musicians. There was no statistically significant difference between amateur and non-musicians on these subtests with one exception, the executive function test, where the amateur musicians performed better than the non-musicians. A regression analysis using age of onset of training and length of music training in relation to fluid intelligence showed that these two factors accounted for almost 30 percent of the variance. Age of onset predicted fluid intelligence but the relationship with length of music education was not significant. As for sub-scores, these two factors accounted for almost 37 percent of the variance for the sub-score speed of processing. Age of starting musical training predicted speed of processing, while the relationship with length of music education was not significant. Regression analyses for the other sub-scores yielded non-significant results.

Silvia and colleagues (2016) adopted a bifactor modelling approach to study data from a sample of 237 young adults who varied substantially in musical expertise. Participants completed a range of tasks that measured several lower-order abilities: fluid intelligence, crystallised intelligence, verbal fluency and auditory discrimination ability. Simple correlations showed that music training correlated with all four lower-order abilities. A bifactor model, however, found that music training had general, a strong association with general intelligence (g), and specific, a moderate association with auditory ability, relationships.

Some research with adults has focused on the relationship between musical and reading skills. For instance, Swaminathan and colleagues (2018) sought to clarify whether the positive association between music lessons and reading ability found in adults was explained better by shared resources for processing pitch and temporal information, or by general cognitive abilities. Participants had varying levels of musical training and were native and non-native speakers of English. The research assessed reading ability, music perception skills, general cognitive ability including non-verbal intelligence, short-term and working memory, and socioeconomic status. The association between reading and music training was significant after socioeconomic status, native language and music perception skills were controlled for. After general cognitive abilities were held constant, there was no longer an association between reading and music training. This suggested that the association between reading ability and music training was a consequence of general cognitive abilities.

Not all of the research has shown positive relationships between musical training and intelligence. For instance, Schellenberg and Moreno (2010) recruited 40 undergraduates on the basis of their musical background. Half had extensive training in music, at least eight years of lessons, and had played regularly up until three years or less before participating. The remaining 20 participants had little or no musical training. The participants responded to tests of pitch processing and completed the Raven's Progressive Matrices to assess non-verbal reasoning. The musicians exhibited superior performance on the musical tests but not on the measure of general intelligence. Similarly, Helmbold and colleagues (2005) compared 70 adult musicians with 70 non-musicians on psychometric performance on verbal comprehension, word fluency, space, flexibility of closure, perceptual speed, reasoning, number and memory. No significant differences were found for either mean full-scale scores or for specific aspects of mental abilities, except flexibility of closure and perceptual speed. In both these subtests, musicians performed reliably better than non-musicians. Also comparing musicians and non-musicians, Brandler and Rammsayer (2003) studied differences in a range of cognitive tasks including verbal comprehension, word fluency, space, closure, perceptual speed, reasoning, number and memory. Significant differences were not found for either mean full-scale scores or for specific aspects of intelligence, except verbal memory and reasoning. While performance on verbal memory was reliably higher for the musicians than for the non-musicians, the non-musicians performed significantly better on all four subscales of Cattell's culture-free intelligence test.

Correlation and Comparative Research with Children

There has long been an interest in the relationship between musical training and intellectual development. Many early studies focused on how general intelligence might underpin musical ability (Beckham, 1942; Fracker and Howard, 1928; Hollingworth, 1926).

Later studies explored the nature of the relationships (Antrim, 1945; Bienstock, 1942; Ross, 1936) but did not address issues of causality, which led to some arguing that the reason for the relationships was because more intelligent children were drawn to participate in musical activities (Farnsworth, 1946; Ross, 1936). Since these early studies, there has been evidence that children who take up a musical instrument frequently have higher-level academic skills prior to participating in musical activities (Feldman and Matjasko, 2005; Fitzpatrick, 2006; Gibson et al., 2009; Hille et al., 2011; Kinney, 2008; 2010; Ruthsatz et al., 2008; Schellenberg, 2011a; Schellenberg and Mankarious, 2012). However, this is not always the case (Habibi et al., 2014). Learning to play a musical instrument is often related to the socioeconomic status of families and family make-up, both of which support opportunities for musical engagement (Bugaj and Brenner, 2011; Costa-Giomi, 2012; Elpus and Abril, 2011; Kinney, 2010; Schellenberg and Weiss, 2013). Only intervention studies can establish the direction of causality.

Overall, there have been a number of correlational and comparative studies with children. Adopting a cross-sectional approach, Schlaug and colleagues (2005) compared nine- to eleven-year-old instrumentalists with an average of four years' training with a control group. The findings showed that the instrumental group performed significantly better than the control group on musical audiation, left-hand index finger tapping rate, and the vocabulary subtest of the WISC-III intelligence test. However, there were non-significant trends in a phonemic awareness test, Raven's Progressive Matrices and a mathematics test. Similarly, Loui and colleagues (2019) showed that children who played a musical instrument for more than half an hour each week had higher scores on verbal ability and intellectual ability, as well as higher axial diffusivity in the left superior longitudinal fasciculus than those who did not play. A correlation between the number of hours of practice each week and axial diffusivity in the left superior longitudinal fasciculus suggested that the relationship between musical practice and intellectual ability was related to the maturation of white-matter pathways in the auditory-motor system.

Some research has focused on multiple intelligences. For instance, Singh and colleagues (2017) studied performance on multiple intelligences in Indian children, comparing them with IQ scores. They recruited 1065 school children between the ages of 12 and 16 from 2 government and 13 private schools in 5 towns, 6 cities and 2 villages across

India. All of the children were administered a multiple-intelligences questionnaire consisting of 30 true-false questions, to assess intelligences in seven domains, including linguistic skills, logical mathematical abilities, musical skills, spatial intelligence, bodily kinaesthetic skills, intrapersonal intelligence and interpersonal intelligence. IQ scores were assessed by Ravens Standard Progressive Matrices. The findings showed that different students possessed different forms of intelligences, and that most students had more than one form of intelligence. Of the seven forms of intelligence, only three—logico-mathematical, musical and spatial—were positively correlated with IQ scores.

Swaminathan and Schellenberg (2020) focused on the links between musical expertise and language ability in a sample of six- to nine-year-old children. Language ability was measured with tests of speech perception and grammar, while musical expertise was assessed with a range of tests of musical ability. Musical training was associated positively with performance on a grammar test, musical ability, IQ, openness and age. Overall, the findings showed that musical ability predicted language ability independent of IQ and other confounding variables, but the links between music and language seemed to arise primarily from pre-existing factors and not from formal training in music.

Schellenberg and colleagues undertook a series of studies exploring the relationships between musical engagement and intelligence in children. For instance, Schellenberg (2006) administered standardised tests of intelligence to approximately 300 children and adults who varied widely in the extent of their musical experiences outside school. The findings showed that, among the children, cognitive performance was positively associated with months of music lessons, even after holding constant parents' education, family income and duration of involvement. Associations were strongest for an aggregate measure of intelligence, with no association between musical activity and particular subtests when general intelligence was held constant. In a later study, Schellenberg (2011a) compared 106 musically trained and untrained nine- to twelve-year-olds on a measure of IQ and five measures of executive function. The musically trained children outperformed the untrained children across the four subtests and three IQ scores of the test used. These findings replicated those reported earlier by Schellenberg (2004; 2006b). However, the association between musical training and executive function was negligible. Further, Corrigal and Schellenberg (2013) collected data from 167 ten- to twelve-year-old children, including demographic information and measured cognitive ability. The duration of music lessons was associated positively with age, socioeconomic status, duration of non-musical extracurricular activities, IQ and school performance. They concluded that the observed associations between musical involvement and cognition were highly unlikely to be solely a consequence of music training.

In a comparative study, Hille and colleagues (2011) explored the impact of different types of musical activities on intelligence. They tested 194 boys aged eight to nine years old, just over half of whom had learned to play a musical instrument. Non-verbal measures of intelligence were higher for boys playing an instrument, with a moderate effect size, but no difference in non-verbal measures of intelligence was found for boys who sang in a choir and those who did not. Overall, active participation in a choir or lessons called 'First Experiences with Music' did not show the benefits associated with learning to play an instrument.

Degé and colleagues (2011a) investigated whether the association between music lessons and intelligence was mediated by executive functions. Intelligence and five different executive functions—set-shifting, selective attention, planning, inhibition and fluency—were assessed in nine- to twelve-year-old children with varying amounts of music lessons. Significant associations emerged between music lessons and all of the measures of executive function. Executive functions mediated the association between music lessons and intelligence, with the measures of selective attention and inhibition being the strongest contributors to the effect. The results suggested that at least part of the association between music lessons and intelligence was explained by the positive influence that music lessons had on executive functions, which in turn improved performance on the intelligence tests. Also focusing on executive functions, Schellenberg (2011) compared musically trained and untrained nine- to twelve-year-olds on a measure of IQ and five measures of executive function. The findings showed that IQ and executive function were correlated. The musically trained group had higher IQs than their untrained counterparts and this advantage extended across the IQ subtests. However, the association between music training and executive function was negligible. These results do not support the hypothesis that the association between music training and IQ is mediated by executive function.

Jaschke and colleagues (2018a) adopted a different approach, assessing exposure to a musically enriched environment, including listening to music at home, during play or when attending concerts. A questionnaire was administered to a sample of 176 primary-school children who also completed the verbal intelligence section of the Wechsler Intelligence Scale (WISC III) and performed executive sub-function tasks such as planning, working memory, inhibition and a short-term memory task. Linear and multiple regression analyses showed no significant relationship between exposure to a musically enriched environment, executive sub-functions, planning, inhibition, working memory and short-term memory. Experiencing a musically enriched environment does not serve as a predictor for higher performance on executive sub functions, although it can influence verbal intelligence.

Intervention Studies

Research which has adopted a retrospective approach to studying the relationship between active engagement with music and intelligence—while showing enhanced performance from musicians on a range of intellectual skills—is not able to address the issue of causality. Those who take up playing musical instruments may have higher IQ scores in the first place, although the evidence regarding this is mixed. Intervention studies can address this issue but have also served to demonstrate the complexity of the issues involved in establishing the relationship between musical engagement and intelligence. In an early study, Hurwitz and colleagues (1975) assigned first-grade children to two groups, one receiving Kodaly music lessons for five days each week for seven months, and one a control group which did not receive musical tuition. At the end of the study, the experimental group scored significantly higher than the control group on three of five sequencing tasks and four of five spatial tasks. No statistically significant differences were found for verbal measures, although the children in the experimental group had higher reading achievement scores than those in the control group. These were maintained after two academic years.

Following this early study, Gromko and Poorman (1998) compared preschool children in a group engaging in weekly musical activities with a control group and found that, for the three-year-olds participating in the study, an intellectually stimulating environment resulted in a gain in the ability to perform the spatial-temporal task element of an intelligence test. Similarly, Bilhartz and colleagues (1999) studied the relationship between participation in a structured music curriculum and cognitive development in four- to six-year-olds. Half of the children participated in a 30-week 75-minute weekly music curriculum with parent involvement. Following this, the children were tested with six subtests of the Stanford-Binet intelligence test and the Young Child Music Skills Assessment test. There were significant gains for the music group on the music test and the Stanford-Binet Bead Memory subtest.

In a series of studies, Costa-Giomi and colleagues (1999; 2004; Costa-Giomi and Ryan, 2007) completed a longitudinal study on the effects of piano instruction on children's cognitive abilities. Children were randomly assigned to an experimental or control group. Each child received free instruction. The two groups of children were comparable at the start of the study in terms of musical ability, cognitive abilities and academic achievement in mathematics, language and motor skills. After two years of instruction, the children in the experimental group obtained significantly higher scores on the cognitive ability tests and spatial scores. However, no differences were found after three years. Additionally, no differences in the quantitative and verbal cognitive abilities of the two groups were found after two years of the study. A follow-up study conducted seven years after the completion of the lessons showed no differences between groups. Similarly, analysis at a ten-year follow-up (Costa-Giomi and Ryan, 2007) showed no differences in IQ or memory. The initial gains became negligible over time. The improvements were small and temporary, and seem to have depended on the level of the children's commitment and effort. After three years, 22 percent of the variance in cognitive improvement was explained by the children's attendance at lessons and time spent practising. Those who were more committed gained more (Costa-Giomi, 1999).

In a carefully controlled study, Schellenberg (2004) randomly assigned a large sample of children to four different groups—two of which received music lessons, standard keyboard or Kodaly voice lessons for a year, while the control groups received instruction in a non-musical artistic activity, drama or no lessons. All four groups exhibited increases in IQ, as would be expected over the time period, but the music groups had reliably larger increases in full-scale IQ, with an effect size of .35. Children in the control groups had average increases of 4.3 points while the music groups had increases of 7 points. On all but two of the 12 subtests, the music group had larger increases than control groups. Notably, the music groups had larger increases on the four indexes that measured specific abilities, verbal ability, spatial ability, processing speed and attention. Catterall and Rauscher (2008), in a review of the literature and a reanalysis of Schellenberg's (2004) data, argue that the gains seen in more general IQ were likely to be the result of specific gains in visuospatial intelligence, although there may also be effects related to the enhanced development of language and literacy skills.

In a more recent study, Moreno and colleagues (2011a; 2011b) devised two interactive computerised training programmes with a focus on music or art. After only 20 days of training, the children in the music group exhibited enhanced performance on a measure of verbal intelligence. These changes were positively correlated with changes in functional brain plasticity during an executive function task, which the authors suggested indicated that the impact of musical engagement on intelligence could be related to executive functions. Similarly, Jaschke and colleagues (2018b) studied 147 primary-school children, aged six to seven years old, who were followed for 2.5 years. Participants were randomised into four groups: two music intervention groups, one active visual arts group, and a no-arts control group. Neuropsychological tests assessed verbal intelligence and executive functions. Additionally, national data on academic performance was available. Children in the visual arts group performed better on visuospatial memory tasks as compared to the three other conditions. However, the test scores on inhibition, planning and verbal intelligence increased significantly in the two music groups over time as compared to the visual art and no-arts controls. Mediation analysis with executive functions and verbal IQ as mediators for academic performance showed a possible far-transfer effect from executive sub-function to academic performance scores.

In Tehran, Iran, Kaviani and colleagues (2014) worked with 154 preschool children from kindergarten. Sixty children aged between five and six years old were randomly assigned to two groups, one receiving twelve 75-minute music lessons and the other—matched for sex, age and mother's educational level—not receiving any music classes. The children were tested before the start of the music lessons and at the end, with four subtests of an intelligence scale. The findings showed a statistically significant increase in IQ in participants receiving music lessons, specifically on verbal reasoning and short-term memory subtests, although there were no differences in numerical and visual abstract reasoning abilities. In Israel, research with children aged six to twelve also found a causal effect of music training on intelligence. Children who were assigned to a two-year music training programme had larger increases in general intelligence compared to a control group with no intervention (Portowitz and Klein, 2007; Portowitz et al., 2009). Working in Spain, Carioti and colleagues (2019) tested 128 students in a middle school at the beginning of the first class and the beginning of the second class. Seventy-two students were able to access a music curriculum, 30 with previous music experience, 42 without, while 56 accessed a standard curriculum. 44 with prior music experience and 12 without. The longitudinal comparison of the four groups of students revealed that students experiencing the music curriculum had better performance in tests of general cognitive abilities, visuospatial skills and memory tests.

Studying children from low socioeconomic backgrounds, Barbaroux et al. (2019) evaluated the impact of a classical music training programme with particular reference to general intelligence, auditory and visual attention, and working and short-term memory. The findings showed that music training improved total IQ and symbol-search scores, as well as concentration abilities.

Rose and colleagues (2019) investigated the effects of musical instrument learning on the development of cognitive skills in 38 seven- to nine-year-old children. Pre- and post-test measures of intelligence and memory were compared in children who received either extracurricular musical training or statutory school music lessons. The results showed a significant association between musical aptitude and intelligence overall. The children receiving extracurricular lessons showed a significant increase in IQ—7 points—in comparison to 4.3 points for those receiving standard school music lessons. No significant differences were found for memory. In a comparison of two different music interventions, James and colleagues (2019) undertook a cluster randomised controlled trial which showed that musical instrumental practice, in comparison to traditional sensitisation to music, led to multiple transfer effects in cognition. Sixty-nine children aged ten to twelve received group music instruction by professional musicians twice a week as part of the regular school curriculum. The intervention group learned to play string instruments, whereas the control group was sensitised to music through listening, theory and some practice. Broad benefits manifested in the intervention group as compared to the control group for working memory, attention, processing speed, cognitive flexibility and matrix reasoning.

Not all of the research has shown increases in IQ relating to active participation in musical activities. For instance, Mehr and colleagues (2013) conducted two randomised controlled trials with American preschool children, on average aged four years old. They compared participation in music classes with participation in visual arts classes. The parents attended classes with their children. The classes ran for six weeks, with a total of 4.5 hours of relatively unstructured musical activity which involved singing, some work with percussion instruments and movement. The children were tested on spatial navigational reasoning, visual form analysis, numerical discrimination and receptive vocabulary. In the first experiment, the children from the music group showed greater spatial navigational ability, while children from the visual arts class showed greater visual form analysis. However, a partial replication with another group of children did not confirm these findings.

Working with secondary- and primary-aged students in two studies, Rickard and colleagues (2012) reported on the impact of an increase in school-based music training on a range of cognitive and psychosocial measures for ten- to thirteen-year-olds. In the first study, the benefits of increased frequency of classroom-based music classes were compared with drama and art lessons. The second study compared the effects of introducing a new classroom-based music programme with a new drama programme for 100 primary-school students. Assessments were obtained at baseline and approximately six months after implementation of each programme. No benefits for school music classes were apparent, although trends of interest were observed in non-verbal intelligence and verbal memory.

Music and Emotional Intelligence

There is evidence that group music-making can support the development of emotional intelligence. For instance, Petrides and colleagues (2006) investigated trait emotional intelligence in a study of 37 music students. They found a positive relationship between trait emotional intelligence scores and length of musical training. The research supported the conceptualisation of trait emotional intelligence as a construct of general emotionality. In contrast, in research assessing ability emotional intelligence, Resnicow and colleagues (2004) worked with 24 undergraduate students. They found that there was a relationship between the ability to recognise emotions in performances of classical piano music and measures of emotional intelligence, which required individuals to identify, understand, reason with and manage emotions using hypothetical scenarios. Emotional intelligence and emotion recognition in the music task were significantly correlated, which suggests that identification of emotion in music performance draws on some of the same sensibilities that make up everyday emotional intelligence. There is also evidence that music training enhances sensitivity to emotions in speech. Thompson and colleagues (2004) revealed that music lessons promoted sensitivity to emotions conveyed by speech prosody. Musically trained adults outperformed untrained adults at identifying sadness, fear or neutral emotion, while six-year-olds randomly assigned to one year of keyboard lessons performed equivalently to a drama group and better than a no-lessons group at identifying anger or fear.

Adopting a different approach, Theorell and colleagues (2014) explored whether musical activities contributed to the prevention of alexithymia, the inability to describe one's own emotions. Eight thousand Swedish twins aged 27 to 54 were studied. They completed the Toronto Alexithymia Scale—a musical achievement scale—and estimated the number of hours of musical practice during different periods of their life. The findings showed that alexithymia was negatively associated with musical creative achievement, having played a musical instrument, total hours of musical training and ensemble-playing. The associations between musical training and alexithymia remained significant when controlling for education, depression and intelligence.

Musical achievement and musical practice were both associated with lower levels of alexithymia. They concluded that musical engagement was associated with higher emotional competence, although the effect sizes were small.

Not all of the research exploring the relationships between music-making and emotional intelligence has found positive relationships. This seems to depend on whether emotional intelligence is measured as a trait, a behavioural disposition or an ability—a skill in processing emotional information and using it in everyday life. Music training seems to be more related to emotional intelligence as a trait (Petrides et al., 2006) rather than as an ability.

Trimmer and Cuddy (2008), working with 100 undergraduates, found that emotional intelligence, not music training or music perception abilities, successfully predicted identification of intended emotion in speech and melodic analogues. The ability to recognise cues of emotion accurately and efficiently across domains may reflect the operation of a cross-modal processor that does not rely on gains in perceptual sensitivity, such as those related to music training. Similarly, Schellenberg (2011b) studied 196 undergraduates ranging in age from 17 to 26 years old with at least eight years of extracurricular private music lessons or no lessons. The musically trained participants scored no higher than their untrained counterparts on a test of emotional intelligence.

Despite this, some research with children has found positive relationships between understanding emotions and music training. For instance, Schellenberg and Mankarious (2012) found that seven- to eight-year-olds with at least eight months of formal musical training, mainly through private individual lessons, showed a positive association between music training and emotional ability, although this seemed to be mediated by higher levels of general intelligence. There is also some evidence that music can enhance emotional competence among children, which then supports their engagement with learning (Adushkina, 2015).

In Korea, two studies—Shin (2006) and Lee (2010)—examined the effect of music therapy on low-income elementary-school children's emotional intelligence. The music programme consisted of singing, listening to music and song-writing. The findings showed that there were statistically significant increases in emotional intelligence compared with a control group. Also in Korea, Kim and Kim (2018) adopted a quasi-experimental design in which 30 children received a weekly group musical instrument performance class with a regular music class, while a control group of 30 children received only a regular music class that was part of the elementary-school curriculum. Emotional intelligence, anxiety and aggression were assessed at the beginning and end of the 24-week intervention. The musical instrument performance programme improved the ability to perceive emotions, and reduced physical and verbal aggression, but had no statistically significant effect on the level of total emotional intelligence, anxiety or aggression.

Studies with Older Adults

Some research has focused on general cognitive functions with older adults. As we saw in Chapters 6 and 7, there is evidence of the impact of music on cognition in older people; for instance, on executive functions, including various aspects of memory, attention, processing speed and planning (Amer et al., 2013; Bugos et al., 2007; Bugos, 2010; Bugos, 2019; Degé and Kerkovius, 2018; Diaz Abrahan et al., 2020; Grassi et al., 2018; Hanna-Pladdy and Gajewski, 2012; Hanna-Pladdy and MacKay, 2011; Hars et al., 2013; Strong and Mast, 2019). There have also been improvements in cognition and working memory in patients with dementia, and evidence that musical activity can prevent cognitive decline (Camic et al., 2013; Maguire et al., 2015; Mansky et al., 2020; Pongan et al., 2017; Särkämö et al., 2014).

In a pilot study with socioeconomically diverse older adults, MacAulay and colleagues (2019) presented interim data on the effect of music training. Thirty-five socioeconomically diverse older adults with a mean age of 70 completed the programme. Participants took part in 12 weekly one-hour recorder lessons and underwent comprehensive pre- and post-intervention neuropsychological assessments. The results indicated improved executive function, global cognition, verbal fluency and visual memory performance following the intervention. The research suggested that music training is a cognitively stimulating activity that has real-life applications for older people.

In a retrospective study, Fancourt and colleagues (2020) examined whether lifetime musical training was associated with neuropsychological performance in a memory-clinic population of older patients. A total of 478 patients, with an average age of almost 74 years old, were included in a cross-sectional analysis. All of the participating patients had been referred to the memory clinic due to cognitive impairments. Participants were assessed using a neuropsychological assessment battery. They also provided information on whether they had played a musical instrument for at least five years during their lives. The outcomes of the neuropsychological test results differed based on the extent of musical training. Overall, there were no differences in any domains of cognitive functioning, other than that patients with musical training performed worse on word-list memory tasks. However, this relationship varied based on the extent of cognitive impairment. Patients who were cognitively unimpaired and had musical training showed better word-list learning, whereas patients with cognitive impairments and musical training performed worse in word-list learning and word-list recall. Overall, there was little evidence of associations between specific neuropsychological test results and musical training. Only in cognitively unimpaired patients was there evidence that musical training had beneficial associations. In patients with cognitive impairment, there were suggestions of negative associations with verbal memory.

In a very large-scale study, Mansens and colleagues (2018) used data from 1101 participants aged 64 and older from the Longitudinal Aging Study Amsterdam. Multivariable linear regression analyses were performed to test the association between time spent making music and cognitive functioning. Making music was significantly positively associated with letter fluency, learning, attention and short-term memory, although time spent making music yielded no significant results. Participants who only played an instrument compared to participants who had not made music performed better on learning, working memory and processing speed. For processing speed, the instrument-only group also had a higher score than participants who only sang. Making music at least once every two weeks—and especially playing a musical instrument—was associated with better attention, episodic memory and executive functions.

Overall, the research to date suggests that music training may protect against age-related decline in working memory and may improve performance among older adults who show some decline in working memory. Music training may also be useful in the prevention and treatment of dementia.

Reviews and Meta-Analyses

Reviews and meta-analyses relating to the role of music in general cognition are inconsistent in their findings. Črnčec and colleagues (2006) concluded that music instruction conferred consistent benefits for spatial-temporal reasoning skills; however, improvements in associated academic domains, such as arithmetic, had not been reliably shown. Similarly, Jaschke and colleagues (2013), in review of research on children aged four to thirteen, suggested that the results of research exploring the effects of active engagement with music on cognitive development were either inconclusive or contradictory, because of the differences in methods adopted and the different types of music education studied. Dumont and colleagues (2017) focused on the role of music in child development. Based on a detailed examination of 46 studies, they argued that research on the impact of music interventions indicated positive effects on a variety of skills which may support educational processes and children's development, although it was not possible to draw definitive conclusions. Seven studies did not have sufficient evidence and the results of a random controlled trial showed no effects, while two experimental studies yielded mixed results. Three quasi-experimental longitudinal studies and a longitudinal development study suggested a partial positive impact of music. Evidence from five experimental longitudinal studies suggested benefits for memory, although there were methodological limitations. Of six quasi-experimental studies exploring the impact on attention and executive functions, only two reported positive outcomes. Five studies focusing on working memory seemed to suggest a positive influence of music.

Protzko and colleagues (2017) reviewed five meta-analyses and 36 randomised controlled trials on the raising of IQ in children. They found that supplementing a deficient child with multivitamins raised IQ, as did providing iodine supplements. Learning to play a musical instrument also enhanced IQ, although the role of iron supplements and executive function training were unreliable. Papageorgi (2021) also concluded that active engagement with music-making, particularly playing a musical instrument, had benefits for cognitive development, while Kraus and Chandrasekaran (2010) argued that, although there is convincing evidence for the overall benefits of engagement with music, many questions remain unanswered. The evidence suggests that music training facilitates cognitive development, but it is not clear whether the improvements are an effect of the music training itself or the cognitive load involved in the process of learning and playing a musical instrument (which facilitates the development of a range of cognitive skills).

Sala and Gobet (2017; 2020) carried out two meta-analyses to establish whether the available data supported an association between music and cognitive skills. The first analysis (2017) examined 38 studies. The results of the random effect models showed a small overall effect size, but with slightly greater effect sizes with regard to intelligence and memory-related outcomes. There was also an inverse relationship between the size of the effects and the methodological quality of the study design. The results suggested that music training does not reliably enhance children and young adolescents' cognitive or academic skills. The later meta-analyses (Sala and Gobet, 2020) reanalysed data from 54 previous studies conducted between 1986 and 2019, and included a total of 6,984 children. The analysis revealed that music training appeared to be ineffective at enhancing cognitive or academic skills, regardless of the type of skill (verbal, non-verbal or speed-related), participants' age or duration of music training. The authors found that studies with high-quality design, such as those which used a group of active controls—like children who learned a different skill, such as dance or sports—showed no effect of music education on cognitive or academic performance. Small effects were found in studies that did not include controls, or where participants were not randomly assigned to intervention or control groups.

Similarly, Cooper (2020) conducted a random effect meta-analysis to measure the overall mean effects of music training on cognitive measures in schoolchildren. The results showed small to medium overall effects. When compared to active control groups, music training yielded more improvement on a range of cognitive measurements. While some studies did result in large effect sizes, significant moderators related to methodological quality rendered the overall findings to non-significant. Additional moderator analysis showed no clear advantage in cognitive function. The findings did not differ in relation to type of music intervention. Overall, they suggested that music training may have a positive impact on cognition in schoolchildren, but may not have advantages when compared with other interventions.

Overview

Overall, taking the findings together, it would appear that active engagement with making music can have an impact on intelligence and cognitive development, although it frequently does not. However, the research highlights a great many issues. Firstly, the nature of intelligence itself is problematic from a research point of view, as it includes many different subskills. Some of these are more likely to benefit from musical interventions than others, as has been demonstrated in this and previous chapters. The nature and relative importance of the relationship between executive functions and measured intelligence is also a problematic area. The type of musical interventions, their duration, intensity and quality continue to be possible confounding factors. There is also an issue in relation to the role of active control groups—for instance, sport, drama, dance and visual art. If there is no difference between the outcomes of musical training and these other activities, or indeed taking dietary supplements, there seems to be an assumption that there is no impact of musical activities where in fact it may be that all of these activities can make a contribution to cognitive development. Just because music has no greater impact on cognition than sport, this does not necessarily mean that music has no impact. Indeed, the preference that an individual has for any of these activities will contribute to their motivation and subsequent propensity to maintain the activity over a long period of time, at high levels of intensity with great commitment, all factors which are important in determining impact on cognition.

It might be expected that active engagement with music would support the development of emotional intelligence. There is no question that music has a profound impact on our moods, emotions and arousal levels, and that, as understanding of music develops, it may support the development of understanding of emotions more generally. The research to date does not entirely support this, although the evidence for the impact of musical training on trait emotional intelligence is stronger than for ability intelligence. Trait emotional intelligence is conceptualised as being aware of one's own emotions. In musicians, how this relates to the performance of music—a key element of which is to convey emotion—is not clear.

9. Musicians and Creativity

Understanding and researching creativity presents many challenges. Several different approaches have been adopted. One strand of research has focused on the characteristics of creative people; a second has considered the process of creativity and its various stages, while some research has been concerned with the outcomes of creativity (in other words, its products). Another strand has considered the environment emphasising social and cultural influences in the development and expression of creativity. Hennessey and Amabile (1988) describe creativity as the process of being original to suit a particular purpose, while others have viewed creativity as the process by which normal cognitive processes lead to a moment of insight in order to discover or produce something new (Perkins, 1981). Torrance (1988) argues that a key component of creativity is the ability to generate something novel or unique, while Guilford (1967) proposed that at the heart of creativity is divergent thinking—the ability to generate new information or solutions from given information. The goal of divergent thinking is to generate as many associations or solutions as possible without relying on guidelines or constraints (Gibson et al., 2009).

There have been many approaches to assessing creativity. For example, Csíkszentmihályi (1996) studied the characteristics of individuals judged to have made significant creative contributions to society. Simonton (1997) differentiated between Big C creativity, which is said to occur when a person solves a problem or creates an object that has a major impact on society, while Little C creativity is seen on a daily basis when someone adapts to change or comes up with new ways of understanding a problem. A measure of Little C divergent thinking is Guilford's (1967) alternative uses task, in which participants list several possible creative uses for common household items, such as a newspaper, a brick or a paperclip. There are no correct answers and participants have to produce as many unique and creative uses as they can.

Domain-specific theories of creativity emphasise the non-transferability of expertise from one creative domain to another (Baer, 2015). These theories are supported by findings that creative individuals are rarely creative in more than a few domains—for instance, an individual known for their creativity in physics is rarely also renowned for their creativity as a musician (Kaufman and Baer, 2004; Baer, 2012). There are also low correlations between an individuals' creative output in different domains (Baer, 1991). Domain-specific theories are consistent with evidence that Big C creativity—ideas that represent a huge leap forward in a field—require specific knowledge and skills in a domain, which in turn requires extensive practice and learning. In contrast, domain-general theories emphasise the generalisability of creative thinking across different domains (Hong and Milgram, 2020). The domain-general view is supported by personality studies, which suggest that there is a creative personality type (Martindale and Daily, 1996; Feist, 1998; Batey and Furnham, 2006) and evidence that when people express themselves in different creative domains, these outputs bear a recognisable style (Gabora et al., 2012).

Attempting to address this issue, Root-Bernstein (2001) focused on scientists who had been musicians and on the ways that they had used their musical knowledge to inform their scientific work. Root-Bernstein argued that music and science are two ways of using a common set of tools for thinking that unify all disciplines. He explored the notion that creative individuals are usually polymaths who think in ways which cross disciplines. Increasingly, scholars are taking a less dichotomous view of creativity, which incorporates both domain-specific and domain-general elements (Kaufman and Baer, 2004b; Gabora, 2017). Some mechanisms for this cross-domain creativity have been suggested and tested in empirical studies: for instance, Palmiero and colleagues (2016; 2019). Even if creative individuals tend to express themselves in one domain, this does not necessarily mean that prior phases of their creative process are domain-specific. For instance, Root-Bernstein (2001) demonstrated how artistic ideas can stimulate creativity in scientists, while Scotney and colleagues (2019) demonstrated how influences for creativity can come from diverse sources. They conducted two studies—one with 151 creative experts recruited over the internet, the other with 463 undergraduate students from diverse academic backgrounds. Participants listed their creative outputs, the things that had influenced them and the sources of inspiration associated with each of these outputs. These were then categorised into groups: within subject domain and outside subject domain. In both studies, cross-domain influences on creativity were found to be widespread, and indeed more frequent than within domain sources of inspiration. These results demonstrate that, even if individuals primarily express their creativity in a single domain, they are often employing cross-domain thinking when they are engaged in creative activities.

Neurological Studies of Creativity

One strand of research has explored the neurological basis of creativity; for instance,

Limb and Braun (2008) studied the neural substrates of spontaneous musical performance in jazz improvisation using functional MRI. They found that improvisation, compared to the production of over-learned musical sequences, was consistently characterised by a dissociated pattern of activity in the prefrontal cortex, and extensive deactivation of dorsolateral prefrontal and lateral orbital regions with focal activation of the medial prefrontal cortex. This may reflect a combination of the psychological processes required for spontaneous improvisation, in which internally motivated, stimulus-independent behaviours unfold in the absence of central processes that typically mediate self-monitoring and conscious volitional control of ongoing performance. Changes in prefrontal activity during improvisation were accompanied by widespread activation of neocortical sensorimotor areas that mediate the organisation and execution of musical performance, as well as deactivation of limbic structures that regulate motivation and emotional tone. This distributed neural pattern may provide a cognitive context that enables the emergence of spontaneous creative activity. Similarly, Liu and colleagues (2012) used functional MRI to study the neural correlates of creativity using freestyle rap, a multidimensional form of creativity at the interface of music and language. Participants were scanned while they performed two tasks, each of which used an identical eight-bar musical background track, a spontaneous, improvised freestyle rap and a conventional performance of an overlearned, well-rehearsed set of lyrics. Task contrast analyses indicated that improvised performance was characterised by dissociated activity in medial and dorsolateral prefrontal cortices, providing a context in which stimulus-independent behaviours may unfold in the absence of conscious monitoring and volitional control. Connectivity analyses revealed widespread improvisation-related correlations between the medial prefrontal, cingulate motor and perisylvian cortices, and the amygdala, suggesting the emergence of a network linking motivation, language, affect and movement. Lyrical improvisation appeared to be characterised by altered relationships between regions coupling intention and action, in which conventional executive control may be bypassed and motor control directed by cingulate motor mechanisms. These functional reorganisations may facilitate the initial improvisatory phase of creative behaviour. Freestyle rap was compared to conventional rehearsed performance, using functional magnetic resonance imaging. The results showed activation of medial and deactivation of dorsolateral cortices, which may provide a context in which self-generated action is freed from the conventional constraints of supervisory attention and executive control, facilitating the generation of novel ideas. Altered relationships within the prefrontal cortex appeared to have widespread functional consequences, affecting motivation, emotion, language as well as motor control. These may generalise to other forms of spontaneous creative behaviour.

Gibson and colleagues (2009) compared classical music students with other similar students on behavioural tasks using near infrared spectroscopy, which uses the near infrared region of the electromagnetic spectrum from 780 nm to 2500 nm. The findings showed that the musicians had increased convergent and divergent thinking compared with non-musicians, while the infrared spectroscopy revealed that they had greater bilateral frontal activity. It may be that non-musicians rely more on the left hemisphere when undertaking divergent thinking than musicians. Using fMRI de Aquino and colleagues (2019) found that there was a different role for the supplementary motor area and the insula between musicians and non-musicians in a controlled musical creativity task. During a rhythmic improvisation task, musicians showed greater activation of the motor supplementary area, the anterior cingulate cortex, the dorsolateral prefrontal cortex and the insula, along with greater deactivation of the default mode network in comparison with non-musicians. There was also a positive correlation between time improvising and the activation of the supplementary motor area in the musicians, while in the non-musicians improvisation time correlated with the activation of the insula. It appears that for musicians the supplementary motor area plays a role in the representation and execution of musical behaviour, while for non-musicians the insula plays a role in the processing of novel musical information. The findings also showed that there were no correlations between a general creativity score, brain activity and performance on the magnetic resonance task. The absence of these correlations suggests that musical creativity, both from a cerebral and behavioural point of view, is specific to the musical field, and not related to creativity capacities in more general domains.

Correlational and Comparative Research on Musicians

One strand of research has compared the performance of musicians and non-musicians on tests of creativity. For instance, in research with higher education musicians and engineers, Charyton and Snelbecker (2007) found that the musicians scored higher on general and artistic creativity, but that there were no significant differences in scientific creativity. The musicians had statistically higher levels of measured general creativity, creative attributes, creative temperament, and cognitive risk tolerance. Similarly, Gibson and colleagues (2009) compared classical music students with other similar students. The musicians scored higher on creativity tasks, including a version of Guilford's (1967) alternative uses task, than non-musicians, while infrared spectroscopy revealed greater bilateral frontal activity in the musicians.

Palmiero and colleagues (2019) studied the relationship between musical expertise which did not involve improvisation training, and divergent thinking. Expert and self-taught musicians were tested in musical, verbal and visual divergent thinking, and were compared with a group of non-musicians in verbal and visual divergent thinking. The musical task required participants to generate different pieces of music, using Happy Birthday as a starting point. The verbal task required participants to list unusual uses for a cardboard box, while the visual task asked them to complete drawings, adding details to basic stimuli. Fluency, flexibility and originality scores were measured for each task. Overall, the expert musicians showed higher creative scores in musical and verbal domains than self-taught musicians. On verbal creative tests, they performed better than non-musicians. No group difference was found in relation to the visual creative task. Musical expertise enhanced not only musical divergent thinking but also verbal divergent thinking. This effect seemed to be specifically supported by formal musical training. Similarly, Sovansky and colleagues (2014) investigated how level of musical expertise and engagement in the creation of music related to divergent thinking in musically trained adults. Sixty participants of varying musical expertise were tested for divergent thinking using a modified version of the alternative uses task, in which participants listed creative uses for two music items and two non-music items. The findings showed that the musicians who created music listed more creative uses for music items than non-musicians, and musicians who did not create music. For non-music items, there were no differences in divergent thinking.

Kleinmintz and colleagues (2014) adopted a different approach, comparing the performance on divergent thinking tasks of three groups of musicians—36 trained in improvisation, 40 not trained in improvisation and a group of non-musicians. Participants were shown a list of five common objects—shoe, button, stapler, drinking glass and cardboard box—and were asked to list as many alternative uses as possible for each object within a period of ten minutes, while trying to think of original uses. Participants were also instructed to evaluate deviance by rating each item on a five-point rating scale, ranging from not at all deviant to highly deviant. The improvisation group scored higher on fluency and originality compared to the other two groups. The authors concluded that deliberate practice of improvisation enhanced creativity. In the non-improvisation group, all of the participants reported playing classical music as well as other styles. The improvisation group was much more diverse in the styles they played, with more than a quarter reporting playing jazz. The findings of this study suggested that musicians who are trained in improvisation are more creative than both musicians without improvisation training and non-musicians.

High school and university music students have been shown to score higher on tests of creativity than non-music majors, this being particularly marked in those with more than ten years of music education (Hamann et al., 1990). Hamann and colleagues (1991) assessed creativity among 144 high-school students to determine whether any significant differences existed between creativity scores, taking account of gender, grade point average and varying degrees of participation in the arts. No significant differences were found among the creativity scores of participants by gender, jazz experience, visual art experience or combined arts experience. Almost all of the variation could be attributed to the influence of grade point average. Significant creative mean score differences, however, were found in relation to participants' musical experience and theatre experience after the influence of grade point average as a covariate was considered. There were no differences between music students and those working in other areas of the arts. However, the greater the musical expertise as assessed by the number of units of music classes taken, the greater the creativity. Students with more than ten years of music education had higher creativity scores than those with fewer than ten years of experience (Hamann et al., 1991). Working with 173 high-school music students and 45 non-music students, Simpson (1969) found that the music students scored higher on several elements of the Guildford tests of creativity.

Working with younger children in Grades Two, Four and Six, Kiehn (2003) compared music improvisation. Eighty-nine randomly selected participants were given two measures of creativity: the Vaughan Test of Musical Creativity and the Torrance Test of Creative Thinking. Two independent judges scored responses on the Vaughan test to determine music improvisational creativity. A significant grade-level difference emerged for music creativity scores, with Grade Two students scoring significantly lower than Grade Four and Six students. This suggests that there may be a musical creativity growth stage between Grades Two to Four, followed by a levelling off, as there were no significant changes in test scores between Grade Four and Six. A weak but statistically significant correlation was found between music creativity and figural creativity.

The Personality of Musicians and Creativity

Domain-general theories of creativity emphasise the generalisability of creative thinking across different domains, suggesting that creativity can transfer across domains (Hong and Milgram, 2010). Personality research supports this, suggesting that there may be a creative personality type (Batey and Furnham, 2006; Feist, 1998; Martindale and Daily, 1996). Additionally, when individuals express themselves in different creative domains, the outputs often have a recognisable style (Gabora et al., 2012). Hughes and colleagues (2013) studied the relationship between personality and self-rated creativity in 222 participants who completed a multidimensional measure of self-estimated creativity, a self-rated personal characteristics questionnaire and a Big Five personality measure. Trait openness predicted all measures of self-estimated creativity. Similarly, Dollinger and colleagues (2004) studied the relationship between personality measures and creativity in 150 college students who completed a test of creative thinking, an inventory of past creative accomplishments and the Big Five personality test. A creative personality adjective check list related to most creativity measures, as did the Big Five 'openness to experience' measure. The findings from the latter were particularly compelling. Together, these studies suggest that there is a general personality characteristic which is related to creativity.

Some research has shown that musicians tend to have personalities with high levels of openness to experience, which means that they have the potential to be creative. Supporting this, Corrigall and colleagues (2013), in a study of 118 adults and 167 ten- to twelve-year-old children, collected demographic information, measured aspects of cognitive ability and administered the Big Five personality test. The findings showed that the personality characteristic 'openness' was associated with duration of musical involvement. Exploring this issue with different types of musicians, Benedek and colleagues (2014) researched 120 college students studying jazz, classical or folk music. They collected data about their musical practice and attainment, and their personalities. The jazz musicians showed higher levels of divergent thinking, were engaged in more creative musical activities and had higher levels of achievement in those activities. The classical musicians spent a great deal of time practising and won more competitions, while the folk musicians were more extroverted. The jazz musicians showed higher ideational creativity as measured by divergent thinking tasks, and tended to be more open to new experiences than the classical musicians. Overall, the jazz musicians showed particularly high creativity with respect to domain-specific musical accomplishments and also in terms of domain-general indicators of divergent thinking ability. This may be related to differences in the formal and informal ways of practising and learning adopted by different musical groups, with jazz musicians attaching more importance to informal practice while placing a lower value on technical perfection and competitions. It may be that individual differences in creative potential may be relevant for the realisation of domain-specific creative activities and achievements (in this case, musical improvisation).

As well as researching personality differences between sub-groups of musicians according to types of employment and instrument group, Vaag and colleagues (2018) investigated differences in personality traits between professional musicians and the general workforce. In 2013, 1,600 members of the Norwegian Musicians' Union answered a questionnaire regarding type of employment, instrument group and a shortened version of the Big Five personality inventory. Their responses were compared to a sample of 6,372 of the general Norwegian workforce, who answered the same personality questionnaire in the Norwegian Generation and Gender Survey of 2007. The findings showed that the musicians displayed higher degrees of 'openness to experience' than the general workforce. This was especially evident among freelance musicians and those who combined freelance work with employment. Within instrument groups, the vocalists scored highest on 'openness to experience'. Similarly, Gjermunds and colleagues (2020) investigated the Big Five personality traits in 509 musicians and 201 non-musicians, and found that the musicians had significantly higher scores on 'openness' than the non-musicians. This was the most typical personality trait for musicians. Focusing on rock and popular musicians, Gillespie and Myors (2000) examined the personality characteristics of 100 rock and popular musicians aged 17 to 49 years old who completed self-report versions of a personality inventory and questionnaires about their musical background. The group as a whole scored significantly above the norm on 'openness'. No background factors—such as instrument played, type of music performed, time spent playing, level of musicianship or commercial success—moderated these findings.

Yondem and colleagues (2017) compared music and art students, and found no differences between the groups in 'openness', while Sandgren (2018) found that musicians did not score more highly on measures of 'openness' than non-musicians.

Intervention Studies

Major national reports on the arts have emphasised their importance in developing a range of transferable skills, including those related to creativity and critical thinking (NACCCE, 1999). This evidence, while demonstrating a relationship between musical skills and creativity, does not address the issue of causality. This requires intervention research, where controls are compared with those participating in musical activities before and after the intervention. There are few intervention studies focusing on the impact of active music-making on general measured creativity.

In an early study, Wolff (1979) studied the effects of 30 minutes of daily music instruction for an entire year on first-graders. Those participating exhibited significant increases in creativity and in perceptual motor skills, compared with controls. Similarly, Kalmar (1982) studied the effects of singing and musical-group play twice weekly for three years on preschool children of three to four years of age, and found that these children scored higher than controls on creativity, had higher levels of abstraction and showed greater creativity in improvised puppet play.

Passanisia and colleagues (2014) conducted a study to determine whether participation in a group musical activity would enhance interpersonal relationships and creativity in nine-year-old students to a significantly greater degree than no participation in musical activities. Performances on the Williams Creative Thinking Test (WCTT) and a test of interpersonal relationships in two class groups—a musical group of 36 and a non-musical group of 32—were compared by measuring changes in pre- and post-test data. The results indicated that the experimental group, compared with the control group, made significant gains in scores for imagination and in interpersonal relationships, particularly with peers. Focusing on improvisation, Lewis and Lovatt

(2013) carried out two experiments and showed that 20 minutes of verbal or musical improvisation significantly improved scores of divergent thinking, as assessed by the alternative uses task. They also showed that novel generation of music increased scores more than playing learned melodies. The development of creative skills seems to be particularly dependent on the type of musical engagement. This is supported by Koutsoupidou and Hargreaves (2009,) who compared two matched groups of six-year-olds over a period of six months. The music lessons for the experimental group were enriched with a variety of improvisatory activities, while those in the control group did not include any improvisation, but were didactic and teacher-centred. Children in the experimental group were offered opportunities to experience improvisation through their voices, their bodies and musical instruments. Webster's Measure of Creative Thinking in Music was administered before and after the six-month teaching programme, to assess children's creative thinking in terms of four musical parameters: extensiveness, flexibility, originality and syntax. The analysis revealed that improvisation significantly improved the development of creative thinking. In particular, it promoted musical flexibility, originality and syntax in children's music-making. Similarly, Sowden and colleagues (2015) focused on the potential for simple, arts-based improvisation activities to enhance divergent thinking skills and creativity in primary-school-aged children. They undertook two experiments. In the first, they compared the effect of children taking part in an improvised versus non-improvised dance class on their subsequent performance on the instances task and on a creative toy design task. In the second experiment, children took part in verbal and acting improvisation games or in matched control games before completing a figural activity. In both experiments, children who took part in the improvisation interventions showed better divergent thinking and creativity.

Fritz and colleagues (2020) attempted to see if making music and physical exercise combined would be beneficial for divergent thinking. They investigated the relationship of physical exertion and being in control of music on divergent thinking, wondering whether there was an interaction effect. Seventy-seven young German participants were tested with measurements of divergent thinking, collected after either physical exercise with music listening, making music without physical effort or undertaking physical exercise with musical feedback. In the music feedback exercise condition, each exercise machine was modified with a movement sensor, which continually transmitted its position to a computer that modified musical material to create musical feedback (Fritz et al., 2013b) based on the current position of the sensor. This effectively transformed each machine into an analogue for a musical instrument. The music produced included harmonically and rhythmically complex components and was described as experimental electronic music. Participants completed three questionnaires assessing demographic information: an alternative uses task, perceived musical control, mood and feelings of being in touch with the music, and perceived creativity. The experiment demonstrated that the music feedback exercise condition significantly increased the participants' scores in the alternative uses task. No effects on divergent thinking were observed for the physical exercise with music listening and music control-only conditions.

Investigating whether background music would have an impact on creative performance, Ritter and Ferguson (2017) tested whether listening to specific pieces of music (four classical music excerpts systematically varying on valence and arousal), as compared to a silence control condition would facilitate divergent and convergent creativity. Creativity was higher for participants who listened to classical music which was high on arousal and positive mood while performing a divergent creativity task, than for participants who performed the task in silence. No effect of music was found for convergent creativity.

Creativity in Later Life

There is much research considering the impact of creative musical activity on wellbeing in later life. Despite this, there is relatively little research considering whether engaging with musical activities specifically enhances creativity more generally. An exception to this is research which has studied song-writing activities. Such studies have reported a range of positive findings relating to wellbeing (Creech et al., 2020). Baker and Ballantyne (2013) found that group song-writing among older adult retirees not only promoted happiness, meaningfulness and engagement, but was perceived to enhance their creativity more broadly.

Although musical creativity can continue throughout the lifespan, it can also develop for the first time in later life. For instance, Varvarigou and colleagues (2013) reported that a 90-year-old with no previous musical training participating in a community music project wrote a song with support from a musical expert, which was subsequently performed publicly.

Reviews and Meta-Analyses

Compared with other areas of research, there have been relatively few reviews relating to the role of music in enhancing creativity. Running (2008) drew no firm conclusions, concluding that more research was needed, while Loui and Guetta (2019) argued that music performance requires perceptual processing (bottom-up and top-down), attention and the integration of executive functions, while creativity entails unconstrained thought processes that yield novel output. They argued that considering these seemingly disparate aspects of cognitive function in tandem might promote a more cohesive conceptualisation of music within cognitive science more generally.

Overview

The evidence shows that musicians as a whole tend to score higher than non-musicians on tests of creativity and on the personality characteristic of 'openness', which is related to creativity. Those whose musical activities are creative, for instance improvisation or composition, tend to respond most positively. However, this does not mean that actively engaging with music enhances creativity. It may be that those who tend towards openness are drawn to those musical activities which require creativity. There is little evidence from intervention research suggesting that making music improves creativity, unless the musical activities themselves are creative in nature. This has implications for music education.

10. General Attainment

There has been considerable research exploring the relationship between actively making music and academic attainment. Most has been correlational in nature, although there are some intervention studies. Researching the impact of musical activity on academic attainment is extremely challenging for a range of reasons. For instance, it may be that not all areas of academic achievement are affected equally by the various ways that music may impact on learning in children and young people. Interactive models are needed to begin to unravel the complexity. One such is Bronfenbrenner's bio-ecological model (Bronfenbrenner and Morris, 2006). This takes account of the interactions between process, person, context and time. In the case of music, this means considering the length of time engaged with music learning, the demands of the musical training, the characteristics of the individual, the immediate learning environment and the broader social environment which the individual inhabits. Research must also take account of the different types of attainment outcomes, general attainment or attainment in particular, subject domains and the nature of the musical activities engaged with and their quality. This implies the need for complex statistical analysis, which can take account of the interactions between these. Earlier chapters have explored the impact on literacy and numeracy and visual and auditory competence. This chapter mainly focuses on attainment across several subjects.

Correlation and Comparative Studies

Kinney (2008) examined sixth- and eighth-grade urban middle-school students' achievement test scores in fourth grade and during sixth- or eighth-grade enrolment in a performing group. Ensemble participation, band, choir or none, as well as socioeconomic status and home environment, were included. Fourth- and sixth-grade achievement tests consisted of reading, mathematics, citizenship and science, while eighth-grade tests included reading, mathematics, social studies, science, and language arts (reading, writing, listening, speaking, viewing and visual representation). Analyses indicated significant differences for socioeconomic status and ensemble participation. Higher socioeconomic status students scored significantly higher on all subtests except fourth-, sixth- and eighth-grade reading. Sixth-grade band students scored significantly higher than choir students and non-participants on every subtest of sixth- and fourth-grade achievement tests. Eighth-grade band students scored significantly higher than non-participants on fourth-grade reading and mathematics and every subtest of the eighth-grade achievement test except social studies. Similar results for both cohorts suggested that playing in a band may attract higher achieving students from the outset, and that test score differences remained stable over time rather than being enhanced by musical activities.

In India, Swaminathan and Gopinath (2013) examined the English second-language abilities of musically trained and untrained primary-school children. Participants were tested on the verbal subscales of an intelligence test designed for Indian children and an English word reading test. The musically trained participants performed significantly better on tests of comprehension and vocabulary. This persisted when comparisons were made with an untrained group. Taking account of more academic subjects, in Hong Kong, Tai and colleagues (2018) investigated the relationship between the extent and outcome of Hong Kong students' musical training, their perceptions of the value of the subjects they studied and their academic achievement. A total of 286 students in Primary Grades Four, Five and Six from a single school reported the extent and outcome of their musical training, including the number of instruments they studied, the number of years spent training and the highest grade and level achieved. The findings showed that music training positively predicted academic achievement in Chinese, English and mathematics. Similarly, Yang and colleagues (2014) examined the relationship between long-term music training and child development based on 250 Chinese elementary school students' academic development of first and second language and mathematics. The findings showed that musician children outperformed non-musician children only on musical achievement and second-language development. Although music training was correlated with children's final academic development of first and second language and mathematics, it did not independently contribute to the development of first language or mathematical skills.

Focusing on attainment across all school subjects, Wetter and colleagues (2009), in a retrospective study, compared the school performance of 53 children engaged in active music-making with 67 controls not engaged in music-making. Overall average marks, as well as the average marks of all school subjects except sport, were significantly higher in children who actively engaged in making music than those who did not. In a multiple regression analysis, musical training, parents' income, and educational level correlated significantly with overall average marks. A slight decrease in overall average marks over four years from Grades Three to Six was found in the control group, while musical training appeared to help maintain school performance at a high level over time.

Schellenberg (2006) studied the relationship between music lessons, intelligence and academic performance in two studies. The first examined the relationship of music lessons to intelligence, academic achievement and social adjustment in six- to eleven-year-olds, while the second examined the association between childhood music lessons and academic achievement in 150 undergraduates. The findings showed music lessons were associated with academic achievement in both studies. Greater exposure to music lessons in childhood was associated with higher scores on a measure of academic achievement, higher elementary school and high school grade point average. These associations held even after taking into account parental education, family income and study participants' involvement in non-musical out-of-school activities.

In England, Hallam and Rogers (2016) drew on nationally available data on attainment at age 11 and 16 relating to 608 students, 115 of whom played a musical instrument to explore the impact of music training on academic progress between ages 11 and 16. The findings showed that the young people playing an instrument showed greater progress and better academic outcomes than those who did not. The impact was greater the longer a young person had been engaged in playing an instrument. The instrumentalists performed at nearly one standard deviation better on almost all measures than those who did not play an instrument at age 16, despite there being negligible differences at age 11. Those who had been learning for four or five years had the best results. When multiple regression analyses were undertaken, length of time playing an instrument was a better predictor than attainment in English at age 11 to a total points score calculated across all examination subjects and the total number of points scored from performance in the best eight examinations at age 16. Playing an instrument made a statistically significant contribution to performance at age 16 across all measures. The musicians showed greater progress between the two examinations than non-musicians. Those who had been learning for the longest period of time made the greatest progress. Also considering the influence of music on progression over time, dos Santos and colleagues (2015) analysed the academic performance of music and non music students from seventh to ninth grade controlling for socioeconomic status, intelligence, motivation and prior academic achievement. Data were collected from 110 adolescents at two time points, once when the students were between eleven and fourteen years old in the seventh grade, and again three years later. The findings showed that music students performed better academically than non music students in the seventh grade and in the ninth grade. This difference was particularly evident in scores in Portuguese language and natural science. The difference was weaker in history and geography and least pronounced in mathematics and English. A longitudinal analysis revealed better academic performance by music students after controlling for prior academic achievement indicating greater progress between the two assessment points. This change remained when intelligence, socioeconomic status and motivation were controlled for.

Not all of the research has had such clear cut results. For instance, Schneider and Klotz (2000) compared the impact of enrolment in music performance classes, band or choir, athletic extracurricular activities or no such activities on the academic achievement of 346 students in grades five through nine. The participating schools adopted a cross section of different types of music programmes. The results showed that although the mean scores for the musicians were higher than the non musicians and non athletes, participation in music was not a conclusive factor in predicting statistically higher academic scores than the other groups, although the musicians did score higher than the athletes and over time this gap widened. The findings indicated that factors other than enrolment in a performing music class affected the outcomes. The findings also indicated an overall drop in standardized test scores in the ninth grade for most students that was not seen for student musicians.

Large-Scale Research

A considerable amount of research has been based on large statewide or national datasets. The evidence from correlation studies in the USA has shown that students who participate in music education do better than their peers on many measures of academic achievement. For instance, using statewide data, Abeles (2007) reported that groups of second grade children who participated in a weekly violin programme having three lessons every two weeks outperformed non violin group controls in performance on mathematics and language arts tests. Morrison (1994) using data from the National Centre for Educational Statistics representing over 13,000 students showed that high school students who participated in music reported higher grades in English, mathematics, history, and science than those who did not participate. Similar outcomes have been reported by Cardarelli (2003), Fitzpatrick (2006) and Trent (1996). A number of doctoral theses have also supported these findings (Cobb, 1997; Gregory. 1988; Miranda, 2001; Schneider, 2000; Underwood, 2000; Zanutto, 1997).

In China, Yang (2015) investigated whether music participation related to academic achievement within the context of representative population level data that adjusted for an array of socio demographic factors as well as early academic achievement. The impact of music practice on educational outcomes was analysed using multivariate regression and individual fixed effects. The findings suggested that childhood musical activity, either playing an instrument or singing, related positively to educational achievements in adolescence. The magnitude and significance of the estimated music coefficients for different music indicators was robust when increasing the amount of individual and family control variables but the size of the music estimates decreased when the effect of parental education, other leisure activities and previous educational achievements were held constant.

In the USA, Fitzpatrick (2006) studied 15,431 students attending Columbus public schools in Ohio and compared the performance on a statewide test of academic attainment of instrumental music students and their non instrumental classmates. The students were in fourth, sixth and ninth grades. Students of like socioeconomic status were compared on their performance on tests of citizenship, mathematics, science and reading. The findings showed that instrumental students outperformed non-instrumental students in every subject and at every grade level. Instrumental students at both levels of socioeconomic status had higher scores than their non-instrumental classmates from the fourth grade, suggesting that instrumental music programmes attracted higher scorers from the outset of instruction. However, the findings also showed a pattern of increased achievement by lower socioeconomic status instrumental students, who surpassed their higher socioeconomic status non-instrumental classmates by the ninth grade in all subjects. Similarly, Thorton (2013) conducted a statewide comparison of test scores for students involved in voluntary music classes or ensembles, and students not involved in such activities. Scores from almost 7,000 students in the three grades tested by the state (Grades Five, Eight and Eleven) were included. Significantly higher scores were found for students involved in music compared with students not involved. It would seem that the additional time spent in music activities did not disadvantage students academically. Also using statewide data, some research has focused on students who participate in statewide ensembles. For instance, Henry and Braucht (2007) found that the most successful young musicians in the USA who participated in statewide ensembles also had higher SAT scores than state averages.

Southgate and Roscigno (2009), using two national data sets (ECLS-K (20,000 US kindergarten students) and NELS:88 (25,000 adolescents)) and three measures of music participation—in school, outside school and parental involvement in the form of concert attendance—found that music involvement varied systematically by class and gender. Involvement had implications for both mathematics and reading achievement for young children and adolescents, and associations between music and achievement persisted even when prior achievement was taken into account. There was evidence of social class variation within school music involvement in adolescents but not in early childhood, while the effects of class on parental music involvement were strong and consistent in both samples. As a mediator of educational outcomes, music involvement was significant for both mathematics and reading achievement. It generally increased achievement levels, although the gains were not distributed equally among all students: a white student advantage existed. This may relate to the type of musical activity engaged in and the opportunities afforded to the students for performance, which may contribute to enhanced self-esteem and increased motivation.

Working with young children and their families in Australia, Williams and colleagues (2015) investigated parent-child home music activities in a sample of 3031 children participating in the programme Growing Up in Australia: The Longitudinal Study of Australian Children. Frequency of shared home music activities was reported by parents when children were two to three years old, and outcomes were measured by parent and teacher report and direct testing two years later (when children were four to five years old). A series of regression analyses controlling for sociodemographic variables found frequency of shared home music activities to have a small significant partial association with measures of children's vocabulary, numeracy, book-reading and shared home music activities. Frequency of shared home music activities maintained small partial associations with measures of attention and numeracy.

Not all of the evidence from large-scale studies has shown positive outcomes for music tuition; for instance, Elpus (2013) examined the college entrance examination scores of music and non-music students in the United States, drawing data from the Education Longitudinal Study of 2002 (a nationally representative education study). Analyses of high-school transcript data showed that 1.127 million students graduated high school having earned at least one course credit in music. Fixed effects regression procedures were used to compare standardised test scores of these music students with their non-music peers, while controlling for demography, prior academic achievement, time use and attitudes toward school. The findings indicated that music students did not outperform non-music students on standard assessment tests once systematic differences had been controlled for statistically. This pattern of results remained consistent and robust through internal replications with another standardised mathematics test, and when disaggregating music students by the type of music studied. Similarly, Miksza (2007)—using data from National Education Longitudinal Study of 1988 and a sample of 5,335—created a composite item which assessed student participation in music for the entire duration of the study from eighth to twelfth grade, and measured academic achievement in mathematics, reading comprehension, science and social studies. There were significant differences for all subtests in the initial testing in favour of those who had participated in a band, choir or orchestra, but rates of change in mathematics, science or social studies were no greater for the music participants, and in reading achievement the music participants increased more slowly than non-participants. In a later study, Miszka (2010), using data from the Educational Longitudinal Study of 2002 and multilevel modelling, was able to take account of a wide range of individual factors including socioeconomic status, minority status, peer influence and music participation and school level factors, including the number of music teachers. Outcome variables were standardised mathematics scores, a composite community ethics score which included strong friendships, helping people in the community and working to correct social and economic inequalities, and a composite school commitment variable including late arrival, skipping class and absence from school. Music participation was related to all outcome variables after controlling for all individual and school-level factors. Students in high-school music ensembles were more likely to have higher standardised mathematics achievement scores, be more concerned about community ethics and be more committed to school.

A study in Germany by Hille and Schupp (2013) used the German socioeconomic panel study longitudinal data to establish the impact of musical training on attainment. The database included a detailed assessment of the intensity and duration of music activities for representative youth cohorts, school results and allowed consideration of a wide range of parental characteristics. The findings on attainment at age 17, taking account of a wide range of individual and family characteristics, showed that children playing an instrument from age eight to seventeen who had taken lessons outside school scored one-sixth of a standard deviation higher than children not playing an instrument. Similarly, in Canada, Gouzouasis and colleagues (2007) found a positive relationship between music achievement in Grade 11 and academic achievement in Grade 12 courses among a representative dataset comprising over 50,000 secondary school students in British Columbia.

Taking account of prior attainment, and thus able to focus on progress, Guhn and colleagues (2020) carried out a multilevel mixed model analysis in British Columbia, Canada of 112,916 students in Grades Seven to Twelve. They compared the mean examination grades of 15,483 students who took school music courses, with 97,433 who took none. Across all courses, English, science and mathematics students who took school music courses had significantly higher raw mean examination grades than students who took no music courses. Mean differences ranged from 4.69 in English to 6.41 in science. Results from the multilevel model, after adjusting for previous academic achievement and socio demographic covariates, cultural background, and neighbourhood showed that exam grade means across all academic subjects were significantly higher for those who took music relative to students who took no music. The adjusted mean differences in grades ranged from 2.47 for English, to 3.76 for science. Comparisons were made between the type of music engagement, instrumental or vocal and academic achievement. Throughout secondary school, Grades ten to twelve the results indicated that differences between the examination means of students who took no school music and those who took school music significantly differed by the type of school music. A significant interaction for music participation, type of music, was observed for all outcomes, English in Grades 10 and 12, science in Grade 10, and mathematics in Grade 10. The students who took instrumental music courses had significantly higher examination mean scores than students who took vocal music courses, across all academic subjects. The instrumental versus vocal music differences in mean examination grades were particularly pronounced for mathematics and science in Grade 10, compared with English in Grades 10 and 12. Additionally, compared with students who took no music classes, students who took vocal music as well as students who took instrumental music had, on average, significantly higher examination means. The vocal music students had examination means that were between 0.80 and 1.40 higher than students who took no music. Students who took instrumental music had examination means that were between 3.10 in Grade 10

English and 5.11 in Grade 10 mathematics, higher than students who took no music. Grades in vocal and instrumental school music classes predicted academic achievement regression results, indicating significant and positive linear associations between grades in vocal, instrumental school music classes and academic grades, adjusting for covariates. The results indicated that associations of music grades with academic achievement examination scores significantly varied by type of school music (solely vocal or solely instrumental) as the interaction between music, grades and type of music was significant for all subjects, English at Grades 10 and 12, science at Grade 10 and mathematics at Grade 10. For vocal music, each one-unit increase in overall mean music vocal grade was associated with predicted increases in examination means in all subjects, ranging from 0.19 for English Grade 10 to 0.38 for mathematics Grade 10. Such associations between music grades and academic examination scores were significantly higher for overall mean instrumental music grades, with coefficients ranging from 0.26 for English Grade 10 to 0.50 for mathematics Grade 10. Higher levels of music engagement, as assessed by the number of courses taken, was related to higher examination scores in all subjects. This pattern was more pronounced for very high engagement in instrumental music, with medium effect sizes compared with vocal music where there were small effect sizes. The effect sizes of these group differences were greater than the effect sizes corresponding to average annual gains in students' academic achievement during high school. In other words, highly engaged instrumental music students were, on average, academically over one year ahead of their peers. The positive relationships between music engagement and academic achievement were independent of students' previous, Grade 7 achievement, sex, cultural background and neighbourhood socioeconomic status, and were of considerable magnitude. The findings suggest that multi-year engagement in music, especially instrumental music, may benefit high school academic achievement.

Although the quality of the music teaching is clearly important in whether music has an impact on academic attainment, relatively little research has taken account of this. An exception is the work of Johnson and Memmott (2006), who studied 4,739 elementary and middle-school students from four states in the USA and showed a strong relationship between third- and fourth-grade students' academic achievement and their participation in music programmes. Analysis of elementary school data indicated that students in exemplary music education programmes scored higher on both English and mathematics standardised tests than their counterparts who did not have this high-quality instruction, although the effect sizes were very small. Analysis of middle-school data indicated that for both English and mathematics, students in exceptional music programmes and deficient instrumental programmes scored better than those who had no music classes or poor-quality choral programmes. The effect sizes were moderate. Overall, the higher the quality of the programme, the higher the academic attainment.

In the USA, exploring issues related to college entrance, Kaufman and Gabler (2004) assessed cultural capital and the extracurricular activities of girls and boys in the college attainment process using data from the National Education Longitudinal Survey. They aimed to assess the specific causal role these activities played in the college attainment process. The research examined extracurricular activities in relation to two different levels of college attainment: enrolment in *any* four-year college or university, and enrolment in one of the nation's elite, or most selective universities. They found that, at the general college level, hands-on training in the arts appeared to improve students' chances of going to college by enhancing their human capital but not their cultural capital. In contrast, direct exposure to the arts did not appear to improve students' chances of going to an elite college, although having parents who were interested in the arts did.

Research with Disadvantaged Populations

Evidence from *El Sistema* and *Sistema*-inspired projects has indicated a positive impact of participating in musical activities on attainment. In the UK, where the programme is based in schools in deprived areas, Smithhurst (2011) reported that after one year of participation in the programme, children in Years One to Four in one school were achieving better scores in mathematics, reading and writing compared with their peers who were not involved. Ninety percent of the children were reaching target grades in maths compared with 68 percent not involved in the programme. Similar trends were evident in reading, with 85 percent of programme children reaching target grades compared with 62 percent not in the programme, and in writing, 65 percent compared with 45 percent. Burns and Bewick (2011) reported that after two years of participating in the programme where children engaged with music for 4.5 hours per week, 43 percent of the children had progressed more than four levels in maths, 53 percent in reading and 42 percent in writing compared with a national average of three levels, despite the fact that the participants included a high proportion of children with special educational needs. However, the rate of improvement slowed as participation continued. In a programme in Chile, Egaña de Sol (2008) showed a positive effect on academic attainment in verbal and mathematics skills. This was attributed in part to participants holding higher expectations of their academic achievements, although evaluations of other programmes in Chile had mixed results, with some programmes having positive results and others no impact (Evaluación de impacto programa prequestas juveniles e infantiles, 2010). Programmes in the USA have indicated increased academic attainment as an outcome of participation, with more children achieving roll of honour status, particularly where children participated for an extended period of time (Creech et al., 2013).

Creech and colleagues (2013), in their review of *El Sistema* and *Sistema*-inspired programmes, concluded that, with few exceptions, the studies demonstrate significant and steady improvement in academic attainment and achieving targets and, in some cases, outperforming comparison groups in maths, reading and writing. There is some evidence that these effects may be cumulative, related to prolonged engagement in the programmes (page 67).

Intervention Research

Most of the research exploring the links between participation in musical activities and attainment has been based on correlation analysis, which precludes the demonstration of causality, particularly as there are many possible confounding factors. There is also the possibility that music programmes may attract students who are already amongst the highest attaining (Arnett-Gary, 1998; Costa-Giomi, 2012; Harrison, 1990; Hodges and O'Connell, 2007; Klinedinst, 1991; Schellenberg,

2014; Shobo, 2001; Yoon, 2000). Overall, the evidence from correlation studies has shown that students who participate in music education tend to do better than their peers on many measures of academic achievement, although there are exceptions. To demonstrate causality requires intervention studies. There have been a small number of experimental studies on the effects of participation in music on general attainment. The findings have been mixed.

Several small-scale doctoral theses have focused on this issue, including Hoffman (1995). Legette (1993) found no effect of music instruction, while Hines (2000), studying students with learning difficulties from kindergarten through to ninth grade, found neither reading nor mathematics achievement was affected by type of music instruction, motoric or non-motoric. In another small-scale study, Cabanac and colleagues (2013) compared the performance of students who participated in a music programme in a single school in Canada with those who did not and found that the music students had consistently higher attainment in all subjects.

Merh and colleagues (2013) conducted two random controlled trials with preschool children investigating the cognitive effects of a brief series of music classes, as compared to a similar but non-musical form of arts instruction, visual arts classes or a no-treatment control. Consistent with typical preschool arts enrichment programmes, parents attended classes with their children, participating in a variety of developmentally appropriate arts activities. After six weeks of classes, children's skills in four distinct cognitive areas were assessed, in which older arts trained students had been reported to excel, spatial navigational reasoning, visual form analysis, numerical discrimination and receptive vocabulary. The findings showed initially that children from the music class showed greater spatial navigational ability than children from the visual arts class, while children from the visual arts class showed greater visual form analysis ability than children from the music class. However, a partial replication attempt comparing music training to a no-treatment control failed to confirm these findings, while the combined results of the two comparisons were negative. Overall, children provided with music classes performed no better than those with visual arts or no classes on any assessment.

Holochwost and colleagues (2017) examined whether music education was associated with improved performance on measures of academic achievement and executive functions with 265 school aged children in Grades 1 through 8. Fifty-eight percent were female, and 86 percent African-American. They were selected by lottery to participate in an out-of-school programme offering individual and large ensemble training on orchestral instruments. Measures of academic achievement, standardised test scores and grades in English language arts and mathematics were taken from participants' academic records. Executive functions were assessed through students' performance on a computerised battery of common executive function tasks. The findings indicated that, relative to controls, students in the music education programme scored higher on standardised tests, earned better grades in English language arts and mathematics, and exhibited superior performance on selected executive function tasks and short-term memory. Further analyses revealed that, although the largest differences in performance were observed between students in the control group and those who had received the music programme for two to three years, conditional effects were also observed on three executive function tasks for students who had been in the programme for one year.

Wallick (1998) examined the effects of a pullout string programme on student achievement in the writing, reading, mathematics, and citizenship sections of the Ohio Proficiency Test. One hundred and forty-eight fourth-grade string students and 148 fourth-grade non-string students from a southwestern Ohio city school district were ability-matched according to their performance on the verbal section of a cognitive abilities test. Scores on the Ohio Proficiency Test were then recorded and compared. The results revealed a significant difference in favour of the string students' achievement in reading and citizenship, although there were no significant differences between the two matched groups in writing or mathematics. Also in the USA, Barr and colleagues (2002) described a programme for the improvement of listening skills in order to increase academic performance. The sample consisted of elementary students in a middle-class community. The problem of ineffective listening skills was documented through data, revealing the number of students whose lowered academic performance was thought to be because of a deficiency in listening skills. Staff reported that students' weaknesses in effective listening skills negatively impacted on their academic performance. Three major categories of intervention were adopted: the direct teaching of effective listening skills, student ownership of self-monitoring, and the effects of using music in the classroom. Over the 16-week period of the interventions, the students showed a notable improvement in academic achievement.

Adopting drama as a comparison group, Haywood and colleagues (2015) evaluated the Act, Sing, Play programme which offered music and drama tuition to Year Two pupils. The aim of the programme was to evaluate whether music workshops had a greater impact than drama workshops in terms of pupils' mathematics and literacy attainment. The programme ran for one academic year; 909 pupils participated in 19 schools in England. In each participating Year Two class, pupils were randomly allocated to one of three groups: violin or cello workshops, singing lessons or drama workshops. Workshops were held once a week over 32 weeks. The findings provided no evidence that the music workshops had a greater impact on maths or literacy attainment than the drama workshops. This also applied to children from disadvantaged families.

An unusual study was undertaken by Schiltz (2016), who researched 93 highly gifted children and adolescents suffering from school failure at the beginning of adolescence. They were treated with an integrated form of music psychotherapy and verbal psychotherapy in five separate groups. The treatment combined active musical improvisation with the writing of stories, or the production of drawings induced by music, followed by verbal elaboration in the cognitive psychodynamic psychotherapeutic tradition. A meta-analysis of the confirmatory results in five subgroups showed a significant increase in concentration and in school marks.

Reviews and Meta-Analyses

Over the years, there have been several reviews of the impact of engagement with music on academic attainment (Arnett-Gary, 1998; Costa-Giomi, 2012; Hodges and O'Connell, 2007; Schellenberg, 2014; Shobo, 2001; Yoon, 2000). These and those undertaken more recently (Benz et al., 2016; Dumont et al., 2017; Sala and Gobet, 2017) have discussed the challenges and limitations of the research and offered explanations for the variability of the empirical findings. The complexity of musical activities and their potential to affect children's social, emotional and cognitive experiences together have made it challenging to formulate theoretical frameworks that account for the wide range of empirical findings.

Miendlarzewska and Trost (2014) synthesised a large body of studies, demonstrating that the benefits of musical training extended beyond the skills which music aims to train, which then last into adulthood. They argued that children who undergo musical training have better verbal memory, second language pronunciation accuracy, reading ability and executive functions. Learning to play an instrument as a child may even predict academic performance and IQ in young adulthood. In addition, the degree of observed structural and functional adaptation in the brain correlates with the intensity and duration of practice. The effects on cognitive development depend on the timing of musical initiation as well as other moderating variables. They suggest that motivation, reward and the social context of musical education are important yet neglected factors which affect the long-term benefits of musical training. They propose the notion of rhythmic entrainment as a mechanism which may support learning, the development of executive functions and temporal processing/orienting of attention in time, which may underlie enhancements observed in reading and verbal memory. Overall, they conclude that musical training uniquely engenders near- and far-transfer effects, preparing a foundation for a range of skills thus fostering cognitive development.

Winner and Cooper (2000) quantified the results of existing research from 1950 to 1998, conducting five meta-analyses of studies assessing the effects of arts education on academic achievement. The studies examined the effects of the arts in general rather than specific art forms (for instance, music or dance). The researchers found evidence for a positive relationship between arts education and academic achievement, but found no increase in verbal or mathematics achievement.

Sala and Gobet (2017) undertook two meta-analyses assessing the effect of chess and music instruction on children's cognitive and academic skills. A third meta-analysis evaluated the effects of working memory training. The findings showed that the effect sizes from the studies were inversely related to the quality of the experimental design. This pattern of results cast serious doubts on the effectiveness of chess, music and working memory training. In a later review, Sala and Gobet (2018) presented a meta-analysis of music intervention studies with 3,780 children and found only a small overall effect size. When active controls were implemented, the effect was practically null. An even later review revealed similar findings (Sala and Gobet (2020). The analysis of data from 6,984 children showed that once the quality of study design was controlled for, the overall effect of music training programmes was null and highly consistent across studies. Small statistically significant overall effects were obtained only in those studies implementing no random allocation of participants and employing non-active controls. They concluded that music training was ineffective regardless of the type of outcome measure (verbal, non-verbal, speed-related, the participants' age, or the duration of training). They concluded that researchers' optimism about the benefits of music training was empirically unjustified and stemmed from misinterpretation of the empirical data and, possibly, confirmation bias. Also adopting a meta-analytic approach, Gordon and colleagues (2015) considered the impact of music engagement on reading with studies that included music training and control groups, pre- and post-comparison measures, and an indication that reading instruction was constant across groups. Thirteen studies were identified including 901 children. Two classes of outcome measures emerged with sufficient overlap to support meta-analysis: phonological awareness and reading fluency. Hours of training, age and type of control intervention were examined as potential moderators. The results supported the hypothesis that music training led to gains in phonological awareness skills. The analyses revealed that transfer effects for rhyming skills tended to grow stronger with increased hours of training. In contrast, no significant aggregate transfer effect emerged for reading fluency measures, although some studies reported large training effects.

Explanations for the Research Findings

Many different explanations for the mixed research findings have been proposed. Some have suggested that the changes that music participation has on the brain are responsible for a range of cognitive and academic benefits. Other explanations relate to enhanced executive functions, the length and types of programme and their quality, and the personality characteristics and motivation of participating children and young people.

Neurological Studies

The kinds of skills gained through learning to play an instrument—including auditory, audiation, reading and executive skills on different instruments (for example, keyboard, string, percussion and wind instruments) have been shown to impact on the auditory and motor regions of the brain (Hyde et al., 2009). As discussed in earlier chapters, music processing and playing instruments are related to activity in many different areas of the brain (Gaser and Schlaug, 2003; Koelsch et al., 2005; Koelsch and Siebel, 2005). Musicians, compared to non-musicians, tend to have enlarged structures in parts of the brain, for instance the left planum temporale and the cerebellum (Gaser and Schlaug, 2003; Hutchinson et al., 2003; Schlaug et al., 1995a; 1995b). These changes have been suggested to have implications for cognitive functions (Chan et al., 1998; Ho et al., 2003). A number of studies have shown structural differences in grey matter and white matter in children who engage in music, particularly in early childhood compared with those who do not (Fernandez, 2018; Groussard et al., 2014; Habibi et al., 2018; Huotilainen and Tervaniemi, 2018; Pantev and Herholz, 2011). Benner and colleagues (2017) found that Heschl's gyrus multiplications occurred much more frequently in musicians than in the general population and constituted a functional unit with Heschl's gyrus, while Schneider and colleagues (2002, 2005) observed that increases in grey-matter volume in the Heschl's gyrus (HG) of musicians, as compared with non-musicians, were linked with greater musical aptitude and audiation (Gordon, 1979; Gouzouasis, 1993). Audiation involves complex internal musical processing, memory and anticipation; and these cognitive processes overlap with executive functions. Some research has reported neural changes alongside significant differences in associated reading skills, sound processing skills and speech (Chobert et al., 2014; Moreno et al., 2009; Trainor et al., 2012). While the structural changes observed in the brain may impact on enhanced cognitive processes which lead to enhanced academic attainment, not all of the evidence supports this. The research findings are mixed (Dumont et al., 2017; Gordon et al., 2015; Jaschke et al., 2013; Sala and Gobet, 2017; 2020).

Adding to the complexity of understanding the findings from the research on the impact of music on attainment, Schlaug (2001) and Tervaniemi (2009) point out that, in the research, musicians have been treated as a unified group, as if the demands of their musical activities are equal in terms of perceptual, cognitive and motor functions. This is clearly not the case. They are differentiated in terms of the instrument that they play, the musical genre that they engage with, as well as their approach to practice. As we saw in Chapter 1, the neuroscientific evidence has shown differences between musicians in the parts of the brain which develop in response to their musical activities. This diversity has generally not been taken into account in the research on general attainment.

Length of Engagement with Music

Several studies have shown that, the longer the engagement with music, the greater the impact on attainment—for instance, Catterall (2000), Corrigal and colleagues (2013), Hallam and Rogers (2016) and Schellenberg (2006; 2019). Despite this, some authors have described changes observed in participants after only one month. In several studies, the effects were largest after two to three years (Holochwost et al., 2017) or only observed after two or more years of learning music (Holmes and Hallam, 2017; Schneider and Klotz, 2000). Overall, most of the evidence suggests that the longer the programme, the greater the impact (Corrigall et al., 2013; Degé et al., 2011a; Hetland, 2000). The time and intensity of programmes have also been pointed out as important (Habibi et al., (2014).

Learning to play an orchestral or band instrument to a high level of expertise involves cumulative learning, with students typically beginning to learn at an early age and putting in many hours of practice. To become a professional musician takes years of dedicated work. During this process, perceptual, cognitive and motor skills are refined to enable musicians to undertake the complex tasks required for solo and ensemble work. Intervention studies cannot mirror this level of engagement, and the subsequent impact on music-related skills or possible transfer to other areas. It is only in comparisons between expert musicians and non-musicians that this is revealed.

Type, Nature and Quality of Musical Training

The type of musical training and its quality are important in determining any impact on academic attainment. There has been significant variation in the quality of training and instruction between studies (Dumont et al., 2017; Foster and Jenkins, 2017; Sala and Gobet, 2017). Musical activities take many forms: composition, improvisation, theory, vocal and instrumental music. These require different forms of learning and practice. For instance, learning to play a musical instrument usually entails reading musical notation, and hand-eye and spatial coordination for physically playing the instrument. These skills are distinct from those involved in vocal training, particularly choral singing. These differences impact on neurological change and may impact on executive functions and other factors such as motivation. Typically, research has not taken account of these differences. However, there are exceptions—for instance, Kinney (2008) considered multiple forms of music education in elementary school and found positive associations between instrumental music participation and academic achievement tests, but no association for choral students. Habibi and colleagues (2014) suggested that playing with others was associated with greater development of auditory skills and executive functioning because of the need to overcome and organise more auditory information, as well as improve attention and concentration. Guhn and colleagues (2020) took into account many of these variables, as well as level of commitment and the interactions between them. They found that higher levels of musical achievement may indicate higher levels of commitment, which may lead to greater exposure to the various cognitive, social, emotional and motivation-related experiences which, in turn, may support academic achievement.

The quality of music interventions has also been raised. For example, Johnson and Memmott (2006) examined the relationship between academic achievement and participation in music activities across nearly 5000 participants and concluded that the higher the quality of the programme, the stronger the relationship. Similarly, Rauscher (2005) experienced difficulties with implementation during the first two years of a music programme and it was only at the end of the study, when the children had received one year of high-quality tuition, that there were any gains for the students.

The Role of Executive Functions in Attainment

One possible explanation for the impact of actively engaging in music-making and enhanced academic attainment is the mediating role of executive functions (Degé et al., 2011; Jaschkeet al., 2018; Slevc et al., 2016). The core competencies of executive functioning include self-regulation, information-monitoring, working memory and flexibility of changing between tasks (Diamond, 2013). These are all required in music-making, particularly in ensembles. Musicians have been shown to outperform non-musicians on various executive functions (Moradzadeh et al., 2015; Zuk et al., 2014). Benefits for memory, particularly aural and verbal memory, have also been demonstrated (Bergman et al., 2014; Oechslin et al., 2013; Roden et al., 2014). The frontal lobe is hypothesised to be particularly salient in executive functions (Miyake et al., 2000; Stuss and Alexander, 2000) and music training in childhood and early adolescence has been found to be related to lasting changes in the corpus callosum, superior temporal gyrus, and middle temporal gyrus (Schlaug et al., 2005; Steele et al., 2013).

Executive functions, as we saw in Chapter 8, have been shown to be linked to academic performance (Best et al., 2011; Cortés Pascual et al., 2019; Slevc et al., 2016; Visu-Petra et al., 2011). Cognitive flexibility, working memory, processing speed and planning (Zuk et al., 2014) may all support academic attainment. Audiation may represent an underlying mechanism through which differences in executive function abilities, as well as various facets of instrumental music learning, are connected. Music learning may enhance executive functions and audiation, which in turn may benefit learning capacity more broadly. Previous research suggests that even though music-related cognitive gains may, to some extent, be domain-specific—for instance, verbal but not visual memory (Ho et al., 2003)—they commonly relate to a range of cognitive domains (Forgeard et al., 2008; Schellenberg, 2004).

Personality Factors

Music students may also be more conscientious than non-music students, which may explain why they are more successful at school than would be indicated by their IQ scores. One personality factor of particular interest in relation to attainment is conscientiousness, as this may be a mediating factor in explaining differences between young musicians and non-musicians. There is certainly evidence that undergraduate music students exhibit conscientious-like traits (Kemp, 1996; Marchant-Haycox and Wilson, 1992), although composers and rock musicians are less conscientious than the general population (Gillespie and Myors, 2000; Kemp, 1996). Corrigall and colleagues (2013) pointed out that participation in music might influence changes in personality and, in this way, interact with better achievement in school. They found that individual differences in conscientiousness helped to explain school grades. It may be that those who are more self-disciplined are more likely to persevere in learning a musical instrument. Costa-Giomi (2006) observed children for three years as they began, continued and discontinued lessons. Those who completed three years of lessons were more responsible, disciplined and able to concentrate. However, these traits characterised the students before they started to learn an instrument and did not change as a result of music instruction. Another explanation comes from research by Butkovic and colleagues (2015), who found that music-specific flow proneness was the best predictor of time spent practising when openness to experience, motivation and intelligence were taken into account.

Motivation

Motivation is clearly a key factor in the development of high-level musical expertise and also in enhancing academic attainment. Motivation will be discussed in depth in Chapter 12. However, the process of music training—which frequently includes hours of practice, typically in solitude, and a lengthy time commitment—might develop the habit of self-discipline and the desire to achieve, both of which are likely to support enhanced academic attainment. Students who learn that hard work can lead to the mastery of complex skills and to desired learning outcomes may develop a sense of self-efficacy and self-belief which will impact on other areas of study. Music-based intervention programmes have shown improvements in self-esteem, confidence, discipline and motivation among young people (Hallam et al., 2017). Students involved in music appear to show high levels of intrinsic motivation

(Diaz, 2010). Higher levels of musical engagement relate to stronger academic self-concept (Degé et al., 2014). Students engaging in musical activities as part of a group may experience a sense of team bonding and accomplishment (Adderley et al., 2003) which can contribute to a positive learning climate. These various elements may interact with each other over time. The context of learning itself is also important in both music and academic work and, if supportive, can enhance attainment. Being rewarded for success, musically and academically, also promotes motivation. Motivational and socioemotional pathways may underlie the associations between music learning and learning in other subjects. A complex interplay of internal and external factors is likely to influence a learner's motivation to participate in and continue long-term engagement with school music-making (Eccles and Wigfield, 2002) and shape an adolescent's conception of their musical ability and the value they place on music (Sichivitsa, 2007). In a large-scale study, McPherson and O'Neill (2010) found that learning to play an instrument or to sing seemed to contribute to higher motivation in other subjects, language, mathematics and science. Participating in musical activities can also affect aspirations, which enhance motivation and subsequently attainment. This is particularly the case with children from deprived areas (Devroop, 2009): for instance, those engaging in *El Sistema* and *Sistema*-inspired programmes (Creech et al., 2013). Participating in musical activities may enhance attainment through providing opportunities to explore and develop different ways of learning, including focused perception, making connections and imagining new possibilities (Burton et al.,, 1999).

Overview

Overall, the evidence regarding the impact of engaging with music on academic attainment is mixed. While the evidence from intervention studies is limited, correlational and comparative studies identify some clear links. While these have been criticised as not demonstrating causality, research which has adopted a retrospective or longitudinal approach has been able to demonstrate that those actively engaged in making music make greater progress academically over time compared with those not actively engaged in making music. What underpins this greater improvement in attainment over time is less clear. The relationship may be mediated by neurological changes relating to aural, phonemic, spatial or memory skills, executive functions, length, type or quality of training, or personality or motivational factors. Only research which is able to take account of all these factors will be able to develop credible explanatory models.

11. Music and Studying

There has been a great deal of research on the impact of music on cognitive activities related to studying. Many different factors can contribute to the outcomes, including the type of music, the nature of the task being undertaken, individual differences and the relationship of the individual to the particular music involved. Each of these will be considered in this chapter. As many studies address several of these issues simultaneously, each study will be considered in relation to its main focus. The theories attempting to explain the various findings will also be outlined. There has been some confusion in the reporting of the research between studies where music is presented prior to the task being undertaken (what has become known as the Mozart effect) and research where music is played in the background while the task is being undertaken. These different approaches are frequently considered as equivalent. Here they are considered separately.

Listening to Music prior to Completing a Task

The positive effect of listening to music prior to undertaking a cognitive task was first associated with the music of Mozart. A group of college students performed a spatial-temporal task after they listened to Mozart's sonata for two pianos in D major, KV 448. Their performance was compared to groups who either listened to a relaxation recording or sat in silence before completing the task. The group listening to Mozart performed significantly better than the other groups (Rauscher et al., 1993). A second study, using the same Mozart composition, repetitive music or a short story, replicated these findings (Rauscher et al., 1995). Since this research, there have been many studies attempting replication. The findings from these have been mixed. Some examples are set out below.

Rideout and Taylor (1997) studied 32 undergraduates who completed two equivalent spatial reasoning tests: one following a control procedure and one following the presentation of Mozart's Sonata for two pianos in D major. Their performance showed a small but significant improvement immediately following presentation of the music. Similarly, Wilson and Brown (1997) studied spatial reasoning in 22 college undergraduates who were exposed to ten minutes of a Mozart piano concerto, repetitive relaxation music or silence prior to undertaking a pencil and paper maze task. The mazes varied in complexity and size. Limited support for the Mozart effect was obtained for the number of maze recursions and the overall quality of maze solutions.

Adopting a neurological perspective, Jaušovec and colleagues (2006), in two experiments, investigated the influence that Mozart's sonata, K. 448, had on brain activity in the process of learning. In the first experiment, individuals were trained in how to solve spatial rotation tasks, and then were required to solve similar tasks. Fifty-six students were divided into four groups: a control group which prior to and after training relaxed, and three experimental groups—one group who prior to and after training listened to Mozart, one who prior to training listened to Mozart and subsequently relaxed, and a fourth group who prior to training relaxed and afterwards listened to Mozart. In the second experiment, 36 respondents were divided into three groups: a control group, a second group who listened to Mozart prior to and after training, and a third group who prior to and after training listened to Brahms' Hungarian Dance No. 5. In both experiments, EEG data were collected during problem-solving. In the first experiment, all of the respondents in the various music groups showed better task performance than the control group, although those experiencing music before and after the task displayed less complex EEG patterns and more alpha-band synchronisation than did respondents in the other three groups. In the second experiment, individuals who listened to Mozart showed better task performance than did the respondents in the other groups. They also displayed less complex EEG patterns and more lower alpha-band synchronisation than did the respondents in the Brahm's music group. The authors argued that Mozart's music, by activating task-relevant brain areas, enhanced the learning of spatial-temporal rotation tasks. The results supported Rauscher and colleagues' (1993) priming explanation of the Mozart effect.

Working with children, Hallam (2001) and Schellenberg and Hallam (2005) replicated Rauscher's study with over 6,000 children in the final year of primary school. The children were randomly allocated within their school to one of three groups: a group listening to the same Mozart piano sonata as in the Rauscher study, one to pop music performed by the pop groups Blur and Oasis, and the third to a talk about experiments. Each of these sessions lasted for ten minutes. Following this, the children completed two spatial reasoning tasks: a paper folding task and a rotational task. The initial analysis (Hallam, 2001) showed no statistically significant difference between the groups on either task. A second analysis by Schellenberg and Hallam (2005) showed a slight statistical advantage for the children listening to popular music. This was interpreted in terms of raised arousal levels and higher motivation because the children liked the popular music. Schellenberg (2005) argued that such short-term effects resulted from the impact of music on changes in arousal level and mood. Following this, Schellenberg and colleagues (2007) undertook two further experiments. In the first, Canadian undergraduates performed better on a symbol-search test after listening to an up-tempo piece of music composed by Mozart in comparison to a slow piece by Albinoni. However, the effect was evident only when the two pieces of music induced reliable differences in arousal and mood. Performance on other intellectual tasks was not affected. In the second experiment, Japanese five-year-olds drew for longer periods of time after singing or hearing familiar children's songs than after hearing Mozart or Albinoni. After hearing the children's songs, their drawings were judged by adults to be more creative, energetic and technically proficient. These findings illustrate that prior exposure to different types of music can enhance performance on a variety of tasks; the effects are mediated by changes in emotional state and can generalise across cultures and age groups.

Exploring whether arousal and mood were responsible for Rauscher's original findings, Thompson and colleagues (2001) studied 24 college students, aged 20 to 60 years old, who completed a test of spatial abilities after either listening to a pleasant and energetic sonata by Mozart, sitting in silence or listening to Albinoni's adagio, a slow reflective piece. Enjoyment, arousal and mood were also assessed. Performance on the spatial task was better following exposure to the composition by Mozart. The two pieces of music induced differential responding to measures of enjoyment, arousal and mood. When these were controlled for, the Mozart effect disappeared. Focusing on the role of mood, Smith and colleagues (2010) carried out two studies. The first explored the effects of prior exposure to office noise on working memory, while the second was a replication of Rauscher and colleagues' (1993) study. The first study showed that mental arithmetic tasks were initially impaired by office noise, but that the effects of the noise disappeared following ten minutes of exposure to office noise between tasks. The second experiment successfully replicated Rauscher and colleagues' (1993) study showing enhanced spatial reasoning following listening to Mozart for 24 young adults, although assessment of the mood of participants demonstrated that the effect was not caused by mood change. Also focusing on the impact of mood and arousal on spatial reasoning, Hussain and colleagues (2002) examined the effects of tempo and mode. A Mozart sonata performed by a skilled pianist was recorded and edited to produce four versions that varied in tempo (fast or slow) and mode (major or minor). Participants listened to a single version and completed measures of spatial ability, arousal and mood. Performance on the spatial task was superior after listening to music at a fast rather than a slow tempo, and when the music was presented in major rather than minor mode. Tempo manipulations affected arousal but not mood, whereas mode manipulations affected mood but not arousal.

Nantais and Schellenberg (1999) found that performance on a spatial-temporal task was better after participants listened to a piece composed by Mozart or by Schubert than after they sat in silence. In a second study, the advantage for the music condition disappeared when the control condition consisted of a narrated story instead of silence. The participants' performance was a function of their preference for either the music or the story, with better performance following the preferred condition. Similarly, Perham and Withey (2012) found that preferred music increased spatial rotation performance regardless of the tempo of the music. Participants listened to both liked and disliked music, in either a fast or slow tempo, prior to completing a series of spatial rotation tasks. At both tempos, liked music was associated with significantly better spatial rotation performance than disliked music.

Some research has focused on music acting as a primer for memory tasks with participants of varied ages. For instance, Hirokawa (2004) examined the effects of preferred music and relaxation instructions on older adults' arousal and working memory. Fifteen female older adults participated in ten minutes of three experimental conditions: participants' preferred music, relaxation instructions or silence. Four subcategories of arousal level, energy, tiredness, tension and calmness were measured before and after experimental treatment using an adjective checklist. After each experimental condition, participants completed a working memory test. The findings showed that music increased participants' energy levels, while relaxation and silence significantly decreased them. Relaxation and silence interventions also increased tiredness and calmness. All experimental conditions decreased tension levels, although working memory performance was not significantly different between the groups. Also focusing on working memory, Steele and colleagues (1997) studied 36 undergraduate students who completed a backwards digit-span task followed by exposure to ten minutes of music composed by Mozart, a recording of rain, or silence and a repetition of the task. No significant differences among treatment conditions were found, although there was a significant effect of practice. In a later study, Steele and colleagues (1999) followed the detailed procedural guidance offered by Rauscher and colleagues needed to produce the Mozart effect. Despite this, Steele and colleagues were unable to produce either a statistically significant Mozart effect or an effect size suggesting practical significance. They concluded that there was little evidence to support the existence of the Mozart effect.

Also offering limited support to the Mozart effect, Twomey and Esgate (2002) compared the performance of 20 musicians and 20 non-musicians on spatial-temporal reasoning tasks following exposure to Mozart's Sonata K. 448. They based their research on the trion model of neural functioning, which is highly structured in time and spatial connections and predicts increased synchrony between musical and spatial temporal centres in the right cerebral hemisphere. Since increased left-hemispheric involvement in music processing occurs as a result of musical training, the possibility of increased synchrony with left-hemispheric areas in the musicians was tested. The results were improved performance on language as well as spatial-temporal tasks. In addition to spatial-temporal tasks, synonym generation and rhyming-word generation tasks were employed. A Mozart effect was demonstrated on the spatial-temporal task, although this was greater for the non-musicians. There was no effect of musical priming for either group on verbal tasks, although the musicians scored higher on rhyming-word generation. No systematic link was found between performance on any task and the number of years spent in musical training. The failure to induce a Mozart effect in the musicians on verbal tasks, as well as the limited impact on their performance on the spatial-temporal tasks, may have been associated with a ceiling effect due to the long-term effects of music training.

Working with 448 younger and older adults with mean ages of 28 and 72 respectively, Giannouli and colleagues (2019) provided participants with novel excerpts by Mozart, Vivaldi and Glass, or silence—after which they completed a forward digit-span test and a word-fluency test to assess verbal working memory and phonologically cued semantic retrieval. Individual preference for each condition was also assessed. Brief exposure to music had no beneficial effect on verbal working memory and there was transient impairment after listening to Vivaldi, although the Vivaldi excerpt did induce a marked enhancement in word fluency, but only in the young adults. In contrast, listening to Mozart's music was followed by decreased word-fluency test scores in both age groups. These findings suggest that, depending on specific musical features, listening to music can selectively facilitate or inhibit ongoing verbal functions. Similarly, Borella and colleagues (2019) examined whether short- and long-term working memory training in older adults could be enhanced by listening to music. Mozart's Sonata K. 448 and Albinoni's Adagio in G minor were played to participants aged 65 to 75 years old before they started working-memory training activities. One group of 19 participants listened to Mozart, another to Albinoni and one to white noise, while eighteen participants served as controls and engaged in other activities. Specific training gains on a task similar to the one used in training and transfer effects to visuo-spatial abilities, executive functioning and reasoning were assessed. Irrespective of the specific listening condition, the trained groups generally outperformed the control group. The white-noise group did not differ in performance from the two music groups, although the group listening to the Albinoni composition showed larger specific training gains in the criterion task in the short-term and on transfer effects in the reasoning task in the short- and long-term compared to the group listening to the composition by Mozart.

Also working with older adults, but in this case with those with mild cognitive impairment, Lake and Goldstein (2011) exposed participants to a music and a silence condition, following which they performed digit-span and coding tasks, both of which require attention for maximal performance. Listening to music did not enhance performance for either group. Researching a wider age range, Carr and Rickard (2016) tested whether listening to emotionally arousing music enhanced memory in 37 participants aged 18 to 50, who listened to two of their own highly enjoyed music tracks, two self-rated neutral tracks from other participants' selections, and a five-minute radio interview. After each listening episode, participants memorised a unique array of 24 images. Subjective and physiological emotional arousal was monitored throughout the experiment and free recall of all images within the five image arrays was tested at the end. Compared to the music and non-music controls, self-selected enjoyed music elicited greater subjective and physiological changes consistent with changes in emotion. More details from images presented were recalled after enjoyed music than after listening to the radio interview. The physiological changes consistent with an emotional arousal response to enjoyed music reliably predicted memory performance.

In a study exploring the impact of music from different cultures, Giroux and colleagues (2020) examined whether listening to pleasant, stimulating or familiar music prior to completing a task improved working-memory performance. One hundred and nineteen Rwandan participants were randomly assigned to a control group, who read a short story prior to completing the task, or to one of four different musical conditions varying on two dimensions: arousing or relaxing music, or Western or Rwandan music. Working memory was measured using the n-back paradigm, where participants are presented with a sequence of stimuli one by one and need to decide if the current stimulus is the same as one presented previously. The gap between current and previous stimuli can be varied. The greater the distance, the harder the task. The findings showed that there were no positive effects of familiar, pleasant or stimulating music on working memory. Performance on the n-back task tended to improve from before and after listening to music across all conditions, but the improvement was less in participants who listened to familiar Rwandan music compared to those who listened to unfamiliar Western music or to a short story.

In contrast, Silva and colleagues (2020) investigated the impact of music on episodic memory. Two potential enhancers of music effects—stopping music before task performance to eliminate music-related distraction, and using preferred music to maximise reward—were adopted. The main study included a sample of 51 healthy younger adults, while a pilot study was conducted with 12 older adults, divided into those classified as low- versus high-functioning according to cognitive performance on a screening test. There was strong evidence that music had no advantage in relation to episodic memory over silence or environmental sounds in younger adults. Preferred music had no advantage either. Among the older adults, low- but not high-functioning participants' item memory was improved by music, particularly by non-preferred music compared to silence. The findings suggest that, in healthy adults, music played prior to a task may be less effective than background music in episodic memory enhancement despite decreased distraction, possibly because reward becomes irrelevant when music is stopped before the task begins. Low-functioning older participants may relate to prior-to-task auditory stimulation in deviant ways when it comes to episodic memory enhancement. Overall, for episodic memory, the arousal, mood or reward effects usually afforded by music played in the background (Blood and Zatorre, 2001; Ferreri and Verga, 2016; Salimpoor et al., 2013; Schellenberg, 2005) may be lost or attenuated when music is stopped before the task begins. Given that preference also had null effects, and preference is strongly linked to reward, it is possible that reward may be a key factor. Music-related reward may no longer favour episodic memory if music is stopped before the task begins. Gilleta and colleagues (2003) studied gender differences working with 26 females and 26 males, who completed a paper folding and cutting task and a mental rotation task following a listening condition (in which a Mozart piano sonata was played or participants sat in silence). A statistically significant three-way interaction among gender, listening condition and task indicated that an effect was present only for female participants on the mental rotations task.

Exploring the differential effects of breaks filled with diverse activities, as is common in everyday life, Kuschpel and colleagues (2015) exposed young adults to breaks involving eyes-open resting, listening to music or playing the video game Angry Birds before performing an n-back working memory task. Playing the Angry Birds video game during a short learning break led to a decline in task performance over the course of the task, as compared to eyes-open resting and listening to music, although overall task performance was not impaired. This effect was associated with high levels of daily mind-wandering and low self-reported ability to concentrate.

Working with children with learning difficulties, Gregoire (1984) focused on the impact of prior listening to music on concentration in subsequent performance on a matching-numbers classroom task with 17 six- to eleven-year-old children. The intervention condition consisted of a brief taped story illustrated on a felt board, a rest period with relaxing music, and five minutes of individual number-matching. The control condition was identical but without the music. There were no significant differences overall, although the older participants exhibited significantly fewer behavioural issues during the music period than during the rest phase.

Overall, the evidence for the priming benefits of music on cognitive tasks is inconclusive. There is some evidence that musical neurological priming can directly enhance performance on spatial reasoning tasks, as proposed by Rauscher and colleagues, although the evidence for this is not consistent. Music can also have priming effects relating to arousal or mood, which may affect performance on a variety of tasks in a range of different ways. To begin to understand these mixed findings, there needs to be a greater focus on the underlying neural priming processes.

Background Music

There is now a substantial body of research which has examined the impact of background music on performance on a range of cognitive tasks in individuals across the lifespan. Music has also been used as a stimulus for creative writing, but this practice needs to be distinguished from music being played as a background to studying (Donlan, 1976). During the 1950s, as radio became more commonplace, concerns were raised as it was feared that listening to the radio while completing homework would negatively affect children's learning. Early studies addressing these issues were not always well controlled, and many did not specify the type of music being played or the nature of the task being undertaken. This made interpreting the findings extremely difficult. The remainder of the chapter is divided into sections which will outline the research, providing more detailed evidence relating to:

- the nature of the music played, including preferred music, familiarity, liking and preference for music of one's own culture;
- the nature of the task to be completed, including memory, attention, reading comprehension, second-language learning and English as a second language;
- individual differences, including musical expertise, gender, personality and metacognition;
- children's behaviour and task performance, including primary-school children and older students;
- children with emotional and behavioural difficulties, ADHD and developmental difficulties;
- older adults and those with cognitive impairment;
- reviews and meta-analyses; and
- explaining the impact of background music on cognitive performance, including an explanatory framework.

The research has been categorised in relation to its main focus, although any single research project may have outcomes related to more than one outcome.

The Nature of the Music

Some research has ignored the characteristics of the music being played, assuming that all music would have a similar impact. For instance, Cockerton and colleagues (1997) simply compared music with no music in a repeated measures design with 30 undergraduates who completed two cognitive tests: one in silence and the other with background music. The students completed more questions and answered more questions correctly when music was playing, although there was no difference in the heart rate of those participating in each condition. Some attempts have been made to address issues relating to the nature of the music by differentiating music on the basis of genre, its perceived potential to stimulate or relax, whether it is vocal or instrumental, and its cognitive complexity. Despite this, such categorisations do not always capture the complexity of music as it is listened to. This particularly applies to Western classical music with its frequent changes of mood, tempo, timbre and volume. To examine the issues further, some research has investigated how exposing participants to different types of music affected their performance on various cognitive tasks. Control groups have listened to music from other genres or spoken text rather than sitting in silence. In an early detailed study in the USA, Henderson and colleagues (1945) explored the effect of music on the reading efficiency of 50 first-year female undergraduates. Participants were divided into three equally matched groups on the basis of psychological examination and reading test scores. One group listened to popular music while completing reading tasks, another classical music, while the third worked in silence. The participants completed a questionnaire which determined whether they were accustomed to studying with the radio on, whether or not they thought that the radio reduced their study efficiency, the amount of studying done with the radio on and the type of programme that they usually listened to when studying. The popular music used was 'Two O'Clock Jump', Harry James; 'That's What You Think', Krupa; 'Sunday, Monday, or Always', Frank Sinatra; 'Mr. Five by Five', Harry James; 'Prince Charming', Harry James; 'Tuxedo Junction', Glenn Miller; 'Idaho', Benny Goodman; 'Crosstown', Glenn Miller; and 'Close to You', Frank Sinatra. The classical music was 'Symphony in D Minor' by Cesar Franck. The tests were administered on three successive afternoons. The participants were asked to assume that they were in their own rooms studying with the radio on. The differences between the averages of the pre-test scores and the final test scores of each group were calculated and the significance of the averages analysed. The findings showed that the popular music acted to distract the students on paragraph comprehension but not on the vocabulary test. The classical music had no negative impact on either test. The authors explained the results in terms of the simpler rhythms and melodies of popular music being easily understood, and therefore listened to, by the participants, diverting their attention from the task in hand. They argued that the classical music was likely to be perceived as vague and not listened to, just providing a background against which the assigned task was accomplished without interference. The popular music may have had a greater impact on the comprehension task, as this task was more complex and required sustained effort, while the vocabulary materials were intermittent and unrelated. Overall, the authors concluded that whether or not music is a real distraction depends on the complexity of the music and the complexity of the test materials. There were no significant differences depending on whether students were accustomed to studying with the radio playing. Also using reading comprehension as the outcome measure, Thompson and colleagues (2012) manipulated changes in tempo and intensity to create four conditions: slow low-intensity, slow high-intensity, fast low-intensity, and fast high-intensity. In each condition, 25 participants were given four minutes to read a passage, followed by three minutes to answer six multiple-choice questions. Baseline performance was established by having control participants complete the reading task in silence. A significant tempo-by-intensity interaction was observed, with comprehension in the fast high-intensity condition falling significantly below baseline. These findings demonstrated that listening to background instrumental music was most likely to disrupt reading comprehension when the music was fast and loud. Similarly, Chou and colleagues (2010), working with 133 Taiwanese college students, studied whether light classical music was more or less distracting than hip-hop music or silence during a comprehension task. The findings showed that music with higher intensity was more distracting and had a greater effect on task performance and concentration.

Yang and colleagues (2016) conducted two experiments: the first tested for differences in perception of distractibility between tonal and atonal music, while the second tested how tonal music and atonal music affected visual working memory by comparing musicians and non-musicians who were placed in contexts with background tonal music, atonal music or silence. Participants were instructed to complete a delayed matching memory task. The results showed that musicians and non-musicians had different evaluations of the distractibility of tonal and atonal music, possibly indicating that long-term training may lead to a higher auditory-perception threshold among musicians. For the working memory task, musicians reacted faster than non-musicians in all background music cases, although the musicians took more time to respond in the tonal background music condition than in the other conditions. The results suggest that, for a visual memory task, background tonal music may occupy more cognitive resources than atonal music or silence for musicians, leaving few resources left for the memory task. Despite this, the musicians outperformed the non-musicians. Similarly, Tze and Chou (2010) explored whether different types of background music affected the performance of a reading comprehension task in 133 Taiwanese college students. The study explored whether listening to music affected the learners' concentration on a reading task and also whether light classical music was more or less distracting than hip-hop music or silence. The findings showed that music with higher intensity was more distracting, and had a greater effect on task performance and concentration.

Using two contrasting tasks, Angel and colleagues (2010) assessed the effects of fast-tempo music on cognitive performance among 56 male and female university students. A linguistic processing task and a spatial processing task were selected to assess verbal and non-verbal performance. Ten excerpts from Mozart's compositions, matched for tempo, were selected to be played in the background. The music increased the speed of spatial processing and the accuracy of linguistic processing. Focusing on performance on arithmetic tasks, Dolegui (2013) used different genres of music, played at different volumes. Thirty-two undergraduate students, ranging in age from 20 to 41 years old, participated on a voluntary basis. Five different arithmetic tests were used, consisting of 20 different operations of similar difficulty: five multiplication, five division, five addition and five subtraction problems. Loud music was defined as heavy rock metal music represented by the song 'Not Ready to Die', Demon Hunters. Soft music was defined as classical piano music, 'Morning Light', Beeson. All participants were exposed to all five conditions. The first test was conducted with soft music at low intensity, the second with loud music at low intensity, the third in complete silence. The fourth and fifth tests were conducted with soft and loud music. The tests were graded for accuracy. Performance scores were significantly higher in silence than in all four music conditions, intensity levels and types of music combined, although overall, performance was significantly worse in the presence of loud music at high intensity. Similarly, Cassidy and MacDonald (2007) investigated the effects of music with high arousal potential and negative affect, music with low arousal potential and positive affect, and everyday noise on the cognitive task performance of introverts and extroverts. Forty participants completed five cognitive tasks: immediate recall, free recall, numerical and delayed recall, and the Stroop test. Ten participants completed each of these tasks in one of the four sound conditions: high arousal and negative affect, low arousal and positive affect, everyday noise, and silence. Participants were also assessed for levels of introversion and extroversion, and reported their preferences for music versus noise while studying. Performance was lessened across all cognitive tasks in the presence of background sound, music or noise, compared to silence. The two music conditions produced differential distraction effects, with performance on all tasks being poorer in the presence of high-arousal, negative-affect music as compared with low-arousal, positive-affect music and silence. Performance was moderated by internal arousal, with introverts performing better overall on each task except the Stroop test, and appearing to be more detrimentally affected by the presence of high arousal negative affect music and noise.

Some research has focused on the differential impact of vocal and instrumental music. For instance, Jäncke and colleagues (2014) studied 226 participants who were randomly assigned to one of five groups, who all completed a verbal learning task. One group served as a control group, working in silence, while four further groups were exposed to vocal or instrumental music during learning, with different subjective intensity and valence. The four music listening conditions were vocal or instrumental music, each with high or low intensity. As the high and low intensity groups did not differ in terms of their rated intensity during the main experiment, these groups were put together. This reduced the sample to three groups: a control group, one listening to vocal music and one listening to instrumental music. Recall of the number of learned words was assessed immediately, after 15 minutes and 14 days later. Verbal learning improved across the recall sessions without any strong differences between the control and experimental groups. Exposure to vocal or instrumental background music during encoding did not influence verbal learning.

Adopting a neuroscientific approach, Nemati and colleagues (2019) investigated the neural correlates of pleasure induced by listening to highly pleasant and neutral musical excerpts using electroencephalography. Analysis of the data showed a distinct gradual change in the power of low-frequency oscillations in response to highly pleasant, but not neutral, musical excerpts. Correlation analysis between behavioural and electrophysiological data revealed that theta power was correlated with subjective assessment of pleasantness. To study the link between attention and positive valence, volunteers performed a delayed match-to-sample memory task while listening to the musical excerpts. Performance was significantly lower under highly pleasant conditions compared to neutral conditions. Listening to pleasant music required high degrees of attention, leading to an observed decline in memory performance. Gradual development of low-frequency oscillations in the frontal and posterior areas may be at least partly due to gradual recruitment of higher levels of attention over time in response to pleasurable music.

Exploring the impact of music on a simple perceptual motor task, Nittono and colleagues (2000) compared the performance of 24 undergraduates on a self-paced line-tracing task with fast or slow classical music or metronome tones in the background. The findings showed that fast music accelerated performance compared with slow music, whereas the tempo of the metronome tones did not affect performance. Similarly, Bottiroli and colleagues (2014) measured how different types of music affected performance on a processing-speed task using no music, white noise, music with positive emotion and high arousal levels (Mozart), or music with negative mood and lower arousal (Mahler). Performance on the processing-speed task improved when listening to Mozart. However, when participants were faced with free-recall and phonemic-fluency tasks, Mahler's music provided the most beneficial conditions. Both types of music were advantageous over white noise or silence for both types of task. In a real-life simulation, Kallinen (2002) studied the effects of the tempo of background music on reading business news in a crowded cafeteria environment. There were three conditions: no music, or fast or slow music. The findings suggested that the type of music (or silence) significantly affected reading performance and the emotional evaluation of the news content. Men evaluated the news most positively in the slow-music condition, whereas women evaluated the news most positively in the no-music condition. Reading rate and efficiency were significantly lower in the slow-music group than in the fast-music group. Also simulating a real-life situation, Mayfield and Moss (1989) undertook two studies to evaluate the effect of music tempo on task performance. In the first study, 44 undergraduate business students were asked to be workers in a stock-market project by collecting closing stock prices and calculating the percentage of change in the price from week to week. Participants were randomly divided into groups, such that they either listened to fast or slow-paced music while they worked, or to no music. The quantity and quality of work was assessed using music-listening habits as a covariate. There were no statistically significant differences between the performance of the two groups. In the second study, the students completed the same task under the same conditions. In this study, the women performed significantly better than the men and performance was significantly higher in a rock-music condition than in a heartbeat condition, although participants in the rock-music condition perceived a higher level of distraction.

Preferred Music, Familiarity and Liking

One strand of research has explored whether participants' familiarity, preference or liking for background music has an impact on task outcomes. For instance, Hilliard and Tolin (1979) studied the effect of familiarity with background music on the performance of 64 undergraduates on simple and difficult reading comprehension tasks. Unsurprisingly, scores on easier sections were higher than on difficult sections, while overall scores were higher when familiar music was playing. In a series of studies, Perham and colleagues explored issues relating to preferred and different types of music. Perham and Vizard (2011) tested serial recall under quiet, liked and disliked music conditions, as well as steady-state and changing-state speech. The findings showed that performance was poorer for both music conditions and the changing-state speech, compared to quiet and steady-state speech conditions. The findings suggested that musical preference did not affect serial recall performance. Similarly, Perham and Sykora (2012) asked participants to serially recall eight item lists in either quiet, liked or disliked music conditions. Performance was poorer when music was played compared with quiet, and in the liked as opposed to the disliked music condition. In addition, participants were inaccurate in perceiving their performance to be roughly equivalent in each of the music conditions when liked music exhibited more task impairment than disliked music. Changing the task to reading comprehension, Perham and Currie (2014) studied 30 undergraduate students, ranging in age from 19 to 65. The background music adopted included disliked lyrical music, thrash metal, liked lyrical music, non-lyrical music, and quiet. The thrash metal music selected were Death's Angel's 'Seemingly Endless Time' and 'The Ultra Violence'. Students who reported liking this genre were omitted from the study. Liked music was selected by the students themselves and included music by One Direction, Frank Ocean and Katy Perry. In the study, participants were told not to attend to the music which they listened to on headphones. A short questionnaire was administered to participants upon completion, which comprised Likert-scale questions that asked participants to rate how likeable, familiar and distracting each sound condition was, as well as how well they thought that they performed in each condition. Students read four passages of text and then answered six multiple-choice questions on each. Reading comprehension performance was greatest for the quiet and non-lyrical music conditions and poorest for the two lyrical music conditions. Participants perceived themselves to have performed best in the liked lyrical, the quiet and the non-lyrical conditions, as well as feeling that they were the most familiar experiences for them. They felt that the liked and disliked lyrical conditions were most distracting to performance, with quiet being much less distracting. It seems that, in the case of reading comprehension and category recall, there is a conflict in processing, as participants attempt to process task-related information and background sound simultaneously.

Chew and colleagues (2016) recruited 165 undergraduate students with a mean age of almost 22 years old who completed arithmetic, reading comprehension and word-memory tasks while exposed to familiar or unfamiliar, foreign or first-language music, or no music. There was a significant impact on the word-memory task for the familiarity of the music, but not in relation to whether it was in a foreign or first language. Overall, depending on the task, familiarity but not the language of the music affected learning and task performance when compared to a no-music condition. Similarly, Sutton and Lowis (2008) studied the effect of musical mode on verbal and spatial task performance. Forty-eight participants completed written verbal and spatial reasoning tests while a piece of music in a major key by Handel was played, and again when the same piece was digitally manipulated to create a version in the minor mode. The findings showed that the music in the major mode was rated more emotionally positive by both sexes than that in the minor mode. Females scored higher than males in performance on the verbal tasks when this was significantly enhanced with the major-mode music, while males scored higher than the females on spatial reasoning when the music was in the major mode.

Smith and Morris (1977) studied the effects of sedative and stimulative music on memory performance, anxiety and concentration. Sixty undergraduate students were exposed to one of five types of music: classical, jazz and blues, country bluegrass, easy listening and rock music. Participants indicated their preferred genre and were requested to repeat a set of numbers backwards while listening to either stimulative, sedative or no music. They were asked about their concerns about the test, their emotionality or physiological affective arousal, their ability to concentrate, their expectations of their performance, and whether they liked or disliked the music. Compared with sedative music, stimulative music increased worry scores, interfered with concentration and resulted in lower performance expectancies. Participants performed best in the no-music condition and worst while listening to their preferred music, with performance to sedative music being between these extremes. The authors argued that preferred music may serve to distract when trying to complete a demanding task, perhaps because fewer cognitive resources are available when attention is drawn to the lyrics, emotions and memories that music can evoke. Complex interactive effects on task performance were reported, suggesting that the effects of music need to be understood in terms of cognitive processes rather than primarily on the basis of physiological affective responses to musical stimuli. Another explanation for the advantage of preferred music is that it is rewarding (Blood and Zatorre, 2001; Ferreri and Verga, 2016). Reward may be one additional mechanism underpinning the positive effects of music on cognition (Ferreri and Verga, 2016).

Preference for Music of One's Own Culture

Preference for music is predominantly determined by an individual's cultural background. For instance, a preference for Indian classical music over Western classical music is seen in Indians from an average socioeconomic background (Schafer et al., 2012). Each individual's way of responding to music is influenced by their liking and preference for that music. For instance, Mohan and Thomas (2020) explored the effect of background music on the performance of 34 Indian adolescents aged 13 to 14 on their comprehension of words and sentences in English. Participants with average verbal ability and a preference for the Indian music comprised the final sample. Two types of music were used: Indian classical music (Raga Shanmukhapriya)—which is said to induce a sense of calm and increase concentration—and Mozart's Symphony No. 35. The findings revealed that playing music in the background resulted in a significant increase in adolescents' performance on the reading comprehension task. The effect was greater when Indian classical music was played, highlighting the importance of culture. Similarly, Kasiri, (2015) studied the impact of non-lyrical Iranian traditional music on the reading comprehension performance of Iranians learning to speak English. Sixty English-as-a-foreign-language learners completed two 50-itemed reading comprehension tests in no-music as well as background-music condition. The results revealed a negative influence of music on reading comprehension.

The Nature of the Task To Be Completed

In addition to research focusing on different types of music, a variety of different tasks have been used—for instance, those related to various different kinds of memory, tasks requiring high levels of attention, reading comprehension and learning a second language.

Background Music and Memory

In research relating to memorisation, the findings have differed when music is played concurrently with material which is to be remembered aurally (Furman, 1978), when the task involves paired associate recall

(Myers, 1979) or phonological short-term memory (Salame & Baddeley, 1989), or when recall is of written sentences presented visually (Hallam et al., 2002). Where background music is vocal in nature, it may have a greater negative impact on reading comprehension and other literacy tasks (Martin et al., 1988). Some research has focused on visual memory, where it might be expected that there would be less interference from the music. For instance, Chraif and colleagues (2014) studied the influence of relaxing music on an abstract visual short-term memory retrieval task. Sixty-eight undergraduate students, aged between 19 and 23 years old, participated. The findings showed that listening to relaxing music had a significant positive effect in increasing the number of correct abstract forms recognised.

Nguyen and Grahn (2017) examined the effect of background music on different types of memory. One hypothesis for the impact of background music on memory is that it modulates mood and arousal, creating optimal levels to enhance memory performance. Another hypothesis is that background music establishes a context that, when reinstated, cues memory performance. The researchers presented music during study time only, test only and both. They also assessed how mood, arousal and context affected performance on recall, recognition and associative memory tasks. Participants recalled more words when they listened to low-arousal music than high-arousal music, regardless of mood or whether context was consistent between study and test. For recognition memory, participants also recognised more words when they listened to low-arousal music than high-arousal music, but only when the music was negative. For associative memory, no significant effects of mood, arousal or context were found on recognition of previously studied word pairs. Across all elements of the research, background music (compared with silence) did not significantly improve verbal memory performance. While mood and arousal affected recall and recognition memory, overall background music did not enhance memory.

Jäncke and Sandmann (2010) used musical excerpts which were specifically composed for the research to ensure that they were unknown to the participants. They were designed to vary in tempo (fast versus slow) and consonance (in tune versus out of tune). Noise was used as a control stimulus. Seventy-five participants were randomly assigned to one of five groups and learned verbal material (non-words with and without semantic connotation, and with and without background music). Each group was exposed to one of five different background stimuli: in-tune fast music, in-tune slow, out-of-tune fast, out-of-tune slow and noise. There was no substantial or consistent influence of background music on verbal learning. However, there were differences in EEG measurements after word presentation for the group exposed to in-tune fast music while they learned the verbal material, and for the group exposed to out-of-tune fast music after word presentation. Although there were different cortical activations in response to the music, these did not relate to behavioural outcomes.

In an unusual study, Liu and colleagues (2012) studied the recognition processes of Chinese characters in background music. Real Chinese characters, upright or rotated, were used as target stimuli, while pseudowords were used as background stimuli. Participants were required to detect real characters while listening to Mozart's Sonata K. 448 or in silence. The findings showed that the music mainly served as a distracter in the recognition processes of real Chinese characters. The impact was greater for the real than the rotated characters.

Some research has focused on episodic memory for verbal materials. Generally, the effects of music are positive (Ferreri et al., 2013; 2014; 2015) and tend to be consistent across younger and older adults (Ferreri et al., 2015). Music facilitates the encoding of printed verbal materials not only when music is compared to a silent context, but also when compared to non-musical auditory contexts, such as environmental sounds or noise. Music has a specific effect rather than a general advantage related to sound.

Other research has extended the range of tasks explored. For instance, Fassbender (2012) explored the use of background music on game technology and its effect on learning. A virtual history lesson was presented to participants with different background stimuli—music or no music—to test the effect of music on memory. To test the role of immersion on memory and its possible relationship to the music, two different display systems (a three-monitor display system or an immersive reality centre) were used. Overall, participants remembered a significantly higher number of facts using the three-monitor display system, particularly if no background music was played. Similarly,

Richards and colleagues (2008) studied the benefits of immersive virtual worlds as a learning environment, and the role that music plays within these environments. They investigated whether background music of the genre typically found in computer-based roleplaying games had an effect on learning in a computer-animated history lesson about the Macquarie Lighthouse within an immersive virtual world. In the first experiment, musical stimuli were created from four different computer-game soundtracks. Seventy-two undergraduate students watched the presentation and completed a survey including biographical details, questions on the historical material presented and questions relating to their perceived level of immersion. While the tempo and pitch of the music was unrelated to learning, music conditions resulted in a higher number of accurately remembered facts than the no-music condition. One soundtrack, in particular, showed a statistically significant improvement in memorisation of facts over the other music conditions. There was also an interaction between the levels of perceived immersion and ability to accurately remember facts. The second experiment involved 48 undergraduate students. The soundtrack that had been most successful in Experiment One (Oblivion) was used again with a silent condition. In this experiment, the participants completed the tasks under both conditions. Only one version of the tempo and pitch manipulations was used: slow tempo, low pitch. The effect of different display systems on feelings of immersion was tested. Half the participants watched the computer-animated history lesson in a cone display system and the other half was allocated to a three-monitor display system on a computer desk. There were no statistically significant differences between the music and no-music conditions. However, the three-monitor display system led to enhanced memory performance. Similarly, Linek and colleagues (2011) investigated the influence of background music within an educational adventure game on motivational and cognitive variables. The results suggested that the music had a high motivational potential. As neither positive nor negative effects on learning were detected, background music may be considered as a motivating design element of educational games.

Using piped music, Langan and Sachs (2013) explored the impact of piping music into an information literacy classroom on student engagement and retention of information literacy concepts. The findings from this study indicated positive relationships between background music and student comfort, confidence and retention. Similarly, Musliu and colleagues (2017) researched whether music could help in the memorisation of different materials, for instance, nonsense syllables, numbers and poems with rhyme. Seventy-four students aged between 17 and 22 years participated. The experiment included four different tests. The first included 50 nonsense syllables. Following this, students were separated into three groups, each with similar outcomes on performance in the first test. The first group took subsequent tests in silence, the second while listening to music with lyrics and the third listening to relaxing music. The students were given five minutes to memorise 50 different nonsense syllables,12 lines from poems and 50 different orders of numbers. They then wrote down what they could remember. The music was the same during the memorising and writing phases. There were significant differences in memorising between students with or without music, in favour of those learning in silence.

Adopting a neuroscientific approach, Ferreri and colleagues (2013) addressed the debate about the link between music and memory for words—in particular, whether music specifically benefits the encoding element of verbal memory tasks by providing a richer context for encoding and, therefore, less demand on the dorsolateral prefrontal cortex. Twenty-two healthy young adults were subjected to functional near-infrared spectroscopy imaging of their bilateral dorsolateral prefrontal cortex while encoding words in the presence of either a musical or silent background. Behavioural data confirmed the facilitating effect of background music during encoding on subsequent item recognition. Functional near-infrared spectroscopy imaging results revealed significantly greater activation of the left hemisphere during encoding and a sustained, bilateral decrease of activity in the dorsolateral prefrontal cortex in the music condition compared to silence. These findings suggest that music modulates the role played by the dorsolateral prefrontal cortex during dorsolateral prefrontal cortex verbal encoding and opens up the possibility for applications in clinical populations with prefrontal impairments, such as elderly adults or Alzheimer's patients. In a later study, Ferreri and colleagues (2015) investigated whether verbal episodic memory could be improved by background instrumental music. Twenty young adults were asked to memorise different lists of words presented against a background of music, environmental sounds or silence. Their episodic memory performance was then tested in terms of item and source-memory scores. The findings revealed better memory performance under the music condition than with environmental sounds or silence in retrieval. These findings indicate that music can specifically act as a facilitating encoding context for verbal episodic memory, which may have implications for music as a rehabilitation tool for episodic memory deficits. Further, Ferreri and colleagues (2015)—based on functional near-infrared spectroscopy imaging studies on music, episodic encoding and the dorsolateral prefrontal cortex—monitored the entire lateral prefrontal cortex during both encoding and retrieval of verbal material. Nineteen participants were asked to encode lists of words presented with either background music or silence, and were subsequently tested during a free-recall task. Meanwhile, their prefrontal cortex was monitored using a 48-channel functional near-infrared spectroscopy system. Behavioural results showed greater chunking of words under the music condition, suggesting the employment of associative strategies for items encoded with music. The functional near-infrared spectroscopy results showed that music provided a less demanding way of modulating both episodic encoding and retrieval, with general prefrontal decreased activity under the music versus silence condition. This suggests that music-related memory processes rely on specific neural mechanisms, and that music can positively influence both episodic encoding and retrieval of verbal information.

Background Music and Attention

There has been considerable research on the impact of music on attention. For instance, Jiang and colleagues (2011) investigated the influence of mood on attentional networks in a normal population. Participants performed an attention-network test, which provided functional measures of alerting, orienting and executive attention. Positive or negative mood was induced by listening to music with a positive or negative valence; neutral mood was induced by reading a collection of basic facts about China. The results revealed that negative mood led to a significantly higher alerting efficiency relative to other moods, while there were no significant mood effects on orienting or executive attention efficiency. Specifically, the increase in the alerting function during negative mood states may be due to the modulation effect of negative mood on the noradrenergic system, and/or to the survival benefit resulting from an increase in automatic vigilance towards negative information.

Another strand of work has been concerned with the impact of music on attentional control—an executive function that allows an individual to focus attention on a specific stimulus, while inhibiting distractors from the environment. For instance, Fernandez and colleagues (2020) reported improved perceptual judgment in young adults on a flanker task (where individuals have to respond to one letter in a group and ignore others) when joyful and arousing or sad and tender music was playing, or they sat in silence. There was no overall effect of background music on attentional control performance per se. Similarly, Burkhard and colleagues (2018) studied the influence of background music on executive functions, particularly inhibitory functions. Participants completed a standardised go/no go task during three conditions: no background music or relaxing or exciting background music. EEG was recorded along with reaction times, omissions and commissions. Event-related potentials revealed no differences between the three conditions in reaction times, omissions or commissions. The findings suggested that background music had no detrimental effects on the performance of a go/no go task and its neural underpinnings. Using a visuo-spatial flanker task, Cloutier and colleagues (2020) studied 19 older and 21 younger adults during three auditory conditions: stimulating music, relaxing music and silence. Participants had to indicate as fast and as accurately as possible the direction of a central arrow, which was flanked by congruent or incongruent arrows. As expected, reaction times were slower for the incongruent compared to congruent trials. This difference was significantly greater under the relaxing-music condition compared to other auditory conditions, for both age groups. Focusing on the impact of mood on attention, Shih and colleagues (2012) studied 102 participants, aged 20 to 24, on concentration and attention with music, with and without lyrics. The findings revealed that background music with lyrics had significant negative effects on concentration and attention. In a later study, Shih and colleagues (2016) studied 75 adults, ranging in age from 20 to 24, who completed an attention test and emotion questionnaire. The findings showed that background music with lyrics adversely impacted attention performance more than that without lyrics. The listeners also self-reported feeling loved while music was playing.

Adopting a neuroscientific approach, using Vivaldi's Four Seasons, Leigh (2013) explored the consequence of music exposure on cognitive event-related potentials. Seventeen participants performed a three-stimulus visual oddball task, where a set of the same stimuli were presented with one different stimulus at various points, the oddball, while event-related potentials were recorded. Participants were required to differentiate between a rare target stimulus, a rare novel stimulus and a frequent non-target stimulus. During task performance, participants listened to the four Vivaldi concertos—'Spring', 'Summer', 'Autumn' and 'Winter'—and experienced a silent control condition. The research also examined the impact of different *tempi*. The data revealed that 'Spring', particularly the first movement, enhanced mental alertness and brain measures of attention and memory. Similarly, Du and colleagues (2020) used event-related potentials to examine the effects of background music on neural responses during reading comprehension and their modulation by musical arousal. Thirty-nine postgraduates judged the correctness of sentences about world knowledge without or with high or low arousal background music. The results showed that the effect elicited by world knowledge violations versus correct controls, was significantly smaller for silence than for high and low arousal-music backgrounds, with no significant difference between the two musical backgrounds.

Reading Comprehension

As reading plays such an important role in the lives of many people, considerable research has used reading comprehension as a task in studies of the impact of background music. For instance, DeMers (1996) compared two classes on their reading prior to the onset of the study to establish equity of performance. The experimental group also practised prior to the study, with Mozart's Concerto No. 21 in C Major, K. 467 playing in the background for several weeks prior to the study to familiarise themselves with working to music. Both groups also practiced undertaking a test prior to the experiment. The findings showed that the group with background music performed significantly better on the reading comprehension test. Similarly, Cooper and colleagues (2008) gave participants three different reading comprehension tests in three different conditions: no music, classical music and lyrical music. The results showed slightly better performance on the reading comprehension test in the no-music condition, but this difference was not statistically significant. In a similar study, Liapis and colleagues (2008) tested the impact of lyrical and non-lyrical music on reading comprehension. Participants in the non-lyrical condition performed better than the other group, although this difference was not statistically significant. Drowns (2002) focused on the effect of classical background music on silent reading comprehension and found an improvement with music in the background, while Harmon and colleagues (2008) showed that there was no significant difference among the three groups who either listened to rock music, Mozart or worked in silence on a reading comprehension test. Martin and colleagues (1988) carried out a series of studies, the first of which demonstrated that speech but not music interfered with reading comprehension, while music had a greater interfering effect than speech on a music identification task. Two further experiments showed that the detrimental effect of the speech background on reading was due to their semantic rather than their phonological properties.

Adopting a different approach Zhang, and colleagues (2018) examined how listening to music affected eye movements when college students read for comprehension. Two studies found that the effects of music depended on word frequency and musical dynamics. The first showed that lexical and linguistic features of the text remained highly robust predictors of looking times, even when listening to music. However, when exposed to music, readers spent more time rereading, and gaze duration on words with very low frequency was less predicted by word length, suggesting disrupted sub-lexical processing. A second study showed that these effects were exacerbated for a short time as soon as a new song was played. The results showed that word recognition was generally unaffected despite music exposure and that extensive rereading could, to some extent, compensate for any disruption.

Second-Language Learning

A further area of interest has been second-language learning. Kang and Williamson (2014) examined the effect of background music on participants taking a beginners' course on a CD in either Mandarin Chinese or Arabic. Groups matched on age, gender, verbal intelligence, musical training and working memory ability were randomly assigned to a CD that contained accompanying music or no music. Individuals who chose to learn Chinese performed better on all outcome tests compared to those who learned Arabic. Within the Chinese learners, those who received music CDs performed significantly better on tests of recall and translation compared to those who received no music CDs. No music effects were observed in the Arabic learners or on pronunciation ability in Chinese.

Küssner and Hillen (2016) investigated individual differences in the effects of background music on foreign-vocabulary learning. They predicted that individuals with a high level of cortical arousal should perform worse when learning with background music compared to silence, whereas individuals with a low level of cortical arousal would be unaffected by background music or may even benefit from it. Participants were tested on a paired associate learning paradigm consisting of three immediate word recall tasks, as well as a delayed recall task one week later. Baseline cortical arousal assessed with spontaneous EEG measurement in silence prior to the learning sessions was used for the analysis. The findings revealed no interaction between cortical arousal and the learning condition with background music versus silence. However, there was a main effect of cortical arousal in the beta band on recall, indicating that individuals with high beta power learned more vocabulary than those with low beta power. To substantiate this finding the study was replicated. A combined analysis of data from both experiments suggested that beta power predicted the performance in the word recall task, but that there was no effect of background music on foreign vocabulary learning.

De Groot and Smedinga (2014) studied participants learning foreign-language vocabulary by means of the paired associates method in silence, with vocal music with lyrics in a familiar language playing in the background, or with vocal music with lyrics in an unfamiliar language playing in the background. The vocabulary to be learned varied in concreteness and phonological typicality of the foreign words. When tested during and immediately after training, learning outcomes were poorer in the familiar language music condition than in the unfamiliar language music and silence conditions. This effect was short-lived, as shown in a delayed test one week after training. Learning outcomes were better for concrete words than for abstract words and better for typical foreign forms than for atypical ones.

Studying the impact of background music on writing rather than learning a second language, Cho (2015) also took account of the writer's-second language proficiency. Twenty-eight students wrote an argumentative essay in music and non-music conditions respectively. The findings were analysed in terms of fluency and writing quality, and showed significant differences in pause frequency between the music and no music conditions. The comparison of high- and low-proficiency groups showed a significant group by condition interaction, indicating marginally different effects of music depending on the writers' proficiency level.

Background Music and English as a Second Language

In Iran, Khaghaninejad and colleagues (2016) evaluated the effect of classical music (a Mozart sonata) on the reading comprehension performance of Iranian students having had four months of tuition in a private college teaching English. The participants were required to learn reading passages and then take two tests of reading comprehension, either in a music (Mozart) condition or a no-music quiet condition. The music group outperformed those with no background music. Also in Iran, Rashidi and Faham, (2011) studied the effect of classical music on students' reading comprehension. A standardised text was used and students answered 20 multiple-choice items. Two groups of students, 60 in total, over a period of three months, were taught reading comprehension with a music background or no music. The group taught with a music background outperformed those taught with no music. Similarly, Sahebdel and Khodadust (2014) studied the effect of background music on reading comprehension in Iranian English for foreign-language learners. The participants were 57 Iranian learners between the ages of 14 and 16 in two third-grade high-school classes at pre-intermediate proficiency level. Before the research, experimental and control groups took a reading comprehension. The researchers played Mozart sonatas as background music to the experimental group and asked them to read the passage silently and then answer the reading comprehension questions. The procedure was the same for the control group but with no music. After ten sessions, the students of both groups were asked to take a parallel form of the same reading comprehension test. The findings showed that the experimental group outperformed the control group in reading comprehension. Listening to background music while reading silently had a significantly positive effect on the reading comprehension of Iranian learners for whom English was a foreign language.

Individual Differences

Research taking account of individual differences has taken account of personality, musical expertise, gender and metacognition.

Musical Expertise

Some research has considered whether having musical expertise makes a difference to the possible enhancing or detrimental effects of music. For instance, Darrow and colleagues (2006) explored whether music compromised selective attention differently in those who were majoring in music to non-music majors. Eighty-seven undergraduate and graduate students participated. They were required to bring to the study music that they typically listened to while driving, studying or engaged in other activities. The music brought represented all musical periods and styles. Participants completed a test of attention under alternating music and no music conditions. There were no significant effects for non-music majors; however, music majors who heard the music first completed significantly fewer total items in the following non-music condition, and music majors who listened to instrumental music completed significantly more total items than those who listened to music with vocals. Overall, the findings showed that participants processed significantly more items under the music condition, and music majors processed significantly more items than non-music majors. There were no significant differences based on music or no music in relation to the number of errors made, the number of items processed minus errors, or concentration performance. However, there were differences for the three measures based on musical training. Music majors made significantly fewer errors than the non-music majors, processed significantly more items correctly and their concentration performance scores were significantly higher than the non-music majors' scores.

Similarly, Yang and colleagues (2016) investigated how background music with different instruments affected trained musicians' performance on cognitive tasks. Participants completed three sets of cognitively demanding intelligence tests in a design where each group listened to a different piece of music, involving their own and other musical instruments. The results showed that musicians' performance on cognitive tasks was more impaired when listening to music featuring their own instruments than when listening to other instruments.

Patston and Tippett (2011) administered a language comprehension task and a visuospatial search task to 36 expert musicians and 36 matched non-musicians in conditions of silence and piano music played correctly or incorrectly. Musicians performed more poorly on the language comprehension task in the presence of background music compared to silence, but there was no effect of background music on the musicians' performance on the visuospatial task. In contrast, the performance of the non-musicians was not affected by music on either task. Additionally, the musicians outperformed the non-musicians on both tasks, reflecting either a general cognitive advantage in musicians or enhancement of more specific cognitive abilities (such as processing speed or executive functioning). Similarly, Haning (2016) studied whether background music impaired language comprehension scores in musicians but not in non-musicians. Thirty-five participants with musical training and 15 without musical training completed a 30-item reading comprehension test. Participants completed the test instrument in silence or in the presence of background music. The findings indicated that there was no significant main effect for either music training or the presence of background music, and no significant interaction between the two conditions.

Gold and colleagues (2013) studied dopamine release in the ventral striatum, as this plays a major role in the rewarding aspect of music listening. Striatal dopamine also influences reinforcement learning, such that people with greater dopamine efficacy better learn to approach rewards, while those with lesser dopamine efficacy better learn to avoid punishments. This research explored the practical implications of musical pleasure through its ability to facilitate reinforcement learning via non-pharmacological dopamine elicitation. Participants from a wide variety of musical backgrounds chose a pleasurable and a neutral piece of music from an experimenter-compiled database, and then listened to one or both of these pieces according to pseudo-random group assignment as they performed a reinforcement learning task dependent on dopamine transmission. Participants' musical backgrounds, as well as typical listening patterns, were assessed. Behaviour for the training and test phases of the learning task was assessed separately. Participants with more musical experience trained better with neutral music and tested better with pleasurable music, while those with less musical experience exhibited the opposite effect. Assessment of results regarding listening behaviours and subjective music ratings indicated that these effects arose from different listening styles: namely, more affective listening in non-musicians and more analytical listening in musicians. In conclusion, musical pleasure was able to influence task performance, and the shape of this effect depended on group and individual factors.

Gender

Palmiero and colleagues (2016) studied gender differences in visuospatial and navigational working memory when background music which was designed to induce positive or negative moods was playing. The findings showed that the positive music group scored significantly higher than other groups and that male participants outperformed females on one task when negative background music was playing.

Personality

Personality factors are implicated in creating optimal arousal levels for completing cognitive tasks. Introverts have higher resting levels of arousal than extroverts and are more susceptible to over-arousal, which impacts on their task performance when there are certain types of background music (Cassidy and MacDonald, 2007). Furnham and colleagues (1999) examined the effects of vocal and instrumental music upon the performance of introverts and extroverts on three cognitive tasks. One hundred and forty-four sixth-form pupils—introverts and extroverts—completed a reading comprehension task, a logic problem and a coding task. An interaction was predicted such that instrumental music would impair and enhance the test performance of introverts and extroverts respectively, and that these effects would be magnified in the vocal music condition. No significant interactions were found, although there was a trend for the introverts to be impaired by the introduction of music to the environment, and extroverts to be enhanced by it, particularly on the reading and coding tasks. A main effect of extroversion was found in the reading comprehension task. There was a condition effect on the logic task, with participants doing best in the presence of instrumental music. Similarly, MacDonald (2013) examined the relationship between music preference and extroversion on complex task performance in a sample of 34 college students. The students were separated into two groups of high and low extroversion. Each participant experienced three different music conditions (preferred, preset and silence) while performing a complex reading comprehension task. The results revealed a significant interaction effect between level of extroversion and music condition. Individuals with higher levels of extroversion performed significantly better listening to preferred music during the complex task compared to silence and a preset music selection. There were no other statistically significant outcomes. Avila and colleagues (2011) investigated the effect of familiar musical distractors on the cognitive performance of introverts and extroverts. Participants completed a verbal, numerical and logic test in three music conditions: vocal music, instrumental music and silence. The findings showed that, during the verbal test, overall performance for all participants was significantly better in silence, suggesting that lyrics interfere with the processing of verbal information. However, no significant music and personality interactions were found.

Dobbs and colleagues (2011) studied the cognitive test performance of introverts and extroverts in the presence of silence, UK garage music and background noise. One hundred and eighteen female secondary-school students carried out three cognitive tests. It was predicted that introverts would perform more badly on all of the tasks than extroverts in the presence of music and noise but, in silence, performance would be the same. A significant interaction was found for all three tasks. It was also predicted that there would be a main effect of background sound. Performance would be worse in the presence of music and noise than silence. The findings confirmed this prediction with one exception.

Furnham and Strbac (2002) extended previous work by examining whether background noise would be as distracting as music. In the presence of silence, background garage music and office noise, 38 introverts and 38 extroverts carried out a reading comprehension task, a prose-recall task and a mental arithmetic task. It was predicted that there would be an interaction between personality and background sound on all three tasks. Introverts would do more badly on all of the tasks than extroverts in the presence of music and noise but, in silence, performance would be the same. A significant interaction was found on the reading comprehension task only, although a trend for this effect was clearly present on the other two tasks. It was also predicted that there would be a main effect for background sound. Performance would be worse in the presence of music and noise than silence. The results confirmed this prediction. These findings support the hypothesis that there is a difference in optimum cortical arousal in introverts and extroverts. Adopting a different approach, Doyle and Furnham (2012) explored the distracting effects of music on the reading comprehension of creative and non-creative individuals. In the presence of musical distraction and silence, 54 individuals participated. No significant interactions were found, although trends indicated that creative individuals performed better than non-creative individuals in the music distraction condition. The creative individuals tended to listen to more music while studying and reported lower distraction levels.

Background Music and Metacognition

The extent to which learners are used to working with music playing in the background may be important in the extent to which it disrupts or enhances their task performance. For instance, Etaugh and Michal, (1975) gave 16 male and 16 female college students tests of reading comprehension which they completed in quiet surroundings or while listening to preferred music. The more frequently students reported studying with music, the less the music impaired their performance. Similarly, Su and Wang (2010) studied the relationship between cognitive memory and background music. According to whether or not the testees were used to listening to background music, the author divided them into two groups. When the participants were exposed to three different music scenes, the impact of different background music on testees' cognitive memory differed. The results showed that pure pop music disturbed both groups and pure soft music improved the performance of those who were used to background music but hindered those who were not. There were no statistically significant differences between groups under no music conditions. Also taking account of familiarity of working with background music, Crawford and Strapp (1994) used three timed visuospatial and verbal tests undertaken while vocal or instrumental music was playing. Vocal music disrupted performance significantly more than instrumental music on maze-tracing speed and logical reasoning tests. Both vocal music and instrumental music disturbed performance more than no music on an object-number test which assessed associative learning and long-term memory but this was moderated by studying preference. On this test, those who typically did not study with music showed deterioration across conditions from no music, through instrumental music to vocal music, while those who typically studied with music performed no better in the no-music condition than either music condition. Although extroversion was not a significant covariate of performance, those who typically studied with music were more extroverted and reported greater skills in focusing attention during distracting situations and reported less sensitivity to noise in general on a test of noise sensitivity.

Some students may be able to control their responses to music better than others. For instance, Christopher and Shelton (2017) explored whether existing differences in working memory might impact on the outcomes of research looking at the effect of music on working-memory performance. Undergraduate students worked on reading comprehension and mathematics tasks under music and silence conditions, before completing a battery of working-memory capacity assessments. Although music led to a significant decline in performance overall, working-memory capacity moderated this effect in the reading comprehension tasks. This suggests that individuals who are better able to control their attention, as indicated by working-memory capacity, may be protected from music-related distraction when completing certain kinds of academically relevant tasks. In addition to this, performance may be influenced by metacognition (the extent to which participants are aware that the music is interfering with task performance and consciously adopt strategies to prevent this). Kotsopoulou and Hallam (2010) administered rating-scale questionnaires to 600 students in three age groups—12 to 13, 15 to 16 and 20 to 21—from Japan, the UK, Greece and the USA. The questionnaires explored the extent of playing music while studying, the kinds of tasks undertaken when music was played, the perceived effects of music on studying, the characteristics and types of music played, and the factors that influenced the decision to play music. Statistical analysis revealed both commonality and differences in playing music while studying, related to both age and culture. Some tasks were more frequently accompanied by music than others, while students reported being able to make decisions about the impact of background music on their performance on various tasks and taking action to arrange music to support their learning. Competence in managing the use of music so it did not interfere with task performance increased with age.

The Impact of Background Music on Children's Behaviour and Task Performance

Historically, research on background music in educational contexts has explored the impact on children at different ages, with special educational needs and undertaking a range of different tasks. For instance, in young children there is evidence that arousing music increases activity. For instance, Rieber (1965) studied the activity of five- and six-year-old children in a specially designed playroom under conditions of silence and two types of music (fast and slow). Activity rates were higher during the intervals when music was played, with fast music having the more marked effect. Music did not affect the variability of activity, which showed a steady decline during the time spent in the room. There is also evidence that the type of play may change. For instance, Gunsberg (1991) found that there was an increase in interactive play when arousing music was playing. Ziv and Goshen (2006) explored the effect of sad and happy background music on the interpretation of a story in five- to six-year-old children. The children heard a story with a background of happy, sad or no melody. The findings showed that background music affected children's interpretation of the story. Happy background music led to positive interpretations, whereas sad background music led to more negative interpretations. The effect of the happy music was stronger than that of sad music.

Koolidge and Holmes (2018) explored the effects of background music on puzzle-assembly task performance in young children. Participants were 87 primarily European-American children aged four to five years old enrolled in early childhood classes. Children were given one minute to complete a 12-piece puzzle task in one of three background music conditions: music with lyrics, music without lyrics and no music. The music selection was 'You're Welcome' from the Disney movie *Moana*. The findings revealed that children who heard the music without lyrics completed more puzzle pieces than children in either the music-with-lyrics or no-music condition. Background music without distracting lyrics may be beneficial and superior to background music with lyrics for young children's cognitive performance, even when they are engaged independently in a non-verbal task. Focusing on drawing, Gur (2009) investigated the effect of classical music on the cognitive content of children's drawings. The sample consisted of 84 six-year-old children from private kindergartens in higher socioeconomic status areas in Ankara in Turkey. The sample was divided into three groups. The first engaged in free drawing while listening to classical music, the second engaged in free drawing with no music and the third group acted as a control. The results showed that there was a positive effect of classical music on the cognitive content of the drawings.

Background Music and Primary-School Children

Mitchell (1949) was interested in the effect of radio programmes on the silent reading achievement of 91 sixth-grade students. At the time of the study, radio had become an integral part of American culture. It seemed pertinent, therefore, to determine whether radio broadcasts had any effect on the ability of pupils to concentrate sufficiently on their studies in order to acquire knowledge and information. Ninety-one students carried out silent reading tests with either a music or a variety radio programme playing in the background, or they worked in silence. Overall, the variety programme disrupted performance more strongly for the boys than the girls. Performance during listening to the music programme was unaffected. In fact, the boys performed slightly better with the music playing. Working in Taiwan, Su and colleagues (2017) tested whether the Mozart Sonata for Two Pianos (K. 448) playing in the background impacted on the learning anxiety, reading rates and reading comprehension of students reading e-books. Sixty-two elementary students participated. The findings showed that, when compared with reading without music, the music had a positive effect in reducing learning anxiety and improved the students' reading rates, reading comprehension and direct process performance. However, the music had a negative effect on the students' attention when they had to interpret what they had read. This was explained in terms of the music taking up attentional resources which were required for the task.

Working in a school setting, Ivanov and Geake (2003) found some evidence of an impact related to playing Mozart in the background with upper-primary-school-aged children. Scores on a paper-folding task for a class which listened to Mozart during testing were significantly higher than the scores of a control class. A similar result was obtained for another class which listened to Bach during testing. The musical educational experience of the children did not significantly contribute to the variance in scores.

Koppelman and Scott (1995) explored the impact of different kinds of music on children's writing content. Nineteen students from a second-grade class participated in ten 15-minute writing sessions, accompanied in each session by one type of background music: classical, jazz, popular, country or silence. The writing was analysed for tone, consistency and number of words. The findings showed that students wrote more words under the classical music condition and there were fewer inconsistencies in writing when listening to jazz. Popular music from the top 40 had a significant negative effect on writing, perhaps because the students were familiar with it. Hallam and Godwin (2015) explored the impact of music on creative writing in primary-school children. Children aged ten to eleven were asked to write an exciting story while listening to arousing, calming or no music. They then completed a questionnaire to establish their awareness of the music and its effects. The music appeared to have little effect on basic literacy skills in the children but stories were rated as more exciting when the calming music was playing. The children had little conception of the detrimental effects of the exciting music on their writing.

Mowsesian and Heyer (1973) studied whether music would distract performance in a testing situation. Four groups of participants were randomly assigned to one of four music conditions. The control group experienced optimal testing conditions as defined by accepted standards. Results on arithmetic, spelling and self-concept measures indicated no differences in mean test scores across groups, regardless of the test condition. The authors suggested that, since a variety of noises is a normal part of the environment, music as a distractor was not an issue. Hallam and colleagues (2002), working with primary-school children aged ten to twelve, undertook two studies exploring the effects of music perceived to be calming and relaxing on performance in arithmetic and on a memory task. They found that calming music led to an improvement in children's performance on memory and mathematics tasks, compared with a no-music condition. Music perceived as arousing, aggressive and unpleasant disrupted performance on the memory task and led to a lower level of reported altruistic behaviour by the children. This suggests that the effects of music on task performance are mediated by arousal and mood rather than directly affecting cognition. Also in the UK, Bloor (2009) administered four tests to three classes in different primary schools, two with music and two with silence, to see if the music had an impact on the behaviour and attainment of the children during testing. The results were then cross-referenced with the children's self-evaluation of their own musicality, to ascertain if those children who experienced disruption of attainment and behaviour were musicians. The findings suggested that the music may have supported performance on reading tests but conversely disrupted mathematics tests. Batur (2016) formed experimental and control groups of students in the fifth and sixth grades on the basis of scores on Turkish language exams. Overall, 80 students participated (40 from each grade), with half participating in the intervention and half acting as controls. The students were given 20 minutes to write about any subject that they wished. Those in the intervention groups worked with background music playing, while the others worked in silence. The findings showed that those who wrote with music in the background used more words in their essays than the control group and wrote more fluently.

Focusing on task behaviour, Davidson and colleagues (1986) determined the effect of background music on 26 pupils in a fifth-grade science class. The children were observed for 42 class sessions over a period of four months. Observational data were recorded every three minutes. Time series analyses were performed to determine the effects. There was a significant increase in task performance for the male students and for the total class when music was playing, although there was a ceiling effect for females.

Background Music and Older Students

There has been considerable research with high-school students, as this is the age when music is often played while homework is completed. Kiger (1989) studied the effects of music information load on a reading comprehension task. Twenty-seven male and 27 female high-school students read a passage of literature in the presence of silence, or low- or high-information-load music. Comprehension was best in the low-information-load music condition and worst when the high-information-load music was playing. Similarly, Fogelson (1973) explored whether music acted as a distracter on reading. Playing popular instrumental music during a test proved to be distracting and lowered the reading test performance of 14 eighth-grade students. The less able students were more adversely affected than those who were of higher levels of competence.

Hall (1952) studied the effect of background music on the reading comprehension of 278 eighth- and ninth-grade students in study-hall conditions. Almost 58 percent of the 245 students tested, exclusive of the control group, showed an increase in score when the test was administered with background music. The difference in means showed a substantial gain with background music during the first lesson in the morning and during the first and second afternoon lessons. Over 67 percent of the students in these periods showed an increase in score with music background. Also studying reading comprehension, Anderson and Fuller (2010) investigated the effect of lyrical music on the performance of adolescents. A reading comprehension test was administered to 334 seventh- and eighth-grade students in a non-music environment or with accompanying music comprising top hit singles from 2006. Following the music portion of the test, students completed a survey to assess their preference for or against listening to music while studying. The findings showed that performance declined significantly when background music was playing. For students exhibiting a strong preference for listening to music while studying, there was a pronounced detrimental effect on comprehension.

At college level, Taylor and Rowe (2010) focused on assessment in mathematics, specifically trigonometry. During six major tests of trigonometry, 69 students were played music by Mozart. The results were compared to the performance of 59 students who took the same tests with no background music. The results indicated that the students performed significantly better when Mozart was being played as background music during the assessment.

Research with Children with Emotional and Behavioural Difficulties, ADHD and Developmental Difficulties

Calming music has a positive impact on the behaviour of children with emotional and behavioural difficulties, reducing their stress and anxiety in a variety of settings, although for some children with learning difficulties—for instance with Attention Deficit Disorder (ADD) or Attention Deficit Hyperactivity Disorder (ADHD)—stimulating music is more effective in improving their behaviour, replacing the children's need for activity and self-stimulation. These differences in response mean that music interventions aimed at changing behaviour need to be tailored to the requirements of specific groups of children.

Children with Attention Deficit Hyperactivity Disorder and Attention Deficit Disorder

Music has been used to help reduce hyperactivity in children with Attention Deficit Disorder (ADD) or Attention Deficit Hyperactivity

Disorder (ADHD) (Scott, 1970). Cripe (1986) proposed that rock music could be used as an adjunctive therapy to other more conventional treatments—rock music has the advantage that it can be 'administered' without the need for training staff. It was hypothesised that rock music would decrease activity level in children with ADD and increase their attention span. Eight males with ADD, aged six to eight years old, were introduced to rock music in a playroom. Activity level, number of activities, attention span and length of time attending to one task were assessed. The results indicated a statistically significant reduction in the number of motor activities during the music periods within the test sessions, although there were no significant differences regarding attention span.

Pelham and colleagues (2011) examined the effects of music and video on the classroom behaviour, and performance of boys with and without ADHD, as well as the effects of the drug methylphenidate. Forty-one boys with ADHD and 26 controls worked in the presence of no distraction, music or video. Video produced significant distraction, particularly for the boys with ADHD, while music improved their performance. There were individual differences in response to the music such that some boys were adversely affected and others benefited relative to no distractor. In a second study, music and methylphenidate were assessed in an additional 86 boys with ADHD to further examine the music results. In the presence or absence of music, methylphenidate improved performance relative to placebo. Similar individual differences were found as in the first experiment. Similarly, Abikoff and colleagues (1996) evaluated the impact of extra task stimulation on the academic performance of children with ADHD. Twenty boys with ADHD and 20 boys without ADHD worked on an arithmetic task during high stimulation, music, low stimulation, speech, and no stimulation (silence). The music distractors were individualised for each child, and the arithmetic problems were set at each child's ability level. The non-ADHD young people performed similarly under all three auditory conditions, while the children with ADHD did significantly better under the music condition than speech or silence conditions. However, arithmetic performance was enhanced only for those children with ADHD who were exposed to music as the first condition. Maloy and Peterson (2014) undertook a meta-analysis of the effectiveness of music interventions for children and adolescents with ADHD. The analysis revealed that music interventions were minimally effective as an intervention for increasing task performance.

Emotional and Behavioural Difficulties

Savan (1989; 1999) observed children with behavioural difficulties during science lessons. She suggested that the behaviour of pupils with special educational needs was, in part, resulting from frustration due to lack of physical coordination and the consequent inability to perform manual tasks effectively and efficiently. She investigated the possibility that specific properties of certain Mozart orchestral compositions might, in combination, improve the coordination skills of pupils with emotional and behavioural difficulties. Audio tapes of Mozart orchestral compositions provided a sound stimulus for ten boys aged twelve and over, identified as having special educational needs and emotional and behavioural difficulties. The tapes were then edited in an attempt to establish which musical qualities produced the effects. Measurements of blood pressure, body temperature and pulse rate were taken to establish which sound stimulus had an effect on the physiology and metabolism of the participants. In each case, an improvement in coordination was observed, accompanied by a corresponding drop in physiological measures and an observed improvement in behaviour. Improvements were also observed in cooperation, aggression was reduced during the lessons immediately following the science lessons.

Hallam and Price (1998) studied the effects of providing background music in the classroom on the behaviour and performance on mathematical tasks of ten children aged nine to ten attending a school for children with emotional and behavioural difficulties, who exhibited a high frequency of disruptive behaviour. The music consisted of songs from children's films and other music which was popular and well known to the children—the music had been previously identified by other children in the school as calming and relaxing. There was a significant improvement in behaviour and mathematics performance for all of the children. The effects were particularly marked for those whose problems were related to constant stimulus-seeking and overactivity.

Reardon and Bell (1970) tested three predictions of the effects of musical stimulation on the activity level of 11 six- to seventeen-year-old institutionalised boys with severe developmental delay. Participants' activity scores during sedative and stimulating music were compared with levels during silent baseline and non-musical, spoken recording conditions. Fourteen behavioural categories were rated by trained observers during eight hours of observations under each of the four conditions. Activity level varied significantly on the day of the experimental work, suggesting that the novelty of the recordings was a significant factor. Differences in activity due to the conditions tended to confirm the prediction of lower activity levels during the more stimulating music.

Older Adults and those with Cognitive Impairment

There has been increasing interest in the ways in which actively making music and listening to it may help older people, and particularly those with dementia. This section focuses on issues related to background music and learning. For instance, Foster and Valentine (2001) studied elderly individuals with mild to moderate, high-ability or moderate low-ability dementia who answered autobiographical memory questions drawn from three life eras (remote, medium-remote and recent) with backgrounds of familiar music, novel music, cafeteria noise or quiet. Recall was significantly better in the high-ability than the low-ability group, in sound than in quiet, and in music than in noise. Recall was significantly related to life era, declining from remote to recent memory. The superiority of recall with music compared with noise was apparent for recall from remote and medium-remote but not recent eras. The findings may be interpreted in terms of enhanced arousal or attention deployment, and a possible subsidiary role for associative facilitation from the particular music.

Thompson and colleagues (2005) investigated the effect of listening to an excerpt of Vivaldi's Four Seasons on category fluency in healthy older-adult controls and Alzheimer's disease patients. Participants completed two one-minute category-fluency tasks whilst listening to an excerpt of Vivaldi and two one-minute category-fluency tasks without music. The findings showed a positive effect of music on category fluency, with performance in the music condition exceeding performance without music in both the healthy older-adult control participants and the Alzheimer's disease patients. The findings suggested that music enhanced attentional processes in healthy adults and those with Alzheimer's disease. Irish and colleagues (2006) studied the enhancing effect of music on autobiographical memory recall in ten individuals with mild Alzheimer's disease and ten healthy elderly matched individuals. Each participant was assessed on two occasions: once in the music condition (listening to 'Spring' from Vivaldi's 'The Four Seasons') and once in silence. Considerable improvement was found for Alzheimer individuals' recall on an autobiographical memory in the music condition. There were no differences in terms of overall arousal using galvanic skin response recordings or attentional errors during a sustained attention to response task. A significant reduction in state anxiety was found in the music condition, suggesting that anxiety reduction may be a potential mechanism underlying the enhancing effect of music on autobiographical memory recall. Also using Vivaldi's 'Four Seasons', Mammarella and colleagues (2007) examined whether listening to music had a positive effect on older adults' cognitive performance on two working-memory tasks. Participants were presented with the forward version of the digit-span task and phonemic-fluency tests accompanied by classical music, white noise or no music. The classical music significantly increased working-memory performance compared with the no-music condition. The effect did not occur with white noise.

It is particularly important to study the effect of background music in older adults, since attentional control can be impaired in normal cognitive ageing. Older adults tend to be more sensitive to distractions in the environment (Darowski et al., 2008), although they also tend to be more accurate in cognitive tasks than their younger counterparts, but slower (Hsieh and Lin, 2014). Reaves and colleagues (2016) investigated the impact of background music on a concurrent paired-associate learning task in healthy young and older adults. Young and older adults listened to music or sat in silence while simultaneously studying face-name pairs. Participants' memory for the pairs was then tested while listening to either the same or different music. Participants also made subjective ratings about how distracting they found each song to be. Despite the fact that all participants rated music as more distracting than silence, only older adults' associative memory performance was impaired by music. These findings are consistent with theories that older adults may fail to inhibit the processing of distracting task-irrelevant information.

Alain and Woods (1999) and Andrés and colleagues (2006) demonstrated that adding irrelevant sounds to a visual discrimination task impaired the reaction times of older adults more than young adults, as well as the amplitude of the event-related potential linked to the processing of distraction. Fernandez and colleagues (2020) demonstrated that, compared to silence or sad and tender music, joyful and highly arousing background music enhanced perceptual judgements in a flanker task in both older and young adults, although no background music effect was found on older adults' attentional control performance. However, this study used a modified version of the flanker task, which measured several components of attention and included cues before the trials. A more challenging task measuring attentional control specifically might have produced different results.

Music has also been found to have an impact on arousal in older people. For instance, Hirokawa (2004) examined the effects of participants' preferred music and relaxation instructions on older adults' arousal and working memory. Fifteen female older adults participated in ten minutes of three experimental conditions: participant preferred music, relaxation instructions and silence. Four subcategories of arousal level,—energy, tiredness, tension and calmness—were measured before and after the experimental treatment. After each condition, participants completed a working-memory test. The findings indicated that music increased participants' energy levels, while relaxation and silence significantly decreased energy levels, and increased tiredness and calmness. All experimental conditions decreased tension. Scores on the working-memory test were not significantly different among the conditions. There were no clear relationships between the four arousal levels and working-memory scores. Overall, the findings indicated that preferred music had the potential to increase older adults' energetic arousal and reduce tension.

The literature on episodic memory suggests that background music may have positive effects on younger and healthy older adults (Bottiroli et al., 2014; Ferreri et al., 2015), although it may be particularly beneficial among older adults with cognitive impairment, contributing to arousal, mood and reward systems. Music may also recruit brain areas spared after degeneration, and elicit compensatory mechanisms (Ferreri and Verga, 2016) which are not activated in healthy participants under the same music stimulation. Alternatively, music may reduce task-related anxiety, which is expected to be higher in cognitively impaired participants. For instance, Ferreri and colleagues (2014) investigated whether music could improve episodic memory in older adults while decreasing prefrontal cortex activity. Sixteen healthy older adults aged 64 to 65 encoded lists of words presented with or without a musical background, while dorsolateral prefrontal cortex activity was monitored using an eight-channel continuous wave near infrared spectroscopy system. Behavioural results indicated a better source-memory performance for words encoded with music compared to words encoded with silence. There was a bilateral decrease of oxyhaemoglobin values in the music-encoding condition compared to the silence condition, suggesting that music modulated the activity of the dorsolateral prefrontal cortex during encoding in a less demanding direction. Overall, the results indicated that music can help older adults in memory performance by decreasing their prefrontal cortex activity.

Reviews and Meta-Analyses

The number of reviews and meta-analyses on the impact of background music on cognitive tasks is relatively limited compared with other areas of research. In a review of studies adopting a priming condition before performance on a cognitive task, Pietschnig and colleagues (2010) observed that the Mozart effect (as first researched by Rauscher and colleagues (1993)) had been difficult to replicate, leading to an abundance of conflicting results. They conducted a meta-analysis of nearly 40 studies involving over 3000 participants, and found a small overall estimated effect for samples exposed to the Mozart sonata K. 448 and samples that had been exposed to a non-musical stimulus or no stimulus at all preceding spatial-task performance. Calculation of effect sizes for samples exposed to other musical stimuli and samples exposed to non-musical stimuli or no stimuli at all yielded effects similar in strength. There was also evidence for confounding publication bias, requiring downward correction of effects. Overall, Pietschnig and colleagues concluded that there were noticeably higher overall effects in studies performed by Rauscher and colleagues than in studies performed by other researchers. Overall, they found little evidence for a specific, performance-enhancing Mozart effect.

In a meta-analysis undertaken by Kämpfe and colleagues (2011), the overall effect of listening to background music was established as null. Further examination led the authors to the conclusion that this finding was most likely caused by the averaging-out of specific effects, such as improved arousal positively influencing achievement in sports, or detrimental effects on reading or memory. Not all of the reviews have come to quite such negative conclusions, in part because their focus was different. For instance, Schwartz and colleagues (2017) undertook a systematic literature review and identified 20 studies between 1970 and 2014 focusing on the role of contingent and noncontingent background music to facilitate task engagement, enhance performance and alter behaviour. They concluded that, although the research addressing background music had mixed results, there was evidence suggesting that this could be an effective strategy for increasing task engagement and performance, and decreasing stimulatory behaviour for individuals with developmental disabilities. As providing musical stimuli is relatively inexpensive and may be less intrusive in comparison to other strategies, they argued that its use merited additional study to explore how and to what extent music could affect behaviour. Similarly, Peck and colleagues (2016) reviewed existing anecdotal and empirical evidence related to the enhancing effects of music exposure on cognitive function and provided a discussion of the potential underlying mechanisms that might explain music's effects. Specifically, they outlined the potential role of the dopaminergic system, the autonomic nervous system and the default network in explaining how music may enhance memory functions in persons with Alzheimer's disease.

De la Mora Velasco and Hirumi (2020) synthesised the findings from 30 studies that examined the effects of background music on learning from 2008 to 2018. Frequencies and percentages were used to describe background music's effects on learning across studies, the methods used and the background music characteristics manipulated. They concluded that the results were inconclusive and the findings from the research were inconsistent. Drawing similar conclusions, Ferreri and Verga (2016) reviewed the evidence for the role of background music on verbal learning and memory. They argued that the existing research provided conflicting findings. Although several studies had shown a positive effect of music on the encoding and retrieval of verbal stimuli, music had also been suggested to hinder mnemonic performance by dividing attention. They argued that the extent to which music boosted cognitive functions relied on the relative complexity of the musical and verbal stimuli employed. Overall, background music has been found to have beneficial, detrimental or no effect on a variety of behavioural and psychological outcome measures. The reasons why this might be the case are discussed below.

Explaining the Impact of Background Music on Cognitive Performance

There are several theories which have attempted to explain how listening to music prior to undertaking a cognitive task may enhance performance. The first is a neural priming effect, associated specifically with spatial-temporal reasoning. The second is the arousal and mood hypothesis (Thompson et al., 2001), which suggests that music enhances arousal and promotes a positive mood, consequently affecting and benefiting attentional processes (Husain et al., 2002). This theory postulates that introducing a preferred auditory background prior to a task makes the task increasingly interesting, thereby enhancing the learner's levels of arousal, and that this level of heightened and increased arousal leads to an increase in attention, thus enhancing performance.

The explanations of the effects of background music in terms of arousal and mood also apply to music played in the background. Research has demonstrated this effect when music is presented simultaneously with a variety of executive tasks, such as cognitive flexibility, working memory and attentional control (Fernandez et al., 2020; Jiang et al., 2011; Shih et al., 2016; Thompson et al., 2005). However, not all of the available research findings fit well within this theoretical relationship between music and cognitive performance. For example, some research suggests that highly pleasant music requires more attentional resources and thus may impair cognitive performance in the context of attentional tasks (Nemati et al., 2019). For instance, music can positively affect working memory (Revelle and Loftus, 1989) which results in more material being processed by the learner consecutively, enhancing their performance, while mood improvement enhances cognitive performance through increased dopamine levels in the brain (Ashby et al., 1999). Explanations relating to arousal also need to take account of anxiety, as some studies have shown that high anxiety is associated with lower task efficiency (Tanaka et al., 2006). Byrne and Eysenck (1995) also found that the task efficiency of participants with high anxiety was lower than that of low-anxiety participants. Where individuals select background music themselves, there may be a rewarding effect in terms of the enjoyment it may bring (Arnett, 1995).

Music may also interfere with cognitive processes. Concentrated listening to music requires cognitive effort for processing, analysis and extracting meaning (Berlyne, 1971). Listening to complex, arousal-evoking music may therefore reduce the attentional space available for task performance. When individuals play music while carrying out a cognitive task, they do not attend to both the music and the task simultaneously; attention switches between the two (Madsen, 1987). Depending on their interest, their focus may be greater on the task or the music.

Another explanation for the impact of music comes from its ability to provide rewards. Salimpoor and colleagues (2013) point out that listening to music is amongst the most rewarding experiences for humans. Music has no functional resemblance to other rewarding stimuli, and has no demonstrated biological value, yet individuals continue listening to music for pleasure. It has been suggested that the pleasurable aspects of music listening are related to changes in emotional arousal, although this link has not been directly investigated. Salimpoor and colleagues (2013), using methods of high temporal sensitivity, investigated whether there was a systematic relationship between dynamic increases in pleasure states and physiological indicators of emotional arousal, including changes in heart rate, respiration, electrodermal activity, body temperature and blood volume pulse. Twenty-six participants listened to self-selected intensely pleasurable music and neutral music that was individually selected for them based on low pleasure ratings they provided based on other participants' music. The 'chills phenomenon' was used to index intensely pleasurable responses to music. During music listening, continuous real-time recordings of subjective pleasure states and simultaneous recordings of sympathetic nervous system activity, an objective measure of emotional arousal, were obtained. The findings revealed a strong positive correlation between ratings of pleasure and emotional arousal. Importantly, a dissociation was revealed, as individuals who did not experience pleasure also showed no significant increases in emotional arousal. There are broader implications for these findings in that strongly felt emotions can be rewarding in the absence of a physically tangible reward or specific functional goal.

Neuroscientific studies have established a relationship between music, emotion and changed brain activity. For instance, Blood and colleagues (1999) used positron emission tomography to examine cerebral blood-flow changes related to affective responses to music. Ten volunteers were scanned while listening to six versions of a novel musical passage varying systematically in degree of dissonance. Reciprocal cerebral blood-flow covariations were observed in several distinct paralimbic and neocortical regions as a function of dissonance and of perceived pleasantness versus unpleasantness. The findings suggested that music may recruit neural mechanisms similar to those previously associated with pleasant or unpleasant emotional states, but different from those underlying other components of music perception, and other emotions such as fear. In a later study, Blood and Zatorre (2001) showed that intensely pleasurable responses to music correlated with activity in the brain regions implicated in reward and emotion. Positron emission tomography was used to study neural mechanisms underlying intensely pleasant emotional responses to music in ten university students aged between 20 and 30, each with at least eight years of music training. Each participant selected one piece of music that consistently elicited intensely pleasant emotional responses, including chills. The music was all in the classical genre, and included pieces such as Rachmaninov's 'Piano Concerto No. 3 in D Minor', 'Opus 30' and 'Intermezzo Adagio' and Barber's 'Adagio for Strings'. These are instrumental works with no lyrics. Participants reported that their emotional responses were intrinsic to the music itself, producing minimal personal associations or memories. Cerebral blood-flow changes were measured in response to participant-selected music that elicited the highly pleasurable experience of shivers down the spine or chills. Subjective reports of chills were accompanied by changes in heart rate, electromyogram measures and respiration. As intensity of chills increased, cerebral blood flow increases and decreases were observed in brain regions thought to be involved in reward and motivation, emotion, and arousal, including the ventral striatum, midbrain, amygdala, orbitofrontal cortex and ventral medial prefrontal cortex. These brain structures are known to be active in response to other euphoria-inducing stimuli, such as food, sex and recreational drugs. This finding links music with biologically relevant, survival-related stimuli via their common recruitment of brain circuitry involved in pleasure and reward. Activity in these regions in relation to reward processes is known to involve dopamine and opioid systems, as well as other neurotransmitters. Dopaminergic activity appears to be the common mechanism underlying reward response to all naturally rewarding stimuli. Support for involvement of opioid systems specifically in response to music comes from a preliminary study that demonstrated that blocking opioid receptors with naloxone decreased or inhibited the chills response in some participants. The possibility of a direct functional interaction between the hippocampus amygdala and midbrain is supported by the exactly opposite correlation of dorsomedial midbrain and left hippocampus amygdala with chills intensity. Thus, activation of the reward system by music may maximise pleasure, not only by activating the reward system but also by simultaneously decreasing activity in brain structures associated with negative emotions. The amygdala and hippocampus both receive inhibitory presynaptic input from cholinergic neurons, suggesting a possible mechanism for decreased activity in these regions as a consequence of activity increases in ventral striatum. Brain structures correlating with intensely pleasant emotion differed considerably from those observed during unpleasant or pleasant responses to musical dissonance or consonance in an earlier study (Blood, 1999). In particular, right parahippocampal activity—previously observed to correlate with unpleasant responses to dissonance—did not correlate with chills intensity, supporting the notion that parahippocampal activity may be specifically related to negative emotion. In addition, regions associated with reward-motivation circuitry, such as the ventral striatum, dorsomedial midbrain, amygdala and hippocampus, were found to correlate with chills intensity but not with the more mildly pleasant emotion associated with consonance. These discrepancies provide further evidence that different emotions are associated with activity in different groups of brain structures.

Nemati and colleagues (2019) also investigated the neural correlates of pleasure induced by listening to highly pleasant and neutral musical excerpts, using electroencephalography. Power-spectrum analysis of the data showed a distinct gradual change in the power of low-frequency oscillations in response to highly pleasant, but not neutral, musical excerpts. Specifically, listening to highly pleasant music was associated with relatively higher oscillatory activity in the theta band over the frontocentral area and in the alpha band over the parieto-occipital area, and a gradual increase in the oscillatory power over time. Correlation analysis between behavioural and electrophysiological data revealed that theta power over the frontocentral electrodes was correlated with subjective assessment of pleasantness while listening to music. To study the link between attention and positive valence, volunteers performed a delayed match-to-sample memory task while listening to the musical excerpts. Their performances were significantly lower under highly pleasant conditions compared to neutral conditions. Listening to pleasant music requires higher degrees of attention, leading to the observed decline in memory performance. Gradual development of low-frequency oscillations in the frontal and posterior areas may be (at least partly) due to gradual recruitment of higher levels of attention over time in response to pleasurable music.

As demonstrated in the earlier sections of this chapter, any single research project generally has a limited focus, and cannot take account of the complexity underlying the impact of background music on task performance. There are also methodological issues relating to the types of task considered. These have included reading comprehension, the completion of mathematical tasks, a range of memory tasks and those relating to attention. There is also an issue relating to how the impact on performance of those tasks is assessed—for instance, physiologically, neurologically, by task performance, observation or rating scales. This is particularly important, as the relationships between these different measures are frequently inconsistent. There are challenges in systematically categorising the nature of the music used in terms of its potential to arouse or generate different moods and the extent to which it is liked or disliked. The music can vary in genre, tempo, timbre, intensity, type (instrumental or vocal), and use of consonance versus dissonance. The relationships between these are complex (Salimpoor et al., 2009), although generally music influences physiological arousal in the expected direction: that is, exciting music leads to increased arousal, calming music the reverse (Abeles and Chung, 1996). These responses are based on pre-wired connections related to the primitive elements of music—for example, loudness, timbre, pitch, and tempo (Peretz, 2010). Favourite music, whether stimulating or relaxing, tends to lower the experience of tension, although not necessarily having a similar impact on physiological responses (Iwanaga and Moroki, 1999). It may also act as a distraction to completion of the task. Finally, there are the subjective aspects of music perception. Individuals respond to the same music in very different ways depending on their musical preferences and their individual characteristics. The structural features of the music (tempo, modality, instrumentation, genre), cultural factors (aspects of the environment including tonality and the way that musical associations are culturally shaped and learned) and associative factors (for example, the personal and subjective meanings placed on a particular piece of music depending on musical experiences) all play a part in responses to music. Where associative factors come into play, the structural and cultural aspects of the music are superseded by personal and associative aspects (see Figure 11.1). Preference may therefore render very different types of music as functionally equivalent. For example, the music which young people may choose to play while studying may differ widely but lead to similar physiological effects. Music may be linked with particular experiences in an individual's life, evoking pleasant or distressing memories (Robazza et al., 1994). It is also related to identity (MacDonald et al., 2009). Quite different music can thus change mood in the same direction (Field et al., 1998). Formal music training, perhaps because of its impact on identity, affects responses but there are no clear patterns relating to gender, age or social class (Abeles and Chung, 1996). The complex and interacting nature of the factors which influence responses mean that it is difficult to predict the exact effects of any particular piece of music on any individual.

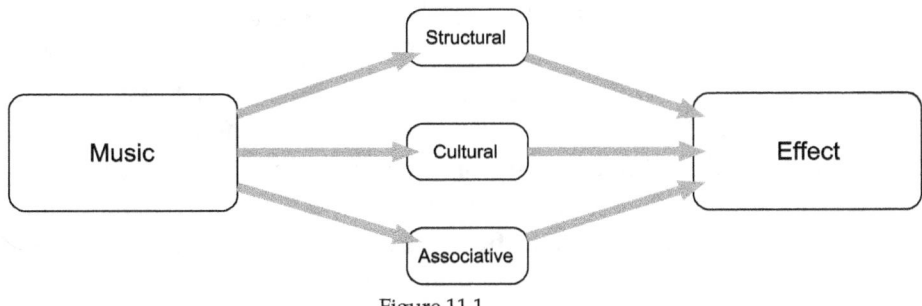

Figure 11.1

There are, of course, interactions between these various factors. In relation to the undertaking of cognitive tasks, a key one is the relationship between the difficulty of the task and the optimal level of arousal needed to undertake it. The Yerkes–Dodson law provides one explanation, stating that arousal levels increase performance up to an optimal level, beyond which overarousal leads to deterioration. Arousal is known to act according to an inverted U shape, where both extremely low and extremely high arousal damages performance, while moderate levels benefit it. This occurs more quickly when the task to be performed is complex or underlearned. Completing a simple task requires a higher level of arousal for concentration to be maintained, while complex tasks require lower arousal levels. Evidence of the way that loud and fast music disrupts reading comprehension (a complex task) supports this explanation (Thompson et al., 2012). Personality factors are also implicated in optimal arousal levels. Introverts have higher resting levels of arousal than extroverts, and are more susceptible to overarousal, which impacts on their task performance when there is background music (Cassidy and MacDonald, 2007; Dobbs et al., 2011). Related to this is the attention drainage effect, which describes attention as a reservoir of mental energy from which resources are drawn to meet situational attentional demands for task processing (Kahneman, 1973; Chou, 2010). Music may, in some circumstances, draw attention away from the task, as it is only possible to pay attention to one thing at a time (Madsen, 1987). For instance, music with lyrics is more likely to interfere with a reading comprehension task than instrumental music if the music is played concurrently with task completion, but this may not apply if the music is used to prime the activity. Music with lyrics may not interfere with task completion if the task is non-verbal. In general, shared attentional resources are involved when processing stimuli from different modalities, including music, and this can lead to impairment in the processing of one or both modalities. Recently, there has been particular interest in the impact of music on the elderly. This has shown that different factors may come into play for this age group, particularly if they are experiencing cognitive impairment. Music played concurrently may distract from task completion, while music played prior to the task may act to enhance motivation and arousal, thus enhancing task performance. Addressing some of these issues, Gonzalez and Aiello (2019) considered the interactions between music-based, task-based, and performer-based characteristics. They hypothesised that music, along with its complexity and volume, would facilitate simple task performance and impair complex task performance, and that an individual's preference for external stimulation (a dimension of boredom proneness) would moderate these effects. To test this, participants completed cognitive tasks either in silence or with music of varying complexity and volume. The findings showed that music generally impaired complex task performance, complex music facilitated simple task performance, and preference for external stimulation moderated these effects.

An Explanatory Framework

Hallam and MacDonald (2016) discussed the subjective aspects of music perception and how individuals benefited from music or not. They considered how this varied and could even fluctuate within the same listener, because individuals respond differently to the same music depending on the features of the music itself, the individual's cultural context and additional experience-driven, associative aspects. Individual preferences and ways of responding to music determine whether music influences mood, level of arousal and the capacity to perform better because of these physiological effects. Overall, the impact of background music on performance on any particular task depends on many interacting factors. Figure 11.2 sets out a model of possible contributory factors including the nature of the music itself: its genre, whether it is stimulating or relaxing, its complexity, whether it is familiar, liked, vocal or instrumental, and has been selected by the individual listening to it or imposed on them by others. The model suggests that the effects of music are mediated by the characteristics of the individual: their age, ability, personality, metacognitive skills, musical expertise, familiarity with the music being played and the frequency with which they normally listen to music when they are studying. The current emotional arousal and mood state of the individual may also be influenced by individual characteristics and recent life events. Individual characteristics also have a direct effect on learning outcomes, and a further indirect effect through metacognitive activity. The environment within which the activity is taking place may also be important—for instance, whether the individual is alone or in a familiar place, and whether there are other distractions. The characteristics of the task (for instance, the nature of the processing required, its difficulty, and whether it is perceived as interesting or boring) will also play a part. Currently, little research takes account of all of these factors. Individuals need to be aware of the impact of music on their task performance and adjust their behaviour accordingly. As a general rule, background music which creates high levels of arousal will disrupt work on complex tasks, although it may prevent boredom if a task is repetitive or boring. Working in silence or with relaxing music may enhance performance on a difficult task. Preferred music is likely to have advantages over disliked music. Music with lyrics may be disruptive, particularly if the task is verbal in nature (see Figure 11.2).

Overview

It is clear that understanding how music can affect task performance is complex and requires many factors to be taken into account. Each individual needs to assess their own situation and the task facing them at any given time, and make a decision as to whether music will assist or disrupt their performance, then act accordingly. In the classroom, unless calming music is used to simply lessen general exuberant behaviour, working in silence is likely to be most beneficial to the majority of students, unless they have particular behavioural difficulties or problems with attention (for instance, ADHD or ADD).

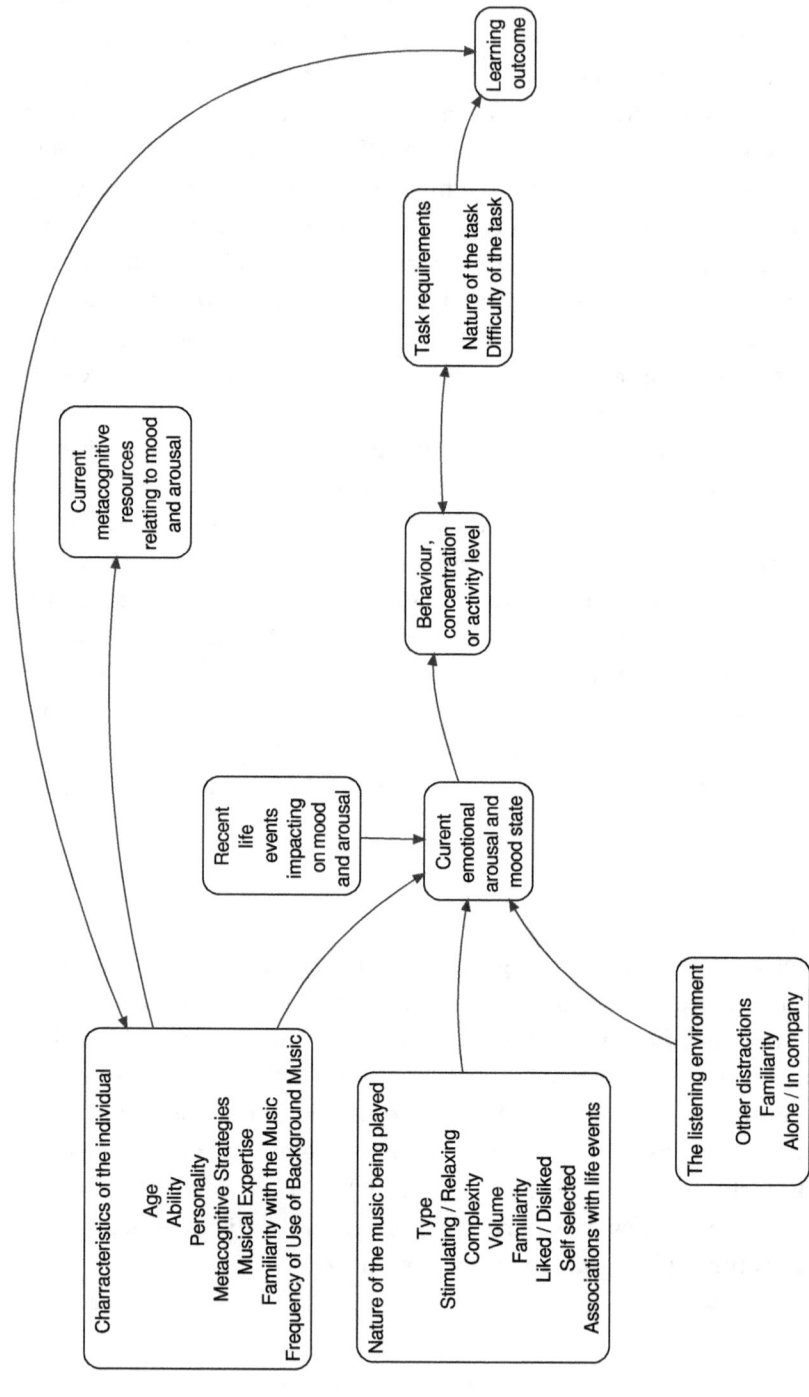

Figure 11.2: A model of the effects of background music on behaviour and learning (derived from Hallam and MacDonald, 2016)

12. Re-Engagement and Motivation

Active engagement with music has been shown to support the positive development of young people who are from areas of high deprivation and may be at risk of disaffection, not fully engaged with education, exhibiting poor behaviour or involved in the criminal justice system. Music has also been found to help with the rehabilitation of prisoners and their successful reintegration into society. This chapter begins by setting out the various influences on an individual's motivation, followed by an exploration of evidence as to how active engagement with music may contribute to bringing about change.

Motivation

Lack of motivation is a problem in formal education across much of the developed world. There is concern about high levels of student boredom and disaffection, high dropout rates, poor attendance and poor behaviour leading to exclusions from school, particularly in urban areas. Some students report viewing school as boring, or as a game where they try to do as well as they can with as little effort as possible. Disaffection increases as students progress through school, particularly in the final years of compulsory education. These issues are particularly acute in boys, some ethnic minorities and those with special educational needs. Young people from lower socioeconomic groups are underrepresented in higher education, and those who take up opportunities to participate in formal education as mature adults tend to be those who have already been relatively successful. There is a substantial group of individuals whose motivation is insufficient to sustain engagement with formal learning in the short-, medium- and long-term.

The complex interactions which occur between the environment and the individual which influence self-development, motivation and ultimately behaviour are set out in Figure 12.1. An individual's identity or self-concept represents the way he or she thinks about him or herself and his or her relationships with others (Mead, 1934; Rogers, 1961; Sullivan, 1964). Identity is developed in response to feedback received from the environment. The desire for social approval, particularly from those we admire and respect, leads us to behave in particular ways. Over time, values and beliefs leading to behaviour associated with praise are internalised. Positive feedback from others raises self-esteem and enhances confidence. Identity develops as a result of these processes. The family has a crucial role to play in this process in the early years but as the child's social contacts broaden, others (including teachers and peers) become important. Individuals set themselves goals, which determine their behaviour. Goals are influenced by identity, ideal and possible selves, as well as environmental factors. Behaviour is the end link in the chain, but at the time of enactment, it too can be influenced and changed by environmental factors. There is interaction between the environment and the individual at every level in the long- and short-term. Individuals can also act upon the environment to change it or seek out new environments more conducive to their needs.

Behaviour is influenced by the individual's interpretation of situations and events, their expectations and the goals that they have, which mediate and regulate behaviour (Mischel, 1973). While each individual has needs and desires, these are tempered by consideration of the consequences of actions prior to attempts to satisfy them. Cognition plays a role in the ways in which we attempt to enhance our self-esteem, leading us to attribute our success or failure to causes which will allow us to maintain a consistent view of ourselves. When a learner has completed a learning task successfully, this will have an impact on self-esteem and motivation which will be carried forward to subsequent learning tasks. Conversely, when learning outcomes are negative, motivation is usually (but not always) impaired.

There are complex interactions between learning and motivation. The more successful and enjoyable our learning in a domain, the more likely we are to be motivated to continue engaging with it. At the same time, the more interested and motivated we are in a domain, the more likely we are to persist when we fail or face difficulties, particularly if we believe that, ultimately, we can be successful. If early engagement with learning in a particular domain is enjoyable and positively rewarded, self-efficacy beliefs are supported and learning continues. This brings further rewards and a positive possible self develops in that domain-enhancing motivation and increasing persistence for the future. Motivation to learn is related to identity and the goals individuals set for themselves in the short-, medium- and long-term. The value attached to learning tasks is related to the extent to which they support this developing identity and the goals derived from it. Throughout life, an individual will engage with learning across several domains and it is inevitable that they will be more successful and interested in some domains than others, and that some will be more closely linked with their personal goals. From time to time, personal goals may be in conflict and individuals may have to make choices based on their relative importance. The difficulty during the years of compulsory schooling, and on occasion after that (when individuals may be required to undertake further training), is that in these circumstances the individual's freedom to choose what and how to learn is removed. If there is little relationship between personal goals and those determined by the educational system and teachers working within it, then motivation is likely to be poor and learners are likely to become disaffected. The more closely the goals of learners, teachers and educational systems are matched, the more likely that effective learning will occur. Motivation is crucial in how well children perform at school and is closely linked to self-perceptions of ability, self-efficacy and aspirations (Hallam, 2005). Actively engaging with music can help enhance motivation and change behaviour through changing self-beliefs and aspirations, and through the transferable skills that it can develop. A study by the Norwegian Research Council for Science and Humanities supported this, finding a connection between having musical competence and high motivation, which led to a greater likelihood of success in school (Lillemyr, 1983). There were high correlations between positive self-perception, cognitive competence, self-esteem, and interest and involvement in school music.

Motivation Developed through Engagement with Music

The process of learning to play an instrument or sing frequently requires hours of practice, typically in solitude, and a commitment to music even when there are competing curricular and extracurricular activities. This may foster motivation-related characteristics (Evans, 2015; Evans and Liu, 2019). Students who learn that repeated music practice can lead to the mastery of complex skills and the achievement of desired outcomes (such as positive examination outcomes or successful performances) develop a mastery-focused learning approach (Degé and Schwarzer, 2017). This may lead to the internalisation of a sense of self-efficacy, which may then be applied to learning in non-musical domains.

Bandura (2005) suggests that efficacy beliefs are multifaceted, although they may covary across distinct domains of functioning. Self-efficacy developed in one area of learning may generalise to other areas. For instance, self-efficacy developed through learning in music may generalise to other areas of learning, particularly when similar subskills are involved. Similarly, self-regulation acquired through music may generalise to other areas. Such transfer of self-efficacy or other motivation-related characteristics is plausible given the parallels between music education and traditional academic subjects. Instruction and feedback are required for both, and there are tangible outcomes in relation to examinations or performance. Self-efficacy is associated with achievement (Caprara et al., 2011), while mastery-learning and self-efficacy develop in an iterative, mutually reinforcing manner (McPherson and Renwich, 2011). Some research has demonstrated how recognition for achievement in music, leading to high levels of self-efficacy, can enhance self-efficacy and self-esteem, which then transfers to motivation for other schoolwork. For instance, McPherson and O'Neill (2010) found that students who were engaged in learning music reported higher competence beliefs and values and lower task difficulty across all school subjects in comparison with those not engaged in making music. Overall, having experience of learning to play an instrument or sing enhanced motivation for other school subjects.

Burnard (2008) explored the attempts of three secondary-school music teachers to re-engage disaffected young people through music lessons. They reported that they democratised music-learning, emphasised creative projects and used digital resources. Similarly, the Musical Futures project was designed to devise new ways of engaging young people (aged 11 to 19) in music activities. Initially, this entailed young people working in small groups, learning to copy recordings of popular music by ear. A large-scale evaluation of the project showed that the music teachers perceived students to be more motivated, better behaved and demonstrating higher levels of participation, greater focus, enhanced musical skills, more confidence, improved small-group and independent-learning skills, and enhanced leadership skills. Those who benefited the most were lower- and middle-ability students (Hallam et al., 2017). The pupils themselves reported improved listening skills and an impact on other schoolwork, including less reliance on the teacher, enhanced concentration and using music to help with other subjects (for instance, making up songs to help with remembering facts). Team-working skills also transferred to other lessons (Hallam et al., 2018). Non-music staff in the participating schools also reported that the Musical Futures approach had had a positive impact on student motivation, wellbeing, self-esteem, concentration, organisation, attitudes towards learning, progression and team-working (Hallam et al., 2016).

Similarly, students randomly assigned to weekly piano lessons over the course of three years demonstrated gains in self-esteem, particularly its academic dimension, whereas a control group showed no such gains (Costa-Giomi, 2004). A quasi-experimental study revealed that students who received a higher number of music lessons over several years reported gains in academic self-concept that were unmatched by those in a comparison group (Rickard et al., 2013). Positive relationships have also been reported between the number of music lessons taken and academic self-concept (Degé et al., 2014) and higher levels of musical engagement (Degé et al., 2014; Degé and Schwarzer, 2017). The experiences of students in musical groups may also contribute to a general sense of accomplishment and collaboration, which may support enhanced interactions in school, leading to a more positive school climate, greater academic achievement and decreased disaffection (Rumberger and Lim, 2008).

Interactions between individual and environmental factors in determining motivation

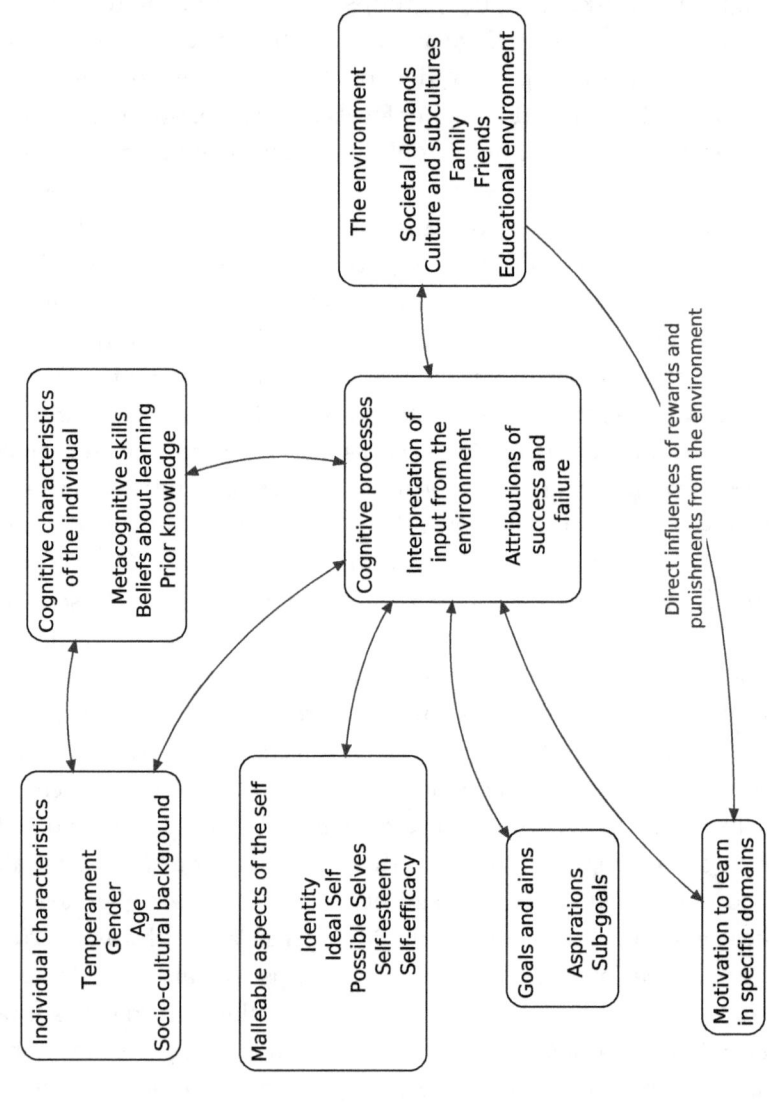

Figure 12.1: Model of motivation

Children and Young People Facing Challenging Life Circumstances

Children born into areas of high deprivation face considerable life challenges. Typically, they only acquire low-level skills and qualifications, and in adulthood they are less likely to be employed and more likely to have lower earnings than those from more affluent areas (Blanden et al., 2008). Other long-term consequences include those relating to health (mental and physical) and involvement in criminal activity (Feinstein and Sabates, 2006). Parental involvement in their child's education, lack of cultural and social capital, negative experiences at school, low aspirations and exposure to multiple risk factors are all implicated in the relationship between deprivation and poor educational outcomes. In relation to music, there is some evidence that children from deprived areas are less likely to have played a musical instrument (Scharff, 2015) and are more likely to have negative experiences with instrumental teachers, interpreting this as their own failure and feeling less comfortable and confident learning classical music (Bull, 2015).

Group music-making offers the opportunity to engage in wider cultural experiences, explore new ideas, places and perspectives, and support social cohesion through broadening experience (Israel, 2012). This not only benefits participants but also increases parents' attendance at cultural events and their exposure to culture more generally (Creech et al., 2016). A range of musical projects have focused on the role that music can play in enhancing the lives of vulnerable children, providing them with a range of transferable skills. Some of these programmes will be discussed here, while others will be addressed in detail in Chapter 16, which addresses issues of social inclusion (for instance, the inclusion of refugee children), while Chapter 14 considers programmes supporting the psychological wellbeing of children from war zones.

Music can be a vehicle for re-engaging young people in education and supporting those who are at risk in making changes in their lives. The context within which projects operate is important for their success, as are the musical genres adopted and the quality of the musical facilitators. Deane and colleagues (2011) found that, whilst music-making acted as a hook in terms of initial project engagement, it was frequently the building of a trusting and a non-judgemental relationship between a young person and their mentor that supported change.

El Sistema and Sistema-inspired Programmes

Internationally, the largest group of programmes supporting children living in deprived areas and at risk of disaffection are *El Sistema* programmes and those inspired by *El Sistema*. *El Sistema* was founded in 1975 as social action for music by Jean Antonio Abreu. It was premised on a utopian dream in which an orchestra represented the ideal society— and the idea was that, if a child was nurtured in that environment, it would be better for society. *El Sistema* has survived through many different administrations and has a large network of youth and children's orchestras. In addition, there are many programmes around the world which have been inspired by *El Sistema* and share its values. The goal of *El Sistema* is to use music for the protection of childhood through training, rehabilitation and the prevention of criminal behaviour. Evaluations of *El Sistema* or *Sistema*-inspired programmes show that they offer a safe and structured environment which ensures that children are occupied and at reduced risk of participating in less desirable activities (Creech et al., 2013; 2016). Evaluations of individual programmes report that children's sense of individual and group identity is enhanced and that children take pride in their accomplishments. They show increased determination and persistence, and become better able to cope with anger and express their emotions more effectively (Creech et al., 2013; 2016).

Raised Aspirations and Motivation for Learning

In England, Lewis and colleagues (2011) showed that participants in a Sistema-inspired programme, *In Harmony*, exhibited more positive attitudes and improved behaviour. Parents and teachers indicated that the pupils had a greater sense of purpose and self-confidence, and their aspirations were raised. This was, in part, attributed to contact with role models in the form of the *In Harmony* teachers and other visiting artists (Lewis et al., 2011). A prominent theme reported in the evaluation of *Big Noise*, Scotland (GCPH, 2015) was the raised aspirations of participants.

The researchers reported qualitative evidence demonstrating enhanced motivation, determination, willingness to be challenged, and the ability to imagine and achieve goals, particularly amongst the secondary-school participants. In particular, the aspirations of the 15- to 16-year-olds were raised (GCPH, 2015). Qualitative interviews with 35 parents of children involved in *Big Noise,* Scotland (Gen, 2011a) provided strong evidence that they considered the programme to have enriched their children's lives. Twenty-nine parents took part in a quantitative survey, which revealed a positive impact attributed to *Big Noise* with regard to confidence, friendships, hope for the future, happiness, concentration and behaviour.

Not all of the research on *Sistema-*inspired projects has been positive. For instance, Rimmer (2018) explored children's reflections on the value of their participation in the English programme, *In Harmony*. Interviews were undertaken with 111 primary-school children aged six to eleven, from three programmes in Newcastle, Telford and Norwich. Parents, siblings and the school environment were all important in the way participating children viewed the programme. The value of engaging with music in the family was particularly important in influencing the children. Challenges in handling or holding instruments—and perceptions of the sounds created as somehow lacking in desirable qualities—emerged. The absence within the programme of some of the valued visual, representational and kinetic aspects of popular music emerged in many accounts. The compulsory nature of *In Harmony* participation contrasted with the valued dimensions of popular music-related activities which were associated with freedom, choice, self-directedness and play.

Raised aspirations were noted by Uy (2010) in the Chicago núcleo of Chacao, where all of the students were enrolled in high school, university or conservatoires, with 40 percent of those studying music while others pursued careers in engineering, medicine or other subjects. In comparison with other underprivileged communities, Uy described this as astounding. Other programmes reported similar raised aspirations and self-beliefs, including *The Boston Conservatory Lab Charter School* (2012), *El Sistema Colorado* (2013), *In Harmony Stockton, Kalamazoo Kids in Tune, KidZNotes,* OrchKids, *The San Diego Community Opus Project, YOLA, The People's Music School Youth Orchestras* and *El Sistema Chicago*. Numerous

USA programmes have included measures in their evaluations which demonstrate the successes they have achieved in realising motivational goals (Case, 2013; Duckworth, 2013; In Harmony Stockton, 2013; Orchestrating Diversity, 2013; Silk et al., 2008; and Smith, 2013—for a review, see Creech et al., 2013; 2016). Other programmes report similar findings. For instance, Devroop (2009) explored the effects of music tuition on the career plans of disadvantaged South-African youth and found positive outcomes, while Galarce and colleagues (2012) reported that academic aspirations had improved as a result of engagement in the programme and that students were less likely to procrastinate in their schoolwork. Similarly, Cuesta (2008) found that 63 percent of participants achieved better outcomes in school compared with 50 percent of non-participants, while Wald (2011) researched two *Sistema*-inspired programmes in Argentina and found evidence of enhanced motivation and commitment. Programmes in Scotland and Ireland also showed enhanced aspirations, engagement with learning and improved behaviour (Kenny and Moore, 2011). In their review, overall, Creech and colleagues (2013; 2016) concluded that raised aspirations were one of the most frequently cited positive outcomes of *El Sistema* and *Sistema*-inspired programmes.

In some programmes (for instance, *In Harmony Liverpool*) changes in aspirations were not restricted to the children participating in the programme but extended across the community. Burns (2016) showed progress in academic attainment at age 11, enhanced musical attainment, and enhanced perceptions of children's social and emotional wellbeing. Parents and carers noted changes in musical ability, communication, confidence, focus, concentration and behaviour. As families engaged with the musical activities and the children took home new skills and shared them with other family members, there was a direct impact on family life. Individual aspiration and community pride changed, creating a virtuous cycle of change. In what was perceived as a severely deprived area, residents now saw some hope. Also working in Liverpool, Robinson (2015) found that parents participating in the research were actively supporting their children and felt that their lives had been transformed, as their children developed new skills and had greater opportunities, experiences of other places and a greater appreciation of music.

In an evaluation of all of the English *Sistema*-inspired programmes, Lord and colleagues (2013) collected evidence through pupil surveys, including a matched-comparison sample drawn from schools not participating in *In Harmony*, as well as case study interviews. The findings showed improvements in pupils' attitudes to learning, self-confidence, self-esteem, wellbeing and aspirations to improve. This was borne out by the national inspection agency for schools, Ofsted, whose reports highlighted pupils' social, emotional and spiritual wellbeing. They attributed this (at least in part) to participation in *In Harmony*. These positive wellbeing outcomes were thought to be influenced by the group work ethic which involved discipline, focus and teamwork. Comparison between the well-established *In Harmony* programmes in England (Liverpool and Lambeth) with more recently established programmes revealed statistically significant differences with regard to children's application of self to learning and their view of their future prospects. Children from the more established *In Harmony* schools who had participated in the programme for longer had more positive scores, suggesting that the programme had had a positive impact with regards to dispositions towards learning and future aspirations. When the established *In Harmony* schools were compared with matched-comparison schools not accessing *In Harmony*, statistically significant differences were also found in relation to application of self to learning and children's views of their future prospects, as well as self-assurance, security and happiness. It seemed that, over time, the programme impacted on children's wellbeing, leading them to become young, confident learners with clear future aspirations.

An evaluation of a summer residential orchestral programme also demonstrated the impact on personal wellbeing amongst participants (NPC, 2012; Hay, 2013). Thirty-five young people aged nine to eighteen, including some with special educational needs, completed a survey of wellbeing before and after the course. While caution must be exercised in interpreting the data—as the sample size was small—there were indications of enhancement in self-esteem, emotional wellbeing, resilience and life satisfaction. A large effect size was reported for each of these measures, although the girls seemed to benefit more than the boys. Compared with national baseline scores for these measures, boys' post course scores for self-esteem and resilience were in the top quartile of what might be expected in a national sample.

Uy (2010) carried out a cross-cultural comparison of *El Sistema* in Venezuela and the USA, and reported consistency with regard to positive outcomes relating to personal development. Overall, parents and students from both contexts reported improvements in focus and discipline, time management, relaxation and coping, communication, ability to work with others, academic performance and aspirations, creative thinking, and self-esteem. In South America, considering the impact of the Batuta, Colombia programmes, which offer strategies for social, educational and cultural development, and support the national system of youth orchestras in Colombia, Cuéllar (2010) drew on key findings from the CreCe report (Matijasevic et al., 2008). Qualitative data provided examples of personal development similar to those reported elsewhere. Students reported positive changes in respect, tolerance, honesty, solidarity, teamwork, sense of responsibility and emotional regulation which helped control aggressiveness, intolerance and impatience. Self-esteem was enhanced, particularly self-efficacy, through feeling competent. Students also reported greater self-care, resilience, happiness and enhanced aspirations. Their social networks were greater and there were enhanced family interactions.

Many USA programmes identified elevated aspirations and goals as key to bringing about change. They included in their evaluations measures to assess these, which demonstrated their success (Case, 2013; Conservatory Lab Charter school, 2012; Duckworth, 2013; In Harmony Stockton, 2013; Orchestrating Diversity, 2013; Renaissance Arts Academy, 2012a; 2012b; 2013; Silk et al., 2008; Smith, 2013; The People's Music School Youth Orchestras - El Sistema Chicago, 2013). For instance, the Renaissance Arts Academy in Los Angeles demonstrated elevated academic and professional aspirations in their students as a result of participating in an academically and musically rigorous intense programme. Their high graduation rate of 100 percent, coupled with the percentage of students who continued their education at university, 95 percent exemplified the huge transformations that occurred, in terms of not only what students believed they could accomplish, but also the goals and expectations that they set for themselves as a result of this realisation. Accomplishments in music and the arts transferred to their beliefs about their academic capabilities, and their elevated goals and achievements in both these areas showed the shifts that can take place in possibilities as a result. Many other programmes have measured and reported raised aspirations and greater self-esteem amongst students. In the Caribbean, *OASIS*—a *Sistema*-inspired orchestral programme established for youth at risk—showed that, after a six-month period of participation, students were significantly less likely to be provoked to anger and display aggressive behaviours including teasing, shoving, hitting, kicking or fighting, or to be involved with delinquent peers. They also had higher educational aspirations. After 18 months, the findings showed positive overall outcomes (Galarce et al., 2012). In terms of academic aspirations, 62 percent of the *OASIS* group, as compared with 41 percent of a control group, expressed hopes to be able to obtain a doctoral degree. Increases in self-regulation were also seen. Seven percent of the *OASIS* group, as compared to 21 percent of the non-*OASIS* students, reported speaking inappropriately to others. They were also less likely to report that pleasurable activities prevented them from achieving their work goals and were less likely to procrastinate in their schoolwork, be involved in fights, or use alcohol or marijuana. After the six-month stage, the results from the Haitian programme were similar to those of Jamaica, with *OASIS* students being significantly less likely to be angered easily, less likely to be involved in aggressive behaviours and to have delinquent peer relationships. Within 18 months, the results for Haitian *OASIS* students mirrored those of Jamaica in terms of academic aspirations, with 80 percent as opposed to 61 percent hoping to attain a doctoral degree. They were also less likely to have disagreements with parents or caregivers, and were more likely to be involved in sports.

Self-Beliefs

Positive self-beliefs regarding what can be achieved (self-efficacy) and what is possible (possible selves) are crucial to motivation. *El Sistema* and *Sistema*-inspired programmes have prioritised the personal and social development of participants, and many evaluations point to the positive impact of the programme on self-beliefs (Esquaea Torres, 2001; 2004; Galarce et al., 2012; Israel, 2012; Uy, 2010). Participation in two Argentinean *Sistema*-inspired orchestras was explored by Wald (2011b) who found that students, parents, coordinators and directors perceived participation in the orchestras as being related to self-esteem, self-worth, self-confidence, and pride about achievements, motivation and commitment. Frequent opportunities for performance helped to raise aspirations (Billaux, 2011) and created safe opportunities for risk-taking (Uy, 2012) which allowed children to experience success on many occasions, enhancing their self-efficacy and self-esteem.

School Attendance and Positive Attitudes towards School

Creech and colleagues (2013; 2016), in their review of *El Sistema* and *Sistema*-inspired programmes, showed that a major area of focus for many American programmes was the impact on students' rates of attendance and punctuality at school. Several programmes documented positive evidence regarding school attendance, including *Austin Soundwaves* (2011-2012), *In Harmony Stockton* (2013), *Kalamazoo Kids in Tune* (2013), *KidZNotes* (2012), *OrchKids* (Potter, 2013), *The Renaissance Arts Academy* (2012a; 2012b; 2013), *The San Diego Community Opus Project* (Smith, 2013), and the *YOURS* programme (2013). Evaluation findings in America showed that *Sistema* participants generally increased their attendance at school. The *B Sharp Programme* (Schurgin, 2012) reported a decrease in absenteeism between 2012 and 2013, from an average of 6.5 days to 4.5 days per child. Many *Sistema* participants attended schools where the majority of students qualified for free or reduced-price school meals. Attendance rates at schools attended by *Sistema* students had higher than state or local average evaluation results in the USA, and showed that *Sistema* students generally had improved attendance at a higher rate than the average for their schools.

In England, the primary school at which *In Harmony Liverpool* is based saw a drop in absence from almost eight percent in 2009 to six percent in 2012 (Burns and Bewick, 2012). This compared with a sector average of five percent. Although absenteeism rose in 2010, an analysis of attendance rates between 2009 and 2013 showed an overall significant improvement, with a school average rate of absence of 6.5 percent by 2013 (Burns and Bewick, 2013). In contrast, in Scotland there was no evidence showing that involvement in *Big Noise* improved attendance (Gen, 2011a), although qualitative data did suggest that the programme was making a difference in this regard. More recently, the 2015 report suggested that the programme was associated with improved school attendance. In Raploch, school attendance was 93 percent among *Big Noise* participants, four percent higher than the eligible population. Govanhill school data showed attendance among *Big Noise* participants to be almost 93 percent—nearly two percent higher than the eligible population (Glasgow Centre for Population Health, 2015). In Canada, Morin (2014) found no improvements in school attendance, although in New Zealand, Wilson and colleagues (2012)—reporting on *Sistema Aorearoa*—indicated that there was a reasonable improvement in overall attainment, engagement and social skills in school, but insufficient data to comment on attendance. Overall, although the data relating to attendance is mixed, there is some evidence of enhanced achievement.

Emotional and Behavioural Difficulties

Alemán and colleagues (2017) assessed the effects of a *Sistema*-inspired music programme on children's developmental functioning in the context of high rates of exposure to violence. The trial was conducted in 16 music centres during 2012 and 2013. In total, 2,914 children aged six to fourteen participated, with approximately half receiving an offer of admission to the programme in September 2012 and half in September 2013. The children in the treatment group participated for one semester more than the control-group children. After one year, there was evidence of improved self-control and reduced behavioural difficulties. The effects were larger among boys and children with less educated mothers, especially those exposed to violence. Following participation in the programme this group exhibited lower levels of aggressive behaviour. The programme improved self-control and reduced behavioural difficulties, with the effects concentrated among subgroups of vulnerable children. In Columbia, Castaneda-Castaneda (2009) explored the impact of intensive guitar workshops offered as part of a rehabilitation programme on young people in a youth detention centre. The findings showed improvements in musical and citizenship skills.

Transferable Skills

Parents and teachers of children participating in some of the *El Sistema* or *Sistema*-inspired programmes referred to the way that the programme developed transferable skills, including concentration (Hallam and Burns. 2018). One parent commented:

> 'The impact on the kids is enormous, the concentration. I've got nephews in other schools and the difference is huge. Our kids can sit there in a massive big place listening to classical music without coughing or fidgeting and sit there and be well behaved for that length of time. There's not many primary kids who can do that. We've got special education kids as well and they can do that.'

Another parent emphasised the impact on learning more generally. *'These children are dedicated to this. Other areas of her learning have come on in leaps and bounds because of this. Without a doubt it is the music.'*

Some parents recognised the impact on confidence. *'Their confidence has gone up sky high. She says she's really nervous but she seems calm.'* Another parent commented: *'The music brought my daughter out of her shell into a confident young lady.'* Some of the older students were able to self-reflect on the wider benefits of participation:

> 'You learn things from it that you don't learn at school. You learn lots of skills for life and you make links with people, like being able to talk to new people, like being able to work on things, so like, team work, listening to others. So even if you don't want to do music for a career, in five years' time you'll have those skills and you'll be able to say I learnt this in orchestra and it will have paid off.'

The young people were also able to develop leadership skills from the mentoring that they were engaged with. This was recognised by staff and parents.

Music Interventions Unrelated to *El Sistema*

There are several music interventions in addition to *El Sistema* or *Sistema*-inspired programmes which have been designed to support disadvantaged children. For instance, Pasiali and Clark (2018) worked with 20 children aged five to eleven years old on a programme that consisted of eight 50-minute music sessions, where teaching social skills through song lyrics and improvisation were central. Social competence, antisocial behaviour and academic competence were assessed, and the outcomes showed that the number of low-performance, high-risk skills decreased significantly, while teacher assessment indicated significant improvement in communication and a decrease in hyperactivity, autistic behavioural tendencies, overall problem behaviours and internalisation. Parent ratings generally mirrored those of teachers. Similarly, Millar and colleagues (2020) reported positive outcomes for the *COOL* project, a 12-month intervention which involved 16 sessions of participatory music-making with 32 hard-to-reach young people aged 12 to 17. The programme aimed to increase confidence and self-esteem, and improve social skills through music that resonated with the young people's lived experience.

One study examined the impact of a singing programme, *Sing Up*, on 48 children and young people (Hampshire and Matthijsse, 2010). The findings indicated that participants' self-confidence and aspirations were enhanced, and that they developed new friendships and better connections with parents. However, Hampshire and Matthijsse cautioned that children and young people from privileged backgrounds benefited more than those from disadvantaged backgrounds, as the latter risked rejection by their existing friends due to the programme being perceived as cheesy or gay. This emphasises the importance of any musical intervention being seen as relevant to the participants.

School music lessons themselves can be therapeutic. For instance, in a case study of a general music class in a Spanish public secondary school, undertaken with disaffected learners who had received a total of 130 reprimands throughout the school year for poor behaviour and systematically rejecting school rules, Rusinek (2008) established that they enjoyed their music lessons. This may have been because the music teacher generated enthusiasm through an inclusive pedagogy in which the principle of 'music for all' was adopted. Arrangements for percussion instruments, in four to twelve parts, of pop, classical and film music were played by each class. The goal of performance was shared by the children and the teacher, and was widely accepted as an important part of school culture. Similarly, an Australian study showed that a group of boys who were identified with behavioural issues who engaged in a proactive music-making activity showed notable improvements in both classroom cooperation and self-esteem. The drumming exercises in the programme were among the most popular and connected closely to the participants' sense of maleness. The activities were fun and provided opportunities for students to enhance positive values such as group cohesion and self-esteem, along with their behavioural and social competence (Smith, 2001).

Drumming seems to be a particularly effective form of musical intervention when children are disaffected. It can support anger management, team-building and substance-abuse recovery, leading to an increase in self-esteem and the development of leadership skills (Mikenas, 2003). Group drumming can foster a sense of cohesion, as it teaches coordination and teamwork, with participants having to assume different roles and work together (Drake, 2003). Faulkner and colleagues (2012) developed a drumming programme as a way of engaging at risk youth, while simultaneously incorporating themes and discussions relating to healthy relationships with others. The evaluation of the programme with a sample of 60 participants in Western Australia's wheatbelt region used quantitative and qualitative methods, including informal discussions with staff and participants, observation, participant and teacher questionnaires, and school attendance and behavioural incident records. The findings showed an increase in scores on a range of social indicators that demonstrated increased connection with the school community. Also in Australia, O'Brien and Donelan (2007) reported on the effectiveness of the creative arts as a diversionary intervention for young people at risk. In this three-year government-funded study, ten arts programmes were conducted across urban and rural areas. The findings demonstrated that arts programmes could have a significant and positive impact on marginalised young people, offering opportunities for skill development and social inclusion, while in Canada, Wright (2012) argued that music education in schools could lead to social transformation

Research on the impact of music-making on children living in care (looked-after children) in the UK has shown that engagement in high-quality music-making projects can support the development of resilience in dealing with challenges. Salmon and Rickaby (2014) researched how developing a musical play could facilitate skills development, improve mental health and strengthen resilience in young people in care. Participants were able to develop new skills, confidence and resilience, and felt more socially connected. In a review, Dillon (2010) showed that music-making could contribute to improved negotiation skills and cooperative working; learning to trust peers; developing the capacity for self-expression and a stronger sense of self-awareness; increased self-discipline and responsibility; a sense of achievement; feelings of belonging and shared identity; and the opportunity to make friends and develop positive relationships with adults. Music-making provided respite from problems and opportunities to have fun. In addition, there was evidence of increased confidence and the acquisition of a wide range of skills. In Norway, Waaktaar and colleagues (2004), in a study of young people who had experienced serious and or multiple life stresses leading to behaviour difficulties, found that a music programme was able to enhance resilience. Positive peer relationships and self-efficacy also improved when the young men demonstrated coherence and creativity as they produced a music video for public viewing. Zanders (2015) also showed how music therapy could support young people in foster care, helping to create stability and find resources and meaning in their lives to promote healing, addressing the displacements, abuse, grief and loss that many had experienced. In England, the evaluation of the *Youth Music* mentoring programme, which included a total of 419 mentees, showed that participants were aware of the musical opportunities available to them and had increased their agency (as assessed by feeling respected, capable and in control). Mentees indicated enhanced ability to work with others, express themselves, respect other people's views and be punctual (Lonie, 2011). Similarly, Brown and Nicklin (2019) explored the impact of a global youth-work project that aimed to engage young people in social issues through the medium of hip hop. Most participants—who were from a range of British ethnic backgrounds—were not in education, employment or training, or were otherwise identified as marginalised, due to having a criminal record or being excluded from mainstream education. The project aimed to challenge the exclusion implied by labels such as 'marginalised', and value participants' experiences, aiming to engage them with global and social issues. The sessions ran over three years and considered financial independence, political identity and mental health, with an overarching focus on money, power and respect. Activities were creative, including lyric-writing, art, interviews and developing tracks to build self-esteem. The outcomes showed that the project built self-esteem and positive attitudes to learning. Participant perceptions suggested that the programme provided them with positive experiences of learning and skills development, thus enhancing self-esteem and reducing risk factors for antisocial behaviour. Hip hop was used to connect young people to social issues and engage them in learning, developing their transferable skills and building confidence, as well as increasing their employability, prosocial behaviour and engagement with social issues. Sessions were interactive, facilitating dialogue and providing peer mentoring. Studio facilities with recording equipment were available. Data included project reports, interviews, field notes, session plans and feedback. The findings suggested that opening informal spaces with opportunities for creative experiential learning (such as hip hop) had positive outcomes for young people and facilitated engagement with prosocial behaviours.

A review of 15 projects funded by *Youth Music* (Qa Research, 2012) showed a range of positive outcomes associated with engaging those not in education, employment or training, or those at risk, in music-making activity. Outcomes included increased motivation to engage in education, employment or voluntary activity, including gaining qualifications, heightened aspirations and a more positive attitude towards learning. Participants also developed a range of transferable skills, including basic academic skills, listening, reasoning and decision-making, concentration, focus, team-working, time-keeping, goal-setting and meeting deadlines. There was also evidence of enhanced wellbeing including increased self-esteem, self-respect, pride, empowerment, sense of achievement and confidence, and an expansion of friendships, trust and improved relationships with adults. Aggression, hyperactivity and impulsivity decreased as participants learned to control their emotions. The projects also broadened horizons, including increased awareness of different cultures and traditions.

An evaluation of the European Social Fund project, *Engaging Disaffected Young People* (Lancashire Learning Skills Council, 2003), found that music and sport activities could encourage participants back into learning by changing negative attitudes and perceptions towards education. Following completion of the project, 85 percent of the 173 project participants were working towards a qualification. Alvaro and colleagues (2010) evaluated the pilot phase of the European Union's *E-motion* project, which was designed to utilise youth-friendly music software in order to engage 14- to 17-year-olds who had dropped out of school, or who were at risk of dropping out. Three experimental pilot programmes were delivered to groups containing between 19 and 26 students in single schools in three different countries: Italy, Romania and the UK. Teachers completed a scorecard for each student at the beginning and end of each programme. Overall, there were improvements in a range of basic academic skills and personal skills including listening, speaking and alcohol avoidance. Interviews also indicated a reduction in offending, antisocial behaviour and substance abuse and, for some participants, enhanced interest in schoolwork, improved school attendance, attention, self-confidence, self-belief, motivation, cultural awareness and communication skills.

School Attendance and Attitudes towards School

Taetle (1999) investigated the relationship between daily school attendance and enrolment in fine arts electives. Three secondary schools participated. Students were divided into three groups according to their elective participation: fine arts courses only, non-fine arts courses only, and a combination of fine arts and non-fine arts courses. Students were then stratified according to grade point average (low or at risk, medium and high). Attendance rates were computed as a percentage of days absent. The findings showed that students with lower absence rates had a higher grade point average, students not enrolled in fine arts electives had significantly higher absence rates than those students with at least one fine arts elective, and students with a low grade point average (at risk) who were not enrolled in fine arts electives had significantly higher absence rates than those students who were enrolled in at least one fine arts elective. Similarly, Oreck and colleagues (1999) reported that participants in an arts-based programme stated that their involvement enabled them to make friends, establish support networks, and feel accepted and valued. Davalos and colleagues (1999) examined extracurricular activity, perception of school, ethnic identification, and the association with school retention rates among Mexican American and white non-Hispanics. Participants engaging in extracurricular activities were considerably more likely to be enrolled in school than were those not participating. Similarly, Lashua (2005) and Lashua and Fox (2007) studied a recreation project that taught young people aged 14 to 20, mainly from Aboriginal backgrounds, to make their own music using computers and studio production software. They showed how participants with literacy problems were able to create complex, spontaneous rhymes through the medium of rap. The participants reported that the programme was meaningful and made school more enjoyable, helping them to stay out of trouble. Activities such as rap battles provided an acceptable outlet for aggression and enabled participants to demonstrate their skills, gain respect and learn humility.

The Integration of Young People with Special Educational Needs into Mainstream Education

Increasingly in Europe, young people with social, emotional and behavioural difficulties are taught in mainstream schools. This presents particular challenges for teachers. Many of these children have difficulties in learning, which may or may not be related to their behaviour. As a result, a prominent area of work in music therapy has become the integration of children with special educational needs. This is particularly the case in Germany and Italy, where government strategies have focused on the integration of children with special educational needs into mainstream schools. In Germany, Hippel and Laabs (2006), Kartz (2000), Koch-Temming (1999), Kok (2006), Mahns (2002), Neels and colleagues (1998) and Palmowski (1979) have explored how music therapy could help children with special educational needs integrate into mainstream classrooms. Similarly, in Italy, Pecoraro (2006) reviewed how music therapy could help young children, some with special educational needs, to learn in mainstream classes, while D'Ulisse and colleagues (2001) also considered how music therapy could be applied in schools. In the UK, some student music therapists have focused on the role of music therapy in supporting children with special educational needs in mainstream schools (Carson, 2007; Crookes, 2012; Hitch, 2010).

Historically, improvisation with individuals has been the principal method adopted in music therapy (Darnley-Smith and Patey, 2003) but increasingly music therapists work in a range of different contexts, including in child and adolescent mental health services, with social services, and in educational settings. Working in schools is a developing area. Carr (2008) undertook a review of 57 relevant papers, 12 of which included outcomes. Although successive governments in the UK have been concerned with the wellbeing of children, in schools music therapy has played a limited role. In a review, Carr and Wigram (2009) found only ten papers which specifically addressed work within mainstream schools. The main recipients were children with mild emotional, behavioural or social problems. Different therapeutic approaches were adopted. For instance, Jenkins (2006) advocated a flexible approach, while Strange (1999; 2012) adopted client-centred music therapy for emotionally disturbed teenagers who had moderate language disabilities. Butterton (1993) used music in the pastoral care of emotionally disturbed children aged 13 to 18 using psychotherapy with music improvisation and drawing, while Nöcker-Ribaupierre and Wölfl (2010) described a preventative approach, introducing music therapy into two secondary boarding schools in Germany with the aim of helping students to express their emotional state and release aggressive tension. The project proved particularly successful in classes with migrant students from diverse cultures, who were able to communicate effectively through shared improvisation.

Pethybridge and Robertson (2010) suggested that music lessons in schools should consist of improvisation, which they believed had the potential to guide the student into areas of learning as a result of experiences acquired through musical interaction. Students from a language and communication unit attached to a mainstream school participated in their study, which involved child-led creative music-making and structured activities to enhance social skills. The findings showed that working in small groups led to greater ability to address educational objectives, both musical and non-musical. Further, Pethybridge (2013) evaluated ways in which music therapists might support teachers to offer interactive group music-making to children with additional support needs. Working with a nursery teacher, Pethybridge planned and delivered an 11-week intervention for three children on the autistic spectrum. The findings showed that experiential music therapy groups offered some level of transferable learning for teaching and support staff, and the potential for developing more indirect approaches. Derrington, in a series of papers (2004; 2005; 2010; 2011, 2012; Derrington and Neale, 2012) also argued for the need to offer music therapy in mainstream schools and pupil referral units to disaffected young people, with an emphasis on creative activities including song-writing, while McFerran (2020) reviewed the research literature in education, mental health and community music, suggesting that grouping knowledge in this way offered new perspectives on the types of programmes offered and the way that they were evaluated.

School-Based Music Therapy Interventions for Children with Emotional and Behavioural Difficulties

There are examples of the use of music therapy with young children. For instance, Brackley (2012) describes the increasingly common need for music therapy work in behavioural support programmes in pupil referral units for children aged between five and nine, who have been excluded from mainstream education. She referred to music therapy's potential to recreate the conditions of the early mother-infant relationship, allowing the music therapist to revisit problematic stages of the pupil's early development and aid their ego development. Similarly, De Silva (2006) also illustrated how music therapy could bring about radical transformation in the behaviour and emotional interaction of younger children, while Thomas (2014) undertook a qualitative case study of two primary-school children with social, emotional and behavioural difficulties, one who exhibited withdrawn behaviour, the other poor behaviour. Music lesson interventions over a period of one year benefited the children in terms of personal competence, self-regulation, self-confidence and self-esteem; task competence, enjoyment, engagement, motivation, social competence, collaboration and social connectedness.

Montello and Coon (1999) also studied the impact of active and passive group music therapy with pre-adolescents with emotional, learning and behavioural disorders. Teachers were asked to rate and confirm changes in the students' attention and motivation. After a period of four months, there were significant changes in aggression, brought about by the facilitation of self-expression, which provided a channel for frustration, anger and aggression. Similarly, Horton (2005) showed that group music therapy with female adolescents in an educational treatment centre—involving stepping, a series of body percussive movements such as foot-stamping and hand-clapping, and chanting or singing—significantly increased group cohesion. The participating adolescents were identified as being at risk of dropping out of school, and were engaged in violent and risky sexual behaviours. The stepping procedure promoted positive social behaviour.

Gold and colleagues (2001) assessed the benefits of music therapy for those with emotional and behavioural difficulties, and showed that children's needs for relationships and opportunities for emotional expression were met by the therapy. In a review, Gold and colleagues (2004) analysed music therapy studies, comprising a total of 188 children and adolescents, and found that the benefits were greater for those who had behavioural problems. Similarly, McIntyre (2007) showed that nine weeks of music therapy with adolescent boys with behavioural and or emotional disorders helped them to develop new skills, enjoy music, experience group cohesion and increase self-esteem. Hirst and Robertshaw (2003) investigated the impact of the Otherwise Creative project, an intervention which involved a wide range of arts activities (including music production and song-writing), targeting young people in pupil referral units with a range of emotional and behavioural difficulties. Following engagement in the project, the participants demonstrated growth in confidence and self-esteem, and an enhanced ability to communicate with staff and to resist negative peer pressure. Chong and Kim (2010) examined how an after-school education-oriented music therapy programme impacted on students. The intervention lasted for 16 weeks and used musical activities to promote academic, social and emotional skills. A rating system completed by teachers assessed change and showed that social skills and problem behaviour improved significantly, although there were no improvements in academic competency.

Using drumming to promote self-expression, Ho and colleagues (2011) compared the effects of 12 weeks of school-counsellor-led drumming on social and emotional behaviour in two fifth-grade intervention classes, with two standard control classes. The children in the intervention classes improved significantly compared with controls on multiple areas of social and emotional behaviour, as assessed by their teachers. Thompson and Tawell (2017) studied the effects of an arts-based intervention on young people deemed at risk of school exclusion because of social, emotional and behavioural difficulties. Eleven young people aged 11 to 16 were studied using observations and interviews. The interventions offered to the young people provided alternatives to their personal, cultural and historical ways of experiencing the world. Experimenting with different arts media and trying out ideas enabled them to develop a new identity for themselves. The findings suggested that imagination, invoked through the intervention, helped the disengaged young people to change their perceptions of their future.

Sausser and Waller (2006) showed that, with proper planning of musical activities, students could benefit from a music therapy programme structured for the success of each individual. They reviewed how music therapy had been used with students with emotional and behavioural difficulties, and proposed a model of music therapy for students in a psychoeducational setting. The model was designed to combine the music therapy process with the nine-week grading period of the school setting. It suggested ways for music therapy and other therapeutic modalities to work collaboratively with students with emotional and behavioural difficulties.

Krüger (2000) set up work in a contemporary secondary school in Norway as part of a new strategy for helping secondary-aged students with emotional and behavioural problems. The students had been labelled as the 'bad guys' and were living up to this name. By gaining attention because of their challenging behaviour, they were able to maintain this role within the school. Krüger found the computer to be a source of new meaning for those who had not learned to play an instrument. Technology led to broad possibilities of exploring, mastering, arranging, creating and improvising music. Participants quickly became confident at using it and being in control. Krüger showed how one child who had threatened other pupils, had very low respect for authority and was difficult to talk to was able to engage in the therapy. Through the shared use of information technology, the process of developing a trusting and communicative relationship was enabled. Krüger reported how he encouraged the boy to master recording techniques but also allowed the child to express anger and shout at him to show that he would always be there. This helped to create a bond and the opportunity to talk about what was wrong in the child's life. Ultimately, the process of using information technology led to a product, and the child became very involved in music-making, burning CDs and creating covers for the CD cases, selling his work and even publishing his music on school radio.

Some research has focused on interventions with children exhibiting highly aggressive behaviour. For instance, Choi and colleagues (2010) investigated 48 such children, who were allocated to either a music intervention or a control group. The music intervention group engaged in 50 minutes of musical activities twice weekly for 15 consecutive weeks. After 15 weeks, the music intervention group showed a significant reduction in aggression and improvement in self-esteem compared with the control group. These findings suggested that music could reduce aggressive behaviour and improve self-esteem in children with highly aggressive behaviours. Similarly, Hashemian and colleagues (2015) studied whether 12 90-minute music therapy sessions could reduce aggression in visually impaired Iranian adolescents compared with a control group matched in relation to age, socioeconomic status and the education level of parents. Two behaviour questionnaires showed a significant decline in aggression in the intervention group. Ye and colleagues (2021) carried out a meta-analysis of research, exploring whether music therapy could reduce aggressive behaviour in children and adolescents. Ten studies were included. The research showed a significant decrease in aggressive behaviour and a significant increase in self-control compared with control groups, whereas there were no differences in a music medicine group and the control group. Music interventions with durations of less than 12 weeks and more sessions per week were more efficient in reducing aggressive behaviour.

Some work has been undertaken with refugee students. For instance, Baker and Jones (2005; 2006) studied the effects of a music therapy programme in stabilising the behaviours of newly arrived refugee students. The research examined the effects of a short-term music therapy programme on changes to behaviour of 31 refugee youths attending an English-language reception centre in Brisbane. Two five-week intervention periods were employed, with group music therapy sessions conducted once or twice a week. The findings indicated that music therapy led to a significant decrease in externalising behaviours, with particular reference to hyperactivity and aggression.

One of the main aims of music therapy for children with emotional and behavioural difficulties is to address behaviour within the classroom. This is particularly prevalent in research in the USA. For instance, Eidson (1989) studied the effect of behavioural music therapy on the generalisation of interpersonal skills from therapy sessions to the classroom by middle-school students with emotional difficulties. Also in the USA, Haines (1989) studied the effects of music therapy on the self-esteem of emotionally disturbed adolescents and showed that music therapy enhanced group cohesion and cooperation. Krout and Mason (1988,) using computers and electronic music resources, worked with behaviourally disordered students aged 12 to 18, either in a self-contained or integrated classroom. Students had the option of enrolling in a music elective class which met three times each week, or of receiving individual music therapy services that focused on learning a musical instrument. Both programmes emphasised targeted social behaviours or skills while learning about music. Kivland (1986) noted the effect of individual music therapy sessions on self-esteem in an adolescent boy with a diagnosis of conduct disorder. Self-esteem was measured by frequency of both positive and negative self-statements, and by his ability to accept positive comments appropriately. By the twelfth week of therapy, he was able to list independently what he had done well at each session, and was able to accept positive comments from others appropriately. In addition, his ability to list what he had done well and what he needed to improve transferred to other disciplines. In Canada, Buchanan (2000), working in mainstream services, studied the effects of music therapy interventions with adolescents aged 15 to 19 who were designated as 'at risk'. The intervention gave them an opportunity for self-expression in a group setting. Similarly, Cheong-Clinch (2009) studied the use of music as a tool to engage young people with English as a second language in a high school and a residential care facility, in particular newly arrived immigrant and refugee students.

Carr and Wigram (2009) identified existing research and clinical activity utilising music therapy with mainstream children, as well as a potential need for music therapy with this group of children. They undertook a systematic review relating to work with children in mainstream schools. Sixty papers were identified, 12 of which were outcome studies. There was evidence that music therapy was used with children in mainstream schools, both in the UK and abroad. They showed that the literature at the time of the review suggested that music therapy was effective in addressing the needs of mainstream schoolchildren — several therapists had documented the benefits of music therapy as a way to increase student's self-esteem, address challenging behaviour, motivate learning and help develop interpersonal relationships (Procter, 2006), although more evidence was needed. Derrington (2012) studied whether music therapy could improve the emotional wellbeing of adolescents who were at risk of exclusion or underachievement. The research took place in a mainstream secondary school and its federated special school for students with emotional and behavioural difficulties. Over 19 months, the intervention group received 20 weekly individual music sessions, while a waiting-list comparison group received the same treatment later. Quantitative data were collected four times during the research from students, teaching staff and school records, while the students were also interviewed. Very few pupils dropped out and the majority of teachers reported improvement in students' social development and overall attitude.

The Role of Rap and Hip Hop in Therapy in School Contexts

The cultural significance of music for youth populations has long been recognised, both in terms of the performance and production of music itself, and the stylised identities surrounding its consumption. Perhaps it is not surprising, therefore, that music-based interventions have been particularly effective at positively impacting the mental health and wellbeing of young people. The kind of music which adolescents prefer is related to their experience of emotional and behavioural difficulties (Took and Weiss, 1994), including expressions of anger (Epstein et al., 1990). Armstrong and Ricard (2016) suggest that rap, hip hop, and rhythm and blues provide a cultural lens, through which many urban adolescents forge identity and express themselves. The music therefore has the potential to combat emotional and interpersonal distress. Creative techniques that incorporate these genres of music can be used to help adolescents understand and regulate coping responses to difficult and emotionally sensitive situations. Schwartz and Fouts

(2003), studying 164 adolescents who preferred light or heavy qualities in music or had eclectic preferences, found that each of the three music preference groups was inclined to demonstrate a unique profile of personality dimensions and developmental issues. Those preferring heavy or light music qualities indicated at least moderate difficulty in negotiating some aspects of personality and/or developmental issues, while those with more eclectic music preferences did not indicate similar difficulties. Despite this, when Gardstrom (1999) examined offenders' perceptions of the relationship between exposure to music and their criminal behaviour, only four percent perceived a connection between their musical preferences and their deviant behaviour, although 72 percent did believe that the music influenced the way that they felt at least some of the time. Most believed that music mirrored their lives rather than being a causative factor in their behaviour. Music was perceived by some as being cathartic, and by some as only harmful when applied to pre-existing states of negative arousal.

In 2000, Elligan introduced rap therapy as a psychotherapeutic intervention for working with at-risk youths, primarily African-American males whose identities were highly influenced by rap music. Rap is able to engage a population of youth who often enter counselling apprehensively (Elligan, 2000; 2004; Allen, 2005). Gonzalez and Grant Hayes (2009) reviewed rap culture, its relationship to inner city youth and the benefits of Elligan's rap therapy with at-risk youth. Kobin and Tyson (2006) also used rap lyrics as the impetus for therapeutic dialogue and the facilitation of empathic connections between clients and therapists. This aided in breaking the ice, encouraging participants to engage in projective narration, and helped the therapist to establish relevant, client-centred treatment goals. In Australia, de Roeper and Savelsberg (2009) showed that taking part in a community-based hip-hop culture project helped at-risk young people to develop confidence, skills, ambition and a stronger sense of identity, although they urged caution in interpreting the findings, as the data were limited.

Cobbett (2007) illustrated an integrative approach to working therapeutically with individual children experiencing emotional and behavioural difficulties, which combined music therapy with other creative therapies, particularly play therapy and drama therapy. In 2009, Cobbett developed the approach, suggesting that such interventions would be more effective if they were available in schools and utilised materials which were relevant to the young people concerned (e.g. rap music or electronic music). In 2016, Cobbett compared 52 young people receiving arts therapy—including music, drama or visual arts—and a control sample of 29 young people on a waiting list over a year-long period in two schools for children with emotional and behavioural difficulties. Two outcome measures were used: a staff-rated Goodman's Strengths and Difficulties Questionnaire and a self-rated scoring system. The Strengths and Difficulties Questionnaire outcomes showed a significant difference in improvement for those in the therapy group compared to the control group for all measures related to emotional and conduct difficulties. The effect sizes were large. Three out of four self-rated categories also showed significant differences in improvement between the groups. Interviews with six young participants suggested that the young people felt that the arts brought benefits that augmented verbal interventions. Examples from the interviews are set out in Box 12.1. In a further paper (2016b), Cobbett outlined a systemic approach which would further support young people.

Box 12.1: Teenagers' comments about music therapy (derived from Cobbett, 2016)

> It helped me find music and I like music a lot now and I can play some instruments. It made me discover a lot of stuff and things I was able to do.
>
> It (music therapy) was easy because I know how to use Fruity Loops (a music software programme) and I can make stick beats.
>
> Sometimes the music helped me get stuff out of my head but sometimes it was just calm too, it helped me cool down. Get myself away from the rest of the world for a bit.
>
> It was a good session because you wouldn't only get to speak about any problems you had in the day. You could also put it into some music.
>
> It made me realize what I wanted to do and then I had to focus more on my future.
>
> If it was just blatant therapy it would put me off, like you need to speak about things that you don't want to talk about maybe, but when you're doing music or something you just feel yourself, it's just expression of yourself.
>
> When we're jamming away, while we're doing it, we could speak about what's kind of bothering me or whatever and it kind of leads on from that.

Parker and colleagues (2018) undertook a small-scale, qualitative interview study in a secondary school over ten weeks with marginalised and at-risk children. The programme was delivered by a team of young people aged 18 to 25, the majority of whom had previous experience of the criminal justice system. They facilitated a single, two-hour music session once a week for approximately 15 pupils. All sessions took place during the course of the normal school day and consisted of a series of activities which involved lyric-writing, usually rap and composing beats, mostly using Logic Pro software on Mac computers, although those pupils who could play musical instruments also did so. The music they composed was recorded and performed. The 32 students aged 13 to 16 were selected to participate because their general behaviour had been disruptive and they had demonstrated defiant, angry, aggressive behaviour towards other pupils and teachers. To remain on the programme, they had to maintain positive interactions with other students and teachers. Some were considered 'at risk' because of previous involvement with the criminal justice system or involvement with gangs. The students revealed in the interviews that music-making increased their confidence, improved their attitudes towards teachers and peers, induced feelings of calm, and improved their communication skills. Parker and colleagues concluded that music-making activities could provide significant psychosocial benefits for young people, particularly when combined with mentoring support.

In a series of papers, Uhlig (2011a; 2011b; 2013; 2015) considered how the voice could be used as a primary therapeutic instrument. Initially, Uhlig worked with children with special educational needs in a public-school setting in New York. She showed that at-risk children demonstrated honesty in expressing their most personal desires and fears through vocal music therapy. Cursing, shouting, singing, rapping, chanting and song-writing helped them to survive their personal and familiar environments, and increased their learning potential. Together with the therapeutic relationship based on sharing rap, behavioural changes occurred. In later research, Uhlig and colleagues (2013) carried out a systematic review and reported that many studies had demonstrated the effects of music on emotion and emotionally evoked processes. In 2015, Uhlig and colleagues investigated the performance of rap-music therapy in a non-clinical, school-based programme to support the development of self-regulative abilities to promote wellbeing and to reduce the risk of low academic performance attributable to troubled mental health. All adolescents in Grade 8 of a public school were invited to participate, and randomly assigned to either rap-music therapy or to regular classes. The rap-music classes took place once a week over a period of four months. Measures of change were taken at four monthly intervals. Primary outcome data included measures of psychological wellbeing, emotion regulation, self-esteem, self-description, language development and executive functioning. Secondary outcome data consisted of the subjective experiences of participants collected in follow-up interviews with members of the experimental group. In 2016, Uhlig and colleagues carried out a survey in the Netherlands of the use of rap and singing by 336 qualified music therapists. The results indicated that rapping and singing applications in music therapy could enhance self-regulative skills during the process of emotional expression. Rapping occurred considerably less frequently than singing but was considered to decrease aggressive behaviour. Singing was applied daily and was associated with the support of deeper emotional involvement. However, the findings suggested the need for more consistent descriptions of therapeutic interventions using rap styles in music therapy practice, and the development of specialised protocols for research studying its effects. In 2018, Uhlig and colleagues investigated 'rap and sing' music therapy in a school-based programme designed to support self-regulative abilities. One-hundred and ninety adolescents in Grade 8 of a public school in the Netherlands were randomly assigned to participate or act as a control group. The intervention took place once a week over a period of four months. Significant differences between groups were found on the teacher Strength and Difficulties Questionnaire, indicating stabilisation in the 'rap and sing' music group as opposed to increased problems in the control group.

Porter (2012) also planned a trial to determine if improvised music therapy could lead to clinically significant improvement in communication and interaction skills in young people experiencing social, emotional or behavioural problems. In 2017, Porter and colleagues studied 251 children aged eight to sixteen with social, emotional, behavioural and developmental difficulties from six child and adolescent mental health service community-care facilities in

Northern Ireland. The children were randomly allocated to 12 weekly sessions of music therapy in addition to their usual care, or acted as a control group. Follow-up occurred at 13 and 26 weeks. For participants aged 13 and over in the intervention group, communication was significantly improved, although this was not the case for their carers. Overall, self-esteem was significantly improved and depression scores were significantly lower at Week 13, although there was no significant difference in family or social functioning at this time point. While the findings provided some evidence for the benefits of the integration of music therapy into clinical practice, differences between subgroups and secondary outcomes indicated that further research was needed.

Olson-McBride and Page (2012) described the implementation of a specialised poetry therapy intervention, which incorporated hip-hop and rap music, with high-risk youths. The programme supported the young people's use of self-disclosure. The intervention involved creative writing and the use of popular music, primarily from the rap and rhythm and blues genres, during the receptive prescriptive component of the session. In some sessions, the facilitator chose the music, but in others group members did so. Group members created a collaborative poem, a structured individual poem or an unstructured individual poem. The symbolic ceremonial component of the session involved group members reading the poems created during the session aloud to the group and soliciting appropriate feedback. Each poetry-therapy group intervention was ten sessions in length, lasting 45 to 60 minutes. Three interventions were conducted with participants selected from two facilities—an alternative school and a transitional living program designed to meet the needs of individuals between the ages of 12 and 21 who were deemed 'at risk' due to problems such as family poverty, family instability, academic problems and behaviour problems. The majority of group participants had histories of serious externalising behaviour problems. Some participants were in state custody as a result of involvement with the juvenile justice system. Data were collected for each group session via video camera. Overall, the intervention fostered a group environment in which guarded, difficult-to-engage, at-risk adolescents felt comfortable and connected enough to engage in surprisingly honest and bold self-disclosure, an initial step in addressing their problems.

Zarobe and Bungay (2017) undertook a rapid review exploring the role of arts activities in promoting the mental wellbeing and resilience of children and young people aged between 11 and 18. Only studies related to activities that took place within community settings, and those related to extracurricular activities based within schools, were included. Eight papers covering a wide range of interventions were included. It was found that participating in arts activities could have a positive effect on self-confidence, self-esteem, relationships and sense of belonging: qualities which are associated with resilience.

Music Programmes for Young Offenders

Adolescents who are in secure residential accommodation are frequently angry, detached, frustrated and in conflict with their peers. They may have experienced trauma, abuse, drug or alcohol use, peer pressure, or gang-related activities. They often lack a structured home environment and may also have learning difficulties or mental health problems. This presents challenges to those attempting to rehabilitate them. Music has been suggested as one possible means of engaging them. McKay (1956) argued that music could benefit young people in juvenile institutions, helping with teamwork and providing a means of letting off steam. In South Africa, Lotter (2006) developed a music programme for adolescents who had been referred by the courts as a means of social rehabilitation. The programme was based on the Circle of Courage which includes four components: belonging, mastery, independence and generosity. The research explored how the Circle of Courage might be integrated into music therapy. Thompson (2016) studied the role of rap music composition in the experience of the incarceration of African-American youth, while Nelson (1997) focused on high-risk adolescent males' self-efficacy in relation to choral performance. A systematic review of research on the impact of active music-making on young people at risk within the criminal justice system in the UK, Australia, the USA, Canada and South Africa—undertaken by Daykin and colleagues (2011)—showed that music offered the potential for improvement in self-efficacy, self-esteem and self-concept. Overall, the review concluded that music projects could help in positive-identity construction, providing a safe means for young offenders to express difficult emotions and anger, although very short projects where participants were unable to meet their goals could lead to frustration (de Roeper and Savelsberg, 2009).

Fouché and Torrance (2005), in South Africa, successfully worked with rival gang members. The young people were brought to the venue by police escort, having volunteered to join the project which met each week. The participants shared their stories and improvised music together. Within the gangs, music was perceived as a cool activity, and rap and hip-hop culture made any musicians heroes. This supported the process. Rapp-Paglicci and colleagues (2012) evaluated the Prodigy cultural arts programme, an early prevention programme for at-risk young people aged five to eighteen. The programme used visual and performing arts to help young people develop life skills including communication, leadership, problem-solving, anger management, career aspirations and goal-setting. Each class was conducted by a professional artist who served as teacher and mentor. Through art, the young people built confidence, learned how to showcase their skills and developed lifelong habits for future success. Over 95 percent of those enrolled did not have contact with law enforcement, and those who did only committed minor offences. Over 89 percent did not reoffend. Prodigy students showed improvement in their ability to control behaviour, affective responsiveness and academic self-efficacy. There was a significant decrease in anger, depression, anxiety, suicidal thoughts, somatic problems, risk behaviours and mental health symptoms, and improved behavioural regulation in addition to increases in academic performance.

Yun (2014) investigated how a music therapy programme was experienced by violent juvenile offenders. Six adolescents participated in 12 consecutive weeks of group music therapy sessions, and were interviewed individually based on open-ended questions which addressed their autonomy, competence and relatedness. The analysis also investigated how the change brought about through the music therapy transferred to their everyday life. Autonomy was promoted by making choices about songs and instruments, deciding how to play, and expressing opinions about music. Competence was associated with developing skills on musical instruments, creating their own music, concentrating on their own project and demonstrating their abilities, while relatedness concerned collaborating, exchanging opinions and playing a part in musical projects. In addition, participants' behaviour changed. They became more self-aware and there was greater mutual exchange and group support. Changes were evident in their school life.

In the UK, De Viggiani and colleagues (2013; 2014) reported on a three-year music project with 118 young people from 19 youth justice programmes. Each music programme had up to ten participants and ran for six half-days, each lasting from one-and-a-half to three hours. The approach was active and participatory including singing, word association, lyrics, artwork, instrumental work, music composition, and the production of a CD or the giving of a live performance. Most participants identified the music as being familiar and safe. For some it brought credibility and celebrity success with peers, but also the expression of criminal identity, genres associated with drugs, guns, gangs and misogyny. There were a great many challenges for the tutors in implementing the programme, including the highly varied demographics of participants, their transience, drop-outs, lack of opportunities for follow-up, dependence on gatekeepers, difficult group dynamics, a lack of decision-making skills in participants, and passivity or resistance as a self-preservation strategy. Despite this, the programme showed the potential to support young people in coping with difficult circumstances and, for some, delivering life-changing benefits. Also in the UK, Anderson and Overy (2010) examined whether music and art classes could engage young offenders in ongoing education. Fourteen young offenders in Scotland voluntarily participated in the ten-week study. Participants were divided into three groups: music, art and a control education group. They completed pre- and post-interviews and measures that examined their emotions, self-esteem, self-control and literacy skills. Behavioural reports and enrolment in education courses were reviewed for three months before and after the project. The findings indicated increased engagement with education during and after the project for individuals in the music and art groups but, overall, the findings were mixed. There were increases in self-esteem for the music intervention and control groups, but not for the art group. All participants felt that they had less control over their behaviour following the project, although emotion scores showed improvement in the music and art groups, but not in the control group. Those in the music and art group indicated that they found the sessions engaging and meaningful. There was a decrease in behaviour-related incidents—for instance, breaking prison rules for the music group—as well as increased engagement with education during and after the project for the music and art groups, with the largest increase in the music group.

In South Africa, Mathiti (2002) and Woodward and colleagues (2008) evaluated a programme that provided instruction in African marimba and djembe ensemble performance on the behaviour of young juvenile offenders. The programme integrated music-teaching, mentoring and intercultural exchanges aimed at the acquisition of musical skills that offered opportunities for diversion from crime and successful reintegration into society. Participants were matched with mentors and reported enjoying the sessions, stating that music-making helped them to stay away from crime, providing them with a sense of purpose and alternative ways to spend their time. Having someone listen to them and to confide in was also important. The programme allowed participants to take on new identities as a result of sharing their skills with others and having them respond positively. The researchers observed that music-making had a therapeutic effect on participants by triggering positive emotions and by giving them a chance for self-expression. In turn, learning a new skill gave mentees a sense of achievement and increased their self-esteem. Interviews with parents revealed that family relationships improved and that the students were more cooperative and helpful, demonstrating respect and acting responsibly. There were also positive outcomes in terms of attitudes towards school. The reoffending rate for the pilot group in the six months post-programme was nine percent, while in the second six months, this dropped to zero, with no repeat offences committed. The programme was successful in aiding the young people to connect with their families, communities and culture.

In the USA, Kennedy (1998) assessed the effects of music activities on the self-esteem and self-efficacy of 45 participants in two homes for at-risk youth and a juvenile detention centre. Musical performance, supported by instrumental coaching, was compared with other interventions, including cognitive behaviour strategies and vicarious experience in the form of observation of videotaped performance by others. The self-efficacy scores, for those involved in musical performance alone and for those with whom this was combined with cognitive behaviour interventions, were significantly higher than for those receiving cognitive behaviour interventions alone or vicarious experience alone. The self-esteem scores for those involved in musical performance also improved significantly following the intervention, although the results did not differ significantly when compared with alternative interventions. Those involved in either the vicarious experience or cognitive intervention alone scored lower than the control group with no intervention, suggesting that these two intervention groups were better without treatment. Some participants showed improvements in mood, reduced anger, increased motivation and improved behaviour. Similarly, Baker and Homan (2007) studied the implementation of a music programme including piano, guitar, rapping, computer-based music sequencing and composition for a group of predominantly black youths within a detention centre, offering a highly practical and direct means of allowing youth offenders to express a particular form of creativity in connection with their existing music and cultural interests. The treatment centre where the programme was based dealt primarily with anger-management and substance-abuse problems. Young people remained in the facility for an average of 90 days, and only those with good behaviour were allowed to participate in the musical activities. Lessons were conducted with individuals or in small groups. While there were many benefits of the programme, there were also considerable challenges, including time pressure, access to lessons which depended on the accumulation of privileges, lack of opportunities for practice and lack of opportunities for continuation on release. The process of writing music can help young people to redefine themselves, especially where projects promote positive expression and seek to challenge lyrics that glorify criminal lifestyles or contain profane, sexist or discriminatory language. The findings showed that such censorship was often met with resistance from young people, who felt that this served to diminish the truth of their feelings and experiences. Lyric-writing allowed those in custody to explore and express thoughts and emotions which may otherwise be repressed—for instance, forgiveness, healing, overcoming and regret.

Also in the USA, Tyson (2002) studied the effects of hip-hop therapy on self-concept and peer relations in a residential setting for at-risk youth. The programme comprised hip hop, bibliotherapy and music therapy that involved discussion of rap lyrics, emphasising positive themes including positive racial identity, group identity, peace and unity. Participants spoke highly of the project, although there were no statistically significant changes in quantitative measures of outcomes. Similar findings were reported by Gann (2010), who assessed the effects of rap therapy on self-concept and peer support in a small sample of 13 at-risk pupils from two urban schools. The results were mixed, with anticipated improvements in self-concept and social support not confirmed in statistical analysis.

Bittman and colleagues (2009) evaluated the effectiveness of a novel creative musical expression protocol with young people in the juvenile justice system. Participants were randomly assigned to participate in an adolescent health RHYTHMS drumming protocol and normal structured routines that included therapeutic and educational programmes focusing on current events, independent living, housing, social skills, grief and loss, health, drug and alcohol use, employment, sexual abuse, sexuality, anger management and conflict resolution. Instruments included hand drums, a variety of auxiliary percussion instruments, bells, maracas, a clavinova and a computerised electronic keyboard. The first session began with a brief welcome, a discussion of expectations and an overview, followed immediately by a five- to ten-minute nonstructured jam session. A total of 52 African-American, Asian, Caucasian and Puerto-Rican participants, ranging in age from 12 to 18, participated. Statistically significant differences between intervention versus control groups emerged, with improvements in schoolwork, role performance, depression, negative self-evaluations and anger. In addition, extended impact was characterised by statistically significant improvements six weeks after completion of the protocol. Other reported benefits included improved social skills, attention span, stress management, anger management, emotional expression, anxiety, depression, coping skills and self-esteem in young people and adults, with a reduction in rates of reoffending. Skills development and employment were further supported by employing people from marginalised groups, such as ex-offenders, to deliver the arts activities to the groups.

Clennon (2013) examined music workshops mainly consisting of group composition through the process of learning to play in a rock band, bass, keys, guitar, vocals, drums and electronic composition, using the software *Logic*. The transformative effect of participating in community music sessions on young people's attitudes towards offending behaviour was assessed. The results suggested that there was a small but measurable improvement in the attitudes towards offending that the young people who participated in the music workshops had, especially relating to their perceptions of their life problems and how these problems could contribute to potential offending behaviour. Similarly, Hickey (2018) undertook a long-term qualitative study to assess the impact of a music composition programme at an urban youth detention centre. Over a period of five years, more than 700 youths participated in the programme and created primarily rap-music compositions. Comments from their feedback, as well as interviews, showed that they enjoyed the programme; it gave them positive feelings and a sense of competence. Creativity emerged as a key element in enhancing competence and autonomy.

Chong and Yun (2020) introduced a music therapy project for young offenders through community collaboration. The project was carried out with collaboration between the educational institution, the district prosecutor's office and a corporate sponsor, forming a tripartite networking system. Project implementation was evaluated with 178 adolescents involved with the juvenile justice system. The music therapy programme was developed with 15 sessions of music-making and song-writing. Three scales, self-concept, resilience and stress coping skills were used, and there was improvement on all following the music intervention. On the basis of 20 interviews, the intervention was reported as helpful in gaining new perspectives, providing courage to challenge and persevere, and self-knowledge.

Ezell and Levy (2003) evaluated the impact of a programme of integrated arts therapy on young female delinquents who experienced emotional and behavioural problems in a correctional institution. The intervention was introduced as part of a curriculum involving art therapy, drama therapy, music therapy and dance movement therapy sessions that were facilitated twice a week during a five-week period. Participants aged 14 to 17 either participated in the intervention or acted as controls. Self-report questionnaires were administered prior to and after the intervention to screen for conduct, emotional and peer problems, hyperactivity, and prosocial behaviour—and to investigate the frequencies of aggressive, withdrawn and prosocial behaviour. There were statistically significant reductions in three of the five emotional and behavioural problems measured by the Strengths and Difficulties Questionnaire including conduct and emotional problems, an increase in prosocial behaviour, and significant differences in the frequency of aggressive behaviour.

Rio and Tenney (2002) developed a programme for juvenile offenders in a residential treatment setting. Many of the clients had difficulty establishing positive relationships, having had severely dysfunctional relationships throughout their lives. The music therapy process was designed to improve social interaction and relatedness, increase self-expression and self-esteem, and decrease hostile and disruptive behaviour. The programme also emphasised the development of empathy and appropriate channels for energy release. The client groups evolved somewhat differently, illustrating how individual personalities and abilities affected the group dynamic and relationships between group members and therapists. In Australia, Barrett and Baker (2012), along with the Australian Children's Music Foundation, implemented a number of music programmes in juvenile detention centres as a means to assist young people to develop their sense of self-worth, build skills in self-discipline and communication, foster resilience, and re-engage with life and the community. In a qualitative case study, participants' perceptions of the learning outcomes were sought—musical and extra-musical—that emerged from participation, the learning and teaching practices, and contextual factors that supported the outcomes. Findings indicated that the programme generated significant musical and extra-musical learning outcomes: in particular, a learning identity.

Skaggs (1997) reported on a music-centred creative arts therapy programme in a residential treatment programme for male juvenile sex offenders, while in Seoul, Korea, the district attorney provided arts programmes instead of social labour hours for youths with conditional suspension. After one year, it was reported that the recidivism rate decreased from 54 percent to 14 percent (Ewha Music Wellness Research Center, 2015).

Music Programmes for Adult Offenders

Music education in prisons has existed since the mid-nineteenth century, but research in the field has been sparse (Lee, 2010). However, recently there has been a surge in activity. Positive outcomes for music interventions have been reported with adult offenders. Participants enhanced their communication and social skills, increased their confidence, became better able to reflect on their situation, and believed that they could change and attain their goals. Early studies were undertaken by Baron (1955) and Benedict (1953). There is evidence that, after participation in such projects, prisoners sought out opportunities for further education and training (Daykin et al., 2012). A number of Master's and doctoral theses have explored these issues—for instance, Apicella (1952)—aimed to establish which music activities were used as part of correctional education in prisons. Similarly, Hodson (1951) carried out a survey of music education programmes in state prisons, as did Littell (1961). Sporny (1941) explored the value of music in correctional settings, while Hess (1956) appraised the music programme in a single institution. In a retrospective study, Richmiller (1992) studied the residual effects of the music education experiences of being in a prison choir 29 years after participation in it. In a doctoral thesis, Cohen (2007) studied choral singing in prison contexts, while Elliot (1981) studied a way of teaching instrumental music to adult offenders. Cohen and Duncan (2015) explored the relationship between restorative and transformative justice and music education in prison and other contexts, while Cohen and Henley (2018) examined music-making in USA and UK prison contexts, pointing out the wide variations in practice and how inmates' opportunities for self-expression could be restricted. However, community music approaches within prisons have improved self-esteem, social support and a sense of accomplishment, and reduced reoffending. The complex power dynamics of prison contexts have emphasised the importance of the welcome and hospitality offered by community music.

Choirs

Many of the interventions and evaluations in prison have focused on choirs. For instance, in the USA Weber (2018) evaluated the Voice of Hope women's prison choir, while Cohen (2007), in Australia, explored inmate and volunteer experiences of singing in a prison-based choir. Similarly, Cohen (2009) carried out two experiments, the first with a choir of ten inmates which only performed within the prison, the second with a larger choir of 48, which included inmates and volunteers and performed externally. There were no significant differences in wellbeing between the two groups overall, but the group who were able to perform externally scored higher on measures of emotional stability, sociability, happiness and joviality. Later, Cohen and Trachsel (2010) discussed voice as the intersection between music and language in the context of the writing component of a prison choir, while Cohen (2010) considered music programmes and restorative practices in prisons across the USA and the UK.

Cohen and Wilson (2017) examined pedagogical strategies for facilitating and developing song-writing skills with 17 males incarcerated in a USA medium-security prison. They investigated the participants' sense of self-worth, purpose and social adjustment related to their participation in a songwriters' workshop. The song-writing sessions spanned two 13-week, 60-minute workshops and one 9-week 90-minute workshop, totalling 35 weeks. The researchers analysed 42 sets of original lyrics, written reflections from three instructors, transcriptions of four workshop sessions and narrative data from participants. The findings showed that the collaborative and social nature of the song-writing workshops provided a supportive atmosphere where participants generated new songs for enjoyment and expression. They wrote about struggles and hardships, especially relationship problems, and the data suggested that the discussions about song topics helped them cope with their incarceration. Cohen (2019) showed that choral singing in prisons could help incarcerated individuals identify as returning citizens instead of felons. Maruna (2010) argued that, while many legal and penal rituals exist to convince individuals to identify as offenders, few such rituals are in place to reconnect formerly incarcerated people to identify as community members outside of prison. Maruna described successful reintegration rituals as symbolic and emotive, repetitive, community-based, and infused with challenge and achievement, while choral singing models are positive reintegration rituals that promote prosocial connections between returning citizens and the societies to which they are restored.

Messerschmidt (2017) explored the effects of singing with incarcerated choir members and the effects of listening to a live prison choir perform on non-incarcerated people—in particular, their attitudes towards prisoners. Forty-one singers from four choirs who sang with prison choirs, a control group of 19 who had no experience of prison choirs, and 78 audience members at a prison choir concert completed an attitude-towards-prisoners scale and answered open-ended questions. The findings showed that it was possible for people to change their attitudes towards prisoners through experiences with a prison choir. Almost 70 percent of those volunteering said that their attitudes towards prisoners were more positive since joining the choir. Audience members were also more positive after attending a concert. Roma (2010) examined a men's prison chorus in a high-security Ohio prison. The research aimed to understand how a men's prison choral community impacted on inmate self-perception, intragroup relationships and external connections. The CD recordings made of the choir were sold and the sales benefited charities of the inmates' choosing. This helped the prisoners connect with the larger society outside prison. The researchers explored how musical performance, especially of inmate-composed choral repertoire, affected the choir as a community.

Projects Using Gamelan

Several programmes have used gamelan for prison interventions, as they do not have affiliations that may alienate anyone and they are generally easy to learn, requiring no previous experience. Groups can learn quickly: in one two-hour session, players can master a composition. There is no leader or conductor and players can swap instruments, and changes in dynamics or tempo are decided as a group. The *Good Vibrations* programme was set up with the aim of trying out gamelan workshops in prisons. Eastburn (2003) evaluated a gamelan Indonesian percussion programme in a prison setting. Data were collected on the participants' self-esteem, basic and key skills. There were questionnaires for prison contacts and workshop leaders. One hundred and twenty-four prisoners participated in taster sessions and 64 completed in-depth workshops. The project helped prisoners to develop basic and key skills, and enhanced their self-esteem. At the start of the programme, about a quarter of the prisoners had very low literacy and numeracy skills. Half had never engaged in any musical activity and nearly 40 percent had never participated in any kind of prison workshop. Prison education staff rated the taster sessions as providing good opportunities for people to deploy basic and key skills including teamwork, communication, listening, concentrating, numeracy and motor skills. They agreed that prisoner self-confidence had grown, as had their teamwork skills. Most agreed that the programme was more effective than other short arts projects. Eighty-nine percent of participants indicated that they felt better about themselves, and had a sense of achievement, pride and increased confidence, while 57 percent of adult respondents and 71 percent of young offenders spontaneously mentioned enjoying and learning from the experience of working in a team. Two prison education managers reported improved behaviour or performance in education, and one reported participants signing up for further prison education activities.

Henley and colleagues (2012) investigated the short-, medium- and long-term impact of a gamelan project and found that participation in a *Good Vibrations* project acted as a catalyst for positive change. The research found that, not only did participants feel more able to communicate with other offenders within the project, they found confidence in their own voice so as to continue to develop their communication and coping skills within prison and as ex-offenders in the community. Furthermore, the project contributed to the development of anger management skills and provided an outlet for self-expression, leading to a feeling of being normal. Henley (2015) investigated the learning processes occurring within a Javanese gamelan project in a young offenders' institution and highlighted the parallels between musical learning processes and the development of certain attributes linked to desistance from crime. The desistance paradigm centres on changing a criminal identity through the development of social and personal attributes. This resonates with recent research on the transformative effects of music and how musical identity can be changed positively through active and successful music-making. The research was carried out in a UK Young Offender's Institution and involved 19 young people between the ages of 18 and 24 over a period of eight weeks. Observation revealed how personal and social development occurred through participation. Mendonça (2010) also focused on the *Good Vibrations* programme, examining the approach from the perspectives of prisoners, administrators and teachers.

Assorted Music Therapies

Wilson and colleagues (2009) argued that there was growing awareness amongst policymakers and those working in the criminal justice system of the contribution that could be made by the arts in prisons—in particular, by innovative projects that offer participants a creative outlet and have a positive impact on offenders, not least by encouraging them to engage with further learning and education. Tuastad and O'Grady (2013) explored the concept of music as a freedom practice in and outside prisons in two studies. Most of the prisoners and ex-prisoners participating reported that music helped them to feel momentarily free from the harsh realities of both prison life and the world outside. The findings described how, through music, prisoners found a free space in an authoritative, suppressing and institutionalised environment, and how music activities helped them in building ties to the world outside prison while connecting to personal emotions and becoming humanised in a dehumanising setting.

Chen and colleagues (2015) investigated the effects of group music therapy on improving anxiety, depression and self-esteem in Chinese prisoners. Two-hundred male prisoners were randomly assigned to music therapy or standard care. The music therapy consisted of 20 sessions of group therapy compared with standard care. Anxiety, depression and self-esteem were measured by standardised scales at baseline, mid- and post-programme. Anxiety and depression in the music therapy condition decreased significantly at mid- and post-test; self-esteem improved significantly at mid-test and at post-test. Improvements were greater in younger participants and in those with a lower level of education. Overall, group music therapy was effective in improving anxiety, depression and self-esteem, particularly for younger and lower educated prisoners. Some programmes employed people from marginalised groups, such as ex-offenders, to deliver the activities, thus supporting skills development and employment. Other reported benefits included improved social skills, attention span, stress management, anger management, emotional expression, anxiety, depression, coping skills and self-esteem, and a reduction in rates of re-offending. Gold and colleagues (2014) also showed how music therapy reduced mental health problems and could be beneficial in the rehabilitation of prisoners. They compared group music therapy with standard care for prisoners in a randomised controlled trial that started with the establishment of music therapy services in a prison near Bergen in Norway in 2008. One hundred and thirteen prisoners agreed to participate. Anxiety, depression and social relationships were assessed at baseline and every two weeks in the intervention group, and after one, three and six months in the control group, then at release. No restrictions were placed on the frequency, duration or contents of the music therapy. Duration of stay in the institution was short, typically less than one month. Only a minority of participants reached clinical cutoffs for anxiety and depression at baseline, but music therapy was well accepted and attractive for prisoners, and there was a reduction in anxiety after two weeks of music therapy. Positive outcomes for music interventions have also been reported in relation to self-harm among women prisoners (Digard et al., 2007). Participants enhanced their communication and social skills, increased their confidence, were better able to reflect on their situation, and believed that they could change and attain their goals. Hakvoort and colleagues (2015) studied the effect of music therapy on anger management, coping skills and dysfunctional behaviour. A pre- and post-test design was used with random assignment of fourteen patients to either treatment or control conditions. All participants received treatment as usual, while nine received a standardised music therapy anger management programme. Five controls received an unplanned aggression management programme. The findings suggested that anger management skills improved for all participants. The improvement of positive coping skills and the diminishing of avoidance as a coping skill were measured, and showed greater changes in music therapy participants. When controlling for the exact number of treatment hours, the outcomes suggested that music therapy might accelerate the process of behavioural change.

Maruna (2010) showed how music teaching, rehearsing, recording, performance, improvisation and composition could aid the rehabilitation of prisoners and ex-prisoners. Participants almost uniformly expressed passionate support for the organisation providing the music intervention, and many insisted that music had changed their lives. The changing tunes logic model developed a sense of collective ownership, responsibility, emotional energy, increased confidence and therapeutic alliance with the facilitator, and led to the management of depression. The programme also led participants to find their own voice and developed creativity, group bonding, mutual support, anger management and an identity separate from being an offender. It provided a way for participants to test their limits, a drug-free way of escape or coping with imprisonment and increased employability. Public performance and acknowledgement led to a calmer prison environment, and praise fostered a sense of achievement. Participants reported that the programme provided them with a form of escape from the cycle of punishment, shame, anger and defiance that prisoners and ex-prisoners found themselves trapped in. Maruna (2010) discovered that increased confidence was the most commonly cited long-term benefit of participation in the *Changing Tunes* project. As a result, many participants felt more optimistic about their futures. A small number of participants reported that taking part in music sessions had improved their symptoms of depression and Post-Traumatic Stress Disorder. Respondents often spoke of the respectful way that they were treated by project leaders and the humanising effect that this had. Participation in arts programmes appears to provide prisoners with new ways of thinking about themselves, allowing them to move away from previously entrenched offender identities by assigning more prosocial labels such as 'musician', which often brought with them new aspirations.

Ascenso (2017) reported the outcomes of *The Lullaby Project*, where the Royal Philharmonic Orchestra worked with refugees, migrant mothers and fathers from a London prison. The programme paired expectant and new mothers with professional musicians to create a lullaby for their children. The programme developed wellbeing through enabling a strong sense of accomplishment, meaning and connectedness, along with the experience of positive emotions. It encouraged proactivity through promoting initiative, both musical and relational, and reflection through stimulating a richer perspective on life and positive coping mechanisms. The project was motivating, offering challenge and a highly valued goal. It was geared towards connecting at a very human level, placing centrality on individuality, a positive agenda, and maintaining two universals at its core: music and parental love. Similarly, Rodrigues and colleagues (2010) studied the *BbBb* project that combined education and artistic performance in a process that was centred on music, babies and their parents. The findings showed that a very strong bonding developed among parents, babies, families and the community. In Alaska, Warfield (2010) reported a study of a 400-bed facility for multi-level adult female offenders which offered a unique educational programme, an orchestra. This was founded in 2003 by a volunteer, and membership grew from eight to twenty-two female offenders between 2003 and 2009.

Bilby and colleagues (2013) considered the possible relationships between the process of abstaining from crime and the influence that taking part in some form of art-based enrichment activity might have on participants. The research specifically explored how arts interventions contributed towards enabling people to form positive identities, build new narratives and build positive relationships with peers, staff and family. It also began to investigate how arts interventions enabled people to make significant behavioural changes. The research team investigated five arts projects in four criminal justice settings, including practising visual arts in a high-security adult male prison; music and DJ-ing skills with young offenders in the community; a music-making project in a resettlement open prison; and creative writing and bookbinding in a closed female prison. The research team spent at least four sessions with each of the projects, observing the activities and interviewing participants, arts practitioners and prison staff. Evidence included participants' written work and evaluations, and examples of the work produced in the arts activities. The findings demonstrated a clear link between taking part in art-based activities and movement towards secondary desistance. Analysis of the data across all five projects showed that participation in arts activities enabled individuals to begin to redefine themselves. Arts projects facilitated high levels of engagement, led to greater participation in education and work-related activities, and could have a positive impact on how people managed themselves during their sentence, particularly on their ability to cooperate with others, including other participants and staff. This was related to increased self-control and better problem-solving skills. Engagement with arts projects facilitated increased compliance with criminal justice orders and regimes, while arts projects could be responsive to participants' individual needs. Overall, art provided a safe space to explore challenging questions and to create, which allowed prisoners to discover what they could do, thus enhancing their confidence.

Cox and Gelsthorpe (2008) evaluated eight *Beats and Bars* projects, including 71 participants. The research showed a reduction in adjudications for rule-breaking during and after the project, an increase in confidence to participate in other educational programmes, and confirmation that music projects can play a role in fulfilling the seven pathways to reducing re-offending. The men's experiences of the project, particularly their feelings of encouragement to try things without judgement and to work together, clearly facilitated the development of their individual competencies and self-esteem. The participants learned to cooperate, relate to others, negotiate and share. These can all lead to improved outcomes following release from prison. Following on from this, Cartwright (2013) evaluated the first phase of the *Sounding Out* ex-prisoner programme, tracking participants over a nine-month period. The research showed that *Sounding Out* was successful in offering a programme of multi-dimensional support to participants. This took the form of financial support, making new friends and contacts, ongoing help to access other training and performing opportunities, a lift in motivation, hope and self-esteem, a clear sense of achievement and a positive use of time. It was found that being paid appropriately for their time and commitment acted as an incentive not to reoffend, and a support in the face of financial hardship. Additionally, being paid engendered a sense of professionalism and pride. Taking part also contributed to rebuilding positive family relationships and being seen in a more positive light by others. Conceived as a year-long intervention, the programme was structured around an initial rehearsal period and concert, followed by two more high-profile performances. Within this period and afterwards, participants were given support to access additional opportunities such as further music training and employment. The *Sounding Out* participants were paid at a rate of £90 per day for all rehearsals and performances. In the case of shorter time periods, this sum was adjusted to an hourly rate of £15. Additionally, travel and food expenses were provided. Built into the programme was the opportunity for a number of the participants to undertake roles as supporting musicians on *Making Tracks*, a programme to support young people at risk of coming into contact with the criminal justice system. *Making Tracks* focused on an intense music-writing and rehearsal period, followed by a performance, but additionally offered weekly sessions to the young people after the intensive project, allowing them to further hone their musical skills. In total, seven former prisoners were recruited for the project. Two had both been out of prison for a number of years. Since their release, they had been involved with various projects and one was on the board of trustees as an advisor. They took on a supporting role as excellent musicians, proven team members and ex-prisoners who had successfully made the challenging transition from prison to release. The remaining five participant members were all recruited within a year of release. They ranged in age from mid-twenties to fifties. The offending histories of the participants were varied. However, all the participants were on licence and had served custodial sentences of a minimum of three years; they had been convicted of relatively serious crimes. Two had spent the previous 20 years periodically offending and returning to prison at regular and frequent intervals. At the time of the *Sounding Out* project, none of the group was in employment or undertaking training or education, and all five were receiving state benefits. Four members were in accommodation regulated by the probation service. *Sounding Out* made a significant impact on reducing participant reoffending levels. Music was found to be a primary motivation, given that the participants were all passionate about playing and performing. The process of creative music-making and preparing for performances fostered participants' teamworking and negotiation skills, self-confidence, achievement and sense of pride. Participants reported that one of the most striking aspects of the programme was the level of trust placed in them from the outset. Being treated in this way led participants to foster a strong sense of responsibility to the organisation and staff. Additionally, this sense of responsibility was a strong motivation not to reoffend, at the risk of letting others down. A later evaluation (Massie et al., 2019) showed similar outcomes.

There have been a number of reviews of the research on music therapy with adult offenders. For instance, Hughes (2005) examined the application and impact of arts practice in the three key areas of criminal justice service provision:

- prevention: arts practice with young people up to 21 years old who are at risk of offending or escalation of existing offending;
- custodial and community sentencing: arts as interventions in sentencing, both in prison and community contexts and resettlement; and
- arts as an intervention made to assist reintegration into society.

The findings showed that, at the time of the review, there was a paucity of high-quality research and evaluation in the field, but the survey findings showed very clearly that the arts had the capacity and potential to offer a range of innovative and practical approaches that could enhance and extend provision of educational, developmental and therapeutic programmes across the criminal justice sector. The review showed that the arts are associated with positive outcomes and can play an important part in changing individual, institutional and social circumstances which sponsor criminal behaviour. The grey literature highlighted the depth and breadth of arts provision, with many examples of interesting, challenging and creative projects in a range of settings. Analysis of the variety of practice identified a series of common effective programme and practice models and features. However, flexibility and responsiveness were key indicators of success. The quantity and consistency of findings from the key areas suggested that there was a strong case to be made for the effectiveness of arts practice across a range of areas. Arts interventions in criminal justice contexts are successful because they offer a non-traditional, non-institutional, social and emotional environment; a non-judgemental and non-authoritarian model of engagement; and an opportunity to participate in a creative process that involves both structure and freedom. At the same time, engagement in the participatory arts requires respect, responsibility, cooperation and collaboration.

Coutinho and colleagues (2015a; 2015b) reviewed 28 articles, mainly qualitative and narrative reports of group music therapy, educational music-making, choir interventions, individual music therapy sessions, and a range of musical projects and case studies. Cohen and Henley (2018) examined music-making in prisons in the UK and USA, contrasting the different approaches and practices of imprisonment and their impact on music therapy, but pointing out that community music within prisons provided a means toward desistance, improved self-esteem, social support and a sense of accomplishment. Cheliotis and Jordanoska (2016) critically reviewed the empirical research literature on the contributions that arts-based programmes make to the process of desistance from crime. They focused on evaluations of programmes run by practitioners inside prisons, and the effects of arts-based prison programmes after participants are released into the community. Kougiali and colleagues (2017) carried out qualitative meta-analyses of 12 articles published worldwide. The findings suggested that music programmes in prison are perceived by participating prisoners as liberating, which encourages participation and allows for noncoercive personal development. The therapeutic potential of music programmes is located in the combination of the benefits emanating from the effect and practice of music and the creation of mental, spatial and temporal zones of free expression, as well as those that derive from the egalitarian and nonauthoritative approach employed by the facilitators.

Chen and colleagues (2016) in a meta-analysis assessed the effectiveness of music therapy on improving the mental health of offenders in correctional settings. Five studies with 409 predominantly male participants were included and showed that music therapy was effective for promoting offenders' self-esteem and social functioning. Effects on anxiety and depression depended on the number of sessions. For both outcomes, the studies with 20 or more sessions had larger effects. No significant effects were found for behaviour management or between different music therapy approaches.

Overview

A great deal has been written about the role of music in supporting young people from disadvantaged backgrounds and helping those who are disengaged back into education or employment, as well as supporting those in the criminal justice system to successfully reintegrate into the community and not reoffend. Across each of these areas, much of the literature is descriptive. Some sets out the details of particular interventions and advocates their use while other papers argue more generally that music therapy has an important role to play and set out a theoretical stance. Some research has assessed the outcomes of interventions, but frequently this is based on single case studies or small group interventions. Nevertheless, it is possible to draw some conclusions. It is clear that making music can have positive benefits: for instance, generating positive attitudes towards school, improving attendance, enhancing motivation for academic schoolwork and helping to improve basic and key skills. Across a range of environments, music offers the potential for enhanced self-efficacy, self-esteem and self-concept, improvements in mood, reduced anger, reduced aggression and improved behaviour. Music programmes can reduce rule-breaking and levels of disruption in institutions, as well as improving relationships. Programmes aimed at resettlement have had some success in supporting ex-offenders into training and employment by helping them to develop a range of personal and social skills which increase employability, as well as facilitating the acquisition of formally accredited educational skills and qualifications. Some participants make a career out of music, becoming mentors or workshop leaders. This means that participants are less likely to reoffend. Some programmes have changed the wider community's views of those in the criminal justice system.

The common elements for success, whatever the nature of the programme, seem to be:

- creating a safe space;
- providing a high-quality musical experience;
- providing highly interactive and enjoyable musical activities;
- using music with which participants can relate and engage;
- having a facilitator who acts as a role model and treats participants with respect;
- enabling trusting and non-judgemental relationships to develop with music facilitators and mentors;
- engendering feelings of belonging in a group;
- encouraging learning to work with others;

- supporting the development of interpersonal bonds and shared goals;
- creating opportunities for developing new skills;
- enabling musical progression;
- providing opportunities to perform;
- maintaining regular and frequent contact;
- recognising and rewarding excellence;
- facilitating positive affirmation from others relating to musical activities, particularly performance;
- providing opportunities to reflect on and articulate emotions;
- providing opportunities to feel a sense of pride;
- providing opportunities for creativity to develop self-efficacy and express feelings;
- facilitating opportunities for participants to gain respect as musicians;
- providing opportunities to learn transferable skills;
- providing opportunities to develop communication skills;
- promoting the giving and receiving of criticism;
- supporting the development of confidence and resilience; and
- allowing time for developing an understanding of self.

There are issues related to how long interventions need to be. Ten mentoring sessions, usually at weekly or fortnightly intervals, seem to be a minimum, although some suggest that a mentoring relationship needs to last for a year to be effective.

13. Personal, Social and Physical Development

This chapter focuses on the way that active engagement with music and listening preferences can affect the way that individuals develop personally, socially and physically.

Personal Development

This section on personal development includes the way that an individual's identity, personality and self-beliefs are shaped by their interactions with the environment, including activities related to music.

Music and Identity

At any point in time, an individual may hold multiple identities depending on their current social context. Identities constantly evolve as they are challenged and reconstructed, based on the feedback that is received from interactions with others. This may be complementary or contradictory. DeNora (2017) identified several properties of personal identity, including status. This infers that identity can be raised or lowered in relation to others. The malleable nature of identities means that they can be combined to form new ones through a form of hybridisation. Music can play an important role in this process. Individuals use music to express themselves and explore their identities (Macdonald et al., 2017). Active listening to music supports this exploration and the integration of identities (Larson, 1995), helping individuals to decide who they are and what they aspire to be. In addition, music assists in sending a message about those decisions to others. Music is used consciously and unconsciously, to demonstrate attitudes, values and beliefs (Larson, 1995; Lull, 1987; North and Hargreaves, 1999). It is also used to gain knowledge about others (Macdonald et al., 2017).

Expression of identity is connected with young people's lifestyle, language, personality development and the music that they listen to (Schwartz and Fouts, 2003). Adolescents' musical identity may be context-specific, and can be different at school and in out-of-school contexts (Rideout et al., 2010). It can be defined through attending concerts, actively making music or listening to specific musical genres. Engagement in musical activities develops several aspects of identity in relation to the family and the school environment, and contributes to physical, cognitive, social, emotional and affective development (Hargreaves and Lamont, 2017). Musical preferences are used for self-identifying as a member of a specific peer group and musical subculture (Miranda and Claes, 2009; North and Hargreaves, 2008), creating social identities and membership of an in-group (Bakagiannis and Tarrant, 2006; Hargreaves et al., 2006; Rentfrow et al., 2009). Adolescents also use musical preferences to acquire valid and reliable information about others (Rentfrow and Gosling, 2006).

Young people spend a great deal of time listening to music (Keen, 2004; North and Hargreaves, 2000). This can be beneficial (Tarrant et al., 2000). It can help them to regulate emotions (North et al., 2000), act as a support when they face problems, help to alleviate loneliness and increase emotional sensitivity (Cook, 2013). Music also helps adolescents to develop a sense of connection and belonging, as they make friends with those with similar musical tastes (Lewis et al., 2012; Selfhout et al., 2009).

Adolescents who belong to minority ethnic groups use music as a means of developing their ethnic identity and resilience (Buffam, 2011; Lundström, 2009; Schweigman et al., 2011). Travis and Bowman (2012) found that having a positive ethnic identity was associated with music, in that music could be empowering. For example, rap music can inspire young people to connect with others, consider the experiences of others, think critically about their environment and want to change their communities. To bring about change requires agency—the ability to act regardless of barriers. This is key to achieving positive outcomes. Dedman (2011) argues that those who actively engage in hip-hop culture are responding to, and continuously resisting, mainstream images and messages from which they feel disconnected. The way that identities can change explains the findings of many studies of the effects of music in migrant communities (Baily and Collyer, 2006; Lenette et al., 2016; Marsh, 2013). Ilari (2017) discusses the role of ethnic identity in the perceptions and interactions of minority groups living among other ethnic and racial groups, such as Mexicans in the USA and South-Eastern Asians and Eastern Europeans in the UK, and how this affects their developing self-perceptions. Ilari argues that an important aspect of the ability to deal with the experience of being an immigrant or refugee is to be able to negotiate multiple identities. Hybrid identities can provide a wider family in which they can feel welcome. One of the main ways this can be achieved is through music. Children's cultural musical heritage cannot be removed as a result of external circumstances (Ilari, 2017). Cultural diversity impacts the development and construction of social and musical identities across the lifespan in a wide range of contexts, including educational settings.

Musical identity, part of the self-system, refers to the self that listens to and creates music (MacDonald et al., 2002). It can support the building of a positive self-identity and effective learning routines (Hallam et al., 2016), As discussed in Chapter 12, disaffected young people and those engaged with juvenile or adult justice systems can develop new identities as musicians, leading to positive changes in their behaviour. Creating possible positive musical selves in this way can lead to broader changes in self-beliefs (Oleś, 2005), aspirations and subsequent career plans (Taylor and Hallam, 2011). Developing a positive possible musical self can occur at any point in the lifespan (Creech et al., 2014).

Music and Personality

There has been considerable research exploring the personalities of musicians. Some has compared musicians with non-musicians, while some has examined differences between musicians playing different instruments or engaging with different genres. The difficulty of interpreting this research in terms of personal development is that it is not possible to determine whether individuals with certain personality types are drawn to playing particular instruments or engaging with particular genres, or whether playing particular instruments or engaging with specific genres develops certain personality characteristics. It may be that elements of both apply and that there are interactions between them.

Musicians require a great many skills to be able to perform: imagination, flexibility, discipline, concentrated attention, emotional expression and intellectual, communication and motor skills (Juslin, 2003; Palmer, 1997). Some of these skills may be related to personality. The evidence from a range of studies shows that, as a group, musicians tend to be open to new experiences. Overall, they are more creative, imaginative and interested in change than the general population (Gibson et al., 2009; Kemp, 1996). Research with ten- to twelve-year-old children by Corrigal and colleagues (2013) showed that duration of music training was associated with openness to experience. It was also associated with conscientiousness. At seven to eight years old, when children frequently begin to take formal music lessons, the best predictors of participating in music training were parents' openness to experiences and the child's agreeableness (Corrigall and Schellenberg, 2014). This may indicate a tendency in very young musicians to comply with parental wishes.

Beyond the evidence regarding openness to experiences, as we saw in Chapter 10, there are differences between musicians on other aspects of personality. In a seminal study, Kemp (1996) identified common personality traits among Western classical musicians. He showed that they were bold introverts who directed energy inwards and appeared outwardly reserved. He argued that the nature of solitary practice may encourage autonomy and independence of thought. String players tended to be introverted, imaginative and radical, while brass players were more extroverted and had lower levels of self-discipline in comparison to other performing groups. Percussionists also tended towards extroversion. These findings suggested that the extent of practice required for these different instruments—typically more for string players, brass, wind and percussion players—either attracted people with personality characteristics suited to these roles or caused these characteristics to develop in response to the particular demands made of them by their chosen roles in the music profession (Kemp, 1996; Wills and Cooper, 1988).

Cribb and Gregory (1999) studied folk fiddle players and Salvation Army brass band members who completed a personality inventory and a questionnaire concerning their opinions about the personality characteristics of orchestral violinists, orchestral brass players, folk fiddlers, and Salvation Army brass band members. The findings showed greater neuroticism among string players but not greater extroversion in brass players (which had been found in previous research). Participants' views about the personality characteristics of orchestral brass players and orchestral violinists echoed those found in previous research, but their views on the Salvation Army brass players and on folk fiddlers did not. The findings showed that personality differences or stereotypes of musicians are probably determined more by the history and traditions of the group in which they are perceived to belong than by the instruments that they play.

Since Kemp's research, many other studies have been undertaken. For instance, Bell and Cresswell (1984) assessed personality traits in a sample of secondary-school musical instrumentalists and student instrumentalists attending a college of music. In both samples, significant differences were found between the musical sample and the normative population from which they were drawn. In the college sample, further differences were found between students whose main instrument of study was strings, woodwind or brass. The authors suggested that some personality characteristics predisposed individuals to pursue instrumental performance studies, whilst others reflected habitual performance on different types of musical instrument. Also studying music students, Shuter-Dyson (2000) found that they scored higher on extroversion than non-musicians, and that female music students were more neurotic and tender-minded than female non-musicians. Undergraduate music students also exhibit conscientious-like traits (Kemp, 1996; Marchant-Haycox and Wilson, 1992), although composers and rock musicians tend to be less conscientious than the general population (Gillespie and Myors, 2000; Kemp, 1996). Buttsworth and Smith (1995), comparing the personality profiles of performing musicians aged 17 to 41 years old with non-musicians, found that the musicians were less intelligent but more emotionally stable, sensitive and conservative. The male musicians were more sensitive and shrewd than their female counterparts, while brass players were more suspicious, imaginative, apprehensive and radical when compared with singers, and more extroverted (but less anxious and creative) when compared with string players. Keyboard players were more warm-hearted, emotionally stable and shrewd than those in the other instrumental groups. MacLellan (2011) explored personality differences among high-school band, string orchestra and choir students according to ensemble membership. The participants were 355 high-school students who had participated in a musical group for one or more years. There were personality differences between the members of the different ensembles, indicating that choir students were more likely to be extroverted when compared to orchestral students. There were no significant differences among the ensembles on the sensing intuition, thinking, feeling or judging/perceiving scales. Compared to high-school norms, the students in each ensemble were significantly more likely to be intuitive and feeling, while the band students were more likely to be perceiving, and the choir students to be extroverted. Hille and Schupp (2015), using a large data set from the German Socioeconomic Panel (SOEP), found that 17-year-old adolescents with music training were more conscientious, open and ambitious than non-musicians. These effects were stronger among adolescents from families with lower socioeconomic status.

Comparing musicians to a representative sample of the general workforce, Vaag and colleagues (2018) found lower levels of conscientiousness but higher levels of neuroticism and openness. There were no significant differences in extroversion or agreeableness. Gjermunds and colleagues (2020) compared the responses of 509 musicians and 201 non-musicians on the Big Five personality traits. The findings confirmed the higher levels of openness for musicians frequently found in previous research. The musicians scored lower on conscientiousness and there were no significant differences between the groups in extroversion, agreeableness, emotional stability or neuroticism. Similarly, Kuckelkorn and colleagues (2021) gathered data from 7,000 respondents: professional, amateur and non-musicians playing different instruments. The findings showed that the professional musicians scored higher than the amateurs, who in turn scored higher than non-musicians on openness to experience. The singers scored higher on extroversion than instrumentalists, while the professional musicians scored higher on neuroticism, lower on agreeableness, and lower on conscientiousness than the amateurs. Although there were personality differences between those playing different instruments, no consistent patterns emerged, which suggested that the differences were not related to instrument choice per se, but were perhaps moderated by musical genre and the social context of music-making in each group. Langendörfer (2008) examined personality differences among 122 professional orchestral groups of six top-level professional orchestras in Germany. The three instrumental groups—strings, woodwind, and brass players—displayed fewer differences in their personality traits than the stereotyped view of them had suggested. Apart from the finding that the string players were more conscientious than the other musicians, differences found in other studies were not replicated. Butkovic and Modrusan (2019) examined whether differences in personality attributed to musicians were based on actual differences or stereotypical views. One hundred and eighty-two string, brass and woodwind students, singers, pianists and music pedagogy students evaluated their own personality traits and the personality traits of the other groups. Comparison of self-reports with in-group and out-group peer reports showed that there were stereotypes of different groups of musicians. The most pronounced differences between self-reports and peer reports were in relation to openness and agreeableness. Similarly, Sandgren (2018) investigated whether there were differences in the personality traits of vocalists and instrumentalists. The findings from the 108 participants indicated that vocalists had significantly higher levels of extroversion, agreeableness and openness than a control group—but the instrumentalists did not.

Exploring motivational intensity and self-esteem, MacIntyre and Potter (2013), in an online survey recruiting an international sample of 599 musicians, examined differences between guitar and piano players and those who composed music, those who planned to compose in the future, and those who did not compose and did not intend to compose. The findings revealed instrument-based differences between pianists' and guitarists' levels of motivational intensity, desire to learn, introjected regulation, perceived competence and willingness to play. The group who composed music also had significantly higher levels of musical self-esteem, willingness to play, motivational intensity, desire to learn and perceived competence. Overall, the findings suggested that pianists and guitarists were both intrinsically motivated, but for different reasons. The authors concluded that the underlying motivational needs that are met by the instrument's culture appear to focus on competence for pianists, and on autonomy and relatedness for guitarists.

Examining differences in genre, Butkovic and Rancic Dopudj (2017) compared 249 musicians playing either classical or heavy-metal music, and found that there were no significant differences in personality traits between the groups, although they differed significantly in personality from population norms, having higher scores on extroversion, agreeableness and intellect. Similarly, comparisons of classical and pop/rock musicians on measures of sensation-seeking found higher levels in the pop/rock musicians (Vuust et al., 2010). Benedek and colleagues (2014) compared students of classical, jazz and folk music with respect to their musical activities, creativity and personality. The jazz musicians were more frequently engaged in extracurricular musical activities, had completed a higher number of creative musical achievements, demonstrated higher ideational creativity and tended to be more open to new experiences than the classical musicians.

Overall, on the basis of the existing evidence it is not possible to say with any certainty that there are systematic personality differences between musicians playing different instruments, although as a group they appear to be more open to new experiences than members of the general population. Emerging differences may be related to the genre within which musicians work—for instance, jazz, pop, rock, or classical music. The research sheds no light on whether the observed differences are influenced by the different environments the musicians play in, or whether they existed prior to choice of instrument or genre.

Kemp (1996) studying young classical musicians found that they were motivated almost to the point of obsession. A high degree of perfectionism and intrinsic motivation seemed to be associated with being a classical musician. This may have indicated greater conscientiousness, although there are mixed findings relating to this. Stoeber and Eismann (2007) found elevated scores for conscientiousness among young musicians, whereas Yöndem and colleagues (2017) found lower scores. In a meta-analysis of studies in the general population, Smith and colleagues (2018) showed that there was a relationship between perfectionistic concerns and conscientiousness, although these were moderated by gender, age and the perfectionism subscale used.

There is considerable evidence that many musicians experience performance anxiety and distress across a variety of musical genres including classical, jazz and popular music (Papageorgi et al., 2013). Vaag and colleagues (2016) also showed that symptoms of anxiety and depression were highly prevalent among professional musicians. These findings have been related to perfectionism. There can be adverse health-related consequences of perfectionistic over-involvement in work. However, Stoeber and Eismann (2007) have shown that only some facets of perfectionism are associated with anxiety and distress, whereas other facets are associated with positive characteristics and outcomes such as motivation and achievement. To investigate how different facets of perfectionism were related to motivation, effort, achievement and distress in musicians, 146 young musicians completed measures of perfectionism: striving for perfection, negative reactions to imperfection, perceived pressure to be perfect, intrinsic and extrinsic motivation, effort, achievement and distress. The findings showed that striving for perfection was associated with intrinsic motivation, higher effort and higher achievement. Perceived pressure from music teachers was also associated with intrinsic motivation, while negative reactions to imperfection were associated with extrinsic motivation and higher distress. The findings demonstrated that perfectionism in musicians can have positive and negative aspects. While negative reactions to imperfection are clearly unhealthy, striving for perfection can be regarded as a healthy pursuit of excellence. Similarly, working with 132 students in music academies in Poland, Lawendowski and colleagues (2020) investigated study addiction. Seven core addiction symptoms related to studying were assessed, along with measures of personality and wellbeing. Study addiction was positively related to learning engagement but also to low extroversion, high social anxiety, longer learning time, lower academic performance and indicators of decreased wellbeing. Overall, the evidence suggests that being a professional musician or preparing for a career as a professional musician can have a negative impact on some aspects of personality.

Self-Beliefs

Historically, the term self-concept has been used to refer to how individuals perceive and evaluate themselves in different areas of their lives. In the same way that an individual can hold multiple identities, the self-system is made up of a number of self-images, including those relating to self-esteem, self-efficacy, ideal selves and possible selves. These are often context- or situation-specific and develop in interaction with the environment (Hallam, 2009; 2016). Active engagement with music can support the development of musical and other identities, and can also impact on self-beliefs. Depending on the feedback received from others, the impact may be positive or negative. Much of the evidence supports the positive impact of music on self-esteem and self-confidence but there are exceptions, typically when feedback is negative. Performance and receiving feedback from it are crucial in this process and can lead to positive or negative responses. Maintaining positive self-esteem is argued to help to maintain positive emotions, which motivates individuals to act and shields them against anxiety (Pyszczynski et al., 1999). Positive self-esteem is essential for individuals to have agency to act, rather than feeling powerless and depressed (Kuhl, 2000).

Bae and Kyungsuk (2020) examined the effects of the creation of a musical play on the self-esteem, self-expression, and social skills of 14 children between first and third grade, and 14 from fourth to sixth grade. Half of the children acted as controls. The activity involved making a script, composing song lyrics and music, and performing the completed musical play. Self-esteem and social-skill scales were administered before and after the intervention. The experimental group exhibited significantly higher scores than the control group on all of the scales except those of self-expression and social skills. The results showed that group music therapy could facilitate children's engagement in groupwork, and that playing an important role in the group could positively impact on self-perceptions. In the UK, Harland (2000) showed that the most frequent overall influences on pupils derived from engagement with the arts in school were related to personal and social development. In music, those who played instruments referred to an increase in self-esteem and sense of identity. Research on the benefits of playing an instrument and participating in extracurricular music groups has been shown to impact on participants' self-confidence and self-esteem. Tolfree and Hallam (2016), in a qualitative study of children in the latter years of primary education and the early years of secondary education, showed that the children had a sense of achievement from playing an instrument. This was most prevalent amongst the younger boys and the older girls, who also expressed having pride in playing well more frequently than the other groups. All age groups reported frustration when they did not achieve. This was mentioned least by the older boys. University music students reflecting on their previous musical experiences at school highlighted the contribution of making music to the development of a strong sense of self-esteem and satisfaction. They reported enhanced personal skills, encouraging the development of self-achievement, self-confidence and intrinsic motivation. A further study with non-music students who had previously participated in musical groups established similar benefits, with a particular preoccupation with the impact of group music-making on self and personal development (Kokotsaki and Hallam, 2007; 2011).

Some early studies exploring the role of music education on self-esteem showed positive relationships between participation in choir, band or formal music instruction and self-esteem (Amchin et al., 1991; Nolin and Vander Ark, 1977; Wood, 1973). Wig and Boyle (1982) studied the effects of a keyboard learning approach and a traditional general music approach on sixth-grade general music students' music achievement, and self-concept regarding music ability. Those in the keyboard group made significantly greater gains in musical attainment and musical self-concept than the control group. Duke and colleagues (1997) administered questionnaires to a large number of children studying piano in various regions of the USA, their parents and their piano teachers, and found that the children, their parents and their piano teachers believed that piano instruction improved the students' lives in many ways, including enhanced self-esteem. Similarly, Austin (1990) found a relationship between music, self-esteem and degree of participation in school and out-of-school music activities among upper elementary students.

In England, the evaluation of a national singing programme involving approximately 6000 children found that those participating had more positive self-concepts than non-participating children (Welch, 2010). There was a positive linear relationship between singing development and self-concept. Similarly, Welch and colleagues (2014), using data from 6087 participants, showed that the higher the normalised singing development rating, the more positive the child's self-concept and sense of being socially included, irrespective of singer age, sex and ethnicity. Also in England, an evaluation of the *Musical Futures* approach—where young people work in the classroom in small groups, copying a popular song and ultimately creating their own—showed that non-music teachers and senior staff in participating schools reported that the approach had a positive impact on students' self-esteem, confidence, motivation and independent learning (Hallam et al., 2015; 2017; 2018).

A study by the Norwegian Research Council for Science and Humanities found high correlations between positive self-perception, cognitive competence scores, self-esteem, interest and involvement in school music (Lillemyr, 1983), while Whitwell (1977) argued that creative participation in music improved self-image and self-awareness, and created positive self-attitudes. Similar findings have been found with urban black middle-school students (Marshall, 1978). Dege and colleagues (2014) showed that the number of music lessons experienced by 12- to 14-year-olds contributed significantly to the prediction of academic self-concept and also motivational characteristics (for instance, perseverance), while Degé and Schwarzer (2018) investigated the influence of an extended music curriculum at school on academic self-concept. They compared the academic self-concept of children between 9 and 11 years old before they started the extended music curriculum and after one year of participation, and compared it with non-participation. Thirty children were assessed in relation to their academic self-concept, with the amount of non-musical out-of-school activities controlled for. The extended music curriculum had a positive influence on academic self-concept following a year of engagement.

Rickard and colleagues (2013) studied the impact on over 350 young children in Grades 1 and 3 of Kodaly music classes (for the youngest children in Grade 1) and instrumental classes, predominantly string-based, for the children in Grade 3, in comparison with control groups. The findings showed that these school-based music classes prevented the decline in global self-esteem measures experienced by the control group in both the younger and older cohorts, and in both general and academic self-esteem for the older cohort. The data suggested that increasing the frequency and quality of arts-based activities can be beneficial for the self-esteem of primary-school-aged children. Clements-Cortes and Chow (2018) also showed that music could prevent a decline in self-esteem. Music interventions have proven to be a protective factor, as positive social experiences instil confidence. Active engagement with music can improve emotional regulation and resilience, and foster identity and self-image, while facilitating social acceptance and a sense of belonging in a nurturing community.

Not all of the research has shown positive outcomes. Several doctoral dissertations have failed to find any impact of engagement with music on self-esteem (Linch, 1994). Legette (1994) compared the effects of two types of music instruction on first- and third-graders' self-concepts, and found no difference in the two types of musical activity or their impact on self-concept. Some research has shown different outcomes for boys and girls. For instance, Lomen (1970) found an increase in one element of self-concept in boys only, while Wamhoff (1972) noticed a decrease in one element of self-concept for girls taking instrumental lessons, as compared to non-participants and girls who dropped out of the lessons.

Self-Beliefs, Deprivation and Disaffection

In Chapter 12, a range of evidence was presented which showed that engagement with musical activities enhanced the self-beliefs, self-esteem and positive possible selves of young people and adults involved with a range of criminal justice systems. It also set out how music could enhance the self-beliefs of those from communities suffering deprivation. For instance, most evaluations of the outcomes of young people participating in *El Sistema* or *Sistema*-inspired programmes have pointed to a positive impact on self-beliefs.

El Sistema and *Sistema*-inspired programmes have prioritised the personal and social development of participants, and many of the evaluations point to the positive impact on self-beliefs (Esqueda Torres, 2001; 2004; Galarce et al., 2012; Israel, 2012; Uy, 2010). However, Lewis and colleagues (2011) found no significant changes in self-esteem over time, although comparisons of the self-esteem of children in the two participating schools where there were differences at the beginning of the project had disappeared by the time of the second survey. Children with low self-esteem at the start of the programme benefited the most. Lopez and Berrios (2007) showed that *El Sistema* orchestras were perceived as providing a positive space for self-affirmation and identity formation. Participation was perceived to show openness to new realities and values, tolerance to diversity, the development of personal identity and self-affirmation. Provenzano and colleagues (2020) studied the effects of an *El-Sistema*-inspired university-partnered after-school music programme on developmental health, social and educational outcomes. The participants were 93 fifth-grade students in a racially and ethnically diverse, low-income elementary school. Over a period of four years, outcomes were assessed with surveys, interviews with music instructors and the school principal, and parent and participant focus groups. There were significant changes in students' perceptions of their music-making ability, their connection to other students and an enhanced sense of school pride. Creech and colleagues (2013; 2016) attributed the impact of *El Sistema* and *Sistema*-inspired programmes on self-esteem to recognition by participants of their own abilities and of these being acknowledged by families and friends.

Shin (2011) investigated how participation in weekly music workshops affected the academic self-concept and self-esteem of middle-school students in low-income communities. The programme lasted for seven weeks and consisted of playing percussion instruments, singing, improvisation, jamming, group dancing, and dynamic and rhythmic exploration. The assessment included a self-description questionnaire, a parent survey and student interviews. The findings demonstrated that there were significant differences in general school self-concept and mathematics self-concept from pre- to post-test. Both parents and students indicated that participation in the programme had positively influenced students' self-esteem. Similarly, Zapata and Hargreaves (2017) researched the impact of a project undertaken in a school located in a deprived neighbourhood of Bogotá, the capital of Colombia. Two groups of 52 six- to eight-year-old children participated. The experimental group followed an 18-week programme of singing workshops of Colombian traditional songs and musical improvisation, whereas the control group had no such experience. Children, teachers and parents were involved in assessing the outcomes. A perceived competence scale for children was administered before and after the singing programme. Analysis revealed that musical activities had a significant impact on children's self-esteem, especially its cognitive component.

Wood and colleagues (2013), in a ten-week intervention that included group drumming, showed that 180 at-risk twelve-year-olds in 19 schools had a ten percent increase in self-esteem scores and improved relationships with peers, as evaluated by teachers. School data showed a decrease in reported behaviour incidents for 29 percent of participants. Overall, the evaluation indicated that the *DRUMBEAT* programme provided a creative medium for working with at-risk young people and helped develop self-esteem and social relationship skills.

Some research found no differences. For instance, Costa-Giomi (2004) randomly assigned nine-year-olds to three years of individual piano lessons or a no-lesson control group. The two groups did not differ in self-esteem at any point in time. Similarly, children who received a two-year music intervention did not differ from control groups at the beginning or end of the study (Portowitz et al., 2009). In these studies, the children received individual music instruction and were not engaged in group music-making. In contrast, Devroop (2012) investigated the social-emotional impact of group instrumental music instruction on 84 disadvantaged South-African students over a period of two years. The findings showed that there were generally increased levels of self-esteem, optimism, happiness and perseverance after participation in an instrumental music programme. It seems that an important element in enhancing self-esteem through music-making may be participation in ensembles.

Children with Special Educational Needs and Disabilities

Some early research with children with low self-esteem or behavioural difficulties showed no impact of musical engagement on self-esteem. For instance, Michel (1971) researched black disadvantaged students with low self-concept who learned to play rhythm guitar through automated instruction. There was no effect on their self-esteem. A second study with students with special educational needs also showed no impact. Similarly, Michel and Farrell (1973) worked with disadvantaged boys aged ten to twelve with a range of problems in an all-black elementary school, and found that the boys—who were taught to play and perform simple chords on a ukulele—showed no enhancement of self-esteem.

Choi and colleagues (2010), working with children exhibiting aggressive behaviour, showed that after participation in a music programme, children showed enhanced self-esteem compared with controls. In a qualitative study with two children with social and behavioural difficulties, Thomas (2014) showed that, after experiencing music lessons for a period of a year, the children demonstrated enhanced self-confidence and self-esteem. Broh (2002) showed that students who participated in musical activities talked more with their parents and teachers, and concluded that these social activities were likely to lead to higher self-esteem and self-efficacy. Keen (2004) worked with troubled adolescents who often have low self-esteem and found that music therapy was successful in raising self-esteem. Various techniques were adopted including song discussion, listening, writing lyrics, composing music and performing.

MacDonald and Miell (2002) demonstrated that educational programmes in music composition and learning to play an instrument could increase self-esteem in children with learning disabilities and developmental disorders. These children face particular challenges as they struggle with intellectual or motor issues, which physically differentiate them from their peers and lead to them being shunned by those around them. Participating in public performances highlighted healthy elements which may have gone unnoticed because of the children being assigned a label of disability. Engaging in music as a rightful member of a musical group can change how disabled people see themselves, enhancing self-esteem and improving relationships with others.

Ensemble Participation

One strand of research has focused on the impact of ensemble participation on self-esteem. In the USA, research has explored the impact of being a member of a school band. For instance, Brown (1980; 1985) found that 91 percent of non-band parents, 79 percent of non-band students, 90 percent of drop-out band parents and 82 percent of drop-out band students agreed that participating in a band built self-esteem, self-confidence and a sense of accomplishment. A study with students who participated in band festivals (Gouzouasis and Henderson, 2012) found that students valued instrumental music and participation in band festivals as a positive, rich educational experience, and experienced a sense of accomplishment after a good performance.

Evans and Liu (2019) examined the impact of psychological need satisfaction and frustration in a high-school orchestra programme. Seven hundred and four participants were surveyed in orchestra programmes in three schools in the midwestern United States. The influence of psychological need satisfaction and frustration were assessed as predictors of time spent practising, intentions to continue participation and self-esteem. Psychological need satisfaction predicted all three outcomes, although psychological need *frustration*, in contrast, showed mixed results and predicted self-esteem negatively.

Musical Preferences and Self-Esteem

Some research has focused on the relationship between self-esteem and musical preferences. Rentfrow and Gosling (2003) failed to uncover significant relationships between self-esteem and musical preferences, suggesting that perceived self-worth had no effect on musical preference, or vice versa. In contrast, Shepherd and Sigg (2015) assessed differences in music preferences and self-esteem in 199 university students and found that music preference scores for clusters of music genres were found to significantly correlate with self-esteem.

In a review including 14 studies, Lawendowski and Bieleninik (2017) examined the evidence regarding music therapy participation and self-esteem. They argued that participation offered opportunities to engage in identity work, defining, developing and reflecting on personal understanding, and cultivating new expressions of self-identity. They suggested that self-understanding developed and led to self-acceptance and personal growth. They also drew attention to the marked variation in research depending on the type of music therapy used, the participants, settings, outcomes and measurement tools. A qualitative analysis showed that expression of emotion and a sense of agency were valuable for both participants and those around them as a way of providing damaged selves with ways to heal, thus improving self-esteem.

Social Development

Music and Early Social Development

In a review, Creighton (2011) argued that early experiences of emotional communication contribute to mother-infant attachment and impact upon an infant's neurological, social and emotional development. Similar conclusions were drawn by Ilari (2016) in a review which examined young children's musical engagement from a social perspective, integrating research from a wide range of fields and theoretical orientations. Children begin to develop social skills with their caregivers from birth. Music can play a role in this development and in the way that mothers bond with their newborn children. For instance, Cevasko (2008) examined the effects of mothers' singing on their adjustment to and bonding with their newborn infants, as well as the use of music in the home environment in the first two weeks after their infants' birth. Fifty-four full-term infants and mothers and 20 premature infants (alongside 16 of their mothers) were randomly assigned to experimental or control conditions. Mothers in both groups were recorded singing songs of their choice for use at home. Recordings of each pre-term mother's voice were played for 20 minutes, three to five times each week, at a time when the mother was not able to visit her infant in hospital. All full-term and pre-term mothers in experimental and control groups completed a post-test survey two weeks after the infants were discharged. There was a significant difference between the mothers' perceived value of music, with the pre-term experimental group valuing music more. They also sang to infants more than the control group. Pre-term mothers more strongly agreed that knowing that their child was listening to their singing helped them to cope with their infants' stay in hospital. In addition, pre-term infants who listened to the CD recording of their mother's singing left the hospital an average of two days earlier than those in the control group, although this difference was not statistically significant.

There is considerable evidence that mother-infant singing leads to increased perceived emotional closeness and strengthening of the mother-infant bond (Fancourt and Perkins; 2018). Fancourt and Perkins (2017) compared the effects of singing to babies with listening to music. Singing to babies on a daily basis was associated with enhanced wellbeing, self-esteem and self-reported mother-infant bonding. Persico and colleagues (2017) compared groups of women who had or had not engaged in singing lullabies at antenatal classes in the 24th week of pregnancy with a follow-up at three months after birth. Postnatal bonding was significantly greater in the singing group three months after birth.

Gerry and colleagues (2012) found that six-month-old infants exposed to active music lessons where they were encouraged to repeat the songs and rhymes every day at home led to superior development of prelinguistic communicative gestures and social behaviour, compared to infants assigned to a passive musical experience. Similarly, Pitt and Hargreaves (2017) investigated the role of and rationale for parent and child, up to three years old, group music-making activities in children's centres. The perceptions of parents and practitioners were sought through a questionnaire which was completed by 49 practitioners and 91 parents. The questionnaire was based on a previous qualitative study which had revealed seven thematic categories of the perceived benefits of music: social, emotional, learning, teaching, links to home, parenting and organisational. Statistical analyses revealed significant differences between the expressed views of parent and practitioner groups, as well as between parents in different broad age groups. Practitioners expressed more positive views about the perceived benefits of music for parents than were expressed by the parents themselves. Parents in the majority age group, 27 to 35 years, expressed significantly more positive opinions on a variety of questionnaire items than did parents in both younger and older age groups.

Researching older children, Williams and colleagues (2015) investigated parent-child home music activities in a sample of 3031 Australian children aged two to five years old, and found that shared home music activities had a small significant partial association with measures of children's prosocial skills. However, Hartas (2011) found no relationship between parents' reported frequency of singing songs and rhymes or playing music at three years old and teacher-rated performance of social emotional development at five years old.

Kawase and colleagues (2018) focused on the age of onset of group music lessons at a music school on children's levels of sociability. A preliminary survey of the association between age of onset and extracurricular musical training or activity in non-music majors implied that musical experience from a very early age positively influenced social skills during adulthood. In the main study, Kawase and colleagues conducted a survey of 276 children aged four to five and six to seven years old who commenced music lessons at ages one, two, four and six. The findings showed that the empathy scores of children aged six to seven who began lessons when they were one year old were greater than those who began lessons at four years old. The communication scores of children aged four to five who began lessons at one year old were greater than those who began lessons when older than one year old. The empathy and extroversion scores were high in those aged six to seven who began lessons in that age range. In the lessons for the very young children, simultaneous parent-child musical activities were also likely to lead to enhanced attachment. Overall, the findings suggested that participation in group music lessons two to four times a month can be effective social training for very young children and foster their later sociability.

Research with disadvantaged children and their parents has also demonstrated the benefits of participation in musical activities. For instance, Nicholson and colleagues (2008) explored the effectiveness of a ten-week group music therapy programme on 358 parents who were socially disadvantaged, young or had a child with a disability. The children were under five years of age. Musical activities were used to promote positive parent-child relationships and children's behavioural, communicative and social development. Significant improvements were found for therapist-observed parent and child behaviours, parent-reported irritable parenting, educational activities in the home, parent mental health, child communication and social play skills. Other research has shown that group music lessons for children can improve accompanying parents' mood (Kawase and Ogawa, 2018).

The Role of Synchronisation

Synchronisation of movement plays an important role in social development. Engagement with musical rhythms at a young age supports synchrony and more altruistic behaviour between children and adults (Trainor and Cirelli, 2015). Parent-child attachment induced by synchronisation increases children's social cognitive skills (Thompson, 2008). Behrends and colleagues (2012), on the basis of the literature, argued that coordinated movement fosters empathy and prosocial behaviour, and synchronous and imitated movement is associated with liking and prosocial behaviour. Supporting this, Cirelli and colleagues (2014) arranged that each of 48 14-month-old infants were held by an assistant and gently bounced to music while facing the experimenter, who bounced either in or out of synchrony with the way that the infant was bounced. The infants were then observed and placed in a situation in which they had the opportunity to help the experimenter by handing to her objects that she had accidentally dropped. The infants were more likely to engage in altruistic behaviour and help the experimenter to pick up the objects after having been bounced to music in synchrony, compared with infants who were bounced asynchronously. A further experiment, using anti-phase bouncing, suggested that this was due to the contingency of the synchronous movements as opposed to movement symmetry. These findings supported the hypothesis that interpersonal motor synchrony might be a key component of musical engagement that encourages social bonds among group members, but also that motor synchrony to music may promote the very early development of altruistic behaviour.

Kirschner and Tomasello (2009) hypothesised that children would spontaneously synchronise their body movements to an external beat at earlier ages and with higher accuracy if the stimulus was presented in a social context. A total of 36 children in three age groups—2.5, 3.5, and 4.5 years old—were invited to drum along with either a human partner, a drumming machine or a drum sound coming from a speaker. When drumming with a social partner, children as young as 2.5 years old were able to adjust their drumming tempo to a beat outside the range of their spontaneous motor tempo. Children of all ages synchronised their drumming with higher accuracy in the social condition. Similarly,

Kirschner and Tomasello (2010) examined the relationship between collaborative music activity and helping behaviour in four-year-old children who engaged in three minutes of musical collaboration, and suggested that the children who synchronised with peers showed more spontaneous cooperative and helpful behaviour, relative to a carefully matched control condition with the same level of social and linguistic interaction but no music. The ability to synchronise with other children in group music lessons also predicts attentional behaviour (Khalil et al., 2013).

Parent-child coordination during musical activity has been shown to be beneficial for good relationships. For instance, Wallace and Harwood (2018) assessed parent-child musical engagement in childhood and adolescence as a predictor of relational quality in emerging adulthood. These findings persisted when controlling for other forms of positive parent-child activity. Since younger children require more support from their parents, attachment might increase through musical engagement in younger classes as compared to older classes.

Synchronising movements with others encourages a collective social identity, leading to increased cooperation within a group. For instance, Good and colleagues (2017) investigated whether movement synchrony impacted on social categorisation and cooperation across intergroup boundaries. Two three-person groups were brought together under movement synchrony conditions designed to emphasise different social categorisations. All individuals moved to the same beat while each minimal group moved to a different beat, or each individual moved to a different beat. The findings demonstrated that movement synchrony influenced social categorisation and cooperation across intergroup boundaries. Valdesolo and colleagues (2010) showed that rocking in synchrony enhanced individuals' perceptual sensitivity to the motion of others and increased their success in a subsequent joint-action task that required the ability to dynamically detect and respond appropriately to a partner's movements. These findings support the view that in addition to fostering social cohesion, synchrony enhances the abilities that allow individuals to functionally direct their cooperative motives. Similarly, Valdesolo and DeSteno (2011) manipulated rhythmic synchrony and showed that synchronous others were not only perceived to be more similar to the participating individual, but also evoked more compassion and altruistic behaviour than asynchronous others having the same experience. These findings support the view that a primary function of synchrony is to mark others as similar to the self and that synchrony-induced affiliation modulates emotional responding and altruism.

Keller and colleagues (2013) reviewed the psychological processes and brain mechanisms that enable rhythmic interpersonal coordination, including an overview of research on the cognitive motor processes that enable individuals to represent joint-action goals and to anticipate, attend and adapt to other's actions in real time. They concluded that music supports social cognitive tendencies including empathy and affects coordination, which affects interpersonal affiliation, trust and prosocial behaviour.

Musical Ensembles and Teamwork

Making music with others in small and large groups requires teamwork, particularly when music is to be performed. Teamwork relies on participating individuals supporting each other and developing trust and respect. Group music-making provides an ideal vehicle for developing prosocial, teamworking skills. Musical ensemble performance constitutes a refined form of joint action that involves the non-verbal communication of information about musical structure and expressive intentions through co-performers' sounds and body movements. From a psychological perspective, ensemble performance necessitates precise yet flexible interpersonal coordination of sensorimotor, cognitive, emotional and social processes. Such interpersonal coordination is facilitated by representations of shared performance goals, which are consolidated during rehearsal. During actual performance, these shared goal representations interact with sensorimotor and cognitive processes that allow co-performers to anticipate, attend to and adapt to each other's actions in real time. Shared representations involve the integration of information related to one's own part, others' parts and the joint-action outcome. Shared musical representations facilitate real-time interpersonal coordination by dynamically embodying intended action outcomes related to the self, others and the ensemble as a whole (Keller, 2014).

Small ensembles, such as string quartets, are argued to be significant examples of self-managed teams, where all members contribute equally to a task. In larger ensembles, such as orchestras, the relationship between conductor and orchestra clearly emerges as they come to know each other (Volpe et al., 2016). Within small musical groups, social relationships and the development of trust and respect are crucial for their functioning (Davidson and Good, 2002; Davidson and King, 2004; Goodman, 2000; Young and Colman, 1979). For long-term success, rehearsals have to be underpinned by strong social frameworks, as interactions are typically characterised by conflict and compromise related mainly to musical content and its coordination, although some interactions are of a more personal nature (for instance, approval; Murninghan and Conlon, 1991; Young and Colman, 1979). The smaller the group, the more important personal friendship seems to be.

Kawase (2015; 2016) studied the relationship between daily social skills, styles of handling interpersonal conflict, non-verbal behaviour and leadership. They requested 68 female music majors to complete questionnaires assessing these different skills and behaviours, and showed that a performer's daily social skills, an integrating style of handling interpersonal conflict, and leadership in daily communication affected the evaluation of ensemble performance through social behaviours during ensemble practice. Overall, daily social skills were correlated with behaviours during ensemble practice. Performers with a high evaluation of their ensemble performance tended to employ two types of social behaviours: an integrating style of handling interpersonal conflict and leadership in daily communication. No correlation was observed between non-verbal skills in daily communication and the evaluation of ensemble performance.

The impact of making music with others has been studied in children. For instance, Pasiali and colleagues (2018) examined the potential benefit of a music therapy social skills development programme to improve the social skills of school-aged children with limited resources in an after-school programme. Twenty students aged five to eleven years old participated. The programme consisted of eight 50-minute sessions. The results showed that music therapy had the potential to promote social competence in school-aged children with limited resources, particularly in the areas of communication and low-performance, high-risk behaviours.

In the UK, peripatetic instrumental teachers working in schools have reported considerable benefits of learning to play an instrument, including the development of social skills, teamwork and a sense of achievement, and enhanced confidence, self-discipline and physical coordination (Hallam and Prince, 2000). Also in the UK, an evaluation of informal music learning where students work in small groups to copy popular songs by ear and ultimately create their own songs showed a positive impact on listening skills and collaborative, peer and teamworking as reported by music and non-music teachers and senior staff in the schools (Hallam et al., 2016; 2017; 2018).

Being involved in the extracurricular rehearsal and performance of a school show has been shown to facilitate the development of friendships with like-minded individuals and make a contribution to social life through a widespread awareness of the show by non-participants (Pitts, 2007). Such participation increased pupils' confidence, social networks and sense of belonging, despite the time commitment which inevitably impinged on other activities. Similarly, Cuadrado and colleagues (2017) researched *Musicalizatech*, a collaborative music production project for secondary and high-school students. Forty-six participants from secondary education and high schools in Seville and Cordoba, grouped in 15 preformed bands, joined the project. The research used questionnaires, a focus group, online diaries and interactions in an online chatroom. The results showed impact on participants' development of social and emotional skills, ability to problem-solve and work in teams, development of technological skills and clear improvements in the process of musical creation.

Research in the USA has shown that involvement in group music activities in high school helped individuals to learn to support each other, maintain commitment and bond together for group goals (Sward, 1989). The benefits of band participation have been reported to include maturing relationships. For instance, band directors talked in general terms about the benefits of teamwork, cooperation, sense of belonging, companionship and social development (Brown, 1980). Adderley and colleagues (2003) investigated the meaning and value that music ensembles engendered for their participants, and the social climate of the music classroom. Structured interviews were conducted with 60 students, 20 each from band, choir and orchestra. Ensemble participation yielded musical, academic, psychological and social benefits. The social climate emerged as an important element, as students noted the importance of relationships for their wellbeing and growth. In the UK, reflecting on previous and current group music-making activities, university music students reported benefits in terms of pride in being an active contributor to a group outcome, developing a strong sense of belonging, gaining popularity, making friends with like-minded people and the enhancement of social skills (Kokosaki and Hallam, 2007; 2011). Similarly, a study of 84 members of a college choral society showed that 87 percent believed that they had benefited socially, 75 percent emotionally, and 49 percent spiritually from participation. Meeting new people, feeling more positive and being uplifted spiritually were all referred to (Clift and Hancox, 2001).

School Climate

Some research has focused on the way that the collaborative and non-competitive elements of ensemble music-making can enhance school climate and social interactions within school contexts (Bastian, 2000; Gouzouasis and Henderson, 2012). In Finland, Eerola and Eerola (2014) explored whether music education could create social benefits in the school environment in ten schools which had an extended music curricular class. The quality of school life was assessed by a representative sample of 735 pupils aged nine to twelve years old. The results showed that extended music education enhanced the quality of school life, particularly in areas related to general satisfaction about the school, and sense of achievement and opportunities for students. A follow-up study examined whether the increase in critical quality of school-life variables was related to music. This analysis utilised data from other classes, with an extended curriculum in sports or visual arts. These classes did not confer similar benefits. Overall, the results suggested that extended music education had a positive effect on the social aspects of schooling. In a major study in Switzerland, Spychiger and colleagues 1993) found that increasing the amount of classroom music within the curriculum increased social cohesion within class and led to greater self-reliance, better social adjustment and more positive attitudes, particularly in low-ability, disaffected pupils.

Sistema Programmes

Evaluations of individual *El Sistema* or *Sistema*-inspired programmes, where children experience intensive and prolonged engagement in an orchestral community, have reported the strengthening of children's sense of individual and group identity, of children taking pride in their accomplishments, and of enhancement in determination and persistence. Children valued their participation as a social activity, a way to enjoy music with others and strengthen friendships with peers, working in teams and acquiring musical skills. Many of the evaluations of *Sistema*-inspired programmes in the USA refer to enhanced peer relationships, demonstrating respect and having consideration for others. Because of their experiences in orchestras and ensembles, participants understood the importance of working cooperatively (Creech et al., 2013; 2016). Intensive ensemble activities are seen as a rich opportunity for nurturing positive citizenship skills, including respect, equality, sharing, cohesion, teamwork and the enhancement of listening as a major constituent of understanding and cooperation (Majno, 2012). Slevin and Slevin (2013) suggested that the programmes offered a safe and nurturing space where children learned what it meant to pursue an ideal. They argued that this type of teamwork, where the goal depended on individual effort, enabled personal development. Similarly, Lewis and colleagues (2011) revealed improvements in social skills and the development of positive group identity in an *ElSistema*-inspired programme. Pupil surveys administered two years apart indicated statistically significant change in relation to social skills and relationships. Children reported how they tried to help others and take turns. Interviews with parents and teachers reinforced these findings. The parents suggested that this was because the children were proud of their musical achievements and because the programme offered opportunities for developing social skills and discipline. Teachers also indicated that pupils had a greater sense of purpose and self-confidence. Smithhurst (2011) and Burns and Berwick (2012) found enhanced confidence and social skills to be outcomes, while programmes in Scotland showed enhanced confidence, happiness and teamworking skills (GEN, 2011a; 2011b). In Ireland, after three years, a *Sistema*-inspired programme was found to foster a strong positive group identity. When asked to design a new school crest, every child produced a design that included a musical symbol (Kenny and Moore, 2011). Parents and others in evaluations by Campe and Kaufman (2013) and Savoie (2012) indicated that playing in *Sistema*-inspired musical groups supported students in their social development, providing an important scaffold for developing collaborative skills. These skills transferred to other school and home settings. Galarce and colleagues (2012), based on findings from focus group data, found that students participating in a *Sistema*-inspired programme in the Caribbean demonstrated improved social skills, cooperation, teamwork, communication and a protective social network after only six months of participation. Quantitative data showed that students were significantly less likely to get angry and be aggressive, and be less involved in teasing, shoving, hitting, kicking or fighting. Similarly, Bergerson and Motto (2013) found that students experienced greater empathy for others who shared their interests. In Argentina, Wald (2011a; 2011b), researching two *Sistema*-inspired programmes, found evidence of enhanced self-esteem, self-worth, self-confidence, pride, motivation, commitment, social responsibility and socialisation. Comparing programmes in Venezuela and the USA, Uy (2010) reported improvements in relaxation and coping, communication, the ability to work with others and self-esteem. Osborne and colleagues (2015) explored the academic and psychosocial impact of *El-Sistema*-inspired music programmes in two low socioeconomic schools, where students experienced generational poverty or had current or first-generation immigrant or refugee status. Ninety-two students in Years 3 to 6 completed audiovisual assessments of psychosocial wellbeing. Comparisons by school and programme participation over a period of 12 months indicated improved psychosocial wellbeing for students in one school. Overall, many positive social outcomes of *Sistema* programmes have been reported internationally (Creech et al., 2013; 2016), although there are exceptions: for instance, Villalba (2010) found that some students did not feel completely integrated and others were bored. This suggests that the nature of the musical activities in these programmes plays an important role in mediating any wider non-musical outcomes.

Prosocial Skills and Empathy

One of the most frequently cited benefits of group music-making is its impact on prosocial behaviour. From an evolutionary perspective, Hagen and Bryant (2003) have argued that group music-making and dancing evolved as ways of demonstrating internal stability in the group and the ability to act collectively in establishing meaningful relationships with other groups. Music and dance can also act as effective tools to maintain bonds within social groups, increasing cooperation and prosocial behaviour (Huron, 2001; 2003). Members of musical groups have to pay attention to the actions and intentions of the other players, and their physical and emotional states (Cross et al., 2012). This promotes states of togetherness (Huron, 2001; 2003; Cross, 2009). Understanding the emotional state of others is key to developing empathy—the ability to produce appropriate responses to the situation of others that approximate their responses and experiences, as well as an awareness and identification of their emotions (Lieberman, 2007). Cross and colleagues (2012) suggest that music has empathy-promoting components which can lead to shared intentionality, understanding of the intentions of others, the adoption of a common object of attention (Tomasello et al., 2005) and intersubjectivity (Rabinowitch et al., 2012).

There is evidence that engagement in making music can enhance children's prosocial behaviour and empathy. Ritblatt and colleagues (2013) examined the effects of a school readiness music programme on preschool children's socioemotional readiness to transition to kindergarten. They found that those participating in musical activities improved on a range of social skills, including social cooperation, social interaction and social independence.

In other research, preschool and primary-school children who participated in a special music empathy programme—which highlighted the importance of empathy through singing and composing songs about empathy, as well as discussing how children empathise—also demonstrated high empathy levels (Kalliopuska and Ruokonen, 1986; 1993; Kalliopuska and Tiitinen, 1991). Schellenberg and Corrigall (2015) investigated whether group music training in childhood was associated with prosocial skills. Children in third and fourth grade who attended ten months of music lessons taught in groups were compared to a control group of children matched for socioeconomic status. All children were administered tests of prosocial skills near the beginning and end of the ten-month period. Compared to the control group, children in the music group had larger increases in sympathy and prosocial behaviour, but this effect was limited to children who had poor prosocial skills before the lessons began. The effect was evident even when the lessons were compulsory, which minimised the role of self-selection. Rabinowitch and colleagues (2013) studied 52 children aged eight to eleven years old who were randomly assigned to musical activities, games or acted as a control group. The musical intervention consisted of a range of musical games which were designed to encourage musical interactions and working together creatively. Entrainment games were designed to encourage rhythmic coordination, and imitation games to highlight imitative and gestural encounters, shared intentionality and intersubjectivity. The children took a battery of tests at the beginning and end of the study, which included three measures of emotional empathy. Two out of three of the empathy measures increased in the children in the music group. Similarly, Hietolahtiansten and Kalliopuska (1991) surveyed 12-year-old children who had been musically active for about six years and same-age control children with no musical activity, and found that the musically trained children scored significantly higher on scores of empathy.

Related to empathy is the concept of emotional sensitivity. As music is closely linked with the emotions, it is possible that active music-making has the capacity to increase emotional sensitivity (Hunter and Schellenberg, 2010). For instance, Resnicow and colleagues (2004) found that there was a relationship between the ability to recognise emotions in performances of classical piano music and measures of emotional intelligence, which required individuals to identify, understand, reason with and manage emotions using hypothetical scenarios. The two were significantly correlated, which suggests that identification of emotion in music performance draws on some of the same skills that make up everyday emotional intelligence. There is also evidence that music training enhances sensitivity to emotions in speech (Thompson et al., 2004). Similarly, Schellenberg and Mankarious (2012) studied the relationship between understanding emotions and music training in 60 seven- to eight-year-olds. The musically trained children had at least eight months of formal musical training out of school, mainly through private individual lessons. The findings showed a positive association between music training and emotional ability.

Comparing the effects of different musical interventions, Rose and Colleagues (2019) investigated the effects of musical instrument learning on the development of 38 seven- to nine-year-old children. Pre- and post-test measures of socioemotional behaviour were compared in children who received either extracurricular musical training or statutory school music lessons. There were no statistically significant differences in socioemotional behaviour between the groups. In a retrospective study, Theorell and colleagues (2014) assessed whether musical creative achievement and musical practice were associated with emotional competence. Eight thousand Swedish twins aged 27 to 54 were studied. Musical achievement and musical practice were related to higher emotional competence, although the effect sizes were small. Focusing on the impact of listening and observation, Haner and colleagues (2010) studied the effects of a children's opera about bullying presented to five classrooms in three schools. Data were available for 104 children in Grades four and five. Knowledge of bullying increased significantly after participation and there was a significant decrease in self-reported victimisation.

Interventions for Children with Special Educational Needs and Disabilities

One strand of research has focused on children with a range of special educational needs and disabilities. For instance, music therapy studies with young autistic children have shown enhanced social, verbal and communication skills and emotional development (Oldfield, 2006). Dezfoolian and colleagues (2013) studied five children with autism who had no previous experience in music or play therapy. Social interaction, verbal communication and repetitive behaviour of the participants were scored before and after the Orff music therapy. All participants improved significantly in their social interactions and verbal communication. Similarly, Kim and colleagues (2009) studied improvisational music therapy and toy-playing sessions using DVD analysis of sessions with children on the autistic spectrum. Improvisational music therapy produced markedly more and longer events of emotional synchronicity and initiation of engagement behaviours in the children than toy-playing sessions. In response to the therapist's interpersonal demands, compliant positive responses were observed more in music therapy than in toy-playing sessions. No responses were twice as frequent in toy-playing sessions as in music therapy. The findings supported the value of music therapy in promoting social, emotional and motivational development in children on the autistic spectrum. Hillier and colleagues (2012) reported the findings of a pilot music programme for adolescents and young adults with Autism Spectrum Disorder. Evaluation of the programme focused on self-esteem, anxiety and attitudes toward/ relationships with peers. Pre- and post-outcome measures showed a significant increase in self-esteem, reduced self-reported anxiety and more positive attitudes toward peers.

Zyga and colleagues (2017) focused on children with intellectual disabilities, as these can cause a child to have significant deficits in social skills and emotional regulation abilities. They investigated the feasibility of delivering a school-based musical theatre programme to students with intellectual disability across a range of school settings. Video recordings were coded for socioemotional ability across each of the 47 participants. The findings showed significant gains across all domains, although these gains related to school- and individual-level student factors such as grade level, severity of disability and baseline social-skill level.

One project explored the impact of musical engagement as part of the *National Orchestra for All* on 35 young people with special educational needs following a summer residential programme. There were statistically significant increases with a large effect size for self-esteem, emotional wellbeing, resilience and life satisfaction. Participating girls seemed to benefit more than boys (Hay, 2013; NPC, 2012).

Physical Development

As we saw in Chapter 2, research in the field of neuroscience has shown that intensive instrumental music training affects the anatomy of the brain, with greater grey-matter volume seen in motor-related areas (Elbert et al., 1995; Hyde et al., 2009; Pascual-Leone, 2001) and greater white-matter volume in motor tracts (Bengtsson et al., 2005), with differences emerging after one year of music training (Hyde et al., 2009; Schlaug et al., 2005). There are also very specific differences in relation to the instruments played (Bangert and Schlaug, 2006). Despite this, there is relatively little research exploring the impact of active engagement with making music on physical development, although children and adults frequently respond to music with movement. For instance, Overy (2014) studied the impact of beat on children's natural responses to music and showed that four-year-old children showed spontaneous, energetic movement responses which were highly periodic and repetitive—such as jumping, swaying and twisting—often in close synchrony with the auditory beat pattern, although not always in time. She concluded that the human motor system responds powerfully to an auditory beat pattern, but that there are large individual differences in preferred movements. Also, individuals frequently use music as a motivator when they are exercising. Research related to this will be discussed fully in Chapter 17.

There is evidence that learning to play an instrument improves fine motor skills (Schlaug et al., 2005). Early training may be important, as Watanabe and colleagues (2007) showed that musicians who trained before the age of seven had better performance in a timed motor sequence task than musicians who began training later. Early- and late-trained musicians were matched for years of musical experience, years of formal training and hours of current practice. The early-trained musicians performed better than the late-trained musicians. This advantage persisted after five days of practice. Performance differences were greatest for a measure of response synchronisation, suggesting that early training has its greatest effect on neural systems involved in sensorimotor integration and timing.

Some research has focused on fine motor abilities. For instance, Costa-Giomi (2005a) compared the fine motor abilities of children who participated in two years of piano instruction and those who had never received formal music training. A significant improvement in fine motor skills was found only for the children who received the music lessons. There was also a significant difference in the speed of response between the two groups at the end of the two years of instruction. Similarly, James and colleagues (2019) carried out a cluster randomised controlled trial which provided evidence that focused musical instrumental practice, in comparison to traditional sensitisation to music, provoked multiple transfer effects in the sensorimotor domain. Over the last two years of primary school, 69 ten- to twelve-year-old children received group music instruction by professional musicians twice a week as part of the regular school curriculum. The intervention group learned to play string instruments, whereas the control group (peers in parallel classes) were sensitised to music through listening, theory and some practice. There were benefits for the intervention group as compared to the control group for sensorimotor hand function and bimanual coordination. Learning to play a complex instrument in a dynamic group setting appears to impact development more strongly than classical sensitisation to music.

Martins and colleagues (2018) conducted a longitudinal training study to examine if collective, Orff-based music training enhanced fine motor abilities when compared to a homogeneous training programme in basketball, or to no specific training. The training programmes in music and sport had the same duration, 24 weeks, and were homogeneous in structure. A design including tests prior to training, post-training and a follow-up was adopted. Seventy-four children attending the third grade, aged eight years old, were pseudo-randomly divided into three groups—music, sport and control—that were matched on demographic and intellectual characteristics. Fine motor abilities relating to hand-eye coordination and motor speed subsumed under manual dexterity, bimanual coordination and manipulative dexterity were tested. All groups improved in manipulative dexterity but the children engaged in the music programme showed an advantage in relation to bimanual coordination and manual dexterity. This persisted for four months after the programme ended.

Music, Locomotor Performance and Coordinated Motor Skills

Some research has explored whether rhythmic accompaniment can improve performance in physical education programmes. In early research, Anshel and Marisi (1978) observed positive results in performance accuracy and endurance when music was rhythmically synchronised with motor performance. Painter (1966) found similar results. Beisman (1967) showed that throwing, catching, jumping and leaping improved when children participated in a programme involving rhythm. Brown and colleagues (1981) studied two approaches to facilitating perceptual motor development in children, aged four to six years old. The experimental group, with 15 children, received 24 sessions of integrated physical education and music instruction, based on the methods developed by Kodaly and Dalcroze. The control group of 15 children received 24 sessions of movement exploration and self-testing instruction. The experimental group showed significant improvement, with changes in motor, auditory, and language aspects of perceptual motor performance, as well as a total score.

Derri and colleagues (2001) investigated the effect of a ten-week music and movement programme on the quality of locomotor performance in 68 four- to six-year-old children. The children were assessed on running, skipping, galloping, hopping, leaping, sliding and horizontal jumping. Thirty-five children participated in the exercise programme twice a week, while the control group did not participate in any organised physical activity programme. The findings showed that the experimental group improved on galloping, leaping, horizontal jumping and skipping. A later study showed that the programme compared favourably with free-play activities (Deli et al., 2006). Similarly, Zachopoupou and colleagues (2004) compared the effect of a developmentally appropriate music and movement programme and a developmentally appropriate physical education programme on the development of jumping and dynamic balance in children aged four to six years old. Ninety children participated. Fifty followed the music and movement programme which lasted for two months. The remainder served as the control group and followed a physical education programme for the same period of time. The results showed that the experimental group improved significantly in jumping and dynamic balance. Rose and Colleagues (2019) investigated the effects of musical instrument learning on the development of 38 seven- to nine-year-old children. Pre- and post-test measures of motor ability and visual motor integration were compared in children who received either extracurricular musical training or statutory school music lessons. The children receiving extracurricular lessons showed a significant increase in visual motor integration and in gross motor ability for aiming and catching measures. It seems that musical activities may support development in a child's ability to judge distance, consider velocity, focus, and use their proprioceptive, interoceptive and exteroceptive nervous system.

Overview

There is clear evidence that music plays an important role in the development and maintenance of identity, although the extent to which this applies may vary among individuals depending on their hobbies and interests. Musicians as a group have been shown to be more open to new experiences than the general population. Beyond this, there are no clear personality differences between musicians and the general population, or between those playing different instruments. However, differences have emerged with more clarity in relation to the genre of music with which musicians are engaged. This suggests that the context in which music is rehearsed and performed influences personality development. There is strong evidence across genres that professional musicians and those training to become professional musicians experience performance anxiety and may experience perfectionistic work tendencies. The latter can have positive benefits in terms of motivation and conscientiousness but may be detrimental when the musician becomes focused on imperfect performances. Music can have a positive impact on self-esteem in children and young people, providing that feedback from peers, teachers and families is positive. This is particularly evident in those from disadvantaged backgrounds or those with special educational needs or disabilities. If feedback on performance, even practising at home, is negative rather than constructive, the impact on self-esteem can be detrimental.

In children and young people, group music-making in large and small groups generally promotes the development of social skills, teamwork and empathy, although there may be exceptions to this (for instance, if a group member does not contribute equitably). Issues can arise in the working of small groups of professional musicians, although the need to prepare for public performance may support the development of skills which help to resolve any challenges—for instance, compromise and leadership skills—in order that the group can perform well. Synchronisation of movement plays a role in supporting group working and may have evolved in order to enhance group cohesion.

Learning to play a musical instrument which requires coordinated complex movements enhances fine motor skills in young children. When children are able to engage in movement to music, this impacts positively on a range of athletic skills including jumping, skipping, throwing and catching.

14. Psychological Wellbeing

Psychological wellbeing is typically viewed as comprising hedonic (feeling good) and eudaimonic (functioning well) components. The emphasis given to each of these varies between conceptualisations. Seligman (2002) proposed the concept of 'authentic happiness', which consists of pleasure, engagement and meaning. More recently, the concepts of relationships and accomplishment have been added (Forgeard et al., 2011; Seligman, 2010; 2011,) leading to the acronym 'PERMA', which stands for positive emotion, engagement, relationships, meaning and accomplishment. Others have argued that positive human experience is only related to hedonic wellbeing, positive emotion, the absence of negative emotions and an evaluative component termed 'life satisfaction' (Diener et al., 1999). More recently, Diener and colleagues (2010) added the concept of 'flourishing', which includes purpose in life, positive relationships, engagement, competence, self-esteem, optimism and contribution to the wellbeing of others. Despite these different conceptualisations, there is agreement that wellbeing is multi-dimensional. Approaching the conceptualisation of wellbeing from a different perspective, Huppert and So (2013) equated high levels of wellbeing with positive mental health. They argue that wellbeing lies at the opposite end of the spectrum to common mental disorders, depression and anxiety. By examining internationally agreed criteria for depression and anxiety and defining the opposite of each symptom, they identified features of positive wellbeing which combined feeling and functioning. The elements that emerged were:

- competence, concentration, attention, decision-making, general competence;
- emotional stability, feeling calm, relaxed, even-tempered;
- engagement, interest, pleasure, enjoyment;

- meaning, purpose, worth, value in life;
- positive relationships, social relationships, positive affirmation;
- optimism, hopeful for the future;
- positive emotion, positive mood, happy, cheerful and contented;
- resilience, managing anxiety and worry, emotional resilience;
- Self-esteem, feelings of self-worth, confidence;
- vitality, feeling energetic, not fatigued or lethargic;
- life satisfaction, positive appraisal of life in general.

Previous chapters have set out the role that music can play in relation to many of these elements, including competence, engagement, positive relationships, self-esteem and (to a lesser extent) resilience and optimism. Some elements can be met by active engagement with music, and others through listening to music, although there is overlap between these. Actively making music offers the most opportunities for supporting competence, self-esteem and resilience, while listening to music is more likely to support emotional stability and positive emotions. Both can support engagement, meaning, optimism, positive relationships and vitality.

There is an ever-increasing body of research on the benefits of engaging with music in relation to psychological wellbeing. This chapter will consider the impact of listening to and actively engaging with music through the different phases of the lifespan. Positive associations between engaging with music and wellbeing have been demonstrated in early childhood (Linnavalli et al., 2018; Trainor et al., 2012), in terms of children's educational outcomes (Guhn et al., 2019), sense of social inclusion (Welch et al., 2014) and social cohesion (Elvers et al., 2016), in adolescence (McFerran et al., 2019), adulthood (Greasley and Lamont, 2006), older age (Laukka, 2007; Lindblad and de Boise, 2020) and overall development (Biasutti et al., 2020). Drawing conclusions about the research is not without its difficulties. For instance, in a recent review, Daykin and colleagues (2018) pointed out that there was a lack of consistency in how wellbeing was assessed and in the range of musical interventions implemented. Overall, they reported that music was associated with reduced anxiety in young adults, enhanced mood and purpose in adults, and mental wellbeing, quality of life, self-awareness and coping in people with diagnosed health conditions. Music listening and singing were shown to be effective in enhancing morale and reducing risk of depression in older people, while a few studies addressed wellbeing in individuals with dementia. Sheppard and Broughton (2020) also reviewed the literature and showed that music and dance were related to key social determinants of health from social, cultural, physical and mental health perspectives. Similarly, O'Donnell and colleagues (2021), in a systematic review which included 32 studies with 1,058 participants focusing on wellbeing in adults over 18 years of age, showed that participatory arts interventions benefited mental health through improved connectedness, emotional regulation, meaning-making and redefining identity, personal growth and empowerment. Benefits relating to wellbeing have been found, whether individuals volunteer to participate or are referred by health or social care professionals. Music has been recognised for its beneficial effects on physical health (Fancourt and Finn, 2019; Hanser, 2010; Jones et al., 2013; MacDonald et al., 2012; Pelletier, 2004; van den Elzen et al., 2019). Research focusing on the way that music has been used in medical contexts will be discussed in Chapter 15. The remainder of this chapter will set out the way in which music can enhance wellbeing and consider its role across the lifespan from infancy, through the school years, adolescence, young adulthood, the adult years and into older age, concluding with a section on music and wellbeing in the COVID-19 pandemic.

The impact of music on psychological wellbeing and good health is largely, although not exclusively, through the emotions it evokes. Music elicits emotions and changes moods through its stimulation of the autonomic nervous system and limbic and related biological systems, including endocrine and hormonal responses (Krout, 2007). Bodily responses linked with emotion include changes in dopamine, serotonin, cortisol, endorphin and oxytocin levels (Kreutz et al., 2012) and cardiovascular indicators, blood pressure and pulse (Lee et al., 2016). Some changes in response to music can occur without an individual's conscious awareness. In two multilevel meta-analyses of 104 studies with 9,617 participants, de Witte and colleagues (2019) showed that interventions using music had an overall significant positive effect on stress reduction, physiologically and psychologically, although greater effects were found for heart rate when compared to blood pressure. Overall, music can reduce stress and increase relaxation (Fukui and Yamashita, 2003; Kreutz et al., 2004) but the outcomes depend on the nature of the music (Kimberley et al., 1995). For instance, Gerra and colleagues (1998) investigated emotional and endocrine changes in response to listening to techno music. Sixteen young people were exposed to techno or classical music for 30 minutes each. Concentrations of plasma norepinephrine, epinephrine, growth hormone, prolactin, adrenocorticotropic hormone, cortisol and β endorphin were assessed before and after the listening activity. Techno music significantly increased heart rate and systolic blood pressure, and led to changes in the assessed neurotransmitters, peptides and hormones related to mental state and emotional involvement. Classical music also enhanced emotional state, but did not lead to significant changes in hormonal concentrations. Similarly, Evers and Suhr (2000), working with adults, investigated the short-term effects of listening to different musical excerpts on serum concentrations of prolactin, adrenocorticotropic hormone and serotonin, the latter contributing to feelings of wellbeing. Some excerpts were characterised as pleasant—for instance, Brahms' 'Symphony No. 3, Opus 90'—while others were perceived as unpleasant (for instance, Penderecki's 'Threnos', which is in part composed in quarter tones to exaggerate the dissonance of the music). Listening to Threnos led to a reduction in concentrations of serotonin, suggesting a negative impact on wellbeing.

The most comprehensive attempt to outline the mechanisms that may underpin music's impact on the emotions is the *BRECVEMA* framework (Juslin, 2013). This features eight mechanisms through which music affects emotions:

- Brain stem reflex: a hard-wired attention response to simple acoustic features such as extreme or increasing loudness or speed (Juslin et al., 2014);
- Rhythmic entrainment: a gradual adjustment of an internal body rhythm—for instance, heart rate—towards an external rhythm in the music (Harrer & Harrer, 1977);

- Evaluative conditioning: a regular pairing of a piece of music and other positive or negative stimuli leading to a conditioned association (Blair and Shimp, 1992);
- Emotional contagion: perception of emotionally relevant expressions in the music which is then copied (Juslin, 2000; Lundqvist et al., 2009);
- Visual imagery: images with emotional qualities evoked by the music (Osborne, 1981);
- Episodic memory: a conscious recollection of a particular event from the listener's past triggered by the music (Baumgartner, 1992);
- Musical expectancy: a reaction to the gradual unfolding of the musical structure and its expected or unexpected continuation (Meyer, 1956); and
- Aesthetic judgment: a subjective evaluation of the aesthetic value of the music based on an individual set of weighted criteria (Juslin and Sloboda, 2010).

The specific way in which emotions are invoked depends on complex interactions between the nature of the music, the individual and the context. Individual preferences play a major role. The more that the individual is familiar with particular genres or pieces of music, the more they are preferred (North and Hargreaves, 2008). This process begins in early childhood. This explains why music that is pleasurable for some individuals may be unpleasant for others. The greatest positive benefits of music on wellbeing and health occur when individuals are able to select the music that they are to listen to (Krause et al., 2015; Mitchell et al. 2006a; 2006b). This is particularly important when music is being used to reduce anxiety or pain (Bernatzky et al., 2012; Mitchell and MacDonald, 2012). If individuals are exposed to music that they do not like in contexts where they have no control, they may remove themselves from the situation, but if that is not possible, the music can cause extreme distress. Although individuals react to music in different ways, there are some musical characteristics which tend to have a relatively consistent effect on arousal levels (which are implicated in emotional responses).

Quiet, slow music tends to lead to a lowering of arousal levels, while fast and loud music tends to increase arousal (North and Hargreaves, 2008).

Music can engender intense, strong emotional experiences. These generally occur when listening to music rather than performing (Gabrielsson, 2001, 2002, 2011; Gabrielsson and Lindström Wik, 2003). Such experiences have overall general characteristics including physical reactions and behaviours; perceptual and cognitive responses; changes in feelings and emotions; existential and transcendental aspects; and personal and social aspects. Individuals report sensations of joy, happiness, rapture, euphoria, calm and peace which have high significance and can lead to long-term benefits, with lives becoming more fulfilling, spiritual and increasingly harmonious (Schäfer et al., 2014) with a positive impact on wellbeing (Lamont, 2011; 2012). Memories of such experiences can be used as sources for self-therapy, inspiration and motivation, and provide insights into alternative ways of being (Gabrielsson, 2011; Gabrielsson and Lindström, 1995). Most occur in adolescence and early adulthood (Gabrielsson and Lindström Wik, 2003).

The Use of Music to Support Emotional Stability and Manage Moods

A key human ability is the capacity to regulate emotion, modifying positive or negative aspects, intensity and time course (Barrett and Gross, 2001; Cole et al., 2004), physiological processes, and emotion-related behaviour (Eisenberg, 2004; Eisenberg and Spinrad, 2004; Gross, 1998). Emotional self-regulation also includes the management of moods which are generally differentiated from emotions in terms of their longer duration, lack of specific cause and greater focus on internal experiences rather than overt behaviour (Gross, 2015). Mood regulation refers to the processes involved in modifying or maintaining the occurrence, duration, and intensity of moods (Cole et al., 2004; Eisenberg and Spinrad, 2004; Gross, 1998).

Music can promote subjective feelings of wellbeing, provide a means of working through difficult emotions, and is often linked to spirituality (Juslin and Sloboda, 2001). It is frequently used as a regulatory strategy for maintaining or changing moods, emotions, arousal levels and to reminisce (DeNora, 1999; Juslin and Laukka, 2004; Parker and Brown, 1982; Rippere, 1977; Schäfer et al., 2013; Silk, 2003; Thayer et al., 1994). It can induce positive affective states (North et al., 2004), help to achieve desired moods—whatever they may be (Vastfjall, 2002) and act as a supporting strategy when coping with negative moods and emotions (Miranda and Claes, 2009; Shifriss and Bodner, 2015). It may be that this is one of the reasons why music plays such an important role in the lives of most people (Sloboda et al., 2009). Certainly, mood regulation is reported to be one of the most important reasons why people listen to music (Christenson and Roberts, 1998; North et al., 2000; Sloboda and O'Neill, 2001; Wells & Hakanen, 1991). Even adolescents who play an instrument report that the best activity for mood regulation is listening to music alone (Saarikallio, 2006). Music is used for self-regulation by adolescents (Behne, 1997; Laiho, 2004; Roe, 1985), adults (Greasley and Lamont, 2006), and the elderly (Davidson et al., 2008). It can be used to maintain positive moods, for revival and energising, to create strong sensations, as a diversion, as discharge, for mental work, for solace and for psyching up (Saarikallio, 2011).

The extent to which music relates to wellbeing has been demonstrated in several reviews. For instance, Schäfer and colleagues (2013) identified 129 functions of listening to music. Ratings by 834 respondents led to the emergence of three underlying dimensions: listening to music to regulate arousal and mood, achieving self-awareness, and as an expression of social relatedness. Similarly, Krause and colleagues (2018) identified 2,075 benefits of music based on a review of 97 published articles. These were reduced to 562 benefits to wellbeing which were perceived to be associated with musical participation. From these, five dimensions were identified: mood and coping, self-esteem and worth, socialisation, cognition and self-actualisation. Saarikallio and colleagues (2018) collected data from 464 online participants and established that the pleasure derived from music was based in part on sensations of relaxation, power and passion, but also feelings of kinship relating to social values and mental contemplation. Reminiscence is also a frequent function of self-chosen music listening. This is particularly prevalent in older adults (Hays and Minichiello, 2005; Juslin and Laukka, 2004), although it is also found in young people (Tolfree and Hallam, 2016). Overall, music is one form of attending to and reappraising emotional experiences (Ruud, 1998; Sloboda and O'Neill, 2001). Van Goethem and Sloboda (2011) carried out diary studies alongside interviews and established that music helped individuals through the use of several regulation strategies. For instance, it could help to distract someone from an emotion or a situation, or help to consider either in a rational way. It plays a major role in assisting relaxation and promoting happiness.

Cognitive reappraisal seems to play an important role in the way that music impacts on wellbeing. If listening to music, making music and social engagement are coupled with a tendency to regulate emotions and thoughts by suppressing emotion, there may be negative outcomes. Suppressing outward expressions of emotions does not decrease negative feelings and emotional arousal. High levels of engagement with music through listening or participating have been associated with a greater use of cognitive reappraisal. This may be because music provides a safe platform for exploring and expressing emotions, positive and negative (Huron, 2006). In this way, the process of emotion regulation may act to mediate the relationship between musical engagement and wellbeing (Chin and Rickard, 2012).

Thoma and colleagues (2012) demonstrated a clear preference for music congruent with the specific emotional situation of the individual at the time, while Randall and colleagues (2014) suggested that listeners adopted particular regulation strategies based on their initial mood, emotional wellbeing and health which would enable them to reach their desired emotional goal. Similarly, Randall and Rickard (2017b), in research with 327 young adults, concluded that music listening was determined by initial mood and emotional health with the aim of fulfilling specific emotional needs. Randall and Rickard (2017a), based on data from research with 195 participants, demonstrated that generally music returned moods to a neutral state, although sometimes music was selected which was congruent with a current mood. Where music was used to cope with very difficult situations or forget problems, it tended to be associated with overall negative affective states and poor emotional health and wellbeing. In a critical analysis, McFerran (2016) suggested that the use of music to maintain negative moods by seriously distressed individuals could lead to increasingly negative outcomes.

As research has developed over time, inconsistencies in terms of conceptualisation and terminology have emerged (Baltazar and

Saarikallio, 2016). It has become clear that the impact of music on wellbeing is not straightforward. For instance, Kantor-Martynuska (2015) suggested that the way that individuals respond to music depends on an interaction between the properties of the music, the relatively stable traits of the listener, his or her current emotional state and their current situation. A considerable body of research has focused on why individuals choose to listen to sad music (Huron and Vuoskoski, 2020; Tahlier et al., 2013; Van den Tol and Edwards, 2015). For instance, Sachs and colleagues (2015) suggest that listening to sad music can bring about positive change by correcting an ongoing homeostatic imbalance. They argue that sadness evoked by music is pleasurable when it is perceived as non-threatening, is aesthetically pleasing and produces psychological benefits such as mood regulation and empathic feelings caused, for instance, by recollection of and reflection on past events. Garrido and colleagues, in several studies, also explored why people listen to sad music (Garrido, 2017; Garrido and Schubert, 2013). Garrido and Schubert (2015a) studied 335 participants who listened to a self-selected piece of sad music. They found that participants' depression increased after listening. Similarly, Garrido and Schubert (2015b), studying 175 university students who listened to a self-selected piece of music on YouTube, found that listening could significantly increase depressive feelings in those with depressive tendencies. In an online survey of 137 participants, Garrido and Schubert (2013) showed that listening to sad music could have adaptive or maladaptive uses. They explained this by the dissociation theory of aesthetic enjoyment, where participants with the capacity to enter states of absorption are able to deactivate displeasure circuits and hence enjoy negative emotions in music. Garrido and colleagues (2017) explored these issues further, investigating whether listening to sad music in group settings provided social benefits for emotionally vulnerable listeners, or whether it further exaggerated depressive tendencies. Six hundred and ninety-seven participants aged 16 to 74 years of age were recruited through online depression groups and mental health websites in the USA, Australia, the UK, South America, Africa, Asia and Europe. A survey of listening habits revealed that participants with depression were more likely to engage in group rumination (the process of continuously thinking the same thoughts, usually sad and dark). Those with depressive tendencies seem to struggle to regulate their emotional responses in musical contexts (McFerran, 2016) and group interactions focusing on sad music exacerbated these difficulties (Miranda et al., 2012). Rose (2002) described this extensive discussion and revisiting of problems among friends as co-rumination. Conversely, the sharing of emotions through music listening may provide individuals with depressive tendencies with social support and thus increase their sense of connection with others. Reflection as opposed to rumination can, it seems, be a useful tool for processing negative emotions (Trapnell and Campbell, 1999). Individuals who have already acquired adaptive coping strategies—for instance, seeking social support—may use group music listening positively to provide support and help them process negative feelings. These findings are important for the use of music in healthcare settings and wellbeing in everyday life (Garrido, 2017).

One strand of research has explored differences between individuals in the ways that music impacts on wellbeing. For instance, Leipold and Loepthien (2015), drawing on data from 521 participants aged 18 to 86 years old and 152 adolescents and young people aged 12 to 23 years old, studied the differences between attentive analytical listening (which was defined as reflective and complex) and emotional listening, and the relationships of these with coping with stress or rumination. They showed that attentive analytical listening to music showed positive relationships to accommodative coping, whereas emotional listening had a positive relationship with rumination. No age differences were found in the nature of listening in adulthood or for the younger age group, although the transition from adolescence to adulthood was important. A comparison between adolescents and young adults revealed that attentive analytical listening was negatively associated with age up to approximately 17 years old, after which the relationship became positive, while adolescents demonstrated age increments in emotional listening.

Similarly, Groarke and Hogan (2016) asked 24 younger people and 19 older adults why they listened to music. The younger adults emphasised affect regulation and social connection, whereas older adults emphasised more eudaimonic (well-functioning) uses of music: for instance, transcendence and personal growth. Saarikallio (2011) found that older people were more aware of how music fitted particular moods and situations. Women have been found to be more likely to use music to regulate emotions and moods than men (Sloboda, 1999). There is evidence that girls are more likely to engage with music to cope with personal problems and interpersonal conflicts, whereas for boys, music is a way of increasing energy levels and positive moods, and creating an impression of being cool (Behne, 1997; Christenson and Roberts, 1998; Larson, 1995; Larson et al., 1989. Music can be effective in decreasing arousal due to stress, particularly for adolescents, females and musicians (Pelletier, 2004). For instance, Lehmann (1997) reported that music majors responded more strongly emotionally to their preferred music than non-music majors, although some studies have reported that the music-related emotional experiences of non-musicians and musicians are broadly similar (Schubert, 2001).

The use of music to regulate moods is related to musical preferences. Diversity in musical preference has been shown to be related to emotionality in listening (Behne, 1997; Schwartz and Fouts, 2003). Preference for harder forms of music has been found to be positively related to emotional problems, including psychological turmoil and behavioural problems (Took and Weiss, 1994) expression of anger (Epstein et al., 1990), feelings of loneliness (Davis and Kraus, 1989) and moodiness, pessimism and impulsiveness (Schwartz and Fouts, 2003). Ter Bogt and colleagues (2020) addressed the potential link between liking goth music and depressive symptoms in a four-year study of 10- to 15 –year-olds. They showed that goth music was liked by a small minority of adolescents, who reported increased levels of depressive symptoms as they grew older. In contrast, preference for upbeat and conventional pop music has been found to be negatively related to depression (Rentfrow and Gosling, 2003). Scheel and Westefeld (1999) investigated the relationship between a preference for heavy-metal music and vulnerability to suicide among 121 tenth- and twelfth-grade high-school students. Participants completed a questionnaire relating to reasons for living, risk of suicide and musical preferences. Heavy-metal fans had less strong reasons for living, especially male fans, and had more thoughts of suicide, especially female fans. For most, listening to all types of music had a positive effect on mood. While preference for heavy-metal music among adolescents may be an indication of increased suicidal vulnerability, the research suggested that the source of the problem was more likely to lie in personal and familial characteristics than in any direct effects of the music. However, group music therapy can support young people at risk of mental health problems and can reduce unhealthy uses of music (Gold et al., 2017).

Saarikallio and Erkkilä (2007), in a large study of 1515 participants with an average age of 15 years old, found that the most preferred musical styles for boys and girls across all age groups were rock, pop, heavy metal and rap. Boys preferred heavy metal and techno music, whereas girls preferred classical music, pop and gospel. Preferences for classical, rock, jazz, folk and gospel music increased with age, while the preference for pop music gradually decreased. Eclectic musical preferences were related to the extent of the use of music to regulate moods. Overall, Saarikallio and Erkkilä demonstrated how personal factors were linked to differences in adolescents' use of music. Those preferring rock and heavy-metal music made greater use of music to regulate their moods. Perhaps the intensity, volume and roughness of these genres reflects the intense emotional experiences which are characteristic of adolescence. In contrast, listening to pop, rap and techno music tended to create positive, feel-good experiences

For many years now it has been possible to use a range of devices to listen to music anywhere and at any time. Skånland (2011; 2013) researching the use of the MP3 player suggested that such availability could be valuable in supporting listeners in coping with crowded and noisy environments, and promoting wellbeing and mental health. Further developments in music technology have meant that people can find expression through creating playlists. These can support the maintenance of mood and recall of memories (Bull, 2005), while Hagen (2015) observing students' use of the playlist function concluded that playlists based on moods, feelings, memories, or biographical, relational representations helped users experience mastery over themselves. Playlists may also support social cohesion as some of the pleasure of creating them may come from owning, customising and trading them (McCourt, 2005).

There are differences in the extent to which listeners are aware of how music affects them. More engaged listeners are acutely aware of how music can change or fit their moods (Greasley and Lamont, 2011). Squirrel listeners (Lamont and Webb, 2010) are better able to access and implement strategies to regulate their moods choosing music to fit any given situation and their own physical, psychological and social needs. Batt-Rawden and DeNora (2005) describe this as 'lay therapeutic practice'.

Singing

One strand of research examining the relationship between wellbeing and music has focused on singing. Reviews of the research on participation in choirs have identified many benefits, including:

- physical relaxation and release of physical tension;
- emotional release and reduction of feelings of stress;
- a sense of happiness, positive mood, joy, elation and feeling high;
- a sense of greater personal, emotional and physical wellbeing;
- an increased sense of arousal and energy;
- stimulation of cognitive capacities, attention, concentration, memory and learning;
- an increased sense of self-confidence and self-esteem;
- a sense of therapeutic benefit in relation to long-standing psychological and social problems;
- a sense of exercising systems of the body through the physical exertion involved, especially the lungs;
- a sense of disciplining of the skeletal-muscular system through the adoption of good posture;
- being engaged in a valued, meaningful worthwhile activity that gives a sense of purpose and motivation (Clift et al., 2008; Clift, 2012; Stacey et al., 2002).

Group singing has been found to reduce anxiety and depression (Houston et al., 1998; Lally, 2009; Wise et al., 1992; Zanini and Leao, 2006), as well as providing opportunities for developing social networks. Singing has a variety of positive effects on both mental and physical health (Fancourt et al., 2019; Irons et al., 2020; Kreutz et al., 2004; Moss and O'Donoghue, 2020).

Kreutz (2014) studied the psychobiological effects of amateur choral singing with a mixed group of 21 novice and experienced singers who completed questionnaires about their psychological wellbeing and gave samples of saliva for measuring levels of salivary oxytocin, cortisol and dehydroepiandrosterone at the beginning of two rehearsal sessions and 30 minutes later. The singing condition included warm-up vocal exercises and repertoire pieces. In a control condition, dyads of participants talked to each other about recent positive life experiences. The findings showed patterns of change favouring singing over chatting. There were no significant interactions for cortisol, dehydroepiandrosterone or the cortisol dehydroepiandrosterone ratio. Overall, the findings suggested that singing enhances individual psychological wellbeing, as well as inducing a sociobiological bonding response.

Grape and colleagues (2003) also used a range of physical markers to explore the possible beneficial effects of singing on wellbeing during a singing lesson. Eight amateur singers aged 28 to 53 years old, and eight professional singers aged 26 to 49 years who had been attending singing lessons for at least six months, participated. Electrocardiogram measures were recorded and computerised spectral analysis was performed. Serum concentrations of TNF alpha, linked to autoimmune systems, prolactin, cortisol and oxytocin were measured before and 30 minutes after the lesson. Five visual scales—sad joyful, anxious calm, worried elated, listless energetic, and tense relaxed—were scored before and after the lesson alongside a semi-structured interview. Heart rate variability analyses showed significant changes over time in the two groups. Power increased during singing for the professionals, whereas there were no changes in the amateurs. This indicated an ability to retain more heart-brain connection, more cardiophysiological fitness for singing in professional singers, compared to amateur singers. Serum concentration of TNF alpha increased in professionals after the singing lesson, whereas the concentration in amateurs decreased. Serum concentrations of prolactin and cortisol increased after the lesson in the group of men and vice versa for women. Oxytocin concentrations increased significantly in both groups after the singing lesson. Amateurs reported increasing joy and elatedness, whereas professionals did not. However, both groups felt more energetic and relaxed. The interviews showed that the professionals were clearly achievement oriented, with a focus on singing technique, vocal apparatus and body during the lesson. In contrast, the amateurs used the singing lessons as a means of self-actualisation and self-expression, as a way to release emotional tensions. Overall, singing lessons seemed to promote wellbeing and reduce arousal for amateurs compared to professional singers, who seemed to experience the reverse.

In a study of young people who were members of a university choir, Clift and Hancox (2001) identified six elements associated with the benefits of singing: wellbeing and relaxation; enhanced breathing and posture; social benefits; spiritual benefits; emotional benefits; and benefits for the heart and immune system. In a later study, Clift and Hancox (2010) surveyed 1124 choral singers drawn from choirs in Australia, England and Germany. Participants completed a questionnaire which measured physical, psychological, social and environmental wellbeing, and a measure of the effects of choral singing. Open questions provided more in-depth understanding. There was a high level of agreement about the positive benefits of choral singing, with women significantly more likely to endorse its value for wellbeing and health compared with men. There was a small significant relationship between psychological wellbeing and the effects of choral singing for women, but not for men. Eighty-five participants with relatively low psychological wellbeing had high scores on the singing scale. Four categories of significant personal and health challenges were disclosed by members of this group: enduring mental health problems; family and relationship problems; physical health challenges and recent bereavement. Their accounts suggested six ways that singing might impact on wellbeing and health: positive affect; focused attention; deep breathing; social support; cognitive stimulation and regular commitment. In a further study Clift and colleagues (2017) studied four community singing groups which met weekly for people with mental health issues. Evaluation took place over a six-month period using two questionnaires. Twenty-six participants completed baseline and follow-up questionnaires. The findings showed that clinical scores reduced, and wellbeing scores increased significantly.

In a comparison of gender differences, Sandgren (2009) examined how emotional states varied on measurements pre- and post- a regular choral rehearsal in 212 participants from eleven choirs. Women reported significantly more positive emotional states than men relating to participation in regular choir rehearsals, although the differences were small. Men and women reported similar levels of negative emotions, but varied more in the extent of positive change after the choir rehearsal.

Some research has focused on the impact of participation in a choir on very specific groups of people. For instance, Bailey and Davidson (2002; 2003) studied whether positive life transformations could occur when homeless men joined a choir. Using semi-structured interviews they found that group singing positively influenced emotional, social and cognitive processes. They concluded that active participation in singing may alleviate depression, increase self-esteem, improve social interaction skills and induce cognitive stimulation. In a later study, Baily and Davidson (2005) explored the effects of group singing and performance with a second choir formed for homeless and other marginalised individuals who had little or no music training or group singing experience, and middle-class singers with low to high levels of music training and choral singing experience. The findings showed that the emotional effects of participation in group singing were similar regardless of training or socioeconomic status, but the interpersonal and cognitive components of the choral experience had different meanings for the two groups. The marginalised individuals appeared to embrace all aspects of the group singing experience, while the middle-class choir members were inhibited by social expectations of musicianship. Also working with a distinctive group, Southcott and Nethsinghe (2019) explored the understandings and meanings of shared music-making held by members of the *Young Hearts* Russian choir in Melbourne, Australia and its impact on their quality of life. The elderly participants were first-generation migrants who spoke most strongly in their first language, Russian. Individual semi-structured interviews were undertaken with nine choir members, while focus group discussion included all 28 members. The interviews revealed two broad themes: maintaining independence and resilience and learning, rehearsing and performing music. Sub-themes included the importance of participation, maintaining face, overcoming illness and disability, and becoming a family. Singing together enhanced quality of life, combatted social isolation, fostered resilience and sense of autonomy, and allowed participants to access inner resources to face life challenges.

Considering issues relating to a range of disabilities, Dingle and colleagues (2012) explored the personal experiences of choir members,

89 percent of whom experienced chronic mental health problems, 28 percent physical disabilities and 11 per cent intellectual disability. Semi-structured interviews were carried out with twenty-one members of the choir at three time points in the choir's inaugural year, at the inception of the choir, after six months, and after twelve months. Three themes emerged:

- personal impact in terms of positive emotions, emotional regulation, spiritual experience, self-perception, finding a voice;
- social impact including connectedness within the choir, connection with audience, social functioning; and
- functional outcomes including health benefits, employment capacity and routine.

Overall, forming a new and valued group identity as a choir member was associated with emotional and health benefits for participants. Fancourt and colleagues (2019) focused on those who were recently bereaved. Fifty-eight adults bereaved in the last five years who had not received treatment of any kind for anxiety or depression in the last month were recruited. Half participated in a choir or acted as a non-intervention control group. Those joining the choir were engaged in 90-minute weekly singing and social sessions for 12 weeks, with a post-intervention assessment after 24 weeks. Those who sang in a choir had more stable symptoms of depression and levels of wellbeing, as well as gradual improvements in their sense of self-efficacy and self-esteem. In contrast, those in the control group showed gradual increases in depressive symptoms, reductions in levels of wellbeing and self-esteem and no improvement in their self-efficacy.

It is not only singing that can have positive benefits for wellbeing. In a review, Perkins and colleagues (2020) identified 46 qualitative studies reporting on participants' subjective views of how participatory music engagement supported their mental wellbeing. Thematic coding revealed four themes: managing and expressing emotions, facilitating self-development, providing respite and facilitating connections. The outcomes of choral singing have also been compared with listening to music. Boyd and colleagues (2020) examined the short-term effects on mood and self-esteem of a novel group singing model that relied exclusively on oral methods of teaching songs to 59 community-recruited adults and compared the effects with group listening. The findings showed that participants' positive emotions and mood improved after singing but declined after listening. Self-esteem increased throughout the sessions regardless of the activity, indicating the importance of the social nature of the singing activities.

Wellbeing in Young Children

Much of the evidence relating to wellbeing in babies, infants and children has been set out in previous chapters. In infancy and early childhood, musical activity largely takes place through interactions with caregivers. Ruud (1997) suggests that the first musical memories often include feelings of being held by parents. Songs are frequently more important than speech in bonding (Nakata and Trehub, 2004; Shenfield et al., 2003). Cirelli and Trehub (2020a) examined the relative efficacy of parents' speech, and singing familiar and unfamiliar songs, in alleviating the distress of 68 eight- and 68 ten-month-old infants. Parent-infant dyads participated in three trials of a still-face procedure, featuring a two-minute play phase, a still-face phase (where parents were immobile and unresponsive for one minute or until infants became visibly distressed), and a two-minute reunion phase in which caregivers attempted to reverse infant distress by singing a highly familiar song, an unfamiliar song, or talking expressively. In the reunion phase, talking led to increased negative affect in both age groups, in contrast to singing familiar or unfamiliar songs, which increased infant attention to parents and decreased negative affect. The favourable consequences were greatest for familiar songs, which also generated increased smiling. Skin conductance recorded from a subset of infants revealed that arousal levels were highest for the talking reunion, lowest for unfamiliar songs, and intermediate for familiar songs. The arousal effects, considered in conjunction with the behavioural effects, confirmed that songs were more effective than speech at mitigating infant distress.

Krueger (2011) argued that, from birth, music is perceived as a structure that offers the possibility of constructing and regulating emotions, expressing and communicating, and shaping relationships and situations. In children's play, symbols, drawings and music can be used thoughtfully but activities are mainly participatory, engaged and active (Bonsdorff, 2017; Karlsen, 2011; Kuuse, 2018). From an early age, using these resources, children develop a sense of agency and self-efficacy. Informal learning of music is frequent in everyday life (Batt-Rawden and DeNora, 2005). This creates memories, patterns, meanings and opportunities for interaction between individuals and their social surroundings. Learning how music can be used empowers the individual to act on their own moods and emotions, wellbeing, health and agency (DeNora, 2000; 2001; Skånland, 2013). Musicality has been argued to be intrinsic to communication between parents and infants (Malloch and Tervarthen, 2009). Parents use music to support other activities and to create a calm and soothing environment prior to sleep times, in addition to participating in child-centred musical activities (Lamont, 2008). Child-parent interactions can be enhanced by music therapy, as can impulse control and self-regulation skills (Pasiali, 2012) and social and communication skills (Mackenzie and Hamlett, 2005; Nicholson et al., 2010; Walworth, 2009). For instance, de Gratzer (1999) showed in a ten-month action research project of group music-making between parents and toddlers that non-verbal communication between parent and child was enhanced. Williams and colleagues (2012) examined the effectiveness of a short-term group music therapy intervention for 201 parents of children with disabilities and found that there were significant improvements for parental mental health, child communication and social skills, parenting sensitivity, parental engagement with and acceptance of their child, child responsiveness to parent, and child interest and participation in programme activities.

As we saw in Chapter 13, moving in time together promotes social bonding. This is important for the social development of infants, as it promotes positive interactions with caregivers. Young infants seem to enjoy listening to and moving to music. For instance, Cirelli and Trehub (2020b) studied an infant who began moving rhythmically to music at six months of age. Across nine sessions, beginning when she was almost 19 months of age and ending eight weeks later, she was video-recorded by her mother during the presentation of 60-second excerpts from two familiar and two unfamiliar songs presented at three tempos: the original tempo and faster and slower versions. The child exhibited a number of repeated dance movements such as head-bobbing, arm-pumping, torso twists and bouncing. She danced most to Metallica's 'Now that We're Dead', a recording that her father played daily in her presence, often dancing with her while it played. Its high pulse clarity, in conjunction with familiarity, may have increased her propensity to dance, as reflected in lesser dancing to familiar music with low pulse clarity and to unfamiliar music with high pulse clarity. She moved faster to faster music but only for unfamiliar music, perhaps because arousal drove her movement to familiar music. Her movement to music was positively correlated with smiling, highlighting the pleasurable nature of the experience. Rhythmic movement to music may have enhanced her pleasure, although the joy of listening may have promoted her movement.

More formal engagement with music may begin in early years education. Certainly, early years educators have positive attitudes towards music and value it, even if they have no formal qualifications in music (Barrett et al., 2019). Parents, grandparents and former child participants of early learning music programmes acknowledge that such programmes enhance musical knowledge and skills (Barrett and Welch, 2020). Active group music-making also enhances pro-social behaviour in young children. For instance, Kirschner and Tomasello (2009; 2010) studied four-year-olds in tasks requiring identical skills in musical and non-musical conditions. Joint music-making enhanced cooperation and helpful behaviour.

Music and Wellbeing in School-Aged Participants

Previous chapters have shown that active engagement with music can enhance intellectual functioning, spatial reasoning, mathematical performance, phonological awareness, literacy, educational attainment and personal, social and physical development. The extent to which these benefits are realised depends on a wide range of factors, not least the nature and quality of the musical education experienced, and the level of commitment and engagement of the child. As musical skills are acquired, a greater sense of purpose and self-confidence can develop (Creech et al., 2013; 2016; Hallam et al., 2017). In this way, music education can have an impact on wellbeing. For instance, Lage-Gómez and Cremades-Andreu (2019) presented the results of a collaborative action research study in Spanish secondary education. Data collected included observations, interviews, classroom diaries, assessments, questionnaires, and video and audio recordings. The findings showed how group improvisation was influenced by:

- active student involvement and wellbeing;
- the students' identification with the music;
- the emergence of group flow and positive emotions, including a high level of motivation; and
- the musical experiences from the students' roles as musicians.

Similarly, informal learning in small groups in the music classroom can benefit wellbeing, leading to enhanced self-esteem, positive relationships, competence and optimism (Hallam et al., 2016; 2017; 2018). Overall, group music-making supports children in improving their social and communication skills, cooperation and teamwork (Creech et al., 2013; 2016).

One strand of research has focused on children perceived as 'at risk'. The *El Sistema* programme and projects inspired by it—where children experience intensive and prolonged engagement in an orchestral community—facilitate pro-social behaviour, and the psychological and physical wellbeing of their students. Evaluations of individual programmes report strengthening children's sense of individual and group identity, causing children to take pride in their accomplishments, enhancing determination and persistence, and making children better able to cope with anger and express their emotions effectively. Children value their participation as a social activity, a way to enjoy music with others, to strengthen friendships with peers, work in teams and acquire musical skills (Creech et al., 2013; 2016).

Some research has focused on children who are marginalised or at risk. For instance, Cain and colleagues (2016) carried out a review of the impact of participatory music programmes, which aimed to promote positive mental and physical health, and wellbeing outcomes for young people from culturally and linguistically diverse communities. The majority of music participation programmes targeted toward young people characterised as 'at risk' have had positive outcomes, including a reduction in anxiety, depression, emotional alienation, truancy and aggression. Participants showed an increase in attendance at school, enhanced self-esteem, cultural empathy, confidence, personal empowerment and healthier nutrition. Similarly, Brown and colleagues (2017) investigated the influence of the arts on cortisol levels in economically disadvantaged children. Three hundred and ten children, aged three to five years old, who attended a Head Start preschool were randomly assigned to participate in different schedules of arts and homeroom classes on different days of the week. Cortisol was sampled at morning baseline and after arts and homeroom classes on two different days at the start, middle and end of the year. For music, dance and visual arts, grouped and separately, the findings showed that cortisol was lower after an arts versus homeroom class at the middle and end of the year, but not at the start of the year. A similar project, where professional musicians worked with school-aged children (Ward et al., 2020) showed through interviews with teachers, musicians, parents and observations that pupils experiencing socioeconomic deprivation enjoyed the benefits of fellowship through group-based music activities. Previously shy pupils began to contribute more in class, and anxious children overcame their fear of performing on stage. Teachers commented that the project had developed pupils' self-confidence.

One strand of research has focused on children's wellbeing in terms of the role that music can play in improving overt behaviour. For instance, Fasano and colleagues (2020) explored whether short orchestral music training could reduce impulsive behaviour. One hundred and thirteen Italian children aged eight to ten years of age participated. Fifty-five attended three months of orchestral training, which included a two-hour lesson each week at school and a final concert. The 58 children in the control group had no orchestral training. The children were assessed in relation to inhibitory control and hyperactivity at the beginning and end of the three-month training period. Children in the music group showed a significant improvement in inhibitory control, while the control group showed an increase in self-reported hyperactivity. This suggests that even an intense and brief period of orchestral training can facilitate the development of inhibitory control by modulating levels of self-reported hyperactivity. Large-scale community-based music programmes for children exposed to violence have also been found to improve self-control and reduce behavioural difficulties. For instance, Alemán and colleagues (2017) assessed the effects of an *El Sistema* music programme on children's developmental functioning in the context of high rates of exposure to violence. The programme emphasised social interactions through group instruction and performance. The research was conducted in 16 music centres and included 2914 children aged six to fourteen years old. Half were admitted to the programme earlier than the remainder. Data collected at the end of the programme indicated improved self-control and reduced behavioural problems. This was particularly the case for children with less educated mothers, and for boys, especially those exposed to violence. Overall, the programme improved self-control and reduced behavioural difficulties.

English and colleagues (2021) explored the viability and effects of a six-week digitally based music outreach programme using *GarageBand* for children in a small rural town who were experiencing difficulties in the upper-primary- and lower-secondary-school years. Focus groups, observations and daily notes showed a significant positive impact on the teachers and children involved. Similarly, Chao-Fernández and colleagues (2020) analysed the benefits of music therapy for six students with disruptive behaviours. A series of activities were designed based on the use of the music video game *Musichao*. There were significant improvements in the development of self-motivation, self-awareness, self-control and social skills. Ye and colleagues (2021) undertook a meta-analysis including ten studies on the effect of music-based interventions on aggressive behaviour in children and adolescents. There was a significant decrease in aggressive behaviour and a significant increase in self-control in the music-based intervention group compared with the control group.

Some research has focused on children experiencing internalised problems. In South Korea, Kim (2017) investigated the effects of community-based group music therapy in children aged seven to twelve who were exposed to ongoing child maltreatment and poverty. Fourteen children experienced music therapy, while twelve acted as controls. Those in the music therapy group received twelve consecutive group music therapy sessions once a week, whereas the control children had no such opportunities. Teacher and child reports assessed behavioural change and showed that children in the music therapy group were less depressed, anxious and withdrawn, and had fewer attention problems than those acting as controls.

In New Zealand, since the 2010-2011 earthquakes, staff and learners at Waitakiri School have participated in daily singing specifically to promote wellbeing. Facilitation of the singing involved no pressure, but rather democratic and participatory conditions, with teachers avoiding judging learners' progress and achievement, and a focus on being together and having fun. Although some teachers lacked confidence about leading singing and the focus was on having fun, learners still developed key competencies and learned musical concepts (Rickson and colleagues, 2018). In England, Chernaik (2021) reported the impact on wellbeing in primary-school children aged eight to ten years old who were exposed to live music provided by professional classical musicians over the period of a school year. The project began with six classroom workshops in each school, progressed to a chamber orchestra workshop for groups of three or four schools in a local venue, and culminated in a symphony orchestra concert. Questionnaires completed following the concerts showed that a range of positive emotions were experienced by the children including excitement, happiness, feeling calm, relaxed, impressed and amazed. Focusing exclusively on extracurricular group percussion activities, Burnard and Dragovic (2015) analysed data from 14 rehearsals, 13 semi-structured interviews and 41 teachers' and pupils' reflective diary entries. The findings showed the potential for such activities to enhance pupil wellbeing by empowering them and enhancing support and decision-making.

Croom (2015) reviewed studies on engagement with music within the PERMA framework to support the claim that music practice and participation could positively contribute to living a flourishing life through positively influencing emotions, engagement, relationships, meaning and accomplishment. Similarly, Lee and colleagues (2017) identified 17 case studies that described successful music programmes in schools in Australia. Content from these case studies was aligned with the five categories of the PERMA wellbeing model. The findings showed that the relationship element of the model was most frequently mentioned. Collaboration and partnership between students, teachers, staff in schools and local people in the community including parents, local entrepreneurs and musicians were repeatedly identified as a highly significant contributing factor to the success of music programmes. Overall, the findings indicated that tailored music and relationship-centred music programmes in schools not only increased the skills and abilities of the students, but also improved their psychosocial wellbeing and that of the community.

Music and Wellbeing in Adolescents and Young People

A great deal of research has been carried out with reference to music and adolescence. As we saw earlier, music plays an important role in teenagers' lives (Bonneville-Roussy et al., 2013; Bosacki and O'Neill, 2013; Greasley and Lamont, 2011). Of all age groups, music seems to be most important for young people (Christenson et al., 1985; Christenson and Roberts, 1998; Gabrielsson and Lindström Wik, 2003; Roe, 1985; Zillmann and Gan, 1997). Music—as it is engaged with in leisure time—contributes to how an individual defines themselves (Hargreaves et al., 2002; Hense and McFerran, 2017; North and Hargreaves, 1999). It is seen to represent personality and is used in impression management, as well as to judge the characteristics of others (Krause and Hargreaves, 2013). In the digital world, this is achieved by controlling what music is shared with others and what is uploaded into personal collections (Voida et al., 2006). By engaging in social comparisons, adolescents are able to portray their own peer groups more positively than other groups in their network, and are thus able to sustain positive self-evaluations. Music facilitates this process (Tarrant et al., 2000). Tarrant and colleagues (2001) investigated English male adolescents aged 14 to 15 years old's perceptions of in-group and out-group. Participants reported greater liking for the in-group and associated it more positively with stereotyped music compared with the out-group. The in-group was viewed as more fun, masculine and sporty and less boring, snobbish and weird. Participants with lower levels of self-esteem showed greater differentiation between groups and greater derogation of the out-group. Van Zalk and colleagues (2009) examined the role of similarity in music preferences in the formation and discontinuation of friendships over a one-year period. Questionnaire data were gathered from 283 Dutch same-sex mutual best friends of almost 13 years of age. The findings showed consistent evidence for high similarity in specific music dimensions among friends at the beginning and end of the year. Moderate similarity was found in the overall patterning of preferences for music genres at both points in time, even after controlling for similarity in social background. Specific music similarity in more non-mainstream music dimensions, and overall music similarity at the beginning were related to selecting a new friend at the end of the time period. However, similarity in music preferences was not related to the discontinuation of existing friendships. Similarity in music preferences seemed to be related to friendship formation but not discontinuation.

Music plays a role in developing and retaining a sense of agency (Saarikallio, 2019). Seeking and exploring a sense of agency through music is particularly relevant for young people but also for those experiencing a reduction in their ability to control their actions and/or their environment due to illness or challenging personal situations (Magee et al., 2017). Sense of agency is important for social-emotional health and can be supported through musical engagement (Saarikallio, 2017; 2019; Saarikallio and Baltazar, 2018). Evaluating the impact of a short music intervention with adolescents, McFerran and colleagues (2018) observed that sense of agency was key. After participation, young people reported an increased awareness of how they could utilise music to reduce distress and promote their own development. Similarly, Saarikallio and colleagues (2020) collected self-reports of personal music listening and their impact on agency from 44 adolescents with an average age of 14 who had received musical training. While there was no general increase in agency over time, there were fluctuations. These were determined by specific contextual factors: for instance, a change in environment, or changes in moods and reasons for listening to music. Elvers (2016; 2018) developed a framework which suggested that increases in feelings of power and control were related to enhanced self-esteem, which could be induced through musical experiences that promoted positive affect, empathy, pleasure and social cohesion. Similarly, music students' wellbeing has been found to improve when their teachers adopt autonomy-supporting strategies (Bonneville-Roussy et al., 2020).

The emotional use of music may not differ according to the type of musical activity, since adolescents' reasons for listening and playing have been shown to be quite similar to one another (North et al., 2000, Saarikallio and Erkkilä, 2007). In a study of 38 adolescents divided into two age groups—9 to 12 and 13 to 17, Tolfree and Hallam (2016) established that, of the four main themes emerging from the data, music in relation to emotions and moods was the strongest. Older girls used music to express anger, stating that it provided a means of acceptable rebelliousness when they were angry with their parents or others in their family. Playing an instrument was not used in relation to managing emotions. Indeed, for most people of any age, listening is the preferred activity for regulating moods, mainly because music is so readily available in the modern world. Lincoln (2005) explored the dynamic relationship between young people, bedroom space and music. Using the concept of zoning, she established that music was used by teenagers spontaneously to create particular atmospheres in their bedrooms, which depended on their age, mood, the time of day, other concurrent activities and other occupants of the space (for instance, friends or siblings). Music blurred the boundaries of public and private space. Music played at a high volume spilled out of the bedroom zone into other rooms in the house. Music was also used as a prequel and a sequel, facilitating getting ready for nights out, setting the right tone and atmosphere.

Teenagers report listening to music to pass time, alleviate boredom, relieve tension and distract themselves from worries. Music is seen as a source of support when they are feeling troubled or lonely, acting as a mood regulator, helping them to maintain a sense of belonging and community (Schwartz and Fouts, 2003; Zillman and Gan, 1997). Music fosters their ability to cope with the challenges that they face, including positive relationships with peers (Papinczak et al., 2015; Selfhout et al., 2009; Ter Bogt et al., 2017), managing emotions (McFerran and Saarikallio, 2014; Saarikallio and Erkkilä, 2007) and developing self-determination (Laiho, 2004). Some have suggested that it is because music plays an important part in these developments that it is so important in adolescents' lives (Laiho 2004; Miranda, 2013; Schwartz and Fouts, 2003). Saarikallio (2019) argued that music is the adolescent's world, their playground and kingdom. They express themselves through it, discover themselves and make their own choices. Studying young adults, Gupta and Kumar (2020) examined the effects of listening to instrumental music over a 20-day period and showed that music listening significantly increased resilience, self-efficacy, optimism, meaning in life and psychosocial flourishing. They concluded that music had the potential for generating positive schemas which could enhance wellbeing and serve as a buffer against increasing negativity in the modern world. Even quite young adolescents use music to manage their moods. For instance, Behne (1997) carried out a longitudinal study of 155 adolescents aged 11 to 17 years old and identified nine listening styles including compensating, concentrated, emotional, distancing, vegetative, sentimental, associative, stimulative and diffused. At ages 11 to 13, the most pronounced listening style was compensating, demonstrating that even young adolescents know how to use music for mood regulation. In general, different strategies for coping with emotions are acquired with age (Seiffge-Krenke, 1995; Mullis and Chapman, 2000).

In a series of studies, Saarikallio and colleagues (Saarikallio, 2006; Saarikallio and Erkkilä, 2007) developed a theoretical model consisting of seven regulatory strategies relating to music: entertainment, revival, strong sensation, diversion, discharge, mental work and solace. They surveyed 1515 adolescents, 652 boys and 820 girls, with an average age of 15. The strategies used most often by boys and girls in all age groups were the same: entertainment, revival and strong sensation. Overall, girls used music for mood regulation more than boys. The use of music for mood regulation increased with age for both sexes but the change occurred later for boys. Singing or playing an instrument as a hobby, valuing music and listening to it were positively related to using music to regulate mood. Composing songs also led to increased regulatory use of music, as did having a family member who sang or played an instrument. Listening alone was chosen by over half of the respondents in all age groups as an influencer of mood. The ways that music was used to regulate mood involved elements that adolescents were often not conscious of in their daily engagement with music (Saarikallio, 2006; Saarikallio and Erkkilä, 2007). Ongoing cognitive development and an increased ability for abstract comprehension may help older adolescents to be more conscious of how they use music to regulate mood. Saarikallio and colleagues (2017) studied 55 adolescents with an average age of 15 who listened to self-selected relaxation music for 20 minutes, once in a laboratory and once at home, and provided written descriptions of their experience. Three major strategies—processing, distraction and induction—and two mechanisms (musical and mental) were identified. Processing was supported by both mechanisms, while distraction and induction were supported predominantly by music. Change from negative to positive mood was generally realised through musical distraction, while the induction of positive emotion was supported by all strategies and mechanisms. In a later study, Baltazar and Saarikallio (2019) studied 571 participants and identified six contrasting strategic uses of music: cognitive work, entertainment, affective work, distraction, revival and focus on the situation. Clear associations between strategies and mechanisms emerged, laying the foundations for a model that integrated regulatory strategies and mechanisms as intrinsic and interrelated components of behaviour (Baltazar, 2019). In an experimental study, Baltazar and colleagues (2019) manipulated the benefits of music and strategy use in reducing stress. Overall, music had a greater impact on short-term outcomes of self-regulation in comparison to strategy use, suggesting that successful affective regulation depends on the adequacy of the chosen strategies and the music, but that the music itself is key in the short term.

An increasing body of research has indicated that listening to music can have very different purposes and outcomes. For instance, McFerran and colleagues (2014) reported an investigation examining how 111 Australian adolescents reported perceived changes in their mood before and after listening to self-selected music. Most reported using music to improve their mood, particularly when their initial state was already positive. However, when feeling sad or stressed, some reported a worsening mood. Those young people who were distressed tended to prefer listening to heavy-metal music but did not report more negative effects on mood for this than for any other genre. They concluded that interpreting such findings was complex, and overly simplistic interpretations needed to be avoided. Miranda (2013; 2019), in two reviews, proposed that music could be both a protective factor and a risk factor in relation to coping in adolescence. McFerran and Saarikallio (2014) explored with 40 Australians aged 13 to 20 years old the beliefs that they held about the power of music to support them during challenging times. They were asked to recall times when music had supported them and times when it had been unhelpful. They considered why young people's beliefs about the positive consequences of music were so strong, even though for those with mental health problems this was not always the case. Miranda and Gaudreau (2011) considered emotional reactions following listening to music, depending on different levels of emotional wellbeing, and also the relationships between social congruence in music tastes with friends or parents and emotional wellbeing. Three hundred and sixteen adolescents with a mean age of 15 years old participated. Three profiles were identified: emotionally negative, limited or positive listeners. These were related to emotional wellbeing, as was social congruence in musical tastes with friends and parents. Also exploring differences between individuals, Gibson and colleagues (2000) divided high-school students into high and low loneliness groups in relation to romantic deprivation, and rated their enjoyment of love-lamenting and love-celebrating videos of popular romantic music. Loneliness proved inconsequential for the enjoyment of love-lamenting songs, although highly lonely males enjoyed love-celebrating songs markedly less than less lonely males. In contrast, highly lonely females enjoyed love-celebrating songs more than less lonely females.

Not all the effects of listening to music are positive. Adolescents may use music as a distraction to avoid thinking about problems (Saarikallio and Erkkilä, 2007). This can have a negative impact on their psychological adjustment (Hutchinson et al., 2006). Listening to music which explores negative themes—for instance, distress, suicide or death—can increase depressive symptoms and suicidal thoughts (Martin et al., 1993; Scheel and Westefeld, 1999). These negative outcomes can be exacerbated through interactions with like-minded peers through music subcultures. For instance, Stewart and colleagues (2020) studied seven Australian young people with a tendency towards depression, exploring their listening habits and their level of awareness of the impact of their music-listening on mood and wellbeing. The findings showed that, while music can have a positive effect on mood, it can also intensify negative moods. They suggested that the relationship between intentions and outcomes is mediated by differing levels of self-awareness and insight into the mood regulation processes which occur during listening to music. Some musical subcultures, such as goth or emo, are focused on music with dark and depressing themes. The blame for some suicides has been laid at the door of such music (Young et al., 2014). In Australia, music therapy carried out over eight weeks was compared with self-directed music-listening in a group of 100 students with self-reported unhealthy music use. There were no differences in outcomes. Both groups showed small improvements over time, although younger participants benefited more from the therapy, and older participants from self-directed listening (Gold et al., 2017).

Specific aspects of music listening can impact on wellbeing. In a small-scale study, Papinczak and colleagues (2015) analysed transcripts from focus groups with 11 participants aged 15 to 25 years old. Four ways in which listening to music linked with wellbeing were revealed: relationship-building, modifying emotions, modifying cognition and emotional immersion. A follow-up questionnaire study with 107 young people showed that music-listening was significantly related to each of these but not directly related to wellbeing. Ter Bogt and colleagues (2017) studied whether adolescents and young adults used music as an agent of consolation when dealing with sorrow and stress, and whether the music itself, its lyrics or experiences of closeness to artists and fans were experienced as comforting. Overall, 1,040 respondents (aged 13 to 30 years old) responded to items assessing listening hours, the importance of music, music preferences, positive and negative effects elicited by music, internalised and externalised problems, and consolation through music. Slightly over 69 percent of respondents reported that they used music as a source of consolation, particularly females and those with higher levels of anxiety and depression. Music's consoling effects were reported as resulting mainly from the sound and texture of the music itself, from attribution of personal meaning to the lyrics, and to a lesser extent from perceptions of closeness to artists and other listeners.

Young people in the Western world spend a great deal of their time listening to music but there is less research globally. Miranda and colleagues (2015), focusing on cultural differences, argued that music can be meaningful in similar and different ways for adolescents living in diverse sociocultural contexts, in which local and global cultures mix and hybridise (Larson et al., 2009). Boer and colleagues (Boer and Fischer, 2012; Boer et al., 2012) proposed two overarching dimensions of music: a contemplative or affective dimension, an individual dimension, and an intrapersonal, interpersonal, a social dimension (collectivism). Adolescents in more collectivist societies used music to convey cultural identity more than those in individualistic societies. Research in six countries (Germany, Kenya, Mexico, New Zealand, the Philippines and Turkey) revealed ten functions of listening to music in late adolescence: as background, focused listening, for venting, related to emotions, for dancing, related to friendship, family, politics, values and cultural identity (Boer et al., 2012). Research in seven countries revealed seven functions: music in the background, memories through music, music as diversion, emotional experiences from music, self-regulation through music, music as a reflection of the self and social bonding (Boer and Fischer, 2012).

Actively Making Music

In addition to listening to music, actively making music can impact on the wellbeing of young people. For instance, in the Netherlands, Uhlig and colleagues (2018) worked with 139 adolescents in schools and showed that engaging in rap and singing music therapy six times a week for four months led to enhanced psychological wellbeing, self-esteem and emotion regulation. Evaluating a similar rap and sing music therapy with 52 adolescents, Uhlig and colleagues (2019) showed a range of benefits for sleep compared with a control group. In the North East of England, Mogro-Wilson and Tredinnick (2020) evaluated the use of visual arts and music on 340 teenagers in a programme designed to enhance social and emotional skill-building. The programme was successful in meeting its aims, and demonstrated that art and music could become a powerful presence in the lives of young people.

Underlying the complexity of the relationship between music and wellbeing, Leung and Cheung (2020) used a process-oriented approach to establish the association between listening to music, playing a musical instrument, musical training and adolescents' wellbeing. One thousand, three hundred and eighteen Chinese adolescents between 12 to 15 years of age from secondary schools in Hong Kong completed questionnaires. Awareness of emotions and emotions themselves were found to mediate between musical training and wellbeing. Positive and negative emotions also mediated between listening to music and wellbeing, although playing an instrument was not associated with emotional awareness, positive or negative emotions, or wellbeing. The findings further reinforce the problems of making direct links between music and wellbeing. Similarly, Clarke and Basillo (2018) investigated the role of the performing arts in 275 secondary-school pupils and demonstrated that the opportunities for playfulness and developing interpersonal relationships afforded by the activities predicted students' wellbeing. The importance of musical context in impacting on wellbeing emerged from research by Baker and colleagues (2018), who studied an artist-led group song-writing programme with 85 young people. They found that contextual factors helped shape the song-writing environment. The young people felt safe, had fun and pushed boundaries, and there was direct and honest feedback, high energy rituals and an emphasis on artistic excellence. Anthony and colleagues (2018), studying the implementation of a music education programme with young people in remote Aboriginal communities, found that the informal learning frameworks (which incorporated music-making shared between educators and community members) provided constructive ways of engaging young people and empowering them in the management of their health and wellbeing. Similarly, in research in Nigeria, Ojukwu (2017) suggested that active engagement in music could promote positive youth development.

Working with at-risk students, Van Rooyen and dos Santos (2020) studied the experiences of teenagers in a children's home who participated in a choir in South Africa. Sixteen weekly choir sessions were held, which included a variety of interactive vocal techniques. A performance marked the end of the process, where songs selected by the teenagers were performed. Qualitative data were collected through 14 semi-structured individual interviews at the end of the process. The findings showed that participation in the choir offered teenagers meaningful intra- and interpersonal experiences. At an intrapersonal level, participants discovered their musical voices, increased their self-awareness, self-esteem and self-confidence, and were able to express and regulate emotions. In terms of interpersonal experiences, the teenagers experienced growth in relationships, improved social skills and greater connection with the broader community. Also working with at-risk young people, Wilson and MacDonald (2020) reported on a ten-week group music programme for young Scottish adults with learning difficulties. Participants enjoyed the programme and participation was generally maintained, with benefits evidenced in increased social engagement, interaction and communication. As we saw in Chapter 12, young people who are disaffected can be re-engaged with their education through music. It can also enhance wellbeing in looked-after children and those in the criminal justice system.

One strand of research has focused on young people presenting issues with academic work. For instance, Sharma and Jagdev (2012) studied 30 adolescents with low self-esteem and high academic stress who engaged with music therapy for a period of 15 days. This reduced anxiety and enhanced self-esteem. Similarly, Schiltz (2016) studied 93 highly gifted adolescents suffering from school failure. They engaged with an integrated form of musical and verbal psychotherapy, musical improvisation with story-writing or the production of drawings with music, followed by verbal elaboration. Participants showed a significant increase in concentration, the capacity for imaginary and symbolic elaboration, pictorial and literary creativity, self-esteem and the quality of coping strategies. There was a significant decrease in defensive functioning and in embitterment and resignation. Music therapy can clearly be beneficial in these circumstances.

Some research has focused on extracurricular school activities. For instance, participating in a school production has been shown to promote friendship groups and support musical, personal and social development (Pitts, 2007; 2008). Kinnunen and colleagues (2020) focused on the social sustainability of music events in adolescents' lives, through their perceptions and own words as they described live music experiences. A web survey of over 1000 adolescents aged 15 to 18 years old demonstrated that cultural content per se was not as meaningful to them as the social networks at such events. Bonding and bridging, as well as the sense of community, produced a range of benefits to wellbeing. Similarly, a thematic analysis by Caleon (2019), including 13 studies aimed at fostering wellbeing in adolescents, identified that music-based activities acted as catalysts for relationship-building, as a means of self-expression and self-regulation, and as a resource for self-transformation. Considering a heritage and related music project, Clennon and Boehm (2014) examined how creative activities that were embedded in a community could serve to enhance the cohesion and wellbeing of the community through the work of its youth groups. In a review, Zarobe and Bungay (2017) concluded that participating in arts activities could have a positive effect on wellbeing through enhancing self-confidence, self-esteem, relationship-building and a sense of belonging.

Music and Wellbeing in Adults

For most people, adulthood is characterised by relative stability and an increase in independence and responsibility, although there are transitions in relation to choices concerning work and family (Levinson, 1986; Levinson et al., 1978). Ageing and retirement bring new challenges, including acceptance of the decline in physical and psychological abilities and the loss of loved ones, while attempting to maintain control over life and sustain interest and motivation (Atchley, 1975; Erikson, 1982). In general, older people report fewer negative emotional experiences (Gross et al., 1997) and retain the ability to regulate their emotions, alongside a desire to derive emotional meaning from their lives (Carstensen et al., 2003). In relation to music, Sloboda and colleagues (2009) have shown that most of music's functions in the everyday lives of adults are related to memories, moods and emotions. Similarly, Greasley and Lamont (2006) reported that adults' use of music included a stress on personal choices, using music for emotional self-regulation and reflection on internal experiences and memories, while Van Goethem (2010) showed that the emotions most typically regulated through music were happiness and calmness. Saarikallio (2011) undertook a qualitative study with 21 participants aged 21 to 70 years old, and revealed that various regulatory goals and strategies were similar throughout adulthood, but that there were also changes related to age, particular events and retirement transition. All participants used music to generate and maintain happy moods, for pleasure and enjoyment. Moods were enhanced by listening to loud music, singing along, starting to play an instrument or even dancing. In addition to using music as a leisure activity, it was used to accompany all kinds of activities, to relax after a working day but also energise to prepare for an activity. When individuals are actively engaged with making music, its effects are greater (Greasley and Lamont, 2006). In adult life, there are many competing demands which affect participation and continuation with music-making. Personal determination and circumstances are key to understanding this (Pitts and Robinson, (2016).

In a very large-scale study in Sweden, Bygren and colleagues (1996) studied 15,198 individuals aged 16 to 74 years old. Of these, 85 percent were interviewed by trained non-medical interviewers about their cultural activities. Eight confounding variables—age, sex, education level, income, long-term disease, social networks, smoking and physical exercise—were controlled for. These influenced survival in the expected direction, except for social networks for men. Taking these into account, the research revealed an influence on mortality in people who rarely attended events compared with those attending most frequently. In another large-scale population study, Cuypers and colleagues (2011) analysed the association between cultural activity and perceived health, anxiety, depression and life satisfaction based on data from the third Nord-Trøndelag Health Study, which included 50,797 adult participants. The findings showed that participation in receptive and creative cultural activities was significantly associated with good health, positive satisfaction with life, and low anxiety and depression scores, especially in men attending the receptive, rather than creative, cultural activities. Similarly, Węziak-Białowolska and Białowolski (2016) investigated the causative impact of attendance at cultural events on self-reported and physical health in the Polish population. Four waves of the biennial longitudinal Polish household panel study representative of the Polish population aged over 16 were used. The findings confirmed that there was a positive association between cultural attendance and self-reported health, although it was not possible to establish a causal link. In another large-scale study, Weinberg and Joseph (2017) explored the connection between habitual music engagement and subjective wellbeing. Data were gathered as part of the 31st survey of the Australian Unity Wellbeing Index, to provide insight into the relationship between music engagement and wellbeing. A sample of 1000 participants were interviewed by telephone. The findings revealed that engaging with music by dancing or attending musical events was associated with higher wellbeing in comparison to those who did not engage with music. The findings also emphasised the importance of engaging with music in the company of others with regard to wellbeing, thus highlighting the interpersonal features of music-making.

In the UK, Tymoszuk and colleagues (2021) explored trends in participatory and receptive engagement with a broad range of arts in 5,338 adults. Over 97 percent of respondents reported engagement in arts activities during 2018 and 2019, with reading and listening to music being the most popular activities. Arts engagement was grouped into three distinct clusters. Almost 20 percent constituted low engagers whose main source of engagement was occasional reading; 44 percent constituted receptive consumers who read and listened to music frequently and engaged with popular receptive arts activities such as going to the cinema, live music, theatre, exhibitions and museums; while almost 36 percent constituted *cultural omnivores* who frequently engaged in almost all arts activities. Greater engagement with the arts was associated with higher levels of wellbeing, social connectedness and a lower possibility of intense social loneliness, although there was a positive association between greater arts engagement, depression and intense emotional loneliness in the most highly engaged omnivores.

Participation in Musical Activities

Pitts (2005) found that musical participation was a potential source of confirmation and confidence, providing opportunities to demonstrate existing skills and acquire new ones. Music can also give a structure to life and offer opportunities to perform with others, develop friendships, engage in social interaction, get relief from family and work pressures and provide spiritual fulfilment and pleasure. It can promote prosocial behaviour, leading to feelings of belonging, social adjustment, trust and cooperation (Anshel and Kipper, 1988; Odena, 2010). People from a range of different backgrounds can experience benefits to their emotional and physical wellbeing from making music, developing an increased sense of self-worth, enhanced social skills and wider social networks (Judd and Pooley, 2014). Lamont and Ranaweera (2020) compared happiness and wellbeing in adults involved in knitting or making music. Eight hundred and thirty-five amateur knitters and 122 amateur musicians completed a measure of happiness and questions about past and current involvement. The knitters scored significantly higher on happiness than the musicians, although no differences were found in relation to subjective wellbeing. Older participants scored more highly on all wellbeing measures, with no effect of time participating in the activity. Despite differences between the activities, participants experienced broadly similar physical, psychological and social benefits. In Australia, Krause and colleagues (2020 administered a questionnaire to 192 residents aged 17 to 85 years old who were participating in a musical activity at the time. The importance of music in individual's lives was positively related to perceived wellbeing including competency, relatedness, autonomous motivation and the social, cognitive and esteem dimensions of wellbeing. These findings were particularly strong for female participants. Overall, there were positive associations between musical activity and psychosocial wellbeing.

As we saw in earlier chapters, positive outcomes have been reported from music interventions with adult offenders (Eastburn, 2003; Digard et al., 2007; Henley et al., 2012). In these studies, participants enhanced their communication and social skills, increased their confidence, were better able to reflect on their situation, and believed that they could change and attain their goals. Overall, their wellbeing was enhanced.

While there can be benefits to participating in music, it can also be stressful. Pitts (2020) studied membership of leisure-time music groups through an online survey of 559 participants in such groups. While there were many benefits to wellbeing through being a member of such groups, there were pressures for some groups as they struggled to maintain their survival in the face of dwindling membership and lack of funding. There can also be a negative impact on wellbeing for those for whom music is a career or potential career. For instance, 126 college students and amateur musicians in a joint Swiss-UK study were assessed in relation to their wellbeing, quality of life and general health (Philippe et al., 2019). Scores were high on general measures of quality of life for both groups and on environment, social relationships, physical health and psychological health. Differences between groups of musicians emerged in terms of overall quality of life and general health, as well as the physical health dimension, where college music students scored lower than the amateur musicians, although the college music students scored higher than the amateurs on social relationships. While music-making can offer some health-protective effects, this may not be the case among those aspiring to become professional musicians. Similarly, MacRitchie and Garrido (2019) studied professional and amateur orchestral musicians using questionnaires and interviews, and found that intellectual stimulation was high for these groups and that there was a balance between perceived challenge, effort and reward of the musical tasks. Emotional engagement increased with age for amateur players but decreased for professionals. Overall, social engagement was high, with players reporting feeling connected as a group whilst making music.

Some research has considered flow experiences in musical participation and their relationship with wellbeing. For instance, Baker and MacDonald (2013) studied flow in non-music-major university students and retirees and their sense of self, achievement, identity, satisfaction and ownership during the creation of personally meaningful songs. There were strong experiences of flow during song-creation when compared with sporting activities, dancing, yoga and performing music. Habe and colleagues (2020) studied 452 elite musicians and top athletes in their early twenties and found that flow was more often experienced in group than individual performance settings, and that life satisfaction was positively related to flow, particularly the challenge-versus-skill balance.

Attendance at Music Festivals

Music festivals offer unique opportunities for engagement with music. The excitement of physical proximity to the performers, social interaction with other attendees and the music itself all contribute to the experience (Oakes, 2003; Paleo and Wijnberg, 2006; Pitts, 2005). Engagement with music in a festival context can contribute to the creation of a sense of community, as it provides opportunities to engage in social activities (Frith, 1996; Gibson and Connell, 2005). It also contributes to the development of identity (Karlsen and Brändström, 2008; Matheson, 2005), although there can be negative outcomes and risks relating to the use of alcohol or drugs, overcrowding, mob behaviour and other public health issues (Earl et al., 2004). Pitts (2005) investigated audience experiences at a chamber music festival, and showed that social and musical enjoyment interacted to generate commitment and a sense of involvement in the event. Similarly, Burland and Pitts (2010) studied the roles that music played in the lives of jazz audiences at the Edinburgh festival. Analysis of a large-scale survey and in-depth interviews revealed a sense of community and atmosphere, within which audience members valued the opportunity to be amongst like-minded jazz enthusiasts.

Similarly, Pitts and Burland (2013) drew on evidence from nearly 800 jazz listeners, surveyed at the Edinburgh Jazz and Blues Festival and in the Spin jazz club, Oxford. Questionnaires, diaries and interviews were used to understand the experiences of listening for a wide range of audience members. The findings illustrated how listening to live jazz had a strongly social element, whereby listeners derived pleasure from attending with others or meeting like-minded enthusiasts in the audience, and welcomed opportunities for conversation and relaxation within venues that helped to facilitate this. Within this social context, live listening was (for some audience members) an intense, sometimes draining experience, while for others it offered a source of relaxation and absorption, through the opportunity to focus on good playing and preferred repertoire. Overall, live listening constituted an individual and social act which varied between listeners, venues and occasions. Packer and Ballantyne (2010) established that a sense of connection between participants and a separation from everyday life distinguished festivals from other musical experiences, providing a sense of disconnection that prompted festival attendees to reflect on their lives and their understanding of themselves. They reported benefits in terms of enhanced interpersonal relationships, a greater sense of belonging, being valued, a deeper understanding of self and emotions, enhanced self-perceptions, confidence, mastery, purpose in life, a greater sense of agency, better strategies for coping with stress, a sense of making a contribution, and being more hopeful. These benefits reflect those reported by those engaged in making music.

Strong experiences of music most commonly occur in live settings (Gabrielsson, 2011; Lamont, 2011). Experiences are enhanced if the performers appear to be enjoying the experience and if they interact with the audience (Brand et al., 2012; Pitts and Burland, 2013; Pitts and Spencer, 2008; Radbourne et al., 2013). Physical proximity between performers and audience can support this (Brand et al., 2012). The quality of the experience is influenced by interactions between audience members and the performers, which transform the experience from being passive to active (Dobson and Sloboda, 2014). Technology has enabled communities of fans to upload set lists and photos to online forums and also use Twitter, which helps non-attending fans to feel involved (Bennett, 2012).

Music and Wellbeing in the Older Generation

Across the world, life expectancy is increasing and there are growing numbers of older people. Many live alone and are vulnerable to experiencing depression. In recent years, there has been an increase in research on the role of music in the lives of the older generation. Overall, music becomes more important for the elderly (Gembris, 2008; Laukka, 2007). Participation in a wide range of musical activities provides a source of enhanced social inclusion, enjoyment, personal development and empowerment supporting group identity, collaborative learning, friendship, social support, a sense of belonging, enhanced wellbeing, and access to new social roles and relationships (Allison, 2008; Coffman, 2002; Coffman and Adamek, 2001; Langston, 2011; Sixsmith and Gibson, 2007; Wood, 2010). It is clear that older people gain cognitive, emotional and social benefits from learning to play a musical instrument in a range of different learning environments (Drummond, 2012; Veblen, 2012), even over short periods of time (Bugos et al., 2016). Music-making contributes to psychological wellbeing. It can alleviate loneliness and offer support in coping with the challenges of ageing, providing opportunities for musical progression and enjoyment, and thus adding meaning to life (Forssen, 2007; Lehmberg and Fung, 2010; Saarikallio, 2011). It can provide contentment, satisfaction and feelings of peace, and reduce anxiety and depression. It can reduce the decline in wellbeing so often experienced by the older generation, and foster positive moods and emotions (Lally, 2009; Livesey et al., 2012; Sandgren, 2009).

There are a number of large-scale studies examining the relationship between wellbeing and musical activity in older people. For instance, Jenkins (2011) derived data from the English Longitudinal Study of Ageing—a large-scale, nationally representative survey of those aged 50 and above which contains several wellbeing measures and information on three types of learning: formal courses, music/arts/evening classes and gym/exercise classes. The key finding from this research was that music, arts and evening classes were significantly associated with positive changes in wellbeing. There was no similar relationship between formal courses, gym or exercise classes, and wellbeing. More recently, also using the English Longitudinal Study of Ageing, Fancourt and Steptoe (2018) analysed data from 2,548 adults aged over 55 during a ten-year period, to explore whether membership of different kinds of community groups was associated with wellbeing. Membership of education, arts or music classes was longitudinally associated with lower negative affect and more life satisfaction, while slightly different positive outcomes were associated with membership of religious groups. In a ten-day diary study of 1,042 people aged 13 to 82 years old with music as a hobby, Koehler and Neubauer (2020) showed that need satisfaction and positive affect were higher when participants reported music-making. The satisfaction of basic psychological needs seemed to act as a mediating mechanism between musical activities and wellbeing.

Since the 1980s, a considerable body of research has demonstrated the relationship between actively making music and subjective wellbeing (Lehmberg and Fung, 2010). Adults who participate in active music-making report that it provides valued and worthwhile experiences, while for those in older age it can provide structure and purpose to daily living, enhancing motivation and providing meaning in life (Hallam et al., 2012). It can reduce depression, promote positive emotions and emotional regulation, and provide spiritual experiences (Creech et al., 2014; Dingle et al., 2012). Those working with the older generation in leading music-making have recognised that the older generation are not a homogenous group. Even those who consider themselves to be novice musicians bring to musical activities a mixture of skills, preferences and cultural backgrounds. While they may have reduced capacity in some areas, as musical groups they have a rich knowledge base, and considerable experience and motivation (Dabback and Smith, 2012). Older people tend to be independent learners who want to control their learning, although the extent to which this applies to musical activities varies across groups and the nature of the activities. Group dynamics are important, as they are frequently key to sustaining motivation (Veblen, 2012). Internationally, music educators are increasingly recognising that the social aspects of music-making are important to older adults (Krause and Davidson, 2018) and that there needs to be a change from pedagogy based on expertise training to pedagogy promoting cultural connectedness and sharing.

Exploring a range of issues, Hays and Minichiello (2005) carried out interviews with 52 older Australians to determine the role of music in their lives. Participants were involved with music for much of the time: for instance, listening to music, actively making music, or volunteering (including working in community radio as broadcasters and programmers, in music administration and concert development, or teaching). Listening, performing or composing enabled expression of their individuality and ways of defining themselves. Listening to specific pieces of music led to the recall of events and experiences in their life, along with the emotions associated with them. Music provided a way for them to maintain positive self-esteem, to feel competent and independent, avoid feelings of isolation or loneliness, be distracted from health problems, feel uplifted physically and psychologically, and feel rejuvenated. They used music as an accompaniment to their daily activities, and reported that music helped them feel more competent and motivated. When they were faced with challenging tasks, music provided support and distraction. It reduced anxiety and stress levels, and increased the threshold for pain endurance. Some indicated that music provided them with inner happiness, contentment and peace. It was therapeutic and made them feel more positive about life, as well as more cheerful, hopeful, contented, relaxed and peaceful. Some were moved to tears by music, and listened for the sheer joy and beauty of the experience. Music was able to calm, excite, thrill and entertain them in ways that other things were not able to. For some it became addictive, a way of escaping reality and stimulating their imagination, while the sense of beauty was spiritual in its effect. While this was associated with specific religious beliefs for some, for others it was a personal feeling of being at one with the world. Music provided many benefits which all contributed to their wellbeing. Similarly, participants in the *Music for Life* project reported engaging in a wide range of musical activities. Questionnaire responses revealed that 96 percent reported listening to recorded music, 81 percent to live music, 80 percent to playing music in the background when they were completing other tasks, 79 percent singing at home, and 49 percent practising at home. They played a wide range of instruments and had a wide range of musical preferences (Creech et al., 2014; Hallam et al., 2012). Laukka (2007) sent a questionnaire to a random sample of 500 community-living older adults aged 65 to 75 years of age in Sweden, to assess their use of music in everyday life including frequency of listening, situations where music was encountered, emotional responses to music and their motives for listening. Different facets of psychological wellbeing were also assessed. The findings showed that listening to music was a common leisure activity and a frequent source of positive emotions. Participants reported using a variety of listening strategies related to emotional functions including pleasure, mood-regulation, and relaxation as well as issues of identity, belonging and agency. Although health status and personality were the most important predictors of wellbeing, some listening strategies were significantly associated with psychological wellbeing.

One strand of research has considered the role of choral singing in promoting wellbeing in older people. For instance, Lamont and colleagues (2018) reported a case study of an older people's choir over a four-year period, using interviews, focus groups, observations and participatory discussion. Choir members highlighted the individual and interpersonal benefits of being part of the choir. They particularly emphasised the importance of developing social relationships within a supportive community, although musical achievement was also central to the ongoing development of the choir. Five main themes emerged from the data: personal investment and reward, an inclusive community, an always evolving yet fundamentally unchanged environment, a desire to connect, and leadership and organisation. Considering these with reference to Seligman's (2010; 2011) PERMA framework from positive psychology, it was apparent that social relationships, meaning and accomplishment were particularly important reasons for older people finding singing in a community choir beneficial for wellbeing.

In Tasmania, Langston and Barrett (2008) explored how social capital was manifested in a community choir. Interviews with 27 choir members revealed that the choir provided shared norms and values, trust, civic and community involvement, networks, knowledge resources, and contact with families and friends. Fellowship was identified as a key component in fostering group cohesion and social capital development. Similarly, in England, Coulton and colleagues (2015) evaluated the effectiveness of community-group-singing for a population of 258 older people aged 60 years old or over who either participated in singing or other activities. After three months, significant differences were observed in relation to the mental health components of quality of life, anxiety and depression. After six months, significant differences were observed in mental health in favour of the group-singing. Similarly, Fung and Lehmberg (2016) found that there was a positive impact on quality of life for people in a retirement community who sang together. Joining a group with singing activities as a new musical hobby in later life can provide mental and physical stimulation, positive benefits to mood and increased social interactions. Davidson and colleagues (2014) developed and evaluated an eight-week singing programme with 26 participants aged 70 years or older. There was little impact on health and wellbeing, although the quality of the programme facilitators was an important factor in how the programme was experienced. Pearce and colleagues (2015) followed newly-formed singing and non-singing (crafts or creative writing) adult education classes over seven months. Participants rated their closeness to their group and their affect, and were given a proxy measure of endorphin release, before and after classes at three timepoints: one, three and seven months. The findings showed that, although singers and non-singers felt equally connected by timepoint three, singers experienced much faster bonding in the form of a significantly greater increase in closeness at timepoint one. It seems that singing can have an icebreaker effect in promoting fast social cohesion between unfamiliar individuals. In a single case study, Southcott (2009) focused on a small choir, the Happy Wanderers, formed by a group of older people to perform to residents in care facilities and to sufferers of dementia. Participation in the group enhanced the lives of the members and those of their audiences. Costa and Ockelford (2019) specifically considered the impact of music on audiences. They evaluated a programme of regular concerts and teas for older people. Interview findings showed that the concerts were effective in evoking positive emotions including happiness, relaxation, inspiration, awe and gratitude, whilst negative emotions (such as anxiety and worry) were lessened. These responses were enhanced by the interaction between performers and audience, the high standard of performance and an appropriate repertoire. The opportunity for social contact and interaction relieved loneliness and contributed to participants' enjoyment.

In a series of studies in the UK, Creech and colleagues (2013; 2014), Hallam and colleagues (2014; Hallam and Creech, 2016) and Varvarigou and colleagues (2012; 2013) researched the relationship between active music-making and subjective wellbeing in older people's lives. The research comprised three UK case-study sites, each offering a wide variety of musical activities including singing, ensemble participation and song composition. At each site, a sample of people aged over 50, a total of 398, some of whom had recently begun musical activities and others who were more experienced, were recruited to complete questionnaires that assessed quality of life. A control group of 100 completed the same measures. In-depth interviews were carried out with a representative sample, followed by observations of musical activities, focus groups and interviews with the music facilitators. Comparisons were made between older people participating in a wide range of musical and other activities in relation to their questionnaire responses and psychological needs, as well as those participating in the musical activities who were in the third and fourth age groups. The factors that emerged from the analysis of the data were: purpose (having a positive outlook on life), autonomy and control, social affirmation, positive social relationships, competence and a sense of recognised accomplishment. Those participating in the music activities responded more positively than those engaged in other activities. There was also no deterioration in responses in the music groups between those in the third and fourth age groups, as might have been expected with the exception of purpose in life. The interviews revealed cognitive benefits including challenge, the acquisition of new skills, a sense of achievement, and improvements in concentration and memory. Health benefits included increased vitality, improved mental health and mobility, and feelings of rejuvenation, while emotional benefits included protection against stress and depression, support following bereavement, a sense of purpose, positive feelings, confidence and opportunities for creativity.

There is considerable evidence that older adults experience a myriad of psychosocial benefits from learning to play a musical instrument, even when starting to play as novices and when receiving training over relatively short-term periods (Jutras, 2006; Roulston et al., 2015). Older adults frequently cite the ensemble nature of musical activities as a motivating factor to continuing engagement in learning to play an instrument (Roulston et al., 2015). The social aspects of ensembles offer wellbeing benefits through the development of new relationships and decreasing isolation. Singing and playing seem to be important to the elderly as they can enhance emotional self-regulation, emotional expression and relaxation. They help to reduce loneliness and provide experiences of togetherness, company and belonging, help to strengthen self-concept and self-understanding, and provide enjoyment, beauty, challenge and meaningful content to life. Focusing on the learning of keyboard, guitar, recorder or djembe drums—taught individually or in small groups—or creative musical activities over a ten-week period with 98 individuals over the age of 50 with no or very little prior musical experience, Perkins and Williamon (2014) concluded that engaging in such activities offered significant wellbeing benefits, particularly enhancing behaviours which promoted good health. Interviews with a subgroup of 21 participants revealed that engaging with the musical activities enhanced wellbeing through subjective experiences of pleasure, enhanced social interactions, musically nuanced engagement in day-to-day life, fulfilment of musical ambition, the ability to make music, and self-satisfaction through making musical progress.

Learning to play a musical instrument may also be effective for improving fine motor skills. Sensorimotor function generally declines with age, and performance of the upper limbs in visuomotor tasks is also subject to this decrease. The tasks required in musical instrument training—employing sensory, motor and multimodal brain regions—have been shown to stimulate brain plasticity (see Chapter 3; Altenmuller and Schlaug, 2015; Rogenmoser et al., 2018). Piano-playing, in particular, trains both coupled movements across the fingers and individuated finger movement (Furuya and Altenmuller, 2013) but it is unclear if this type of training is useful for maintenance or improvement in the context of ageing. Preservation of domain-general fine motor skills may also benefit healthy older adults, supporting the maintenance of the skills required for numerous daily tasks involved in independent living.

In a series of studies, Bugos and colleagues (2007; 2016; Bugos and Kochar, 2017) demonstrated that healthy older adults experienced significant improvements in cognitive measures, particularly trail-making tasks and digit-span tests, as a result of piano training programmes. They also showed that the intense piano training of 17 healthy community-dwelling adults aged 60 to 85 years old enhanced musical self-efficacy, although not general self-efficacy or cortisol levels.

Bugos and Cooper (2019) examined the effects of music interventions on bimanual coordination and cognitive performance in healthy older adults aged 60 to 80 years old. One hundred and thirty-five participants completed motor measures and a battery of standardised cognitive measures, before and after a 16-week music training programme with a three-hour practice requirement. Participants were allocated to either piano, fine motor training or percussion instruction, gross motor training, or music listening. There were significant enhancements in bimanual synchronisation and visual scanning working memory abilities for fine- and gross-motor training groups, as compared to listening to music. Piano training significantly improved motor synchronisation skills as compared to percussion instruction or music-listening. Reflecting on the existing research, Bugos (2014) developed a model suggesting how community music programmes and musical training could be integrated to lead to successful ageing. Similarly, Seinfeld and colleagues (2013) showed significant improvement in cognitive measures for a group of older adults involved in piano training programmes as compared to other leisure activities (for instance, exercise or painting). Thirteen participants received piano lessons and undertook daily training for four months, compared to 16 age-matched participants who acted as a control group and participated in other types of leisure activities (physical exercise, computer lessons or painting lessons). There was a significant improvement in the piano training group in relation to executive functions, inhibitory control and divided attention. There was also a trend indicating an enhancement in visual scanning and motor ability. Piano lessons also decreased depression, induced positive mood states, and improved the psychological and physical quality of life. Overall, playing the piano and learning to read music can be a useful intervention in older adults to promote cognitive reserve and improve subjective wellbeing. In an ongoing study, James and colleagues (2020) explored the outcomes of piano instruction or musical listening awareness on two sites in Hannover and Geneva with 155 retired healthy adults aged 64 to 78 years old. Participants receive weekly training for one hour over a 12-month period. The outcomes being assessed relate to cognitive and perceptual motor aptitudes, as well as structural neuroimaging and blood-sampling. MacRitchie and colleagues (2020) examined the effects of a ten-week piano training programme on healthy older adult novices' cognitive and motor skills, in comparison to an inactive waiting-list control group. Fifteen participants completed piano training, led by a music facilitator in small groups. Quantitative data from a battery of cognitive and motor tests was collected before and after training, with further post-test data from the control group. Qualitative data included weekly facilitator observations, participant practice diaries, and an individual, semi-structured, post-experiment interview. The findings demonstrated evidence of a strong positive impact of training on a trail-making test, indicating improved visuomotor skills. Moderate evidence for the negative impact of training on a different section of the trail-making test was also found, suggesting no benefit of cognitive switching. Qualitative results revealed that the group learning environment motivated participants to play in musical ensembles and to socialise. Motivation was optimal when all participants were happy with the chosen repertoire. Participants reported that they were motivated by learning to play familiar music and when the facilitator observed that groups had formed cohesive bonds.

As we saw in Chapter 2, brain plasticity is possible in adulthood and in the elderly, following relatively short-term musical training (Herdener et al., 2010; Lappe et al., 2008; 2011). Training programmes requiring intensive multisensory, cognitive and motor activities (for instance, piano lessons) can improve working memory, perceptual and motor skills, and delay age-related decline in speech perception (Parbery-Clark et al., 2011; 2012), non-verbal memory, executive processes (Hanna-Pladdy and MacKay, 2011) and dementia (Verghese et al., 2003). Supporting this, comparisons of 42 professional, 45 amateur and 38 non-musicians by Rogenmoser and colleagues (2018), using brain imaging to calculate a brain age for each participant, found that being a musician had a positive impact on brain-age scores. Musicians in general exhibited lower brain-age scores than non-musicians, suggesting a general age-decelerating effect of music-making on the brain. Further, there was a stronger age-decelerating effect in the amateur musicians, perhaps because the multisensory, motor and socioaffective experiences of musical activity enriched their lives in addition to other activities. For the professional musicians, brain plasticity may be maladaptive. The extensively rehearsed and highly specialised repetitive sensorimotor activities and stressful public performances may result in a less enriched environment and lead to negative health effects.

There has been a focus in some research on creative activities, usually song composition. For instance, Waddington-Jones and colleagues (2019) analysed video-recall interviews and questionnaires, to evaluate the impact of participation in collaborative composition workshops on the subjective and psychological wellbeing of older adults. The analysis revealed that all of the dimensions of the PERMA framework for subjective and psychological wellbeing were met. For older adults, collaborative composition encouraged social interaction with others with shared interests, increased positive affect, enhanced self-esteem and allowed older people to express themselves. Similarly, Baker and Ballantyne (2013) investigated whether group song-writing and performing affected perceptions of quality of life and feelings of connectedness in a community of retirees. Thematic analysis of data transcripts from focus groups and written questionnaires from participants and the students involved in the project indicated that the programme stimulated enjoyment, positively affected emotions and improved wellbeing. Participants experienced enhanced connection with one another, as well as with others in the broader community, and a sense of accomplishment, meaning and engagement in creating and performing their own songs. In a similar project, where professional musicians worked with a small group of older people to compose individual pieces of music, Habron and colleagues (2013) demonstrated enhanced wellbeing through facilitated control over musical materials, opportunities for creativity and the development of identity, the validation of life experiences, and social engagement with other participants and the professional musicians. The results emphasised the importance of occupation as essential to health and wellbeing in the later stages of life. Creech and colleagues (2020) focused on the role of creativity in promoting wellbeing. In a review of 23 articles, they concluded that creativity in participatory music-making was underpinned by social engagement, collaboration and inclusivity. Opportunities for creative expression offered a range of benefits relating to quality of life, including positive emotions, engagement, relationships, a sense of meaning and accomplishment.

An innovative programme in rural Ontario was designed to address social isolation among older people through matching participants with trained volunteers. Both then worked together over ten sessions in their home setting to create expressive art, which may have involved music. Evaluating the programme using interviews, MacLeod and colleagues (2016) found enhanced wellbeing in the older adults and the volunteers, particularly in terms of relationships, personal development and creating meaning. The impact of the intervention extended beyond the programme's duration. In an exclusively musical programme which used similar methods, Dassa (2018) analysed 43 interviewers' essays, documenting meetings between an interviewer and an elderly person written over four years. The mutual musicking elicited remote memories from childhood, adolescence and adulthood, and emotionally impacted both parties. Mutual musicking revealed new and unfamiliar facets of the participants. The findings suggested that creating a musical autobiography interview through a process of music and reminiscence strengthened the older person's sense of self-identity, illuminated hidden aspects and also changed attitudes toward the elderly. Also studying the concept of reminiscence, Kruse (2021) explored the ways that older adults reminisced about music participation over the course of their lives. Six community musicians participated in the interviews and worked with a life-review tool. Two hundred and twenty-five reminiscences reflected healthy ageing and satisfaction, including self-acceptance, valuable life lessons and the reconciliation of life events, although some participants were troubled by strained parental relationships and bittersweet associations with music.

Some research has focused more broadly on music-related activities: for instance, dancing. Focusing on depression in the elderly, Rummy and colleagues (2020) carried out a systematic review of 13 articles. Some studies used individual therapy, while others combined music therapy with other activities such as singing, dancing and lyric-writing. The time spent varied from two weeks to six months, with one or two sessions weekly, each with a duration of 30 to 60 minutes. They concluded that music therapy was effective in reducing depression. Also studying the impact of music indirectly through dance, Murrock and Graor (2016) found that the 16 disadvantaged adult participants who completed a 12-week dance intervention developed a sense of belonging and group identity, which may have maintained group involvement and contributed to reducing depression and social isolation.

There has been some interest in the way that music technology might support wellbeing in the older generation. For instance, Engelbrecht and Shoemark (2015) carried out a mixed-method feasibility study investigating the acceptability and efficacy of using iPads compared to traditional musical instruments with older adults living privately in the community. Five women aged 71 to 96 years of age were recruited from a community-based day-respite centre in Brisbane, Australia. Participants were randomly assigned to either a traditional musical instrument or an iPad group, and engaged in five sessions of activity-based music therapy. Participants completed journal entries following each session to detail their experiences, and were assessed for levels of perceived social isolation and global self-esteem before and after the intervention. The use of iPads was acceptable to the group. Learning was central to all sessions, but there were differences in mood outcomes and emotional communications. Playing on an iPad resulted in greater creativity and freedom. There were no significant differences in social isolation or self-esteem between groups or over time. Both iPad and traditional instrument interventions developed social cohesion group identity and positive self-concept. Overall, the findings showed that technology can be an acceptable and potentially successful tool for use in music therapy with older people living in the community. Creech (2019) supported these findings in a literature review of the intersection between music, technology and ageing. Of the 144 papers screened, 18 were retained. Ten focused on using technology to support musicking in the form of listening, reflecting and interpreting, while five explored the utility of technology in promoting singing or playing instruments, and a further three were focused on music and movement. Overall, the literature suggested that older people, even those with complex needs, were capable of and interested in using music technologies to access and create personally meaningful music. Similarly, Poscia and colleagues (2018) reviewed the effectiveness of existing interventions for alleviating loneliness and social isolation among older people. The findings from 15 quantitative and five qualitative studies suggested that new technologies and community-engaged arts might be able to tackle social isolation and loneliness among older individuals.

While the wellbeing of older people is important, it is also important to consider the wellbeing of those caring for them. Considering the role of carers and their patients, Ascenso and colleagues (2018) studied 39 participants in a series of community drumming programmes. The outcomes were assessed through semi-structured interviews and focus groups at the end of each programme. Emotional, psychological and social dimensions of wellbeing emerged for both patients and carers.

Music, Wellbeing and the COVID-19 Pandemic

There have been a number of research projects which have considered the role of music in offering support to people during the COVID-19 pandemic. One strand of research has explored the use of music in families during lockdowns. For instance, in the USA, Cho and Ilari (2021) studied how parents with young children used recorded music in their everyday lives during the pandemic. Nineteen mothers of children aged 18 months to five years strategically managed the sonic home environment over a period of one week, based on resources provided by the researchers in response to their children's mood and state. A total of 197 episodes were collected of children's engagement with recorded music. The findings showed that, while mothers utilised music to fulfil various emotional needs, they tended to use it most to maintain or reinforce their child's positive mood, rather than to improve a negative mood. Mothers reported various ways that their young children engaged with music and stated that their strategic approaches to using recorded music seemed to help their children feel less distressed and more happy, thus reducing the stresses of parenting. Similarly, in the USA and Canada, Steinberg and colleagues (2021) utilised an online questionnaire to assess the use of music in the homes of young children and their parents, and its relationship with parents' attachment to their child. Musical activity was high for both parents and children. Parents reported using music for emotional regulation and to socially connect with their children. The extent of parent-child musical engagement was associated with attachment. Overall, music may be an effective tool for building and maintaining parent-child relationships during a period of uncertainty and change. In Brazil, Ribeiro and colleagues (2021) explored how social distancing during the COVID-19 pandemic altered families' music-related behaviours with children aged three to six years old, as well as caregivers' levels of wellbeing and stress. One hundred and eighty-eight caregivers participated in an online survey which showed significant changes in families' dynamics: parents, especially mothers, spent more time in childcare, with a substantial decrease in caregivers' wellbeing. There were changes in caregivers' and children's musical activities at home during social distancing, including an increase in child-only and shared caregiver-child musical activities. Sociodemographic factors and the child's disability status significantly influenced musical engagement.

Through a transhistorical comparison of the musical activities of the Milanese during an outbreak of plague in 1576 and the musical activities observed during the COVID lockdowns in 2020 (including balcony-singing and playlist-making), Chiu (2020) discussed how music fulfils its functions of mood regulation and social cohesion in times of pandemic and social isolation. There is much evidence from the internet and news outlets of the important role that music, communicated through social media, has played in supporting people during the COVID-19 pandemic. A number of research projects have also been undertaken, typically through the use of online questionnaires. For instance, Granot and colleagues (2021) administered an online questionnaire in 11 countries: Argentina, Brazil, China, Colombia, Italy, Mexico, the Netherlands, Norway, Spain, the UK and the USA. They received 5,619 responses. Participants rated the relevance of wellbeing goals during the pandemic, and the effectiveness of different activities in obtaining these goals: enjoyment, venting negative emotions and self-connection. For diversion, music was as effective as entertainment, while it was second best in creating a sense of togetherness, after socialisation. This was evident across different countries and genders, with minor effects of age on specific goals, and a clear effect of the importance of music in people's lives. Cultural effects were generally small and occurred mainly in the use of music to obtain a sense of togetherness. Culture moderated the use of negatively-valenced and nostalgic music for those with higher levels of distress.

Carlson and colleagues (2021) also used an online survey with a Likert scale and free-text responses, to establish how participants were engaging with music during the first wave of the pandemic. The findings showed that the extent of music-listening behaviours were either unaffected or increased. This was especially true of listening to self-selected music and watching live-streamed concerts. There was a relationship between participants' use of music for mood regulation, their musical engagement, and their levels of anxiety and worry. A small number of participants described having negative emotional responses to music, the majority of whom also reported severe levels of anxiety. In Spain, also using an online survey disseminated to the general population and groups of musicians, Martinez-Castilla and colleagues (2021) analysed the impact of personal and contextual factors on the perceived efficacy of musical behaviours in fulfilling wellbeing-related goals during lockdown. Responses were received from 507 people. Personal factors had an impact on music's efficacy, but not contextual variables related to COVID-19 itself. The youngest respondents and those with musical training reported the highest efficacy of music for enhancing wellbeing, but overall, music's importance was the main predictor of its perceived efficacy. People who were emotionally more vulnerable during lockdown, due to either a strong impact on their daily lives or lower resilience, perceived greater benefits from engagement with music. In Brazil, also using an online questionnaire, Ribeiro and colleagues (2021) explored how music was used during lockdowns and whether it helped individuals, especially those with severe depression. Nearly 500 people aged 18 and over responded. Four types of music-listening functions were identified: negative mood management, cognitive functioning, positive mood management and physical involvement. Those with severe depression were more likely to use music for each of these functions—in particular, to manage negative moods. Most respondents used music-listening to cope with and regulate their moods. Again, using an online questionnaire, Gibbs and Egermann (2021) explored the nature of music-induced nostalgia. Five hundred and seventy participants listened to a self-selected piece of music designed to induce nostalgia, which they had listened to three months prior to lockdown. They reported the emotions and the memories induced. There were significant differences in the affective and narrative content of nostalgic music-listening in relation to which emotional regulation strategy was used. Employing nostalgic music-listening as a form of approaching difficult emotions was shown to have a positive impact on wellbeing.

In Italy, Corvo and De Caro (2020) studied spontaneous singing during the COVID-19 pandemic. Overall the Italians spent a great deal of time in lockdown. From a mental wellbeing point of view, it was difficult to adapt to internment and movement controls. The lack of freedom and opportunities to meet with friends and relatives had a serious impact on wellbeing. Almost immediately after the first lockdown began, the silence in Italian cities was broken by singing. It was carried out in various ways. In some places, quite recent songs with a strong emotional impact were sung, while in others, old songs strongly connected to Italian culture (such as the national anthem) were chosen. The balconies and windows in the streets of the cities were animated with people of all ages enjoying these moments of social cohesion and emotional exchange. Videos were made instinctively and shared through social media by individuals, showing moments of strong union, in which the sense of loneliness was (to some extent) forgotten. These singing networks were completely spontaneous and showed singing used as a coping strategy and to improve the sense of cohesion. The songs chosen reflected individuals' identities and helped avoid feelings of loneliness and enhance mood. After two or three weeks, the number of people singing reduced, but revived later. Music clearly provided a means of demonstrating social solidarity which helped communities in a time of crisis. Similarly, Calvo and Bejarano (2020) reported on music in Spain during the crisis, where during the first weekend of confinement, a growing number of individuals started to play music after the collective applause to express gratitude towards health workers and doctors. This involved professional musicians but also many amateurs. Performances were posted on social media. Singalongs, balcony to balcony, classical music duos or serenading with traditional instruments expressed a social message that transcended the quality of the music performed. They set up a database of 150 individuals who had played or sung on their balconies at least twice. They identified performers in places with strong regional identities, such as Galicia or the Basque Country, and also with strong traditions of band music, such as Valencia. They also undertook 51 telephone interviews. They asked about confinement, why people played, the selection of repertoire and how neighbours reacted. In many cases, performers reacted to informal or formal petitions to sing or play by close relatives, next-door neighbours, or even by brass bands and orchestras. A professional association of music teachers set up an online challenge which invited music teachers to simultaneously play a different score each day. Music teachers spoke about these challenges as a very persuasive reason to keep on playing, perhaps through fear of breaking relationships of trust and respect with peers in their profession. Despite differences in professional background, respondents quoted personal reasons for playing from balconies. They talked about the need to provide a break to the tedious life of confinement. Musicking provided children with activities and gave students a reason to continue practising. Local media reported that a music teacher organised balcony-to-balcony study sessions of txistu—a traditional instrument popular in the Basque Country that resembles a flute—with students who happened to live nearby. The dominant theme emerging from the data was the need to create bonds with neighbours and also to help others. Professional musicians saw this as their duty as artists. In other cases, performers simply wanted to do something for other people. A further theme was the presentation of music as a stress reliever, a way to cope with anxiety, loneliness and the pain associated with not being able to meet loved ones. Many musicians started playing on March 19th, Father's Day in Spain, as a way to express love and affection. Musicking helped with the celebration of birthdays in an interesting process where private rituals became a vehicle to connect with neighbours. Helping others was the most common expression. Performers wanted to cheer up people hospitalised in nearby mental health centres, to remind senior neighbours that there was someone out there and to cheer children up. The realisation that music had the potential to do good transformed what was meant as a one-off act into a daily routine.

Also in Spain, Cabedo-Mas and colleagues (2021) carried out a survey on the use of music during the pandemic. A total of 1868 Spanish citizens responded. The findings indicated that, during lockdown, respondents perceived an increase in the time they devoted to musical activities such as listening, singing, dancing or playing an instrument. They also reported using music to cope with the lockdown, finding that it helped them to relax, escape, raise their mood or keep them company. The findings suggested an improvement in their perception of the value of music in personal and social wellbeing during the lockdown, although there were significant differences in the use and perceptions of music according to respondents' personal situations. Age and feelings of vulnerability may have led to more conservative uses of musical practice and to more moderate perceptions of the positive values of music.

Cabedo-Mas and colleagues also pointed out the importance of playlists during isolation because of their social functions. As more and more countries entered lockdown, Spotify reported on March 30th an increase in collaborative playlist-making, which allowed people to connect over shared music and have virtual jam sessions together. In the same media release, Spotify also noted that their users were sharing more content on their social networks than usual, so friends and followers would know what they were doing. One group of songs that saw spikes in streaming figures were those used in balcony performances, the recordings of which circulated widely on social media. According to the March 20th report by Spotify, streams of two of the songs sung by Italian flash mobs Abbracciame and Azzurro had increased over 700 percent. In Spain, streams of the song Resistiré increased by over 400 percent. 'Abbracciame' ('Embrace Me') by Andrea Sannino first released in 2015, has since earned the gold certification by Federazione Industria Musicale Italiana in 2020, with 35,000 copies sold. At that time, it had received over 41 million views on YouTube and seven million streams on Spotify. Undoubtedly, balcony-singing had an immense impact on musical culture during the lockdowns and will remain, for many, one of the musical practices indelibly associated with that period.

During lockdowns, participants in musical activities such as flash mobs or online ensembles, as well as their spectators, frequently reported the alleviation of stress and the feeling of connectedness as a result of their musical engagement. Erica Marino was a participant in one of the earliest balcony flash mobs in Benevento, the video of which went viral in early March (Cozzolino, 2020). When asked about the messages flooding in from all over Italy after the video of the music-making was widely shared on social media, Marino reported that viewers expressed gratitude because they perceived a message of hope and positivity from viewing it, as most social networks only contained devastating news. Balcony-singing has deep roots in Italy. In 1576, when the Milanese plague grew more deadly and public processions came to an end, Borromeo relocated the ritual inside private homes, decreeing that church bells across the city were to be rung seven times a day and, while the bell was rung, litanies or supplications were to be sung or recited at the direction of the bishop. This was to be performed in such a way that one group sang from the windows or the doors of their homes, and then another group sang and responded in turn. COVID-19 seems to have revived this tradition. Mak and colleagues (2021) collected data from 19,384 participants participating in the UK COVID-19 social study at University College London to investigate who engaged with the arts at home during lockdown, how this engagement differed from patterns of arts engagement prior to COVID-19, and whether home-based arts engagement was related to people's ability to cope with their emotions during lockdown. Demographic factors, socioeconomic status, psychosocial wellbeing, health conditions, adverse events, worries and coping styles were considered. Four types of home-based arts engagement were identified: digital arts and writing, musical activities, crafts and reading for pleasure. The strongest predictors of engagement were age, educational attainment, social support, and emotion-focused or supportive coping styles. Younger adults aged 18 to 29, non-key workers, people with greater social support, people who had lost work, those who were worried about catching the virus, and those with an emotion-focused, problem-focused or supportive coping style were more likely to have increased arts engagement during lockdown. Arts activities were used as approach and avoidance strategies to help cope with emotions, as well as to help improve self-development. Overall, the findings suggested that, while some people who engaged in the arts during the pandemic were those who typically engaged under normal circumstances, the pandemic created new incentives and opportunities for others to engage virtually. The research also highlighted the value of the arts as coping tools during stressful situations.

Some research has explored how online music-making has developed as a result of the lack of opportunities for live music-making during the pandemic. For instance, MacDonald and colleagues (2021) studied the Glasgow Improvisers Orchestra's virtual, synchronous improvisation sessions through interviews with 29 participants. Sessions included an international, gender-balanced and cross-generational group of over 70 musicians, all of whom were living under conditions of social distancing. The sessions were recorded using Zoom. The findings showed that the sessions provided opportunities for artistic development, enhanced mood, reduced feelings of isolation, and sustained and developed community. Improvisation facilitated interaction and also allowed the technological affordances of software and hardware to become part of the artistic collaboration. The domestic environment merged with the technology to create what the authors described as 'The Theatre of Home'. Similarly, Daffern and colleagues (2021) studied virtual choirs in the UK through an online survey of 3,948 choir members and facilitators. The findings showed that three virtual choir models were employed: multi-track, whereby individuals recorded a solo which was mixed into a choral soundtrack; live-streamed, where individuals took part in sessions streamed live over social media; and live teleconferencing, for spoken interaction and or singing using teleconferencing software. Responses to open questions revealed several issues, including the practicalities of participation, the continuation of the choir, the responsibility of maintaining the choir, how the choir contributed to a sense of wellbeing, and social aspects reflecting a sense of community and social identity. Musical elements were also reported, particularly how the value of the musical experience changed with the virtual models, the possibility of co-creation through singing, but also a sense of loss of singing together in real time.

Sacred Harp singers from all over the world gather weekly to sing a collection of shape-note songs first published in 1844, *The Sacred Harp* (Morgan-Ellis, 2021). This tradition is highly ritualised, and plays an important role in the lives of participants. As lockdowns were implemented, groups of Sacred Harp singers independently devised a variety of means by which they could sing together online using Zoom, zinging, Jamulus, jamzinging, and Facebook Live stringing. These developments were undertaken rapidly and creatively, indicating the importance participants attached to singing. Twenty-two interviews were conducted with participants and revealed that online singing practices had reshaped the Sacred Harp community. Many singers who previously did not have the opportunity to participate now did so, while others lost access. As geographical barriers disintegrated, singing organisers had to find ways to maintain local identity. The online community of singers in the digital realm was stable but not identical to the community that predated the pandemic. Online singing was meaningful to participants, and provided continuity in their personal and communal practice. It allowed participants to access and celebrate their collective memories of the Sacred Harp community, carry out significant rituals and continue to grow as singers. No single modality replicated the complete Sacred

Harp singing experience, but each allowed individual participants to access many aspects that were most meaningful to them. Also focusing on communal singing, Dowson and colleagues (2021) studied the impact of the pandemic on existing dementia singing groups and choirs. Over 50 examples of online musical activities were identified. Sessions had to be adapted to the limitations of the technology rather than technological difficulties being overcome. Accessibility, digital safety and the wellbeing of participants were important considerations, but overall the pandemic prompted innovative approaches to delivering activities and interventions. People with dementia and their carers adapted rapidly to the changes. Online music met a clear need for social connection and cognitive stimulation. It also offered some advantages which will remain even when COVID-19 restrictions are relaxed.

In a cross-sectional survey of 257 adults who participated in instrumental, singing or dance groups, Draper and Dingle (2021) explored the impact of face-to-face versus virtual music-making during the pandemic. Participants rated the extent of their group identification and the extent to which their psychological need satisfaction was met retrospectively for their music group in face-to-face mode, and then in adapted online mode, along with their mental health. The findings showed that instrumental groups were less commonly adapted to virtual mode than singing and dance groups. Group identification and average psychological need satisfaction scores were significantly lower for groups in virtual mode than in face-to-face mode. However, group identification and psychological need satisfaction remained high, which suggests that virtual music groups may be beneficial when face-to-face music-making is not possible.

As concerts have been recorded rather than live during the pandemic, Belfi and Colleagues (2021) investigated differences in aesthetic judgments of live as opposed to recorded concerts, and whether these responses varied based on congruence between the musical artist and the piece. Thirty-two individuals made continuous ratings of the pleasure that they experienced during a live concert or while viewing an audiovisual recorded version of the same concert given by a university band and a United States army band. Each band played two pieces: a United States patriotic composition and a non-patriotic one. The findings showed that, on average, participants reported more pleasure while listening to pieces that were congruent with the band playing them (patriotic for the army band and non-patriotic for the university band). These findings did not change whether the performance was live or recorded. It seems that virtual concerts are a reasonable way to elicit pleasure from audiences when live performances are not possible. Focusing on the use of collaborative playlists, during the pandemic Harris and Cross (2021) developed an experimental procedure to study whether the perceived presence of a partner during playlist-making could elicit the observable correlates of social processing. Preliminary findings suggested that, for younger individuals, some of the social processes involved in joint music-making were elicited even by an assumption of a virtual co-presence.

One strand of research has focused on the way that undergraduates used music during the pandemic. Hurwitz and Krumhansi (2021) discussed the concept of listening-niche referrals to the contexts in which people listen to music, including the music they are listening to, with whom, when, where and with what media. They investigated undergraduate students' music-listening niches in the initial COVID-19 lockdown period, four weeks immediately after the campus shut down, and then when returning for a hybrid semester. Participants provided a list of their most frequently listened to songs and identified one that seemed most associated with that time period and why it was relevant. Three clusters of themes emerged from the data: emotional responses, memory associations and discovery of new music. Overall, the pandemic led to more frequent listening in general and on Spotify, with no differences between lockdown and the new normal. Listening companions shifted from family members to significant others, and finally to other friends and roommates. Overall, the implementation of strategies to manage COVID-19 increased listening and changed its context.

Vidas and colleagues (2021) surveyed 402 first-year Australian university students, domestic and international, to examine the effectiveness of music-listening during COVID-19. Songs that participants were asked to nominate as helping them to cope with pandemic stress tended to be negative in mood. Listening to music was among the most effective coping strategies, and was as effective as exercise, sleep and changing location. Its effectiveness was related to enhanced wellbeing but not specifically to the level of stress caused by the pandemic. International students experienced higher pandemic stress levels, but similar levels of wellbeing to domestic students. Overall, listening to music remained an effective strategy for maintaining wellbeing. Also in Australia, Krause and colleagues (2021) assessed students' media use throughout the early stages of the COVID-19 pandemic and determined whether media use was related to changes in life satisfaction. One hundred and twenty-seven participants were asked to complete online questionnaires, capturing pre- and during-pandemic experiences. The findings indicated that media use varied substantially throughout the study period, and at the within-person level. Life satisfaction was positively associated with listening to music and negatively with watching TV, videos or movies. The findings highlighted the potential benefits of listening to music during periods of social isolation.

The Impact of the Pandemic on Music Professionals

A further strand of research has focused on the ways that musicians have coped during the pandemic. For instance, Onderdijk and colleagues (2021) collected responses from 234 musicians in Belgium or the Netherlands. The findings showed a decrease of 79 percent of live music-making in social settings during lockdown and an increase of 264 percent for online joint music-making. Respondents depending on music-making as their main source of income explored online methods significantly more than those relying on other income sources. Most respondents were largely or even completely unaccustomed to using specialised platforms for online joint music-making, and mainly used video conferencing platforms such as Zoom and Skype when playing together virtually. These were not often employed for synchronised playing and were generally reported to be unable to deal with latency issues. There was an increase of 93 percent in the use of alternative remote joint music-making methods—for instance, recording parts separately and subsequently circulating these digital recordings.

In the UK, Spiro and colleagues (2021) collected data from 385 performing-arts professionals. The pandemic led to a substantial reduction in work and income, leading 53 percent to report financial hardship. Eighty-five percent reported increased anxiety and 63 percent being lonelier than before the crisis. While 61 percent sought financial support, only 45 percent asked for support for health and wellbeing. Perceived financial hardship was associated with lower wellbeing and higher depression and loneliness scores. There were positive associations between self-rated health and wellbeing and lower depression scores. Responses to open questions identified several overarching themes characterising the effects of lockdown:

- loss of work and income, financial concerns, and uncertainties for the future;
- the constraints of lockdown working, including challenges of working at home, struggles with online work and skill maintenance, and caring responsibilities;
- loss and vulnerability, including reduced social connections, lack of support, feelings of loss and grief, and concern for others;
- detrimental effects on health and wellbeing, including anxiety, low or unstable mood, poorer physical health and lack of motivation; and
- professional and personal opportunities, including coping well or living more healthily, more time and less pressure, new possibilities and activities, enhanced social connections and new skills.

Overall, lockdown had profound negative effects on performing-arts professionals, but also presented some opportunities. Also in the UK, Cohen and Ginsborg (2021) studied the impact of COVID-19 on professional freelance musicians, comparing those in the middle of their performing careers (aged 35 to 45) with older players (aged 53 and over). Semi-structured interviews were carried out over Zoom with 24 freelance, self-employed orchestral musicians. Thematic analysis identified common issues: the loss of a much-loved performing career, missing music-making and colleagues, and anxiety about the future of the music profession—although there were differences in relation to identity as a musician, the extent of anxiety about finance, the extent of emotional distress, attitudes toward practising and engaging in collaborative music-making, and confusion over future career plans. Music students seemed to be less affected by the pandemic than professional musicians and showed no significant differences in satisfaction with life, studying or the impact of the pandemic when compared with students studying sports (Habe and colleagues, 2021).

Focusing on music teachers in Australia, De Bruin (2021) studied how COVID-19 impacted on the way they taught, engaged and interacted with students across online platforms. The findings from interviews showed that the adopted teaching approaches fostered connection, empathy and relationship-building, guiding students in slower and deeper learner-centred approaches, using pedagogical practices that reinforced and promoted interpersonal connectedness in and through musical experience and discovery.

The COVID-19 pandemic has impacted on the way that music therapists across the world have undertaken their work, particularly in relation to the use of technology (Agres et al., 2021). Cole and colleagues (2021) investigated the transition of neurological music therapy services from in-person to telehealth. An online survey was distributed to neurological music therapy affiliates worldwide. Sixty-nine therapists fully participated in the survey. The findings showed that there was no change in the overall number of clinical hours retained over telehealth, and there was an association between more frequent telehealth usage and the perceived likelihood of using telehealth in the future. All types of therapy transferred to telehealth, although there were some specific implementation changes. Overall, therapists spent fewer hours working with telehealth compared to in-person therapy, regardless of the employment setting. Technological challenges were drawbacks, but major benefits included the ability to continue providing therapy when in-person sessions were not possible, increased accessibility for remote clients, and positive outcomes relating to increased caregiver involvement.

Overview

The evidence set out in this and previous chapters shows clearly that music can benefit the hedonic (feeling good) and eudaimonic (functioning well) components of wellbeing throughout the lifespan, although it has particular impact in adolescence and older age. Overall, there are many possible benefits to wellbeing and physical health from engaging with music, either through listening to or actively making music. These benefits occur through the impact of music on arousal levels, moods and emotions, the social aspects of group music-making, its role in personal development, and in some cases, directly through music therapy. For the benefits of listening to be realised, the listener needs to like the music. Music imposed by others, if not to an individuals' taste, can create tension and distress. For those prone to depression, engaging deeply with music which is sad or focuses on negative life experiences, particularly when shared with others, can have negative effects. For the social and personal benefits of making music to be realised, the quality of the interpersonal interactions between participants and those facilitating the musical activities is crucial. The quality of the teaching, the extent to which individuals are successful, and whether overall it is a positive experience contribute to whether there are positive outcomes. If the musical experience is negative in any respect, any possible positive effects will be marginal or non-existent. The way that music has been used in the COVID-19 pandemic illustrates clearly how important it is in people's lives and the extent to which it can support wellbeing in a myriad of ways in stressful situations. Ongoing technological advances continue to make listening to or making music more accessible to a greater number of people, providing more opportunities for promoting wellbeing.

15. Music and Physical and Mental Health

There is increasing evidence suggesting that mind-body interactions play an important role in good physical health. Psychological factors play a causal role in the onset, course and speed of recovery in many illnesses, and non-medical interventions can sometimes be as effective as medical ones (Pelletier, 1992). Emotions impact on health and can play a role in clinical outcomes (Yael et al., 2000). They may also indirectly influence health-related behaviours (Diefenbach et al., 2008). Trudel-Fitzgerald and colleagues (2019) suggest that psychological wellbeing is associated with lower disease and mortality risk, while Diržytė and Perminas (2021) studied 1001 healthy and unhealthy Lithuanian adults, and showed that those who were physically healthy had significantly higher scores on measures of wellbeing. This does not unequivocally demonstrate causality, although overall, there is strong evidence that positive emotions are associated with better health and health behaviours.

The role of stress in ill health has increasingly been acknowledged. From an evolutionary perspective, the capacity to respond to environmental threats is important for survival. In mammals, responses to threats include changes in the delivery of oxygen and glucose to the heart and the large skeletal muscles, providing physiological support for fight or flight. Each of these carries the risk of injury and subsequent infection, so immune system responses may also be included in adaptive responses to help prevent infections from taking hold. While such threats are rare in the modern world, the human physiological system continues to respond in the same way. Threats that do not require physical action (for instance, work pressures) can still have physical consequences, including changes in the immune system. Segerstrom and Miller (2004) reviewed hundreds of studies and demonstrated that psychological challenges could modify immune responses. They found that acute stressors lasting for minutes were associated with changes in immunity. Brief naturalistic stressors (for instance, taking an examination) tended to suppress cellular immunity while preserving humoral immunity, while chronic stressors are associated with the suppression of cellular and humoral immunity. Picard and McEwen (2018) proposed that chronic psychological stress induces metabolic and neuroendocrine mediators that cause structural and functional changes in mitochondria, leading to mitochondrial allostatic load which, in turn, affects the brain, endocrine and immune systems. These play a role in psychosomatic processes, suggesting shared underlying mechanisms. Many health problems occur as a result of long-term stress, including depression, cancer, anger and cardiovascular disease (Davidson et al., 2003, Steptoe et al., 2001). Mroczek and colleagues (2015), in a diary study with 181 men aged 58 to 88 years old, showed that a decrease in positive emotions in response to daily stressors increased the risk of mortality.

The Role of Music in Psychological and Physical Health

For many years, research has focused on trying to understand how and to what extent music can impact physical health (MacDonald et al., 2012). As we saw in Chapter 14, the impact of music on psychological wellbeing and subsequently good health is largely, although not exclusively, through the emotions it evokes (Juslin and Sloboda, 2010). Music stimulates the cortical and subcortical neural networks in the brain which are associated with activity in the autonomic nervous system (Panksepp and Bernatzky, 2002). Responses related to emotion include changes in dopamine, serotonin, cortisol, endorphin and oxytocin levels (van Eck et al., 1996). These can all affect physical health. Evidence from observational and experimental animal studies supports this (Kubzansky, 2009). The physiological effects of music include changes in heart rate, respiration, blood pressure, skin conductivity, skin temperature, muscle tension and various biochemical responses (Kreutz and Lotze, 2008). Finn and Fancourt (2018), in a review, found that listening to music mainly displayed effects through stress responses, irrespective of musical genre, self-selection of music or duration of listening. Also in a review, Chanda and Levitin (2013) showed that music improved health and wellbeing through the engagement of the neurochemical systems for reward, motivation, pleasure, stress and arousal, immunity and social affiliation.

Neuroscientific and clinical studies of music in the recent past have substantially increased our understanding of how music supports therapy. Music is able to influence complex neurobiological processes in the brain and, through this, can play an important role in therapy (Lin et al., 2011). Altenmüller and Schlaug (2015) argue that the power of music to support mental and physical health lies in its potential to support and facilitate neurorehabilitation. They point out that music provides emotional, sensorimotor and cognitive experiences involving listening, watching, feeling, moving, coordinating, remembering and expecting musical elements. It is frequently accompanied by strong emotions which in themselves can lead to physical reactions: for instance, tears in the eyes or shivers down the spine. A large number of cortical and subcortical regions of the brain are involved in all musical activities (Altenmüller and McPherson, 2007; Tramo, 2001). Primary and secondary regions in the cerebral cortex are involved in all sensory perception including music, but music also impacts on multisensory and motor integration in the frontal, parietal and temporo-occipital brain regions. The frontal lobe is involved in controlling attention, planning and motor preparation, in integrating auditory and motor information, and in imitation and empathy. The multisensory integration regions in the parietal lobe and temporo-occipital areas integrate sensory inputs from auditory, visual and somatosensory systems into a combined sensory impression. The multisensory brain activation of these different systems is typical when we engage with music through listening to it or actively making it. The cerebellum is important in motor coordination and tasks which require timing. It is activated during the processing of rhythm or keeping time rhythmically—for instance, in tapping in time with an external stimulus. In addition, the emotional network in the brain (which includes the cingulate gyrus and the older parts of the brain such as the amygdala, hippocampus and midbrain) is crucial to the way that music is perceived emotionally and, subsequently, leading to motivation to engage with music. As we have seen in earlier chapters, engaging in musical activities changes the brain. This has contributed to demonstrating the extent of neural plasticity (Bangert and Altenmuller, 2003; Hyde et al., 2009; Wan and Schlaug, 2010). As a result of this plasticity, music can assist in restoring damaged sensorimotor brain networks, and have an impact on neurohormonal status and cognitive and emotional processes. Overall, a wide range of sensorimotor, coordination and emotional problems can be improved with therapy that includes music. Overall, music has many functions, roles, and psychological and physical applications. Participating in making music can help to overcome issues relating to lung function, language, mobility and fine motor coordination. Music can help to decrease anxiety, enhance the immune system and alleviate depression (Schäfer and colleagues, 2013). It can offer support to those with a range of clinical problems, from Alzheimer's disease to those on the autism spectrum. Yap and colleagues (2017), in a review of 4,198 studies on the impact of drumming and percussion music in promoting personal and interpersonal wellbeing, found benefits for physical, psychological and social health. Perceived health benefits identified by those singing in choirs include stress reduction, therapeutic benefit in relation to long-standing psychological and social problems, and the exercising of the body through the physical exertion involved (especially the lungs) and the disciplining of the skeletal-muscular system through the adoption of good posture (Clift, 2012).

Although the healing powers of music have been acknowledged for centuries, it was only after the 2nd World War that the American Services recognised the power of music as capable of helping those with physical and psychological injuries. This represented a major shift in the relationship between music and medicine, and led to the development of modern music therapy (Rorke, 1996). Since then, music therapists have worked with a wide range of people across the lifespan, and have developed many different strategies to support health and wellbeing. As we have seen, listening to and making music engages multisensory and motor networks in the brain, inducing change and fostering links between them. These functions, alongside the ability of music to tap into human emotion and reward systems, can be used to facilitate and enhance therapeutic approaches which support the rehabilitation and restoration of neurological functions and other neurological disorders (Altenmüller and Schlaug, 2015). Music therapy contributes to the treatment of a range of long-term psychiatric conditions including anxiety, schizophrenia, sleep disorders, depression and dementia (Boss et al., 2015; Wang and Agius, 2018). Kamioka and colleagues (2014) summarised evidence from 21 studies, including those focused on mental and behavioural disorders and diseases of the nervous, respiratory, endocrine, nutritional, metabolic and circulatory systems, as well as pregnancy, childbirth and the puerperium, while Stige and colleagues (2010) focused on how music helped those struggling with illness, disability, social and cultural disadvantage, or injustice. Clinical studies have shown that music therapy can be used to treat depression, autism, schizophrenia and dementia, as well as problems of agitation, anxiety, sleeplessness and substance misuse. It can also delay age-related decline in speech perception (Parbery-Clark et al., 2011), non-verbal memory and executive processes (Hanna-Pladdy and MacKay, 2011). Detailed examples of music therapy research will be presented later in the chapter.

Recently, there have been developments in what has become known as 'music medicine', where music is used to promote good health and support patients, particularly in reducing anxiety and pain. Performing-arts medicine has a similar focus, with musicians going into hospitals to entertain and engage patients of all ages in music-making to promote their recovery and psychological wellbeing following treatment. As we saw in Chapter 14, there has been considerable interest in the way that music can promote wellbeing in everyday life, through listening to or actively making music. The boundaries between these different areas of work have become blurred and continue to change over time. For instance, work with Alzheimer sufferers in care homes was initiated by music therapists, but as its effectiveness was demonstrated and its practice spread, it has tended to be delivered by community musicians. They differ in the way that they apply music in therapy, perhaps including musical composition, discussion of song lyrics or participation in joint singing or musical games. There is no consensus as to which specific approaches are more effective. Listening is the one constant among all applications. This suggests that music itself is therapeutic.

Music has been used in a range of medical contexts (Le Roux et al., 2007; Spintge, 2012). Listening to music can reduce the amount of sedative drugs required in hospital (Conrad et al., 2007) and support recovery after surgery, in particular reducing the need for pain medication (Nelson et al., 2017; Vollert et al., 2003), in some cases by up to 50 percent (Spintge 2012; Spintge and Droh, 1992). This is particularly the case when patients select the music themselves (Mitchell and McDonald, 2006a; 2006b; 2012). Music can support improvement in speech impairment following strokes (Kaser et al., 2017), support the rehabilitation of motor movements in a range of conditions, and improve the quality, range and speed of movement. There are benefits for stroke patients (Särkämö et al., 2008) and those with neurodegenerative disorders, such as Parkinson's disease and dementia (Spaulding et al., 2013; Verghese et al., 2003). Detailed examples of research in medical contexts will be presented later in this chapter.

Music, Stress and the Immune System

Stress is a major worldwide health issue leading to exhaustion, burnout, anxiety, a weak immune system and possibly organ damage. Creative-arts interventions, including those based on musical activities, have been suggested as ways to prevent stress and improve its management. In a review of 37 studies on creative-arts interventions, Martin and colleagues (2018) concluded that they were relatively effective in reducing stress. Kreutz and colleagues (2012) developed a psychoneuroendocrine approach to explore how musical activity was related to psychological and physical health, using cortisol levels as a psychophysiological measure of stress. Listening to particular types of music has been shown to lead to significant reductions in cortisol, including classical choral (Kreutz et al., 2004), meditative (Möckel, 1994) and folk music (Fukui and Yamashita, 2003). However, not all music has this effect. Significant increases in cortisol have been noted in listeners exposed to technomusic, along with increased heart rate, systolic blood pressure and emotional state (Gerra et al., 1998). Increases in cortisol have also been found in those listening to upbeat pop and rock music (Brownley et al., 1995).

Singing and other participatory musical activities can bring about positive changes in cortisol levels. Beck and colleagues (2000) observed decreases of cortisol of 30 percent on average in members of a professional choir during a rehearsal, although there was a 37 percent increase during a performance. In an experimental study, Bittman and colleagues (2005) exposed participants to a one-hour stress-induced protocol, followed by a novel recreational music-making programme which successfully modulated stress. Music also has an effect on cortisol levels in the context of tango dancing. Murcia and colleagues (2009) observed that the presence of music during dance led to decreases in cortisol levels, although there was no impact on the presence or absence of a dance partner. Keeler (2015) explored the neurochemistry and social flow of group singing in four participants from a vocal jazz ensemble, who sang together in two separate performances: one pre-composed, the other improvised. Group singing reduced stress and arousal, and induced social flow in both conditions.

Some research has focused on the impact of music on the immune system. Making and listening to music can have a positive impact on the immune system (Chida et al., 2008; Wilkinson and Marmot, 2003). To assess immunity, samples of secretory immunoglobulin A in saliva are measured. This is used as an indicator of the local immune system in the upper respiratory tract, the first line of defence against bacterial and viral infections. There have been reported increases in secretory immunoglobulin A, suggesting enhanced immune system activity, after singing (Beck et al., 2000; 2006; Kuhn, 2002; Kreutz et al., 2004). No such increases have been found in those listening to choral music (Kuhn, 2002). A study exploring active drumming or singing compared with watching a live performance also found a more pronounced effect on the immune system in those actively participating in making music. In contrast, McCraty and colleagues (1996) found that listening to relaxing music that created a positive emotional state led to increases in secretory immunoglobulin A concentrations, while rock or new-age music had no effect. Similarly, Hirokawa and Ohira (2003) examined the impact of listening to more or less relaxing music on immune functions, neuroendocrine responses and the emotional state of eighteen Japanese college students after they had carried out a stressful task. The findings were inconclusive in relation to the impact on the immune system. In a review of 63 studies on the effects of music on neurotransmitters, hormones, cytokines, lymphocytes, vital signs and immunoglobulins, as well as psychological assessments, Fancourt and colleagues (2014) indicated that there was a pivotal role for stress pathways in linking music and immune responses, although there were a range of methodological difficulties in the existing research.

Active Music-Making and the Promotion of General Good Health

There has been relatively little research focusing on the general physical-health benefits of participation in musical activities. Early reviews of research with adult singers concluded that there could be health and wellbeing benefits of participating in a choir (Clift et al., 2008; Stacey et al., 2002), although subsequent reviews have been more cautious (Clift, 2012). Perceived benefits include:

- physical relaxation and release of physical tension;
- emotional release and reduction of feelings of stress;
- a sense of happiness, positive mood, joy, elation and feeling high;
- a sense of greater personal, emotional and physical wellbeing;
- an increased sense of arousal and energy;
- stimulation of cognitive capacities, attention, concentration, memory and learning;
- an increased sense of self-confidence and self-esteem;
- a sense of therapeutic benefit in relation to long-standing psychological and social problems;
- a sense of exercising systems of the body through the physical exertion involved, especially the lungs;
- a sense of disciplining the skeletomuscular system through the adoption of good posture; and
- being engaged in a valued, meaningful, worthwhile activity that gives a sense of purpose and motivation.

In the UK, Hillman (2002) surveyed 75 participants who had participated in a community singing project since reaching the statutory retirement age. The long-term benefit attributed to participation in music was a lack of deterioration in physical health. Reagon and colleagues (2016) reviewed 18 papers studying the effect of group singing on health-related quality of life. The patients included were suffering from chronic respiratory disease, neurological conditions or mental ill-health. The findings showed some evidence for improved quality of life, while participants reported directly on their enhanced confidence, mood and levels of social support. Also focusing on choral singing, Więch and colleagues (2020) assessed the nutritional status and quality of life of 200 healthy adults aged 19 to 70 years old. Those involved in singing had significantly lower body weight and body mass index in comparison with a control group. They also had significantly lower basal metabolic rate and metabolic age, and reported greater life quality. Drumming has been the focus of some research. For instance, Smith and colleagues (2014) examined the impact of djembe-drumming in a comparison of middle-aged experienced drummers and a younger novice group who each participated in 40-minute sessions, preceded and followed by measurements of blood pressure, blood lactate, stress, anxiety and ongoing measures of heart rate. Drumming decreased stress and anxiety in both age groups, and blood pressure in the older participants. Assessment of lactate and heart rate suggested that drumming can be considered as low- to moderate-intensity exercise.

One strand of research has investigated the impact of creative song-writing. For instance, Baker and MacDonald (2014) studied 13 students and 13 retirees who engaged in song-writing activities. Each participant created a song parody, original lyrics and an original song describing a positive, negative or neutral experience. Positive outcomes included listening to personal creations, exploring self, the relationship with the therapist, the way that being fully immersed altered perception of time, and the experience of balancing ability and effort. The younger participants were more likely to continue to use their songs for further therapeutic benefit.

The role of attendance at cultural events on health and wellbeing has been studied. For instance, in Poland, Węziak-Białowolska and Białowolski (2016) used data from the biennial longitudinal Polish household study which represented the Polish population over the age of 18, and found a positive association between cultural attendance and self-reported health, although no causal link was established. In Norway, Cuypers and colleagues (2011) examined the association between cultural activity and perceived health, anxiety, depression and satisfaction with life in 50,797 adult participants. Data on cultural activities (receptive and creative), perceived health, anxiety, depression and satisfaction with life were collected. The findings showed that participation in receptive and creative cultural activities was significantly associated with good health, life satisfaction, and low anxiety and depression. For men, attending receptive, rather than creative, cultural activities was more strongly associated with all health-related outcomes. Similarly, in the UK, Fancourt and Steptoe (2018) compared data from 2,548 adults aged over 55 years old—drawn from the *English longitudinal study of ag[i]ng* modelling change over a ten-year period—in relation to membership of different community groups, while controlling for potential confounding variables. Membership of two types of community groups was associated with enhanced wellbeing: attending education, arts or music classes, and church or religious group membership.

Music, Health and the Older Generation

There are general health benefits of participating in making music for older people, including lower mortality rates (Johansson et al., 2001). Music-making contributes to perceived good health, quality of life and mental wellbeing (Coffman and Adamek, 1999; 2001; Kahn, 1998; Wise et al., 1992), while playing the piano exercises the heart as much as a brisk walk (Parr, 1985), although studies on the impact of lung function have had mixed outcomes (Clift, 2012). In the USA, Cohen and colleagues (2006; 2007) carried out studies with 166 participants with an average age of 80 who participated in 30 singing workshops and ten performances over a one-year period. The choir group reported a higher overall rating of physical health, fewer visits to the doctor, less medication use, fewer falls, and fewer other health problems in comparison with a control group, who had carried on with their usual activities and did not participate in the choir. There was evidence of higher morale, a reduction in loneliness and increased activity, while the comparison group experienced a significant decline in activities. Cohen and colleagues argued that sense of control, as well as social engagement, were the most likely mechanisms responsible for the positive outcomes. Coulton and colleagues (2015) studied the value of community singing on the mental-health-related quality of life of older people with 258 participants in five centres in the UK. Group singing was compared with usual activities in those aged 60 years or over. Significant differences were observed in mental-health-related quality of life, anxiety and depression in favour of group singing. Similarly,

Zanini and Leao (2006) studied a therapeutic choir for the elderly and found that singing provided a means of self-expression and fulfilment, and instilled self-confidence in the participants' expectations about the future.

Depression in older adults has increased recently, and will continue to rise as the number and proportion of older adults in the population rises worldwide. Dunphy and colleagues (2019) carried out a review of how art, dance movement, drama and music could help to alleviate depression in the elderly, and established common mechanisms of change. These included:

- physical changes, such as muscle strength;
- neurochemical effects, such as endorphin release;
- intrapersonal change, such as enhanced self-concept, sense of agency and mastery;
- improved processing and communication of emotions;
- the provision of opportunities for creative expression and aesthetic pleasure;
- cognitive stimulation, including memory; and
- social benefits, such as increased social skills and connection.

Each of these were considered to contribute to a reduction in depression. Alzheimer's patients can benefit from engagement with music, as it encourages reminiscence and improves moods and behaviour, although it does not have any long-term impact on underlying cognitive deterioration (Creech et al., 2014). Despite this, some activities are preserved and are relatively resistant to decline. One such activity is engagement with music (Sacks, 2007). Baird and Thompson (2019) point out that musical skills can be preserved in some people with Alzheimer's and dementia, including memory for familiar music and the ability to produce music by singing or playing an instrument. They studied a 77-year-old woman with severe Alzheimer's disease and her husband's use of music in her care. Her behaviour and verbal communication were observed when she read a newspaper article or familiar song lyrics, or sang familiar song lyrics, or listened to the original version of the familiar song. Over time, there was a gradual deterioration in her expressive language abilities, whereas her musical skills were comparatively preserved.

Residents in Care Homes

Care homes support people with a range of difficulties who cannot live independently. With the increase in the older population, many care homes cater for those who need support or who may need additional care following a stroke or other serious illness. Many residents in such homes have dementia, a group of symptoms that typically includes problems with memory, thinking, problem-solving, language and perception. Dementia has a number of different causes, including Alzheimer's disease, vascular dementia and dementia with Lewy Body. Anyone with dementia, whatever its underpinnings, can benefit from engaging with music, as it encourages reminiscence and can improve moods and behaviour. Much of the research on the impact of music in relation to dementia has occurred in residential care or nursing homes (Elliott and Gardner, 2018). Active participation in making music has been found to have broadly positive effects. For instance, Biasutti and Mangiacotti (2018) compared outcomes for older people with mild to moderate cognitive impairment, who were either assigned to a group receiving cognitive music training for 12 twice-weekly 70-minute music sessions or acted as a control group who attended a similar number of gymnastic sessions. A neuropsychological test battery, administered at the beginning and end of treatment, showed a significant improvement for the music group in relation to general mental state, verbal fluency and a clock-drawing test, while the control group showed no significant improvements. In a later study, Biasutti and Mangiacotti (2021) studied the effectiveness of musical improvisation on depressed mood and general cognitive function in 45 elderly care residents. The findings revealed a significant improvement in cognition and a reduction in depression and cognition for the music group, while the control group showed no change in relation to depression and a deterioration in cognition. Also focusing on depression, Werner and colleagues (2017) examined the effect of interactive group music therapy, as opposed to recreational group singing, on symptoms in elderly nursing-home residents. A total of 117 participants from two German nursing homes were allocated to 20 interactive group music therapy sessions of 40 minutes each twice a week, or recreational group singing on ten occasions for 90 minutes weekly. Levels of depressive symptoms were assessed at baseline and follow-up in the sixth and twelfth weeks. The level of depressive symptoms improved significantly more in those assigned to music therapy than recreational singing.

In Australia, Brancatisano and colleagues (2020) reported the outcomes of a music, mind and movement programme for 20 people in their eighties with mild to moderate dementia. The programme involved seven 45-minute weekly group sessions, and individual 15-minute booster sessions. Assessments of global cognition, mood, identity and fine motor skills were conducted at the start of the programme, immediately following the intervention and one month after its close. The majority of participants in the programme showed an improvement in overall cognition, attention and verbal fluency, while the majority of those in the control group showed a decline. Hämäläinen and colleagues (2021) focused on the impact of *yoik*, a traditional vocal music of the indigenous Sami people of Fennoscandia, with elderly and dementia residents in a care home. In-depth interviews with close relatives of participants and healthcare professionals revealed that they had observed positive effects when *yoik* was introduced, even in persons unfamiliar with the genre. Improvements in memory, orientation, depression and anxiety in both mild and moderate cases of Alzheimer's disease, and hallucinations, agitation, irritability and language disorders in those with moderate Alzheimer's disease have been found in patients after six weeks of music therapy. The effect on cognitive aspects was notable after only four music therapy sessions (Gallego and García, 2017)

Focusing on agitation and anxiety in older people with dementia, Cooke and colleagues (2010) investigated the impact of participation in a 40-minute group music-making programme involving facilitated engagement with singing songs and listening three times a week for eight weeks. Forty-seven participants with mild to moderate dementia from two care facilities in Australia participated. A sub-analysis of 24 participants who attended less than half of the music sessions found a significant increase in the frequency of verbal aggression over time. Participation in the music programme did not significantly reduce agitation and anxiety, although music and reading group activities gave some participants a voice and increased their level of verbalisation. Also focusing on agitation and anxiety, Sung and colleagues (2012) set up a group music intervention using percussion instruments with familiar music to reduce the anxiety and agitation of 60 institutionalised older adults with dementia. The experimental group received a 30-minute music intervention using percussion instruments with familiar music in a group setting twice weekly for six weeks. In comparison with a normal-care control group, those in the music group had significantly lower levels of anxiety following the intervention, although there was no difference between the groups in the reduction of agitation. Aiming to reduce agitation, Vink and colleagues (2013) undertook a study of 94 residents with dementia who were allocated to either music therapy or recreational activities twice weekly for four months. Data from 77 residents showed a decrease in agitated behaviours from one hour before to four hours after each session. This decrease was greater in the music therapy group but disappeared completely after adjustment for general level of deterioration. There were no other reported benefits.

Castillejos and Godoy-Izquierdo (2021) explored the outcomes of a music intervention which was integrated into the therapeutic activities of institutionalised elderly people. Fifty residents in a care home were studied at baseline, postintervention, and after two weeks. The music intervention had a positive impact on physical health, cognitive functioning, emotional wellbeing, pain and happiness compared with stability in controls, although the benefits decreased progressively after the discontinuation of the music programme. Similarly, Paolantonio and colleagues (2020) examined the effects of group music-making on the health and wellbeing of 22 nursing-home residents aged 72 to 95 years of age in Switzerland. Professional and student musicians delivered ten weekly music sessions in four nursing homes, focusing on singing, rhythm-based activities with percussion instruments and listening to short, live performances. Being involved in musical activities offered engagement and novelty, providing learning opportunities and facilitating interpersonal relationships. Residents particularly appreciated the opportunity to listen to live performances.

McDermott and colleagues (2014) undertook a qualitative study to explore how care-home residents with dementia and their families, day-hospital clients with dementia, care-home staff, and music therapists perceived the role of music therapy. Music was viewed as being accessible for people at all stages of dementia. There were perceived to be close links between music, personal identity and life events, while music was seen as being useful for building relationships. The effects of music were viewed as going beyond the reduction of behavioural and psychological symptoms, in part because individual preferences for music were preserved in spite of dementia. This helped others to value the dementia sufferer as a person and to support and maintain the quality of their life.

In a case study, Giovagnoli and colleagues (2014) described the effects of active music therapy on cognition and behaviour in one individual with chronic vascular encephalopathy who suffered with memory, attention and verbal fluency deficits. A four-month programme of 16 sessions was implemented based on creative and interactive music-making, in addition to pharmacological therapy. At baseline, the patient reported a tendency to feel tense, nervous and angry, and had difficulties with memory and visuospatial performance, frequently accompanied by loss of attention. Following music therapy, there were improvements in attention, visuomotor coordination, verbal and spatial memory, an increase in interpersonal interactions and a reduction in anxiety.

In an acute hospital setting, Cheong et al. (2016) evaluated the impact of a creative music therapy programme on mood and engagement in older patients with delirium and or dementia. Twenty-five patients of approximately 80 years of age were observed before and after music therapy, which included improvisation and playing songs of the patient's choice. There was a significant positive change in patients in relation to constructive and passive engagement, pleasure and general alertness. Also focusing on hospital stays for people with dementia, Daykin and colleagues (2018) examined the effects of ten weeks of music sessions on patients' wellbeing and the environment in an acute elderly care service in a UK hospital. Observational data, semi-structured interviews and focus groups with patients, visitors, musicians and staff showed that patients generally enjoyed the activity and that there was a reduction in the prescription of antipsychotic drugs, enhanced patient and staff experiences, and an improvement in care. Feeding difficulties can be a problem as dementia progresses, resulting in malnutrition which, in turn, can compromise physical and cognitive functioning. Fifteen participants in a care facility, who were not malnourished at the start, participated in 12 music sessions lasting for 25 minutes just before lunch, with songs likely to be known by residents. Unfortunately, there were too many confounding variables for any conclusions to be drawn (McHugh et al., 2012).

Some research has attempted to identify the most effective type of music. For instance, Lem (2015) studied the levels of engagement with music of 12 people with dementia who participated in 20 weekly music therapy sessions, and found that engagement increased midway through the programme when a more intuitive approach was adopted, with more challenging musical experiences and less structure. An evaluation of an intervention based on group singing activities—developed by the Alzheimer's Society for people with dementia and their carers—showed that social inclusiveness and improvements in relationships, memory and mood were particularly important to participants, who enjoyed the sessions and found that they helped in accepting and coping with dementia (Osman and colleagues, 2016). Pavlicevic and colleagues (2015) explored music therapists' strategies for creating musical communities in dementia care settings. Six experienced music therapists identified a ripple effect of music from person-to-person music-making to that which continued beyond session time, within the care home and beyond. Ongoing qualitative research by Skinner and colleagues (2018) is examining the potential for dance to improve social inclusion for people living with dementia in care facilities.

Some programmes have focused on training care-home staff to deliver music sessions. For instance, Tapson and colleagues (2018) evaluated an intervention comprising an 11-session interactive weekly music programme in five care homes in the UK, which included training for staff. The programme focused on singing and the use of voice, and was led by pairs of trained professional musicians for 45 minutes each week. The programme provided positive social experiences, creative engagement, fun and a sense of achievement, and enhanced the working and living environment for care-home residents and staff, playing a crucial role in developing a sense of identity and empowerment for residents, facilitated by musicians and care teams working together. The role of those delivering such programmes cannot be overestimated. Tuckett and colleagues (2015), in evaluating the effectiveness of a group music therapy intervention, concluded that the impact was mediated by the older person's dementia state, its psychosomatic effect on the participants and the nature of the session. The therapy evoked memories and facilitated reminiscence, and acted as a diversion, but the independent effects of the music and the therapist could not be determined.

While most research has focused on active engagement with making music, some has concentrated on the impact of listening to music. For instance, Costa and colleagues (2018a) assessed the effect of listening to preferred music on pain, depression and anxiety in older care-home residents. One hundred and thirteen participants either continued with their usual routine or listened to a daily 30-minute programme of preferred music over a three-week period. Levels of pain, depression and anxiety were assessed and showed decreases, although these were less for pain. Those who regarded music as important listened most, and those whose preferences were accommodated benefited most. In a similar study, Costa and colleagues (2018b) studied the effects of listening to preferred music on 117 participants from nine care homes. In addition to their usual routine, each participant listened to a daily 30-minute programme of their preferred music for three weeks. Findings showed that listening to preferred music resulted in relaxation, positive reminiscence, reduced depression and boredom, and a range of physical reactions including chills, tears or emotional arousal. Some reactions, such as foot-tapping, were beneficial to the most disabled participants. The use of preferred and favourite music was the principal factor in the intervention's effectiveness.

Some interventions have combined active music-making with listening activities. For instance, Särkämö and colleagues (2014) determined the efficacy of a novel music intervention based on coaching the caregivers of patients with dementia to use either singing or music-listening regularly as a part of everyday care. Eighty-nine patient caregiver dyads were randomised to a ten-week singing coaching group, a ten-week music-listening coaching group or a usual-care control group. The coaching sessions consisted mainly of singing or listening to familiar songs, with some vocal exercises and rhythmic movements for the singing group, and reminiscence and discussions for the music-listening group. The intervention also included regular musical exercises at home. The findings showed that, compared with usual care, singing and music listening improved mood, orientation and remote episodic memory, and to a lesser extent attention, executive function and general cognition. Singing also enhanced short-term and working memory, and caregiver wellbeing, whereas music-listening had a positive effect on quality of life. Särkämö and colleagues (2014) concluded that regular musical leisure activities could have long-term cognitive, emotional and social benefits in those with mild to moderate dementia. Although music can be considered as a leisure activity enjoyed for its own sake, there is some evidence which highlights the benefits of prescribed therapy that can be personalised to meet the needs and skill level of each individual (Genoe and Dupuis, 2012). Menne and colleagues (2012) also point out that, when designing interventions for people with dementia, it is important to ensure that they enjoy the activities.

Live music performances have been shown to have a positive effect on human contact, care relationships, positive emotions and negative emotions in people with dementia in nursing homes (van der Vleuten et al., 2012). Shibazaki and Marshall (2017) explored the effects of live music concerts on dementia sufferers, their families, nursing staff and caregivers. Interviews and researcher attendance at concerts in care facilities showed that concerts were beneficial to patients and staff, even when they did not attend the concerts. Those with mild to mid-stage dementia showed increased levels of cooperation, interaction and conversation, while those with more advanced forms exhibited decreased levels of agitation and anti-social behaviour. Staff members reported increased cooperation and opportunities for assessment, while family members noted an increase in levels of wellbeing. The concerts revealed that knowledge of music and its rules (as well as musical preferences) remained when other cognitive skills and abilities had disappeared. De Wit (2020) also explored the impact of live music-making on hospital nurses and nursing-home caregivers working with vulnerable elderly patients. The healthcare professionals collaborated with the musicians to connect with residents, taking time to become engaged with them in musical situations. This enabled new understandings to develop, supporting the delivery of person-centred care.

Music, Dementia and Care in the Home

Most of the research relating to music and dementia has been undertaken in residential, nursing and hospital settings despite estimates that, in the UK, two thirds of those living with dementia continue to live in their own homes (Wittenberg et al., 2019), a practice known as 'ageing in place' (Wiles et al., 2012). Those with Alzheimer's and related dementias who live at home have unique advantages in terms of being in a familiar place with people they are close to, but carers and those cared for are at risk of depression, isolation and decreased contact with peers and the networks that normally help to maintain social, intellectual, physical, sensory and spiritual needs. As memory declines, the person with dementia loses life skills and sense of self, while their caregiver is increasingly burdened physically and emotionally. Services are now developing to support those who are ageing in place (Dawson et al., 2015). For instance, the BUDI Orchestra was created as a music-based initiative for people with dementia and their family carers living in the community. The initiative comprised ten weekly sessions, facilitated by professional musicians and supported by university students. At the end of the programme, participants showcased their achievements at a public performance. There were a range of positive outcomes, including enjoyment for participants, a sense of social inclusion for musicians and participants alike, and (for the dementia sufferers) increased engagement, a sense of achievement, confidence and enhanced mood. Carers reported improved mood, feelings of relaxation and improvements in their relationships with the cared-for. Musicians' preconceptions of musical learning were challenged and they learnt more about themselves through facilitating the sessions. In addition, the performance positively impacted audience members' perceptions of dementia. The findings challenged assumptions of the capacity of people with dementia to learn new skills and play instruments, and highlighted the power of performance to challenge negative perceptions of dementia (BUDI Orchestra, 2015). Similarly, Lee and colleagues (2020) explored how a community-based group singing intervention impacted the wellbeing of people with early-stage dementia and their family carers. Participants engaged in a six-week group singing intervention facilitated by a music therapist in a community arts centre. Semi-structured interviews revealed enhanced social connection, happiness and rejuvenation, reconnection with the self and support for the relationship between carer and cared-for. Overall, community-based music therapy can be effective in supporting carers and those they care for (Rio, 2018).

Prattini (2016) examined music's effects on levels of agitation in people with Alzheimer's disease or other dementias. The research focused on those living at home who were cared for by an informal caregiver. The participants either participated in active music-making or listened to music. Only active participation had an impact on agitation. Smith and colleagues (2021) arranged ten music-making sessions for community-dwelling people living with dementia and their care partners, once a month over a period of seven months. Eighteen participants consented to take part, including seven people living with dementia, five care partners and six former care partners. Baseline semi-structured interviews explored the lived experience of music, and expectations of the upcoming music-making cafés. Self-report questionnaires captured the experiences of each music-making café, while follow-up semi-structured interviews explored the impact of music-making on participants' self-reported wellbeing. The findings demonstrated that participating in a music-making cafe benefited the wellbeing of participants, providing a sense of camaraderie that facilitated connections with others, creating opportunities to level the playing field, drawing on a person's strengths and abilities, and providing meaningful musical experiences. Participating in music-making promoted the wellbeing of community-dwelling people living with dementia and their care partners, offering opportunities for peer support and a reduction in feelings of isolation through a shared love of music, as well as providing meaningful musical experiences in a supportive, enabling environment.

In a home-based programme, participants with major or minor depressive disorder learned how to use music to reduce stress. They either received a weekly home visit by a music therapist, participated in a self-administered programme where they applied the same techniques with moderate therapist intervention, received a weekly telephone call, or were part of a wait-list control group. Participants in the music conditions performed significantly better than controls on standardised tests of depression, distress, self-esteem and mood. These improvements were maintained nine months after the end of the project (Hanser and Thompson, 1994). In a community-based arts programme in Canada, Moody and Phinney (2012) found that participating older adults experienced enhanced capacity to connect to the community and a stronger sense of community through collaboration as a group, as they worked together on the project towards a final demonstration to the larger community.

Reviews of the Relationship between Music Therapy and Dementia

There has been little agreement between reviews of the literature pertaining to the role of music therapy with the older generation and its effectiveness. Some reviews have drawn relatively positive conclusions, although sometimes with caveats. For instance, Abraha and colleagues (2017) provided an overview of 142 non-pharmacological interventions for behavioural and psychological symptoms in dementia, including music therapy, and concluded that overall, music therapy and behavioural management techniques were effective for reducing the behavioural and psychological symptoms of dementia. Zeilig and colleagues (2014) also reviewed a range of interventions and reported that music could generate feelings of peace for patients with dementia. A range of arts projects have been identified as promoting social engagement, but it has been difficult to establish if the effects related to the role of the arts specifically or could have been attained by any form of social engagement, although the emphasis in the arts on creation and play may have supported patients with dementia, as may the emphasis in the arts on emotion. Istvandity (2017) reviewed intervention studies that utilised music and reminiscence activities in elderly adult populations, and found positive effects in four out of five studies, while Zhao and colleagues (2016) (in a meta-analysis of 19 articles) suggested that music therapy plus standard treatment reduced depressive symptoms to some extent.

Dowlen and colleagues (2018), in a review of 18 studies, identified benefits in terms of taking part, being connected, affirming identity and immersion in the moment, while Zhang and colleagues (2017)—in a review of 34 studies with 1575 participants—showed that disease subtype, intervention method, nature of the control or comparison group, participant location, trial design, trial period and outcome measure instruments made little difference to outcomes. Overall, there was positive evidence to support the use of music therapy to treat disruptive behaviour and anxiety, and positive trends supporting the use of music therapy for the treatment of cognitive function, depression and quality of life. Raglio and colleagues (2012), reviewing clinically controlled trials focusing on the use of music and music therapy in the context of dementia, found that (with some limitations) the findings were consistent in showing the efficacy of music therapy in impacting positively on the behavioural and psychological symptoms of dementia. However, the ability of the music therapist to directly interact with the participants appeared to be crucial for success.

No difference was found in cognitive function between dementia sufferers receiving interactive or receptive music therapy or usual care in one review of 38 trials involving 1418 participants aged 75 to 90 years old. Those receiving receptive therapy showed a significant decrease in agitation and behavioural problems, although there was no significant difference between those engaged in interactive music therapy and usual care in relation to behavioural and psychiatric problems (Tsoi et al., 2018). McDermott and colleagues (2012) found consistent improvement in behavioural disturbance in the short term, in a review of 18 studies adopting a diverse range of active music-making activities, with singing often being used as a medium of change. However, the review did not find any high-quality longitudinal studies that demonstrated long-term benefits. Focusing on the impact of music therapy on anxiety in a review of studies where the severity of dementia varied from mild to severe, Ing-Randolph and colleagues (2015) found variation in the nature of the interventions and the group sizes. While the findings seemed promising, the small number of studies and the variability in methods made it impossible to draw firm conclusions. Also taking account of variations in the quality of the research and how it was reported, van der Steen and colleagues (2018) reviewed 22 studies with 1097 dementia patients in nursing homes or hospitals, and concluded that people with dementia in institutional care participating in at least five sessions of a music-based therapeutic intervention probably experienced reduced depression and anxiety, improved overall behaviour and possible enhanced emotional wellbeing and quality of life, although there was no impact on agitation, aggression or cognition. The effect on social behaviour and the long-term impact of the interventions was unclear.

In a scoping review, Elliott and Gardner (2018) summarised what was known about the role and impact of music in the lives of community-dwelling older adults with dementia, and reported that music could reduce agitation, improve cognition and enhance social wellbeing, while Bamford and Bowell (2018) also concluded that music could promote a range of benefits for people with dementia when used appropriately and in a meaningful way. In contrast, Vink and colleagues (2003) reviewed ten music therapy interventions designed to treat the behavioural, social, cognitive and emotional problems of older people with dementia, criticised the methodological quality of the research and reported that it was not possible to draw any firm conclusions. In a later review, Vink and Hanser (2018) reported that most descriptions of music therapy interventions lacked sufficient detail to enable researchers to compare and replicate studies, or for clinicians to apply the techniques. Definitions of music therapy and music-based interventions were inconsistent, and practitioners varied in the extent of their professional training and preparation for implementing music-based clinical strategies. Fusar-Poli and colleagues (2018) carried out a meta-analysis of six studies including 330 participants with an age range of 79 to 86 years old, and found no significant effects of music therapy on any outcomes. Similarly, Hui-Chi and colleagues (2015) conducted a review of music therapy interventions with older people in nursing homes, hospitals or communities, and indicated that (in the short-term) music therapy did not improve the cognitive function of older people. Considering the role of the arts in relation to dementia more broadly, Schneider and colleagues (2018) included 11 relevant studies and concluded that there was insufficient evidence demonstrating causality to draw any firm conclusions.

Music, Public Health and Music on Prescription

Music has been used to communicate public health messages. For instance, Cournoyer Lemaire (2020) report how the Quebec government promoted adherence to COVID-19 measures through the use of music, taking advantage of its capacity to reach a large population, capture the population's attention quickly regardless of age, language or cultural barriers, effectively communicate messages and thus change behaviour.

Clift and Camic (2016) provided an evidence base supporting the role of the creative arts in public health, bringing together contributions from practitioners and researchers to provide a comprehensive account of the field and the approaches that had successfully led to improvements. They showed that several countries had moved towards offering a range of arts interventions on prescription. Similarly, Jensen and colleagues (2016) reviewed current practice relating to arts and culture on prescription in Sweden, Norway, Denmark and the UK, considering the evidence supporting social prescription and potential barriers to its implementation. In a later article, Jensen and Bonde (2018) illustrated the variety and multitude of studies, showing that participation in arts activities could be beneficial for those with mental and physical health problems, and demonstrating the possible impact on reducing physical symptoms and improving mental health.

Some research has focused on showing how arts on prescription can be effective. For instance, Batt-Rawden and Tellnes (2011) explored the role and significance of making music in the lives of men and women with long-term illnesses in different life phases, facing different challenges. In a longitudinal study that included eight interviews with each of the 22 participants, aged between 35 and 65, they found that music could promote movement, release anger or aggression, and transcend pain. Personal listening preferences were important. Crone and colleagues (2018) presented findings from a longitudinal follow-up study of an arts-on-referral programme in UK general practice over a seven-year period, including 1,297 patients who were referred to an eight- or ten-week intervention. Of all referrals, just over half completed their course of prescribed art. Of those that attended, 75 percent were observed to be engaged with the intervention. A significant increase in wellbeing was observed from pre- to post-intervention for those that engaged with or completed their programme. Some had multiple health issues. In the main, this group completed the programme, were rated as engaged and showed a significant increase in wellbeing. Poulos and colleagues (2019) targeted community-dwelling older people with a wide range of health and wellness needs who were referred to a programme by their healthcare practitioner. The courses, led by professional artists in a range of artistic activities, included dance, singing and music. Classes were held weekly for eight to ten weeks with six to eight participants in each group, culminating with a showing of work or a performance. Data from 127 participants aged 65 years old and over showed that *Arts on Prescription* had a positive impact on wellbeing, self-reported creativity and the frequency of undertaking creative activities. The activities on offer were challenging, created a sense of purpose and direction, enabled personal growth and achievement, and empowered participants in an environment which fostered the development of meaningful relationships with others. Similarly, Murabayashi and colleagues (2019) studied 115 frail elderly individuals aged between 65 and 89 years of age, who were divided into two groups. The music therapy group participated in group sessions of 45 to 50 minutes conducted by a music therapist for 12 weeks. A control group waited for 12 weeks before participation. Cognitive, physical and psychophysical functions were assessed. Improvements were observed in physical function, depressive mood and quality of life.

Overall, there is evidence that art interventions can be effective in the promotion of wellbeing, whether individuals choose to participate or are referred through social prescribing (Bungay and Clift, 2010; Jones et al., 2013). Engaging with the arts can reduce loneliness and social isolation (Poscia et al., 2017), particularly for those living in rural or disadvantaged areas (MacLeod et al., 2016; Murrock and Graor, 2016; Pearce and Lillyman, 2015).

The Role of Community Music and Creative Workshops

In developed countries, there are high levels of mental and physical illness associated with long-term health conditions, unhealthy lifestyles and an ageing population. Community music activities can address these issues (Jones et al., 2013). Increasing numbers of mental health organisations are developing music-making interventions for patients. To demonstrate whether such programmes could be effective, Fancourt and colleagues (2016) studied a ten-week group drumming programme and found significant decreases in depression and increases in social resilience, anxiety and wellbeing. These changes were maintained three months later. Participants also provided saliva samples to test for immune responses. These showed underlying biological effects, supporting the programme's potential for enhancing mental health. Similarly, Ascenso and colleagues (2018) studied 39 participants engaged in a community drumming programme. There were a range of benefits for patients and carers, including enhanced emotions, initiative and sense of control, accomplishment, redefinition of self and social wellbeing. Perkins and colleagues (2016) researched group djembe-drumming and found that the drumming itself was important as a form of non-verbal communication, providing a connection with life through rhythm, and generating and liberating energy. The group setting facilitated feelings of acceptance, safety and care, and enabled new social interactions. Inclusivity, musical freedom and the acceptance of making mistakes supported by the music facilitator were important for learning. Solli and colleagues (2013), in a review, explored service users' experiences of music therapy in the development of recovery-oriented provision. Key factors were having a good time, being together, exploring feelings and self-concept. Music therapy supported the development of strengths and resources that contributed to the growth of positive identity and hope.

Stickley and colleagues (2018) established that a range of arts activities could support recovery through enhancing connectedness and improving hope. Van Lith and colleagues (2013), in a review, concluded that arts could play a substantial role in mental health recovery, while Stevens and colleagues (2018) reported significant increases in self-reported mental wellbeing, social inclusion and the ongoing use of skills learned for some, but not all participants, depending on the in-course experience of artistic growth. Community-based creative workshops have supported those experiencing severe and persistent mental illness. Workshops typically aim to build the skills and capacities of participants, providing alternative ways to communicate identity and recovery stories through visual arts, writing, dance and music, facilitated by practising artists. Participants typically enjoy the workshops and being involved in creative activities with others, which improves their confidence and understanding of their illness (Stewart et al., 2018; Slatterly et al., 2020).

Bolger (2015) investigated the process of collaboration between a music therapist and community participants in three music projects in

Australia. The projects were undertaken with three separate communities which supported groups of marginalised young people. The findings provided an understanding of the conditions required to optimise the potential for positive growth in collaborators in participatory music projects. MacGlone and colleagues (2020) investigated a community music intervention for a population with varied disabilities—physical, learning or both—who took part in weekly music workshops. Although the findings showed improvements in individuals' self-expression, confidence, mood and social skills, there were differences in outcomes in different centres. Participants in one centre improved their musical skills; in another, some participated with enthusiasm but others chose other art activities over music; while in another there was a lasting positive impact. Despite this, all groups showed improvement in communication, interaction with others and joint attention.

Music, Brain Plasticity and Movement

Motor skills tend to deteriorate with age. Activities which support lifelong neuroplasticity, such as making music, can counteract these processes and allow for the reacquisition of motor and cognitive skills in the elderly following brain-tissue damage (for instance, after a stroke). Playing a keyboard can improve fine motor functions through neurophysiological changes in audiomotor networks. Rhythmic cueing has a positive effect on gait disorders, improving stride length, speed and overall mobility. Melodic intonation therapy can improve recovery from non-fluent aphasia through the activation of right-hemisphere networks. Importantly, the rewarding effects of music-making and listening provoke neurochemical effects which, in combination with music-induced brain plasticity, can facilitate neurorehabilitation (Altenmüller and James, 2020). Much of the research on mobility has focused on rhythm. Clinical evidence has shown that the use of external rhythmic auditory cueing can aid in the rehabilitation of motor movements such as gait in patients with Parkinson's disease, traumatic brain injury, spinal cord injury and Huntington's disease (Thaut et al., 2015). Neurological music therapy techniques can promote sensorimotor rehabilitation (Mainka et al., 2016). Music can support improvement in movement in a range of conditions, improving individuals' quality, range and speed of movement. In acute medical settings or neurological rehabilitation, music can facilitate and target specific therapeutic goals. Making music can be beneficial for those who have partial paralysis following a stroke (LaGasse and Thaut, 2012). While the motivational aspects of music may account for some gains made, there is evidence of increased activation of the motor cortex and improved cortical connectivity (Altenmuller et al., 2009). Särkämö and colleagues (2014) carried out a voxel-based morphometry analysis on acute and six-month post-stroke patients. Structural magnetic resonance imaging data from 49 patients who listened to either their favourite music, verbal material or no listening material during the six-month recovery period showed that listening to music enhanced behavioural recovery and also induced fine-grained neuroanatomical changes in the recovering brain.

Also working with stroke patients, Schneider and colleagues (2007) evaluated a music-supported training programme designed to induce an auditory sensorimotor co-representation of movements. Patients without any previous musical experience participated in intensive step-by-step training, first of the paretic extremity, followed by training of both extremities. Training was given 15 times over three weeks in addition to conventional treatment. Fine as well as gross motor skills were addressed by using either a MIDI piano or electronic drum pads. Pre- and post-treatment motor functions were monitored using a computerised movement analysis system and established motor tests. Patients showed significant improvement after treatment with respect to speed, precision and smoothness of movement and motor control in everyday activities. Similarly, Villeneuve and colleagues (2014) engaged 13 stroke patients in three weeks of piano training comprising nine 60-minute supervised sessions and home practice. Fine and gross manual dexterity, movement coordination and functional use of the upper extremity were assessed pre- and post-intervention at a three-week follow-up. Significant improvements were observed for all outcomes, particularly in those with a higher initial level of motor recovery at the beginning of the intervention. Also working with stroke patients, Särkämö and colleagues (2008) studied 60patients in the acute recovery phase who were either assigned to a music, language or control group. During the following two months, the music and language groups listened daily to self-selected music or audiobooks respectively, while the control group received no listening material. All patients received standard medical care and rehabilitation. The findings showed that recovery in the domains of verbal memory and focused attention improved significantly more in the music group than the other groups. The music group also experienced a less depressed and confused mood.

Working with patients with Parkinson's disease, Pantelyat and colleagues (2016) assessed the feasibility and effects of twice-weekly group West African drum-circle classes for six weeks. Compared with controls, those in the drumming group showed significantly improved walking performance and quality of life. Studying patients with cerebral palsy, Ghai and colleagues (2017) reviewed 547 records of the effects of rhythmic auditory cueing on spatiotemporal and kinematic parameters of gait in people with cerebral palsy, and concluded that there was converging evidence towards the application of rhythmic auditory cueing to enhance gait performance and stability. Alves-Pinto and colleagues (2016) also reviewed the evidence supporting the use of musical-instrument-playing for rehabilitation in cerebral palsy. They proposed that active musical-instrument-playing could be an efficient way of triggering the neuroplastic processes necessary for the development of sensorimotor skills in patients with early brain damage. In a later study, Alves-Pinto and colleagues (2017) studied adolescents and adult patients with cerebral palsy, as well as a group of typically developing children, who learned to play the piano for four consecutive weeks, completing a total of eight hours of training. For ten of the participants, learning was supported by a special technical system aimed at helping people with sensorimotor deficits to better discriminate fingers and orient themselves along the piano keyboard. The potential effects of piano training were assessed with tests of finger-tapping at the piano and perception of vibratory stimulation of fingers, as well as neuronal correlates of motor learning in the absence of and after piano training. Although the findings were highly variable, there were significant effects of training on the ability to perceive the localisation of vibrations over fingers, but there was no effect of training on the performance of simple finger-tapping sequences at the piano or on motor-associated brain responses.

Some work has focused on children. For instance, Marrades-Caballero and colleagues (2018) studied 18 children between 4 and 16 years of age with severe bilateral cerebral palsy, who received music therapy for 16 weeks. Significant improvements were observed in overall and specific arm and hand position, as well as activities from standard locomotor stages. The improvements persisted at a four-month follow-up. Also working with children, Peng and colleagues (2011) explored the effects of patterned sensory enhancement music on muscle power and movement control in children with spastic diplegia during loaded sit-to-stands. Twenty-three children with spastic diplegia, aged five to twelve years old, participated. Individual patterned sensory-enhanced music was composed by a music therapist based on each participant's sit-to-stand movement, with 50 percent one repetition maximum load. Each participant performed sit-to-stands continuously for eight repetitions under randomly assigned music or no music conditions, while kinematic and kinetic data were measured simultaneously. In the music condition, the music was played only during the first five repetitions. The following three repetitions were referred to as the 'continuation condition'. Compared to the control condition, greater peak knee extensor power, greater total extensor power and better centre of mass smoothness, but less movement time was found in the music condition. Significant effects of the music were also found for the continuation condition.

Auditory stimulation has been shown to improve upper-extremity skills. Ben-Pazi and colleagues (2018) studied nine matched pairs of children aged 7.5 years old. The children listened to auditory stimulation embedded in music or music alone for at least ten minutes, four times a week for four weeks. The children with auditory stimulation achieved more goals than children who listened to music alone. Parents reported improved care and comfort in the children in the intervention group, compared to a slight deterioration in the control group. Bringas and colleagues (2015) tested the effectiveness of a music therapy intervention for children with severe neurological disorders. The control group received only a standard neurorestoration programme, while the experimental group received an additional music therapy auditory attention plus communication protocol immediately before the usual occupational and speech therapy. Overall, the findings showed improved attention and communication, as well as changes in brain plasticity, in children with severe neurological impairments who experienced adjunct music therapy.

Another strand of research has focused on individuals with Huntingdon's disease, a neurodegenerative condition that leads to progressive loss of motor and cognitive functions. Metzler-Baddley and colleagues (2014) devised an intervention involving drumming and rhythm exercises to target early executive problems, such as difficulties in sequence and reversal learning, response speed, timing and dual-tasking. Five people completed the two-month music intervention. The effects of rhythm exercises on executive function, basal ganglia volume and white-matter microstructure in the anterior corpus callosum, the anterior thalamic radiation and the corticospinal tract were assessed. After two months of training, there were improvements in executive function and white-matter microstructure, notably in the genus of the corpus callosum (which connects the prefrontal cortices of both hemispheres). There were no changes in basal ganglia volume.

Some research has focused on whether music therapy can support those suffering from multiple sclerosis. Aldridge and colleagues (2005) aimed to see which components of multiple sclerosis would respond to music therapy. Twenty adult multiple sclerosis patients participated, half receiving music therapy, over the course of one year. Measurements were taken before therapy began and subsequently every three months, then at a six-month follow-up without music therapy. Tests included indicators of clinical depression and anxiety, a self-acceptance scale and a life-quality assessment. Data were also collected on cognitive and functional measures. Significant improvements were found for the therapy group over time in relation to self-esteem, depression and anxiety but these worsened when the therapy stopped.

Breathing

Several studies have investigated whether singing has a beneficial effect on aspects of breathing. Overall, the findings are mixed (Clift, 2012). For instance, Schorr-Lesnick and colleagues (1985) compared singers with instrumentalists and reported no difference between participants aged 25 to 83 in choir, string, percussion or wind ensembles in pulmonary function. Studies of patients with chronic pulmonary disease have also had mixed results, with some research on singing showing improvements compared with controls (Bonilha et al., 2009), while some has shown limited impact (Lord et al., 2010). Despite this, those participating in singing activities frequently report that singing has exercised body systems through the physical exertion involved, especially the lungs (Clift et al., 2008; Stacey et al., 2002). Skingley and colleagues (2018) established the views of participants with chronic obstructive pulmonary disease who took part in a ten-month 'singing for better breathing' programme. The findings showed that participants learned about breath control, relaxation, exercises for breathing and using singing as a means to deflect attention away from breathing problems. The programme led to increased activity levels, was seen as fun, provided friendship, increased motivation to participate in further activities and offered support. For some, it was the highlight of the week. The majority of participants reported improvements in respiratory symptoms and mental and social wellbeing.

Speech Impairment

Music can play a therapeutic role in supporting improvement in speech impairments. Rhythmic cueing has been used to reduce speech rate and increase speech intelligibility in patients with severe dysarthria and problems with the muscles that support speech due to traumatic brain injury (for instance, as the result of a stroke; Pilon et al., 1998). Similar results have been found for increasing the intelligibility of the speech of patients with Parkinson's disease (Thaut et al., 2001). Hays and Minichiello (2005) found that music provided a means of communication with spouses, friends or others, where language-based communication was restricted due to Parkinson's disease, dementia or other illnesses affecting verbal communication.

Matthews (2018) compared two groups of people with Parkinson's disease who participated in voice and choral singing or a music appreciation activity. Both groups attended once a week for nine weeks. There was significant improvement for those in the choir for voice volume and quality, maximum sustained phonation time and functional symptom severity. At the end of the intervention, significant group differences were observed in average and maximum voice volume, voice quality and glottal function. Attendance for both groups was over 96 percent, suggesting that both groups found the nature and format of the activities enjoyable and worthwhile. Quinn and colleagues (2021) worked with post-verbal people with strokes, learning difficulties, acquired brain injury, dementia or autism. The findings showed how post-verbal people could use music to communicate and demonstrate their capacities, and how those working with them used music to foster a sense of inclusion and belonging.

The surgical removal of the larynx (i.e. the voice box) has a profound psychosocial impact, often leading to depression and social isolation. After laryngectomy, breathing, voicing, articulation and tongue movement are important in restoring communication, and require exercises which can be challenging motivationally. Moors and colleagues (2020) explored the use of basic beatboxing techniques to create a wide variety of fun and interactive exercises that maximised the use of the structures important in alaryngeal phonation to maintain motivation. An instructional online video was created to support patients working on their own or with support from speech therapists. For patients, the approach was engaging, useful, informative and motivating. O'Donoghue and colleagues (2021) studied whether music therapy—including song-writing, improvisation and singing—could help adolescents who stuttered. The findings revealed participants' experiences of living with stuttering, the importance of music in their everyday lives and how music could help them.

Music in Hospital Settings

Music and Hospitalised Babies, Infants and Children

Babies born premature or underweight can benefit from the stimulation of music in neonatal intensive care units. Music can enhance heart rate, respiration, oxygen saturation, mean arterial pressure, sucking, feeding ability and behavioural state. It has also been linked with overall reductions in the length of stay in intensive care (Caine, 1991; Cassidy and Standley, 1995; Keith et al., 2009; Standley, 2002; 2011; 2012). Music can significantly reduce the frequency and duration of episodes of inconsolable crying (Keith et al., 2009; Loewy, 2014) and have longer-term benefits, reducing reactions to fear and anger at 12 and 24 months (LeJeune et al., 2019). Some research has found reductions in the number of negative critical events (Filippa et al., 2013) and the regulation of salivary cortisol levels (Shenfield et al., 2003). In a meta-analysis of 14 studies involving 964 infants and 266 parents, Bieleninik and colleagues (2016) found significant large effects, indicating the positive effects of music therapy on infant respiratory rate and maternal anxiety. There was insufficient evidence to confirm or refute other effects. Walworth (2009) examined the effect of music therapy on premature and full-term infants' developmental responses and the responsiveness of parents. Sixty-five parent-infant dyads either attended music groups or a control group. Infants participating in musical activities with their parents demonstrated significantly more social toy-play than the control group.

Music therapy with hospitalised infants has shown positive effects on infants' capacity to self-regulate and engage in social interaction with adults compared to controls (Malloch et al., 2012). Music has been effective in promoting the wellbeing of young patients, enhancing relaxation, providing distraction and helping them to cope with their hospital experiences. In some cases, music-making can reduce or remove the need for sedation. Listening to music can increase oxygenation levels in the blood of long-term paediatric patients and have a positive psychological impact on the chronically ill (Longhi and Pickett, 2008). Patients react better to music therapy than other therapies (Hendon and Bohon, 2008; Longhi and Pickett, 2008; Longhi et al., 2015), perhaps because it is frequently perceived as fun (O'Callaghan et al., 2013).

Music is used in paediatric settings to enhance the wellbeing of young patients (Klassen et al., 2008; Preti, 2013; Preti and McFerran, 2016). It can help children and young people relax (Daveson, 2001; Longhi and Pickett, 2008; Malone, 1996), be used as a distraction (Caprilli et al., 2007; Hendon and Bohon, 2008) and help children and young people to talk about their hospital experiences and develop coping strategies (Brodsky, 1989; Froehlich, 1984; Robb, 2000). Familiar music can reduce anxiety associated with the hospital environment (Preti and Welch, 2011) and can reduce children's stress during painful procedures (Caprilli et al., 2007; Klassen et al., 2008; Nguyen et al., 2010; Vohra and Nilsson, 2011; Whitehead-Pleaux et al., 2006;). In some cases, music-making can reduce or remove the need for sedation (DeLoach Walworth, 2005). In a recent review of research with participants aged 0 to 21 years old, Johnson and colleagues (2021) showed consistent and significant evidence that music could reduce anxiety before and during medical procedures, although the findings relating to pain and vital signs were mixed. Several studies have highlighted the importance of patient preference in selecting music. This can be achieved easily through the use of headphones. Group music-making can also benefit teenagers in hospital (Bittman et al., 2001; Burns et al., 2005; Nicholson et al., 2008).

Nguyen and colleagues (2010) studied whether music interventions could influence pain and anxiety in children undergoing lumbar punctures. Forty children aged seven to twelve years of age with leukaemia participated, half experiencing a music intervention and half acting as controls. Measures were taken before, during and after the procedure. The findings showed lower anxiety, pain scores and heart and respiratory rate in the music group during and after the procedure. Similarly, Giordano and colleagues (2020) found that music therapy reduced preoperative anxiety in children affected by leukaemia when undergoing invasive diagnostic procedures. Barrera and colleagues (2002) studied the impact of music therapy on paediatric haematology and oncology patients. Data from 65 children and parents showed a significant improvement in children's emotions and wellbeing, while parents perceived improved play performance in preschoolers and adolescents but not school-aged children. In a review of 19 music therapy studies with 596 participants, Facchini and Ruini (2020) noted a significant reduction in psychological distress and an increase in wellbeing. Eight articles evaluated the effects on pain and other biological parameters, but the findings were inconclusive.

Patients undergoing haematopoietic stem cell transplants are at risk of developing post-traumatic stress disorder (PTSD). This may explain the extent of music therapy research in this area. For instance, Uggla and colleagues (2016) examined the effect of expressive and receptive music therapy delivered twice weekly on 24 patients up to the age of 16 undergoing haematopoietic stem cell transplants. The music therapy significantly reduced evening heart rate compared to controls, indicating reduced stress, although there were no significant differences in saturation or blood pressure between the groups. In a later study (Uggla et al., 2018), 29 patients aged 0 to 17 years of age were studied, 14 of whom received music therapy twice a week for four to six weeks during hospitalisation. Those experiencing music therapy had higher estimated physical function at the time of discharge and improved quality of life.

In a further study, Uggla and colleagues (2019) explored six families' experiences of music therapy and found that it became a significant and helpful experience, an important element in coping with and managing treatment. In 2020, Uggla and Bond studied 38 patients, aged from two months to 17 years old, who were receiving haematopoietic stem cell transplantation and who participated in expressive and receptive music therapy. The sessions took place in the child's hospital room, and the child was invited to play different musical instruments, sing and listen to music with the music therapist. Parents and siblings could also participate. The increasing physical functioning reported by the children at discharge and the overall increased quality of life at the six-month follow-up suggested that the music therapy intervention was effective. Similarly, Robb and colleagues (2014) examined the efficacy of a therapeutic music video intervention on adolescents and young adults who were in the acute phase of having a haematopoietic stem cell transplant. Participants were allocated to the video intervention or an audiobook group for six sessions over a three-week period. After the intervention, the music video group reported significantly better social integration and family environment. Haase and colleagues (2020) also reported adolescents' and young adults' experiences of a therapeutic music video intervention during hospitalisation for haematopoietic stem cell transplants. Fourteen participants were interviewed and revealed that the video provided an opportunity for reflection, self-expression and meaning-making: it helped them to tell their story and to overcome the negative aspects of cancer. It supported participants in overcoming distress and challenges by providing opportunities to reflect on what was meaningful, connect with others, and explore and identify personal strengths.

Other research has focused on the effect of listening to music in the recovery period following a range of surgery. Preethy and Gurunathan (2020) studied the effects on the vital signs and behaviour of 62 children, and showed that those listening to music demonstrated more positive behaviour, significantly lower pulse rate and diastolic and systolic blood pressure, and significantly higher oxygen saturation. Focusing on burn injuries, Eid and colleagues (2020) evaluated the effect of a physical therapy rehabilitation programme combined with music therapy on children with lower limb burns, compared with controls. Both groups improved, but the music therapy group showed greater improvement in terms of pain, range of motion and gait parameters.

There are benefits of music therapy for the families of children in hospital (Preti and McFerran, 2016). Parents value being able to participate in musical activities with their child. Music can open up communication between family members (Lindenfelser et al., 2012). In addition to supporting children during stressful procedures, parents are indirectly supported by music, creating a more relaxed environment (Preti and Welch, 2004; 2011). Music can also contribute to the overall hospital environment, modulating patient and staff mood (Rossetti, 2020).

Music Therapy and Cancer

There are an increasing number of music interventions focused on supporting those with cancer. For instance, Boldt (1996) assessed the effects of music therapy on bone-marrow-transplant patients who needed to exercise to prevent muscle atrophy (although this was difficult due to treatment effects). The long-term findings indicated that music was effective in increasing participants' self-reported relaxation and comfort. Endurance increased, as did cooperative behaviour and participation levels. Robb and colleagues (2003) examined the impact of music therapy on anxiety and depression following bone-marrow transplants. Three patients experienced music therapy for one hour a week over six weeks, while three did not. Analysis of the content of patient-generated songs revealed hope, positive coping, control and appreciation. The findings provided insight into the individualised experience of each patient and their coping strategies. Focusing on Chinese female patients with breast cancer, Zhou and colleagues (2015) examined the effects of music therapy and progressive muscle relaxation on depression, anxiety and length of hospital stay following radical mastectomy. A group of 170 patients either received music therapy and muscle-relaxation training, or acted as controls who only received nursing care. The 30-minute intervention was implemented twice a day within 48 hours of surgery. Those participating showed significant improvement in depression and anxiety, and spent less time in hospital. A single session of patient-preferred live music has been shown to have a significantly positive impact on pain following surgery in patients in a post-surgical oncology ward (Merry and Silverman, 2021).

Fancourt and colleagues (2016) carried out a multicentre study to assess the impact of singing on mood, stress and immune response in three groups affected by cancer: carers, bereaved carers and patients. Participants sang regularly in five choirs across South Wales. Before and after singing, mood and stress were assessed, and saliva samples were taken to test for cortisol, beta-endorphin, oxytocin and cytokines. All participants associated singing with reductions in negative affect and increases in positive affect, alongside significant increases in cytokines. Singing was associated with reductions in cortisol, beta-endorphin and oxytocin levels. Overall, it improved mood and modulated elements of the immune system. Köhler and colleagues (2020) synthesised the evidence for the effectiveness of music therapy in different oncological treatment phases with adult cancer patients. The narrative synthesis included 30 studies and showed that, overall, music therapy had positive effects on a broad range of outcomes, with techniques and effects varying in different phases. During curative treatment, the results were most promising with regard to anxiety, depression and pain-medication intake, while in palliative settings, improvements with regard to quality of life, spiritual wellbeing, pain and stress were reported. Twenty-one studies were included in a meta-analysis, which showed small but significant effects of music therapy on psychological wellbeing, physical symptom distress and quality of life. In contrast, Daykin and colleagues (2007) drew attention to the challenges and complexity of using music with cancer patients because of the wide variation in responses. They suggested that identity and creativity were key to understanding the impact of music interventions.

Music and Surgery

Music has been used in a range of ways to support people who are having surgery. Exposure to music has been shown to reduce cortisol levels during medical treatment (Le Roux et al., 2007). For instance, in pre-operative settings in hospitals, where patients are often experiencing pain, anxiety, distress and even aggressive non-compliance, meta-analytic analyses have demonstrated that music can help to reduce anxiety (Spintge, 2012). Conrad and colleagues (2007) played critically ill patients slow movements of Mozart's piano sonatas and found that the use of music significantly reduced the amount of sedative drugs needed to achieve the degree of sedation, comparable to controls who received standard treatment. In the music group, plasma concentrations of growth hormone increased, whereas concentrations of interleukin-6 (a component of the immune system) and adrenaline decreased. Significantly lower levels of blood pressure and heart rate also indicated reductions in stress. Overall, calming music activated neurohumoral pathways associated with psychophysiological sedation. In Sweden, Nilsson (2009) found that patients who had undergone heart surgery and were allocated on the following day to 30 minutes of uninterrupted bed rest with music, followed by 30 minutes of bed rest——or alternatively 60 minutes of uninterrupted bed rest—— showed a difference in cortisol levels after the initial 3030 minutes but not after 6060 minutes. The music was presented through a music pillow connected to an MP3 player. There was no difference in heart rate, respiratory rate, mean arterial pressure, arterial oxygen tension or saturation, pain or anxiety levels.

Music and Pain

There has been considerable interest in the use of music to reduce pain. Stress and anxiety exacerbate the experience of pain. Music therapy or musical stimulation can reduce the perception of pain in post-surgical patients, alone or as part of a pain management programme. Music chosen by the patient is usually more effective than music chosen by others. Patients also need to be able to control the volume at which the music is played, when and for how long (Bernatzky et al., 2011; 2012). Hole and colleagues (2015), in a review, reinforced these findings, showing that music was effective in reducing pain and anxiety, even when patients were under general anaesthetic. Pothoulaki and colleagues (2008) investigated the effects of preferred-music-listening on anxiety and pain perception in patients undergoing haemodialysis. Sixty people diagnosed with end-stage renal failure and undergoing haemodialysis treatment participated. Anxiety and pain were measured pre- and post-intervention. The control group scored significantly higher on state anxiety than the experimental group and experienced significantly higher pain intensity. In a study where pain was induced experimentally, Basiński and colleagues (2018) showed that average pain ratings were significantly lower when any music was played, but increasingly so when the music selected was arousing or complex. Focusing on pain and stress management in everyday life, Linnemann and colleagues (2015) studied 30 women with fibromyalgia syndrome, a condition characterised by chronic pain. Participants rated their pain intensity, perceived control over pain, perceived stress level and music-listening behaviour five times a day for 14 consecutive days. At each assessment, participants provided a saliva sample for the analysis of cortisol and alpha amylase, as biomarkers of stress response systems. The findings showed that music-listening increased perceived control over pain. Listening to music in combination with guided imagery has also been found to lead to significant reductions of the β-endorphin, which the body uses to numb or dull pain (McKinney et al., 1997), although music-listening or guided imagery alone did not have this effect. Vollert and colleagues (2003) used relaxing music with coronary patients during rehabilitation and found significant decreases of β-endorphin during physical exercise, suggesting that the music compensated for the need for natural pain relief. In addition, systolic blood pressure, anxiety and worry were reduced. These decreases were not found in patients who performed the exercises without music. Gerra and colleagues (1998) extended these observations, showing that listening to upbeat techno music led to increases in β-endorphins, demonstrating that upbeat music led to different outcomes.

Some research has focused on pain reduction in terms of active engagement with music. For instance, Irons and colleagues (2020) carried out a systematic review of 13 studies on the impact of group singing on pain. There were psychological, physical and social benefits. Most interventions reduced pain intensity. Overall, music does seem to be able to contribute to the management of pain. This is gradually being recognised and the processes involved more fully understood so that treatment techniques can be refined to meet patients' needs more effectively (Mainka et al., 2016).

Music and Palliative Care

Coelho and colleagues (2017) carried out a scoping review to examine and map non-pharmacological interventions implemented to provide comfort in palliative care in home care, hospices and palliative care units. Eighteen studies were included, covering ten non-pharmacological interventions implemented in one to fourteen sessions which lasted for five to sixty minutes. The most common were music and massage therapy. The characteristics of these differed significantly across and within interventions. They were mostly implemented in palliative care units and hospices, and for patients with a cancer diagnosis. The use of music as therapy in multidisciplinary end-of-life care dates back to the 1970s. Music therapy is now one of the most frequently used complementary therapies in palliative care in the USA. Schmid and colleagues (2018) provided an overview of users' and providers' perspectives, and showed that music therapy was viewed positively. Similarly, Nyashanu and colleagues (2020) undertook a scoping review to explore the efficacy of music interventions in palliative care. Music therapy supported the management of pain, anxiety and depression, and promoted relaxation, happiness and hope, enhanced spirituality and quality of life. Leow and colleagues (2010) also reviewed terminally ill patients' experiences of using music therapy in a hospital, an inpatient hospice, a nursing home or their own homes. They concluded that music therapy could promote social interaction and communication with family, friends, other patients and healthcare workers, and provide support for patients' holistic needs. McConnell and Porter (2017), in a review of 51 articles of music therapy in palliative care, found that music had a therapeutic effect on the physical, psychological, emotional and spiritual suffering of palliative-care patients and that group music therapy might be an effective way to support staff caring for palliative-care patients.

Music and Mental Health: Stress, Anxiety and Depression

Current levels of psychosocial distress in society are significant, as evidenced by the number of prescribed antidepressants and working days lost as a result of stress and anxiety. There is a growing body of evidence that active involvement in creative activities promotes wellbeing, quality of life and health. In adults with a mental illness, activities such as singing in a choir, creating art, expressive writing and group drumming can reduce mental distress, depression and anxiety, while simultaneously enhancing individual and social wellbeing. In the UK, there are currently a number of projects that offer creative-arts activities on prescription for those experiencing mental health issues or social isolation. The projects adopt different approaches but all take place in the community, are facilitated by professional artists and have a referral process (Bungay and Clift, 2010). Engaging with music can promote relaxation and reduce stress. Using a representative sample of the Swedish population, Juslin and colleagues (2011) found that 78 percent reported that they listened to music at least once every day and that one of the reasons for doing so was that it helped them to relax (Juslin et al., 2011). Using music was reported as beneficial because it was easily available at any time or place, and could be tailored to personal taste. Linnemann and colleagues (2016) assessed whether the presence of others while listening enhanced music's stress-reducing effect. Participants responded to questions on stress, the presence of others and music-listening five times each day, 30 minutes after waking and at 1100, 1400, 1800 and 2100 hours for seven consecutive days. They also collected a saliva sample after each data collection to enable a biological assessment of stress. Music had the greatest impact on stress reduction when listening took place with others or when it was deliberately listened to for relaxation. In a later study, Linnemann and colleagues (2018) studied 60 participants aged eight to 34 years old, who answered questions on music-listening and stress six times each day for a week using an electronic diary device, which reported the time and duration of listening. Self-reports of music-listening were associated with lower reported stress levels but this was not corroborated by the objective data. Participants had to listen for 20 minutes before stress was reduced.

In an experimental study, Jiang and colleagues (2013) examined the effects of sedative and stimulative music and music preference on stress reduction, following induced stress. One hundred and forty-four female music-education students performed a stressful mental arithmetic test, and were then assigned to listen to preferred or non-preferred sedative or stimulative music. Sedative music lowered tension and anxiety, but there was no difference between preferred and non-preferred music. Gold and colleagues (2013) researched the effectiveness of three months of biweekly individual resource-oriented music therapy with 144 adults with non-organic mental disorders in Norway, Austria and Australia. The findings showed that music therapy was an effective addition to usual care for those who were not motivated to engage with other therapies.

Reviews relating to music and stress have had broadly positive outcomes. For instance, Panteleeva and colleagues (2017) conducted a meta-analysis of 19 trials on the effects of music on anxiety and showed an overall decrease in self-reported anxiety, while music also had an impact on blood pressure, cortisol level and heart rate. De Witte and colleagues (2019), in a review of 104 trials with 9,617 participants, showed that music interventions had a positive effect on stress reduction, with larger effects for heart rate compared to blood pressure and hormone levels. Also in a meta-analysis, Pelletier (2004) reviewed 22 articles which used music to decrease arousal due to stress. Music alone and music-assisted relaxation techniques significantly decreased arousal, but the extent of reduction was mediated by age, type of stress, the relaxation technique adopted, musical preference, previous musical experience and the type of intervention. Leckey (2011), reviewing 11 studies, suggested that creative activities could have a healing and protective effect on mental wellbeing through promoting relaxation, providing a means of self-expression and reducing blood pressure, while boosting the immune system and reducing stress. Overall, however, the evidence was weak. Williams and colleagues (2018) systematically reviewed 13 articles with 667 participants. The findings of seven longitudinal studies showed that,, when people with mental health conditions participated in choral singing, their mental health and wellbeing significantly improved,, with moderate to large effect sizes. Qualitative studies showed that group singing provided enjoyment, enhanced emotional states, a a developed sense of belonging and enhanced self-confidence.

In the modern world, depression is common, leading to a loss of social function, reduced quality of life and increased mortality. Music interventions have been used as an alternative to therapy or antidepressant drugs. Leubner and Hinterberger (2017) reviewed 28 studies with 1,810 participants distinguishing between passive listening to music and active singing, playing, or improvising with instruments. In almost all studies, there was a significant reduction in depression levels over time in response to musical activities, particularly in the elderly. Group settings had slightly better outcomes than individual sessions. There were improvements in participants' confidence, self-esteem and motivation. In a meta-analysis, Aalbers and colleagues (2017) found that music therapy, in addition to usual treatment, reduced depressive symptoms and anxiety, and helped to improve functioning, including maintaining employment, activities and relationships. They concluded that music therapy was likely to be effective for people by decreasing symptoms of depression and anxiety and helping them to function in everyday life, although they were reluctant to draw firm conclusions because of the small number of studies and the lack of detailed descriptions of the nature of the interventions. Fancourt and colleagues (2016) studied the reaction of pro-inflammatory cytokines to music interventions, as these decrease in individuals with depression as they recover. The impact of group drumming on a broad array of inflammatory measures was assessed over a six-week intervention. Thirty-one participants with mild or moderate depression completed psychological scales related to depression, anxiety, wellbeing, social resilience and social inclusion before and after participation. The drumming sessions lasted for 90 minutes over a period of six weeks, with groups of 15 to 20 playing together. The sessions consisted of call-and-response exercises and the learning of drumming patterns that were built up into larger pieces. Significant improvements were found for depression, wellbeing and social resilience. Stress and tiredness levels decreased from the beginning to the end of each session, while happiness, relaxation and energy levels increased. There was no impact on blood pressure, but a decrease in heart rate. Overall, the drumming had a positive impact on mental and physical health.

Postnatal depression can be reduced when mothers sing to their babies on a daily basis or listen to music (Fancourt and Perkins, 2017). In comparison with other mother-infant interactions, singing is associated with greater increases in emotional closeness, positive emotions and decreases in psychological and biological markers of anxiety (Fancourt and Perkins, 2018). Music therapy can also be used to support those who are grieving. Smeijsters and van den Hurk (1999) described a single case study of the treatment of a woman experiencing grief after the death of her husband. They described how she was able to express a part of her personality which she had been suppressing since childhood through playing the piano and vocalising during improvisational music therapy.

People with depression are more likely to engage in group rumination related to music, which can amplify negative emotions (Garrido et al., 2017), although Sakka and Juslin (2018)—in a comparison of the everyday use of music for mood regulation in depressed and non-depressed individuals aged 19 to 65 years of age—found few differences between depressed and non-depressed participants.

Mental Health Care in Children, Adolescents and Young People

Children and young people can experience mental illness, and music can sometimes act to support them. McFerran and colleagues (2018) studied whether involvement in a brief music-based intervention engaged young people, was appropriate, decreased distress and increased their understanding of ways to use music positively. The findings showed that at least some of the measurable decreases in distress were related to participation in the music sessions. Similarly, arts engagement, including music therapy and dance, can reduce internalising symptoms such as anxiety and depression in children and adolescents (Geipel et al., 2018). Henderson (1983) studied 13 hospitalised young people, diagnosed with adjustment reactions to adolescence, who either received 18 one-hour sessions of music therapy or acted as controls. The music sessions involved discussion about emotions in music, expression, the identification of body language, story composition to recorded music and drawing to music. Participants showed greater emotional awareness and felt a greater sense of inclusion. In Hong Kong, Kwok (2019) examined the effectiveness of an intervention integrating positive psychology and elements of music therapy in increasing sense of hope, emotional competence and happiness, and decreasing anxiety in 106 students in Grades Eight to Nine who were suffering from anxiety. There was an improvement, with changes in hope acting as a significant mediator in the relationship between the intervention, a decrease in anxiety and an increase in subjective happiness.

In Northern Ireland, Porter and colleagues (2017) examined the efficacy of active music therapy with 251 children aged eight to sixteen years old—who had social, emotional, behavioural and developmental difficulties—and their parents. They either participated in usual care or had an additional 12 sessions of music therapy delivered weekly. Those in the music group showed improvements in communication, social skills, social functioning, self-esteem, depression and family-functioning. In Austria, Grebosz-Haring and Thun-Hohenstein (2018) assessed the potential neuroendocrine, immune and psychological efficacy of group singing and group music-listening in children and adolescents with mental disorders. Seventeen patients aged 11 to 18 in a department for child and adolescent psychiatry participated in a singing or music-listening programme in five daily, 45-minute sessions in one week. Saliva samples were taken to assess cortisol. Mood was also measured before and after the music activities. Singing led to a significantly higher reduction in cortisol than music-listening, while listening led to significantly higher positive change in feelings of calmness and wellbeing. Group music therapy also positively affected the mood states of 352 adolescents aged 12 to 21 who were inpatients in a psychiatric hospital (Shuman et al., 2016). Individual music therapy has also been found to slightly improve the quality of life for some children with psychopathology in an outpatient department, although the impact on symptoms depended on the severity of comorbid medical conditions (Gold et al., 2007b). Promoting positive identities and social participation has been shown to help recovery from mental illness in a range of studies (Hense and McFerran, 2017).

Some interventions have used music through the medium of dance. For instance, Jeong and colleagues (2005) assessed psychological health and changes in the neurohormones of adolescents with mild depression after 12 weeks of dance movement therapy. Forty middle-school seniors participated and were randomly assigned to a dance movement group or acted as controls. Following treatment there was a reduction in psychological distress. Plasma serotonin concentration increased and dopamine concentration decreased. It seems that dance movement therapy can stabilise the sympathetic nervous system. Similarly, Gandhi and colleagues (2021) are studying 36 institutionalised adolescents with depression who will either engage in a therapeutic listening programme or traditional music therapy for 30 minutes a day, two days each week for eight weeks, while participants in a dance group will perform for 30 minutes a day, three days each week for six weeks.

Music has been found to help alleviate depression in university students. For instance, Wu (2002) studied the effect of 20 hours of music therapy on the anxiety, depression and self-esteem of 24 Taiwanese undergraduates. There were positive outcomes in relation to anxiety immediately following music therapy and after a two-month follow-up. The effects on depression were less positive, although the music therapy did lead to enhanced confidence, ability to relax and decreased negative emotions. Also studying university students, Thomson and colleagues (2014) explored how the use of music to regulate moods was associated with depression, anxiety and stress. One hundred and forty-six university students aged between 17 and 24 years of age completed an online questionnaire addressing levels of psychopathology, music-related mood regulation behaviours, and personal music-related information. Overall, music-related mood regulation predicted levels of psychopathology. High use of music for the venting of negative emotions predicted high levels of depression, anxiety and stress. Diversion (distraction from worries and stress) predicted high levels of anxiety and stress, while music for entertainment or maintaining or enhancing a happy mood predicted low levels of depression. For some individuals, using music to regulate mood may be maladaptive, although it may be that young people experiencing psychopathology are more likely to use music to help to reduce their symptoms. Indeed, Miranda and colleagues (2012) suggested that music-listening might influence internalising psychopathology because of its role in emotion regulation and coping.

Insomnia

Losing sleep is a widespread problem which can have serious physical and economic consequences. Music's impact on physical, psychological and emotional states may explain why it has helped people with sleeping disorders. Music can improve sleep quality, sleep efficiency and time-to-sleep onset, with greater effectiveness than a range of other interventions, including acupuncture and medication. Trahan and colleagues (2018) investigated music as a sleep aid amongst the general public using an online survey that assessed musicality, sleep habits and which music helped sleep (and why). Of the 651 responses, 62 percent of respondents stated that they used music to help them sleep. Fourteen musical genres and 545 different artists were reported to be used as sleep aids. Stress, age and music use were significant predictors of sleep quality. Younger people with higher musical engagement were significantly more likely to use music to aid sleep. Respondents reported that music helped them sleep because of its unique sleep-inducing properties, its role as part of their normal sleep routine, and the way it blocked internal or external stimuli that would otherwise disrupt sleep. Jespersen and Vuust (2012) studied the use of relaxing music at bedtime with 15 traumatised refugees experiencing difficulties in sleeping. The intervention group heard relaxing music played at night through a music player nested in a pillow. There was a significant improvement in sleep quality and wellbeing but no changes in trauma symptoms. In a later study, Jespersen and colleagues (2019) studied 57 people with insomnia who either listened to music or were given audiobooks to listen to. The severity of insomnia decreased and participants perceived an improvement in sleep and quality of life, but there were no changes in objective measures of sleep.

Reviews of the role of music in supporting sleep have had broadly positive results. Feng and colleagues (2018) reviewed 20 studies involving 1339 patients and 12 interventions. All interventions were statistically more effective than usual care, but patients ranked listening to music as the best method for overall sleep quality. In terms of sleep onset latency, music-associated relaxation and listening to music had significant advantages. Listening to music and music with exercise also tended to improve sleep efficiency. Wang and colleagues (2014) reviewed ten studies involving 557 participants, and showed that sleep quality was improved significantly by music and that there was a cumulative effect for chronic sleep disorders. Jespersen and colleagues (2015) reviewed six publications involving 314 participants across a variety of settings including the participant's own home, a sleep laboratory and an inpatient rehabilitation facility. Sample sizes varied between 15 to 65 participants aged from 19 to 83 years of age. Some trials used music only, others music with relaxation. The music included

Eastern and Chinese classical music, new age, electric, popular oldies, and jazz. The music was played for 25 to 60 minutes once a day over three to 35 days. Sleep quality improved with music-listening in almost all studies. Similarly, De Niet and colleagues (2009) conducted a meta-analysis with data from 170 adults, including older people, to evaluate the efficacy of music-assisted relaxation to improve sleep quality. Music had a moderate effect. In ongoing research, Lund and colleagues (2020) are trialling how music might help people with depression who suffer from insomnia by asking them to listen to music for a minimum of 30 minutes at bedtime for four weeks.

Music, Trauma and Abuse

Music therapists around the world work in a wide range of settings with those who are traumatised or abused (Pavlicevic and Ansdell, 2004). Music has been shown to be cost-effective and powerful in supporting sustainable community development, mental and physical health, and peace initiatives (Hesser and Heinemann, 2010). It can help to reduce symptoms and improve general functioning among those exposed to trauma (McFerran et al., 2020), acting as an adjunct to conventional therapy and promoting emotional regulation, increased pleasure and anxiety reduction. It can be particularly helpful when individuals struggle with the stigma associated with asking for professional help (Landis-Shack et al., 2017), or when cognitive behavioural therapy has had limited success. Rhythm may be particularly important in supporting recovery. Research in neurobiology has shown that rhythmic music has a specific impact on the brain. Therapy models using rhythm have been used since 2003 in centres for young people at risk, in refugee trauma centres, forensic psychiatric wards in prisons, and child and adult mental health services. Its benefits include increased levels of social integration, improvements in affect and mood stabilisation, reductions in anxiety and depression, and increases in self-esteem (Faulkner, 2017).

Post-Traumatic Stress Disorder

Post-traumatic stress disorder can be caused by a wide range of incidents, the most common following engagement in severe combat-related emotional trauma. Symptoms include distressing memory intrusions, avoidance, emotional disturbance and hyperarousal, and lead to a significantly reduced quality of life. In recent years, there has been increasing demand for music therapy services within military treatment facilities, partly due to the increased research output, but also the increased prevalence of injuries—including traumatic brain injury and post-traumatic stress disorder—for which interdisciplinary patient-centred care is required. The complexity of traumatic brain injury and post-traumatic stress in the context of military service presents particular challenges for music therapists as they try to develop effective interventions (Bronson et al., 2018). Pezzin and colleagues (2018) examined the feasibility and potential effectiveness of an active music-instruction intervention in improving psychological health and social functioning among veterans suffering from moderate to severe post-traumatic stress disorder. Sixty-eight veterans were self- or provider-referred to the programme. Participants were aged 22 to 76 years old, mainly male, African-American or black. Almost a third were in employment, while almost half were retired due to disability. The research assessed symptomatology, depression, perceptions of cognitive failure, social functioning, isolation and health-related quality of life. Participation led to a significant reduction in post-traumatic stress symptoms and depression, with a trend towards improvement in the other assessed areas. Carr and colleagues (2012) assessed whether group music therapy had an effect on post-traumatic stress disorder symptoms and depression in 17 patients who had already participated in cognitive behavioural therapy. Participants received ten weeks of group music therapy, following which there was a significant reduction in the severity of symptoms and a reduction in depression. Participants reported the group music therapy as helpful. Vaudreuil and colleagues (2020) used public performance to support the social transformation and reintegration of US military service members. Two case studies of service members who received music therapy as part of their treatment for post-traumatic stress disorder, brain injury and other psychological health concerns were presented. The participants wrote, learned and refined songs over a number of sessions, and created songs to perform to audiences. Interviews showed evidence of beneficial psychological effects of this procedure. Similarly, Bensimon and colleagues (2012) studied six soldiers who had been diagnosed as suffering from combat- or terror-related post-traumatic stress disorder, who participated in a series of 90-minute weekly sessions of music therapy. The sessions were filmed and in-depth interviews were undertaken with participants. Analysis of musical and verbal content revealed the importance of group engagement with issues related to trauma and non-trauma matters, decreasing reflection on traumatic emotions and increasing expressions of non-traumatic feelings. In a single case study of a 36-year-old army veteran, Wellman and Pinkerton (2015) described how a ten-week music therapy intervention enhanced motivation, decreased stress, anxiety and depression, and led to reported feelings of wholeness. Medication was reduced, which led to increased reengagement with previously enjoyed activities and enhanced quality of life following four years of medical disability and significant social phobias. The use of music for therapeutic purposes can also occur in more informal ways. For instance, one US soldier rapped about his experiences in Iraq to cope with the aftermath of his deployment there, while in Uganda, one young man constantly played a stringed instrument but was too traumatised to talk about his role as a resistance army commander (Bergh and Sloboda, 2010). Military sexual trauma is an issue for some returning veterans. Story and Beck (2017) studied five veteran women who participated in up to ten music and imagery sessions and a post-session focus group over the course of three months. Participants reported using music and imagery to manage and reduce their symptoms.

Civilians can also experience post-traumatic stress after being subject to combat events. Following the 2014 Israel Gaza conflict, Bensimon and colleagues (2017) examined the emotional effects of listening to happy and sad national songs on young and older adults and the relationship to exposure to missile attacks, post-traumatic stress symptoms and negative emotions. In young adults with low post-traumatic stress symptoms, sad national songs were related to higher negative emotions, whereas in older adults it was those with higher post-traumatic stress disorder symptoms that exhibited higher negative emotions in response to sad national songs.

Music, Asylum Seekers, Refugees and Survivors

Music therapists have become increasingly interested in the role of music in relation to war, peace, refugees and trauma (Akombo,, 2000; Edwards,, 2005; Hunt,, 2005; Kennedy,, 2001; Lopez,, 2008; Ng,, 2005). Following the attack on the USA in September 2001, many have been—and continue to be—traumatised by war, acts of terrorism and violence worldwide. Some music therapists have sought to respond actively to these events and the resulting trauma, by reaching out to trauma survivors.

Refugees have to move involuntarily from their country of residence, often having witnessed disasters, wars and the deaths of immediate family members prior to leaving. These traumatic situations provoke strong reactions and emotions. often exacerbated by challenging refugee-processing system,—for instance, detention and waiting in refugee camps—which make migration and resettlement processes for refugees and asylum-seekers much more challenging than for other migrants. The psychological effects of trauma experienced by refugees tend to be long-lasting. Multicultural arts programmes can allow for sensitivity to different identities, heritage and experience, and can be important in healing and promoting wellbeing (Gopalkrishnan, 2016). In refugee camps, the arts can support the preservation of religious identity through the celebration of festivals and events, help to alleviate psychosocial distress and trauma, and reduce stigmatisation.

Among children who have experienced trauma, including sexual abuse, terrorism, war and domestic violence, there have been promising findings for the value of the arts in supporting grief, depression and post-traumatic stress disorder, as well as supporting the communication of experiences (Andemicael, 2011). Clini and colleagues (2019) assessed the impact of arts interventions on forcibly displaced people, and identified several key issues concerning the perceived benefits of such programmes. The findings showed that participants reported the impact of creative activities in relation to skills, social engagement and personal emotions. Artistic and cultural activities impacted positively by helping participants to find a voice, creating support networks and providing opportunities to learn practical skills which were useful in gaining employment. In a review, Lenette and Sunderland (2016) mapped the potential for participatory music practices to support the health and wellbeing of asylum-seekers and refugees in three contexts: conflict settings, refugee camps and resettlement settings. The review highlighted the different roles that music could have in people's lives as they moved away from their home countries towards resettlement. Overall, they found that the growing body of research on music and wellbeing for asylum-seekers provided a strong foundation for investment in music as a key positive social and cultural determinant of health for this group of people. Music can reduce the symptoms of post-traumatic stress disorder through reducing anxiety and depressive symptoms, increasing pleasure, helping with emotional regulation, and supporting the building of communities and support networks, thus enhancing resilience, reducing stigma and improving general functioning (Sutton, 2002). This has been demonstrated in community arts projects in Sri Lanka following the civil war and the tsunami. The arts can help people to regain control of their lives (Huss et al., 2016).

Beck and colleagues (2018) researched the impact of guided imagery with music alongside standard medication with 16 adult refugees who completed 16 one-hour individual sessions. Pre- and post-measures of post-traumatic stress symptoms, sleep quality, wellbeing and social function demonstrated significant positive changes with large effect sizes. Evaluation of single sessions showed that participants found the therapy acceptable and helpful. All of the participants used music-listening for self-care in their homes between sessions and responded positively to the intervention overall. In Australia, Lenette and colleagues (2016) studied music facilitators who regularly attended an immigration transit accommodation facility to share music and singing activities with detained asylum-seekers, to ameliorate significant mental and emotional distress resulting from indefinite detention. Drawing on the facilitators' monthly written observations, a number of key themes emerged which linked music and singing to the health and wellbeing of detained asylum-seekers. Overall, it was clear that there was the potential for participatory music-making to counter the impact of traumatic experiences and detention on asylum-seekers' health and wellbeing. Similarly, Hesser and Heinemann (2010) provided examples of music projects which supported the social inclusion of refugees and others who had experienced severe trauma. The Rwandan Genocide of

1994 killed over a million people and led to enormous distress for those who survived. D'Ardenne and Kiyendeye (2015) used focus-group interviews with 13 survivors who participated in a music programme and found that the music had changed their past, given them a safe place in the present, fellowship and prayer, and provided them with the personal resources to face the future. Research looking at the lasting impact of trauma (for example, in Holocaust survivors after 70 years) has found higher levels of resilience among those who have engaged in the arts over the course of their lives relative to those who have not, suggesting the value of the arts both in the immediate aftermath of trauma and in the decades that follow (Diamond and Shrira, 2018).

There is also evidence that music can support victims of torture. Alanne (2010) studied three traumatised men from Central Africa, South Asia and the Middle East who lived as asylum-seekers or refugees in Finland. They received weekly or bimonthly music therapy sessions over one to two years as part of their rehabilitation, using projective listening, guided imagery and free association within a psychoanalytic frame of reference. Analysis of data from the sessions revealed that music therapy approaches were effective in promoting verbalisation as well as the regulation and expression of emotions. Participants responded positively and demonstrated some improvement, although with varying degrees of satisfaction. The therapy increased the consciousness of patients regarding their traumatic experiences, and was perceived as supporting calm and relaxation. The findings suggested that music psychotherapy methods may be effective in treating patients who are survivors of torture and related traumatic experiences. Music can support the healing of children who have been traumatised through war, those forced to fight, serve as spies, soldier wives or camp followers, and who are now refugees. Using their own cultural music and creative compositions can help young people to overcome their fears and challenges, promote healing and the development of self-esteem, trust and identity. Osborne (2012) provided examples of the way that music neuroscience can provide a means of evaluating the success of music therapy with traumatised children in post-conflict societies including North Uganda, Palestine and South Thailand. Felsenstein (2013) studied the impact of a short-term music therapy intervention on three groups of preschool children in the aftermath of a forced evacuation from their homes during the unilateral Israeli disengagement from the Gaza Strip in 2005, and the post-trauma treatment of the evacuees. The findings suggested that music could build post-trauma resilience and reduce the vulnerability of preschoolers to traumatic events, although community and family could also strengthen the way that individual children coped.

Several authors have documented the benefits of creative musical activity for children who have experienced war (Bergmann, 2002; Heidenrich, 2005; Osborne, 2009; Sutton, 2002) as a means of developing self-esteem, trust, identity and social cohesion in a range of countries including Bosnia-Herzegovina, Georgia, Sierra Leone, Rwanda and Palestine. These projects have enabled reflection and the expression of feelings. Some programmes supporting refugees or displaced young people in Sierra Leone, Ghana and Slovenia have included dance. These programmes supported the development of communication, empowered young people, gave them a sense of belonging and relief, and supported identity development (Harris, 2007; Jones et al., 2004; Lederach and Lederach, 2010; Pesek, 2009).

Zharinova-Sanderson (2004) reported work with traumatised refugees in Berlin at the Centre for the Treatment of Torture Victims. Music therapy in this context helped young people to use their own cultural music to adjust to their new culture, while performance opportunities allowed audience members to see beyond traumatised refugees to real people. In Sierra Leone, Gonsalves (2010) worked with traumatised young girls who had been forced to fight and serve as spies, soldier wives and camp followers. Through song, the girls communicated their emotional and material needs, histories, fears and current difficulties. Creative musical interaction supported increased understanding, reengagement and connections with others, and promoted healing, thus empowering the participants. In post-conflict Kosovo, Gerber and colleagues (2014) evaluated the work of a charity which aimed to promote a culture of peace and unity, as well as the development and recovery of children. Groups of non-participating students were compared with new programme participants, those participating for twelve months and those who had graduated from the programme. Overall, children who participated in the programme for at least one year had fewer emotional and cognitive problems than recently enrolled children. In Ireland, Kenny (2018) examined the musical lives of the children of asylum-seekers living in a state system of communal housing while they waited for their refugee applications to be processed. Data were collected through six participatory music workshops, video observations, a reflective log and focus-group interviews. Eleven children aged seven to twelve years old, of six different nationalities, participated. The findings revealed the importance and relevance of the contexts of music-making in temporary accommodation settings, as well as the broader national and international contexts for children living in asylum-seeking systems.

A review of 21 school- and community-based interventions for approximately 1800 refugee and asylum-seeking children, carried out in high-income countries or refugee camps, with a focus on verbal processing of past experiences or a range of creative arts activities, suggested that interventions delivered within the school setting could be successful in helping children overcome difficulties associated with forced migration. Feelings of powerlessness, humiliation and anger were reduced and social inclusion, mental health, social acceptance and belonging were enhanced (Tyrer and Fazel, 2014).

Music and Victims of Abuse

Child sexual exploitation is a major international problem and victims need to be rehabilitated and reintegrated into society. They can be supported through the creative arts. Schrader and Wendland (2012) described how music therapists working in Phnom Penh, Cambodia—in a centre that provided care for young girls rescued from sexual violence or commercial sexual exploitation—trained staff in the centre, teaching them to play instruments, participate in ensembles and lead large group music activities so that they could support the girls. Rogers (1992) highlighted a number of factors that appear to be common to sexually abused individuals, including the participants' manipulation of music therapy, the symbolic use of instruments, the preoccupation with mess and containers, the use of boundaries, and the power of secrets. Material from case studies illuminated these points.

In the USA, there are over five million crimes involving violence to partners annually. Victims experience a lifetime of increased risk for depression, anxiety, addiction, suicide attempts and post-traumatic stress disorder. Additionally, women's experience of abuse is a risk factor for incarceration. Palidofsky and Stolbach (2012) describe the therapeutic benefits to incarcerated adolescent girls of working collaboratively with theatre professionals to create, develop and perform musicals based on their own traumatic experiences. Similarly, Neupane and Taylor (2011) described how a gender-sensitive music intervention was able to facilitate healing and recovery in incarcerated abused women. Also working with victims of abuse, Slotoroff (1994) developed a technique in an inpatient short-term psychiatric setting using improvisational drumming and cognitive behavioural methods to address issues of power. A middle-aged woman and an eleven-year-old boy participated, and increased their sense of power and self-control, leading to long-term positive behavioural, cognitive and emotional changes. Flores and colleagues (2016) used African drumming to enhance the emotional and social wellbeing of 16 children in residential care, most of whom had been exposed to some form of neglect or abuse and displayed high levels of anger, anxiety, depression or disruptive behaviour. Participants attended weekly sessions of African djembe-drumming over a period of four months. The intervention did not appear to significantly impact the participants' long-term self-concept or levels of depression, anger or disruptive behaviour, while anxiety increased. Despite this, findings from interviews and observations suggested that the workshops did enhance the children's emotional and social functioning in terms of their self-esteem and self-confidence, prosocial behaviour, enjoyment, concentration and manifestation of musical capacity, even though these did not transfer to the children's everyday functioning. This may have been because of the severity of their socioemotional difficulties, as well as the limitations of the intervention itself. Hannigan and McBride (2011) investigated therapists' perspectives on the value of using drumming, along with other percussion instruments, as therapeutic tools in family violence treatment groups. Overall, drumming was perceived as useful in fostering group cohesion and cooperation, helping clients with a passive communication style become more involved in groupwork, facilitating emotional expression and offering participants a way to experience active relaxation and engagement in the group process.

Another approach to supporting trauma victims has been through song-writing. For instance, Fairchild and McFerran (2019) studied 15 children aged eight to fourteen years old who had experienced homelessness and family violence. Participants collaborated in writing a song about what music meant to them. Throughout the process of song-writing, the children described how music provided an escape from what was happening in their lives and offered hope for a better future. Similarly, Clendenon-Wallen (1991) studied 11 adolescents who had been sexually abused who participated in a music group where activities included song- or rap-writing, rhythm-playing, improvisation, lyric analysis and creative movement. The adolescents also designed record-album covers. The music-based activities increased participants' sense of self-worth and self-confidence. Not only did the music ease their anxiety, but it was also useful in the process of socialisation and verbalisation, and served as a starting point for discussing personal matters. Group improvisation also enhanced group cohesion and cooperation. Christenbury (2017) combined song-writing and art to promote healing in a child who had been traumatised. The child controlled the process, as the therapist composed songs in response to the child's drawings. Both related to the emotions that the child chose as being important for her healing. This increased self-esteem and provided a healthy emotional outlet. Also using song-writing, along with improvisational instrument-playing, lyric analysis and musical games where participants were asked to encode and decode various emotions, Graham (2011) determined the effects of music on the emotional expressivity of children and adolescents who had experienced abuse or neglect. All 22 participants had been removed from their homes and placed in group foster homes. The findings showed an increase in emotional expressivity and in the degree and appropriateness of the emotions expressed by participants.

Rudstam and colleagues (2017) employed group music and imagery with ten women who had been exposed to physical, psychological or sexual abuse—often with a history of childhood abuse and neglect—who were suffering from post-traumatic stress disorder. All participants completed the treatment, indicated that it was helpful and showed a decrease in post-traumatic stress and dissociative symptoms, alongside an increase in quality of life. These changes were maintained when the programme ended. Adopting a different approach, Strehlow (2009) focused on the use of analytical music therapy to treat sexually abused children, showing how an eight-year-old rebellious girl who had suppressed her feelings after being sexually abused by her mother's partner responded positively. Similarly, Sutton and De Backer (2009) drew on case material from work with a young boy and an adult attending a psychiatric outpatient department, to show how a form of musical listening and thinking could help to understand the issues faced by those who are traumatised.

Fairchild (2018) highlighted the creative resources that children experiencing homelessness and family violence can bring to research, as well as the range of resources that they can draw upon in the face of adversity. The research challenged the view of such children as being at risk, and explored their resources and what helped them to do well. Fairchild and colleagues (2017) used song-writing and interviews to collaborate with children, focusing on what music meant to them. Music offered an escape from the outside world and provided hope that the future would be better. The children described a range of support from friends, family, sport, pets, writing a journal and creativity. They wanted to feel safe and cared for, and protect themselves and others, and exhibited considerable self-determination. A collaborative article written with one 11-year-old revealed that he believed that learning to play the drums through music therapy had changed his life.

Music therapy has been used to support parenting. For instance, Day and colleagues (2009) reported the reflections of five women who had experienced childhood abuse as they participated in a group parenting programme that incorporated song-writing. Three years after completion of the programme, all participants reflected positively on the process of creating their songs, and most reported that they continued to engage with their song creations. Parents who have experienced childhood trauma often experience challenges when parenting an adolescent as this can trigger memories of abuse, which can intensify conflict, resulting in negative relationship cycles. Colegrove and colleagues (2018) devised a dyadic music therapy for parents and adolescents which increased responsive parent-adolescent interactions and parental emotion coaching, while reducing conflict and adolescent mental health difficulties.

Children who have been exposed to ongoing maltreatment and poverty frequently experience behaviour problems. In South Korea, Kim (2013) used music therapy for 15 weeks with four such children. There was a reduction in externalising and internalising behavioural problems overall, although there was considerable individual variation. In a later study, Kim (2017) showed that, although children in the music therapy group were less depressed, anxious and withdrawn, and had less attention problems than children in standard-care waiting groups, there were many confounding factors. The *El Sistema* programme, a large-scale community-based music programme which includes children exposed to violence, showed in research conducted in 16 music centres with 2914 children aged six to fourteen years old that participating children had improved self-control and reduced behavioural difficulties (Alemán et al., 2017).

Severe Mental Ill-Health

The following sections provide examples of the way that music can be used to support recovery from severe mental ill-health, providing supplementary support to traditional pharmacological and psychological approaches. For patients with psychosis, music therapy and music-listening have both been reported to improve symptoms of general psychopathology, psychoticism, aggressiveness and interpersonal hostility, paranoid ideation, phobic anxiety, somatisation, anxiety and depression, as well as catatonic symptoms such as lack of participation, cooperation, relaxation, interaction and psychosocial functioning (Silverman, 2003). However, not all of the research has confirmed these findings (Attard and Larkin, 2016). An interesting line of enquiry has focused on the use of music individually tailored to match patients' brain rhythms. For instance, Müller and colleagues (2014) examined whether long-term exposure of psychiatric patients to music that was individually adapted to brain rhythm disorders associated with psychoticism could act to ameliorate symptoms. A total of 50 patients with various psychiatric diagnoses were randomised to listen to CDs either containing music adapted to brain-rhythm anomalies associated with psychoticism as measured by specific spectral analysis, or standard classical music. Participants were instructed to listen to the CDs for 18 months. Psychiatric symptoms were assessed at the start of the intervention and at four, eight and eighteen months. Patients in the experimental group showed significantly decreased symptoms compared to control patients for psychoticism, paranoia, anxiety, phobic anxiety and somatisation. These changes may have resulted from the modulation of neurochemical interactions which improved brain function and enhanced neuroplasticity. Feng and colleagues (2019) explored whether music therapy could improve the brain function of patients with major depressive disorder using near-infrared spectroscopy. Fifteen mild or moderate major depressive disorder patients were compared with healthy controls, who were all treated with continuous music therapy for ten days. Verbal fluency task performance of the participants yielded significantly higher scores after music therapy. The near-infrared spectroscopy data showed increases in some channels which were significant for both groups. The major depressive disorder group showed significant activation in the dorsolateral prefrontal cortex, orbitofrontal cortex and ventromedial prefrontal cortex after music therapy, suggesting that the music therapy had been effective.

One strand of research has considered the impact of music on acute mental health. For instance, Silverman (2017) explored the effects of different levels of structure within educational music therapy interventions on knowledge of illness management, and recovery and affect in adult acute-care mental health inpatients. One hundred and fifteen participants were randomly assigned to either high- or low-structured educational music therapy or a waiting-list control. There were significant differences in relation to knowledge of illness management and recovery between the high-structure condition and the other groups. Overall, highly structured music therapy seemed to be best for efficiently and effectively imparting knowledge concerning illness management and recovery in acute mental health settings. Stefani and Biasutti (2016) studied the impact of group music therapy alongside drug care in comparison with drug care alone, in addition to other non-expressive group activities in the treatment of psychiatric outpatients. Twenty-seven patients with diagnoses of schizophrenia, schizoaffective disorders, bipolar affective disorder, depressive episode and specific personality disorders were allocated to receive group music therapy and standard care in 48 weekly sessions of two hours, or standard care only. Those participating in the group music therapy demonstrated improvement in neuroleptic drug dosage. Although antidepressant drug usage increased for both groups, the difference was only significant for the control group. Benzodiazepines and mood stabilisers showed no significant change in either group. Overall, group music therapy combined with standard drug care was effective for controlling neuroleptic drug dosage in adult psychiatric outpatients

Grocke and colleagues (2014) studied 99 individuals with severe mental illness who experienced weekly group music therapy, including singing familiar songs and composing original songs in a professional studio. Focus group interviews and lyric analyses, along with quantitative data, were collected at 13, 26 and 39 weeks. Music therapy improved the quality of life and self-esteem of participants, with those participating in a greater number of sessions experiencing the greatest benefits. Focusing on singing, Williams and colleagues (2018) reviewed 13 articles including 667 participants on the efficacy of group singing as a mental health intervention for individuals living with a mental health condition in a community setting. The findings showed that, when people with mental health conditions participated in a choir, their mental health and wellbeing significantly improved, with moderate to large effect sizes. Group singing provided enjoyment, improved emotional states, developed a sense of belonging and enhanced self-confidence. Working with young people in a youth mental health service in Australia, Hense and McFerran (2017) showed that promoting young people's musical identities could facilitate their recovery from mental illness.

Reviews of the evidence for the effectiveness of music therapy for those with psychopathology across a range of different age groups have had mixed findings. Silverman (2003) carried out a meta-analysis including 19 studies, and showed that music could effectively suppress and combat psychotic symptoms. There were no differences between live and recorded music, structured music therapy and passive listening, or between preferred versus therapist-selected music. However, classical music was less effective than popular music. Gold and colleagues (2004) reviewed the overall efficacy of music therapy for children and adolescents with psychopathology, and examined how the size of the effect of music therapy was influenced by the nature of the pathology, the client's age, the music therapy approach adopted, and the way that outcomes were assessed. Of the 11 studies included, with a total of 188 participants, music therapy had a medium to large positive effect on clinically relevant outcomes. The effects tended to be greater for behavioural and developmental disorders than for emotional disorders, social skills or self-concept, particularly when eclectic, psychodynamic or humanistic approaches, rather than behavioural models, were adopted. In a later review focusing on adults, Gold and colleagues (2009) found that music therapy, when supplementing standard care, had a strong and significant effect on global state, general and negative symptoms, depression, anxiety and general functioning. Small effect sizes were achieved after three to ten sessions, while 16 to 51 sessions were needed to achieve large effects. Overall, the findings suggested that music therapy was an effective treatment which could help people with psychotic and non-psychotic severe mental disorders to improve their functioning. In a review of 35 studies focusing on acute psychiatric disorders, Carr and colleagues (2013) found that drawing firm conclusions was limited by methodological shortcomings and small sample sizes. Studies with significant positive effects used active, structured musical participation and were delivered in four or more sessions. No clearly defined effective model emerged but greater frequency of therapy, actively structured music-making with verbal discussion, consistency of contact, clear boundaries and an emphasis on building a therapeutic relationship and building patient resources seemed to be of particular importance. Yinger and Gooding (2014) summarised the research on music therapy for children and adolescents, including disorders usually diagnosed in childhood (for instance, substance abuse, mood and anxiety difficulties, and eating disorders). They outlined a range of music therapy techniques and their strengths and weaknesses. Some research has considered how music might support those having electroconvulsive therapy. Graff and colleagues (2016) examined 30 patients' preferences for music prior to treatment. Most enjoyed listening to music through speakers or headphones, although 17 percent preferred no music. Gleadhill and Ferris (2010) developed a framework for evaluating the impact of music therapy on people with dissociative identity disorder. This debilitating disorder, acquired due to severe ongoing neglect or abuse, is characterised by the presence of two or more identities that frequently control the individual's behaviour. The framework suggested that symptom relief, destigmatisation, increased self-esteem and prevention of future abuse were important outcomes.

Eating Disorders

The role of music in ameliorating eating disorders has been examined in a number of studies and reviews. Free and structured improvisation, song-writing and listening to pre-composed music can all be used to help sufferers to address specific aspects of their eating disorder, including being able to recognise and tolerate their feelings, connect with others, and make links between thoughts, feelings and their body. Music can support the development of a sense of self and facilitate understanding of the symbolic functions of the illness. Robarts and Sloboda (1994) explored the process of music therapy in the treatment of people suffering from anorexia nervosa. Individual cases have illustrated the ways in which music therapy can support the individual while addressing frequently deeply rooted problems: for instance, issues with identity, negative self-image, distorted body image, autonomy, control, avoiding facing difficult emotions and difficulty in relationships. There is a relationship between listening to music for cathartic purposes and emotional eating. Van den Tol and colleagues (2018) argued that enjoyment of food and music share similar neural activations in the brain and are both used to regulate feelings. They investigated the associations between emotional eating, disordered mood and music-related mood regulation, and found associations with depression, anxiety and stress. Music-listening for releasing anger or sadness and emotional eating were positively associated. Other music-listening strategies—including entertainment, diversion or mental work—were associated in people who had low levels of disordered mood. High levels of disordered mood were associated with high levels of emotional eating but not with music-listening strategies. This suggests that some music-listening strategies might be able to be used as healthier alternatives to emotional eating. In a retrospective analysis of songs written by adolescents with anorexia nervosa, McFerran and colleagues (2006) revealed identity as the most common theme. Mealtime is an anxious time for people with anorexia, and music therapy has been used successfully to significantly reduce post-meal-related anxiety (Bibb et al., 2015).

Addiction

Chronic drug abuse leads to a dopamine-deficient state in the mesolimbic system, causing dysphoria in abstinence, leading to craving and, subsequently, a return to drug use. Functional imaging studies have shown that listening to personally pleasing music activates the mesolimbic reward system in a fashion similar to that of drug abuse. Such activation could therefore ameliorate dysphoria and the craving of the hypodopaminergic state. Mathis and Han (2017) found that listening to personally pleasing or moving music could reduce craving in abstinent alcoholics. Twelve participants with alcohol-use disorder in a residential substance rehabilitation unit reported on their level of craving before and after listening to either a participant-selected song or white noise. The music intervention had a significant advantage in reducing craving compared to noise. Other studies on addiction have reported that music therapy can improve perceived control, thus reducing cravings. Silverman (2011) researched the effect of music therapy on readiness to change and craving in patients in a detoxification unit. One hundred and forty-one participants were allocated to a rockumentary music therapy intervention, verbal therapy or a recreational music therapy condition. There were significant differences between groups in readiness to change, contemplation and action, with participants in both music conditions having higher scores than those in the verbal therapy condition. They also tended to have lower mean craving scores, and perceived the intervention as helpful and enjoyable.

Group music-making activities such as choirs can enhance social connections and provide a positive diversion for people overcoming addiction. For instance, Liebowitz and colleagues (2015) investigated how participation in a music-based performance and instruction programme influenced the sense of engagement experienced by participants in a residential setting for at-risk veterans. Participants had opportunities to connect with others through shared interests, and the connections forged with other residents extended beyond relationships established in the choir through increased recognition associated with performances. The choir provided a diversion from other concerns and may have served as a means of facilitating adjustment to change at a measured speed.

Reviews of the impact of music therapy in relation to addiction report a lack of consistency in research outcomes (Hohmann et al., 2017; Mays et al., 2008). A scoping review of 3697 articles on the impact of music in the lives of young adult drug users found that they valued music for meeting emotional, psychological and social needs, particularly when they were homeless. However, the research included in the review was limited to considering the harmful consequences of music rather than considering potential benefits (Lemaire et al., 2021).

Obsessive-Compulsive Disorder and Social Anxiety Disorder

Music can play a role in ameliorating the symptoms of obsessive-compulsive disorder alongside pharmacotherapy and cognitive behavioural therapy. In Iraq, Abdulah and colleagues (2018) evaluated the impact of passive music-listening as an adjunct therapy with 36 patients aged from 19 to 65 years old. The experimental group received seven 50-minute relaxing music tracks to listen to daily, in addition to regular pharmacological treatment for a three-month period. Controls received regular treatment only. The findings showed improvement in the severity of the behaviours for the experimental group. Similarly, Shiranibidabadi and Mehryar (2015) randomly assigned 30 patients with obsessive-compulsive disorder to standard treatment, pharmacotherapy and cognitive behaviour therapy, in addition to 12 sessions of individual music therapy or standard treatment for one month. Music therapy resulted in a greater decrease in checking and slowness but not for washing or responsibility. Overall, music therapy as an adjunct to standard care was effective in reducing obsessions, as well as comorbid anxiety and depressive symptoms.

Listening to music has been found to reduce time spent dwelling on threats in people experiencing social anxiety disorder. Lazarov and colleagues (2017) examined the efficacy of a gaze-contingent music reward therapy for social anxiety disorder, designed to reduce the extent of dwelling on threats. Forty patients were randomly assigned to eight sessions of either gaze-contingent music reward therapy (designed to divert patients' gaze toward neutral stimuli rather than threat stimuli) or to a control condition. The music therapy yielded greater reductions in symptoms than the control condition. These effects were maintained after the intervention, which also revealed reduced time spent dwelling on threats and socially threatening faces which had not been used in training, suggesting that the outcomes transferred to other situations.

Schizophrenia

Music therapy can reduce some of the symptoms of mild schizophrenia, including hostility, hallucinations, suspiciousness, emotional withdrawal, poor rapport and difficulty in abstract thinking. Compared with controls, those with schizophrenia receiving adjunct music therapy have shown improvement regardless of the duration, frequency or number of therapy sessions (Tseng et al., 2016). In a review of 18 studies with a total of 1,215 participants, undertaken during 7 to 240 sessions, Geretsegger and colleagues (2017) showed that in the medium term, there were positive effects for adjunct music therapy on a range of negative symptoms, social functioning and quality of life, although the effects were inconsistent across studies and depended on the number of sessions and the quality of the therapy. Working in a hospital emergency psychiatric ward with 61 patients with psychosis, Volpe and colleagues (2018) found that structured music therapy led to a decrease in anxiety, depression and affective symptoms.

Liao and colleagues (2020) explored the factors which were important for the effectiveness of group singing when social robots interacted with individuals with schizophrenia. Nine participants aged 28 to 62 years old participated in four group singing therapy sessions provided by a social robot and an occupational therapist. Group cohesiveness, universality and altruism were the most important factors related to the efficacy of the programme. Similarly, Odell-Miller (2016) considered how music therapists could use the music created by patients to better understand their emotions and how they interacted with others.

Music Therapy for Those with Autistic Spectrum Disorder or Severe Learning Difficulties

Music therapists have worked with children on the autistic spectrum disorder for many years, typically as a means to improve verbal and non-verbal communication. Music can be particularly effective in supporting the development of communication, as in itself it is a kind of language (Ockelford, 2012). Using functional magnetic resonance imaging, Sharda and colleagues (2015) showed that those with autistic spectrum disorder had alternate mechanisms for speech and music processing, and established that song could overcome the structural deficit for speech. In a later study, Sharda and colleagues (2018) evaluated the neurobehavioural outcomes of an eight- to twelve-week music intervention with 51 autistic children aged six to twelve years old. Song and rhythm improvisation improved communication and the resting state brain functional connectivity between auditory and subcortical regions and auditory and frontomotor regions, although connectivity was lower between the auditory and visual regions, areas known to be overconnected in those with autistic spectrum disorder.

Some children with autistic spectrum disorder excel at creative activities, particularly music, having superior memory for pitch and timbre and a high-level capacity for processing melodic and rhythmic complexity (Janzen and Thaut, 2018). A survey of adults with autistic spectrum disorder studied their special interests, the intensity of and motivation for those interests, and their impact on quality of life. Approximately two thirds of the sample reported having a special interest, including computers, music, nature and gardening. Most engaged with more than one. Having such interests was associated with enhanced wellbeing, including social contact and leisure. However, very high intensity of engagement with special interests was negatively related to wellbeing (Grove et al., 2018). Even those on the autistic spectrum without special musical skills can benefit from music therapy as a means of enhancing social interaction, sensory perception, language and eye contact (LaGasse, 2017). Musically enriched interactions can reduce anxiety and aggressive behaviour and improve listening, attention span and social interaction (Campbell, 2010), while auditory motor rhythmic training can improve language acquisition and processing, as well as speech control (Janzen and Thaut, 2018). However, not all interventions have successful long-term outcomes. For instance, Dvir and colleagues (2020) videoed the synchrony of body rhythms between four-to-six-year-old children with autistic spectrum disorder and their music therapists over a 20-week period. Higher levels of synchrony were found when repetitive rhythmicity that occurred twice or more times per second was used, but there was no long-term impact.

Although individuals with autistic spectrum disorder commonly have deficits in processing complex emotional cues, the ability to identify the emotional content of music is generally preserved. In Sweden, Theorell and colleagues (2014) established that playing a musical instrument, particularly in an ensemble, was associated with higher emotional competence. There is further support for this from a review conducted by Molnar-Szakacs and Heaton (2012), who pointed out that many individuals with autistic spectrum disorder showed an early preference for music and were able to understand simple and complex musical emotions in childhood and adulthood, despite the difficulties that they experienced with communication and understanding of emotions within the social domain. One study has even suggested that antenatal music training and maternal talk could reduce the risk of children developing autistic-like behaviours. In China, a study of 34,749 parents of kindergarten children completed questionnaires which revealed that antenatal music training and maternal talk to the foetus was associated with a reduction in autistic-like behaviours (Ruan et al., 2018). Parent-child integrated music activities can support the relationships between children with autistic spectrum disorder and their parents or caregivers (Lense et al., 2020), as can music-based parent coaching (Hernandez-Ruiz, 2020), while musical activities which include children with autistic spectrum disorder can reduce their being victimised by neurotypical peers (Cook et al., 2018).

Some research has considered how music might help children with learning difficulties more broadly. For instance, Mendelson and colleagues (2016) studied a classroom-based music intervention for improving communication skills in children with autistic spectrum disorder or other intellectual disabilities in four elementary school special education classrooms. The findings showed that 45-minute weekly music therapy sessions promoted improvements in verbal responsiveness. Working with young adults with severe learning difficulties, Pavlicevic and colleagues (2014) found that long-term music-making provided them with ongoing opportunities for gaining confidence and enhancing self-esteem, with feelings of shared acceptance and success. In a case study of an individual with profound learning difficulties, McFerran and Shoemark (2013) found that the success of the therapy lay in a combination of attentive, responsive and creative behaviour over time, with the music therapist listening and taking responsibility for the structure of the activities, and the young person spontaneously initiating activities—withboth participants building a relationship over time. Biological markers of stress have also shown a reduction following music therapy in individuals with intellectual disabilities and autistic spectrum disorder (Poquérusse et al., 2018). Community music activities can also benefit those with mild to profound learning difficulties, increasing their self-confidence and enabling wider recognition of their musicality (Wilson and MacDonald, 2019).

Reviews of the impact of music on individuals with autistic spectrum disorder have generally shown positive outcomes, including improved non-verbal and verbal communication, motor development, coordination, body awareness, sensory perception, social emotional reciprocity and a wide range of social skills (Geretsegger et al., 2014; Janzen and Thaut, 2018; Shi et al., 2016; Srinivasan and Bhat, 2013; Vaiouli and Andreou, 2018). In addition to the impact on these functions, De Vries and colleagues (2015) showed that music reduced anxiety and improved cognitive skills, attention to task, enhanced body awareness, self-care skills, and the expression, recognition, understanding and processing of emotions. Ragone and colleagues (2021), focusing on the use of technology with children with autistic spectrum disorder, showed a relationship between sound-based activities and improvement of motor and social skills. The reviews all point out the limitations of the research, particularly in terms of the small sample sizes and variation in the kinds of therapy and outcome measures, while still acknowledging the benefits. In contrast, Simpson and Keen (2011) gave limited support for the use of song-writing or improvisational therapy to facilitate social, communicative and behavioural skills in young children with autism spectrum disorder. Music has been successful in increasing exercise intensity and important in reducing the risk of obesity, sleep disorders and stereotypical behaviours common in children with autism spectrum disorder, although the effects are mediated by the extent to which the exercise is structured, the nature of the music and the characteristics of the child (Woodman et al., 2018).

Some research has focused on the nature of effective music teaching for children with a range of learning difficulties and autism. Gerrity and colleagues (2013) showed that the use of repetition, giving students choice and allowing for longer response time were important teaching strategies, while children themselves found it important to have clear directions and expectations, a behaviour plan, and fostering a positive atmosphere that was free of distractions. Thompson and colleagues (2020) gathered the perspectives of autistic individuals aged 18 to 25 years old to inform the design of music-making workshops using an online survey and structured interviews, and showed that participants expected a welcoming atmosphere and an acceptance of diversity.

Overview

Psychological wellbeing and physical health are closely linked. The former can enhance recovery from illness and limit its occurrence, while stress and anxiety can contribute to ill health. Music can enhance wellbeing, but equally it can contribute negatively to psychological health (if depressing or aggressive music is listened to constantly, particularly in the presence of others). Music-making in ensembles activates many regions of the brain, enhancing the connections between them, while listening to music—which constitutes an aspect of making music—impacts on brain regions associated with arousal, the emotions, reward and pleasure. The rhythmic aspects of music impact on movement, while whether music is slow, fast, quiet or loud affects arousal, mood and emotion. Musical preferences have a major influence on whether music therapy is effective. In these different ways, music can influence mental and physical health positively or negatively. In addition to the direct effects of music, therapy interventions typically involve interactions with other people, the therapist and other participants. The social interactions involved in music-making and listening with others are important in the impact of music on mental and physical health, and can be more or less positive. The therapist or facilitator and the approaches that they adopt are also important mediators. It is not possible for research to untangle the differential impact of music itself and the social interactions with others that may accompany it. Overall, predicting the outcome of any musical intervention on mental or physical health is complex because of the interaction of these factors. This complexity can also account for the different research outcomes.

16. Music, Inclusion and Social Cohesion

Music has a wide range of functions. These were set out in detail in Chapter 1. One of the most important functions is the role of actively making music in encouraging social bonding. This function has been argued to have an evolutionary basis (Huron, 2001). Harvey (2018) suggests that music and music-related behaviours, along with language and speech, were important for early evolution in helping to promote emotional synergy and social bonding, and foster group-level cooperation and coordination. Savage and colleagues (2020) argue that the evolution of musicality involved gene and cultural coevolution, where proto-musical behaviours that began as cultural inventions had effects on biological evolution through their impact on social bonding. Repetition, synchronisation and the combination of harmony, rhythm and pitch provided social rewards through linking brain networks, physiological systems and behaviours. Cross (2003) argues that music may be particularly suited for supporting social bonding, as it is generally free of risk and its meaning can be interpreted in different ways, allowing humans to interact and share experiences, even though each participating individual may have different perspectives, goals and relationships. Music can promote survival through the way it synchronises the moods of many individuals, who can then collectively take action to protect and defend themselves from attack (Dowling and Harwood, 1986). Moving together rhythmically seems to reinforce this process (Hove and Risen, 2009; Kogan, 1997; Trainor, 2014). Further support for the role of music in social bonding is the fact that music occurs in every human culture and subculture, unless it is deliberately suppressed. It is the most universal human behaviour on record (Merker et al., 2015). Mehr and colleagues (2020) support the evolutionary role of music in relation to coalitional interactions, but also emphasise its importance in infant care.

Humans, as a species, face considerable challenges compared with primates as to how to maintain social bonds with groups much larger than those of primates. Music might provide a way of achieving this (Freeman, 2000). Rhythmic activities induced by drum beats or music can lead to altered states of consciousness, through which mutual trust among members of societies can be engendered. This proposition has been supported by empirical research. For instance, Weinstein and colleagues (2016) recruited individuals from a community choir that met in small groups (20 to 80 people) and large groups (232 people). Feelings of inclusion, connectivity and positive affect increased after each 90-minute singing rehearsal in the small choir, but greater increases were reported for those in the large choir, suggesting that singing together fosters social closeness—even in large group contexts where individuals are not known to each other. Similarly, Pearce and colleagues (2015) followed newly-formed singing and non-singing adult education classes over a period of seven months. Participants rated their closeness to their group before and after classes at three timepoints: one, three and seven months. Singers and non-singers felt equally connected after seven months, but much faster bonding occurred in the singing group after only one month. Singing may have evolved specifically to bond together large human groups of relative strangers quickly, their willingness to coordinate with others supported by the way that music generates positive emotions.

All group music-making involves a strong element of sociability (Finnegan, 1989). The links between music, social bonding (Cross, 2009; Hagen and Bryant, 2003) and emotion (Juslin and Sloboda, 2001) may explain why group music-making enhances wellbeing. Sloboda (1985) suggests that music-making is rewarding, in part because it generates social bonding and cultural coherence. Its role in a range of ceremonies supports this (Roederer, 1984). Social networks developed through music-making support group identity, collective thinking, collaborative learning, friendship, social support, a sense of belonging, synchronisation, catharsis, and the collective expression and experience of emotion (Brown, 1991; Faulkner and Davidson, 2004; Coffman, 2002; Creech et al., 2013a; Lehmberg and Fung, 2010). In a recent example, Arditi (2020) suggests that when musicians in popular bands perceive their performance identity as linked to the identity of the band, the group has greater solidarity and is more likely to remain together. While music can support the formation and maintenance of group identity, and promote cooperative behaviour, conversely it can create the potential for hostility towards outgroups. For children and young people, group music-making offers the opportunity to engage in wide cultural experiences, explore new ideas, places and perspectives, and support social cohesion (Israel, 2012). This not only benefits participants but also increases the involvement of parents and carers, and their attendance at cultural events and exposure to culture more generally (Creech et al., 2013).

The biological underpinnings of social bonding in primates involve endorphins and the endogenous opioid system. These are released during synchronised exertion (Tarr et al, 2014) and are associated with several human behaviours, including laughing and synchronised sports, as well as singing and dancing. Passively listening to music also engages the endogenous opioid system. Identifying self as part of a group, combined with the activity of the endogenous opioid system, may be important in the way that music promotes social bonding. Endorphins are released during synchronised movements which also have an effect on social bonding, social behaviours and oxytocin levels (Weinstein et al., 2016). Kreutz (2014), studying the psychobiological effects of amateur choral singing in comparison with dyads chatting to each other, showed patterns of change favouring singing over chatting, suggesting that singing enhanced individual psychological wellbeing, as well as inducing a sociobiological response. Similarly, Grape and colleagues (2003) observed significant increases of oxytocin—which plays a fundamental role in social behaviours—in both professional and amateur singers after a singing lesson.

Participating in musical groups requires attention to be paid to the actions and intentions of other group members and their physical and emotional states, in addition to being able to communicate emotions and respond to those of others (Cross et al., 2012). Group music-making promotes the activity of neural networks that connect areas of the brain associated with social cognition and music production (Sanger et al., 2012). This is key to the development of empathy. Musical participation can enhance empathy in children (Rabinowitch et al., 2013) and may also increase emotional sensitivity (Resnicow et al., 2004). In young people, music preferences can indicate similar or different values, with similarity contributing to social attraction, explaining how musical bonding can occur in a range of different cultures (Boer et al., 2011).

Human interactions sometimes require that behaviour is coordinated (Keller et al., 2014). Such synchrony promotes positive social behaviour. For instance, infants who were bounced in synchrony with an experimenter were subsequently more likely to help the experimenter when they dropped objects which were needed to complete a task than those bounced out of synchrony (Trainor and Cirelli, 2015). The pleasure of performing in temporal synchrony with others may also have wide-ranging consequences for wellbeing and overall functioning (McNeill, 1995). For instance, Hove and Risen (2009) showed that degree of synchrony in tapping tasks predicted subsequent affiliation ratings.

One of the most frequently cited benefits of group music-making is its impact on prosocial behaviour. Young children have shown enhanced cooperation and helpful behaviour in musical as opposed to non-musical conditions (Kirschner and Tomasello, 2009; 2010). The *El Sistema* programme and projects inspired by it facilitate prosocial behaviour (Creech et al., 2013; 2016). Intensive ensemble activities are seen as providing opportunities for nurturing positive citizenship, including respect, equality, sharing, cohesion, teamwork, and the enhancement of listening skills as an important element in promoting understanding and cooperation (Majno, 2012). Research in the USA has shown that involvement in group music activities in high school helps individuals learn to support each other, maintain commitment and bond together to achieve group goals (Sward, 1989). Band participation has positive benefits on maturing relationships, teamwork, cooperation, sense of belonging, companionship and social development (Brown, 1980). In adolescence and young adulthood, music-listening in families and peer groups contributes to family and peer cohesion. This applies across a range of cultures including Kenya, the Philippines, New Zealand and Germany (Boer and Abubakar, 2014). In a large study of 30,476 people in the UK, Van de Vyver and Abrams (2018) found that greater engagement with the arts, including musical activities, predicted greater prosociality, volunteering and charitable giving.

Joint music-making provides opportunities for developing skills relating to citizenship. It can encourage tolerance and the development of social ethics, increase acceptance of children with intellectual impairments (Humpal, 1991; Jellison et al., 1984) and enhance concern with wider community issues (Miksza, 2010). Wiltermutt and Heath (2009) showed that students in the USA scored higher on a coordination exercise and a public-good game after singing along with a song played on headphones compared to no singing or forced asynchronous singing. Music-making can also be used to teach leadership skills to children in primary and secondary schools (Hallam, 2017), where they learn to communicate verbally and musically with other children.

Music and Conflict

There can be no greater illustration of the power of music than its role in conflict situations. The relationship between music and conflict is complex. Music has not always been used to promote peace. It can be—and has been used by—those who desire to create or maintain conflict. Bergh and Sloboda (2010), in a review of the literature, outlined the ways in which music can support conflict. They give examples of how music has been used to support preparations for war. For instance, in Nazi Germany, music was used to accompany large rallies, with the purpose of developing a sense of cohesion (Reinert, 1997). In Croatia, music was used to develop nationalist feelings before the start of the war (Pettan, 1998), while Serbians used folk music to bolster the concept of Serbian uniqueness (Hudson, 2003; Bohlman, 2003). Similarly, Albanians used music videos to attempt to create a national identity in preparation for war (Sugarman, 2006). For centuries, music has been used to support militia as they face battle, drums offering rhythm to support marching together, while drums, bugles and bagpipes have been used to bolster courage (McNeill, 1995). More recently, in Iraq, American soldiers played loud, aggressive music while engaging in dangerous activities (Gittoes, 2006). In some countries, music has been used to promote revolution. Songs can be used as calls for action. For instance, congregational music represents solidarity and a sense of collective identity in the civil rights movement (Ward, 1998). Boulanger Martel (2020), drawing on data relating to the production of music between 1988 to 2019 of the Fuerzas

Armadas Revolucionarias de Colombia, argued that cultural production was employed to bolster rebel-group legitimacy: internally by justifying the existing hierarchical relationships between leaders and fighters, and externally by identifying the rebel group as a legitimate alternative to the existing establishment and a rightful representative of the people.

Typically, in conflict situations, music is employed with multiple purposes. For instance, in the 2nd World War, in the ghettos and concentration camps, music played a complex role in daily life. It was used to help to alleviate distress among those who were incarcerated (Gilbert, 2005) but at the same time to intimidate and demonstrate power (Pettan, 1998). Moreno (1999) reviewed the meaning and sometimes therapeutic role of music for victims and perpetrators during the Holocaust, demonstrating the importance of music in times of stress. Music was used for humiliation and torment. Musical censorship was applied and music was used for deception, distraction and masking. The prisoner orchestras demonstrate how musically induced humane feelings were separated out, with sentiment and nostalgia coexisting alongside denial and indifference to the way that others were suffering.

Recently, loud noise and music have been used as a means of torture, to challenge beliefs (Cloonan and Johnson, 2002), or to torment and humiliate prisoners of war (Cusick, 2006). Bayoumi (2005) reported how detainees have been subjected to music at high volume which has been designed to destroy their minds. In Guantánamo Bay, Eminem, Britney Spears, Limp Bizkit, Rage Against the Machine, Metallica and Bruce Springsteen have been played at excessive volume for long periods of time. Detainees indicated that music was used as a weapon designed to deprive them of sleep, cause overstimulation and be psychologically intolerable.

In contrast to promoting conflict and causing distress, music has been used over many years in attempts to resolve conflict and support peace. For instance, the Buwaya Kalingga people established peace pacts that were consolidated through feasts and the use of specific songs (Prudente, 1984). Bergh and Sloboda (2010), in a review, point out that since the early 1990s there has been increasing use of music and arts to reduce conflict. In the Balkans and between Israel and Palestine, music and the arts have frequently been used in mediation efforts. In the Sudan, music was used as a meeting place between 29 different ethnic groups who had been displaced as a result of the 22-year civil war (Bergh, 2007). Other initiatives have included the recording of joint Israeli-Palestinian CDs, music therapy with children (Ng, 2005) and brass-band performances for children from different ethnic groups (Veledar, 2008). Bornstein (2008) has researched artistic and religious contributions to peace building in Indonesia, while music and poetry have been used to attempt to resolve conflict in Cyprus (Ungerleider, 1999) and elsewhere (Epskamp, 1999). Bang (2016), in a review of the literature, investigated how artistic engagement could facilitate transformative learning and the development of skills and capacities for more constructive engagement with conflict, fostering new perspectives and, ultimately, cooperative relationships. Zelizer (2003; 2004), working in Bosnia, Herzegovina, focused on the process of artistic interventions, suggesting that conflict could be resolved by expanding the identity of participants beyond current group identities. Also focusing on process, Weaver (2001) argued that reconciliation between parties in conflict should be viewed as a creative process, while Zelizer (2003; 2004) suggested that changing emotions, not rational thought, was necessary to achieve reconciliation after civil war.

Much of the research on conflict reduction has been criticised because outcomes have been based on the perceptions of those organising the programmes and the musicians delivering them, rather than the participants (Cohen, 2005a). This may have distorted the reported effectiveness of programmes. For instance, Fock (2004) found that teachers in a Danish multicultural music project were more cautious when reporting change in pupils than they were in responses given in questionnaires which had to be returned to the organisers. Cohen (2005a) suggested that, to be effective, projects should connect with other conflict resolution interventions and take greater account of the context. Lederach (2005) also considered how artists could contribute to peacebuilding, while in a review (but also using empirical data collected from conflict transformation projects in Sudan and Norway—Bergh, 2007; Bergh, 2008; Bergh, 2011), Bergh and Sloboda (2010) concluded that most interventions were ineffective in the long term because they did not relate to participants' daily lives. It seems that, to be effective and make sustainable changes, programmes need to take place over many years. Some multicultural projects, where music from other cultures is shared, can emphasise differences between groups rather than the similarities. This can exacerbate the issues which the programme intended to address. The imbalance in power between organisers, those delivering the programme and participants can also be a problem in establishing efficacy (Zelizer, 2004). Haskell (2005) suggests that issues of power and control need to be taken into account in all interventions, as weaker parties may agree to avoid future negative consequences. Academic research in this area has been criticised for sometimes having too great an emphasis on theory rather than practice (Robertson, 2006). Despite these difficulties, there continue to be discussions about how music might help in supporting the resolution of conflict (Lopez, 2008; Urbain, 2007). As considered in Chapter 15, there has been increasing interest from music therapists in developing interventions to support those traumatised by conflict (Edwards, 2005; Ng, 2005).

Some research has focused on the relationship between social cohesion and patriotism. Hamzah and colleagues (2021) studied the impact of music in Malaysia, which became independent in 1957. The national anthem and patriotic songs were mobilised by the state to foster a sense of national cohesion and collective identity. These songs were popular and accepted by Malaysian citizens from diverse backgrounds as a part of their national identity. This was supported by their repetition on national radio, television and social media platforms. Group discussions were conducted and revealed that patriotic songs, rather than commercial popular songs, were more popular and wide-reaching in appeal across different professions, ethnicities, religions and geographic locations. Patriotic music provided a means for social cohesion through the personal, intimate and affective associations that such songs solicited from individual citizens. Johan (2020)—drawing on cases of intercultural intimacy found in the production, performance and studio recordings of Malaysian artists and groups—revealed how Malaysian popular music, specifically from the stage of maturing nationhood during the 1970s and 1980s, provided an important means of intercultural cohesion among citizens from a range of ethnicities, religions and social classes. It offered intimate, creative expression that facilitated the process of everyday social cohesion.

In the same way that music can be used to promote conflict, it can also be used to increase prejudice. For instance, Corte and Edwards

(2008) researched the use of punk music by white power activists. At the end of the 1970s, a racist rock music movement known as White Power music emerged in Great Britain connected to political parties of the extreme right. Throughout the 1990s, it expanded significantly into a multi-million-dollar international enterprise, promoting White Power musicians performing in a wide range of musical genres. The music had a particular role in recruiting new adherents, especially young people. The authors concluded that White Power music continued to play a significant role in the mobilisation of racist political and social movements by drawing in new recruits, cultivating a racist collective identity, and generating substantial sums of money to finance a range of racist endeavours. In contrast, Roberts (2009) provided examples of punk involvement in left-wing social movements, including the Rock Against Racism movement in the UK and the Peace movement in the US. The punk ethic of independent media construction at the centre of the punk movement made it possible for punks to make connections to various social movements, in addition to altering the dynamics of those social movements. Eyerman (2002), drawing on research on the Civil Rights movement in the United States, the memory of slavery in the formation of African-American identity and the place of white-power music in contemporary neo-fascist movements, outlined how music can act as a political mediator.

Some research has focused specifically on using music to reduce prejudice. For instance, in Northern Ireland, Odena (2010) studied the perceptions of 14 practitioners engaged in musical activities in cross-community settings, working with Protestant and Catholic groups. Interview data showed that cross-community music education projects were an effective means of addressing prejudice amongst young people, but the specific contexts of each setting put limits on what could be achieved. Similarly, folk songs have been used in Israel to bring Palestinian and Jewish children and their families together during cross-community school visits (Lichman, 2006; Lichman and Sullivan, 2000). Songs promoting social inclusion can reduce prejudice, discrimination and aggression between groups and promote cultural understanding. For instance, Greitemeyer and Schwab (2014), in a series of experiments, showed that participants who had listened to songs with pro-integration relative to neutral lyrics expressed less prejudice and were less aggressive and more helpful towards an outgroup member. These effects were unaffected by liking the song or the mood and arousal properties of the songs employed, suggesting that it was the pro-integration content of the lyrics that achieved the effects. Clarke and colleagues (2015) reported the outcome of an empirical study demonstrating that passive listening to music of an unfamiliar culture could significantly change the cultural attitudes of listeners who had high levels of empathy. Research in other areas relating to the way that music can bring about change has shown that sustainable change tends to occur where participation is active and involves participants in the regular use of musical skills over a period of months as opposed to days (Spychiger et al., 1993; Harland et al., 2000).

Music and Refugees

For many years, Australia has been one of the most multicultural countries in the world, although globalisation increased the number of people arriving from countries with vastly different backgrounds, experiences, ideologies, values and belief systems. Gifford and colleagues (2009) carried out a longitudinal study to explore the experiences of 120 newly arrived young people with refugee backgrounds. In their first year at a school focused on developing their English language skills, with the exception of instances of teasing and bullying, their experience was positive, but on transition to mainstream school they felt that they had inadequate English language skills to engage fully with educational requirements. They felt less supported by teachers, their academic work declined, as did their feelings of belonging and safety, and there was a significant increase in experiences of discrimination. Most did not complete secondary education, instead seeking further technical training or employment. Many were not part of an intact family, and family instability was a feature of their lives, with family support weakening over time. This may be why they valued their wider ethnic community. Most experienced discrimination or violence because of their ethnicity, religion or colour. Despite their often traumatic lives prior to arrival, they exhibited considerable personal strengths, but nevertheless faced many challenges. This, coupled with the burdens shouldered by their families, had an impact on their ability to reach their full potential in the early years of settlement in Australia. Perhaps because of the large number of immigrants, there has been considerable research in Australia about the possible impact of music in supporting their integration. For young children, playground games provide a mechanism through which they can be included in the school environment while retaining connections with their home cultures (Marsh and Dieckmann, 2016; 2017). Marsh (2016) explored how music participation, specifically participation in musical play, could contribute to the wellbeing of newly-arrived refugee and migrant children, providing new musical and social beginnings. Specific reference was made to children from Iraq, South Sudan and Sierra Leone in Australia, Punjabi children in the UK and newly arrived Central and South American immigrants in the USA. In a school catering for newly-arrived immigrants, music was used to support acculturation and integration (Marsh, 2012a; 2012b). Young people aged 12 to 18 years old participated in musical activities designed to provide opportunities for cultural maintenance, cross-cultural transmission and verbal and non-verbal communication, with a view to developing interpersonal connections, social cohesion and empowerment through varied learning, teaching and performance opportunities. Participation in performance in a major school concert was important in achieving these aims. The key outcomes for students included feelings of belonging to the school community, the wider Australian community, as well as to a global music community, reached through various technological media (Marsh, 2012a; 2012b). Marsh (2015) focused on the collaborative music and dance activities of a Sierra Leone youth group attending an intensive English language centre for newly arrived students. For these marginalised young people, the music and dance activities, conceived within a socially just framework, provided opportunities for participatory parity, cultural justice and social inclusion within communities from both the home and host cultures.

Also in Australia, Crawford (2017; 2019) reported the findings of a case study that investigated the impact of music education on students in a school in Victoria. Music education was used as a vehicle to engage young people with a refugee background. The findings indicated that classroom music which fostered socially inclusive practices resulted in a positive transcultural learning space, which supported young refugees, fostering a sense of wellbeing and belonging and an enhanced engagement with learning. While some of these benefits were not always clearly distinguished from the more general experience of school, the students did identify some elements of music-learning and teaching that they linked to these outcomes. In a multiple case study of three schools in Victoria, Crawford (2020) explored the perceptions, experiences and practices of teachers directly or indirectly involved with music education in schools that had a high percentage of young people with a refugee background. Intercultural competence and socially inclusive behaviours were seamlessly embedded in the music learning activities on offer. These were student-centred, active, practical, experiential and authentic.

Also in Australia, Lenette and colleagues studied a group of music facilitators who regularly attended an immigration transit accommodation facility to share music and singing activities with detained asylum seekers. The monthly written observations of the facilitators were analysed and revealed links between music and singing and the health and wellbeing of detained asylum-seekers related to humanisation, community, resilience and agency. Sunderland and colleagues (2015) reported the outcomes of an exploratory narrative study on the impact of participatory music-making on the social determinants of health and wellbeing of refugees in Brisbane. They mapped reported outcomes for five refugee and asylum-seeker members of a participatory Brisbane-based music initiative, the Scattered People. Three key aspects were critical for wellbeing: cultural expression, music-making, and the consolidation of personal and social identity. Cain and colleagues (2020), using qualitative methods, explored how participatory music-making within immigrant communities could influence wellbeing. Three broadly defined cultural groups living in the region participated: people of Baltic origin, from Latin American and Caribbean backgrounds, and newly arrived immigrants and refugees. Individual interviews were analysed and showed how musical involvement affected mental, social and emotional wellbeing. Focusing on the staff of a refugee and asylum-seeker music programme, Sunderland and colleagues (2016) showed that they shared a common concern for promoting social justice using music participation, creation and dissemination.

Some research in Australia has been concerned with the experiences of migrant musicians. Mani (2020) investigated the multiple and often marginalised ways of being, knowing, educating and performing in migrant musicians in South East Queensland. The wide range of activities that they undertook in their new homes not only built their capacity but also added culturally derived value to their lives and the lives of those that they encountered. Three key features were central to their lives and livelihoods: connectedness, self-identity, and wellbeing. Magowan (2019) considered how complex emotional dynamics emerged between music facilitators, music producers and asylum-seekers as they variously navigated experiences of dislocation and replacement. The recounting of painful journeys immersed singers and music producers in reciprocal recognition and reimagining of events in an empathic process, empowering asylum-seekers and Aboriginal Australians through their songs.

As in Australia, a considerable body of research has been undertaken in Norway. In 2020 just over four percent (238,291) of the Norwegian population had a refugee background. In the region of 21,000 of these refugees were children between six and fifteen years of age (Statistics Norway, 2020). In 1989, the Norwegian concert agency initiated a three-year programme of introducing multicultural music-teaching in Norwegian primary schools. Eighteen schools in and around the capital took part in a research project to determine the effects of immigrant musicians introducing the music of their countries of origin to fourth-grade children. Positive results emerged, particularly with regard to reduced harassment and ethnic tension. Multicultural music is now regularly on the school concert agenda, with a total of 3,000 such concerts having been presented to more than a quarter of the total Norwegian school population (Skyllstad (1995; 1997). Skyllstad (2000) initiated a three-year research project aimed at understanding the cultural traditions of immigrant communities in Oslo, and preventing discriminatory attitudes. The project also aimed at releasing and promoting the artistic talents and resources in immigrant communities through cooperation with leading artists from countries of origin in the fields of music and dance. Participating schools benefited from the programme through improved interethnic relationships, a reduction in incidents of harassment and the enhanced self-image of immigrant children, who were more easily accepted. Other intercultural initiatives followed. A multicultural music centre was founded, which arranged a yearly world music festival. Similar projects have been established—for instance, Einarsen (1998) and Fock (2004)—but have generally had less positive outcomes than those reported by Skyllstad (1995; 1997). Bergh (2007) followed up the performances of traditional folk and classical music by musicians from the home countries of immigrant groups 13 years later and found that, although participants recalled the programme and enjoyed it at the time, it had had little impact on their daily lives and their relationships with other groups as they did not see any connections between the musical performances, the musicians or the populations of these countries. In contrast, Enge and Stige (2021) explored music therapy in a public primary school in a rural area of Western Norway which focused on refugee children's social wellbeing, with an emphasis on their peer community. The children who were offered music therapy faced various challenges, including living in difficult home situations or struggling academically or socially. The music therapy had a participatory and exploratory character, and successfully nurtured the children's capacity to regulate their emotions and engage in social participation.

Studying a refugee camp in Greece where people from Iraq and Syria had been living for up to a year, Millar and Warwick (2018) aimed to improve understanding of the relationship between music and the wellbeing of young refugees aged 11 to 18. Data were collected over a five-week period through observation of individual music lessons and group music workshops involving between three to twelve participants and semi-structured interviews. The findings showed that actively making music could impact positively on young people's wellbeing, enabling the development of emotional expression, improved social relations, self-knowledge, positive self-identification and a sense of agency. In London, Clini and colleagues (2019) undertook a collaborative study using focus groups and in-depth semi-structured interviews with asylum-seekers and refugees, and showed that participants articulated the impact of creative activities around three main themes: skills, social engagement and personal emotions. The activities helped participants to find a voice, create support networks and learn practical skills useful in the labour market.

In Wales, Vougioukalou and colleagues (2019), using observations and interviews, explored the effect of participating in weekly structured musical activities and improvisation, as well as at public performances.

They observed that improvisation encouraged individual unscripted performances, instilled confidence in solo performance, gave individuals who had experienced displacement and marginalisation a chance to lead in a safe, performative space, gave other participants a chance to follow and accompany these compositions instrumentally or vocally (drawing on their own cultural traditions, thus creating innovative cross-cultural pieces), and provided participants and audience members with a unique and irreplicable experience that triggered their imaginations, prompting questions and further discussion between participants. These findings suggest that the combination of structured and improvisational musical activity can help to foster a sense of wellbeing and social inclusion, change power dynamics, create opportunities for cross-cultural dialogue and create a community out of people from different locations and situations. The Welsh choral tradition and arts in the local community provided a receptive environment for this diverse group of performers, connecting them to the wider local community arts scene that led to individual, collective and wider societal benefits. In the USA, Muriithi (2020), using interviews and observations of performances, explored the lived experience of six refugee musicians who had been involved in music prior to entering the USA. Traumatic experiences resulted in their fleeing from their homes to seek refuge elsewhere. After being resettled in the United States, they continued to suffer from the experience of loss, the need to adapt and change, and the struggle with trauma and negative emotions. Music was their method of healing trauma and facilitating integration. It supported healing, enabling them to forget problems, communicate a message of hope and integrate, thus reducing isolation and loneliness.

In a review, Henderson and colleagues (2017) identified the possible positive health and wellbeing outcomes of participatory music activities for culturally and linguistically diverse people who could be described as vulnerable or at risk in particular migrant populations. They concluded that there was insufficient evidence from the existing research to draw clear conclusions. Similarly, Lennette and Sunderland (2016) mapped the potential for participatory music practices to support health and wellbeing outcomes for asylum-seekers and refugees in conflict settings, refugee camps and resettlement contexts. The findings highlighted the different roles that music had in people's lives as they moved towards resettlement, and how music might support health and wellbeing in this population.

Social Inclusion

There have been several approaches to defining social inclusion. An overarching approach considers it in terms of the interaction between psychological and sociological factors, including:

- motivation;
- loneliness;
- self-efficacy;
- anxiety;
- self-esteem;
- self-regulation;
- identity;
- development;
- feelings of contentment and belonging;
- social relationships and networks;
- group coherence and dynamics;
- marginalisation;
- integration;
- interaction;
- social sharing; and
- enabling social relations (Baumeister et al., 2005).

As considered in earlier chapters, music can play a role in enhancing social inclusion in many everyday situations rather than being limited to those relating to large-scale conflict. Music-making has been used to support children and young people who are at risk through poverty, prejudice, disaffection or involvement with the judicial system. For instance, Ho and colleagues (2011) reported positive changes in wellbeing and mental health following a drumming intervention with low-income children, while Barrett and Bond (2015) found that participation in a music programme enhanced the musical, academic and social competence and confidence, connection, character and caring of students in four socioeconomically disadvantaged school settings. Similarly, Fanian and colleagues (2015) evaluated a creative arts workshop for Tłı̨chǫ youth in circumpolar, arctic and subarctic regions which enabled young people perceived as 'at risk' to explore critical community issues and find solutions together using the arts. Observations, focus groups, questionnaires and reflective practice were adopted. Participating young people reported gaining confidence and new skills, artistic and personal. Many found the workshops to be engaging, enjoyable and culturally relevant, and they expressed an interest in continuing their involvement with the arts and spreading their messages through art to other young people and others in their communities. However, the short-term nature of some programmes makes drawing conclusions about their efficacy difficult. For instance, Millar and colleagues (2020) reported on a project involving 16 sessions of participatory music-making with 32 hard-to-reach young people aged 12 to 17, which aimed to engage them on their own terms through music that resonated with their lived experience, but their need for stability required more long-term engagement.

In the UK, positive benefits for self-efficacy and self-esteem have been found for looked-after children (Dillon, 2010) and those in the criminal justice system (Daykin et al., 2012). Programmes for juvenile offenders have successfully addressed complex mental health symptoms and behavioural regulation difficulties, and increased academic performance and family functioning (Bittman et al., 2009; Rapp-Paglicci et al., 2012) Coutinho and colleagues (2015a; 2015b), in two reviews, showed the possible benefits of a range of music interventions with adult offenders, while in Norway, Waakter and colleagues (2004) researched the impact of music on young people who had experienced serious and multiple life stresses. Cain and colleagues (2016) carried out a review to explore whether participatory music activities could promote positive outcomes for young people from culturally and linguistically diverse communities characterised as 'at risk', and reported a range of positive wellbeing and health outcomes, in addition to enhanced cultural empathy.

Delgado (2018) argued that the performing arts can be implemented effectively to attract young people in schools, out-of-school settings, or what has been referred to as the 'third area' between school and family. The latter are non-stigmatising, community-based venues that can supplement or enhance formal education, providing a counter-narrative for young people to enable them to resist the labels placed on them, serving as a vehicle for reactivity and self-expression. The performing arts can support creative expression that can be transformative for individuals and communities. Group music-making offers the opportunity to engage in wider cultural experiences and explore new ideas, places and perspectives; it supports social cohesion through broadening experiences (Israel, 2012). Benefits can extend beyond those for participants to include families and whole communities (Creech et al., 2016)

Some research has been undertaken in the context of school music education. Early research in Switzerland showed that increasing the amount of class music within the curriculum did not have a detrimental effect on language and reading skills, despite a reduction in time in these lessons (Spychiger, et al., 1993; Zulauf, 1993), but led to increased social cohesion within class, greater self-reliance, better social adjustment and more positive attitudes. These effects were particularly marked in low-ability, disaffected pupils (Spychiger et al., 1993). In Finland, Eerola and Eerola (2013) studied 735 children, some of whom participated in extended music education classes from age nine for four hours each week, compared with just over 80 minutes for the remaining children. By the end of the programme, the children receiving additional classes reported a more positive classroom climate and more satisfaction with school life. However, those attending the additional classes were selected because of their strong musical skills. This may have influenced the outcomes, although other factors may have been important, including shared musical interests, positive feedback from public performance, intense emotional experiences, feelings of affiliation and the prosocial effects of joint musical activities.

In a national study of 2000 children in the UK, *Sing Up*, those who were relatively more musically skilled were more likely to report themselves as being more socially included (Welch et al., 2010). Later analysis (Welch et al., 2014) matched data from 6087 participants following three years of the *Sing Up* project, and suggested that engagement in musical activities impacted on sense of self and sense of social integration irrespective of age, sex and ethnicity. Similarly, Rinta and colleagues (2011) explored the connections between children's musical backgrounds and their feelings of social inclusion. Data were gathered from 110 eight- to eleven-year-old children in the UK and Finland. The findings showed that those children who played a musical instrument or sang with their family or friends regularly felt more socially included.

In Spain, Almau (2005) found that extracurricular musical activities contributed towards increased school attendance and social inclusion in Roma children. Also in Spain, *Musicalizatech* (a project that promoted musical creativity in secondary and high-school students) showed a clear impact on participants in relation to the development of social and emotional skills, problem-solving and teamwork, the development of technological skills, and creative processes (Cuadrado et al., 2017). In contrast, in the USA, Gerrard (2021) found through interviews with students, band leaders, teachers, parents and administrators that a middle-school band programme with Latinx students did not meet their needs as they were uncomfortable with the band model and wanted more creative work with music that was familiar to them.

Music teachers face a range of challenges related to social inclusion. They have to decide whether it is part of their role to address such issues. For instance, Evron (2007), working as an art educator in Israel, considered whether teachers of the arts should ignore the violent experiences of their students, relate the curriculum to address such problems, or simply expect creative activities to enable students to express their fears and life experiences, avoiding political issues. A further issue is whether teachers of the arts should respond to the challenges of re-engaging disaffected young people through inclusive teaching practices or go beyond this in some way (Burnard, 2008). In a review, Karlsen and Westerlund (2010) argued that the musical education of immigrant students could be seen as a healthy test for any educational context in terms of how democracy is enacted. Bates (2012) considered issues relating to social class in school music, and concluded that there is a need to provide free and equitable music education for all students, understand and respect their cultural backgrounds, and also recognise the social forces that perpetuate poverty. Several authors have commented on the lack of equity in opportunities for different groups.

In England, Griffiths (2020) found that female, black and minority-ethnic students were well represented in elite music education, but were very poorly represented in the professional repertoire, where 99 percent of performed pieces were by white composers and 98 percent by men. Treacy (2020) found that the challenges female musician teachers encountered in pursuit of their careers in Nepal were not addressed in shared visions of music education. In the USA, Palmer (2017) considered how music educators could address issues of discrimination that appeared to be beyond their control. Also in the USA, Baird (2001) interviewed nine teachers to investigate how they engaged preschool- and elementary-aged children in singing and talking about social justice issues, the barriers that they perceived to this practice in schools and society, and how parents, educators and song-makers could bring about changes that would improve the ability of children to sing for social justice in American schools and the wider society.

In the relatively recent past, the arts in general have been used to attempt to address social inequality, the uneven distribution of wealth or resources and inequity, unfair differences in society, and the environment in wealthy and poor countries around the world (Parkinson et al., 2013). For instance, in Ireland, a study in a deprived area of Cork explored the impact of a wide music education project on the feelings of social inclusion exhibited by local residents. The findings indicated that music could be used as a tool to tackle social exclusion and educational disadvantage (Minguella and Buchanan, 2009). In Tasmania, Langston and Barrett (2008) examined social capital in a community choir using a survey, field notes and semi-structured interviews. Many social capital indicators were evident in the choir: shared norms and values, trust, civic and community involvement, networks, knowledge resources, and contact with families and friends. Fellowship was identified as a key component in fostering group cohesion and the development of social capital. Laing and Mair (2015) studied the role of music festivals in helping to build strong and cohesive communities and found that the organisation of festivals might contribute to social inclusion through providing opportunities for local participation, learning new skills, and access to education about social justice, although organisers tended to direct their social inclusion efforts towards attendees rather than reaching out to local residents, limiting the impact on the local community and social inclusion more generally.

Overview

The evidence relating to the role of music in social cohesion demonstrates only too clearly the power of music. It has been successfully used to promote prejudice and enhance national identities for political purposes. It has been used to bolster the morale of those engaged in warfare and to humiliate and terrorise opponents. Attempts to use music positively to promote social cohesion in those already or previously engaged in conflict have had limited success and, in some cases, have highlighted differences between groups, exacerbating problems. Active music-making may offer some support in breaking down barriers between different ethnic or religious groups, but its effectiveness in any given situation depends on the depth and strength of existing prejudices and the current political climate. As we have seen in Chapters 14 and 15, music therapy can offer support to those traumatised by conflict and can enhance the self-beliefs of members of marginalised groups. Those engaged in music education are faced with challenges in deciding whether they should overtly address issues relating to prejudice in their classes, consistently adopt inclusive teaching strategies, or narrowly focus their teaching on musical issues.

17. Music in Everyday Life

The development of the electronic media in the latter part of the 20th century revolutionised access to and the use of music in our everyday lives. In the Western world, music pervades every aspect of our lives (Clarke et al., 2010). Music is played in supermarkets, shopping precincts, restaurants, places of worship, schools, on the radio and television, and through the medium of recordings. Music plays an important role in the theatre, TV, films, video and advertising. Music is now available in a wide variety of formats, not only through radio and recordings but through smartphones and computers, which can stream music on demand. These new technologies have changed the way that people are able to interact with music (Nill and Geipel, 2010) making music easily accessible at any time and in a wide variety of contexts (Heye and Lamont, 2010; Juslin et al., 2008). Individuals are able to control what, when and how they listen to music. This has led to complex patterns of everyday music usage and storage, leading to the highly personalised categorisation of music (Greasley and Lamont, 2006). Users adopt different ways of managing playlists which fuse new ways of collecting music with practices from pre-digital collecting (Hagen, 2015). Digital music has facilitated greater interactivity between user, device, and music (Kibby, 2009) and moved from collecting music being a tangible experience to a more ephemeral one (McCourt, 2005).

A reflection of the extent to which people engage with music is the size of the music industry. In the UK and the USA, it is amongst the top generators of income. Prior to these developments, music was only accessible for most people if they made it themselves or attended religious or social events. Alongside the increased availability of music for listening, there are also greater opportunities for actively making music. Many more people of all ages now learn to play instruments or sing and participate in musical groups, although the degree of participation to some extent depends on financial resources (ABRSM, 2014).

Music and Leisure

Listening to music is a top leisure activity for many people (Rentfrow and Gosling, 2003). Engaging in leisure activities has a long history, going back to at least the fourth century BCE, when Aristotle referred to it as constituting an important element in the life of the citizens of Athens (including the experience of melody, drama, poetry and dance). These were perceived as important in supporting happiness (Hallam et al., 2017). More recently, Stebbins (1992) has distinguished between casual leisure—which mainly includes enjoyable social interactions and self-gratification behaviours—and serious leisure, which requires significant effort. Those participating in serious leisure fall into three groups: amateurs, hobbyists and volunteers. Amateurs share similar expectations with professionals and rely on the general public to appreciate and support their activities. Hobbyists are dedicated, but to a lesser extent. Their activities are frequently undertaken alone. Volunteers provide help, formally or informally, while dabblers or dilettantes only participate in any specific leisure activity for a brief period of time or to a limited extent. Amateur musicians can engage in musical activities for personal amusement or as a serious leisure activity. Many of the activities that they engage with are indistinguishable from those undertaken by professional musicians. Music constitutes a key part of their identity, and they invest much time and energy in it. At the start of active engagement with music, motivations may vary. Dabblers or dilettantes have no great commitment and spend little time practising, which limits their musical development and the benefits that they may derive from it, while others may be totally committed and aspire to amateur or professional status. Hobbyists (Stebbins, 1992) or enthusiasts (Keown, 2015) tend to focus on listening, have large music collections and high-quality equipment, and invest considerable time in learning about and adding to their collections. Regular attenders at concerts or festivals tend to have higher levels of musical experience and rate music as important in their lives. Less committed listeners, dabblers, dilettantes and recreationists enjoy music, but it is not a major focus in their lives, although it is important to them.

Relatively little research attention has been given to understanding the behaviours of music enthusiasts and sound-recording collectors (Keown, 2015). They, mainly men, may actively participate in collecting sound-recording albums to fulfil multiple motivational desires including love of music, obsessive-compulsive behaviour, accumulation and completism, selectivity and discrimination or self-education and scholarship (Shuker, 2004). Lacher and Mizerski (1994) describe their behaviour in terms of affective responses, experiential responses, the ability to be swept up in the music, and the need to re-experience the music. Other influential factors include perceived knowledge (an illusion of knowing), objective knowledge (knowing based on data-supported information), opinion leadership (allowing other individuals' opinions to influence purchasing behaviours), and enduring involvement (relating to a product in support of self-image). These are better predictors of motivation to purchase particular recordings than demographic variables such as age, social class and marital status (Flynn et al., 1995), although record-collecting in general has been identified as a male characteristic (Straw, 1997). Technological developments have led to further distinctions in terms of technology users and technology consumers, and different downloading profiles: occasional downloaders, online listeners, explorer pioneers, curious and duplicators (Molteni and Ordanini, 2003).

Related to the concept of enthusiasts is that of fandom, which has been conceptualised as a psychological symptom of a presumed social dysfunction (Jenson, 1992) although also as a logical consumer strategy focusing on pleasure and identity development in association with an identifiable capital (Stevens, 2010). Fandom is also related to seeking out interpersonal relationships with other music fans (Duffett, 2013). Whatever the musical activity, the level of commitment and time spent engaging with music impacts on the benefits which can be derived from it. To be a dedicated fan requires having sufficient finance to attend concerts and pay for recordings and, for the really dedicated, travel to distant performances. Higher incomes are required for this (Bennett et al., 2009).

Listening to Music

Listening to music is a key leisure activity for many people (Rentfrow and Gosling, 2003). The easy availability of music nowadays means that people are able to interact with music at any time and in a variety of contexts. Listening can be motivated by the desire for aesthetic experience, the regulation of moods and emotions (Groake and Hogan, 2018), to promote wellbeing in those with long-term illness (Batt-Rawden et al., 2005) or to help in accessing new ways of being (Krueger, 2018). As considered in depth in Chapter 14, music is frequently used as a regulatory strategy for maintaining or changing moods (Silk, 2003; Thayer et al., 1994). This is one of the most common reasons for listening to music. While people generally use music to enhance positive emotions, it can be used to explore negative themes: for instance, distress, suicide and death. This can subsequently increase depressive symptoms and suicidal thoughts (Scheel and Westefeld, 1999). These negative outcomes can be exacerbated through interactions with like-minded others. Music can also have a negative impact when individuals are exposed to music that they dislike in contexts where they have no control and are unable to remove themselves from the situation. This can cause extreme distress.

There is variation in the extent to which listeners are aware of the impact of music on their moods. Typically, older people and women are more aware while, amongst young people, girls are more likely to use music to cope with personal problems as a kind of lay-therapeutic practice (Batt-Rawden and DeNora, 2005), while boys tend to use it to increase energy and promote their image (North et al., 2000; Wells and Hakanen, 1991). Open and intellectually engaged individuals and those with higher levels of intelligence tend to use music in a rational cognitive way, while neurotic, introverted and non-conscientious individuals are more likely to use music for emotional regulation. Extroverts tend to adopt an emotional approach to listening and to use it as a background to other activities (Chamorro-Premuzic and Furnham, 2007; Chamorro-Premuzic et al., 2009). The use of music to regulate moods may be related to musical preferences. For instance, eclectic preferences have been shown to correlate with emotionality in listening (Behne, 1997; Wells and Hakanen, 1991) and flexibility in using music for mood-related needs (Schwartz and Fouts, 2003). Arnett (1995) discusses how individuals set about selecting and using music to serve their needs, wants and purposes.

For many years now there has been controversy over the extent to which engaging with depictions of violence in a range of media—or listening to music which has violent lyrics—impacts on behaviour. Violent media exposure is a risk factor for aggression and there are short- and long-term harmful effects, including increases in aggressive thoughts and behaviour, desensitisation to violence, and a decrease in prosocial behaviour and empathy. However, it is the accumulation of risk factors and the relative lack of protective factors which leads to violence rather than one single factor (Anderson et al., 2017; Bender et al., 2018; Browne and Hamilton-Giachritsis, 2005). In the case of music, there are relationships between certain types of music (for instance, hard rock, heavy metal, hip hop, rap and punk) and alcohol and substance abuse, violent behaviour and delinquency (Lozon and Bensimon, 2014). An experimental study has shown that when misogynous aggressive song lyrics are played, male and females respond more negatively to the opposite sex and recall more of their negative attributes than when neutral lyrics are played (Fischer and Greitmeyer, 2006). Teenage sexual attitudes, norms, desires and intentions are impacted by the kind of music that they prefer to listen to (Agbo-Quaye, 2006), while sexual and violent slang and expressions of Nigerian hip hop are reflected in Nigerian higher-education students' linguistic expressions of sexuality and violence (Onanuga and Onanuga, 2020). Appreciation of the rhythmic flow, melodic structure and particular artists of some genres, but revulsion at the misogynistic and sexist messages can lead to internal conflict in young women (Zichermann, 2009). Overall, the lyrics of some music may be a risk factor for violent or misogynistic behaviour, but other factors determine whether this translates into actual behaviour, although it is clear that its influence on language and attitudes has a more subtle effect, which may impact on behaviour in everyday life.

Attending Live Musical Events

Attendance at a live music event indicates a greater level of commitment to music than listening to recorded music and typically is motivated by hearing a particular artist or style of music, learning about new music, or personal and social reasons (for example, going with friends or being part of a community; Pitts and Burland, 2013). Strong experiences of music most commonly occur in live settings. These tend to be enhanced if the performers interact with the audience and appear to be enjoying the experience. This transforms the experience from being passive to active. Music festivals offer unique opportunities for intense musical experiences, the physical proximity to the performers, social interactions and the music itself all making a contribution. The festival context can provide a sense of community and help support the development of identity, although there can be risks associated with alcohol or drug abuse, and other negative behaviours. The sense of separation from everyday life distinguishes festivals from other musical experiences, leading participants to reflect on their lives. Clubbing also creates a distinctive musical environment where mobile phones play an important role in managing the experience, helping to develop clubbing friendships and supporting the friendly vibe of club culture (Bull, 2006).

Actively Making Music

Many more people of all ages learn to play instruments, sing and participate in musical groups than in the past, although the extent and types of opportunity vary and participation frequently depends on financial resources (ABRSM, 2014). In some cultures, music-making is a central activity. The Mekranoti Indians, primarily hunter-gatherers, living in the Amazon rainforest in Brazil spend up to two hours each day making music. The women sing for up to two hours in the morning and evening, while the men sing very early each day and frequently for half an hour before sunset. Historically this activity related to the need for vigilance in case of attack but nowadays it continues probably because it is intrinsically rewarding (Werner, 1984). In Western cultures, music-making does not play a central role in everyday life for most people. Listening to music is the most common way of engaging with music. The reasons for adults' participation in music have been grouped into three broad categories: music-making as a musical act, deepening musical knowledge and understanding; as a social act, developing a sense of belonging, making friends with like-minded people; and for personal reasons, skill development, self-esteem and satisfaction (Kokotsaki and Hallam, 2007). Music-making is generally pleasurable and relaxing, and provides opportunities for self-expression and the opportunity to demonstrate musical skills. It can give structure to life and offer opportunities to develop friendships, get relief from family and work pressures, and provide spiritual fulfilment. Being a member of a musical group can also lead to feelings of belonging, trust and cooperation. Adult participation in music-making is frequently an extension of engagement with active music-making in childhood in the home or at school. The pattern of engagement generally changes over the course of life, diminishing in the middle years and increasing in retirement. Life-changing events sometimes provide an impetus for re-engagement.

Socioeconomic Status

Bennett and colleagues (2009) examined the relationships between class, gender and ethnicity and a range of activities including music, film, television, literary and arts consumption. They also considered the organisation of sporting and culinary practices and self-maintenance. They found that social class was the most powerful indicator of the nature of cultural consumption, but other factors such as age and gender were important. The primary distinction was not between high or popular, legitimate or ordinary cultural forms but rather between participation and non-participation, although there were some very subtle differences related to class: for instance, the distinction between jazz and Dixieland jazz, and Radio Three and Classic FM. North and Hargreaves (2007a; b; c), in an examination of the relationships between musical preferences and factors relating to the lifestyles of different social groups, found numerous associations showing that fans of high- or low-art musical styles demonstrated a preference for other high- or low-art media (for instance, in reading, TV, radio and leisure activities). In relation to interpersonal relationships, living arrangements, moral and political beliefs, and criminal behaviour there tended to be an association between a commonly accepted liberal conservative divide and musical preferences. Social class aspects of lifestyle (for instance, travel, personal finances, education, employment, health, drinking and smoking) indicated that liking for high-art music was indicative of the upper-middle and upper classes, whereas liking for low-art music was indicative of a lifestyle of the lower-middle and lower classes.

The Audience Agency (2013) studied the impact of socioeconomic status and geographical location on engagement with cultural activities, and identified ten distinct groups based on cultural values:

- metroculturals—prosperous, liberal, urbanites interested in a very wide cultural spectrum;
- commuterland culture buffs—affluent and professional consumers of culture;
- experience seekers—highly active, diverse, social and ambitious, engaging with arts on a regular basis;
- dormitory dependables—from suburban and small towns with an interest in heritage activities and mainstream arts;
- trips and treats—enjoy mainstream arts and popular culture influenced by children, family and friends;
- home and heritage—from rural areas and small towns, engaging in daytime activities and historic events;
- up our street—modest in habits and means with occasional engagement in popular arts, entertainment and museums;
- Facebook families—younger suburban and semi-urban who enjoy live music, eating out and popular entertainment such as pantomime;
- Kaleidoscope creativity—mix of backgrounds and ages, occasional visitors or participants, particularly in community-based events and festivals;
- Heydays—older, often limited by mobility to engage with arts and cultural events.

These categorisations highlight the issues that people face in accessing live music related to finance and geographical location.

Music in the Arts

Music plays a major role in film and other media. Without it, drama would be much less interesting. For instance, the shower scene in Psycho, which is disturbing without music, is much more terrifying with it. Music contributes to our enjoyment of films or TV programmes in many ways. Most film music is designed to influence our emotions subconsciously. If the action is ambiguous, the music can provide clues as to what is going on. When there is no other information, music can help to define characters, sometimes with a character being given a theme. It is frequently more effective than dialogue in providing information to the audience: for instance, indicating the time when the action is taking place. It can indicate urgency, building up tension when something frightening is going to happen, while increasing volume creates the impression of fast-moving sequences. Music can give certain passages continuity or divide a film into segments. If music accompanies actions, the mood of the event will be better remembered, as the music deepens the emotional experience. Some messages are culturally specific: for instance, the music that indicates bravery in one culture might indicate evil in another (Cohen, 2016).

Listening to Support Everyday Activities

People rarely listen to music as a specific activity. It more usually accompanies other activities, although at the same time it can induce feelings of being more alert, positive and focused, particularly when the music is self-selected (Sloboda et al., 2001). Although in everyday life much music-listening takes place alongside other activities, this does not mean that it is not listened to with full attention (Lamont et al., 2016). People listen to music when travelling, carrying out boring tasks (for instance, housework) or routine intellectual tasks, or when engaged in physical activity. Music can distract, energise, facilitate moving in time and enhance meaning. It has the greatest impact on behaviour when it is selected for a particular purpose (Lamont et al., 2016). The most common use of music is when travelling, where it helps the individual to isolate themselves from other travellers, pass the time and make preparation for whatever activity is to be engaged with on arrival at the destination (Bull, 2005; Lamont et al., 2016).

Music and Driving

The effects of music on driving vary depending on the type of music, the context and the characteristics of the driver. A survey of 1,780 British drivers revealed that approximately two thirds listened to recorded music or music on the radio while driving. Reasons for listening included relaxation and concentration. Music was seen as less distracting than conversation. There were associations between possession of a motor insurance no-claims bonus and a preference for silence, although the genre of music affected driving performance. Driver age may have been a mediating factor, as older drivers who listened to classical music may have been less likely to be involved in a road accident, simply because they were safer drivers with lower levels of sensation-seeking, risk-taking or drink-driving. For the youngest age group, house and dance music were associated with a higher incidence of accidents, but this may have been associated with times when groups of friends were travelling together and driving at night, introducing other potential distractions and challenges (for instance, poor visibility, driver drowsiness, distractions from passengers, or the influence of drugs or alcohol—Dibben and Williamson, 2007). However, it is possible that different genres may affect driving safety because of their musical characteristics. Dance and house music tend to be characterised by fast tempo, high volume, complex rhythmic patterns and layered textures. These are highly arousing and can increase alertness or, alternatively, divert attention away from driving (Brodsky, 2002; Recarte and Nunes, 2002). They may also result in greater aggression at the wheel (Wiesenthal et al., 2003). Using a driving simulator, Catalina and colleagues (2020) investigated the extent to which listening to music could affect young drivers' emotions and their driving performance. They found that driving with music increased the tendency to increase speed level, particularly if happy music was playing. Relaxing music or no music reduced the probability of speeding. Also using simulated driving, Navarro and colleagues (2018) manipulated musical background using preferred and researcher-selected music played at different *tempi*. Listening to music influenced drivers' performance but its tempo did not. Arousing music improved drivers' responsiveness to changes in the speed of the vehicle that they were following, but this was cancelled out by a reduction in intervehicle safety margin. Also simulating driving, Arafat and colleagues (2017) investigated the effects of natural sounds, classical music and hard rock on driving performance. Driving was most efficient with natural sounds and most inaccurate with hard rock. Participants' perceptions of the impact of the music on their driving reflected these findings.

Studying young adults in a broader travelling context, Heye and Lamont (2008) showed that listeners consciously chose their music, depending on current goals which may have been linked to their destination. Listeners created an auditory bubble which enhanced their awareness of their surroundings, although it was partly permeable. DeNora (2013) also suggested that personal listening created an environment of asylum which provided space to explore inner reality, but at the same time removed connection with other human beings.

Music at Work and to Accompany Mental Activity

Music has always played a major part in work activities and continues to do so. It has been used to coordinate movement, alleviate boredom, develop team spirit and speed up the pace of work. Nowadays, singing to accompany work is uncommon in the developed world, but in the office environment, those who listen to recorded music report improved mood, providing that they are able to select the music themselves. When tasks are routine and solitary music can improve concentration and focus, relieve boredom, reduce stress and block out unwanted noise (Lamont et al., 2016). Increasing access to music has contributed to changes in listening to music in offices, where employees can listen to music through personal listening devices. A survey of music-listening in office settings in the UK found that employees listened to music for a third of their working week. They listened to a wide variety of styles and artists. Music helped them to both engage in and escape from work, and they often used it to seal themselves off from the office environment. They managed listening so that they did not disturb colleagues or appear unprofessional in front of clients (Haake, 2011). Companies have come to recognise that music can support job performance and foster ethical conduct (Meyer, 2019).

Generally, cognitive work is enhanced with the playing of calming, relaxing music, although if a task is very boring, more stimulating music may be required to maintain concentration. However, tasks involving rote memorisation tend to be disrupted by music, although it can act as a mnemonic to support memory for factual information (Hallam and MacDonald, 2016; Hallam and Rogers, 2016). As we saw in Chapter 11, schoolchildren and students frequently play music when completing academic work. As with driving, the effect of the music depends on a range of factors which interact together, including the complexity of the task and the nature of the music. Children with behavioural difficulties who may have particular difficulties with concentration can be helped by calming music playing in the background (Hallam and MacDonald, 2016).

Music and Exercise

Regular physical activity has benefits for physical and mental health. Music is a common accompaniment to exercise, whether in the gym or outside in the park or on the streets. Music played before exercise has been shown to optimise arousal, facilitate task-relevant imagery and improve performance in simple motoric tasks. During repetitive endurance activities, preferred motivational, stimulative music reduces levels of perceived exertion, improves energy efficiency and leads to increased work output. In high-intensity exercise, carefully selected music can promote ergogenic and psychological benefits, although it does not appear to help in reducing perceptions of exertion beyond the anaerobic threshold. Medium-tempo music can enhance positive feelings during high-intensity exercise and in recovery periods, while medium and fast music can increase zoning out, enjoyment and remembered pleasure (Karageorghis et al., 2021). In high humidity and high temperature conditions, time to exhaustion when music is playing is longer and perceived exhaustion lower (Nikol et al., 2019). Music is most effective when it accompanies self-paced exercise or when it is selected as being motivational (Karageorghis and Priest, 2012). Schneider and colleagues (2010) also showed that an adequate choice of music during exercise-enhanced performance output and mood, while Potteiger and colleagues (2000) found that different types of music acted as distractors during exercise and were associated with lower ratings of perceived exertion. Differences in musical preferences while exercising are most influenced by age. When working out in gyms, older people prefer quieter, slower and less stimulative motivational music (Priest et al., 2004). In a review, Terry and colleagues (2020) concluded that music was associated with significant beneficial effects on affect, physical performance, perceived exertion and oxygen consumption, but not heart rate. The effects were moderated by context, exercise as opposed to sport, and the tempo of the music.

Music, Commerce and Consumption

Recorded music is played extensively in workplaces, shops, airports, restaurants and hotels. The commercial and industrial uses of music constitute major industries. As a general rule, people tend to avoid music that they do not like, and are attracted to places where they find the music appealing. This has led various authorities to use music to persuade people they consider undesirable to relocate from specific public places. Typically, opera or other classical music is used for this purpose. The police have also used music to try to reduce aggressive behaviour in groups of people who have been drinking heavily by playing children's songs or other calming, pleasant music. In everyday life, music is used to manipulate what is purchased through advertising and create an appropriate ambience in retail settings. Music achieves this through its capacity to change arousal and emotions, and the way that it is associated with particular events or items.

One strand of research has focused on the role of music in store ambience. For instance, Ishar and colleagues (2017) studied consumer purchasing behaviour at self-service convenience stores in Sri Lanka and found that music was one of several factors that influenced purchasing, along with scent and light. Singh and colleagues (2014) found that appropriate background music helped retailers to create a desirable store atmosphere, which contributed to the image of the store and allied with consumer preferences. Playing the right kind of music has a direct impact on consumer behaviour within a store (Farias et al., 2014). When preferred music is played, customers stay longer, are more comfortable and relaxed, and likely to purchase more. If background music is fast, loud and causing discomfort, less time is spent shopping. An appropriate level of arousal induced by music increases pleasure, which positively influences satisfaction with the shopping experience (Moran et al., 2013). Music can also affect perceptions of the atmosphere in banks and bars (North et al., 2000). The speed at which people shop is positively related to the tempo and volume of background music. Milliman (1982) found that slow music led to supermarket customers shopping more slowly and spending more money, perhaps because they took more time to browse available products, while Smith and Curnow (1966) found that customers spent less time in store when loud music was playing, although there was no difference in the amount of money spent.

The type of music can influence what is bought. In one study, stereotypical French or German music was played in a store and influenced whether French or German wine was purchased, although customers were unaware of the influence of the music (North et al., 1997; 1999a). Similarly, a soundtrack depicting nature-influenced perceptions of the country of origin of orange juice, its cost, whether the oranges were genetically modified and beliefs about the health benefits of drinking it (North et al., 2016). Lacher and Mizerski (1994) examined the purchasing of new rock music and found that sensorial, emotional, imaginal and analytical responses to the music all had direct effects on responses to it, which in turn influenced purchase intention. The strongest indicator of purchase intention was the need to re-experience the music. The COVID-19 pandemic has led to a major increase in online purchasing. Within this context, Hwang and colleagues (2020) found that interactive (as opposed to static) background or no music enhanced the experiential value of e-commerce for consumers.

Music is used to entice people into retail establishments. North and Hargreaves (1996a) demonstrated this by setting up an advice stall in a café on a university campus, which offered leaflets with advice to students on a range of issues. Pop music was played at three levels of complexity. Moderately complex music positively influenced approach towards the stall, although not actually visiting it. Preferred music was better at attracting students to the stall than no music, although disliked music acted as a deterrent.

Different kinds of music not only have an impact on perceptions of ambience but can also affect the amount of money spent. For instance, North and Hargreaves (1998) played pop, classical, easy listening or no music in a café for four days. Customers rated the ambience of the café and also indicated how much they were prepared to spend on typical items: for instance, a slice of pizza or a canned drink. When popular music was playing, the café was seen as lively and youthful; classical music led to perceptions of it being upmarket and sophisticated, while stereotypical piped music led to perceptions of it being downmarket. Customers were prepared to pay more money when any kind of music was playing in contrast to silence, but classical music led to customers being prepared to pay the most. Areni and Kim (1993) played classical or pop music in a wine cellar and found that, although the two different types of music did not lead to customers buying any more wine, classical music led to customers buying more expensive wine. They suggested that the classical music primed customers to feel more affluent and to act accordingly. In a restaurant setting, North and colleagues (2003) also found that customers spent more money when classical music was played as opposed to pop or no music. The positive effects of classical music on spending were particularly marked for non-essential items, such as a starter or coffee afterwards.

The sounds made in consuming food can affect how it is perceived. For instance, potato crisps are perceived as tasting fresher when the sound of biting into them is louder (Zampini and Spence, 2004), while discontinuous or uneven sounds influence perceptions of how crispy they are (Vickers and Wasserman, 1979). Music can influence perceptions of flavour. Music selected to reflect the descriptors often used to describe wine (for instance, heavy, subtle and refined, zingy and refreshing, or mellow and soft) influenced the perceived taste of the wine in the direction of the emotions symbolised by the music (North, 2012).

Some research has focused on the impact of music on the speed of the consumption of food and drink. For instance, Milliman (1986) studied restaurant customers and found that slow music led to customers eating more slowly, completing their meal in just under an hour on average, compared with three quarters of an hour when fast music was played. In a café setting, Roballey and colleagues (1985) found that fast music led to customers eating at more bites per minute than when slow music was playing. Spending may also be affected, with slow music leading to greater spending on drinks (Milliman, 1986). In a student cafe, diners were asked to say how much they liked the music (North and Hargreaves, 1996b), with data showing that moderately complex music was most popular. It was also clear that the more music was disliked, the more noticeable it became.

Music plays a key role in advertising. To persuade customers to buy particular products, the music needs to be appropriate. Customers need to understand the advertising message but also be able to relate to the emotional elements of the music. The most successful advertisements are those that provide information and have emotional power. The attitudes of potential customers can be changed if music conforms to their conception of the nature of the product: for instance, exciting classical music might be used to advertise an expensive sports car. Food adverts tend to be accompanied by cheerful songs, which may include the product name in their lyrics. North and colleagues (2004) prepared radio adverts for five brands: an online bank, a people carrier, a bathroom cleaner, a chocolate bar and a high sugar drink. In addition to the voiceover, music was played that did or did not fit with the characteristics of the brand. Recall of the product was higher when the adverts featured music that fitted the advertised product. When music is well-matched with the product, it is better remembered. Audio branding in the form of jingles or signature tunes can support memory for a brand. Overall, music is effective in helping to enhance the appeal of products and promote memory for them (Çupi and Morma, 2020; Deaville et al., 2020; North et al., 2016; Rathee and Pallavi, 2020).

The Economics of Music

Music makes a major contribution to economies locally, nationally and internationally, including recordings, radio, live-music venues, production and distribution, applications including ringtones, computer games, films, children's toys, as background in business environments and through the employment of musicians. The music economy is spread across most categories of economic activity: construction, manufacturing, wholesaling, retailing, consumer services, and the public sector. Musicians work as employees and in self-employment, the largest groups in music and dance, education, broadcasting, software and computer services (Beyers et al., 2008; UK Music, 2020). The introduction of streaming services presented particular challenges to the industry (Molteni and Ordanini, 2003). Musicians and the music industries are generally concentrated in a relatively small number of large regional centres (or at least this is the case in the USA and the UK;Florida et al., 2010), although music festivals of all kinds can have a major impact on local economies. Even when entrance to events is free, there are considerable benefits to the local economy more generally (Bracalente et al., 2011; Tohmo, 2005). In the USA, the music industry recently accounted for $514 billion (Music Market Research, 2021), while in the UK it accounted for £5.8 billion, employed almost 200,000 people and accounted for £2.9 billion of exports and £4.7 billion in music tourism (UK Music, 2020).

Music and Non-Human Species

Music can have an impact on animals and plants. Music as part of an enriched environment has been shown to have a positive impact on many non-human species, including domestic animals, those reared on farms and those in captivity in zoos and wildlife parks. The aim of playing music is generally to enhance wellbeing, although there has been some research exploring the benefits to cognition. For instance, music has been shown to have a positive effect on rats' maze-learning capacity. Rauscher (1998) reported that, when rats were exposed to Mozart's sonata K448 they completed a maze faster and with fewer errors than if minimalist music, white noise or silence was in the background, suggesting that repeated exposure to complex music improved spatial-temporal reasoning. Similarly, Tonon do Amaral and colleagues (2020) assessed the effect of both classical and heavy-metal music on short- and long-term memory of rats exposed to music for eight hours a day for 61 days. After exposure, the rats were familiarised with two objects, and their memory for them was tested after ninety minutes and 28 days. Rats exposed to either type of music performed better than controls with regard to short-term memory, although there was no impact on long-term memory, suggesting a temporary effect.

Within an agricultural context, one strand of research has focused on the impact of playing music to cows when they are being milked. For instance, North and MacKenzie (2001) found that dairy cows increased their milk production by three quarters of a litre a day when listening to slow rather than fast or no music over a nine-week period. Exposure to a pleasant auditory environment alleviated stress and encouraged relaxation, which resulted in greater milk yields. Similarly, Mallick and colleagues (2020) studied the amount of milk produced by aged crossbred cows following instrumental music playing in the background during milking. Milk production increased particularly in the evening, which may have been a more stressful time for the cows prior to exposure to the music. Also in an agricultural context, Jiafang and colleagues (2021) found that repeated sound stimulation, Mozart, a mechanical noise or natural sound background affected the behaviour, physiology and immunity of 72 hybrid piglets who were exposed to six hours of sound stimulation per day. In the short term, the music reduced stress responses and, in the long term, enhanced immune responses, while noise increased aggressive behaviour and reduced immunity.

Music can also benefit domestic animals, particularly dogs and cats, when they are hospitalised, receiving veterinary care or in a rescue centre. Wells and colleagues (2002) explored the influence of five types of auditory stimulation—human conversation, classical, heavy metal, pop or no music—on the behaviour of 50 dogs living in a rescue shelter. The dogs were exposed to each type of auditory stimulation for four hours, with one day between conditions. Classical music led to more time spent resting, while heavy metal encouraged barking. The other stimuli had no effects. In a review, McDonald and Zaki (2020) showed that classical music could influence behaviour and physiological measures associated with canine stress responses such as heart rate variability, level of vocalisation and time spent resting in animal hospital settings, while Boone and Quelch (2003) showed that harp therapy decreased restless behaviour, anxiety and respiration rate in hospitalised dogs or those in post-surgical care. In research focusing on domestic cats, Hampton and colleagues (2020) found that music reduced stress in a veterinary context. The most effective music was that designed specifically for cats, not classical music.

In relation to music and plants, Retallack (1973) claimed that plants exposed to soothing music showed better growth and were healthier than those without music, while Ramekar and Gurjar (2016) showed that vedic chanting had a positive effect on plant growth, leaf size and internodes (the parts of the plant carrying water, hormones and food between nodes). Chowdhury and Gupta (2015) studied the effects of different types of sound on the health and growth of marigolds using light Indian and meditative music, as well as noise. They also monitored the germination of chickpea exposed to light Indian music. Music promoted the growth and development of the plants, including germination, whereas noise hindered it. Focusing on the role of sound on the germination of okra and zucchini seeds, Creath and Schwartz (2004) used musical sound, pink noise and healing energy. Musical sound had a highly significant effect on the number of seeds which germinated, compared to an untreated control. This effect was independent of temperature, seed type, position in room, specific petri dish and the person doing the scoring.

Overview

Music plays a major role in everyday life. It is a major leisure activity but also supports the undertaking of many everyday tasks, including travelling, exercise and intellectual work. People listen to music for pleasure but also to manipulate or consolidate their moods. In some cases, this can have negative effects. There are individual differences in the extent to which people are aware of the effects of music. Fewer people are actively engaged in making music or attending live events, perhaps because of lack of opportunity or financial constraints. The types of music listened to and the musical activities engaged with depend broadly on economic factors, age and individual dispositions. Music plays a crucial role in all of the arts and in commerce, purchasing and advertising. It also makes a major contribution to local and national economies. The benefits of music can also be seen in non-human species, including the growth and productivity of animals in the agricultural sector, and the growth and germination process in plants.

Reflections on an Exploration of the Evidence for the Power of Music

Perhaps the most surprising aspect of this exploration of the evidence relating to the power of music is the fact that there is so much research. Related to this, a very wide range of methods have been adopted to study the impact of many different musical activities. Most people do not need scientific evidence to demonstrate the power of music. They recognise its power in their everyday activities and use it to manage their moods and emotions, although they may not be consciously aware of the extent of its power—for instance, in influencing what they buy, their consumption of food and drink, or the way it is used in advertising, drama and films. Certainly, those engaged in commerce are aware of music's impact as they use it to manipulate our behaviour, as are some who hold political power, who have deliberately used music to generate prejudice or violence, or approved its application in torture. At the other extreme, some have recognised the power of music by controlling or banning it.

The possible benefits of listening to and making music for health and wellbeing have broadly been recognised, although often in conjunction with other more conventional treatments and, even then, not for all conditions. It can be particularly helpful in reducing stress, anxiety and pain through the way it directly affects opioid systems in the brain. However, at the individual level, we should not only think of the power of music in terms of its benefits to health and wellbeing, as for some individuals it may reinforce existing negative emotions, exacerbating mental ill health. This is not a reflection of its lack of power: quite the reverse. It demonstrates that it can have powerful negative effects.

Assessing the impact of actively making music or music therapy is challenging, because the effects of the music itself cannot easily be disentangled from its social elements. This does not necessarily mean that the music itself does not make a contribution, as clearly in many cases it does, but there may be exceptions; for instance, if individuals do not like particular musical genres or specific musical activities. Relationships with those facilitating musical activities play a key role in bringing about change, as does the quality of the facilitation. In some cases, such relationships and the quality of the musical experience may be more important than the actual musical activities. Making or creating music with others is a social event, and its social nature is an important factor in its success or failure. The impact of any activity on self-efficacy, self-esteem and overall self-beliefs depends on feedback from others. Musical activity leads to feedback being given, but it may not always be positive. If feedback is negative, it is likely to have negative effects and lead to the individual looking for more rewarding ways to spend their time.

The major controversies in relation to the research, which have not lessened but escalated over time, concern the impact of music on various aspects of cognition, particularly in children and young people, but also in older age. The evidence from neuroscience has clearly shown that learning to play a musical instrument leads to changes in the brain. The extent to which these changes transfer to other activities is hotly debated, although the evidence for the impact on a range of aural skills is strong, as might be expected from activities which require high levels of aural perception and the analysis of sound. These skills in turn are important for the development of language. The evidence for transfer to other skills—for instance, spatiotemporal reasoning, executive functioning, literacy, mathematics, intelligence, aspects of memory and academic attainment—is mixed. Some of the possible causes for this have been outlined above. Some have argued that the gold standard in research requires the random allocation of participants to intervention and control groups, the latter being an alternative activity rather than no activity. This paradigm has gained its credibility from its routine use in medical research. However, medical research does not typically take account of individual differences or involve human interaction at any level, which is likely to affect the outcomes. This is not the case with research involving musical activity. The outcomes of listening to music depend on many individual differences including personality, gender, musical preferences and musical experience, and also vary depending on whether listening is undertaken alone or with others. When considering actively making music, the possible confounding factors are even greater. While the research evidence might be stronger when control groups participate in alternative activities, there is no reason why other activities should not be equally successful in bringing about positive change. The fact that sport or visual art (for instance) may generate positive change does not undermine the possible impact of music. Some types of musical engagement may have advantages over other interventions because of the complex demands that they make on participating individuals aurally, emotionally, intellectually, physically and socially. As the evidence stands at the moment, it is not clear which musical activities might be beneficial for promoting any particular outcome. Currently, much of the evidence is mixed, to some extent explicable in terms of the different musical activities studied and the research methods used. As research into the wider benefits of music is not a high priority for research funders, it may be many years before it is possible to provide clear guidance on which musical interventions might lead to particular outcomes, and what qualities in the delivery of those interventions are key to success.

Bibliography

Aalbers, S., Fusar-Poli, L., Freeman, R. E., Spreen, M., Ket, J. C., Vink, A. C., Maratos, A., Crawford, M., Chen, X.-J., & Gold, C. (2017). Music therapy for depression. *Cochrane Database of Systematic Reviews, 2017*(11). https://doi.org/10.1002/14651858.cd004517.pub3

Abdulah, D. M., Alhakem, S. S. M., & Piro, R. S. (2018). Effects of music as an adjunctive therapy on severity of symptoms in patients with obsessive-compulsive disorder: Randomized controlled trial. *Nordic Journal of Music Therapy, 28*(1), 27–40. https://doi.org/10.1080/08098131.2018.1546222

Abeles, H. F. (2007). The effect of string instruction on students' performance on state-mandated achievement tests in mathematics and language arts. *Eastern Division MENC Meeting*.

Abeles, H. F., & Chung, J. W. (1996). Responses to music. In D. A. Hodges (Ed.), *Handbook of music psychology* (pp. 285–342). IMR Press.

Aben, B., Stapert, S., & Blokland, A. (2012). About the Distinction between Working Memory and Short-Term Memory. *Frontiers in Psychology, 3*. https://doi.org/10.3389/fpsyg.2012.00301

Abikoff, H., Courtney, M. E., Szeibel, P. J., & Koplewicz, H. S. (1996). The Effects of Auditory Stimulation on the Arithmetic Performance of Children with ADHD and Nondisabled Children. *Journal of Learning Disabilities, 29*(3), 238–246. https://doi.org/10.1177/002221949602900302

Abraha, I., Rimland, J. M., Trotta, F. M., Dell'Aquila, G., Cruz-Jentoft, A., Petrovic, M., Gudmundsson, A., Soiza, R., O'Mahony, D., Guaita, A., & Cherubini, A. (2017). Systematic review of systematic reviews of non-pharmacological interventions to treat behavioural disturbances in older patients with dementia. The SENATOR-OnTop series. *BMJ Open, 7*(3), e012759. https://doi.org/10.1136/bmjopen-2016-012759

A.B.R.S.M. (2014). *Making music: Teaching, learning and playing in the UK*. Associated Board of the Royal Schools of Music.

Academy, R. A. (2013). *Final Report for 2012 National Endowment for the Arts (NEA) Grant*.

Adderley, C., Kennedy, M., & Berz, W. (2003). "A Home away from Home": The World of the High School Music Classroom. *Journal of Research in Music Education, 51*(3), 190–205. https://doi.org/10.2307/3345373

Adushkina, K. V. (2015). Development of emotional intelligence of adolescents in institutions of additional education by means of music therapy. *Pedagog Educ Russia*[MP1, 9, 47–51.

Agbo-Quaye, S. (2006). *Teenage sexual attitudes, norms, desires and intentions: The impact of preferred musical genres. Unpublished doctoral dissertation.* Brunel University.

Agency, A. (2013). *Audience Spectrum.* https://www.theaudienceagency.org/audience-spectrum.

Agres, K. R., Foubert, K., & Sridhar, S. (2021). Music Therapy During COVID-19: Changes to the Practice, Use of Technology, and What to Carry Forward in the Future. *Frontiers in Psychology, 12.* https://doi.org/10.3389/fpsyg.2021.647790

Ahissar, M., Protopapas, A., Reid, M., & Merzenich, M. M. (2000). Auditory processing parallels reading abilities in adults. *Proceedings of the National Academy of Sciences, 97*(12), 6832–6837. https://doi.org/10.1073/pnas.97.12.6832

Akombo, D. O. (2001). Reporting on Music Therapy in Kenya. *Voices: A World Forum for Music Therapy, 1*(1). https://doi.org/10.15845/voices.v1i1.45

Alain, C., Moussard, A., Singer, J., Lee, Y., Bidelman, G. M., & Moreno, S. (2019). Music and Visual Art Training Modulate Brain Activity in Older Adults. *Frontiers in Neuroscience, 13.* https://doi.org/10.3389/fnins.2019.00182

Alain, C., & Woods, D. L. (1999). Age-related changes in processing auditory stimuli during visual attention: Evidence for deficits in inhibitory control and sensory memory. *Psychology and Aging, 14*(3), 507–519. https://doi.org/10.1037/0882-7974.14.3.507

Alanne, S. (2010). *Music Psychotherapy with Refugee Survivors of Torture: Interpretations of three Clinical Case Studies.* University of the Arts Helsinki.

Aldridge, D., Schmid, W., Kaeder, M., Schmidt, C., & Ostermann, T. (2005). Functionality or aesthetics? A pilot study of music therapy in the treatment of multiple sclerosis patients. *Complementary Therapies in Medicine, 13*(1), 25–33. https://doi.org/10.1016/j.ctim.2005.01.004

Aleman, A., Nieuwenstein, M. R., Böcker, K. B. E., & Haan, E. H. F. de. (2000). Music training and mental imagery ability. *Neuropsychologia, 38*(12), 1664–1668. https://doi.org/10.1016/s0028-3932(00)00079-8

Alemán, X., Duryea, S., Guerra, N. G., McEwan, P. J., Muñoz, R., Stampini, M., & Williamson, A. A. (2016). The Effects of Musical Training on Child Development: A Randomized Trial of El Sistema in Venezuela. *Prevention Science, 18*(7), 865–878. https://doi.org/10.1007/s11121-016-0727-3

Alexander, J. A., Wong, P. C. M., & Bradlow, A. R. (2005, September). Lexical tone perception in musicians and non-musicians. *Interspeech 2005*. https://doi.org/10.21437/interspeech.2005-271

Allen, T. N. M. (2005). Exploring hip-hop therapy with high-risk youth. *Praxis*, 5, 30–36.

Allison, T. A. (2011). *Songwriting and Transcending Institutional Boundaries in the Nursing Home*. Oxford University Press. https://doi.org/10.1093/oxfordhb/9780199756261.013.0010

Almau, A. (2005). Music is why we come to school. *Improving Schools*, 8(2), 193–197. https://doi.org/10.1177/1365480205057707

Altenmüller, E., & James, C. E. (2020). The impact of music interventions on motor rehabilitation following stroke in elderly. In *Music and the Aging Brain* (pp. 407–432). Elsevier. https://doi.org/10.1016/b978-0-12-817422-7.00016-x

Altenmüller, E., Marco-Pallares, J., Münte, T. F., & Schneider, S. (2009). Neural Reorganization Underlies Improvement in Stroke-induced Motor Dysfunction by Music-supported Therapy. *Annals of the New York Academy of Sciences*, 1169(1), 395–405. https://doi.org/10.1111/j.1749-6632.2009.04580.x

Altenmüller, E. O. (2001). How Many Music Centers Are in the Brain? *Annals of the New York Academy of Sciences*, 930(1), 273–280. https://doi.org/10.1111/j.1749-6632.2001.tb05738.x

Altenmüller, E. O. (2003). How many Music Centres are in the Brain? In *The Cognitive Neuroscience of Music* (pp. 346–353). Oxford University Press. https://doi.org/10.1093/acprof:oso/9780198525202.003.0022

Altenmuller, E. O., Gruhn, W., & Parlitz, D. (1997). Music learning produces changes in brain activation patterns: A longitudinal DC-EEG-study unit. *International Journal of Arts Medicine*, 5, 28–34.

Altenmüller, E., O., & McPherson, G. (2007). Motor learning and instrumental training. In F. R. Gruhn (Ed.), *Neurosciences in Music Pedagogy* (pp. 145–155). Nova Science Publisher.

Altenmüller, E., & Schlaug, G. (2015). Apollo's gift. In *Progress in Brain Research* (pp. 237–252). Elsevier. https://doi.org/10.1016/bs.pbr.2014.11.029

Alvaro, F., A.F., S., Viti, A., Simone, R., Miranda, E., Kirke, A., Badia, T., Helling, G., & Istrate, O. (2010). E-motion Project: Electronic Music and use of ICT for young at risk of exclusion. In *Final Report of Classroom Testing. Lifelong Learning Programme, Education and Culture DG*.

Alves-Pinto, A., Ehrlich, S., Cheng, G., Turova, V., Blumenstein, T., & Lampe, R. (2017). Effects of short-term piano training on measures of finger tapping, somatosensory perception and motor-related brain activity in patients with cerebral palsy. *Neuropsychiatric Disease and Treatment, Volume 13*, 2705–2718. https://doi.org/10.2147/ndt.s145104

Alves-Pinto, A., Turova, V., Blumenstein, T., & Lampe, R. (2016). The Case for Musical Instrument Training in Cerebral Palsy for Neurorehabilitation. *Neural Plasticity, 2016*, 1–9. https://doi.org/10.1155/2016/1072301

Amaral, J. A., Souza Faria, R., Faraco, A., Coli, A. C. M., & Los Rios Leal, L. (2020). Auditory stimulation with Mozart sonata k-448 and heavy metal music improves short term memory in rats. *Open Science Journal, 5*(4).

Amchin, R., Kopf, T., & Weaver, M. (1991). Effects of arts education on high school student self-concept. In *Convention of the Ohio Music Education Association*.

Amer, T., Kalender, B., Hasher, L., Trehub, S. E., & Wong, Y. (2013). Do Older Professional Musicians Have Cognitive Advantages? *PLoS ONE, 8*(8), e71630. https://doi.org/10.1371/journal.pone.0071630

Amunts, K., Schlaug, G., Jäncke, L., Steinmetz, H., Schleicher, A., Dabringhaus, A., & Zilles, K. (1997). Motor cortex and hand motor skills: Structural compliance in the human brain. *Human Brain Mapping, 5*(3), 206–215. https://doi.org/10.1002/(sici)1097-0193(1997)5:3<206::aid-hbm5>3.0.co;2-7

An, S. A., Tillman, D. A., Boren, R., & Wang, J. (2014). Fostering Elementary Students' Mathematics Disposition through Music Mathematics Integrated Lessons. *International Journal for Mathematics Teaching and Learning, 15*(3), 1–18 3.

Anaya, E. M., Pisoni, D. B., & Kronenberger, W. G. (2016). Visual-spatial sequence learning and memory in trained musicians. *Psychology of Music, 45*(1), 5–21. https://doi.org/10.1177/0305735616638942

Andemicael, A. (2011). *Positive energy: A review of the role of artistic activities in refugee camps*. Office of the United Nations High Commissioner for Refugees.

Anderson, C. A., Bushman, B. J., & Bartholow, B. D. (2017). Screen violence and youth behaviour. *Paediatrics, 140*(2), 142–147.

Anderson, K., & Overy, K. (2010). Engaging Scottish young offenders in education through music and art. *International Journal of Community Music, 3*(1), 47–64. https://doi.org/10.1386/ijcm.3.1.47/1

Anderson, P. J. (2014). Neuropsychological outcomes of children born very preterm. *Seminars in Fetal and Neonatal Medicine, 19*(2), 90–96. https://doi.org/10.1016/j.siny.2013.11.012

Anderson, S. A., & Fuller, G. B. (2010). Effect of music on reading comprehension of junior high school students. *School Psychology Quarterly, 25*(3), 178–187. https://doi.org/10.1037/a0021213

Anderson, S., Fast, J., Keating, N., Eales, J., Chivers, S., & Barnet, D. (2016). Translating Knowledge. *Health Promotion Practice, 18*(1), 15–25. https://doi.org/10.1177/1524839915625037

Andrés, P., Parmentier, F. B. R., & Escera, C. (2006). The effect of age on involuntary capture of attention by irrelevant sounds: A test of the frontal hypothesis of aging. *Neuropsychologia, 44*(12), 2564–2568. https://doi.org/10.1016/j.neuropsychologia.2006.05.005

Angel, L. A., Polzella, D. J., & Elvers, G. C. (2010). Background Music and Cognitive Performance. *Perceptual and Motor Skills, 110*(3_suppl), 1059–1064. https://doi.org/10.2466/pms.110.c.1059-1064

Anshel, A., & Kipper, D. A. (1988). The Influence of Group Singing on Trust and Cooperation. *Journal of Music Therapy, 25*(3), 145–155. https://doi.org/10.1093/jmt/25.3.145

Anshel, M. H., & Marisi, D. Q. (1978). Effect of Music and Rhythm on Physical Performance. *Research Quarterly. American Alliance for Health, Physical Education and Recreation, 49*(2), 109–113. https://doi.org/10.1080/10671315.1978.10615514

Anthony, B., Weston, D., & Vallen, S. (2018). Thumbs Up: The effective use of music in health and well-being education for Australian Aboriginal youth in remote communities. *International Journal of Community Music, 11*(1), 71–89. https://doi.org/10.1386/ijcm.11.1.71_1

Antrim, D. K. (1945). Do musical talents have higher intelligence? *Etude, 63*, 127–128.

Anvari, S. H., Trainor, L. J., Woodside, J., & Levy, B. A. (2002). Relations among musical skills, phonological processing, and early reading ability in preschool children. *Journal of Experimental Child Psychology, 83*(2), 111–130. https://doi.org/10.1016/s0022-0965(02)00124-8

Apicella, A. (1952). *Survey of music activities in the penal institutions of the Northeastern United States* [PhD Thesis]. Boston University.

Aquino, M. P. B. de, Verdejo-Román, J., Pérez-García, M., & Pérez-García, P. (2019). Different role of the supplementary motor area and the insula between musicians and non-musicians in a controlled musical creativity task. *Scientific Reports, 9*(1). https://doi.org/10.1038/s41598-019-49405-5

Arafat, F., Wu, C., Zhong, M., Hu., Z., & Zhang, H. (2017). The Effect of Natural Sounds and Music on Driving Performance and Physiological. *Engineering Letters, 25*(4), 13.

Arditi, D. (2020). We're Getting the Band Back Together: Social Cohesion and Solidarity in Bands. In D. Arditi (Ed.), *Getting Signed: Record Contracts, Musicians, and Power in Society* (pp. 151–178 ,). Palgrave Macmillan. https://doi.org/10.1007/978-3-030-44587-4_6.

Areni, C. S., & Kim, D. (1993). The influence of background music on shopping behaviour: Classical versus top-forty music in a wine store. *Advances in Consumer Research, 20*, 336–340.

Armstrong, S. N., & Ricard, R. J. (2016). Integrating Rap Music Into Counseling With Adolescents in a Disciplinary Alternative Education Program. *Journal of Creativity in Mental Health, 11*(3–4), 423–435. https://doi.org/10.1080/15401383.2016.1214656

Arnaud.Cabanac, Perlovsky, L., Bonniot-Cabanac, M.-C., & Cabanac, M. (2013). Music and academic performance. *Behavioural Brain Research, 256,* 257–260. https://doi.org/10.1016/j.bbr.2013.08.023

Arnett, J. J. (1995). Adolescents' uses of media for self-socialization. *Journal of Youth and Adolescence, 24*(5), 519–533. https://doi.org/10.1007/bf01537054

Arnett-Gary, D. (1998). The effects of the arts on academic achievement. *Masters Abstracts International, 42*(1), 22.

Ascenso, S. (2017a). *The Lullaby Project: Areas of Change and Mechanisms of Impact.*

Ascenso, S. (2017b). *The Lullaby Project: Areas of Change and Mechanisms of Impact.* The Irene Taylor Trust. https://irenetaylortrust.files.wordpress.com/2018/06/the-lullaby-project_areas-of-change-and-mechanisms-of-impact-_research-by-sara-ascenso.pdf.

Ascenso, S., Perkins, R., Atkins, L., Fancourt, D., & Williamon, A. (2018). Promoting well-being through group drumming with mental health service users and their carers. *International Journal of Qualitative Studies on Health and Well-Being, 13*(1), 1484219. https://doi.org/10.1080/17482631.2018.1484219

Ashby, F. G., Isen, A. M., & Turken, A. U. (1999). A neuropsychological theory of positive affect and its influence on cognition. *Psychological Review, 106*(3), 529–550. https://doi.org/10.1037/0033-295x.106.3.529

Atchley, R. C. (1975). Adjustment to loss of job or retirement. *International Journal of Ageing and Development, 5*(1), 17–27. https://doi.org/10.2190/EHU3-VCRVJ-04NU.

Attard, A., & Larkin, M. (2016). Art therapy for people with psychosis: A narrative review of the literature. *The Lancet Psychiatry, 3*(11), 1067–1078. https://doi.org/10.1016/s2215-0366(16)30146-8

Atterbury, B. W. (1985). Musical Differences in Learning-Disabled and Normal-Achieving Readers, Aged Seven, Eight and Nine. *Psychology of Music, 13*(2), 114–123. https://doi.org/10.1177/0305735685132005

Austin, J. R. (1990). The relationship of music self-esteem to degree of participation in school and out-of-school music activities among upper-elementary students. *Contributions to Music Education, 17,* 20–31.

Avila, C., Furnham, A., & McClelland, A. (2011). The influence of distracting familiar vocal music on cognitive performance of introverts and extraverts. *Psychology of Music, 40*(1), 84–93. https://doi.org/10.1177/0305735611422672

Aydin, K. K. C., & Terzibasioglu, E. (2005). Quantitative proton MR spectroscopic findings of cortical reorganization in the auditory cortex of musicians. *American Journal of Neuroradiology, 26,* 128–136.

Azaryahu, L., Courey, S. J., Elkoshi, R., & Adi-Japha, E. (2019). 'MusiMath' and 'Academic Music' – Two music-based intervention programs for fractions learning in fourth grade students. *Developmental Science*, 23(4). https://doi.org/10.1111/desc.12882

Bae, S., & Kyungsuk, K. (2020). Group music therapy involving the creation of a musical play to improve self esteem. *Journal of Music and Human Behaviour*, 17(1), 51–70.

Baer, J. (1991). Generality of creativity across performance domains. *Creativity Research Journal*, 4(1), 23–39. https://doi.org/10.1080/10400419109534371

Baer, J. (2012). Domain Specificity and the Limits of Creativity Theory. *The Journal of Creative Behavior*, 46(1), 16–29. https://doi.org/10.1002/jocb.002

Baer, J. (2015). The Importance of Domain-Specific Expertise in Creativity. *Roeper Review*, 37(3), 165–178. https://doi.org/10.1080/02783193.2015.1047480

Baharloo, S., Johnston, P. A., Service, S. K., Gitschier, J., & Freimer, N. B. (1998). Absolute Pitch: An Approach for Identification of Genetic and Nongenetic Components. *The American Journal of Human Genetics*, 62(2), 224–231. https://doi.org/10.1086/301704

Bahna-James, T. (1991). The Relationship Between Mathematics and Music: Secondary School Student Perspectives. *The Journal of Negro Education*, 60(3), 477. https://doi.org/10.2307/2295499

Bahr, N., & Christensen, C. (2000). Inter-domain transfer between mathematical skill and musicianship. *Journal of Structural Learning and Intelligent Systems*, 14, 187–197.

Bailey, B. A., & Davidson, J. W. (2002). Adaptive Characteristics of Group Singing: Perceptions from Members of a Choir Forhomeless Men. *Musicae Scientiae*, 6(2), 221–256. https://doi.org/10.1177/102986490200600206

Bailey, B. A., & Davidson, J. W. (2003). Amateur Group Singing as a Therapeutic Instrument. *Nordic Journal of Music Therapy*, 12(1), 18–32. https://doi.org/10.1080/08098130309478070

Bailey, B. A., & Davidson, J. W. (2005). Effects of group singing and performance for marginalized and middle-class singers. *Psychology of Music*, 33(3), 269–303. https://doi.org/10.1177/0305735605053734

Bailey, J. A., & Penhune, V. B. (2010). Rhythm synchronization performance and auditory working memory in early- and late-trained musicians. *Experimental Brain Research*, 204(1), 91–101. https://doi.org/10.1007/s00221-010-2299-y

Bailey, J. A., Zatorre, R. J., & Penhune, V. B. (2014). Early Musical Training Is Linked to Gray Matter Structure in the Ventral Premotor Cortex and Auditory–Motor Rhythm Synchronization Performance. *Journal of Cognitive Neuroscience*, 26(4), 755–767. https://doi.org/10.1162/jocn_a_00527

Bailey, J., & Penhune, V. B. (2012). A sensitive period for musical training: Contributions of age of onset and cognitive abilities. *Annals of the New York Academy of Sciences, 1252*(1), 163–170. https://doi.org/10.1111/j.1749-6632.2011.06434.x

Baily, J., & Collyer, M. (2006). Introduction: Music and Migration. *Journal of Ethnic and Migration Studies, 32*(2), 167–182. https://doi.org/10.1080/13691830500487266

Baird, A., & Samson, S. (2015). Music and dementia. *Progress in Brain Research, 217*, 207–235. https://doi.org/10.1016/bs.pbr.2014.11.028Get.

Baird, A., & Thompson, W. F. (2018). When music compensates language: A case study of severe aphasia in dementia and the use of music by a spousal caregiver. *Aphasiology, 33*(4), 449–465. https://doi.org/10.1080/02687038.2018.1471657

Baird, P. J. (2001). *Children's song-makers as messengers of hope: Participatory research with implications for teacher educators. Unpublished doctoral dissertation.* University of San Francisco.

Bakagiannis, S., & Tarrant, M. (2006). Can music bring people together? Effects of shared musical preference on intergroup bias in adolescence. *Scandinavian Journal of Psychology, 47*(2), 129–136. https://doi.org/10.1111/j.1467-9450.2006.00500.x

Baker, F. A., & Ballantyne, J. (2013). "You've got to accentuate the positive": Group songwriting to promote a life of enjoyment, engagement and meaning in aging Australians. *Nordic Journal of Music Therapy, 22*(1), 7–24. https://doi.org/10.1080/08098131.2012.678372

Baker, F. A., Jeanneret, N., & Clarkson, A. (2017). Contextual factors and wellbeing outcomes: Ethnographic analysis of an artist-led group songwriting program with young people. *Psychology of Music, 46*(2), 266–280. https://doi.org/10.1177/0305735617709520

Baker, F. A., & MacDonald, R. A. R. (2013a). Flow, identity, achievement, satisfaction and ownership during therapeutic songwriting experiences with university students and retirees. *Musicae Scientiae, 17*(2), 131–146. https://doi.org/10.1177/1029864913476287

Baker, F. A., & MacDonald, R. A. R. (2013b). Experiences of creating personally meaningful songs within a therapeutic context. *Arts & Health, 6*(2), 143–161. https://doi.org/10.1080/17533015.2013.808254

Baker, F., & Jones, C. (2005). Holding a Steady Beat: The Effects of a Music Therapy Program on Stabilising Behaviours of Newly Arrived Refugee Students. *British Journal of Music Therapy, 19*(2), 67–74. https://doi.org/10.1177/135945750501900205

Baker, F., & Jones, C. (2006). The effect of music therapy services on classroom behaviours of newly arrived refugee students in Australia—A pilot study. *Emotional and Behavioural Difficulties*, 11(4), 249–260. https://doi.org/10.1080/13632750601022170

Baker, S., & Homan, S. (2007). Rap, Recidivism and the Creative Self: A Popular Music Programme for Young Offenders in Detention. *Journal of Youth Studies*, 10(4), 459–476. https://doi.org/10.1080/13676260701262566

Balbag, M. A., Pedersen, N. L., & Gatz, M. (2014). Playing a Musical Instrument as a Protective Factor against Dementia and Cognitive Impairment: A Population-Based Twin Study. *International Journal of Alzheimer's Disease*, 2014, 1–6. https://doi.org/10.1155/2014/836748

Baltazar, M. (2019). Musical affect regulation in adolescents: A conceptual model. In *Handbook of Music, Adolescents, and Wellbeing* (pp. 65–74). Oxford University Press. https://doi.org/10.1093/oso/9780198808992.003.0006

Baltazar, M., & Saarikallio, S. (2016). Toward a better understanding and conceptualization of affect self-regulation through music: A critical, integrative literature review. *Psychology of Music*, 44(6), 1500–1521. https://doi.org/10.1177/0305735616663313

Baltazar, M., & Saarikallio, S. (2017). Strategies and mechanisms in musical affect self-regulation: A new model. *Musicae Scientiae*, 23(2), 177–195. https://doi.org/10.1177/1029864917715061

Baltazar, M., Västfjäll, D., Asutay, E., Koppel, L., & Saarikallio, S. (2019). Is it me or the music? Stress reduction and the role of regulation strategies and music. *Music & Science*, 2, 205920431984416. https://doi.org/10.1177/2059204319844161

Bamford, S. M., & Bowell, S. (2018). What would life be—Without a song or a dance, what are we? In *Report from the commission on dementia and music, International Longevity Centre—UK (ILC-UK*. https://ilcuk.org.uk/wp-content/uploads/2018/10/

Banai, K., & Ahissar, M. (2013). Musical Experience, Auditory Perception and Reading-Related Skills in Children. *PLoS ONE*, 8(9), e75876. https://doi.org/10.1371/journal.pone.0075876

Banai, K., Hornickel, J., Skoe, E., Nicol, T., Zecker, S., & Kraus, N. (2009). Reading and Subcortical Auditory Function. *Cerebral Cortex*, 19(11), 2699–2707. https://doi.org/10.1093/cercor/bhp024

Bandura, A. (2005). *Guide for creating self-efficacy scales*. Information Age Publishing.

Bang, A. H. (2016). The Restorative and Transformative Power of the Arts in Conflict Resolution. *Journal of Transformative Education*, 14(4), 355–376. https://doi.org/10.1177/1541344616655886

Bangert, M., & Altenmüller, E. O. (2003). Mapping perception to action in piano practice: A longitudinal DC-EEG study. *BMC Neuroscience*, 4(1), 26. https://doi.org/10.1186/1471-2202-4-26

Bangert, M., Haeusler, U., & Altenmüller, E. (2001). On Practice: How the Brain Connects Piano Keys and Piano Sounds. *Annals of the New York Academy of Sciences, 930*(1), 425–428. https://doi.org/10.1111/j.1749-6632.2001.tb05760.x

Bangert, M., & Schlaug, G. (2006). Specialization of the specialized in features of external human brain morphology. *European Journal of Neuroscience, 24*(6), 1832–1834. https://doi.org/10.1111/j.1460-9568.2006.05031.x

Barbaroux, M., Dittinger, E., & Besson, M. (2019). Music training with Démos program positively influences cognitive functions in children from low socio-economic backgrounds. *PLOS ONE, 14*(5), e0216874. https://doi.org/10.1371/journal.pone.0216874

Baron, R. (1955). Music in penal institutions. *Bulletin of the National Association for Music Therapy, 4*, 5–6.

Barr, L., Dittmar, M., Roberts, E., & Sheraden, M. (2002). *Enhancing student achievement through the improvement of listening skills.*

Barrera, M. E., Rykov, M. H., & Doyle, S. L. (2002). The effects of interactive music therapy on hospitalized children with cancer: A pilot study. *Psycho-Oncology, 11*(5), 379–388. https://doi.org/10.1002/pon.589

Barrett, K. C., Ashley, R., Strait, D. L., & Kraus, N. (2013). Art and science: How musical training shapes the brain. *Frontiers in Psychology, 4*. https://doi.org/10.3389/fpsyg.2013.00713

Barrett, L. F., & Gross, J. J. (2001). Emotional intelligence: A process model of emotion representation and regulation. In T. J. Mayne & G. A. Bonanno (Eds), *Emotions and social behavior. Emotions: Current issues and future directions* (pp. 286–310). Guilford Press.

Barrett, M. S., & Baker, J. S. (2012). Developing learning identities in and through music: A case study of the outcomes of a music programme in an Australian juvenile detention centre. *International Journal of Music Education, 30*(3), 244–259. https://doi.org/10.1177/0255761411433721

Barrett, M. S., & Bond, N. (2014). Connecting through music: The contribution of a music programme to fostering positive youth development. *Research Studies in Music Education, 37*(1), 37–54. https://doi.org/10.1177/1321103x14560320

Barrett, M. S., Flynn, L. M., Brown, J. E., & Welch, G. F. (2019). Beliefs and Values About Music in Early Childhood Education and Care: Perspectives From Practitioners. *Frontiers in Psychology, 10*. https://doi.org/10.3389/fpsyg.2019.00724

Barrett, M. S., & Welch, G. F. (2020). Music early learning programs: Enduring outcomes for children and their families. *Psychology of Music, 49*(5), 1226–1241. https://doi.org/10.1177/0305735620944232

Barroso, C., Ganley, C. M., Hart, S. A., Rogers, N., & Clendinning, J. P. (2019). The relative importance of math- and music-related cognitive and affective factors in predicting undergraduate music theory achievement. *Applied Cognitive Psychology, 33*(5), 771–783. https://doi.org/10.1002/acp.3518

Barrow, J. D. (1995). *The Artful Universe*. Clarendon Press.

Barwick, J., Valentine, E., West, R., & Wilding, J. (1989). Relations between reading and musical abilities. *British Journal of Educational Psychology, 59*(2), 253–257. https://doi.org/10.1111/j.2044-8279.1989.tb03097.x

Basiński, K., Zdun-Ry\textbackslash.zewska, A., & Majkowicz, M. (2018). The Role of Musical Attributes in Music-Induced Analgesia: A Preliminary Brief Report. *Frontiers in Psychology, 9*. https://doi.org/10.3389/fpsyg.2018.01761

Bastian, H. G. (Ed.). (2002). *Musik(erziehung) und ihre Wirkung. Eine Langzeitstudie an Berliner Grundschulen* [Music education and its effects. A long-term study in elementary schools in. Schott.

Bates, V. C. (2012). Social Class and School Music. *Music Educators Journal, 98*(4), 33–37. https://doi.org/10.1177/0027432112442944

Batey, M., & Furnham, A. (2006). Creativity, Intelligence, and Personality: A Critical Review of the Scattered Literature. *Genetic, Social, and General Psychology Monographs, 132*(4), 355–429. https://doi.org/10.3200/mono.132.4.355-430

Batt-Rawden, K. B., DeNora, T., & Ruud, E. (2005). Music Listening and Empowerment in Health Promotion: A Study of the Role and Significance of Music in Everyday Life of the Long-term Ill. *Nordic Journal of Music Therapy, 14*(2), 120–136. https://doi.org/10.1080/08098130509478134

Batt-Rawden, K., & Denora, T. (2005). Music and informal learning in everyday life. *Music Education Research, 7*(3), 289–304. https://doi.org/10.1080/14613800500324507

Batt-Rawden, K., & Tellnes, G. (2011). How music may promote healthy behaviour. *Scandinavian Journal of Public Health, 39*(2), 113–120. https://doi.org/10.1177/1403494810393555

Batur, Z. (2016). The contribution of music to the fluent writing skills: MAYAZ technique. *Education, 137*(1), 82–92.

Baumeister, R. F., DeWall, C. N., Ciarocco, N. J., & Twenge, J. M. (2005). Social exclusion impairs self-regulation. *Journal of Personality and Social Psychology, 88*(4), 589–604. https://doi.org/10.1037/0022-3514.88.4.589

Baumgartner, H. (1992). Remembrance of things past: Music, autobiographical memory, and emotion. *Advances in Consumer Research, 19*, 613–620.

Bayoumi, M. (2005). Disco Inferno. *The Nation, 26*. http://www.thenation.com/doc/20051226/bayoumi.

Beck, B. D., Messel, C., Meyer, S. L., Cordtz, T. O., Søgaard, U., Simonsen, E., & Moe, T. (2017). Feasibility of trauma-focused Guided Imagery and Music with adult refugees diagnosed with PTSD: A pilot study. *Nordic Journal of Music Therapy, 27*(1), 67–86. https://doi.org/10.1080/08098131.2017.1286368

Beck, R. J., Cesario, T. C., Yousefi, A., & Enamoto, H. (2000). Choral Singing, Performance Perception, and Immune System Changes in Salivary Immunoglobulin A and Cortisol. *Music Perception, 18*(1), 87–106. https://doi.org/10.2307/40285902

Beckham, A. S. (1942). A study of social background and music ability of superior Negro children. *Journal of Applied Psychology, 26*(2), 210–217. https://doi.org/10.1037/h0054822

Behne, K. (1997). The development of "musicerleben" in adolescence: How and why young people listen to music. In I. Deliége & J. A. Sloboda (Eds), *Perception and cognition of music* (pp. 143–159). Psychology Press.

Behrends, A., Müller, S., & Dziobek, I. (2012). Moving in and out of synchrony: A concept for a new intervention fostering empathy through interactional movement and dance. *The Arts in Psychotherapy, 39*(2), 107–116. https://doi.org/10.1016/j.aip.2012.02.003

Beisman, G. L. (1967). Effect of Rhythmic Accompaniment upon Learning of Fundamental Motor Skills. *Research Quarterly. American Association for Health, Physical Education and Recreation, 38*(2), 172–176. https://doi.org/10.1080/10671188.1967.10613376

Belfi, A. M., Samson, D. W., Crane, J., & Schmidt, N. L. (2021). Aesthetic Judgments of Live and Recorded Music: Effects of Congruence Between Musical Artist and Piece. *Frontiers in Psychology, 12*. https://doi.org/10.3389/fpsyg.2021.618025

Bell, C. R., & Cresswell, A. (1984). Personality Differences among Musical Instrumentalists. *Psychology of Music, 12*(2), 83–93. https://doi.org/10.1177/0305735684122002

Bella, S. D., Berkowska, M., & Sowiński, J. (2011). Disorders of Pitch Production in Tone Deafness. *Frontiers in Psychology, 2*. https://doi.org/10.3389/fpsyg.2011.00164

Benasich, A. A., & Tallal, P. (2002). Infant discrimination of rapid auditory cues predicts later language impairment. *Behavioural Brain Research, 136*(1), 31–49. https://doi.org/10.1016/s0166-4328(02)00098-0

Bender, P. K., Plante, C., & Gentile, D. A. (2018). The effects of violent media content on aggression. *Current Opinion in Psychology, 19*, 104–108. https://doi.org/10.1016/j.copsyc.2017.04.003

Benedek, M., Borovnjak, B., Neubauer, A. C., & Kruse-Weber, S. (2014). Creativity and personality in classical, jazz and folk musicians. *Personality and Individual Differences, 63*, 117–121. https://doi.org/10.1016/j.paid.2014.01.064

Benedict, L. (1953). Survey of music in correctional institutions for adults. In E. G. Gilliland (Ed.), *Music Therapy 1952: Second book of Proceedings of the*

National Association for Music Therapy: Papers from the Third Annual Convention (pp. 119–121). National Association for Music Therapy.

Bengtsson, S. L., Nagy, Z., Skare, S., Forsman, L., Forssberg, H., & Ullén, F. (2005). Extensive piano practicing has regionally specific effects on white matter development. *Nature Neuroscience, 8*(9), 1148–1150. https://doi.org/10.1038/nn1516

Benner, J., Wengenroth, M., Reinhardt, J., Stippich, C., Schneider, P., & Blatow, M. (2017). Prevalence and function of Heschl's gyrus morphotypes in musicians. *Brain Structure and Function, 222*(8), 3587–3603. https://doi.org/10.1007/s00429-017-1419-x

Bennett, L. (2012). Patterns of listening through social media: Online fan engagement with the live music experience. *Social Semiotics, 22*(5), 545–557. https://doi.org/10.1080/10350330.2012.731897

Bennett, T., Savage, M., Silva, E. B., Warde, A., Gayo-Cal, M., & Wright, D. (2009). *Culture, Class, Distinction.* Routledge. https://doi.org/10.4324/9780203930571

Ben-Pazi, H., Aran, A., Pandyan, A., Gelkop, N., Ginsberg, G., Pollak, Y., & Elnatan, D. (2018). Auditory stimulation improves motor function and caretaker burden in children with cerebral palsy- A randomized double blind study. *PLOS ONE, 13*(12), e0208792. https://doi.org/10.1371/journal.pone.0208792

Bensimon, M., Amir, D., & Wolf, Y. (2012). A pendulum between trauma and life: Group music therapy with post-traumatized soldiers. *The Arts in Psychotherapy, 39*(4), 223–233. https://doi.org/10.1016/j.aip.2012.03.005

Bensimon, M., Bodner, E., & Shrira, A. (2016). The emotional impact of national music on young and older adults differing in posttraumatic stress disorder symptoms. *Aging & Mental Health, 21*(10), 1090–1098. https://doi.org/10.1080/13607863.2016.1196338

Benyamini, Y., Leventhal, E. A., & Leventhal, H. (2000). Gender Differences in Processing Information for Making Self-Assessments of Health. *Psychosomatic Medicine, 62*(3), 354–364. https://doi.org/10.1097/00006842-200005000-00009

Benz, S., Sellaro, R., Hommel, B., & Colzato, L. S. (2016). Music Makes the World Go Round: The Impact of Musical Training on Non-musical Cognitive Functions—A Review. *Frontiers in Psychology, 6.* https://doi.org/10.3389/fpsyg.2015.02023

Bergee, M. J., & Weingarten, K. M. (2020). Multilevel Models of the Relationship Between Music Achievement and Reading and Math Achievement. *Journal of Research in Music Education, 68*(4), 398–418. https://doi.org/10.1177/0022429420941432

Bergerson, D., & Motto, E. (2013). *Assessing the power of music.* Advocates for Community through Musical Excellence and Breck School's Advanced Mathematics Research.

Bergh, A. (2007). I'd like to Teach the World to Sing: Music and Conflict Transformation. *Musicae Scientiae*, *11*(2_suppl), 141–157. https://doi.org/10.1177/10298649070110s207

Bergh, A. (2008). *Everlasting love: The sustainability of top-down vs bottom-up approaches to music and conflict transformation* (S. Kagan & V. Kirchberg, Eds.). Higher Education for Sustainability.

Bergh, A. (2011). Emotions in motion: Transforming conflict and music. In *Music and the Mind* (pp. 363–378). Oxford University Press. https://doi.org/10.1093/acprof:osobl/9780199581566.003.0018

Bergmann, K. (2002). The sound of trauma: Music therapy in a post-war environment. *Australian Journal of Music Therapy*, *13*, 3–16.

Berlyne, D. E. (1971). *Aesthetics and Psychobiology*. Appleton-Century–Crofts.

Bermudez, P., Lerch, J. P., Evans, A. C., & Zatorre, R. J. (2008). Neuroanatomical Correlates of Musicianship as Revealed by Cortical Thickness and Voxel-Based Morphometry. *Cerebral Cortex*, *19*(7), 1583–1596. https://doi.org/10.1093/cercor/bhn196

Bernatzky, G., Presch, M., Anderson, M., & Panksepp, J. (2011). Emotional foundations of music as a non-pharmacological pain management tool in modern medicine. *Neuroscience & Biobehavioral Reviews*, *35*(9), 1989–1999. https://doi.org/10.1016/j.neubiorev.2011.06.005

Bernatzky, G., Strickner, S., Presch, M., Wendtner, F., & Kullich, W. (2012). Music as Non-Pharmacological Pain Management in Clinics\textbackslashast. In *Music, Health, and Wellbeing* (pp. 258–275). Oxford University Press. https://doi.org/10.1093/acprof:oso/9780199586974.003.0019

Besson, M., Chobert, J., & Marie, C. (2011). Transfer of Training between Music and Speech: Common Processing, Attention, and Memory. *Frontiers in Psychology*, *2*. https://doi.org/10.3389/fpsyg.2011.00094

Besson, M., Faïta, F., & Requin, J. (1994). Brain waves associated with musical incongruities differ for musicians and non-musicians. *Neuroscience Letters*, *168*(1–2), 101–105. https://doi.org/10.1016/0304-3940(94)90426-x

Best, J. R., Miller, P. H., & Naglieri, J. A. (2011). Relations between executive function and academic achievement from ages 5 to 17 in a large, representative national sample. *Learning and Individual Differences*, *21*(4), 327–336. https://doi.org/10.1016/j.lindif.2011.01.007

Bever, T. G., & Chiarello, R. J. (1974a). Cerebral Dominance in Musicians and Nonmusicians. *Science*, *185*(4150), 537–539. https://doi.org/10.1126/science.185.4150.537

Bever, T. G., & Chiarello, R. J. (1974b). Cerebral Dominance in Musicians and Nonmusicians. *Science*, *185*(4150), 537–539. https://doi.org/10.1126/science.185.4150.537

Beyers, W. B., Fowler, C., & Andreoli, D. (2008). *The economic impact of Seattle's music industry: A report for the Mayor's Office of Economic Development*. City of Seattle Office of Economic Development.

Bhat, A. N., & Srinivasan, S. (2013). A review of "music and movement" therapies for children with autism: Embodied interventions for multisystem development. *Frontiers in Integrated Neuroscience, 7*, 22.

Bhatara, A., Tirovolas, A. K., Duan, L. M., Levy, B., & Levitin, D. J. (2011). Perception of emotional expression in musical performance. *Journal of Experimental Psychology: Human Perception and Performance, 37*(3), 921–934. https://doi.org/10.1037/a0021922

Bhide, A., Power, A., & Goswami, U. (2013). A Rhythmic Musical Intervention for Poor Readers: A Comparison of Efficacy With a Letter-Based Intervention. *Mind, Brain, and Education, 7*(2), 113–123. https://doi.org/10.1111/mbe.12016

Bialystok, E., & DePape, A.-M. (2009). Musical expertise, bilingualism, and executive functioning. *Journal of Experimental Psychology: Human Perception and Performance, 35*(2), 565–574. https://doi.org/10.1037/a0012735

Biasutti, M., & Mangiacotti, A. (2017a). Assessing a cognitive music training for older participants: A randomised controlled trial. *International Journal of Geriatric Psychiatry, 33*(2), 271–278. https://doi.org/10.1002/gps.4721

Biasutti, M., & Mangiacotti, A. (2017b). Assessing a cognitive music training for older participants: A randomised controlled trial. *International Journal of Geriatric Psychiatry, 33*(2), 271–278. https://doi.org/10.1002/gps.4721

Biasutti, M., & Mangiacotti, A. (2019). Music Training Improves Depressed Mood Symptoms in Elderly People: A Randomized Controlled Trial. *The International Journal of Aging and Human Development, 92*(1), 115–133. https://doi.org/10.1177/0091415019893988

Bibb, J., Castle, D., & Newton, R. (2015). The role of music therapy in reducing post meal related anxiety for patients with anorexia nervosa. *Journal of Eating Disorders, 3*(1). https://doi.org/10.1186/s40337-015-0088-5

BibTeX generic citation style. (n.d.).

Bidabadi, S. S., & Mehryar, A. (2015). Music therapy as an adjunct to standard treatment for obsessive compulsive disorder and co-morbid anxiety and depression: A randomized clinical trial. *Journal of Affective Disorders, 184*, 13–17. https://doi.org/10.1016/j.jad.2015.04.011

Bidelman, G. M., & Alain, C. (2015). Musical Training Orchestrates Coordinated Neuroplasticity in Auditory Brainstem and Cortex to Counteract Age-Related Declines in Categorical Vowel Perception. *Journal of Neuroscience, 35*(3), 1240–1249. https://doi.org/10.1523/jneurosci.3292-14.2015

Bidelman, G. M., Gandour, J. T., & Krishnan, A. (2011a). Cross-domain Effects of Music and Language Experience on the Representation of Pitch in the

Human Auditory Brainstem. *Journal of Cognitive Neuroscience, 23*(2), 425–434. https://doi.org/10.1162/jocn.2009.21362

Bidelman, G. M., Gandour, J. T., & Krishnan, A. (2011b). Cross-domain Effects of Music and Language Experience on the Representation of Pitch in the Human Auditory Brainstem. *Journal of Cognitive Neuroscience, 23*(2), 425–434. https://doi.org/10.1162/jocn.2009.21362

Bidelman, G. M., Hutka, S., & Moreno, S. (2013). Tone Language Speakers and Musicians Share Enhanced Perceptual and Cognitive Abilities for Musical Pitch: Evidence for Bidirectionality between the Domains of Language and Music. *PLoS ONE, 8*(4), e60676. https://doi.org/10.1371/journal.pone.0060676

Bidelman, G. M., & Krishnan, A. (2010). Effects of reverberation on brainstem representation of speech in musicians and non-musicians. *Brain Research, 1355,* 112–125. https://doi.org/10.1016/j.brainres.2010.07.100

Bidelman, G. M., Weiss, M. W., Moreno, S., & Alain, C. (2014). Coordinated plasticity in brainstem and auditory cortex contributes to enhanced categorical speech perception in musicians. *European Journal of Neuroscience, 40*(4), 2662–2673. https://doi.org/10.1111/ejn.12627

Bieleninik, Ł., Ghetti, C., & Gold, C. (2016). Music therapy for preterm infants and their parents: A meta-analysis. *Pediatrics, 138*(3). https://doi.org/10.1542/peds2016-0971.

Bienstock, S. F. (1942). A Predictive Study of Musical Achievement. *The Pedagogical Seminary and Journal of Genetic Psychology, 61*(1), 135–145. https://doi.org/10.1080/08856559.1942.10534660

Bigand, E., & Poulin-Charronnat, B. (2006). Are we "experienced listeners"? A review of the musical capacities that do not depend on formal musical training. *Cognition, 100*(1), 100–130. https://doi.org/10.1016/j.cognition.2005.11.007

Bilby, C., Caufield, L., & Ridley, L. (2013). *Re-imagining futures: Exploring arts interventions and the process of desistance*. The Arts Alliance.

Bilhartz, T. D., Bruhn, R. A., & Olson, J. E. (1999). The Effect of Early Music Training on Child Cognitive Development. *Journal of Applied Developmental Psychology, 20*(4), 615–636. https://doi.org/10.1016/s0193-3973(99)00033-7

Billaux, N. (2011). *New directions for classical music in Venezuela*. Hochschulefür Musik.

Binet, A., & Simon, T. (1916). *The development of intelligence in children*. Williams & Wilkins.

Bisanz, J., Sherman, J. L., Rasmussen, C., & Ho, E. (2005). Development of arithmetic skills and knowledge in preschool children. In J. I. D. Campbell (Ed.), *Handbook of Mathematical Cognition* (p. 14). Psychology Press Ltd.

Biscaldi, M., Fischer, B., & Hartnegg, K. (2000). Voluntary Saccadic Control in Dyslexia. *Perception, 29*(5), 509–521. https://doi.org/10.1068/p2666a

Bittman, B. B., Berk, L. S., Felten, D. L. W., J., S., O.C., P., J., & Ninehouser, M. (2001). Composite effects of group drumming music therapy on modulation of neuroendocrine-immune parameters in normal subjects. *Alternative Therapies in Health and Medicine, 7*(1), 38–47.

Bittman, B., Berk, L., Shannon, M., Sharaf, M., Westengard, J., & Guegler, K. J. (2005). Recreational music-making modulates the human stress response: A preliminary individualized gene expression strategy. *Medical Science Monitor, 11*(2), 31–40.

Bittman, B., Dickson, L., & Coddington, K. (2009). Creative musical expression as a catalyst for quality-of-life improvement in inner-city adolescents placed in a court-referred residential treatment program. *Advances in Mind-Body Medicine, 24*(1), 8–19.

Blair, M. E., & Shimp, T. A. (1992). Consequences of an Unpleasant Experience with Music: A Second-Order Negative Conditioning Perspective. *Journal of Advertising, 21*(1), 35–43. https://doi.org/10.1080/00913367.1992.10673358

Blakemore, S. J., & Frith, U. (2000). *The implications of recent developments in neuroscience for research on teaching and learning.* Institute of Cognitive Neuroscience.

Blanden, J., Hansen, K., & Machin, S. (2008a). *The GDP cost of the lost earning potential of adults who grew up in poverty.*

Blanden, J., Hansen, K., & Machin, S. (2008b). *The GDP cost of the lost earning potential of adults who grew up in poverty.*

Blood, A. J., & Zatorre, R. J. (2001). Intensely pleasurable responses to music correlate with activity in brain regions implicated in reward and emotion. *Proceedings of the National Academy of Sciences, 98*(20), 11818–11823. https://doi.org/10.1073/pnas.191355898

Blood, A. J., Zatorre, R. J., Bermudez, P., & Evans, A. C. (1999). Emotional responses to pleasant and unpleasant music correlate with activity in paralimbic brain regions. *Nature Neuroscience, 2*(4), 382–387. https://doi.org/10.1038/7299

Bloor, A. J. (2009). The rhythm's gonna get ya' – background music in primary classrooms and its effect on behaviour and attainment. *Emotional and Behavioural Difficulties, 14*(4), 261–274. https://doi.org/10.1080/13632750903303070

Boer, D., & Abubakar, A. (2014). Music listening in families and peer groups: Benefits for young people's social cohesion and emotional well-being across four cultures. *Frontiers in Psychology, 5.* https://doi.org/10.3389/fpsyg.2014.00392

Boer, D., & Fischer, R. (2011). Towards a holistic model of functions of music listening across cultures: A culturally decentred qualitative approach. *Psychology of Music, 40*(2), 179–200. https://doi.org/10.1177/0305735610381885

Boer, D., Fischer, R., Strack, M., Bond, M. H., Lo, E., & Lam, J. (2011). How Shared Preferences in Music Create Bonds Between People. *Personality and Social Psychology Bulletin, 37*(9), 1159–1171. https://doi.org/10.1177/0146167211407521

Boer, D., Fischer, R., Tekman, H. G., Abubakar, A., Njenga, J., & Zenger, M. (2012). Young people's topography of musical functions: Personal, social and cultural experiences with music across genders and six societies. *International Journal of Psychology, 47*(5), 355–369. https://doi.org/10.1080/00207594.2012.656128

Bogt, T., Hale, W. W., & Canale, N. (2020). Goth Music and Depressive Symptoms among Adolescents: A Longitudinal Study. *Journal of Youth and Adolescence*.

Bogt, T. F. M. ter, Vieno, A., Doornwaard, S. M., Pastore, M., & Eijnden, R. J. J. M. van den. (2016). "You're not alone": Music as a source of consolation among adolescents and young adults. *Psychology of Music, 45*(2), 155–171. https://doi.org/10.1177/0305735616650029

Bohlman, P. (2003). *The music of European nationalism: Cultural identity and modern history*. ABC-CLIO.[MP15.

Boldt, S. (1996). The Effects of Music Therapy on Motivation, Psychological Well-Being, Physical Comfort, and Exercise Endurance of Bone Marrow Transplant Patients. *Journal of Music Therapy, 33*(3), 164–188. https://doi.org/10.1093/jmt/33.3.164

Bolduc, J. (2008). The Effects of Music Instruction on Emergent Literacy Capacities among Preschool Children: A Literature Review. *Early Childhood Research & Practice, 10*(1), 16.

Bolger, L. (2015). Being a player: Understanding collaboration in participatory music projects with communities supporting marginalised young people. *Qualitative Inquiries in Music Therapy, 10*, 77–126.

Boll-Avetisyan, N., Bhatara, A., & Höhle, B. (2020). Processing of Rhythm in Speech and Music in Adult Dyslexia. *Brain Sciences, 10*(5), 261. https://doi.org/10.3390/brainsci10050261

Bonacina, S., Cancer, A., Lanzi, P. L., Lorusso, M. L., & Antonietti, A. (2015). Improving reading skills in students with dyslexia: The efficacy of a sublexical training with rhythmic background. *Frontiers in Psychology, 6*. https://doi.org/10.3389/fpsyg.2015.01510

Bonneville-Roussy, A., Hruska, E., & Trower, H. (2020). Teaching Music to Support Students: How Autonomy-Supportive Music Teachers Increase Students' Well-Being. *Journal of Research in Music Education, 68*(1), 97–119. https://doi.org/10.1177/0022429419897611

Bonneville-Roussy, A., Rentfrow, P. J., Xu, M. K., & Potter, J. (2013). Music through the ages: Trends in musical engagement and preferences from adolescence through middle adulthood. *Journal of Personality and Social Psychology, 105*(4), 703–717. https://doi.org/10.1037/a0033770

Bonsdorff, P. V. (2017). Transformations of the everyday: The social aesthetics of childhood. In S. Schinkel & I. Herrmann (Eds), *Ästhetiken in Kindheit und Jugend: Sozialisationim Spannungsfeld von Kreativität, Konsum und Distinktion Edition Kulturwissenschaft, Transcript Verlag*[MP17 (pp. 319–334 ,). https://doi.org/10.14361/9783839434833-018.

Boone, A., & Quelch, V. (2003). Effects of harp music therapy on canine patients in the veterinary hospital setting. *The Harp Therapy Journal, 8*(2), 4–5, 15.

Booth, J. L., & Siegler, R. S. (2008). Numerical Magnitude Representations Influence Arithmetic Learning. *Child Development, 79*(4), 1016–1031. https://doi.org/10.1111/j.1467-8624.2008.01173.x

Borella, E., Carretti, B., Meneghetti, C., Carbone, E., Vincenzi, M., Madonna, J. C., Grassi, M., Fairfield, B., & Mammarella, N. (2017). Is working memory training in older adults sensitive to music? *Psychological Research, 83*(6), 1107–1123. https://doi.org/10.1007/s00426-017-0961-8

Bornstein, J. L. (2008). *Religion and Art as Peacebuilding Tools, A Case Study Of The Education of Arts Appreciation Program.*

Bosacki, S. L., & O'Neill, S. A. (2013). Early adolescents' emotional perceptions and engagement with popular music activities in everyday life. *International Journal of Adolescence and Youth, 20*(2), 228–244. https://doi.org/10.1080/02673843.2013.785438

Bosnyak, D. J. (2004). Distributed Auditory Cortical Representations Are Modified When Non-musicians Are Trained at Pitch Discrimination with 40 Hz Amplitude Modulated Tones. *Cerebral Cortex, 14*(10), 1088–1099. https://doi.org/10.1093/cercor/bhh068

Boss, L., Kang, D.-H., & Branson, S. (2015). Loneliness and cognitive function in the older adult: A systematic review. *International Psychogeriatrics, 27*(4), 541–553. https://doi.org/10.1017/s1041610214002749

Bosseler, A. N., Teinonen, T., Tervaniemi, M., & Huotilainen, M. (2016). Infant Directed Speech Enhances Statistical Learning in Newborn Infants: An ERP Study. *PLOS ONE, 11*(9), e0162177. https://doi.org/10.1371/journal.pone.0162177

Bottiroli, S., Rosi, A., Russo, R., Vecchi, T., & Cavallini, E. (2014). The cognitive effects of listening to background music on older adults: Processing speed improves with upbeat music, while memory seems to benefit from both upbeat and downbeat music. *Frontiers in Aging Neuroscience, 6*. https://doi.org/10.3389/fnagi.2014.00284

Bouissac, P. (2004). *How plausible is the motherese hypothesis? Behav Brain Sci.* [MP20. https://doi.org/10.1017/S0140525X04250117.

Bowles, S. A. (2003). *Tune up the mind: The effect of orchestrating music as a reading intervention* [Doctoral dissertation.]. Indiana University of Pennsylvania.

Bowmer, A., Mason, K., Knight, J., & Welch, G. (2018). Investigating the impact of a musical intervention on preschool children's executive function. *Front.*

Boyd, M., Ranson, K. M. von, Whidden, C., & Frampton, N. M. A. (2020). Short-term effects of group singing versus listening on mood and state self-esteem. *Psychomusicology: Music, Mind, and Brain, 30*(4), 178–188. https://doi.org/10.1037/pmu0000266

Bracalente, B., Chirieleison, C., Cossignani, M., Ferrucci, L., Gigliotti, M., & Ranalli, M. G. (2011). The Economic Impact of Cultural Events: The Umbria Jazz Music Festival. *Tourism Economics, 17*(6), 1235–1255. https://doi.org/10.5367/te.2011.0096

Brackley, J. (2012). Music Therapy and The Expression of Anger and Aggression: Working with aggressive behaviour in children aged five to nine who risk mainstream exclusion. In J. Tomlinson, P. Derrington, & A. Oldfield (Eds), *Music Therapy in Schools. Working with children of all ages in mainstream and special education* (p. 23). Jessica Kingsley.

Bradley, L., & Bryant, P. E. (1983). Categorizing sounds and learning to read—A causal connection. *Nature, 301*(5899), 419–421. https://doi.org/10.1038/301419a0

Brancatisano, O., Baird, A., & Thompson, W. F. (2019). A `Music, Mind and Movement' Program for People With Dementia: Initial Evidence of Improved Cognition. *Frontiers in Psychology, 10.* https://doi.org/10.3389/fpsyg.2019.01435

Brand, G., Sloboda, J., Saul, B., & Hathaway, M. (2012). The reciprocal relationship between jazz musicians and audiences in live performances: A pilot qualitative study. *Psychology of Music, 40*(5), 634–651. https://doi.org/10.1177/0305735612448509

Brandler, S., & Rammsayer, T. H. (2003). Differences in Mental Abilities between Musicians and Non-Musicians. *Psychology of Music, 31*(2), 123–138. https://doi.org/10.1177/03057356030031002290

Brandt, A., Gebrian, M., & Slevc, L. R. (2012). Music and Early Language Acquisition. *Frontiers in Psychology, 3.* https://doi.org/10.3389/fpsyg.2012.00327

Brattico, E., Tupala, T., Glerean, E., & Tervaniemi, M. (2013). Modulated neural processing of Western harmony in folk musicians. *Psychophysiology, 50*(7), 653–663. https://doi.org/10.1111/psyp.12049

Breen, M., Fitzroy, A. B., & Ali, M. O. (2019). Event-Related Potential Evidence of Implicit Metric Structure during Silent Reading. *Brain Sciences, 9*(8), 192. https://doi.org/10.3390/brainsci9080192

Bregman, A. S. (1990). *Auditory Scene Analysis.* The MIT Press. https://doi.org/10.7551/mitpress/1486.001.0001

Bringas, M. L., Zaldivar, M., Rojas, P. A., Martinez-Montes, K., Chongo, D. M., Ortega, M. A., Galvizu, R., Perez, A. E., Morales, L. M., Maragoto, C., Vera, H., Galan, L., Besson, M., & Valdes-Sosa, P. A. (2015). Effectiveness of music therapy as an aid to neurorestoration of children with severe neurological disorders. *Frontiers in Neuroscience, 9*. https://doi.org/10.3389/fnins.2015.00427

Brochard, R., Dufour, A., & Després, O. (2004). Effect of musical expertise on visuospatial abilities: Evidence from reaction times and mental imagery. *Brain and Cognition, 54*(2), 103–109. https://doi.org/10.1016/s0278-2626(03)00264-1

Brodsky, W. (1989). Music Therapy as an Intervention for Children with Cancer in Isolation Rooms. *Music Therapy, 8*(1), 17–34. https://doi.org/10.1093/mt/8.1.17

Brodsky, W. (2001). The effects of music tempo on simulated driving performance and vehicular control. *Transportation Research Part F: Traffic Psychology and Behaviour, 4*(4), 219–241. https://doi.org/10.1016/s1369-8478(01)00025-0

Brodsky, W., & Sulkin, I. (2011). Handclapping songs: A spontaneous platform for child development among 5–10-year-old children. *Early Child Development and Care, 181*(8), 1111–1136. https://doi.org/10.1080/03004430.2010.517837

Broh, B. A. (2002). Linking Extracurricular Programming to Academic Achievement: Who Benefits and Why? *Sociology of Education, 75*(1), 69. https://doi.org/10.2307/3090254

Bronfenbrenner, U., & Morris, P. A. (2007). *The Bioecological Model of Human Development*. John Wiley & Sons, Inc. https://doi.org/10.1002/9780470147658.chpsy0114

Bronson, H., Vaudreuil, R., & Bradt, J. (2018). Music Therapy Treatment of Active Duty Military: An Overview of Intensive Outpatient and Longitudinal Care Programs. *Music Therapy Perspectives, 36*(2), 195–206. https://doi.org/10.1093/mtp/miy006

Brown, D. (1991). *Human Universals*. McGraw-Hill.

Brown, E. D., Benedett, B., & Armistead, M. E. (2010). Arts enrichment and school readiness for children at risk. *Early Childhood Research Quarterly, 25*(1), 112–124. https://doi.org/10.1016/j.ecresq.2009.07.008

Brown, E. D., Garnett, M. L., Anderson, K. E., & Laurenceau, J.-P. (2016). Can the Arts Get Under the Skin? Arts and Cortisol for Economically Disadvantaged Children. *Child Development, 88*(4), 1368–1381. https://doi.org/10.1111/cdev.12652

Brown, E. D., & Sax, K. L. (2013). Arts enrichment and preschool emotions for low-income children at risk. *Early Childhood Research Quarterly, 28*(2), 337–346. https://doi.org/10.1016/j.ecresq.2012.08.002

Brown, E. J., & Nicklin, L. L. (2019). Spitting rhymes and changing minds: Global youth work through hip-hop. *International Journal of Development Education and Global Learning, 11*(2), 159–174, https://doi.org/10.18546/IJDEGL.11.2.

Brown, J. D. (1980). *Identifying problems facing the school band movement.* Gemeinhardt Co. Ltd.

Brown, J. D. (1985). *Strategic marketing for music educators.* Gemeinhardt Co. Ltd.

Brown, J., Sherrill, C., & Gench, B. (1981). Effects of an Integrated Physical Education/Music Program in Changing Early Childhood Perceptual-Motor Performance. *Perceptual and Motor Skills, 53*(1), 151–154. https://doi.org/10.2466/pms.1981.53.1.151

Browne, K. D., & Hamilton-Giachritsis, C. (2005). The influence of violent media on children and adolescents: A public-health approach. *The Lancet, 365*(9460), 702–710. https://doi.org/10.1016/s0140-6736(05)17952-5

Brownley, K. A., McMurray, R. G., & Hackney, A. C. (1995). Effects of music on physiological and affective responses to graded treadmill exercise in trained and untrained runners. *International Journal of Psychophysiology, 19*(3), 193–201. https://doi.org/10.1016/0167-8760(95)00007-f

Bruck, M. (1992). Persistence of dyslexics' phonological awareness deficits. *Developmental Psychology, 28*(5), 874–886. https://doi.org/10.1037/0012-1649.28.5.874

Bruin, L. R. de. (2021). Instrumental Music Educators in a COVID Landscape: A Reassertion of Relationality and Connection in Teaching Practice. *Frontiers in Psychology, 11.* https://doi.org/10.3389/fpsyg.2020.624717

Buchsbaum, B., Pickell, B., Love, T., Hatrak, M., Bellugi, U., & Hickok, G. (2005). Neural substrates for verbal working memory in deaf signers: FMRI study and lesion case report. *Brain and Language, 95*(2), 265–272. https://doi.org/10.1016/j.bandl.2005.01.009

Buckner, R. L. (2004). Memory and Executive Function in Aging and AD. *Neuron, 44*(1), 195–208. https://doi.org/10.1016/j.neuron.2004.09.006

Buffam, B. (2011). Can't hold us back! Hip-hop and the racial motility of aboriginal bodies in urban spaces. *Social Identities, 17*(3), 337–350. https://doi.org/10.1080/13504630.2011.570973

Bugaj, K., & Brenner, B. (2011). The Effects of Music Instruction on Cognitive Development and Reading Skills—An Overview. *Bulletin of the Council for Research in Music Education, 189,* 89–104. https://doi.org/10.5406/bulcouresmusedu.189.0089

Bugos, J. A. (2010). The benefits of music instruction on processing speed, verbal fluency, and cognitive control in aging. *Music Education Research International, 4,* 1–9.

Bugos, J. A. (2014). Community music as a cognitive training program for successful ageing. *Int. J. Commun. Music*[MP29, 7, 319–331, https://doi.org/10.1386/ijcm.7.3.319_1.

Bugos, J. A. (2019). The Effects of Bimanual Coordination in Music Interventions on Executive Functions in Aging Adults. *Frontiers in Integrative Neuroscience*, 13. https://doi.org/10.3389/fnint.2019.00068

Bugos, J. A., & Cooper, P. (2019). The effects of mallet training on self-efficacy and processing speed in beginning adult musicians. *Res. Perspect. Music Educ*[MP30, 20, 21–32.

Bugos, J. A., & DeMarie, D. (2017). The effects of a short-term music program on preschool children's executive functions. *Psychology of Music*, 45(6), 855–867. https://doi.org/10.1177/0305735617692666

Bugos, J. A., & Jacobs, E. (2012). Composition instruction and cognitive performance: Results of a pilot study. *Res. Issues Music Educ.*[MP31, 10(2). http://ir.stthomas.edu/rime/vol10/iss1/2.

Bugos, J. A., Kochar, S., & Maxfield, N. (2015). Intense piano training on self-efficacy and physiological stress in aging. *Psychology of Music*, 44(4), 611–624. https://doi.org/10.1177/0305735615577250

Bugos, J. A., & Mostafa, W. (2011). Musical training enhances information processing speed. *Bulletin of the Council for Research in Music Education*, 187, 7–18.

Bugos, J. A., Perlstein, W. M., McCrae, C. S., Brophy, T. S., & Bedenbaugh, P. H. (2007). Individualized Piano Instruction enhances executive functioning and working memory in older adults. *Aging & Mental Health*, 11(4), 464–471. https://doi.org/10.1080/13607860601086504

Bugos, J., & Kochar, S. (2017). Efficacy of a short-term intense piano training program for cognitive aging: A pilot study. *Musicae Scientiae*, 21(2), 137–150. https://doi.org/10.1177/1029864917690020

Bull, A. (2015). *The musical body: How gender and class are reproduced among young people playing classical music in England. Unpublished doctoral dissertation.* Goldsmiths College.

Bull, M. (2005). No Dead Air! The iPod and the Culture of Mobile Listening. *Leisure Studies*, 24(4), 343–355. https://doi.org/10.1080/0261436052000330447

Bull, M. (2006). Investigating the culture of mobile listening: From Walkman to iPod. In K. O'Hara & B. Brown (Eds), *Consuming Music Together: Social and Collaborative Aspects of Music Consumption Technologies* (pp. 131–149 ,). Springer. https://doi.org/10.1007/1-4020-4097-0_7.

Bungay, H., & Clift, S. (2010). Arts on Prescription: A review of practice in the UK. *Perspectives in Public Health*, 130(6), 277–281. https://doi.org/10.1177/1757913910384050

Burkhard, A., Elmer, S., Kara, D., Brauchli, C., & Jäncke, L. (2018). The Effect of Background Music on Inhibitory Functions: An ERP Study. *Frontiers in Human Neuroscience, 12.* https://doi.org/10.3389/fnhum.2018.00293

Burland, K., & Pitts, S. E. (2010). Understanding Jazz Audiences: Listening and Learning at the Edinburgh Jazz and Blues Festival. *Journal of New Music Research, 39*(2), 125–134. https://doi.org/10.1080/09298215.2010.493613

Burnard, P. (2008). A phenomenological study of music teachers' approaches to inclusive education practices among disaffected youth. *Research Studies in Music Education, 30*(1), 59–75. https://doi.org/10.1177/1321103x08089890

Burnard, P., & Dragovic, T. (2014). Collaborative creativity in instrumental group music learning as a site for enhancing pupil wellbeing. *Cambridge Journal of Education, 45*(3), 371–392. https://doi.org/10.1080/0305764x.2014.934204

Burns, D. S., Sledge, R. B., Fuller, L. A., Daggy, J. K., & Monahan, P. O. (2005). Cancer Patients' Interest and Preferences for Music Therapy. *Journal of Music Therapy, 42*(3), 185–199. https://doi.org/10.1093/jmt/42.3.185

Burns, S. (2016). *In Harmony Liverpool Special Report: Impact on Early Years Education.* In Harmony Liverpool.

Burns, S., & Bewick, P. (2011). *In Harmony Liverpool: Interim Report Year Two.* Royal Liverpool Philharmonic; Department for Education; In Harmony Sistema England.

Burns, S., & Bewick, P. (2012). *In Harmony Liverpool Interim Report: Year Three.* In Harmony Liverpool.

Burns, S., & Bewick, P. (2014). *In Harmony Liverpool Interim Report: Year Four.* In Harmony Liverpool.[MP36.

Burton, J., Horowitz, R., & Abeles, H. (1999). Learning in and through the arts. In E. Fiske (Ed.), *Partnership and The President's Committee on the Arts and the Humanities* (p. 37). The Arts Education.

Butkovic, A., & Dopudj, D. R. (2016). Personality traits and alcohol consumption of classical and heavy metal musicians. *Psychology of Music, 45*(2), 246–256. https://doi.org/10.1177/0305735616659128

Butkovic, A., & Modrusan, I. (2019). Personality differences among musicians: Real differences or stereotypes? *Psychology of Music, 49*(2), 216–226. https://doi.org/10.1177/0305735619849625

Butkovic, A., Ullén, F., & Mosing, M. A. (2015). Personality related traits as predictors of music practice: Underlying environmental and genetic influences. *Personality and Individual Differences, 74,* 133–138. https://doi.org/10.1016/j.paid.2014.10.006

Butterton, M. (1993). Music in the Pastoral Care of Emotionally Disturbed Children. *Journal of British Music Therapy, 7*(2), 12–22. https://doi.org/10.1177/135945759300700203

Buttsworth, L. M., & Smith, G. A. (1995). Personality of australian performing musicians by gender and by instrument. *Personality and Individual Differences, 18*(5), 595–603. https://doi.org/10.1016/0191-8869(94)00201-3

Butzlaff, R. (2000). Can Music Be Used to Teach Reading? *Journal of Aesthetic Education, 34*(3/4), 167. https://doi.org/10.2307/3333642

Bygren, L. O., Konlaan, B. B., & Johansson, S.-E. (1996). Attendance at cultural events, reading books or periodicals, and making music or singing in a choir as determinants for survival: Swedish interview survey of living conditions. *BMJ, 313*(7072), 1577–1580. https://doi.org/10.1136/bmj.313.7072.1577

Byrne, A., & Eysenck, M. W. (1995). Trait anxiety, anxious mood, and threat detection. *Cognition & Emotion, 9*(6), 549–562. https://doi.org/10.1080/02699939508408982

Cabedo, A. (2008). La educación musical comomodelo para una cultura de paz. In *Catorzenes Jornades de Foment de la investigació, Universitá Jaumei, Castellón*.

Cabedo-Mas, A., Arriaga-Sanz, C., & Moliner-Miravet, L. (2021). Uses and Perceptions of Music in Times of COVID-19: A Spanish Population Survey. *Frontiers in Psychology, 11*. https://doi.org/10.3389/fpsyg.2020.606180

Cain, M., Istvandity, L., & Lakhani, A. (2019). Participatory music-making and well-being within immigrant cultural practice: Exploratory case studies in South East Queensland, Australia. *Leisure Studies, 39*(1), 68–82. https://doi.org/10.1080/02614367.2019.1581248

Cain, M., Lakhani, A., & Istvandity, L. (2015). Short and long term outcomes for culturally and linguistically diverse (CALD) and$\textbackslash$i$\textbackslashgreater$at-risk$\textbackslash$/i$\textbackslashgreater$communities in participatory music programs: A systematic review. *Arts & Health, 8*(2), 105–124. https://doi.org/10.1080/17533015.2015.1027934

Caine, J. (1991). The Effects of Music on the Selected Stress Behaviors, Weight, Caloric and Formula Intake, and Length of Hospital Stay of Premature and Low Birth Weight Neonates in a Newborn Intensive Care Unit. *Journal of Music Therapy, 28*(4), 180–192. https://doi.org/10.1093/jmt/28.4.180

Caleon, I. S. (2019). The Role of Music-Based Activities in Fostering Well-Being of Adolescents: Insights from a Decade of Research (2008–2018. In P. Costes-Onishi (Ed.), *Artistic Thinking in the Schools* (p. ,). Springer.

Calvo, K., & Bejarano, E. (2020). *Music, solidarities and balconies in Spain. Interface: A journal for and about social movements Sharing stories of struggles*. https://www.interfacejournal.net/wp-content/uploads/2020/05/Calvo-and-Hernandez.pdf.

Camic, P. M., Williams, C. M., & Meeten, F. (2011). Does a `Singing Together Group' improve the quality of life of people with a dementia and their carers? A pilot evaluation study. *Dementia, 12*(2), 157–176. https://doi.org/10.1177/1471301211422761

Campbell, P. S. (2010). *Songs in their heads: Music and its meaning in children's lives.* Oxford University Press.

Campe, K., & Kaufman, B. (2013). *El Sistema: Development Beyond the Orchestra.* El Sistema at Conservatory Lab.

Caprara, G. V., Vecchione, M., Alessandri, G., Gerbino, M., & Barbaranelli, C. (2011). The contribution of personality traits and self-efficacy beliefs to academic achievement: A longitudinal study. *British Journal of Educational Psychology, 81*(1), 78–96. https://doi.org/10.1348/2044-8279.002004

Caprilli, S., Anastasi, F., Grotto, R. P. L., Abeti, M. S., & Messeri, A. (2007). Interactive Music as a Treatment for Pain and Stress in Children During Venipuncture: A Randomized Prospective Study. *Journal of Developmental & Behavioral Pediatrics, 28*(5), 399–403. https://doi.org/10.1097/dbp.0b013e31811ff8a7

Carbo, N., Fiese, R., & Boyle, D. (1990). A profile of all-state instrumentalists. *Research Perspectives in Music Education, 1,* 32–40.

Carcagno, S., & Plack, C. J. (2010). Subcortical Plasticity Following Perceptual Learning in a Pitch Discrimination Task. *Journal of the Association for Research in Otolaryngology, 12*(1), 89–100. https://doi.org/10.1007/s10162-010-0236-1

Cardarelli, D. M. (2003). *The effects of music instrumental training on performance on the reading and mathematics portions of the Florida Comprehensive Achievement Test for 3rd grade students* [Doctoral dissertation.]. University of Central Florida.

Carioti, D., Danelli, L., Guasti, M. T., Gallucci, M., Perugini, M., Steca, P., Stucchi, N. A., Maffezzoli, A., Majno, M., Berlingeri, M., & Paulesu, E. (2019). Music Education at School: Too Little and Too Late? Evidence From a Longitudinal Study on Music Training in Preadolescents. *Frontiers in Psychology, 10.* https://doi.org/10.3389/fpsyg.2019.02704

Carlisle, R. C. (1975). Women Singers in Darfur, Sudan Republic. *The Black Perspective in Music, 3*(3), 253. https://doi.org/10.2307/1214011

Carlson, E., Wilson, J., Baltazar, M., Duman, D., Peltola, H.-R., Toiviainen, P., & Saarkallio, S. H. (2021). The role of music in everyday life during the first wave of the COVID-19 pandemic: A mixed methods exploratory study. *Front. Psychol, P41*(ttps://doi.org/10.3389/fpsyg.2021.647756).

Carpentier, S. M., Moreno, S., & McIntosh, A. R. (2016). Short-term Music Training Enhances Complex, Distributed Neural Communication during Music and Linguistic Tasks. *Journal of Cognitive Neuroscience, 28*(10), 1603–1612. https://doi.org/10.1162/jocn_a_00988

Carr, C. (2008). Music Therapy with Children and Adolescents within mainstream schools. *Literature Review.*

Carr, C., d'Ardenne, P., Sloboda, A., Scott, C., Wang, D., & Priebe, S. (2011). Group music therapy for patients with persistent post-traumatic stress disorder—An exploratory randomized controlled trial with mixed methods evaluation. *Psychology and Psychotherapy: Theory, Research and Practice, 85*(2), 179–202. https://doi.org/10.1111/j.2044-8341.2011.02026.x

Carr, C., Odell-Miller, H., & Priebe, S. (2013). A Systematic Review of Music Therapy Practice and Outcomes with Acute Adult Psychiatric In-Patients. *PLoS ONE, 8*(8), e70252. https://doi.org/10.1371/journal.pone.0070252

Carr, C., & Wigram, T. (2009). Music Therapy with Children and Adolescents in Mainstream Schools: A Systematic Review. *British Journal of Music Therapy, 23*(1), 3–18. https://doi.org/10.1177/135945750902300102

Carr, S. M., & Rickard, N. S. (2016). The use of emotionally arousing music to enhance memory for subsequently presented images. *Psychology of Music, 44*(5), 1145–1157. https://doi.org/10.1177/0305735615613846

Carson, K. (2007). *Fank u for da musik... 4 givin it 2 me: How successful is music therapy as a supporting intervention for increased inclusion within British mainstream secondary education? Unpublished Master's dissertation.* City University.

Carstensen, L. L., Fung, H. H., & Charles, S. T. (2003). Socioemotional Selectivity Theory and the Regulation of Emotion in the Second Half of Life. *Motivation and Emotion, 27*(2), 103–123. https://doi.org/10.1023/a:1024569803230

Carterette, E. C., & Kendall, R. A. (1999). Comparative Music Perception and Cognition. In *The Psychology of Music* (pp. 725–791). Elsevier. https://doi.org/10.1016/b978-012213564-4/50019-6

Case, A. (2013). *Valley vibes orchestras participant evaluation form (questionnaire for teachers): Valley Vibes Orchestras, Sonoma Valley Education Foundation.*

Cassidy, G., & MacDonald, R. A. R. (2007). The effect of background music and background noise on the task performance of introverts and extraverts. *Psychology of Music, 35*(3), 517–537. https://doi.org/10.1177/0305735607076444

Cassidy, J. W., & Standley, J. M. (1995). The Effect of Music Listening on Physiological Responses of Premature Infants in the NICU. *Journal of Music Therapy, 32*(4), 208–227. https://doi.org/10.1093/jmt/32.4.208

Castañeda-Castañeda, J. C. (2009). *Percepciónsobre un taller de educación musical, de jóvenesenreclusiónen el Marceliano Ossa Lázaro Nicholls 'Créeme'.* Universidad Tecnológica de Pereira.

Castillejos, C., & Godoy-Izquierdo, D. (2020). "Music Makes My Old Heart Beat": A Randomised Controlled Study on the Benefits of the Use of Music in Comprehensive Care for Institutionalised Older Adults. *Applied Psychology: Health and Well-Being, 13*(1), 84–108. https://doi.org/10.1111/aphw.12217

Catalina, C. A., García-Herrero, S., Cabrerizo, E., Herrera, S., García-Pineda, S., Mohamadi, F., & Mariscal, M. A. (2020). Music Distraction among Young Drivers: Analysis by Gender and Experience. *Journal of Advanced Transportation, 2020*, 1–12. https://doi.org/10.1155/2020/6039762

Catanzaro, S., & Mearns, J. (1990). Measuring Generalized Expectancies for Negative Mood Regulation: Initial Scale Development and Implications. *Journal of Personality Assessment*, 54(3), 546–563. https://doi.org/10.1207/s15327752jpa5403&4_11

Catterall, J., Chapleau, R., & Iwanaga, J. (2000). Involvement in the arts and human development: General involvement and intensive involvement in music and theater arts. In MENC, *National Association for Music Education (ed.), Music makes a difference: Music, brain development and learning* (pp. 74–100). MENC.

Catterall, J. S. (1998). Involvement in the arts and success in secondary school. *America for the Arts*, 9([MP47).

Catterall, J. S., & Rauscher, F. H. (2008). Unpacking the impact of music on intelligence. In W. Gruhn & F. H. Rauscher (Eds), *Neurosciences in music pedagogy* (pp. 171–201). Nova Science Publishers.

Center, E. M. W. R. (2015). *Young & Great Music Project Annual Report*. Ewha Music Wellness Research Center.

Ceretti, A., & Cornelli, R. (2013). *Cinque riflessioni su criminalità, societ à e politica*. Feltrinelli.

Cevasco, A. M. (2008). The Effects of Mothers' Singing on Full-term and Preterm Infants and Maternal Emotional Responses. *Journal of Music Therapy*, 45(3), 273–306. https://doi.org/10.1093/jmt/45.3.273

Chamberlain, J. R. (2003). *The relationship between beat competency and reading abilities of third and fifth grade students* [Doctoral dissertation.]. The University of North Carolina at Greensboro.

Chamorro-Premuzic, T., & Furnham, A. (2007). Personality and music: Can traits explain how people use music in everyday life? *British Journal of Psychology*, 98(2), 175–185. https://doi.org/10.1348/000712606x111177

Chamorro-Premuzic, T., Gomà-i-Freixanet, M., Furnham, A., & Muro, A. (2009). Personality, self-estimated intelligence, and uses of music: A Spanish replication and extension using structural equation modeling. *Psychology of Aesthetics, Creativity, and the Arts*, 3(3), 149–155. https://doi.org/10.1037/a0015342

Chan, A. S., Ho, Y.-C., & Cheung, M.-C. (1998). Music training improves verbal memory. *Nature*, 396(6707), 128–128. https://doi.org/10.1038/24075

Chanda, M. L., & Levitin, D. J. (2013). The neurochemistry of music. *Trends in Cognitive Sciences*, 17(4), 179–193. https://doi.org/10.1016/j.tics.2013.02.007

Chandrasekaran, B., & Kraus, N. (2010). Music, Noise-Exclusion, and Learning. *Music Perception*, 27(4), 297–306. https://doi.org/10.1525/mp.2010.27.4.297

Chandrasekaran, B., Krishnan, A., & Gandour, J. (2009). Relative influence of musical and linguistic experience on early cortical processing of pitch contours. *Brain and Language*, *108*(1), 1–9. https://doi.org/10.1016/j.bandl.2008.02.001

Chao-Fernández, R., Gisbert-Caudeli, V., & Vázquez-Sánchez, R. (2020). Emotional Training and Modification of Disruptive Behaviors through Computer-Game-Based Music Therapy in Secondary Education. *Applied Sciences*, *10*(5), 1796. https://doi.org/10.3390/app10051796

Charyton, C., & Snelbecker, G. E. (2007). General, Artistic and Scientific Creativity Attributes of Engineering and Music Students. *Creativity Research Journal*, *19*(2–3), 213–225. https://doi.org/10.1080/10400410701397271

Cheek, J. M., & L.R, S. (1999). Music training and mathematics achievement. *Adolescence*, *34*, 759–761.

Cheliotis, L., & Jordanoska, A. (2015). The Arts of Desistance: Assessing the Role of Arts-based Programmes in Reducing Reoffending. *The Howard Journal of Crime and Justice*, *55*(1–2), 25–41. https://doi.org/10.1111/hojo.12154

Chen, J. L., Rae, C., & Watkins, K. E. (2012). Learning to play a melody: An fMRI study examining the formation of auditory-motor associations. *NeuroImage*, *59*(2), 1200–1208. https://doi.org/10.1016/j.neuroimage.2011.08.012

Chen, J., Zhou, Y., & Chen, J. (2020). The relationship between musical training and inhibitory control: An ERPs study. *Acta Psychologica Sinica*, *52*(12), 1365. https://doi.org/10.3724/sp.j.1041.2020.01365

Chen, X. J., Leith, H., Aarø, L. E., Manger, T., & Gold, C. (2016). Music therapy for improving mental health problems of offenders in correctional settings: Systematic review and meta-analysis. *Journal of Experimental Criminology*, *12*(2), 209–228. https://doi.org/10.1007/s11292-015-9250-y

Chen, X.-J., Hannibal, N., & Gold, C. (2015). Randomized Trial of Group Music Therapy With Chinese Prisoners. *International Journal of Offender Therapy and Comparative Criminology*, *60*(9), 1064–1081. https://doi.org/10.1177/0306624x15572795

Cheng, Y.-L., & Mix, K. S. (2013). Spatial Training Improves Children's Mathematics Ability. *Journal of Cognition and Development*, *15*(1), 2–11. https://doi.org/10.1080/15248372.2012.725186

Cheong, C. Y., Tan, J. A. Q., Foong, Y.-L., Koh, H. M., Chen, D. Z. Y., Tan, J. J. C., Ng, C. J., & Yap, P. (2016). Creative Music Therapy in an Acute Care Setting for Older Patients with Delirium and Dementia. *Dementia and Geriatric Cognitive Disorders Extra*, *6*(2), 268–275. https://doi.org/10.1159/000445883

Cheong-Clinch, C. (2009). Music for engaging young people in education. *Youth Studies Australia*, *28*(2), 50–57.

Chernaik, D. (2021). *Apollo music projects*. Apollo Music.

Chew, A. S.-Q., Yu, Y.-T., Chua, S.-W., & Gan, S. K.-E. (2016). The effects of familiarity and language of background music on working memory and language tasks in Singapore. *Psychology of Music, 44*(6), 1431–1438. https://doi.org/10.1177/0305735616636209

Chida, Y., Hamer, M., Wardle, J., & Steptoe, A. (2008). Do stress-related psychosocial factors contribute to cancer incidence and survival? *Nature Clinical Practice Oncology, 5*(8), 466–475. https://doi.org/10.1038/ncponc1134

Chin, T., & Rickard, N. S. (2013). Emotion regulation strategy mediates both positive and negative relationships between music uses and well-being. *Psychology of Music, 42*(5), 692–713. https://doi.org/10.1177/0305735613489916

Chiu, R. (2020). Functions of Music Making Under Lockdown: A Trans-Historical Perspective Across Two Pandemics. *Frontiers in Psychology, 11.* https://doi.org/10.3389/fpsyg.2020.616499

Cho, E., & Ilari, B. S. (2021). Mothers as Home DJs: Recorded Music and Young Children's Well-Being During the COVID-19 Pandemic. *Frontiers in Psychology, 12.* https://doi.org/10.3389/fpsyg.2021.637569

Cho, H. (2015). Is Background Music a Distraction or Facilitator?: An Investigation on the Influence of Background Music in L2 Writing. *Multimedia-Assisted Language Learning, 18*(2), 37–58. https://doi.org/10.15702/mall.2015.18.2.37

Chobert, J., Francois, C., Velay, J.-L., & Besson, M. (2012). Twelve Months of Active Musical Training in 8- to 10-Year-Old Children Enhances the Preattentive Processing of Syllabic Duration and Voice Onset Time. *Cerebral Cortex, 24*(4), 956–967. https://doi.org/10.1093/cercor/bhs377

Chobert, J., Marie, C., François, C., Schön, D., & Besson, M. (2011). Enhanced Passive and Active Processing of Syllables in Musician Children. *Journal of Cognitive Neuroscience, 23*(12), 3874–3887. https://doi.org/10.1162/jocn_a_00088

Choi, A.-N., Lee, M. S., & Lee, J.-S. (2010). Group Music Intervention Reduces Aggression and Improves Self-Esteem in Children with Highly Aggressive Behavior: A Pilot Controlled Trial. *Evidence-Based Complementary and Alternative Medicine, 7*(2), 213–217. https://doi.org/10.1093/ecam/nem182

Choi, U.-S., Sung, Y.-W., Hong, S., Chung, J.-Y., & Ogawa, S. (2015). Structural and functional plasticity specific to musical training with wind instruments. *Frontiers in Human Neuroscience, 9.* https://doi.org/10.3389/fnhum.2015.00597

Chong, H. J., & Kim, S. J. (2010). Education-oriented Music Therapy as an after-school program for students with emotional and behavioral problems. *The Arts in Psychotherapy, 37*(3), 190–196. https://doi.org/10.1016/j.aip.2010.03.004

Chong, H. J., & Yun, J. (2020). Music Therapy for Delinquency Involved Juveniles Through Tripartite Collaboration: A Mixed Method Study. *Frontiers in Psychology, 11.* https://doi.org/10.3389/fpsyg.2020.589431

Chou, M.-Y., Chang, N.-W., Chen, C., Lee, W.-T., Hsin, Y.-J., Siu, K.-K., Chen, C.-J., Wang, L.-J., & Hung, P.-L. (2019). The effectiveness of music therapy for individuals with Rett syndrome and their families. *Journal of the Formosan Medical Association, 118*(12), 1633–1643. https://doi.org/10.1016/j.jfma.2019.01.001

Chou, P. T. (2010). Attention drainage effect: How background music affects concentration in Taiwanese college students. *Journal Scholar. Teach, Learn[MP52], 10*, 36–46.

Chowdhury, A. R., & Gupta, A. (2015). Effect of Music on Plants – An Overview. *International Journal of Integrative Sciences, Innovation and Technology, 4*(6), 30–34.

Chraif, M., Mitrofan, L., Golu, F., & Gâtej, E. (2014). The Influence of Relaxation Music on Abstract Visual Short Term Memory Retrieval Task at Young Students at Psychology. *Procedia - Social and Behavioral Sciences, 127*, 852–857. https://doi.org/10.1016/j.sbspro.2014.03.367

Christenbury, K. R. (2015). I Will Follow You: The Combined Use of Songwriting and Art to Promote Healing in a Child Who Has Been Traumatized. *Music Therapy Perspectives, 35*(1), 1–12. https://doi.org/10.1093/mtp/miv005

Christenson, P. G., DeBenedittis, P., & Lindlof, T. R. (1985). CHILDREN'S USE OF AUDIO MEDIA. *Communication Research, 12*(3), 327–343. https://doi.org/10.1177/009365085012003005

Christenson, P. G., & Roberts, D. F. (1998). *It's not only rock & roll: Popular music in the lives of adolescents.* Hampton Press.

Christiner, M., & Reiterer, S. (2018). Early Influence of Musical Abilities and Working Memory on Speech Imitation Abilities: Study with Pre-School Children. *Brain Sciences, 8*(9), 169. https://doi.org/10.3390/brainsci8090169

Christopher, E. A., & Shelton, J. T. (2017). Individual differences in working memory predict the effect of music on student performance. *Journal of Applied Research in Memory and Cognition, 6*(2), 167–173. https://doi.org/10.1016/j.jarmac.2017.01.012

Chung, H. L., Monday, A., & Perry, A. (2017). Promoting the Well-being of Urban Youth through Drama-based Peer Education. *American Journal of Health Behavior, 41*(6), 728–739. https://doi.org/10.5993/ajhb.41.6.7

Cirelli, L. K., Einarson, K. M., & Trainor, L. J. (2014). Interpersonal synchrony increases prosocial behavior in infants. *Developmental Science, 17*(6), 1003–1011. https://doi.org/10.1111/desc.12193

Cirelli, L. K., & Trehub, S. E. (2019). Dancing to Metallica and Dora: Case Study of a 19-Month-Old. *Frontiers in Psychology, 10.* https://doi.org/10.3389/fpsyg.2019.01073

Cirelli, L. K., & Trehub, S. E. (2020). Familiar songs reduce infant distress. *Developmental Psychology, 56*(5), 861–868. https://doi.org/10.1037/dev0000917

Clarke, E., DeNora, T., & Vuoskoski, J. (2015). Music, empathy and cultural understanding. *Physics of Life Reviews*, *15*, 61–88. https://doi.org/10.1016/j.plrev.2015.09.001

Clarke, E., Dibben, N., & Pitts, S. (2009). *Music and mind in everyday life*. Oxford University Press. https://doi.org/10.1093/acprof:oso/9780198525578.001.0001

Clarke, T., & Basilio, M. (2018). Do arts subjects matter for secondary school students wellbeing? The role of creative engagement and playfulness. *Thinking Skills and Creativity*, *29*, 97–114, https://doi.org/10.1016/j.tsc.10

Clayton, K. K., Swaminathan, J., Yazdanbakhsh, A., Zuk, J., Patel, A. D., & Kidd, G. (2016). Executive Function, Visual Attention and the Cocktail Party Problem in Musicians and Non-Musicians. *PLOS ONE*, *11*(7), e0157638. https://doi.org/10.1371/journal.pone.0157638

Clements-Cortès, A. (2012). Can music be used to help a person who stutters? *Canadian Music Educator*, *53*(4), 45–48.

Clements-Cortes, A., & Chow, S. (2018). Enhancing self-esteem in the music classroom. *The Canadian Music Educator; Edmonton*, *59*(2), 23–26.

Clendenon-Wallen, J. (1991). The Use of Music Therapy to influence the Self-Confidence and Self-Esteem of Adolescents Who Are Sexually Abused. *Music Therapy Perspectives*, *9*(1), 73–81. https://doi.org/10.1093/mtp/9.1.73

Clennon, O., & Boehm, C. (2014). Young Musicians for Heritage Project: Can a music-based heritage project have a positive effect on well-being? *Music Education Research*, *16*(3), 307–329. https://doi.org/10.1080/14613808.2014.909395

Clennon, O. D. (2013). How effective are music interventions in the criminal youth justice sector? Community music making and its potential for community and social transformation: A pilot study. *Journal of Music, Technology and Education*, *6*(1), 103–130. https://doi.org/10.1386/jmte.6.1.103_1

Clift, S. (2012). Singing, Wellbeing, and Health. In *Music, Health, and Wellbeing* (pp. 114–124). Oxford University Press. https://doi.org/10.1093/acprof:oso/9780199586974.003.0009

Clift, S., & Camic, P. M. (Eds). (2015). *Oxford Textbook of Creative Arts, Health, and Wellbeing*. Oxford University Press. https://doi.org/10.1093/med/9780199688074.001.0001

Clift, S., & Hancox, G. (2010). The significance of choral singing for sustaining psychological wellbeing: Findings from a survey of choristers in England, Australia and Germany. *Music Performance Research*, *3*, 79–96.

Clift, S., Hancox, G., Staricoff, R., & Whitmore, C. (2008). *Singing and Health: A systematic mapping and review of non-clinical research*. Sidney de Haan Research Centre for Arts and Health: Canterbury Christ Church University.

Clift, S. M., & Hancox, G. (2001). The perceived benefits of singing. *Journal of the Royal Society for the Promotion of Health*, 121(4), 248–256. https://doi.org/10.1177/146642400112100409

Clift, S., Manship, S., & Stephens, L. (2017). Further evidence that singing fosters mental health and wellbeing: The West Kent and Medway project. *Mental Health and Social Inclusion*, 21(1), 53–62. https://doi.org/10.1108/mhsi-11-2016-0034

Clini, C., Thomson, L. J. M., & Chatterjee, H. J. (2019). Assessing the impact of artistic and cultural activities on the health and well-being of forcibly displaced people using participatory action research. *BMJ Open*, 9(2), e025465. https://doi.org/10.1136/bmjopen-2018-025465

Cloonan, M., & Johnson, B. (2002). Killing me softly with his song: An initial investigation into the use of popular music as a tool of oppression. *Popular Music*, 21(1), 27–39. https://doi.org/10.1017/s0261143002002027

Cloutier, A., Fernandez, N. B., Houde-Archambault, C., & Gosselin, N. (2020). Effect of Background Music on Attentional Control in Older and Young Adults. *Frontiers in Psychology*, 11. https://doi.org/10.3389/fpsyg.2020.557225

Cobb, T. A. (1997). *A comparison of the academic achievement of students who have a musical background versus students who do not have a musical background* [PhD Thesis]. University: The University of Mississippi.

Cobbett, S. (2007). Playing at the Boundaries. *British Journal of Music Therapy*, 21(1), 3–11. https://doi.org/10.1177/135945750702100102

Cobbett, S. (2009). Including the Excluded. *British Journal of Music Therapy*, 23(2), 15–24. https://doi.org/10.1177/135945750902300203

Cobbett, S. (2016a). Context and relationships: Using the systemic approach with music therapy in work with children, adolescents and their families. *British Journal of Music Therapy*, 30(2), 65–73. https://doi.org/10.1177/1359457516662474

Cobbett, S. (2016b). Reaching the hard to reach: Quantitative and qualitative evaluation of school-based arts therapies with young people with social, emotional and behavioural difficulties. *Emotional and Behavioural Difficulties*, 1–13. https://doi.org/10.1080/13632752.2016.1215119

Cockerton, T., Moore, S., & Norman, D. (1997). Cognitive Test Performance and Background Music. *Perceptual and Motor Skills*, 85(3_suppl), 1435–1438. https://doi.org/10.2466/pms.1997.85.3f.1435

Coelho, A., Parola, V., Cardoso, D., Bravo, M. E., & Apóstolo, J. (2017). Use of non-pharmacological interventions for comforting patients in palliative care: A scoping review. *JBI Database of Systematic Reviews and Implementation Reports*, 15(7), 1867–1904. https://doi.org/10.11124/jbisrir-2016-003204

Coffman, D. D. (2002). Music and quality of life in older adults. *Psychomusicology: A Journal of Research in Music Cognition, 18*(1–2), 76–88. https://doi.org/10.1037/h0094050

Coffman, D. D., & Adamek, M. S. (1999). The contribution of wind band participation to quality of life of senior adult band members. *Dialogue in Instrumental Music Education, 20*(1), 25–34.

Coffman, D. D., & Adamek, M. S. (2001). Perceived social support of New Horizons Band participants. *Contributions to Music Education, 28*(1), 27–40.

Cogo-Moreira, H., Andriolo, R. B., Yazigi, L., Ploubidis, G. B., Ávila, C. R. B. de, & Mari, J. J. (2012). Music education for improving reading skills in children and adolescents with dyslexia. *Cochrane Database of Systematic Reviews*. https://doi.org/10.1002/14651858.cd009133.pub2

Cogo-Moreira, H., Ávila, C. R. B. de, Ploubidis, G. B., & Mari, J. de J. (2013). Effectiveness of Music Education for the Improvement of Reading Skills and Academic Achievement in Young Poor Readers: A Pragmatic Cluster-Randomized, Controlled Clinical Trial. *PLoS ONE, 8*(3), e59984. https://doi.org/10.1371/journal.pone.0059984

Cohen, A. J. (2016). Music in performance arts: Film, theatre and dance. In S. Hallam, I. Cross, & M. Thaut (Eds), *The Oxford handbook of music psychology* (pp. 725–743). Oxford University Press.

Cohen, G. D., Perlstein, S., Chapline, J., Kelly, J., Firth, K. M., & Simmens, S. (n.d.). The impact of professionally conducted cultural programs on the physical health, mental health and social functioning of older adults–2-year results. *Journal of Aging, Humanities and the Arts, 1*(1), 5–22.

Cohen, G. D., Perlstein, S., Chapline, J., Kelly, J., Firth, K. M., & Simmens, S. (2006). The Impact of Professionally Conducted Cultural Programs on the Physical Health, Mental Health, and Social Functioning of Older Adults. *The Gerontologist, 46*(6), 726–734. https://doi.org/10.1093/geront/46.6.726

Cohen, M. A., Evans, K. K., Horowitz, T. S., & Wolfe, J. M. (2011). Auditory and visual memory in musicians and nonmusicians. *Psychonomic Bulletin & Review, 18*(3), 586–591. https://doi.org/10.3758/s13423-011-0074-0

Cohen, M. L. (2007a). *Christopher Small's concept of musicking: Toward a theory of choral singing pedagogy in prison contexts* [PhD Thesis]. https://doi.org/10.13140/RG.2.1.5098.2643.

Cohen, M. L. (2007b). Explorations of inmate and volunteer choral experiences in a prison-based choir. *Australian Journal of Music Education, 1*, 61–72.

Cohen, M. L. (2009). Choral singing and prison inmates: Influences of singing in a prison choir. *Journal of Correctional Education, 60*(1), 52–65.

Cohen, M. L. (2010). Select musical programs and restorative practices in prisons across the US and the UK. *Community Music Activity Commission of the International Society for Music Education Conference*.

Cohen, M. L. (2012). Harmony within the walls: Perceptions of worthiness and competence in a community prison choir. *International Journal of Music Education, 30*(1), 46–56. https://doi.org/10.1177/0255761411431394

Cohen, M. L. (2019). Choral Singing in Prisons: Evidence-Based Activities to Support Returning Citizens. *The Prison Journal, 99*(4_suppl), 106S-117S. https://doi.org/10.1177/0032885519861082

Cohen, M. L., & Duncan, S. P. (2015). Restorative and transformative justice and its relationship to music education within and beyond prison contexts. In C. Benedict, P. Schmidt, G. Spruce, & P. Woodford (Eds), *Oxford Handbook of Social Justice in Music Education* (pp. 554–566). Oxford University Press.

Cohen, M. L., & Henley, J. (2018). Music-making behind bars: The many dimensions of community music in prisons. In B. Bartleet & L. Higgins (Eds), *The Oxford Handbook of Community Music* (pp. 153–171). Oxford University Press.

Cohen, M. L., & Trachsel, M. (2010). Voice as intersection between music and language: The writing component of the Oakdale Prison Community Choir. *International Society for Music Education Conference.*

Cohen, M. L., & Wilson, C. M. (2017). Inside the fences: Pedagogical practices and purposes of songwriting in an adult male U.S. state prison. *International Journal of Music Education, 35*(4), 541–553. https://doi.org/10.1177/0255761416689841

Cohen, S., & Ginsborg, J. (2021). The Experiences of Mid-career and Seasoned Orchestral Musicians in the UK During the First COVID-19 Lockdown. *Frontiers in Psychology, 12.* https://doi.org/10.3389/fpsyg.2021.645967

Cole, L. P., Henechowicz, T. L., Kang, K., Pranjić, M., Richard, N. M., Tian, G. L. J., & Hurt-Thaut, C. (2021). Neurologic Music Therapy via Telehealth: A Survey of Clinician Experiences, Trends, and Recommendations During the COVID-19 Pandemic. *Frontiers in Neuroscience, 15.* https://doi.org/10.3389/fnins.2021.648489

Cole, P. M., Martin, S. E., & Dennis, T. A. (2004). Emotion Regulation as a Scientific Construct: Methodological Challenges and Directions for Child Development Research. *Child Development, 75*(2), 317–333. https://doi.org/10.1111/j.1467-8624.2004.00673.x

Colegrove, V. M., Havighurst, S. S., Kehoe, C. E., & Jacobsen, S. L. (2018). Pilot randomized controlled trial of Tuning Relationships with Music: Intervention for parents with a trauma history and their adolescent. *Child Abuse & Neglect, 79,* 259–268. https://doi.org/10.1016/j.chiabu.2018.02.017

Colorado. (2013). *Boulder, Colorado.*

Conrad, C., Niess, H., Jauch, K.-W., Bruns, C. J., Hartl, W. H., & Welker, L. (2007). Overture for growth hormone: Requiem for interleukin-6?\textbackslashast. *Critical Care Medicine, 35*(12), 2709–2713. https://doi.org/10.1097/01.ccm.0000291648.99043.b9

Conservatory Lab Charter School: A Public School for Learning Through Music. (2012). [Annual Report 2012.].

Cook, A., Ogden, J., & Winstone, N. (2018). The impact of a school-based musical contact intervention on prosocial attitudes, emotions and behaviours: A pilot trial with autistic and neurotypical children. *Autism, 23*(4), 933–942. https://doi.org/10.1177/1362361318787793

Cook, N. (2013). *Improving the therapeutic alliance with adolescents using music* [PhD Thesis]. Pacific University[MP64.

Cooke, M. L., Moyle, W., Shum, D. H. K., Harrison, S. D., & Murfield, J. E. (2010). A randomized controlled trial exploring the effect of music on agitated behaviours and anxiety in older people with dementia. *Aging & Mental Health, 14*(8), 905–916. https://doi.org/10.1080/13607861003713190

Cooper, A., M., C., & Goss, S. (2008). *The effect of music on reading comprehension.* Hanover College.

Cooper, A., & Wang, Y. (2010). Can musical aptitude and experience predict success in non-native tone word learning? *The Journal of the Acoustical Society of America, 128*(4), 2478–2478. https://doi.org/10.1121/1.3508890

Cooper, P. K. (2019a). It's all in your head: A meta-analysis on the effects of music training on cognitive measures in schoolchildren. *International Journal of Music Education, 38*(3), 321–336. https://doi.org/10.1177/0255761419881495

Cooper, P. K. (2019b). It's all in your head: A meta-analysis on the effects of music training on cognitive measures in schoolchildren. *International Journal of Music Education, 38*(3), 321–336. https://doi.org/10.1177/0255761419881495

Cooper, R. P., & Aslin, R. N. (1989). The language environment of the young infant: Implications for early perceptual development. *Canadian Journal of Psychology/Revue Canadienne de Psychologie, 43*(2), 247–265. https://doi.org/10.1037/h0084216

Cooper, T. L. (2001). Adults' Perceptions of Piano Study: Achievements and Experiences. *Journal of Research in Music Education, 49*(2), 156–168. https://doi.org/10.2307/3345867

Corrigall, K. A., & Schellenberg, E. G. (2013). Music: The language of emotion. In C. Mohiyeddini, M. Eysenck, & S. Bauer (Eds), *Handbook of psychology of emotions: Recent theoretical perspectives and novel empirical findings* (pp. 299–325). Nova.

Corrigall, K. A., & Schellenberg, E. G. (2015). Predicting who takes music lessons: Parent and child characteristics. *Frontiers in Psychology, 6.* https://doi.org/10.3389/fpsyg.2015.00282

Corrigall, K. A., Schellenberg, E. G., & Misura, N. M. (2013). Music Training, Cognition, and Personality. *Frontiers in Psychology, 4.* https://doi.org/10.3389/fpsyg.2013.00222

Corrigall, K. A., & Trainor, L. J. (2009). Effects of Musical Training on Key and Harmony Perception. *Annals of the New York Academy of Sciences, 1169*(1), 164–168. https://doi.org/10.1111/j.1749-6632.2009.04769.x

Corrigall, K. A., & Trainor, L. J. (2011). Associations Between Length of Music Training and Reading Skills in Children. *Music Perception, 29*(2), 147–155. https://doi.org/10.1525/mp.2011.29.2.147

Corriveau, K. H., & Goswami, U. (2009). Rhythmic motor entrainment in children with speech and language impairments: Tapping to the beat. *Cortex, 45*(1), 119–130. https://doi.org/10.1016/j.cortex.2007.09.008

Corriveau, K., Pasquini, E., & Goswami, U. (2007). Basic Auditory Processing Skills and Specific Language Impairment: A New Look at an Old Hypothesis. *Journal of Speech, Language, and Hearing Research, 50*(3), 647–666. https://doi.org/10.1044/1092-4388(2007/046)

Corte, U., & Edwards, B. (2008). White Power music and the mobilization of racist social movements. *Music and Arts in Action, 1*(1), 4–20.

Corvo, E., & Caro, W. D. (2020). COVID-19 and spontaneous singing to decrease loneliness, improve cohesion, and mental well-being: An Italian experience. *Psychological Trauma: Theory, Research, Practice, and Policy, 12*(S1), S247–S248. https://doi.org/10.1037/tra0000838

Costa, F., & Ockelford, A. (2018). Why Music? An Evaluation of a Music Programme for Older People in the Community. *INTERNATIONAL JOURNAL OF MUSIC AND PERFORMING ARTS, 6*(2). https://doi.org/10.15640/ijmpa.v6n2a4

Costa, F., Ockelford, A., & Hargreaves, D. J. (2017). The effect of regular listening to preferred music on pain, depression and anxiety in older care home residents. *Psychology of Music, 46*(2), 174–191. https://doi.org/10.1177/0305735617703811

Costa, F., Ockelford, A., & Hargreaves, D. J. (2018). Does regular listening to preferred music have a beneficial effect on symptoms of depression and anxiety amongst older people in residential care? The qualitative findings of a mixed methods study. *Music and Medicine, 10*(2), 54. https://doi.org/10.47513/mmd.v10i2.567

Costa-Giomi, E. (1999). The Effects of Three Years of Piano Instruction on Children's Cognitive Development. *Journal of Research in Music Education, 47*(3), 198–212. https://doi.org/10.2307/3345779

Costa-Giomi, E. (2000). The relationship between absolute pitch and spatial abilities. In C. Woods, G. Luck, R. Brochard, F. Seddon, & J. A. Sloboda (Eds), *Proceedings of the Sixth International Conference on Music Perception and Cognition* (p. 67). Keele University, Department of Psychology.

Costa-Giomi, E. (2004). Effects of Three Years of Piano Instruction on Children's Academic Achievement, School Performance and Self-Esteem. *Psychology of Music, 32*(2), 139–152. https://doi.org/10.1177/0305735604041491

Costa-Giomi, E. (2005a). *Does Music Instruction Improve Fine Motor Abilities? Annals of the New York Academy of Sciences,* [MP68.

Costa-Giomi, E. (2005b). I do not want to study piano! Early predictors of student dropout behavior. *Bulletin of the Council for Research in Music Education, 161*(162), 57–64.

Costa-Giomi, E. (2006). The personality of children who study piano, drop out of piano lessons or never play a note: A longitudinal study. *Meeting of the Texas Music Educators Association.*

Costa-Giomi, E. (2012). Music instruction and children's intellectual development: The educational context of music participation. In R. MacDonald, G. Kreutz, & L. Mitchell (Eds), *Music, health and well-being* (pp. 337–355). Oxford University Press.

Costa-Giomi, E. (2013). Music instruction and children's intellectual development: The educational context of music participation. In R. A. R. MacDonald, G. Kreutz, & L. Mitchell (Eds), *Music, Health, and Wellbeing* (pp. 339–355 69). Oxford University Press.

Costa-Giomi, E., & Ryan, C. (2007). The benefits of music instruction: What remains years later. *Symposium for Research in Music Behaviour.*

Coulton, S., Clift, S., Skingley, A., & Rodriguez, J. (2015). Effectiveness and cost-effectiveness of community singing on mental health-related quality of life of older people: Randomised controlled trial. *British Journal of Psychiatry, 207*(3), 250–255. https://doi.org/10.1192/bjp.bp.113.129908

Council, L. L. S. (2003). *Evaluation of European Social Fund Project, Engaging Disaffected Young People.* Lancashire County Council.

Courey, S. J., Balogh, E., Siker, J. R., & Paik, J. (2012). Academic music: Music instruction to engage third-grade students in learning basic fraction concepts. *Educational Studies in Mathematics, 81*(2), 251–278. https://doi.org/10.1007/s10649-012-9395-9

Cowan, N. (2013). Working Memory Underpins Cognitive Development, Learning, and Education. *Educational Psychology Review, 26*(2), 197–223. https://doi.org/10.1007/s10648-013-9246-y

Cox, A., & Gelsthorpe, L. (2008). *Beats and Bars, Music in Prisons: An Evaluation.* The Irene Taylor Trust.

Cox, H. A., & Stephens, L. J. (2006). The effect of music participation on mathematical achievement and overall academic achievement of high school students. *International Journal of Mathematical Education in Science and Technology, 37*(7), 757–763. https://doi.org/10.1080/00207739050013 7811

Cozzolino, G. (2020). *A Benevento una Tammurriata sui Balconi per Uscire Dall'isolamento.* Napoli Fanpage.

Cranmore, J., & Tunks, J. (2015). High School Students' Perceptions of the Relationship between Music and Math. *Mid-Western Educational Researcher, 27*(1), 51–69.

Crawford, R. (2017). Creating unity through celebrating diversity: A case study that explores the impact of music education on refugee background students. *International Journal of Music Education, 35*(3), 343–356, https://doi.org/10.1177/02557614

Crawford, R. (2019). Socially inclusive practices in the music classroom: The impact of music education used as a vehicle to engage refugee background students. *Research Studies in Music Education, 42*(2), 248–269. https://doi.org/10.1177/1321103x19843001

Crawford, R. (2020). Beyond the dots on the page: Harnessing transculturation and music education to address intercultural competence and social inclusion. *International Journal of Music Education, 38*(4), 537–562. https://doi.org/10.1177/0255761420921585

Creath, K., & Schwartz, G. E. (2004). Measuring Effects of Music, Noise, and Healing Energy Using a Seed Germination Bioassay. *The Journal of Alternative and Complementary Medicine, 10*(1), 113–122. https://doi.org/10.1089/107555304322849039

Creech, A. (2019). Using Music Technology Creatively to Enrich Later-Life: A Literature Review. *Frontiers in Psychology, 10.* https://doi.org/10.3389/fpsyg.2019.00117

Creech, A. G.-M., P., L., L., W., G., S., E., & S, F. (2016). *El Sistema and Sistema inspired programmes: A literature review of research, evaluation and critical debates* (2nd ed.). Sistema Global.

Creech, A., Gonzalez-Moreno, P., Lorenzino, L., & Waitman, G. (2013). *El Sistema and Sistema-Inspired Programmes: A literature review of research, evaluation and critical debates.* Sistema Global.

Creech, A., Hallam, S., McQueen, H., & Varvarigou, M. (2013). The power of music in the lives of older adults. *Research Studies in Music Education, 35*(1), 87–102. https://doi.org/10.1177/1321103x13478862

Creech, A., Hallam, S., Varvarigou, M., & McQueen, H. (2014). *Active Ageing with Music: Supporting Wellbeing in the Third and Fourth Ages.* Institute of Education Press.

Creech, A., Larouche, K., Generale, M., & Fortier, D. (2020). Creativity, music, and quality of later life: A systematic review. *Psychology of Music,* 030573562094811. https://doi.org/10.1177/0305735620948114

Creighton, A. (2011). Mother-infant musical interaction and emotional communication: A literature review. *Australian Journal of Music Therapy, 22,* 37–56.

Cribb, C., & Gregory, A. H. (1999). Stereotypes and Personalities of Musicians. *The Journal of Psychology, 133*(1), 104–114. https://doi.org/10.1080/00223989909599725

Cripe, F. F. (1986). Rock Music as Therapy for Children with Attention Deficit Disorder: An Exploratory Study. *Journal of Music Therapy, 23*(1), 30–37. https://doi.org/10.1093/jmt/23.1.30

Criscuolo, A. B., L., S., Kliuchko, T., M., & Brattico, E. (2019). On the Association Between Musical Training. *Intelligence and Executive Functions in Adulthood, Frontiers in Psychology, 10,* 1704, https://doi.org/10.3389/fpsyg.2019.01704DOI

Črnčec, A. W., S.J., & Prior, M. (2006). The Cognitive and Academic Benefits of Music to Children: Facts and fiction. *Educational Psychology: An International Journal of Experimental Educational Psychology, 26*(4), 579–594.

Crone, D. M., Sumner, R. C., Baker, C. M., Loughren, E. A., Hughes, S., & James, D. V. B. (2018). `Artlift' arts-on-referral intervention in UK primary care: Updated findings from an ongoing observational study. *European Journal of Public Health, 28*(3), 404–409. https://doi.org/10.1093/eurpub/cky021

Crookes, L. (2012). *What are the key features of music therapy work with mainstream adolescents in mainstream secondary schools? Unpublished Master's dissertation.* Guildhall School of Music and Drama.

Croom, A. M. (2014). Music practice and participation for psychological well-being: A review of how music influences positive emotion, engagement, relationships, meaning, and accomplishment. *Musicae Scientiae, 19*(1), 44–64. https://doi.org/10.1177/1029864914561709

Cross, I. (2001). Music, Cognition, Culture, and Evolution. *Annals of the New York Academy of Sciences, 930*(1), 28–42. https://doi.org/10.1111/j.1749-6632.2001.tb05723.x

Cross, I. (2003). Music and Evolution: Consequences and Causes. *Contemporary Music Review, 22*(3), 79–89. https://doi.org/10.1080/0749446032000150906

Cross, I. (2009). The evolutionary nature of musical meaning. *Musicae Scientiae, 13*(2_suppl), 179–200. https://doi.org/10.1177/1029864909013002091

Cross, I. (2016). The nature of music and its evolution. In S. Hallam, I. Cross, & M. Thaut (Eds), *The Oxford Handbook of Music Psychology* (pp. 3–18). Oxford University Press.

Cross, I. L., F., & Rabinowitch, T.-C. (2012). Empathetic creativity in music group practices. In G. McPherson & G. Welch (Eds), *The Oxford Handbook of Music Education* (pp. 337–353). Oxford University Press.

Csíkszentmihályi, M. (1996). *Creativity: Flow and the psychology of discovery and invention.* Harper Collins.

Cuadrado, F., Lopez-Cobo, I., Valverde, B., & Varona, D. (2017). Musicalizatech: A collaborative music production project for secondary and high-school students. *Journal of Music, Technology and Education, 10*(1), 93–116. https://doi.org/10.1386/jmte.10.1.93_1

CUDDY, L. L. (2005). Musical Difficulties Are Rare: A Study of 'Tone Deafness' among University Students. *Annals of the New York Academy of Sciences, 1060*(1), 311–324. https://doi.org/10.1196/annals.1360.026

Cuéllar, J. A. (2010). Fundación nacional Batuta: El impacto de la práctica musical educativa. *EGOBRevista de Asuntos Públicos, 6*, 61–64.

Cuesta, J. (2011). Music to my ears: The (many) socioeconomic benefits of music training programmes. *Applied Economics Letters, 18*(10), 915–918. https://doi.org/10.1080/13504851.2010.517187

Cumming, R., Wilson, A., & Goswami, U. (2015). Basic auditory processing and sensitivity to prosodic structure in children with specific language impairments: A new look at a perceptual hypothesis. *Frontiers in Psychology, 6*. https://doi.org/10.3389/fpsyg.2015.00972

Currie, J., Ramsden, B., McArthur, C., & Maruff, P. (1991). Validation of a Clinical Antisaccadic Eye Movement Test in the Assessment of Dementia. *Archives of Neurology, 48*(6), 644–648. https://doi.org/10.1001/archneur.1991.00530180102024

Cusick, S. G. (2006). Music as Torture. *Music as Weapon. Transcultural Music Review, 10*([MP80).

Cuypers, K., Krokstad, S., Holmen, T. L., Knudtsen, M. S., Bygren, L. O., & Holmen, J. (2011). Patterns of receptive and creative cultural activities and their association with perceived health, anxiety, depression and satisfaction with life among adults: The HUNT study, Norway. *Journal of Epidemiology and Community Health, 66*(8), 698–703. https://doi.org/10.1136/jech.2010.113571

d'Ardenne, P., & Kiyendeye, M. (2014). An initial exploration of the therapeutic impact of music on genocide orphans in Rwanda. *British Journal of Guidance & Counselling, 43*(5), 559–569. https://doi.org/10.1080/03069885.2014.954237

Dabback, W. M., & Smith, D. S. (2012). Elders and music: Empowering, learning, valuing life experience and considering the needs of aging adult learners. In G. E. McPherson & G. F. Welch (Eds), *The Oxford Handbook of Music Education* (pp. 229–242). Oxford University Press.

Daffern, H., Balmer, K., & Brereton, J. (2021). Singing Together, Yet Apart: The Experience of UK Choir Members and Facilitators During the Covid-19 Pandemic. *Frontiers in Psychology, 12*. https://doi.org/10.3389/fpsyg.2021.624474

Daikoku, T. (2018). Neurophysiological Markers of Statistical Learning in Music and Language: Hierarchy, Entropy, and Uncertainty. *Brain Sciences, 8*(6), 114. https://doi.org/10.3390/brainsci8060114

Dalla Bella, S. (2016). Music and Brain Plasticity. In S. Hallam, I. Cross, & M. Thaut (Eds), *The Oxford Handbook of Music Psychology* (pp. 325–342). Oxford University Press.

Daneman, M., & Carpenter, P. A. (1980). Individual differences in working memory and reading. *Journal of Verbal Learning and Verbal Behavior, 19*(4), 450–466. https://doi.org/10.1016/s0022-5371(80)90312-6

Darnley-Smith, R., & Patey, H. (2003). *Music Therapy.* SAGE Publications Ltd. https://doi.org/10.4135/9781446218006

Darowski, E. S., Helder, E., Zacks, R. T., Hasher, L., & Hambrick, D. Z. (2008). Age-related differences in cognition: The role of distraction control. *Neuropsychology, 22*(5), 638–644. https://doi.org/10.1037/0894-4105.22.5.638

Darrow, A.-A., Johnson, C., Agnew, S., Fuller, E. R., & Uchisaka, M. (2006). Effect of preferred music as a distraction on music majors' and nonmusic majors' selective attention. *Bull. Counc. Res. Music. Educ, MP83]170*, 21–31.

Dassa, A. (2018). Musical Auto-Biography Interview (MABI) as promoting self-identity and well-being in the elderly through music and reminiscence. *Nordic Journal of Music Therapy, 27*(5), 419–430. https://doi.org/10.1080/08098131.2018.1490921

Davalos, D. B., Chavez, E. L., & Guardiola, R. J. (1999). The Effects of Extracurricular Activity, Ethnic Identification, and Perception of School on Student Dropout Rates. *Hispanic Journal of Behavioral Sciences, 21*(1), 61–77. https://doi.org/10.1177/0739986399211005

Daveson, B. A. (2001). Music Therapy and Childhood Cancer: Goals, Methods, Patient Choice and Control During Diagnosis, Intensive Treatment, Transplant and Palliative Care. *Music Therapy Perspectives, 19*(2), 114–120. https://doi.org/10.1093/mtp/19.2.114

Davidson, C. W., & Powell, L. A. (1986). The Effects of Easy-Listening Background Music on the On-Task-Performance of Fifth-Grade Children. *The Journal of Educational Research, 80*(1), 29–33. https://doi.org/10.1080/00220671.1986.10885717

Davidson, J. R. T., Weisler, R. H., Butterfield, M. I., Casat, C. D., Connor, K. M., Barnett, S., & Meter, S. van. (2003). Mirtazapine vs. Placebo in posttraumatic stress disorder: A pilot trial. *Biological Psychiatry, 53*(2), 188–191. https://doi.org/10.1016/s0006-3223(02)01411-7

Davidson, J. W., & Good, J. M. M. (2002). Social and Musical Co-Ordination between Members of a String Quartet: An Exploratory Study. *Psychology of Music, 30*(2), 186–201. https://doi.org/10.1177/0305735602302005

Davidson, J. W., & King, E. C. (2004). Strategies for ensemble practice. In A. Williamon (Ed.), *Musical Excellence* (pp. 105–122). Oxford University Press.

Davidson, J. W., McNamara, B., Rosenwax, L., Lange, A., Jenkins, S., & Lewin, G. (2013). Evaluating the potential of group singing to enhance the well-being of older people. *Australasian Journal on Ageing, 33*(2), 99–104. https://doi.org/10.1111/j.1741-6612.2012.00645.x

Davis, M. H., & Kraus, L. A. (1989). Social Contact, Loneliness, and Mass Media Use: A Test of Two Hypotheses1. *Journal of Applied Social Psychology, 19*(13), 1100–1124. https://doi.org/10.1111/j.1559-1816.1989.tb01242.x

Dawson, A., Bowes, A., Kelly, F., Velzke, K., & Ward, R. (2015). Evidence of what works to support and sustain care at home for people with dementia: A literature review with a systematic approach. *BMC Geriatrics, 15*(1). https://doi.org/10.1186/s12877-015-0053-9

Day, T., Baker, F., & Darlington, Y. (2009). Experiences of song writing in a group programme for mothers who had experienced childhood abuse. *Nordic Journal of Music Therapy, 18*(2), 133–149. https://doi.org/10.1080/08098130903062405

Daykin, N., Mansfield, L., Meads, C., Julier, G., Tomlinson, A., Payne, A., Duffy, L. G., Lane, J., D'Innocenzo, G., Burnett, A., Kay, T., Dolan, P., Testoni, S., & Victor, C. (2017). What works for wellbeing? A systematic review of wellbeing outcomes for music and singing in adults. *Perspectives in Public Health, 138*(1), 39–46. https://doi.org/10.1177/1757913917740391

Daykin, N., McClean, S., & Bunt, L. (2007). Creativity, identity and healing: Participants' accounts of music therapy in cancer care. *Health: An Interdisciplinary Journal for the Social Study of Health, Illness and Medicine, 11*(3), 349–370. https://doi.org/10.1177/1363459307077548

Daykin, N., Moriarty, Y., Viggiani, N., & Pilkington, P. (2011). *Evidence review: Music making with young offenders and young people at risk of offending.* University of West of England/Youth Music.

Daykin, N., Parry, B., Ball, K., Walters, D., Henry, A., Platten, B., & Hayden, R. (2017). The role of participatory music making in supporting people with dementia in hospital environments. *Dementia, 17*(6), 686–701. https://doi.org/10.1177/1471301217739722

Daykin, N., Viggiani, N. de, Pilkington, P., & Moriarty, Y. (2012). Music making for health, well-being and behaviour change in youth justice settings: A systematic review. *Health Promotion International, 28*(2), 197–210. https://doi.org/10.1093/heapro/das005

Deane, K., Hunter, R., & Mullen, P. (2011). *Move On Up—An evaluation of Youth Music Mentors.* Youth Music.

Deaville, J., Tan, S.-L., & Rodman, R. (Eds). (2021). *The Oxford Handbook of Music and Advertising.* Oxford University Press. https://doi.org/10.1093/oxfordhb/9780190691240.001.0001

DeCasper, A. J., & Fifer, W. P. (1980). Of Human Bonding: Newborns Prefer Their Mothers' Voices. *Science, 208*(4448), 1174–1176. https://doi.org/10.1126/science.7375928

DeCasper, A. J., & Sigafoos, A. D. (1983). The intrauterine heartbeat: A potent reinforcer for newborns. *Infant Behavior and Development, 6*(1), 19–25. https://doi.org/10.1016/s0163-6383(83)80004-6

DeCasper, A. J., & Spence, M. J. (1986). Prenatal maternal speech influences newborns' perception of speech sounds. *Infant Behavior and Development, 9*(2), 133–150. https://doi.org/10.1016/0163-6383(86)90025-1

Dedman, T. (2011). Agency in UK hip-hop and grime youth subcultures – peripherals and purists. *Journal of Youth Studies, 14*(5), 507–522. https://doi.org/10.1080/13676261.2010.549820

Deere, K. B. (2010). *The Impact of Music Education on Academic Achievement in Reading and Math* [PhD Thesis]. Union University.

Degé, F., & Kerkovius, K. (2018). The effects of drumming on working memory in older adults. *Annals of the New York Academy of Sciences, 1423*(1), 242–250. https://doi.org/10.1111/nyas.13685

Degé, F., Kubicek, C., & Schwarzer, G. (2011). Music Lessons and Intelligence: A Relation Mediated by Executive Functions. *Music Perception, 29*(2), 195–201. https://doi.org/10.1525/mp.2011.29.2.195

Degé, F., & Schwarzer, G. (2011). The Effect of a Music Program on Phonological Awareness in Preschoolers. *Frontiers in Psychology, 2*. https://doi.org/10.3389/fpsyg.2011.00124

Degé, F., & Schwarzer, G. (2017a). The influence of an extended music curriculum at school on academic self-concept in 9- to 11-year-old children. *Musicae Scientiae, 22*(3), 305–321. https://doi.org/10.1177/1029864916688508

Degé, F., & Schwarzer, G. (2017b). Music lessons and verbal memory in 10- to 12-year-old children: Investigating articulatory rehearsal as mechanism underlying this association. *Psychomusicology: Music, Mind, and Brain, 27*(4), 256–266. https://doi.org/10.1037/pmu0000201

Degé, F., Wehrum, S., Stark, R., & Schwarzer, G. (2011). The influence of two years of school music training in secondary school on visual and auditory memory. *European Journal of Developmental Psychology, 8*(5), 608–623. https://doi.org/10.1080/17405629.2011.590668

Degé, F., Wehrum, S., Stark, R., & Schwarzer, G. (2014). Music lessons and academic self-concept in 12- to 14-year-old children. *Musicae Scientiae, 18*(2), 203–215. https://doi.org/10.1177/1029864914523283

Deguchi, C., Boureux, M., Sarlo, M., Besson, M., Grassi, M., Schön, D., & Colombo, L. (2012). Sentence pitch change detection in the native and unfamiliar language in musicians and nonmusicians. *Behavioral, Electrophysiological and Psychoacoustic Study. Brain Research, 1455*, 75–89.

Delgado, M. (2018). *Music, song, dance, and theatre: Broadway meets social justice youth community practice.* Oxford University Press.

Deli, E., Bakle, I., & Zachopoulou, E. (2006). Implementing intervention movement programs for kindergarten children. *Journal of Early Childhood Research*, 4(1), 5–18. https://doi.org/10.1177/1476718x06059785

Delogu, F., Lampis, G., & Belardinelli, M. O. (2010). From melody to lexical tone: Musical ability enhances specific aspects of foreign language perception. *European Journal of Cognitive Psychology*, 22(1), 46–61. https://doi.org/10.1080/09541440802708136

DeMers, A. S. (1996). *The Effect of Background Music on Reading Comprehension Test Scores* [PhD Thesis]. https://digitalcommons.brockport.edu/ehd_theses/111.

Demorest, S. M., & Morrison, S. J. (2000). Does Music Make You Smarter? *Music Educators Journal*, 87(2), 33–58. https://doi.org/10.2307/3399646

DeNora, T. (2000). *Music in Everyday Life*. Cambridge University Press. https://doi.org/10.1017/cbo9780511489433

DeNora, T. (2001). Aesthetic agency and musical practice: New directions in the sociology of music and emotion. In P. N. Juslin & J. A. Sloboda (Eds), *Music and Emotion: Theory and Research* (pp. 161–180). Oxford University Press.

DeNora, T. (2016). *Music Asylums: Wellbeing Through Music in Everyday Life*. Routledge. https://doi.org/10.4324/9781315596730

DeNora, T. (2017). Music-ecology and everyday action: Creating, changing and contesting identities. In R. A. R. MacDonald, D. J. Hargreaves, & D. E. Miell (Eds), *Handbook of musical identities* (pp. 46–62). Oxford University Press.

DeNora, T., & Ansdell, G. (2014). What can't music do? *Psychology of Well-Being*, 4(1). https://doi.org/10.1186/s13612-014-0023-6

Derri, V., Tsapakidou, A., Zachopoulou, E., & Kioumourtzoglou, E. (2001). Effect of a Music and Movement Programme on Development of Locomotor Skills by Children 4 to 6 Years of Age. *European Journal of Physical Education*, 6(1), 16–25. https://doi.org/10.1080/1740898010060103

Derrington, P. (2004). Music therapy on the time-table. Working with students in mainstream secondary schools. In *Paper given at the 6th European Music Therapy Congress*.

Derrington, P. (2005). *Teenagers and songwriting: Supporting students in a mainstream secondary school* (F. Baker & T. Wigram, Eds.). Jessica Kingsley.

Derrington, P. (2006). *Music therapy in a mainstream secondary school: A study of its role. Unpublished Master's dissertation*. Anglia Ruskin University.

Derrington, P. (2010). Yeah I'll do music! Looking at ways to engage with teenage hoodies and X-factor hopefuls. *Paper given at the 8th European Conference*.

Derrington, P. (2011). *Improvisation—Exploring the art and science of clinical practice*.

Derrington, P. (2012a). *Music Therapy for youth at risk: An exploration of clinical practice through research. Unpublished doctoral dissertation.* Anglia Ruskin University.

Derrington, P. (2012b). Yeah I'll do music! Working with secondary-aged students who have complex emotional and behavioural difficulties. In J. Tomlinson, P. Derrington, & A. Oldfield (Eds), *Music Therapy in Schools. Working with children of all ages in mainstream and special education* (p. 91). Jessica Kingsley.

Derrington, P., & Neale, L. (2012). Music therapy for youth at risk. *Key Changes Annual Conference: Music Therapy - Proving the Case.*

Deshmukh, A. D., Sarvaiya, A. A., Seethalakshmi, R., & Nayak, A. S. (2009). Effect of Indian classical music on quality of sleep in depressed patients: A randomized controlled trial. *Nordic Journal of Music Therapy, 18*(1), 70–78. https://doi.org/10.1080/08098130802697269

Devroop, K. (2009). The effect of instrumental music instruction on disadvantaged South African student's career plans. *Musicus, 37*(2), 7–12.

Devroop, K. (2012). The social-emotional impact of instrumental music performance on economically disadvantaged South African students. *Music Education Research, 14*(4), 407–416. https://doi.org/10.1080/14613808.2012.685456

Dezfoolian, L., Zarei, M., Ashayeri, H., & Looyeh, M. Y. (2013). A Pilot Study on the Effects of Orff-Based Therapeutic Music in Children With Autism Spectrum Disorder. *Music and Medicine, 5*(3), 162–168. https://doi.org/10.1177/1943862113491502

Diamond, A. (1990). The development and neural bases of higher cognitive functions. Introduction. *Annals of the New York Academy of Sciences, 608*, https://doi.org/10.1111/j.1749-6632.1990.tb48888.

Diamond, A. (2002). Normal Development of Prefrontal Cortex from Birth to Young Adulthood: Cognitive Functions, Anatomy, and Biochemistry. In *Principles of Frontal Lobe Function* (pp. 466–503). Oxford University Press. https://doi.org/10.1093/acprof:oso/9780195134971.003.0029

Diamond, A. (2013). Executive Functions. *Annual Review of Psychology, 64*(1), 135–168. https://doi.org/10.1146/annurev-psych-113011-143750

Diamond, A., Barnett, W. S., Thomas, J., & Munro, S. (2007). Preschool Program Improves Cognitive Control. *Science, 318*(5855), 1387–1388. https://doi.org/10.1126/science.1151148

Diaz, A. V., Shifres, F., & Justel, N. (2020). *Impact of music-based intervention on verbal memory: An experimental behavioral study with older adults.*

Diaz, F. M. (2010). Intrinsic and extrinsic motivation among collegiate instrumentalists. *Contributions to Music Education, 37*, 23–35.

Dibben, N., & Williamson, V. J. (2007). An exploratory survey of in-vehicle music listening. *Psychology of Music*, *35*(4), 571–589. https://doi.org/10.1177/0305735607079725

Diefenbach, M. A., Miller, S. M., Porter, M., Peters, E., Stefanek, M., & Leventhal, H. (2008). Emotions and health behaviour: A self-regulation perspective. In M. Lewis, J. M. Haviland-Jones, & L. F. Barrett (Eds), *The Handbook of Emotions* (pp. 645–660). Guilford Press.

Diener, E., Suh, E. M., Lucas, R. E., & Smith, H. L. (1999). Subjective well-being: Three decades of progress. *Psychological Bulletin*, *125*(2), 276–302. https://doi.org/10.1037/0033-2909.125.2.276

Diener, E., Wirtz, D., Tov, W., Kim-Prieto, C., Choi, D., Oishi, S., & Biswas-Diener, R. (2009). New Well-being Measures: Short Scales to Assess Flourishing and Positive and Negative Feelings. *Social Indicators Research*, *97*(2), 143–156. https://doi.org/10.1007/s11205-009-9493-y

Dieringer, S. T., & Porretta, D. L. (2013). Using music to decrease off-task behaviors in young children with Autism Spectrum Disorders. *Palaestra*, *27*(1), 7–9.

Digard, L., Sponeck, A. G., & Liebling, A. G. (2007). All together now: The therapeutic potential of a prison-based music programme. *Prison Service Journal*, *170*, 3–14.

Dillon, L. (2010). *Looked after children and music making: An evidence review*. Youth Music.

Ding, Y., Gray, K., Forrence, A., Wang, X., & Huang, J. (2018). A behavioral study on tonal working memory in musicians and non-musicians. *PLOS ONE*, *13*(8), e0201765. https://doi.org/10.1371/journal.pone.0201765

Dingle, G. A., Brander, C., Ballantyne, J., & Baker, F. A. (2012). `To be heard': The social and mental health benefits of choir singing for disadvantaged adults. *Psychology of Music*, *41*(4), 405–421. https://doi.org/10.1177/0305735611430081

Diržytė, A. e, & Perminas, A. (2021). Self-reported health-related experiences, psychological capital, and psychological wellbeing in Lithuanian adults sample. *Health Psychology Open*, *8*(1), 205510292199616. https://doi.org/10.1177/2055102921996164

Dissanayake, E. (1988). *What is art for?* University of Washington Press.

Dissanayake, E. (2004). Motherese is but one part of a ritualized, multimodal, temporally organized, affiliative interaction. *Behavioral and Brain Sciences*, *27*(4), 512–513. https://doi.org/10.1017/s0140525x0432011x

Dittinger, E., Barbaroux, M., D'Imperio, M., Jäncke, L., Elmer, S., & Besson, M. (2016). Professional Music Training and Novel Word Learning: From Faster Semantic Encoding to Longer-lasting Word Representations. *Journal* of Cognitive Neuroscience, 28(10), 1584–1602. https://doi.org/10.1162/jocn_a_00997

Dobbs, S., Furnham, A., & McClelland, A. (2011). The effect of background music and noise on the cognitive test performance of introverts and extraverts. *Applied Cognitive Psychology*, 25(2), 307–313. https://doi.org/10.1002/acp.1692

Dobson, M., & Sloboda, J. (2014). Staying Behind: Explorations in Post-performance Musician–Audience Dialogue. In K. Burland & S. Pitts (Eds), *Coughing and clapping: Investigating audience experience* (p. 95). Routledge.

Doelling, K. B., & Poeppel, D. (2015). Cortical entrainment to music and its modulation by expertise. *Proceedings of the National Academy of Sciences*, 112(45). https://doi.org/10.1073/pnas.1508431112

Dolegui, A. S. (2013). The impact of listening to music on cognitive performance. *Inquiries Journal*, 5(1), 1 1 97.

Dollinger, S. J., Urban, K. K., & James, T. A. (2004). Creativity and Openness: Further Validation of Two Creative Product Measures. *Creativity Research Journal*, 16(1), 35–47. https://doi.org/10.1207/s15326934crj1601_4

Donlan, D. (1976). The Effect of Four Types of Music on Spontaneous Writings of High School Students. *Research in the Teaching of English*, 10(2), 116–126.

Douglas, S., & Willatts, P. (1994). The relationship between musical ability and literacy skills. *Journal of Research in Reading*, 17(2), 99–107. https://doi.org/10.1111/j.1467-9817.1994.tb00057.x

Dowlen, R., Keady, J., Milligan, C., Swarbrick, C., Ponsillo, N., Geddes, L., & Riley, B. (2017). The personal benefits of musicking for people living with dementia: A thematic synthesis of the qualitative literature. *Arts & Health*, 1–16. https://doi.org/10.1080/17533015.2017.1370718

Dowling, W. J., & Harwood, D. (1986). *Music Cognition*. Academic Press.

Dowson, B., Atkinson, R., Barnes, J., Barone, C., Cutts, N., Donnebaum, E., Hsu, M. H., Coco, I. L., John, G., Meadows, G., O'Neill, A., Noble, D., Norman, G., Pfende, F., Quinn, P., Warren, A., Watkins, C., & Schneider, J. (2021). Digital Approaches to Music-Making for People With Dementia in Response to the COVID-19 Pandemic: Current Practice and Recommendations. *Frontiers in Psychology*, 12. https://doi.org/10.3389/fpsyg.2021.625258

Doyle, M., & Furnham, A. (2012). The distracting effects of music on the cognitive test performance of creative and non-creative individuals. *Thinking Skills and Creativity*, 7(1), 1–7. https://doi.org/10.1016/j.tsc.2011.09.002

Drake, C., & Palmer, C. (2000). Skill acquisition in music performance: Relations between planning and temporal control. *Cognition*, 74(1), 1–32. https://doi.org/10.1016/s0010-0277(99)00061-x

Drake, M. (2003). *Drum therapy: Excerpt from the book The Shamanic Drum*. http://

Draper, G., & Dingle, G. A. (2021). "It's Not the Same": A Comparison of the Psychological Needs Satisfied by Musical Group Activities in Face to Face and Virtual Modes. *Frontiers in Psychology, 12.* https://doi.org/10.3389/fpsyg.2021.646292

Drayna, D., Manichaikul, A., Lange, M. de, Snieder, H., & Spector, T. (2001). Genetic Correlates of Musical Pitch Recognition in Humans. *Science, 291*(5510), 1969–1972. https://doi.org/10.1126/science.291.5510.1969

Drew, T. W., McCollough, A. W., & Vogel, E. K. (2006). Event-Related Potential Measures of Visual Working Memory. *Clinical EEG and Neuroscience, 37*(4), 286–291. https://doi.org/10.1177/155005940603700405

Drowns, M. R. (2002). *The effect of classical background music on fourth-grade silent reading comprehension* [PhD Thesis]. Truman State University.

Drummond, J. (2012). An international perspective on music education for adults. In G. E. McPherson & G. F. Welch (Eds), *Oxford Handbook of Music Education* (pp. 303–315). Oxford University Press.

D'Souza, A. A., Moradzadeh, L., & Wiseheart, M. (2018). Musical training, bilingualism, and executive function: Working memory and inhibitory control. *Cognitive Research: Principles and Implications, 3*(1). https://doi.org/10.1186/s41235-018-0095-6

Duffett, M. (2013). *Understanding Fandom: An Introduction to the Study of Media Fan Culture.* Bloomsbury.

D'Ulisse, M., Ferrara, C., Walter, D., & Valentina, M. V. (2001). Music therapy and integration: Application within schools. In *5th European Music Therapy Congress.*

Dunphy, K., Baker, F. A., Dumaresq, E., Carroll-Haskins, K., Eickholt, J., Ercole, M., Kaimal, G., Meyer, K., Sajnani, N., Shamir, O. Y., & Wosch, T. (2019). Creative Arts Interventions to Address Depression in Older Adults: A Systematic Review of Outcomes, Processes, and Mechanisms. *Frontiers in Psychology, 9.* https://doi.org/10.3389/fpsyg.2018.02655

Dvir, T., Lotan, N., Viderman, R., & Elefant, C. (2020). The body communicates: Movement synchrony during music therapy with children diagnosed with ASD. *The Arts in Psychotherapy, 69,* 101658. https://doi.org/10.1016/j.aip.2020.101658

Eccles, J. S., & Wigfield, A. (2002). Motivational Beliefs, Values, and Goals. *Annual Review of Psychology, 53*(1), 109–132. https://doi.org/10.1146/annurev.psych.53.100901.135153

Eccles, R., Linde, J. van der, Roux, M. le, Holloway, J., MacCutcheon, D., Ljung, R., & Swanepoel, D. W. (2020). Effect of music instruction on phonological awareness and early literacy skills of five- to seven-year-old children. *Early Child Development and Care, 191*(12), 1896–1910. https://doi.org/10.1080/03004430.2020.1803852

Eck, M. van, Berkhof, H., Nicolson, N., & Sulon, J. (1996). The Effects of Perceived Stress, Traits, Mood States, and Stressful Daily Events on Salivary Cortisol. *Psychosomatic Medicine*, 58(5), 447–458. https://doi.org/10.1097/00006842-199609000-00007

Edwards, B. M., Smart, E., King, G., Curran, C. J., & Kingsnorth, S. (2018). Performance and visual arts-based programs for children with disabilities: A scoping review focusing on psychosocial outcomes. *Disability and Rehabilitation*, 42(4), 574–585. https://doi.org/10.1080/09638288.2018.1503734

Edwards, J. (2005). *War and Music*. A World Forum for Music Therapy.[MP105.

Eerola, P.-S., & Eerola, T. (2013). Extended music education enhances the quality of school life. *Music Education Research*, 16(1), 88–104. https://doi.org/10.1080/14613808.2013.829428

Eid, M. M., Abdelbasset, W. K., Abdelaty, F. M., & Ali, Z. A. (2021). Effect of physical therapy rehabilitation program combined with music on children with lower limb burns: A twelve-week randomized controlled study. *Burns*, 47(5), 1146–1152. https://doi.org/10.1016/j.burns.2020.11.006

Eidson, C. E. (1989). The Effect of Behavioral Music Therapy on the Generalization of Interpersonal Skills From Sessions to the Classroom by Emotionally Handicapped Middle School Students. *Journal of Music Therapy*, 26(4), 206–221. https://doi.org/10.1093/jmt/26.4.206

Einarsen, H. P. (1998). *Møtet Som Ikke Tok Sted. Unpublished doctoral dissertation.* University of Oslo.

Einarsen, H. P. (2002). Musikkens roller ikulturmøtet. *Nord Nytt*, 83, 17–34.

Eisenberg, N., Champion, C., & Ma, Y. (2004). Emotion-Related Regulation: An Emerging Construct. *Merrill-Palmer Quarterly*, 50(3), 236–259. https://doi.org/10.1353/mpq.2004.0016

Eisenberg, N., & Spinrad, T. L. (2004). Emotion-Related Regulation: Sharpening the Definition. *Child Development*, 75(2), 334–339. https://doi.org/10.1111/j.1467-8624.2004.00674.x

Elbert, T., Pantev, C., Wienbruch, C., Rockstroh, B., & Taub, E. (1995). Increased Cortical Representation of the Fingers of the Left Hand in String Players. *Science*, 270(5234), 305–307. https://doi.org/10.1126/science.270.5234.305

Elligan, D. (2000). Rap therapy: A culturally sensitive approach to psychotherapy with young african american men. *Journal of African American Men*, 5(3), 27–36. https://doi.org/10.1007/s12111-000-1002-y

Elligan, D. (2004). *Rap Therapy: A Practical Guide to Communicating with Youth and Young Adults through Rap Music*. Kensington Publishing.

Elliot, S., & Mikulas, C. (2014). A Study of the Effectiveness of Music Technology Integration on the Development of Language and Literacy Skills. In M.

Searson & M. Ochoa (Eds), *Proceedings of Society for Information Technology & Teacher Education International Conference 2014* (pp. 1883–1890). AACE.

Elliot, T. G. (1981). A study of the psychology of a non-verbal methodology in the teaching of instrumental music as observed in a program for adult offenders. *Doctoral Dissertation.* [MP107]*Dissertation Abstracts International*, 42(06), 2352.

Elliott, M., & Gardner, P. (2016). The role of music in the lives of older adults with dementia ageing in place: A scoping review. *Dementia, 17*(2), 199–213. https://doi.org/10.1177/1471301216639424

Ellis, R. J., Bruijn, B., Norton, A. C., Winner, E., & Schlaug, G. (2013). Training-mediated leftward asymmetries during music processing: A cross-sectional and longitudinal fMRI analysis. *NeuroImage, 75,* 97–107. https://doi.org/10.1016/j.neuroimage.2013.02.045

Ellis, R. J., Norton, A. C., Overy, K., Winner, E., Alsop, D. C., & Schlaug, G. (2012). Differentiating maturational and training influences on fMRI activation during music processing. *NeuroImage, 60*(3), 1902–1912. https://doi.org/10.1016/j.neuroimage.2012.01.138

Elmer, S., Dittinger, E., & Besson, M. (2019). One Step Beyond: Musical Expertise and Word Learning. In S. Frühholz & P. Belin (Eds), *The Oxford Handbook of Voice Perception* (pp. 209–234). Oxford University Press.

Elmer, S., Klein, C., Kühnis, J., Liem, F., Meyer, M., & Jäncke, L. (2014). Music and Language Expertise Influence the Categorization of Speech and Musical Sounds: Behavioral and Electrophysiological Measurements. *Journal of Cognitive Neuroscience, 26*(10), 2356–2369. https://doi.org/10.1162/jocn_a_00632

Elmer, S., Meyer, M., & Jancke, L. (2011). Neurofunctional and Behavioral Correlates of Phonetic and Temporal Categorization in Musically Trained and Untrained Subjects. *Cerebral Cortex, 22*(3), 650–658. https://doi.org/10.1093/cercor/bhr142

Elpus, K. (2013). Is It the Music or Is It Selection Bias? A Nationwide Analysis of Music and Non-Music Students' SAT Scores. *Journal of Research in Music Education, 61*(2), 175–194. https://doi.org/10.1177/0022429413485601

Elpus, K., & Abril, C. R. (2011). High School Music Ensemble Students in the United States. *Journal of Research in Music Education, 59*(2), 128–145. https://doi.org/10.1177/0022429411405207

Elvers, P. (2016). Songs for the Ego: Theorizing Musical Self-Enhancement. *Frontiers in Psychology, 7.* https://doi.org/10.3389/fpsyg.2016.00002

Elvers, P., Fischinger, T., & Steffens, J. (2017). Music listening as self-enhancement: Effects of empowering music on momentary explicit and implicit self-esteem. *Psychology of Music, 46*(3), 307–325. https://doi.org/10.1177/0305735617707354

Elzen, N. van den, Daman, V., Duijkers, M., Otte, K., Wijnhoven, E., Timmerman, H., & Rikkert, M. O. (2019). The Power of Music: Enhancing Muscle Strength in Older People. *Healthcare, 7*(3), 82. https://doi.org/10.3390/healthcare7030082

Enge, K. E. A., & Stige, B. (2021a). Musical pathways to the peer community: A collective case study of refugee children's use of music therapy. *Nordic Journal of Music Therapy, 31*(1), 7–24. https://doi.org/10.1080/08098131.2021.1891130

Enge, K. E. A., & Stige, B. (2021b). Musical pathways to the peer community: A collective case study of refugee children's use of music therapy. *Nordic Journal of Music Therapy, 31*(1), 7–24. https://doi.org/10.1080/08098131.2021.1891130

Engel, C., Bueno, C. D., & Sleifer, P. (2019). Music training and auditory processing skills in children: A systematic review. *Audiology Communication Research, 24.*

Engelbrecht, R., & Shoemark, H. (2015). The acceptability and efficacy of using iPads in music therapy to support wellbeing with older adults: A pilot study. *Australian Journal of Music Therapy, 26,* 52–73.

English, H. J., Lumb, M., & Davidson, J. W. (2021). What are the affordances of the digital music space in alternative education? A reflection on an exploratory music outreach project in rural Australia. *International Journal of Music Education, 39*(3), 275–288. https://doi.org/10.1177/0255761421999731

Epskamp, K. (1999). Introduction—Healing Divided Societies. In *European Centre for Conflict Prevention (ed.), People building peace: 35 inspiring stories from around the world,* Utrecht: European Centre for Conflict Prevention (p. 112).

Epstein, J. S., Pratto, D. J., & Skipper, J. K. (1990). Teenagers, behavioral problems, and preferences for heavy metal and rap music: A case study of a southern middle school. *Deviant Behavior, 11*(4), 381–394. https://doi.org/10.1080/01639625.1990.9967860

Erickson, L. C., & Thiessen, E. D. (2015). Statistical learning of language: Theory, validity, and predictions of a statistical learning account of language acquisition. *Developmental Review, 37,* 66–108. https://doi.org/10.1016/j.dr.2015.05.002

Erikson, E. (1982). *The Life Cycle Completed.* Norton.

Escobar, J., Mussoi, B. S., & Silberer, A. B. (2019). The Effect of Musical Training and Working Memory in Adverse Listening Situations. *Ear & Hearing, 41*(2), 278–288. https://doi.org/10.1097/aud.0000000000000754

Esqueda Torres, L. (2001). *Execution of phase 1 of the monitoring and evaluation plan of the impact of the orchestras national system: Final report.* Los Andes University, Médicine Faculty, Centre of Psychological Research.

Esqueda Torres, L. (2004). *Ejecución de la Fase 3 del Plan de Seguimiento y Evaluación de Impacto del Sistema Nacional de Orquestas de Venezuela: Informe final*. Centro de Investigaciones Psicológicas, Universidad de Los Andes.

Etaugh, C., & Michals, D. (1975). Effects on Reading Comprehension of Preferred Music and Frequency of Studying to Music. *Perceptual and Motor Skills, 41*(2), 553–554. https://doi.org/10.2466/pms.1975.41.2.553

Europe, S. (2019). Sistema Europe. https://www.sistemaeurope.

Evaluación de impacto Programa Orquestas Juveniles e Infantiles: Informe de Resultados. (2010). Observatorio Social, Universidad Alberto Hurtado.

Evans, P., & Liu, M. Y. (2018). Psychological Needs and Motivational Outcomes in a High School Orchestra Program. *Journal of Research in Music Education, 67*(1), 83–105. https://doi.org/10.1177/0022429418812769

Evans, P., McPherson, G. E., & Davidson, J. W. (2012). The role of psychological needs in ceasing music and music learning activities. *Psychology of Music, 41*(5), 600–619. https://doi.org/10.1177/0305735612441736

Evans, S. E., Beauchamp, G., & John, V. (2014). Learners' experience and perceptions of informal learning in Key Stage 3 music: A collective case study, exploring the implementation of$\textbackslashless$i$\textbackslashgreater$Musical Futures$\textbackslashless$/i$\textbackslashgreater$in three secondary schools in Wales. *Music Education Research, 17*(1), 1–16. https://doi.org/10.1 080/14613808.2014.950212

Evers, S., & Suhr, B. (2000). Changes of the neurotransmitter serotonin but not of hormones during short time music perception. *European Archives of Psychiatry and Clinical Neuroscience, 250*(3), 144–147. https://doi.org/10.1007/s004060070031

Evron, N. C. (n.d.). Conflict and Peace: Challenges for Arts Educators. In *International Handbook of Research in Arts Education* (pp. 1031–1054). Springer Netherlands. https://doi.org/10.1007/978-1-4020-3052-9_71

Eyerman, R. (2002). Music in Movement: Cultural Politics and Old and New Social Movements. *Qualitative Sociology, 25*(3), 443–458. https://doi.org/10.1023/a:1016042215533

Ezell, M., & Levy, M. (2003). An evaluation of an arts program for incarcerated juvenile offenders. *Journal of Correct, MP115]Education, 54*, 108–114.

Facchini, M., & Ruini, C. (2021). The role of music therapy in the treatment of children with cancer: A systematic review of literature. *Complementary Therapies in Clinical Practice, 42*, 101289. https://doi.org/10.1016/j.ctcp.2020.101289

Fairchild, R. E. (2018). *Collaborative Songwriting with Children Experiencing Homelessness and Family Violence to Understand Their Resources*. The University of Melbourne.

Fairchild, R., & McFerran, K. S. (2018). "Music is everything": Using collaborative group songwriting as an arts-based method with children experiencing homelessness and family violence. *Nordic Journal of Music Therapy, 28*(2), 88–107. https://doi.org/10.1080/08098131.2018.1509106

Fairchild, R., Thompson, G., & McFerran, K. S. (2016). Exploring the Meaning of a Performance in Music Therapy for Children and Their Families Experiencing Homelessness and Family Violence. *Music Therapy Perspectives*, miw004. https://doi.org/10.1093/mtp/miw004

Falk, D. (2004). Prelinguistic evolution in early hominins: Whence motherese? *Behavioral and Brain Sciences, 27*(4), 491–503. https://doi.org/10.1017/s0140525x04000111

Fancourt, D., & Finn, S. (2019). What is the Evidence on the Role of the Arts in Improving Health and Well-being? A Scoping Review. *Health Evidence Network Synthesis Report, 67.*

Fancourt, D., Finn, S., Warran, K., & Wiseman, T. (2019). Group singing in bereavement: Effects on mental health, self-efficacy, self-esteem and well-being. In *BMJ Supportive and Palliative Care*[MP118. https://doi.org/10.1136/bmjspcare-2018-001642.

Fancourt, D., Geschke, K., Fellgiebel, A., & Wuttke-Linnemann, A. (2020). Lifetime musical training and cognitive performance in a memory clinic population: A cross-sectional study. *Musicae Scientiae, 26*(1), 71–83. https://doi.org/10.1177/1029864920918636

Fancourt, D., Ockelford, A., & Belai, A. (2014). The psychoneuroimmunological effects of music: A systematic review and a new model. *Brain, Behavior, and Immunity, 36*, 15–26. https://doi.org/10.1016/j.bbi.2013.10.014

Fancourt, D., & Perkins, R. (2017). Associations between singing to babies and symptoms of postnatal depression, wellbeing, self-esteem and mother-infant bond. *Public Health, 145*, 149–152. https://doi.org/10.1016/j.puhe.2017.01.016

Fancourt, D., & Perkins, R. (2018). The effects of mother–infant singing on emotional closeness, affect, anxiety, and stress hormones. *Music & Science, 1*, 205920431774574. https://doi.org/10.1177/2059204317745746

Fancourt, D., Perkins, R., Ascenso, S., Atkins, L., Kilfeather, S., Carvalho, L., Steptoe, A., & Williamon, A. (2015). Group Drumming Modulates Cytokine Response in Mental Health Services Users: A Preliminary Study. *Psychotherapy and Psychosomatics, 85*(1), 53–55. https://doi.org/10.1159/000431257

Fancourt, D., Perkins, R., Ascenso, S., Carvalho, L. A., Steptoe, A., & Williamon, A. (2016). Effects of Group Drumming Interventions on Anxiety, Depression, Social Resilience and Inflammatory Immune Response among Mental Health Service Users. *PLOS ONE, 11*(3), e0151136. https://doi.org/10.1371/journal.pone.0151136

Fancourt, D., & Steptoe, A. (2018). Community group membership and multidimensional subjective well-being in older age. *Journal of Epidemiology and Community Health*, 72(5), 376–382. https://doi.org/10.1136/jech-2017-210260

Fancourt, D., Williamon, A., Carvalho, L. A., Steptoe, A., Dow, R., & Lewis, I. (2016). Singing modulates mood, stress, cortisol, cytokine and neuropeptide activity in cancer patients and carers. *Ecancermedicalscience*, 10. https://doi.org/10.3332/ecancer.2016.631

Fanian, S., Young, S. K., Mantla, M., Daniels, A., & Chatwood, S. (2015). Evaluation of the Kts'iiht\textbackslashla ("We Light the Fire") Project: Building resiliency and connections through strengths-based creative arts programming for Indigenous youth. *International Journal of Circumpolar Health*, 74(1), 27672. https://doi.org/10.3402/ijch.v74.27672

Farias, S. A. de, Aguiar, E. C., & Melo, F. V. S. (2014). Store Atmospherics and Experiential Marketing: A Conceptual Framework and Research Propositions for An Extraordinary Customer Experience. *International Business Research*, 7(2). https://doi.org/10.5539/ibr.v7n2p87

Farnsworth, P. R. (1946). School Instruction in Music. *Review of Educational Research*, 16(2), 182. https://doi.org/10.2307/1168501

Fasano, M. C., Semeraro, C., Cassibba, R., Kringelbach, M. L., Monacis, L., Palo, V. de, Vuust, P., & Brattico, E. (2019). Short-Term Orchestral Music Training Modulates Hyperactivity and Inhibitory Control in School-Age Children: A Longitudinal Behavioural Study. *Frontiers in Psychology*, 10. https://doi.org/10.3389/fpsyg.2019.00750

Fassbender, E., Richards, D., Bilgin, A., Thompson, W. F., & Heiden, W. (2012). VirSchool: The effect of background music and immersive display systems on memory for facts learned in an educational virtual environment. *Computers & Education*, 58(1), 490–500. https://doi.org/10.1016/j.compedu.2011.09.002

Faulkner, R., & Davidson, J. (2004). Men's Vocal Behaviour and the Construction of Self. *Musicae Scientiae*, 8(2), 231–255. https://doi.org/10.1177/102986490400800206

Faulkner, S. (2017). Rhythm2Recovery: A Model of Practice Combining Rhythmic Music with Cognitive Reflection for Social and Emotional Health within Trauma Recovery. *Australian and New Zealand Journal of Family Therapy*, 38(4), 627–636. https://doi.org/10.1002/anzf.1268

Faulkner, S., Wood, L., Ivery, P., & Donovan, R. (2012). It Is Not Just Music and Rhythm. . . Evaluation of a Drumming-Based Intervention to Improve the Social Wellbeing of Alienated Youth. *Children Australia*, 37(1), 31–39. https://doi.org/10.1017/cha.2012.5

Fauvel, B., Groussard, M., Chételat, G., Fouquet, M., Landeau, B., Eustache, F., Desgranges, B., & Platel, H. (2014). Morphological brain plasticity induced by musical expertise is accompanied by modulation of functional connectivity at rest. *NeuroImage*, 90, 179–188. https://doi.org/10.1016/j.neuroimage.2013.12.065

Fauvel, B., Groussard, M., Mutlu, J., Arenaza-Urquijo, E. M., Eustache, F., Desgranges, B., & Platel, H. (2014). Musical practice and cognitive aging: Two cross-sectional studies point to phonemic fluency as a potential candidate for a use-dependent adaptation. *Frontiers in Aging Neuroscience, 6.* https://doi.org/10.3389/fnagi.2014.00227

Feinstein, L., & Sabates, R. (2006). *The prevalence of multiple deprivation for children in the UK: analysis of the Millennium Cohort and Longitudinal Survey of Young People in England.* Institute of Education, University of London.

Feist, G. J. (1998). A Meta-Analysis of Personality in Scientific and Artistic Creativity. *Personality and Social Psychology Review, 2*(4), 290–309. https://doi.org/10.1207/s15327957pspr0204_5

Feldman, A. F., & Matjasko, J. L. (2005). The Role of School-Based Extracurricular Activities in Adolescent Development: A Comprehensive Review and Future Directions. *Review of Educational Research, 75*(2), 159–210. https://doi.org/10.3102/00346543075002159

Feldman, A. F., & Matjasko, J. L. (2007). Profiles and portfolios of adolescent school-based extracurricular activity participation. *Journal of Adolescence, 30*(2), 313–332. https://doi.org/10.1016/j.adolescence.2006.03.004

Felsenstein, R. (2013). From uprooting to replanting: On post-trauma group music therapy for pre-school children. *Nordic Journal of Music Therapy, 22*(1), 69–85. https://doi.org/10.1080/08098131.2012.667824

Feng, F., Zhang, Y., Hou, J., Cai, J., Jiang, Q., Li, X., Zhao, Q., & Li, B. (2018). Can music improve sleep quality in adults with primary insomnia? A systematic review and network meta-analysis. *International Journal of Nursing Studies, 77,* 189–196. https://doi.org/10.1016/j.ijnurstu.2017.10.011

Feng, K., Shen, C.-Y., Ma, X.-Y., Chen, G.-F., Zhang, M.-L., Xu, B., Liu, X.-M., Sun, J.-J., Zhang, X.-Q., Liu, P.-Z., & Ju, Y. (2019). Effects of music therapy on major depressive disorder: A study of prefrontal hemodynamic functions using fNIRS. *Psychiatry Research, 275,* 86–93. https://doi.org/10.1016/j.psychres.2019.03.015

Fennell, A. M., Bugos, J. A., Payne, B. R., & Schotter, E. R. (2020). Music is similar to language in terms of working memory interference. *Psychonomic Bulletin & Review, 28*(2), 512–525. https://doi.org/10.3758/s13423-020-01833-5

Fernald, A. (1989). Intonation and Communicative Intent in Mothers' Speech to Infants: Is the Melody the Message? *Child Development, 60*(6), 1497. https://doi.org/10.2307/1130938

Fernandez, N. B., Trost, W. J., & Vuilleumier, P. (2019). Brain networks mediating the influence of background music on selective attention. *Social Cognitive and Affective Neuroscience, 14*(12), 1441–1452. https://doi.org/10.1093/scan/nsaa004

Fernandez, S. (2018). Music and Brain Development. *Pediatric Annals, 47*(8). https://doi.org/10.3928/19382359-20180710-01

Ferreri, L., Aucouturier, J.-J., Muthalib, M., Bigand, E., & Bugaiska, A. (2013). Music improves verbal memory encoding while decreasing prefrontal cortex activity: An fNIRS study. *Frontiers in Microbiology, 7*. https://doi.org/10.3389/fnhum.2013.00779

Ferreri, L., Bigand, E., Bard, P., & Bugaiska, A. (2015). The Influence of Music on Prefrontal Cortex during Episodic Encoding and Retrieval of Verbal Information: A Multichannel fNIRS Study. *Behavioural Neurology, 2015*, 1–11. https://doi.org/10.1155/2015/707625

Ferreri, L., Bigand, E., & Bugaiska, A. (2015). The positive effect of music on source memory. *Musicae Scientiae, 19*(4), 402–411. https://doi.org/10.1177/1029864915604684

Ferreri, L., Bigand, E., Perrey, S., Muthalib, M., Bard, P., & Bugaiska, A. (2014). Less Effort, Better Results: How Does Music Act on Prefrontal Cortex in Older Adults during Verbal Encoding? An fNIRS Study. *Frontiers in Human Neuroscience, 8*. https://doi.org/10.3389/fnhum.2014.00301

Ferreri, L., & Verga, L. (2016). Benefits of Music on Verbal Learning and Memory. *Music Perception, 34*(2), 167–182. https://doi.org/10.1525/mp.2016.34.2.167

Field, T., Martinez, A., Nawrocki, T., Pickens, J., Fox, N. A., & Schanberg, S. (1998). Music shifts frontal EEG in depressed adolescents. *Adolescence, 33*(129), 109–116.

Fields, R. D. (2005). Making Memories Stick. *Scientific American, 292*(2), 74–81. https://doi.org/10.1038/scientificamerican0205-74

Filippa, M., Devouche, E., Arioni, C., Imberty, M., & Gratier, M. (2013). Live maternal speech and singing have beneficial effects on hospitalized preterm infants. *Acta Paediatrica, 102*(10), 1017–1020. https://doi.org/10.1111/apa.12356

Finn, S., & Fancourt, D. (2018). The biological impact of listening to music in clinical and nonclinical settings: A systematic review. In *Progress in Brain Research* (pp. 173–200). Elsevier. https://doi.org/10.1016/bs.pbr.2018.03.007

Finnegan, R. (1989). *The Hidden Musicians: Music-Making in an English Town*. Cambridge University Press.

Fischer, M. H., Riello, M., Giordano, B. L., & Rusconi, E. (2013). Singing Numbers\textbackslashldots in Cognitive Space—A Dual-Task Study of the Link Between Pitch, Space, and Numbers. *Topics in Cognitive Science, 5*(2), 354–366. https://doi.org/10.1111/tops.12017

Fischer, P., & Greitemeyer, T. (2006). Music and Aggression: The Impact of Sexual-Aggressive Song Lyrics on Aggression-Related Thoughts, Emotions, and Behavior Toward the Same and the Opposite Sex. *Personality and Social Psychology Bulletin, 32*(9), 1165–1176. https://doi.org/10.1177/0146167206288670

Fitzpatrick, K. R. (2006). The Effect of Instrumental Music Participation and Socioeconomic Status on Ohio Fourth-, Sixth-, and Ninth-Grade Proficiency Test Performance. *Journal of Research in Music Education*, 54(1), 73–84. https://doi.org/10.1177/002242940605400106

Fiveash, A., & Pammer, K. (2012). Music and language: Do they draw on similar syntactic working memory resources? *Psychology of Music*, 42(2), 190–209. https://doi.org/10.1177/0305735612463949

Flaugnacco, E., Lopez, L., Terribili, C., Montico, M., Zoia, S., & Schön, D. (2015). Music Training Increases Phonological Awareness and Reading Skills in Developmental Dyslexia: A Randomized Control Trial. *PLOS ONE*, 10(9), e0138715. https://doi.org/10.1371/journal.pone.0138715

Flohr, J. W., Miller, D. C., & deBeus, R. (2000). EEG Studies with Young Children. *Music Educators Journal*, 87(2), 28–54. https://doi.org/10.2307/3399645

Flores, K., Niekerk, C. van, & Roux, L. le. (2015). Drumming as a medium to promote emotional and social functioning of children in middle childhood in residential care. *Music Education Research*, 18(3), 254–268. https://doi.org/10.1080/14613808.2015.1077798

Florida, R., Mellander, C., & Stolarick, K. (2010). Music Scenes to Music Clusters: The Economic Geography of Music in the US, 1970–2000. *Environment and Planning A: Economy and Space*, 42(4), 785–804. https://doi.org/10.1068/a4253

Flynn, L. R., Eastman, J. K., & Newell, S. J. (1995). An Exploratory Study of the Application of Neural Networks to Marketing: Predicting Rock Music Shopping Behavior. *Journal of Marketing Theory and Practice*, 3(2), 75–85. https://doi.org/10.1080/10696679.1995.11501686

Fock, E. (2004). *World.dk-erfaringerfraverdensmusikprojekteriskolerogpåspillesteder*. Center for Kulturpolitiske Studier, Danmarks Biblioteksskole.

Fogel, A. R., Rosenberg, J. C., Lehman, F. M., Kuperberg, G. R., & Patel, A. D. (2015). Studying Musical and Linguistic Prediction in Comparable Ways: The Melodic Cloze Probability Method. *Frontiers in Psychology*, 6. https://doi.org/10.3389/fpsyg.2015.01718

Fogelson, S. (1973). Music as a Distractor on Reading-Test Performance of Eighth Grade Students. *Perceptual and Motor Skills*, 36(3_suppl), 1265–1266. https://doi.org/10.2466/pms.1973.36.3c.1265

Fonseca-Mora, M. C., Jara-JimÃ©nez, P., & GÃ^3mez-DomÃ\textbackslash-nguez, M. (2015). Musical plus phonological input for young foreign language readers. *Frontiers in Psychology*, 6. https://doi.org/10.3389/fpsyg.2015.00286

Forgeard, M., Schlaug, G., Norton, A., Rosam, C., Iyengar, U., & Winner, E. (2008). The relation between music and phonological processing in normal-reading children and children with dyslexia. *Music Perception*, 25(4), 383–390. https://doi.org/10.1525/mp.2008.25.4.383

Forgeard, M., Winner, E., Norton, A., & Schlaug, G. (2008). Practicing a Musical Instrument in Childhood is Associated with Enhanced Verbal Ability and Nonverbal Reasoning. *PLoS ONE*, *3*(10), e3566. https://doi.org/10.1371/journal.pone.0003566

Forssén, A. S. K. (2007). Humour, beauty, and culture as personal health resources: Experiences of elderly Swedish women. *Scandinavian Journal of Public Health*, *35*(3), 228–234. https://doi.org/10.1080/14034940601160680

Francois, C., Chobert, J., Besson, M., & Schon, D. (2012). Music Training for the Development of Speech Segmentation. *Cerebral Cortex*, *23*(9), 2038–2043. https://doi.org/10.1093/cercor/bhs180

Freeman, W. J. (2000). A neurobiological role of music in social bonding. In N. Wallin, B. Merkur, & S. Brown (Eds), *The Origins of Music* (pp. 411–424). MIT Press.

Frith, S. (1996). *Performing rites: On the value of popular music*. Oxford University Press.

Froehlich, M. A. R. (1984). A Comparison of the Effect of Music Therapy and Medical Play Therapy on the Verbalization Behavior of Pediatric Patients. *Journal of Music Therapy*, *21*(1), 2–15. https://doi.org/10.1093/jmt/21.1.2

Fukui, H., & Yamashita, M. (2003). The effects of music and visual stress on testosterone and cortisol in men and women. *Neuro Endocrinology Letters*, *24*(3–4), 173–180.

Fung, C. V., & Lehmberg, L. J. (2016). *Music for Life*. Oxford University Press. https://doi.org/10.1093/acprof:oso/9780199371686.001.0001

Furuya, S., & Altenmuller, E. (2013). Flexibility of movement organization in piano performance, Front. *Hum*.

Fusar-Poli, L., Bieleninik, \textbackslashLucja, Brondino, N., Chen, X.-J., & Gold, C. (2017). The effect of music therapy on cognitive functions in patients with dementia: A systematic review and meta-analysis. *Aging & Mental Health*, *22*(9), 1103–1112. https://doi.org/10.1080/13607863.2017.1348474

Gaab, N., & Schlaug, G. (2003). The effect of musicianship on pitch memory in performance matched groups. *Neuroreport*, *14*(18), 2291–2295. https://doi.org/10.1097/00001756-200312190-00001

Gabrielsson, A. (2001a). Emotions in strong experiences with music. In P. N. Juslin & J. A. Sloboda (Eds), *Music and emotion: Theory and research* (pp. 431–449). Oxford University Press.

Gabrielsson, A. (2001b). Emotion perceived and emotion felt: Same or different? *Musicae Scientiae*, *5*(1_suppl), 123–147. https://doi.org/10.1177/10298649020050s105

Gabrielsson, A. (2011). *Strong Experiences with MusicMusic is much more than just music*. Oxford University Press. https://doi.org/10.1093/acprof:oso/9780199695225.001.0001

Gabrielsson, A., & Lindström, E. (1995). Emotional expression in synthesizer and sentograph performance. *Psychomusicology: A Journal of Research in Music Cognition, 14*(1–2), 94–116. https://doi.org/10.1037/h0094089

Gabrielsson, A., & Wik, S. L. (2003). Strong Experiences Related to Music: Adescriptive System. *Musicae Scientiae, 7*(2), 157–217. https://doi.org/10.1177/102986490300700201

Gallego, G. M., & García, G. J. (2017). Music therapy in Alzheimer's disease: Cognitive, psychological and behavioural effects. *Neurology, 32*(5), 300–308.

Gandhi, K., B., P., J., & Gokulakannan, K. (2021). A Single-center, Single Blinded, Randomized Controlled Trial Protocol of Therapeutic Listening Programme Versus Traditional Music Therapy on Depression and Quality of Life in Institutionalized Adolescents. *Medico-Legal Update, 21.*

Garlin, F. V., & Owen, K. (2006). Setting the tone with the tune: A meta-analytic review of the effects of background music in retail settings. *Journal of Business Research, 59*(6), 755–764. https://doi.org/10.1016/j.jbusres.2006.01.013

Garrido, S. (2017). *Why Are We Attracted to Sad Music?* Springer International Publishing. https://doi.org/10.1007/978-3-319-39666-8

Garrido, S., Eerola, T., & McFerran, K. (2017). Group Rumination: Social Interactions Around Music in People with Depression. *Frontiers in Psychology, 8.* https://doi.org/10.3389/fpsyg.2017.00490

Garrido, S., & Schubert, E. (2013a). Adaptive and maladaptive attraction to negative emotions in music. *Musicae Scientiae, 17*(2), 147–166. https://doi.org/10.1177/1029864913478305

Garrido, S., & Schubert, E. (2013b). Moody melodies: Do they cheer us up? A study of the effect of sad music on mood. *Psychology of Music, 43*(2), 244–261. https://doi.org/10.1177/0305735613501938

Garrido, S., & Schubert, E. (2015). Music and People with Tendencies to Depression. *Music Perception, 32*(4), 313–321. https://doi.org/10.1525/mp.2015.32.4.313

Geipel, J., Koenig, J., Hillecke, T. K., Resch, F., & Kaess, M. (2018). Music-based interventions to reduce internalizing symptoms in children and adolescents: A meta-analysis. *Journal of Affective Disorders, 225,* 647–656. https://doi.org/10.1016/j.jad.2017.08.035

Gembris, H. (2008). Musical activities in the third age: An empirical study with amateur musicians. *Second European Conference on Developmental Psychology of Music.*

Genoe, M. R., & Dupuis, S. L. (2012). The role of leisure within the dementia context. *Dementia, 13*(1), 33–58. https://doi.org/10.1177/1471301212447028

Gerber, M. M., Hogan, L. R., Maxwell, K., Callahan, J. L., Ruggero, C. J., & Sundberg, T. (2014). Children after war: A novel approach to promoting resilience through music. *Traumatology: An International Journal, 20*(2), 112–118. https://doi.org/10.1037/h0099396

Geretsegger, M., Elefant, C., Mössler, K. A., & Gold, C. (2014). Music therapy for people with autism spectrum disorder. *Cochrane Database of Systematic Reviews, 2016*(3). https://doi.org/10.1002/14651858.cd004381.pub3

Geretsegger, M., Mossler, K. A., Bieleninik, L., Chen, X.-J., Heldal, T. O., & Gold, C. (2017). Music therapy for people with schizophrenia and schizophrenia-like symptoms. *Cochrane Database Systemic Reviews, 29*(5), 004025.

Gerra, G., Zaimovic, A., Franchini, D., Palladino, M., Giucastro, G., Reali, N., Maestri, D., Caccavari, R., Delsignore, R., & Brambilla, F. (1998). Neuroendocrine responses of healthy volunteers to \textbackslashtextasci igravetechno-music': Relationships with personality traits and emotional state. *International Journal of Psychophysiology, 28*(1), 99–111. https://doi.org/10.1016/s0167-8760(97)00071-8

Gerrard, C. L. (2021). It's more than playing music: Exploring band in a predominantly Latinx community. *Bulletin of the Council for Research in Music Education, 227*([MP153].

Gerrity, K. W., Hourigan, R. M., & Horton, P. W. (2013). Conditions That Facilitate Music Learning Among Students With Special Needs. *Journal of Research in Music Education, 61*(2), 144–159. https://doi.org/10.1177/0022429413485428

Ghai, S., Ghai, I., & Effenberg, A. O. (2017). Effect of rhythmic auditory cueing on gait in cerebral palsy: A systematic review and meta-analysis. *Neuropsychiatric Disease and Treatment, Volume 14*, 43–59. https://doi.org/10.2147/ndt.s148053

Gibbs, H., & Egermann, H. (2021). Music-Evoked Nostalgia and Wellbeing During the United Kingdom COVID-19 Pandemic: Content, Subjective Effects, and Function. *Frontiers in Psychology, 12*. https://doi.org/10.3389/fpsyg.2021.647891

Gibson, C., & Connell, J. (2005). *Music and Tourism*. Multilingual Matters. https://doi.org/10.21832/9781873150948

Gibson, R., Aust, C. F., & Zillmann, D. (2000). Loneliness of Adolescents and Their Choice and Enjoyment of Love-Celebrating versus Love-Lamenting Popular Music. *Empirical Studies of the Arts, 18*(1), 43–48. https://doi.org/10.2190/b51g-8u0w-n0eq-mjuu

Gilbert, S. (2005). *Music in the Holocaust: Confronting Life in the Nazi Ghettos and Camps*. Oxford University Press.

Giordano, F., Zanchi, B., Leonardis, F. D., Rutigliano, C., Esposito, F., Brienza, N., & Santoro, N. (2020). The influence of music therapy on preoperative anxiety in pediatric oncology patients undergoing invasive procedures. *The Arts in Psychotherapy, 68*, 101649. https://doi.org/10.1016/j.aip.2020.101649

Giovagnoli, A. R., Oliveri, S., Schifano, L., & Raglio, A. (2014). Active music therapy improves cognition and behaviour in chronic vascular encephalopathy: A case report. *Complementary Therapies in Medicine, 22*(1), 57–62. https://doi.org/10.1016/j.ctim.2013.11.001

Glasgow Centre for Population Health (GCPH. (2015). Education Scotland; Glasgow Caledonian University.

Gleadhill, L., & Ferris, K. (2010). A theoretical music therapy framework for working with people with dissociative identity disorder. *Australian Journal of Music Therapy, 21,* 42–55.

Goethem, A. (2010). *Affect regulation in everyday life: Strategies, tactics, and the role of music* [PhD Thesis].

Goethem, A. van, & Sloboda, J. (2011). The functions of music for affect regulation. *Musicae Scientiae, 15*(2), 208–228. https://doi.org/10.1177/1029864911401174

Gold, C., Saarikallio, S., Crooke, A. H. D., & McFerran, K. S. (2017). Group Music Therapy as a Preventive Intervention for Young People at Risk: Cluster-Randomized Trial. *Journal of Music Therapy, 54*(2), 133–160. https://doi.org/10.1093/jmt/thx002

Gold, C., Solli, H. P., Krüger, V., & Lie, S. A. (2009). Dose–response relationship in music therapy for people with serious mental disorders: Systematic review and meta-analysis. *Clinical Psychology Review, 29*(3), 193–207. https://doi.org/10.1016/j.cpr.2009.01.001

Gold, C., Voracek, M., & Wigram, T. (2004). Effects of music therapy for children and adolescents with psychopathology: A meta-analysis. *Journal of Child Psychology and Psychiatry, 45*(6), 1054–1063. https://doi.org/10.1111/j.1469-7610.2004.t01-1-00298.x

Gold, C., Wigram, T., & Voracek, M. (2007). Effectiveness of music therapy for children and adolescents with psychopathology: A quasi-experimental study. *Psychotherapy Research, 17*(3), 289–296. https://doi.org/10.1080/10503300600607886

Gonsalves, M. (2010). *Restoring connection and personal capacities for healing music therapy in Sierra Leone* (M. E. N. Ouedraogo, M. Meyer, & J. Atiri, Eds.). Africa World Press.

Gonzalez, M. F., & Aiello, J. R. (2019). More than meets the ear: Investigating how music affects cognitive task performance. *Journal of Experimental Psychology: Applied, 25*(3), 431. https://doi.org/10.1037/xap0000202

Good starts for recently arrived youth with refugee backgrounds: Promoting wellbeing in the first three years of settlement in Melbourne, Australia. (2009). La Trobe Refugee Research Centre, La Trobe University.

Gopalkrishnan, N. (2016). Multicultural Arts and Integrative Medicine: Empowering Refugees in the Healing Process. ETropic electronic journal of studies in the Tropics, 12(2. *Special Issue: Refereed Proceedings of the Tropics of the Imagination Conference.*

Goriounova, N. A., & Mansvelder, H. D. (2019). Genes, Cells and Brain Areas of Intelligence. *Frontiers in Human Neuroscience, 13.* https://doi.org/10.3389/fnhum.2019.00044

Goswami, U. (2011). A temporal sampling framework for developmental dyslexia. *Trends in Cognitive Sciences, 15*(1), 3–10. https://doi.org/10.1016/j.tics.2010.10.001

Goswami, U. (2019). A neural oscillations perspective on phonological development and phonological processing in developmental dyslexia. *Language and Linguistics Compass, 13*(5), e12328. https://doi.org/10.1111/lnc3.12328

Goswami, U., Thomson, J., Richardson, U., Stainthorp, R., Hughes, D., Rosen, S., & Scott, S. K. (2002). Amplitude envelope onsets and developmental dyslexia: A new hypothesis. *Proceedings of the National Academy of Sciences, 99*(16), 10911–10916. https://doi.org/10.1073/pnas.122368599

Gouzouasis, P. (1993). Music audiation: A comparison of the music abilities of kindergarten children of various ethnic backgrounds. *The Quarterly Journal of Music Teaching and Learning, 4,* 70–76.

Gouzouasis, P. (2014). What matters most: Using contemporary research to support music education policies in schools (a performative autoethnography). In P. Gouzouasis (Ed.), *Proceedings of the commission on music policy: Culture, education, and media of the International Society for Music Education.*

Gouzouasis, P., Guhn, M., & Kishor, N. (2007). The predictive relationship between achievement and participation in music and achievement in core Grade 12 academic subjects. *Music Education Research, 9*(1), 81–92. https://doi.org/10.1080/14613800601127569

Gouzouasis, P., & Henderson, A. (2012). Secondary student perspectives on musical and educational outcomes from participation in band festivals. *Music Education Research, 14*(4), 479–498. https://doi.org/10.1080/14613808.2012.714361

Gouzouasis, P., Henrey, J., & Belliveau, G. (2008). Turning points: A transitional story of grade seven music students' participation in high school band programmes. *Music Education Research, 10*(1), 75–90. https://doi.org/10.1080/14613800701871397

Graff, V., Wingfield, P., Adams, D., & Rabinowitz, T. (2016). An Investigation of Patient Preferences for Music Played Before Electroconvulsive Therapy. *The Journal of ECT, 32*(3), 192–196. https://doi.org/10.1097/yct.0000000000000315

Graham, S. (2011). *Effect of Music Therapy on the Emotional Expressivity of Children and Adolescents Who Have Experienced Abuse or Neglect.* Florida State University.

Granert, O., Peller, M., Gaser, C., Groppa, S., Hallett, M., Knutzen, A., Deuschl, G., Zeuner, K. E., & Siebner, H. R. (2011). Manual activity shapes structure and function in contralateral human motor hand area. *NeuroImage, 54*(1), 32–41. https://doi.org/10.1016/j.neuroimage.2010.08.013

Granier-Deferre, C., Ribeiro, A., Jacquet, A.-Y., & Bassereau, S. (2011). Near-term fetuses process temporal features of speech. *Developmental Science, 14*(2), 336–352. https://doi.org/10.1111/j.1467-7687.2010.00978.x

Granot, R., Spitz, D. H., Cherki, B. R., Loui, P., Timmers, R., Schaefer, R. S., Vuoskoski, J. K., Cárdenas-Soler, R.-N., Soares-Quadros, J. F., Li, S., Lega, C., Rocca, S. L., Martínez, I. C., Tanco, M., Marchiano, M., Martínez-Castilla, P., Pérez-Acosta, G., Martínez-Ezquerro, J. D., Gutiérrez-Blasco, I. M., ... Israel, S. (2021). "Help! I Need Somebody": Music as a Global Resource for Obtaining Wellbeing Goals in Times of Crisis. *Frontiers in Psychology, 12*. https://doi.org/10.3389/fpsyg.2021.648013

Grape, C., Sandgren, M., Hansson, L.-O., Ericson, M., & Theorell, T. (2002). Does singing promote well-being?: An empirical study of professional and amateur singers during a singing lesson. *Integrative Physiological & Behavioral Science, 38*(1), 65–74. https://doi.org/10.1007/bf02734261

Grassi, M., Meneghetti, C., Toffalini, E., & Borella, E. (2018). Correction: Auditory and cognitive performance in elderly musicians and nonmusicians. *PLOS ONE, 13*(2), e0192918. https://doi.org/10.1371/journal.pone.0192918

Grätzer, D. P. D. (1999). Can music help to improve parent-child communication? Learning music with parents – an Argentine experience. *International Journal of Music Education, os-34*(1), 47–56. https://doi.org/10.1177/025576149903400105

Graven, S. N., & Browne, J. V. (2008). Auditory development in the fetus and infant. *Newborn Infant Nurs Review, 8*(4), 187–93, https://doi.org/10.1016/j.jpeds2016.12.072.

Graziano, A. B., Peterson, M., & Shaw, G. L. (1999). Enhanced learning of proportional math through music training and spatial-temporal training. *Neurological Research, 21*(2), 139–152. https://doi.org/10.1080/01616412.1999.11740910

Greasley, A. E., & Lamont, A. (2006). Music preference in adulthood: Why do we like the music we do? In M. Baroni, A. R. Adessi, R. Caterina, & M. Costa (Eds), *Proceedings of the 9th International Conference on Music Perception and Cognition* (pp. 960–966). University of Bologna.

Greasley, A. E., & Lamont, A. (2011). Exploring engagement with music in everyday life using experience sampling methodology. *Musicae Scientiae, 15*(1), 45–71. https://doi.org/10.1177/1029864910393417

Grebosz-Haring, K., & Thun-Hohenstein, L. (2018). Effects of group singing versus group music listening on hospitalized children and adolescents with mental disorders: A pilot study. *Heliyon, 4*(12), e01014. https://doi.org/10.1016/j.heliyon.2018.e01014

Gregory, A. H. (1997). The Roles of Music in Society. In D. J. Hargreaves & A. C. North (Eds), *The Social Psychology of Music* (pp. 123–140). Oxford University Press.

Gregory, A. H., & Varney, N. (1996). Cross-Cultural Comparisons in the Affective Response to Music. *Psychology of Music*, 24(1), 47–52. https://doi.org/10.1177/0305735696241005

Greitemeyer, T., & Schwab, A. (2014). Employing music exposure to reduce prejudice and discrimination. *Aggressive Behavior*, 40(6), 542–551. https://doi.org/10.1002/ab.21531

Griffiths, A. (2019). Playing the white man's tune: Inclusion in elite classical music education. *British Journal of Music Education*, 37(1), 55–70. https://doi.org/10.1017/s0265051719000391

Grinspun, N., Nijs, L., Kausel, L., Onderdijk, K., Sepúlveda, N., & Rivera-Hutinel, A. (2020). Selective Attention and Inhibitory Control of Attention Are Correlated With Music Audiation. *Frontiers in Psychology*, 11. https://doi.org/10.3389/fpsyg.2020.01109

Groarke, J. M., & Hogan, M. J. (2015). Enhancing wellbeing: An emerging model of the adaptive functions of music listening. *Psychology of Music*, 44(4), 769–791. https://doi.org/10.1177/0305735615591844

Grocke, D., Bloch, S., Castle, D., Thompson, G., Newton, R., Stewart, S., & Gold, C. (2013). Group music therapy for severe mental illness: A randomized embedded-experimental mixed methods study. *Acta Psychiatrica Scandinavica*, 130(2), 144–153. https://doi.org/10.1111/acps.12224

Gromko, J. E. (2005). The Effect of Music Instruction on Phonemic Awareness in Beginning Readers. *Journal of Research in Music Education*, 53(3), 199–209. https://doi.org/10.1177/002242940505300302

Gromko, J. E., & Poorman, A. S. (1998). The Effect of Music Training on Preschoolers' Spatial-Temporal Task Performance. *Journal of Research in Music Education*, 46(2), 173–181. https://doi.org/10.2307/3345621

Groot, A. M. B. de, & Smedinga, H. E. (2014). LET THE MUSIC PLAY! *Studies in Second Language Acquisition*, 36(4), 681–707. https://doi.org/10.1017/s0272263114000059

Gross, J., Hoogenboom, N., Thut, G., Schyns, P., Panzeri, S., Belin, P., & Garrod, S. (2013). Speech Rhythms and Multiplexed Oscillatory Sensory Coding in the Human Brain. *PLoS Biology*, 11(12), e1001752. https://doi.org/10.1371/journal.pbio.1001752

Gross, J. J. (1998). Sharpening the Focus: Emotion Regulation, Arousal, and Social Competence. *Psychological Inquiry*, 9(4), 287–290. https://doi.org/10.1207/s15327965pli0904_8

Gross, J. J. (2015). Emotion Regulation: Current Status and Future Prospects. *Psychological Inquiry,* 26(1), 1–26. https://doi.org/10.1080/1047840x.2014.940781

Gross, J. J., Carstensen, L. L., Pasupathi, M., Tsai, J., Skorpen, C. G., & Hsu, A. Y. C. (1997). Emotion and aging: Experience, expression, and control. *Psychology and Aging,* 12(4), 590–599. https://doi.org/10.1037/0882-7974.12.4.590

Gross, J. J., & John, O. P. (2003). Individual differences in two emotion regulation processes: Implications for affect, relationships, and well-being. *Journal of Personality and Social Psychology,* 85(2), 348–362. https://doi.org/10.1037/0022-3514.85.2.348

Groussard, M., Viader, F., Landeau, B., Desgranges, B., Eustache, F., & Platel, H. (2014). The effects of musical practice on structural plasticity: The dynamics of grey matter changes. *Brain and Cognition,* 90, 174–180. https://doi.org/10.1016/j.bandc.2014.06.013

Grove, R., Hoekstra, R. A., Wierda, M., & Begeer, S. (2018). Special interests and subjective wellbeing in autistic adults. *Autism Research,* 11(5), 766–775. https://doi.org/10.1002/aur.1931

Gruhn, W., Litt, F., Scherer, A., Schumann, T., Weiß, E. M., & Gebhardt, C. (2006). Suppressing reflexive behaviour: Saccadic eye movements in musicians and non-musicians. *Musicae Scientiae,* 10(1), 19–32. https://doi.org/10.1177/102986490601000102

Guhn, M., Emerson, S. D., & Gouzouasis, P. (2020). A population-level analysis of associations between school music participation and academic achievement. *Journal of Educational Psychology,* 112(2), 308–328. https://doi.org/10.1037/edu0000376

Gunderson, E. A., Ramirez, G., Beilock, S. L., & Levine, S. C. (2012). The relation between spatial skill and early number knowledge: The role of the linear number line. *Developmental Psychology,* 48(5), 1229–1241. https://doi.org/10.1037/a0027433

Gunsberg, A. S. (1991). Play as improvisation: The benefits of music for developmentally delayed young children's social play. *Early Child Development and Care,* 66(1), 85–91. https://doi.org/10.1080/0300443910660108

Guo, X., Ohsawa, C., Suzuki, A., & Sekiyama, K. (2018). Improved Digit Span in Children after a 6-Week Intervention of Playing a Musical Instrument: An Exploratory Randomized Controlled Trial. *Frontiers in Psychology,* 8. https://doi.org/10.3389/fpsyg.2017.02303

Gupta, U., & and, and V. K. S. (2020). Effects of Music Listening on Resilience, Self-Efficacy and Positivity in Healthy Young Adults. *Journal of Psychosocial Research,* 15(1), 1–24. https://doi.org/10.32381/jpr.2020.15.01.1

Gur, C. (2009). Is there any positive effect of classical music on cognitive content of six year-old children in Turkey? *European Journal of Scientific Research,* 36(2), 251–259.

Haake, A. B. (2011). Individual music listening in workplace settings. *Musicae Scientiae*, *15*(1), 107–129. https://doi.org/10.1177/1029864911398065

Haase, J. E., Robb, S. L., Burns, D. S., Stegenga, K., Cherven, B., Hendricks-Ferguson, V., Roll, L., Docherty, S. L., & Phillips, C. (2019). Adolescent/Young Adult Perspectives of a Therapeutic Music Video Intervention to Improve Resilience During Hematopoietic Stem Cell Transplant for Cancer\textbackslashast. *Journal of Music Therapy*, *57*(1), 3–33. https://doi.org/10.1093/jmt/thz014

Habe, K., Biasutti, M., & Kajtna, T. (2019). Flow and Satisfaction With Life in Elite Musicians and Top Athletes. *Frontiers in Psychology*, *10*. https://doi.org/10.3389/fpsyg.2019.00698

Habe, K., Biasutti, M., & Kajtna, T. (2021). Wellbeing and flow in sports and music students during the COVID-19 pandemic. *Thinking Skills and Creativity*, *39*, 100798. https://doi.org/10.1016/j.tsc.2021.100798

Habib, M., & Besson, M. (2009). What do Music Training and Musical Experience Teach Us About Brain Plasticity? *Music Perception*, *26*(3), 279–285. https://doi.org/10.1525/mp.2009.26.3.279

Habib, M., Lardy, C., Desiles, T., Commeiras, C., Chobert, J., & Besson, M. (2016). Music and Dyslexia: A New Musical Training Method to Improve Reading and Related Disorders. *Frontiers in Psychology*, *7*. https://doi.org/10.3389/fpsyg.2016.00026

Habibi, A., Cahn, B. R., Damasio, A., & Damasio, H. (2016). Neural correlates of accelerated auditory processing in children engaged in music training. *Developmental Cognitive Neuroscience*, *21*, 1–14. https://doi.org/10.1016/j.dcn.2016.04.003

Habibi, A., Damasio, A., Ilari, B., Sachs, M. E., & Damasio, H. (2018). Music training and child development: A review of recent findings from a longitudinal study. *Annals of the New York Academy of Sciences*, *1423*(1), 73–81. https://doi.org/10.1111/nyas.13606

Habibi, A., Ilari, B., Crimi, K., Metke, M., Kaplan, J. T., Joshi, A. A., Leahy, R. M., Shattuck, D. W., Choi, S. Y., Haldar, J. P., Ficek, B., Damasio, A., & Damasio, H. (2014). An equal start: Absence of group differences in cognitive, social, and neural measures prior to music or sports training in children. *Frontiers in Human Neuroscience*, *8*. https://doi.org/10.3389/fnhum.2014.00690

Habron, J., Butterly, F., Gordon, I., & Roebuck, A. (2013). Being Well, Being Musical: Music Composition as a Resource and Occupation for Older People. *British Journal of Occupational Therapy*, *76*(7), 308–316. https://doi.org/10.4276/030802213x13729279114933

Haecker, V., & Ziehen, T. (1922). ZurVererbung und Entwicklung der musikalischen Begabung. In *Inheritance and development of musical talent*. J.A. Barth.

Hagen, A. N. (2015). The Playlist Experience: Personal Playlists in Music Streaming Services. *Popular Music and Society, 38*(5), 625–645. https://doi.org/10.1080/03007766.2015.1021174

Hagen, E. H., & Bryant, G. A. (2003). Music and dance as a coalition signaling system. *Human Nature, 14*(1), 21–51. https://doi.org/10.1007/s12110-003-1015-z

Haimson, J., Swain, D., & Winner, E. (2011a). Do Mathematicians Have Above Average Musical Skill? *Music Perception, 29*(2), 203–213. https://doi.org/10.1525/mp.2011.29.2.203

Haimson, J., Swain, D., & Winner, E. (2011b). Do Mathematicians Have Above Average Musical Skill? *Music Perception, 29*(2), 203–213. https://doi.org/10.1525/mp.2011.29.2.203

Haines, J. H. (1989). The Effects of Music Therapy on the Self-Esteem of Emotionally-Disturbed Adolescents. *Music Therapy, 8*(1), 78–91. https://doi.org/10.1093/mt/8.1.78

Hakvoort, L., Bogaerts, S., Thaut, M. H., & Spreen, M. (2013). Influence of Music Therapy on Coping Skills and Anger Management in Forensic Psychiatric Patients. *International Journal of Offender Therapy and Comparative Criminology, 59*(8), 810–836. https://doi.org/10.1177/0306624x13516787

Haley, J. A. (2001). *The relationship between instrumental music instruction and academic achievement in fourth grade students* [Doctoral dissertation.]. Pace University.

Hall, J. C. (1952). The Effect of Background Music on the Reading Comprehension of 278 Eighth and Ninth Grade Students. *The Journal of Educational Research, 45*(6), 451–458. https://doi.org/10.1080/00220671.1952.10881962

Hallam, S. (2000). The effects of listening to music on children's spatial task performance. *British Psychological Society Education Review, 25*(2), 22–26.

Hallam, S. (2001). The Effects of Listening to Music on Children's Spatial Task Performance. *Psychology of Education Review, 25*(2), 22–26 175.

Hallam, S. (2005). *Enhancing learning and motivation through the lifespan*. Institute of Education, University of London.

Hallam, S. (2010). The power of music: Its impact on the intellectual, social and personal development of children and young people. *International Journal of Music Education, 28*(3), 269–289. https://doi.org/10.1177/0255761410370658

Hallam, S. (2012a). *Motivation to learn* (S. Hallam, I. Cross, & M. Thaut, Eds.). Oxford University Press. https://doi.org/10.1093/oxfordhb/9780199298457.013.0027

Hallam, S. (2012b). *Motivation to learn* (S. Hallam, I. Cross, & M. Thaut, Eds.). Oxford University Press. https://doi.org/10.1093/oxfordhb/9780199298457.013.0027

Hallam, S. (2015). *The power of music: A research synthesis of the impact of actively making music on intellectual, social and personal development of children and young people*. International Music Education Research Centre; Institute of Education.

Hallam, S. (2017a). *Evaluation of Young Music Leader Programme*. VCM Foundation.

Hallam, S. (2017b). Musical Identity, Learning, and Teaching. In *Handbook of Musical Identities* (pp. 475–492). Oxford University Press. https://doi.org/10.1093/acprof:oso/9780199679485.003.0026

Hallam, S. (2017c). The impact of making music on aural perception and language skills: A research synthesis. *London Review of Education*. https://doi.org/10.18546/lre.15.3.05

Hallam, S. (2018). Can a rhythmic intervention support reading development in poor readers? *Psychology of Music*, 47(5), 722–735. https://doi.org/10.1177/0305735618771491

Hallam, S., Burnard, P., Robertson, A., Saleh, C., Davies, V., Rogers, L., & Kokatsaki, D. (2009). Trainee primary-school teachers' perceptions of their effectiveness in teaching music. *Music Education Research*, 11(2), 221–240. https://doi.org/10.1080/14613800902924508

Hallam, S., & Burns, S. (2018a). *Progression in instrumental music making for learners from disadvantaged communities: A literature review*. Opera North/Arts Council England.

Hallam, S., & Burns, S. (2018b). *Research into support for musical progression for young people from In Harmony programmes and other disadvantaged communities*. Opera North/Arts Council England.

Hallam, S., & Creech, A. (2016). Can active music making promote health and well-being in older citizens? Findings of the music for life project. *London Journal of Primary Care*, 8(2), 21–25. https://doi.org/10.1080/17571472.2016.1152099

Hallam, S., Creech, A., & McQueen, H. (2015). Teachers' perceptions of the impact on students of the Musical Futures approach. *Music Education Research*, 19(3), 263–275. https://doi.org/10.1080/14613808.2015.1108299

Hallam, S., Creech, A., & McQueen, H. (2016a). The perceptions of non music staff and senior management of the impact of the implementation of the Musical Futures approach on the whole school. *British Journal of Music Education*, 33(2), 133–157. https://doi.org/10.1017/s0265051716000139

Hallam, S., Creech, A., & McQueen, H. (2016b). Pupils' perceptions of informal learning in school music lessons. *Music Education Research*, 20(2), 213–230. https://doi.org/10.1080/14613808.2016.1249358

Hallam, S., Creech, A., & Papageorgi, I. (2009). *EMI Music Sound Foundation: Evaluation of the Impact of Additional Training in the Delivery of Music at Key Stage 1*. Institute of Education. https://discovery.ucl.ac.uk/id/eprint/10002299/.

Hallam, S., Creech, A., & Varvarigou, M. (2017). Well-being and music leisure activity through the lifespan: A psychological perspective. In R. Mantie & G. D. Smith (Eds), *Oxford Handbook of Music Making and Leisure* (pp. 31–60). Oxford University Press.

Hallam, S., Creech, A., Varvarigou, M., & McQueen, H. (2012). Perceived benefits of active engagement with making music in community settings. *International Journal of Community Music*, 5(2), 155–174. https://doi.org/10.1386/ijcm.5.2.155_1

Hallam, S., Creech, A., Varvarigou, M., McQueen, H., & Gaunt, H. (2013). Does active engagement in community music support the well-being of older people? *Arts & Health*, 6(2), 101–116. https://doi.org/10.1080/17533015.2013.809369

Hallam, S., Cross, I., & Thaut, M. (Eds). (2012). *Oxford Handbook of Music Psychology*. Oxford University Press. https://doi.org/10.1093/oxfordhb/9780199298457.001.0001

Hallam, S., & Godwin, C. (2015). Actual and perceived effects of background music on creative writing in the primary classroom. *Psychology of Education Review*, 39(2), 15–21.

Hallam, S., & MacDonald, R. (2012). *The effects of music in community and educational settings* (S. Hallam, I. Cross, & M. Thaut, Eds.). Oxford University Press. https://doi.org/10.1093/oxfordhb/9780199298457.013.0044

Hallam, S., & Price, J. (2003). Research Section: Can the use of background music improve the behaviour and academic performance of children with emotional and behavioural difficulties? *British Journal of Special Education*, 25(2), 88–91. https://doi.org/10.1111/1467-8527.t01-1-00063

Hallam, S., Price, J., & Katsarou, G. (2002). The Effects of Background Music on Primary School Pupils' Task Performance. *Educational Studies*, 28(2), 111–122. https://doi.org/10.1080/03055690220124551

Hallam, S., & Prince, V. (2000). *Research into instrumental music services*. Department for Education and Employment.

Hallam, S., & Rogers, K. (2016). The impact of instrumental music learning on attainment at age 16: A pilot study. *British Journal of Music Education*, 33(3), 247–261, https://doi.org/10.1017/S0265051716000371.155.

Hallberg, K. A., Martin, W. E., & McClure, J. R. (2017). The impact of music instruction on attention in kindergarten children. *Psychomusicology: Music, Mind, and Brain*, 27(2), 113–121. https://doi.org/10.1037/pmu0000177

Halpern, A. R., & Bower, G. H. (1982). Musical Expertise and Melodic Structure in Memory for Musical Notation. *The American Journal of Psychology*, 95(1), 31. https://doi.org/10.2307/1422658

Hämäläinen, J. A., Salminen, H. K., & Leppänen, P. H. T. (2012). Basic Auditory Processing Deficits in Dyslexia. *Journal of Learning Disabilities, 46*(5), 413–427. https://doi.org/10.1177/0022219411436213

Hämäläinen, S., Salamonsen, A., Mehus, G., Schirmer, H., Graff, O., & Musial, F. (2021). Yoik in Sami elderly and dementia care – a potential for culturally sensitive music therapy? *Nordic Journal of Music Therapy, 30*(5), 404–423. https://doi.org/10.1080/08098131.2020.1849364

Hamann, D., & Aderman, M. (1991). Arts experiences and creativity scores of high school students. *Contributions to Music Education, 18*, 36–47.

Hamann, D., Bourassa, R., & Aderman, M. (1991). Arts experiences and creativity scores of high school students. *Contribution to Music Education, 14*, 35–47.

Hamann, D. L., Bourassa, R., & Aderman, M. (1990). Creativity and the arts. Dialogue in Instrumental Music. *Music[MP179] Education, 14*(2), 59–68.

Hamilton, T. J., Doai, J., Milne, A., Saisanas, V., Calilhanna, A., Hilton, C., Goldwater, M., & Cohn, R. (2018, December). Teaching Mathematics with Music: A Pilot Study. *2018 IEEE International Conference on Teaching, Assessment, and Learning for Engineering (TALE)*. https://doi.org/10.1109/tale.2018.8615262

Hampshire, K. R., & Matthijsse, M. (2010). Can arts projects improve young people's wellbeing? A social capital approach. *Social Science & Medicine, 71*(4), 708–716. https://doi.org/10.1016/j.socscimed.2010.05.015

Hampton, A., Ford, A., Cox, R. E., Liu, C., & Koh, R. (2019). Effects of music on behavior and physiological stress response of domestic cats in a veterinary clinic. *Journal of Feline Medicine and Surgery, 22*(2), 122–128. https://doi.org/10.1177/1098612x19828131

Hamza, S. A., & Johan, A. (2020). MALAYSIAN MUSIC AND SOCIAL COHESION: CONTEMPORARY RESPONSES TO POPULAR PATRIOTIC SONGS FROM THE 1950s – 1990s. *Journal of Southeast Asian Studies, 25*(1), 191–209. https://doi.org/10.22452/jati.vol25no1.10

Han, Y., Yang, H., Lv, Y.-T., Zhu, C.-Z., He, Y., Tang, H.-H., Gong, Q.-Y., Luo, Y.-J., Zang, Y.-F., & Dong, Q. (2009). Gray matter density and white matter integrity in pianists' brain: A combined structural and diffusion tensor MRI study. *Neuroscience Letters, 459*(1), 3–6. https://doi.org/10.1016/j.neulet.2008.07.056

Haner, D., Pepler, D., Cummings, J., & Rubin-Vaughan, A. (2009). The Role of Arts-Based Curricula in Bullying Prevention: Elijah's Kite—A Children's Opera. *Canadian Journal of School Psychology, 25*(1), 55–69. https://doi.org/10.1177/0829573509349031

Haning, M. (2016). The association between music training, background music, and adult reading comprehension. *Contributions to Music Education, 41*, 131–143.

Hanna-Pladdy, B., & Gajewski, B. (2012). Recent and Past Musical Activity Predicts Cognitive Aging Variability: Direct Comparison with General Lifestyle Activities. *Frontiers in Human Neuroscience, 6*. https://doi.org/10.3389/fnhum.2012.00198

Hanna-Pladdy, B., & MacKay, A. (2011). The relation between instrumental musical activity and cognitive aging. *Neuropsychology, 25*(3), 378–386. https://doi.org/10.1037/a0021895

Hannigan, P. D., & McBride, D. L. (2011). Drumming with Intimate Partner Violence Clients: Getting into the Beat$\textbackslashmathsemicolon$ Therapists' Views on the Use of Drumming in Family Violence Treatment Groups. *Canadian Art Therapy Association Journal, 24*(1), 2–9. https://doi.org/10.1080/08322473.2011.11434787

Hannon, E. E., & Trainor, L. J. (2007). Music acquisition: Effects of enculturation and formal training on development. *Trends in Cognitive Sciences, 11*(11), 466–472. https://doi.org/10.1016/j.tics.2007.08.008

Hansen, M., Wallentin, M., & Vuust, P. (2012). Working memory and musical competence of musicians and non-musicians. *Psychology of Music, 41*(6), 779–793. https://doi.org/10.1177/0305735612452186

Hanser, S. B. (1993). Music, Health, and Well-Being. In *Handbook of Music and Emotion: Theory, Research, Applications* (pp. 849–877). Oxford University Press. https://doi.org/10.1093/acprof:oso/9780199230143.003.0030

Hanser, S. B., & Thompson, L. W. (1994). Effects of a Music Therapy Strategy on Depressed Older Adults. *Journal of Gerontology, 49*(6), P265–P269. https://doi.org/10.1093/geronj/49.6.p265

Hanson, M. (2003). Effects of sequenced Kodaly literary based music instructions on the spatial reasoning skills of kindergarten students. *Research and Issues in Music Education, 1*(1), 4.

Harding, E. E., Sammler, D., Henry, M. J., Large, E. W., & Kotz, S. A. (2019). Cortical tracking of rhythm in music and speech. *NeuroImage, 185*, 96–101. https://doi.org/10.1016/j.neuroimage.2018.10.037

Hargreaves, D. J., MacDonald, R. A. R., & Miell, D. E. (2002). What are musical identities, and why are they important? In R. A. R. MacDonald, D. J. Hargreaves, & D. E. Miell (Eds), *Musical Identities* (pp. 1–20). Oxford University Press.

Hargreaves, D. J., North, A. C., & Tarrant, M. (2006). Musical Preference and Taste in Childhood and Adolescence. In *The Child as Musician* (pp. 135–154). Oxford University Press. https://doi.org/10.1093/acprof:oso/9780198530329.003.0007

Hargreaves, D., & Lamont, A. (2017). *The Psychology of Musical Development*. Cambridge University Press. https://doi.org/10.1017/9781107281868

Harland, J., Kinder, K., Lord, P., Stott, A., Schagen, I., & Haynes, J. (2000). *Arts education in secondary schools: Effects and effectiveness*. The Arts Council of.

Harmon, L., Pelosi, G., Pickwick, T., & Troester, K. (2008). The effects of different types of music on cognitive abilities. *Journal of Undergraduate Psychological Research, 3*, 41–46.

Harrer, G., & Harrer, H. (1977). Music, emotion and autonomous function. In M. Critchley & R. A. Henson (Eds), *Music and the brain: Studies in the neurology of music* (pp. 202–216). William Heinemann.

Harris, D. A. (2007). Dance/movement therapy approaches to fostering resilience and recovery among African adolescent torture survivors. *Torture, 17*(2), 134–155.

Harris, I., & Cross, I. (2021). Investigating Everyday Musical Interaction During COVID-19: An Experimental Procedure for Exploring Collaborative Playlist Engagement. *Frontiers in Psychology, 12*. https://doi.org/10.3389/fpsyg.2021.647967

Harrison, C. S. (1990). Predicting Music Theory Grades: The Relative Efficiency of Academic Ability, Music Experience, and Musical Aptitude. *Journal of Research in Music Education, 38*(2), 124–137. https://doi.org/10.2307/3344932

Hars, M., Herrmann, F. R., Gold, G., Rizzoli, R., & Trombetti, A. (2013). Effect of music-based multitask training on cognition and mood in older adults. *Age and Ageing, 43*(2), 196–200. https://doi.org/10.1093/ageing/aft163

Harvey, A. R. (2018). Music and the Meeting of Human Minds. *Frontiers in Psychology, 9*. https://doi.org/10.3389/fpsyg.2018.00762

Hashemian, P., Mashoogh, N., & Jarahi, L. (2015). Effectiveness of Music Therapy on Aggressive Behavior of Visually Impaired Adolescents. *Journal of Behavioral and Brain Science, 05*(03), 96–100. https://doi.org/10.4236/jbbs.2015.53009

Haskell, E. (2005). International Cultural Aid and the Case of Guca Gora, Bosnia. *ICTM World Conference 2005*.

Haslinger, B., Erhard, P., Altenmüller, E., Hennenlotter, A., Schwaiger, M., Einsiedel, H. G. von, Rummeny, E., Conrad, B., & Ceballos-Baumann, A. O. (2004). Reduced recruitment of motor association areas during bimanual coordination in concert pianists. *Human Brain Mapping, 22*(3), 206–215. https://doi.org/10.1002/hbm.20028

Hausmann, M., Ergun, G., Yazgan, Y., & Güntürkün, O. (2002). Sex differences in line bisection as a function of hand. *Neuropsychologia, 40*(3), 235–240. https://doi.org/10.1016/s0028-3932(01)00112-9

Hay, M. (2013). Summary of nPC/noFA research findings. In *Unpublished Personal notes*. New Philanthropy Capital (NPC) with National Orchestra for All (NOFA.

Hays, T., & Minichiello, V. (2005). The meaning of music in the lives of older people: A qualitative study. *Psychology of Music, 33*(4), 437–451. https://doi.org/10.1177/0305735605056160

Haywood, S., Griggs, J., Lloyd, C., Morris, S., Kiss, Z., & Skipp, A. (2015). *Creative futures: Act, sing, play. Evaluation report and executive summary*. Educational Endowment Foundation.

Heidenrich, V. (2005). Music therapy in war-affected areas. *Intervention, 3*(2), 129–134.

Helmbold, N., Rammsayer, T., & Altenmüller, E. (2005). Differences in Primary Mental Abilities Between Musicians and Nonmusicians. *Journal of Individual Differences, 26*(2), 74–85. https://doi.org/10.1027/1614-0001.26.2.74

Henderson, M. T., Crews, A., & Barlow, J. (1945). A study of the effect of music distraction on reading efficiency. *Journal of Applied Psychology, 29*(4), 313–317. https://doi.org/10.1037/h0056128

Henderson, S., Cain, M., Istvandity, L., & Lakhani, A. (2016). The role of music participation in positive health and wellbeing outcomes for migrant populations: A systematic review. *Psychology of Music, 45*(4), 459–478. https://doi.org/10.1177/0305735616665910

Henderson, S. M. (1983). Effects of a Music Therapy Program Upon Awareness of Mood in Music, Group Cohesion, and Self-Esteem Among Hospitalized Adolescent Patients. *Journal of Music Therapy, 20*(1), 14–20. https://doi.org/10.1093/jmt/20.1.14

Hendon, C., & Bohon, L. M. (2008). Hospitalized children's mood differences during play and music therapy. *Child: Care, Health and Development, 34*(2), 141–144. https://doi.org/10.1111/j.1365-2214.2007.00746.x

Henley, D. (2011). *Importance of Music: The National Plan for Music Education*. Department for Education Publications. https://www.gov.uk/government/uploads/system/uploads/attachment_data/file/180973/DFE-00086-2011.pdf.

Henley, J. (2014). Musical learning and desistance from crime: The case of a 'Good Vibrations' Javanese gamelan project with young offenders. *Music Education Research, 17*(1), 103–120. https://doi.org/10.1080/14613808.2014.933791

Henley, J., Caulfield, L. S., Wilson, D., & Wilkinson, D. J. (2012). Good Vibrations: Positive change through social music-making. *Music Education Research, 14*(4), 499–520. https://doi.org/10.1080/14613808.2012.714765

Henley, J., & Parks, J. (2020). The pedagogy of a prison and community music programme: Spaces for conflict and safety. *International Journal of Community Music, 13*(1), 7–27. https://doi.org/10.1386/ijcm_00008_1

HENNESSEY, B. A., & AMABILE, T. M. (1988). Story-telling: A Method For Assessing Children's Creativity. *The Journal of Creative Behavior*, 22(4), 235–246. https://doi.org/10.1002/j.2162-6057.1988.tb00502.x

Henry, M., & Braucht, M. (2007). Are all-state musicians our future music educators? *Southwestern Musician*, 186 36-37.

Hense, C., & McFerran, K. S. (2017). Promoting young people's musical identities to facilitate recovery from mental illness. *Journal of Youth Studies*, 20(8), 997–1012. https://doi.org/10.1080/13676261.2017.1287888

Hepper, P. G. (1991). An Examination of Fetal Learning Before and After Birth. *The Irish Journal of Psychology*, 12(2), 95–107. https://doi.org/10.1080/03033910.1991.10557830

Herbert, R. (2011). Musical and non-musical involvement in daily life: The case of absorption. *Musicae Scientiae*, 16(1), 41–66. https://doi.org/10.1177/1029864911423161

Herdener, M., Esposito, F., Salle, F. di, Boller, C., Hilti, C. C., Habermeyer, B., Scheffler, K., Wetzel, S., Seifritz, E., & Cattapan-Ludewig, K. (2010). Musical Training Induces Functional Plasticity in Human Hippocampus. *Journal of Neuroscience*, 30(4), 1377–1384. https://doi.org/10.1523/jneurosci.4513-09.2010

Herdener, M., Humbel, T., Esposito, F., Habermeyer, B., Cattapan-Ludewig, K., & Seifritz, E. (2012). Jazz Drummers Recruit Language-Specific Areas for the Processing of Rhythmic Structure. *Cerebral Cortex*, 24(3), 836–843. https://doi.org/10.1093/cercor/bhs367

Herholz, S. C., & Zatorre, R. J. (2012). Musical Training as a Framework for Brain Plasticity: Behavior, Function, and Structure. *Neuron*, 76(3), 486–502. https://doi.org/10.1016/j.neuron.2012.10.011

Hernandez-Ruiz, E. (2019). Feasibility of Parent Coaching of Music Interventions for Children With Autism Spectrum Disorder. *Music Therapy Perspectives*, 38(2), 195–204. https://doi.org/10.1093/mtp/miz016

Hess, C. D. (1956). *An appraisal of the program of music education at the California Institute for Men* [PhD Thesis]. Claremont College.

Hesser, B., & Heinemann, H. (Eds). (2010). *Music as a natural resource: Solutions for social and economic issues*. United Nations.

HESTER, R. L., KINSELLA, G. J., & ONG, B. (2004). Effect of age on forward and backward span tasks. *Journal of the International Neuropsychological Society*, 10(4), 475–481. https://doi.org/10.1017/s1355617704104037

Hetland, L. (2000a). Learning to make music enhances spatial reasoning. *Journal of Aesthetic Education*, 34(3/4).

Hetland, L. (2000b). Listening to Music Enhances Spatial-Temporal Reasoning: Evidence for the 'Mozart Effect'. *Journal of Aesthetic Education*, 34(3/4), 105. https://doi.org/10.2307/3333640

Heye, A., & Lamont, A. (2010). Mobile listening situations in everyday life: The use of MP3 players while travelling. *Musicae Scientiae, 14*(1), 95–120. https://doi.org/10.1177/102986491001400104

Hickey, M. (2018). "We all Come Together to Learn About Music": A Qualitative Analysis of a 5-Year Music Program in a Juvenile Detention Facility. *International Journal of Offender Therapy and Comparative Criminology, 62*(13), 4046–4066. https://doi.org/10.1177/0306624x18765367

Hickok, G. (2012). Computational neuroanatomy of speech production. *Nature Reviews Neuroscience, 13*(2), 135–145. https://doi.org/10.1038/nrn3158

Hickok, G., & Poeppel, D. (2000). Towards a functional neuroanatomy of speech perception. *Trends in Cognitive Sciences, 4*(4), 131–138. https://doi.org/10.1016/s1364-6613(00)01463-7

Hickok, G., & Poeppel, D. (2007). The cortical organization of speech processing. *Nature Reviews Neuroscience, 8*(5), 393–402. https://doi.org/10.1038/nrn2113

Hietolahti-Ansten, M., & Kalliopuska, M. (1990). Self-Esteem and Empathy among Children Actively Involved in Music. *Perceptual and Motor Skills, 71*(3_suppl), 1364–1366. https://doi.org/10.2466/pms.1990.71.3f.1364

Higgins, W. (1972). A study of the effect of participation in a high school band on academic achievement and social adjustment. *Journal of Band Research, 9,* 12–16.

Hille, A., & Schupp, J. (2015). How learning a musical instrument affects the development of skills. *Economics of Education Review, 44,* 56–82. https://doi.org/10.1016/j.econedurev.2014.10.007

Hille, K., Gust, K., Bitz, U., & Kammer, T. (2011a). Associations between music education, intelligence, and spelling ability in elementary school. *Advances in Cognitive Psychology, 7*(1), 1–6. https://doi.org/10.2478/v10053-008-0082-4

Hille, K., Gust, K., Bitz, U., & Kammer, T. (2011b). Associations between music education, intelligence, and spelling ability in elementary school. *Advances in Cognitive Psychology, 7*(1), 1–6. https://doi.org/10.2478/v10053-008-0082-4

Hilliard, O. M., & Tolin, P. (1979). Effect of Familiarity with Background Music on Performance of Simple and Difficult Reading Comprehension Tasks. *Perceptual and Motor Skills, 49*(3), 713–714. https://doi.org/10.2466/pms.1979.49.3.713

Hillier, A., Greher, G., Poto, N., & Dougherty, M. (2011). Positive outcomes following participation in a music intervention for adolescents and young adults on the autism spectrum. *Psychology of Music, 40*(2), 201–215. https://doi.org/10.1177/0305735610386837

Hillman, S. (2002). Participatory singing for older people: A perception of benefit. *Health Education, 102*(4), 163–171. https://doi.org/10.1108/09654280210434237

Hines, S. W. (2000). *The effects of motoric and non-motoric music instruction on reading and mathematics achievements of learning disabled students in kindergarten through ninth grade* [Doctoral dissertation.]. The University of North Carolina at Greensboro.

Hippel, N., & Laabs, F. (2006). Musiktherapie in der Schule – ein neues Arbeitsfeld Für Musiktherapeuten? *Musiktherapeutische Umschau, 27*(3), 280–289.

Hirokawa, E. (2004). Effects of Music Listening and Relaxation Instructions on Arousal Changes and the Working Memory Task in Older Adults. *Journal of Music Therapy, 41*(2), 107–127. https://doi.org/10.1093/jmt/41.2.107

Hirokawa, E., & Ohira, H. (2003). The Effects of Music Listening after a Stressful Task on Immune Functions, Neuroendocrine Responses, and Emotional States in College Students. *Journal of Music Therapy, 40*(3), 189–211. https://doi.org/10.1093/jmt/40.3.189

Hirshkowitz, M., Earle, J., & Paley, B. (1978). EEG alpha asymmetry in musicians and non-musicians: A study of hemispheric specialization. *Neuropsychologia, 16*(1), 125–128. https://doi.org/10.1016/0028-3932(78)90052-0

Hirst, E., & Robertshaw, D. (2003). *Breaking the Cycle of Failure: Examining the Impact of Arts Activity on Young People Attending Pupil Referral Units in Doncaster*. Darts.

Hirt-Mannheimer, J. (1995). Making Music Big for Little Folks. *Teaching Music, 3*(2), 38–39, 62.

Hitch, R. (2010). *Removing 'Roadblocks': What is the role of music therapy in mainstream schools in promoting inclusion of children with special educational needs? And does this environment impact practice?* Unpublished Master's dissertation. Roehampton University.

Ho, P., Tsao, J. C. I., Bloch, L., & Zeltzer, L. K. (2011). *The impact of group drumming on social-emotional behavior in low-income children.* https://doi.org/10.1093/ecam/neq072.

Ho, Y.-C., Cheung, M.-C., & Chan, A. S. (2003a). Music training improves verbal but not visual memory: Cross-sectional and longitudinal explorations in children. *Neuropsychology, 17*(3), 439–450. https://doi.org/10.1037/0894-4105.17.3.439

Ho, Y.-C., Cheung, M.-C., & Chan, A. S. (2003b). Music training improves verbal but not visual memory: Cross-sectional and longitudinal explorations in children. *Neuropsychology, 17*(3), 439–450. https://doi.org/10.1037/0894-4105.17.3.439

Ho, Y.-C., Cheung, M.-C., & Chan, A. S. (2003c). Music training improves verbal but not visual memory: Cross-sectional and longitudinal explorations in children. *Neuropsychology, 17*(3), 439–450. https://doi.org/10.1037/0894-4105.17.3.439

Ho, Y.-C., Cheung, M.-C., & Chan, A. S. (2003d). Music training improves verbal but not visual memory: Cross-sectional and longitudinal explorations in children. *Neuropsychology, 17*(3), 439–450. https://doi.org/10.1037/0894-4105.17.3.439

Hodges, D. A., & O'Connell, D. S. (2007). The impact of music education on academic achievement. In *Sounds of Learning Report*. NAMM Foundation Sounds of Learning.[MP193.

Hodson, R. G. (1951). *A survey of music education programs in state prisons* [PhD Thesis]. University of Denver.

Hoffman, D. S. (1995). *Relationships between Academic Achievement and Participation in a comprehensive and sequential keyboard-based public school music education programme* [Doctoral dissertation.]. University of South Carolina.

Hohmann, L., Bradt, J., Stegemann, T., & Koelsch, S. (2017). Effects of music therapy and music-based interventions in the treatment of substance use disorders: A systematic review. *PLOS ONE, 12*(11), e0187363. https://doi.org/10.1371/journal.pone.0187363

Hole, J., Hirsch, M., Ball, E., & Meads, C. (2015). Music as an aid for postoperative recovery in adults: A systematic review and meta-analysis. *The Lancet, 386*(10004), 1659–1671. https://doi.org/10.1016/s0140-6736(15)60169-6

Hollingworth, L. (1926). Musical sensitivity of children who test above 135 IQ (Standford Binet. *Journal of Educational Psychology, 17*, 95–105.

Holmes, S. (2017). *The impact of participation in music on learning mathematics. Unpublished doctoral dissertation*. University College London.

Holmes, S. (2021). The wider cognitive benefits of engagement with music. In *Routledge International Handbook of Music Psychology in Education and the Community* (pp. 38–51). Routledge. https://doi.org/10.4324/9780429295362-5

Holmes, S., & Hallam, S. (2017). The impact of participation in music on learning mathematics. *London Review of Education*. https://doi.org/10.18546/lre.15.3.07

Holochwost, S. J., Propper, C. B., Wolf, D. P., Willoughby, M. T., Fisher, K. R., Kolacz, J., Volpe, V. V., & Jaffee, S. R. (2017). Music education, academic achievement, and executive functions. *Psychology of Aesthetics, Creativity, and the Arts, 11*(2), 147–166. https://doi.org/10.1037/aca0000112

Hong, E., & Milgram, R. M. (2010). Creative Thinking Ability: Domain Generality and Specificity. *Creativity Research Journal, 22*(3), 272–287. https://doi.org/10.1080/10400419.2010.503535

Horton, M. M. (2005). *The Effect of Stepping as a Group Music Therapy Intervention on Group Cohesion and Positive Oral Statements of African-American Female Adolescents Attending an Educational Treatment Center* [PhD Thesis]. Florida State University.

HOUSTON, D. M., MCKEE, K. J., CARROLL, L., & MARSH, H. (1998). Using humour to promote psychological wellbeing in residential homes for older people. *Aging & Mental Health*, 2(4), 328–332. https://doi.org/10.1080/13607869856588

Hove, M. J., & Risen, J. L. (2009). It's All in the Timing: Interpersonal Synchrony Increases Affiliation. *Social Cognition*, 27(6), 949–960. https://doi.org/10.1521/soco.2009.27.6.949

Hsieh, S., & Lin, Y.-C. (2014). The boundary condition for observing compensatory responses by the elderly in a flanker-task paradigm. *Biological Psychology*, 103, 69–82. https://doi.org/10.1016/j.biopsycho.2014.08.008

Hudson, R. (2003). Songs of seduction: Popular music and Serbian nationalism. *Patterns of Prejudice*, 37(2), 157–176. https://doi.org/10.1080/0031322032000084688

Hudziak, J. J., Albaugh, M. D., Ducharme, S., Karama, S., Spottswood, M., Crehan, E., Evans, A. C., & Botteron, K. N. (2014). Cortical Thickness Maturation and Duration of Music Training: Health-Promoting Activities Shape Brain Development. *Journal of the American Academy of Child & Adolescent Psychiatry*, 53(11), 1153–1161.e2. https://doi.org/10.1016/j.jaac.2014.06.015

Hughes, D. J., Furnham, A., & Batey, M. (2013). The structure and personality predictors of self-rated creativity. *Thinking Skills and Creativity*, 9, 76–84. https://doi.org/10.1016/j.tsc.2012.10.001

Hughes, J. (2005). *Doing the Arts Justice: A Review of Research Literature, Practice and Theory*. http://webarchive.nationalarchives.gov.uk/+/

Humpal, M. (1991). The Effects of an Integrated Early Childhood Music Program on Social Interaction Among Children with Handicaps and Their Typical Peers. *Journal of Music Therapy*, 28(3), 161–177. https://doi.org/10.1093/jmt/28.3.161

Humpal, M. E., & Wolf, J. (2007). Music in the inclusive classroom. *Young Children*, 58(2), 103–107.

Hund-Georgiadis, M., & Cramon, D. Y. von. (1999). Motor-learning-related changes in piano players and non-musicians revealed by functional magnetic-resonance signals. *Experimental Brain Research*, 125(4), 417–425. https://doi.org/10.1007/s002210050698

Hunt, M. (2005). Action Research and Music Therapy: Group Music Therapy with Young Refugees in a School Community. *Voices: A World Forum for Music Therapy*, 5(2). https://doi.org/10.15845/voices.v5i2.223

Hunter, P. G., & Schellenberg, E. G. (2010). Music and Emotion. In *Music Perception* (pp. 129–164). Springer New York. https://doi.org/10.1007/978-1-4419-6114-3_5

Huotilainen, M. (2010). Building blocks of fetal cognition: Emotion and language. *Infant and Child Development*, 19(1), 94–98. https://doi.org/10.1002/icd.658

Huotilainen, M., & Tervaniemi, M. (2018). Planning music-based amelioration and training in infancy and childhood based on neural evidence. *Annals of the New York Academy of Sciences*, *1423*(1), 146–154. https://doi.org/10.1111/nyas.13655

Huppert, F. A., & So, T. T. C. (2011). Flourishing Across Europe: Application of a New Conceptual Framework for Defining Well-Being. *Social Indicators Research*, *110*(3), 837–861. https://doi.org/10.1007/s11205-011-9966-7

HURON, D. (2001a). Is Music an Evolutionary Adaptation? *Annals of the New York Academy of Sciences*, *930*(1), 43–61. https://doi.org/10.1111/j.1749-6632.2001.tb05724.x

HURON, D. (2001b). Is Music an Evolutionary Adaptation? *Annals of the New York Academy of Sciences*, *930*(1), 43–61. https://doi.org/10.1111/j.1749-6632.2001.tb05724.x

Huron, D. (2006). *Sweet Anticipation*. The MIT Press. https://doi.org/10.7551/mitpress/6575.001.0001

Huron, D., & Vuoskoski, J. K. (2020). On the Enjoyment of Sad Music: Pleasurable Compassion Theory and the Role of Trait Empathy. *Frontiers in Psychology*, *11*. https://doi.org/10.3389/fpsyg.2020.01060

Hurwitz, E. R., & Krumhansl, C. L. (2021). Shifting Listening Niches: Effects of the COVID-19 Pandemic. *Frontiers in Psychology*, *12*. https://doi.org/10.3389/fpsyg.2021.648413

Hurwitz, I., Wolff, P. H., Bortnick, B. D., & Kokas, K. (1975). Nonmusicol Effects of the Kodaly Music Curriculum in Primary Grade Children. *Journal of Learning Disabilities*, *8*(3), 167–174. https://doi.org/10.1177/002221947500800310

Husain, G., Thompson, W. F., & Schellenberg, E. G. (2002). Effects of Musical Tempo and Mode on Arousal, Mood, and Spatial Abilities. *Music Perception*, *20*(2), 151–171. https://doi.org/10.1525/mp.2002.20.2.151

Huss, E., Kaufman, R., Avgar, A., & Shuker, E. (2015). Arts as a vehicle for community building and post-disaster development. *Disasters*, *40*(2), 284–303. https://doi.org/10.1111/disa.12143

Huss, M., Verney, J. P., Fosker, T., Mead, N., & Goswami, U. (2011). Music, rhythm, rise time perception and developmental dyslexia: Perception of musical meter predicts reading and phonology. *Cortex*, *47*(6), 674–689. https://doi.org/10.1016/j.cortex.2010.07.010

Hutchinson, S. (2003). Cerebellar Volume of Musicians. *Cerebral Cortex*, *13*(9), 943–949. https://doi.org/10.1093/cercor/13.9.943

Hutchinson, S. L., Baldwin, C. K., & Oh, S.-S. (2006). Adolescent Coping: Exploring Adolescents' Leisure-Based Responses to Stress. *Leisure Sciences*, *28*(2), 115–131. https://doi.org/10.1080/01490400500483984

Hutka, S., Bidelman, G. M., & Moreno, S. (2015). Pitch expertise is not created equal: Cross-domain effects of musicianship and tone language experience on neural and behavioural discrimination of speech and music. *Neuropsychologia, 71*, 52–63. https://doi.org/10.1016/j.neuropsychologia.2015.03.019

Hwang, A. H.-C., Oh, J., & Scheinbaum, A. C. (2020). Interactive music for multisensory e-commerce: The moderating role of online consumer involvement in experiential value, cognitive value, and purchase intention. *Psychology & Marketing, 37*(8), 1031–1056. https://doi.org/10.1002/mar.21338

Hyde, K. L., Lerch, J., Norton, A., Forgeard, M., Winner, E., Evans, A. C., & Schlaug, G. (2009). Musical Training Shapes Structural Brain Development. *Journal of Neuroscience, 29*(10), 3019–3025. https://doi.org/10.1523/jneurosci.5118-08.2009

Hyyppä, M. T., & Mäki, J. (2001). Individual-Level Relationships between Social Capital and Self-Rated Health in a Bilingual Community. *Preventive Medicine, 32*(2), 148–155. https://doi.org/10.1006/pmed.2000.0782

Ilari, B. (2016). Music in the early years: Pathways into the social world. *Research Studies in Music Education, 38*(1), 23–39. https://doi.org/10.1177/1321103x16642631

Ilari, B. (2017). Children's ethnic identity, cultural diversity, and music education. In R. A. R. MacDonald, D. J. Hargreaves, & D. E. Miell (Eds), *Handbook of Musical Identities* (pp. 527–542). Oxford University Press.

Ing-Randolph, A. R., Phillips, L. R., & Williams, A. B. (2015). Group music interventions for dementia-associated anxiety: A systematic review. *International Journal of Nursing Studies, 52*(11), 1775–1784. https://doi.org/10.1016/j.ijnurstu.2015.06.014

Ireland, K., Parker, A., Foster, N., & Penhune, V. (2018). Rhythm and Melody Tasks for School-Aged Children With and Without Musical Training: Age-Equivalent Scores and Reliability. *Frontiers in Psychology, 9*. https://doi.org/10.3389/fpsyg.2018.00426

Irish, M., Cunningham, C. J., Walsh, J. B., Coakley, D., Lawlor, B. A., Robertson, I. H., & Coen, R. F. (2006). Investigating the Enhancing Effect of Music on Autobiographical Memory in Mild Alzheimer's Disease. *Dementia and Geriatric Cognitive Disorders, 22*(1), 108–120. https://doi.org/10.1159/000093487

Irons, J. Y., Sheffield, D., Ballington, F., & Stewart, D. E. (2019). A systematic review on the effects of group singing on persistent pain in people with long-term health conditions. *European Journal of Pain, 24*(1), 71–90. https://doi.org/10.1002/ejp.1485

Ishar, M. S., Mubarak, K. M., & Shameem, A. (2017). Interior atmosphere: Does it really have an impact on consumer purchasing behaviour at self-serving convenience stores. *Journal of Marketing and Consumer Research, 31*, 28 205.

Israel, E. P. (2012). *Instructor perception of El Sistema-based programs in the United States* [Unpublished Master's thesis.]. Faculty of the College of the Arts and Sciences, American University.

Istvandity, L. (2017). Combining music and reminiscence therapy interventions for wellbeing in elderly populations: A systematic review. *Complementary Therapies in Clinical Practice, 28,* 18–25. https://doi.org/10.1016/j.ctcp.2017.03.003

Ivanov, V. K., & Geake, J. G. (2003). The Mozart Effect and Primary School Children. *Psychology of Music, 31*(4), 405–413. https://doi.org/10.1177/03057356030314005

Iwanaga, M., & Moroki, Y. (1999). Subjective and Physiological Responses to Music Stimuli Controlled Over Activity and Preference. *Journal of Music Therapy, 36*(1), 26–38. https://doi.org/10.1093/jmt/36.1.26

J., C. H., & M, S. C. (1994). Effects of vocal and instrumental music on visuospatial and verbal performance as moderated by studying preference and personality. *Personality and Individual Differences, 16,* 237–245, https://doi.org/10.1016/0191-8869(94)90162-.

Jakobson, L. S., Cuddy, L. L., & Kilgour, A. R. (2003). Time Tagging: A Key to Musicians' Superior Memory. *Music Perception, 20*(3), 307–313. https://doi.org/10.1525/mp.2003.20.3.307

Jakobson, L. S., Lewycky, S. T., Kilgour, A. R., & Stoesz, B. M. (2008). Memory for Verbal and Visual Material in Highly Trained Musicians. *Music Perception, 26*(1), 41–55. https://doi.org/10.1525/mp.2008.26.1.41

James, C. E., Altenmüller, E., Kliegel, M., Krüger, T. H. C., Ville, D. V. D., Worschech, F., Abdili, L., Scholz, D. S., Jünemann, K., Hering, A., Grouiller, F., Sinke, C., & Marie, D. (2020). Train the brain with music (TBM): Brain plasticity and cognitive benefits induced by musical training in elderly people in Germany and Switzerland, a study protocol for an RCT comparing musical instrumental practice to sensitization to music. *BMC Geriatrics, 20*(1). https://doi.org/10.1186/s12877-020-01761-y

James, C. E., Oechslin, M. S., Ville, D. V. D., Hauert, C.-A., Descloux, C., & Lazeyras, F. (2013). Musical training intensity yields opposite effects on grey matter density in cognitive versus sensorimotor networks. *Brain Structure and Function, 219*(1), 353–366. https://doi.org/10.1007/s00429-013-0504-z

James, C. E., Zuber, S., Dupuis-Lozeron, E., Abdili, L., Gervaise, D., & Kliegel, M. (2020). Formal String Instrument Training in a Class Setting Enhances Cognitive and Sensorimotor Development of Primary School Children. *Frontiers in Neuroscience, 14.* https://doi.org/10.3389/fnins.2020.00567

Jäncke, L. (2009). The plastic human brain. *Restorative Neurology and Neuroscience, 27*(5), 521–538. https://doi.org/10.3233/rnn-2009-0519

Jäncke, L. (2012). The Relationship between Music and Language. *Frontiers in Psychology, 3.* https://doi.org/10.3389/fpsyg.2012.00123

Jäncke, L., Brügger, E., Brummer, M., Scherrer, S., & Alahmadi, N. (2014). Verbal learning in the context of background music: No influence of vocals and instrumentals on verbal learning. *Behavioral and Brain Functions, 10*(1), 10. https://doi.org/10.1186/1744-9081-10-10

Jäncke, L., Gaab, N., Wüstenberg, T., Scheich, H., & Heinze, H.-J. (2001). Short-term functional plasticity in the human auditory cortex: An fMRI study. *Cognitive Brain Research, 12*(3), 479–485. https://doi.org/10.1016/s0926-6410(01)00092-1

Jäncke, L., & Sandmann, P. (2010). Music listening while you learn: No influence of background music on verbal learning. *Behavioral and Brain Functions, 6*(1), 3. https://doi.org/10.1186/1744-9081-6-3

Jäncke, L., Shah, N. J., & Peters, M. (2000). Cortical activations in primary and secondary motor areas for complex bimanual movements in professional pianists. *Cognitive Brain Research, 10*(1–2), 177–183. https://doi.org/10.1016/s0926-6410(00)00028-8

Jantzen, M. G., Howe, B. M., & Jantzen, K. J. (2014). Neurophysiological evidence that musical training influences the recruitment of right hemispheric homologues for speech perception. *Frontiers in Psychology, 5.* https://doi.org/10.3389/fpsyg.2014.00171

Jantzen, M. G., Large, E. W., & Magne, C. (2016a). Editorial: Overlap of Neural Systems for Processing Language and Music. *Frontiers in Psychology, 7.* https://doi.org/10.3389/fpsyg.2016.00876

Jantzen, M. G., Large, E. W., & Magne, C. (2016b). Editorial: Overlap of Neural Systems for Processing Language and Music. *Frontiers in Psychology, 7.* https://doi.org/10.3389/fpsyg.2016.00876

Janus, M., Lee, Y., Moreno, S., & Bialystok, E. (2016). Effects of short-term music and second-language training on executive control. *Journal of Experimental Child Psychology, 144,* 84–97. https://doi.org/10.1016/j.jecp.2015.11.009

Janzen, T. B., & Thaut, M. H. (2018). *Rethinking the role of music in the neurodevelopment of autism spectrum disorder.* Music Science.

Jaschke, A. C., Eggermont, L. H. P., Honing, H., & Scherder, E. J. A. (2013). Music education and its effect on intellectual abilities in children: A systematic review. *Reviews in the Neurosciences, 24*(6). https://doi.org/10.1515/revneuro-2013-0023

Jaschke, A. C., Honing, H., & Scherder, E. J. A. (2018a). Longitudinal Analysis of Music Education on Executive Functions in Primary School Children. *Frontiers in Neuroscience, 12.* https://doi.org/10.3389/fnins.2018.00103

Jaschke, A. C., Honing, H., & Scherder, E. J. A. (2018b). Exposure to a musically-enriched environment; Its relationship with executive functions, short-term memory and verbal IQ in primary school children. *PLOS ONE, 13*(11), e0207265. https://doi.org/10.1371/journal.pone.0207265

JAUSOVEC, N., JAUSOVEC, K., & GERLIC, I. (2006). The influence of Mozart's music on brain activity in the process of learning. *Clinical Neurophysiology, 117*(12), 2703–2714. https://doi.org/10.1016/j.clinph.2006.08.010

Jefferies, L. N., Smilek, D., Eich, E., & Enns, J. T. (2008). Emotional Valence and Arousal Interact in Attentional Control. *Psychological Science, 19*(3), 290–295. https://doi.org/10.1111/j.1467-9280.2008.02082.x

Jellison, J. A., Brooks, B. H., & Huck, A. M. (1984). Structuring Small Groups and Music Reinforcement to Facilitate Positive Interactions and Acceptance of Severely Handicapped Students in the Regular Music Classroom. *Journal of Research in Music Education, 32*(4), 243–264. https://doi.org/10.2307/3344923

Jenkins, A. (2011). Participation in learning and wellbeing among older adults. *International Journal of Lifelong Education, 30*(3), 403–420. https://doi.org/10.1080/02601370.2011.570876

Jenkins, C. (2006). *Music therapy with adolescents with emotional and behavioural difficulties: A flexible approach. Unpublished postgraduate diploma dissertation.* Guildhall School of Music and Drama.

Jensen, A., & Bonde, L. O. (2018). The use of arts interventions for mental health and wellbeing in health settings. *Perspectives in Public Health, 138*(4), 209–214. https://doi.org/10.1177/1757913918772602

Jensen, A., Stickley, T., Torrissen, W., & Stigmar, K. (2016). Arts on prescription in Scandinavia: A review of current practice and future possibilities. *Perspectives in Public Health, 137*(5), 268–274. https://doi.org/10.1177/1757913916676853

Jensen, J. (1992). *Fandom as pathology: The consequences of characterization* (L. A. Lewis, Ed.). Routledge.

Jentschke, S. (2016). The relationship between music and language. In I. S. Hallam, I. Cross, & M. Thaut (Eds), *The Oxford Handbook of music psychology* (pp. 343–355). Oxford University Press.

Jentschke, S., & Koelsch, S. (2009). Musical training modulates the development of syntax processing in children. *NeuroImage, 47*(2), 735–744. https://doi.org/10.1016/j.neuroimage.2009.04.090

Jentzsch, I., Mkrtchian, A., & Kansal, N. (2014). Improved effectiveness of performance monitoring in amateur instrumental musicians. *Neuropsychologia, 52,* 117–124. https://doi.org/10.1016/j.neuropsychologia.2013.09.025

Jeong, Y.-J., Hong, S.-C., Lee, M. S., Park, M.-C., Kim, Y.-K., & Suh, C.-M. (2005). Dance movement therapy improves emotional responses and modulates neurohormones in adolescents with mild depression. *International Journal of Neuroscience, 115*(12), 1711–1720. https://doi.org/10.1080/00207450590958574

Jespersen, K. V., Koenig, J., Jennum, P., & Vuust, P. (2015). Music for insomnia in adults. *Cochrane Database of Systematic Reviews.* https://doi.org/10.1002/14651858.cd010459.pub2

Jespersen, K. V., Otto, M., Kringelbach, M., Someren, E. V., & Vuust, P. (2019). A randomized controlled trial of bedtime music for insomnia disorder. *Journal of Sleep Research, 28*(4), e12817. https://doi.org/10.1111/jsr.12817

Jespersen, K. V., & Vuust, P. (2012). The Effect of Relaxation Music Listening on Sleep Quality in Traumatized Refugees: A Pilot Study. *Journal of Music Therapy, 49*(2), 205–229. https://doi.org/10.1093/jmt/49.2.205

Jiang, J., Scolaro, A. J., Bailey, K., & Chen, A. (2011). The effect of music-induced mood on attentional networks. *International Journal of Psychology, 46*(3), 214–222. https://doi.org/10.1080/00207594.2010.541255

Jiang, J., Zhou, L., Rickson, D., & Jiang, C. (2013). The effects of sedative and stimulative music on stress reduction depend on music preference. *The Arts in Psychotherapy, 40*(2), 201–205. https://doi.org/10.1016/j.aip.2013.02.002

Johan, A. (2020). Intercultural Intimacy: Malaysian Popular Music as an Expression of Social Cohesion (1970s and 1980s. *Malaysian Journal of History, Politics and Strategic Studies, 47*(3).

Johansson, R., Holmqvist, K., Mossberg, F., & Lindgren, M. (2011). Eye movements and reading comprehension while listening to preferred and non-preferred study music. *Psychology of Music, 40*(3), 339–356. https://doi.org/10.1177/0305735610387777

Johansson, S. E. (2001). Sustaining habits of attending cultural events and maintenance of health: A longitudinal study. *Health Promotion International, 16*(3), 229–234. https://doi.org/10.1093/heapro/16.3.229

John, O. P., Naumann, L. P., & Soto, C. J. (2008). Paradigm shift to the integrative big-five trait taxonomy: History, measurement, and conceptual Issues. In O. P. John, R. W. Robins, & L. A. Pervin (Eds), *Handbook of personality: Theory and research* (pp. 114–158). Guilford.

Johnson, A. A., Berry, A., Bradley, M., Daniell, J. A., Lugo, C., Schaum-Comegys, K., Villamero, C., Williams, K., Yi, H., Scala, E., & Whalen, M. (2021). Examining the Effects of Music-Based Interventions on Pain and Anxiety in Hospitalized Children: An Integrative Review. *Journal of Pediatric Nursing, 60*, 71–76. https://doi.org/10.1016/j.pedn.2021.02.007

Johnson, C. M., & Memmott, J. E. (2006). Examination of Relationships between Participation in School Music Programs of Differing Quality and Standardized Test Results. *Journal of Research in Music Education, 54*(4), 293–307. https://doi.org/10.1177/002242940605400403

Johnson, D. C., & Davis, V. W. (2016). The effects of musical ensembles-in-residence on elementary students' auditory discrimination and spatial reasoning skills: A longitudinal study. *Visions of Research in Music Education, 28*. http://www.rider.edu/~vrme

Johnson, G. L., & Edelson, R. J. (2003). Integrating Music and Mathematics in the Elementary Classroom. *Teaching Children Mathematics, 9*(8), 474–479. https://doi.org/10.5951/tcm.9.8.0474

Jones, C. (2004). From healing rituals to music therapy: Bridging the cultural divide between therapist and young Sudanese refugees. *The Arts in Psychotherapy*. https://doi.org/10.1016/s0197-4556(04)00024-3

Jones, J. L., Lucker, J., Zalewski, C., Brewer, C., & Drayna, D. (2009). Phonological processing in adults with deficits in musical pitch recognition. *Journal of Communication Disorders*, 42(3), 226–234. https://doi.org/10.1016/j.jcomdis.2009.01.001

Jones, M., Kimberlee, R., Deave, T., & Evans, S. (2013). The Role of Community Centre-based Arts, Leisure and Social Activities in Promoting Adult Wellbeing and Healthy Lifestyles. *International Journal of Environmental Research and Public Health*, 10(5), 1948–1962. https://doi.org/10.3390/ijerph10051948

Jones, M. R. (2009). Musical time. In S. Hallam, I. Cross, & M. Thaut (Eds), *The Oxford Handbook of Music Psychology* (pp. 125–142). Oxford University Press.

Jones, M. R. (2019). *Time Will Tell: A Theory of Dynamic Attending*. Oxford University Press.

Jones, M. R., Johnston, H. M., & Puente, J. (2006). Effects of auditory pattern structure on anticipatory and reactive attending. *Cognitive Psychology*, 53(1), 59–96. https://doi.org/10.1016/j.cogpsych.2006.01.003

Jordan, N. C., Glutting, J., & Ramineni, C. (2008). A Number Sense Assessment Tool for Identifying Children at Risk for Mathematical Difficulties. In *Mathematical Difficulties* (pp. 45–58). Elsevier. https://doi.org/10.1016/b978-012373629-1.50005-8

Judd, M., & Pooley, J. A. (2013). The psychological benefits of participating in group singing for members of the general public. *Psychology of Music*, 42(2), 269–283. https://doi.org/10.1177/0305735612471237

Jung, H., Sontag, S., Park, Y. S., & Loui, P. (2015). Rhythmic Effects of Syntax Processing in Music and Language. *Frontiers in Psychology*, 6. https://doi.org/10.3389/fpsyg.2015.01762

Jung, R. E., & Haier, R. J. (2007). The Parieto-Frontal Integration Theory (P-FIT) of intelligence: Converging neuroimaging evidence. *Behavioral and Brain Sciences*, 30(2), 135–154. https://doi.org/10.1017/s0140525x07001185

Juslin, P. N. (1993). *Handbook of Music and Emotion: Theory, Research, Applications*. Oxford University Press. https://doi.org/10.1093/acprof:oso/9780199230143.001.0001

Juslin, P. N. (2000). Vocal expression and musical expression: Parallels and contrasts. In A. Kappas (Ed.), *Proceedings of the 16th Conference of the International Society for Research on Emotions* (pp. 281–284). ISRE Publications.

Juslin, P. N. (2003). Five Facets of Musical Expression: A Psychologist's Perspective on Music Performance. *Psychology of Music*, 31(3), 273–302. https://doi.org/10.1177/03057356030313003

Juslin, P. N. (2013). From everyday emotions to aesthetic emotions: Towards a unified theory of musical emotions. *Physics of Life Reviews*, *10*(3), 235–266. https://doi.org/10.1016/j.plrev.2013.05.008

Juslin, P. N., Harmat, L., & Eerola, T. (2013). What makes music emotionally significant? Exploring the underlying mechanisms. *Psychology of Music*, *42*(4), 599–623. https://doi.org/10.1177/0305735613484548

Juslin, P. N., & Laukka, P. (2004). Expression, Perception, and Induction of Musical Emotions: A Review and a Questionnaire Study of Everyday Listening. *Journal of New Music Research*, *33*(3), 217–238. https://doi.org/10.1080/0929821042000317813

Juslin, P. N., Liljeström, S., Laukka, P., Västfjäll, D., & Lundqvist, L.-O. (2011). Emotional reactions to music in a nationally representative sample of Swedish adults. *Musicae Scientiae*, *15*(2), 174–207. https://doi.org/10.1177/1029864911401169

Juslin, P. N., Liljeström, S., Västfjäll, D., Barradas, G., & Silva, A. (2008). An experience sampling study of emotional reactions to music: Listener, music, and situation. *Emotion*, *8*(5), 668–683. https://doi.org/10.1037/a0013505

Juslin, P. N., Liljeström, S., Västfjäll, D., & Lundqvist, L.-O. (2010). How does music evoke emotions? Exploring the underlying mechanisms. In P. N. Juslin & J. A. Sloboda (Eds), *Handbook of music and emotion: Theory, research, applications* (pp. 605–642). Oxford University Press.

Juslin, P. N., & Sloboda, J. A. (Eds). (2001). *Music and Emotion: Theory and Research*. Oxford University Press.

Jutras, P. J. (2006). The Benefits of Adult Piano Study as Self-Reported by Selected Adult Piano Students. *Journal of Research in Music Education*, *54*(2), 97–110. https://doi.org/10.1177/002242940605400202

Kahn, A. P. (1998). Healthy aging: A study of self-perceptions of well-being. Doctoral dissertation. *Dissertation[MP224] Abstracts International*, *58*, 4740.

Kahneman, D. (1973). *Attention and effort*. Prentice Hall Inc.

Kallinen, K. (2002). Reading news from a pocket computer in a distracting environment: Effects of the tempo of background music. *Computers in Human Behavior*, *18*(5), 537–551. https://doi.org/10.1016/s0747-5632(02)00005-5

Kalliopuska, M., & Ruókonen, I. (1986). Effects of Music Education on Development of Holistic Empathy. *Perceptual and Motor Skills*, *62*(1), 187–191. https://doi.org/10.2466/pms.1986.62.1.187

Kalliopuska, M., & Ruokonen, I. (1993). A Study with a Follow-up of the Effects of Music Education on Holistic Development of Empathy. *Perceptual and Motor Skills*, *76*(1), 131–137. https://doi.org/10.2466/pms.1993.76.1.131

Kalliopuska, M., & Tiitinen, U. (1991). Influence of Two Developmental Programmes on the Empathy and Prosociability of Preschool Children.

Perceptual and Motor Skills, 72(1), 323–328. https://doi.org/10.2466/pms.1991.72.1.323

Kalmar, M. (1982). The effects of music education based on Kodaly's directives in nursery school children. *Psychology of Music*.

Kamioka, H., Mutoh, Y., Tsutani, K., Yamada, M., Park, H., Okuizumi, H., Tsuruoka, K., Honda, T., Okada, S., Park, S.-J., Kityuguchi, J., Abe, T., Handa, S., & Oshio, T. (2014). Effectiveness of music therapy: A summary of systematic reviews based on randomized controlled trials of music interventions. *Patient Preference and Adherence*, 727. https://doi.org/10.2147/ppa.s61340

Kämpfe, J., Sedlmeier, P., & Renkewitz, F. (2010). The impact of background music on adult listeners: A meta-analysis. *Psychology of Music*, 39(4), 424–448. https://doi.org/10.1177/0305735610376261

Kang, H. J., & Williamson, V. J. (2013). Background music can aid second language learning. *Psychology of Music*, 42(5), 728–747. https://doi.org/10.1177/0305735613485152

Kantor-Martynuska, J. (2015). Emotional responses to music and their musical, individual, and situational factors: An integrative approach. *Psychological Studies*, 53, 30–45, https://doi.org/10.2478/V10167-010-

Karageorghis, C. I. (2020). Music-related interventions in sport and exercise. In G. Tenenbaum & R. C. Eklund (Eds), *Handbook of sport psychology* (pp. 929–949). Wiley.

Karageorghis, C. I., Jones, L., Howard, L. W., Thomas, R. M., Moulashis, P., & Santich, S. J. (2021). When It HIITs, You Feel No Pain: Psychological and Psychophysiological Effects of Respite–Active Music in High-Intensity Interval Training. *Journal of Sport & Exercise Psychology*, 43(1), 41–52. https://doi.org/10.1123/jsep.2019-0335

Karageorghis, C. I., & Priest, D.-L. (2012). Music in the exercise domain: A review and synthesis (Part I). *International Review of Sport and Exercise Psychology*, 5(1), 44–66. https://doi.org/10.1080/1750984x.2011.631026

Karlsen, S. (2011). Using musical agency as a lens: Researching music education from the angle of experience. *Research Studies in Music Education*, 33(2), 107–121. https://doi.org/10.1177/1321103x11422005

Karlsen, S., & Brändström, S. (2008). Exploring the music festival as a music educational project. *International Journal of Music Education*, 26(4), 363–373. https://doi.org/10.1177/0255761408096077

Karlsen, S., & Westerlund, H. (2010). Immigrant students' development of musical agency – Exploring democracy in music education. *British Journal of Music Education*, 27(3), 225–239, https://doi.org/10.1017/s026505170000203.

Kartz, B. (2000). *Grenzen. Heilpädagogische Musiktherapie an einer Schule für Erziehungshilfe*. Unpublished diploma. Conservatorium Saxion Hogeschool.

Karzon, R. G. (1985). Discrimination of polysyllabic sequences by one- to four-month-old infants. *Journal of Experimental Child Psychology, 39*(2), 326–342. https://doi.org/10.1016/0022-0965(85)90044-x

Kaser, M., Zaman, R., & Sahakian, B. J. (2016). Cognition as a treatment target in depression. *Psychological Medicine, 47*(6), 987–989. https://doi.org/10.1017/s0033291716003123

Kasiri, F. (2015). The Impact of Non-lyrical Iranian Traditional Music on Reading Comprehension Performance of Iranian EFL Learners: The Case of Gender, Attitude, and Familiarity. *Procedia - Social and Behavioral Sciences, 199*, 157–162. https://doi.org/10.1016/j.sbspro.2015.07.500

Kaufman, J. C., & Baer, J. (2004). The amusement park theoretical (APT) model of creativity. *Int. J. Creat. Probl, Solving*[MP232], *14*, 15–25.

Kaufman, J., & Gabler, J. (2004). Cultural capital and the extracurricular activities of girls and boys in the college attainment process. *Poetics, 32*(2), 145–168. https://doi.org/10.1016/j.poetic.2004.02.001

Kaufmann, L. (2008). Neural correlates of number processing and calculation: Developmental trajectories and educational implications. In A. Dowker (Ed.), *Mathematical Difficulties: Psychology and Intervention* (p. 233). Elsevier.

Kausel, L., Zamorano, F., Billeke, P., Sutherland, M. E., Larrain-Valenzuela, J., Stecher, X., Schlaug, G., & Aboitiz, F. (2020). Neural Dynamics of Improved Bimodal Attention and Working Memory in Musically Trained Children. *Frontiers in Neuroscience, 14*. https://doi.org/10.3389/fnins.2020.554731

Kaviani, H., Mirbaha, H., Pournaseh, M., & Sagan, O. (2013). Can music lessons increase the performance of preschool children in IQ tests? *Cognitive Processing, 15*(1), 77–84. https://doi.org/10.1007/s10339-013-0574-0

Kawase, S. (2015a). Associations among music majors' personality traits, empathy, and aptitude for ensemble performance. *Psychology of Music, 44*(2), 293–302. https://doi.org/10.1177/0305735614568697

Kawase, S. (2015b). Relationships between performers' daily social skills, social behaviors in ensemble practice, and evaluations of ensemble performance. *Musicae Scientiae, 19*(4), 350–365. https://doi.org/10.1177/1029864915590171

Kawase, S., & Ogawa, J. (2018). *Group music lessons for children aged 1–3 improve accompanying parents' moods∗*. Psychology of Music.

Kawase, S., Ogawa, J., Obata, S., & Hirano, T. (2018). An Investigation Into the Relationship Between Onset Age of Musical Lessons and Levels of Sociability in Childhood. *Frontiers in Psychology, 9*. https://doi.org/10.3389/fpsyg.2018.02244

Keeler, J. R., Roth, E. A., Neuser, B. L., Spitsbergen, J. M., Waters, D. J. M., & Vianney, J.-M. (2015). The neurochemistry and social flow of singing: Bonding and oxytocin. *Frontiers in Human Neuroscience, 9*. https://doi.org/10.3389/fnhum.2015.00518

Keen, A. W. (2005). Using Music as a Therapy Tool to Motivate Troubled Adolescents. *Social Work in Health Care*, *39*(3–4), 361–373. https://doi.org/10.1300/j010v39n03_09

Keenan, J. P., Thangaraj, V., Halpern, A. R., & Schlaug, G. (2001). Absolute Pitch and Planum Temporale. *NeuroImage*, *14*(6), 1402–1408. https://doi.org/10.1006/nimg.2001.0925

Keith, D. R., Russell, K., & Weaver, B. S. (2009). The Effects of Music Listening on Inconsolable Crying in Premature Infants. *Journal of Music Therapy*, *46*(3), 191–203. https://doi.org/10.1093/jmt/46.3.191

Keller, P. (2014). Ensemble Performance. In *Expressiveness in music performance* (pp. 260–282). Oxford University Press. https://doi.org/10.1093/acprof:oso/9780199659647.003.0015

Keller, P. E., Novembre, G., & Hove, M. J. (2014). Rhythm in joint action: Psychological and neurophysiological mechanisms for real-time interpersonal coordination. *Philosophical Transactions of the Royal Society B: Biological Sciences*, *369*(1658), 20130394. https://doi.org/10.1098/rstb.2013.0394

Kemmerer, K. P. (2003). *Relationship between the number of hours spent in general music class and reading skills in kindergarten through grade 3. Doctoral dissertation.* Lehigh University.

Kemp, A. E. (1996). *The Musical temperament: Psychology and Personality of Musicians*. Oxford University Press.

Kempert, S., Gotz, R., Blatter, K., Tibken, C., Artelt, C., Schneider, W., & Stanat, P. (2016). *Training early literacy related skills: To which degree does musical training contribute to phonological awareness development?* https://doi.org/10.3389/fpsyg.2016.01803.

Kennedy, J. R. (1998). *The effects of musical performance, rational emotive therapy and vicarious experience on the self-efficacy and self-esteem of juvenile delinquents and disadvantaged children* [PhD Thesis]. University of Kansas.

Kennedy, P. (2001). Working with survivors of torture in Sarajevo with Reiki. *Complementary Therapies in Nursing and Midwifery*, *7*(1), 4–7. https://doi.org/10.1054/ctnm.2000.0516

Kenny, A. (2018). Voice of Ireland? Children and music within asylum seeker accommodation. *Research Studies in Music Education*, *40*(2), 211–225. https://doi.org/10.1177/1321103x18794197

Kenny, A., & Moore, G. (2011). *Sing Out with Strings Evaluation Report*. Irish Chamber Orchestra, University of Limerick.

Keown, D. J. (2015). *A descriptive analysis of film music enthusiasts' purchasing and consumption behaviours of soundtrack albums: An exploratory study*. Psychology of Music.

Khaghaninejad, M. S., Motlagh, H. S., & Chamacham, R. (2016). How does Mozart's music affect the reading comprehension of Iranian EFL learners of both genders. *International Journal of Human Cultural Studies*, 238 489–499.

Khalil, A. K., Minces, V., McLoughlin, G., & Chiba, A. (2013). Group rhythmic synchrony and attention in children. *Frontiers in Psychology*, 4. https://doi.org/10.3389/fpsyg.2013.00564

Kibby, M. (2009). COLLECT YOURSELF. *Information, Communication & Society*, 12(3), 428–443. https://doi.org/10.1080/13691180802660644

KidZNotes. (2012). *El Sistema in Durham: Progress and Possibilities*. Kidznotes.

Kiehn, M. T. (2003). Development of Music Creativity among Elementary School Students. *Journal of Research in Music Education*, 51(4), 278–288. https://doi.org/10.2307/3345655

Kiger, D. M. (1989). Effects of Music Information Load on a Reading Comprehension Task. *Perceptual and Motor Skills*, 69(2), 531–534. https://doi.org/10.2466/pms.1989.69.2.531

Kilgour, A. R., Jakobson, L. S., & Cuddy, L. L. (2000). Music training and rate of presentation as mediators of text and song recall. *Memory & Cognition*, 28(5), 700–710. https://doi.org/10.3758/bf03198404

Kim, H.-S., & Kim, H.-S. (2017). Effect of a musical instrument performance program on emotional intelligence, anxiety, and aggression in Korean elementary school children. *Psychology of Music*, 46(3), 440–453. https://doi.org/10.1177/0305735617729028

Kim, J. (2013). Music therapy with children who have been exposed to ongoing child abuse and poverty: A pilot study. *Nordic Journal of Music Therapy*, 24(1), 27–43. https://doi.org/10.1080/08098131.2013.872696

Kim, J. (2017). Effects of community-based group music therapy for children exposed to ongoing child maltreatment & poverty in South Korea: A block randomized controlled trial. *The Arts in Psychotherapy*, 54, 69–77. https://doi.org/10.1016/j.aip.2017.01.001

Kim, J., Wigram, T., & Gold, C. (2009). Emotional, motivational and interpersonal responsiveness of children with autism in improvisational music therapy. *Autism*, 13(4), 389–409. https://doi.org/10.1177/1362361309105660

Kim, K. H., Chong, H. J., & Yun, J. (2015). Use of arts as the strategic medium for restorative justice: Restorative function of music. *Korean Journal of Youth Studies*, 22, 275–300.

Kimmig, H. (1986). *Express-sakkadenbeim menschen: Die rolle der aufmerksamkeit in der vorbereitungsphase zielgerichteter blicksprünge* [PhD Thesis]. Universität Freiburg.

Kinney, D. W. (2008). Selected Demographic Variables, School Music Participation, and Achievement Test Scores of Urban Middle School

Students. *Journal of Research in Music Education, 56*(2), 145–161. https://doi.org/10.1177/0022429408322530

Kinney, D. W. (2009). Selected Nonmusic Predictors of Urban Students' Decisions to Enroll and Persist in Middle School Band Programs. *Journal of Research in Music Education, 57*(4), 334–350. https://doi.org/10.1177/0022429409350086

Kinnunen, M., Homi, H., & Honkanen, A. (2020). Social Sustainability in Adolescents' Music Event Attendance. *Sustainability, 12*(22), 9419. https://doi.org/10.3390/su12229419

Kinsler, V., & Carpenter, R. H. S. (1995). Saccadic eye movements while reading music. *Vision Research, 35*(10), 1447–1458. https://doi.org/10.1016/0042-6989(95)98724-n

Kirnarskaya, D., & Teeter, M. H. (2009). *The Natural Musician*. Oxford University Press. https://doi.org/10.1093/acprof:oso/9780199560134.001.0001

Kirschner, S., & Tomasello, M. (2009). Joint drumming: Social context facilitates synchronization in preschool children. *Journal of Experimental Child Psychology, 102*(3), 299–314. https://doi.org/10.1016/j.jecp.2008.07.005

Kirschner, S., & Tomasello, M. (2010). Joint music making promotes prosocial behavior in 4-year-old children\textbackslashding73\textbackslashding73\textbackslashding73. *Evolution and Human Behavior, 31*(5), 354–364. https://doi.org/10.1016/j.evolhumbehav.2010.04.004

Kishon-Rabin, L., Amir, O., Vexler, Y., & Zaltz, Y. (2001). Pitch Discrimination: Are Professional Musicians Better than Non-Musicians? *Journal of Basic and Clinical Physiology and Pharmacology, 12*(2). https://doi.org/10.1515/jbcpp.2001.12.2.125

Kisilevsky, B. S., & Hains, S. M. (2009). Onset and maturation of fetal heart rate response to the mother's voice over late gestation. *Dev. Science[MP240, 14*, 214–223.

Kisilevsky, B. S., Hains, S. M. J., Jacquet, A.-Y., Granier-Deferre, C., & Lecanuet, J. P. (2004). Maturation of fetal responses to music. *Developmental Science, 7*(5), 550–559. https://doi.org/10.1111/j.1467-7687.2004.00379.x

Kisilevsky, B. S., Hains, S. M. J., Lee, K., Xie, X., Huang, H., Ye, H. H., Zhang, K., & Wang, Z. (2003). Effects of Experience on Fetal Voice Recognition. *Psychological Science, 14*(3), 220–224. https://doi.org/10.1111/1467-9280.02435

Kivland, M. J. (1986). The Use of Music to Increase Self-Esteem in a Conduct Disordered Adolescent. *Journal of Music Therapy, 23*(1), 25–29. https://doi.org/10.1093/jmt/23.1.25

Klassen, J. A., Liang, Y., Tjosvold, L., Klassen, T. P., & Hartling, L. (2008). Music for pain and anxiety in children undergoing medical procedures: A systematic review of randomized controlled trials. *Acute Pain, 10*(2), 106. https://doi.org/10.1016/j.acpain.2008.05.038

Kleber, B., Veit, R., Birbaumer, N., Gruzelier, J., & Lotze, M. (2009). The Brain of Opera Singers: Experience-Dependent Changes in Functional Activation. *Cerebral Cortex*, *20*(5), 1144–1152. https://doi.org/10.1093/cercor/bhp177

Kleinmintz, O. M., Goldstein, P., Mayseless, N., Abecasis, D., & Shamay-Tsoory, S. G. (2014). Expertise in Musical Improvisation and Creativity: The Mediation of Idea Evaluation. *PLoS ONE*, *9*(7), e101568. https://doi.org/10.1371/journal.pone.0101568

Klinedinst, R. E. (1991). Predicting Performance Achievement and Retention of Fifth-Grade Instrumental Students. *Journal of Research in Music Education*, *39*(3), 225–238. https://doi.org/10.2307/3344722

Kobin, C., & Tyson, E. (2006). Thematic analysis of hip-hop music: Can hip-hop in therapy facilitate empathic connections when working with clients in urban settings? *The Arts in Psychotherapy*, *33*(4), 343–356. https://doi.org/10.1016/j.aip.2006.05.001

Koch-Temming, H. (1999). Von der Behandlung der Krankheitzur Sorge um die Gesundheit. Musiktherapie in integrativen Kindergärten. *Musiktherapeutische Umschau*, *20*(1), 5–13.

Koehler, F., & Neubauer, A. B. (2020). From music making to affective well-being in everyday life: The mediating role of need satisfaction. *Psychology of Aesthetics, Creativity, and the Arts*, *14*(4), 493–505. https://doi.org/10.1037/aca0000261

Koelsch, S. (2011). Toward a Neural Basis of Music Perception – A Review and Updated Model. *Frontier in Psychology*, *2*. https://doi.org/10.3389/fpsyg.2011.00110

Koelsch, S., Grossmann, T., Gunter, T. C., Hahne, A., Schröger, E., & Friederici, A. D. (2003). Children Processing Music: Electric Brain Responses Reveal Musical Competence and Gender Differences. *Journal of Cognitive Neuroscience*, *15*(5), 683–693. https://doi.org/10.1162/jocn.2003.15.5.683

Koelsch, S., Gunter, T. C., Cramon, D. Y. v, Zysset, S., Lohmann, G., & Friederici, A. D. (2002). Bach Speaks: A Cortical "Language-Network" Serves the Processing of Music. *NeuroImage*, *17*(2), 956–966. https://doi.org/10.1006/nimg.2002.1154

Koelsch, S., Gunter, T. C., Wittfoth, M., & Sammler, D. (2005). Interaction between Syntax Processing in Language and in Music: An ERP Study. *Journal of Cognitive Neuroscience*, *17*(10), 1565–1577. https://doi.org/10.1162/089892905774597290

Koelsch, S., Schmidt, B., & Kansok, J. (2002). Effects of musical expertise on the early right anterior negativity: An event-related brain potential study. *Psychophysiology*, *39*(5), 657–663. https://doi.org/10.1111/1469-8986.3950657

Koelsch, S., Schröger, E., & Tervaniemi, M. (1999). Superior pre-attentive auditory processing in musicians. *NeuroReport*, *10*(6), 1309–1313. https://doi.org/10.1097/00001756-199904260-00029

Koelsch, S., & Siebel, W. A. (2005). Towards a neural basis of music perception. *Trends in Cognitive Sciences, 9*(12), 578–584. https://doi.org/10.1016/j.tics.2005.10.001

Koelsch, S., Vuust, P., & Friston, K. (2019). Predictive Processes and the Peculiar Case of Music. *Trends in Cognitive Sciences, 23*(1), 63–77. https://doi.org/10.1016/j.tics.2018.10.006

Koeneke, S., Lutz, K., Wüstenberg, T., & Jäncke, L. (2004). Long-term training affects cerebellar processing in skilled keyboard players. *NeuroReport, 15*(8), 1279–1282. https://doi.org/10.1097/01.wnr.0000127463.10147.e7

Kogan, N. (1997). Reflections on aesthetics and evolution. *Critical Review, 11*(2), 193–210. https://doi.org/10.1080/08913819708443453

Köhler, F., Martin, Z.-S., Hertrampf, R.-S., Gäbel, C., Kessler, J., Ditzen, B., & Warth, M. (2020). Music Therapy in the Psychosocial Treatment of Adult Cancer Patients: A Systematic Review and Meta-Analysis. *Frontiers in Psychology, 11*. https://doi.org/10.3389/fpsyg.2020.00651

Kok, M. (2006). Neue Wege der Musiktherapie an der Musikschule–Kooperation Allgemeinbildenden Schulen. *Musiktherapeutische Umschau, 27*(3), 269–274.

Kokotsaki, D., & Hallam, S. (2007). Higher education music students' perceptions of the benefits of participative music making. *Music Education Research, 9*(1), 93–109. https://doi.org/10.1080/14613800601127577

Kokotsaki, D., & Hallam, S. (2011). The perceived benefits of participative music making for non-music university students: A comparison with music students. *Music Education Research, 13*(2), 149–172. https://doi.org/10.1080/14613808.2011.577768

Konlaan, B. B., Bygren, L. O., & Johansson, S.-E. (2000). Visiting the cinema, concerts, museums or art exhibitions as determinant of survival: A Swedish fourteen-year cohort follow-up. *Scandinavian Journal of Public Health, 28*(3), 174–178. https://doi.org/10.1177/14034948000280030501

Koolidge, L., & Holmes, R. M. (2018). Piecing It Together: The Effect of Background Music on Children's Puzzle Assembly. *Perceptual and Motor Skills, 125*(2), 387–399. https://doi.org/10.1177/0031512517752817

Kopiez, R., & Galley, N. (2002). The musicians' glance: A pilot study comparing eye movement parameters in musicians and non-musicians. In C. Stevens, D. Burnham, G. McPherson, E. Schubert, & J. Renwick (Eds), *Proceedings of the 7th International Conference on Music Perception and Cognition* (pp. 683–686). Causal Productions.

Koppelman, D., & Scott, I. (1995). *The effect of music on children's writing content.*

Koshimori, Y., & Thaut, M. H. (2019). New Perspectives on Music in Rehabilitation of Executive and Attention Functions. *Frontiers in Neuroscience, 13*. https://doi.org/10.3389/fnins.2019.01245

Kotilahti, K., Nissilä, I., Näsi, T., Lipiäinen, L., Noponen, T., Meriläinen, P., Huotilainen, M., & Fellman, V. (2009). Hemodynamic responses to speech and music in newborn infants. *Human Brain Mapping*, NA-NA. https://doi.org/10.1002/hbm.20890

Kotsopoulou, A., & Hallam, S. (2010). The perceived impact of playing music while studying: Age and cultural differences. *Educational Studies, 36*(4), 431–440. https://doi.org/10.1080/03055690903424774

Kotz, S. A., Ravignani, A., & Fitch, W. T. (2018). The Evolution of Rhythm Processing. *Trends in Cognitive Sciences, 22*(10), 896–910. https://doi.org/10.1016/j.tics.2018.08.002

Kotz, S. A., & Schmidt-Kassow, M. (2015). Basal ganglia contribution to rule expectancy and temporal predictability in speech. *Cortex, 68*, 48–60. https://doi.org/10.1016/j.cortex.2015.02.021

Kotz, S. A., & Schwartze, M. (2010). Cortical speech processing unplugged: A timely subcortico-cortical framework. *Trends in Cognitive Sciences, 14*(9), 392–399. https://doi.org/10.1016/j.tics.2010.06.005

Kougiali, Z., Einat, T., & Liebling, A. (2017). Rhizomatic affective spaces and the therapeutic potential of music in prison: A qualitative meta-synthesis. *Qualitative Research in Psychology, 15*(1), 1–28. https://doi.org/10.1080/14780887.2017.1359710

Koutsoupidou, T., & Hargreaves, D. J. (2009). An experimental study of the effects of improvisation on the development of children's creative thinking in music. *Psychology of Music, 37*(3), 251–278. https://doi.org/10.1177/0305735608097246

Krajewski, K., & Schneider, W. (2009). Exploring the impact of phonological awareness, visual–spatial working memory, and preschool quantity–number competencies on mathematics achievement in elementary school: Findings from a 3-year longitudinal study. *Journal of Experimental Child Psychology, 103*(4), 516–531. https://doi.org/10.1016/j.jecp.2009.03.009

Kraus, N., & Chandrasekaran, B. (2010). Music training for the development of auditory skills. *Nature Reviews Neuroscience, 11*(8), 599–605. https://doi.org/10.1038/nrn2882

Kraus, N., Hornickel, J., Strait, D. L., Slater, J., & Thompson, E. (2014). Engagement in community music classes sparks neuroplasticity and language development in children from disadvantaged backgrounds. *Frontiers in Psychology, 5*. https://doi.org/10.3389/fpsyg.2014.01403

Kraus, N., & Nicol, T. (2014). The cognitive auditory system. In R. Fay & A. Popper (Eds), *Perspectives on auditory research* (pp. 299–319). Springer.

Kraus, N., & Slater, J. (2016). Beyond Words: How Humans Communicate Through Sound. *Annual Review of Psychology, 67*(1), 83–103. https://doi.org/10.1146/annurev-psych-122414-033318

Kraus, N., Slater, J., Thompson, E. C., Hornickel, J., Strait, D. L., Nicol, T., & White-Schwoch, T. (2014). Music Enrichment Programs Improve the Neural Encoding of Speech in At-Risk Children. *Journal of Neuroscience, 34*(36), 11913–11918. https://doi.org/10.1523/jneurosci.1881-14.2014

Kraus, N., & Strait, D. L. (2015). Emergence of biological markers of musicianship with school-based music instruction. *Annals of the New York Academy of Sciences, 1337*(1), 163–169. https://doi.org/10.1111/nyas.12631

Kraus, N., Strait, D. L., & Parbery-Clark, A. (2012). Cognitive factors shape brain networks for auditory skills: Spotlight on auditory working memory. *Annals of the New York Academy of Sciences, 1252*(1), 100–107. https://doi.org/10.1111/j.1749-6632.2012.06463.x

Kraus, N., & White-Schwoch, T. (2016). Neurobiology of Everyday Communication: What Have We Learned From Music? *The Neuroscientist, 23*(3), 287–298. https://doi.org/10.1177/1073858416653593

Krause, A. E., & Davidson, J. W. (2018). Effective Educational Strategies to Promote Life-Long Musical Investment: Perceptions of Educators. *Frontiers in Psychology, 9*. https://doi.org/10.3389/fpsyg.2018.01977

Krause, A. E., Davidson, J. W., & North, A. C. (2018). Musical Activity and Well-being. *Music Perception, 35*(4), 454–474. https://doi.org/10.1525/mp.2018.35.4.454

Krause, A. E., Dimmock, J., Rebar, A. L., & Jackson, B. (2021). Music Listening Predicted Improved Life Satisfaction in University Students During Early Stages of the COVID-19 Pandemic. *Frontiers in Psychology, 11*. https://doi.org/10.3389/fpsyg.2020.631033

Krause, A. E., & Hargreaves, D. J. (2012). myTunes: Digital music library users and their self-images. *Psychology of Music, 41*(5), 531–544. https://doi.org/10.1177/0305735612440612

Krause, A. E., Kirby, M. L., Dieckmann, S., & Davidson, J. W. (2020). From dropping out to dropping in: Exploring why individuals cease participation in musical activities and the support needed to reengage them. *Psychology of Aesthetics, Creativity, and the Arts, 14*(4), 401–414. https://doi.org/10.1037/aca0000268

Krause, A. E., North, A. C., & Hewitt, L. Y. (2013). Music-listening in everyday life: Devices and choice. *Psychology of Music, 43*(2), 155–170. https://doi.org/10.1177/0305735613496860

Kreutz, G. (2014). Does Singing Facilitate Social Bonding? *Music and Medicine, 6*(2), 51. https://doi.org/10.47513/mmd.v6i2.180

Kreutz, G., Bongard, S., Rohrmann, S., Hodapp, V., & Grebe, D. (2004). Effects of Choir Singing or Listening on Secretory Immunoglobulin A, Cortisol, and Emotional State. *Journal of Behavioral Medicine, 27*(6), 623–635. https://doi.org/10.1007/s10865-004-0006-9

Kreutz, G., & Lotze, M. (2008). Neuroscience of music and emotion. In W. Gruhn & R. Rauscher (Eds), *The Neuroscience of Music Education* (pp. 145–169). Nova Publishers.

Kreutz, G., Quiroga Murcia, C., & Bongard, S. (2012). Psychoneuroendocrine research on music and health. In R. MacDonald, G. Kreutz, & L. Mitchell (Eds), *Music, health and wellbeing* (pp. 457–490). Oxford University Press.

Krings, T., Töpper, R., Foltys, H., Erberich, S., Sparing, R., Willmes, K., & Thron, A. (2000a). Cortical activation patterns during complex motor tasks in piano players and control subjects. A functional magnetic resonance imaging study. *Neuroscience Letters*, 278(3), 189–193. https://doi.org/10.1016/s0304-3940(99)00930-1

Krings, T., Töpper, R., Foltys, H., Erberich, S., Sparing, R., Willmes, K., & Thron, A. (2000b). Cortical activation patterns during complex motor tasks in piano players and control subjects. A functional magnetic resonance imaging study. *Neuroscience Letters*, 278(3), 189–193. https://doi.org/10.1016/s0304-3940(99)00930-1

Krishnan, A., Xu, Y., Gandour, J., & Cariani, P. (2005). Encoding of pitch in the human brainstem is sensitive to language experience. *Cognitive Brain Research*, 25(1), 161–168. https://doi.org/10.1016/j.cogbrainres.2005.05.004

Krizman, J., Marian, V., Shook, A., Skoe, E., & Kraus, N. (2012). Subcortical encoding of sound is enhanced in bilinguals and relates to executive function advantages. *Proceedings of the National Academy of Sciences*, 109(20), 7877–7881. https://doi.org/10.1073/pnas.1201575109

Krout, R. E. (2007). Music listening to facilitate relaxation and promote wellness: Integrated aspects of our neurophysiological responses to music. *The Arts in Psychotherapy*, 34(2), 134–141. https://doi.org/10.1016/j.aip.2006.11.001

Krout, R. E., & Mason, M. (1988a). Using Computer and Electronic Music Resources in Clinical Music Therapy with Behaviorally Disordered Students, 12 to 78 Years Old. *Music Therapy Perspectives*, 5(1), 114–118. https://doi.org/10.1093/mtp/5.1.114

Krout, R. E., & Mason, M. (1988b). Using Computer and Electronic Music Resources in Clinical Music Therapy with Behaviorally Disordered Students, 12 to 78 Years Old. *Music Therapy Perspectives*, 5(1), 114–118. https://doi.org/10.1093/mtp/5.1.114

Krueger, J. (2019). Music as affective scaffolding. In *Music and Consciousness 2* (pp. 55–70). Oxford University Press. https://doi.org/10.1093/oso/9780198804352.003.0004

Krüger, V. (2000). The use of information technology in music therapy: Behavioural problems in contemporary schools. *Nordic Journal of Music Therapy*, 9(2), 77–83.

Kruse, N. B. (2021). Reminiscence and Music Participation Among Older Adults. *Bulletin of the Council for Research in Music Education, 228,* 40–58. https://doi.org/10.5406/bulcouresmusedu.228.0040

Kruse, N. B., & Veblen, K. K. (2012). Music teaching and learning online: Considering YouTube instructional videos. *Journal of Music, Technology and Education, 5*(1), 77–87. https://doi.org/10.1386/jmte.5.1.77_1

Kubzansky, L. D. (2009). Health and emotion. In D. Sander & K. R. Scherer (Eds), *Oxford companion to emotion and the affective sciences* (pp. 204–205). Oxford University Press.

Kuckelkorn, K. L., Manzano, Ö. de, & Ullén, F. (2021). Musical expertise and personality – differences related to occupational choice and instrument categories. *Personality and Individual Differences, 173,* 110573. https://doi.org/10.1016/j.paid.2020.110573

Kuhl, J. (2000). A Functional-design approach to motivation and self-regulation: The dynamics of personality systems Interactions. In M. Boekaerts, P. R. Pintrich, & M. Zeidner (Eds), *Handbook of Self-Regulation* (pp. 111–169). Academic Press. https://doi.org/10.1016/B978-012109890-2/50034-2.

Kuhl, P. K. (2004). Early language acquisition: Cracking the speech code. *Nature Reviews Neuroscience, 5*(11), 831–843. https://doi.org/10.1038/nrn1533

Kuhn, D. (2002). The Effects of Active and Passive Participation in Musical Activity on the Immune System as Measured by Salivary Immunoglobulin A (SlgA). *Journal of Music Therapy, 39*(1), 30–39. https://doi.org/10.1093/jmt/39.1.30

Kühnis, J., Elmer, S., Meyer, M., & Jäncke, L. (2013). The encoding of vowels and temporal speech cues in the auditory cortex of professional musicians: An EEG study. *Neuropsychologia, 51*(8), 1608–1618. https://doi.org/10.1016/j.neuropsychologia.2013.04.007

Kujala, T. (2007). The Role of Early Auditory Discrimination Deficits in Language Disorders. *Journal of Psychophysiology, 21*(3–4), 239–250. https://doi.org/10.1027/0269-8803.21.34.239

Kujala, T., LepistÄk̦, T., & NÄÏÄÏtÄÏnen, R. (2013). The neural basis of aberrant speech and audition in autism spectrum disorders. *Neuroscience & Biobehavioral Reviews, 37*(4), 697–704. https://doi.org/10.1016/j.neubiorev.2013.01.006

Kunert, R., & Slevc, L. R. (2015). A Commentary on: "Neural overlap in processing music and speech". *Frontiers in Human Neuroscience, 9.* https://doi.org/10.3389/fnhum.2015.00330

Kuriansky, J., & Nemeth, D. G. (2020). Rebuilding executive functions in environmentally traumatized children and adolescents. In G. Darlyne, D. G. Nemeth, & J. Glozman (Eds), *Evaluation and treatment of neuropsychologically compromised children* (pp. 221–247). Academic Press. https://doi.org/10.1016/B978-0-12-819545-1.00012-6.

Kuschpel, M. S., Liu, S., Schad, D. J., Heinzel, S., Heinz, A., & Rapp, M. A. (2015). Differential effects of wakeful rest, music and video game playing on working memory performance in the n-back task. *Frontiers in Psychology, 6*. https://doi.org/10.3389/fpsyg.2015.01683

Küssner, M. B., Groot, A. M. B. de, Hofman, W. F., & Hillen, M. A. (2016). EEG Beta Power but Not Background Music Predicts the Recall Scores in a Foreign-Vocabulary Learning Task. *PLOS ONE, 11*(8), e0161387. https://doi.org/10.1371/journal.pone.0161387

Kuuse, A.-K. (2018). "We will fight Goliath": Negotiation of space for musical agency in children's music education. *Research Studies in Music Education, 40*(2), 140–156. https://doi.org/10.1177/1321103x18771796

Kuusi, T., Haukka, J., Myllykangas, L., & Järvelä, I. (2019). Causes of Death of Professional Musicians in the Classical Genre. *Medical Problems of Performing Artists, 34*(2), 92–97. https://doi.org/10.21091/mppa.2019.2016

Kvet, E. J. (1985). Excusing Elementary School Students from Regular Classroom Activities for the Study of Instrumental Music: The Effect on Sixth-Grade Reading, Language, and Mathematics Achievement. *Journal of Research in Music Education, 33*(1), 45–54. https://doi.org/10.2307/3344757

Kwok, S. Y. C. L. (2018). Integrating Positive Psychology and Elements of Music Therapy to Alleviate Adolescent Anxiety. *Research on Social Work Practice, 29*(6), 663–676. https://doi.org/10.1177/1049731518773423

Lacey, M. (2004). Nyala Journal; Singers of Sudan Study War No More. *New York Times*. http://www.nytimes.com/2004/07/12/world/nyala-journal-singers-of-sudan-study-war-no-more.html.

Lacher, K. T., & Mizerski, R. (1994). An Exploratory Study of the Responses and Relationships Involved in the Evaluation of, and in the Intention to Purchase New Rock Music. *Journal of Consumer Research, 21*(2), 366. https://doi.org/10.1086/209404

LaCroix, A. N., Diaz, A. F., & Rogalsky, C. (2015). The relationship between the neural computations for speech and music perception is context-dependent: An activation likelihood estimate study. *Frontiers in Psychology, 6*. https://doi.org/10.3389/fpsyg.2015.01138

Ladányi, E., Persici, V., Fiveash, A., Tillmann, B., & Gordon, R. L. (2020). Is atypical rhythm a risk factor for developmental speech and language disorders? *WIREs Cognitive Science, 11*(5). https://doi.org/10.1002/wcs.1528

LaGasse, A. B., & Thaut, M. H. (2012). Music and Rehabilitation: Neurological Approaches. In *Music, Health, and Wellbeing* (pp. 153–163). Oxford University Press. https://doi.org/10.1093/acprof:oso/9780199586974.003.0012

LaGasse, B. (2017). Social outcomes in children with autism spectrum disorder: A review of music therapy outcomes. *Patient Related Outcome Measures, Volume 8*, 23–32. https://doi.org/10.2147/prom.s106267

Lage-Gómez, C., & Cremades-Andreu, R. (2019). Group improvisation as dialogue: Opening creative spaces in secondary music education. *Thinking Skills and Creativity, 31*, 232–242. https://doi.org/10.1016/j.tsc.2018.12.007

Lagrois, M.-É., Palmer, C., & Peretz, I. (2019). Poor Synchronization to Musical Beat Generalizes to Speech. *Brain Sciences, 9*(7), 157. https://doi.org/10.3390/brainsci9070157

Lahav, A., Saltzman, E., & Schlaug, G. (2007). Action Representation of Sound: Audiomotor Recognition Network While Listening to Newly Acquired Actions. *Journal of Neuroscience, 27*(2), 308–314. https://doi.org/10.1523/jneurosci.4822-06.2007

Laiho, S. (2004). The Psychological Functions of Music in Adolescence. *Nordic Journal of Music Therapy, 13*(1), 47–63. https://doi.org/10.1080/08098130409478097

Laing, J., & Mair, J. (2015). Music Festivals and Social Inclusion – The Festival Organizers' Perspective. *Leisure Sciences, 37*(3), 252–268. https://doi.org/10.1080/01490400.2014.991009

Lakatos, P., Gross, J., & Thut, G. (2019). A New Unifying Account of the Roles of Neuronal Entrainment. *Current Biology, 29*(18), R890–R905. https://doi.org/10.1016/j.cub.2019.07.075

Lake, J. I., & Goldstein, F. C. (2011). An Examination of an Enhancing Effect of Music on Attentional Abilities in Older Persons with Mild Cognitive Impairment. *Perceptual and Motor Skills, 112*(1), 267–278. https://doi.org/10.2466/04.10.15.pms.112.1.267-278

Lally, E. (2009). The power to heal us with a smile and a song: Senior Well-being, Music-based Participatory Arts and the Value of Qualitative Evidence. *Journal of Arts and Communities, 1*(1), 25–44. https://doi.org/10.1386/jaac.1.1.25_1

Lamb, S. J., & Gregory, A. H. (1993). The Relationship between Music and Reading in Beginning Readers. *Educational Psychology, 13*(1), 19–27. https://doi.org/10.1080/0144341930130103

Lamont, A. (2008). Young children's musical worlds. *Journal of Early Childhood Research, 6*(3), 247–261. https://doi.org/10.1177/1476718x08094449

Lamont, A. (2011a). University students' strong experiences of music. *Musicae Scientiae, 15*(2), 229–249. https://doi.org/10.1177/1029864911403368

Lamont, A. (2011b). The beat goes on: Music education, identity and lifelong learning. *Music Education Research, 13*(4), 369–388. https://doi.org/10.1080/14613808.2011.638505

Lamont, A. (2012). Emotion, engagement and meaning in strong experiences of music performance. *Psychology of Music, 40*(5), 574–594. https://doi.org/10.1177/0305735612448510

Lamont, A., Greasley, A., & Sloboda, J. (2016). Choosing to hear music: Motivation, process and effect. In S. Hallam, I. Cross, & M. Thaut (Eds), *The Oxford handbook of music psychology* (pp. 711–724). Oxford University Press.

Lamont, A., Murray, M., Hale, R., & Wright-Bevans, K. (2017). Singing in later life: The anatomy of a community choir. *Psychology of Music, 46*(3), 424–439. https://doi.org/10.1177/0305735617715514

Lamont, A., & Ranaweera, N. A. (2019). Knit One, Play One: Comparing the Effects of Amateur Knitting and Amateur Music Participation on Happiness and Wellbeing. *Applied Research in Quality of Life, 15*(5), 1353–1374. https://doi.org/10.1007/s11482-019-09734-z

Lamont, A., & Webb, R. (2009). Short- and long-term musical preferences: What makes a favourite piece of music? *Psychology of Music, 38*(2), 222–241. https://doi.org/10.1177/0305735609339471

Landis-Shack, N., Heinz, A. J., & Bonn-Miller, M. O. (2017). Music therapy for posttraumatic stress in adults: A theoretical review. *Psychomusicology: Music, Mind, and Brain, 27*(4), 334–342. https://doi.org/10.1037/pmu0000192

Langan, K. A., & Sachs, D. E. (2013). Opening Pandora's Stream: Piping Music into the Information Literacy Classroom. *Public Services Quarterly, 9*(2), 89–109. https://doi.org/10.1080/15228959.2013.785876

Langendörfer, F. (2008). Personality differences among orchestra instrumental groups: Just a stereotype? *Personality and Individual Differences, 44*(3), 610–620. https://doi.org/10.1016/j.paid.2007.09.027

Langston, T. (2011). It is a life support, isn't it? Social capital in a community choir. *International Journal of Community Music, 4*(2), 163–184. https://doi.org/10.1386/ijcm.4.2.163_1

Langston, T. W., & Barrett, M. S. (2008). Capitalizing on community music: A case study of the manifestation of social capital in a community choir. *Research Studies in Music Education, 30*(2), 118–138. https://doi.org/10.1177/1321103x08097503

Lappe, C., Herholz, S. C., Trainor, L. J., & Pantev, C. (2008). Cortical Plasticity Induced by Short-Term Unimodal and Multimodal Musical Training. *Journal of Neuroscience, 28*(39), 9632–9639. https://doi.org/10.1523/jneurosci.2254-08.2008

Lappe, C., Trainor, L. J., Herholz, S. C., & Pantev, C. (2011). Cortical Plasticity Induced by Short-Term Multimodal Musical Rhythm Training. *PLoS ONE, 6*(6), e21493. https://doi.org/10.1371/journal.pone.0021493

Large, E. W., Herrera, J. A., & Velasco, M. J. (2015). Neural Networks for Beat Perception in Musical Rhythm. *Frontiers in Systems Neuroscience, 9*. https://doi.org/10.3389/fnsys.2015.00159

Large, E. W., & Jones, M. R. (1999). The dynamics of attending: How people track time-varying events. *Psychological Review, 106*(1), 119–159. https://doi.org/10.1037/0033-295x.106.1.119

Larson, R. (1995). Secrets in the bedroom: Adolescents' private use of media. *Journal of Youth and Adolescence, 24*(5), 535–550. https://doi.org/10.1007/bf01537055

Larson, R., Kubey, R., & Colletti, J. (1989). Changing channels: Early adolescent media choices and shifting investments in family and friends. *Journal of Youth and Adolescence, 18*(6), 583–599. https://doi.org/10.1007/bf02139075

Larson, R. W., Wilson, S., & Rickman, A. (2009). *Globalization, Societal Change, and Adolescence Across the World*. John Wiley & Sons, Inc. https://doi.org/10.1002/9780470479193.adlpsy002018

Lashua, B. (2005). *Making music, remaking leisure in the Beat of Boyle St* [PhD Thesis]. University of Alberta.

Lashua, B. D., & Fox, K. (2007). Defining the Groove: From Remix to Research in The Beat of Boyle Street. *Leisure Sciences, 29*(2), 143–158. https://doi.org/10.1080/01490400601160796

Laukka, P. (2006). Uses of music and psychological well-being among the elderly. *Journal of Happiness Studies, 8*(2), 215–241. https://doi.org/10.1007/s10902-006-9024-3

Lawendowski, R., Bereznowski, P., Wróbel, W. K., Kierzkowski, M., & Atroszko, P. A. (2019). Study addiction among musicians: Measurement, and relationship with personality, social anxiety, performance, and psychosocial functioning. *Musicae Scientiae, 24*(4), 449–474. https://doi.org/10.1177/1029864918822138

Lawendowski, R., & Bieleninik, \textbackslashLucja. (2017). Identity and self-esteem in the context of music and music therapy: A review. *Health Psychology Report, 2*, 85–99. https://doi.org/10.5114/hpr.2017.64785

Lazarov, A., Pine, D. S., & Bar-Haim, Y. (2017). Gaze-Contingent Music Reward Therapy for Social Anxiety Disorder: A Randomized Controlled Trial. *American Journal of Psychiatry, 174*(7), 649–656. https://doi.org/10.1176/appi.ajp.2016.16080894

L.E., P., Larson, E. R., Lorber, W., McGinley, E. L., & Dillingham, T. R. (2018). Music-instruction intervention for treatment of post-traumatic stress disorder: A randomized pilot study. *BMC Psychology, 6*(1), 60 360.

Leamy, M., Bird, V., Boutillier, C. L., Williams, J., & Slade, M. (2011). Conceptual framework for personal recovery in mental health: Systematic review and narrative synthesis. *British Journal of Psychiatry, 199*(6), 445–452. https://doi.org/10.1192/bjp.bp.110.083733

LECKEY, J. (2011). The therapeutic effectiveness of creative activities on mental well-being: A systematic review of the literature. *Journal* of Psychiatric and Mental Health Nursing, 18(6), 501–509. https://doi.org/10.1111/j.1365-2850.2011.01693.x

Lederach, J. P. (2005). *The moral imagination: The art and soul of building peace.* Oxford University Press. https://doi.org/10.1093/0195174542.001.0001.

Lederach, J. P., & Lederach, A. J. (2010). *When blood and bones cry out: Journeys through the soundscape of healing and reconciliation.* St Lucia.

Lee, C.-Y., & Hung, T.-H. (2008). Identification of Mandarin tones by English-speaking musicians and nonmusicians. *The Journal of the Acoustical Society of America, 124*(5), 3235–3248. https://doi.org/10.1121/1.2990713

Lee, D. J., Chen, Y., & Schlaug, G. (2003). Corpus callosum: Musician and gender effects. *NeuroReport, 14*(2), 205–209. https://doi.org/10.1097/00001756-200302100-00009

Lee, H., & Noppeney, U. (2014). Music expertise shapes audiovisual temporal integration windows for speech, sinewave speech, and music. *Frontiers in Psychology, 5.* https://doi.org/10.3389/fpsyg.2014.00868

Lee, J., Krause, A. E., & Davidson, J. W. (2017). The PERMA well-being model and music facilitation practice: Preliminary documentation for well-being through music provision in Australian schools. *Research Studies in Music Education, 39*(1), 73–89. https://doi.org/10.1177/1321103x17703131

Lee, Jung, & Loui. (2019). Attention Modulates Electrophysiological Responses to Simultaneous Music and Language Syntax Processing. *Brain Sciences, 9*(11), 305. https://doi.org/10.3390/brainsci9110305

Lee, K. M., Skoe, E., Kraus, N., & Ashley, R. (2009a). Selective Subcortical Enhancement of Musical Intervals in Musicians. *Journal of Neuroscience, 29*(18), 5832–5840. https://doi.org/10.1523/jneurosci.6133-08.2009

Lee, K. M., Skoe, E., Kraus, N., & Ashley, R. (2009b). Selective Subcortical Enhancement of Musical Intervals in Musicians. *Journal of Neuroscience, 29*(18), 5832–5840. https://doi.org/10.1523/jneurosci.6133-08.2009

Lee, K. S., Jeong, H. C., Yim, J. E., & Jeon, M. Y. (2016). Effects of Music Therapy on the Cardiovascular and Autonomic Nervous System in Stress-Induced University Students: A Randomized Controlled Trial. *The Journal of Alternative and Complementary Medicine, 22*(1), 59–65. https://doi.org/10.1089/acm.2015.0079

Lee, L., & Lin, S.-C. (2015). The impact of music activities on foreign language, English learning for young children. *Journal of the European Teacher Education Network, 10,* 13–23.

Lee, R. (2010). Music education in prisons: A historical overview. *International Journal of Community Music, 3*(1), 7–18. https://doi.org/10.1386/ijcm.3.1.7/1

Lee, S. H. (2010). *The effects of group music therapy for emotional intelligence and sociability of the lower grades in lower-income groups* [PhD Thesis]. Chungnam.

Lee, S., O'Neill, D., & Moss, H. (2020). Promoting well-being among people with early-stage dementia and their family carers through community-based group singing: A phenomenological study. *Arts & Health*, *14*(1), 85–101. https://doi.org/10.1080/17533015.2020.1839776

Lee, Y., Lu, M., & Ko, H. (2007). Effects of skill training on working memory capacity. *Learning and Instruction*, *17*(3), 336–344. https://doi.org/10.1016/j.learninstruc.2007.02.010

Legette, R. M. (1994). *The effect of a selected use of music instruction on the self-concept and academic achievement to the musical problem solving abilities of high school students* [PhD Thesis]. Case Western Reserve University.

Lehmann, A. C. (1997). Research Note: Affective Responses to Everyday Life Events and Music Listening. *Psychology of Music*, *25*(1), 84–90. https://doi.org/10.1177/0305735697251007

Lehmberg, L. J., & Fung, V. C. (2010). Benefits of music participation for senior citizens: A review of the literature. *Music Education Research International*, *4*, 19–30.

Lehto, J. E., Juujärvi, P., Kooistra, L., & Pulkkinen, L. (2003). Dimensions of executive functioning: Evidence from children. *British Journal of Developmental Psychology*, *21*(1), 59–80. https://doi.org/10.1348/026151003321164627

Leigh, J., Dettman, S., Dowell, R., & Briggs, R. (2013). Communication Development in Children Who Receive a Cochlear Implant by 12 Months of Age. *Otology & Neurotology*, *34*(3), 443–450. https://doi.org/10.1097/mao.0b013e3182814d2c

Leipold, B., & Loepthien, T. (2015). Music reception and emotional regulation in adolescence and adulthood. *Musicae Scientiae*, *19*(1), 111–128. https://doi.org/10.1177/1029864915570354

Lejeune, F., Lordier, L., Pittet, M. P., Schoenhals, L., Grandjean, D., Hüppi, P. S., Filippa, M., & Tolsa, C. B. (2019). Effects of an Early Postnatal Music Intervention on Cognitive and Emotional Development in Preterm Children at 12 and 24 Months: Preliminary Findings. *Frontiers in Psychology*, *10*. https://doi.org/10.3389/fpsyg.2019.00494

Lem, A. (2015). The evaluation of musical engagement in dementia: Implications for self-reported quality of life. *Australian Journal of Music Therapy*, *26*, 30–51.

Lemaire, E. C. (2020). Extraordinary times call for extraordinary measures: The use of music to communicate public health recommendations against the spread of COVID-19. *Canadian Journal of Public Health*, *111*(4), 477–479. https://doi.org/10.17269/s41997-020-00379-2

Lemaire, E. C., Loignon, C., & Bertrand, K. (2020). A critical scoping review about the impact of music in the lives of young adults who use drugs. *Drug and Alcohol Review*, *40*(1), 135–154. https://doi.org/10.1111/dar.13136

Lenette, C., & Sunderland, N. (2014). "Will there be music for us?" Mapping the health and well-being potential of participatory music practice with asylum seekers and refugees across contexts of conflict and refuge. *Arts & Health*, *8*(1), 32–49. https://doi.org/10.1080/17533015.2014.961943

Lenette, C., Weston, D., Wise, P., Sunderland, N., & Bristed, H. (2015a). Where words fail, music speaks: The impact of participatory music on the mental health and wellbeing of asylum. *Arts & Health*, *8*(2), 125–139. https://doi.org/10.1080/17533015.2015.1037317

Lenette, C., Weston, D., Wise, P., Sunderland, N., & Bristed, H. (2015b). Where words fail, music speaks: The impact of participatory music on the mental health and wellbeing of asylum seekers. *Arts & Health*, *8*(2), 125–139. https://doi.org/10.1080/17533015.2015.1037317

Lense, M. D., Beck, S., Liu, C., Pfeiffer, R., Diaz, N., Lynch, M., Goodman, N., Summers, A., & Fisher, M. H. (2020). Parents, Peers, and Musical Play: Integrated Parent-Child Music Class Program Supports Community Participation and Well-Being for Families of Children With and Without Autism Spectrum Disorder. *Frontiers in Psychology*, *11*. https://doi.org/10.3389/fpsyg.2020.555717

Lepistö, T., Kujala, T., Vanhala, R., Alku, P., Huotilainen, M., & Näätänen, R. (2005). The discrimination of and orienting to speech and non-speech sounds in children with autism. *Brain Research*, *1066*(1–2), 147–157. https://doi.org/10.1016/j.brainres.2005.10.052

Leubner, D., & Hinterberger, T. (2017). Reviewing the Effectiveness of Music Interventions in Treating Depression. *Frontiers in Psychology*, *8*. https://doi.org/10.3389/fpsyg.2017.01109

Leung, M. C., & Cheung, R. Y. M. (2020). Music engagement and well-being in Chinese adolescents: Emotional awareness, positive emotions, and negative emotions as mediating processes. *Psychology of Music*, *48*(1), 105–119, https://doi.org/10.1177/03057356

Levinson, D. J. (1986). A conception of adult development. *American Psychologist*, *41*(1), 3–13. https://doi.org/10.1037/0003-066x.41.1.3

Levinson, D. J., Darrow, C. N., Klein, E. B., Levinson, M. H., & McKee, B. (1978). *The Seasons of a Man's Life*. Alfred A. Knopf.

Levitin, D. J., & Rogers, S. E. (2005). Absolute pitch: Perception, coding, and controversies. *Trends in Cognitive Sciences*, *9*(1), 26–33. https://doi.org/10.1016/j.tics.2004.11.007

Lewis, C., & Lovatt, P. J. (2013). Breaking away from set patterns of thinking: Improvisation and divergent thinking. *Thinking Skills and Creativity*, *9*, 46–58. https://doi.org/10.1016/j.tsc.2013.03.001

Lewis, K., Demie, F., & Rogers, L. (2011). *In Harmony Lambeth: An Evaluation*. Lambeth Children and Young People's Service with the Institute of Education, University of London.

Lewis, K., Gonzalez, M., & Kaufman, J. (2011). Social selection and peer influence in an online social network. *Proceedings of the National Academy of Sciences*, *109*(1), 68–72. https://doi.org/10.1073/pnas.1109739109

Lezak, M. D. (Ed.). (2004). *Neuropsychological assessment*. Oxford University Press.

Li, H.-C., Wang, H.-H., Chou, F.-H., & Chen, K.-M. (2015). The Effect of Music Therapy on Cognitive Functioning Among Older Adults: A Systematic Review and Meta-Analysis. *Journal of the American Medical Directors Association*, *16*(1), 71–77. https://doi.org/10.1016/j.jamda.2014.10.004

Li, J., Li, X., Liu, H., Li, J., Han, Q., Wang, C., Zeng, X., Li, Y., Ji, W., Zhang, R., & Bao, J. (2021). Effects of music stimulus on behavior response, cortisol level, and horizontal immunity of growing pigs. *Journal of Animal Science*, *99*(5). https://doi.org/10.1093/jas/skab043

Li, S., Han, Y., Wang, D., Yang, H., Fan, Y., Lv, Y., Tang, H., Gong, Q., Zang, Y., & He, Y. (2009). Mapping Surface Variability of the Central Sulcus in Musicians. *Cerebral Cortex*, *20*(1), 25–33. https://doi.org/10.1093/cercor/bhp074

Liapis, Z., Giddens, Z., & Uhlenbrock, M. (2008). *Effects of lyrical music on reading comprehension*. Hanover College.

Lichman, S. (2006). *Perception and Experience: The Application of Folklore to Coexistence Education in Israeli and Palestinian School-Communities*. Queen's University Belfast.

Lichman, S., & Sullivan, K. (2000). Harnessing folklore and traditional creativity to promote better understanding between Jewish and Arab children in Israel. In M. Leicester, S. Modgil, & C. Modgil (Eds), *Education, Culture and Values* (Vol. 6, pp. 66–77). The Falmer Press.

Lieberman, M. D. (2007). Social Cognitive Neuroscience: A Review of Core Processes. *Annual Review of Psychology*, *58*(1), 259–289. https://doi.org/10.1146/annurev.psych.58.110405.085654

Liebowitz, M., Tucker, M. S., Frontz, M., & Mulholland, S. (2015a). Participatory choral music as a means of engagement in a veterans' mental health and addiction treatment setting. *Arts & Health*, *7*(2), 137–150. https://doi.org/10.1080/17533015.2014.999246

Liebowitz, M., Tucker, M. S., Frontz, M., & Mulholland, S. (2015b). Participatory choral music as a means of engagement in a veterans' mental health and addiction treatment setting. *Arts & Health*, *7*(2), 137–150. https://doi.org/10.1080/17533015.2014.999246

Lillemyr, O. F. (1983). Achievement motivation as a factor in self-perception. In *Norwegian Research Council for Science and the Humanities* (p. 274 245–248).

Lim, T., Lee, S., & Ke, F. (2017). Integrating Music into Math in a Virtual Reality Game. *International Journal of Game-Based Learning, 7*(1), 57–73. https://doi.org/10.4018/ijgbl.2017010104

Lima, C. F., & Castro, S. L. (2011). Speaking to the trained ear: Musical expertise enhances the recognition of emotions in speech prosody. *Emotion, 11*(5), 1021–1031. https://doi.org/10.1037/a0024521

Limb, C. J., & Braun, A. R. (2008). Neural Substrates of Spontaneous Musical Performance: An fMRI Study of Jazz Improvisation. *PLoS ONE, 3*(2), e1679. https://doi.org/10.1371/journal.pone.0001679

Lin, S.-T., Yang, P., Lai, C.-Y., Su, Y.-Y., Yeh, Y.-C., Huang, M.-F., & Chen, C.-C. (2011). Mental Health Implications of Music: Insight from Neuroscientific and Clinical Studies. *Harvard Review of Psychiatry, 19*(1), 34–46. https://doi.org/10.3109/10673229.2011.549769

Linch, S. A. (1994). Differences in Academic Achievement and Level of Self-Esteem among High School Participants in Instrumental Music, Non-Participants, and Students Who Discontinue Instrumental Music Education. *Doctoral Dissertation. Dissertation[MP276] Abstracts International, 54*(9), 3362.

Lincoln, S. (2005). Feeling the Noise: Teenagers, Bedrooms and Music. *Leisure Studies, 24*(4), 399–414. https://doi.org/10.1080/02614360500199544

Lindblad, K., & Boise, S. de. (2019). Musical engagement and subjective wellbeing amongst men in the third age. *Nordic Journal of Music Therapy, 29*(1), 20–38. https://doi.org/10.1080/08098131.2019.1646791

Lindenfelser, K. J., Hense, C., & McFerran, K. (2011). Music Therapy in Pediatric Palliative Care. *American Journal of Hospice and Palliative Medicine®, 29*(3), 219–226. https://doi.org/10.1177/1049909111429327

Linnakyla, P., & Malin, A. (1997). Oppilaidenprofiloituminenkouluviihtyvyyde narvuiubbussa(Student profiles in the light of school engagement. *Kasvatus, 28*(2), 583–602.

Linnavalli, T., Putkinen, V., Lipsanen, J., Huotilainen, M., & Tervaniemi, M. (2018). Music playschool enhances children's linguistic skills. *Scientific Reports, 8*(1). https://doi.org/10.1038/s41598-018-27126-5

Linnemann, A., Kappert, M. B., Fischer, S., Doerr, J. M., Strahler, J., & Nater, U. M. (2015). The effects of music listening on pain and stress in the daily life of patients with fibromyalgia syndrome. *Frontiers in Human Neuroscience, 9*. https://doi.org/10.3389/fnhum.2015.00434

Linnemann, A., Strahler, J., & Nater, U. M. (2016). The stress-reducing effect of music listening varies depending on the social context. *Psychoneuroendocrinology, 72*, 97–105. https://doi.org/10.1016/j.psyneuen.2016.06.003

Linnemann, A., Wenzel, M., Grammes, J., Kubiak, T., & Nater, U. M. (2017). Music Listening and Stress in Daily Life—A Matter of Timing. *International*

Journal of Behavioral Medicine, 25(2), 223–230. https://doi.org/10.1007/s12529-017-9697-5

Lipscomb, S. D., Lundell, D., Sevett, C., & Scripp, L. (2008). Rhythm and reading: Improvement of reading fluency using a rhythm based pedagogical technique. *Presentation at the 10th International Conference on Music Perception and Cognition.*

Lischetzke, T., & Eid, M. (2003). Is Attention to Feelings Beneficial or Detrimental to Affective Well-Being? Mood Regulation as a Moderator Variable. *Emotion, 3*(4), 361–377. https://doi.org/10.1037/1528-3542.3.4.361

Lith, T. V., Schofield, M. J., & Fenner, P. (2012). Identifying the evidence-base for art-based practices and their potential benefit for mental health recovery: A critical review. *Disability and Rehabilitation, 35*(16), 1309–1323. https://doi.org/10.3109/09638288.2012.732188

Littell, W. J. (1961). *A survey of the uses of music in correctional institutions in the United States* [PhD Thesis]. University of Kansas.

Liu, B., Huang, Y., Wang, Z., & Wu, G. (2012). The influence of background music on recognition processes of Chinese characters: An ERP study. *Neuroscience Letters, 518*(2), 80–85. https://doi.org/10.1016/j.neulet.2012.04.055

Liu, S., Chow, H. M., Xu, Y., Erkkinen, M. G., Swett, K. E., Eagle, M. W., Rizik-Baer, D. A., & Braun, A. R. (2012). Neural Correlates of Lyrical Improvisation: An fMRI Study of Freestyle Rap. *Scientific Reports, 2*(1). https://doi.org/10.1038/srep00834

Livesey, L., Morrison, I., Clift, S., & Camic, P. (2012). Benefits of choral singing for social and mental wellbeing: Qualitative findings from a cross-national survey of choir members. *Journal of Public Mental Health, 11*(1), 10–26, https://doi.org/10.1108/17465721211201275.

Lloyd, B. T., & Mendez, J. L. (2001). Batswana 1 Adolescents' Interpretation of American Music Videos: So that's What that Means! *Journal of Black Psychology, 27*(4), 464–476. https://doi.org/10.1177/0095798401027004005

Loehr, J. D., Kourtis, D., Vesper, C., Sebanz, N., & Knoblich, G. (2013). Monitoring Individual and Joint Action Outcomes in Duet Music Performance. *Journal of Cognitive Neuroscience, 25*(7), 1049–1061. https://doi.org/10.1162/jocn_a_00388

Loehr, J. D., & Palmer, C. (2011). Temporal Coordination between Performing Musicians. *Quarterly Journal of Experimental Psychology, 64*(11), 2153–2167. https://doi.org/10.1080/17470218.2011.603427

Loewy, J. (2014). First sounds: NICU Rhythm, breath and lullaby research and practice. *Neurosciences and Music V: Cognitive Stimulation and Rehabilitation Conference.*

Logue, S. F., & Gould, T. J. (2014). The neural and genetic basis of executive function: Attention, cognitive flexibility, and response inhibition.

Pharmacology Biochemistry and Behavior, 123, 45–54. https://doi.org/10.1016/j.pbb.2013.08.007

Lolli, S. L., Lewenstein, A. D., Basurto, J., Winnik, S., & Loui, P. (2015). Sound frequency affects speech emotion perception. *Front.*

Lomen, D. O. (1970). Changes in Self-Concept Factors: A Comparison of Fifth-Grade Instrumental Music Participants and Nonparticipants in Target and Nontarget Schools in Des Moines, Iowa. *Doctoral Dissertation.* [MP281] *Dissertation Abstracts International, 31,* 3962.

Long, M. (2014). `I can read further and there's more meaning while I read': An exploratory study investigating the impact of a rhythm-based music intervention on children's reading. *Research Studies in Music Education*, 36(1), 107–124. https://doi.org/10.1177/1321103x14528453

Long, M., & Hallam, S. (2012). Rhythm for reading: A rhythm-based approach to reading intervention. [MP282]*Proceedings of Music Paedeia, 30th ISME World Conference on Music Education, MP283]*(pp, 221–232.

Longhi, E., & Pickett, N. (2007). Music and well-being in long-term hospitalized children. *Psychology of Music*, 36(2), 247–256. https://doi.org/10.1177/0305735607082622

Longhi, E., Pickett, N., & Hargreaves, D. J. (2013). Wellbeing and hospitalized children: Can music help? *Psychology of Music*, 43(2), 188–196. https://doi.org/10.1177/0305735613499781

Lonie, D. (2011). *Attuned to Engagement: The Effects of a Music Mentoring Programme on the Agency and Musical Ability of Children and Young People.* Youth Music.

López, G. L., & Berríos, E. R. (2007). *Impacto de las orquestas en la formación de escolares chilenos.* Fundación de Orquestas Juveniles e Infantiles de Chile Universidad de Chile.

Lopez, M. E. (2008). Music Therapy: Healing, Growth, Creating a Culture of Peace. In O. Urbain (Ed.), *Music and Conflict Transformation: Harmonies and Dissonances in Geopolitics* (pp. 147–171). I.B.

Lord, P., Sharp, C., Dawson, A., Mehta, P., White, R., & Jeffes, J. (2013). *Evaluation of In Harmony: Year 1 Interim Report.* National Foundation for Educational Research.

Lord, V. M., Cave, P., Hume, V. J., Flude, E. J., Evans, A., Kelly, J. L., Polkey, M. I., & Hopkinson, N. S. (2010). Singing teaching as a therapy for chronic respiratory disease—A randomised controlled trial and qualitative evaluation. *BMC Pulmonary Medicine*, 10(1). https://doi.org/10.1186/1471-2466-10-41

Loth, H. (2016). Music therapy with people who have eating disorders. In J. Edwards (Ed.), *The Oxford handbook of music therapy* (p. 285). Oxford University Press.

Lotter, C. B. (2003). *Circles of Courage: Music therapy with adolescents in conflict with the law at a community-based setting* [PhD Thesis]. University of Pretoria.

Loui, P., & Guetta, R. (2019). Music and attention, executive function, and creativity. In M. H. Thaut & D. A. Hodges (Eds), *The Oxford Handbook of Music and Neuroscience*. Oxford University Press. https://doi.org/0.1093/oxfordhb/9780198804123.013.12

Loui, P., Kroog, K., Zuk, J., Winner, E., & Schlaug, G. (2011). Relating Pitch Awareness to Phonemic Awareness in Children: Implications for Tone-Deafness and Dyslexia. *Frontiers in Psychology*, 2. https://doi.org/10.3389/fpsyg.2011.00111

Loui, P., Li, H. C., Hohmann, A., & Schlaug, G. (2011). Enhanced Cortical Connectivity in Absolute Pitch Musicians: A Model for Local Hyperconnectivity. *Journal of Cognitive Neuroscience*, 23(4), 1015–1026. https://doi.org/10.1162/jocn.2010.21500

Loui, P., Raine, L. B., Chaddock-Heyman, L., Kramer, A. F., & Hillman, C. H. (2019). Musical Instrument Practice Predicts White Matter Microstructure and Cognitive Abilities in Childhood. *Frontiers in Psychology*, 10. https://doi.org/10.3389/fpsyg.2019.01198

Loui, P., Wu, E. H., Wessel, D. L., & Knight, R. T. (2009). A Generalized Mechanism for Perception of Pitch Patterns. *Journal of Neuroscience*, 29(2), 454–459. https://doi.org/10.1523/jneurosci.4503-08.2009

Loui, P., Zamm, A., & Schlaug, G. (2012). Enhanced functional networks in absolute pitch. *NeuroImage*, 63(2), 632–640. https://doi.org/10.1016/j.neuroimage.2012.07.030

Lozon, J., & Bensimon, M. (2014). Music misuse: A review of the personal and collective roles of "problem music". *Aggression and Violent Behavior*, 19(3), 207–218. https://doi.org/10.1016/j.avb.2014.04.003

Lu, D. T. (1986). *The effects of teaching music skills on the development of reading skills among first graders: An experimental study* [Doctoral dissertation.]. University Washington.

Luders, E., Gaser, C., Jancke, L., & Schlaug, G. (2004). A voxel-based approach to gray matter asymmetries. *NeuroImage*, 22(2), 656–664. https://doi.org/10.1016/j.neuroimage.2004.01.032

Ludke, K. M., Ferreira, F., & Overy, K. (2013). Singing can facilitate foreign language learning. *Memory & Cognition*, 42(1), 41–52. https://doi.org/10.3758/s13421-013-0342-5

Lukács, B., & Honbolygó, F. (2019). Task-Dependent Mechanisms in the Perception of Music and Speech: Domain-Specific Transfer Effects of Elementary School Music Education. *Journal of Research in Music Education*, 67(2), 153–170. https://doi.org/10.1177/0022429419836422

Lull, J. (1987). *Listeners' communicative properties of music* (J. Lull, Ed.). Sage Publications.

Lund, H. N., Pedersen, I. N., Johnsen, S. P., Heymann-Szlachcinska, A. M., Tuszewska, M., Bizik, G., Larsen, J. I., Kulhay, E., Larsen, A., Grønbech, B., Østermark, H., Borup, H., Valentin, J. B., & Mainz, J. (2020). Music to improve sleep quality in adults with depression-related insomnia (MUSTAFI): Study protocol for a randomized controlled trial. *Trials, 21*(1). https://doi.org/10.1186/s13063-020-04247-9

Lundqvist, L.-O., Carlsson, F., Hilmersson, P., & Juslin, P. N. (2008). Emotional responses to music: Experience, expression, and physiology. *Psychology of Music, 37*(1), 61–90. https://doi.org/10.1177/0305735607086048

Lundström, C. (2009). 'People take for granted that you know how to dance Salsa and Merengue': Transnational diasporas, visual discourses and racialized knowledge in Sweden's contemporary Latin music boom. *Social Identities, 15*(5), 707–723. https://doi.org/10.1080/13504630903205340

M., B., D., S., S., M., A., S., & C, M. (2007). Influence of musical expertise and musical training on pitch processing in music and language. *Restorative Neurology and Neurosciences, 25*, 399–410.

Mabel, L. Q. H., Drury, V. B., & Hong, P. W. (2010). The experience and expectations of terminally ill patients receiving music therapy in the palliative setting: A systematic review. *JBI Library of Systematic Reviews, 8*(27), 1088–1111. https://doi.org/10.11124/jbisrir-2010-155

MacAulay, R. K., Edelman, P., Boeve, A., Sprangers, N., & Halpin, A. (2019). Group music training as a multimodal cognitive intervention for older adults. *Psychomusicology: Music, Mind, and Brain, 29*(4), 180–187. https://doi.org/10.1037/pmu0000239

MacDonald, R. A. R., Hargreaves, D. J., & Miell, D. (2009). Musical identities. In S. Hallam, I. Cross, & M. Thaut (Eds), *Oxford Handbook of Music Psychology* (pp. 462–470). Oxford University Press.

MacDonald, R. A. R., & Miell, D. J. (2002). Music for individuals with special needs: A catalyst for developments in identity, communication, and musical ability. In R. A. R. MacDonald, D. J. Hargreaves, & D. Miell (Eds), *Musical Identities* (pp. 163–178). Oxford University Press.

MacDonald, R., Burke, R., Nora, T. D., Donohue, M. S., & Birrell, R. (2021). Our Virtual Tribe: Sustaining and Enhancing Community via Online Music Improvisation. *Frontiers in Psychology, 11.* https://doi.org/10.3389/fpsyg.2020.623640

MacDonald, R., Hargreaves, D. J., & Miell, D. (Eds). (2017). *Handbook of Musical Identities*. Oxford University Press. https://doi.org/10.1093/acprof:oso/9780199679485.001.0001

MacDonald, R., Kreutz, G., & Mitchell, L. (Eds). (2012). *Music, Health, and Wellbeing.* Oxford University Press. https://doi.org/10.1093/acprof:oso/9780199586974.001.0001

MacGlone, U. M., Vamvakaris, J., Wilson, G. B., & MacDonald, R. A. R. (2020). Understanding the Wellbeing Effects of a Community Music Program for People With Disabilities: A Mixed Methods, Person-Centered Study. *Frontiers in Psychology, 11.* https://doi.org/10.3389/fpsyg.2020.588734

MacIntyre, P. D., & Potter, G. K. (2013). Music motivation and the effect of writing music: A comparison of pianists and guitarists. *Psychology of Music, 42*(3), 403–419. https://doi.org/10.1177/0305735613477180

Mackenzie, J., & Hamlett, K. (2005). The Music Together Programme: Addressing the needs of well families with young children. *Australian Journal of Music Therapy, 16,* 43–59.

MacLellan, C. R. (2011). Differences in Myers-Briggs Personality Types Among High School Band, Orchestra, and Choir Members. *Journal of Research in Music Education, 59*(1), 85–100. https://doi.org/10.1177/0022429410395579

MacLeod, A., Skinner, M. W., Wilkinson, F., & Reid, H. (2016). Connecting Socially Isolated Older Rural Adults with Older Volunteers through Expressive Arts. *Canadian Journal on Aging / La Revue Canadienne Du Vieillissement, 35*(1), 14–27. https://doi.org/10.1017/s071498081500063x

MacRitchie, J., Breaden, M., Milne, A. J., & McIntyre, S. (2020). Cognitive, Motor and Social Factors of Music Instrument Training Programs for Older Adults' Improved Wellbeing. *Frontiers in Psychology, 10,* 2868, https://doi.org/10.3389/fpsyg.2019.

MacRitchie, J., & Garrido, S. (2019). Ageing and the orchestra: Self-efficacy and engagement in community music-making. *Psychology of Music, 47*(6), 902–916. https://doi.org/10.1177/0305735619854531

Madsen, C. K. (1987). Background music: Competition for focus of attention. In C. K. Madsen & C. A. Prickett (Eds), *Applications of research in music behaviour* (p. 288). The University of Alabama Press.

Magee, W. L., Clark, I., Tamplin, J., & Bradt, J. (2017). Music interventions for acquired brain injury. *Cochrane Database of Systematic Reviews, 2017*(1). https://doi.org/10.1002/14651858.cd006787.pub3

Magne, C., Schön, D., & Besson, M. (2006). Musician Children Detect Pitch Violations in Both Music and Language Better than Nonmusician Children: Behavioral and Electrophysiological Approaches. *Journal of Cognitive Neuroscience, 18*(2), 199–211. https://doi.org/10.1162/jocn.2006.18.2.199

Magowan, F. (2019). Resonance, Resilience and Empathy in Music Production with Asylum Seekers in Australia. *Music and Arts in Action, 7*(1).

Maguire, L. E., Wanschura, P. B., Battaglia, M. M., Howell, S. N., & Flinn, J. M. (2015). Participation in Active Singing Leads to Cognitive Improvements in

Individuals with Dementia. *Journal of the American Geriatrics Society, 63*(4), 815–816. https://doi.org/10.1111/jgs.13366

Mahdhaoui, A., Chetouani, M., Cassel, R. S., & Cohen, D. (2011). *Computerized home video detection for motherese may help to study impaired interaction between infants who become autistic and their parents.*[MP291. https://doi.org/10.1002/mpr.332.

Mahdhaoui, A., Chetouani, M., Zong, C., Cassel, R. S., Saint-Georges, C., Laznik, M.-C., Maestro, S., Apicella, F., Muratori, F., & Cohen, D. (2009). Automatic Motherese Detection for Face-to-Face Interaction Analysis. In *Multimodal Signals: Cognitive and Algorithmic Issues* (pp. 248–255). Springer Berlin Heidelberg. https://doi.org/10.1007/978-3-642-00525-1_25

Mahns, W. (2002). The psychodynamic function of music in analytical music therapy with children. In T. J. Eschen (Ed.), *Analytical Music Therapy* (p. 292). Jessica Kingsley Publishers.

Mainka, S., Spintge, R., & Thaut, M. (2016). Music therapy in medical and neurological rehabilitation settings. In S. Hallam, I. Cross, & M. Thaut (Eds), *Oxford Handbook of Music Psychology* (pp. 857–873). Oxford University Press.

Majno, M. (2012). From the model of El Sistema in Venezuela to current applications: Learning and integration through collective music education. *Annals of the New York Academy of Sciences, 1252*(1), 56–64. https://doi.org/10.1111/j.1749-6632.2012.06498.x

Mak, H. W., Fluharty, M., & Fancourt, D. (2021). Predictors and Impact of Arts Engagement During the COVID-19 Pandemic: Analyses of Data From 19,384 Adults in the COVID-19 Social Study. *Frontiers in Psychology, 12*. https://doi.org/10.3389/fpsyg.2021.626263

Mallick, K. A. D., N., K., A.K., M., A.P.K., P., N., & Mohanty, G. P. (2020). Music helps in inducing more milk yield. *International Journal of Current Science and Multidisciplinary Research, 3*(7), 293.

Malloch, S., Shoemark, H., Črnčec, R., Newnham, C., Paul, C., Prior, M., Coward, S., & Burnham, D. (2012). Music therapy with hospitalized infants-the art and science of communicative musicality. *Infant Mental Health Journal, 33*(4), 386–399. https://doi.org/10.1002/imhj.21346

Malloch, S., & Trevarthen, C. (2009). Musicality: Communicating the Vitality and Interests of life. In S. Malloch & C. Trevarthen (Eds), *Communicative Musicality: Exploring the basis of human companionship* (Vol. 1, pp. 1–10). Oxford University Press.

Malone, A. B. (1996). The Effects of Live Music on the Distress of Pediatric Patients Receiving Intravenous Starts, Venipunctures, Injections, and Heel Sticks. *Journal of Music Therapy, 33*(1), 19–33. https://doi.org/10.1093/jmt/33.1.19

Maloy, M., & Peterson, R. (2014). A meta-analysis of the effectiveness of music interventions for children and adolescents with attention-deficit/

hyperactivity disorder. *Psychomusicology: Music, Mind, and Brain*, 24(4), 328–339. https://doi.org/10.1037/pmu0000083

Mammarella, N., Fairfield, B., & Cornoldi, C. (2007). Does music enhance cognitive performance in healthy older adults? The Vivaldi effect. *Aging Clinical and Experimental Research*, 19(5), 394–399. https://doi.org/10.1007/bf03324720

Mampe, B., Friederici, A. D., Christophe, A., & Wermke, K. (2009). Newborns' Cry Melody Is Shaped by Their Native Language. *Current Biology*, 19(23), 1994–1997. https://doi.org/10.1016/j.cub.2009.09.064

Mani, C. (2020). Livelihoods as a kaleidoscope of distributed lifeworlds: Towards a nuanced understanding of music-making and identity in migrants in South-East Queensland. *Music Education Research*, 22(5), 581–595. https://doi.org/10.1080/14613808.2020.1840536

Mansens, D., Deeg, D. J. H., & Comijs, H. C. (2017). The association between singing and/or playing a musical instrument and cognitive functions in older adults. *Aging & Mental Health*, 22(8), 970–977. https://doi.org/10.1080/13607863.2017.1328481

Mansky, R., Marzel, A., Orav, E. J., Chocano-Bedoya, P. O., Grünheid, P., Mattle, M., Freystätter, G., Stähelin, H. B., Egli, A., & Bischoff-Ferrari, H. A. (2020). Playing a musical instrument is associated with slower cognitive decline in community-dwelling older adults. *Aging Clinical and Experimental Research*, 32(8), 1577–1584. https://doi.org/10.1007/s40520-020-01472-9

Marchant-Haycox, S. E., & Wilson, G. D. (1992). Personality and stress in performing artists. *Personality and Individual Differences*, 13(10), 1061–1068. https://doi.org/10.1016/0191-8869(92)90021-g

Margulis, E. H., Mlsna, L. M., Uppunda, A. K., Parrish, T. B., & Wong, P. C. M. (2009). Selective neurophysiologic responses to music in instrumentalists with different listening biographies. *Human Brain Mapping*, 30(1), 267–275. https://doi.org/10.1002/hbm.20503

Marie, C., Delogu, F., Lampis, G., Belardinelli, M. O., & Besson, M. (2011). Influence of Musical Expertise on Segmental and Tonal Processing in Mandarin Chinese. *Journal of Cognitive Neuroscience*, 23(10), 2701–2715. https://doi.org/10.1162/jocn.2010.21585

Marie, C., Magne, C., & Besson, M. (2011). Musicians and the Metric Structure of Words. *Journal of Cognitive Neuroscience*, 23(2), 294–305. https://doi.org/10.1162/jocn.2010.21413

Marques, C., Moreno, S., Castro, S. L., & Besson, M. (2007). Musicians Detect Pitch Violation in a Foreign Language Better Than Nonmusicians: Behavioral and Electrophysiological Evidence. *Journal of Cognitive Neuroscience*, 19(9), 1453–1463. https://doi.org/10.1162/jocn.2007.19.9.1453

Marrades-Caballero, E., Santonja-Medina, C. S., Sanz-Mengibar, J. M., & Santonja-Medina, F. (2019). Neurologic music therapy in upper-limb rehabilitation in children with severe bilateral cerebral palsy: A randomized controlled trial. *European Journal of Physical and Rehabilitation Medicine, 54*(6). https://doi.org/10.23736/s1973-9087.18.04996-1

Marsh, K. (2012a). "The beat will make you be courage": The role of a secondary school music program in supporting young refugees and newly arrived immigrants in Australia. *Research Studies in Music Education, 34*(2), 93–111. https://doi.org/10.1177/1321103x12466138

Marsh, K. (2012b). *Music in the Lives of Refugee and Newly Arrived Immigrant Children in Sydney, Australia*. Oxford University Press. https://doi.org/10.1093/oxfordhb/9780199737635.013.0030

Marsh, K. (2012c). *Music in the Lives of Refugee and Newly Arrived Immigrant Children in Sydney, Australia*. Oxford University Press. https://doi.org/10.1093/oxfordhb/9780199737635.013.0030

Marsh, K. (2015). Music, social justice, and social inclusion: The role of collaborative music activities in supporting young refugees and newly arrived immigrants in Australia. In C. Benedict, P. Schmidt, G. Spruce, & P. Woodford (Eds), *The Oxford handbook of social justice in music education* (pp. 173–189). Oxford University Press.

Marsh, K. (2016). Creating bridges: Music, play and well-being in the lives of refugee and immigrant children and young people. *Music Education Research, 19*(1), 60–73. https://doi.org/10.1080/14613808.2016.1189525

Marsh, K., & Dieckmann, S. (2016). Interculturality in the playground and playgroup: Music as shared space for young immigrant children and their mothers. In P. Burnard, E. Mackinlay, & K. Powell (Eds), *The Routledge International Handbook of Intercultural Arts Research* (pp. 358–368). Routledge.

Marsh, K., & Dieckmann, S. (2017). Contributions of playground singing games to the social inclusion of refugee and newly arrived immigrant children in Australia. *Education 3–13, 45*(6), 710–719. https://doi.org/10.1080/03004279.2017.1347128

Marshall, A. T. (1978). An analysis of music curricula and its relationship to the self image of urban black middle school age children. *Doctoral Dissertation.* [MP295]*Dissertation Abstracts International, A, 38,* 6594–6595.

Martel, S. P. B. (2020). Cultural Production, Music and the Politics of Legitimacy: The Case of the FARC in Colombia. *Civil Wars, 23*(1), 104–126. https://doi.org/10.1080/13698249.2021.1846351

Martens, M. A., Jungers, M. K., & Steele, A. L. (2011). Effect of musical experience on verbal memory in Williams syndrome: Evidence from a novel word learning task. *Neuropsychologia, 49*(11), 3093–3102. https://doi.org/10.1016/j.neuropsychologia.2011.07.016

Martens, M. A., Wilson, S. J., & Reutens, D. C. (2008). Research Review: Williams syndrome: A critical review of the cognitive, behavioral, and neuroanatomical phenotype. *Journal of Child Psychology and Psychiatry, 49*(6), 576–608. https://doi.org/10.1111/j.1469-7610.2008.01887.x

Martens, S., Wierda, S. M., Dun, M., Vries, M. de, & Smid, H. G. O. M. (2015). Musical Minds: Attentional Blink Reveals Modality-Specific Restrictions. *PLOS ONE, 10*(2), e0118294. https://doi.org/10.1371/journal.pone.0118294

MARTIN, G., CLARKE, M., & PEARCE, C. (1993). Adolescent Suicide: Music Preference as an Indicator of Vulnerability. *Journal of the American Academy of Child & Adolescent Psychiatry, 32*(3), 530–535. https://doi.org/10.1097/00004583-199305000-00007

Martin, L., Oepen, R., Bauer, K., Nottensteiner, A., Mergheim, K., & Gruber, H. (2018). Creative arts interventions for stress management and prevention–A systematic review. *Behaviour Science (Basel, 8*(2), 28 296.

Martin, L., & Segrave, K. (1988). *Anti-Rock: The opposition to Rock 'n' Roll.* Archon.

Martin, R. C., Wogalter, M. S., & Forlano, J. G. (1988). Reading comprehension in the presence of unattended speech and music. *Journal of Memory and Language, 27*(4), 382–398. https://doi.org/10.1016/0749-596x(88)90063-0

Martindale, C., & Dailey, A. (1996). Creativity, primary process cognition and personality. *Personality and Individual Differences, 20*(4), 409–414. https://doi.org/10.1016/0191-8869(95)00202-2

Martinez, J. (2008). Effects of singing classes on pulmonary function and quality of life of COPD patients. *International Journal of Chronic Obstructive Pulmonary Disease*, 1. https://doi.org/10.2147/copd.s4077

Martínez-Castilla, P., Gutiérrez-Blasco, I. M., Spitz, D. H., & Granot, R. (2021). The Efficacy of Music for Emotional Wellbeing During the COVID-19 Lockdown in Spain: An Analysis of Personal and Context-Related Variables. *Frontiers in Psychology, 12*. https://doi.org/10.3389/fpsyg.2021.647837

Martínez-Montes, E., Hernández-Pérez, H., Chobert, J., Morgado-Rodríguez, L., Suárez-Murias, C., Valdés-Sosa, P. A., & Besson, M. (2013). Musical expertise and foreign speech perception. *Frontiers in Systems Neuroscience, 7*. https://doi.org/10.3389/fnsys.2013.00084

Martins, M., Neves, L., Rodrigues, P., Vasconcelos, O., & Castro, S. L. (2018). Orff-Based Music Training Enhances Children's Manual Dexterity and Bimanual Coordination. *Frontiers in Psychology, 9*. https://doi.org/10.3389/fpsyg.2018.02616

Maruna, S. (2010). *The Great Escape: Exploring the Rehabilitative Dynamics Involved in Changing Tunes.* http://www.changingtunes.org.uk.

Masataka, N. (1999). Preference for infant-directed singing in 2-day-old hearing infants of deaf parents. *Developmental Psychology, 35*(4), 1001–1005. https://doi.org/10.1037/0012-1649.35.4.1001

Massie, R., Jolly, A., & Caulfield, L. (2019). *An Evaluation of the Irene Taylor Trust's 'Sounding Out' Programme 2016–2019*. Institute for Community Research & Development, University of Wolverhampton.

Matheson, C. M. (2005). Festivity and sociability: A study of a Celtic music festival. *Tourism Culture & Communication*, 5(3), 149–163. https://doi.org/10.3727/109830405774545035

Mathias, B., Gehring, W., & Palmer, C. (2019). Electrical Brain Responses Reveal Sequential Constraints on Planning during Music Performance. *Brain Sciences*, 9(2), 25. https://doi.org/10.3390/brainsci9020025

Mathis, W. S., & Han, X. (2017). The acute effect of pleasurable music on craving for alcohol: A pilot crossover study. *Journal of Psychiatric Research*, 90, 143–147. https://doi.org/10.1016/j.jpsychires.2017.04.008

Mathiti, V. (2002). An evaluation of a diversion into music education (DIME) programme for at-risk youth: Implications for programme development. In *14th International congress on Child Abuse and Neglect.[MP299]*.

Matijasevic, M. T. C., Buitrago, G. E., Ramírez, M., & Villada, C. (2008). Evaluación Cualitativa de resultados del proyecto 'Educación musical para niños y jóvenes: Déjate Tocar por la música'. In *Realizado por la Fundación Batuta y Acción Social. Colombia[MP300]: Centro de estudios regionales, Cafeteros y empresariales CreCe*.

Matthews, R. (2018). *Acoustic, respiratory, cognitive and wellbeing comparisons of two groups of people with Parkinson's disease participating in voice and choral singing group therapy versus a music appreciation activity* [PhD Thesis]. University of Auckland.

Mayberry, R. I., Lock, E., & Kazmi, H. (2002). Linguistic ability and early language exposure. *Nature*, 417(6884), 38–38. https://doi.org/10.1038/417038a

Mayer, J. D., Salovey, P., & Caruso, D. R. (2004a). TARGET ARTICLES: 'Emotional Intelligence: Theory, Findings, and Implications'. *Psychological Inquiry*, 15(3), 197–215. https://doi.org/10.1207/s15327965pli1503_02

Mayer, J. D., Salovey, P., & Caruso, D. R. (2004b). TARGET ARTICLES: 'Emotional Intelligence: Theory, Findings, and Implications'. *Psychological Inquiry*, 15(3), 197–215. https://doi.org/10.1207/s15327965pli1503_02

Mayer, J. D., Salovey, P., Caruso, D. R., & Sitarenios, G. (2001). Emotional intelligence as a standard intelligence. *Emotion*, 1(3), 232–242. https://doi.org/10.1037/1528-3542.1.3.232

Mayfield, C., & Moss, S. (1989). Effect of Music Tempo on Task Performance. *Psychological Reports*, 65(3_suppl2), 1283–1290. https://doi.org/10.2466/pr0.1989.65.3f.1283

Mays, K. L., Clark, D. L., & Gordon, A. J. (2008). Treating Addiction with Tunes: A Systematic Review of Music Therapy for the Treatment of

Patients with Addictions. *Substance Abuse, 29*(4), 51–59. https://doi.org/10.1080/08897070802418485

McConnell, T., & Porter, S. (2016). Music therapy for palliative care: A realist review. *Palliative and Supportive Care, 15*(4), 454–464. https://doi.org/10.1017/s1478951516000663

McCourt, T. (2005). Collecting music in the digital realm. *Popular Music Soc, 28*, 249–252.

McCraty, R., Atkinson, M., Rein, G., & Watkins, A. D. (1996). Music enhances the effect of positive emotional states on salivaryIgA. *Stress Medicine, 12*(3), 167–175. https://doi.org/10.1002/(sici)1099-1700(199607)12:3<167::aid-smi697>3.0.co;2-2

McDermott, O., Crellin, N., Ridder, H. M., & Orrell, M. (2012). Music therapy in dementia: A narrative synthesis systematic review. *International Journal of Geriatric Psychiatry, 28*(8), 781–794. https://doi.org/10.1002/gps.3895

McDermott, O., Orrell, M., & Ridder, H. M. (2014). The importance of music for people with dementia: The perspectives of people with dementia, family carers, staff and music therapists. *Aging & Mental Health, 18*(6), 706–716. https://doi.org/10.1080/13607863.2013.875124

McDonald, C. I., & Zaki, S. (2020). A role for classical music in veterinary practice: Does exposure to classical music reduce stress in hospitalised dogs? *Australian Veterinary Journal, 98*(1–2), 31–36. https://doi.org/10.1111/avj.12905

McDonald, J. (2013). The Effect of Music Preference on Complex Task Performance. *Global Tides, 7*, 10 303.

McFerran, K., Baker, F., Patton, G. C., & Sawyer, S. M. (2006). A Retrospective lyrical analysis of songs written by adolescents with anorexia nervosa. *European Eating Disorders Review, 14*(6), 397–403. https://doi.org/10.1002/erv.746

McFerran, K., Derrington, P., & Saarikallio, S. (Eds). (2019). *Handbook of Music, Adolescents, and Wellbeing*. Oxford University Press. https://doi.org/10.1093/oso/9780198808992.001.0001

McFerran, K. S. (2016). Contextualising the relationship between music, emotions and the well-being of young people: A critical interpretive synthesis. *Musicae Scientiae, 20*(1), 103–121. https://doi.org/10.1177/1029864915626968

McFerran, K. S. (2019). Adolescents and Music Therapy: Contextualized Recommendations for Research and Practice. *Music Therapy Perspectives, 38*(1), 80–88. https://doi.org/10.1093/mtp/miz014

McFerran, K. S., Garrido, S., O'Grady, L., Grocke, D., & Sawyer, S. M. (2014). Examining the relationship between self-reported mood management and music preferences of Australian teenagers. *Nordic Journal of Music Therapy, 24*(3), 187–203. https://doi.org/10.1080/08098131.2014.908942

McFerran, K. S., Hense, C., Koike, A., & Rickwood, D. (2018). Intentional music use to reduce psychological distress in adolescents accessing primary mental health care. *Clinical Child Psychology and Psychiatry*, 23(4), 567–581. https://doi.org/10.1177/1359104518767231

McFerran, K. S., Lai, H. I. C., Chang, W.-H., Acquaro, D., Chin, T. C., Stokes, H., & Crooke, A. H. D. (2020a). Music, Rhythm and Trauma: A Critical Interpretive Synthesis of Research Literature. *Frontiers in Psychology*, 11. https://doi.org/10.3389/fpsyg.2020.00324

McFerran, K. S., Lai, H. I. C., Chang, W.-H., Acquaro, D., Chin, T. C., Stokes, H., & Crooke, A. H. D. (2020b). Music, Rhythm and Trauma: A Critical Interpretive Synthesis of Research Literature. *Frontiers in Psychology*, 11. https://doi.org/10.3389/fpsyg.2020.00324

McFerran, K. S., Rickard, N. S., & McFerran, K. S. (2011). *Music and adolescents* (eds, Ed.). Nova Science Publishers.

McFerran, K. S., & Saarikallio, S. (2014). Depending on music to feel better: Being conscious of responsibility when appropriating the power of music. *The Arts in Psychotherapy*, 41(1), 89–97. https://doi.org/10.1016/j.aip.2013.11.007

McFerran, K. S., & Shoemark, H. (2013). How musical engagement promotes well-being in education contexts: The case of a young man with profound and multiple disabilities. *International Journal of Qualitative Studies on Health and Well-Being*, 8(1), 20570. https://doi.org/10.3402/qhw.v8i0.20570

McHugh, L., Gardstrom, S., Hiller, J., Brewer, M., & Diestelkamp, W. S. (2012). The Effect of Pre-Meal, Vocal Re-Creative Music Therapy on Nutritional Intake of Residents with Alzheimer's Disease and Related Dementias: A Pilot Study. *Music Therapy Perspectives*, 30(1), 32–42. https://doi.org/10.1093/mtp/30.1.32

McIntyre, J. (2007). Creating order out of chaos: Music therapy with adolescent boys diagnosed with a behaviour disorder and / or emotional disorder. *Music Therapy Today*, VIII(1), 308.

McKAY, F. R. (2009). Music in the Correction of Juvenile Delinquency. *Juvenile Court Judges Journal*, 7(4), 24–30. https://doi.org/10.1111/j.1755-6988.1956.tb00139.x

McKinney, C. H., Tims, F. C., Kumar, A. M., & Kumar, M. (1997). The Effect of Selected Classical Music and Spontaneous Imagery on Plasma β-Endorphin. *Journal of Behavioral Medicine*, 20(1), 85–99. https://doi.org/10.1023/a:1025543330939

MCMullen, E., & Saffran, J. R. (2004). Music and Language: A Developmental Comparison. *Music Perception*, 21(3), 289–311. https://doi.org/10.1525/mp.2004.21.3.289

McNeill, W. H. (1997). *Keeping Together in Time*. Harvard University Press. https://doi.org/10.4159/9780674040878

McPherson, G. E., & Lehmann, A. C. (2012). Exceptional musical abilities: Musical Prodigies. In G. E. McPherson & G. F. Welch (Eds), *The Oxford Handbook of Music Education* (Vol. 2, pp. 31–50 ,). Oxford University Press. https://doi.org/10.1093/oxfordhb/9780199928019.013.0003_update_001.

McPherson, G. E., & O'Neill, S. A. (2010). Students' motivation to study music as compared to other school subjects: A comparison of eight countries. *Research Studies in Music Education*, 32(2), 101–137. https://doi.org/10.1177/1321103x10384202

McPherson, G. E., & Renwick, J. M. (2001). A Longitudinal Study of Self-regulation in Children's Musical Practice. *Music Education Research*, 3(2), 169–186. https://doi.org/10.1080/14613800120089232

Mead, G. H., Joas, H., Huebner, D. R., & Morris, C. W. (2015). *Mind, Self, and Society*. University of Chicago Press. https://doi.org/10.7208/chicago/9780226112879.001.0001

Medina, D., & Barraza, P. (2019). Efficiency of attentional networks in musicians and non-musicians. *Heliyon*, 5(3), e01315. https://doi.org/10.1016/j.heliyon.2019.e01315

Mehr, S. A., Krasnow, M. M., Bryant, G. A., & Hagen, E. H. (2020). Origins of music in credible signaling. *Behavioral and Brain Sciences*, 44. https://doi.org/10.1017/s0140525x20000345

Mehr, S. A., Schachner, A., Katz, R. C., & Spelke, E. S. (2013a). Two Randomized Trials Provide No Consistent Evidence for Nonmusical Cognitive Benefits of Brief Preschool Music Enrichment. *PLoS ONE*, 8(12), e82007. https://doi.org/10.1371/journal.pone.0082007

Mehr, S. A., Schachner, A., Katz, R. C., & Spelke, E. S. (2013b). Two Randomized Trials Provide No Consistent Evidence for Nonmusical Cognitive Benefits of Brief Preschool Music Enrichment. *PLoS ONE*, 8(12), e82007. https://doi.org/10.1371/journal.pone.0082007

Meinz, E. J., & Hambrick, D. Z. (2010). Deliberate Practice Is Necessary but Not Sufficient to Explain Individual Differences in Piano Sight-Reading Skill. *Psychological Science*, 21(7), 914–919. https://doi.org/10.1177/0956797610373933

Meister, I., Krings, T., Foltys, H., Boroojerdi, B., Müller, M., Töpper, R., & Thron, A. (2005). Effects of long-term practice and task complexity in musicians and nonmusicians performing simple and complex motor tasks: Implications for cortical motor organization. *Human Brain Mapping*, 25(3), 345–352. https://doi.org/10.1002/hbm.20112

Mendelson, J., White, Y., Hans, L., Adebari, R., Schmid, L., Riggsbee, J., Goldsmith, A., Ozler, B., Buehne, K., Jones, S., Shapleton, J., & Dawson, G. (2016). A Preliminary Investigation of a Specialized Music Therapy Model for Children with Disabilities Delivered in a Classroom Setting. *Autism Research and Treatment*, 2016, 1–8. https://doi.org/10.1155/2016/1284790

Mendona, M. (2010). Prison, music and the rehabilitation revolution: The case of Good Vibrations. *Journal of Applied Arts & Health*, *1*(3), 295–307. https://doi.org/10.1386/jaah.1.3.295_1

Menne, H. L., Johnson, J. D., Whitlatch, C. J., & Schwartz, S. M. (2012). Activity Preferences of Persons With Dementia. *Activities, Adaptation & Aging*, *36*(3), 195–213. https://doi.org/10.1080/01924788.2012.696234

Menning, H., Roberts, L. E., & Pantev, C. (2000). Plastic changes in the auditory cortex induced by intensive frequency discrimination training. *NeuroReport*, *11*(4), 817–822. https://doi.org/10.1097/00001756-200003200-00032

Merchant, H., Grahn, J., Trainor, L., Rohrmeier, M., & Fitch, W. T. (2015). Finding the beat: A neural perspective across humans and non-human primates. *Philosophical Transactions of the Royal Society B: Biological Sciences*, *370*(1664), 20140093. https://doi.org/10.1098/rstb.2014.0093

Merker, B., Morley, I., & Zuidema, W. (2015). Five fundamental constraints on theories of the origins of music. *Philosophical Transactions of the Royal Society B: Biological Sciences*, *370*(1664), 20140095. https://doi.org/10.1098/rstb.2014.0095

Merrett, D. L., Peretz, I., & Wilson, S. J. (2013). Moderating variables of music training-induced neuroplasticity: A review and discussion. *Frontiers in Psychology*, *4*. https://doi.org/10.3389/fpsyg.2013.00606

Merriam, A. P. (1964). *The anthropology of music*. Northwestern University Press.

Merry, M., & Silverman, M. J. (2021). Effects of patient-preferred live music on positive and negative affect and pain with adults on a post-surgical oncology unit: A randomized study. *The Arts in Psychotherapy*, *72*, 101739. https://doi.org/10.1016/j.aip.2020.101739

Messerschmidt, T. (2017). *Change is gonna come: A mixed methods examination of people's attitudes toward prisoners after experiences with a prison choir*. Boston University.

Metzler-Baddeley, C., Cantera, J., Coulthard, E., Rosser, A., Jones, D. K., & Baddeley, R. J. (2014). Improved Executive Function and Callosal White Matter Microstructure after Rhythm Exercise in Huntington's Disease. *Journal of Huntington's Disease*, *3*(3), 273–283. https://doi.org/10.3233/jhd-140113

Meyer, J., Oguz, P. G., & Moore, K. S. (2018). Superior fluid cognition in trained musicians. *Psychology of Music*, *48*(3), 434–447. https://doi.org/10.1177/0305735618808089

Meyer, L. B. (1961). *Emotion and Meaning in Music*. University of Chicago Press. https://doi.org/10.7208/chicago/9780226521374.001.0001

Meyer, M. (2019). The Power of Music: Can Music at Work Help to Create more Ethical Organizations? *Humanistic Management Journal*, *4*(1), 95–99. https://doi.org/10.1007/s41463-019-00053-x

Michel, D. E. (1971). Self-Esteem and Academic Achievement in Black Junior High School Students: Effects of Automated Guitar Instruction. *Council for Research in Music Education, 24*, 15–23.

Michel, D. E., & Farrell, D. M. (1973). Music and Self-Esteem: Disadvantaged Problem Boys in an All-Black Elementary School. *Journal of Research in Music Education, 21*(1), 80–84. https://doi.org/10.2307/3343983

Micheyl, C., Delhommeau, K., Perrot, X., & Oxenham, A. J. (2006). Influence of musical and psychoacoustical training on pitch discrimination. *Hearing Research, 219*(1–2), 36–47. https://doi.org/10.1016/j.heares.2006.05.004

Miendlarzewska, E. A., & Trost, W. J. (2014). How musical training affects cognitive development: Rhythm, reward and other modulating variables. *Frontiers in Neuroscience, 7*. https://doi.org/10.3389/fnins.2013.00279

Mikenas, E. (2003). Drumming on the edge of leadership: Hand drumming and leadership skills for the new millennium. *Percussive Notes, 41*(1), 42–45.

Mikkola, K., Kushnerenko, E., Partanen, E., Serenius-Sirve, S., Leipälä, J., Huotilainen, M., & Fellman, V. (2007). Auditory event-related potentials and cognitive function of preterm children at five years of age. *Clinical Neurophysiology, 118*(7), 1494–1502. https://doi.org/10.1016/j.clinph.2007.04.012

Miksza, P. (2007a). Music participation and socioeconomic status on correlates of change: A longitudinal analysis of academic achievement. *Bulletin of the Council for Research in Music Education, 172*, 41–57.

Miksza, P. (2007b). Effective Practice. *Journal of Research in Music Education, 55*(4), 359–375. https://doi.org/10.1177/0022429408317513

Miksza, P. (2010). Investigating relationships between participation in high school music ensembles and extra-musical outcomes: An analysis of the Education Longitudinal Study of 2002 using bio-ecological development models. *Bulletin of the Council for Research in Music Education, 186*, 7–25.

Miles, S. A., Miranda, R. A., & Ullman, M. T. (2016). Sex Differences in Music: A Female Advantage at Recognizing Familiar Melodies. *Frontiers in Psychology, 7*. https://doi.org/10.3389/fpsyg.2016.00278

Millar, O., & Warwick, I. (2018). Music and refugees' wellbeing in contexts of protracted displacement. *Health Education Journal, 78*(1), 67–80. https://doi.org/10.1177/0017896918785991

Millar, S., Stiner, A., Calo, F., & Teasdate, S. (2020). COOL music: A bottom up music intervention for hard to reach young people in Scotland. *British Journal of Music Education, 37*(1), 87-98, https://doi.org/10.1017/S02851719000226.

Miller, G. (2000). Evolution of human music through sexual selection. In N. L. Wallin, B. Merker, & S. Brown (Eds), *The Origins of Music* (pp. 329–360). MIT Press.

Milliman, R. E. (1982). Using background music to affect the behaviour of supermarket shoppers. *Journal of Marketing, 46,* 86–91.

Milliman, R. E. (1986). The Influence of Background Music on the Behavior of Restaurant Patrons. *Journal of Consumer Research, 13*(2), 286. https://doi.org/10.1086/209068

Milovanov, R., Huotilainen, M., Välimäki, V., Esquef, P. A. A., & Tervaniemi, M. (2008). Musical aptitude and second language pronunciation skills in school-aged children: Neural and behavioral evidence. *Brain Research, 1194,* 81–89. https://doi.org/10.1016/j.brainres.2007.11.042

Milovanov, R., & Tervaniemi, M. (2011). The Interplay between Musical and Linguistic Aptitudes: A Review. *Frontiers in Psychology, 2.* https://doi.org/10.3389/fpsyg.2011.00321

Minguella, M., & Buchanan, C. (2009). *The use of music as a tool for social inclusion.* Research Report for Cork City Council.

Miranda, D. (2013). The role of music in adolescent development: Much more than the same old song. *International Journal of Adolescence and Youth, 18*(1), 5–22. https://doi.org/10.1080/02673843.2011.650182

Miranda, D. (2019). A review of research on music and coping in adolescence. *Psychomusicology: Music, Mind, and Brain, 29*(1), 1–9. https://doi.org/10.1037/pmu0000229

Miranda, D., Blais-Rochette, C., Vaugon, K., Osman, M., & Arias-Valenzuela, M. (2013). Towards a cultural-developmental psychology of music in adolescence. *Psychology of Music, 43*(2), 197–218. https://doi.org/10.1177/0305735613500700

Miranda, D., & Claes, M. (2009). Music listening, coping, peer affiliation and depression in adolescence. *Psychology of Music, 37*(2), 215–233. https://doi.org/10.1177/0305735608097245

Miranda, D., & Gaudreau, P. (2011). Music listening and emotional well-being in adolescence: A person- and variable-oriented study. *European Review of Applied Psychology, 61*(1), 1–11. https://doi.org/10.1016/j.erap.2010.10.002

Miranda, D., Gaudreau, P., Debrosse, R., Morizot, J., & Kirmayer, L. (2012). Music listening and mental health: Variations on internalizing psychopathology. In R. A. R. MacDonald, G. Kreutz, & L. Mitchell (Eds), *Music, Health and Wellbeing* (pp. 513–530). Oxford University Press.

Miranda, J. Y. (2001). *A study of the effect of school-sponsored, extra-curricular activities on high school students' cumulative grade point average, SAT score, ACT score, and core curriculum subject grade point average* [PhD Thesis]. University of North Texas.

Miranda, R. A., & Ullman, M. T. (2007). Double dissociation between rules and memory in music: An event-related potential study\

textbackslashding73. *NeuroImage, 38*(2), 331–345. https://doi.org/10.1016/j.neuroimage.2007.07.034

Mischel, W. (1973). Toward a cognitive social learning reconceptualization of personality. *Psychological Review, 80*(4), 252–283. https://doi.org/10.1037/h0035002

Mitchell, A. H. (1949). The Effect of Radio Programs on Silent Reading Achievement of Ninety-One Sixth Grade Students. *The Journal of Educational Research, 42*(6), 460–470. https://doi.org/10.1080/00220671.1949.10881709

Mitchell, L. A., & MacDonald, R. A. R. (2006). An Experimental Investigation of the Effects of Preferred and Relaxing Music Listening on Pain Perception. *Journal of Music Therapy, 43*(4), 295–316. https://doi.org/10.1093/jmt/43.4.295

Mitchell, L. A., MacDonald, R. A. R., & Brodie, E. E. (2006). A comparison of the effects of preferred music, arithmetic and humour on cold pressor pain. *European Journal of Pain, 10*(4), 343–343. https://doi.org/10.1016/j.ejpain.2005.03.005

Mitchell, L., & MacDonald, R. (2012). Music and Pain: Evidence from Experimental Perspectives. In *Music, Health, and Wellbeing* (pp. 231–238). Oxford University Press. https://doi.org/10.1093/acprof:oso/9780199586974.003.0017

Mithen, S. (1996). *The Prehistory of the mind*. Thames and Hudson.

Miyake, A., & Friedman, N. P. (2012). The Nature and Organization of Individual Differences in Executive Functions. *Current Directions in Psychological Science, 21*(1), 8–14. https://doi.org/10.1177/0963721411429458

Miyake, A., Friedman, N. P., Emerson, M. J., Witzki, A. H., Howerter, A., & Wager, T. D. (2000). The Unity and Diversity of Executive Functions and Their Contributions to Complex "Frontal Lobe" Tasks: A Latent Variable Analysis. *Cognitive Psychology, 41*(1), 49–100. https://doi.org/10.1006/cogp.1999.0734

Möckel, M., Röcker, L., Störk, T., Vollert, J., Danne, O., Eichstädt, H., Müller, R., & Hochrein, H. (1994). Immediate physiological responses of healthy volunteers to different types of music: Cardiovascular, hormonal and mental changes. *European Journal of Applied Physiology and Occupational Physiology, 68*(6), 451–459. https://doi.org/10.1007/bf00599512

Mogro-Wilson, C., & Tredinnick, L. (2020). Influencing Social and Emotional Awareness and Empathy with a Visual Arts and Music Intervention for Adolescents. *Children & Schools, 42*(2), 111–119. https://doi.org/10.1093/cs/cdaa008

Mohan, A., & Thomas, E. (2019). Effect of background music and the cultural preference to music on adolescents' task performance. *International Journal of Adolescence and Youth, 25*(1), 562–573. https://doi.org/10.1080/02673843.2019.1689368

Mohan, G., Sivakumaran, B., & Sharma, P. (2013). Impact of store environment on impulse buying behavior. *European Journal of Marketing, 47*(10), 1711–1732. https://doi.org/10.1108/ejm-03-2011-0110

Molnar-Szakacs, I., & Heaton, P. (2012). Music: A unique window into the world of autism. Annals of the New York Academy of Sciences: The Neurosciences and Music IV. *Learning and Memory, 318,* 318–324.

Molteni, L., & Ordanini, A. (2003). Consumption Patterns, Digital Technology and Music Downloading. *Long Range Planning, 36*(4), 389–406. https://doi.org/10.1016/s0024-6301(03)00073-6

Mom, P., & Zu, O. D. (2012). Effects of Tone Merging and Musical Training on Cantonese Tone Perception in Speech Prosody. *Sixth International Conference.*

Montello, L., & Coons, E. E. (1998). Effects of Active Versus Passive Group Music Therapy on Preadolescents with Emotional, Learning, and Behavioral Disorders. *Journal of Music Therapy, 35*(1), 49–67. https://doi.org/10.1093/jmt/35.1.49

Montgomery, A. J. (1997). *The influence of movement activities on achievement in melodic pitch discrimination and language arts reading readiness skills of selected kindergarten music classes* [Doctoral dissertation.]. University of Southern Mississippi.

Moody, E., & Phinney, A. (2012). A Community-Engaged Art Program for Older People: Fostering Social Inclusion. *Canadian Journal on Aging / La Revue Canadienne Du Vieillissement, 31*(1), 55–64. https://doi.org/10.1017/s0714980811000596

Moon, C., Cooper, R. P., & Fifer, W. P. (1993). Two-day-olds prefer their native language. *Infant Behavior and Development, 16*(4), 495–500. https://doi.org/10.1016/0163-6383(93)80007-u

Moon, C., Lagercrantz, H., & Kuhl, P. K. (2013). Language experienced$\textbackslash$i$\textbackslashgreater$in utero$\textbackslash$i$\textbackslashgreater$affects vowel perception after birth: A two-country study. *Acta Paediatrica, 102*(2), 156–160. https://doi.org/10.1111/apa.12098

Moon, C. M., & Fifer, W. P. (2000). Evidence of Transnatal Auditory Learning. *Journal of Perinatology, 20*(S1), S37–S44. https://doi.org/10.1038/sj.jp.7200448

Moore, G. P., & Chen, J. (2010). Timings and interactions of skilled musicians. *Biological Cybernetics, 103*(5), 401–414. https://doi.org/10.1007/s00422-010-0407-5

Moors, T., Silva, S., Maraschin, D., Young, D., Quinn, J. M., Carpentier, J. de, Allouche, J., & Himonides, E. (2020). Using Beatboxing for Creative Rehabilitation After Laryngectomy: Experiences From a Public Engagement Project. *Frontiers in Psychology, 10.* https://doi.org/10.3389/fpsyg.2019.02854

Moradzadeh, L., Blumenthal, G., & Wiseheart, M. (2014). Musical Training, Bilingualism, and Executive Function: A Closer Look at Task Switching and Dual-Task Performance. *Cognitive Science, 39*(5), 992–1020. https://doi.org/10.1111/cogs.12183

Moreno, J. (1999). Orpheus in hell: Music and therapy in the Holocaust. *The Arts in Psychotherapy, 26*(1), 3–14. https://doi.org/10.1016/s0197-4556(98)00040-9

Moreno, S., & Besson, M. (2006). Musical training and language-related brain electrical activity in children. *Psychophysiology, 43*(3), 287–291. https://doi.org/10.1111/j.1469-8986.2006.00401.x

Moreno, S., Bialystok, E., Barac, R., Schellenberg, E. G., Cepeda, N. J., & Chau, T. (2011). Short-Term Music Training Enhances Verbal Intelligence and Executive Function. *Psychological Science, 22*(11), 1425–1433. https://doi.org/10.1177/0956797611416999

Moreno, S., & Bidelman, G. M. (2014). Examining neural plasticity and cognitive benefit through the unique lens of musical training. *Hearing Research, 308*, 84–97. https://doi.org/10.1016/j.heares.2013.09.012

Moreno, S., & Farzan, F. (2015). Music training and inhibitory control: A multidimensional model. *Annals of the New York Academy of Sciences, 1337*(1), 147–152. https://doi.org/10.1111/nyas.12674

Moreno, S., Lee, Y., Janus, M., & Bialystok, E. (2014). Short-Term Second Language and Music Training Induces Lasting Functional Brain Changes in Early Childhood. *Child Development, 86*(2), 394–406. https://doi.org/10.1111/cdev.12297

Moreno, S., Marques, C., Santos, A., Santos, M., Castro, S. L., & Besson, M. (2008). Musical Training Influences Linguistic Abilities in 8-Year-Old Children: More Evidence for Brain Plasticity. *Cerebral Cortex, 19*(3), 712–723. https://doi.org/10.1093/cercor/bhn120

Moreno, S., Wodniecka, Z., Tays, W., Alain, C., & Bialystok, E. (2014). Inhibitory Control in Bilinguals and Musicians: Event Related Potential (ERP) Evidence for Experience-Specific Effects. *PLoS ONE, 9*(4), e94169. https://doi.org/10.1371/journal.pone.0094169

Morgan-Ellis, E. M. (2021). "Like Pieces in a Puzzle": Online Sacred Harp Singing During the COVID-19 Pandemic. *Frontiers in Psychology, 12.* https://doi.org/10.3389/fpsyg.2021.627038

Morin, F. (2014). From Caracas to the Canadian prairies: Executive summary of the pilot evaluation of an el sistema-inspired after-school orchestral program. *Canadian Music Educator / Musicien Educateur Au Canada, 56*(1).

Moritz, C., Yampolsky, S., Papadelis, G., Thomson, J., & Wolf, M. (2012). Links between early rhythm skills, musical training, and phonological awareness. *Reading and Writing, 26*(5), 739–769. https://doi.org/10.1007/s11145-012-9389-0

Morrison, S. J. (1994). Music Students and Academic Growth. *Music Educators Journal, 81*(2), 33–36. https://doi.org/10.2307/3398812

Moser, D. K., Chung, M. L., McKinley, S., Riegel, B., An, K., Cherrington, C. C., Blakely, W., Biddle, M., Frazier, S. K., & Garvin, B. J. (2003). Critical care nursing practice regarding patient anxiety assessment and management. *Intensive and Critical Care Nursing, 19*(5), 276–288. https://doi.org/10.1016/s0964-3397(03)00061-2

Mosing, M. A., Madison, G., Pedersen, N. L., & Ullén, F. (2015). Investigating cognitive transfer within the framework of music practice: Genetic pleiotropy rather than causality. *Developmental Science, 19*(3), 504–512. https://doi.org/10.1111/desc.12306

Moss, H., & O'Donoghue, J. (2019). An evaluation of workplace choir singing amongst Health Service staff in Ireland. *Health Promotion International, 35*(3), 527–534. https://doi.org/10.1093/heapro/daz044

Moussard, A., Bermudez, P., Alain, C., Tays, W., & Moreno, S. (2016). Lifelong music practice and executive control in older adults: An event-related potential study. *Brain Research, 1642*, 146–153. https://doi.org/10.1016/j.brainres.2016.03.028

Moussard, A., Bigand, E., Belleville, S., & Peretz, I. (2012). Music as an Aid to Learn New Verbal Information in Alzheimer's Disease. *Music Perception, 29*(5), 521–531. https://doi.org/10.1525/mp.2012.29.5.521

Mroczek, D. K., Stawski, R. S., Turiano, N. A., Chan, W., Almeida, D. M., Neupert, S. D., & Spiro, A. (2013). Emotional Reactivity and Mortality: Longitudinal Findings From the VA Normative Aging Study. *The Journals of Gerontology Series B: Psychological Sciences and Social Sciences, 70*(3), 398–406. https://doi.org/10.1093/geronb/gbt107

Müllensiefen, D., Gingras, B., Musil, J., & Stewart, L. (2014). The Musicality of Non-Musicians: An Index for Assessing Musical Sophistication in the General Population. *PLoS ONE, 9*(2), e89642. https://doi.org/10.1371/journal.pone.0089642

Müller, W., Haffelder, G., Schlotmann, A., Schaefers, A. T. U., & Teuchert-Noodt, G. (2014). Amelioration of psychiatric symptoms through exposure to music individually adapted to brain rhythm disorders – a randomised clinical trial on the basis of fundamental research. *Cognitive Neuropsychiatry, 19*(5), 399–413. https://doi.org/10.1080/13546805.2013.879054

Mullis, R. L., & Chapman, P. (2000). Age, Gender, and Self-Esteem Differences in Adolescent Coping Styles. *The Journal of Social Psychology, 140*(4), 539–541. https://doi.org/10.1080/00224540009600494

Murabayashi, N., Akahoshi, T., Ishimine, R., Saji, N., Takeda, C., Nakayama, H., Noro, M., Fujimoto, H., Misaki, M., Miyamoto, K., Yamada, Y., Kohya, I., Kondo, M., Yamaguchi, H., Sasaki, D., & Murai, Y. (2019). Effects of Music Therapy in Frail Elderlies: Controlled Crossover Study. *Dementia and Geriatric Cognitive Disorders Extra, 9*(1), 87–99. https://doi.org/10.1159/000496456

Murcia, C. Q., Bongard, S., & Kreutz, G. (2009). Emotional and Neurohumoral Responses to Dancing Tango Argentino: The Effects of Music and Partner. *Music and Medicine, 1*(1), 14–21. https://doi.org/10.1177/1943862109335064

Muriithi, B. A. K. (2020). Music as the Medicine of Trauma among Refugees in Arizona. *Voices: A World Forum for Music Therapy, 20*(2). https://doi.org/10.15845/voices.v20i2.2891

Murnighan, J. K., & Conlon, D. E. (1991). The Dynamics of Intense Work Groups: A Study of British String Quartets. *Administrative Science Quarterly, 36*(2), 165. https://doi.org/10.2307/2393352

Murrock, C. J., & Graor, C. H. (2016). Depression, Social Isolation, and the Lived Experience of Dancing in Disadvantaged Adults. *Archives of Psychiatric Nursing, 30*(1), 27–34. https://doi.org/10.1016/j.apnu.2015.10.010

Musacchia, G., Sams, M., Skoe, E., & Kraus, N. (2007). Musicians have enhanced subcortical auditory and audiovisual processing of speech and music. *Proceedings of the National Academy of Sciences, 104*(40), 15894–15898. https://doi.org/10.1073/pnas.0701498104

Musacchia, G., Strait, D., & Kraus, N. (2008). Relationships between behavior, brainstem and cortical encoding of seen and heard speech in musicians and non-musicians. *Hearing Research, 241*(1–2), 34–42. https://doi.org/10.1016/j.heares.2008.04.013

Music as a technology of self. (2000). In *Music in Everyday Life* (pp. 46–74). Cambridge University Press. https://doi.org/10.1017/cbo9780511489433.004

Music, U. K. (2013). *The Economic Contribution of the Core UK Music Industry*. UK Music.

Music, U. K. (2020). *Music by Numbers 2020*. UK Music.

Musik als begleitende Therapie bei koronarer Herzkrankheit. (2003). *DMW - Deutsche Medizinische Wochenschrift, 128*(51/52), 2712–2716. https://doi.org/10.1055/s-2003-812546

Musliu, A., Berisha, B., & Latifi, D. (2017). The Impact of Music in Memory. *European Journal of Social Sciences Education and Research, 10*(2), 222. https://doi.org/10.26417/ejser.v10i2.p222-227

Myers, B., Lense, M., & Gordon, R. (2019). Pushing the Envelope: Developments in Neural Entrainment to Speech and the Biological Underpinnings of Prosody Perception. *Brain Sciences, 9*(3), 70. https://doi.org/10.3390/brainsci9030070

Myers, E. G. (1979). The Effect of Music on Retention in a Paired-Associate Task with EMR Children. *Journal of Music Therapy, 16*(4), 190–198. https://doi.org/10.1093/jmt/16.4.190

Nachev, P., Kennard, C., & Husain, M. (2008). Functional role of the supplementary and pre-supplementary motor areas. *Nature Reviews Neuroscience, 9*(11), 856–869. https://doi.org/10.1038/nrn2478

Nakata, T., & Trehub, S. E. (2004). Infants' responsiveness to maternal speech and singing. *Infant Behavior and Development, 27*(4), 455–464. https://doi.org/10.1016/j.infbeh.2004.03.002

Nan, Y., Liu, L., Geiser, E., Shu, H., Gong, C. C., Dong, Q., Gabrieli, J. D. E., & Desimone, R. (2018). Piano training enhances the neural processing of pitch and improves speech perception in Mandarin-speaking children. *Proceedings of the National Academy of Sciences, 115*(28). https://doi.org/10.1073/pnas.1808412115

Nantais, K. M., & Schellenberg, E. G. (1999). The Mozart Effect: An Artifact of Preference. *Psychological Science, 10*(4), 370–373. https://doi.org/10.1111/1467-9280.00170

Narme, P., Clément, S., Ehrlé, N., Schiaratura, L., Vachez, S., Courtaigne, B., Munsch, F., & Samson, S. (2013). Efficacy of Musical Interventions in Dementia: Evidence from a Randomized Controlled Trial. *Journal of Alzheimer's Disease, 38*(2), 359–369. https://doi.org/10.3233/jad-130893

Navarro, J., Osiurak, F., & Reynaud, E. (2018). Does the Tempo of Music Impact Human Behavior Behind the Wheel? *Human Factors: The Journal of the Human Factors and Ergonomics Society, 60*(4), 556–574. https://doi.org/10.1177/0018720818760901

Nederlanden, C. M., Joanisse, M. F., & Grahn, J. A. (2020). Music as a Scaffold for Listening to Speech: Better Neural Phase-Locking to Song than Speech. *Neuroimage, 214,* 116767 473.

Nee, D. E., Brown, J. W., Askren, M. K., Berman, M. G., Demiralp, E., Krawitz, A., & Jonides, J. (2012). A Meta-analysis of Executive Components of Working Memory. *Cerebral Cortex, 23*(2), 264–282. https://doi.org/10.1093/cercor/bhs007

Neels, M., Lang, S., & Wegener, W. (1998). Therapeutisches Musizieren an der Musikschule. *Musiktherapeutische Umschau, 19*(3), 216–217.

Nelson, D. L. (1997). High-risk adolescent males, self-efficacy, and choral performance: An investigation of affective intervention. Doctoral dissertation. *MP328]Dissertation Abstracts International, 58*(3A), 0791.

Nelson, K., Adamek, M., & Kleiber, C. (2017). Relaxation Training and Postoperative Music Therapy for Adolescents Undergoing Spinal Fusion Surgery. *Pain Management Nursing, 18*(1), 16–23. https://doi.org/10.1016/j.pmn.2016.10.005

Nemati, S., Akrami, H., Salehi, S., Esteky, H., & Moghimi, S. (2019). Lost in music: Neural signature of pleasure and its role in modulating attentional resources. *Brain Research, 1711,* 7–15. https://doi.org/10.1016/j.brainres.2019.01.011

Nes, F. van, & Doorman, M. (2011). Fostering Young Children's Spatial Structuring Ability. *International Electronic Journal of Mathematics Education, 6*(1), 27–39. https://doi.org/10.29333/iejme/259

Nes, F. van, & Lange, J. de. (2007). Mathematics Education and Neurosciences: Relating Spatial Structures to the Development of Spatial Sense and Number Sense. *The Mathematics Enthusiast*, 4(2), 210–229. https://doi.org/10.54870/1551-3440.1072

Neupane, S., & Taylor, J. Y. (2011). *Music Therapy for Incarcerated Women Recovering from Trauma and Abuse*. The University of Iowa.

Ng, W. F. (2005). Music Therapy, War Trauma, and Peace: A Singaporean Perspective. *Voices: A World Forum for Music Therapy*, 5(3). https://doi.org/10.15845/voices.v5i3.231

Nguyen, T., & Grahn, J. A. (2017). Mind your music: The effects of music-induced mood and arousal across different memory tasks. *Psychomusicology: Music, Mind, and Brain*, 27(2), 81–94. https://doi.org/10.1037/pmu0000178

Nguyen, T. N., Nilsson, S., Hellström, A.-L., & Bengtson, A. (2010). Music Therapy to Reduce Pain and Anxiety in Children With Cancer Undergoing Lumbar Puncture: A Randomized Clinical Trial. *Journal of Pediatric Oncology Nursing*, 27(3), 146–155. https://doi.org/10.1177/1043454209355983

Nicholson, J., & Davies, L. (2013). Patients' experiences of the PICC insertion procedure. *British Journal of Nursing*, 22(Sup9), S16–S23. https://doi.org/10.12968/bjon.2013.22.sup9.s16

Nicholson, J. M., Berthelsen, D., Abad, V., Williams, K., & Bradley, J. (2008). Impact of Music Therapy to Promote Positive Parenting and Child Development. *Journal of Health Psychology*, 13(2), 226–238. https://doi.org/10.1177/1359105307086705

Nicholson, J. M., Berthelsen, D., Williams, K. E., & Abad, V. (2010). National Study of an Early Parenting Intervention: Implementation Differences on Parent and Child Outcomes. *Prevention Science*, 11(4), 360–370. https://doi.org/10.1007/s11121-010-0181-6

Niet, G., Tiemens, B., Lendemeijer, B., & Hutschenaekers, G. (2009). Music assisted relaxation to improve sleep. *Database of Abstracts of Reviews of Effects (DARE) Quality-Assessed Reviews*, 65(7), 1356–1364.

Nikol, L., Kuan, G., Ong, M., Chang, Y.-K., & Terry, P. C. (2018). The Heat Is On: Effects of Synchronous Music on Psychophysiological Parameters and Running Performance in Hot and Humid Conditions. *Frontiers in Psychology*, 9. https://doi.org/10.3389/fpsyg.2018.01114

Nill, A., & Geipel, A. (2009). Sharing and Owning of Musical Works. *Journal of Macromarketing*, 30(1), 33–49. https://doi.org/10.1177/0276146709352217

Nilsson, U. (2009). The effect of music intervention in stress response to cardiac surgery in a randomized clinical trial. *Heart & Lung*, 38(3), 201–207. https://doi.org/10.1016/j.hrtlng.2008.07.008

Nittono, H., Tsuda, A., Akai, S., & Nakajima, Y. (2000). Tempo of Background Sound and Performance Speed. *Perceptual and Motor Skills*, *90*(3_suppl), 1122–1122. https://doi.org/10.2466/pms.2000.90.3c.1122

Nöcker-Ribaupierre, M., & Wölfl, A. (2010). Music to counter violence: A preventative approach for working with adolescents in schools. *Nordic Journal of Music Therapy*, *19*(2), 151–161. https://doi.org/10.1080/08098131.2010.489997

Nolin, W., & Vanderark, S. (1977). A pilot study of patterns of attitudes toward school music experiences, self-esteem and socio-economic status in elementary and junior high students. *Contributions to Music Education*, *5*, 31–46.

Norgaard, M., Stambaugh, L. A., & McCranie, H. (2019). The Effect of Jazz Improvisation Instruction on Measures of Executive Function in Middle School Band Students. *Journal of Research in Music Education*, *67*(3), 339–354. https://doi.org/10.1177/0022429419863038

Norman-Haignere, S., Kanwisher, N. G., & McDermott, J. H. (2015). Distinct Cortical Pathways for Music and Speech Revealed by Hypothesis-Free Voxel Decomposition. *Neuron*, *88*(6), 1281–1296. https://doi.org/10.1016/j.neuron.2015.11.035

North, A. C. (2011). The effect of background music on the taste of wine. *British Journal of Psychology*, *103*(3), 293–301. https://doi.org/10.1111/j.2044-8295.2011.02072.x

North, A. C., & Hargreaves, D. J. (1996a). Responses to Music in a Dining Area1. *Journal of Applied Social Psychology*, *26*(6), 491–501. https://doi.org/10.1111/j.1559-1816.1996.tb02727.x

North, A. C., & Hargreaves, D. J. (1996b). The effects of music on responses to a dining area. *Journal of Environmental Psychology*, *16*(1), 55–64. https://doi.org/10.1006/jevp.1996.0005

North, A. C., & Hargreaves, D. J. (1998). The Effect of Music on Atmosphere and Purchase Intentions in a Cafeteria1. *Journal of Applied Social Psychology*, *28*(24), 2254–2273. https://doi.org/10.1111/j.1559-1816.1998.tb01370.x

North, A. C., & Hargreaves, D. J. (1999). Music and Adolescent Identity. *Music Education Research*, *1*(1), 75–92. https://doi.org/10.1080/1461380990010107

North, A. C., & Hargreaves, D. J. (2007a). Lifestyle correlates of musical preference: 1. Relationships, living arrangements, beliefs, and crime. *Psychology of Music*, *35*(1), 58–87. https://doi.org/10.1177/0305735607068888

North, A. C., & Hargreaves, D. J. (2007b). Lifestyle correlates of musical preference: 2. Media, leisure time and music. *Psychology of Music*, *35*(2), 179–200. https://doi.org/10.1177/0305735607070302

North, A. C., & Hargreaves, D. J. (2007c). Lifestyle correlates of musical preference: 3. Travel, money, education, employment and health. *Psychology of Music, 35*(3), 473–497. https://doi.org/10.1177/0305735607072656

North, A. C., Hargreaves, D. J., & Hargreaves, J. J. (2004). Uses of Music in Everyday Life. *Music Perception, 22*(1), 41–77. https://doi.org/10.1525/mp.2004.22.1.41

North, A. C., Hargreaves, D. J., & Krause, A. E. (2016). Music and consumer behaviour. In S. Hallam, I. Cross, & M. Thaut (Eds), *The Oxford Handbook of Music Psychology* (2nd ed., pp. 789–803). Oxford University Press.

North, A. C., Hargreaves, D. J., & McKendrick, J. (1997). In-store music affects product choice. *Nature, 390*(6656), 132–132. https://doi.org/10.1038/36484

North, A. C., Hargreaves, D. J., & McKendrick, J. (1999). The influence of in-store music on wine selections. *Journal of Applied Psychology, 84*(2), 271–276. https://doi.org/10.1037/0021-9010.84.2.271

North, A. C., Hargreaves, D. J., & Mckendrick, J. (2000a). The Effects of Music on Atmosphere in a Bank and a Bar1. *Journal of Applied Social Psychology, 30*(7), 1504–1522. https://doi.org/10.1111/j.1559-1816.2000.tb02533.x

North, A. C., Hargreaves, D. J., & Mckendrick, J. (2000b). The Effects of Music on Atmosphere in a Bank and a Bar1. *Journal of Applied Social Psychology, 30*(7), 1504–1522. https://doi.org/10.1111/j.1559-1816.2000.tb02533.x

North, A. C., Hargreaves, D. J., & O'Neill, S. A. (2000). The importance of music to adolescents. *British Journal of Educational Psychology, 70*(2), 255–272. https://doi.org/10.1348/000709900158083

North, A. C., Hewitt, L., & Dzidic, P. (2014). *Concurrent audio, taste perceptions, and consumer attitudes concerning orange juice (cited in North.*

North, A. C., Mackenzie, L. C., Law, R. M., & Hargreaves, D. J. (2004). The Effects of Musical and Voice 'Fit' on Responses to Advertisements1. *Journal of Applied Social Psychology, 34*(8), 1675–1708. https://doi.org/10.1111/j.1559-1816.2004.tb02793.x

North, A. C., Shilcock, A., & Hargreaves, D. J. (2003). The Effect of Musical Style on Restaurant Customers' Spending. *Environment and Behavior, 35*(5), 712–718. https://doi.org/10.1177/0013916503254749

North, A., & Hargreaves, D. (2008). *The Social and Applied Psychology of Music*. Oxford University Press. https://doi.org/10.1093/acprof:oso/9780198567424.001.0001

North, A., & MacKenzie, L. (2001). Psychologists' trials find music tempo affects productivity in cows. *June, 67*. http://www.le.ac.uk/press/press/moosicstudy.html.

Norton, A., Winner, E., Cronin, K., Overy, K., Lee, D. J., & Schlaug, G. (2005). Are there pre-existing neural, cognitive, or motoric markers for musical ability? *Brain and Cognition*, *59*(2), 124–134. https://doi.org/10.1016/j.bandc.2005.05.009

Norway, S. (2020). *This is Norway*.

Nozaradan, S., Peretz, I., & Keller, P. E. (2016). Individual Differences in Rhythmic Cortical Entrainment Correlate with Predictive Behavior in Sensorimotor Synchronization. *Scientific Reports*, *6*(1). https://doi.org/10.1038/srep20612

N.P.C. (2012). *The results of NPC's Well-being Measure for Music First: National Orchestra for All 2012 Follow Up*. New Philanthropy Capital.

Nutley, S. B., Darki, F., & Klingberg, T. (2013). Music practice is associated with development of working memory during childhood and adolescence. *Frontiers in Human Neuroscience*, *7*, 926 335.

Nutley, S. B., Darki, F., & Klingberg, T. (2014). Music practice is associated with development of working memory during childhood and adolescence. *Frontiers in Human Neuroscience*, *7*. https://doi.org/10.3389/fnhum.2013.00926

Nyashanu, M., Ikhile, D., & Pfende, F. (2020). Exploring the efficacy of music in palliative care: A scoping review. *Palliative and Supportive Care*, *19*(3), 355–360. https://doi.org/10.1017/s1478951520001042

Oakes, S. (2003). Demographic and Sponsorship Considerations for Jazz and Classical Music Festivals. *The Service Industries Journal*, *23*(3), 165–178. https://doi.org/10.1080/714005121

O'Brien, A., & Donelan, K. (2007). Risky Business: Engaging Marginalised Young People in the Creative Arts. *The International Journal of the Arts in Society: Annual Review*, *1*(6), 15–24. https://doi.org/10.18848/1833-1866/cgp/v01i06/35277

O'Callaghan, C., Dun, B., Baron, A., & Barry, P. (2013). Music's Relevance for Children With Cancer: Music Therapists' Qualitative Clinical Data-Mining Research. *Social Work in Health Care*, *52*(2–3), 125–143. https://doi.org/10.1080/00981389.2012.737904

Ockelford, A. (2012). Songs Without Words: Exploring How Music Can Serve as a Proxy Language in Social Interaction with Autistic Children. In *Music, Health, and Wellbeing* (pp. 289–323). Oxford University Press. https://doi.org/10.1093/acprof:oso/9780199586974.003.0021

Odell-Miller, H. (2016). Music therapy for people with a diagnosis of personality disorder: Considerations of thinking and feeling. In J. Edwards (Ed.), *The Oxford handbook of music therapy* (p. 337). Oxford University Press.

Odena, O. (2010). Practitioners' views on cross-community music education projects in Northern Ireland: Alienation, socio-economic factors and educational potential. *British Educational Research Journal*, *36*(1), 83–105. https://doi.org/10.1080/01411920902878909

O'Donnell, S., Lohan, M., Oliffe, J. L., Grant, D., & Galway, K. (2021). The acceptability, effectiveness and gender responsiveness of participatory arts interventions in promoting mental health and Wellbeing: A systematic review. *Arts & Health*, 1–18. https://doi.org/10.1080/17533015.2021.1894463

O'Donoghue, J., Moss, H., Clements-Cortes, A., & Freeley, C. (2020). Therapist and individual experiences and perceptions of music therapy for adolescents who stutter: A qualitative exploration. *Nordic Journal of Music Therapy*, 29(4), 353–370. https://doi.org/10.1080/08098131.2020.1745872

Oechslin, M. S., Ville, D. V. D., Lazeyras, F., Hauert, C.-A., & James, C. E. (2012). Degree of Musical Expertise Modulates Higher Order Brain Functioning. *Cerebral Cortex*, 23(9), 2213–2224. https://doi.org/10.1093/cercor/bhs206

O.F.S.T.E.D. (2009). *Making More of Music: Improving the Quality of Teaching Music in Primary Schools*. HMSO.

Ogg, M., & Slevc, R. (2019). Neural Mechanisms of Music and Language. In G. I. Zubicaray & N. O. Schiller (Eds), *The Oxford Handbook of Neurolinguistics* (p. 338). Oxford University Press.

Ohnishi, T., Matsuda, H., Asada, T., Hirakata, M., Aruga, M., Imabayashi, E., Imabayashi, E., & Nishikawa, M. (2001). Functional anatomy of musical perception in musicians. *NeuroImage*, 13(6), 923. https://doi.org/10.1016/s1053-8119(01)92265-7

Ojukwu, E. V. (1970). Music Education: A Vehicle for Fostering Positive Youth Development. *UJAH: Unizik Journal of Arts and Humanities*, 18(2), 489–506. https://doi.org/10.4314/ujah.v18i2.28

Okada, B. M. (2016). *Musical Training and Executive Functions* [PhD Thesis]. University of Maryland.

Okada, B. M., & Slevc, L. R. (2018a). Musical training: Contributions to executive function. In M. Bunting, J. Novick, M. Dougherty, & R. W. Engle (Eds), *An integrative approach to cognitive and working memory training: Perspectives from psychology, neuroscience, and human development* (p. 340). Oxford University Press.

Okada, B. M., & Slevc, L. R. (2018b). Individual differences in musical training and executive functions: A latent variable approach. *Memory & Cognition*, 46(7), 1076–1092. https://doi.org/10.3758/s13421-018-0822-8

Okada, B. M., & Slevc, L. R. (2018c). Individual differences in musical training and executive functions: A latent variable approach. *Memory & Cognition*, 46(7), 1076–1092. https://doi.org/10.3758/s13421-018-0822-8

Okhrei, A., Kutsenko, T., & Makarchuk, M. (2017). Performance of working memory of musicians and non-musicians in tests with letters, digits, and geometrical shapes. *Biologija*, 62(4). https://doi.org/10.6001/biologija.v62i4.3408

Oldfield, A. (2006). Investigation into music therapy for ten pre-school children with autistic spectrum disorder and their parents. In A. Oldfield (Ed.),

Interactive music therapy: A positive approach (pp. 157–188). Jessica Kingsley Publishers.

Oleś, P. K. (2005). *Wprowadzenie do psychologii osobowości* [*An introduction to personality psychology*. Wydawnictwo Naukowe Scholar.

Oliveri, M., Rausei, V., Koch, G., Torriero, S., Turriziani, P., & Caltagirone, C. (2004). Overestimation of numerical distances in the left side of space. *Neurology, 63*(11), 2139–2141. https://doi.org/10.1212/01.wnl.0000145975.58478.6d

Olson-McBride, L., & Page, T. F. (2012). Song to Self: Promoting a Therapeutic Dialogue with High-Risk Youths Through Poetry and Popular Music. *Social Work with Groups, 35*(2), 124–137. https://doi.org/10.1080/01609513.2011.603117

Onanuga, P. A., & Onanuga, A. O. (2020). Violence, Sexuality and Youth Linguistic Behaviour: An Exploration of Contemporary Nigerian Youth Music. *Contemporary Music Review, 39*(1), 137–166. https://doi.org/10.1080/07494467.2020.1753478

Onderdijk, K. E., Acar, F., & Dyck, E. V. (2021). Impact of Lockdown Measures on Joint Music Making: Playing Online and Physically Together. *Frontiers in Psychology, 12.* https://doi.org/10.3389/fpsyg.2021.642713

Orchestra, B. U. D. I. (2015). *Evaluation of a music-based initiative for people with dementia and their carers.* Bournemouth University Dementia Institute & Bournemouth Symphony Orchestra.

Oreck, B., Baum, S., & McCartney, H. (1999). Artistic Development for Urban Youth: The Promise and Challenge. In B. Fiske (Ed.), *Champions of Change: The Impact of the Arts on Learning* (p. 341). University of Michigan Libraries.

Orsmond, G. I., & Miller, L. K. (1999). Cognitive, Musical and Environmental Correlates of Early Music Instruction. *Psychology of Music, 27*(1), 18–37. https://doi.org/10.1177/0305735699271003

Orton, A. (2004). *Learning Mathematics: Issues, Theory and Classroom Practice.* Continuum.

Osborne, J. W. (1980). The mapping of thoughts, emotions, sensations and images as responses to music. *Journal of Mental Imagery, 5,* 133–136.

Osborne, M. S., McPherson, G. E., Faulkner, R., Davidson, J. W., & Barrett, M. S. (2015). Exploring the academic and psychosocial impact of El Sistema-inspired music programs within two low socio-economic schools. *Music Education Research, 18*(2), 156–175. https://doi.org/10.1080/14613808.2015.1056130

Osborne, N. (2009). Music for children in zones of conflict and post conflict: A psychobiological approach. In S. Malloch & C. Trevarthen (Eds), *Communicative musicality: Exploring the basis of human companionship* (pp. 331–356). Oxford University Press.

Osborne, N. (2012). Neuroscience and "real world" practice: Music as a therapeutic resource for children in zones of conflict. *Annals of the New York Academy of Sciences, 1252*(1), 69–76. https://doi.org/10.1111/j.1749-6632.2012.06473.x

Osman, S. E., Tischler, V., & Schneider, J. (2016). `Singing for the Brain': A qualitative study exploring the health and well-being benefits of singing for people with dementia and their carers. *Dementia, 15*(6), 1326–1339. https://doi.org/10.1177/1471301214556291

Ott, C. (2011). Processing of voiced and unvoiced acoustic stimuli in musicians. *Frontiers in Psychology, 2*. https://doi.org/10.3389/fpsyg.2011.00195

Overy, K. (2000). Dyslexia, Temporal Processing and Music: The Potential of Music as an Early Learning Aid for Dyslexic Children. *Psychology of Music, 28*(2), 218–229. https://doi.org/10.1177/0305735600282010

Overy, K. (2003). Dyslexia and Music. *Annals of the New York Academy of Sciences, 999*(1), 497–505. https://doi.org/10.1196/annals.1284.060

Overy, K. (2014). Motor responses to a steady beat. *Neurosciences and Music–V: Cognitive Stimulation and Rehabilitation Conference*.

Overy, K., Nicolson, R. I., Fawcett, A. J., & Clarke, E. F. (2003). Dyslexia and music: Measuring musical timing skills. *Dyslexia, 9*(1), 18–36. https://doi.org/10.1002/dys.233

Owen, A. M., McMillan, K. M., Laird, A. R., & Bullmore, E. (2005). N-back working memory paradigm: A meta-analysis of normative functional neuroimaging studies. *Human Brain Mapping, 25*(1), 46–59. https://doi.org/10.1002/hbm.20131

Ozernov-Palchik, O., & Patel, A. D. (2018). Musical rhythm and reading development: Does beat processing matter? *Annals of the New York Academy of Sciences, 1423*(1), 166–175. https://doi.org/10.1111/nyas.13853

Öztürk, A. H., Taşçıoğlu, B., Aktekin, M., Kurtoglu, Z., & Erden, I. (2002). Morphometric comparison of the human corpus callosum in professional musicians and non- musicians by using in vivo magnetic resonance imaging. *Journal of Neuroradiology, 29*, 29–34.

Packer, J., & Ballantyne, J. (2010). The impact of music festival attendance on young people's psychological and social well-being. *Psychology of Music, 39*(2), 164–181. https://doi.org/10.1177/0305735610372611

Painter, G. (1966). The Effect of a Rhythmic and Sensory Motor Activity Program on Perceptual Motor Spatial Abilities of Kindergarten Children. *Exceptional Children, 33*(2), 113–116. https://doi.org/10.1177/001440296603300206

Paleo, I. O., & Wijnberg, N. M. (2006). Classification of popular music festivals: A typology of festivals and an inquiry into their role in the construction of music genres. *International Journal of Arts Management, 8*(2), 50–81.

Palidofsky, M., & Stolbach, B. C. (2012). Dramatic Healing: The Evolution of a Trauma-Informed Musical Theatre Program for Incarcerated Girls. *Journal of*

Child & Adolescent Trauma, 5(3), 239–256. https://doi.org/10.1080/19361521.2012.697102

Pallesen, K. J., Brattico, E., Bailey, C. J., Korvenoja, A., Koivisto, J., Gjedde, A., & Carlson, S. (2010). Cognitive Control in Auditory Working Memory Is Enhanced in Musicians. *PLoS ONE, 5*(6), e11120. https://doi.org/10.1371/journal.pone.0011120

Palmer, C. (1997). Music Performance. *Annual Review of Psychology, 48*(1), 115–138. https://doi.org/10.1146/annurev.psych.48.1.115

Palmer, C. (2013). Music performance: Movement and coordination. In D. Deutsch (Ed.), *The psychology of music* (pp. 405–422). Academic Press.

Palmer, C., & Pfordresher, P. Q. (2003). Incremental planning in sequence production. *Psychological Review, 110*(4), 683–712. https://doi.org/10.1037/0033-295x.110.4.683

Palmer, E. S. (2017). Literature Review of Social Justice in Music Education: Acknowledging Oppression and Privilege. *Update: Applications of Research in Music Education, 36*(2), 22–31. https://doi.org/10.1177/8755123317711091

Palmiero, M., Giulianella, L., Guariglia, P., Boccia, M., D'Amico, S., & Piccardi, L. (2019). The Dancers' Visuospatial Body Map Explains Their Enhanced Divergence in the Production of Motor Forms: Evidence in the Early Development. *Frontiers in Psychology, 10.* https://doi.org/10.3389/fpsyg.2019.00768

Palmiero, M., Guariglia, P., Crivello, R., & Piccardi, L. (2020). The relationships between musical expertise and divergent thinking. *Acta Psychologica, 203,* 102990. https://doi.org/10.1016/j.actpsy.2019.102990

Palmiero, M., Nori, R., & Piccardi, L. (2016). Visualizer cognitive style enhances visual creativity. *Neuroscience Letters, 615,* 98–101. https://doi.org/10.1016/j.neulet.2016.01.032

Palmiero, M., Nori, R., Rogolino, C., D'amico, S., & Piccardi, L. (2016). Sex differences in visuospatial and navigational working memory: The role of mood induced by background music. *Experimental Brain Research, 234*(8), 2381–2389. https://doi.org/10.1007/s00221-016-4643-3

Palmowski, W. (1979). Music therapy for students with behaviour problems. *Zeitschrift Für Heilpädagogik, 30*(8), 546–550.

Palomar-García, M.-Á., Zatorre, R. J., Ventura-Campos, N., Bueichekú, E., & Ávila, C. (2017). Modulation of functional connectivity in auditory–motor networks in musicians compared with nonmusicians. *Cerebral Cortex, 27,* 2768–2778.

Panksepp, J., & Bernatzky, G. (2002). Emotional sounds and the brain: The neuro-affective foundations of musical appreciation. *Behavioural Processes, 60*(2), 133–155. https://doi.org/10.1016/s0376-6357(02)00080-3

Pannenborg, H. J., & Pannenborg, W. A. (1915). Die Psychologie der Musiker (The psychology of musicians. *Zeitschrift Für Psychologie, 73,* 91–136.

Panteleeva, Y., Ceschi, G., Glowinski, D., Courvoisier, D. S., & Grandjean, D. (2017). Music for anxiety? Meta-analysis of anxiety reduction in non-clinical samples. *Psychology of Music, 46*(4), 473–487. https://doi.org/10.1177/0305735617712424

Pantelyat, A., Syres, C., Reichwein, S., & Willis, A. (2015). DRUM-PD: The Use of a Drum Circle to Improve the Symptoms and Signs of Parkinson's Disease (PD). *Movement Disorders Clinical Practice, 3*(3), 243–249. https://doi.org/10.1002/mdc3.12269

Pantev, C., Engelien, A., Candia, V., & Elbert, T. (2001a). Representational Cortex in Musicians. *Annals of the New York Academy of Sciences, 930*(1), 300–314. https://doi.org/10.1111/j.1749-6632.2001.tb05740.x

Pantev, C., Engelien, A., Candia, V., & Elbert, T. (2001b). Representational Cortex in Musicians. *Annals of the New York Academy of Sciences, 930*(1), 300–314. https://doi.org/10.1111/j.1749-6632.2001.tb05740.x

Pantev, C., & Herholz, S. C. (2011). Plasticity of the human auditory cortex related to musical training. *Neuroscience & Biobehavioral Reviews, 35*(10), 2140–2154. https://doi.org/10.1016/j.neubiorev.2011.06.010

Pantev, C., Oostenveld, R., Engelien, A., Ross, B., Roberts, L. E., & Hoke, M. (1998). Increased auditory cortical representation in musicians. *Nature, 392*(6678), 811–814. https://doi.org/10.1038/33918

Pantev, C., Roberts, L. E., Schulz, M., Engelien, A., & Ross, B. (2001). Timbre-specific enhancement of auditory cortical representations in musicians. *Neuroreport, 12*(1), 169–174. https://doi.org/10.1097/00001756-200101220-00041

Paolantonio, P., Cavalli, S., Biasutti, M., Pedrazzani, C., & Williamon, A. (2020). Art for Ages: The Effects of Group Music Making on the Wellbeing of Nursing Home Residents. *Frontiers in Psychology, 11.* https://doi.org/10.3389/fpsyg.2020.575161

Papageorgi, I. (2021). The role of music performance through the life course. In *Routledge International Handbook of Music Psychology in Education and the Community* (pp. 269–285). Routledge. https://doi.org/10.4324/9780429295362-23

Papageorgi, I., Creech, A., & Welch, G. (2011). Perceived performance anxiety in advanced musicians specializing in different musical genres. *Psychology of Music, 41*(1), 18–41. https://doi.org/10.1177/0305735611408995

Papinczak, Z. E., Dingle, G. A., Stoyanov, S. R., Hides, L., & Zelenko, O. (2015). Young people's uses of music for well-being. *Journal of Youth Studies, 18*(9), 1119–1134. https://doi.org/10.1080/13676261.2015.1020935

Paraskevopoulos, E., Kuchenbuch, A., Herholz, S. C., & Pantev, C. (2012). Evidence for Training-Induced Plasticity in Multisensory Brain Structures:

An MEG Study. *PLoS ONE, 7*(5), e36534. https://doi.org/10.1371/journal.pone.0036534

Parbery-Clark, A., Skoe, E., & Kraus, N. (2009). Musical Experience Limits the Degradative Effects of Background Noise on the Neural Processing of Sound. *Journal of Neuroscience, 29*(45), 14100–14107. https://doi.org/10.1523/jneurosci.3256-09.2009

Parbery-Clark, A., Skoe, E., Lam, C., & Kraus, N. (2009). Musician Enhancement for Speech-In-Noise. *Ear & Hearing, 30*(6), 653–661. https://doi.org/10.1097/aud.0b013e3181b412e9

Parbery-Clark, A., Strait, D. L., Anderson, S., Hittner, E., & Kraus, N. (2011). Musical Experience and the Aging Auditory System: Implications for Cognitive Abilities and Hearing Speech in Noise. *PLoS ONE, 6*(5), e18082. https://doi.org/10.1371/journal.pone.0018082

Parbery-Clark, A., Tierney, A., Strait, D. L., & Kraus, N. (2012). Musicians have fine-tuned neural distinction of speech syllables. *Neuroscience, 219,* 111–119. https://doi.org/10.1016/j.neuroscience.2012.05.042

Parker, A., Marturano, N., O'Connor, G., & Meek, R. (2018). Marginalised youth, criminal justice and performing arts: Young people's experiences of music-making. *Journal of Youth Studies, 21*(8), 1061–1076. https://doi.org/10.1080/13676261.2018.1445205

Parker, G. B. (1982). Coping Behaviors That Mediate Between Life Events and Depression. *Archives of General Psychiatry, 39*(12), 1386. https://doi.org/10.1001/archpsyc.1982.04290120022004

Parkinson, B., Toterdell, P., Briner, R. B., & Reynolds, S. (1996). *Changing moods. The psychology of mood and mood regulation.* Addison Wesley Longman Publishing Company.

Parkinson, C., & White, M. (2013). Inequalities, the arts and public health: Towards an international conversation. *Arts & Health, 5*(3), 177–189. https://doi.org/10.1080/17533015.2013.826260

Parncutt, R. (2009). In I. S. Hallam, I. Cross, & M. Thaut (Eds), *Oxford Handbook of Psychology of Music* (pp. 219–228). Oxford University Press.

Parr, S. M. (1985). The effects of graduated exercise at the piano on the pianist's cardiac output, forearm blood flow, heart rate, and blood pressure. *Doctoral Dissertation.* [MP347]*Dissertation Abstracts International, 46*(6), 1436.

Partanen, E., Kujala, T., Näätänen, R., Liitola, A., Sambeth, A., & Huotilainen, M. (2013). Learning-induced neural plasticity of speech processing before birth. *Proceedings of the National Academy of Sciences, 110*(37), 15145–15150. https://doi.org/10.1073/pnas.1302159110

Partanen, E., Kujala, T., Tervaniemi, M., & Huotilainen, M. (2013). Prenatal Music Exposure Induces Long-Term Neural Effects. *PLoS ONE, 8*(10), e78946. https://doi.org/10.1371/journal.pone.0078946

Pascual, A. C., Muñoz, N. M., & Robres, A. Q. (2019). The Relationship Between Executive Functions and Academic Performance in Primary Education: Review and Meta-Analysis. *Frontiers in Psychology*, 10. https://doi.org/10.3389/fpsyg.2019.01582

Pascual-Leone, A. (2001). The Brain That Plays Music and Is Changed by It. *Annals of the New York Academy of Sciences*, 930(1), 315–329. https://doi.org/10.1111/j.1749-6632.2001.tb05741.x

Pascual-Leone, A., Nguyet, D., Cohen, L. G., Brasil-Neto, J. P., Cammarota, A., & Hallett, M. (1995). Modulation of muscle responses evoked by transcranial magnetic stimulation during the acquisition of new fine motor skills. *Journal of Neurophysiology*, 74(3), 1037–1045. https://doi.org/10.1152/jn.1995.74.3.1037

Pasiali, V. (2012). Supporting Parent-Child Interactions: Music Therapy as an Intervention for Promoting Mutually Responsive Orientation. *Journal of Music Therapy*, 49(3), 303–334. https://doi.org/10.1093/jmt/49.3.303

Pasiali, V., & Clark, C. (2018). Evaluation of a Music Therapy Social Skills Development Program for Youth with Limited Resources. *Journal of Music Therapy*, 55(3), 280–308. https://doi.org/10.1093/jmt/thy007

Passanisi, A., Nuovo, S. D., Urgese, L., & Pirrone, C. (2015). The Influence of Musical Expression on Creativity and Interpersonal Relationships in Children. *Procedia - Social and Behavioral Sciences*, 191, 2476–2480. https://doi.org/10.1016/j.sbspro.2015.04.308

Patel, A. D. (2003). Language, music, syntax and the brain. *Nature Neuroscience*, 6(7), 674–681. https://doi.org/10.1038/nn1082

Patel, A. D. (2007). *Music, Language, and the Brain*. Oxford University Press. https://doi.org/10.1093/acprof:oso/9780195123753.001.0001

Patel, A. D. (2011). Why would Musical Training Benefit the Neural Encoding of Speech? The OPERA Hypothesis. *Frontiers in Psychology*, 2. https://doi.org/10.3389/fpsyg.2011.00142

Patel, A. D. (2016). Using music to study the evolution of cognitive mechanisms relevant to language. *Psychonomic Bulletin Review*, 24(1), 177–180. https://doi.org/10.3758/s13423-016-1088-4

Patel, A. D., & Daniele, J. R. (2003). An empirical comparison of rhythm in language and music. *Cognition*, 87(1), B35–B45. https://doi.org/10.1016/s0010-0277(02)00187-7

Patel, A. D., & Iversen, J. R. (2007). The linguistic benefits of musical abilities. *Trends in Cognitive Sciences*, 11(9), 369–372. https://doi.org/10.1016/j.tics.2007.08.003

Patscheke, H., Degé, F., & Schwarzer, G. (2018). The effects of training in rhythm and pitch on phonological awareness in four- to six-year-old children. *Psychology of Music*, 47(3), 376–391. https://doi.org/10.1177/0305735618756763

Patston, L., Kirk, I., Rolfe, M., Corballis, M., & Tippett, L. (2007). The unusual symmetry of musicians: Musicians have equilateral interhemispheric transfer for visual information. *Neuropsychologia, 45*(9), 2059–2065. https://doi.org/10.1016/j.neuropsychologia.2007.02.001

Patston, L. L. M., Corballis, M. C., Hogg, S. L., & Tippett, L. J. (2006). The Neglect of Musicians. *Psychological Science, 17*(12), 1029–1031. https://doi.org/10.1111/j.1467-9280.2006.01823.x

Patston, L. L. M., Hogg, S. L., & Tippett, L. J. (2007). Attention in musicians is more bilateral than in non-musicians. *Laterality: Asymmetries of Body, Brain and Cognition, 12*(3), 262–272. https://doi.org/10.1080/13576500701251981

Patston, L. L. M., & Tippett, L. J. (2011). The Effect of Background Music on Cognitive Performance in Musicians and Nonmusicians. *Music Perception, 29*(2), 173–183. https://doi.org/10.1525/mp.2011.29.2.173

Pavlicevic, M., & Ansdell, G. (Eds). (2004). *Community Music Therapy*. Jessica Kingsley Publishers.

Pavlicevic, M., O'Neil, N., Powell, H., Jones, O., & Sampathianaki, E. (2013). Making music, making friends: Long-term music therapy with young adults with severe learning disabilities. *Journal of Intellectual Disabilities, 18*(1), 5–19. https://doi.org/10.1177/1744629513511354

Pavlicevic, M., Tsiris, G., Wood, S., Powell, H., Graham, J., Sanderson, R., Millman, R., & Gibson, J. (2013). The `ripple effect': Towards researching improvisational music therapy in dementia care homes. *Dementia, 14*(5), 659–679. https://doi.org/10.1177/1471301213514419

Pearce, E., Launay, J., & Dunbar, R. I. M. (2015). The ice-breaker effect: Singing mediates fast social bonding. *Royal Society Open Science, 2*(10), 150221. https://doi.org/10.1098/rsos.150221

Pearce, R., & Lillyman, S. (2015). Reducing social isolation in a rural community through participation in creative arts projects. *Nursing Older People, 27*(10), 33–38. https://doi.org/10.7748/nop.27.10.33.s22

Peck, K. J., Girard, T. A., Russo, F. A., & Fiocco, A. J. (2016). Music and Memory in Alzheimer's Disease and The Potential Underlying Mechanisms. *Journal of Alzheimer's Disease, 51*(4), 949–959. https://doi.org/10.3233/jad-150998

Pecoraro, E. P. (2006). The pleasure of being differently able: Integration through music therapy in primary schools. *Music Therapy Today, 7*(2), 413–429.

Pelham, W. E., Waschbusch, D. A., Hoza, B., Gnagy, E. M., Greiner, A. R., Sams, S. E., Vallano, G., Majumdar, A., & Carter, R. L. (2011). Music and Video as Distractors for Boys with ADHD in the Classroom: Comparison with Controls, Individual Differences, and Medication Effects. *Journal of Abnormal Child Psychology, 39*(8), 1085–1098. https://doi.org/10.1007/s10802-011-9529-z

Pelletier, C. L. (2004). The Effect of Music on Decreasing Arousal Due to Stress: A Meta-Analysis. *Journal of Music Therapy*, 41(3), 192–214. https://doi.org/10.1093/jmt/41.3.192

Pelletier, K. R. (1992). Mind-body health: Research, Clinical and Policy Applications. *American Journal of Health Promotion*, 6(5), 345–358, https://doi.org/10.4278/0809-1171-6.5.345.

Peng, Y.-C., Lu, T.-W., Wang, T.-H., Chen, Y.-L., Liao, H.-F., Lin, K.-H., & Tang, P.-F. (2011). Immediate effects of therapeutic music on loaded sit-to-stand movement in children with spastic diplegia. *Gait & Posture*, 33(2), 274–278. https://doi.org/10.1016/j.gaitpost.2010.11.020

Penhune, V. B. (2011). Sensitive periods in human development: Evidence from musical training. *Cortex*, 47(9), 1126–1137. https://doi.org/10.1016/j.cortex.2011.05.010

Perani, D., Saccuman, M. C., Scifo, P., Anwander, A., Spada, D., Baldoli, C., Poloniato, A., Lohmann, G., & Friederici, A. D. (2011). Neural language networks at birth. *Proceedings of the National Academy of Sciences*, 108(38), 16056–16061. https://doi.org/10.1073/pnas.1102991108

Peretz, I., Aubé, W., & Armony, J. L. (2013). Toward a neurobiology of musical emotions. In *Evolution of Emotional Communication* (pp. 277–299). Oxford University Press. https://doi.org/10.1093/acprof:oso/9780199583560.003.0017

Peretz, I., & Coltheart, M. (2003). Modularity of music processing. *Nature Neuroscience*, 6(7), 688–691. https://doi.org/10.1038/nn1083

Peretz, I., Cummings, S., & Dubé, M.-P. (2007). The Genetics of Congenital Amusia (Tone Deafness): A Family-Aggregation Study. *The American Journal of Human Genetics*, 81(3), 582–588. https://doi.org/10.1086/521337

Peretz, I., & Hyde, K. L. (2003). What is specific to music processing? Insights from congenital amusia. *Trends in Cognitive Sciences*, 7(8), 362–367. https://doi.org/10.1016/s1364-6613(03)00150-5

Peretz, I., Vuvan, D., Lagrois, M.-É., & Armony, J. L. (2015). Neural overlap in processing music and speech. *Philosophical Transactions of the Royal Society B: Biological Sciences*, 370(1664), 20140090. https://doi.org/10.1098/rstb.2014.0090

Peretz, I., & Zatorre, R. J. (Eds). (2003). *The Cognitive Neuroscience of Music*. Oxford University Press. https://doi.org/10.1093/acprof:oso/9780198525202.001.0001

Peretz, I., & Zatorre, R. J. (2005). Brain Organization for Music Processing. *Annual Review of Psychology*, 56(1), 89–114. https://doi.org/10.1146/annurev.psych.56.091103.070225

Perfetti, C., & Stafura, J. (2013). Word Knowledge in a Theory of Reading Comprehension. *Scientific Studies of Reading*, *18*(1), 22–37. https://doi.org/10.1080/10888438.2013.827687

Perfors, A., & Ong, J. (2012). Musicians are better at learning non-native sound contrasts even in non-tonal languages. In N. Miyake, D. Peebles, & R. P. Cooper (Eds), *Proceedings of the 34th Annual Conference of the Cognitive Science Society* (pp. 839–844). Cognitive Science Society.

Perham, N., & Currie, H. (2014). Does listening to preferred music improve reading comprehension performance? *Applied Cognitive Psychology*, *28*(2), 279–284. https://doi.org/10.1002/acp.2994

Perham, N., & Sykora, M. (2012). Disliked Music can be Better for Performance than Liked Music. *Applied Cognitive Psychology*, *26*(4), 550–555. https://doi.org/10.1002/acp.2826

Perham, N., & Vizard, J. (2010). Can preference for background music mediate the irrelevant sound effect? *Applied Cognitive Psychology*, *25*(4), 625–631. https://doi.org/10.1002/acp.1731

Perham, N., & Withey, T. (2012). Liked Music Increases Spatial Rotation Performance Regardless of Tempo. *Current Psychology*, *31*(2), 168–181. https://doi.org/10.1007/s12144-012-9141-6

Perkins, D. N. (1981). *The mind's best work*. Harvard University Press.

Perkins, R., Ascenso, S., Atkins, L., Fancourt, D., & Williamon, A. (2016). Making music for mental health: How group drumming mediates recovery. *Psychology of Well-Being*, *6*(1). https://doi.org/10.1186/s13612-016-0048-0

Perkins, R., Mason-Bertrand, A., Fancourt, D., Baxter, L., & Williamon, A. (2020). How Participatory Music Engagement Supports Mental Well-being: A Meta-Ethnography. *Qualitative Health Research*, *30*(12), 1924–1940. https://doi.org/10.1177/1049732320944142

Perkins, R., & Williamon, A. (2013). Learning to make music in older adulthood: A mixed-methods exploration of impacts on wellbeing. *Psychology of Music*, *42*(4), 550–567. https://doi.org/10.1177/0305735613483668

Perruchet, P., & Poulin-Charronnat, B. (2012). Challenging prior evidence for a shared syntactic processor for language and music. *Psychonomic Bulletin & Review*, *20*(2), 310–317. https://doi.org/10.3758/s13423-012-0344-5

Persico, G., Antolini, L., Vergani, P., Costantini, W., Nardi, M. T., & Bellotti, L. (2017). Maternal singing of lullabies during pregnancy and after birth: Effects on mother–infant bonding and on newborns' behaviour. Concurrent Cohort Study. *Women and Birth*, *30*(4), e214–e220. https://doi.org/10.1016/j.wombi.2017.01.007

Pesek, A. (2009). War on the former Yugoslavian territory. Integration of refugee children into the school system and musical activities as an important factor for overcoming war trauma. In B. Clausen, U. Hemetek, & E. Saether (Eds),

Music in Motion: Diversity and Dialogue in Europe (pp. 359–370). Transcript Verlag.

Pethybridge, E. (2013). "That's the Joy of Music!" An Evaluation of Partnership Working with a Teacher in Planning and Delivering a Music Therapy Group for Three Children with Autistic Spectrum Conditions. *British Journal of Music Therapy, 27*(2), 24–39. https://doi.org/10.1177/135945751302700203

Pethybridge, E., & Robertson, J. (2010). Educational music therapy: Theoretical foundations explored in time-limited group work projects with children. In V. Karkou (Ed.), *Arts Therapies in Schools: Research and Practice* (pp. 129–144). Jessica Kingsley Publishers.

Petition, R. A. A. C. (2013). *Renaissance Arts Academy. Renaissance Arts Academy: California Distinguished Schools Exemplary Arts Programme-Arts Education Synopsis.*

Petrides, K. V. (2013). Ability and Trait Emotional Intelligence. In *The Wiley-Blackwell Handbook of Individual Differences* (pp. 656–678). Wiley-Blackwell. https://doi.org/10.1002/9781444343120.ch25

Petrides, K. V., & Furnham, A. (2001). Trait emotional intelligence: Psychometric investigation with reference to established trait taxonomies. *European Journal of Personality, 15*(6), 425–448. https://doi.org/10.1002/per.416

Petrides, K. V., Niven, L., & Mouskounti, T. (2006). The trait emotional intelligence of ballet dancers and musicians. *Psicothema, 18*, 101–107.

Pettan, S. (1998). Music, politics and war in Croatia in the 1990s: An introduction. In S. Pettan (Ed.), *Music, Politics, and War: Views From Croatia* (pp. 9–27). Institute of Ethnology and Folklore Research.

Peynircioglu, Z. F., Durgunoglu, A. Y., & Uney-Kusefoglu, B. (2002). Phonological awareness and musical aptitude. *Journal of Research in Reading, 25*(1), 68–80. https://doi.org/10.1111/1467-9817.00159

Philippe, R. A., Kosirnik, C., Vuichoud, N., Williamon, A., & Roten, F. C. (2019). *Understanding wellbeing Among College Music Students and Amateur musicians in Western Switzerland.*

Phillips, R. D., Gorton, R. L., Pinciotti, P., & Sachdev, A. (2010). Promising Findings on Preschoolers' Emergent Literacy and School Readiness In Arts-integrated Early Childhood Settings. *Early Childhood Education Journal, 38*(2), 111–122. https://doi.org/10.1007/s10643-010-0397-x

Picard, M., & McEwen, B. S. (2018). Psychological Stress and Mitochondria: A Conceptual Framework. *Psychosomatic Medicine, 80*(2), 126–140. https://doi.org/10.1097/psy.0000000000000544

Pietsch, S., & Jansen, P. (2012). Different mental rotation performance in students of music, sport and education. *Learning and Individual Differences, 22*(1), 159–163. https://doi.org/10.1016/j.lindif.2011.11.012

Pietschnig, J., Voracek, M., & Formann, A. K. (2010). Mozart effect–Shmozart effect: A meta-analysis. *Intelligence, 38*(3), 314–323. https://doi.org/10.1016/j.intell.2010.03.001

Pilon, M. A., McIntosh, K. W., & Thaut, M. H. (1998). Auditory vs visual speech timing cues as external rate control to enhance verbal intelligibility in mixed spastic ataxic dysarthric speakers: A pilot study. *Brain Injury, 12*(9), 793–803. https://doi.org/10.1080/026990598122188

Pinheiro, A. P., Vasconcelos, M., Dias, M., Arrais, N., & Gonçalves, Ó. F. (2015). The music of language: An ERP investigation of the effects of musical training on emotional prosody processing. *Brain and Language, 140*, 24–34. https://doi.org/10.1016/j.bandl.2014.10.009

Pinker, S. (2010). How the Mind Works. In *Philosophy after Darwin* (pp. 275–288). Princeton University Press. https://doi.org/10.1515/9781400831296-033

Piro, J. M., & Ortiz, C. (2009). The effect of piano lessons on the vocabulary and verbal sequencing skills of primary grade students. *Psychology of Music, 37*(3), 325–347. https://doi.org/10.1177/0305735608097248

Pitt, J., & Hargreaves, D. (2017). Exploring the rationale for group music activities for parents and young children: Parents' and practitioners' perspectives. *Research Studies in Music Education, 39*(2), 177–194. https://doi.org/10.1177/1321103x17706735

Pitts, S. (2016). *Valuing Musical Participation*. Routledge. https://doi.org/10.4324/9781315548432

Pitts, S. E. (2005). What Makes an Audience? Investigating the Roles and Experiences of Listeners at a Chamber Music Festival. *Music and Letters, 86*(2), 257–269. https://doi.org/10.1093/ml/gci035

Pitts, S. E. (2007). Anything goes: A case study of extra-curricular musical participation in an English secondary school. *Music Education Research, 9*(1), 145–165. https://doi.org/10.1080/14613800601127627

Pitts, S. E. (2008). Extra-curricular music in UK schools: Investigating the aims, experiences and impact of adolescent musical participation. *International Journal of Education & the Arts, 9*(10). http://www.ijea.org/v9n10/.

Pitts, S. E. (2016). Music, language and learning: Investigating the impact of a music workshop project in four English early years settings. *International Journal of Education & the Arts, 17*(20). http://www.ijea.org/v17n20/.

Pitts, S. E. (2020). Leisure-Time Music Groups and Their Localities: Exploring the Commercial, Educational, and Reciprocal Relationships of Amateur Music-Making. *Music and Letters, 101*(1), 120–134. https://doi.org/10.1093/ml/gcz044

Pitts, S. E., & Burland, K. (2013). Listening to live jazz: An individual or social act? *Arts Marketing: An International Journal, 3*(1), 7–20. https://doi.org/10.1108/20442081311327138

Pitts, S. E., & Robinson, K. (2016). Dropping in and dropping out: Experiences of sustaining and ceasing amateur participation in classical music. *British Journal of Music Education*, 33(3), 327–346. https://doi.org/10.1017/s0265051716000152

Pitts, S. E., & Spencer, C. P. (2008). Loyalty and Longevity in Audience Listening: Investigating Experiences of Attendance at a Chamber Music Festival. *Music and Letters*, 89(2), 227–238. https://doi.org/10.1093/ml/gcm084

Platel, H. (1997). The structural components of music perception. A functional anatomical study. *Brain*, 120(2), 229–243. https://doi.org/10.1093/brain/120.2.229

Poeppel, D., & Assaneo, M. F. (2020). Speech rhythms and their neural foundations. *Nature Reviews Neuroscience*, 21(6), 322–334. https://doi.org/10.1038/s41583-020-0304-4

Politimou, N., Bella, S. D., Farrugia, N., & Franco, F. (2019). Born to Speak and Sing: Musical Predictors of Language Development in Pre-schoolers. *Frontiers in Psychology*, 10. https://doi.org/10.3389/fpsyg.2019.00948

Pongan, E., Tillmann, B., Leveque, Y., Trombert, B., Getenet, J. C., Auguste, N., Dauphinot, V., Haouari, H. E., Navez, M., Dorey, J.-M., Krolak-Salmon, P., Laurent, B., & and, I. R. (2017). Can Musical or Painting Interventions Improve Chronic Pain, Mood, Quality of Life, and Cognition in Patients with Mild Alzheimer's Disease? Evidence from a Randomized Controlled Trial. *Journal of Alzheimer's Disease*, 60(2), 663–677. https://doi.org/10.3233/jad-170410

Poquérusse, J., Azhari, A., Setoh, P., Cainelli, S., Ripoli, C., Venuti, P., & Esposito, G. (2017). Salivary $\textbackslash alpha$-amylase as a marker of stress reduction in individuals with intellectual disability and autism in response to occupational and music therapy. *Journal of Intellectual Disability Research*, 62(2), 156–163. https://doi.org/10.1111/jir.12453

Porter, S., Holmes, V., McLaughlin, K., Lynn, F., Cardwell, C., Braiden, H.-J., Doran, J., & Rogan, S. (2012). Music in mind, a randomized controlled trial of music therapy for young people with behavioural and emotional problems: Study protocol. *Journal of Advanced Nursing*, 68(10), 2349–2358. https://doi.org/10.1111/j.1365-2648.2011.05936.x

Porter, S., McConnell, T., McLaughlin, K., Lynn, F., Cardwell, C., Braiden, H.-J., Boylan, J., & and, V. H. (2016). Music therapy for children and adolescents with behavioural and emotional problems: A randomised controlled trial. *Journal of Child Psychology and Psychiatry*, 58(5), 586–594. https://doi.org/10.1111/jcpp.12656

Portowitz, A., & Klein, P. S. (2007). MISC-MUSIC: a music program to enhance cognitive processing among children with learning difficulties. *International Journal of Music Education*, 25(3), 259–271. https://doi.org/10.1177/0255761407087263

Portowitz, A., Lichtenstein, O., Egorova, L., & Brand, E. (2009). Underlying mechanisms linking music education and cognitive modifiability. *Research Studies in Music Education*, 31(2), 107–128. https://doi.org/10.1177/1321103x09344378

Portowitz, A., Peppler, K. A., & Downton, M. (2014). In Harmony: A technology-based music education model to enhance musical understanding and general learning skills. *International Journal of Music Education*, 32(2), 242–260. https://doi.org/10.1177/0255761413517056

Poscia, A., Stojanovic, J., Milia, D. I. L., Duplaga, M., Grysztar, M., Moscato, U., Onder, G., Collamati, A., Ricciardi, W., & Magnavita, N. (2018). Interventions targeting loneliness and social isolation among the older people: An update systematic review. *Experimental Gerontology*, 102, 133–144. https://doi.org/10.1016/j.exger.2017.11.017

Pothoulaki, M., MacDonald, R. A. R., Flowers, P., Stamataki, E., Filiopoulos, V., Stamatiadis, D., & Stathakis, C. P. (2008). An Investigation of the Effects of Music on Anxiety and Pain Perception in Patients Undergoing Haemodialysis Treatment. *Journal of Health Psychology*, 13(7), 912–920. https://doi.org/10.1177/1359105308095065

Potteiger, J. A., Schroeder, J. M., & Goff, K. L. (2000). Influence of Music on Ratings of Perceived Exertion during 20 Minutes of Moderate Intensity Exercise. *Perceptual and Motor Skills*, 91(3), 848–854. https://doi.org/10.2466/pms.2000.91.3.848

Poulos, R. G., Marwood, S., Harkin, D., Opher, S., Clift, S., Cole, A. M. D., Rhee, J., Beilharz, K., & Poulos, C. J. (2018). Arts on prescription for community-dwelling older people with a range of health and wellness needs. *Health & Social Care in the Community*, 27(2), 483–492. https://doi.org/10.1111/hsc.12669

Pratt, A. C., & Brady, S. (1988). Relation of phonological awareness to reading disability in children and adults. *Journal of Educational Psychology*, 80(3), 319–323. https://doi.org/10.1037/0022-0663.80.3.319

Prattini, R. J. (2016). *Participation in active and passive music interventions by individuals with Alzheimer's disease and related dementias: Effects on agitation* [Doctoral dissertation.]. Louisiana State University.

Preethy, N. A., & Gurunathan, D. (2020). Effect of Music on the Vital Signs and Behaviour of Children During the Recovery Period after General Anaesthesia Procedure-A Randomized Controlled Trial. *Indian Journal of Forensic Medicine & Toxicology*, 14(4), 336–341.

Preti, C. (2013). Live music as a bridge between hospitals and outside communities: A proposed research framework and a review of the literature. UNESCO Refereed E-Journal. *Multi-Disciplinary Research in the Arts*, 3(3), 1–18.

Preti, C., & McFerran, K. (2016). Music to promote children's well-being during illness and hospitalization. In G. E. McPherson (Ed.), *The Child as Musician* (pp. 373–385). Oxford University Press.

Preti, C., & Welch, G. F. (2004). Music in a hospital setting: A multifaceted experience. *British Journal of Music Education*, 21(3), 329–345. https://doi.org/10.1017/s0265051704005893

Preti, C., & Welch, G. F. (2011). Music in a Hospital: The Impact of a Live Music Program on Pediatric Patients and Their Caregivers. *Music and Medicine*, 3(4), 213–223. https://doi.org/10.1177/1943862111399449

Priest, D. L., Karageorghis, C. I., & Sharp, N. C. C. (2004). The characteristics and effects of motivational music in exercise settings: The possible influence of gender, age, frequency of attendance, and time of attendance. *Journal of Sports Medicine and Physical Fitness*, 44(1), 77–86.

Procter, S. (2006). Music Therapy: Why not in education? In A. Paterson & S. Zimmerman (Eds), *No Needs for Words: Special Needs in Music Education*. National Association of Music Educators.

Protzko, J. (2017). Raising IQ among school-aged children: Five meta-analyses and a review of randomized controlled trials. *Developmental Review*, 46, 81–101. https://doi.org/10.1016/j.dr.2017.05.001

Provenzano, A. M., Spencer, M. S., Hopkins, M., Ellis, J., Reischl, C. H., Karr, K., & Savas, S. A. (2020). Effects of a University–School Partnered After-School Music Program on Developmental Health, Social, and Educational Outcomes. *Journal of the Society for Social Work and Research*, 11(3), 443–462. https://doi.org/10.1086/709175

Prudente, F. A. (1984). *Musical Process in the Gasumbi Epic of the Buwaya Kalingga People of Northern Philippines* [PhD Thesis]. Ann.

Przybylski, L., Bedoin, N., Krifi-Papoz, S., Herbillon, V., Roch, D., Léculier, L., Kotz, S. A., & Tillmann, B. (2013). Rhythmic auditory stimulation influences syntactic processing in children with developmental language disorders. *Neuropsychology*, 27(1), 121–131. https://doi.org/10.1037/a0031277

Puschmann, S., Baillet, S., & Zatorre, R. J. (2018). Musicians at the Cocktail Party: Neural Substrates of Musical Training During Selective Listening in Multispeaker Situations. *Cerebral Cortex*, 29(8), 3253–3265. https://doi.org/10.1093/cercor/bhy193

Putkinen, V., Huotilainen, M., & Tervaniemi, M. (2019). Neural Encoding of Pitch Direction Is Enhanced in Musically Trained Children and Is Related to Reading Skills. *Frontiers in Psychology*, 10. https://doi.org/10.3389/fpsyg.2019.01475

Putkinen, V., Saarikivi, K., & Tervaniemi, M. (2013). Do informal musical activities shape auditory skill development in preschool-age children? *Frontiers in Psychology*, 4. https://doi.org/10.3389/fpsyg.2013.00572

Putkinen, V., Tervaniemi, M., & Huotilainen, M. (2012). Informal musical activities are linked to auditory discrimination and attention in 2–3-year-old children: An event-related potential study. *European Journal of Neuroscience*, *37*(4), 654–661. https://doi.org/10.1111/ejn.12049

Putkinen, V., Tervaniemi, M., Saarikivi, K., & Huotilainen, M. (2015a). Promises of formal and informal musical activities in advancing neurocognitive development throughout childhood. *Annals of the New York Academy of Sciences*, *1337*(1), 153–162. https://doi.org/10.1111/nyas.12656

Putkinen, V., Tervaniemi, M., Saarikivi, K., & Huotilainen, M. (2015b). Promises of formal and informal musical activities in advancing neurocognitive development throughout childhood. *Annals of the New York Academy of Sciences*, *1337*(1), 153–162. https://doi.org/10.1111/nyas.12656

Putkinen, V., Tervaniemi, M., Saarikivi, K., Ojala, P., & Huotilainen, M. (2013). Enhanced development of auditory change detection in musically trained school-aged children: A longitudinal event-related potential study. *Developmental Science*, *17*(2), 282–297. https://doi.org/10.1111/desc.12109

Putkinen, V., Tervaniemi, M., Saarikivi, K., Vent, N. de, & Huotilainen, M. (2014). Investigating the effects of musical training on functional brain development with a novel Melodic MMN paradigm. *Neurobiology of Learning and Memory*, *110*, 8–15. https://doi.org/10.1016/j.nlm.2014.01.007

Pyszczynski, T., Greenberg, J., & Solomon, S. (1999). A dual-process model of defense against conscious and unconscious death-related thoughts: An extension of terror management theory. *Psychological Review*, *106*(4), 835–845. https://doi.org/10.1037/0033-295x.106.4.835

Quinn, J., Blandon, C., & Batson, A. (2019). Living beyond words: Post-human reflections on making music with post-verbal people. *Arts & Health*, *13*(1), 73–86. https://doi.org/10.1080/17533015.2019.1652194

Rabinowitch, T. C., Cross, I., & Burnard, P. (2013). Musical group interaction, intersubjectivity and merged subjectivity. In D. Reynolds & M. Reason (Eds), *Kinaesthetic Empathy in Creative and Cultural Practices*. Intellect Press.

Rabinowitch, T.-C., Cross, I., & Burnard, P. (2012). Long-term musical group interaction has a positive influence on empathy in children. *Psychology of Music*, *41*(4), 484–498. https://doi.org/10.1177/0305735612440609

Radbourne, J., Glow, H., & Johanson, K. (2013). *The audience experience*. University of Chicago Press.

Radocy, R. E., & Boyle, J. D. (1988). *Psychological foundations of musical behaviour*. Charles C. Thomas.

Rafferty, K. N. (2003). *Will a music and spatial-temporal math program enhance test scores? An analysis of second-grade students' mathematics performance on the Stanford-9 Test and the Capistrano Unified School District CORE level test* [Doctoral dissertation.]. University of Southern Carolina.

Ragert, M., Fairhurst, M. T., & Keller, P. E. (2014). Segregation and Integration of Auditory Streams when Listening to Multi-Part Music. *PLoS ONE, 9*(1), e84085. https://doi.org/10.1371/journal.pone.0084085

Raglio, A., Bellelli, G., Mazzola, P., Bellandi, D., Giovagnoli, A. R., Farina, E., Stramba-Badiale, M., Gentile, S., Gianelli, M. V., Ubezio, M. C., Zanetti, O., & Trabucchi, M. (2012). Music, music therapy and dementia: A review of literature and the recommendations of the Italian Psychogeriatric Association. *Maturitas, 72*(4), 305–310. https://doi.org/10.1016/j.maturitas.2012.05.016

Raglio, A., & Oasi, O. (2015). Music and health: What interventions for what results? *Frontiers in Psychology, 6.* https://doi.org/10.3389/fpsyg.2015.00230

Ragone, G., Good, J., & Howland, K. (2021). How Technology Applied to Music-Therapy and Sound-Based Activities Addresses Motor and Social Skills in Autistic Children. *Multimodal Technologies and Interaction, 5*(3), 11. https://doi.org/10.3390/mti5030011

Ramekar, U. V., & Gurjar, A. A. (2016). Empirical study of the effect of music on plant growth. *Tenth International Conference on Intelligent Systems and Control (ISCO,* 1–369 4.

Randall, W. M., & Rickard, N. S. (2016). Reasons for personal music listening: A mobile experience sampling study of emotional outcomes. *Psychology of Music, 45*(4), 479–495. https://doi.org/10.1177/0305735616666939

Randall, W. M., & Rickard, N. S. (2017). Personal Music Listening. *Music Perception, 34*(5), 501–514. https://doi.org/10.1525/mp.2017.34.5.501

Randall, W. M., Rickard, N. S., & Vella-Brodrick, D. A. (2014). Emotional outcomes of regulation strategies used during personal music listening: A mobile experience sampling study. *Musicae Scientiae, 18*(3), 275–291. https://doi.org/10.1177/1029864914536430

Rapp-Paglicci, L., Stewart, C., & Rowe, W. (2012). Improving Outcomes for at-risk Youth: Findings from the Prodigy Cultural Arts Program. *Journal of Evidence-Based Social Work, 9*(5), 512–523. https://doi.org/10.1080/15433714.2011.581532

Rashidi, N., & Faham, F. (2011). The Effect of Classical Music on the Reading Comprehension of Iranian Students. *Theory and Practice in Language Studies, 1*(1). https://doi.org/10.4304/tpls.1.1.74-82

Rasmussen, C., & Bisanz, J. (2005). Representation and working memory in early arithmetic. *Journal of Experimental Child Psychology, 91*(2), 137–157. https://doi.org/10.1016/j.jecp.2005.01.004

Rasmussen, C., Ho, E., & Bisanz, J. (2003). Use of the mathematical principle of inversion in young children. *Journal of Experimental Child Psychology, 85*(2), 89–102. https://doi.org/10.1016/s0022-0965(03)00031-6

Rathee, R., & Pallavi, R. (2020). Influence of Music on Consumer Behaviour: An Experimental Study. *Abhigyan, 38*(1), 30 371.

Rauschecker, J. P. (2001). Cortical Plasticity and Music. *Annals of the New York Academy of Sciences*, *930*(1), 330–336. https://doi.org/10.1111/j.1749-6632.2001.tb05742.x

Rauscher, F. H. (1999). Music exposure and the development of spatial intelligence in children. *Bulletin of the Council for Research in Music Education*, *142*, 35–47.

Rauscher, F. H. (2002). Mozart and the mind: Factual and fictional effects of musical enrichment. In J. Aronson (Ed.), *Improving academic achievement: Impact of psychological factors on education* (pp. 269–278). Academic Press.

Rauscher, F. H. (2003). Effects of piano, rhythm and singing instruction on the spatial reasoning of at-risk children. In R. Kopiez, A. C. Lehmann, I. Wolther, & C. Wolf (Eds), *Proceedings of the Fifth European Society for the Cognitive Sciences of Music* (pp. 190–194). Hannover University Press.

Rauscher, F. H. (2005). Musical influences on children's cognitive development. In *Royal College of Music*.

Rauscher, F. H. (2009). The impact of music instruction on other skills. In S. Hallam, I. Cross, & M. Thaut (Eds), *The Oxford Handbook of Music Psychology* (pp. 244–252). Oxford University Press.

Rauscher, F. H. (2014). *Effects of Piano, Singing and Rhythm Instruction on the Spatial Reasoning of At-Risk Children*.

Rauscher, F. H., & Gruhn, W. (Eds). (2007). *Neurosciences in Music Pedagogy*. Nova Science Publishers Inc.

Rauscher, F. H., & Hinton, S. C. (2006). The Mozart Effect: Music Listening is Not Music Instruction. *Educational Psychologist*, *41*(4), 233–238. https://doi.org/10.1207/s15326985ep4104_3

Rauscher, F. H., & Hinton, S. C. (2011). Music Instruction and its Diverse Extra-Musical Benefits. *Music Perception*, *29*(2), 215–226. https://doi.org/10.1525/mp.2011.29.2.215

Rauscher, F. H., LeMieux, M., & Hinton, S. C. (2005). Selective effects of music instruction on cognitive performance of at–risk children. *Bi-Annual Meeting of the European Conference on Developmental Psychology*.

Rauscher, F. H., & LeMieux, M. T. (2003). Piano, Rhythm, and Singing Instruction Improve Different Aspects of Spatial-temporal Reasoning in Head Start Children. *Annual Meeting of the Cognitive Neuroscience Society*.

Rauscher, F. H., Mosley, J., & Almane, D. (2008). The effects of music instruction on phonemic awareness in kindergarten children. *European Conference on Music Development*.

Rauscher, F. H., Shaw, G. L., & Ky, C. N. (1993). Music and spatial task performance. *Nature*, *365*, 611, 374. https://doi.org/10.1038/365611.

Rauscher, F. H., Shaw, G. L., & Ky, K. N. (1995). Listening to Mozart enhances spatial-temporal reasoning: Towards a neurophysiological basis. *Neuroscience Letters, 185*(1), 44–47. https://doi.org/10.1016/0304-3940(94)11221-4

Rauscher, F. H., & Zupan, M. A. (2000). Classroom keyboard instruction improves kindergarten children's spatial-temporal performance: A field experiment. *Early Childhood Research Quarterly, 15*(2), 215–228. https://doi.org/10.1016/s0885-2006(00)00050-8

Rauscher, F., Robinson, D., & Jens, J. (1998). Improved maze learning through early music exposure in rats. *Neurological Research, 20*(5), 427–432. https://doi.org/10.1080/01616412.1998.11740543

Rauscher, F., Shaw, G., Levine, L., Wright, E., Dennis, W., & Newcomb, R. (1997). Music training causes long-term enhancement of preschool children's spatial–temporal reasoning. *Neurological Research, 19*(1), 2–8. https://doi.org/10.1080/01616412.1997.11740765

Rautenberg, I. (2013). The effects of musical training on the decoding skills of German-speaking primary school children. *Journal of Research in Reading, 38*(1), 1–17. https://doi.org/10.1111/jrir.12010

Raven, J. (1981). Manual for Raven's Progressive Matrices and Vocabulary Scales. In *Research Supplement No.1: The 1979 British Standardisation of the Standard Progressive Matrices and Mill Hill Vocabulary Scales,*[MP375.

Reagon, C., Gale, N., Enright, S., Mann, M., & Deursen, R. van. (2016). A mixed-method systematic review to investigate the effect of group singing on health related quality of life. *Complementary Therapies in Medicine, 27*, 1–11. https://doi.org/10.1016/j.ctim.2016.03.017

Reardon, D., & Bell, G. (1970). Effects of sedative and stimulative music on activity levels of severely retarded boys. *American Journal of Mental Deficiency, 75*, 156–159.

Reaves, S., Graham, B., Grahn, J., Rabannifard, P., & Duarte, A. (2015). Turn Off the Music! Music Impairs Visual Associative Memory Performance in Older Adults. *The Gerontologist, 56*(3), 569–577. https://doi.org/10.1093/geront/gnu113

Recarte, M. A., & Nunes, L. (2002). Mental load and loss of control over speed in real driving. *Transportation Research Part F: Traffic Psychology and Behaviour, 5*(2), 111–122. https://doi.org/10.1016/s1369-8478(02)00010-4

Reeves, P. D. (2013). *How Music and Lyrics Protect and Heal the Souls of African American Women Who Have Experienced Domestic-Violence Trauma, Sexual Abuse, or Depression: A Phenomenological Study*. Pacifica Graduate Institute.

Register, D. (2001). The Effects of an Early Intervention Music Curriculum on Prereading/Writing. *Journal of Music Therapy, 38*(3), 239–248. https://doi.org/10.1093/jmt/38.3.239

Register, D. (2004). The Effects of Live MUSIC Groups Versus an Educational Children's Television Program on the Emergent Literacy of Young Children. *Journal of Music Therapy, 41*(1), 2–27. https://doi.org/10.1093/jmt/41.1.2

Reinert, K. C. (1997). *Music and the Nazi Party Congresses, its role in spectacle, festival and ritual* [PhD Thesis]. University of Alberta.

Rentfrow, P. J., & Gosling, S. D. (2003). The do re mi's of everyday life: The structure and personality correlates of music preferences. *Journal of Personality and Social Psychology, 84*(6), 1236–1256. https://doi.org/10.1037/0022-3514.84.6.1236

Rentfrow, P. J., & Gosling, S. D. (2006). Message in a Ballad. *Psychological Science, 17*(3), 236–242. https://doi.org/10.1111/j.1467-9280.2006.01691.x

Rentfrow, P. J., McDonald, J. A., & Oldmeadow, J. A. (2009). You Are What You Listen To: Young People's Stereotypes about Music Fans. *Group Processes & Intergroup Relations, 12*(3), 329–344. https://doi.org/10.1177/1368430209102845

Report, M. M. (2021).

Research, Q. A. (2012). *Young people not in education, employment or training (NEET) and music making*. Youth Music.

Resnicow, J. E., Salovey, P., & Repp, B. H. (2004). Is Recognition of Emotion in Music Performance an Aspect of Emotional Intelligence? *Music Perception, 22*(1), 145–158. https://doi.org/10.1525/mp.2004.22.1.145

Retallack, D. L. (1973). *The sound of music and plants*. http://www.dovesong.com/positive_music/plant_experiments.asp

Revelle, W., & Loftus, D. A. (1990). Individual Differences and Arousal: Implications for the Study of Mood and Memory. *Cognition & Emotion, 4*(3), 209–237. https://doi.org/10.1080/02699939008410797

Revesz, G. (1954). *Introduction to the Psychology of Music*. University of Oklahoma Press.

Reybrouck, M., & Podlipniak, P. (2019). Preconceptual Spectral and Temporal Cues as a Source of Meaning in Speech and Music. *Brain Sciences, 9*(3), 53. https://doi.org/10.3390/brainsci9030053

Ribeiro, F. S., Janzen, T. B., Passarini, L., & Vanzella, P. (2021). Exploring Changes in Musical Behaviors of Caregivers and Children in Social Distancing During the COVID-19 Outbreak. *Frontiers in Psychology, 12*. https://doi.org/10.3389/fpsyg.2021.633499

Ribeiro, F. S., Lessa, J. P. A., Delmolin, G., & Santos, F. H. (2021). Music Listening in Times of COVID-19 Outbreak: A Brazilian Study. *Frontiers in Psychology, 12*. https://doi.org/10.3389/fpsyg.2021.647473

Ribeiro, F. S., & Santos, F. H. (2017). Enhancement of numeric cognition in children with low achievement in mathematic after a non-instrumental musical training. *Research in Developmental Disabilities, 62,* 26–39. https://doi.org/10.1016/j.ridd.2016.11.008

Riby, L. M. (2013). The Joys of Spring. *Experimental Psychology, 60*(2), 71–79. https://doi.org/10.1027/1618-3169/a000166

Richards, D., Fassbender, E., Bilgin, A., & Thompson, W. F. (2008). An investigation of the role of background music in IVWs for learning. *Research in Learning Technology, 16*(3). https://doi.org/10.3402/rlt.v16i3.10901

Richards, S., & Goswami, U. (2019). Impaired Recognition of Metrical and Syntactic Boundaries in Children with Developmental Language Disorders. *Brain Sciences, 9*(2), 33. https://doi.org/10.3390/brainsci9020033

Richmiller, M. G. (1992). *Study of the residual effects of music education experiences of a prison choir, twenty-nine years after participation* [PhD Thesis]. Southeast Missouri State University.

Rickard, N. S., Appelman, P., James, R., Murphy, F., Gill, A., & Bambrick, C. (2012). Orchestrating life skills: The effect of increased school-based music classes on children's social competence and self-esteem. *International Journal of Music Education, 31*(3), 292–309. https://doi.org/10.1177/0255761411434824

Rickard, N. S., Bambrick, C. J., & Gill, A. (2012). Absence of widespread psychosocial and cognitive effects of school-based music instruction in 10–13-year-old students. *International Journal of Music Education, 30*(1), 57–78. https://doi.org/10.1177/0255761411431399

Rickard, N. S., & McFerran, K. (2012). *Lifelong engagement with music: Benefits for mental health and wellbeing*. Nova Science Publishers, Inc.

Rickard, N. S., Vasquez, J. T., Murphy, F., Gill, A., & Toukhsati, S. R. (2010). Benefits of a classroom based music program on verbal memory of primary school children: A longitudinal study. *Australian Journal of Music Education, 1,* 36–47.

Rickson, D., Legg, R., & Reynolds, D. (2018). Daily Singing in a School Severely Affected by Earthquakes. *Teachers' Work, 15*(1), 63–84. https://doi.org/10.24135/teacherswork.v15i1.243

Rideout, B. E., & Taylor, J. (1997). Enhanced Spatial Performance following 10 Minutes Exposure to Music: A Replication. *Perceptual and Motor Skills, 85*(1), 112–114. https://doi.org/10.2466/pms.1997.85.1.112

Rideout, V. J., Foehr, U. G., & Roberts, D. F. (2010). *Generation M2: Media in the lives of 8- to 18-year-olds*. Henry J. Kaiser Family Foundation.

Rieber, M. (1965). The effect of music on the activity level of children. *Psychonomic Science, 3*(1–12), 325–326. https://doi.org/10.3758/bf03343162

Rimmer, M. (2017). Harmony or Discord? Understanding children's valuations of a Sistema-inspired initiative. *British Journal of Music Education, 35*(1), 43–55. https://doi.org/10.1017/s0265051717000146

Rincón Prat, C. (2013). Promoting personal development through music participation: A case study of youth orchestras in Columbia. In S. O'Neill (Ed.), *Personhood and Music Learning*. Canadian Music Educators Association.

Rinta, T., Purves, R., Welch, G., Elmer, S. S., & Bissig, R. (2011). Connections between children's feelings of social inclusion and their musical backgrounds. *Journal of Social Inclusion*, 2(2), 34. https://doi.org/10.36251/josi.32

Rio, R. (2018). A Community-Based Music Therapy Support Group for People With Alzheimer's Disease and Their Caregivers: A Sustainable Partnership Model. *Frontiers in Medicine*, 5. https://doi.org/10.3389/fmed.2018.00293

Rio, R. E., & Tenney, K. S. (2002). Music Therapy for Juvenile Offenders in Residential Treatment. *Music Therapy Perspectives*, 20(2), 89–97. https://doi.org/10.1093/mtp/20.2.89

Rippere, V. (1977). `What's the thing to do when you're feeling depressed?'—A pilot study. *Behaviour Research and Therapy*, 15(2), 185–191. https://doi.org/10.1016/0005-7967(77)90104-8

Ritblatt, S., Longstreth, S., Hokoda, A., Cannon, B.-N., & Weston, J. (2013). Can Music Enhance School-Readiness Socioemotional Skills? *Journal of Research in Childhood Education*, 27(3), 257–266. https://doi.org/10.1080/02568543.2013.796333

Ritter, S. M., & Ferguson, S. (2017). *Happy Creativity: Listening to happy music facilitates divergent thinking*. https://doi.org/10.1371/journal.pone.0182210.

Roballey, T. C., McGreevy, C., Rongo, R. R., Schwantes, M. L., Steger, P. J., Wininger, M. A., & Gardner, E. B. (1985). The effect of music on eating behavior. *Bulletin of the Psychonomic Society*, 23(3), 221–222. https://doi.org/10.3758/bf03329832

Robarts, J. Z., & Sloboda, A. (1994). Perspectives on Music Therapy with People Suffering from Anorexia Nervosa. *Journal of British Music Therapy*, 8(1), 7–14. https://doi.org/10.1177/135945759400800104

Robazza, C., Macaluso, C., & D'Urso, V. (1994). Emotional Reactions to Music by Gender, Age, and Expertise. *Perceptual and Motor Skills*, 79(2), 939–944. https://doi.org/10.2466/pms.1994.79.2.939

Robb, S. L. (2000). The Effect of Therapeutic Music Interventions on the Behavior of Hospitalized Children in Isolation: Developing a Contextual Support Model of Music Therapy. *Journal of Music Therapy*, 37(2), 118–146. https://doi.org/10.1093/jmt/37.2.118

Robb, S. L. (2003). Designing Music Therapy Interventions for Hospitalized Children and Adolescents Using a Contextual Support Model of Music Therapy. *Music Therapy Perspectives*, 21(1), 27–40. https://doi.org/10.1093/mtp/21.1.27

Robb, S. L., Burns, D. S., Stegenga, K. A., Haut, P. R., Monahan, P. O., Meza, J., Stump, T. E., Cherven, B. O., Docherty, S. L., Hendricks-Ferguson, V. L.,

Kintner, E. K., Haight, A. E., Wall, D. A., & Haase, J. E. (2014). Randomized clinical trial of therapeutic music video intervention for resilience outcomes in adolescents/young adults undergoing hematopoietic stem cell transplant: A report from the Children's Oncology Group. *Cancer, 120*(6), 909–917. https://doi.org/10.1002/cncr.28355

Robb, S. L., & Ebberts, A. G. (2003). Songwriting and Digital Video Production Interventions for Pediatric Patients Undergoing Bone Marrow Transplantation, Part II: An Analysis of Patient-Generated Songs and Patient Perceptions Regarding Intervention Efficacy. *Journal of Pediatric Oncology Nursing, 20*(1), 16–25. https://doi.org/10.1053/jpon.2003.4

Robert, J. B., Terry, L. G., David, J. H., Caitlin, A. C., & Kenneth, W. B. (2006). Supporting the Health of College Solo Singers: The Relationship of Positive Emotions and Stress to Changes in Salivary IgA and Cortisol during Singing. *Journal for Learning through the Arts, 2*(1). https://doi.org/10.21977/d92110079

Roberts, M. J. (2009). Peace Punks and Punks Against Racism: Resource Mobilization and Frame Construction in the Punk Movement. *Music and Arts in Action, 1*(2).

Roberts, N. (2016). *The school curriculum and SATs in England: Reforms since.* House of Commons Library.

Robertson, C. (2006). *The Potential Role of Collaborative Music-Making in Conflict Resolution: An Exploratory Enquiry.* Unpublished dissertation[MP383. Goldsmiths University.

Robinson, J. (2015). *Playing at Home: How Families Engage with In Harmony Liverpool.* University of Liverpool.

Rochette, F., Moussard, A., & Bigand, E. (2014). Music Lessons Improve Auditory Perceptual and Cognitive Performance in Deaf Children. *Frontiers in Human Neuroscience, 8.* https://doi.org/10.3389/fnhum.2014.00488

Roden, I., Grube, D., Bongard, S., & Kreutz, G. (2013). Does music training enhance working memory performance? Findings from a quasi-experimental longitudinal study. *Psychology of Music, 42*(2), 284–298. https://doi.org/10.1177/0305735612471239

Roden, I., Könen, T., Bongard, S., Frankenberg, E., Friedrich, E. K., & Kreutz, G. (2014). Effects of music training on attention, processing speed and cognitive music abilities—Findings from a longitudinal study.

Roden, I., Kreutz, G., & Bongard, S. (2012). Effects of a School-Based Instrumental Music Program on Verbal and Visual Memory in Primary School Children: A Longitudinal Study. *Frontiers in Psychology, 3.* https://doi.org/10.3389/fpsyg.2012.00572

Rodrigues, A., C., G., L., & Loureiro, M. (2007). Visual attention in musicians and non-musicians: A comparative study; CIM07. *Proceedings of the 3rd*

International Conference on Interdisciplinary Musicology, 15–19. http://www-gewi.uni-graz.at/cim07/index2.htm.

Rodrigues, A. C., Loureiro, M. A., & Caramelli, P. (2013). Long-term musical training may improve different forms of visual attention ability. *Brain and Cognition, 82*(3), 229–235. https://doi.org/10.1016/j.bandc.2013.04.009

Rodrigues, H., Leite, A., Faria, C., Monteiro, I., & Rodrigues, P. M. (2010). Music for mothers and babies living in a prison: A report on a special production of `BebéBabá'. *International Journal of Community Music, 3*(1), 77–90. https://doi.org/10.1386/ijcm.3.1.77/1

ROE, K. (1985). SWEDISH YOUTH AND MUSIC: Listening Patterns and Motivations. *Communication Research, 12*(3), 353–362. https://doi.org/10.1177/009365085012003007

Roederer, J. G. (1984). The Search for a Survival Value of Music. *Music Perception, 1*(3), 350–356. https://doi.org/10.2307/40285265

Roeper, J. de, & Savelsberg, H. J. (2009). Challenging the youth policy imperative: Engaging young people through the arts. *Journal of Youth Studies, 12*(2), 209–225. https://doi.org/10.1080/13676260802672820

Rogalsky, C., Rong, F., Saberi, K., & Hickok, G. (2011). Functional Anatomy of Language and Music Perception: Temporal and Structural Factors Investigated Using Functional Magnetic Resonance Imaging. *Journal of Neuroscience, 31*(10), 3843–3852. https://doi.org/10.1523/jneurosci.4515-10.2011

Rogenmoser, L., Kernbach, J., Schlaug, G., & Gaser, C. (2017). Keeping brains young with making music. *Brain Structure and Function, 223*(1), 297–305. https://doi.org/10.1007/s00429-017-1491-2

Rogers, C. R. (1957). Becoming a Person. In *Healing: Human and divine: Man's search for health and wholeness through science, faith, and prayer.* (pp. 57–67). Association Press. https://doi.org/10.1037/10811-003

Rogers, P. (1992). Issues in Working with Sexually Abused Clients in Music Therapy. *Journal of British Music Therapy, 6*(2), 5–15. https://doi.org/10.1177/135945759200600202

Rolka, E. J., & Silverman, M. J. (2015). A systematic review of music and dyslexia. *The Arts in Psychotherapy, 46,* 24–32. https://doi.org/10.1016/j.aip.2015.09.002

Rolvsjord, R. (2016). Resource-oriented perspectives in music therapy. In J. Edwards (Ed.), *Oxford Library of Psychology.The Oxford Handbook of Music Therapy* (pp. 557–576). Oxford University Press.

Roma, C. (2010). Re-sounding: Refuge and reprise in a prison choral community. *International Journal of Community Music, 3*(1), 91–102. https://doi.org/10.1386/ijcm.3.1.91/1

Román-Caballero, R., Martín-Arévalo, E., & Lupiáñez, J. (2020). Attentional networks functioning and vigilance in expert musicians and non-musicians.

Psychological Research, 85(3), 1121–1135. https://doi.org/10.1007/s00426-020-01323-2

Root-Bernstein, R. S. (2001). Music, Creativity and Scientific Thinking. *Leonardo*, 34(1), 63–68. https://doi.org/10.1162/002409401300052532

Rooyen, A. van, & Santos, A. dos. (2020). Exploring the lived experiences of teenagers in a children's home participating in a choir: A community music therapy perspective. *International Journal of Community Music*, 13(1), 81–101. https://doi.org/10.1386/ijcm_00011_1

Rorke, M. A. (1996). Music and the Wounded of World War II. *Journal of Music Therapy*, 33(3), 189–207. https://doi.org/10.1093/jmt/33.3.189

Rose, A. J. (2002). Co–Rumination in the Friendships of Girls and Boys. *Child Development*, 73(6), 1830–1843. https://doi.org/10.1111/1467-8624.00509

Rose, D., Bartoli, A. J., & Heaton, P. (2017). Measuring the impact of musical learning on cognitive, behavioural and socio-emotional wellbeing development in children. *Psychology of Music*, 47(2), 284–303. https://doi.org/10.1177/0305735617744887

Ross, V. R. (1936). Relationship between intelligence, scholastic achievement and musical talent. *Journal of Juvenile Research*, 20, 47–64.

Rossetti, A. (2020). Environmental Music Therapy (EMT): Music's Contribution to Changing Hospital Atmospheres and Perceptions of Environments. *Music and Medicine*, 12(2), 130. https://doi.org/10.47513/mmd.v12i2.742

Rossi, S., Gugler, M. F., Rungger, M., Galvan, O., Zorowka, P. G., & Seebacher, J. (2020). How the Brain Understands Spoken and Sung Sentences. *Brain Sciences*, 10(1), 36. https://doi.org/10.3390/brainsci10010036

Roulston, K., Jutras, P., & Kim, S. J. (2015). Adult perspectives of learning musical instruments. *International Journal of Music Education*, 33(3), 325–335. https://doi.org/10.1177/0255761415584291

Roux, F. H. le, Bouic, P. J. D., & Bester, M. M. (2007). The Effect of Bach's Magnificat on Emotions, Immune, and Endocrine Parameters During Physiotherapy Treatment of Patients with Infectious Lung Conditions. *Journal of Music Therapy*, 44(2), 156–168. https://doi.org/10.1093/jmt/44.2.156

Rowe, G., Hirsh, J. B., & Anderson, A. K. (2007). Positive affect increases the breadth of attentional selection. *Proceedings of the National Academy of Sciences*, 104(1), 383–388. https://doi.org/10.1073/pnas.0605198104

Ruan, Z.-L., Liu, L., Strodl, E., Fan, L.-J., Yin, X.-N., Wen, G.-M., Sun, D.-L., Xian, D.-X., Jiang, H., Jing, J., Jin, Y., Wu, C.-A., & Chen, W.-Q. (2018). Antenatal Training with Music and Maternal Talk Concurrently May Reduce Autistic-Like Behaviors at around 3 Years of Age. *Frontiers in Psychiatry*, 8. https://doi.org/10.3389/fpsyt.2017.00305

Rudnick, M., Sterritt, G. M., & Flax, M. (1967). Auditory and Visual Rhythm Perception and Reading Ability. *Child Development*, *38*(2), 581. https://doi.org/10.2307/1127312

Rudstam, G., Elofsson, U., Søndergaard, H. P., Bonde, L. O., & Beck, B. D. (2017). Trauma-focused group music and imagery with women suffering from PTSD/complex PTSD: A feasibility study. *Approach*, *9*, 202–216.

Rumberger, R. W., & Sun Ah Lim, S. (2008). *Why students drop out of school: A review of 25 years of research* [California dropout research project report 15.]. University of California.

Rummy, N. S. J., Rumaolat, W., & Trihartity, T. (2020). A Systematic Review of Effectiveness of Music Therapy on Depression in the Elderly. *Jurnal Ners*, *15*(2), 101–106, https://doi.org/10.20473/jn.v15i2.18974.

Rusinek, G. (2008). Disaffected learners and school musical culture: An opportunity for inclusion. *Research Studies in Music Education*, *30*(1), 9–23. https://doi.org/10.1177/1321103x08089887

Ruthsatz, J., Detterman, D., Griscom, W. S., & Cirullo, B. A. (2008). Becoming an expert in the musical domain: It takes more than just practice. *Intelligence*, *36*(4), 330–338. https://doi.org/10.1016/j.intell.2007.08.003

Ruud, E. (1997a). Music and identity. *Norsk Tidsskrift for Musikkterapi*, *6*(1), 3–13. https://doi.org/10.1080/08098139709477889

Ruud, E. (1997b). Music and the Quality of Life. *Norsk Tidsskrift for Musikkterapi*, *6*(2), 86–97. https://doi.org/10.1080/08098139709477902

Saarikallio, S. (2006a). Differences in adolescents' use of music in mood regulation. In M. Baroni, A. R. Addessor, R. Caterina, & M. Costa (Eds), *Proceedings of the 9th International Conference on Music Perception and Cognition* (p. 391). Alma Mater Studiorum, University of Bologna.

Saarikallio, S. (2006b). The strategies for regulating mood by musical activities in adolescence. *Proceedings of the 21st International Seminar on Research in Music Education*.

Saarikallio, S. (2010). Music as emotional self-regulation throughout adulthood. *Psychology of Music*, *39*(3), 307–327. https://doi.org/10.1177/0305735610374894

Saarikallio, S. (2017). Musical Identity in Fostering Emotional Health. In *Handbook of Musical Identities* (pp. 602–623). Oxford University Press. https://doi.org/10.1093/acprof:oso/9780199679485.003.0033

Saarikallio, S. (2019). Access-Awareness-Agency (AAA) Model of Music-Based Social-Emotional Competence (MuSEC). *Music & Science*, *2*, 205920431881542. https://doi.org/10.1177/2059204318815421

Saarikallio, S., & Baltazar, M. (2018). Music as a Forum for Social-Emotional Health. In L. O. Bonde & T. Theorell (Eds), *Music and Public Health: A Nordic*

Perspective,: Springer [MP392]International Publishing (pp. 101–113 ,). https://doi.org/10.1007/978-3-319-76240-1_7.

Saarikallio, S., Baltazar, M., & Västfjäll, D. (2017). Adolescents' musical relaxation: Understanding related affective processing. *Nordic Journal of Music Therapy, 26*(4), 376–389. https://doi.org/10.1080/08098131.2016.1276097

Saarikallio, S., & Erkkilä, J. (2007). The role of music in adolescents' mood regulation. *Psychology of Music, 35*(1), 88–109. https://doi.org/10.1177/0305735607068889

Saarikallio, S. H., Maksimainen, J. P., & Randall, W. M. (2018). Relaxed and connected: Insights into the emotional–motivational constituents of musical pleasure. *Psychology of Music, 47*(5), 644–662. https://doi.org/10.1177/0305735618778768

Saarikallio, S. H., Randall, W. M., & Baltazar, M. (2020). Music Listening for Supporting Adolescents' Sense of Agency in Daily Life. *Frontiers in Psychology, 10.* https://doi.org/10.3389/fpsyg.2019.02911

Saarikivi, K. A., Houtilainen, M., Tervaniemi, M., & Putkinen, V. (2019). Selectively enhanced development of working memory in musically trained children and adolescents. *Frontiers in Integrative Neuroscience, 13*, 62, https://doi.org/10.3389/finint.2019.00062.

Saarikivi, K., Putkinen, V., Tervaniemi, M., & Huotilainen, M. (2016). Cognitive flexibility modulates maturation and music-training-related changes in neural sound discrimination. *European Journal of Neuroscience, 44*(2), 1815–1825. https://doi.org/10.1111/ejn.13176

Sachs, M. E., Damasio, A., & Habibi, A. (2015). The pleasures of sad music: A systematic review. *Frontiers in Human Neuroscience, 9.* https://doi.org/10.3389/fnhum.2015.00404

Sachs, M., Kaplan, J., Sarkissian, A. D., & Habibi, A. (2017). Increased engagement of the cognitive control network associated with music training in children during an fMRI Stroop task. *PLOS ONE, 12*(10), e0187254. https://doi.org/10.1371/journal.pone.0187254

Sacks, O. (2007). *Musicophilia: Tales of Music and the Brain.* Alfred A. Knopf.

Sadakata, M., & Sekiyama, K. (2011). Enhanced perception of various linguistic features by musicians: A cross-linguistic study. *Acta Psychologica, 138*(1), 1–10. https://doi.org/10.1016/j.actpsy.2011.03.007

Sahebdel, S., & Khodadust, M. (2014). The effect of background music while silent reading on EFL Learners' reading comprehension. *The Journal of Applied Linguistics, 7*(14), 102–119.

Saint-Georges, C., Chetouani, M., Cassel, R., Apicella, F., Mahdhaoui, A., Muratori, F., Laznik, M.-C., & Cohen, D. (2013). Motherese in Interaction:

At the Cross-Road of Emotion and Cognition? (A Systematic Review). *PLoS ONE, 8*(10), e78103. https://doi.org/10.1371/journal.pone.0078103

Sakka, L. S., & Juslin, P. N. (2018). Emotion regulation with music in depressed and non-depressed individuals. *Music & Science, 1*, 205920431875502. https://doi.org/10.1177/2059204318755023

Sala, G., & Gobet, F. (2017a). When the music's over: Does music skill transfer to children's and young adolescent's cognitive and academic skills? A meta-analysis. *Educational Research Review, 20*, 55–67, https://doi.org/10.1016/j.edutev.2016.11.005.

Sala, G., & Gobet, F. (2017b). Does Far Transfer Exist? Negative Evidence From Chess, Music, and Working Memory Training. *Current Directions in Psychological Science, 26*(6), 515–520. https://doi.org/10.1177/0963721417712760

Sala, G., & Gobet, F. (2018). *Elvis Has Left the Building: Correlational but Not Causal Relationship between Music Skill and Cognitive Ability*. https://doi.org/10.31234/osf.io/auzry

Sala, G., & Gobet, F. (2020). Cognitive and academic benefits of music training with children: A multilevel meta-analysis. *Memory & Cognition, 48*(8), 1429–1441. https://doi.org/10.3758/s13421-020-01060-2

Salamé, P., & Baddeley, A. (1989). Effects of Background Music on Phonological Short-Term Memory. *The Quarterly Journal of Experimental Psychology Section A, 41*(1), 107–122. https://doi.org/10.1080/14640748908402355

Salimpoor, V. N., Benovoy, M., Longo, G., Cooperstock, J. R., & Zatorre, R. J. (2009). The Rewarding Aspects of Music Listening Are Related to Degree of Emotional Arousal. *PLoS ONE, 4*(10), e7487. https://doi.org/10.1371/journal.pone.0007487

Salmon, D., & Rickaby, C. (2012). City of One: A Qualitative Study Examining the Participation of Young People in Care in a Theatre and Music Initiative. *Children & Society, 28*(1), 30–41. https://doi.org/10.1111/j.1099-0860.2012.00444.x

Salomon, G., & Perkins, D. N. (1989). Rocky Roads to Transfer: Rethinking Mechanism of a Neglected Phenomenon. *Educational Psychologist, 24*(2), 113–142. https://doi.org/10.1207/s15326985ep2402_1

Salovey, P., & Mayer, J. D. (1990). Emotional Intelligence. *Imagination, Cognition and Personality, 9*(3), 185–211. https://doi.org/10.2190/dugg-p24e-52wk-6cdg

Salovey, P., Mayer, J. D., Goldman, S. L., Turvey, C., & Palfai, T. P. (1995). Emotional attention, clarity, and repair: Exploring emotional intelligence using the Trait Meta-Mood Scale. In *Emotion, disclosure, & health.* (pp. 125–154). American Psychological Association. https://doi.org/10.1037/10182-006

Salthouse, T. A. (2010). Is flanker-based inhibition related to age? Identifying specific influences of individual differences on neurocognitive variables. *Brain and Cognition, 73*(1), 51–61. https://doi.org/10.1016/j.bandc.2010.02.003

Sammler, D., & Elmer, S. (2020). Advances in the Neurocognition of Music and Language. *Brain Sciences*, *10*(8), 509. https://doi.org/10.3390/brainsci10080509

Sammler, D., Grigutsch, M., Fritz, T., & Koelsch, S. (2007). Music and emotion: Electrophysiological correlates of the processing of pleasant and unpleasant music. *Psychophysiology*, *44*(2), 293–304. https://doi.org/10.1111/j.1469-8986.2007.00497.x

San Diego Youth Symphony Community Opus Project. (2011).

Sandgren, M. (2009). Evidence of strong immediate well–being effects of choral singing–with more enjoyment for women than for men. *7th Triennial Conference of European Society for the Cognitive Sciences of Music (ESCOM 2009.*

Sandgren, M. (2018). Exploring personality and musical self-perceptions among vocalists and instrumentalists at music colleges. *Psychology of Music*, *47*(4), 465–482. https://doi.org/10.1177/0305735618761572

Sänger, J., Müller, V., & Lindenberger, U. (2012). Intra- and interbrain synchronization and network properties when playing guitar in duets. *Frontiers in Human Neuroscience*, *6*. https://doi.org/10.3389/fnhum.2012.00312

Santos-Luiz, C. dos, Mónico, L. S. M., Almeida, L. S., & Coimbra, D. (2016). Exploring the long-term associations between adolescents' music training and academic achievement. *Musicae Scientiae*, *20*(4), 512–527. https://doi.org/10.1177/1029864915623613

Särkämö, T., Ripollés, P., Vepsäläinen, H., Autti, T., Silvennoinen, H. M., & Salli, E. (2014). Structural changes induced by daily music listening in the recovering brain after middle cerebral artery stroke: A voxel-based morphometry study. *Frontiers in Human Neuroscience*, *8*, 245 398.

Sarkamo, T., Tervaniemi, M., Laitinen, S., Forsblom, A., Soinila, S., Mikkonen, M., Autti, T., Silvennoinen, H. M., Erkkila, J., Laine, M., Peretz, I., & Hietanen, M. (2008). Music listening enhances cognitive recovery and mood after middle cerebral artery stroke. *Brain*, *131*(3), 866–876. https://doi.org/10.1093/brain/awn013

Särkämö, T., Tervaniemi, M., Laitinen, S., Numminen, A., Kurki, M., Johnson, J. K., & Rantanen, P. (2013). Cognitive, Emotional, and Social Benefits of Regular Musical Activities in Early Dementia: Randomized Controlled Study. *The Gerontologist*, *54*(4), 634–650. https://doi.org/10.1093/geront/gnt100

Sauce, B., & Matzel, L. D. (2018). The paradox of intelligence: Heritability and malleability coexist in hidden gene-environment interplay. *Psychological Bulletin*, *144*(1), 26–47. https://doi.org/10.1037/bul0000131

Sausser, S., & Waller, R. J. (2006). A model for music therapy with students with emotional and behavioral disorders. *The Arts in Psychotherapy*, *33*(1), 1–10. https://doi.org/10.1016/j.aip.2005.05.003

Savage, P., Loui, P., Tarr, B., Schachner, A., Glowacki, L., Mithen, S., & Fitch, W. (2020). Music as coevolved system for social bonding. *Behavioural and Brain Sciences*, *1*[MP399]-36. https://doi.org/10.1017/SO140525X20000333.

Savan, A. (1998). A study of the effect of background music on the behaviour and physiological responses of children with special educational needs. *The Psychology of Education Review*, *22*(1), 32–36.

Savan, A. (1999). The Effect of Background Music on Learning. *Psychology of Music*, *27*(2), 138–146. https://doi.org/10.1177/0305735699272005

Savoie, I. (2012). *Evaluation Report: Evaluation of Sistema*. Department of Healthy and Inclusive Communities & Sistema New Brunswick.

Schäfer, T., Sedlmeier, P., Städtler, C., & Huron, D. (2013). The psychological functions of music listening. *Frontiers in Psychology*, *4*. https://doi.org/10.3389/fpsyg.2013.00511

Schäfer, T., Smukalla, M., & Oelker, S.-A. (2013). How music changes our lives: A qualitative study of the long-term effects of intense musical experiences. *Psychology of Music*, *42*(4), 525–544. https://doi.org/10.1177/0305735613482024

Schäfer, T., Tipandjan, A., & Sedlmeier, P. (2012). The functions of music and their relationship to music preference in India and Germany. *International Journal of Psychology*, *47*(5), 370–380. https://doi.org/10.1080/00207594.2012.688133

Scharff, C. (2015). *Equality and Diversity in the Classical Music Profession*. Kings College London.

Scheel, K. R., & Westefeld, J. S. (1999). Heavy metal music and adolescent suicidality: An empirical investigation. *Adolescence*, *34*, 253–273.

Schellenberg, E. G. (2001). Music and Nonmusical Abilities. *Annals of the New York Academy of Sciences*, *930*(1), 355–371. https://doi.org/10.1111/j.1749-6632.2001.tb05744.x

Schellenberg, E. G. (2003). Does Exposure to Music Have Beneficial Side Effects? In *The Cognitive Neuroscience of Music* (pp. 430–448). Oxford University Press. https://doi.org/10.1093/acprof:oso/9780198525202.003.0028

Schellenberg, E. G. (2004). Music Lessons Enhance IQ. *Psychological Science*, *15*(8), 511–514. https://doi.org/10.1111/j.0956-7976.2004.00711.x

Schellenberg, E. G. (2005). Music Listening and Cognitive Abilities in 10- and 11-Year-Olds: The Blur Effect. *Annals of the New York Academy of Sciences*, *1060*(1), 202–209. https://doi.org/10.1196/annals.1360.013

Schellenberg, E. G. (2006). Long-term positive associations between music lessons and IQ. *Journal of Educational Psychology*, *98*(2), 457–468. https://doi.org/10.1037/0022-0663.98.2.457

Schellenberg, E. G. (2011a). Examining the association between music lessons and intelligence. *British Journal of Psychology, 102*(3), 283–302. https://doi.org/10.1111/j.2044-8295.2010.02000.x

Schellenberg, E. G. (2011b). Music Lessons, Emotional Intelligence, and IQ. *Music Perception, 29*(2), 185–194. https://doi.org/10.1525/mp.2011.29.2.185

Schellenberg, E. G. (2015). Music training and speech perception: A gene-environment interaction. *Annals of the New York Academy of Sciences, 1337*(1), 170–177. https://doi.org/10.1111/nyas.12627

Schellenberg, E. G. (2016). Music training and non-musical abilities. In S. Hallam, I. Cross, & M. Thaut (Eds), *The Oxford Handbook of Music Psychology* (pp. 415–432). Oxford University Press.

Schellenberg, E. G. (2020). Correlation = causation? Music training, psychology, and neuroscience. *Psychology of Aesthetics, Creativity, and the Arts, 14*(4), 475–480. https://doi.org/10.1037/aca0000263

Schellenberg, E. G., Corrigall, K. A., Dys, S. P., & Malti, T. (2015). Group Music Training and Children's Prosocial Skills. *PLOS ONE, 10*(10), e0141449. https://doi.org/10.1371/journal.pone.0141449

Schellenberg, E. G., & Mankarious, M. (2012). Music training and emotion comprehension in childhood. *Emotion, 12*(5), 887–891. https://doi.org/10.1037/a0027971

Schellenberg, E. G., & Moreno, S. (2009). Music lessons, pitch processing, and g. *Psychology of Music, 38*(2), 209–221. https://doi.org/10.1177/0305735609339473

Schellenberg, E. G., Nakata, T., Hunter, P. G., & Tamoto, S. (2007). Exposure to music and cognitive performance: Tests of children and adults. *Psychology of Music, 35*(1), 5–19. https://doi.org/10.1177/0305735607068885

Schellenberg, E. G., & Peretz, I. (2008). Music, language and cognition: Unresolved issues. *Trends in Cognitive Sciences, 12*(2), 45–46. https://doi.org/10.1016/j.tics.2007.11.005

Schellenberg, E. G., & Weiss, M. W. (2013a). Music and Cognitive Abilities. In *The Psychology of Music* (pp. 499–550). Elsevier. https://doi.org/10.1016/b978-0-12-381460-9.00012-2

Schellenberg, E. G., & Weiss, M. W. (2013b). Music and Cognitive Abilities. In *The Psychology of Music* (pp. 499–550). Elsevier. https://doi.org/10.1016/b978-0-12-381460-9.00012-2

Schiltz, L. (2016). Treating the emotional and motivational inhibition of highly gifted underachievers with music psychotherapy: Meta-analysis of an evaluation study based on a sequential design. *Bull Soc Sci Med Grand DucheLuxemb[MP402, 1,* 7–26.

Schlaug, G. (2001). The Brain of Musicians. *Annals of the New York Academy of Sciences, 930*(1), 281–299. https://doi.org/10.1111/j.1749-6632.2001.tb05739.x

Schlaug, G. (2005). Effects of Music Training on the Child's Brain and Cognitive Development. *Annals of the New York Academy of Sciences, 1060*(1), 219–230. https://doi.org/10.1196/annals.1360.015

Schlaug, G. (2009). Music, musicians and brain plasticity. In S. Hallam, I. Cross, & M. Thaut (Eds), *Oxford Handbook of Music Psychology* (pp. 197–207). Oxford University Press.

Schlaug, G. (2015). Musicians and music making as a model for the study of brain plasticity. In *Progress in Brain Research* (pp. 37–55). Elsevier. https://doi.org/10.1016/bs.pbr.2014.11.020

Schlaug, G., Jäncke, L., Huang, Y., Staiger, J. F., & Steinmetz, H. (1995). Increased corpus callosum size in musicians. *Neuropsychologia, 33*(8), 1047–1055. https://doi.org/10.1016/0028-3932(95)00045-5

Schlaug, G., Jäncke, L., Huang, Y., & Steinmetz, H. (1995). In Vivo Evidence of Structural Brain Asymmetry in Musicians. *Science, 267*(5198), 699–701. https://doi.org/10.1126/science.7839149

Schmid, W., Rosland, J. H., Hofacker, S., Hunskår, I., & Bruvik, F. B. (2018). Patient's and health care provider's perspectives on music therapy in palliative care-An integrative review. *Palliative Care, 17*(1), 32 404.

Schmidt, R., & Lee, T. (2011). *Motor control and learning: A behavioral emphasis.* Human Kinetics.

Schmithorst, V. J., & Holland, S. K. (2003). The effect of musical training on music processing: A functional magnetic resonance imaging study in humans. *Neuroscience Letters, 348*(2), 65–68. https://doi.org/10.1016/s0304-3940(03)00714-6

Schneider, C. E., Hunter, E. G., & Bardach, S. H. (2018). Potential Cognitive Benefits From Playing Music Among Cognitively Intact Older Adults: A Scoping Review. *Journal of Applied Gerontology, 38*(12), 1763–1783. https://doi.org/10.1177/0733464817751198

Schneider, J. (2018). The Arts as a Medium for Care and Self-Care in Dementia: Arguments and Evidence. *International Journal of Environmental Research and Public Health, 15*(6), 1151. https://doi.org/10.3390/ijerph15061151

Schneider, P., Scherg, M., Dosch, H. G., Specht, H. J., Gutschalk, A., & Rupp, A. (2002). Morphology of Heschl's gyrus reflects enhanced activation in the auditory cortex of musicians. *Nature Neuroscience, 5*(7), 688–694. https://doi.org/10.1038/nn871

Schneider, P., Sluming, V., Roberts, N., Scherg, M., Goebel, R., Specht, H. J., Dosch, H. G., Bleeck, S., Stippich, C., & Rupp, A. (2005). Structural and functional asymmetry of lateral Heschl's gyrus reflects pitch perception preference. *Nature Neuroscience, 8*(9), 1241–1247. https://doi.org/10.1038/nn1530

Schneider, S., Askew, C. D., Abel, T., & Strüder, H. K. (2010). Exercise, music, and the brain: Is there a central pattern generator? *Journal of Sports Sciences*, *28*(12), 1337–1343. https://doi.org/10.1080/02640414.2010.507252

Schneider, S., Schönle, P. W., Altenmüller, E., & Münte, T. F. (2007). Using musical instruments to improve motor skill recovery following a stroke. *Journal of Neurology*, *254*(10), 1339–1346. https://doi.org/10.1007/s00415-006-0523-2

Schneider, T. W. (2000). *The effects of music education on academic achievement. Unpublished doctoral dissertation*. The University of Southern Mississippi.

Schneider, T. W., & Klotz, J. (2000). *The impact of music education and athletic participation on academic achievement*.

Schon, D. (2014). Short and long-term rhythmic interventions in language rehabilitation. *Neurosciences and Music–V: Cognitive Stimulation and Rehabilitation Conference*.

Schön, D., Anton, J. L., Roth, M., & Besson, M. (2002). An fMRI study of music sight-reading. *NeuroReport*, *13*(17), 2285–2289. https://doi.org/10.1097/00001756-200212030-00023

Schön, D., Magne, C., & Besson, M. (2004). The music of speech: Music training facilitates pitch processing in both music and language. *Psychophysiology*, *41*(3), 341–349. https://doi.org/10.1111/1469-8986.00172.x

Schön, D., & Tillmann, B. (2015). Short- and long-term rhythmic interventions: Perspectives for language rehabilitation. *Annals of the New York Academy of Sciences*, *1337*(1), 32–39. https://doi.org/10.1111/nyas.12635

Schorr-Lesnick, B., Teirstein, A. S., Brown, L. K., & Miller, A. (1985). Pulmonary Function in Singers and Wind-Instrument Players. *Chest*, *88*(2), 201–205. https://doi.org/10.1378/chest.88.2.201

Schrader, E. M., & Wendland, J. M. (2012). Music therapy programming at an aftercare center in Cambodia for survivors of child sexual exploitation and rape and their caregivers. *Soc. Work Christ, MP407]39*, 390–406.

Schubert, E. (2001a). Continuous measurement of self-report emotional response to music. In P. N. Juslin & J. A. Sloboda (Eds), *Music and Emotion: Theory and Research* (pp. 393–414). Oxford University Press.

Schubert, E. (2001b). Continuous measurement of self-report emotional response to music. In P. N. Juslin & J. A. Sloboda (Eds), *Music and emotion: Theory and research* (pp. 393–414). Oxford University Press.

Schulte, M., Knief, A., Seither-Preisler, A., & Pantev, C. (2002). Different Modes of Pitch Perception and Learning-Induced Neuronal Plasticity of the Human Auditory Cortex. *Neural Plasticity*, *9*(3), 161–175. https://doi.org/10.1155/np.2002.161

Schulze, K., Zysset, S., Mueller, K., Friederici, A. D., & Koelsch, S. (2011). Neuroarchitecture of verbal and tonal working memory in nonmusicians and musicians. *Human Brain Mapping*, 32(5), 771–783. https://doi.org/10.1002/hbm.21060

Schurgin, E. (2012). *B Sharp Youth Music: Annual Report and Report on Musical Accomplishments January-May 2012*. Goff Family Foundation.

Schwabe, C. (2005). Resource-Oriented Music Therapy—The Developement of a Concept. *Nordic Journal of Music Therapy*, 14(1), 49–56. https://doi.org/10.1080/08098130509478125

Schwartz, K. D., & Fouts, G. T. (2003). Music Preferences, Personality Style, and Developmental Issues of Adolescents. *Journal of Youth and Adolescence*, 32(3), 205–213. https://doi.org/10.1023/a:1022547520656

Schwartz, R. W., Ayres, K. M., & Douglas, K. H. (2017). Effects of music on task performance, engagement, and behavior: A literature review. *Psychology of Music*, 45(5), 611–627. https://doi.org/10.1177/0305735617691118

Schweigman, K., Soto, C., Wright, S., & Unger, J. (2011). The Relevance of Cultural Activities in Ethnic Identity Among California Native American Youth. *Journal of Psychoactive Drugs*, 43(4), 343–348. https://doi.org/10.1080/02791072.2011.629155

Schweizer, C., Knorth, E. J., & Spreen, M. (2014). Art therapy with children with Autism Spectrum Disorders: A review of clinical case descriptions on 'what works'. *The Arts in Psychotherapy*, 41(5), 577–593. https://doi.org/10.1016/j.aip.2014.10.009

Scotney, V. S., Weissmeyer, S., Carbert, N., & Gabora, L. (2019). The Ubiquity of Cross-Domain Thinking in the Early Phase of the Creative Process. *Frontiers in Psychology*, 10. https://doi.org/10.3389/fpsyg.2019.01426

Scott, T. J. (1970). The use of music to reduce hyperactivity in children. *American Journal of Orthopsychiatry*, 40(4), 677–680. https://doi.org/10.1111/j.1939-0025.1970.tb00725.x

Segerstrom, S. C., & Miller, G. E. (2004). Psychological Stress and the Human Immune System: A Meta-Analytic Study of 30 Years of Inquiry. *Psychological Bulletin*, 130(4), 601–630. https://doi.org/10.1037/0033-2909.130.4.601

Seiffge-Krenke, I. (2013). *Stress, Coping, and Relationships in Adolescence*. Psychology Press. https://doi.org/10.4324/9780203773123

Seinfeld, S., Figueroa, H., Ortiz-Gil, J., & Sanchez-Vives, M. V. (2013). Effects of music learning and piano practice on cognitive function, mood and quality of life in older adults. *Frontiers in Psychology*, 4. https://doi.org/10.3389/fpsyg.2013.00810

Seither-Preisler, A., Parncutt, R., & Schneider, P. (2014). Size and Synchronization of Auditory Cortex Promotes Musical, Literacy, and Attentional Skills in Children. *Journal of Neuroscience*, 34(33), 10937–10949. https://doi.org/10.1523/jneurosci.5315-13.2014

Selfhout, M. H. W., Branje, S. J. T., Bogt, T. F. M. ter, & Meeus, W. H. J. (2009a). The role of music preferences in early adolescents' friendship formation and stability. *Journal of Adolescence, 32*(1), 95–107. https://doi.org/10.1016/j.adolescence.2007.11.004

Selfhout, M. H. W., Branje, S. J. T., Bogt, T. F. M. ter, & Meeus, W. H. J. (2009b). The role of music preferences in early adolescents' friendship formation and stability. *Journal of Adolescence, 32*(1), 95–107. https://doi.org/10.1016/j.adolescence.2007.11.004

Seligman, M. E. P. (2002). *Authentic happiness.* Free Press.

Seligman, M. E. P. (2010). Flourish: Positive psychology and interventions. In T[MP409]*he Tanner Lectures on Human Values, Ann Arbor: University of Michigan* (pp. 1–243).

Seligman, M. E. P. (2011). *Flourish.* Simon & Schuster.

Seligman, M. E. P., Forgeard, M. J. C., Jayawickreme, E., & Kern, M. L. (2011). Doing the Right Thing: Measuring Well-Being for Public Policy. *International Journal of Wellbeing, 1*(1). https://doi.org/10.5502/ijw.v1i1.15

Selkirk, E. (1984). *Phonology and Syntax: The Relation between Sound and Structure.* MIT Press.

Sereno, A. B., & Holzman, P. S. (1995). Antisaccades and smooth pursuit eye movements in schizophrenia. *Biological Psychiatry, 37*(6), 394–401. https://doi.org/10.1016/0006-3223(94)00127-o

Serpell, Z. N., & Esposito, A. G. (2016). Development of Executive Functions. *Policy Insights from the Behavioral and Brain Sciences, 3*(2), 203–210. https://doi.org/10.1177/2372732216654718

Sesma, H. W., Mahone, E. M., Levine, T., Eason, S. H., & Cutting, L. E. (2009). The Contribution of Executive Skills to Reading Comprehension. *Child Neuropsychology, 15*(3), 232–246. https://doi.org/10.1080/09297040802220029

Shahin, A., Bosnyak, D. J., Trainor, L. J., & Roberts, L. E. (2003). Enhancement of Neuroplastic P2 and N1c Auditory Evoked Potentials in Musicians. *The Journal of Neuroscience, 23*(13), 5545–5552. https://doi.org/10.1523/jneurosci.23-13-05545.2003

Shahin, A. J. (2011). Neurophysiological Influence of Musical Training on Speech Perception. *Frontiers in Psychology, 2.* https://doi.org/10.3389/fpsyg.2011.00126

Shahin, A. J., Roberts, L. E., Chau, W., Trainor, L. J., & Miller, L. M. (2008). Music training leads to the development of timbre-specific gamma band activity. *NeuroImage, 41*(1), 113–122. https://doi.org/10.1016/j.neuroimage.2008.01.067

Shahin, A., Roberts, L. E., Pantev, C., Trainor, L. J., & Ross, B. (2005). Modulation of P2 auditory-evoked responses by the spectral complexity of musical sounds. *NeuroReport*, *16*(16), 1781–1785. https://doi.org/10.1097/01.wnr.0000185017.29316.63

Shahin, A., Roberts, L. E., & Trainor, L. J. (2004). Enhancement of auditory cortical development by musical experience in children. *NeuroReport*, *15*(12), 1917–1921. https://doi.org/10.1097/00001756-200408260-00017

Sharda, M., Midha, R., Malik, S., Mukerji, S., & Singh, N. C. (2014). Fronto-Temporal Connectivity is Preserved During Sung but Not Spoken Word Listening, Across the Autism Spectrum. *Autism Research*, *8*(2), 174–186. https://doi.org/10.1002/aur.1437

Sharda, M., Tuerk, C., Chowdhury, R., Jamey, K., Foster, N., & Custo-Blanch, M. (2018). Music improves social communication and auditory–motor connectivity in children with autism. *Translat, iatry*[*MP411*], *8*, 1–13.

Sharma, M., & Jagdev, T. (2012). Use of Music Therapy for Enhancing Self-esteem among Academically Stressed Adolescents. *University Journal of Psychological Research*, *27*(1), 53–64.

Sharon, A., Levav, I., Brodsky, J., Shemesh, A. A., & Kohn, R. (2009). Psychiatric disorders and other health dimensions among Holocaust survivors 6 decades later. *British Journal of Psychiatry*, *195*(4), 331–335. https://doi.org/10.1192/bjp.bp.108.058784

Shaw, G. L. (2000). *Keeping Mozart in Mind*. Academic Press.

Shen, Y., Lin, Y., Liu, S., Fang, L., & Liu, G. (2019a). Sustained Effect of Music Training on the Enhancement of Executive Function in Preschool Children. *Frontiers in Psychology*, *10*. https://doi.org/10.3389/fpsyg.2019.01910

Shen, Y., Lin, Y., Liu, S., Fang, L., & Liu, G. (2019b). Sustained Effect of Music Training on the Enhancement of Executive Function in Preschool Children. *Frontiers in Psychology*, *10*. https://doi.org/10.3389/fpsyg.2019.01910

Shenfield, T., Trehub, S. E., & Nakata, T. (2003). Maternal Singing Modulates Infant Arousal. *Psychology of Music*, *31*(4), 365–375. https://doi.org/10.1177/03057356030314002

Shepherd, D., & Sigg, N. (2015). Music Preference, Social Identity, and Self-Esteem. *Music Perception*, *32*(5), 507–514. https://doi.org/10.1525/mp.2015.32.5.507

Sheppard, A., & Broughton, M. C. (2020). Promoting wellbeing and health through active participation in music and dance: A systematic review. *International Journal of Qualitative Studies on Health and Well-Being*, *15*(1), 1732526. https://doi.org/10.1080/17482631.2020.1732526

Shi, Z.-M., Lin, G.-H., & Xie, Q. (2016). Effects of music therapy on mood, language, behavior, and social skills in children with autism: A meta-analysis. *Chinese Nursing Research*, *3*(3), 137–141. https://doi.org/10.1016/j.cnre.2016.06.018

Shibazaki, K., & Marshall, N. A. (2015). Exploring the impact of music concerts in promoting well-being in dementia care. *Aging & Mental Health*, 21(5), 468–476. https://doi.org/10.1080/13607863.2015.1114589

Shifriss, R., Bodner, E., & Palgi, Y. (2014). When you're down and troubled: Views on the regulatory power of music. *Psychology of Music*, 43(6), 793–807. https://doi.org/10.1177/0305735614540360

Shih, Y.-N., Chien, W.-H., & Chiang, H. (2016). Elucidating the relationship between work attention performance and emotions arising from listening to music. *Work*, 55(2), 489–494. https://doi.org/10.3233/wor-162408

Shih, Y.-N., Huang, R.-H., & Chiang, H.-Y. (2012). Background music: Effects on attention performance. *Work*, 42(4), 573–578. https://doi.org/10.3233/wor-2012-1410

Shih, Y.-N., Liao, Y.-H., Wu, C.-C., & Yang, E.-L. (2020). Therapeutic Factors in the Group Singing Therapy by Social Robot for Patients with Schizophrenia: A Pilot Study. *Taiwanese Journal of Psychiatry*, 34(4), 196. https://doi.org/10.4103/tpsy.tpsy_38_20

Shin, J. (2011). An investigation of participation in weekly music workshops and its relationship to academic self-concept and self esteem of middle school students in low-income. *Contributions to Music Education*, 38(2), 29–42.

Shin, Y. H. (2006). *The effect of music therapy on low-income children's emotional intelligence* [PhD Thesis]. Jeonbuk.

Shobo, Y. (2001). *Arts, Recreation and Children and Arkansas*.

Shuker, R. (2004). Beyond the `high fidelity' stereotype: Defining the (contemporary) record collector. *Popular Music*, 23(3), 311–330. https://doi.org/10.1017/s0261143004000224

Shuman, J., Kennedy, H., DeWitt, P., Edelblute, A., & Wamboldt, M. Z. (2016). Group music therapy impacts mood states of adolescents in a psychiatric hospital setting. *The Arts in Psychotherapy*, 49, 50–56. https://doi.org/10.1016/j.aip.2016.05.014

Shuter-Dyson, R. (2000). Profiling Music Students: Personality and Religiosity. *Psychology of Music*, 28(2), 190–196. https://doi.org/10.1177/0305735600282008

Sichivitsa, V. O. (2007). The influences of parents, teachers, peers and other factors on students' motivation in music. *Research Studies in Music Education*, 29(1), 55–68. https://doi.org/10.1177/1321103x07087568

Siegel, L. S. (2006). Perspectives on dyslexia. *Paediatrics & Child Health*, 11(9), 581–587. https://doi.org/10.1093/pch/11.9.581

Silk, J. S. (2003). *Emotion regulation in the daily lives of adolescents: Links to adolescent adjustment* [Doctoral dissertation.].

Silk, Y., Griffin, N., & Chow, K. (2008). *Youth Orchestras LA: Theory of Action and Proposed Evaluation Plan*. Los Angeles Philharmonic & National Center for Research on Evaluation, Standards and Student Testing (CRESST.

Silva, S. (2006). Music therapy. In M. Hunter-Carsch, Y. Tiknaz, P. Cooper, & R. Sage (Eds), *The handbook of Social, Emotional and Behavioural Difficulties* (pp. 199–204). Continuum.

Silva, S., Belim, F., & Castro, S. L. (2020). The Mozart Effect on the Episodic Memory of Healthy Adults Is Null, but Low-Functioning Older Adults May Be an Exception. *Frontiers in Psychology, 11*. https://doi.org/10.3389/fpsyg.2020.538194

Silva, S., Dias, C., & Castro, S. L. (2019). Domain-Specific Expectations in Music Segmentation. *Brain Sciences, 9*(7), 169. https://doi.org/10.3390/brainsci9070169

Silverman, M. J. (2003). The Influence of Music on the Symptoms of Psychosis: A Meta-Analysis. *Journal of Music Therapy, 40*(1), 27–40. https://doi.org/10.1093/jmt/40.1.27

Silverman, M. J. (2011). Effects of Music Therapy on Change Readiness and Craving in Patients on a Detoxification Unit. *Journal of Music Therapy, 48*(4), 509–531. https://doi.org/10.1093/jmt/48.4.509

Silverman, M. J. (2016). Comparison of two educational music therapy interventions on recovery knowledge and affect: A cluster-randomized study. *Nordic Journal of Music Therapy, 26*(4), 359–375. https://doi.org/10.1080/08098131.2016.1259646

Silvia, P. J., Thomas, K. S., Nusbaum, E. C., Beaty, R. E., & Hodges, D. A. (2016). How does music training predict cognitive abilities? A bifactor approach to musical expertise and intelligence. *Psychology of Aesthetics, Creativity, and the Arts, 10*(2), 184–190. https://doi.org/10.1037/aca0000058

Simmons-Stern, N. R., Budson, A. E., & Ally, B. A. (2010). Music as a memory enhancer in patients with Alzheimer's disease. *Neuropsychologia, 48*(10), 3164–3167. https://doi.org/10.1016/j.neuropsychologia.2010.04.033

Simonton, D. K. (1997). Creative productivity: A predictive and explanatory model of career trajectories and landmarks. *Psychological Review, 104*(1), 66–89, https://doi.org/10.1037/0033

Simonton, D. K. (2017). Creative Geniuses, Polymaths, Child Prodigies, and Autistic Savants: The Ambivalent Function of Interests and Obsessions. In P. O'Keefe & J. Harackiewicz (Eds), *The Science of Interest* (pp. 175–185 ,). Springer. https://doi.org/10.1007/978-3-319-55509-6_9.

Simpson, D. J. (1969). The effect of selected musical studies on growth in general creative potential. *Dissertation Abstracts, 30*, 502–503.

Simpson, K., & Keen, D. (2011). Music Interventions for Children with Autism: Narrative Review of the Literature. *Journal of Autism and Developmental Disorders*, *41*(11), 1507–1514. https://doi.org/10.1007/s10803-010-1172-y

Singh, P., Katiyar, N., & Verma, G. (2014). Retail Shoppability: The Impact Of Store Atmospherics & Store Layout On Consumer Buying Patterns. *International Journal of Scientific and Technology Research*, *3*(8), 15–23.

Singh, Y., Makharia, A., Sharma, A., Agrawal, K., Varma, G., & Yadav, T. (2017). A study on different forms of intelligence in Indian school-going children. *Industrial Psychiatry Journal*, *26*(1), 71. https://doi.org/10.4103/ipj.ipj_61_16

Siponkoski, S.-T., Martínez-Molina, N., Kuusela, L., Laitinen, S., Holma, M., Ahlfors, M., Jordan-Kilkki, P., Ala-Kauhaluoma, K., Melkas, S., Pekkola, J., Rodriguez-Fornells, A., Laine, M., Ylinen, A., Rantanen, P., Koskinen, S., Lipsanen, J., & Särkämö, T. (2020). Music Therapy Enhances Executive Functions and Prefrontal Structural Neuroplasticity after Traumatic Brain Injury: Evidence from a Randomized Controlled Trial. *Journal of Neurotrauma*, *37*(4), 618–634. https://doi.org/10.1089/neu.2019.6413

Sistema, E. & Louis. (2013). *Orchestrating Diversity: Programme overview and evaluation indicators*.

Sixsmith, A., & Gibson, G. (2006). Music and the wellbeing of people with dementia. *Ageing and Society*, *27*(1), 127–145. https://doi.org/10.1017/s0144686x06005228

Skaggs, R. (1997). Music-Centered Creative Arts in a Sex Offender Treatment Program for Male Juveniles. *Music Therapy Perspectives*, *15*(2), 73–78. https://doi.org/10.1093/mtp/15.2.73

Skånland, M. S. (2011). Use of MP3-players as a coping resource. *Music Arts Action*, *3*, 15–33.

Skånland, M. S. (2013). Everyday music listening and affect regulation: The role of MP3 players. *International Journal of Qualitative Studies on Health and Well-Being*, *8*(1), 20595. https://doi.org/10.3402/qhw.v8i0.20595

Skingley, A., Clift, S., Hurley, S., Price, S., & Stephens, L. (2017). Community singing groups for people with chronic obstructive pulmonary disease: Participant perspectives. *Perspectives in Public Health*, *138*(1), 66–75. https://doi.org/10.1177/1757913917740930

Skinner, M. W., Herron, R. V., Bar, R. J., Kontos, P., & Menec, V. (2018). Improving social inclusion for people with dementia and carers through sharing dance: A qualitative sequential continuum of care pilot study protocol. *BMJ Open*, *8*(11), e026912. https://doi.org/10.1136/bmjopen-2018-026912

Skoe, E., & Kraus, N. (2013). Musical training heightens auditory brainstem function during sensitive periods in development. *Frontiers in Psychology*, *4*. https://doi.org/10.3389/fpsyg.2013.00622

Skyllstad, K. (1997). Music in conflict management – a multicultural approach. *International Journal of Music Education*, *os-29*(1), 73–80. https://doi.org/10.1177/025576149702900111

Skyllstad, K. (2000). Creating a culture of peace. The performing arts in interethnic negotiations. *Intercultural Communication*, *4*(4). http://www.immi.se/intercultural/.

Slater, J., Azem, A., Nicol, T., Swedenborg, B., & Kraus, N. (2017). Variations on the theme of musical expertise: Cognitive and sensory processing in percussionists, vocalists and non-musicians. *European Journal of Neuroscience*, *45*(7), 952–963. https://doi.org/10.1111/ejn.13535

Slater, J., Skoe, E., Strait, D. L., O'Connell, S., Thompson, E., & Kraus, N. (2015). Music training improves speech-in-noise perception: Longitudinal evidence from a community-based music program. *Behavioural Brain Research*, *291*, 244–252. https://doi.org/10.1016/j.bbr.2015.05.026

Slater, J., Strait, D. L., Skoe, E., O'Connell, S., Thompson, E., & Kraus, N. (2014). Longitudinal Effects of Group Music Instruction on Literacy Skills in Low-Income Children. *PLoS ONE*, *9*(11), e113383. https://doi.org/10.1371/journal.pone.0113383

Slatterly, M., Attard, H., Stewart, V., & Wheeler, A. (2020). Participation in creative workshops supports mental health consumers to share their stories of recovery: A one-year qualitative follow-up study. *PloS ONE*, *15*(12), 0243284.

Slevc, L. R., Davey, N. S., Buschkuehl, M., & Jaeggi, S. M. (2016). Tuning the mind: Exploring the connections between musical ability and executive functions. *Cognition*, *152*, 199–211. https://doi.org/10.1016/j.cognition.2016.03.017

Slevc, L. R., & Miyake, A. (2006). Individual differences in second-language proficiency: Does musical ability matter? *Psychological Science*, *17*, 675–681, https://doi.org/10.1111/j.1467

Slevc, L. R., & Okada, B. M. (2014a). Nonmusical abilities. In W. Thompson (Ed.), *Music in the social and behavioral sciences: An encyclopedia* (Vol. 12, pp. 815–817). SAGE Publications, Inc.

Slevc, L. R., & Okada, B. M. (2014b). Processing structure in language and music: A case for shared reliance on cognitive control. *Psychonomic Bulletin & Review*, *22*(3), 637–652. https://doi.org/10.3758/s13423-014-0712-4

Slevc, L. R., Rosenberg, J. C., & Patel, A. D. (2009). Making psycholinguistics musical: Self-paced reading time evidence for shared processing of linguistic and musical syntax. *Psychonomic Bulletin & Review*, *16*(2), 374–381. https://doi.org/10.3758/16.2.374

Slevin, M., & Slevin, P. (2013). Psychoanalysis and El Sistema: Human Development through Music. *International Journal of Applied Psychoanalytic Studies*, *10*(2), 132–140. https://doi.org/10.1002/aps.1355

Sloboda, J. (2004). Everyday Uses of Music Listening: A Preliminary Study. In *Exploring the Musical MindCognition, emotion, ability, function* (pp. 318–331). Oxford University Press. https://doi.org/10.1093/acprof:oso/9780198530121.003.0018

Sloboda, J. A. (1976). Visual Perception of Musical Notation: Registering Pitch Symbols in Memory. *Quarterly Journal of Experimental Psychology, 28*(1), 1–16. https://doi.org/10.1080/14640747608400532

Sloboda, J. A. (1985). *The Musical Mind: The Cognitive Psychology of Music*. Oxford University Press.

Sloboda, J. A., Lamont, A., & Greasley, A. (2009). Choosing to hear music: Motivation process and effect. In S. Hallam, I. Cross, & M. Thaut (Eds), *The Oxford Handbook of Music Psychology* (pp. 431–440). Oxford University Press.

Sloboda, J. A., & O'Neill, S. A. (2001). Emotions in everyday listening to music. In P. N. Juslin & J. A. Sloboda (Eds), *Music and Emotion: Theory and Research* (pp. 71–104). Oxford University Press.

Sloboda, J. A., O'Neill, S. A., & Ivaldi, A. (2001). Functions of Music in Everyday Life: An Exploratory Study Using the Experience Sampling Method. *Musicae Scientiae, 5*(1), 9–32. https://doi.org/10.1177/102986490100500102

Slotoroff, C. (1994). Drumming technique for assertiveness and anger management in the short-term psychiatry setting for adult and adolescent survivors of trauma. *Music Ther, Perspectives*[MP424], *12*, 111–116.

Sluming, V., Barrick, T., Howard, M., Cezayirli, E., Mayes, A., & Roberts, N. (2002). Voxel-Based Morphometry Reveals Increased Gray Matter Density in Broca's Area in Male Symphony Orchestra Musicians. *NeuroImage, 17*(3), 1613–1622. https://doi.org/10.1006/nimg.2002.1288

Sluming, V., Brooks, J., Howard, M., Downes, J. J., & Roberts, N. (2007). Broca's Area Supports Enhanced Visuospatial Cognition in Orchestral Musicians. *Journal of Neuroscience, 27*(14), 3799–3806. https://doi.org/10.1523/jneurosci.0147-07.2007

Smart, E., Edwards, B., Kingsnorth, S., Sheffe, S., Curran, C. J., Pinto, M., Crossman, S., & King, G. (2016). Creating an inclusive leisure space: Strategies used to engage children with and without disabilities in the arts-mediated program Spiral Garden. *Disability and Rehabilitation, 40*(2), 199–207. https://doi.org/10.1080/09638288.2016.1250122

Smeijsters, H., & Hurk, J. van den. (1999). Music Therapy Helping to Work Through Grief and Finding a Personal Identity. *Journal of Music Therapy, 36*(3), 222–252. https://doi.org/10.1093/jmt/36.3.222

Smigelsky, M. A., Neimeyer, R. A., Murphy, V., Brown, D., Brown, V., Berryhill, A., & Knowlton, J. (2016). Performing the Peace: Using Playback Theatre in the Strengthening of Police–Community Relations. *Progress in Community Health Partnerships: Research, Education, and Action, 10*(4), 533–539. https://doi.org/10.1353/cpr.2016.0061

Smith, A., Waters, B., & Jones, H. (2010). Effects of prior exposure to office noise and music on aspects of working memory. *Noise and Health*, *12*(49), 235. https://doi.org/10.4103/1463-1741.70502

Smith, C. A., & Morris, L. W. (1977). Differential Effects of Stimulative and Sedative Music on Anxiety, Concentration, and Performance. *Psychological Reports*, *41*(3_suppl), 1047–1053. https://doi.org/10.2466/pr0.1977.41.3f.1047

Smith, C., Viljoen, J. T., & McGeachie, L. (2014). African drumming. *Journal of Cardiovascular Medicine*, *15*(6), 441–446. https://doi.org/10.2459/jcm.0000000000000046

Smith, D. (2013). *Community opus project–Year three update*. San Diego Youth Symphony and Conservatory.

Smith, J. M., & Szathmary, E. (1995). *The major transitions in evolution*. Oxford University Press.

Smith, M. M., Sherry, S. B., Vidovic, V., Saklofske, D. H., Stoeber, J., & Benoit, A. (2019). Perfectionism and the Five-Factor Model of Personality: A Meta-Analytic Review. *Personality and Social Psychology Review*, *23*(4), 367–390. https://doi.org/10.1177/1088868318814973

Smith, R. J. (2001). *Boys' business: Documenting boys' engagement with music education in two Top End schools*.

Smith, S. K., Innes, A., & Bushell, S. (2021a). Exploring the impact of live music performances on the wellbeing of community dwelling people living with dementia and their care partners. *Wellbeing, Space and Society*, *2*, 100032. https://doi.org/10.1016/j.wss.2021.100032

Smith, S. K., Innes, A., & Bushell, S. (2021b). *Music making in the community with people living with dementia and care partners–'I'm leaving feeling on top of the world*.

Smithurst, S. (2011). *In Harmony Norwich Final Pilot Evaluation Report–April 2011*. Priory Research Services.

Snijders, T. M., Benders, T., & Fikkert, P. (2020). Infants Segment Words from Songs—An EEG Study. *Brain Sciences*, *10*(1), 39. https://doi.org/10.3390/brainsci10010039

Sol, P. (2008). *Relevancia e impacto de las actividades artísticas sobre los resultados escolares: El caso de la Orquesta Curanilahue* [PhD Thesis]. Universidad de Chile.

Solli, H. P., Rolvsjord, R., & Borg, M. (2013). Toward Understanding Music Therapy as a Recovery-Oriented Practice within Mental Health Care: A Meta-Synthesis of Service Users' Experiences. *Journal of Music Therapy*, *50*(4), 244–273. https://doi.org/10.1093/jmt/50.4.244

Soundwaves, A. (2011). *MP5]Austin Soundwaves Results and Findings*.

Southcott, J. E. (2009). And as I go, I love to sing: The Happy Wanderers, music and positive aging. *International Journal of Community Music*, 2(2), 143–156. https://doi.org/10.1386/ijcm.2.2-3.143_1

Southcott, J., & Nethsinghe, R. (2018). Resilient Senior Russian-Australian Voices: "We Live to Sing and Sing to Live". *Applied Research in Quality of Life*, 14(1), 39–58. https://doi.org/10.1007/s11482-017-9580-1

Southgate, D. E., & Roscigno, V. J. (2009). The Impact of Music on Childhood and Adolescent Achievement. *Social Science Quarterly*, 90(1), 4–21. https://doi.org/10.1111/j.1540-6237.2009.00598.x

Sovansky, E. E., Wieth, M. B., Francis, A. P., & McIlhagga, S. D. (2014). Not all musicians are creative: Creativity requires more than simply playing music. *Psychology of Music*, 44(1), 25–36. https://doi.org/10.1177/0305735614551088

Sowden, P. T., Clements, L., Redlich, C., & Lewis, C. (2015). Improvisation facilitates divergent thinking and creativity: Realizing a benefit of primary school arts education. *Psychology of Aesthetics, Creativity, and the Arts*, 9(2), 128–138. https://doi.org/10.1037/aca0000018

Sparks, R., Helm, N., & Albert, M. (1974). Aphasia Rehabilitation Resulting from Melodic Intonation Therapy. *Cortex*, 10(4), 303–316. https://doi.org/10.1016/s0010-9452(74)80024-9

Spaulding, S. J., Barber, B., Colby, M., Cormack, B., Mick, T., & Jenkins, M. E. (2013). Cueing and Gait Improvement Among People With Parkinson's Disease: A Meta-Analysis. *Archives of Physical Medicine and Rehabilitation*, 94(3), 562–570. https://doi.org/10.1016/j.apmr.2012.10.026

Spearman, C. (1927). The Measurement of Intelligence. *Nature*, 120(3025), 577–578. https://doi.org/10.1038/120577a0

Spelke, E. S. (2008). Effects of music instruction on developing cognitive systems at the foundations of mathematics and science. In C. Asbury & B. Rich (Eds), *Learning, Arts and the Brain* (p. 431). Dana Press.

Sperber, D. (1996). *Explaining Culture*. Blackwell.

Spintge, R. (2012). Clinical Use of Music in Operating Theatres. In *Music, Health, and Wellbeing* (pp. 277–286). Oxford University Press. https://doi.org/10.1093/acprof:oso/9780199586974.003.0020

Spintge, R., & Droh, R. (1992). *Musik Medizin–Physiologische Grundlagen und praktische Anwendungen*. Fischer.

Spiro, N., Perkins, R., Kaye, S., Tymoszuk, U., Mason-Bertrand, A., Cossette, I., Glasser, S., & Williamon, A. (2021). The Effects of COVID-19 Lockdown 1.0 on Working Patterns, Income, and Wellbeing Among Performing Arts Professionals in the United Kingdom (April–June 2020). *Frontiers in Psychology*, 11. https://doi.org/10.3389/fpsyg.2020.594086

Sporny, V. W. (1941). *The value of music in correctional institutions* [PhD Thesis]. Duquesne University.

Spychiger, M., Patry, J., Lauper, G., Zimmerman, E., & Weber, E. (1993). Does more music teaching lead to a better social climate? In R. Olechowski & G. Svik (Eds), *Experimental research in teaching and learning* (p. 432). Peter Lang.

Stacy, R., Brittain, K., & Kerr, S. (2002). Singing for health: An exploration of the issues. *Health Education*, 102(4), 156–162. https://doi.org/10.1108/09654280210434228

Standley, J. (2012). Music Therapy Research in the NICU: An Updated Meta-Analysis. *Neonatal Network*, 31(5), 311–316. https://doi.org/10.1891/0730-0832.31.5.311

Standley, J. M. (2002). A meta-analysis of the efficacy of music therapy for premature infants. *Journal of Pediatric Nursing*, 17(2), 107–113. https://doi.org/10.1053/jpdn.2002.124128

Standley, J. M. (2008). Does Music Instruction Help Children Learn to Read? Evidence of a Meta-Analysis. *Update: Applications of Research in Music Education*, 27(1), 17–32. https://doi.org/10.1177/8755123308322270

Standley, J. M. (2011). Efficacy of music therapy for premature infants in the neonatal intensive care unit: A meta-analysis. *Arch Dis Child Fetal*[MP433, 96(supplement 1). https://doi.

Standley, J. M., & Hughes, J. E. (1997). Evaluation of an early intervention music curriculum for enhancing prereading/writing skills. *Music Therapy, Perspectives,15*(2, 79–85.

Starke, K. (2012). Encouraging creativity in children. *The Education Digest, Ann Arbor*, 78(4), 57–59.

Stebbins, R. A. (1992). *Amateurs, professionals and serious leisure.* McGill-Queen's University Press.

Steele, C. J., Bailey, J. A., Zatorre, R. J., & Penhune, V. B. (2013). Early Musical Training and White-Matter Plasticity in the Corpus Callosum: Evidence for a Sensitive Period. *Journal of Neuroscience*, 33(3), 1282–1290. https://doi.org/10.1523/jneurosci.3578-12.2013

Steele, K. M., Ball, T. N., & Runk, R. (1997). Listening to Mozart does not enhance backwards digit span performance. *Percept Mot Skills*[MP436, 3(2), 1179-1184, https://doi.org/10.2466/pms.1997.84.3c.1179.PMID:

Steele, K. M., Bass, K. E., & Crook, M. D. (1999). The Mystery of the Mozart Effect: Failure to Replicate. *Psychological Science*, 10(4), 366–369. https://doi.org/10.1111/1467-9280.00169

Steen, J. T. van der, Smaling, H. J., Wouden, J. C. van der, Bruinsma, M. S., Scholten, R. J., & Vink, A. C. (2018). Music-based therapeutic interventions for people with dementia. *Cochrane Database of Systematic Reviews*, 2018(7). https://doi.org/10.1002/14651858.cd003477.pub4

Stefani, M. D., & Biasutti, M. (2016). Effects of Music Therapy on Drug Therapy of Adult Psychiatric Outpatients: A Pilot Randomized Controlled Study. *Frontiers in Psychology*, 7. https://doi.org/10.3389/fpsyg.2016.01518

Steinberg, S., Liu, T., & Lense, M. D. (2021). Musical Engagement and Parent-Child Attachment in Families With Young Children During the Covid-19 Pandemic. *Frontiers in Psychology*, 12. https://doi.org/10.3389/fpsyg.2021.641733

Steptoe, A., Willemsen, G., Owen, N., Flower, L., & Mohamed-Ali, V. (2001). Acute mental stress elicits delayed increases in circulating inflammatory cytokine levels. *Clinical Science*, 101(2), 185–192. https://doi.org/10.1042/cs1010185

Sternberg, R. J. (1985). *Beyond IQ: A Triarchic Theory of Intelligence*. Cambridge University Press.

Sterritt, G. M., & Rudnick, M. (1966). Auditory and Visual Rhythm Perception in Relation to Reading Ability in Fourth Grade Boys. *Perceptual and Motor Skills*, 22(3), 859–864. https://doi.org/10.2466/pms.1966.22.3.859

Stevens, C. S. (2010). You Are What You Buy: Postmodern Consumption and Fandom of Japanese Popular Culture. *Japanese Studies*, 30(2), 199–214. https://doi.org/10.1080/10371397.2010.497578

Stevens, J., Butterfield, C., Whittington, A., & Holttum, S. (2018). Evaluation of Arts based Courses within a UK Recovery College for People with Mental Health Challenges. *International Journal of Environmental Research and Public Health*, 15(6), 1170. https://doi.org/10.3390/ijerph15061170

Stewart, J., Garrido, S., Hense, C., & McFerran, K. (2019). Music Use for Mood Regulation: Self-Awareness and Conscious Listening Choices in Young People With Tendencies to Depression. *Frontiers in Psychology*, 10. https://doi.org/10.3389/fpsyg.2019.01199

Stewart, L. (2006). Congenital amusia. *Current Biology*, 16(21), R904–R906. https://doi.org/10.1016/j.cub.2006.09.054

Stewart, L., Henson, R., Kampe, K., Walsh, V., Turner, R., & Frith, U. (2003). Becoming a Pianist. *Annals of the New York Academy of Sciences*, 999(1), 204–208. https://doi.org/10.1196/annals.1284.030

Stewart, V., Roennfeldt, H., Slattery, M., & Wheeler, A. J. (2019). Generating mutual recovery in creative spaces. *Mental Health and Social Inclusion*, 23(1), 16–22. https://doi.org/10.1108/mhsi-08-2018-0029

Stickley, T., Wright, N., & Slade, M. (2018). The art of recovery: Outcomes from participatory arts activities for people using mental health services. *Journal of Mental Health*, 27(4), 367–373. https://doi.org/10.1080/09638237.2018.1437609

Stige, B., Ansdell, G., Elefant, C., & Pavlicevic, M. (2017). *Where Music Helps: Community Music Therapy in Action and Reflection*. Routledge. https://doi.org/10.4324/9781315084084

Stoeber, J., & Eismann, U. (2007). Perfectionism in young musicians: Relations with motivation, effort, achievement, and distress. *Personality and Individual Differences*, *43*(8), 2182–2192. https://doi.org/10.1016/j.paid.2007.06.036

Stoesz, B. M., Jakobson, L. S., Kilgour, A. R., & Lewycky, S. T. (2007). Local Processing Advantage in Musicians: Evidence from Disembedding and Constructional Tasks. *Music Perception*, *25*(2), 153–165. https://doi.org/10.1525/mp.2007.25.2.153

Story, K. M., & Beck, B. D. (2017). Guided Imagery and Music with female military veterans: An intervention development study. *The Arts in Psychotherapy*, *55*, 93–102. https://doi.org/10.1016/j.aip.2017.05.003

Strait, D., & Kraus, N. (2011). Playing Music for a Smarter Ear: Cognitive, Perceptual and Neurobiological Evidence. *Music Perception*, *29*(2), 133–146. https://doi.org/10.1525/mp.2011.29.2.133

Strait, D. L., Chan, K., Ashley, R., & Kraus, N. (2012). Specialization among the specialized: Auditory brainstem function is tuned in to timbre. *Cortex*, *48*(3), 360–362. https://doi.org/10.1016/j.cortex.2011.03.015

Strait, D. L., Hornickel, J., & Kraus, N. (2011). Subcortical processing of speech regularities underlies reading and music aptitude in children. *Behavioral and Brain Functions*, *7*(1). https://doi.org/10.1186/1744-9081-7-44

Strait, D. L., & Kraus, N. (2011). Can You Hear Me Now? Musical Training Shapes Functional Brain Networks for Selective Auditory Attention and Hearing Speech in Noise. *Frontiers in Psychology*, *2*. https://doi.org/10.3389/fpsyg.2011.00113

Strait, D. L., & Kraus, N. (2014). Biological impact of auditory expertise across the life span: Musicians as a model of auditory learning. *Hearing Research*, *308*, 109–121. https://doi.org/10.1016/j.heares.2013.08.004

Strait, D. L., Kraus, N., Parbery-Clark, A., & Ashley, R. (2010a). Musical experience shapes top-down auditory mechanisms: Evidence from masking and auditory attention performance. *Hearing Research*, *261*(1–2), 22–29. https://doi.org/10.1016/j.heares.2009.12.021

Strait, D. L., Kraus, N., Parbery-Clark, A., & Ashley, R. (2010b). Musical experience shapes top-down auditory mechanisms: Evidence from masking and auditory attention performance. *Hearing Research*, *261*(1–2), 22–29. https://doi.org/10.1016/j.heares.2009.12.021

Strait, D. L., Kraus, N., Skoe, E., & Ashley, R. (2009a). Musical experience and neural efficiency—Effects of training on subcortical processing of vocal expressions of emotion. *European Journal of Neuroscience*, *29*(3), 661–668. https://doi.org/10.1111/j.1460-9568.2009.06617.x

Strait, D. L., Kraus, N., Skoe, E., & Ashley, R. (2009b). Musical experience and neural efficiency—Effects of training on subcortical processing of vocal expressions of emotion. *European Journal of Neuroscience, 29*(3), 661–668. https://doi.org/10.1111/j.1460-9568.2009.06617.x

Strait, D. L., Kraus, N., Skoe, E., & Ashley, R. (2009c). Musical Experience Promotes Subcortical Efficiency in Processing Emotional Vocal Sounds. *Annals of the New York Academy of Sciences, 1169*(1), 209–213. https://doi.org/10.1111/j.1749-6632.2009.04864.x

Strait, D. L., O'Connell, S., Parbery-Clark, A., & Kraus, N. (2013). Musicians' Enhanced Neural Differentiation of Speech Sounds Arises Early in Life: Developmental Evidence from Ages 3 to 30. *Cerebral Cortex, 24*(9), 2512–2521. https://doi.org/10.1093/cercor/bht103

Strait, D. L., Parbery-Clark, A., Hittner, E., & Kraus, N. (2012). Musical training during early childhood enhances the neural encoding of speech in noise. *Brain and Language, 123*(3), 191–201. https://doi.org/10.1016/j.bandl.2012.09.001

Strait, D. L., Parbery-Clark, A., O'Connell, S., & Kraus, N. (2013). Biological impact of preschool music classes on processing speech in noise. *Developmental Cognitive Neuroscience, 6*, 51–60. https://doi.org/10.1016/j.dcn.2013.06.003

Strange, J. (1999). Client-centred music therapy for emotionally disturbed teenagers having moderate learning disability. In T. Wigram & J. Backer (Eds), *Clinical applications of music therapy in developmental disability, paediatrics and neurology* (pp. 134–154). Jessica Kingsley Publishers.

Strange, J. (2012). Psychodynamically-informed Music Therapy Groups with Teenagers with Severe Special Needs in a College Setting: Working Jointly with Teaching Assistants. In J. Tomlinson, P. Derrington, & A. Oldfield (Eds), *Music Therapy in Schools. Working with Children of All Ages in Mainstream and Special Education* (p. 441). Jessica Kingsley.

Straw, W. (1997). Sizing up Record Collections: Gender and Connoisseurship in Rock Music Culture. In S. Whiteley (Ed.), *Sexing the Groove: Popular Music and Gender* (pp. 3–16). Routledge.

Strehlow, G. (2009). The use of music therapy in treating sexually abused children. *Nordic Journal of Music Therapy, 18*(2), 167–183. https://doi.org/10.1080/08098130903062397

Strong, J. V., & Mast, B. T. (2018). The cognitive functioning of older adult instrumental musicians and non-musicians. *Aging, Neuropsychology, and Cognition, 26*(3), 367–386. https://doi.org/10.1080/13825585.2018.1448356

Stupar, R. (2012). *Superar–Chancen Für Volksschulkinder Durch Musikalische Förderung*. ARGE Bildungsmanagement Wien.

Stuss, D. T., & Alexander, M. P. (2000). Executive functions and the frontal lobes: A conceptual view. *Psychological Research, 63*(3–4), 289–298. https://doi.org/10.1007/s004269900007

Su, Q., & Wang, F. (2010). Study the Effect of Background Music on Cognitive Memory. *Applied Mechanics and Materials, 37–38*, 1368–1371. https://doi.org/10.4028/www.scientific.net/amm.37-38.1368

Su, Y. N., Kao, C.-C., Hsu, C.-C., Pan, L.-C., Cheng, S.-C., & Huang, Y.-M. (2017). How does Mozart's music affect children's reading? The evidence from learning anxiety and reading rates with e-books. *Journal of Educational Technology and Society, 20*(2), 101–112.

Suárez, L., Elangovan, S., & Au, A. (2016). Cross-sectional study on the relationship between music training and working memory in adults. *Australian Journal of Psychology, 68*(1), 38–46. https://doi.org/10.1111/ajpy.12087

Sugarman, J. (2010). Kosova Calls for Peace: Song, Myth, and War in an Age of Global Media. In J. O'Connell & S. E. Castelo-Branco (Eds), *Music and Conflict: Ethnomusicological Perspectives* (p. 442). University of Illinois Press.

Sullivan, H. S. (1964). *The fusion of psychiatry and social science*. Norton.

Summary, H. S. P., & Plan, E. (2013). *Stockton: University of the Pacific*.

Sun, Y., Lu, X., Ho, H. T., & Thompson, W. F. (2017). Pitch discrimination associated with phonological awareness: Evidence from congenital amusia. *Scientific Reports, 7*(1). https://doi.org/10.1038/srep44285

Sunderland, N., Graham, P., & Lenette, C. (2016). Epistemic communities: Extending the social justice outcomes of community music for asylum seekers and refugees in Australia. *International Journal of Community Music, 9*(3), 223–241. https://doi.org/10.1386/ijcm.9.3.223_1

Sunderland, N., Istvandity, L., Lakhani, A., Lenette, C., Procopis, B., & Caballero, P. (2015). They [do more than] Interrupt Us from Sadness: Exploring the impact of participatory music making on social determinants of health and wellbeing for refugees in Australia. *Health, Culture and Society, 8*(1), 1–19. https://doi.org/10.5195/hcs.2015.195

Sung, H., Lee, W., Li, T., & Watson, R. (2011). A group music intervention using percussion instruments with familiar music to reduce anxiety and agitation of institutionalized older adults with dementia. *International Journal of Geriatric Psychiatry, 27*(6), 621–627. https://doi.org/10.1002/gps.2761

Sutcliffe, R., Du, K., & Ruffman, T. (2020). Music Making and Neuropsychological Aging: A Review. *Neuroscience & Biobehavioral Reviews, 113*, 479–491. https://doi.org/10.1016/j.neubiorev.2020.03.026

Sutton, C. J. C., & Lowis, M. J. (2008). The Effect of Musical Mode on Verbal and Spatial Task Performance. *Creativity Research Journal, 20*(4), 420–426. https://doi.org/10.1080/10400410802391884

Sutton, J., & Backer, J. D. (2009). Music, trauma and silence: The state of the art. *The Arts in Psychotherapy, 36*(2), 75–83. https://doi.org/10.1016/j.aip.2009.01.009

Sutton, J. P. (Ed.). (2002). *Music, music therapy and trauma*. Jessica Kingsley.

Swaminathan, S., & Gopinath, J. K. (2013). Music Training and Second-Language English Comprehension and Vocabulary Skills in Indian Children. *Psychological Studies, 58*(2), 164–170. https://doi.org/10.1007/s12646-013-0180-3

Swaminathan, S., & Schellenberg, E. G. (2019). Music training and cognitive abilities: Associations, causes, and consequences. In M. H. Thaut & D. A. Hodges (Eds), *The Oxford Handbook of Music and the Brain* (pp. 645–670). Oxford University Press.

Swaminathan, S., & Schellenberg, E. G. (2020). Musical ability, music training, and language ability in childhood. *Journal of Experimental Psychology: Learning, Memory, and Cognition, 46*(12), 2340–2348. https://doi.org/10.1037/xlm0000798

Swaminathan, S., Schellenberg, E. G., & Khalil, S. (2017). Revisiting the association between music lessons and intelligence: Training effects or music aptitude? *Intelligence, 62*, 119–124. https://doi.org/10.1016/j.intell.2017.03.005

Swaminathan, S., Schellenberg, E. G., & Ventatesan, K. (2018). Explaining the association between music training and reading in adults. *Journal of Experimental Psychology: Learning, Memory and Cognition, 44*(6), 992–999, https://doi.org/10.1037/xml0000493.

Sward, R. (1989). Band is a family. *Today's Music Educator*, 448 26–27.

Taetle, L. (1999). The relationship between fine arts participation and daily school attendance at the secondary level. *Contributions to Music Education, 26*(1), 50–66.

Tahlier, M., Miron, A. M., & Rauscher, F. H. (2012). Music choice as a sadness regulation strategy for resolved versus unresolved sad events. *Psychology of Music, 41*(6), 729–748. https://doi.org/10.1177/0305735612446537

Tai, D. M., Phillipson, S. N., & Phillipson, S. (2018). Music training and the academic achievement of Hong Kong students. *Research Studies in Music Education, 40*(2), 244–264. https://doi.org/10.1177/1321103x18773099

Takacs, Z. K., & Kassai, R. (2019). The efficacy of different interventions to foster children's executive function skills: A series of meta-analyses. *Psychological Bulletin, 145*(7), 653–697. https://doi.org/10.1037/bul0000195

Talamini, F., Altoè, G., Carretti, B., & Grassi, M. (2017). Musicians have better memory than nonmusicians: A meta-analysis. *PLOS ONE, 12*(10), e0186773. https://doi.org/10.1371/journal.pone.0186773

Talamini, F., Carretti, B., & Grassi, M. (2016). The Working Memory of Musicians and Nonmusicians. *Music Perception, 34*(2), 183–191. https://doi.org/10.1525/mp.2016.34.2.183

Tallal, P., & Gaab, N. (2006). Dynamic auditory processing, musical experience and language development. *Trends in Neurosciences*, *29*(7), 382–390. https://doi.org/10.1016/j.tins.2006.06.003

Tallal, P., Miller, S., & Fitch, R. H. (1993). Neurobiological Basis of Speech: A Case for the Preeminence of Temporal Processing. *Annals of the New York Academy of Sciences*, *682*(1 Temporal Info), 27–47. https://doi.org/10.1111/j.1749-6632.1993.tb22957.x

Tanaka, A., Takehara, T., & Yamauchi, H. (2006). Achievement goals in a presentation task: Performance expectancy, achievement goals, state anxiety, and task performance. *Learning and Individual Differences*, *16*(2), 93–99. https://doi.org/10.1016/j.lindif.2005.06.005

Tapson, C., Noble, D., Daykin, N., & Walters, D. (2018). *Live Music in Care: The Impact of Music Interventions for People Living and Working in Care Home Settings*. University of Winchester. https://achoirineverycarehome.files.wordpress.com/2018/11/live-music-in-care.pdf.

Tarr, B., Launay, J., & Dunbar, R. I. M. (2014). Music and social bonding: "Self-other" merging and neurohormonal mechanisms. *Frontiers in Psychology*, *5*. https://doi.org/10.3389/fpsyg.2014.01096

Tarrant, M., North, A. C., & Hargreaves, D. J. (2000). English and American Adolescents' Reasons for Listening to Music. *Psychology of Music*, *28*(2), 166–173. https://doi.org/10.1177/0305735600282005

Tarrant, M., North, A. C., & Hargreaves, D. J. (2001). Social Categorization, Self-Esteem, and the Estimated Musical Preferences of Male Adolescents. *The Journal of Social Psychology*, *141*(5), 565–581. https://doi.org/10.1080/00224540109600572

Tatler, B. W., & Wade, N. J. (2003). On Nystagmus, Saccades, and Fixations. *Perception*, *32*(2), 167–184. https://doi.org/10.1068/p3395

Taylor, A. (2010). Participation in a master class: Experiences of older amateur pianists. *Music Education Research*, *12*(2), 199–217. https://doi.org/10.1080/14613801003746576

Taylor, A. C., & Dewhurst, S. A. (2017). Investigating the influence of music training on verbal memory. *Psychology of Music*, *45*(6), 814–820. https://doi.org/10.1177/0305735617690246

Taylor, A., & Hallam, S. (2008). Understanding what it means for older students to learn basic musical skills on a keyboard instrument. *Music Education Research*, *10*(2), 285–306. https://doi.org/10.1080/14613800802079148

Taylor, A., & Hallam, S. (2011). From leisure to work: Amateur musicians taking up instrumental or vocal teaching as a second career. *Music Education Research*, *13*(3), 307–325. https://doi.org/10.1080/14613808.2011.603044

Taylor, J. M., & Rowe, B. J. (2012). The "Mozart Effect" and the Mathematical Connection. *Journal of College Reading and Learning*, 42(2), 51–66. https://doi.org/10.1080/10790195.2012.10850354

Terman, L. M. (1916). *The measurement of intelligence*. Houghton, Mifflin and Company. https://doi.org/10.1037/10014-000

Terry, P. C., Karageorghis, C. I., Curran, M. L., Martin, O. V., & Parsons-Smith, R. L. (2020). Effects of music in exercise and sport: A meta-analytic review. *Psychological Bulletin*, 146(2), 91–117. https://doi.org/10.1037/bul0000216

Tervaniemi, M. (2009). *Musicians–Same or different? Annals of the New York Academy of Science.*

Tervaniemi, M. (2017). Music in learning and relearning: The life-span approach. *Psychomusicology: Music, Mind, and Brain*, 27(3), 223–226. https://doi.org/10.1037/pmu0000185

Tervaniemi, M., Castaneda, A., Knoll, M., & Uther, M. (2006a). Sound processing in amateur musicians and nonmusicians: Event-related potential and behavioral indices. *NeuroReport*, 17(11), 1225–1228. https://doi.org/10.1097/01.wnr.0000230510.55596.8b

Tervaniemi, M., Castaneda, A., Knoll, M., & Uther, M. (2006b). Sound processing in amateur musicians and nonmusicians: Event-related potential and behavioral indices. *NeuroReport*, 17(11), 1225–1228. https://doi.org/10.1097/01.wnr.0000230510.55596.8b

Tervaniemi, M., Ilvonen, T., Karma, K., Alho, K., & Näätänen, R. (1997). The musical brain: Brain waves reveal the neurophysiological basis of musicality in human subjects. *Neuroscience Letters*, 226(1), 1–4. https://doi.org/10.1016/s0304-3940(97)00217-6

Tervaniemi, M., Janhunen, L., Kruck, S., Putkinen, V., & Huotilainen, M. (2016). Auditory Profiles of Classical, Jazz, and Rock Musicians: Genre-Specific Sensitivity to Musical Sound Features. *Frontiers in Psychology*, 6. https://doi.org/10.3389/fpsyg.2015.01900

Tervaniemi, M., Rytkönen, M., Schröger, E., Ilmoniemi, R. J., & Näätänen, R. (2001). Superior Formation of Cortical Memory Traces for Melodic Patterns in Musicians. *Learning & Memory*, 8(5), 295–300. https://doi.org/10.1101/lm.39501

Tervaniemi, M., Tao, S., & Huotilainen, M. (2018). Promises of Music in Education? *Frontiers in Education*, 3. https://doi.org/10.3389/feduc.2018.00074

Thaut, M. (2013). *Rhythm, Music, and the Brain*. Routledge. https://doi.org/10.4324/9780203958827

Thaut, M. H., & Hodges, D. A. (Eds). (2018). *The Oxford Handbook of Music and the Brain*. Oxford University Press. https://doi.org/10.1093/oxfordhb/9780198804123.001.0001

Thaut, M. H., McIntosh, G. C., & Hoemberg, V. (2015). Neurobiological foundations of neurologic music therapy: Rhythmic entrainment and the motor system. *Frontiers in Psychology, 5*. https://doi.org/10.3389/fpsyg.2014.01185

Thaut, M. H., McIntosh, K. H., McIntosh, G. C., & Hoemberg, V. (2001). Auditory rhythmicity enhances movement and speech motor control in patients with Parkinson's disease. *Functional Neurology, XVI*(2), 163–172.

Thayer, R. E. (1996). *The Origins of Everyday Moods*. Oxford University Press.

Thayer, R. E., Newman, J. R., & McClain, T. M. (1994). Self-regulation of mood: Strategies for changing a bad mood, raising energy, and reducing tension. *Journal of Personality and Social Psychology, 67*(5), 910–925. https://doi.org/10.1037/0022-3514.67.5.910

The People's Music School Youth Orchestras. (2013).

The People's Music School Youth Orchestras—El Sistema Chicago. (2013). *Evaluation Tools and Strategy*.

Theorell, T. P., Lennartsson, A.-K., Mosing, M. A., & Ullà©n, F. (2014). Musical activity and emotional competence – a twin study. *Frontiers in Psychology, 5*. https://doi.org/10.3389/fpsyg.2014.00774

Thoma, M. V., Ryf, S., Mohiyeddini, C., Ehlert, U., & Nater, U. M. (2012). Emotion regulation through listening to music in everyday situations. *Cognition & Emotion, 26*(3), 550–560. https://doi.org/10.1080/02699931.2011.595390

Thomas, J. M. (2014). *To what extent do intervention music classes impact on seven and eight year old children presenting with social, emotional and behavioural difficulties: A study of student learning in a deprived school setting* [PhD Thesis]. University of Bath, Department of Education.

Thompson, G. A., Raine, M., Hayward, S. M., & Kilpatrick, H. (2020). Gathering community perspectives to inform the design of autism-friendly music-making workshops for wellbeing. *International Journal of Wellbeing, 10*(5), 117–143. https://doi.org/10.5502/ijw.v10i5.1497

Thompson, I., & Tawell, A. (2017). Becoming other: Social and emotional development through the creative arts for young people with behavioural difficulties. *Emotional and Behavioural Difficulties, 22*(1), 18–34. https://doi.org/10.1080/13632752.2017.1287342

Thompson, J. D. (2016). *The role of rap music composition in the experience of incarceration for African American youth* [PhD Thesis]. Northwestern University.

Thompson, R. A. (2008). Early attachment and later development: Familiar questions, new answers. In J. Cassidy, P. R. Shaver, & eds (Eds), *Handbook of Attachment: Theory, Research, and Clinical Applications* (pp. 348–365). Guilford Press.

Thompson, R. G., Moulin, C. J. A., Hayre, S., & Jones, R. W. (2005). Music Enhances Category Fluency In Healthy Older Adults And Alzheimer's Disease Patients. *Experimental Aging Research, 31*(1), 91–99. https://doi.org/10.1080/03610730590882819

Thompson, W. F., Schellenberg, E. G., & Husain, G. (2001). Arousal, Mood, and The Mozart Effect. *Psychological Science, 12*(3), 248–251. https://doi.org/10.1111/1467-9280.00345

Thompson, W. F., Schellenberg, E. G., & Husain, G. (2003). Perceiving Prosody in Speech. *Annals of the New York Academy of Sciences, 999*(1), 530–532. https://doi.org/10.1196/annals.1284.067

Thompson, W. F., Schellenberg, E. G., & Husain, G. (2004). Decoding speech prosody: Do music lessons help? *Emotion, 4*(1), 46–64. https://doi.org/10.1037/1528-3542.4.1.46

Thompson, W. F., Schellenberg, E. G., & Letnic, A. K. (2011). Fast and loud background music disrupts reading comprehension. *Psychology of Music, 40*(6), 700–708. https://doi.org/10.1177/0305735611400173

Thomson, C. J., Reece, J. E., & Benedetto, M. D. (2014). The relationship between music-related mood regulation and psychopathology in young people. *Musicae Scientiae, 18*(2), 150–165. https://doi.org/10.1177/1029864914521422

Thomson, J. (2014). Rhythm and literacy abilities: What is the relationship and can rhythm-based interventions help students with dyslexia. *Neurosciences and Music–V: Cognitive Stimulation and Rehabilitation Conference.*

Thomson, M. (1993). Teaching the dyslexic child: Some evaluation studies. In G. Hales (Ed.), *Meeting Points in Dyslexia: Proceedings of the first International Conference of the British Dyslexia Association* (p. 455).

Thorndike, E. L. (1920). Intelligence and its use. *Harper's Magazine, 140,* 227–235.

Thornton, L. (2013). A Comparison of State Assessment Scores Between Music and Nonmusic Students. *Update: Applications of Research in Music Education, 32*(1), 5–11. https://doi.org/10.1177/8755123313502339

Thurstone, L. L. (1973). Primary Mental Abilities. In *The Measurement of Intelligence* (pp. 131–136). Springer Netherlands. https://doi.org/10.1007/978-94-011-6129-9_8

Tierney, A., & Kraus, N. (2013a). Music training for the development of reading skills. In M. M. Merzenich, M. Nahum, & T. M. Vleet (Eds), *Progress in Brain Research, 207* (pp. 209–241 ,). Academic Press. https://doi.org/10.1016/B978-0-444-63327-9.00008-4.

Tierney, A., & Kraus, N. (2013b). The Ability to Move to a Beat Is Linked to the Consistency of Neural Responses to Sound. *Journal of Neuroscience, 33*(38), 14981–14988. https://doi.org/10.1523/jneurosci.0612-13.2013

Tierney, A., & Kraus, N. (2014). Auditory-motor entrainment and phonological skills: Precise auditory timing hypothesis (PATH). *Frontiers in Human Neuroscience, 8*. https://doi.org/10.3389/fnhum.2014.00949

Tierney, A., Krizman, J., Skoe, E., Johnston, K., & Kraus, N. (2013). High school music classes enhance the neural processing of speech. *Frontiers in Psychology, 4*. https://doi.org/10.3389/fpsyg.2013.00855

Tierney, A. T., & Kraus, N. (2013). The ability to tap to a beat relates to cognitive, linguistic, and perceptual skills. *Brain and Language, 124*(3), 225–231. https://doi.org/10.1016/j.bandl.2012.12.014

Tierney, A. T., Krizman, J., & Kraus, N. (2015). Music training alters the course of adolescent auditory development. *Proceedings of the National Academy of Sciences, 112*(32), 10062–10067. https://doi.org/10.1073/pnas.1505114112

Tohmo, T. (2005). Economic Impacts of Cultural Events on Local Economies: An Input—Output Analysis of the Kaustinen Folk Music Festival. *Tourism Economics, 11*(3), 431–451. https://doi.org/10.5367/000000005774352980

Tol, A. J. M., Coulthard, H., & Hanser, W. E. (2018). Music listening as a potential aid in reducing emotional eating: An exploratory study. *Musicae Scientiae, 24*(1), 78–95.

Tol, A. J. M. V. den, & Edwards, J. (2014). Listening to sad music in adverse situations: How music selection strategies relate to self-regulatory goals, listening effects, and mood enhancement. *Psychology of Music, 43*(4), 473–494. https://doi.org/10.1177/0305735613517410

Tolfree, E., & Hallam, S. (2016). Children and young people's uses of and responses to music in their everyday lives: A pilot study. *Psychology of Education Review, 40*(2), 44–50.

Tomasello, M., Carpenter, M., Call, J., Behne, T., & Moll, H. (2005). Understanding and sharing intentions: The origins of cultural cognition. *Behavioral and Brain Sciences, 28*(5), 675–691. https://doi.org/10.1017/s0140525x05000129

Took, K. J., & Weiss, D. S. (1994). The relationship between heavy metal and rap music and adolescent turmoil: Real or artifact? *Adolescence, 29*(115), 613–621.

Torppa, R., Faulkner, A., Huotilainen, M., Järvikivi, J., Lipsanen, J., Laasonen, M., & Vainio, M. (2014). The perception of prosody and associated auditory cues in early-implanted children: The role of auditory working memory and musical activities. *International Journal of Audiology, 53*(3), 182–191. https://doi.org/10.3109/14992027.2013.872302

Torppa, R., & Huotilainen, M. (2019). Why and how music can be used to rehabilitate and develop speech and language skills in hearing-impaired children. *Hearing Research, 380*, 108–122. https://doi.org/10.1016/j.heares.2019.06.003

Torppa, R., Huotilainen, M., Leminen, M., Lipsanen, J., & Tervaniemi, M. (2014). Interplay between singing and cortical processing of music: A longitudinal study in children with cochlear implants. *Frontiers in Psychology, 5.* https://doi.org/10.3389/fpsyg.2014.01389

Torrance, E. P. (1988). The nature of creativity as manifest in its testing. In R. J. Sternberg (Ed.), *The nature of creativity: Contemporary psychological perspectives* (pp. 43–75). Cambridge University Press.

Trahan, T., Durrant, S. J., Müllensiefen, D., & Williamson, V. J. (2018). The music that helps people sleep and the reasons they believe it works: A mixed methods analysis of online survey reports. *PLOS ONE, 13*(11), e0206531. https://doi.org/10.1371/journal.pone.0206531

Trainor, L. (2014). The importance of rhythm and interpersonal synchrony in social development. *Neurosciences and Music–V: Cognitive Stimulation and Rehabilitation Conference.*

Trainor, L. J. (1996). Infant preferences for infant-directed versus noninfant-directed playsongs and lullabies. *Infant Behavior and Development, 19*(1), 83–92. https://doi.org/10.1016/s0163-6383(96)90046-6

Trainor, L. J., & Cirelli, L. (2015). Rhythm and interpersonal synchrony in early social development. *Annals of the New York Academy of Sciences, 1337*(1), 45–52. https://doi.org/10.1111/nyas.12649

Trainor, L. J., Desjardins, R. N., & Rockel, C. (1999). A comparison of contour and interval processing in musicians and nonmusicians using event-related potentials. *Australian Journal of Psychology, 51*(3), 147–153. https://doi.org/10.1080/00049539908255352

Trainor, L. J., Lee, K., & Bosnyak, D. J. (2011). Cortical Plasticity in 4-Month-Old Infants: Specific Effects of Experience with Musical Timbres. *Brain Topography, 24*(3–4), 192–203. https://doi.org/10.1007/s10548-011-0177-y

Trainor, L. J., Marie, C., Gerry, D., Whiskin, E., & Unrau, A. (2012). Becoming musically enculturated: Effects of music classes for infants on brain and behavior. *Annals of the New York Academy of Sciences, 1252*(1), 129–138. https://doi.org/10.1111/j.1749-6632.2012.06462.x

Trainor, L. J., Shahin, A. J., & Roberts, L. E. (2009). Understanding the Benefits of Musical Training. *Annals of the New York Academy of Sciences, 1169*(1), 133–142. https://doi.org/10.1111/j.1749-6632.2009.04589.x

Trainor, L. J., Shahin, A., & Roberts, L. E. (2003). Effects of Musical Training on the Auditory Cortex in Children. *Annals of the New York Academy of Sciences, 999*(1), 506–513. https://doi.org/10.1196/annals.1284.061

Tramo, M. J. (2001). Music of the Hemispheres. *Science, 291*(5501), 54–56. https://doi.org/10.1126/science.10.1126/science.1056899

Trapnell, P. D., & Campbell, J. D. (1999). Private self-consciousness and the five-factor model of personality: Distinguishing rumination from reflection. *Journal of Personality and Social Psychology, 76*(2), 284–304. https://doi.org/10.1037/0022-3514.76.2.284

Travis, F., Harung, H. S., & Lagrosen, Y. (2011). Moral development, executive functioning, peak experiences and brain patterns in professional and amateur classical musicians: Interpreted in light of a Unified Theory of Performance. *Consciousness and Cognition*, 20(4), 1256–1264. https://doi.org/10.1016/j.concog.2011.03.020

Travis, R., & Bowman, S. W. (2012). Ethnic identity, self-esteem and variability in perceptions of rap music's empowering and risky influences. *Journal of Youth Studies*, 15(4), 455–478. https://doi.org/10.1080/13676261.2012.663898

Treacy, D. S. (2019). "Because I'm a girl": Troubling shared visions for music education. *Research Studies in Music Education*, 42(3), 310–325. https://doi.org/10.1177/1321103x19845145

Trehub, S. E. (2014). Singing interventions for managing infant distress. *Neurosciences and Music–V: Cognitive Stimulation and Rehabilitation Conference*.

Trehub, S. E., & Trainor, L. (1998). Singing to infants: Lullabies and playsongs. *Adv. Infancy Research*[MP457, 12, 43–77.

Trent, D. E. (1996). *The impact of instrumental education on academic achievement* [Doctoral dissertation.]. East Texas State University. Dissertation Abstracts International.

Trimmer, C. G., & Cuddy, L. L. (2008). Emotional intelligence, not music training, predicts recognition of emotional speech prosody. *Emotion*, 8(6), 838–849. https://doi.org/10.1037/a0014080

Trondalen, G. (2016). The future of music therapy for persons with eating disorders. In C. Dileo (Ed.), *Envisioning the future of music therapy* (pp. 31–44). Temple University.

Trudel-Fitzgerald, C., Millstein, R. A., Hippel, C. von, Howe, C. J., Tomasso, L. P., Wagner, G. R., & VanderWeele, T. J. (2019). Psychological well-being as part of the public health debate? Insight into dimensions, interventions, and policy. *BMC Public Health*, 19(1). https://doi.org/10.1186/s12889-019-8029-x

Tsai, C.-G., & Li, C.-W. (2019). Is It Speech or Song? Effect of Melody Priming on Pitch Perception of Modified Mandarin Speech. *Brain Sciences*, 9(10), 286. https://doi.org/10.3390/brainsci9100286

Tsang, C. D., & Conrad, N. J. (2011). Music Training and Reading Readiness. *Music Perception*, 29(2), 157–163. https://doi.org/10.1525/mp.2011.29.2.157

Tseng, P.-T., Chen, Y.-W., Lin, P.-Y., Tu, K.-Y., Wang, H.-Y., Cheng, Y.-S., Chang, Y.-C., Chang, C.-H., Chung, W., & Wu, C.-K. (2016). Significant treatment effect of adjunct music therapy to standard treatment on the positive, negative, and mood symptoms of schizophrenic patients: A meta-analysis. *BMC Psychiatry*, 16(1). https://doi.org/10.1186/s12888-016-0718-8

Tsoi, K. K. F., Chan, J. Y. C., Ng, Y.-M., Lee, M. M. Y., Kwok, T. C. Y., & Wong, S. Y. S. (2018). Receptive Music Therapy Is More Effective than Interactive Music Therapy to Relieve Behavioral and Psychological Symptoms of

Dementia: A Systematic Review and Meta-Analysis. *Journal of the American Medical Directors Association, 19*(7), 568–576.e3. https://doi.org/10.1016/j.jamda.2017.12.009

Tuastad, L., & O'Grady, L. (2013). Music therapy inside and outside prison – A freedom practice? *Nordic Journal of Music Therapy, 22*(3), 210–232. https://doi.org/10.1080/08098131.2012.752760

Tuckett, A. G., Hodgkinson, B., Rouillon, L., Balil-Lozoya, T., & Parker, D. (2014). What carers and family said about music therapy on behaviours of older people with dementia in residential aged care. *International Journal of Older People Nursing, 10*(2), 146–157. https://doi.org/10.1111/opn.12071

Tune, K. K. (2013). *Mid-Year Evaluation Report*. Communities in schools.

Turk, I. (Ed.). (1997). *Mousterian 'Bone Flute' and Other Finds from Divje Babe I Cave Site in Slovenia*. Zalozba ZRC.

Turner, M. L., & Engle, R. W. (1989). Is working memory capacity task dependent? *Journal of Memory and Language, 28*(2), 127–154. https://doi.org/10.1016/0749-596x(89)90040-5

Twomey, A., & Esgate, A. (2002). The Mozart Effect May Only Be Demonstrable in Nonmusicians. *Perceptual and Motor Skills, 95*(3), 1013–1026. https://doi.org/10.2466/pms.2002.95.3.1013

Tyler, H. M. (2002). In the music prison: The story of Pablo. In J. P. Sutton (Ed.), *Music, music therapy and trauma: International perspectives* (pp. 175–192). Jessica Kingsley Publishers.

Tymoszuk, U., Spiro, N., Perkins, R., Mason-Bertrand, A., Gee, K., & Williamon, A. (2021). *Arts engagement trends in the United Kingdom and their mental and social wellbeing implications: HEartS Survey*. https://doi.org/10.1371/journal.pone.0246078.

Tyrer, R. A., & Fazel, M. (2014). School and Community-Based Interventions for Refugee and Asylum Seeking Children: A Systematic Review. *PLoS ONE, 9*(2), e89359. https://doi.org/10.1371/journal.pone.0089359

Tyson, E. H. (2002). Hip Hop Therapy: An Exploratory Study of a Rap Music Intervention with At-Risk and Delinquent Youth. *Journal of Poetry Therapy, 15*(3), 131–144. https://doi.org/10.1023/a:1019795911358

Tze, P., & Chou, P. T. (2010). Attention drainage effect: How background music effects concentration in Taiwanese college students. *Journal of the Scholarship of Teaching and Learning, 10*(1), 36–46.

Uggla, L., Blom, K. M., Bonde, L., Gustafsson, B., & Wrangsjö, B. (2019). An Explorative Study of Qualities in Interactive Processes with Children and Their Parents in Music Therapy during and after Pediatric Hematopoietic Stem Cell Transplantation. *Medicines, 6*(1), 28. https://doi.org/10.3390/medicines6010028

Uggla, L., & Bonde, L. O. (2020). In L. O. Bonde & K. Johansson (Eds), *Music in Paediatric Hospitals–Nordic Perspectives*. Oslo: Norges musikkhøgskole (pp. 141–147 ,). https://hdl.handle.net/11250/2719973.

Uggla, L., Bonde, L. O., Svahn, B. M., Remberger, M., Wrangsjö, B., & Gustafsson, B. (2016). Music therapy can lower the heart rates of severely sick children. *Acta Paediatrica*, *105*(10), 1225–1230. https://doi.org/10.1111/apa.13452

Uggla, L., Bonde, L.-O., Hammar, U., Wrangsjö, B., & Gustafsson, B. (2018). Music therapy supported the health-related quality of life for children undergoing haematopoietic stem cell transplants. *Acta Paediatrica*, *107*(11), 1986–1994. https://doi.org/10.1111/apa.14515

Uhlig, S. (2011a). From violent rap to lovely blues: The transformation of aggressive behavior through vocal music therapy. In A. Meadows (Ed.), *Developments in Music Therapy Practice: Case Study Perspectives* (p. 466). Barcelona Publishers.

Uhlig, S. (2011b). Rap and singing for the emotional and cognitive development of at risk children. In F. Baker & S. Uhlig (Eds), *Voicework in music therapy* (pp. 63–83). Jessica Kingsley Publishers.

Uhlig, S., Dimitriadis, T., Hakvoort, L., & Scherder, E. (2017). Rap and singing are used by music therapists to enhance emotional self-regulation of youth: Results of a survey of music therapists in the Netherlands. *The Arts in Psychotherapy*, *53*, 44–54. https://doi.org/10.1016/j.aip.2016.12.001

Uhlig, S., Groot, J., Jansen, E., & Scherder, E. (2018). Rap & Sing Music Therapy and sleep in adolescents: A single-blind cluster randomized controlled trial. *Nordic Journal of Music Therapy*, *28*(1), 60–70. https://doi.org/10.1080/08098 131.2018.1542613

Uhlig, S., Jansen, E., & Scherder, E. (2016). Study protocol RapMusicTherapy for emotion regulation in a school setting. *Psychology of Music*, *44*(5), 1068–1081. https://doi.org/10.1177/0305735615608696

Uhlig, S., Jansen, E., & Scherder, E. (2017). "Being a bully isn't very cool\textbackslashdots": Rap & Sing Music Therapy for enhanced emotional self-regulation in an adolescent school setting – a randomized controlled trial. *Psychology of Music*, *46*(4), 568–587. https://doi.org/10.1177/0305735617719154

Uhlig, S., Jaschke, A., & Scherder, E. (2013). Effects of music on emotion regulation: A systematic literature review. *Pr[MP467]Oceedings of the 3rd International Conference on Music and Emotion,[MP468]: University of Jyväskylä. Department of Music*, 469.

Ullal-Gupta, S., Nederlanden, C. M. V. B. der, Tichko, P., Lahav, A., & Hannon, E. E. (2013). Linking prenatal experience to the emerging musical mind. *Frontiers in Systems Neuroscience*, *7*. https://doi.org/10.3389/fnsys.2013.00048

Ullman, M. T. (2001). The Declarative/Procedural Model of Lexicon and Grammar. *Journal of Psycholinguistic Research*, 30(1), 37–69. https://doi.org/10.1023/a:1005204207369

Underwood, E. B. (2000). *An analysis of the achievement patterns of high school students who participate in instrumental music and those who do not participate in instrumental music* [PhD Thesis].

Ungerleider, J. (1999). Music and Poetry Build Bi-communal Peace Culture in Cyprus. *People Building Peace*. http://www.gppac.net/documents/pbp/7/4_mpcypr.htm

Urbain, O. (2007). *Music and Conflict Transformation: Harmonies and Dissonances in Geopolitics*. I. B.

Uy, M. (2010). *Positive Behavioral and Academic Outcomes in Students Participating in Two After School Music Programs: The Harmony Project and El Sistema. Unpublished manuscript*. Berkeley College of Letters and Sciences, University of California.

Uy, M. (2012). Venezuela's National Music Education Programme El Sistema: Its Interactions with Society and Its Participants' Engagement in Praxis. *Music & Arts in Action*, 4(1), 5–21.

Vaag, J., Bjørngaard, J. H., & Bjerkeset, O. (2015). Symptoms of anxiety and depression among Norwegian musicians compared to the general workforce. *Psychology of Music*, 44(2), 234–248. https://doi.org/10.1177/0305735614564910

Vaag, J., Sund, E. R., & Bjerkeset, O. (2017). Five-factor personality profiles among Norwegian musicians compared to the general workforce. *Musicae Scientiae*, 22(3), 434–445. https://doi.org/10.1177/1029864917709519

Vaiouli, P., & Andreou, G. (2017). Communication and Language Development of Young Children With Autism: A Review of Research in Music. *Communication Disorders Quarterly*, 39(2), 323–329. https://doi.org/10.1177/1525740117705117

Valdesolo, P., & DeSteno, D. (2011). Synchrony and the social tuning of compassion. *Emotion*, 11(2), 262–266. https://doi.org/10.1037/a0021302

Valdesolo, P., Ouyang, J., & DeSteno, D. (2010). The rhythm of joint action: Synchrony promotes cooperative ability. *Journal of Experimental Social Psychology*, 46(4), 693–695. https://doi.org/10.1016/j.jesp.2010.03.004

Vanderark, S., Newman, I., & Bell, S. (1983). The Effects of Music Participation on Quality of Life of the Elderly. *Music Therapy*, 3(1), 71–81. https://doi.org/10.1093/mt/3.1.71

Varvarigou, M., Creech, A., Hallam, S., & McQueen, H. (2012). Benefits experienced by older people in group music-making activities. *Journal of Applied Arts & Health*, 3(2), 183–198. https://doi.org/10.1386/jaah.3.2.183_1

Varvarigou, M., Hallam, S., Creech, A., & McQueen, H. (2013). Different ways of experiencing music-making in later life: Creative music sessions for older learners in East London. *Research Studies in Music Education*, 35(1), 103–118. https://doi.org/10.1177/1321103x13478863

Västfjäll, D. (2001). Emotion induction through music: A review of the musical mood induction procedure. *Musicae Scientiae*, 5(1_suppl), 173–211. https://doi.org/10.1177/10298649020050s107

Vaudreuil, R., Bronson, H., & Bradt, J. (2019). Bridging the Clinic to Community: Music Performance as Social Transformation for Military Service Members. *Frontiers in Psychology*, 10. https://doi.org/10.3389/fpsyg.2019.00119

Vaughn, K. (2000). Music and Mathematics: Modest Support for the Oft-Claimed Relationship. *Journal of Aesthetic Education*, 34(3/4), 149. https://doi.org/10.2307/3333641

Veblen, K. (2012). Community music making: Challenging the stereotypes of conventional music education. In C. A. Baynon & K. K. Veblen (Eds), *Critical perspectives in Canadian music education* (pp. 123–133). WLU Press.

Velasco, E. de la M., & Hirumi, A. (2020). The effects of background music on learning: A systematic review of literature to guide future research and practice. *Educational Technology Research and Development*, 68(6), 2817–2837. https://doi.org/10.1007/s11423-020-09783-4

Veledar, A. (2008). Tutti Concert in Mostar. In *The Royal Norwegian Embassy in Sarajevo*. http://www.norveska.ba/News_and_events/Culture/Music/Tutti_Concert_in_Mostar.

Verghese, J., Lipton, R. B., Katz, M. J., Hall, C. B., Derby, C. A., Kuslansky, G., Ambrose, A. F., Sliwinski, M., & Buschke, H. (2003). Leisure Activities and the Risk of Dementia in the Elderly. *New England Journal of Medicine*, 348(25), 2508–2516. https://doi.org/10.1056/nejmoa022252

Vickers, Z. M., & Wasserman, S. S. (1980). Sensory Qualities of Food Sounds Based on Individual Perceptions. *Journal of Texture Studies*, 10(4), 319–332. https://doi.org/10.1111/j.1745-4603.1980.tb00863.x

Vidas, D., Larwood, J. L., Nelson, N. L., & Dingle, G. A. (2021). Music Listening as a Strategy for Managing COVID-19 Stress in First-Year University Students. *Frontiers in Psychology*, 12. https://doi.org/10.3389/fpsyg.2021.647065

Viggiani, N. (2014). A study of young people in the justice system engaged with a creative music programme. *BPS Developmental Section Conference*.

Viggiani, N., Daykin, N., Moriarty, Y., & Pilkington, P. (2013). *Musical pathways: An exploratory study of young people in the criminal justice system, engaged with a creative music programme*. University of the West of England.

Viggiani, N., Macintosh, S., & Lang, P. (2010). *Music in time: An evaluation of a participatory creative music programme for older prisoners*. University of the West of England.

Villalba, M. (2010). La política pública de las orquestas infanto-juveniles. *Revista Latino Americana de Ciencias Sociales, Niñez y Juventud, 8*(1), 131–149.

Villeneuve, M., Penhune, V., & Lamontagne, A. (2014). A Piano Training Program to Improve Manual Dexterity and Upper Extremity Function in Chronic Stroke Survivors. *Frontiers in Human Neuroscience, 8.* https://doi.org/10.3389/fnhum.2014.00662

Vink, A. C., Bruinsma, M. S., & Scholten, R. J. (2003a). *Music therapy for people with dementia* (A. C. Vink, Ed.). John Wiley & Sons, Ltd. https://doi.org/10.1002/14651858.cd003477.pub2

Vink, A. C., Bruinsma, M. S., & Scholten, R. J. (2003b). *Music therapy for people with dementia* (A. C. Vink, Ed.). John Wiley & Sons, Ltd. https://doi.org/10.1002/14651858.cd003477.pub2

Vink, A. C., Zuidersma, M., Boersma, F., Jonge, P. de, Zuidema, S. U., & Slaets, J. P. J. (2012). The effect of music therapy compared with general recreational activities in reducing agitation in people with dementia: A randomised controlled trial. *International Journal of Geriatric Psychiatry, 28*(10), 1031–1038. https://doi.org/10.1002/gps.3924

Vink, A., & Hanser, S. (2018). Music-Based Therapeutic Interventions for People with Dementia: A Mini-Review. *Medicines, 5*(4), 109. https://doi.org/10.3390/medicines5040109

Virtala, P., & Partanen, E. (2018). Can very early music interventions promote at-risk infants' development? *Annals of the New York Academy of Sciences, 1423*(1), 92–101. https://doi.org/10.1111/nyas.13646

Visu-Petra, L., Cheie, L., Benga, O., & Miclea, M. (2011). Cognitive control goes to school: The impact of executive functions on academic performance. *Procedia - Social and Behavioral Sciences, 11,* 240–244. https://doi.org/10.1016/j.sbspro.2011.01.069

Vleuten, M. van der, Visser, A., & Meeuwesen, L. (2012). The contribution of intimate live music performances to the quality of life for persons with dementia. *Patient Education and Counseling, 89*(3), 484–488. https://doi.org/10.1016/j.pec.2012.05.012

Vohra, S., & Nilsson, S. (2011). Does music therapy reduce pain and anxiety in children with cancer undergoing lumbar puncture? *Focus on Alternative and Complementary Therapies, 16*(1), 66–67. https://doi.org/10.1111/j.2042-7166.2010.01070_15.x

Voida, S., Edwards, W. K., Newman, M. W., Grinter, R. E., & Ducheneaut, N. (2006, April). Share and share alike. *Proceedings of the SIGCHI Conference on Human Factors in Computing Systems.* https://doi.org/10.1145/1124772.1124806

Volpe, G., D'Ausilio, A., Badino, L., Camurri, A., & Fadiga, L. (2016). *Measuring social interaction in music ensembles* (P. R, Trans.). https://doi.org/10.1098/rstb.2015.0377.

Volpe, U., Gianoglio, C., Autiero, L., Marino, M. L., Facchini, D., Mucci, A., & Galderisi, S. (2018). Acute Effects of Music Therapy in Subjects With Psychosis During Inpatient Treatment. *Psychiatry, 81*(3), 218–227. https://doi.org/10.1080/00332747.2018.1502559

Vougioukalou, S., Dow, R., Bradshaw, L., & Pallant, T. (2019). Wellbeing and Integration through Community Music: The Role of Improvisation in a Music Group of Refugees, Asylum Seekers and Local Community Members. *Contemporary Music Review, 38*(5), 533–548. https://doi.org/10.1080/07494467.2019.1684075

Vries, D., Beck, T., Stacey, B., Winslow, K., & Meines, K. (2015). Music as a Therapeutic Intervention with Autism: A Systematic Review of the Literature. *Therapeutic Recreational Journal, 49*(3), 220–237.

Vuust, P., Brattico, E., Seppänen, M., Näätänen, R., & Tervaniemi, M. (2012). The sound of music: Differentiating musicians using a fast, musical multi-feature mismatch negativity paradigm. *Neuropsychologia, 50*(7), 1432–1443. https://doi.org/10.1016/j.neuropsychologia.2012.02.028

Vuust, P., Gebauer, L., Hansen, N. C., Jørgensen, S. R., Møller, A., & Linnet, J. (2010). Personality influences career choice: Sensation seeking in professional musicians. *Music Education Research, 12*(2), 219–230. https://doi.org/10.1080/14613801003746584

Vuust, P., Pallesen, K. J., Bailey, C., Zuijen, T. L. van, Gjedde, A., Roepstorff, A., & Østergaard, L. (2005). To musicians, the message is in the meter. *NeuroImage, 24*(2), 560–564. https://doi.org/10.1016/j.neuroimage.2004.08.039

Vuust, P., Roepstorff, A., Wallentin, M., Mouridsen, K., & Østergaard, L. (2006). It don't mean a thing\textbackslashldots. *NeuroImage, 31*(2), 832–841. https://doi.org/10.1016/j.neuroimage.2005.12.037

Vuust, P., Wallentin, M., Mouridsen, K., Østergaard, L., & Roepstorff, A. (2011). Tapping polyrhythms in music activates language areas. *Neuroscience Letters, 494*(3), 211–216. https://doi.org/10.1016/j.neulet.2011.03.015

Vyver, J. V. de, & Abrams, D. (2017). The Arts as a Catalyst for Human Prosociality and Cooperation. *Social Psychological and Personality Science, 9*(6), 664–674. https://doi.org/10.1177/1948550617720275

Waaktaar, T., Christie, H. J., Borge, A. I. H., & Torgersen, S. (2004). How Can Young People's Resilience be Enhanced? Experiences from a Clinical Intervention Project. *Clinical Child Psychology and Psychiatry, 9*(2), 167–183. https://doi.org/10.1177/1359104504041917

Waddington-Jones, C., King, A., & Burnard, P. (2019). Exploring Wellbeing and Creativity Through Collaborative Composition as Part of Hull 2017 City of Culture. *Frontiers in Psychology, 10*. https://doi.org/10.3389/fpsyg.2019.00548

Wade-Woolley, L., & Heggie, L. (2016). The Contributions of Prosodic and Phonological Awareness to Reading. In *Linguistic Rhythm and Literacy* (pp.

3–24). John Benjamins Publishing Company. https://doi.org/10.1075/tilar.17.01wad

Wahn, B., & König, P. (2017). Is Attentional Resource Allocation Across Sensory Modalities Task-Dependent? *Advances in Cognitive Psychology*, *13*(1), 83–96. https://doi.org/10.5709/acp-0209-2

Wald, G. (2011a). Los usos de los programas sociales y culturales: El caso de dos orquestas juveniles de la Ciudad de Buenos Aires. *Questión: Revista Especializadaen Periodismo y Comunicación*, *1*(29), 1–13.

Wald, G. (2011b). Promoción de la salud integral a través del arte con jóvenes situación de vulnerabilidad social: Estudio comparativo de dos orquestas juveniles de la Ciudad de Buenos Aires. *Revista de Humanidades Médicas & Estudios Sociales de La Ciencia y La Tecnología*, *3*(1), 1–31.

Wallace, S. D., & Harwood, J. (2018). Associations Between Shared Musical Engagement and Parent–Child Relational Quality: The Mediating Roles of Interpersonal Coordination and Empathy. *Journal of Family Communication*, *18*(3), 202–216. https://doi.org/10.1080/15267431.2018.1466783

Wallentin, M., Nielsen, A. H., Friis-Olivarius, M., Vuust, C., & Vuust, P. (2010). The Musical Ear Test, a new reliable test for measuring musical competence. *Learning and Individual Differences*, *20*(3), 188–196. https://doi.org/10.1016/j.lindif.2010.02.004

Wallick, M. D. (1998). A Comparison Study of the Ohio Proficiency Test Results between Fourth-Grade String Pullout Students and Those of Matched Ability. *Journal of Research in Music Education*, *46*(2), 239–247. https://doi.org/10.2307/3345626

Walsh, S., Causer, R., & Brayne, C. (2019). Does playing a musical instrument reduce the incidence of cognitive impairment and dementia? A systematic review and meta-analysis. *Aging & Mental Health*, *25*(4), 593–601. https://doi.org/10.1080/13607863.2019.1699019

Walworth, D. D. (2005). Procedural-Support Music Therapy in the Healthcare Setting: A Cost–Effectiveness Analysis. *Journal of Pediatric Nursing*, *20*(4), 276–284. https://doi.org/10.1016/j.pedn.2005.02.016

Walworth, D. D. (2009). Effects of Developmental Music Groups for Parents and Premature or Typical Infants Under Two Years on Parental Responsiveness and Infant Social Development. *Journal of Music Therapy*, *46*(1), 32–52. https://doi.org/10.1093/jmt/46.1.32

Wamhoff, M. J. (1972). A Comparison of Self-concept of Fourth Grade Students Enrolled and Not Enrolled in Instrumental Music in Selected Schools in the Barstow, California School District. *Doctoral Dissertation*. [MP481]*Dissertation Abstracts International*, *33*, 626.

Wan, C. Y., Rüber, T., Hohmann, A., & Schlaug, G. (2010). The Therapeutic Effects of Singing in Neurological Disorders. *Music Perception*, *27*(4), 287–295. https://doi.org/10.1525/mp.2010.27.4.287

Wan, C. Y., & Schlaug, G. (2010). Music Making as a Tool for Promoting Brain Plasticity across the Life Span. *The Neuroscientist, 16*(5), 566–577. https://doi.org/10.1177/1073858410377805

Wang, C.-F., Sun, Y.-L., & Zang, H.-X. (2014). Music therapy improves sleep quality in acute and chronic sleep disorders: A meta-analysis of 10 randomized studies. *International Journal of Nursing Studies, 51*(1), 51–62. https://doi.org/10.1016/j.ijnurstu.2013.03.008

Wang, S., & Agius, M. (2018). The use of music therapy on the treatment of mental illness and the enhancement of societal wellbeing. *Psychiatria Danubina, 30*(7), 595–600.

Ward, B. (1998). *Just my soul responding: Rhythm and blues, Black consciousness and race relations*. Routledge. https://doi.org/10.1016/j.ijnurstu.2013.03.008.

Ward, S., James, S. J., James, K., Brown, C., Kokotsaki, D., & Wigham, J. (2020). *The benefits of music workshop participation for pupils' wellbeing and social capital; the In2 music project*. Durham University.

Warfield, D. (2010). Bowing in the right direction: Hiland Mountain Correctional Center women's string orchestra programme. *International Journal of Community Music, 3*(1), 103–110. https://doi.org/10.1386/ijcm.3.1.103/7

Watanabe, D., Savion-Lemieux, T., & Penhune, V. B. (2007). The effect of early musical training: Evidence for a sensitive period in motor learning. *Brain and Cognition, 176*, 332–340.

Weaver, H. (2001). *Travellin' home and back, Exploring the psychological processes of reconciliation* [PhD Thesis]. Union Institute and University.

Weber, A. (2018). *Choral Singing and Communal Mindset: A Program Evaluation of the Voices of Hope Women's Prison Choir*. Unpublished DMA dissertation. University of Minnesota.

Weber, M., Martindale, D., Riedel, J., & Neuwirth, G. (1958). *The Rational and Social Foundations of Music*. Southern Illinois University Press.

Wechsler, D. (1997). *WAIS-III, Wechsler Adult Intelligence Scale: Administration and Scoring Manual*. Psychological Corporation.

Wechsler, D. (2008). *Wechsler Adult Intelligence Scale*. Psychological Corporation.

Weidema, J. L., Roncaglia-Denissen, M. P., & Honing, H. (2016). Top–Down Modulation on the Perception and Categorization of Identical Pitch Contours in Speech and Music. *Frontiers in Psychology, 7*. https://doi.org/10.3389/fpsyg.2016.00817

Weinberg, M. K., & Joseph, D. (2016). If you're happy and you know it: Music engagement and subjective wellbeing. *Psychology of Music, 45*(2), 257–267. https://doi.org/10.1177/0305735616659552

Weinstein, D., Launay, J., Pearce, E., Dunbar, R. I. M., & Stewart, L. (2016). Singing and social bonding: Changes in connectivity and pain threshold as a function of group size. *Evolution and Human Behavior, 37*(2), 152–158. https://doi.org/10.1016/j.evolhumbehav.2015.10.002

Welch, G. F., Biasutti, M., MacRitchie, J., McPherson, G. E., & Himonides, E. (2020). Editorial: The Impact of Music on Human Development and Well-Being. *Frontiers in Psychology, 11.* https://doi.org/10.3389/fpsyg.2020.01246

Welch, G. F., Himonides, E., Saunders, J., & Papageorgi, I. (2010). *Researching the impact of the national singing programme 'Sing Up' in England: Main findings from the first three years.* International Music Education Research Centre (iMerc), Institute of Education, University of London.

Welch, G. F., Himonides, E., Saunders, J., Papageorgi, I., & Sarazin, M. (2014). Singing and social inclusion. *Frontiers in Psychology, 5.* https://doi.org/10.3389/fpsyg.2014.00803

Welch, G. F., Papageorgi, I., Vraka, M., Himonides, E., & Saunders, J. (2011). *The Chorister Outreach Programme: A research evaluation 2008–2009.* iMerc, Institute of Education, University of London.

Welch, G. F., Saunders, J., Hobsbaum, A., & Himonides, E. (2012). *Literacy through music: A research evaluation of the New London Orchestra's Literacy through Music Programme.* iMerc, Institute of Education, University of London.

Welch, G. F., Saunders, J., Papageorgi, I., Joyce, H., & E, H. (2009). *An instrument for the assessment of children's attitudes to singing, self and social inclusion.* Institute of Education, University of London.

Welch, G., Purves, R., Saunders, J., Mason, K., Bowmer, A. R., & Wright, A. (2020). Sing Every Day: The wider benefits of a school-based singing project with disadvantaged children. In P. González & R. Omolo-Ongati (Eds), *Proceedings of the 28th International Society for Music Education (ISME) Seminar on Research in Music Education.*[MP482.

Wellman, R., & Pinkerton, J. (2015). The Development of a Music Therapy Protocol: A Music 4 Life® Case Report of a Veteran with PTSD. *Music and Medicine, 7*(3), 24–39. https://doi.org/10.47513/mmd.v7i3.408

Wells, A., & Hakanen, E. A. (1991). The Emotional Use of Popular Music by Adolescents. *Journalism Quarterly, 68*(3), 445–454. https://doi.org/10.1177/107769909106800315

Wells, D. L., Graham, L., & Hepper, P. G. (2002). The influence of auditory stimulation on the behaviour of dogs housed in a rescue shelter. *Animal Welfare, 11*(4), 385–393.

Wengenroth, M., Blatow, M., Heinecke, A., Reinhardt, J., Stippich, C., Hofmann, E., & Schneider, P. (2013). Increased Volume and Function of Right Auditory Cortex as a Marker for Absolute Pitch. *Cerebral Cortex, 24*(5), 1127–1137. https://doi.org/10.1093/cercor/bhs391

Wentworth, E. R. (2019). *Mathematics and Music: The Effects of an Integrated Approach on Student Achievement and Affect* [PhD Thesis]. Columbia University.

Werker, J. F., Lloyd, V. L., Pegg, J. E., & Polka, L. (1996). Putting the baby in the bootstraps: Toward a more complete understanding of the role of the input in infant speech processing. In J. L. Morganand & K. Demuth (Eds), *Signal to Syntax: Bootstrapping from speech to grammar in early acquisition, Mahwah, NJ: Lawrence Erlbaum* (pp. 427–447).

Werner, D. (1984). *Amazon journey; An anthropologist's year among Brazil's Mekranoti Indians.* Simon and Schuster.

Werner, J., Wosch, T., & Gold, C. (2015). Effectiveness of group music therapy versus recreational group singing for depressive symptoms of elderly nursing home residents: Pragmatic trial. *Aging & Mental Health, 21*(2), 147–155. https://doi.org/10.1080/13607863.2015.1093599

Wetter, O. E., Koerner, F., & Schwaninger, A. (2008). Does musical training improve school performance? *Instructional Science, 37*(4), 365–374. https://doi.org/10.1007/s11251-008-9052-y

Węziak-Białowolska, D., & Białowolski, P. (2016). Cultural events – does attendance improve health? Evidence from a Polish longitudinal study. *BMC Public Health, 16*(1). https://doi.org/10.1186/s12889-016-3433-y

White, E. J., Hutka, S. A., Williams, L. J., & Moreno, S. (2013). Learning, neural plasticity and sensitive periods: Implications for language acquisition, music training and transfer across the lifespan. *Frontiers in Systems Neuroscience, 7*. https://doi.org/10.3389/fnsys.2013.00090

Whitehead, B. J. (2001). *The effect of music-intensive intervention on mathematics scores of middle and high school students* [Doctoral dissertation.]. Capella University. Dissertation Abstracts International.

Whitehead-Pleaux, A. M., Baryza, M. J., & Sheridan, R. L. (2006). The Effects of Music Therapy on Pediatric Patients' Pain and Anxiety During Donor Site Dressing Change. *Journal of Music Therapy, 43*(2), 136–153. https://doi.org/10.1093/jmt/43.2.136

White-Schwoch, T., Carr, K. W., Anderson, S., Strait, D. L., & Kraus, N. (2013). Older Adults Benefit from Music Training Early in Life: Biological Evidence for Long-Term Training-Driven Plasticity. *Journal of Neuroscience, 33*(45), 17667–17674. https://doi.org/10.1523/jneurosci.2560-13.2013

Whitwell, D. (1977). *Music learning through performance.* Texas Music Educators Association.

Więch, P., Sa\textbackslashlacińska, I., Walat, K., Kózka, M., & Bazaliński, D. (2020). Can Singing in a Choir Be a Key Strategy for Lifelong Health? A Cross-sectional Study. *Journal of Voice.* https://doi.org/10.1016/j.jvoice.2020.11.010

Wiesendanger, M., & Serrien, D. J. (2004). The quest to understand bimanual coordination. In *Progress in Brain Research* (pp. 491–505). Elsevier. https://doi.org/10.1016/s0079-6123(03)43046-x

Wiesenthal, D. L., Hennessy, D. A., & Totten, B. (2003). The influence of music on mild driver aggression. *Transportation Research Part F: Traffic Psychology and Behaviour, 6*(2), 125–134. https://doi.org/10.1016/s1369-8478(03)00020-2

Wig, J. A., & Boyle, J. D. (1982). The Effect of Keyboard Learning Experiences on Middle School General Music Students' Music Achievement and Attitudes. *Journal of Research in Music Education, 30*(3), 163–172. https://doi.org/10.2307/3345083

Wiles, J. L., Wild, K., Kerse, N., & Allen, R. E. S. (2012). Resilience from the point of view of older people: `There's still life beyond a funny knee'. *Social Science & Medicine, 74*(3), 416–424. https://doi.org/10.1016/j.socscimed.2011.11.005

Wilkinson, R. G., & Marmot, M. (2003). *Social determinants of health: The solid facts*. WHO Regional Office for Europe.

Williams, E., Dingle, G. A., & Clift, S. (2018). A systematic review of mental health and wellbeing outcomes of group singing for adults with a mental health condition. *European Journal of Public Health, 28*(6), 1035–1042. https://doi.org/10.1093/eurpub/cky115

Williams, K. E., Barrett, M. S., Welch, G. F., Abad, V., & Broughton, M. (2015). Associations between early shared music activities in the home and later child outcomes: Findings from the Longitudinal Study of Australian Children. *Early Childhood Research Quarterly, 31*, 113–124. https://doi.org/10.1016/j.ecresq.2015.01.004

Williams, K. E., Berthelsen, D., Nicholson, J. M., Walker, S., & Abad, V. (2012). The Effectiveness of a Short-Term Group Music Therapy Intervention for Parents Who Have a Child with a Disability. *Journal of Music Therapy, 49*(1), 23–44. https://doi.org/10.1093/jmt/49.1.23

Wills, G., & Cooper, C. L. (1988). *PressuresSensitive: Popular musicians under stress*. Sage.

Wilson, D., Caulfield, L. S., & S, A. (2009). Good vibrations: The long-term impact of a prison based music project. *The Prison Service Journal, 182*, 27–32.

Wilson, D., & Logan, M. (2006). *Breaking down walls-The good vibrations project in prison*. Centre for Criminal Justice Policy and Research.

Wilson, D., McKegg, K., Goodwin, D., Black, X., Sauni, P., & Toumua, R. (2012). *Evaluation of Sistema Aotearoa*. Institute of Public Policy, AUT University.

Wilson, G. B., & MacDonald, R. A. R. (2019). The Social Impact of Musical Engagement for Young Adults With Learning Difficulties: A Qualitative Study. *Frontiers in Psychology, 10*. https://doi.org/10.3389/fpsyg.2019.01300

Wilson, S. J., Lusher, D., Martin, C. L., Rayner, G., & McLachlan, N. (2011). Intersecting Factors Lead to Absolute Pitch Acquisition That is

Maintained in a "Fixed $\textbackslash$i$\textbackslashgreater$do$\textbackslash$/i$\textbackslashgreater$" Environment. *Music Perception, 29*(3), 285–296. https://doi.org/10.1525/mp.2012.29.3.285

Wilson, S. J., Lusher, D., Wan, C. Y., Dudgeon, P., & Reutens, D. C. (2008). The Neurocognitive Components of Pitch Processing: Insights from Absolute Pitch. *Cerebral Cortex, 19*(3), 724–732. https://doi.org/10.1093/cercor/bhn121

Wilson, T. L., & Brown, T. L. (1997). Reexamination of the Effect of Mozart's Music on Spatial-Task Performance. *The Journal of Psychology, 131*(4), 365–370. https://doi.org/10.1080/00223989709603522

Wiltermuth, S. S., & Heath, C. (2009). Synchrony and Cooperation. *Psychological Science, 20*(1), 1–5. https://doi.org/10.1111/j.1467-9280.2008.02253.x

Winner, E., & Cooper, M. (2000). Mute Those Claims: No Evidence (Yet) for a Causal Link between Arts Study and Academic Achievement. *Journal of Aesthetic Education, 34*(3/4), 11. https://doi.org/10.2307/3333637

Winsler, A., Ducenne, L., & Koury, A. (2011). Singing One's Way to Self-Regulation: The Role of Early Music and Movement Curricula and Private Speech. *Early Education & Development, 22*(2), 274–304. https://doi.org/10.1080/10409280903585739

Wise, G. W., Hartmann, D. J., & Fisher, B. J. (1992). Exploration of the Relationship between Choral Singing and Successful Aging. *Psychological Reports, 70*(3_suppl), 1175–1183. https://doi.org/10.2466/pr0.1992.70.3c.1175

Wit, K. (2020). *Legacy: Participatory music practices with elderly people as a resource for the wellbeing of healthcare professionals* [PhD Thesis]. Hanze University of Applied Sciences.

Witte, M. de, Spruit, A., Hooren, S. van, Moonen, X., & Stams, G.-J. (2019). Effects of music interventions on stress-related outcomes: A systematic review and two meta-analyses. *Health Psychology Review, 14*(2), 294–324. https://doi.org/10.1080/17437199.2019.1627897

Wittenberg, R., Hu, B., Barraza-Araiza, L., & Rehil, A. (2019). Projections of older people with dementia and costs of dementia care in the United Kingdom, 2019–2040. *Care Policy and Evaluation Centre. Research at LSE CPEC Working Paper, 5*([MP485).

Wolf, J. (1992). Let's sing it again: Creating music with young children. *Young Children, 47*(2), 56–61.

Wolff, K. (1979). The non-musical outcomes of music education: A review of the literature. *Bulletin of the Council for Research in Music Education, 55*, 1–27.

Wolff, P. H., Michel, G. F., & Ovrut, M. (1990). The Timing of Syllable Repetitions in Developmental Dyslexia. *Journal of Speech, Language, and Hearing Research, 33*(2), 281–289. https://doi.org/10.1044/jshr.3302.281

WONG, P. C. M., & PERRACHIONE, T. K. (2007). Learning pitch patterns in lexical identification by native English-speaking adults. *Applied Psycholinguistics, 28*(4), 565–585. https://doi.org/10.1017/s0142716407070312

Wong, P. C. M., Perrachione, T. K., & Parrish, T. B. (2007). Neural characteristics of successful and less successful speech and word learning in adults. *Human Brain Mapping, 28*(10), 995–1006. https://doi.org/10.1002/hbm.20330

Wong, P. C. M., Skoe, E., Russo, N. M., Dees, T., & Kraus, N. (2007). Musical experience shapes human brainstem encoding of linguistic pitch patterns. *Nature Neuroscience, 10*(4), 420–422. https://doi.org/10.1038/nn1872

Wood, A. (2010). Singing Diplomats: The Hidden Life of a Russian-speaking Choir in Jerusalem. *Ethnomusicology Forum, 19*(2), 165–190. https://doi.org/10.1080/17411912.2010.507360

Wood, A. L. (1973). *The relationship of selected factors to achievement motivation and self-esteem among senior high school band members* [Doctoral dissertation.]. Louisiana State University and Agricultural & Mechanical College. Dissertation Abstracts International.

Wood, L., Ivery, P., Donovan, R., & Lambin, E. (2013). "To the beat of a different drum": Improving the social and mental wellbeing of at-risk young people through drumming. *Journal of Public Mental Health, 12*(2), 70–79. https://doi.org/10.1108/jpmh-09-2012-0002

Woodman, A., Breviglia, E., Mori, Y., Golden, R., Maina, J., & Wisniewski, H. (2018). The Effect of Music on Exercise Intensity among Children with Autism Spectrum Disorder: A Pilot Study. *Journal of Clinical Medicine, 7*(3), 38. https://doi.org/10.3390/jcm7030038

Woodward, S. C., Sloth-Nielsen, J., & Mathiti, V. (2007). South Africa, the arts and youth in conflict with the law. *International Journal of Community Music, 1*(1), 69–88. https://doi.org/10.1386/ijcm.1.1.69_0

Wright, R. (2012). Music education and social transformation: Building social capital through music. *The Canadian Music Educator, Edmonton, 53*(3), 12–13.

Wristen, B. (2006). Demographics and motivation of adult group piano students. *Music Education Research, 8*(3), 387–406. https://doi.org/10.1080/14613800600957503

Wu, C. C., Hamm, J. P., Lim, V. K., & Kirk, I. J. (2017). Musical training increases functional connectivity, but does not enhance mu suppression. *Neuropsychologia, 104*, 223–233. https://doi.org/10.1016/j.neuropsychologia.2017.08.029

Wu, S. M. (2002). Effects of music therapy on anxiety, depression and self-esteem of undergraduates. *PSYCHOLOGIA, 45*(2), 104–114. https://doi.org/10.2117/psysoc.2002.104

Yang, H., Lu, J., Gong, D., & Yao, D. (2016). How do musical tonality and experience affect visual working memory? *NeuroReport*, 27(2), 94–98. https://doi.org/10.1097/wnr.0000000000000503

Yang, H., Ma, W., Gong, D., Hu, J., & Yao, D. (2014). A Longitudinal Study on Children's Music Training Experience and Academic Development. *Scientific Reports*, 4(1). https://doi.org/10.1038/srep05854

Yang, J., McClelland, A., & Furnham, A. (2016). The effect of background music on the cognitive performance of musicians: A pilot study. *Psychology of Music*, 44(5), 1202–1208. https://doi.org/10.1177/0305735615592265

Yang, M.-T., Hsu, C.-H., Yeh, P.-W., Lee, W.-T., Liang, J.-S., Fu, W.-M., & Lee, C.-Y. (2015). Attention deficits revealed by passive auditory change detection for pure tones and lexical tones in ADHD children. *Frontiers in Human Neuroscience*, 9. https://doi.org/10.3389/fnhum.2015.00470

Yang, P. (2015). The impact of music on educational attainment. *Journal of Cultural Economics*, 39(4), 369–396. https://doi.org/10.1007/s10824-015-9240-y

Yap, A. F., Kwan, Y. H., & Ang, S. B. (2017). A systematic review on the effects of active participation in rhythm-centred music making on different aspects of health. *European Journal of Integrative Medicine*, 9, 44–49. https://doi.org/10.1016/j.eujim.2016.11.011

Yazejian, N., & Peisner-Feinberg, E. S. (2009). Effects of a Preschool Music and Movement Curriculum on Children's Language Skills. *NHSA Dialog*, 12(4), 327–341. https://doi.org/10.1080/15240750903075255

Ye, P., Huang, Z., Zhou, H., & Tang, Q. (2021). Music-based intervention to reduce aggressive behavior in children and adolescents. *Medicine*, 100(4), e23894. https://doi.org/10.1097/md.0000000000023894

Yinger, O. S., & Gooding, L. (2014). Music Therapy and Music Medicine for Children and Adolescents. *Child and Adolescent Psychiatric Clinics of North America*, 23(3), 535–553. https://doi.org/10.1016/j.chc.2013.03.003

Yöndem, S., Yöndem, Z. D., & Per, M. (2017). Personality Traits and Psychological Symptoms of Music and Art Students. *Journal of Education and Training Studies*, 5(7), 53. https://doi.org/10.11114/jets.v5i7.2431

Yoon, J. N. (2000). Music in the classroom: Its influence on children's brain development, academic performance, and practical life skills. *ERIC Document Reproduction Service, ED442707.[MP489.*

Young, R., Sproeber, N., Groschwitz, R. C., Preiss, M., & Plener, P. L. (2014). Why alternative teenagers self-harm: Exploring the link between non-suicidal self-injury, attempted suicide and adolescent identity. *BMC Psychiatry*, 14(1). https://doi.org/10.1186/1471-244x-14-137

Young, V. M., & Colman, A. M. (1979). Some Psychological Processes in String Quartets. *Psychology of Music*, 7(1), 12–18. https://doi.org/10.1177/030573567971002

Yun, J. (2014). Juvenile offenders' experience of music therapy within the framework of self-determination: A modified grounded theory study. *Journal of Music and Human Behavior, 11*(1), 63–82.

Yurgil, K. A., Velasquez, M. A., Winston, J. L., Reichman, N. B., & Colombo, P. J. (2020). Music Training, Working Memory, and Neural Oscillations: A Review. *Frontiers in Psychology, 11.* https://doi.org/10.3389/fpsyg.2020.00266

Zachopoulou, E., Tsapakidou, A., & Derri, V. (2004). The effects of a developmentally appropriate music and movement program on motor performance. *Early Childhood Research Quarterly, 19*(4), 631–642. https://doi.org/10.1016/j.ecresq.2004.10.005

Zafranas, N. (2021). Piano keyboard training and the spatial-temporal development of young children attending kindergarten classes in Greece. In *Music in the Lives of Young Children* (pp. 261–273). Routledge. https://doi.org/10.4324/9781003090311-19

Zampini, M., & Spence, C. (2004). The role of auditory cues in modulating the perceived crispness and staleness of potato chips. *Journal of Sensory Studies, 19*(5), 347–363. https://doi.org/10.1111/j.1745-459x.2004.080403.x

Zanders, M. L. (2015). Music Therapy Practices and Processes with Foster-Care Youth: Formulating an Approach to Clinical Work. *Music Therapy Perspectives, 33*(2), 97–107. https://doi.org/10.1093/mtp/miv028

Zanini, C. R. de O., & Leao, E. (2006). Therapeutic Choir—A Music Therapist Looks at the New Millenium Elderly. *Voices: A World Forum for Music Therapy, 6*(2). https://doi.org/10.15845/voices.v6i2.249

Zanutto, D. R. (1997). *The effect of instrumental music instruction on academic achievement* [PhD Thesis]. University of California.

Zapata, G. P., & Hargreaves, D. J. (2017). The effects of musical activities on the self-esteem of displaced children in Colombia. *Psychology of Music, 46*(4), 540–550. https://doi.org/10.1177/0305735617716756

Zarobe, L., & Bungay, H. (2017). The role of arts activities in developing resilience and mental wellbeing in children and young people a rapid review of the literature. *Perspectives in Public Health, 137*(6), 337–347. https://doi.org/10.1177/1757913917712283

Zatorre, R. (2005). Music, the food of neuroscience? *Nature, 434*(7031), 312–315. https://doi.org/10.1038/434312a

Zatorre, R. J. (2001). Spectral and Temporal Processing in Human Auditory Cortex. *Cerebral Cortex, 11*(10), 946–953. https://doi.org/10.1093/cercor/11.10.946

Zatorre, R. J. (2003). Absolute pitch: A model for understanding the influence of genes and development on neural and cognitive function. *Nature Neuroscience, 6*(7), 692–695. https://doi.org/10.1038/nn1085

Zatorre, R. J. (2013). Predispositions and Plasticity in Music and Speech Learning: Neural Correlates and Implications. *Science*, *342*(6158), 585–589. https://doi.org/10.1126/science.1238414

Zatorre, R. J., Belin, P., & Penhune, V. B. (2002). Structure and function of auditory cortex: Music and speech. *Trends in Cognitive Sciences*, *6*(1), 37–46. https://doi.org/10.1016/s1364-6613(00)01816-7

Zatorre, R. J., Chen, J. L., & Penhune, V. B. (2007). When the brain plays music: Auditory–motor interactions in music perception and production. *Nature Reviews Neuroscience*, *8*(7), 547–558. https://doi.org/10.1038/nrn2152

Zatorre, R. J., Delhommeau, K., & Zarate, J. M. (2012). Modulation of Auditory Cortex Response to Pitch Variation Following Training with Microtonal Melodies. *Frontiers in Psychology*, *3*. https://doi.org/10.3389/fpsyg.2012.00544

Zatorre, R. J., Fields, R. D., & Johansen-Berg, H. (2012). Plasticity in gray and white: Neuroimaging changes in brain structure during learning. *Nature Neuroscience*, *15*(4), 528–536. https://doi.org/10.1038/nn.3045

Zeevi, L. S., Regev, D., & Guttmann, J. (2018). The Efficiency of Art-Based Interventions in Parental Training. *Frontiers in Psychology*, *9*. https://doi.org/10.3389/fpsyg.2018.01495

Zeilig, H., Killick, J., & Fox, C. (2014). The participative arts for people living with a dementia: A critical review. *International Journal of Ageing and Later Life*, *9*(1), 7–34. https://doi.org/10.3384/ijal.1652-8670.14238

Zelazo, P. D. (2004). The development of conscious control in childhood. *Trends in Cognitive Sciences*, *8*(1), 12–17. https://doi.org/10.1016/j.tics.2003.11.001

Zelizer, C. M. (2003). The Role of Artistic Processes in Peacebuilding in Bosnia-Herzegovina. *Peace and Conflict Studies*, *10*(2), 62–75.

Zelizer, C. M. (2004). *The role of artistic processes in peacebuilding in Bosnia-Herzegovina. Unpublished doctoral dissertation*. George Mason University.

Zendel, B. R., & Alain, C. (2009). Concurrent Sound Segregation Is Enhanced in Musicians. *Journal of Cognitive Neuroscience*, *21*(8), 1488–1498. https://doi.org/10.1162/jocn.2009.21140

Zhang, H., Miller, K., Cleveland, R., & Cortina, K. (2018). How listening to music affects reading: Evidence from eye tracking. *Journal of Experimental Psychology: Learning, Memory, and Cognition*, *44*(11), 1778–1791. https://doi.org/10.1037/xlm0000544

Zhang, J. D., Susino, M., McPherson, G. E., & Schubert, E. (2018). The definition of a musician in music psychology: A literature review and the six-year rule. *Psychology of Music*, *48*(3), 389–409. https://doi.org/10.1177/0305735618804038

Zhang, Y., Cai, J., An, L., Hui, F., Ren, T., Ma, H., & Zhao, Q. (2017). Does music therapy enhance behavioral and cognitive function in elderly dementia patients? A systematic review and meta-analysis. *Ageing Research Reviews*, 35, 1–11. https://doi.org/10.1016/j.arr.2016.12.003

Zhao, K., Bai, Z. G., Bo, A., & Chi, I. (2016). A systematic review and meta-analysis of music therapy for the older adults with depression. *International Journal of Geriatric Psychiatry*, 31(11), 1188–1198. https://doi.org/10.1002/gps.4494

Zhao, T. C., & Kuhl, P. K. (2016). Musical intervention enhances infants' neural processing of temporal structure in music and speech. *Proceedings of the National Academy of Sciences*, 113(19), 5212–5217. https://doi.org/10.1073/pnas.1603984113

Zhao, T. C., Lam, H. T. G., Sohi, H., & Kuhl, P. K. (2017). Neural processing of musical meter in musicians and non-musicians. *Neuropsychologia*, 106, 289–297. https://doi.org/10.1016/j.neuropsychologia.2017.10.007

Zharinova-Sanderson, O. (2004). Promoting integration and socio-cultural change: Community music therapy with traumatized refugees in Berlin. In M. Pavlicevic & G. Ansdell (Eds), *Community Music Therapy, London. Jessica Kingsley* (pp. 233–248).

Zhenxiong, G., Quingyi, Z., & Yuzhen, J. (1995). On the Musical Instruments of Chinese Nationalities. [MP491] *Proceedings of the International Symposium on Musical Acoustics, Le Normont*, 546–550.

Zhou, K., Li, X., Li, J., Liu, M., Dang, S., Wang, D., & Xin, X. (2015). A clinical randomized controlled trial of music therapy and progressive muscle relaxation training in female breast cancer patients after radical mastectomy: Results on depression, anxiety and length of hospital stay. *European Journal of Oncology Nursing*, 19(1), 54–59. https://doi.org/10.1016/j.ejon.2014.07.010

Zichermann, S. C. (2009). *The effects of hip hop and rap on young women in academia* [PhD Thesis]. University of Toronto.

Zillman, D., & Gan, S. (1997). Musical taste in adolescence. In D. J. Hargreaves & A.C. (Eds), *North, The Social Psychology of Music* (pp. 161–187). Oxford University Press.

Ziv, N., & Goshen, M. (2006). The effect of `sad' and `happy' background music on the interpretation of a story in 5 to 6-year-old children. *British Journal of Music Education*, 23(3), 303–314. https://doi.org/10.1017/s0265051706007078

Zuijen, T. L. van, Sussman, E., Winkler, I., Näätänen, R., & Tervaniemi, M. (2005). Auditory organization of sound sequences by a temporal or numerical regularity—A mismatch negativity study comparing musicians and non-musicians. *Cognitive Brain Research*, 23(2–3), 270–276. https://doi.org/10.1016/j.cogbrainres.2004.10.007

Zuk, J., Benjamin, C., Kenyon, A., & Gaab, N. (2014). Behavioral and Neural Correlates of Executive Functioning in Musicians and Non-Musicians. *PLoS ONE*, 9(6), e99868. https://doi.org/10.1371/journal.pone.0099868

Zuk, J., & Gaab, N. (2018). Evaluating predisposition and training in shaping the musician's brain: The need for a developmental perspective. *Annals of the New York Academy of Sciences, 1423*(1), 40–50. https://doi.org/10.1111/nyas.13737

Zuk, J., Ozernov-Palchik, O., Kim, H., Lakshminarayanan, K., Gabrieli, J. D. E., Tallal, P., & Gaab, N. (2013). Enhanced Syllable Discrimination Thresholds in Musicians. *PLoS ONE, 8*(12), e80546. https://doi.org/10.1371/journal.pone.0080546

Zulauf, M. (1993). Three year experiment in extended music teaching in Switzerland: The different effects observed in a group of French speaking pupils. *Bulletin of the Council for Research in Music Education, 119,* 111–121.

Zyga, O., Russ, S. W., Meeker, H., & Kirk, J. (2017). A preliminary investigation of a school-based musical theater intervention program for children with intellectual disabilities. *Journal of Intellectual Disabilities, 22*(3), 262–278. https://doi.org/10.1177/1744629517699334

Çupı, B., & Morına, S. (2020). The influential poser and the importance of music in advertising and marketing. *Journal of Life Economics, 7*(1), 17–28.

Index

β-endorphin 518

ABRSM 574, 578
abuse 527, 530, 534–537, 541–542, 577–578
accommodation 164, 531, 533, 562
accompaniment 31, 92–93, 164, 408, 455, 584
accuracy 20, 23, 32, 42, 51, 57, 70, 73, 80, 89, 92–93, 97–98, 104, 395, 408
acoustic 21, 30, 33, 45, 48, 50, 52, 61, 64, 72, 104, 126, 142, 156, 416
activation 20, 22, 24, 26–31, 36, 38–39, 41
active 15, 18–20, 24, 28, 33, 36, 42
acute 424, 480, 493, 505–506, 514, 539, 541
adaptive 4, 421–422, 479
addiction 180, 383, 455, 534, 543
ADHD 180, 270, 301–303, 317
adolescence 3, 5–6, 70, 75, 156, 171, 241, 251, 257, 396, 414–415, 418, 422, 424, 437, 441, 444, 463, 477, 523, 554. *See* adolescent
adolescent 419, 422–424, 435, 437–444, 446. *See* adolescence
adrenocorticotropic hormone 416
adulthood 19, 75, 160, 252, 394, 396, 414–415, 418, 422, 447, 461, 463, 547, 554
advantage 21, 56–57, 60, 65, 80, 87, 123, 126, 136, 138–139, 142–144, 146, 148, 150–151, 157–159, 167, 169, 175, 177, 185, 194, 197, 203, 209, 220–221, 243
aesthetic 417, 421, 473
affective 5, 47, 50, 81, 114, 376, 419–420, 441, 443, 461, 467, 539, 545, 558, 575

affirmation 12, 414, 458
Africa 7, 421, 445, 507, 532, 535
African-American 250, 528, 559
after-school 35, 118, 155, 188, 388, 398
age-decelerating 461
ageing 61, 159–160, 162, 191, 193, 196, 447, 453–454, 459–460, 463–464, 497, 503
age-matched 73, 96, 118, 460
agency 376, 384, 391, 431, 438, 452, 456, 489, 562, 564
 organisation 563, 580
age-related 23, 36, 160, 167, 184–185, 201, 218, 461, 483
aggression 217, 303, 340, 342, 345, 366, 373, 390, 402, 433, 435, 491, 500, 502, 516, 538, 546, 549, 555, 559, 577, 582, 590
aggressive 585
agitation 483, 491–492, 496, 498, 500–501
agreeableness 378, 380–382
agricultural 589–591
aims 444, 561
alcohol 167, 451, 577–578, 582
alcoholics 543
alertness 493, 582
alexithymia 215–216
 Toronto Alexithymia Scale 215
altruism 2, 395, 397, 545
Alzheimer's disease 163, 165–166, 304, 482–483, 489–491, 494, 497–498
Alzheimer's disease 163, 165–166, 304–305, 308, 482, 489–491, 498
amateur 12, 21–22, 34, 57, 149, 151, 175, 180, 191, 204–205, 380–381, 426–427, 449–451, 461, 468, 553, 574

America 112, 199, 214, 421, 482, 528, 555, 561–562, 570
amplitude 20, 32, 52, 68, 75, 95, 98–100
amusement 12, 574
amusia 37, 97
  congenital 37, 97
amygdala 226, 481
analogue scale 166
anatomical 21, 25–26, 31, 37, 47–48, 181, 202, 506
anger 59, 215, 326, 331, 336, 342, 344, 347, 350, 353–354, 357–358, 364, 366–367, 373, 402, 423, 433, 439, 480, 493, 502, 511, 534–535, 542
anorexia 542
antenatal 393, 547
anterior 17, 21, 32, 35, 60, 153, 175, 202, 227, 509
anthem 468, 558
antidepressant 519, 521, 539
anxiety 162–163, 165, 217, 278, 298, 301, 305, 307, 310, 354, 358, 365–366, 372, 380, 383–384, 406, 410, 413–414, 417, 425, 426, 429, 433–435, 443, 446, 448, 453, 455, 457, 467, 469, 475–476, 482–484, 487–488, 491–493, 495, 499–500, 503, 509, 511–513, 515–525, 527, 529, 531, 534–536, 538, 541–542, 544–546, 548–549, 566, 590, 593
aphasia 74, 505
appreciation 11, 71, 148, 192, 510, 515, 577
aptitude 54, 58, 70, 82, 94, 102, 112, 121–122, 140, 154, 156–161, 167, 169, 189, 203, 213, 254, 460
architecture 76, 164
arithmetic 107–108, 115, 117–121, 124, 130, 200, 219, 520
army 473–474, 529. *See* military
arterial 511, 517
articulation 47, 99, 164, 511
articulatory 47–48, 157
articulatory suppression 157
artist 12, 167, 443, 445, 469, 473, 502, 504, 520, 525, 557–558, 563, 577–578, 583

artistic 16, 27, 211, 224, 227, 445, 471–472, 502, 504, 530, 557, 563, 567
arts-based 233, 387
Asia 145, 377, 421, 532
assessment 10, 17, 67, 88, 102, 113, 154–155, 159, 162–163, 166, 176–179, 189, 197, 211, 214, 217–218, 240, 243–244, 249, 388, 402, 429, 433, 485, 487, 491, 496, 509, 518, 520
assignment 63, 86, 196
associative 139
asylum-seeker 530–534, 562–565
asymmetry 25, 36, 58, 152
  leftward 25, 36
athlete 240–241, 451
athletic 240, 411
atmosphere 439, 452, 548, 585–586
atonal 153
at-risk 89, 117–118, 389, 445, 543
attention 135–138, 142–143, 146–147, 150, 153–154, 156–157, 159, 164, 173–174, 176–177, 181–182, 184–185, 189, 191–193, 195–196
  attentional abilities 177
  attentional processes 135–136, 146, 154
  attentional system 176
attentional control impairment 305
attentive analytical listening 422
attitudes 7, 125, 326, 347, 350, 376, 400, 406, 568, 588
  cultural 560
  discriminatory 563
  towards learning 243, 323, 329, 338, 356, 373
  towards music 432, 476
  towards offending 359
  towards prisoners 363
  towards self 386
  towards sex 577
  towards the elderly 463
audiation 189, 207, 254, 257
audiobook 506, 514, 526
audiovisual 57, 151, 402, 473
audition 47, 72, 95

auditory-motor 32, 38, 207
aural 21, 42, 46, 55, 57, 61, 69, 76–77, 104–105, 116, 140–141, 169, 257, 260, 279, 594–595
Australia 64, 113, 243, 335–336, 348, 353, 360, 362, 393, 421, 427–428, 436, 441–442, 448, 450, 455, 464, 474–475, 477, 491, 504, 520, 531, 540, 560–563
Austria 520, 524
authentic cadence 53
autism spectrum disorder 76, 335, 341, 405–406, 482–483, 510, 545–548
autobiographical memory 304–305
automation
  of instruction 389
  of processes 26
  of skills 7, 25, 42
autonomic nervous system 308, 415, 480
autonomy 354, 359, 378, 382, 428, 438, 458, 542
axial diffusivity 207

babies 43–45, 48, 368, 392–393, 430, 511, 522
basal ganglia 29, 47, 99, 509
basal metabolic rate 487
baseline 41, 83, 109, 124, 156, 163, 166, 181, 193, 214, 272, 288, 304, 329, 365–366, 406, 427, 434, 491–493, 498
Basque Country 468–469
beat-making 128
behavioural modelling 52
behavioural problems 165–166, 269–270, 301, 303, 317
bereavement 427, 429, 458, 515
beta-endorphin 516
bias 10, 136, 144, 195, 253, 307
Big Five personality test 230–231, 380
bilateral 20, 23–24, 28, 30, 38, 48, 137, 153, 174, 188, 226–227, 283, 307, 507
bilingualism 88, 151, 177–178
bimanual
  coordination 26, 29, 157, 185, 192, 408, 460
  movements 26–27, 29
  patterns 148

synchronisation 193, 460
  training 137, 182
biological 4, 58, 99, 142, 167, 194, 310, 312, 415, 426, 481, 503, 513, 520, 522, 547, 551, 553
birth 3, 45, 61, 74, 325, 392–393, 430, 511
blending 50, 79, 83, 97, 101
blood flow 18, 25, 28, 311–312
blood oxygenation 27–28, 153
blood pressure 109, 303, 415–416, 480, 484, 487, 513–514, 517–518, 521–522
blues 278, 347, 352, 452
bonding 3–4, 6, 259, 344, 367–368, 374, 392–393, 395, 399, 403, 426, 430–431, 444, 446, 457, 461, 469, 551–554
boredom 5, 316–317, 319, 402, 439, 495, 583
bottom-up processes 34, 49, 53, 195, 235
boundaries 100, 396, 439, 445, 483, 534, 541
boy 103, 145, 209, 247, 298, 302–304, 319, 329, 333, 335, 343–344, 346, 385, 387, 389–390, 406, 423–424, 435, 440, 535–536, 576
brain damage
  and music 46, 74, 482, 505, 507
brain injury 505, 510, 527–528
brainstem 16–17, 20, 32–33, 47, 57, 61, 67, 156
bravery 6, 581
Brazil 94, 465–467, 578
breathing 427, 509–511
British Columbia 245
bullying 405, 560

cadence 53
calmness 265, 279, 298–299, 301, 303, 306, 314, 317, 334, 349–350, 367, 413, 418, 426, 431, 436, 447, 455, 517, 524, 532, 583–585
Canada 244–245, 249, 333, 336, 346, 353, 465, 498
cancer 480, 514–516, 519
Cantonese 145
cardiovascular 415, 480
career plans 328, 377, 476

caregiver 62, 165–166, 169, 328, 331, 352, 392, 430–431, 464–466, 473, 477, 494–498, 504, 515, 547, 553
care home 483, 490–492, 494–495
carer. *See* caregiver
Caribbean 331, 402, 562
catharsis 3, 348, 542, 552
cats 590
causality 9, 37–38, 61–62, 64, 83, 114, 121, 146, 159, 196, 202, 206–207, 210, 213, 232, 247–249, 259, 448, 479, 487, 501
CDs 1, 288, 345, 538, 557
cell
   nerve cell 18, 24
   transplant 514
   transplants 513–514
cell transplants 513–514
cellular immunity 480
censorship 7, 357, 556
cerebellum 16, 28–29, 31, 254, 481
cerebral
   activation 27
   areas 135
   cortex 15, 481
   functions 17
   hemispheres 23, 265
   palsy 507
   processing 139
ceremonies 3, 6, 352, 552
change readiness 543
chanting 86, 92–93, 343, 350, 590
chess 252
Chicago 327, 330
chills phenomenon 310–312, 495
China 2, 7, 13, 70, 81, 129, 139–141, 146, 179, 182, 238, 241, 281, 284, 288, 365, 444, 466, 515, 526, 547
choir 4, 103, 160, 165, 209, 237–238, 240, 244, 247, 256, 353, 361–363, 371, 380, 385, 399–400, 425–429, 445, 456–457, 472–473, 482, 484–489, 509–510, 516, 519, 521, 540, 543, 552–553, 565, 570
chord 21, 32, 41, 390
chronic illness 163, 165, 429, 480, 486, 493, 509, 512, 518

chronic sleep disorder 526
chronic stressors 109, 480
cingulate 22, 153, 175, 226–227, 481
circuitry 29–30, 46–47, 49, 54, 312, 421
citizenship 238, 242, 250, 333, 401, 554–555
civil war 531, 557
clapping 86, 92–93, 127, 148, 343
classical 7, 19, 22, 30, 32, 58, 88, 157, 167, 180, 213, 215, 226–228, 230–231, 234, 271–273, 275, 278–279, 287, 289, 297–298, 305, 311, 325, 334–335, 378, 382–383, 404, 408, 416, 424, 436, 468, 484, 526, 538, 540, 564, 582–583, 585–590
classroom-based training 86, 141, 214, 547
close relatives 411, 468, 491
closure 112, 115, 143, 150, 178, 206
cluster analysis 124
cluster randomised controlled trial 157, 213, 407
coaching 164, 356, 495, 537, 547
coarse temporal scales 69–70
cochlea 20, 45, 73
cochlear implant 73–74
cognitive control 50, 142, 153, 159–160, 176, 178, 185, 188
cognitive impairment 74, 163, 169, 180, 193, 218, 267, 270, 306–307, 316, 490, 555
cognitively unimpaired 218
cognitive maturation 48
cognitive processing 7, 23, 26, 39, 44, 50, 79, 134, 145, 154, 195, 197, 223, 254, 278, 310, 397, 428
coherence 3, 151, 337, 552, 566
collaboration 323, 342, 344, 352, 354, 359, 362, 371, 396, 399–400, 402, 432, 436, 453, 462, 470, 472, 474, 476, 496, 499, 504, 534–535, 537, 552, 561, 564
college attainment 247
college students 109, 121, 139, 230, 261–263, 272–273, 287, 293–294, 450, 485
coloured blocks 111, 137

Columbia 333
comfort 3, 283, 325, 352, 443, 508, 515, 518, 569, 585
communication
 and music 3–4, 6, 32–33, 43–44, 63, 73, 76, 169, 328, 330, 335, 339, 341, 343, 350–352, 354, 360–361, 364, 366, 374, 378, 394, 397–398, 402, 405, 430–431, 433, 446, 450, 489, 501, 504–505, 508, 510, 515, 519, 523, 530, 533, 535, 545, 547–548, 553, 555, 561, 565
communicative gestures 63, 393
community-based 348, 363, 434–435, 464, 497–498, 504, 534, 538, 568, 580
comorbidity 524, 544
comparative study 69, 207, 209, 259
composers 258, 379, 570
composite 178, 203, 244
composition 22–23, 149, 263–265, 280, 350, 363, 381, 416, 462, 485, 508, 536, 541
comprehensive neuropsychological battery 162, 190
computer
 music 234, 282, 340, 344, 350, 357
computerised 68, 152, 183, 186, 212, 250, 358, 426, 506
concertos 109, 262, 286
concerts 210, 242, 363, 369, 376, 434, 436, 455, 457, 466, 473–474, 496, 561, 563, 574–575
conductor 30, 136, 363, 398
conflict 3, 180, 187, 194–195, 277, 321, 353, 358, 398, 529–530, 532–533, 537, 555–558, 565–566, 571, 577
conflict-monitoring abilities 180, 195
conformity to social norms 4, 6
confounding factors 9, 125, 140, 163, 177, 197, 203–204, 208, 221, 248, 307, 448, 488, 494, 537, 595
confusion 128, 261, 476, 506
connectedness 342, 367, 415, 429, 449, 454, 462, 470, 477, 504, 563
connectivity 29, 37, 108, 137, 226, 506, 545–546, 552
conscientiousness 258, 378, 380–383, 410

consciousness 17, 532, 552
consonance 280, 312–314
consonant-based word discrimination 65, 87, 146
contour 21, 26, 32, 40–41, 44, 53, 58–59, 61, 74, 92, 144
contralateral 28, 39
cooperation 433
 and music 303, 336–337, 346, 356, 369, 371, 396, 399, 401–403, 432, 449, 496, 515, 535–536, 538, 551, 553–554, 557, 579
coordinated movement 395, 411, 583
coping
 and music 5, 191, 326, 330, 347, 355, 358–359, 362, 364, 366–368, 392, 402, 415, 419–420, 422–424, 433, 439–441, 446, 452–453, 467–469, 471, 474, 476, 494, 512–513, 515, 525, 529, 576
corpus callosum 16, 24, 35–36, 257, 509
correctional institution 359, 361, 372
correlation 9, 24, 33, 36, 58, 70, 81–82, 88, 94, 102–103, 109, 113, 121–123, 137, 158, 175, 195–197, 202–203, 205, 207, 224, 226–227, 229, 237, 241, 248–249, 259, 275, 311–313, 321, 386, 398
cortical thickness maturation 19, 35, 174, 187
cortices 25, 28–29, 37, 41, 202, 226, 509
corticospinal 24, 509
cortisol 415–416, 426, 434, 459, 480, 484–485, 511, 516–518, 521, 524
courage 359, 555
 Circle of Courage 353
covariate 179, 229, 245–246, 276, 295
COVID-19 415, 465–467, 471, 473–478, 501, 586
cows 589–590
creative behaviour 226
creative thinking 224, 229–230, 232–233
creativity 11, 14, 16, 223–235, 337, 357, 367, 374, 382, 446, 458, 462, 464, 503, 516, 537, 569, 580
crime

and music 319, 325–326, 337, 348, 350, 353, 355–357, 364–365, 368–373, 387, 446, 534, 567, 579
cross-community 559
cross-cultural 43, 330, 561, 565
cross-domain 4, 47, 224–225
cross-sectional 80
cross-sectional survey 36–37, 41, 64, 138, 144, 158, 196, 207, 218, 473
cultural capital 247, 325
cultural omnivores 449
culture
  adjustment and music 533
  and music interpretation 63, 98, 267, 279, 296, 581
  and music-making 2, 6–7, 43, 63, 578
  awareness and music 325, 338, 553, 557, 560
  cross-communication and music 341, 356, 443, 554, 561
  of music 57, 297, 335, 348, 354, 376–377, 382, 442, 470
culture-free intelligence test 143, 206
cytokines 485, 516, 522

dancing 163, 182, 388, 403, 432, 444, 447–448, 451, 463, 469, 485, 553
deactivation 225–227
deafness 72, 98
decision-making 22, 175, 338, 355, 413, 436
decoding 79–80, 82–84, 90, 97, 105, 174, 187
dehydroepiandrosterone 426
dementia 163–167, 169, 217, 219, 304, 415, 457, 461, 473, 483–484, 489–501, 510. *See also* Alzheimer's disease; *See* Alzheimer's disease
depression 161–162, 165, 215, 352, 354, 358, 365–367, 372, 383–384, 413, 415, 421–423, 425, 428–429, 433, 435, 442–443, 448–449, 453–454, 457–458, 460, 463, 467, 476, 478, 480, 482–483, 487–491, 495, 497–500, 503, 506, 509, 511, 515–516, 519, 521–525, 527–531, 534–535, 537–539, 541–542, 544–545, 576
detention centre 333, 356–357, 359–360
determination 128, 326–327, 401, 433, 439, 448, 537
developmental difficulties / disabilities / delays 51, 64, 74–76, 94, 96, 270, 304, 308, 348, 351, 390, 523, 540
developmental functioning
  and music 333, 435
developmental responses
  and music 512
deviant stimuli 21, 32–33, 40, 59, 134, 150, 228, 268, 348
dexterity 104, 159, 191–192, 408, 506
differential 28, 31, 79, 165, 194, 196, 264, 268, 274, 549
diffusivity 207
digit-span task 73, 149–151, 154–156, 158, 165–166, 173, 175, 184, 188, 265–267, 305, 459
disabilities 74–75, 166, 308, 341, 390, 394, 405–406, 410, 428–429, 431, 466, 483, 505, 528–529, 547
disadvantage 86, 103, 119, 129, 242, 251, 567, 570
disaffection 319, 321–323, 326, 335–336, 342, 377, 400, 446, 566, 568–569
disorder
  behavioural 166, 342, 346, 483
  brain 76
  eating 541–542
  gait 505
  language 51, 75, 491
  mood 542
  neurodegenerative 484
  neurological 482, 508
  obsessive-compulsive 180, 544
  psychiatric 180, 413, 498, 513, 520, 524, 527–530, 534, 536, 538–539, 541
  rhythm 538
  schizophrenia 483, 539, 544–545
  sleep 483, 525–526, 548
  social anxiety 544
disruptive behaviour 303, 360, 499, 535

dissociation 60, 311, 421
dissonance 311–312, 314, 416
distractibility 34, 64, 272
distraction 268, 272, 274, 276, 294, 296, 302, 305–306, 314, 317, 440–442, 455, 512, 525, 548, 556, 582
distress 13, 347, 383, 417, 420, 430, 438, 441–442, 465–466, 476, 478, 498, 513–514, 516, 519, 523–524, 530–531, 556, 576
divergent thinking 223, 226–228, 230–231, 233–234
diversion 356, 419, 440, 444, 466, 495, 525, 542–543
diversity 12, 61, 69–70, 217, 224–225, 228, 255, 268, 341, 377, 388, 423, 433, 443, 500, 548, 558, 565, 567, 580
doctoral theses 241, 249
dogs 590
domain-general 47, 51–54, 168, 176, 194, 224, 230–231, 459
domain-specific 4, 52, 69–70, 224, 231, 257
dopamine 291–292, 310, 312, 415, 480, 524, 542
dorsal 25, 28, 38, 41, 47–48, 99, 153
dorsolateral 23, 58, 174, 225–227, 283–284, 307, 539
dorsomedial 312
drama 129, 211, 214–215, 221, 251, 348–349, 359, 489, 574, 581, 593
drawing 111, 118, 137–138, 140, 164, 193, 228, 251, 263, 297, 341, 430, 446, 490, 523, 536
driving 290, 582–584
drug dosage 539
drugs 483, 493, 516, 521, 539
drumming 127, 160, 336, 343, 358, 389, 395, 464, 482, 485, 487, 503–504, 507–508, 519, 522, 535, 566
dysphoria 542–543

economically disadvantaged 103, 129, 434, 567
educated mothers 333, 435

elderly 166, 197, 283, 304–305, 316, 419, 428, 453, 459, 461, 463, 489–493, 496, 499, 503, 505, 521
electroencephalography 17, 39–40, 60, 69–70, 75, 109, 262, 281, 285, 288
electrophysiological 17, 33, 144, 275, 313
elementary students 81, 89, 116, 125, 129, 189, 216–217, 238–239, 247, 250, 256, 298, 385, 388, 390, 547, 570
elite 247, 451, 570
El Sistema 72, 118, 155, 247–248, 259, 326–334, 387–388, 401–402, 433–434, 537, 554
emission tomography 311
emotional listening 422–423
emotional self-regulation 64, 182, 330, 387, 406, 415, 418, 422, 429, 447, 454, 459, 465, 467, 527, 531, 576
emotional stability 362, 380, 413–414
empathy 175, 201, 348, 360, 394–395, 397, 402–404, 410, 421, 434, 438, 477, 481, 553–554, 560, 563, 567, 577
empirical study 189, 224, 251–253, 308, 372, 552, 557, 560
empowerment 338, 415, 434, 453, 494, 503, 533, 561
endocrine 415–416, 480, 483–485, 524
endogenous opioid system 553
endorphin 6, 415–416, 457, 480, 489, 516, 518, 553
England 239, 251, 326, 329, 332, 337, 385–386, 427, 436, 444, 456, 570
enjoyment 4–5, 33, 110, 126, 197–198, 263–264, 267, 310, 320–321, 335, 340, 342–343, 356, 359, 362, 364, 373, 401, 413, 421, 431, 433–434, 442, 445, 447, 451–453, 457, 459, 462, 466, 468, 493–494, 496–497, 504, 510, 521, 529, 535, 540–543, 564, 567, 574, 578, 580–581, 584
ensemble 11, 30, 83, 114, 116, 136, 173–174, 186, 197–198, 215, 238, 242, 244, 250, 255, 257, 356, 380, 389–390, 397–401, 458, 461, 470, 485, 509, 534, 546, 549, 554

entertainment 4, 98, 440–441, 466, 525, 542, 580
entrainment 50–53, 75, 83, 92, 98–99, 195, 252, 404, 416
envelope tracking 52
episodic memory 133, 191, 204, 218, 268, 281, 283–284, 306–307, 417, 495
ethnicity 117, 319, 337, 339, 376–377, 386, 557–558, 560, 563, 569–571, 579
eudaimonic 413, 422, 477
Europe 297, 340, 377, 421
event-related potential 17–18, 38–39, 59, 65, 70, 180, 306
evolution 2, 4, 50, 403, 479, 551
exhaustion 484, 584
ex-offenders 358, 364–367, 370, 373
expert 6, 9–10, 19, 21, 23, 25, 32–33, 42, 57–60, 70, 83, 111, 144, 149–151, 154, 167–169, 175, 177–178, 194, 197, 203–205, 208, 224–225, 227–229, 235, 255, 258, 270, 290–291, 317, 454
expressivity 50, 536
ex-prisoners. *See* ex-offenders
extensor 39, 508
extensor muscles 39
extroverts 231, 274, 292–295, 315, 378, 380, 576

familiarity 22, 30, 48, 55, 59–60, 136, 142, 144, 164, 182, 199, 263, 267, 270, 276–277, 288–289, 293, 295, 298, 304, 316–317, 350, 355, 417, 430–432, 461, 489, 491–492, 495, 497, 540, 569
fasciculus 207
fear 215, 311, 350, 434, 469, 511, 532–533, 569
feelings of belonging 5, 14, 337, 353, 373, 376, 387, 399–400, 439, 447, 449, 452–453, 456, 459, 463, 510, 521, 533–534, 540, 552, 554, 560–561, 566, 578–579
female 3, 43, 109, 121, 139, 161, 167, 250, 265, 268, 271, 273, 278, 292–294, 300, 306, 343, 359, 368, 379, 398, 423, 442–443, 450, 515, 520, 570, 577. *See also* girls

festival 391, 451–452, 530, 563, 570, 574, 578, 580, 589
fibromyalgia syndrome 518
financial hardship 369, 475, 476. *See also* economically disadvantaged
finger flexor 39
flash mobs 470
fMRI 18, 22, 28, 36, 38, 226
foetus 3, 43, 547
folk 32, 57, 164, 230–231, 379, 382, 424, 484, 555, 559, 564
folk fiddlers 379
food 312, 370, 542, 587, 591, 593
fraction computation 126
France 69–70, 144, 187, 199, 586
Frank Sinatra 271
freedom 321, 327, 365, 371, 464, 468, 504
freelance 231, 476
friendship 244, 327, 335, 337–339, 369, 376, 388, 398–401, 422, 433, 437–439, 442, 444, 446, 449, 453, 456, 468, 470, 474, 510, 519, 537, 552, 569–570, 578–580, 582
frontal 16, 20, 22–23, 25, 32, 38, 48, 55, 153, 162, 181, 186, 193–194, 202, 226–227, 257, 275, 313, 481
frontocentral 194, 313
frontoparietal 30, 137, 185
frustration 303, 342, 353–354, 385, 391

gamelan 363–364
gamma-band activity 17, 31, 34, 41, 65
gangs 350, 354–355
gender 138, 144, 152, 180, 203, 229, 242, 268, 270, 288, 290, 292, 314, 383, 427, 466, 471, 534, 579, 595
gene 201–202, 551
generalisability 10, 224, 230
genetic 37–38, 42, 61, 76, 171, 201–202
genre 21, 32, 77, 164, 255, 271, 273, 277–278, 282, 311, 314, 316, 325, 347, 352, 355, 376–378, 381–383, 391, 410, 417, 424, 438, 441, 480, 491, 525, 559, 577, 582, 594

Germany 7, 61, 89, 97, 103, 155, 233, 244, 340–341, 381, 427, 444, 490, 554–555, 586
germination 591
gifted 251, 446
girls 116, 247, 298, 329, 385, 387, 406, 423–424, 439–440, 533–534, 536, 576
Glasgow 333, 471
Glenn Miller 271
glucose 24, 479
gospel 424
government 7, 207, 336, 340–341, 501
Greece 13, 296, 564
grey matter 21–23, 35, 37, 139, 155, 194, 202, 254, 406
grief 337, 358, 476, 522, 530
growth hormone 416, 517
gyrus 20–21, 23–25, 31, 36, 38, 153, 181, 186, 254, 257, 481

haematopoietic 513–514
haemodynamic 18, 27, 29
Haiti 331
hallucinations 491, 544
happiness 59, 234, 297, 327, 329–330, 362, 389, 401, 413–414, 418, 420, 425, 436, 447, 449, 455, 457, 461, 465, 486, 492, 497, 519, 522–523, 525, 529, 574, 582
harmonic 40–41, 50, 53–54, 56, 60, 81, 83, 142
harmony 21, 55, 59, 139, 194, 551
healing 13, 337, 357, 482, 521, 530, 532–534, 536, 565, 591
healthcare professionals 491, 496, 502, 519
hearing
  in noise 141
  spatial 176
hearing music 6, 20, 43
hearing speech 141–142, 167
heart rate 270, 310, 312, 416, 426, 480, 484, 487, 511, 513, 517, 521–522, 585, 590
heavy metal 382, 423–424, 441, 577, 589–590
hedonic 4, 413, 477

hemisphere 16, 23, 31, 36, 46, 48, 58–59, 69, 74, 136–137, 147, 152–153, 226, 265, 283, 505, 509
heritability 201
heritage 377, 446, 530, 580
high-functioning 57, 203, 268
high risk 335, 352–353, 398
high school 71, 87, 114, 122–124, 128, 130, 229, 239, 241, 243–244, 246, 300, 327, 346, 380, 391, 399, 423, 442, 554, 569
hip hop 272–273, 337–338, 347–348, 352, 354, 357, 376, 577
hippocampus 22, 312, 481
hobby 12, 66, 410, 440, 454, 457
hobbyists 574
holistic 126, 195, 519
Holocaust 531, 556
homelessness 428, 535, 537, 543
Hong Kong 139, 238, 444, 523
hormonal 415–416
hormones 416, 485, 517, 521, 524, 591
hospices 518–519
hospital 13, 74, 392, 469, 483, 492–493, 496, 500–501, 512–516, 519, 523–524, 545, 590
hostility 360, 538, 544, 553
human capital 247
humoral immunity 480
hyperactivity 180, 301, 335, 338, 345, 360, 434
hyperconnectivity 24

identification
  emotion 215–216, 404
  language unit 56, 69, 77, 80, 84, 87, 100, 141
  logo 91, 104
  music 20, 40, 49, 68, 70, 97, 100, 287, 355
  self 553, 564
identity 1, 3, 5–6, 314, 320–321, 326, 337, 344, 347–348, 353, 355–356, 358, 360, 364, 367–368, 375–377, 384, 387–388, 391, 396, 401, 410, 415, 429, 433, 443–444, 451, 453, 456, 462–464, 468,

472, 476, 491–492, 494, 499, 504, 516, 524, 530, 532–533, 540–542, 552–553, 555, 557–559, 562–563, 566, 571, 574–575, 578
illness 163, 428, 438, 479, 483, 486, 490, 502–504, 510, 519, 523–524, 538–540, 542, 549, 576
imagery
  and music 107, 135, 417, 518, 529, 531–532, 536, 584
imagination 232, 344, 378, 455
imaging 18, 22, 25–27, 30, 32, 35–36, 41, 46, 138, 149–150, 155, 167, 174–175, 181, 185, 188, 202, 226, 283–284, 460–461, 506, 542, 545
imitation 3, 34, 54, 154, 395, 404, 481
immersion 281–282, 443, 487, 499, 563
immigrant 341, 346, 367, 377, 402, 428, 530, 561–565, 569
immigration 201, 531, 562
immunity 480–481, 485, 590
immunoglobulin 485
immunty 427, 479–480, 482, 484–485, 503, 515–517, 521, 524, 590
improvisation 42, 86, 129, 161, 173, 182, 189–190, 193, 204, 225–229, 231–233, 235, 251, 256, 335, 340–341, 344, 351, 354, 367, 388, 405, 433, 446, 471, 485, 490, 493, 511, 521–522, 535–536, 541, 545, 548, 564–565
incarceration 353, 362–363, 534, 556
inclusion 10, 143, 179, 325, 335–336, 414, 453, 456, 462, 494, 497, 504, 510, 522–523, 531, 534, 552, 559, 561–562, 565–566, 569–571
India 13, 207–208, 238, 279, 591
infant 3, 33, 43–45, 48, 62–63, 71, 74–75, 98, 114, 197, 342, 392–393, 395, 430–431, 511–512, 522, 552, 554. *See* babies
infant-directed 44–45, 71
informal musical activities 11, 33–34, 63, 77, 81, 84, 173, 231, 338, 399, 431, 433, 445, 468, 529
infrared spectroscopy 226–227, 283–284, 307, 539
infrequent deviant stimuli 134, 150

In Harmony 326–330, 332
inhibitory control 85, 92–93, 151, 171, 173, 175, 179–180, 182–184, 186, 189, 195, 434, 460
insomnia 526–527
institutionalised 304, 365, 492, 524
instrumentalists 31, 207, 239, 379–381, 509
intensive care 74, 511
intensive training 84, 89, 95, 104, 141, 157, 185, 333, 406, 506
intercultural 356, 558, 562–563
interference 144, 149, 162, 180, 194, 272, 278, 280, 287, 293, 296, 310, 315
interpersonal intelligence 3, 200, 208, 443, 445, 448
interval 21, 26, 29, 59, 61, 100, 150, 296, 351, 370, 374
intonation 59, 74, 100, 144, 505
  therapy 74, 505
intrapersonal intelligence 200, 208, 443, 445
introverts 274, 292–294, 315, 378, 576
iPad 464
Iran 7, 212, 279, 289–290, 345
Iraq 529, 544, 555, 561, 564
Ireland 156, 328, 352, 401, 523, 533, 559, 570
Israel 118, 213, 529, 532, 556–557, 559, 569
Italy 144, 339–340, 434, 466–468, 470

Jamaica 331
jamming 349, 358, 388, 470
joy 418, 425–426, 432, 455, 486
judgement 54, 56, 76, 80, 187, 191, 306, 326, 369, 371, 373

Kalamazoo Kids 327, 332
kinaesthetic 200, 208
kindergarten 84, 88, 90–91, 115–116, 118–119, 129, 146, 154, 182, 212, 242, 249, 403, 547
kinematic 507–508
kinetic 327, 508
Korea 216–217, 360, 435, 537

language impairment 75–76, 94–96, 99
latency 137, 152, 475, 526
lateralisation 58, 60, 137
late-trained 407
leadership 323, 334, 336, 354, 398, 410, 456, 555, 575
learning climate 259, 323, 400, 568
leukaemia 513
life satisfaction 329, 406, 413–414, 448, 451, 454, 475, 488
limbic 225, 415
linguistically diverse 433, 565, 567
Liverpool 328, 332
lobe 16, 20, 24, 48, 55, 148, 202, 257, 481
localisation 26, 36, 112, 139, 148, 507
lockdown 465–472, 474–476
locomotor 409, 507
loneliness 5, 376, 423, 439, 442, 449, 453, 455, 457, 459, 464, 468–469, 476, 488, 503, 565–566
longitudinal study 9, 35, 64–66, 68–69, 72, 75, 86, 88, 121, 154, 156, 182–183, 187, 207, 211, 213, 219, 240, 244, 259, 408, 440, 448, 487–488, 500, 502, 521, 560
Los Angeles 71, 88, 330
loudness 272–274, 314–315, 416, 418, 447, 549, 555–556, 585–586
love 6, 12, 33, 368, 442, 469, 498, 575
low-arousal music 274, 280
low-frequency oscillations 275, 313
low-income 88, 104, 118, 128, 182, 216, 388, 566. *See also* economically disadvantaged
lullabies 3, 367, 393
lungs 425, 482, 486, 488, 509
lyrical 226, 277, 279, 287, 300
lyric-writing 338, 350, 463

magnetic resonance 18, 22–23, 25–28, 30, 35–36, 149, 174–175, 181, 185, 188, 226–227, 506, 545
magnetoencephalography 18, 20, 31, 33, 44, 64, 147
mainstream education 337, 340–342, 346–347, 560

maladaptive 421, 461, 525
Malaysia 558
male 3, 23–24, 109, 112, 121, 139, 167, 273, 292, 294, 300, 360, 365, 368, 372, 379, 423, 437, 528, 575, 577
manipulative dexterity 408
manual dexterity 408, 506
marginalised 336–337, 350, 358, 366, 428, 433, 504, 561–562, 571
mastery 4, 13, 258, 322, 344, 353, 363, 424, 452, 489
maternal 44, 187, 511, 547
maturation 19, 23, 35–36, 48, 71, 87, 174, 182, 184, 187, 207
mean arterial pressure 511, 517
meaning 4, 6, 48, 50, 54–55, 310, 314, 337, 344, 367, 399, 413–415, 428, 431, 436, 439, 443, 447, 453–454, 456, 462–463, 514, 551, 556, 581
medication 484, 488, 516, 525, 531
medicine 327, 345, 482–483
Mekranoti Indians 578
melodic 21–22, 34, 36, 44, 50, 53, 66, 74, 76, 83, 100–101, 147, 164, 203, 216, 546, 577
melodies 22, 33, 38, 41, 43, 53–55, 59–60, 74, 150, 175, 233, 271
memories 16, 22, 133, 169, 278, 311, 314, 424, 430–431, 444, 447, 463, 467, 472, 495, 537
  working memory 23, 26, 34, 36, 54, 67, 73, 81–82, 86–87, 101, 120, 133–135, 138, 141, 144–146, 148–162, 164–169, 171, 173–179, 182, 184–187, 191–197, 200, 204–205, 210, 214, 217–219, 252–253, 257, 264–267, 269, 272, 288, 292, 295, 306, 309, 460–461, 496
memorisation 8, 55, 59, 139, 149, 153, 157, 267, 279, 282–284, 584
memory impairment 305
memory performance 146, 150, 152–153, 159, 161, 165, 167, 169, 192, 217, 265, 267, 275, 278, 280, 282, 284, 295, 305, 307, 313
men 275–276, 337, 363, 369, 423, 426–428, 448, 480, 488, 502, 532, 570, 575, 578

mental health 13, 337, 341–342, 347, 351, 353–354, 366, 372, 394, 413, 415, 421, 424, 427, 429, 431, 441, 457–458, 469, 473, 502–504, 520–521, 527, 534, 537, 539–540, 566–567, 584
mental rotation 111, 121, 268
mentor 326, 354, 356, 373
mesolimbic 542
meta-analytic analyses 10, 253, 516
metabolic 480, 483, 487
metabolism 24, 202, 303
metacognition 270, 290, 296, 317
metal music 273, 277, 382, 423–424, 441, 577, 589–590
methylphenidate 302
Mexico 339, 444, 466
midbrain 312, 481
middle-aged 178, 487, 535
middle-class 250, 428
middle school 189, 213, 237, 246–247, 346, 386, 388, 524, 569
Milanese 466, 470
military 6, 527–528
military service 528
mirror neurons 73
misogynism 577
mobility 458, 482, 505, 580
Modern Language Association 112
modulation 39, 51, 57, 75, 150, 280, 283, 285–286, 307, 397, 485, 516, 538
monolingual 69, 151, 177
morale 415, 488, 571
morphometry 18, 23, 25, 181, 506
mortality 167, 448, 479–480, 488, 521
motherese 44, 48
mothers 3, 43–44, 48, 83, 212, 333, 342, 367, 392–393, 431, 435, 465–466, 522, 536
motivation 6, 8, 77, 101, 110, 119, 125, 128, 140, 157, 197, 200, 221, 225–226, 240, 243, 252, 254, 256, 258–260, 263, 282, 312, 316, 319–324, 327–328, 331–332, 338–339, 342, 357, 368–370, 373, 381–383, 385–386, 402, 406, 410, 418, 425, 433, 435, 447, 450, 454–455, 458, 461, 476, 481, 486, 505, 510–511, 521–522, 529, 546, 566, 575–577, 584–585
motoric 249, 584
Mozart effect 8, 110, 261–262, 264–266, 307–308
Mozart, W. 8, 109–110, 261–266, 268, 273, 275, 279, 281, 286–287, 289–290, 298, 301, 303, 307–308, 516, 589–590
MP3 player 424, 517
multicultural 126, 530, 557, 560, 563
multimodal 16, 37, 39–40, 62, 76, 459
multiple sclerosis 509
muscles 22, 24, 39, 479–480, 489, 508, 510, 515
musicality 2–3, 112, 299, 525, 547, 551
musicianship 6, 112, 123, 176–177, 190, 232, 428
myelination 15, 24, 137, 172

national anthem. *See* anthem
Nazi Germany 7, 555
negativity
   brain activity 17–18, 21, 32, 34, 60
   feeling 440
negligible 188, 209, 211, 240
neighbourhood 118, 245–246, 388
neocortical 65, 225, 311
neonatal 44–45, 511
nerve impulses 15
nervous system 72, 135, 156, 308, 311, 410, 415, 480, 524
neurocognitive 60, 74
neurodegenerative 167, 484, 508
neuroimaging investigations 35, 155
neuroleptic drug 539
neurological 25, 33, 38, 42, 44, 75, 87, 99, 180–181, 225, 256, 260, 262, 269, 392, 477, 482, 486, 505, 508
neurological impairment 49, 508
neuron 15, 17–19, 21–22, 24–25, 27–31, 40–41, 44, 50–53, 73, 75, 153, 176, 202, 312, 507
neuroplasticity 21, 31, 37, 40, 505, 507, 538

neuropsychological 135, 138, 155, 162, 181, 183, 190–191, 193, 196–197, 212, 217–218, 490
neurorehabilitation 481, 505
neuroscience 9–10, 15–17, 46, 104, 108, 110, 148, 193, 202, 255, 274, 283, 286, 311, 406, 481, 532, 594
neuroticism 379–381, 576
neurotransmitter 172, 312, 416, 485
New Zealand 333, 436, 444, 554
Nigeria 445, 577
noise 20, 33–34, 45, 56–57, 60–61, 64, 67, 80, 101, 141–142, 147, 157–158, 161, 167, 264, 266, 274–275, 280–281, 293–295, 299, 304–305, 326–327, 332–333, 543, 556, 583, 589–591
noisy 67, 72, 142, 424
non-human species 589, 591
non-medical interventions 479
non-musicians 9, 19–34, 37–40, 42, 46, 55–61, 65, 67, 70, 80–81, 110–112, 114, 134–145, 149–153, 157–158, 160–162, 168–169, 175–179, 186, 190–191, 193–194, 196–197, 204–206, 226–228, 231–232, 235, 240, 254–255, 257–258, 265–266, 272–273, 291–292, 377, 379–380, 423, 461
non-trained 67, 184–185
Northern Ireland 352, 523, 559
Norway 337, 344, 366, 466, 487, 502, 520, 557, 563–564, 567
Norwegian 231, 321, 386, 563
nostalgia 164, 466–467, 556
novice 21, 426, 454, 458, 461, 487
numerical magnitude representations 121
nursery 116, 190, 341
nurture 326, 387, 401, 554, 564

occipital 16, 35, 155, 187, 313, 481
oculomotor 135
offender 348, 353–362, 364–366, 368, 371–373, 450, 567
offending 339, 359, 366, 369–371
Ohio 242, 250, 363
Ohio Proficiency Test 250

openness 82, 208, 230–232, 235, 258, 378, 380–381, 388
opera 405, 585
optimism 253, 389, 413–414, 433, 439
Opus Project 327, 332
orbitofrontal 174, 312, 539
orchestra 23, 111, 113, 118, 135, 139–140, 186, 191, 244, 250, 255, 303, 326, 329–331, 334, 367–368, 379–381, 388, 391, 398–399, 401, 406, 433–434, 436, 451, 468, 471, 476, 497, 556
oscillation 34, 47, 50, 100, 148, 275, 313
out-of-key 59–60
out-of-tune 281
overarousal 315
overstimulation 556
oxygenation 27–28, 153, 174, 512
oxygen saturation 511, 514
oxytocin 415, 426, 480, 516, 553

paediatric 512–513
palliative 516, 518–519
parahippocampal 312
parent 11, 33, 63–64, 75, 82, 113, 129, 181, 189, 203, 208, 211, 214, 239, 243, 247, 249, 325–328, 330–331, 334–335, 345, 356, 368, 378, 385, 388, 390, 393–394, 396, 401–402, 430–432, 434, 436, 439, 442, 465, 508, 511–515, 523, 537, 547, 553, 569–570
parietal 16, 20, 27, 29, 41, 139, 153, 175, 202, 481
Parkinson's disease 76, 484, 505, 507, 510
participatory 33, 63, 335, 355, 371, 415, 429, 431, 433, 436, 449, 456, 462, 484, 504, 530–531, 533, 561–562, 564–565, 567
patriotism 6–7, 164, 473–474, 558
patterning 51, 98, 108, 120, 122, 437
pattern-matching 36, 98
peace 358, 418, 453, 455, 499, 527, 529, 533, 555–557
pedagogy 335, 381, 454
peer pressure 343, 353

percussion 84, 114, 129, 160, 193–194, 214, 254, 335, 343, 358, 363, 378, 388, 436, 460, 482, 491–492, 509, 535
perfectionism 382–383, 410
performance 12, 39, 123, 154, 215, 313, 322, 369–370, 390, 404, 410, 461, 470, 474, 485, 488, 492, 496, 543, 557, 564–565, 575
performer 31, 173, 316, 397–398, 410, 451–452, 457, 468–469, 565, 578
perseverance 101, 119, 258, 359, 386, 389
persistence 69, 95, 138–139, 143, 163, 195, 238, 242, 321, 326, 396, 401, 407–408, 433, 504, 507
personal development 1, 330, 372, 375, 377, 385, 401, 453, 463, 478
personality 9, 157, 200, 203, 224, 230–231, 235, 254, 257–258, 260, 270, 290, 293–294, 317, 348, 360, 375–383, 410, 437, 456, 522, 539, 595
pharmacological 292, 493, 499, 518, 538, 544
pharmacotherapy 544
Philippines 444, 554
phobic 538
phonation 510–511
phoneme 45, 52, 79–80, 84–85, 89, 94
phonemic awareness 81, 84–86, 95, 207
phonetic 54, 56, 61, 72–73, 80, 154
phonetic contrasts 56, 80
physical development 407, 432
physiological 13, 21, 50, 60–61, 72, 134, 142, 150, 267, 278, 303, 310, 313–314, 316, 416, 418, 479–480, 505, 551, 590
pitch 8, 20, 24–25, 29–30, 32–33, 36, 39–41, 44, 48–49, 56–59, 62–63, 65, 67–68, 71, 81, 85, 90, 93–94, 96–98, 100, 102, 139, 144–145, 180, 183, 205–206, 282, 314, 546, 551
pitch impairment 97
planum temporale 25, 36, 58, 254
plasma 416, 516, 524
plasticity 16–17, 28, 32, 36, 40, 42, 47, 49, 171, 183, 185, 195, 202, 212, 459, 461, 482, 505, 508
playlist 1, 424, 466, 470, 474, 573

playschool 33, 64, 73, 85, 182
pleasure 4, 12, 14, 169, 263, 267, 274–275, 292, 309–314, 331, 413, 416–417, 419, 421, 424, 432, 438, 447, 449, 452, 456, 459, 471, 473–474, 481, 489, 493, 527, 531, 549, 554, 575, 579, 584–585, 590–591
poetry 283, 352, 557, 574
Poland 383, 448, 487
police 354, 585
pop 58, 110, 263, 271–272, 295, 323, 327, 335, 352, 382–383, 399, 423–424, 484, 540, 558, 586–587, 590
posterior 20, 22, 25, 36, 58, 60, 153, 275, 313
post-traumatic stress disorder 513, 527–528, 530–531, 534, 536
poverty 352, 402, 435, 537, 566, 569
pre-attentive 33, 66, 69, 76, 96
precentral gyrus 31
predictive 45, 50–51, 53, 75, 121, 191
predictive coding 50, 53
predictor 70, 80, 82, 98, 114, 121, 210, 240, 258, 287, 378, 391, 396, 456, 467, 471, 525, 575
predisposition 37–38, 42, 159, 201
preference 43, 221, 264, 266, 268, 270, 276, 279, 293, 295, 301, 316, 348, 391, 420, 423–424, 512, 520–521, 546, 579, 582
pregnancy 43–44, 393, 483
prejudice 558–559, 566, 571, 593
prelinguistic 63, 393
pre-literacy 91, 103
premotor 26–29, 36, 38, 41
prepotent 177, 194
preschool 62–63, 80–81, 84–85, 89, 97, 115, 117, 124–125, 127, 154, 182, 189–190, 210, 212, 214, 232, 249, 403, 434, 513, 532, 570
pride 326, 328, 332, 338, 364, 369–370, 374, 385, 388, 400–402, 433
priming 262, 266, 269, 307, 309, 587
prison 356, 361–372, 527
prisoners 319, 361, 363–367, 369–370, 372, 556

problem-solving 120, 134, 173, 262, 354, 369, 399, 490, 569
procrastination 328, 331
proficiency 104, 113, 153, 289–290
prolactin 416, 426
proneness 258, 316
prosocial 6, 64, 338, 360, 363, 367, 393, 395, 397, 403–404, 449, 535, 554, 568, 577
prosodic 47–48, 50–53, 59, 74–75, 92, 97, 100, 215
prosody 50
protective factors/effects 167, 387, 441, 521, 577
protein 24, 202
proximity 451–452, 578
pseudo-words 93, 95, 144, 281
psychiatric 180, 483, 500, 524, 527, 535–536, 538–539, 541, 545
psychiatry 524
psychodynamic 251, 540
psychometric 143, 178, 206
psychopathology 524–525, 538, 540
psychophysical 144, 503
psychophysiological 484, 517
psychosis 538, 545
psychosocial 214, 350, 402, 437, 439, 450, 458, 471, 511, 519, 530, 538
psychosomatic 480, 494
psychotherapy 251, 341, 348, 446, 532
psychoticism 538, 540–541
pulmonary 509–510
punk 559, 577
pupil referral units 342–343
putamen 47, 153

qualitative 123, 165, 327, 332, 336, 342, 350, 359–360, 371–372, 385, 390–391, 393, 429, 447, 464, 492, 494, 562
quality of life 165–166, 172, 415, 428, 450, 457–458, 460, 462, 486–488, 496, 500, 503, 507, 513–514, 516, 519, 521, 524, 526–529, 536, 540, 545–546
quantitative 129, 211, 327, 336, 358, 464, 540

race 358, 377
racism 559
randomised controlled trial 10, 71, 94–95, 157, 165–166, 169, 213–214, 219, 366, 407
rap 225–226, 340, 347–354, 357–359, 376, 424, 444, 536, 577
rapport 12, 544
rats 589
receptive activities 2, 63, 73, 76, 83, 100, 189, 204, 214, 249, 352, 448–449, 487–488, 500, 513–514, 565
refugee 325, 345–346, 367, 377, 402, 526–527, 529–534, 560–565
regression analysis 9, 23, 52, 64, 73, 97, 113, 155, 176, 190, 205, 210, 218, 239–240, 243
rehabilitation 73–74, 159, 284, 319, 326, 333, 353, 366–367, 482, 484, 505–507, 514, 518, 526, 532, 534, 543
rehearsal 6, 136, 151, 157, 369–370, 397–399, 426–428, 436, 484, 552
reintegration 319, 356, 363, 371–372, 528
relationship-building 443, 446–447, 477
relaxation 426
relaxing 1, 5, 11–12, 27, 109, 261–262, 265, 271, 306, 330, 402, 413, 416, 419–420, 425–427, 436, 440, 447, 452, 455–457, 459, 469, 473, 486, 495, 497, 510, 512, 515, 519–522, 525–526, 532, 535, 538, 582, 585, 590
relief 449, 469, 518, 533, 541, 579
religion 1, 5–6, 454–455, 488, 530, 557–558, 560, 571, 573
reminiscence 419, 463, 489–490, 495, 499
reoffend 354, 356, 358, 361, 369–370, 372–373
repetition 15, 18, 27, 41, 48, 54, 62–64, 80, 95, 109, 129, 144, 157, 173, 261–262, 265, 270, 278, 317, 322, 356, 363, 393, 405, 407, 431, 436, 461, 508, 546, 548, 551, 558, 584, 589–590
reproduction of music 98, 161
residential home 193, 346, 490. *See* care home

resilience 329–330, 336–337, 353, 359–360, 374, 376, 387, 406, 414, 428, 439, 467, 503, 522, 531–532, 562
resonance 18, 22, 25–28, 30, 35–36, 149, 164, 174–175, 181, 185, 188, 226–227, 506, 545
respect 320, 330, 337–338, 340, 344, 356, 367, 371, 373–374, 397–398, 401, 469, 554, 569
respiration 310, 312, 480, 511, 590
respiratory 164, 483, 485–486, 510–511, 513, 517
responsiveness 354, 369, 371, 431, 512, 537, 547, 582
retention 16, 23, 88, 107, 133–134, 145–146, 150, 153, 180, 282–283, 339, 426, 438, 447, 464, 477, 561
retirement 234, 447, 451, 457, 460, 462, 486–487, 528, 579
retrospective 210, 217, 239, 259, 361, 405, 542
Rett syndrome 76
rewarding 3, 14, 77, 278, 291, 310–312, 374, 505, 552, 578, 594
rewards 5, 252, 259, 268, 278, 292, 306, 310–312, 321, 451, 456, 481–482, 542, 544, 549, 551
rhyme 79, 83, 86, 94, 97, 102, 117, 253, 265–266, 283, 340, 393–394
rhythm 30, 33–34, 36, 43, 47–48, 50–54, 60, 66, 68, 70–71, 74–76, 81–87, 90, 92–102, 105, 107, 114, 116–118, 122–123, 126–127, 130–131, 144, 151, 156, 158, 160–162, 164, 173, 175, 183, 193, 195, 203, 226, 252, 271, 347, 352, 388–389, 395–397, 404, 408–409, 416, 481, 492, 495, 504–505, 507–509, 527, 536, 538, 545–546, 549, 551, 555, 577, 582
  cueing 505, 510
  impairment 90
  prosodic cues 51, 75
rhythmic prosodic cues 51, 75
rituals 5–6, 362–363, 445, 469–470, 472

rock 7, 32, 58, 231, 258, 273, 276, 278, 287, 302, 358, 379, 382, 424, 484–485, 559, 577, 583, 586
romantic music 442
rostral 28
rules 17, 42, 55, 59–60, 120, 173, 335, 356, 496

saccadic 135
sadness 215, 285, 297, 306, 421–422, 426, 441, 478, 529, 542
saliva 426, 485, 503, 511, 516, 518, 520
Salvation Army 379
San Diego 327, 332
scanning 18, 27, 35, 138, 152, 159–160, 193, 460
school readiness 83, 403
secretory 485
sedation 278, 304, 483, 512, 516–517, 520
segmentation 50, 69, 82–84, 88, 95, 99–101
segregation 43, 45, 83, 141
self-acceptance 391, 509
self-actualisation 419, 427
self-affirmation 388
self-awareness 386
self-belief 258, 321, 327, 331, 339, 375, 377, 384, 387, 571, 594
self-care 330, 531, 548
self-concept 259, 299, 320, 323, 353, 357–359, 373, 384–389, 459, 464, 489, 504, 535, 540
self-confidence 13, 326, 329, 332, 335, 339, 342, 353, 364, 370, 384–385, 390–391, 401–402, 425, 432, 434, 445, 447, 486, 489, 521, 535–536, 540, 547
self-control 22, 333, 345, 355, 369, 434–435, 535, 538
self-description 351, 388
self-development 320, 429, 471
self-directed 443
self-discipline 258, 329–330, 337, 360, 378, 399, 401
self-disclosure 352
self-efficacy 119, 128, 200, 258, 321–322, 330–332, 337, 353–354, 356, 373–374,

384, 390, 429, 431, 439, 459, 566–567, 594
self-esteem 6, 243, 258, 320–323, 329–332, 335–336, 338, 342–343, 345–347, 351–353, 355–358, 360–361, 364–366, 369, 372–373, 381, 384–393, 402, 406, 410, 413–414, 419, 425, 428–429, 433–434, 437–438, 444–447, 455, 462, 464, 486, 498, 509, 521, 524, 527, 532–533, 535–536, 540–541, 547, 566–567, 579, 594
self-estimated 230
self-evaluation 5, 299, 358, 437
self-expression 12, 337, 342–343, 346, 356, 360–361, 364, 384, 427, 446, 489, 505, 514, 521, 568, 579
self-identity 5, 377, 391, 463, 563
self-image 384, 386–387, 542, 563, 575
self-knowledge 359, 564
self-monitoring 225, 251
self-paced 27, 275, 584
self-perception 200, 321, 363, 377, 384, 386, 429, 452
self-rated 230, 267, 349, 476
self-regulation 181, 188, 257, 322, 331, 342, 351, 418–419, 431, 440–441, 444, 446–447, 459, 566, 576
self-reliance 400, 568
self-report 112, 158, 163, 180, 191–192, 200, 231, 269, 286, 359, 381, 393, 405–406, 434, 438, 443, 448, 487, 498, 503–504, 515, 520–521
self-satisfaction 459
self-select 9, 112, 183–184, 267, 310, 404, 421, 440–441, 466–467, 480, 506, 581
self-system 377, 384
self-taught 227–228
self-understanding 391, 459
semantic 54, 59, 71, 133, 143, 160, 175, 187, 266, 281, 287
sensation-seeking 382, 582
sensitisation 157, 185, 214, 408
sensor 234
sensorimotor 23, 26, 29, 31, 36–37, 39–42, 76, 98, 157, 175, 185, 225, 397, 407–408, 461, 481–482, 505–507

sensory 15–17, 22, 47, 50, 55, 74, 95, 99, 133, 151, 196, 459, 481, 497, 508, 546, 548
sequencing 89, 99, 107, 147–148, 204, 210, 357
serotonin 415–416, 480, 524
set-shifting 172, 181, 184–185, 209
sex 23, 69, 87, 112, 163, 212, 246, 278, 312, 360, 386, 437, 440, 448, 569, 577
sexism 357, 577
sexuality 3, 343, 358, 529–530, 534, 536, 577
sexually abused 358, 530, 534–536
Sierra Leone 533, 561
sight-reading 174, 197, 204
Sing Up 335, 568
sleep 45, 180, 431, 444, 474, 483, 525–526, 531, 548, 556
smoking 448, 580
sociability 362, 394, 552
social capital 325, 456, 570
social climate 399–400
socialisation 402, 419, 466, 536
social isolation 6, 428, 455, 459, 462–464, 466, 470–471, 475, 497–498, 503, 511, 520, 528, 565
social media 466, 468, 470, 472, 558
socioeconomic status 69, 82, 87–88, 113–114, 140, 157, 161, 188, 203, 205, 207, 209, 237–238, 240, 242, 244, 246, 297, 345, 380, 404, 428, 471, 580
socioemotional 259, 403, 405–406, 535
sociomoral reflection 180
software 94, 339–340, 349–350, 359, 471–472, 588
soldier 528–529, 532–533, 555
solidarity 2, 330, 468, 553, 555
solitude 258, 322, 378, 583
somatisation 538
somatosensory 19, 22, 24, 30, 95, 481
sonata 109, 261–266, 268, 281, 289–290, 298, 307, 516, 589
song-writing 216, 234, 342–343, 350, 359, 362, 445, 462, 487, 511, 535–537, 541, 548

soothing 3, 431, 590
sound discrimination 43, 45, 64, 86, 97, 100, 119, 154, 507
soundtrack 282, 472, 586
South Africa 7, 328, 353–354, 356, 389, 445
South America 330, 421, 561
Spain 67, 88, 213, 335, 432, 466–470, 569
spatiotemporal 507, 594
special educational needs 90, 248, 296, 303, 319, 329, 340, 350, 389, 405–406, 410
spectroscopy 226–227, 283–284, 307, 539
speech deficits 76
speech impairment 484, 510
spinal cord 16, 505
spiritual fulfilment 449, 579
spirituality 5, 329, 400, 418, 427, 429, 449, 454–455, 497, 516, 519, 579
spontaneous 7, 98, 148, 154, 225–226, 288, 340, 364, 395–396, 407, 439, 467–468, 547
Sri Lanka 531, 585
stem cell 513–514
stereotype 17, 379, 381, 437
stigma 527, 531
stimulation 1, 5–6, 18, 39, 50, 67, 76, 224, 268, 271, 278, 301–303, 307, 316, 415, 425, 427–428, 440, 451, 457, 459, 473, 486, 489, 507–508, 511, 517, 520, 584–585, 590
story development 164
stress 45, 51, 53, 73, 76, 147, 166, 301, 337, 358–359, 366–367, 416, 422–423, 425, 441, 443, 446–447, 450, 452, 455, 458, 461, 465, 469–471, 474–475, 478–482, 484–487, 498, 512–513, 515–522, 525, 527–531, 534, 536, 542, 547, 549, 556, 567, 583, 590, 593
striatum 291, 312
stroke 484, 490, 505–506, 510
Stroop test 172, 182, 193, 204, 274
stutter 76, 511
subcortical 19, 27, 29, 48, 57, 60, 71, 87, 99, 142, 156, 480–481, 546
  consonant discrimination 57, 60

subculture 376, 551
substance abuse 336, 357
suicidal 354, 423, 442, 576
suicide 423, 442, 534, 576
superior longitudinal fasciculus 207
surgery 484, 514–517
survivor 530–532
Suzuki method 34, 146, 154
Sweden 215, 405, 448, 456, 502, 517, 520, 546
Switzerland 400, 450, 492, 568
syllable 45, 51–52, 56, 60–62, 69, 80, 82, 87, 92, 95–96, 98–99, 101, 147, 283
symbol 4, 6, 55, 85–86, 121, 123, 126–127, 141, 159, 161, 192, 213, 263, 352, 363, 402, 430, 446, 534, 542
sympathetic nervous system 311, 524
synapse 15, 17, 24, 65, 172, 202
synchronisation 3, 6, 17, 37, 50, 62, 93, 98–99, 156, 160, 193, 262, 395–396, 407–408, 460, 475, 551–553
synchrony 92, 265, 395–397, 407, 546, 554
systematic 26, 72, 84, 101, 131, 182, 188, 234, 242–243, 266, 308, 310–311, 313, 335, 346, 350, 353, 382, 415, 463, 518, 521
systematic review 10, 101, 131, 346, 350, 353, 415, 463, 518
systolic blood pressure 416, 484, 514, 518

Taiwan 272–273, 298, 524
task-switching 174, 177, 185, 195
Tasmania 456, 570
taste 12, 133, 376, 442, 478, 520, 587
teamwork 329–330, 336, 353, 364, 397, 399, 401–402, 410, 433, 554, 569
tears 455, 481, 495
technology 1, 7, 17, 44, 46, 281, 344–345, 399, 424, 452, 463–464, 471–473, 477–478, 548, 561, 569, 573, 575
teenager 5, 341, 437, 439, 444–445, 512
tempi 88, 286, 582
tempo 98, 114, 263–264, 271–273, 275–276, 280, 282, 314, 363, 395, 431, 582, 584–586
temporo-occipital 35, 155, 187, 481

tension 5, 265, 306, 314, 341, 425–426, 439, 478, 480, 486, 493, 517, 520, 563, 581
terrorism 529–530
therapeutic 13, 76, 335, 341, 344, 348, 350–351, 356, 358, 367, 371–372, 425, 455, 482–483, 486–487, 489, 492, 500, 505, 510, 514, 519, 524, 529, 534–535, 541, 556, 576
therapist 340–342, 347–348, 351, 360, 394, 406, 477, 482–483, 487, 492, 494–495, 497–498, 500, 503–504, 508, 511, 514, 527–529, 534–536, 540, 545–547, 549, 558
thrash metal 277
threats 344, 421, 479, 544
timbre 8, 21, 32, 65, 100, 271, 314, 546
timing 8, 29, 32, 39, 50, 56, 58, 60, 62, 94–95, 98–99, 142, 252, 407, 481, 509
tiredness 265, 306, 522
togetherness 403, 459, 466
tolerance 227, 330, 388, 555
tomography 311
tonality 63, 150, 314
tone 19–21, 24, 33–34, 37, 40–41, 49, 56, 58–59, 62–65, 80, 82, 97, 144–145, 147, 152–153, 225, 275, 298, 416, 439
tone deaf 37, 82
top-down processes 34, 49, 52–53, 195, 235
torment 556
torture 532, 556, 593
Tower of Hanoi test 173, 186
transcranial magnetic stimulation 18, 39
transferable 232, 321, 325, 334, 338, 341, 374
transformation 36, 121, 330, 336, 342, 428, 446, 528, 557
transformative 359, 361, 364, 557, 568
transplant 513–515
trauma 180–181, 353, 505, 510, 513, 526–537, 558, 560, 565, 571
trust 326, 337–338, 344, 370, 373, 397–398, 449, 456, 469, 532–533, 552, 570, 579
twins 163, 171, 202, 215, 405

unconscious awareness 11, 55, 77, 133–134, 415, 440, 593
undergraduate 109, 114, 143, 179, 203–204, 206, 215–216, 225, 239, 258, 262–263, 265, 270–271, 273, 275–278, 280, 282, 290, 474, 525
unhealthy 383, 424, 443, 479, 503
United States 13, 114, 243, 391, 473, 559, 565. *See* America
untrained 40, 64, 69, 95, 100, 127, 147, 156–157, 159, 161, 184–185, 188, 202–203, 208–209, 215–216, 238
urban 114, 237, 319, 336, 347, 358–359, 386, 580

valence 234, 274–275, 284, 313
variability 10, 44, 98, 142, 153, 191, 251, 296, 426, 500, 590
variables 10, 26, 50, 95, 109, 129, 140, 156, 160, 177, 180, 191, 203–204, 208, 241, 243–244, 252, 256, 282, 400, 448, 467, 488, 494, 507, 575
variation 49, 54, 183, 229, 242, 256, 391, 500, 516, 537, 548, 576
vascular 163, 490, 493
ventral striatum 291, 312
verbalisation 491, 532, 536
veterans 528–529, 543
victim 405, 532–535, 547, 556
vigilance 177, 285, 578
violations 17, 59–60, 62, 286
violence 333, 343, 354, 434–435, 529–530, 534–535, 537–538, 560, 569, 577, 593
virtual 41, 128, 281–282, 470–474
visual analogue scale 166
visual impairment 345
visual memory
    and behaviour 134
visuomotor 28, 136, 459, 461, 493
vital signs 485, 512, 514
Vivaldi 266, 286, 304–305
vocally expressed emotion 57, 59
voice 43, 58, 68–69, 76, 87, 96, 183, 194, 211, 350, 362, 364, 367, 392, 429, 491, 494, 510–511, 530, 564

volume 20–23, 25–26, 35, 155, 181, 187, 202, 254, 271, 310, 316, 406–407, 424, 439, 509–510, 517, 556, 581–582, 586
volunteer 31, 47, 164, 242, 273, 275, 311, 313, 338, 362–363, 368, 415, 455, 462–463, 554, 574
vowel 49, 56, 61, 65, 69–70, 87, 146, 164
voxel 18, 22–23, 27, 36, 175, 181, 506
voxel-based morphometry 23, 506
vulnerability 325, 333, 421, 423, 453, 467, 469, 476, 496, 532, 565

weapon
  of music 556
Wechsler Adult Intelligence Scale 200, 204
wellbeing 1, 5, 8, 11, 13, 92, 165, 167, 196, 234, 323, 325, 328–329, 338, 341, 347, 351, 353, 362, 367, 383, 393, 400, 402, 406, 413–422, 424–427, 429–434, 436–438, 440, 442–451, 453–460, 462–469, 471–483, 486–488, 492–493, 496–498, 500–504, 510, 512–513, 516, 519, 521–522, 524, 526, 530–531, 535, 540, 546, 549, 552–554, 561–567, 576, 589, 593

Western 7, 19, 32–33, 63, 139, 267, 271, 279, 336, 378, 443, 564, 573, 578
white-matter microstructure 509
Williams syndrome 148
willingness 128, 327, 381, 552
womb 3, 43, 46
women 275–276, 362, 366, 393, 426–428, 464, 502, 518, 529, 534, 536–537, 576–578
word discrimination 65, 82, 87, 146
working memory
  and behaviour 148, 150
workshop 64, 251, 333, 358–359, 362–364, 373, 388, 436, 462, 488, 504–505, 533, 535, 548, 564, 567
World War 482, 556
worry 5, 278, 414, 426, 439, 457, 467, 471, 518, 525

youth 6, 121, 186, 244, 326, 328, 330–331, 333, 336–337, 339, 345, 347–348, 352–353, 355–357, 359–360, 445–446, 540, 561, 567

About the Team

Alessandra Tosi was the managing editor for this book.

Rosalyn Sword and Melissa Purkiss performed the copy-editing and proofreading. Rosalyn indexed the volume.

Anna Gatti designed the cover. The cover was produced in InDesign using the Fontin font.

Luca Baffa typeset the book in InDesign and produced the paperback and hardback editions. The text font is Tex Gyre Pagella; the heading font is Californian FB. Luca produced the EPUB, AZW3, PDF, HTML, and XML editions — the conversion is performed with open source software such as pandoc (https://pandoc.org/) created by John MacFarlane and other tools freely available on our GitHub page (https://github.com/OpenBookPublishers).

This book need not end here...

Share

All our books — including the one you have just read — are free to access online so that students, researchers and members of the public who can't afford a printed edition will have access to the same ideas. This title will be accessed online by hundreds of readers each month across the globe: why not share the link so that someone you know is one of them?

This book and additional content is available at:

https://doi.org/10.11647/OBP.0292

Donate

Open Book Publishers is an award-winning, scholar-led, not-for-profit press making knowledge freely available one book at a time. We don't charge authors to publish with us: instead, our work is supported by our library members and by donations from people who believe that research shouldn't be locked behind paywalls.

Why not join them in freeing knowledge by supporting us: https://www.openbookpublishers.com/section/104/1

Like Open Book Publishers

Follow @OpenBookPublish

Read more at the Open Book Publishers BLOG

You may also be interested in:

A Philosophy of Cover Songs
P.D. Magnus

https://doi.org/10.11647/OBP.0293

Classical Music
Contemporary Perspectives and Challenges
Michael Beckerman and Paul Boghossian (eds)

https://doi.org/10.11647/OBP.0242

Rethinking Social Action through Music
The Search for Coexistence and Citizenship in Medellín's Music Schools
Geoffrey Baker

https://doi.org/10.11647/OBP.0243

www.ingramcontent.com/pod-product-compliance
Lightning Source LLC
Chambersburg PA
CBHW050522300426
44113CB00012B/1917